Jew and Gentile
in the Ancient World

———————————

Jew and Gentile in the Ancient World

ATTITUDES AND INTERACTIONS
FROM ALEXANDER TO JUSTINIAN

Louis H. Feldman

PRINCETON UNIVERSITY PRESS

PRINCETON, NEW JERSEY

Copyright © 1993 by Princeton University Press
Published by Princeton University Press, 41 William Street,
Princeton, New Jersey 08540
In the United Kingdom: Princeton University Press,
Chichester, West Sussex

Library of Congress Cataloging-in-Publication Data

Feldman, Louis H.
Jew and Gentile in the ancient world : attitudes and interactions
from Alexander to Justinian / Louis H. Feldman.
p. cm.
Includes bibliographical references and indexes.
ISBN 0-691-07416-x
1. Judaism—Relations. 2. Jews—Public opinion—History.
3. Jews—History—586 B.C.–70 A.D. 4. Jews—History—70–638.
5. Antisemitism—History. 6. Judaism—Controversial literature—
History and criticism. 7. Proselytes and proselyting, Jewish—
History. 8. Philosemitism—History. I. Title.
BM534.F45 1992
296.3′872′09015—dc20 92-11952

Publication of this book has been aided by a grant from the
Lucius N. Littauer Foundation, Inc.

This book has been composed in Adobe Janson

Princeton University Press books are printed on
acid-free paper, and meet the guidelines
for permanence and durability of the Committee on
Production Guidelines for Book Longevity of
the Council on Library Resources

Printed in the United States of America

2 4 6 8 10 9 7 5 3 1

To the Memory
of my mother,
of blessed memory,
whose lullaby
still rings
in my ears:
"Vos iz di beste schorah?
Das kind vet lernen
Torah."

CONTENTS

PREFACE

THIS BOOK began with a question: How can we explain why the Jews in antiquity—so bitterly hated, as so many scholars have insisted—succeeded in winning so many adherents, whether as "sympathizers" who observed one or more Jewish practices or as full-fledged proselytes?

Of course, we might conclude that they were not so bitterly hated after all, though that seems to contradict deep-seated assumptions and stereotypes. Some years ago, when I wrote an article entitled "Philo-Semitism among Ancient Intellectuals," a colleague of mine at Yeshiva University indignantly objected to the very idea that non-Jews ever failed to hate Jews. He had quite clearly adopted the "lachrymose" conception of Jewish history as a narration of uninterrupted suffering; thus he felt uncomfortable with the notion that Jews were sometimes strong, self-confident, and influential, winning many to their cause.

Alternatively, we might deny that they had really been so successful in winning adherents, or in any case adopt a "show me" attitude, asking for hard evidence for large-scale proselytizing by Jews. How could the Jews have converted so many when we do not have a single missionary tract and when the only missionaries that we know of by name are those such as Paul, Peter, and Barnabas, who preached the Gospel? Indeed, it would seem that the proper question is, How, in view of the tremendous strength and attractiveness of Hellenism and of the various pagan cults, the Jews managed to avoid assimilation both in the Land of Israel and especially in the Diaspora.

The missing link that precipitated this book was the publication in 1987 of the Aphrodisias inscriptions from Asia Minor. These seemed to establish once and for all the existence of a large class of "G-d-fearers" or "sympathizers," people who adopted certain practices of Judaism without actually converting. I had always assumed that Judaism's "outreach" to Gentiles had ended for all practical purposes with the Bar Kochba rebellion (132–135 c.e.), one result of which was to make proselytism a capital crime. And yet, in the third century, in an area where Christianity was supposedly making tremendous inroads, Judaism seemed to be counterattacking, as it were, with great success. This led me to re-examine the whole picture of the relationship between Jew and Gentile in the Hellenistic and Roman world.

Portions of this work have appeared in preliminary form in the following publications: Chapter 1: "Hengel's *Judaism and Hellenism* in Retrospect," *Journal of Biblical Literature* 96 (1977): 371–82; "How Much Hellenism in Jewish Palestine?" *Hebrew Union College Annual* 57 (1986): 83–111; Chapter 2: "The Orthodoxy of the Jews in Hellenistic Egypt," *Jewish Social Studies* 22 (1960): 212–37; Chapters 3–5: "Philo-Semitism among Ancient Intellectuals," *Tradition* 1 (1958–59): 27–39; "Anti-Semitism in the Ancient World," in David Berger, ed., *History and Hate: The Dimensions of Anti-Semitism* (Philadelphia: Jewish Publication Society, 1986), 15–42; "The Jews in Greek and Roman Literature" [in Hebrew], in Menaham Stern and Zvi Baras, eds., *World History of the Jewish People*, First Series: *The Diaspora in the Hellenistic-Roman World* (Jerusalem: Am Oved, 1984), 265–85, 361–65, 383–84; Chapter 6: "Origen's *Contra Celsum* and Josephus's *Contra Apionem*: The Issue of Jewish Origins," *Vigiliae Christianae* 44 (1990): 105–35; Chapter 7: "Use, Authority, and Exegesis of Mikra in the Writings of Josephus," in Jan Mulder and Harry Sysling, eds., *Mikra: Text, Translation, Reading and Interpretation of the Hebrew Bible in Ancient Judaism and Early Christianity (Compendia Rerum Iudaicarum ad Novum Testamentum* [Assen: Van Gorcum, 1988], Sect. 2, vol. 1), 455–518; Chapter 8: "Josephus's Portrait of Moses," *Jewish Quarterly Review* 82 (1991–92), forthcoming; Chapter 9: "Proselytism and Syncretism" [in Hebrew], in Menaham Stern and Zvi Baras, eds., *World History of the Jewish People*, First Series: *The Diaspora in the Hellenistic-Roman World* (Jerusalem: Am Oved, 1984), 188–207, 340–45, 378–80; Chapter 10: "Proselytes and 'Sympathizers' in the Light of the New Inscriptions from Aphrodisias," *Revue des Études juives* 148 (1989): 265–305; Chapter 11: "Proselytism by Jews in the Third, Fourth, and Fifth Centuries," *Journal for the Study of Judaism* 23 (1992), forthcoming. All are republished here with the permission of the publishers, though most have been altered very substantially.

I am most grateful to the following for assistance: William Adler, Bezalel Bar-Kochva, Christopher T. Begg, Herbert W. Benario, Frederick F. Bruce, Randall D. Chesnutt, Naomi G. Cohen, Shaye J. D. Cohen, David Daube, Robert Doran, Zvi Erenyi, Wolfgang Fauth, Paula Fredriksen, Gilad J. Gevaryahu, Jonathan A. Goldstein, Martin Goodman, Joan Haahr, Howard Jacobson, Aryeh Kasher, A. Thomas Kraabel, William Lee, David Levenson, Amy-Jill Levine, Thomas F. McDaniel, James T. McDonough, Jr., Scot McKnight, Ronald H. Martin, Eric M. Meyers, Richard Nochimson, David Olster, Charles Persky, Michael B. Poliakoff, Charlotte Roueché, Lawrence H. Schiffman, Daniel R. Schwartz, Seth Schwartz, Alan F. Segal, Carole Silver, Morton Smith (of blessed memory), Marta Steele, Robert Tannenbaum, Ben Zion Wacholder, Manfred Weidhorn, and Robert L. Wilken.

I am deeply grateful to the Lucius N. Littauer Foundation and to its president, Mr. William Frost, for helping to make this work possible.

Jew and Gentile
in the Ancient World

CHAPTER 1

CONTACTS BETWEEN JEWS AND
NON-JEWS IN THE
LAND OF ISRAEL

1. CONTACTS PRIOR TO ALEXANDER THE GREAT

It always comes as a surprise—perhaps even a shock—that the two peoples who have most profoundly influenced Western civilization, the Jews and the Greeks, seem to have been just about unaware of each other, at least in a cultural sense, until the fifth century B.C.E. at the very earliest.

Apparently, however, the Pentateuch is aware of a relationship between Semites and Greeks, because it declares that Shem, the ancestor of the Semites, and Japheth, almost certainly the ancestor of the Greeks, are brothers. The very name of Japheth reminds us strongly of the Greek Iapetos, the father of Prometheus, and the Hebrew letters for Japheth's son Javan are YWN, the equivalent of the Greek Ion, the ancestor of the Ionians (though Greek mythology knows of no relationship between Iapetos and Ion).

Even a glance at a map of antiquity will indicate that the land of Javan, Ionia, is not far from the land of Shem, Israel, while the Biblical references (2 Sam 20:23, 1 Kgs 1:38) make it probable that King David in the tenth century B.C.E. employed Cretan mercenaries. Moreover, the brother of the famous Greek poet Alcaeus at the end of the seventh century B.C.E. served as a mercenary in the army of the Babylonians and apparently took part in the capture of the city of Ashkelon in the Land of Israel, indicating probable military contact between the two peoples.[1] During the fourth century B.C.E., military affairs, particularly the continued struggle of the Greeks against the Persian empire, called the attention of the Athenians to the Land of Israel.

Finds of Greek pottery on such sites as Samaria reveal commercial ties at least as early as the eighth century B.C.E.[2] As early as the fifth century B.C.E., the Jews minted coins on the Attic standard and with the characteristic Athenian emblem of the owl, similarly indicating commercial contact.[3] Likewise, Herodotus's mention in the fifth century B.C.E. of Ashkelon (1.105.2–4) and of Cadytis (presumably Gaza) (3.5.1–2) suggests Greek acquaintance with Philistia, the coast of the Land of Israel.

We also find that several Greek words have penetrated the Hebrew

Bible itself, notably Hebrew *darkemonim* (Ezra 2:69, Nehemiah 7:69–71), where, in view of the context, it must mean Greek drachmas; *qiteros* (Daniel 3:5, 3:7) = Greek κιθάρα ("lyre"), *pesanterin* (Daniel 3:5, 3:7, 3:10, 3:15) = ψαλτήριον ("harp"), *sumponeya* (Daniel 3:5, 3:15) = συμφωνία ("harmony," "orchestra"), and *sabbeka* (Daniel 3:7, 3:10, 3:15) = σαμβύκη (a triangular musical instrument with four strings). But most such words reflect commercial rather than cultural contacts between the Israelites and the Greeks during the sixth and fifth centuries B.C.E., the period of Ezra, Nehemiah, and Daniel. In fact, Greek words in the Hebrew Bible and, for that matter, in the Hebrew texts of the Apocrypha, Pseudepigrapha, and extra-biblical Qumran manuscripts prove strikingly few.[4]

Demosthenes (52.20) and Isaeus (4.7) imply that Athenians inhabited the coast of the Land of Israel at Acre in the fourth century B.C.E. During that century the Athenians certainly maintained close commercial contacts with Sidon and with other Phoenician cities. Thus, Xenophon (*Hellenica* 3.4.1) tells of the visit of Herodas of Syracuse to Phoenicia in 399 B.C.E.[5] The presence of Phoenicians in Athens during this period is well attested; and these Phoenicians, we may guess, knew something about their Jewish neighbors.[6] The mention by Pseudo-Scylax,[7] in the middle of the fourth century B.C.E., of Acre, Dor, Carmel, Ashkelon, and Jaffa along the coast of the Land of Israel again indicates possible commercial contact, though we must not forget that in this period and indeed for centuries thereafter, according to Josephus (*Against Apion* 1.60), the Jews were not living along the coast and were not a maritime people. The famous myth of Perseus and Andromeda, which is so frequently cited by ancient writers,[8] may well have aroused interest in the place, Joppa, where this episode supposedly occurred, but again this was along the coast, where the Jews were not yet living.

The earliest reference to the Jews in Greek literature would appear to be in Herodotus, if we accept Josephus's view that Herodotus's mention of the circumcised Syrians of Palestine refers to the Jews. Even if it does refer to Jews, however, Herodotus never refers to any exchange of ideas.[9]

Another fifth century B.C.E. writer, the historian Hellanicus, together with the third century B.C.E. historian Philochorus, is quoted by the third century Pseudo-Justin (*Cohortatio ad Gentiles* 9) as mentioning Moses as a very ancient leader of the Jews; but the *Cohortatio* contains some of the most glaring forgeries of Hellenistic Jewish literature.[10] In that light, it would appear significant that Josephus, who was seeking high and low for references to Jews in early Greek writers and who does mention Hellanicus (*Against Apion* 1.16), does not cite this passage mentioning Moses.[11] Moreover, it is most probable that the *Cohortatio* draws on a passage in Africanus (quoted in Eusebius, *Praeparatio Evangelica* 10.10.7–

9) that mentions Hellanicus and Philochorus but does not refer to Moses. Africanus is unlikely to have drawn on the *Cohortatio*, for it is hardly imaginable that he would have closely paraphrased the *Cohortatio* yet ignored the reference to Moses.

The poet Choerilus, who lived in the second half of the fifth century B.C.E., is cited by Josephus (*Against Apion* 1.172–73) as referring to Jews in the army of Xerxes during his invasion of Greece. Choerilus does not mention the Jews by name, however; rather, he speaks of people living in the Solymian hills. Most likely he is alluding to the Solymoi referred to by Homer (*Iliad* 6.184). Choerilus describes the hair on the heads of the warriors as shorn in a circle, a practice forbidden by the Torah (Lev 19:27), further militating against an identification with Jews. At best this source indicates relations between Persians and Jews, referring in any case to military, not cultural, contact.[12]

The first cultural contact between Greeks and Jews is said to have occurred in the fourth century B.C.E., when a learned Jew from Coele-Syria supposedly met Aristotle in Asia Minor. This meeting, which took place about 340 B.C.E., is reported by Clearchus of Soli (about 300 B.C.E.), as quoted in Josephus (*Against Apion* 1.176–83). The passage is extremely complimentary to the Jews, who are said to be descended from the philosophers of India. This particular Jew, we are told, not only spoke Greek but had the soul of a Greek. He had come to test Aristotle's learning but, in the end, it was he who imparted to Aristotle knowledge of his own. Clearchus marvels, in particular, at the astonishing endurance and sobriety displayed by this Jew in his way of life.

Lewy, however, cites cogent reasons for concluding that the Jew whom Aristotle met is a figment of Clearchus's imagination similar to those representatives of Oriental priestly wisdom who are often depicted as superior in wisdom to the great Greek philosophers. Admittedly, Clearchus's attempt to approximate the Hebrew name for Jerusalem (*Against Apion* 1.179) is an indication that he had met a real Jew.[13] But even if the meeting did take place, it represents the contact of a single Jew, rather than of groups of Jews, with a single Greek philosopher; and it took place in Asia Minor, not in the Land of Israel. Even if we assume that he existed, the Jew might have learned his Greek in Asia Minor, where he met Aristotle. We must beware of imitating Aristotle, who apparently was so impressed with this one Jew that he forgot his celebrated logic and generalized from this one case to the Jews as a race of philosophers. In actuality, the whole story appears to be imaginary and stereotyped, relayed secondhand through Clearchus of Soli. We can conclude that Aristotle had not met Jews before, inasmuch as Clearchus has to explain to his readers who the Jews are and remarks that their city has an unusually odd name, Hierusaleme.

In Aristotle's own writings (*Meteorologica* 2.359A) there is one reference to a bitter and salty lake in Palestine, presumably the Dead Sea, in which it is impossible to sink; but that he locates it not in Judaea but in Palestine, which in this period refers to the area along the Mediterranean coast,[14] so called because it had been inhabited by the Philistines, would indicate that he derived his information secondhand. In any case, again, this hardly indicates cultural contact.

2. Literary Contacts between the Time of Alexander and the Maccabean Revolt

The usual picture of the era following the death of Alexander is one of the universal missionary propagation of Greek culture, in all its aspects—language, literature, art, religion, and, indeed, total way of life—for the benefit of the unenlightened backward peoples. If so, we should expect the Jews also to be deeply affected. But Green has convincingly demonstrated that this is a most pernicious myth, compounded of anachronistic Christian evangelicism and Plutarch-inspired wishful thinking.[15] Rather, what motivated the Greeks and Macedonians was the power-hungry imperialist lure of conquest, commercial profits, and general land grants; and their contempt for the non-Greeks—the "barbarians" as they termed them—was met at almost every turn by the stubborn refusal of the conquered peoples to accept the enlightenment thrust on them.[16] Indeed, in such lands as India, especially where there was a religious and ideological and ethnic basis to the opposition, we find real hostility; and this is precisely what we should expect in the Land of Israel, with its religious and ideological uniqueness. In fact, the dissemination of Hellenism, when it finally came, was usually incidental rather than conscious and deliberate.

Moreover, the agents of this alleged Hellenization were, to a considerable degree, soldiers and businessmen—hardly the kind of people that we would term intellectuals or a cultural elite. Those who were impressed and influenced by Hellenism were either puppet rulers who sought social and political advancement thereby or collaborators who served as administrators for the occupying power and wanted to rise in the bureaucracy, starting as petty clerks and tax collectors. And even they did not constitute more than 2.5 percent of the official class, and that only after two generations.[17]

Furthermore, what Alexander and his successors set up were islands of Graeco-Macedonian culture for a ruling elite and their professional or commercial adherents in a sea of alien native cultures. Green draws a parallel with the relationship in India between the British and the natives; there, too, we find some natives who, in their ambition for power, even of a petty sort, went to England for their higher education. And yet, even after adopting the mores of the British clubs, they did not sever themselves from their deep cultural and religious roots.[18]

To be sure, after Alexander the evidence for contact between Greeks and Jews, far from remaining scarce and dubious, gradually becomes more impressive, but not if we confine ourselves to the period before the Hasmoneans (167 B.C.E.).

An examination of the earliest Greek literature for this period reveals seven references to Jews or to their land in the works of Aristotle's pupil and successor Theophrastus (372–287 B.C.E.). Five of them, however, come from his *Historia Plantarum* (2.6.2–8, 4.4.14, 7.4.8–9, 9.1.6, and 9.6.1–4), where he mentions plants and trees that grow in Coele-Syria. Nowhere does he mention Judaea or Jerusalem, and it is most likely that his information is secondhand. Nor does such information indicate a cultural encounter. With regard to the other two passages, Josephus (*Against Apion* 1.166–67), as evidence that various cities were acquainted with the existence of the Jews and that many Jewish customs had found their way to some of them, cites a passage from Theophrastus's *On Laws* which states that the laws of the Tyrians prohibit the use of foreign oaths, including the oath "Korban." But it is clear that Josephus himself has drawn the conclusion that the reference is to a Jewish oath, inasmuch as he adds that this oath is found nowhere except among the Jews. Theophrastus himself does not here mention Jews at all: Although the oath "Korban" exists among the Jews, it seems that Theophrastus thought that it was a word in the Phoenician language, not its near neighbor, Hebrew.[19]

Finally, the most substantial passage, from a lost work *On Piety*, as quoted by Porphyry (*De Abstinentia* 2.26), describes the method by which "the Syrians, of whom the Jews constitute a part," conduct their sacrifices. He speaks of these Syrians with the highest praise, referring to them as philosophers by race. But it is clear that Theophrastus had not visited the Land of Israel and was not conveying firsthand information about Jewish sacrifices, for he makes the egregious error of claiming that the sacrifices include living beings as well as self-immolation.[20] Likewise, his statement that honey and wine are poured on the sacrifices is inconsistent with what we know of Jewish sacrifices from the Bible (Lev 2:11), as well as from Plutarch (*Quaestiones Convivales* 4.6.2.672B). A closer look at the passage reveals that Theophrastus does not say that this is specifically the Jewish method of sacrifice; what he does say is that this is the way that the *Syrians*, of whom the Jews constitute a part, offer their sacrifices.

About the year 290 B.C.E., a certain Megasthenes (quoted in Clement of Alexandria, *Stromata* 1.15.72.5) in his work *Indica* states that all of the ancients' opinions concerning nature can also be found in, and presumably were derived from, the philosophers outside Greece, some among the Indian Brahmans and others in Syria among those called Jews. We can immediately call to mind the statement ascribed to Aristotle (quoted in Josephus, *Against Apion* 1.179) that the Jews are descendants of the Indian philosophers, and that philosophers are called Calani in India and Jews in Syria, as well as the remark of Theophrastus (quoted in Porphyry, *De Abstinentia* 2.26) that during the time that they engage in sacrifices, the Syrians, of whom the Jews constitute a part, being philosophers by race, converse with each other about the deity. This view of Jews as philosophers and the theory connecting them with the Indians would seem to link all three references; but it would also seem to indicate that what we have here is not direct knowledge of the Jews by the Greeks but rather a commonplace view of the Orientals as philosophers from whom the Greeks drew their wisdom.[21]

The longest and most important of these earliest extant references to the Jews lies among the fragments of Hecataeus of Abdera. According to Josephus (*Against Apion* 1.183), Hecataeus wrote a book entirely about Jews in which he mentions, approvingly, that the Jews have a high regard for their laws, that they razed pagan temples in their land, that their population is vast, that their capital city, Jerusalem, and, in particular, their temple have great beauty, and that they proved themselves excellent fighters in the armies of Alexander and of his successors. But there is good reason to doubt that Hecataeus wrote such a work.[22] We know of at least one book, about Abraham, fabricated by Jewish apologetic writers and attached to the name of Hecataeus. Doubt about its authenticity had already been expressed by Herennius Philo (quoted in Origen, *Against Celsus* 1.15) at the beginning of the second century c.e., and its panegyrical tone is considerably different from the detached tone in the passage cited by Diodorus (40.3).[23]

As for the passage cited by Diodorus, if Hecataeus had been well informed, he could hardly have remarked (quoted in Diodorus 40.3.5) that the Jews have never had a king, though, to be sure, centuries had passed by without a king. That Hecataeus locates the Temple in almost the center of Jerusalem (quoted in *Against Apion* 1.198) shows that he had never visited Jerusalem (unless, of course, he is thinking of the ideal Jerusalem) and that his source was not well informed. Again, the statement (cited in *Against Apion* 2.43) that, as a reward for Jewish loyalty, Alexander the Great assigned Samaria to the Jews free of tribute would seem to be an anachronism, reflecting the second century b.c.e., when Demetrius II (1 Mac 11:34) awarded three Samaritan districts to Jonathan the Hasmonean.[24] All of this indicates lack of firsthand contact with Jews.[25] Moreover, the passage in Diodorus (40.3) comes from a brief digression within Hecataeus's *Aegyptiaca*, which, of course, focused on Egypt. It is highly probable that Hecataeus received his information in Egypt, which he had visited (Diodorus 1.46.8). Hence, this passage tells us nothing directly about cultural contact between Greeks and Jews in the Land of Israel.[26]

The third century B.C.E. Hermippus of Smyrna (cited in Josephus, *Against Apion* 1.164–65) refers to Pythagoras, the semilegendary philosopher of the sixth century B.C.E., as imitating and appropriating the doctrines of Jews and Thracians. Stern points out that the passage hardly redounds to the glory of the Jewish people, because the Jews are put on a level with the Thracians;[27] but Josephus, who cited the text in an apologetic context, certainly thought that it did enhance the reputation of the Jews. Significantly, he follows up this statement in more decisively glowing terms: "In fact, it is actually said that that great man [i.e., Pythagoras] introduced many points of Jewish law into his philosophy."[28] Hermippus, as a pupil of the famous Callimachus, must have worked in Alexandria; and the possibility should not be excluded that he himself had been influenced by Jewish theories, which were probably already widespread at that time in Alexandrian circles.[29] Even so, this influence certainly does not reflect contact between Greek and Jewish thought in the Land of Israel. Similar contacts of Pythagoras with Jewish thought are alleged by Antonius Diogenes (cited in Porphyry, *Life of Pythagoras* 11) at the end of the first century C.E. and by Origen (*Against Celsus* 1.15, citing Hermippus) in the third century; but this seems merely to reflect the romantic tendency during the Hellenistic period to have Greek thinkers come into contact with Eastern ideas. Indeed, all of these alleged encounters between Greeks and Jewish philosophers are part of a stereotyped theme of Hellenistic literature—the encounter of a Greek with a barbarian philosopher in which the non-Greek shows his superiority.[30]

Thus, we may well ask why cultural contacts between Greeks and Jews were so few and so late, especially when we consider that the everyday language spoken by the Jews, from the sixth century B.C.E. onward, was Aramaic, which was also the common international language of the entire Near East from India to Egypt, so that any Greek expecting commercial or cultural contact with this entire area probably had to know Aramaic or had to employ an interpreter who understood it.[31] One answer is that the Jews apparently lived inland rather than along the coast,[32] because even at a much later date, the first century, according to Josephus (*Against Apion* 1.60), the Jews were not a "maritime" people. Rather, they were a relatively minuscule tribe lost, as it were, in the immensity of the Persian Empire.[33] Ancient travelers did not find it easy to enter into the interior of countries, so that even Herodotus, who (in the context of the fifth century B.C.E.) traveled so widely, seems never to have penetrated beyond the coast. Indeed, Josephus, who labors to explain why the Greeks should have dismissed the Jews in silence and who, as we have emphasized, searched everywhere for references to the Jews in Greek literature, was able to find no indirect references earlier than Herodotus and Choerilus in the fifth century B.C.E. As for these two Greek authors, it is possible, as we have indicated, that neither is referring to the Jews. The *Letter of Aristeas* (313–16), resorting, so to speak, to a *deus ex machina*—an artifical device introduced suddenly to resolve the problem—explains that the reason for the silence is that when, in the fourth century B.C.E., the historian Theopompus and the tragedian Theodectes attempted to introduce references to the Torah into their works, they were smitten with illness, presumably because of the very holiness of the Writ. All that this argues, however, is that fruitless efforts had been made to find references to the Jews in Greek literature dating from before the time of Alexander. Apparently, pagan writers had come to contest the Jewish claims to antiquity—so important in the ancient period. Josephus, too (*Against Apion* 1.60–65), feels constrained to explain why they had been ignored by Greek writers for so long. According to him, as we have noted, the Jews did not live along the coast and hence, unlike the Egyptians and the Phoenicians, did not have extensive commercial contacts with the Greeks. But the chief reason why the Greeks ignored the Jews may well have been this: From the Greek point of view, the Jews were obscurantists who had not contributed significantly to the arts and sciences.[34]

As a parallel to the Greeks' silence about the Jews we may cite, as does Josephus (*Against Apion* 1.66), their silence about the Romans until a relatively late date. Thus, though Thucydides writes at length about the Athenians' expedition to Sicily in 415 B.C.E., he says not a word about the Romans. Indeed, not until Theopompus in the fourth century B.C.E. do we find a Greek writer who mentions an event in Roman history, the capture of Rome by the Gauls in 387 B.C.E. The Greeks seem to have been enormously self-centered, throwing all others into one common denominator, "barbarians."

The lack of cultural contact between Greeks and Jews is surely not due to the immunity of the Jews to foreign influence, because, after all, they had often succumbed to it during the biblical period. Nothing indicates, however, that Jews worshipped Greek gods or combined their G-d with the Olympians prior to the Hellenistic period. Perhaps the explanation is that the Greek intelligentsia felt that they had little or nothing to learn from the Jews, who had produced only a single important work, the Bible, and who certainly had nothing comparable to the Homeric epics or lyric poetry or tragedy or philosophy or scientific critical history. After all, the great heroes of Judaism from Moses on down in the Bible are farmers and shepherds and warriors, not intellectuals. Moreover, it would appear, the Jews deliberately sought to isolate themselves; the Greeks, on the other hand, often attempted to disturb the peace of the Persian Empire, on which the reconstruction of Judaism depended so heavily.

We must, however, explain why there is Jewish literature in Greek, perhaps from the Land of Israel,[35] notably the anonymous Samaritan (pseudo-Eupolemus), who probably wrote, between 200 and the Maccabean revolt in 167 B.C.E., a history, fragments of which have survived, identifying Noah, Nimrod, Bel, and Kronos, and describing Abraham as the discoverer of astrology. But we may counter that the Talmud, Josephus, and the New Testament, at any rate, would have us believe (though, admittedly, the reality may have been more ambiguous than this) that the Jews avoided contact with the Samaritans; and hence it is unlikely that the anonymous Samaritan, pseudo-Eupolemus, had any significant influence on Jews. Moreover, because we know that there was a Samaritan colony in Greek-speaking Egypt, it is more likely that he wrote there than in the Land of Israel.

3. Military, Political, and Economic Contacts between Greeks and Jews from the Time of Alexander to the Maccabean Revolt

During the period between 330 and 200 B.C.E., Greek armies frequently marched through the Land of Israel and must have had contact with the Jewish inhabitants. Furthermore, there is evidence (Josephus, *Against Apion* 1.192) that Jewish mercenaries served in the armies of Alexander and of his successors. Moreover, the Jews were greatly impressed with the Macedonian techniques of war. The apocalypses of the Jews are consequently couched in military terms. The Zeno papyri show that the Greek language was known in aristocratic and military circles of Palestinian Jewry between 260 and 250 B.C.E.[36] But we have no evidence in either Greek or Jewish sources, literary or epigraphical, of any influence exercised by Greek armies marching through the Land of Israel; and, to judge from admittedly much later comments in the Talmudic writings, the Jews' reaction to such soldiers was contempt.[37]

In particular, we may note the claim, in 1 Maccabees (12:6–23) and 2 Maccabees (5:9), as well as in Josephus (*Ant.* 12.226–27, 13.166–67), based on correspondence between the Spartan king Areus and the Jewish high priest Onias I about 300 B.C.E. and renewed by Jonathan the Hasmonean in the middle of the second century B.C.E., that the Jews and the Spartans are related. Though the Spartans at this time had little military power, such a claim, if authenticated, would have lent much prestige to the Jews in view of the high regard in which the Spartans were held in antiquity. Indeed, the high priest Jason, the author of the Hellenistic reform in Jerusalem, ended his life in Sparta.[38] But we may here suggest that the theory of a connection between Jews and Spartans may have come about through the association with the mythical founder of Thebes, Cadmus, whose very name is probably Semitic (from *qedem*, "east") and who, indeed, is reported to have come to Thebes from Phoenicia; Cadmus is said to have sown a serpent's teeth in the ground, from which sprang armed men who were called $\Sigma\pi\alpha\rho\tauo\acute{\iota}$, that is, "sown men." Though there is apparently no connection between $\sigma\pi\alpha\rho\tau\acute{o}\varsigma$, "sown," and $\Sigma\pi\acute{\alpha}\rho\tau\eta$, "Sparta," the words are very similar, and folk etymologists may well have connected them, thus bringing Cadmus of Phoenicia into juxtaposition with Sparta. The next step would be to connect the Phoenicians' neighbors, the Judaeans, with Sparta.

To be sure, there were a large number of "free" or "semi-free" cities in Palestine with constitutions following the Greek models.[39] Hence, Judaea would appear to have been a temple-state similar to other temple-states of the period. But we must insist that it is an error to assume that what was true of the non-Jewish Palestinian cities was also true of the Jewish cities. Moreover, the relationship between the Jews and the Hellenistic cities during the Second Temple period was, on the whole, one of profound religious hostility, based, as it was, on a long history of conflict, aggravated by the fact that the Hellenistic cities were built on the foundation of the old Canaanite and Philistine cities, with neither side willing to consider the option of peaceful coexistence.[40] This tension, furthermore, had an economic basis in that the Hellenistic cities had a purely urban population, whereas the Jews were primarily a rural society. It was the cities that minted currency, that controlled imports and exports, and that set prices and standards for goods. In addition, the Hellenistic cities were protected by foreign conquerors, whether Ptolemies or Seleucids. Finally, the Jewish population, both through natural increase and through conversions to Judaism, became much more numerous than the non-Jewish population of the cities. This undoubtedly added to the fear of the cities that they would be overwhelmed by the Jewish religion, which left no room for other gods. The fear increased particularly after the triumph of the Hasmoneans and the establishment of an independent Jewish state and contrived to transform Judaea into a sort of demographic pressure cooker.[41]

During the Ptolemaic rule of Palestine in the third century B.C.E., the Jews developed an aristocratic ruling body known as the *gerousia*, modeled, it has been argued, on the Greek system and limiting the authority of the high priest.[42] Yet, with regard to the *gerousia* or the Sanhedrin, for that matter, although there can be no doubt that the name was borrowed from the Greek, more borrowing than that has not yet been proved.[43] To be sure, during this early Hellenistic period the Jews would appear to have held positive views toward the foreign state and its rulers, making them more susceptible to influence.[44] But we can see in the prophet Isaiah and in the books of Ezra and Nehemiah that even before the Hellenistic period the Jews were favorably inclined toward the Persians, presumably because they opted for the Persian policy of granting religious autonomy to their subject states rather than war with a highly dubious outcome. Inasmuch as Alexander and his successors continued this policy of laissez-faire in religious matters, the Jews later continued to pray for the welfare of the secular government, as we see in the statement attributed to the first-century Ḥanina Segan Ha-Kohanim in the Mishnah (*Avoth* 3:2). But this was a purely pragmatic relationship, as we see from the advice, also in *Avoth* (1:10), that no Jew should seek intimacy with the ruling power. Moreover, to judge from the pages of Josephus, to be sure from his first-century point of view, the attitudes of the Jews toward non-Jews in the Land of Israel ranged from disagreement to disdain.

Hengel would have us believe that the Hellenization imposed forcibly by Antiochus Epiphanes in 167 B.C.E. was actually the natural consequence of the process that had been going on for at least a century and a half, explaining in that way how the Hellenizers in Jerusalem came to be strong enough to force the hand of Antiochus in the first place.[45] But Diodorus (34.5.1), Tacitus (*Histories* 5.8.2), and 2 Maccabees indicate that Antiochus did not continue a process of syncretism that was in motion but rather attempted to abolish Jewish observance completely, thereby ensuring substantial resistance.[46] Although the Maccabees (1 Mac 2:46) did have to circumcise by force many children of those who had feared to disobey Antiochus, many Jews resisted Antiochus's decrees even at the cost of martyrdom. By contrast, the Samaritan leaders, according to Josephus (*Ant.* 12.257–64), who was admittedly no great friend of theirs, petitioned Antiochus to name their temple after Zeus Hellenios and promised to apply themselves seriously to their work so as to increase Antiochus's revenues. Meanwhile, the abrupt abandonment of the attempt forcibly to convert the Jews to paganism suggests either that the original decision of Antiochus was a whim rather than the climax of a gradual movement or that Jewish resistance was successful, or both.

As for economic influence, the Egyptian Ptolemies employed the Greek system of tax-farming in the Land of Israel during their century-long rule prior to their displacement by the Syrian Seleucids in 200 B.C.E. During this period the Ptolemies introduced Greek weights, coins, and trade usage. Finds of coins and pottery indicate that there was a commercial boom in the land favored by the long period of relative peace in the third century B.C.E. Economic ties led to social relations, as we see in the story of the Tobiad family in Josephus (*Ant.* 12.158–236).[47] However, aside from the highly assimilated—and truly exceptional—family of the Tobiads, there is little indication of Greek influence among the masses. It would be as if someone were to draw conclusions about the extent of assimilation of American Jews by considering only the wealthiest German Jewish families in the United States at the end of the nineteenth century. Nor is there much to indicate that the Jewish communities of Egypt and Palestine had more contact with each other and drew closer together even though during the third century the Ptolemies ruled both lands.

4. Linguistic Contacts between Greeks and Jews before the Maccabean Revolt

In language, as in culture generally, the degree to which Hellenism spread after Alexander has been much exaggerated. Thus, even in the most heavily Hellenized portions of Syria, Phoenicia, and Cyprus, bilingual inscriptions and coins for this period are common.[48] In Antioch, the capital of the Seleucid empire, for example, Aramaic remained as the second language and continued thus even after the Roman conquest. Hence, if the Greek language emerged clearly triumphant in the Land of Israel, this would be the exception to the general pattern.

Inscriptions, though admittedly there are few in any language prior to the third century B.C.E., should give us a clue of the extent to which the Jews had absorbed the Greek language. Hengel, in his latest publication on the subject, stresses that as early as the third century B.C.E. in various parts of the Land of Israel we have a whole series of testimonies to Greek as a language, and that the evidence is slowly but steadily increasing.[49] The earliest Greek text in the Land of Israel, found in 1971, is a bilingual Edomite-Greek ostracon dating from 277 B.C.E. Previously the earliest known Greek inscription was one set up by a priest of Ptolemy IV dating from 217 B.C.E. But as Fitzmyer correctly concludes, these inscriptions at best tell us about the use of Greek by Greek foreigners in Israel; they say little about its use by the Jews of Judaea.[50] Moreover, the bilingual character of the Edomite-Greek ostracon would appear to indicate that Greek was not the primary language of the inhabitants. In addition, the level of Greek in these inscriptions is very elementary (though it is true that the Greek usage in many contemporary funerary inscriptions and papyri in other parts of the Greek world is hardly more grammatical); usually it consists of little more than the names of the deceased and their age at death.[51] If we ask why Greek was employed at all, we may reply that perhaps it was intended to deter non-Jewish passers-by from molesting the graves. Not until the second century C.E. do we find the letter in

Greek of Bar Kochba to his lieutenants, and there the handwriting is much less than elegant and the spelling rather reminiscent of present-day teenagers.

To be sure, we must note the increasing prevalence of Greek names among Jews. The adoption of Greek names by Phoenicians as early as the century before Alexander, followed by the adoption of double names (Semitic and Greek) by Phoenicians in the third century, may have spread from them to the Jews;[52] but the mere fact that the Phoenicians in the third century adopted Greek names does not mean that the Jews also did so. Indeed, little can be said about Jewish names in the Land of Israel during the third century B.C.E., as almost no Jewish material from the Land from that century has survived. To be sure, from the moment when the sources for Judaism in the Land become fuller, we come across an abundance of Greek names, such as Antigonus of Socho (Mishnah, *Avoth* 1:3), at the end of the third century B.C.E., as well as a number of the seventy-two elders among the translators of the Septuagint in the third century B.C.E. and of the ambassadors sent by the Hasmoneans Jonathan and Simon to Sparta in the second century B.C.E. That the name Simeon (which is almost identical with the Greek name Simon) is the most frequent name in the Land of Israel during the Hellenistic-Roman period up to about 200 C.E. seems clearly to point to Greek influence. And yet there is no meaningful correlation between pagan versus Jewish naming and the extent of allegiance to and attitude toward Judaism and Jewish observance.[53]

Because Alexandria is geographically close to the Land of Israel, it has been assumed that the connections between the two were also cultural.[54] In particular, we may note the traditional claim that there were seventy or seventy-two elders in Jerusalem in approximately the year 270 B.C.E. who were said to know Greek well enough to translate the Torah into that language.[55]

But joining previous scholars, we may express our doubt about Aristeas's statement that there were seventy or seventy-two Palestinian Greek specialists, especially because the number seems a deliberate attempt to parallel the number of elders whom Moses chose to assist him (Num 11:24).[56] In addition, if we hear that seventy-two elders in the third century B.C.E. knew enough Greek to be able to translate the Torah into that language, the question still remains how many others possessed such knowledge. Furthermore, there is some reason to think that the translators were not from the Land of Israel at all but rather were Alexandrians.[57] Even if they were from Judaea, the level of their knowledge of Greek, to judge from the style of the Septuagint, is far from that of a Philo.

Moreover, to say that the translators of the Septuagint knew enough of the cosmological vocabulary to avoid it completely in rendering Genesis and that they did so in order to avoid the charge that they had plagiarized from the Greek philosophers[58] is a case of *argumentum ex silentio*. On that basis we could argue that they knew the political theories of Thucydides, because they avoid them in rendering the Pentateuch.

5. INFLUENCE OF GREEK IDEAS BEFORE THE MACCABEES

Hengel suggests that there is Greek influence on ideas in the Bible, the Apocrypha, and the Pseudepigrapha.[59] Thus the book of Ecclesiastes, which some have dated to 270–220 B.C.E., is said to reflect the spirit of Hellenism in both ideas and mood.[60] In particular, the breach with faith in the efficacy of divine righteousness in reward and punishment had already been introduced into Greece a considerable time earlier, as we see in the views of Thrasymachus in Plato's *Republic*, Book 1. Ecclesiastes contains parallels with the third century B.C.E. comic poet Menander and Cercidas (ca. 290–220 B.C.E.), a politician and poet influenced by Cynic philosophy, in the opinion, for example, that one should not fight against G-d (Eccl 6:10). The concepts of *miqre* (=τύχη, "chance") and of *ḥeleq* (=μοῖρα, "portion") are said to have influenced the author of Ecclesiastes, who absorbed not the school opinions of the philosophers but the popular views of the Greek bourgeoisie. Moreover, even in syntax the author of Ecclesiastes would seem to have been influenced by Greek style. For example, the complex and cumbersome sentence that comprises the first seven verses of chapter 12 is far from the paratactic norms of Hebrew. But we may counter that the question of theodicy, at any rate, need not go back to the Greeks, because it is found in the book of Job.

The Book of Daniel is said to show that Hellenistic sources mediated themes that were originally Near Eastern.[61] For example, the idea of four world kingdoms is Greek, common in Orphic as well as in Hermetic writings. Striking also is the analogy between Hesiod's three times ten thousand immortal watchers of men, "who observe decisions of law and unwholesome deeds and go about the whole earth clothed in air" (*Works and Days* 252–53) and watcher-angels in Daniel (4:10, 14, 20) and in 1 Enoch (1:5; 12:2, 3; 20:1). The idea that four metals of increasingly inferior quality correspond to the ages of man finds its nearest parallel in Hesiod (*Works and Days* 109–201), according to Hengel, who likewise adopts from Schlatter the view that Daniel took over from the Greeks a reverence for the power created by knowledge.[62]

Nevertheless, to trace back to the Greeks the reverence in Daniel for the power created by knowledge is to disregard the commandment in the Torah (Deut 6:7) to study and teach. Moreover, the kingdoms in Daniel differ considerably from Hesiod's five ages; in particular, Daniel's fourth kingdom is partly of iron and partly of clay, indicating a divided state. In addition, a fifth kingdom, symbolized by a stone, shall never be destroyed, whereas the fifth age in Hesiod is the worst age, that of iron. Indeed, Flusser argues for a Persian source for the four metals and the four ages in Daniel.[63] As for the analogy between Hesiod's watcher-angels and those in Daniel and 1 Enoch, many in scholarly circles believe that Hesiod drew on Near Eastern sources in that case as in others.[64]

Though Ben Sira (ca. 180–175 B.C.E.) is said to wage war with Hellenism and though he refutes the denial of free will and "Epicureanism," Hengel still claims that he falls under Greek influence.[65] In his theodicy, notably in his great confidence in the possibility of a rational understanding of the world, a spirit seems to emerge that draws on Hellenistic popular philosophy. Ben Sira apparently has close parallels with Stoic conceptions, especially the purposefulness of individual phenomena and the phrase "He is all." In fact, the hymn to Zeus of the Stoic Cleanthes (*SVF* 1.122, no. 537) could well have come from Ben Sira. Ben Sira likewise shares with the Stoics the notion that the whole world is a single cosmos that a rational power has permeated and shaped down to its smallest part. He is alleged to have rediscovered a number of other important elements found in Stoic thought: a drive toward ethical conduct, an attempt at a balance between human freedom and divine providence, the value of man as G-d's first creation, and even the identity of the divine reason (or wisdom) of the world and the moral law that binds all people. Supposedly, this borrowing was all the easier for him, because the Stoics had grown up on Semitic soil.[66] The statements made by Wisdom about herself (Ben Sira 24:3–7) parallel similar discussions of the qualities of Isis. In view of archaeological finds in Jerusalem pertaining to the Isis cult,[67] we cannot exclude the possibility that in the third century B.C.E. this cult had attempted to penetrate Jerusalem itself.

However, Ben Sira's understanding of the world as rational, down to the smallest detail, is implicit not only in Stoic sources but also in the latter chapters of the book of Job. Likewise, the phrase "He is all" may hark back to Jeremiah 23:29 and Psalm 139:7–12. The ethical ideas in Ben Sira, as well as the delicate balance between human freedom and divine providence, pervade the Bible and the oral Torah; they need hardly be traced back to the Greeks. That it was easy for Ben Sira to borrow from the Stoics because several of the important Stoic thinkers had grown up on Semitic soil might imply that the Stoics had borrowed from the Bible, at least indirectly, and that Ben Sira had thereafter borrowed from the Stoics. But why not say that Ben Sira did what the Stoics had done before him, namely, borrow directly from the Bible? Furthermore, the claim that the descriptions of Isis parallel Ben Sira and that archaeologists corroborate the possibility that Isis had penetrated even Jerusalem rests on the assumption, hardly proved, that the human remains are those of Jews, whereas they may very well be those of Ptolemaic administrators or soldiers.

In short, the evidence for appreciable influence of Greek thought on the Jews of Palestine prior to the Hasmoneans is slight. What about the Hasmonean and Roman periods?

6. POLITICAL CONTACTS BETWEEN GREEKS AND JEWS DURING THE HASMONEAN AND ROMAN PERIODS

Ostensibly, the Maccabean revolt against the Syrian Greeks was a reaction against the attempt of the latter to enforce Hellenization on the Jews. Yet Antiochus Epiphanes had not the slightest interest, any more than his father had had, in stamping out local culture as such, let alone in proselytizing for Hellenism, a role that, ab initio, was alien to the Greek mind and seems to be a modern invention.[68] Nevertheless, considerable evidence indicates that the successors of Judah Maccabee succumbed increasingly to the very Hellenization that they had originally opposed so vehemently. Simon, the last of the Hasmonean brothers, built a mausoleum that was completely in the Hellenistic style of his time.[69] Moreover, it is most striking that the Hasmonean king Aristobulus I, who ruled from 104 to 103 B.C.E., adopted the surname Philhellene, which was popular among Eastern monarchs.[70] His successor, Alexander Jannaeus, hired mercenaries from Asia Minor to preserve and extend his realm.

A claim of a friendship between the people of Pergamum and the Hebrews in the time of Abraham similar to that between the Spartans and the Jews that we have noted above is made in a document quoted by Josephus (*Ant.* 14.255), dating from the reign of John Hyrcanus in the latter part of the second century B.C.E., when Pergamum renewed this friendship formally. Such a treaty undoubtedly lent prestige to the fledgling state of the Hasmoneans, inasmuch as Pergamum was a brilliant center of culture, especially of sculpture, particularly during this period, and ranked second only to Alexandria in this respect. Yet there is no evidence that the treaty led to any kind of cultural exchange between their respective peoples.

That the masses of the people strongly resisted paganism can be seen from the passion with which they resisted the attempts of the procurator Pontius Pilate early in the first century C.E. to introduce busts of the emperor into Jerusalem, so that even Pilate was astonished at the strength of the devotion of the Jews to their laws and straightway removed the images (Josephus, *War* 2.169–74; *Ant.* 18. 55–59).[71] We see

similar zeal on the part of large numbers of Jews a few years later when, we are told (*Ant.* 18.263), many tens of thousands of Jews came to the Roman governor Petronius at Ptolemais asking that he slay them rather than set up an image of the Emperor Gaius Caligula in the Temple in Jerusalem. When many additional tens of thousands similarly faced Petronius at Tiberias (*Ant.* 18.270), he realized their stubborn determination and decided to write the emperor asking him to revoke his orders (*Ant.* 18.278).

7. CULTURAL CONTACTS BETWEEN GREEKS AND JEWS DURING THE HASMONEAN AND ROMAN PERIODS: THE ALLEGED INFLUENCE OF THE GREEK LANGUAGE

Josephus's admission (*Against Apion* 1.50) that he needed assistants in composing the version in Greek of the *Jewish War* illustrates that few attained the competence in the language necessary for reading and understanding Greek literature. Another indication that real knowledge of Greek was not widespread is the fact that Josephus, a mere youngster of twenty-six, was chosen in the year 64 to go on a mission to the Roman emperor, presumably, in part, because he knew Greek well, though also perhaps because he had connections at the Imperial Court.[72] It is Josephus himself, certainly not a modest person (cf. *Ant.* 20.264), who says that knowledge of foreign languages is a skill common to freedmen and even slaves.[73] From this Sevenster concludes that every man, even a slave, if he put his mind to it, could learn to speak good Greek; but the point of the passage is that learning Greek was frowned on, so that only the lowest classes of the population acquired the skill.[74] To be sure, because slaves and freedmen knew and used Greek, we may wonder whether people in the middle and upper classes may not have had to know some Greek in order to deal with them and whether, indeed, the upper classes may not have been influenced by popular culture, because culture can and often does trickle up. Indeed, Hengel assumes that Jesus, who, as a building craftsman, belonged to the middle class, was capable of carrying on a conversation in Greek, inasmuch as the synoptic tradition presupposes without further ado that he could talk with the captain from Capernaum, with Pilate, and with the Syro-Phoenician woman (Mark 7:26).[75] And yet the language in which slaves communicated with their masters was apparently Aramaic, so that slaves probably knew Greek mostly because they had to act as interpreters in business transactions. As to Jesus' knowledge of Greek, there is no specific indication in the Gospels that he lapsed into Greek as he did into Aramaic from time to time; and, in any case, in antiquity, as we can see from conversations between Greeks and

Trojans in Homer and between Greeks and Persians in such writers as Herodotus, there is generally no indication that interpreters were needed, even though it is quite clear that they must have been present. As late as the third century c.e., Joḥanan ben Nappaḥa, who taught in Sepphoris and Tiberias in Galilee, is quoted (Jerusalem Talmud, *Pe'ah* 1.1.15c) as stating that one may have one's daughter taught Greek, for it serves her as an ornament, whereas one may not teach one's son Greek, according to the Mishnah (*Sotah* 9:14). Similarly, in the third century, admittedly in a polemical passage, Origen (*Against Celsus* 2.34) declares that Jews are not very well [or at all] versed in Greek literature.[76]

It has been suggested that the upper classes, such as the Tobiads or the Herodian princes[77] or Josephus, spoke Greek, and the uneducated, particularly in the rural areas, spoke Aramaic. But the poor quality of the Greek on ossuaries and the continued use of Aramaic by Josephus in the first century and by the rabbis long thereafter indicate that no such clear-cut distinction is defensible. Moreover, when Bar Kochba or one of his officers in the second century c.e. declares that he is writing in Greek because "we have no one here capable of writing Hebrew," the implication is that normally one would write in Hebrew rather than in Greek.[78] Incidentally, it is not aversion to adopting the language of a conqueror that led the Jews to retain their ancestral language so stubbornly. After all, Aramaic itself was the language of a conqueror in the sixth century b.c.e. Moreover, within two centuries after the conquest of the Land of Israel by the Arabs in 640 c.e., Arabic displaced Aramaic as the chief language of the Jews.[79] Clearly, under certain conditions the Jews proved willing to adopt the language of a conqueror.

Letters, contracts, documents, ossuary inscriptions, Pseudepigrapha, Dead Sea Scrolls, the New Testament, rabbinic works—all indicate that the predominant language of the Jews of the Land of Israel throughout the Hellenistic and Roman periods—in fact, from the time of the Babylonian captivity in 586 b.c.e. until approximately two centuries after the Arab conquest of the Land—was not Greek but Aramaic, though Hebrew, it appears, continued to be spoken, certainly throughout the Mishnaic period.[80] Thus, we hear that when Titus sought to convince the Jews to surrender Jerusalem, he sent Josephus to speak with them in their "ancestral language," presumably Aramaic (Josephus, *War* 5.361). Likewise, when Paul (Acts 21:40, 22:2) addresses the Jews in Jerusalem, he does not speak in Greek but in Hebrew (or in Aramaic). To be sure, during the War of Quietus (115–17 c.e.) Jews were forbidden (Mishnah, *Sotah* 9:14) to teach their sons Greek (ironically, the very word used in the decree is the Greek πόλεμος, rather than the usual Hebrew word for war, *milḥamah*), so that prior to the decree Greek must have been taught to some degree in Jewish circles. Yet as late as the end of the second century C.E., Rabbi Judah the Prince recognized the predominant place of Aramaic as the language of the Jews when he asked rhetorically, "Why use the Syriac [i.e., Aramaic] language in the Land of Israel? [Use] either the Holy Language or Greek" (*Baba Qamma* 82b–83a, *Sotah* 49b). If this condemnation of Aramaic indicates its popularity, why does the edict prohibiting Greek not imply a similar popularity? In the case of Aramaic, the leader of the Palestinian Jewish community, the patriarch Judah the Prince, expresses a preference and gives advice, apparently realizing that to ban Aramaic totally would be useless because it was so widely spoken, whereas the rabbis issue an outright prohibition against Greek. True, edicts against an activity imply scores of people in favor of an activity, but we may again note that it is the masses, not the rabbis, that Josephus and Paul choose to address in Aramaic (or Hebrew), and that it is the masses, not the rabbis, whom Judah the Prince berates for using Aramaic. Moreover, though we may well suppose that some non-Jewish soldiers and merchants must have picked up a certain amount of Hebrew or Aramaic, we have no evidence that any non-Jew in antiquity[81] ever mastered Hebrew or any other Near Eastern language in order to study the sacred books of the East in the original. Hence, the use of Aramaic and of Hebrew served as a constant barrier against assimilation.

Consider once again the significance of the decree issued during the war of Quietus (115 C.E.) forbidding the teaching of Greek. Actually, it tells us nothing about the extent of the knowledge of Greek at an earlier period. Bear in mind that the Talmud mentions the patriarch, Rabban Gamaliel II (*Baba Qamma* 83a, *Sotah* 49b), as an exception in that he was permitted during the previous century to teach Greek culture to his students.[82] Further, the rabbis challenge the patriarch himself for teaching Greek, implying the strength of their discontent.

As for the Greek coins that have been found in the Land of Israel, those of the Hasmoneans in the second and first centuries B.C.E. bear legends in Greek and in Hebrew,[83] whereas those of the Herodians in the first century B.C.E. and the first century C.E. feature Greek alone. Coins with both languages may mean only that the rulers realized that the coins would be handled not only by Jews but also by non-Jews, who must have been numerous in the Land of Israel. If Herod and his sons, as well as the Roman procurators, placed only Greek inscriptions on their coins, this illustrates either their disregard of the sentiments of the Jewish masses or the degree to which the Greek language had penetrated the economic, but not necessarily the cultural and religious, structure of Jewish life.

Furthermore, the fact that two-thirds of the graffiti on ossuaries are in Greek would seem to show that Greek had entered into everyday life—or death, at any rate. Hengel cites a climactic bit of evidence—a *graffito* in the form of a love poem from Marisa, in which a courtesan exults over a lover to whom she has shown the door, keeping his coat as a pledge.[84] Hengel likewise cites the two famous warning inscriptions found in Jerusalem which prohibit Gentiles from entering the inner precincts of the Temple (*CII* 2.1400), the inscription dedicated to a donor from Rhodes who paid for a stone pavement on or near the Temple Mount in Jerusalem,[85] and the inscription presumed to be from Seleucid military settlers in the Acra in Jerusalem.[86] Moreover, at a cemetery in Beth Shearim, Greek dominates in a majority of epitaphs for rabbis.

As for the ossuaries, they range in date up to the third century C.E., and the very earliest are from the second century B.C.E., a full century after Hengel claims the Land of Israel had been thoroughly Hellenized.[87] To confirm his point that Jews in the first century were trilingual, Hengel cites a new discovery of an ossuary found near Jerusalem belonging to the granddaughter of Theophilus, who was high priest between 37 and 41; but the inscription itself is in Aramaic, and the only Greek element in it is the Greek origin of the name Theophilus.[88] As for the scandalous graffito from Marisa, it turns out to be not Jewish but Sidonian; and to suggest that proximity to another people's immorality would necessarily have corrupted Jews is extravagant, especially when the Jews looked with such contempt upon the Sidonians. As for the warning inscriptions, they tell us nothing about the degree to which Greek had penetrated Jewish life, inasmuch as they are clearly directed to non-Jews. The inscription from the Rhodian Jew can tell us what we already know, namely that the predominant language of the Jews in Rhodes was Greek. Furthermore, the inscription of Seleucid military settlers, as Bar-Kochva has demonstrated, is not of Jews but of Hellenistic soldiers, as the oath by Ares would seem to indicate.[89] As for the rabbinic cemetery at Beth Shearim, not until the end of the second century C.E. did it become an important center for burials.[90] Moreover, of the synagogue inscriptions found thus far in the Land of Israel, though they range in date from the first to the seventh centuries, by which time Greek should really have become predominant, less than a quarter (about 30 of 140) are in Greek, the rest being in Hebrew or Aramaic.

Goldstein has suggested that one of the routes of contact with Hellenism was through Greek tourists with philosophic training and that these tourists found the Jews so interesting that Jews may have been pestered for some time by visiting "philosophers" just as modern primitives are by anthropologists today.[91] Yet the only citable examples of such "philosophers" are Hecataeus of Abdera and Megasthenes; and the latter is so similar to Theophrastus and to Clearchus of Soli in his views that we may guess that he derived his information from them without necessarily visiting Judaea.[92]

What about Hellenization through contact with the multitudes of Diaspora Jews, most of whom were Greek-speaking from at least 270 B.C.E. and who came to Jerusalem each year for the three pilgrimage festivals? Two of these festivals lasted a full week, and pilgrims generally planned to arrive early. According to Josephus (*War* 6.425), at any rate, there were approximately 2,700,000 Jews[93] in Jerusalem who partook of the Passover lambs when the war against the Romans began in 66 C.E. The overwhelming majority of these were certainly not from Jerusalem, estimates of whose population vary from 25,000 to 82,500 or 220,000.[94] In addition, because of the tremendous success of the Jewish proselytizing movement, as we shall see,[95] there must have been many Greek-speaking proselytes in the Land of Israel. Indeed, according to Philo (*De Specialibus Legibus* 1.12.69), "countless multitudes from countless cities come, some over land, others over sea, from east and west and north and south at every feast." Moreover, Hengel postulates that the court of Herod, which was surely dominated by the spirit of Hellenism with its game hunting, gymnastics, musical and dramatic performances, and chariot races, must have attracted visitors.[96]

However, we must allow for exaggeration on the part of Philo[97] and Josephus, and we must assume that most of the pilgrims came from the Land of Israel itself,[98] whose Jewish population was at least 700,000, with 5,000,000 as an overly generous maximum and 2,000,000[99] as the most reasonable estimate. Doubtless many Diaspora Jews were reluctant to make a pilgrimage, especially in view of the precarious conditions of travel. Indeed, even Philo, wealthy as he was and living in comparative proximity in Alexandria, came only once, so far as we know (*De Providentia* 2.64). In any case, our figures in Josephus, for whatever they are worth, are for the year 66, not necessarily for an earlier period and surely not for the period after the destruction of the Temple, when the numbers of Diaspora Jews coming to Jerusalem surely decreased. Furthermore, we have no firm figures for the number of proselytes. Moreover, as for the attractions that Herod's court allegedly had for visitors, we have no evidence at all of this in Josephus; and, in view of Herod's religious deviations and personal misbehavior, we may guess that he was hardly an attraction for Jews who took all the trouble to come to Jerusalem to pay their respects to the Temple.

Geographically, the Jews of the Land of Israel were surrounded by non-Jewish lands where Greek was widely, though hardly exclusively,[100] spoken; and even within the Land there were some thirty Greek cities[101] where Hellenization was, as the archaeologists have shown, far advanced. But, as Tcherikover[102] has noted, not a single Greek urban community was founded in Judaea, nor did Hellenism, with few exceptions, become deeply rooted in Samaria or Idumaea. Only a relatively small percentage of the Jews lived in the larger cities, such as Jerusalem or Caesarea, where contacts with non-Jews in commercial and governmental matters, and hence with the Greek language and perhaps with Greek culture, were more frequent. The average Jew had little if anything to do with overseas commerce, because, as Josephus (*Against Apion* 1.60) remarks and as we have noted, "Ours is not a maritime country; neither commerce nor the intercourse which it promotes with the outside world has any attraction for us." The great majority of Jews, as he goes on to say, and as is clear from rabbinic literature, were farmers, most of whom had very small plots of land.

8. Hellenization in Lower vs. Upper Galilee during the Hasmonean and Roman Periods

Apparently, the most densely populated area of the Land of Israel was Galilee, according to Josephus (*Life* 235), who, as a general there, should have known a good deal, even if he exaggerates, about the make-up of the Land and its population. There were 204 villages, the smallest with 15,000 inhabitants (*War* 3.43). This leads to a minimum of 3,060,000 people, the attractions of urban life notwithstanding.[103] It is not surprising that most of the inscriptions from the Galilean region come from such Greek cities as Ptolemais, Tyre, Carmel, and Scythopolis.[104] Not until the second century c.e. do we begin to find Greek inscriptions from synagogues.

There seems good reason to draw a distinction in degree of Hellenization between Lower Galilee and Upper Galilee, because the latter is almost devoid of Greek epigraphy and its art is limited mainly to menorahs, eagles,[105] and simple decorative elements.[106] Here we find no zodiacs with Greek inscriptions nor mosaics with richly ornamented designs.[107] Lower Galilee had several sizable urban centers that were linked to the more pagan, cosmopolitan (and Greek-speaking) West;[108] and it was in Lower Galilee, significantly, that Jesus spent most of his career. Meyers is probably wrong to speculate that the negative reflections of the later Talmudic sages on first-century Galilee and some of the clichés in the New Testament about Galilee (e.g., John 7:52) stem more from the degree of accommodation to Hellenism than from a presumed rural and agricultural Judaism;[109] for the rabbis do not focus their attacks on places that were really Hellenized, such as Caesarea. Indeed, genuine contact with the pagans must have been slight, because on only one occasion (Matt 6:7, whose historicity is suspect) does Jesus refer to pagan practices, namely when he criticizes the Gentiles heaping up empty phrases in their prayers. Even this thought might have come to him from his reading of the biblical account (1 Kgs 18:26–27) of the contest be-tween Elijah and the prophets of Baal. As Meyers has noted, not only is representational art more conservative in Upper Galilee than in Lower Galilee even as late as the third and fourth centuries c.e., and not only is there a striking paucity of depictions of the Torah shrine in particular,[110] but there is also a prevailing attachment to Hebrew and Aramaic and a unique ceramic repertory, such as is lacking in Judaea and is present to a lesser degree in Lower Galilee.

Even during the procuratorial period in the first century, as Avi-Yonah[111] has argued, Upper Galilee and apparently the western Golan were not, for practical purposes, under Roman control. The explanation for the transfer of Jewish settlers to Upper Galilee after the wars with Rome may be that they wished to escape the Hellenization that had by that time begun to overtake Jewish settlements elsewhere,[112] just as in our own day Hasidic communities have begun to leave the "Pale of Settle-ment" in Brooklyn for such relatively remote areas as Monroe County, New York. But even in Lower Galilee, the people, as portrayed by Jo-sephus, were deeply religious in theory and in practice, and presumably only minimally affected by Hellenism.

9. Cultural Contacts between Greeks and Jews during the Hasmonean and Roman Periods: Education and Literature

The existence of gymnasiums in Phoenician and in other cities of Pal-estine must have abetted the intellectual influence of Hellenism in non-Jewish Palestine, especially in Gadara, where we find such names as Meleager the poet in the mid-second century b.c.e., Philodemus the phi-losopher in the mid-first century b.c.e., Theodore the orator who in-structed the future emperor Tiberius (Suetonius, *Tiberius* 57) at the end of the first century b.c.e., and Oenomaus the Cynic philosopher at the beginning of the second century c.e. Stephanus of Byzantium mentions that the great Platonist Antiochus who lived during the first century b.c.e., as well as three Stoic philosophers, two grammarians, and two historians,[113] lived in the coastal city of Ashkelon. According to Hengel, Applebaum's claim that a gymnastic education must have necessitated the betrayal of Judaism is probably too sweeping; but inasmuch as atten-dance in the gymnasium entailed observing pagan festivals, it is hard not to agree with Applebaum.[114]

And yet the presence of gymnasiums in Phoenician and other cities of the Land of Israel does not mean that Jews attended them; indeed, there is no evidence that they did, except during the brief period of the high priesthood of Jason (2 Mac 4:9–12). Moreover, to argue that because

Hellenism profoundly influenced several non-Jewish writers in Palestine, it must have influenced Jews is to rely on the unproven assumption that there were meaningful cultural contacts between Gentiles and Jews; we know of such contacts only with Oenomaus (*Hagigah* 15b).

In a recent book Harris notes that Josephus refers in passing to eight sports buildings in the Land of Israel and argues that there were hardly enough Gentiles there to fill them.[115] Inasmuch as the rabbis (*'Avodah Zarah* 18b) inveigh against those who visit stadia, the apparent popularity of athletics would seem to be an instance of pagan influence. But when we consider that in 66 the Gentile inhabitants of Caesarea (*War* 2.457) massacred twenty thousand Jews, we must presuppose a large non-Jewish population; many thousands of Roman troops, moreover, were ready at all times to view athletic contests. Likewise, the presence of theaters and amphitheaters in such cities as Jerusalem and Jericho is hardly evidence that sizable numbers of Jews attended them, because Josephus (*Ant.* 15.268) describes theaters and amphitheaters as "alien to Jewish custom."[116]

In fact, Morton Smith, after contending that Greek influence had commenced long before Alexander and that it was already deep-seated through repeated military conquests and economic and administrative penetration, is forced to admit that the factors behind the changes called Hellenization were not universally, or even primarily, Greek, but rather Persian.[117] After enumerating seven major differences between classical and Hellenistic culture, he concludes that except for one, the importance of written law, the Hellenistic world more closely resembled Persia or Egypt than it did classical Greece. In particular, we may note a Persian parallel to the motif that there will be six thousand years from the beginning of time to the final judgment of humanity by fire, and its Talmudic counterpart (*Sanhedrin* 97a–b), which quotes the *Tanna de-vei Eliyahu* as declaring that the world is to exist for six thousand years, the last two thousand of which will be the Messianic era; and this, according to tradition, will culminate in the Last Judgment.[118]

Narrative romance with erotic motifs, such as the stories of Esther, Tobit, and Judith, and the *Testament of Joseph*, is said to derive its form from the Hellenistic period. In particular, the *Testament of Joseph*, dating in its original form from perhaps the second or first century B.C.E., supposedly shows the influence of Euripides' *Hippolytus*.[119] It has also been alleged that the account of the rebellion and fall of the watchmen angels in the Ethiopian Enoch 6–11 shows the influence of the Greek story of Prometheus;[120] but it is more likely that a common Oriental source had influenced Hesiod in his account.[121] Similarly, the pseudepigraphon, a typical Hellenistic product, has abundant Greek parallels. Yet Greek influence on erotic motifs of certain books of the Bible, Apocrypha, and

Pseudepigrapha is unprovable, because such motifs are found in Egyptian and Iranian sources also and may have influenced the Bible by that route.

Furthermore, in the Slavonic Apocalypse of Enoch (30.3–5) we find the Greek names of the planets, and the order preserved is in partial agreement with that of the Greek physicists (cf. Cicero, *De Divinatione* 2.43.91), as Matthews[122] notes; but we may remark that astronomy was a science that knew no bounds, geographical or theological, and Greek influence is not necessarily implied.

It has likewise been postulated that Alexandrian wisdom speculation, which we meet for the first time in the Graeco-Jewish philosopher Aristobulus, who lived during the middle of the second century B.C.E., had its origins in the Land of Israel. But we hear amazingly little in Philo, Josephus, or the Talmud of contact between Alexandria and the Land.

Indeed, we may well speculate that if we had the writings of the revolutionaries who opposed Rome rather than those of Josephus, we might well conclude that there was much less Hellenization than there actually was. After all, even the procurator Pontius Pilate was shocked at the power of the Jewish resistance to his attempt to introduce busts of the emperor (*War* 2.169–74, *Ant.* 18.55–62).

Even such ultra-pious Jewish sects as the Essenes and the Dead Sea Sect are said to have had contact with Hellenism. Thus, the Essenes' stress on the ordering of the world, even before creation, and in the divine plans points to analogies with the hymn to Zeus of Cleanthes.[123] Noting that astrological fragments have been found among the Dead Sea fragments, Hengel declares that astral and solar theologizing could never have gained such significance had it not been for the victorious progress of astrology in the Hellenistic era. He furthermore argues that there are direct points of contact in the military technique of the War Scroll, which he postulates is based on a Hellenistic book of tactics.[124] Moreover, the form of the Essene community reminds us of the law of associations in the Hellenistic period.[125]

Indeed, the presence of Greek documents in the Dead Sea caves would indicate that knowledge of Greek had penetrated even the most fanatical religious groups. Most strikingly, a manuscript of the Minor Prophets in Greek has been found in the Dead Sea caves. It is possible, however, that the scroll was brought by a more worldly person, who had decided to join the sect and who presented the scroll to the sect's library so that the leaders of the sect might be able to refute their opponents. In any case, as we can see increasingly as the manuscripts found in the caves are published, the library of the sect contained a wide diversity of views and not merely those of the sect itself. Moreover, the vast majority of Qumran texts are in Hebrew or Aramaic and contain no Greek loanwords. It is at least as likely that the Essenes' idea of dualism was derived from Iranian influence as that it came from the Greeks or from an Alexandrian Jewish source; after all, the library at Alexandria included two million lines of the writings of Zarathustra.[126]

What about the astrological fragments?[127] Astrology predates the Greeks; in particular, the Babylonians cultivated it. Isaiah (47:12–13), moreover, already attacks astrologers. As for the monastic-like form of the Essene community, it seems most likely that the Essenes would have avoided drawing on Hellenistic laws of association because they abhorred all alien influences.[128] They may well have owed their monastic ideals to the tradition of the Rechabites mentioned by the prophet Jeremiah (chapter 35). Finally, even if there was Hellenistic influence on the Essenes, we must recall that Philo and Josephus agree in giving the total number of Essenes as a mere four thousand;[129] despite the attention Josephus devotes to them, their influence on the rest of the Jews was not great.

The Jewish historian Eupolemus (to be distinguished from pseudo-Eupolemus), who wrote a history of the Jews in the middle of the second century B.C.E., composed a work in Greek, fragments of which have come down to us. Its linguistic and stylistic deficiences are so serious that, according to Hengel, it can hardly have been composed in Alexandria.[130] Holladay, in his recent edition, lays stress on Eupolemus's use of Hebrew measuring units, notably *cors*.[131] Furthermore, Fallon has noted that Eupolemus's rendering of the name of Hiram and his translation of terms that the Septuagint has merely transliterated argue for his use of the Hebrew text and hence for a provenance from the Land of Israel.[132] To argue that Eupolemus must have composed his work in Judaea rather than in Alexandria because his Greek is deficient, however, is to assume that every Alexandrian Jew wrote Greek as well as Philo did and that everyone in the Land of Israel wrote it as poorly as did the authors of the graffiti. If, as Hengel asserts, the Jews of the Land of Israel were so deeply Hellenized, they should have written Greek much better than Eupolemus did. Moreover, the *cors* appear in the Septuagint (1 Kgs 5:11), which Eupolemus certainly knew, and they reflect commercial contact with the Land of Israel. As for Eupolemus's rendering of the name Hiram and his translation of terms that are merely transliterated in the Septuagint, we may suggest that such data may have been available to the author separately. After all, we have found papyri that give the same etymologies of Hebrew names as are found in Philo.[133]

Finally, it seems hard to believe that if Eupolemus was a Jew, a priest, a historian of the biblical period, a friend of the Hasmoneans, and an inhabitant of the Land of Israel, Josephus, who was all of these, should not have drawn on him as a source. In fact, when Josephus mentions

Eupolemus (*Against Apion* 1.218), Josephus cites him together with Demetrius of Phalerum and the Elder Philo, apparently as non-Jews, because he speaks of them as not accurately following the meaning of "our" records. Likewise, those who identify this Eupolemus with the Eupolemus, the ambassador of Judah the Maccabee to Rome who is mentioned in 1 Maccabees 8:17–18 and 2 Maccabees 4:11, have to explain how a Jew from the Land of Israel could have referred to David, the most famous of all Jewish kings and the ancestor of the awaited Messiah, as the son of Saul (quoted in Eusebius, *Praeparatio Evangelica* 9.30.3).[134] Of course, Josephus could be wrong with regard to Eupolemus, or he might be guilty of misrepresenting the facts. But this is unlikely in a work as well crafted as the treatise *Against Apion*, clearly Josephus's most careful work. He had to be especially diligent in his research because he had taken upon himself the burden of defending his people against the attacks of the numerous and vicious anti-Jewish bigots of his day, who would have reduced him to absurdity if they could have found him either less than accurate in his citations or guilty of misrepresentation.

Because the contents of the five books of Jason of Cyrene, whose history is summarized in 2 Maccabees, refer completely to Judaea, it has been conjectured that the author had a lengthy stay there and knew Aramaic and Hebrew.[135] But most scholars, though admittedly there is no definitive evidence, regard Jason of Cyrene as having received his rhetorical training in Alexandria.[136] The evidence that he spent a lengthy period in the Land of Israel is at best circumstantial.

Some have suggested that the Second Book of Maccabees, which dates most probably during the early years of the reign of John Hyrcanus (135–104 B.C.E.) and which is written in an ornate Greek style, rich in poetic metaphor, pathos, drama, and rhetoric, and reminiscent of the flowery, ornate style of many Hellenistic Greek historians, was composed in Jerusalem.[137] Whereas the fervor for the Jerusalem Temple is said to be a strong argument for composition in Jerusalem,[138] a similar fervor for the Temple is found in the *Letter of Aristeas*, which, in all probability, was written by an Alexandrian Jew about 100 B.C.E. (or somewhat earlier), not long after the probable date of the Second Book of Maccabees. At about the same time, we may conjecture, Philo the Elder, in all probability an Alexandrian Jew, composed a lengthy epic on Jerusalem in fourteen (or four) books in rhetorical Homeric hexameters.[139]

Granted, a few books in Greek were composed in Palestine. Thus, the colophon of the Greek book of Esther indicates that the translation was done in Jerusalem in the latter part of the second century B.C.E. Moreover, it is against this background that we can understand the transformation of Haman into a Macedonian who sought to betray the Persian kingdom to the Macedonians. Furthermore, Hengel points out that the

Greek of the additions to this book is substantially better than that of the translated passages.[140] Likewise, in the first century B.C.E., the infamous Herod the Great wrote memoirs in Greek, now completely lost, cited by Josephus (*Ant.* 15.174) as the source of one account of the execution of the high priest Hyrcanus.[141] Furthermore, in the first century C.E., Josephus's rival, Justus of Tiberias, wrote *A Chronicle of the Jewish Kings* and *A History of the Jewish War*, neither of which is extant; and even Josephus, grudgingly (*Life* 40) to be sure, has to admit that Justus was not unversed in Greek culture, a fact confirmed by Justus's later elevation to the role of private secretary to King Agrippa II of Judaea in the latter part of the first century.

Of course, the supreme example of Hellenization in literature of a Jew from the Land of Israel is Josephus himself, particularly in his paraphrase of the Bible.[142] Yet we must emphasize that he wrote all his works in Rome and not in Jerusalem; that, as we have noted, he needed assistants (*Against Apion* 1.50) to help him with the Greek of the *Jewish War*; and that when he did not have these assistants, as apparently was the case in the *Antiquities*, his style suffered considerably. Indeed, Josephus, who is not known for modesty, theorizes (*Ant.* 20.263) that the habitual use of his native tongue prevented his attaining precision in the pronunciation of Greek. It is important, moreover, to realize that Josephus addresses his *magnum opus*, the *Antiquities*, to non-Jews primarily, as is clear from the statement that his work was undertaken in the belief that the whole Greek world would find it worthy of attention (*Ant.* 1.5) and from the precedent he cites, namely, the Septuagint (*Ant.* 1.10), which, according to the traditional version in the *Letter of Aristeas*, was undertaken about 270 B.C.E. at the behest of a non-Jewish king, Ptolemy II Philadelphus. We may well ask why he did not address it to Jews (except incidentally, in such a passage as *Antiquities* 4.197), if Hellenization cut as deep as Hengel asserts it did. We may also ask why, if Hellenization was so profound, Philo never refers to the Hellenized writers of the Land of Israel and why Josephus refers only once to Philo as a writer (*Ant.* 18.259) and fails to refer to the Hellenistic Jewish historians as Jewish (*Against Apion* 1.218).

On the other hand, an impressive series of works in Hebrew and in Aramaic emanate from the Land of Israel, the only Near Eastern land that, so far as we know, produced such a range of works in its own language(s). Even such natives of Egypt and Babylonia as Manetho and Berossus, as early as the beginning of the third century B.C.E., wrote their histories in Greek. No other people had a sacred book comparable to the Bible as a national history, as a decisive influence on its national consciousness, and as a means to maintain continuity with the past. If

Egypt maintained its national identity and even "counterattacked" by spreading the worship particularly of Isis and Osiris and Sarapis to Greece and to Italy, and produced a literature to show that the Greek gods, literature, and inventions all came from Egypt, this is not so remarkable in view of the sheer number of Egyptians and the long and almost uninterrupted (except for the Hyksos) history of national independence until the Persian era. But in the case of Israel, such factors were not present, and yet the Jews were remarkably successful in winning converts and "sympathizers."

10. Alleged Greek Influence on the Talmudic Rabbis in the First Five Centuries c.e.

The coup de grâce of those who, like Hengel, argue that Hellenization in the Land of Israel was profound is that even the Talmudic rabbis themselves were deeply influenced by the language and thought of the Greeks. The argument depends on the assumption that although the rabbis themselves date from a later period, namely the first five centuries c.e., the language and methodology of their discussions reflect a much earlier era. A number of tales about the late first-century b.c.e. Hillel recall Socratic and Cynic anecdotes.[143] Joshua ben Ḥananiah's discussions with Athenians, Alexandrians, and Roman philosophers at the end of the first century c.e.,[144] Rabbi Meir's reported disputations during the second century c.e. with the Cynic Oenomaus of Gadara (*Genesis Rabbah* 68.20),[145] as well as Judah ha-Nasi's discussions at the end of the second century with the emperor "Antoninus," would seem to reflect rabbinic interest in and concern about Hellenism. Countless examples have been marshaled by a host of writers—notably Saul Lieberman, David Daube, Yitzhak Baer, Elimelekh E. Halevi, and Henry Fischel[146]—to show that the rabbis were influenced not merely in their vocabulary (approximately twenty-five hundred to three thousand different words in the Talmudic corpus are of Greek origin) but also in their method of Platonic-like dialectic, as well as in their techniques of analysis and in their motifs.

Fischel has noted a number of changes that took place in the Hebrew language during the rabbinic period and suggests that they are due to Greek influence: the gradual weakening of laryngeals, the dissolution of the construct case into a prepositional phrase, and the frequency of an absolute nominative before conditional clauses resembling the Greek genitive absolute. He has postulated the same explanation for certain parallels in phraseology (for example, Greek κακογλωσσία, "evil tongue," and Hebrew *lashon ha-ra*), in semantics (for example, Greek σχολαστικός, "scholar," and Hebrew *batlan*, both referring to one who has leisure;

Greek οἰκουμένη, "habitation," and Hebrew *yishuv*), in change of gender (for example, Greek βακτηρία and ῥάβδος, "staff," influence Hebrew *maqqel* to become feminine), in the increase of reflexive verbs, and in new properties of prepositions. Moreover, new Hebrew roots are created from Greek, notably *k-r-z*, "proclaim," from κηρύσσω; *h-g-n*, "be proper," from ἀξιόω; *p-y-s*, "pacify," from παύω; *t-g-n*, "fry," from ταγηνίζω; *t-k(k)-s*, "arrange," from τάσσω; *s-m-n*, "signify," from σημαίνω; and *q-t-r-g*, "accuse," from κατηγορέω.[147]

It is significant, however, that the words borrowed from Greek appear in such realms as military affairs, politics, law, administration, trade, items of food, clothing, household utensils, and building materials, and almost never in religious, philosophical, or literary passages. In addition, although there is no indication as to when these words were borrowed, they appear in the Talmudic corpus, which was not finally codified until the end of the fourth and fifth centuries C.E., and in midrashic works, which, for the most part, were composed even later. Goldstein has stressed the significance of the absence in Jewish texts of verbs comparable to Latin *pergraecare* or nouns such as *graeculus*, which show disdain for the Greeks.[148] If they were really disturbed by Hellenization, the rabbis could have used the verb Ἑλληνίζειν ("to speak Greek, Hellenize") as the church fathers did and could have employed *yavan* ("Greece") or *yevanim* ("Greeks") as terms of reproach. Yet there is no trace of such expressions. Moreover, the rabbis would hardly have said such favorable things about Alexander the Great if, in their opinion, his arrival had marked the beginning of assimilation.

To be sure, analogies have been noted between rabbinic thought and Greek philosophy, especially Platonism and Stoicism, in cosmology, in the doctrine of the immortality of the soul, and in ethics.[149] We may cite, for example, the parallel between the rabbinic view (*Niddah* 30b) that the embryo in the womb of its mother has been taught all the Torah from beginning to end and the Platonic view (*Meno* 81–86) that before one is born one has true knowledge and that this knowledge is subject to recollection (ἀνάμνησις) through skillful questioning. But the nature of the knowledge, namely of the Forms, that the Platonic embryo has is very different from the knowledge possessed by the embryo described by the rabbis, namely the text of the Torah. Moreover, Plato insists that the knowledge possessed by the embryo can be recalled through skillful questioning, whereas the rabbis do not speak at all of recalling this knowledge.

Likewise, Stoic rules for health, for the table, and for the toilet seem to be similar. Other parallels may be found in the emphasis on the simple life, fortitude, the ethos of work, generosity, the contrast between theory and practice, the contrast between the good and the merely valuable, and new interpretations of suffering. The rabbis are also said to be influenced by the Stoic-rhetorical literary forms, such as catalogues of virtues and vices, sorites (that is, heaps of syllogisms, where the predicate of the first becomes the subject of the second, until the last predicate is equated with the first subject), consolation formulae (for example, that life is a deposit to be returned to the original owner, G-d), eristic dialogues, diatribic sequences, certain similes (for example, with athletics and with civic life; life as a deposit from G-d) and comparisons (for example, G-d is to the world as the soul is to the body), speculation as to the origin of the soul, the concept of Divine providence and of man as a colleague of G-d, the notion of *imitatio D-i*, an attempt to explain suffering as a sign of Divine love, the belief that it is sin but not the sinner that is to be eliminated, the maxim that one should not judge others until one is in the other's place, the emphasis on action in order to improve life, the stress on marriage and family life, the stress on filial piety, the concept of the merits of ancestors, the conflict between self-preservation and love of one's fellow, the advice to follow the middle path, the injunction not to act because of a possible reward, the avoidance of swearing, the stress on cleanliness of body, the notion that the soul is a guest, the advice that one should constantly think of death, the premium on the moral life as of the highest worth, and the ideal of wisdom.[150] That there was contact between Jews and Stoics would seem to be supported by the fact that the first-century Stoic philosopher, Epictetus, is aware (quoted in Arrian, *Dissertationes* 1.11.12–13, 1.22.4) of the Jewish dietary laws, as well as (quoted in Arrian, *Dissertationes* 2.9.19–21) of the requirement of immersion in a ritual pool for those who wish to convert to Judaism. The very fact that Josephus, who allied himself with the Pharisees (*Life* 12), declares that the Pharisees, with whom the Talmudic rabbis are most closely associated, nearly resemble the Stoics in their views (ibid.) and that he states (*Against Apion* 2.168) that the Stoic view of the nature of G-d was similar to that of Moses further appears to argue for a connection between the Stoics and the rabbis.

Nevertheless, as for Stoic influence on the rabbis, Lieberman rightly states that many of the ethical aphorisms alleged to be derived from the Stoics might have been formulated by any intelligent person raised on the teachings of the Bible.[151] Others are commonplaces found independently among various peoples. Moreover, even Bergmann admits that the Stoic philosophy lacks the warmth of religiosity which permeates the rabbinic teachings, that its religion is the pantheism so abhorrent to Judaism, that its ethics is based on intellectual sanction rather than on divine authority, and that its notions of sin and of charity are radically different from those held by the rabbis.[152]

There would also appear to be a number of parallels between Epicurean and rabbinic dicta, notably the concept of study for its own sake (Epicurus, Vatican fragment 45 and *Avoth* 6:1), the removal of doubt (Epicurus, *Life* 121b and *Avoth* 1:16), mortality and urgency (Vatican fragment 10 and *Avoth* 2:15), the acquisition of a companion (Epicurus, *To Menoeceus*, end, and *Avoth* 1:6), a diet of bread and water (Bailey, fragments of Epicurus 37 and *Avoth* 4:1), satisfaction with one's lot (Bailey, fragments 69–70 and *Avoth* 4:1), avoidance of public office (Bailey, fragments of Epicurus 85–87 and *Avoth* 1:10–11, 2:3), and, indeed, the very concept of the centrality of the sage.[153] But although the rabbis know the term *Apiqoros* (that is, Epicurean), and Rabbi Eleazar ben Arakh (*Avoth* 2:14) in the second half of the first century c.e. says that one should "know what to reply to an Epicurean," the specific doctrines that are equated would seem to be commonplaces.

Fischel has noted a number of parallels between witty anecdotes told about the Cynics, especially Diogenes, and those related about such first- and second-century rabbis as Hillel, Eliezer ben Hyrcanus, Joshua ben Hananiah, Meir, and Akiva, particularly those emphasizing such values as endurance, poverty, lowly toil, strenuous effort, and avoidance of worry.[154] To be sure, Rabbi Meir's colloquy (*Hagigah* 15b) with the second-century Cynic philosopher Oenomaus of Gadara may reflect personal contacts between the Cynics and the rabbis; and, indeed, the term *Qinuqos* (*Qoniqos*, that is "Cynic"; Jerusalem Talmud, *Gittin* 7.1.48c), referring to a destructive person, similarly indicates contacts with this popular philosophy, which was preached from street corners. But again the parallels would appear to be commonplaces that are insufficiently distinctive.

Lieberman feels that Baer has misinterpreted the passages cited as indicating Platonic influence.[155] Both Wolfson and Lieberman, who, in our generation, knew both the Greek philosophical and rabbinic traditions with great thoroughness, say that they are unable to find any purely philosophical Greek term in rabbinic literature.[156] Nowhere in the rabbinic corpus do we find the names of Socrates, Plato, or Aristotle. We may well wonder about the Greek philosophic influence on people who regard Oenomaus of Gadara (ca 120 c.e.) as the greatest Gentile philosopher of all time (*Genesis Rabbah* 68.20). Comparing the attitude of the rabbis in medieval Babylonia and Spain toward Greek philosophy, we see a striking difference; in the Middle Ages many of the writings of Plato and Aristotle were translated into Arabic and Hebrew and annotated. On the other hand, not a single Jew from the Land of Israel in antiquity distinguished himself in philosophy. The nameless one who impressed Aristotle in Asia Minor, as we have suggested above, inhabits an anecdote clearly wrapped in legend.

As for parallels in the field of law, although there are nearly two hundred Greek and Latin terms of law, narrowly defined, in rabbinic literature, the vast majority appear only in aggadic texts (containing homiletic expositions of the Bible), less than fifty appear in halakhic (legal) contexts, and remarkably few actually entered the rabbis' legal vocabulary.[157] Of the handful that did become an integral part of rabbinic Hebrew—for example, *perozebbol*, which is associated with Hillel—the strange fact is that they were all absorbed early in the rabbinic period. In other words, as time went on, far from becoming more susceptible to Greek and Latin influence, the rabbis became more resistant. Most amazingly, despite the development of the great system of Roman law at almost the exact time as the development of the great system of Talmudic law, and though a much larger percentage of the legal terms in the Talmudic corpus come from Latin than had been previously thought, not a single one entered the rabbis' active legal vocabulary.[158] Indeed, as Katzoff points out, efforts to find traces of the influence of Roman law on Jewish legal institutions have failed to reach firm conclusions.[159]

As for the methods of rabbinic exegesis, the use of allegory in scriptural interpretation is hardly due to Greek influence, inasmuch as parables are found in the Bible (e.g., Nathan's parable, 1 Sam 12:1–7). Even if we say, as does Matthews, that the Greeks, starting with Theagenes of Rhegium in the sixth century B.C.E., were unique in seeing a universal application in their method of application, the rabbis do not go beyond the biblical model in their application of the method.[160]

As for logical methods of exegesis, *gezerah shavah*, the comparison of similar expressions, seems to translate literally the strange phrase κατὰ τὸ ἴσον or σύγκρισις πρὸς ἴσον, "decree with the equal."[161] In fact, the Greek phrase, in contrast to the term σύγκρισις alone, is found for the first time in extant Greek literature in the second century in Hermogenes,[162] whereas Hillel (Tosefta, *Sanhedrin* 7, end) used the Hebrew term in the second half of the first century B.C.E. Further, the Greek and the Hebrew terms are used in totally different ways. Moreover, the distinction between the written and oral law (found both in Greek thought, in Sophocles' *Antigone* [454–55], for example, and in rabbinic writings) and attempts to reconcile authority and reason are commonplace in various systems of law. We must also note that the term *oral law* has a different meaning for Greeks and for Jews: For the former it refers to natural law, whereas for the latter it signifies the oral exegesis of written law.

Most recently, Shaye Cohen has noted parallels between the names of the rabbinic and philosophic schools (such as between the Garden of Epicurus, the Porch of Zeno the Stoic, and the Walk of the Peripatetics and the Vineyard of Yavneh), between the disciple circles of the rabbis and those of the Greek philosophers, and, in particular, between the testament of Rabbi Judah the Prince and those of the Greek philosophers Plato, Aristotle, Theophrastus, Strato, Lyco, and Epicurus, as cited by Diogenes Laertius.[163] He likewise notes a parallel between the entrance requirement to Rabban Gamaliel's study hall, namely that a student's inside should be like his outside, and the entrance requirement to Plato's Academy, "He who is without geometry may not enter."[164] Admittedly, we cannot find exact counterparts in extant ancient literature, but some of these parallels would seem to be insufficiently precise (for example, between a garden and a vineyard), or they would appear to be commonplace and mere common sense (that the older members of the school are considered superior to the youths, that the students sit on benches arranged in a circle, that a high official of the school is termed "wise," that the school's name is derived from the place where its sessions are held, that the will of the leader designates his successor and gives instructions regarding his funeral and offers an injunction on behalf of his widow). As for the parallel in the entrance requirements to Rabban Gamaliel's study hall and Plato's Academy, even if we adopt the explanation of the scholiast on Plato, which is rather far from the simple meaning of the original and is, in any case, several centuries after Rabban Gamaliel, namely that to be without geometry means to be unjust, there is still quite a gap between the entrance requirements of the two schools. And, as Cohen himself admits in passing, the parallels may tell us more about the Hellenization of the period when the texts were redacted, the fourth and fifth centuries, than they do about the rabbis, notably Rabbi Judah the Prince (end of the second century), of whom they speak.

The concept of a chain of authoritative transmitters of tradition, such as is found in the Mishnah of *Avoth* 1:1 ff., does parallel the chains of tradition of the heads of the Greek philosophical schools and the Roman law schools, as Hengel has noted.[165] Yet, as Momigliano has remarked, the functions of these chains are totally different, because in the Mishnah the list is used to eliminate differences of opinion between schools and, above all, to establish the existence of an originally revealed truth.[166] Furthermore, even if parallelomania (to use the term that Samuel Sandmel made famous) were to prove influence, the rabbis about whom we are speaking functioned long after the time when Hellenization was supposedly profound, that is, according to Hengel, prior to Antiochus Epiphanes. Moreover, we do not know of a single rabbi of the Talmudic period (and we know of hundreds by name) who ever composed a single original work in Greek. The one rabbi who was deeply influenced by Hellenism, Elisha ben Abuyah, is roundly condemned by the other Talmudic rabbis (*Ḥagigah* 15b). In his case, the other rabbis asked why the study of Torah did not save him from eternal condemnation, and the answer was that "Greek song did not cease from his mouth." Compare with this the Middle Ages, when Saadia, Judah Halevi, Maimonides, and many others composed important works in Arabic.

Moreover, Hengel suggests that the Talmudic curse on those who instruct their sons in Greek wisdom goes back to the period of Antiochus Epiphanes in the second century B.C.E. and indicates that before that time Greek wisdom was studied.[167] But the context in all three passages in the Talmud (*Baba Qamma* 82b, *Sotah* 49b, and *Menaḥoth* 64b) where it occurs is the civil war between Hyrcanus II and Aristobulus II in 65 B.C.E., that is, a century after the Hasmonean revolt; and the parallel passage in Josephus (*Ant.* 14.25–28), although differing in a number of details, agrees in referring the incident to the same civil war. Moreover, if we find that the patriarch Rabban Gamaliel II of Yavneh in the latter part of the first century had a thousand students, five hundred of whom studied Torah and five hundred of whom studied Greek wisdom, the passage goes on specifically to note that this seemed incomprehensible to the other scholars (*Sotah* 49b, *Baba Qamma* 82b). They later explained this as a clear aberration in the light of the patriarch's need to maintain good relations with the Roman government, with whom it was necessary to converse in Greek. If we find (*Megillah* 9b, 18a) the statement that the books of the Scripture may be written only in Greek (in addition to the original Hebrew), it is Rabban Gamaliel's son Simeon to whom this is ascribed. Moreover, it is clear that the Greek culture is not to be studied in pagan gymnasiums and academies but rather under the careful guidance and in the Torah atmosphere of the patriarch himself. In any case, the norm, as expressed in the Talmud (*Sotah* 49b, *Baba Qamma* 82b) in the very passage referring to Rabban Gamaliel's academy for the study of Greek, is expressed by the proclamation issued by the rabbis during the civil war between Hyrcanus and Aristobulus: "Cursed be the man who would teach his son Greek wisdom." Finally, the rabbis differentiated strongly between the Greek language, the beauty of which they recognized (*Megillah* 9b), and Greek culture, which they proscribed.

To be sure, Jewish circles in the Land of Israel apparently recognized Homer's epic poetry as the authoritative "book" of Greek education. Hengel cites the statement made by the Sadducees in the first century C.E. in the Mishnah (*Yadaim* 4:6) that the books of Homer do not make the hands unclean.[168] The "books of Homer" were regarded by the Greeks as their Bible, in effect;[169] and we may perhaps see here a sign that the phrase had found its way into the everyday language of Jews in the Land of Israel a long time before, perhaps going back to the period of Hellenization after 175 B.C.E. We may perhaps conjecture that in the later rabbinic period (third and fourth centuries) Homer was read in more exalted circles close to Graeco-Roman civilization.[170] And yet, even if our reading, which is disputed, is correct, and even if the reference is to the famous epic poet, the mention in the Mishnah of the books of Homer does not show that the books were known earlier than the period of the Mishnah (ca 200).[171] Indeed, despite all his efforts, Lieberman is forced to admit that it is very hard to prove that the rabbis made direct use of the *Iliad* or of the *Odyssey*.[172]

In the last analysis, Hengel's diminution of the distinction between the Land of Israel and the Diaspora fails to explain why at a later period the Land of Israel produced so many academies whereas the Diaspora in the Roman Empire produced only one academy of which we know, that of Matthiah ben Ḥeresh in Rome (*Sanhedrin* 32b), which is nowhere else referred to in classical or, for that matter, rabbinic literature. Nor does it explain why among the hundreds of rabbis mentioned in the Talmudim and in the midrashim there is not a single one from so large a Jewish community as that of Egypt. The answer would seem to be that the rabbinic influence in the Land of Israel was indeed great; and the rabbis ultimately—whether Simeon ben Shetaḥ at the beginning of the first century B.C.E. (Jerusalem Talmud, *Kethuboth* 8.11.32c) or Joshua ben Gamla in the first century C.E. (*Baba Bathra* 21a)—succeeded in setting up a system of universal elementary education for Jewish males.[173] When the Talmudic tradition delineated the greatness of a town, it gave the number of schools and schoolchildren, so that we hear that on the eve of the destruction of the Temple Jerusalem had 480 synagogues, each of which had facilities for study of the Written Torah and a school for the study of the Oral Torah (Jerusalem Talmud, *Megillah* 3.73d, *Kethuboth* 13.35c).

Certainly the sources here cited, notably Josephus and the rabbis, reflect a certain point of view and indeed create, sometimes quite consciously, a particular image of Judaism. May we not have lost the literature reflecting other views? Is it not true that one man's apostasy may be another's orthodoxy? But the question is not what the Sadducees or the Essenes, whose literature is lost, thought, because history's verdict is that they are not the mainstream of Judaism. To argue that the literature that is lost may have contradicted what has remained is the *argumentum ex silentio*, which must be used with caution.

In short, those few intellectuals, whether Jewish or non-Jewish, who did take the trouble to investigate Greek culture tended, at most, to borrow its style or scholarly techniques and methodology or logic, as perhaps the Pharisees did. They were not interested in theoretical insights, and they discarded the substance of Greek thought as irrelevant.[174]

11. GREEK INFLUENCE ON JEWISH ART

It is often alleged that at least in the realms of art and architecture the native populations in the lands ruled by Alexander and his successors assimilated Greek building styles in their temples and theaters, in their statues and pottery. But, as Green has contended, where we do find Greek styles, these appear in artificial islands of Greek settlers who were, in effect, isolated from the native populations. Hence, any Jewish adoption of Greek styles in art would be exceptional.[175]

Goodenough, however, has propounded the thesis that paganism deeply influenced Judaism during the Hellenistic period, that the rabbis had much less control over the people than Moore had postulated, and that, in fact, there was a "popular" Judaism with a mystic bent, as indicated by the symbolism of Hellenistic Jewish art, which cannot be regarded as merely decorative and which corresponds on the artistic plane to Philo on the literary and philosophical level; Goodenough further suggests that the literature that accompanied this artistic expression was proscribed by the rabbis at the time (ca 500) when the Talmud was completed.[176] That this art, indeed, reflects a Hellenization that was already deep-seated may be deduced from the haphazard, rather than careful, character, in many cases, of the drawings of pagan symbols, as, for example, in the synagogue at Beth Shearim. Goodenough would thus explain the rapid Hellenization of Christianity, which has usually been posed as a paradox, namely, the triumph of Christianity despite its Jewish origins, by declaring that Christianity was the natural heir of a deeply Hellenized Judaism. In a recent article, moreover, Shaye Cohen upholds Goodenough's claim that the rabbis in the Land of Israel did not exercise effective control over the synagogue.[177]

Though Goodenough himself made no claims that this art indicated Hellenization prior to the Maccabees, Hengel theorizes that the influence must have started at a prior period. On the contrary, however, the Jews, at least in the time of Hecataeus (ca 300 B.C.E.; cited in Josephus, *Against Apion* 1.193), avoided contact with paganism, to the extent that when pagan temples and altars were erected in Judaea "the Jews razed them all to the ground, paying, in some cases, a fine to the satraps and, in others, obtaining pardon."[178] If this is the case, once Jews who took their religion seriously were in effective control, non-Jews could hardly have resided in Judaea, inasmuch as they would not have been free to practice their religion.[179]

The archaeological evidence indicates that during the Hasmonean-Herodian period (150 B.C.E.–70 C.E.) the Jews were so completely under the spiritual domination of the Pharisees, who were so careful in the

observance of both the written and the oral law (Josephus, *Ant.* 18.12),
that they refrained from any attempt at painting and sculpture, religious
or secular, whereas after that date rabbinical control ceased to be as effective both in the Diaspora and in Palestine. This would contradict the
theory of Smith and Neusner that the differences in the portrayal of the
Pharisees in the *Jewish War*, as against the later *Antiquities*, may be explained as Josephus's attempt to portray in the *Antiquities* the Pharisees
as so influential among the people after 70 that it was impossible to gov-
ern the land of Israel without their support.[180] Goodenough postulates
increased Hellenization after the destruction of the Temple in Jerusalem
in the year 70; yet it is precisely after that date that the Pharisees,
through the establishment of the academy at Yavneh and other centers of
study, increased in power and influence among their students, yet apparently exercised less control over the masses, at least in the realm of painting and sculpture. To be sure, one reason for the difference in the
amount of symbolic art between the period before and the period after
the destruction of the Temple may be the relative paucity of excavations
for the period before 70. With regard to the supposed Hellenization
in the art of Dura-Europos in Babylonia, the paintings there show the
influence of Jewish mysticism and eschatology more than they show
Greek influence.

Did Christianity spread because Judaism had already become so thoroughly Hellenized? If so, why was this dissemination so slow, certainly at
first, as compared with the spread of Mithraism, for example, or of Judaism itself? The view that the rabbis did not control synagogues because
they permitted pagan symbols does not necessarily follow. At least as
likely is the hypothesis that the rabbis were more flexible than we often
suppose, just as they were more flexible in interpreting the laws prohibiting divination and the occult, for they had less fear of syncretism and
assimilation than we think they had. Thus, we have the tradition (*Yoma*
69b, *Sanhedrin* 64a), cited in the name of Rabbi Judah (second century)
or Rabbi Jonathan (beginning of the third century), that all idolatrous
impulses had been eradicated from among the people of Israel as early as
the beginning of the Second Temple under Ezra in the fifth century
B.C.E., as well as the corroborative statement in Judith (8:18), dating
probably from the Maccabean period in the second century B.C.E., that
idol worship had disappeared "in our generation."[181] Indeed, Lieberman
has observed that the one tractate of the Talmud which deals with idol
worship, *'Avodah Zarah*, actually features very little ridiculing of idols
and that in this respect the rabbis differ drastically from the church fathers, such as Clement of Alexandria, Athenagoras, Theophilus of Antioch, Tertullian, Arnobius, and Lactantius, who engage in violent denun-
ciations of graven images.[182] The explanation may be, to be sure, that the

Jews were afraid to indulge in such polemics. More likely, however, they felt no need to do so in view of their confidence that idol-worship by Jews was not an immediate problem or threat.

Alternatively, we may suggest, as does Smith, that the lack of decoration before 70 stems from the influence wielded by the Sadducean aristocracy, which, in the absence of concrete evidence, we may speculate, interpreted the prohibition of all artistic representation (Exod 20:4) literally.[183] In that case, the increase after 70 may reflect the heightened influence of the Pharisees, who were more liberal in their outlook. We may also note, moreover, that decoration increased in Roman art after 70.[184]

The main point here is that the thirty-three "epigraphical rabbis" noted by Cohen all date from the period 100 to 400 C.E., long after the "profound Hellenization" period before Antiochus Epiphanes.[185] Moreover, as Cohen himself admits, none of these rabbis can be identified definitely with a Talmudic rabbi; hence, we can say nothing about the influence of Greek on the Talmudic rabbis, let alone on their predecessors.

Surely the references to idolatry in Josephus indicate fierce opposition in the first century B.C.E. to Herod's introduction of pagan athletic contests, and especially to trophies containing three-dimensional images (*Antiquities* 15.267–91), and to Herod's placing of an image of an eagle at the gate of the Temple (*Ant.* 17.149–54, *War* 1.641–50).[186] Josephus (*Ant.* 15.267) claims that the Jews suffered considerable harm because Herod had corrupted their ancient way of life which had long been inviolable. Even if Josephus is exaggerating, this fact indicates that the Jews had, up until that time, resisted such practices, which Herod had introduced, as athletic contests and spectacles in an amphitheater. We may also call attention to the avoidance of divine or even of human representations of any kind on the coins of Herod Antipas, ruler of Galilee from 4 B.C.E. to 39 C.E., which were, for the most part, minted in Tiberias in Galilee.[187] Opposition to idolatry turned bitter during the first century C.E.: remember the widespread uproar against Pilate's marching his troops into Jerusalem with portraits of the emperor (*Ant.* 18.55–59, *War* 1.648–50); the opposition (*Ant.* 18.121–22) to allowing images such as were attached to Roman military standards to be brought on the soil of the Land of Israel by Vitellius, the Roman governor of Syria; the readiness to die rather than to allow the statue of the Emperor Caligula to be brought into the Temple (*Ant.* 18.257–309; *War* 2.184–203); and the destruction of the palace of Herod Antipas in Tiberias upon the outbreak of the war with the Romans in 66, simply because it contained representations of animals (*Life* 66–67).

That the Greek style of architecture was adopted for the Temple of

Jerusalem does indicate Greek influence (perhaps from Greek intellectuals, such as Nicolaus of Damascus, in Herod's court), but of a more innocuous sort. In any case that building was erected by Herod in the first century B.C.E., and there is no evidence that Greek styles were adopted earlier or later for ordinary houses. Indeed, Tacitus (*Histories* 5.5.4) remarks on the absence of images from cities and temples as one of the distinguishing marks of the Jews. The art of the ossuaries is of flat, stylized plants and birds; and it is not until the third century C.E. that we find art with three-dimensional representation, including Helios and Medusa. When this type of art does appear, it is found only in certain areas of the Land of Israel, such as the coast and Judaea, where, we may suggest, there was a maximum amount of political and commercial contact between Jews and non-Jews and a great deal of urbanization.

12. SUMMARY

In a recent work Bowersock has pointed out that the persistence of local traditions indicates that there was no more than a superficial Hellenization in much of Asia Minor, the Near East, and Egypt.[188] Even cities that seem to have all the external trappings of Greek urbanism have been shown, as he remarks, to contain within them indigenous forms of urbanization. Indeed, he concludes, the very word *Hellenization* is a useless barometer for assessing Greek culture; significantly enough, there is not even a word for it in classical or Byzantine Greek. To the extent that there was Greek influence, it was not antithetical to local traditions but rather provided a new and perhaps more eloquent way to give voice to them.

In day-to-day life in the Holy Land throughout the Hellenistic and Roman periods, however, relatively little Greek influence of importance impressed itself on the Jews. Yes, the concept of public baths may show Greek influence, as is indicated by the fact that the bathing master is known in the Mishnah (*Shevi'ith* 8:5, *Shabbath* 4:2) by a Greek name, *balan* (Greek βαλανεύς). Indeed, the rabbis realized the pagan origin of the baths, as we see perhaps in the story of Rabban Gamaliel II (Mishnah, *'Avodah Zarah* 3:4), who is criticized for bathing in the bathhouse of Aphrodite. Similarly, inns derive from Greek origins, as their name *pundak* (Greek πανδοκεῖον) would indicate. But such institutions did not bring with them indiscriminate social intermingling and assimilation, as is clear from the recurring charge in pagan literature of the Jews' unsocial character (ἀπάνθρωπόν τινα) and hostility to foreigners (μισόξενον),[189] and from Josephus's defense against this charge, for example, in King Solomon's denial (*Ant.* 8.117) that the Jews are inherently inhuman (ἀπάνθρωποι).

The very fact that tension, and even open conflict, between Jews and non-Jews was a major causative factor in the war with the Romans (66–74) would indicate that opposition to non-Jewish culture, which was an important element in this conflict, was crucial to the preservation of Jewish identity.[190] In truth, the war could hardly have lasted as long as it did (66–70, and, in the case of the Sicarii at Masada, until 74) if the revolutionaries had not had widespread popular support.

That there were so many sects of Jews (twenty-four according to the Jerusalem Talmud, *Sanhedrin* 10.6.29c)[191] may, from one point of view, be viewed as a sign of the vitality of Judaism, just as the multiplicity of Christian heresies may likewise, in a certain sense, be viewed as a sign of strength; and that the Pharisees were able to triumph over all challengers shows their power and popularity—a point made by Josephus (*Ant.* 13.288). Finally, rather than look for external factors to explain the changes in Pharisaism, one should perhaps examine internal factors in Judaism.

Is it possible to live in a sea of foreign culture without being enveloped by it? Analogies are always dangerous, and one must note that in the Land of Israel in antiquity there was no governmentally imposed Pale of Settlement such as was the case in Czarist Russia in the nineteenth century. Still, one cannot avoid developing the comparison suggested by Samuel Sandmel.[192] For hundreds of years the Jews lived in Eastern Europe surrounded by Poles, Russians, and Lithuanians. They carried on commercial dealings with them, and they even incorporated a certain number of words—*borscht*, *kasha*, and the like—from the languages spoken by the peoples among whom they lived; but, in general, they did not learn foreign languages (not even a genius such as the Gaon of Vilna, so far as we can tell, bothered to do so), or in any case they learned them in only a perfunctory way. On the other hand, they maintained their own distinctive language, Yiddish (like Aramaic, a derivative from the people among whom they once lived), together with their religious laws and customs. Occasionally, they would incorporate a non-Jewish melody into the synagogue or home service and insert Hebrew words. Why was there so little assimilation for so long, at least until the nineteenth century? The answer would seem to lie in part in the probability that the alien surroundings in Eastern Europe were not seductive, though contempt did not prevent some assimilation. Furthermore, until fairly recent times the Jews lived almost exclusively in their townlets—their *shtetlach*—analogous to the 204 villages of Galilee mentioned by Josephus (*Life* 235), maintained a strong system of education for males, heeded rabbinic leadership, and scorned the life-style of their neighbors; and all of these tendencies increased with every outbreak of anti-Judaism. In countries such as Germany, Hungary, and Czechoslovakia, Orthodox Jews did learn the language of the land, because they had an admiration for its culture, whereas most of the Jews of the Land of Israel in the Hellenistic period did not respect the non-Jewish culture of their land.

The question, then, is not how thoroughly Jews and Judaism in the Land of Israel were Hellenized, but how strongly they resisted Hellenization. In other words, what was the power of Judaism that enabled it to remain strong despite the challenge of Hellenism and later of Christianity and even to counterattack through conversion of non-Jews to Judaism? The answers may lie in its paradoxical self-confidence and defensiveness, its unity and diversity, its stubbornness and flexibility.

CHAPTER 2

THE STRENGTH OF JUDAISM
IN THE DIASPORA

1. PAGAN VIEWS ON JEWISH UNITY
AND DIVERSITY

If Judaism outside the Land of Israel was to maintain its numbers and even vastly increase, as apparently happened during the Hellenistic period (323 to 31 B.C.E.), the Jews living in the Diaspora had to be strong in their Jewish allegiance and had to prevent defections. Did this, in fact, happen?

It is perhaps hazardous to judge from pagan writers, inasmuch as they are generally poorly informed and in many cases are guilty of exaggeration as satirists and rhetoricians. Moreover, we usually depend on fragments and lack their original literary context. As for Jewish writers, Philo is primarily a philosopher and a theologian of what he sees as eternal truth and hence has remarkably little to say about the degree of observance of the contemporary Jewish community. Josephus, on the other hand, is primarily a political historian and has relatively little to say about religious and sociological currents, ancient or contemporary, and, in any case, is concerned chiefly with events in the Land of Israel.

Nevertheless, it is clear that in comments on every detail of Jewish observance the pagans, throughout the entire period of antiquity, viewed the Jews as a group, making almost no differentiation among subgroups of Jews. Thus, though the Samaritans are mentioned, they are regarded, by writers such as Quintus Curtius Rufus (*History of Alexander* 4.8.34.9), Tacitus (*Annals* 12.54.2), the author of the *Historia Augusta* (*Antoninus Heliogabalus* 3.5; *Quadrigae Tyrannorum* 7.5), and Damascius (*Vita Isidori*, cited in Photius, *Bibliotheca* 242, p. 345B) as a religious movement totally separate from the Jews. However, when it comes to the Jews, aside from the Essenes, who are singled out for their peculiar asceticism by Pliny the Elder (*Natural History* 5.73), Dio Chrysostom (cited in Synesius, *Vita Dionis*), Solinus (*Collectanea Rerum Memorabilium* 35.9–12), Porphyry (*De Abstinentia* 4.11–13), and Martianus Capella (*De Nuptiis Philologiae et Mercurii* 6.679), there is hardly any mention of division of opinion or differences in practice among them.

We find, in the very earliest mentions of Jews, that there is always a facile generalization about *the* Jews. In fact, when Aristotle, as quoted by

Clearchus of Soli and later by Josephus (quoted in *Against Apion* 1.179), tells of a Jew whom he had met in Asia Minor, he says that these people are descended from Indian philosophers and that the philosophers in Syria are called Jews, taking their name from the place. Again, Theophrastus (quoted in Porphyry, *De Abstinentia* 2.26) speaks of the Jews as being philosophers by birth, without in any way indicating that this was true of only a portion of the people.

Indeed, as we shall see, the charge of misanthropy against the Jews is based on the perception, found even in a writer as favorably disposed toward the Jews as Hecataeus (quoted in Diodorus 40.3.4), about 300 B.C.E. that Moses introduced to his Jewish followers a way of life that was hostile to foreigners (μισόξενον), that is, so that they might not have social contact with non-Jews. A similar sentiment is found in Apollonius Molon (cited in Josephus, *Against Apion* 2.258) in the first century B.C.E., when he declares that the Jews are unwilling to associate (κοινωνεῖν, "share," "form a community") with those who have chosen to live a different mode (συνήθειαν, "habit," "custom," "practice," "usage") of life. Diodorus (34[35].1.2) says that the Jews refuse to eat with other people because of their observance of their dietary laws. "The Jews," says Tacitus (*Histories* 5.5.1) in the early second century C.E., again generalizing, "are extremely loyal toward one another, and always ready to show compassion toward their fellow Jews, but toward every other people they feel only hate and enmity." In particular, he remarks (*Histories* 5.5.2) that their males abstain from intercourse with foreign women.

To be sure, Hecataeus (quoted in Diodorus 40.3.8), writing about the year 300 B.C.E., draws a distinction between the laws promulgated by Moses and those that prevailed at a later time. He says that when the Jews became subject to foreign rule, as a result of their intermingling (ἐπιμιξίας) with people of foreign nations (ἀλλοφύλων), both under Persian rule and under that of the Macedonians who succeeded them, many of their traditional practices (πατρίων νομίμων) were disturbed (ἐκινήθη, "removed," "changed"). It would appear that Hecataeus is here referring to the period of Babylonian captivity and thereafter, when many of the traditional laws were apparently forgotten or fell into disuse; but here again Hecataeus is speaking of the Jews generally and does not indicate whether some, many, or most of the Jews failed to observe the old laws. Strabo in the early part of the first century C.E. (16.2.37.761) asserts that it was Moses' successors who became more fanatic in introducing the dietary laws and circumcision, but he gives no inkling that there were differences in attitude or in degree of observance among the Jews on these or other questions. In the third century C.E. Dio Cassius (37.17.2) summarizes it all by remarking that *the* Jews are distinguished from the rest of humankind in practically every detail of life (δίαιταν, "mode of life," "regimen," "diet").[1]

What, however, must be stressed is that in all of these passages the author generalizes about *the* Jews without indicating that there are some Jews who do not fit into the stereotype or that there are various movements within the Jewish people. The only distinction, aside from the Samaritans and the special, eccentric group known as the Essenes, is between Moses's constitution and the practices introduced by his followers; but the implication is clear that in the time of the writer all Jews think and act alike, so far as their religious beliefs and practices are concerned, whether in the Land of Israel or in the Diaspora. Indeed, it is not until the end of the third century C.E. that we meet a pagan writer, Porphyry (*De Abstinentia* 4.11), who, citing Josephus's discussion, mentions the division within the Jews among the Pharisees, the Sadducees, and the Essenes.

Similarly, when we hear of the expulsion of Jews from Rome in 139 B.C.E. (Valerius Maximus, 1.3.3), there is no distinction made between those Jews who were guilty of the offense of transmitting their sacred rites to the Romans[2] and those Jews who abstained from such activities. Despite the fact that the Romans were, as a people, generally careful to observe such distinctions in law, the *praetor peregrinus* banished *the* Jews.[3]

Likewise, the Emperor Tiberius, who was known to be a stickler for legal procedure (cf., e.g., Suetonius, *Tiberius* 33), expelled the entire (πᾶν, Josephus, *Ant.* 18.83) Jewish community from Rome because four Jewish embezzlers had taken for their own personal expenses the gifts that they had induced a certain Fulvia, a woman of high rank who had become a proselyte, to send to the Temple in Jerusalem.[4] In Tacitus's version (*Annals* 2.85.4), which refers to the proscription of Egyptian and Jewish rites, it is clear that the expulsion applies to all the Jews, inasmuch as we read that four thousand descendants of enfranchised slaves were shipped to Sardinia, and that the rest (*ceteri*, presumably all the rest) were ordered to leave Italy unless they renounced their rites by a certain date. In Suetonius's version (*Tiberius* 36), Tiberius assigned to provinces with a less healthy climate those of the Jews who were of military age, while he banished from the city others of the same people or of similar beliefs, again without drawing any distinctions among the Jews. It is only in Dio Cassius's much later third-century account (57.18.5a) that we read that Tiberius banished most—presumably not all—of the Jews, the grounds being that the Jews were converting many of the natives to their ways.

Finally, we read (Suetonius, *Claudius* 25.4) that because the Jews constantly made disturbances at the instigation of a certain Chrestus, the Emperor Claudius expelled them—and not merely the followers of Chrestus (presumably the Christians)[5]—from Rome. Again, the reference is to the Jews generally as a group; and indeed the New Testament (Acts 18:2) specifically states that Claudius—the reason is not given—commanded *all* the Jews (πάντας τοὺς Ἰουδαίους) to leave Rome.

This unity of the Jews was undoubtedly enhanced by the fact that all adult male Jews between the ages of twenty and fifty were expected to contribute a half shekel (two drachmas in Greek or two denarii in Roman currency) each year. We would not, it seems, be unjustified in assuming that Jews generally did contribute to the Temple, to judge from the huge sum of eight hundred talents that, according to Strabo (quoted in Josephus, *Antiquities* 14.112), the Jews had collected on the island of Cos off the coast of Asia Minor for transmission to the Temple and that was sent annually and not allowed to accumulate from year to year.[6] That Jews did not avoid making this contribution is clear from Cicero's remark (*Pro Flacco* 28.67; the trial is dated in the year 59 B.C.E.) that it was customary to send gold to Jerusalem every year on the order of the Jews from Italy and from all the Roman provinces. That in each of the relatively small towns of Apamea and Adramyttium (*Pro Flacco* 28.68) approximately a hundred pounds of gold were collected is an indication that the Jews were conscientious in making their contributions (a pound of gold at this time was worth about a thousand denarii or drachmas; hence this would indicate approximately 50,000 adult male Jews in each of these two cities, unless, of course, we assume that some contributed more than was required). To be sure, Cicero is a lawyer for a client who had been accused of confiscating this money, and he may be exaggerating when he remarks on how the Jews stick together (*quanta concordia*); but surely we have here more than a glimpse of the *Sitz-in-Leben*.

Again, when speaking about the specific beliefs and practices of Jews, the Greek and Roman writers give no indication that there were differences within the Jewish people on these points. Thus, when speaking of the theological views of the Jews, Varro (cited in Augustine, *De Civitate D-i* 4.31) cites as a parallel to the imageless worship of the Romans the testimony of the Jewish people (*gentem Iudaeam*).

The impression given is that the Jews, as a people, were universally observant of the laws of the Torah. In fact, Hecataeus (quoted in Josephus, *Against Apion* 1.191) declares that all (πάντες) of the Jews, though slandered by their neighbors and by foreign visitors and though subjected to frequent outrages by Persian kings and satraps, remained firm in their determination and were ready to face torture and death rather than repudiate the faith of their forefathers. As an example of this obstinacy, he relates the incident (*Against Apion* 1.192) that Alexander the Great gave orders to all his soldiers without distinction to bring materials for the earthworks of a temple that he proposed to restore; in that case, the Jews alone—again with the clear implication that all the Jews were in agreement—refused and even submitted to severe chastisement and heavy fines until the king pardoned them.[7]

Furthermore, when the pagans refer to the most distinctive Jewish practices, namely circumcision and observance of the Sabbath and of the dietary laws, they clearly imply that these are characteristic of the Jews in general that are universally observed by Jews. Thus, when Strabo (17.2.5.824) notes that the Egyptians circumcise their males and excise their females, he adds that this is also customary among *the* Jews. Though he could have cited others, such as the Ethiopians, who likewise practice circumcision, apparently it was most commonly identified with the Jews, and thus the casual reference. The satirist Petronius (fragment 37) likewise knows that circumcision is the sine qua non for Jewish identity and remarks that unless a Jew is circumcised he is removed from his people, implying that such an ostracism is hardly a frequent occurrence. Tacitus (*Histories* 5.5.2) speaks of the Jews as a group adopting circumcision "to distinguish themselves from other peoples by this difference."

Likewise, in their numerous references to the Sabbath the pagan writers assume its universal observance by Jews. Thus, Agatharchides (quoted in Josephus, *Against Apion* 1.209), who lived in the second century B.C.E., says that the people known as Jews are accustomed to abstain from work on the seventh day. That strict observance of the Sabbath by Jews was proverbial may be seen by the remark attributed to the Emperor Augustus (quoted in Suetonius, *Augustus* 76.2) that not even a Jew fasts on the Sabbath as diligently as he (Augustus) did on a certain day. We may draw a similar conclusion from the allusions in Ovid (*Ars Amatoria* 1.75–76 and 1.413–16) to the seventh day that the Syrian Jews hold sacred. Such satirical references as Horace's (*Satires* 1.9.69) to the thirtieth Sabbath of the Jews imply that the Sabbath was universally observed by Jews and that it was therefore naturally identified with them. Similarly, Tacitus (*Histories* 5.4.3) speaks of the Jews as a group being led by the charms of indolence to observe the Sabbath day and even the Sabbatical year, which occurs at seven-year intervals.[8]

That the dietary laws and, in particular, the abstention from eating pork, were universally observed by Jews seems clear from the statement of the first-century Erotianus (*Vocum Hippocraticarum Collectio cum Fragmentis*, F 33), the glossator of Hippocrates, that if someone is afflicted with epilepsy the physician should ask whether he is a Jew so that he may refrain from prescribing pork. Likewise, his contemporary Epictetus (*Dissertationes* 1.11.12–13) speaks of the different attitudes toward diet among the Jews, the Syrians, the Egyptians, and the Romans, the implication being that Jews as a group have distinct views that are clearly identifiable. That the Emperor Caligula in the year 40 asks the Jewish delegation from Alexandria, "Why do you not eat pork?" (Philo, *Legatio ad Gaium* 45.361) shows that in his mind this abstention was universally practiced among Jews. Tacitus (*Histories* 5.5.2), too, generalizes when he says that they (i.e., the Jews as a people) sit apart at meals (i.e., separate themselves from non-Jews because of their food laws). Furthermore, in the second century Sextus Empiricus (*Hypotyposeis* 3.24.223) says that a Jew would rather die than eat pork, the clear implication being that all Jews held such a view.

We may counter by saying that many of the writers citing Jewish observance of these commandments are speaking of the Roman Jewish community; although there was probably not much difference in observance in the various parts of the Diaspora, the Roman Jewish community does not seem to have had the liberal attitude toward Greek culture which marked the Alexandrian Jewish intelligentsia, nor was the Roman community apparently so eager for citizenship and social advancement. Furthermore, the Roman writers may have based their comments more on ethnographic tradition than on actual—and flawed—observation. In addition, we may note that Horace and Petronius are satirists and that Tacitus is, in effect, a satirical historian of the Roman Empire; they are all obviously exaggerating because they are eager, to make a satiric point, to show how greatly the Jews hate strangers. Finally, the Roman writers are poorly informed about Judaism; thus, for example, several of them actually state that the Jews fasted on the Sabbath. But in reply we may remark that the same generalizations are to be found among such non-Latin writers as Agatharchides, Strabo, Erotianus, and Sextus Empiricus.

Liberal views of Jewish law are implied, as we shall see, in the *Letter of Aristeas* and in certain passages in Philo; these attitudes, according to Goodenough (though he supplies little hard evidence), were shared by a large group of Jews both in Alexandria and in the rest of the Diaspora.[9] Tcherikover, on the other hand, though admittedly with similarly little conclusive evidence, argues that these are the views of restricted groups of wealthy people and of the intelligentsia in particular who were more deeply influenced by Greek thought.[10] Works such as Jason of Cyrene's version of the Maccabean revolt, the Greek versions of Esther and Judith, the Third Book of Maccabees, and the *Wisdom of Solomon*, all of which probably date from the second and first centuries B.C.E. and which are opposed to assimilation of foreign thought, may more closely reflect the view of the masses. There may be evidence for this in Philo's remark (*De Specialibus Legibus* 1.12.69) that countless multitudes from countless cities come, some over land, some over sea, from every direction to the Temple in Jerusalem for the pilgrimage festivals; whether or not Philo is exaggerating, he expected at the very least that his readers would believe that the Egyptian Jews, as a group, were enormously loyal to the Temple.

A further indication of the loyalty of the Egyptian Jews to Judaean religious leadership may be found in the Second Book of Maccabees (1:1–6), which opens with a letter, dated in the year 124 B.C.E., refer-

ring to a previous letter with the same purpose dating from the year
143 B.C.E. This letter from the Jews of Judaea to their fellow Jews in
Egypt invites them to institute the celebration of Hanukkah.[11] In any
case, the very fact that in 102 B.C.E. Ananias, the Jewish commander-in-
chief of the Ptolemaic army, could tell his sovereign, Cleopatra, that if
she went to war against Alexander Jannaeus, the king of Judaea, *all* the
Jews in her kingdom would become her foes shows (*Ant.* 13.353–55) that
the Egyptian Jews had very strong sentimental feelings toward their Palestinian brethren and toward the Judaism with which they were so
closely identified. Likewise, half a century later, in the year 55 B.C.E., that
the Jewish soldiers in the Ptolemaic army who were guarding the frontier
allowed the Roman proconsul of Syria, Gabinius, to enter Egypt because
the head of the Jewish state, Antipater, urged them to do so indicates
their close association with Judaea (*Ant.* 14.99). A similar incident, in the
year 48 B.C.E., when the Jewish soldiers at the frontier allowed a force of
Julius Caesar's allies to relieve him, again demonstrates the close connection of the Egyptian Jews' with Judaea, inasmuch as they were persuaded
by a letter from the high priest Hyrcanus (*Ant.* 14.131–32).

2. ASSIMILATION OF THE JEWS TO GREEK LANGUAGE AND THOUGHT

That there was no pervasive spread of Greek thought among the masses
with whom Alexander and his successors came into contact has been
amply demonstrated by Green.[12] In Egypt, as Avi-Yonah has stressed, the
impact of Hellenism on the natives was to impose a thin Greek veneer on
a still strong and vital native tradition.[13] The one shining exception is
Rome, which welcomed Greek culture. But this was perhaps true because
the Romans were almost morbidly conscious of being cultural parvenus,
which was certainly not true of the Jews, who had an ancient culture and
a book, the Bible, to demonstrate this.

We may now ask to what degree there was assimilation to Greek ways
in the Jewish Diaspora during the Hellenistic-Roman period. Of course,
we must consider differences in local conditions, as the recent discoveries at Sardis and Aphrodisias have demonstrated.

The earliest Jewish community of Hellenistic Egypt is in the most
important region of the Diaspora, rivaled only by the Jewish community
of Babylonia, and is the one about which we have the most information.
Dating from the fourth century B.C.E., immediately after the founding of
the city by Alexander, the Jews there probably spoke Aramaic; indeed,
our papyri from that place and period are in that language.[14] Within less
than a century, however, the papyri indicate that the Jews had become
Greek-speaking, and, as Deissmann remarks, Hellenistic Jews spoke

Greek, prayed in Greek, sang Greek psalms, wrote in Greek, produced Greek literature, and with their best minds thought in Greek.[15] Consequently, the Egyptian Jews now found it necessary to have the Torah translated into Greek for their liturgical and educational needs and perhaps also to combat the incipient anti-Jewish bigotry as seen in the work of the Egyptian priest Manetho, who apparently lived at the time the Septuagint was translated.[16] One might have expected a priori that at least the leaders of the Jewish community in Alexandria would realize the limitations and dangers of a translation and that they would have done their best to encourage the study of Hebrew in their schools.[17] Yet, aside from the Greek translator of Ecclesiasticus, who rendered it into Greek in Egypt in 132 B.C.E. and who, in his Prologue, citing the example of the Septuagint, admits that "things originally spoken in Hebrew have not the same force in them when they are translated into another tongue," there is no indication that Alexandrian Jewry bewailed the loss of its competence to consult the Bible in the original. In fact, as we learn from Philo (*De Vita Mosis* 2.7.41), they actually celebrated the date of the completion of the Septuagint as a holiday, and they regarded the translation itself as much more than a translation: It was looked on as a creation of importance comparable to the Hebrew original. This version was regarded as perfect—in some respects even more correct than the original.[18]

There has been much debate as to whether the Septuagint shows the influence of Greek philosophy and even Greek mythology. Most investigators, on the whole, agree that there is no systematic pattern of Hellenizing and that the Greek elements tend to be superficial and decorative rather than deep-seated and significant.[19] Moreover, these Greek elements, such as the references to Titans (2 Sam 5:18, 22) and Sirens (Job 30:29; Mic 1:8; Isa 13:21, 34:13, 43:20; Jer 27:39) and the horn of Amalthia (Job 42:14), as well as the metrics of the Book of Proverbs,[20] occur in books outside the Pentateuch. Indeed, the reference to Titans is not an indication of the acceptance of Greek mythological beliefs, inasmuch as the word Titan then, as now, had non-theological connotations as well.[21]

It has been argued that the very translation of the word *Torah* by the Greek νόμος ("law," "custom") represented the introduction of a basic Greek and un-Jewish concept, namely the notion that the Torah is legalistic, in contrast to φύσις, nature or natural law, and that Judaism is controlled by custom (νόμος), as reflected in Herodotus's famous story (3.38) comparing the way the Greeks and the Indians are guided by it in their methods of disposing of the dead.[22] However, one might argue that there is also considerable evidence of the divine origin and nature of the concept of νόμος in Greek literature of the classical period (e.g., in Sophocles' *Antigone*, 454–55) and thereafter, as we see in the hymn of the third century B.C.E. Stoic philosopher Cleanthes (*SVF* 1.121, fragment no. 537), who asserts that the all-powerful Zeus controls the world through νόμος.[23] Moreover, the very fact that the Septuagint uses the singular νόμος to render Torah, whereas pagans would always speak of νόμοι in the plural when speaking of Mosaic legislation, is an indication that the translators looked on the Torah as unique and not just another code of law.[24] Indeed, not even Aquila, though committed to an absolutely literal translation of the Scriptures, could find a better translation for the word *Torah*.

In addition, the Septuagint generally avoids, in discussions of the Jewish religion, Greek terms that are used in pagan worship.[25] It speaks of βωμός (altar), σηκός (sacred enclosure), and ἄδυτον (innermost sanctuary), which are pagan terms, only with reference to heathen worship; on the contrary, when referring to the altar of G-d, for example, the Septuagint uses the term θυσιαστήριον, which has no precedent in pagan literature. Again, the Septuagint never uses the terms ἄγαλμα and εἰκών when referring to pagan images but uses the word εἴδολον to convey the idea that the images were completely worthless. Likewise, inasmuch as the words μόνος and πρῶτος are common in Greek prayers where they stress the superiority of the god who is being invoked over other deities, the Septuagint generally avoids these words and instead prefers the word εἷς ("one"). Furthermore, the Septuagint changes the meaning of certain Greek religious terms; thus ἀνάθημα, which for the pagans refers to a votive offering, is used by the Septuagint in the sense of a vow, whereas it employs the word δῶρον for a votive offering. In addition, whereas εὐλογία for the Greeks means "praise," for the Septuagint it is the word for "blessing." Likewise, the Septuagint has a separate word (but not coined by it), μάντις, for a heathen soothsayer as opposed to a true prophet, for which it uses the word προφήτης. Finally, in order to indicate the special nature of the Israelites as chosen, the translators generally use the word λαός for the Jewish people, whereas they use the word ἔθνος to refer to pagan peoples.[26]

Alleged Platonisms, such as the translation of *tohu va-vahu* (Genesis 1:2) by ἀόρατος καὶ ἀκατασκεύαστος ("unseen and unformed"), hardly prove that the translators believed with Plato that prior to the visible world there existed an invisible world; rather, they were confronted with a phrase whose meaning was very obscure. Again, the translation of *gehonekha* (Genesis 3:14), "your belly," by τῷ στήθει σου καὶ τῇ κοιλίᾳ ("upon your chest and belly") hardly proves that the translators were aware of the Platonic division of the human faculties into the rational, spirited, and appetitive, assigned respectively to the head, the chest, and the abdomen. Indeed, if they had been influenced by Platonism, it would seem more likely that they would have shown it throughout and, in particular, introduced the most famous Platonic theory, that of Forms.

For the period from the third century B.C.E. until the period of the late Roman Empire (about 400 C.E.), we have found some 520 papyri pertaining to the Jews. And yet so thoroughgoing was the victory of the Greek over the Hebrew language that for this period only one papyrus fragment with any Hebrew or Aramaic has been found—the Nash Papyrus, in Hebrew, dating from the second or first century B.C.E. (containing the Decalogue and the Shema), of unknown provenance (although allegedly from the Fayum district in northern Egypt west of the Nile). People often tend to be more conservative in their inscriptions on tombstones than in their attitudes on other matters, but here again, out of 122 inscriptions of Jews from Egypt, 116 are in Greek.[27] There are only six inscriptions (5 percent) extant in Hebrew or Aramaic, plus two others that contain the word *shalom* after an inscription in Greek. Of course, there is always the *argumentum ex silentio*, for perhaps we have the papyri and the tombstones of the more assimilated Jews in Hellenistic Egypt and not of the more religious Jews. Nevertheless, the mass of papyri and inscriptions is sufficient to assign the burden of proof to the scholar who asserts that Alexandrian Jewry knew and used Hebrew rather than to the scholar who makes the contrary assertion. We may add that a similar picture emerges when we examine the inscriptions of Jews in ancient Rome. Of the 534 inscriptions, 405 (76 percent) are in Greek, 123 (23 percent) are in Latin, three are in Hebrew, one is in Aramaic, one is a bilingual Greek and Latin inscription, and one is a bilingual Aramaic and Greek inscription.[28] From this we may, at least tentatively, conclude that the Jews in the Diaspora had overwhelmingly adopted the Greek language and thus were equipped in many cases to communicate with non-Jews in terms of spreading Jewish ideas.

Furthermore, we have fragments in Greek from a number of writers, whom most scholars believe to have been Jews and who probably lived in Egypt. Thus, Demetrius, who mentions (quoted in Clement of Alexandria, *Stromata* 1.21.141.2) the Egyptian king Ptolemy IV Philopator and who apparently flourished in Alexandria during the latter half of the third century B.C.E., is the author of a chronicle of Jewish history which extends from the period of the patriarchs until the fall of the kingdom of Judah and shows an awareness, to be sure on an elementary level, of Greek historiography.[29] An Egyptian provenance is virtually certain for the historian Artapanus, who lived perhaps in the second century B.C.E. and who is so liberal and syncretistic in his glorification of Jewish biblical history that some scholars have seriously questioned whether he was a

Jew.[30] As to poetry in Greek, we may here call attention to a certain otherwise unknown Sosates, who is termed the Hebrew Homer (*Ebraicus Omirus*) in the *Excerpta Latina Barbari*, a seventh- or eighth-century Latin translation of a lost Greek chronicle written in the early fifth century. Sosates is specifically said there to have flourished in Alexandria during either the second or first century B.C.E.[31] Most likely, according to his latest editor, Holladay, Philo the epic poet, who wrote a poem *On Jerusalem* about 100 B.C.E., came from Alexandria, in view of his close affinity with other Hellenistic epics.[32] Likewise, an Alexandrian provenance is most likely for Ezekiel the tragedian,[33] whose date is most probably the latter part of the second century B.C.E.[34] Finally, the philosopher Aristobulus of Paneas, noted for his allegorical interpretation of the Bible, is described by the author of 2 Maccabees (1:10) as the teacher of King Ptolemy, presumably Ptolemy Philometor VI (181–145 B.C.E.).

Indeed, there is a real question as to whether Philo, clearly the greatest of the Alexandrian Jewish writers, who wrote a series of essays expounding biblical themes, knew more than a modicum of Hebrew. Wolfson thinks that Philo knew enough Hebrew to be able to check, in the original when necessary, the Greek translation of a given passage,[35] but in view of the fact that in Philo's time Hebrew was almost unknown in Egypt the burden of proof rests on those who assert that he did know Hebrew.[36] In any case, it seems hard to believe that one who knew Hebrew and wrote in such detail about biblical episodes would not have consulted the original text and at least occasionally have quoted from it, especially where it differed from the Septuagint translation. In particular, we note that Philo (*De Decalogo* 24.121–22 and *De Specialibus Legibus* 3.2.8) follows the Septuagint in placing the prohibition of adultery as the sixth commandment, rather than the extant Hebrew text, which places it seventh. As to the occasional places where Philo has etymologies of Hebrew names that are not found in the biblical text, he may have derived them from an onomasticon such as has been discovered in a papyrus at Oxyrhynchus.[37] Finally, it would seem significant that we may infer much, from his citations, about Philo's Greek education but nothing about his Hebrew education.

This attitude toward Greek thought, if we are to believe the author of the *Letter of Aristeas*, was set by the Jewish elders who were responsible for the Septuagint. Aristeas says (*Letter of Aristeas* 40) that he is a non-Jewish official of Ptolemy Philadelphus (285–245 B.C.E.) and that he is writing this letter to his brother (*Letter of Aristeas* 7) to tell him how deeply impressed he was with these elders.[38] There is general agreement that this work was written in the second century B.C.E. by an Alexandrian Jew who is a propagandist for the notion of the synthesis of Hellenism and Judaism.[39] Such writings were addressed by the Jewish intelligentsia primarily to non-Jews, as we can see from the author's statement that he is a non-Jew.[40] In an effort to impress the king and the non-Jewish intelligentsia, the seventy-two elders are depicted as having had a good Greek education and as having "released themselves from the harsh and barbarian traits of character" (*Letter of Aristeas* 121–22) which, according to this view, describes those Jews who have not received a secular education. Even the high priest, Eleazar, to whom the application had been made for the translators, is called καλοκἀγαθός (*Letter of Aristeas* 3), a term describing a perfect Greek gentleman, noble in character and athletic as well.

There would also seem to be Greek influence in the Apocryphal *Book of Wisdom*, probably composed in Alexandria during the first century B.C.E. or the first century C.E. The book has seemingly adopted from Plato and his followers the doctrine that matter is eternal (11:17), that it is essentially evil (1:4), and that the soul pre-exists (8:20) and finds in the body a temporary prison-house (9:15).[41] The author's account of the origin of idol-worship (14) is apparently taken from Euhemerus. From the Stoics he is said to have borrowed the idea of the world-soul (7:24, 11:7, 12:1), the penetrating quality of wisdom (7:24), and the doctrine of Providence (14:3). And yet, although Greek influence cannot be denied, the first six chapters of the book, extolling the beauties of Judaism, are directed against recalcitrant and apostate Jews, who have succumbed to materialism; and the last ten chapters are a ringing denunciation of idolatry.[42]

That the rank and file of the Jews in Egypt, nevertheless, felt strong in their knowledge of and their identification with Judaism, and in particular with the central institution of the Sabbath, may be seen from Philo's proud boast (*De Specialibus Legibus* 2.15.62) that on every Sabbath thousands of places stand wide open for teaching the cardinal virtues. There the students, apparently mature adults, presumably in the tens if not hundreds of thousands, sit attentively, together with potential proselytes, it would seem, eager to hear the words of teachers.

Indeed, though the Jews were apparently living side by side with Greeks and, in the Mediterranean climate, must have passed Greeks frequently on the street, the evidence reveals almost no direct contact between the two peoples, certainly in the third century B.C.E. and arguably for a much longer period of time.[43] Moreover, there is no mention, in either pagan or Jewish writers, of contact between non-Jewish scholars, critics, and poets, such as Callimachus, Apollonius of Rhodes, Aristophanes of Byzantium, Theocritus, Aristarchus, and Didymus, and Jewish scholars, even Philo.[44]

3. Secular Education of Jews in
the Diaspora

We can see how positively secular education was viewed by those who had come into contact with Greek culture from Josephus's rewriting of the biblical narrative. In particular, Josephus (*Ant.* 2.39) adds to the biblical narrative (Genesis 39:1) not only that Potiphar held Joseph in the highest esteem but also that he gave him a liberal education (παιδείαν . . . ἐλευθέριον), presumably in the seven liberal arts. Similarly, Philo (*De Vita Mosis* 1.5.23–24) declares that Moses was taught the seven liberal arts by Egyptian and Greek teachers.

Moreover, any instruction in Judaism which Jewish children received might well have been nullified if the Jews had succeeded in entering their children of secondary school age in Greek gymnasiums. But the Alexandrian Greeks were eager to exclude Jewish children from these pagan schools, which were highly selective and exclusive clubs, and were finally able (London Papyrus 1912) to convince the Roman Emperor Claudius in 41 c.e. to expel them from the gymnasiarchic games, which, in effect, meant exclusion from the gymnasium. We know from several sources (e.g., Philo, *Legatio ad Gaium* 44.349) how eager the Jews were to obtain citizenship in Alexandria; this was apparently granted only to those who had received a gymnasium education.[45]

Philo speaks often of the gymnasiums, in particular when he declares (*De Specialibus Legibus* 2.40.229) that the goal of education of children is not only life but a good life. He elaborates (2.40.230) by stating that this goal is achieved through physical training in the gymnasium and through mental training in the liberal arts and philosophy. Moreover, it is thought that at least one papyrus (*CPJ* 2, no. 151) mentions that an Alexandrian Jew and his father had a gymnasium education.[46] It seems fair to conclude, therefore, that, at any rate, some members of the upper classes had such an education.[47] There was, moreover, a close connection between the gymnasiums and the army. The papyri leave no doubt[48] that many non-Greeks, especially Jews (despite the apparent difficulties involved in observing the Sabbath and the dietary laws), served in the armies of the Ptolemies; and consequently it would not be surprising if non-Greeks were also admitted to the gymnasiums.[49] An examination of these schools, and especially of their curricula, will reveal to us the kind of education to which the Alexandrian Jews of these classes wished to expose their adolescents.

Though many gymnasiums are mentioned in the Egyptian papyri, we know little of their organization. The gymnasium was the place where young men, starting at the age of fourteen, received their training for manhood, that is, to become ephebes. Though we have little information about Jews in Egyptian gymnasiums, we do have a list of ephebes from the town of Iasos in Asia Minor, dating from the early Roman period, in which the distinctly Jewish names of Judah, Dositheos, and Theophilos appear.[50] Moreover, an inscription, dating from the second or third century c.e., found at Hypaipa near Sardis in Asia Minor (*CII* 2.755) indicates that a group of young Jews called themselves νεώτεροι, thus showing that the usual system existed of grouping ephebes into juniors, intermediates, and seniors.[51] Marrou, whose history of ancient education includes the first systematic survey of Hellenistic education yet attempted by a scholar, notes that the chief function of this training was not so much career preparation as initiation of youth into the Greek way of life, above all athletics, arguably its most characteristic feature.[52] In Egypt, in particular, where the Greeks were numerically a minority group, this education served to differentiate those who were truly "civilized" from those who were "barbarians." On completion of this training, the ephebe often continued to attend the gymnasium, where he joined a closely knit club of alumni. For these alumni, the gymnasium was more than a postgraduate school: It was also a social center equivalent to the modern country club.[53] It is these alumni who seem to have administered and financially maintained the gymnasiums in Egypt during the Ptolemaic period.[54] As is true of most country clubs today, the membership fee in gymnasiums was so high as to permit only the wealthy to enroll;[55] and apparently then, as in modern times, the gymnasiums excluded Jews and others perceived as outsiders.

That Philo had firsthand knowledge of the gymnasium seems likely from his reference (*De Migratione Abrahami* 20.116) to the methods of reproaches and punishments used by the σωφρονισταί, who were officials appointed to look after the morals of the ephebes in general and particularly in the gymnasiums.[56] Marcus, in his survey of Philo's views on education, expresses amazement that Philo (*De Specialibus Legibus* 2.40.230) should praise the gymnasium, an institution that Marcus admits is in spirit opposed to the Jewish tradition.[57] It is a mistake to assume that the gymnasium was in the main an academic institution, because the evidence for what went on there concerns athletic, social, and religious life.[58] Wolfson recognizes the religious nature of the gymnasiums, but he asserts that Jews did not attend them.[59] If, as indicated above, Jews did attend them, they would have had to make several compromises with their orthodoxy. In the first place, all the gymnasiums had numerous busts of deities, particularly of Hermes and Heracles, the patron gods of the gymnasium. The gymnasium itself was dedicated to one or more of these deities; for example, we hear of one that was dedicated to Ammon, Pan, Apollo, Hermes, and Heracles.[60] These statues were not mere

adornments in the gymnasium; we know that in Hellenistic cities generally the ephebes joined in religious processions, sang hymns to gods, and
even participated in pagan sacrifices.[61]

The question, however, remains whether a gymnasium education must
have been purchased with the betrayal of Judaism.[62] If so, we would have
expected a condemnation of the institution by Philo; not only is this
nowhere to be found in his extant essays, but, as we have noted, there is
praise instead.

4. JEWS AND ATHLETICS

Elsewhere in the Hellenistic world, the importance of athletics in the
gymnasium curriculum declined, and that of literature increased. But in
Egypt, and particularly in the countryside, athletics continued to be the
focal point of the curriculum, for this interest represented the distinguishing mark of the true Greek in contrast to the barbarian—a contrast
that was beginning to be blurred, especially in the rural districts, where
the Greeks were much less numerous than the native Egyptians.[63]

Moreover, to the Greeks, as Marrou has remarked, "Sport was not
merely a pleasant form of relaxation; it was a highly serious business,
involving a whole complex of affairs concerned with hygiene and medicine, aesthetics and ethics."[64] Wolfson, obviously disturbed at the possibility of Jewish participation in athletics, notes a reference in an inscription (*CII* 2.755) from Asia Minor dating from the second or third century
C.E. to a Jewish young men's sporting organization and thinks that organizations of this kind may also have existed in Alexandria during the
time of Philo.[65] However, in the absence of any evidence of such a separate organization, we must assume that Jews participated in the athletic
activities of the pagan Greek gymnasiums.

The games in which the students of the gymnasiums participated were
pagan religious festivals, and more and more of them were founded
throughout the Hellenistic world on the model of the old pan-Hellenic
games, the champions being sent to participate at the great games of
Olympia and Delphi.[66] Gardiner, the greatest authority on Greek athletics, has remarked on the religious significance of the games: "Sports were
definitely placed under the patronage of the gods, and the victorious athlete felt that he was well pleasing to the gods and owed his success to
them. Further, the athlete felt that any violation of the rules of the
games, especially any unfairness or corruption, was an act of sacrilege
and displeasing to the gods. . . . It was to religion that Greek athletics
and Greek athletic festivals owed their vitality."[67] Because of the religious associations of these contests, even participation as a spectator involved a compromise with Jewish orthodoxy.[68]

And yet Philo himself, who certainly gives every appearance of being an observant Jew in the traditional sense, presents ample evidence of knowledge of athletics, particularly in his similes and metaphors.[69] Thus, in a single passage (*De Agricultura* 25.111–27.121) he gives details about contests in running, boxing, wrestling, the *pankration* (an athletic contest involving both boxing and wrestling), and the long jump. In some cases he has given us information we find in few other sources, for example, that one official announced the victor and another presented the wreath (*De Agricultura* 25.112), that there were second and third prizes (*De Specialibus Legibus* 1.7.38), that boxers rained blows not only on the head but on other parts of the body (*De Agricultura* 26.114), that there were many cases of tripping—some intentional, some accidental (*Quod Deus Immutabilis Sit* 16.75)—in running. Indeed, we get a fuller picture in Philo (*De Migratione Abrahami* 30.166) than in any other extant literary source, of a trainer coaching a young runner, running alongside at exactly the same speed and with exactly the same length of stride. He is the only writer who has given us (*De Fuga et Inventione* 18.97–98) a picture of a stadium adapted for the races that were shortened for women and for boys. Likewise, he is the only writer who mentions (*De Vita Contemplativa* 5.43) the presence of referees physically separating contestants in boxing. Furthermore, the portrayal of the boxer (*De Cherubim* 24.80–81) weaving with his neck to avoid punches, rising on tiptoe and pulling himself up to his full height, crouching and tucking up and thus compelling his opponent to miss repeatedly as if he were shadowboxing—all this is, it would seem, too detailed to be drawn from books. The portrait (*De Somniis* 1.21.129) of the trainer who fastens the gloves on his pupil and then forces him to wrestle until he has developed in him an irresistible strength seems to be drawn from real experience. Indeed, at one point (*Quod Omnis Probus Liber Sit* 6.26) Philo actually says that he once saw a *pankration* fight in which one of the contestants delivered his blows and kicks with hands and feet well aimed and yet was compelled to admit defeat because his opponent was so tough and solid. He likewise recounts an incident he witnessed (*De Providentia* 2.58) in which the spectators took a position in the middle of the course and were crushed by the wheels of passing chariots and by the hoofs of the horses as they rushed past them. He also seems to have firsthand knowledge of the methods used by athletes to attain the proper weight through dry sweating (*De Specialibus Legibus* 2.19.91), that is, through getting rid of extra fat and leaving only muscle.[70] Again, of the few references in Greek literature to the process by which competitors for athletic events were selected, Philo supplies the majority.[71] That Philo is drawing on firsthand experience with athletes is clear from his statement (*Quod Omnis Probus Liber Sit* 17.110) that he knows many cases of wrestlers and pancratiasts so eager for victory that though their bodies had lost their strength yet they persevered to the actual point of death.

That Philo looked favorably on gymnastic competitions may be seen from his comment (*De Specialibus Legibus* 3.31.176) commending the managers of gymnastic competitions for excluding women from the spectacle because of the immodesty of seeing men stripping themselves naked. There is no hint here that Philo had any reservation in principle about the competitions themselves, and the fact that he praises the managers here is an indication of his favorable attitude.[72]

If we may judge from the Emperor Claudius's famous letter to the Alexandrians (London Papyrus 1912; *CPJ* 2, no. 153, lines 92–93), the Jews of Alexandria, as we have noted, apparently aspired to participate in the games run by the gymnasiarchs and the cosmetae.[73] Inasmuch as Claudius speaks of "the Jews" agitating for more privileges than they had enjoyed in the past, including this privilege of participating in the games, he apparently indicates that the Jewish community generally was behind this request even though the Jews had sent two delegations, each composed, presumably, of different factions.[74]

Indeed, in recounting the benefits bestowed by parents on children (*De Specialibus Legibus* 2.40.229–230), Philo specifies that they improve their children's bodies through gymnastic training and anointing (γυμναστικῆς καὶ ἀλειπτικῆς), thus producing muscular vigor and good condition, so that the children stand and move gracefully, with rhythm and good carriage. Inasmuch as this passage appears in a treatise dealing with the norms of Jewish life, as regulated by the Torah, it is clear that Philo not only saw no contradiction between the fulfillment of the commandments of the Torah and athletic training but even actually regarded the latter as itself part of the requirements placed by the Torah on parents. Furthermore, the fact that he says (*De Vita Mosis* 2.39.211) that the Sabbath should not be spent in bursts of laughter or sports or shows of mimes and dancers would seem to indicate that such activities were permitted during the rest of the week and were common forms of entertainment among Philo's audience.

5. JEWS AND THE THEATER

It was not only through their attendance at gymnasiums and their participation in athletic festivals that Jews were apparently guilty of compromising their Judaism and perhaps even worshipping idols. Attendance at theaters was declared by Rabbi Meir (*'Avodah Zarah* 18b) in the second century to be prohibited because entertainments were arranged there in honor of idols; the other sages also prohibited attendance at theaters even when the entertainment was not accompanied by idol worship, on the ground that it involved neglect of Torah. In prohibiting attendance at theaters, the rabbis were presumably aware not only of the vulgarity of the comic performances,[75] but also of the association of the drama with pagan religion, in particular with the worship of Dionysus. In both classical and Hellenistic times, these plays were performed only at festivals of the gods, in theaters adjacent to the temples of the gods (because the temples themselves were too small to accommodate the huge audiences), in the presence of the altar and priests of the gods.[76] Even the χορηγοί, who bore the expenses of the performance, as well as the poets, the actors, and the chorus, "were looked upon as ministers of religion, and their persons were sacred and inviolable."[77]

And yet, despite the religious associations of drama, we read in the *Letter of Aristeas* (284) that when King Ptolemy Philadelphus asked one of the seventy-two translators of the Septuagint what he should make his pastime in his hours of relaxation, the translator replied, "To watch plays performed with propriety and to set before one's eyes scenes from life presented with decency and restraint is profitable to one's life and appropriate, for even in such things there is some edification." Philo (*De Ebrietate* 43.177) himself remarks that he has often been to the theater, where he has noticed the diverse effects of the same music on various people. He also notes (*Quod Omnis Probus Liber Sit* 20.141) how enthusiastically the audience in a theater, some of whom were presumably Jewish like himself, received a play of Euripides. That Jews attended the theater is also to be seen from an inscription (*CII* 2.748) found at Miletus in Asia Minor which indicates that a special place was reserved for them.[78]

We know of one Jewish playwright, Ezekiel, whose drama seems a manifest attempt to show both Gentiles and fellow Jews that the Jews too had heroic subjects for tragedy and could present them in the best style of Euripides, the favorite playwright of the Hellenistic era. If Ezekiel's play was composed for the stage and was actually presented, we have still further evidence for deviation from orthodoxy: In one of the extant fragments, Ezekiel actually has G-d (or His voice) addressing Moses on stage from the burning bush.[79] That this was not the only tragedy that he wrote seems to be indicated by the reference (quoted in Clement of Alexandria, *Stromata* 1.23.155.1, and Eusebius, *Praeparatio Evangelica* 9.28.1) to "Ezekiel, the poet of the tragedies."

Wolfson, troubled by such deviations from orthodoxy on the part of the Alexandrian Jewish community, suggests that the Jews may have had young men's dramatic organizations where Greek plays, as well as plays on Biblical themes, were presented.[80] Philo, he thinks, may have attended performances in such a Jewish milieu; or he may simply have been curious to see the plays performed and did not participate at all in the cultural life of Alexandria. The burden of proof rests, however, with Wolfson to cite evidence that there were such Jewish organizations; and thus far the papyri have yielded no support for his view. Moreover, Philo speaks as a habitué of the theater, and, in fact, of all phases of Greek cultural life; he says, as we have noted, that he has visited the theater often, and it would seem fair to conclude that he did so not merely out of curiosity but because of real interest.

6. The Organization of the Jewish Community

It would seem axiomatic that if the Jews were to resist the temptations of assimilation, it would be necessary that they be organized as a community in the various places in which they lived. To be sure, in neither the papyri nor in the inscriptions do we have evidence of Jewish communities in Egypt in the Ptolemaic period; we hear of only one community, Oxyrhynchus (*CPJ* 3.473), in a papyrus dated 291 C.E. in the Roman period. However, inasmuch as in this papyrus the community is referred to as a synagogue (*CPJ* 3.473, line 7) and inasmuch as synagogues in this period were much more than houses of prayer and study and actually served as the centers of Jewish social, cultural, and even political life, we may assume that an organized Jewish community existed wherever we can establish the existence of a synagogue.[81] In the case of Egypt we hear of synagogues dating from as early as the third century B.C.E. (*CII* 2.1432, 2.1440, 2.1532A). Indeed, there is evidence that synagogues even served as hostels.[82] The existence of a synagogue implies a community of a certain size and religious leadership, as well as, though admittedly this is less certain, a court, archives, community foundations for various purposes, and a ritual bath.[83] In a country as carefully controlled as Ptolemaic Egypt, such organizations must have had the approval of the government; and that the relations between these synagogues and the king were cordial seems clear from the dedication of synagogues "to the king's welfare."[84] We know this from the papyri and inscriptions of ten such communities;[85] and, in the case of the most important of these, Alexandria, we are told by Philo (*Legatio ad Gaium* 20.132) that there were many synagogues in each of the five sections of the city. Rabbinic sources (*Sukkah* 51b, Jerusalem *Sukkah* 5.55a, Tosefta *Sukkah* 4.6) say, in obvious exaggeration to be sure, that the main synagogue of the city was so huge that it sometimes held twice the number of people that went forth from Egypt (i.e., 1,200,000) and that he who has not seen it has not beheld the glory of Israel. We are told there that when the time came to answer "Amen!" a functionary would wave a scarf, presumably because the size of the building made it virtually impossible to hear the precentor.

That Jewish children in Egypt did receive a religious education would seem to be clear from Philo's statement (*Legatio ad Gaium* 16.115) that

Jews were taught "from their very cradles, as it were, by their parents, tutors (παιδαγωγῶν), and teachers (ὑφηγητῶν), and—more than that—by their holy Laws and even by their unwritten customs, to believe that the Father and Creator of the universe is one G-d." The reference here to the unwritten customs is probably to the oral law and would seem to be evidence that children were taught the rudiments of the oral law that was later to be codified in the Mishnah.[86]

Whether or not the Jews of Egypt were organized in more or less autonomous quasi-independent political units called *politeumata*[87]—a claim contested by Zuckerman[88] in view of the silence about *politeumata* in the papyri, Philo, and Josephus—or whether the Jews were organized in private voluntary associations similar to the ancient Greek θίασοι or Roman collegia or the Jewish *ḥavuroth* of Renaissance and modern times, the important point, for our purposes, is that the Jews were organized. Strabo (quoted in Josephus, *Ant.* 14.117), writing in the early part of the first century, states that the Jews in Egypt had an ethnarch[89] who, he says, governed the Jews and adjudicated suits and supervised contracts and ordinances in a manner reminiscent of a head of state, much like the later patriarchs of Palestine and exilarchs of Babylonia. When the ethnarch died in the year 10 or 11, the Emperor Augustus created a council of elders, called a *gerousia*, either to replace the ethnarch or, as is more likely, to reduce his power and to submit him to a system of checks and balances.[90]

That the Jews had their own courts is indicated by the rabbinic reference (Tosefta *Kethuboth* 3.1, *Peah* 4.6) to a Jewish court in Alexandria,[91] just as we hear that the Jews of Ephesus (or, according to the variant reading, Sardis) in Asia Minor (Josephus, *Ant.* 14.235) are said to have had a place of their own "in which they decide their affairs and controversies with one another" similar to extraterritorial courts in modern times.

Although there were no ghettos in antiquity and although the Jews were consequently free to settle wherever they pleased, the Jews were socially so close to one another that they were concentrated in two of the five quarters of the city of Alexandria (Philo, *In Flaccum* 8.55); similarly, in Edfu (Apollinopolis Magna) in Upper Egypt we hear (*CPJ* 2.194, 200, 202, 209, 213) that the Jews were concentrated in one of the quarters. According to Josephus (*War* 2.488), the reason why the Jews chose to sunder themselves off from non-Jews was so that "through mixing less with aliens they might be free to observe their rules more strictly," in other words to avoid assimilation—a phenomenon Gentiles sometimes criticize as Jewish "clannishness."

The fact that in the riots of 38 and 66 in Alexandria we hear of no division of opinion among the Jews and that, in the latter case, we are told (*War* 2.492) that when three Jews were caught by the Alexandrians and dragged off to be burned alive the *whole* Jewish community rose to their rescue would indicate the cohesion of the Jewish community. Indeed, so united, apparently, was the community that, in the end, no fewer than fifty thousand (*War* 2.497) were killed—surely a large percentage of the Jewish population if the number is at all accurate.

As Green[92] has indicated in his sociological analysis, the fact that the Jews in Egypt developed their own institutional structures would imply a definite sense of Jewish identity, whether secular or religious. We may add that these bonds of social solidarity were reinforced by the requirement that every adult male Jew was to contribute a half-shekel annually to the Temple in Jerusalem,[93] as well as by the economic and political rivalry with non-Jews and by the anti-Jewish bigotry that it engendered. These strictures affected all classes, including, as we see in the riot of 38, those of the highest socioeconomic status.

We must emphasize, of course, that, despite the attempts, which we have noted above, on the part of non-Jewish writers to generalize about *the* Jews, each of the excavated Diaspora synagogues is so different from the others as to make generalizations about Diaspora Judaism hazardous indeed, let alone to talk about *the* Jews without differentiating Palestinian from Diaspora Judaism. Thus, the design, at least, of the synagogues at Dura, Sardis, Priene, Delos, Stobi, and Ostia is quite varied and seems to depend largely on the overall context of the area in which they are found or on the functions they were to serve.[94] And yet, though the form of each building may have been heavily influenced by the local situation, this does not necessarily mean that the kind of Judaism represented at each site was likewise molded by such local influences, except in superficial ways. Indeed, as Kraabel[95] concludes, "This diversity [in synagogue buildings] does not mean that they [the Jews of the various Diaspora communities] were Jews any less. They acted as though their form of Judaism was authentic; the burden of proof is now on those who would argue that it was otherwise." In the case of Sardis, from which we now have over seventy Greek inscriptions from the synagogue, we see the Jews in the third century as a powerful, perhaps even a wealthy, community in a major city, with a huge, lavishly decorated building on a main thoroughfare.[96]

7. SYNCRETISM AMONG THE JEWS

To what degree did religious deviations among the Jews lead to assimilation, syncretism, intermarriage, and apostasy?

We may suggest that the very size of the Jewish community in Egypt must have militated against assimilation. If Philo's figure (*In Flaccum* 6.43) of one million Jews in the first century out of a total population of seven million (Diodorus Siculus 1.31.8 and 17.52.6) or seven and a half million (Josephus, *War* 2.385) is at all accurate, and if the Jews were concentrated in certain areas, such as two of the five quarters of the city of Alexandria (Philo, *In Flaccum* 8.55), their social contacts must have been predominantly with other Jews.

And yet that there was some concern about assimilation seems likely from Philo's comment (*De Josepho* 42.254) that the biblical Joseph, who is the obvious prototype of the Jew living in a non-Jewish environment, realized "how natural it is for youth to lose its footing and what license to sin belongs to the stranger's life." This danger is particularly great, he adds, in Egypt, "where things created and mortal are deified," and where, in consequence, "the land is blind to the true G-d." In remarking that the danger of assimilation increases with wealth and fame especially, as was the case with Joseph, and that there is a gap (whether physical or intellectual, we may presume) between the younger generation and their parents, Philo, it would appear, is commenting on the contemporary situation of Egyptian Jewry, particularly in his native Alexandria. This passage is notably poignant precisely because there is no biblical parallel to it.[97]

Philo also apparently saw a lesson for his own time in the account of Moses, who, like Joseph, managed to remain true to his ancestral heritage despite having been brought up in an alien atmosphere. Moreover, Mendelson insightfully notes the unusual interpretation that Philo (*De Specialibus Legibus* 4.28.149) gives to the biblical prohibition (Deut 19:14) against removing one's neighbor's landmark that one's forefathers has erected, namely that this applies not only to boundaries of land but also to the safeguarding of ancient customs.[98] This comment, too, it would seem, is intended for his fellow Jews who are tempted to neglect the ancient laws and customs.

Fuchs contends, to be sure, that the inner strength of Judaism on Egyptian soil was so great that only seldom was there admixture with pagan cults.[99] And yet there would seem to be syncretistic elements in several Graeco-Jewish writers. Thus, the *Letter of Aristeas* (16) declares that the Jews worship the same god as do the Greeks (Zeus or Dis) under another name. Again, Artapanus (quoted in Eusebius, *Praeparatio Evangelica* 9.27.3–5) identifies Moses with the semilegendary Greek poet Musaeus, the teacher of Orpheus, founder of the great Orphic religion so popular at this time. Artapanus also identifies Moses with the Egyptian equivalent of the god Hermes. Aristobulus (quoted in Eusebius, *Praeparatio Evangelica* 13.12.5–6), though not identifying any Greek deity with G-d, nonetheless cites the holy scripture (ἱερὸς λόγος) of Orpheus as a witness to G-d's rule over the world, thus by implication lending a certain legitimacy to Orpheus.

Again, the fact that even the great Philo (*De Sobrietate* 4.20) refers to

Moses as a hierophant (the term that designates the highest officer of the heathen mysteries) who initiated the Jews into the mysteries (μυσταγω-γῶν) (*De Virtutibus* 33.178) would appear to be another point of connection between Judaism and paganism in his mind. Indeed, Philo (*De Cherubim* 14.49), in a rare autobiographical note, himself claims to have been initiated by Moses into the greater mysteries; in fact, the very distinction between the greater and the lesser mysteries has been borrowed from the Eleusinian Mysteries, the most prominent of all the mysteries among the Greeks.[100] Moreover, we may mention some undoubtedly Jewish documents from Egypt which show deviations from the Jewish tradition of monotheism.[101] Thus, there are a number of documents dating from the second century B.C.E. in which the contracting parties, as well as witnesses, are Jews and in which there are references to the Ptolemies as gods.[102] We also have some inscriptions dating from the Ptolemaic period found in the Temple of Pan at Resediyeh in Upper Egypt.[103] One of them reads, "Praise to G-d. Theodorus, son of Dorion, saved from the sea." Another reads, "Ptolemaios, son of Dionysios, the Jew, praises G-d." The other inscriptions in this temple, all of which are similarly worded, mention Pan by name; these, to be sure, do not, but inasmuch as inscriptions in a temple are normally to the god of that temple, such inscriptions would seem to indicate a real compromise with Jewish monotheism.

Furthermore, there are three inscriptions on Jewish tombstones dating from the first century B.C.E. and the first century C.E. which mention that the departed has arrived in the realm of Hades, one of the names in pagan mythology for the Lower World and for the ruler, the god Pluto, who presided there.[104] The last of these, in the best style of pagan epitaphs, is a dialogue between the deceased and the passer-by in which the latter asks how old the deceased was when he "slipped down to the shadowy region of Lethe" and whether he had children. The deceased replies that he was twenty and that he went childless to the house of Hades. It may be thought that Hades and Lethe are nothing more than poetic terms for death, and that therefore their use may not indicate any real deviation from Jewish tradition; but these terms did have significance in the pagan religions that were still very much alive during this period, and they therefore do apparently indicate pagan infiltration.[105] Again, a papyrus (ca. 295 C.E.) mentions a Jew named Jacob ben Achilles, who was a guard in the temple of the Egyptian god Sarapis (the Hellenized Osiris) at Oxyrhynchus.[106]

Finally, we may cite certain pagan elements in some charms (that is, verbal incantations) and apotropaic amulets (or the material objects themselves containing graphic symbols), which are apparently Jewish but which contain pagan elements and which Goodenough has systematically examined for the first time.[107] Before Goodenough, the combination in charms of Jewish and pagan elements had usually been interpreted as indicating that these were pagan or Gnostic formulae into which the Jewish divine names had been borrowed; and scholars, relying on the conventional picture of the Egyptian Jewish community as an orthodox one, seldom ventured to suggest that the Jews might have done much of the borrowing.[108] Goodenough, however, by examining the many hundreds of charms and amulets with Jewish elements, has been able to set forth a criterion for determining whether a charm is Jewish, namely, whether the Jewish elements are central or merely tangential.[109] Using this criterion, Goodenough presents many charms that are in all probability Jewish, in which, nonetheless, various Egyptian and Greek gods are invoked together with the Jewish G-d. Thus, we have one that calls on the Egyptian gods Ammon, Ptah, and Thoth, together with the Jewish G-d (by several names) and a number of unrecognizable names. Another charm, which is probably Jewish, has a prayer to Zeus and Sarapis, as well as to the Jewish G-d. Another refers to Apollo side by side with G-d, Michael, and Gabriel.[110] Another syncretistic charm, which appears, by Goodenough's criterion, to be Jewish, addresses the Egyptian deity Osiris and "Moses, thy prophet, to whom thou hast given thy mysteries that Israel celebrates." The charm continues with a number of Jewish divine names.[111]

Moreover, there is a charm, apparently Jewish, which calls upon the sun god Helios, the father of the world.[112] Another amulet, which is very likely Jewish, asks that the wearer be guarded by the angels Michael, Gabriel, Ouriel, and Raphael; but it contains busts of Helios, the sungod, and Selene, the moon-goddess, as well as the eye of Horus, the son of Isis and Osiris and the Egyptian god of the sun.[113] Another charm by a man who was, in all probability, a Jew, addresses, in addition to the Jewish divine names, the Greek deities Helios, Aphrodite, and Kronos, as well as the two chief Egyptian deities, Isis and Osiris.[114]

Among the Jews seeking to win their beloved, Aphrodite and Cupid are particular favorites because they are concerned with erotic love.[115] The appearance of Cupid on such amulets is not a mere decorative device, as it might be construed in modern art, because the cupids in ancient times were deeply symbolic and meaningful.[116] Similarly, the Gorgon's head or Medusa from pagan mythology, so common in Jewish amulets, is not a mere decoration but a meaningful symbol.[117] A charm dedicated to Apollo mentions Sabaoth and Ad-nai and has Moses (though not mentioned by name) proclaim himself as "him who met you and you gave to me as a gift the knowledge of your greatest name."[118] Furthermore, a papyrus, purporting to include an excerpt from a work entitled *The Diadem of Moses*, contains a charm telling the user how to render himself invisible in order to obtain the love of a woman; the magical words to be spoken include *Iao* (a version of the Tetragrammaton), *Sa-baoth* ("Hosts"), and Ad-nai ("L-rd").[119]

As to the many magical papyri and charms that have been found in Egypt, there is a keen debate in most instances as to whether they are of Jewish or pagan origin. A third possibility, we may add, is that they belonged to "G-d-fearers." Goodenough, who discusses this question at length, concludes that it is impossible to determine which way the borrowing went.[120] Some names, such as Iao, Ad-nai, Sa-baoth, and Moses, became so much part of the syncretistic magical vocabulary that their Jewish origin was probably eventually forgotten.[121]

The Jews seem to have been attracted, in particular, to the pagan deity Chnoubis, who was himself a combination of the Greek gods Agathos Daimon and Chnun, the ram-headed god of the city of Elephantine in southern Egypt, and who thus served as one of the favorite magical symbols on amulets among Jews, particularly when it came to seeking good luck or healing.[122] Thus, one amulet shows a snake, presumably Chnoubis, between the words *Sabao* and *Iao*, with *Moyse* ("Moses") on the reverse.

Moreover, at Dura in Mesopotamia in the third century, there are a number of pagan influences. For example, there are felines, which are generally associated with Cybele. There is a portrayal of Orpheus playing a lyre. Moses leads the Jews out of Egypt holding a knobby club of Heracles. In the depiction of Ezekiel and the valley of the dry bones, the souls of the dead are portrayed as Greek Psyches.

In summary, even if the Jewish divine names and that of Moses had been widely appropriated in pagan circles for magical purposes, and even if almost every one of Goodenough's attempts to identify a given charm or amulet as Jewish may consequently be questioned, still the cumulative effect of all the evidence is considerable in indicating a high level of syncretism. And yet this was all at the level of folklore and hardly diminished the loyalty to Judaism of the Jewish possessors of these amulets.

8. The Strength of Judaism in Asia Minor

There is good reason to think that there were strong Jewish communities in Asia Minor at least as early as the second century B.C.E. A letter written by Antiochus III (quoted in Josephus, *Ant.* 12.148–53) to Zeuxis, the governor of Lydia, some time between 212 and 204 B.C.E. concerning the settlement, with special privileges, of two thousand Jewish families in Lydia and Phrygia in Asia Minor for security purposes, would indicate a large, well-established, and affluent Jewish community.[123] In the middle of the second century B.C.E., letters sent by the Roman Senate to a number of kings and cities in Asia Minor in support of the Jews there indicate a sizable Jewish population. A number of documents quoted by Josephus (*Ant.* 14.185–267; 16.160–78), dating from the first century B.C.E., indicate that, despite local opposition, the Roman authorities insisted on confirming the privileges of the Jews of Asia Minor to live in accordance with their national customs (that is, the Torah), to be permitted to build synagogues and to assemble for their religious services,[124] to be accorded a reduction in taxes, to be excused from military service because of the problem of Sabbath and dietary observance, and to transmit funds to the Temple in Jerusalem.[125] The fact that the Jews of Asia Minor in the year 59 B.C.E., as we see from Cicero (*Pro Flacco* 28.66–69), apparently were ready to defy a Roman edict in order to send huge funds to the Temple in Jerusalem is an indication of the strength of their loyalty to their Jewish identity.[126] The fact that the Jews of Sardis, for example (*Ant.* 14.259–61) appealed to the council and people of the city to confirm their right to observe the Sabbath would indicate that such observance was to them an important part of Jewish identity. Likewise, Augustus's edict (*Ant.* 16.163) exempting Jews from the requirement to appear in court on Friday afternoon after the ninth hour shows that the Jews were deeply concerned with Sabbath observance. There is, furthermore, evidence of the Jews' concern for observance of the dietary laws in the decree of the people of Sardis (*Ant.* 14.261) ordering market officials to arrange to have suitable food brought in for the Jews. The vigorous opposition that Paul, according to the Book of Acts, encountered in his preaching in Asia Minor would similarly suggest that the Jews, as a group, during the first century were zealous defenders of the law.[127]

The newly discovered inscriptions from Aphrodisias raise the question of the inherent strength of Judaism in Asia Minor in the third century, the presumed date of the inscriptions.[128] One major conclusion of Reynolds and Tannenbaum is that the Jews of Asia Minor were close to Palestinian and Babylonian Talmudic Judaism, proved by their adoption of the institution of the *tamḥui* (soup kitchen).[129] They conclude that "by at least the third century the Jews in Asia Minor think in the same institutional and educational terms, and organize associations for the pursuit of the same goals, along the same lines, as their co-religionists in Palestine."[130] And this despite the total lack in the inscriptions of any indication of knowledge of Hebrew.

To support the conclusion of Reynolds and Tannenbaum, there is scattered evidence of rabbinic interest in Asia Minor. Thus, we hear (*Megillah* 18b) that in the middle of the second century Rabbi Meir, the teacher of the patriarch Rabbi Judah the Prince, went to "Asia" (presumably one of the cities of Asia Minor), apparently having been sent by the patriarch, whose prerogative it was, in order to announce an intercalary month. It was perhaps on this occasion that Rabbi Akiva (*Yevamoth* 121a), who was traveling on another ship, noted that Rabbi Meir's ship was in distress. When they landed in Cappadocia, the two scholars were said to have discussed matters of *halakhah* together. Indeed, Naomi Cohen suggests, on the basis of both onomastic considerations and the Talmudic portrayal of Nero, who is said to have escaped to Asia Minor, that Rabbi Meir was of Anatolian origin.[131] Asia Minor may also have been a place of refuge for those who fled after the Bar Kochba rebellion, if we may judge from the instance of Rabbi Jose ben Ḥalafta (*Baba Metzia* 84a), who fled there at that time.

We hear, moreover, that in the district of Lydda (*Pesaḥim* 50a, cf. *Ta'anith* 18b) in Asia Minor, to which the city of Laodicea belonged, two Jews were martyred during the second century. Furthermore, a mission (*Sanhedrin* 26a) in connection with the calendar brought Rabbi Ḥiyya ben Zarnuki and Rabbi Simeon ben Jehozadak to Asia Minor in the third century, where they were met by the great sage Resh Lakish.

In further support of the thesis of Reynolds and Tannenbaum that the Jews of Asia Minor were close to Talmudic Judaism, we may be tempted to add that the power of the Palestinian patriarch in the Diaspora generally seems to have been considerable. We hear, for example, from a third-century inscription (contemporary, it would seem, therefore, with the Aphrodisias inscriptions) found in a synagogue in Stobi in Macedonia, that a certain Claudius Tiberius Polycharmus demanded that he who violated the terms of his testament should pay the patriarch 250,000 denarii.[132] In the earlier part of the fourth century, we read (Eusebius, *Commentary on Isaiah* 18.1 [*PG* 14.212]) of "apostles" (the literal translation, we may note, of *sheluḥim*) "who bear encyclical letters from their rulers" (presumably the patriarchs). In the mid-fourth century, we have definite evidence of payments to the patriarch in a letter addressed by the Emperor Julian to "the community of the Jews," because Julian advises the patriarch, whom he addresses as "most venerable" (αἰδεσιμώτατον), to abolish the collection of the ἀποστολή, a tax that the Jews apparently found onerous.[133] Shortly thereafter, in the latter part of the century, John Chrysostom (*Contra Iudaeos et Gentiles* 16 [*PG* 48.835]) remarks that the patriarch was growing rich from the levies that he received from Diaspora Jews. The fact that this tax was the subject of legislation in 399 and 404 (*Codex Theodosianus* 16.8.14, 17) and was not abolished until 429 indicates that it was still being collected by the patriarch's emissaries. There is some reason to think, moreover, in the light of a letter from Libanius to his friend Priscianus in 364, that the chief archonship of the Jews of Antioch was at the disposal of the patriarch of the Land of Israel.[134] Similarly, in the following decade, Epiphanius (*Panarion* 30.11.4

[*PG* 41.424 = *GCS* 25.346]) writes that the emissary of the patriarch had the authority to remove such synagogue functionaries as "archsynagogues, priests, elders, and precentors." In the following decade, Jerome (*Commentary on Galatians* 1:1 [*PL* 26.335]) declares that the patriarchs dispatched apostles who instructed the Jews how to behave. The power of the patriarch is confirmed by the fact that even the Christian emperor Arcadius in 397 (*Codex Theodosianus* 16.8.13) declares that the privileges bestowed on the chief Christian clerics were also to be granted to those Jews who were subject to the power of the illustrious patriarchs. Nevertheless, although most of the rabbinic references to the patriarch derive from the third century, precisely the period when other sources are silent, none of the rabbinic references claim that the patriarch controlled Diaspora synagogues or that he collected taxes from them.[135]

And yet the Judaism of Asia Minor was hardly learned; and the Jews there, like those of Egypt, had relatively few contacts with Palestinian Judaism. There is no mention in the entire rabbinic corpus of even a single Torah academy in all of Asia Minor. Nor is there any mention in the Talmudic and midrashic writers of a single student from Asia Minor who studied in the academies of either Palestine or Babylonia during the entire Talmudic period (first through fifth centuries C.E.), when rabbinic Judaism was at its height, even though the Talmud usually gives the place of origin of those from abroad. A further clue to the lack of learning in Asia Minor is that when Rabbi Meir in the mid-second century (*Megillah* 18b) visited the area there was not a single copy of the *Megillah* (the Book of Esther) in Hebrew to be found there. He consequently had to write it out from memory.

The archaeological and epigraphical evidence that has come to light thus far would seem to indicate that in contrast to the constant commercial traffic between Palestine and Alexandria, there was much less between Palestine and Asia Minor.[136] Moreover, if there was any contact between the Jews of Asia Minor and those of Palestine, it would seem to have been largely confined to the coast of Asia Minor, because travel to the interior was relatively difficult.[137] In addition, the rabbis would have had less incentive to visit the inland communities, because these were apparently much smaller than those on the coast. Furthermore, in inland cities, such as Iconium, Akmonia, Apamea, and Eumenia, though perhaps not in Aphrodisias, to judge from the inscriptions, the Greek element in the population was a definite minority, and the level of culture was probably lower than it was on the coast. In these inland cities, we find few menorahs and Jewish cult objects as compared to many in the coastal areas, suggesting a lower degree of Jewish identity and presumably of Pharisaic influence. Moreover, there is nothing in the Jewish inscriptions from Asia Minor of the pious Jewish sentiments so frequently found elsewhere in the Diaspora; nothing to indicate love of Torah, of the Holy Land and of Jerusalem, or longing for the rebuilding of the Temple.[138] In particular, we find no depiction of the ark, so frequent in the Land of Israel and in other parts of the Diaspora, where Torah scrolls were kept.

This difference between the Jewish communities of the coast and those of the interior may also perhaps account for the different responses to the message of Christianity. The relative lack of contact between the Jews of Asia Minor and the fountainhead in the Land of Israel may explain why Christianity seems to have made relatively great progress in Asia Minor, presumably among Jews, by the beginning of the second century, because we find fledgling Christian groups generally in cities— Pergamum, Thyateira, Smyrna, Philadelphia, Ephesus, Tralles, Hierapolis, Magnesia, Laodicea, Colossae, and Miletus—where we usually know that there are Jewish communities.[139] And yet the actual number of Christians in Asia Minor, at least in the earlier period, was small, compared with the number of Jews; and by the third century the counterattack by Jews had remarkably and successfully begun.

Sardis seems to be a major exception to the lower degree of Jewish identity that we generally find inland in Asia Minor. Perhaps because of the very size of the Jewish population, it shows, in the many depictions of menorahs, for example, a much higher degree of Jewish consciousness.[140] As a result of the excavations at Sardis, we now realize that the Jewish community had far greater wealth, power, and self-confidence, especially in the third century, than the usual views of ancient Judaism would give us any right to expect.[141] In particular, the fierceness of the second-century Bishop Melito of Sardis's polemic against the Jews in his homily *On Pascha* is evidence of a sense of powerlessness he felt in the presence of the Jews.[142] As he points out, when finally, in the middle of the fourth century—and after, we may add, Christianity has attained licit status in the Roman Empire—the Christians build a church there, it is far smaller than the synagogue that had recently been rebuilt and enlarged.

Moreover, Goodenough's work dealing with Jewish art during this period, which shows such divergences from halakhic norms, has convinced most scholars that the degree of rabbinic control, especially in the Diaspora and even in the Land of Israel itself, was far from dominant.[143] The fact that the Diaspora Jewish communities were more remote from one another than were the early Christian communities may have contributed to this sense of isolation. If, however, no other province became so completely Christianized by the beginning of the fourth century as did Asia Minor,[144] we may suggest that this happened not because Judaism was weak but rather because there was a unique combination of Greek and Oriental elements in the area. Indeed, Asia Minor was a crucial area for the Church's expansion, because the density of its population was apparently the greatest in the empire; and it was from here that the apostle John and the book of Revelation were said to have originated, and here also, most probably, the four Gospels were canonized.[145] There is little evidence, however, of actual syncretism among Jews in Asia Minor. Some scholars have sought to find evidence of such syncretism in the references in both Jewish and non-Jewish inscriptions to ὕψιστος and Θεὸς ὕψιστος.[146] Further evidence of such syncretism has been seen in the fact that the term Θεὸς ὕψιστος was used of the deity Sabazius, whose cult was thought to have originated in Asia Minor. We do have one inscription (*CII* 2.749, second century B.C.E.) that cites a Jew named Niketes who contributed to the festival of Dionysus. Moreover, two second-century coins from the town of Sale bear the names of two Jewish officials, one of whom was a high priest in one of the local cults.[147] These appear to be exceptional; otherwise the community, though highly Hellenized, shows little evidence of actual defection from Judaism and, in fact, as we shall see, exhibits considerable vitality in securing proselytes and especially "sympathizers." Indeed, it is significant that the use of the term ὕψιστος as a title for the Jewish G-d actually declined, most of the occurrences being found in inscriptions dating from the second century B.C.E. to the first century C.E., whereas the bulk of Jewish inscriptions date from the period after that.[148] This suggests that the dangers of the title were recognized, and hence it was avoided; this will also explain the very limited use of the term by Philo and Josephus, who wrote primarily for pagan audiences.[149] As to syncretism with the cult of Sabazius, Kraabel has demonstrated that, although Sabazius was worshipped in Sardis from the fourth century B.C.E. through at least the second century C.E. none of the more than eighty Jewish inscriptions from Sardis show any knowledge of Sabazius, nor is there any evidence in the otherwise sharp attacks on the Jews by Melito, the second-century bishop of Sardis, that Jews were guilty of syncretism or that they were apostates to any degree.[150]

9. EXCESSES IN INTERPRETATION OF THE LAW: LITERALISTS AND ALLEGORISTS

To what degree was there deviation in practice from the traditional norms of Judaism? One group of deviants consisted of literalists, who refused to allegorize the Scriptures and hence were forever encountering serious theological difficulties.[151] Shroyer, in his study of this group, has given a list of difficulties that they found especially puzzling.[152] In spirit they were naturally contemptuous of those investigators of Scripture whom they called "straw-splitters" (Philo, *De Somniis* 2.45.301). On the other hand, they are condemned (*De Cherubim* 12.42) for engaging in petty quibbling (γλισχρότητι, "stickiness") about expressions and words and for having no other standard for measuring what is pure and pious. They scoffed particularly at the story of the Tower of Babel (*De Confusione Linguarum* 4.9–10), for they asked what good G-d had accomplished by the confusion of tongues. These intellectuals are accused by Philo of godlessness, inasmuch as they asserted that the Bible contains myths that the Jews deride in others while accepting them in their own case without question. Thus, Jews will ridicule the piling of Mount Pelion on Mount Ossa atop Mount Olympus in Greek mythology without realizing, according to the literalists (*De Confusione Linguarum* 2.2), that the story of the Tower of Babel is very similar. Again, they are puzzled (*Quod Deus Sit Immutabilis* 5.21, 11.52) by G-d's repentance and by His anger. In reply, Philo (*De Virtutibus* 3.10) says that the literalists are full of inconsistencies. Moreover, only through allegorical interpretation can one explain why Scripture employs synonymous but different words for the same term, for example, "husbandman" ($\gamma \varepsilon \omega \rho \gamma \acute{o} \varsigma$) and "soil-worker" ($\gamma \tilde{\eta} \varsigma \ \dot{\varepsilon} \rho \gamma \acute{\alpha} \tau \eta \varsigma$).

We do not know how numerous the literalists were, but Philo refers to only one literalist whom he knew. This one, whom Philo (*De Mutatione Nominum* (8.61) classifies as an atheistic and impious person, scoffed that G-d should have added an alpha to Abram's name or a rho to Sara's. Eventually he hanged himself (*De Mutatione Nominum* 8.62). It is clear from Philo's tone that this was an isolated case, and the sharpness of his attack indicates condemnation in the strongest terms.

The second group of intellectuals who deviated from traditional Jewish observance according to Philo were the extreme allegorists, who, although not constituting a distinct sect, were forerunners of antinomianism, the attack on Jewish legalism associated with Paul.[153] Philo (*De Migratione Abrahami* 16.89) is critical of them for being overpunctilious about seeing symbolism in the laws while they treat the literal sense of the laws with easygoing neglect. It is clear that he has these excessive allegorists in mind when he excoriates (*De Migratione Abrahami* 16.91), in immediate juxtaposition with this passage, those who violate the rules of the Sabbath by lighting fires, tilling the ground, carrying loads, instituting proceedings in court, acting as jurors, and demanding the restoration of deposits or recovering loans. Among the examples that he here gives are rules drawn from the oral Torah, as later codified in the Talmud, which were apparently treated with less seriousness than those from the written Torah. Philo (*De Posteritate Caini* 12.42) calls these allegorists "sons of Cain" who deviated from Judaism on the pretext that the ceremonial laws are only a parable and that one who understands the allegorical idea behind them need no longer obey them. These allegorists were thoroughgoing individualists. It is, he says (*De Migratione Abrahami* 16.90), as though they were living alone by themselves in a wilderness with no social community able to satisfy them.[154] That such excessive allegorists are a minority, at least in Philo's eyes, we may infer from the statement (*De Migratione Abrahami* 16.93) that they incur the censure of the many (τῶν πολλῶν); and that they are not an organized group we may infer from the statement (16.90) that they live alone by themselves. But, in any case, nowhere are the extreme allegorists denounced as apostates, even though Philo excoriates them.[155]

10. DEVIATIONS FROM JEWISH LAW

That the deviations of the Hellenistic Jews are not restricted to matters of theology may be seen from the number of extant documents in which the contracting parties, as well as the witnesses, are Jews and in which there are references to the Ptolemies as gods. But perhaps this may be as little indicative of deviation from orthodoxy as "A.D." in documents of Jews today.

If the laws described in Philo's treatise *De Specialibus Legibus* were in actual practice in Philo's day, we find that there were deviations even in the Jewish courts.[156] Thus, the practice of having an oath administered to a judge is based not on Jewish but on Roman practice (Philo, *De Decalogo* 27.138–41). Again, those who endeavor to show that Philo's law is in accord with rabbinic *halakhah* admit that Philo does diverge occasionally from this law, as he does, for example, in his statement that unmarried daughters who have no fixed dowries share equally in the inheritance with the sons (Philo, *De Specialibus Legibus* 2.25.124–26).

But even if Philo does not represent the actual practices of the law courts of Alexandrian Jewry,[157] the papyri surely do offer some evidence—admittedly slight, though their unanimity is impressive—of the halakhic practices of the community. That the deviations of the Hellenistic Jews are not restricted to matters of theology may be seen from the fact that of six papyri mentioning loans by Jews to Jews, one is at interest although we do not know the rate, and four are at the usual rate of interest during the Ptolemaic period of 24 percent per year, and only one is without interest; and even that one is subject to the overtime interest rate of 24 percent if not repaid within a year.[158] To lend money to a Jew at interest is strictly forbidden by the Bible (Exod 22:24, Deut 23:20); and even a hint of interest is forbidden by the rabbis (Mishnah, *Baba Metzia* 5:1 ff.). Indeed, Philo (*De Specialibus Legibus* 2.17.75), to judge by his indignation, seems to be thinking of violators of this law in Alexandria when he says, "I ask you, Sir Moneylender, why do you disguise your want of a partner's feeling (ἀκοινώνητον) by pretending to act as a partner (κοινωνίᾳ)?[159] Why do you assume outwardly a kindly and charitable appearance but display in your actions inhumanity and a savage brutality, exacting more than you lend, sometimes double, reducing the pauper to further depths of poverty?"

Again, we see that the one Jewish divorce document we have on a papyrus dating from 13 B.C.E., when compared with the other twenty-five divorce documents thus far discovered involving non-Jews, follows non-Jewish formulae and violates the Jewish law (Deut 24:1) that the husband is the one who divorces the wife, because it states that the husband and wife agree to be divorced.[160]

It may be argued that our documents, referring, for example, to the Jewish soldiers of the Fayûm in northern Egypt, reflect the more Hellenized element of the Jewish community; that they are drawn up in gentile courts, in accordance with Greek rather than with Jewish law, may be due to the Jews' lack of a Beth Din (religious court), and, at any rate, they are not necessarily significant indicators of the attitude toward *halakhah* of the rest of the Egyptian Jewish community. But we know from the Talmud (*Kethuboth* 25a) that Alexandria itself did have a Beth Din; and the papyri from the region of Alexandria, in their reliance on Gentile courts, reveal the same state of affairs as do those from rural Egypt.[161] Thus, we have a manifest violation of the Talmudic declaration (*Gittin* 88b) that it is forbidden for a Jew to summon another Jew before tribunals of idolators. And we are aware of no decree in Hellenistic times, such as that which existed in the days of Rabbenu Tam,[162] which permitted this by mutual agreement.

Moreover, we know from Josephus (*War* 1.33, 7.423–32; *Ant.* 12.387–88, 13.62–73, 13.285, 20.236–37) and from the Talmud (Mishnah, *Menaḥoth* 13:10; *'Avodah Zarah* 52b; *Megillah* 10a; Jerusalem *Yoma* 6.3) that the high priest Onias IV in the second century B.C.E. established, ostensibly in violation of the law of the Torah (Deut 12:13–14),[163] a small replica of the Temple of Jerusalem at Leontopolis in Egypt. Here sacrifices were offered until 74 C.E., when Vespasian (see Josephus, *War* 7.421) ordered it to be closed. It is clear, however, from Philo's complete silence about this temple and from the fact that, according to Josephus (*Ant.* 14.110), the Jews from throughout the world had been contributing to the Temple in Jerusalem for a very long time, that the Egyptian Jews as a community continued to remain loyal to the Temple in Jerusalem.[164]

11. INTERMARRIAGE

In view of this evidence, we may well ask how much actual intermarriage and apostasy there was. Indeed, even the *Letter of Aristeas*, which is so liberal as to equate the Jewish G-d with Zeus (16), makes it clear (139) that intermarriage is forbidden, because G-d gave the Torah so that "we should mingle in no way with any of the other nations."

If intermarriage had been frequent, we would expect it to be mentioned often by Philo, especially because he played such a leading role in the Jewish community. Yet Philo adopts a surprisingly gentle tone in discussing the instances of biblical intermarriage, especially when we consider the harsh condemnation of these practices in Deuteronomy 7:3–6.[165] Thus, though Hagar, Abraham's concubine, was, we are told (*De Abrahamo* 43.251) in an extra-biblical comment, an Egyptian by birth, yet she was a Hebrew by her rule of life (προαίρεσιν, "deliberate choice," "conduct," "character"), that is, she was a convert or a proto-convert to Judaism. Likewise, without scriptural basis (cf. Gen 30:3, 9), Philo (*De Virtutibus* 40.223) elevates the Babylonian handmaids Bilhah and Zilpah to the name and position of wedded wives who "were treated no longer as handmaids, but as almost equal in rank to their mistresses, who, indeed, incredible as it seems, promoted them to the same dignity as themselves." Again, when Philo mentions Moses' intermarriage with Zipporah (*De Vita Mosis* 1.11.59), he says nothing about her Midianite origin and the fact that this was an intermarriage; he describes her simply as the fairest of Jethro's daughters. As to Moses' marriage with the Ethiopian woman (Num 12:1), far from condemning it as a case of intermarriage, Philo (*Legum Allegoria* 2.17.67) says, in effect, that this was a marriage made in heaven, and that it was G-d Himself who wedded Moses to the Ethiopian woman, who stands for the supremely laudable virtue of unalterable, intense, and fixed resolve.

On the contrary, when Philo (*De Specialibus Legibus* 3.5.29) does mention the biblical prohibition of intermarriage, he speaks of its consequences not in his own day but rather at some vague time in the future, "lest some day (ποτε), conquered by the forces of opposing customs, you surrender and stray unawares from the path that leads to piety and turn aside into a pathless wild." He specifically indicates that he is not worried about the current generation, because they have been carefully instructed by their parents in the holy laws of the Torah. Rather, he indicates his fear for the next generation, lest they be enticed to prefer spurious to genuine customs. If intermarriage were, indeed, the terrible scourge that one might expect in view of the syncretism noted above, we might well ask why Philo, who surely is a devoted and observant Jew, fails to state the biblically prescribed punishment for such an infraction, namely (Deut 7:4) that the anger of G-d will be kindled against those who intermarry and that they will be speedily destroyed. Perhaps Philo's silence may be an indication that intermarriage was so common that he felt that the wiser course was not to condemn it but rather to encourage the conversion of the non-Jewish partner.[166] But this seems unlikely in view of the statement, noted above, that intermarriage might someday lead to the abandonment of the prescriptions of the Torah.

Tcherikover, on the basis of Philo's extra-biblical exposition (*De Vita Mosis* 1.27.147) that the mixed multitude (Exod 12:38) who accompanied the Israelites during their exodus from Egypt were actually the children of the intermarriage of Egyptian women and Hebrew men, suggests that Philo may be describing the conditions of his own time.[167] That he speaks in such derogatory terms of the products of these marriages, referring to them as "a promiscuous (μιγάδων, "mixed pell-mell"), nondescript (συγκλύδων, "washed together by the waves"), and menial crowd, a bastard host, so to speak, associated with the true-born," would seem, to be sure, to be a sharp attack on intermarriage, but Philo avoids any comment on the contemporary situation, though this was certainly an excellent opening.

Most likely, intermarriage was not frequent. For one thing the sheer number of Jews[168] and their concentration in certain areas must have made such unions less likely.[169] To be sure, Baron postulates that intermarriage must have increased in direct ratio with the intimacy of social contacts with Gentiles, and he asserts that even in Philo's Alexandria, where the Jews constituted the largest single religious and ethnic group in the city's cosmopolitan population, marriage with non-Jews was apparently quite common.[170] In support of his statement, Baron cites a passage in Philo (De Specialibus Legibus 3.4.25 which states that "intermarriages with outsiders create new kinships not a wit inferior to blood-relationships." But the context here is explaining why the Torah forbids the union of a brother with a sister and is surely not justifying marriage of Jew and non-Jew, as we can see from the prohibition a very few paragraphs later (De Specialibus Legibus 3.5.29) of entering into "the partnership of marriage with a member of a foreign nation." Tcherikover says that "we shall not be far wrong in stating that intermarriage was frequent, particularly among the rural population, which lived in direct proximity to the natives; here, perhaps the Egyptian element attracted the Jews more strongly than did the Greek."[171] Moreover, it may be true, as Tcherikover remarks, that Greek and Macedonian soldiers married women of the local population, that with the women Egyptian names, language, religion, and customs entered into their family life, and that when the Romans arrived in the first century B.C.E. they found in the Egyptian villages not Greeks but Graeco-Egyptians.[172] In support of his hypothesis, Tcherikover calls attention to Egyptian names taken by many Jews;[173] but we may counter by remarking that although this may indicate a degree of assimilation, among the by now many thousands of papyri we have there is only one unambiguous mention, dating from the second century B.C.E., of an intermarriage between a Jew and a non-Jew.[174]

12. APOSTASY

Wolfson, who defines apostates as those who actually adopted another religion, distinguishes three types.[175] In the first place, there are those rebels (ἀποστάντας) from the holy laws who are condemned (De Virtuti-

bus 34.182) as "incontinent, shameless, unjust, frivolous, petty-minded, quarrelsome, friends of falsehood and perjury, who have sold their freedom for dainties and strong liquor and cakes and the enjoyment of another's beauty, thus ministering to the delights of the belly and the organs below it." These are, however, not apostates but Jews who are no longer observant of the commandments of the Torah, as we can see from the concern with repentance in the essay in which this passage appears; and Philo has here just described (*De Virtutibus* 33.179) the greatest form of repentance, namely turning from polytheism to monotheism, after which he says (*De Virtutibus* 33.179), "We have described the first and most essential form of repentance." But, he then adds, a man should show repentance not only in matters of theology but also in his pattern of life, in particular diet and sexual freedom. It is in this context that the passage about rebels from the laws appears. According to Wolfson, the breaking of these laws proved, in general experience, to be the beginning of the breakdown of social barriers generally between Jew and non-Jew and ultimately led to the abandonment of Judaism.[176] Consequently, Philo should have raised these laws to the status of fundamental religious principles; but, if so, Philo nowhere in his voluminous works draws this corollary. Mere failure to observe the commandments did not then, as it does not now, in itself constitute apostasy, because a Jew, though a sinner, remains a Jew (*Sanhedrin* 44a), and if he should revert to observance of the commandments, he would require no special ritual act, because technically he never left Judaism.

A second passage that Wolfson believes refers to apostasy is the one where Philo speaks (*De Praemiis et Poenis* 26.152) of the nobly born (εὐπατρίδης) who has falsified (παρακόψας, "strike falsely," "counterfeit") the sterling (νόμισμα, "current coin," "custom") of his high lineage (εὐγενείας, "nobility of birth").[177] This metaphor, which appears frequently in Philo,[178] is used in connection with the breaking of any established law, but with the connotation that this breaking of the law involves adulteration of something that is pure by nature or birth. Wolfson then concludes that the reference is to an apostate who has not only been disloyal to the laws of his fathers but has also been led to his disloyalty by his intermarriage to a non-Jew. But an examination of the context in Philo shows no reference to intermarriage; moreover, a person may be false to his lineage not only through actual apostasy but also through nonobservance of the commandments.

That it was lack of observance rather than actual apostasy that was the chief problem of Alexandrian Jewish community in Philo's day would seem to be indicated by the passage (*De Specialibus Legibus* 1.35.186) in which Philo states that the fast of the Day of Atonement is carefully observed (ἐσπουδάκασιν, "be serious," "be earnest," "pursue zealously") not only by those who are zealous for piety and holiness but also by those who never act religiously (εὐαγές, "holy," "lawful," "free from defilement") in the rest of their life. All, he says, stand in awe, overcome by the sanctity of the day, and at least for that one day, he adds, "the worse vie with the better in self-denial and virtue." The clear implication, then, is that no one in the community goes so far as to cut himself off utterly from identification with the Jewish way of life, and that Philo and his circle continued to count such people as Jews.

A second class of apostates discerned by Wolfson in Philo's works (*De Vita Mosis* 1.6.30–31) are the nouveaux riches, who have despised their erstwhile friends, have given up the laws under which they were born and bred, have subverted their ancestral traditions, and have changed their mode of life (ἐκδεδιῃτημένοι). In their contentment with the present, they are said to lose all memory of the past. From this Wolfson deduces that they have become completely severed from the body of Israel; but the more likely explanation is that they have changed their mode of life in the sense that they have ceased to observe the commandments.[179]

A third class of apostates mentioned by Philo, according to Wolfson, consists of those who have dropped out of Judaism through an unconscious shifting of intellectual interest.[180] Goodenough, however, would seem to be justified in objecting to this conclusion on the ground that a change in thinking that leads to apostasy is hardly likely to be unconscious, especially when it leads to such actions as those Tiberius Julius Alexander, Philo's nephew, undertook against the Jews.[181] An example of this third group is, indeed, usually said to be the same Tiberius Julius Alexander, with whom Philo, in his treatise *De Providentia*, debated the problem of divine providence.[182] Alexander eventually rose to be procurator of Judaea (46–48 C.E.), even (66 C.E.) attained the governorship of the most important province in the Roman Empire, Egypt, and (69 C.E.) became the highest-ranking officer, next to Titus himself, in the Roman army besieging Jerusalem. Nevertheless, the one passage on which the ascription of apostasy to Alexander rests (Josephus, *Ant.* 20.100) does not actually say that he was an apostate. Rather, it states that his father differed (διήνεγκε, "excelled") from him in piety (εὐσεβείᾳ) toward G-d, for Alexander did not abide by the ancestral practices (πατρίοις ... ἔθεσιν). The implication here is that Alexander's father was more pious than the son and that the son ceased to abide by the commandments; but there is no indication that the son became a complete apostate.[183]

Another possible apostate is Helicon, described by Philo (*Legatio ad Gaium* 26.166–70) as a damnable and abominable slave who, as a skilled jester, had wormed his way into an influential position in the household of the Emperor Gaius Caligula. Philo says (*Legatio ad Gaium* 26.170) that from his very cradle Helicon learned the false charges against Jews and

against the Jewish customs; and it would seem possible from this statement that he was actually a Jew by birth. Philo (*Legatio ad Gaium* 27.174)
adds that for a time the delegation to Rome headed by himself did not
know about "the enemy lurking in our midst, and so we were on our
guard against outside enemies only." But it is more likely that Helicon
was a Gentile Alexandrian who had heard these charges simply because
he lived in Alexandria, where there was such a large Jewish community.
In fact, Philo (*Legatio ad Gaium* 26.166) calls him the chorus leader of the
whole Egyptian troupe at the imperial court and states (*Legatio ad Gaium*
30.205) that he had vented his Egyptian venom on the Jews; and it is clear
that the context seeks to contrast the Egyptians with the Jews. As to the
identification of Helicon as the enemy lurking within, the simplest explanation is not that he was a Jew by birth but rather that he had pretended,
with his indirect and crafty methods, as Philo (*Legatio ad Gaium* 27.171)
remarks, to be friendly to the Jews, when actually he was on the side of
the enemy.

The only definite apostates of whom we hear are Dositheos, son of
Drimylos, and Antiochus of Antioch, and the great-grandchildren of Alexander, Herod the Great's son. The first, a courtier of King Ptolemy IV
Philopator (reigned 221–205 B.C.E.), whose very life he saved, according
to 3 Maccabees (1:3), "changed (μεταβαλὼν) his faith (τὰ νόμιμα, "customs," "usages") and became alienated (ἀπηλλοτριωμένος, "estranged,"
"separated") from the beliefs of his fathers (τῶν πατρίων δογμάτων)." The
name Dositheos was particularly favored by Jews and is a rare name
among pagans; hence it is very likely that he was a Jew by birth.[184] That
he was an apostate is clear from the papyri (*CPJ* 1.127d and 127e) that
mention him in the year 222 B.C.E. as the eponymous priest of Alexander
and the deified Ptolemies, the highest priesthood in Hellenistic Egypt.[185]

As to Antiochus of Antioch, Josephus (*War* 7.47) states that at the
outbreak of the war against the Romans in 66 C.E., when Vespasian had
recently landed in Syria and hatred of the Jews was everywhere at its
height, Antiochus, one of their number (εἷς ἐξ αὐτῶν), the son of the chief
magistrate (ἄρχων) of the Jews of Antioch, denounced his father and the
other Jews, accusing them of plotting to burn the whole city. Antiochus,
we are told (*War* 7.50), in his eagerness to give proof of his conversion
(μεταβολῆς, "transition," "change") and of his detestation (μεμισηκέναι,
"hatred") for Jewish customs (ἔθη, "habits"), sacrificed in the Greek manner and recommended that the other Jews be compelled to do likewise.
A few, we are told, submitted, and the rest were massacred. Antiochus
then, with the aid of Roman troops, attempted to force the Jews to violate
the Sabbath.[186]

As to the grandchildren of Alexander, Herod's son, Josephus (*Ant.*
18.141) reports that they abandoned (ἐξέλιπε) from birth the observance

(θεραπείαν) of the ways of the Jews and ranged (μεταταξάμενοι) with the Greek ancestral ways (τὰ Ἕλλησι πάτρια). Their father, also called Alexander, had married a non-Jewish princess, Jotape, the daughter of Antiochus, the king of Commagene. We do hear, in an unusual inscription (*CII* 2.742), of a group of "former Jews" (οἱ ποτὲ Ἰουδαῖοι) in Smyrna in the second century who had made benefactions to the city.[187] Presumably, these are Jews who had acquired Greek citizenship at the price of repudiating their Jewish allegiance;[188] and, apparently, in the view of non-Jews (though, of course, not in the view of Jewish law), a Jew who no longer observed the commandments of Judaism had ceased to be a Jew. But we must stress that such an inscription referring to "former" Jews is utterly unique in the corpus of inscriptions.

In practice, the more common method in the Diaspora of expressing deviation from the Jewish tradition was probably not intermarriage, apostasy, or freethinking but simply nonobservance. In the third century B.C.E., we know through Josephus (*Ant.* 12.186–87) of a wealthy Transjordanian Jew, Joseph, the son of Tobias, who, in frequent visits to the Egyptian court, ate forbidden food and fell in love with a pagan dancing-girl; and we read in 3 Maccabees (7:11) about others who ate forbidden food. The Wisdom of Solomon (2:1-20), dating apparently from the first century B.C.E.,[189] mentions some prosperous Jews who, probably under the influence of the popular form of Epicureanism, adopted the philosophy of "eat, drink, and be merry" and who oppressed poor people and widows. From the fact that Philo never mentions the names of any rabbis who lived in Egypt or even visited there and from the fact that the Talmudic writings mention few rabbis who took the initiative to visit the huge Egyptian Jewish community, we may guess that rabbinic authority there was weak and that there was, as we see from the amulets, a good deal of compromising and syncreticism with paganism. But although there may have been many "Yom Kippur Jews," who never acted religiously during the rest of calendar year, intermarriage and apostasy were apparently deterred by the high level of anti-Judaism on the part of the masses; and Jews maintained their identity with the Jewish people and, as shown by their warm greeting of Agrippa I in Alexandria (Philo, *In Flaccum* 5.30), with Judaea as an independent state. Hence, the net effect of the assimilation of the Greek language and culture by the Jews was not defection from Judaism but rather, on the contrary, the creation of a common bond of communication with Gentiles, through which at least some non-Jews were won over to Judaism.

CHAPTER 3

OFFICIAL ANTI-JEWISH BIGOTRY: THE RESPONSES OF GOVERNMENTS TO THE JEWS

1. ANTI-JEWISH BIGOTRY BEFORE THE ERA OF ALEXANDER THE GREAT

The survival of the Jews would appear to depend not only on their inner strength and the degree to which they were able to resist the forces of assimilation, such as we have discussed above, but also on the degree to which their neighbors admired or hated or tolerated them.

Has hatred of Jews been universally prevalent?[1] Perhaps it will be appropriate to start with a discussion of the very word *anti-Semitism*. The word *Semitic* is derived from Shem, the son of Noah in the Bible (Gen 7:13), but the term is commonly understood as a linguistic term referring to a family of related languages rather than to a race or a nation of people.[2]

The term *anti-Semitism*, clearly a misnomer, was introduced by the German Wilhelm Marr in 1879 and entered into English usage in the period from 1880 to 1884, presumably to base hatred of the Jews not on mere religious grounds but on race, because many Jews by that time were no longer identified with the Jewish religion in practice or, like several of Moses Mendelssohn's children, had actually become Christians. Though clearly inappropriate, the term has, however, come into such wide use that more appropriate terms, such as Jew-hatred or anti-Judaism, have failed to gain comparable currency. Nevertheless, whatever term is used, the definition of this attitude is based on the belief that Jews are uniquely inferior, evil, or deserving of condemnation by their very nature or according to historical or supernatural dictates.

The earliest instance of Jew-hatred is found in the Bible, where we read (Exod 1:8–10) that a new king arose in Egypt who did not know Joseph and who said to his people, "Behold the people of Israel are too many (*rav*) and too mighty (*'atzum*) for us." He then expresses the fear that they will multiply and will join themselves with the enemies of the Egyptians in war. It is almost as if the Pharaoh who had spoken these words had set a two-fold major theme for the anti-Judaism that was to follow throughout antiquity, namely fear of expansion of the numbers of

Jews and belief that the Jews would not be loyal to the regime but, because they constitute a nation, would be torn by dual loyalties. Indeed, the Midrash (*Genesis Rabbah* 79.1) has a tradition that at the death of Jacob the seventy persons he had brought down to Egypt with him had grown to six hundred thousand; furthermore, we are told that the Israelites filled the theaters and all the places of amusement; that is, not only were they populous, but they were also visibly numerous and ostentatious. It was this mixture of exaggerated hatred, jealousy, and fear that led Pharaoh to take drastic measures against them. In view of the fact that the Egyptians had recently experienced the invasion of the Hyksos from Asia in the seventeenth century B.C.E., who had actually managed to seize the kingship itself of Egypt,[3] and in view of the threat posed at this time by the Hittites, whose power the Pharaoh Rameses could not break, one can understand his fear, even if one cannot, of course, justify the measures that he promulgated against the Hebrews. In any case, the action he took was not prompted by disdain for the Israelite religion or even for the Israelite people as such, but rather was against foreigners who, he thought, were a threat to Egyptian independence as a nation.

A second case of Jew-hatred may be seen in the attack on the Israelites by King Amalek (Exod 17:8–14, Deut 25:17–19). But this attack was not prompted by the feeling that the Israelites were uniquely inferior or evil or deserving of condemnation by their very nature. Rather, they were viewed by the Amalekites as invaders or potential invaders of their territory.

A third case in the Bible of Jew-hatred may be seen in the Book of Esther (3:8), where Haman, who was, in effect, the prime minister of King Ahasuerus of Persia, furious that Mordecai the Jew did not bow down to him, decided to destroy all of Mordecai's people and thus declared to Ahasuerus, "There is a certain people scattered abroad and dispersed among the people in all the provinces of your kingdom; their laws are different from those of every other people, and they do not keep the king's laws, so that it is not for the king's profit to tolerate them." The historicity of the whole episode has been challenged on the grounds that we know of no official named Haman and no queens named Vashti and Esther; but this is really irrelevant. The important point is that this scene contains the elements that were viewed by the author of the Book of Esther as integral to Jew-hatred: the dispersion and homelessness of the Jews, the generalization by the bigot from one person to the entire people, the suspicions aroused by strange customs that engender dislike for those who are unlike oneself, and, finally and most importantly, the accusation that there is an alien element that is potentially harmful to the State (as in the case of Pharaoh noted above) and that, in any case, the Jews are politically disloyal. Here again, as in the case of the Israelites in

Egypt, the fear is in the sheer number of Jews, who are alleged to be in all 127 provinces of the Persian Empire. And again, in view of the recent creation of this empire and its fragility because the Persians themselves (as later Alexander in his, the Ptolemies and Seleucids in theirs, the Romans in theirs, and the Arabs in theirs) constituted a small percentage of the population in their own empire, they feared the Jews as a subversive fifth column who would feel a double loyalty. Indeed, the Persians had experienced one revolt after another in their vast empire. Moreover, if Ahasuerus is to be identified with Xerxes,[4] as he generally is, his resources had been exhausted by the abortive invasion of Greece, and hence Haman's offer to give him ten thousand talents, which, according to Herodotus (3.95), was approximately equal to the annual revenue of the entire Persian Empire during the reign of Darius half a century earlier, must have been very tempting. But if, indeed, this incident has historical validity, it would seem to be exceptional, inasmuch as the policy of the Persian Empire was throughout almost all of its history one of toleration toward its many minorities, an attitude dictated, undoubtedly, by the hard realism that the ruling Persians were, as we have noted, a small minority in their own empire.

A final incident prior to Alexander which some have interpreted as anti-Jewish is the destruction in 411 b.c.e. by the Egyptians of the temple of the Jewish mercenaries who had been stationed by the Persians at Elephantine in southern Egypt. Rather, this should be viewed as revenge by the native Egyptians against the Persians, whose rule they had bitterly resented, against whom they had frequently revolted, and whose interests these Jews had represented for over a century.

2. Jews under Egyptian Ptolemies and Syrian Seleucids

With Alexander, who reigned from 336 to 323 b.c.e., a new era dawned for the Jews; they were now encouraged to settle in the cities that he established, most notably Alexandria in Egypt. Alexander was enough of a realist to understand that he could not rule his vast, newly acquired empire containing so few Greeks and Macedonians unless he continued the attitude of tolerance toward native peoples that had been practiced by his predecessors, the Persians. He and his successors in Egypt, the Ptolemies, realized that they would never be able to control the native Egyptians, who still remembered their glorious kingdom of the past, unless they could count on a group of "middlemen," a position readily filled by the Jews and other non-Egyptians. From the Jewish point of view, this "vertical" alliance with their rulers, which, of course, was not unique to the Jews but extended to other minorities, likewise appeared advantageous. Within a very short period, Alexandria had displaced Athens as the cultural and commercial center of the Mediterranean world, and the Jews flocked to the city in large numbers.[5] The self-rule granted to them and their ability to enter various fields, including (perhaps because of their higher degree of literacy) the civil service as well as the army, served as considerable inducements.[6] The papyri now show conclusively that Jews did serve in the armies of the Ptolemies and that there is no basis for the skepticism of those who had wondered how Jews could have served as soldiers when they were not allowed by the Torah to work on the Sabbath.[7] Inasmuch as the Ptolemies felt, for good reason, that they could not trust the native Egyptians, who vastly outnumbered them, they especially welcomed the Jews, and so they continued the Persian tradition of settling the Jews in frontier fortresses. The children of these soldiers, called the *Epigone*, served as a permanent source of new enlistments and, in effect, as a reserve army.

Moreover, there was soon need, as we have noted, for a translation of the Pentateuch into Greek because Hebrew and Aramaic had become largely forgotten and because some sought to use the knowledge of Greek gained through the translation as a ticket of admission into the world of Greek culture and Greek society.[8] Furthermore, there was need for a text to combat the anti-Jewish statements of the Egyptian priest Manetho. In addition, at least as implied in the *Letter of Aristeas* (38), King Ptolemy Philadelphus in 270 B.C.E. wished to flatter the Jewish community by including a copy of their sacred book in his great new library. With the Ptolemies' loss of the Land of Israel in 198 B.C.E. to the Syrian Seleucids, the Jews of Egypt were now, to a greater degree than ever, cut off from Judaea and more open to the Greek culture in the midst of which they found themselves; and the Ptolemies may well have sought to make the Egyptian Jews religiously as well as politically independent of Jerusalem.

Significantly, during the dispute surrounding the high priesthood at the beginning of the reign of Antiochus Epiphanes in 175 B.C.E., it is in Egypt that Onias IV, the legitimate successor to the high priesthood, found refuge. Indeed, so hospitable was the Egyptian king, Ptolemy VI Philometor, that Onias, though he apparently had no previous military experience, was made commander-in-chief of Ptolemy's armed forces (Josephus, *Against Apion* 2.49) and was permitted to build his own temple at Leontopolis (*Ant.* 13.62–73, *War* 7.426–32). One assumes that Ptolemy was not utterly disinterested in showing such favor to Onias, but rather that he looked on him as a key to restoring his influence in the Land of Israel and viewed the temple as a means of anti-Seleucid propaganda among the Jews of Judaea. He may also have considered the economic advantage of having a temple in his own country so as to prevent the export to Jerusalem of the annual half-shekel from every adult male Jew. In any case, the Land of Onias, where Onias settled, was of strategic importance for the defense of Egypt. It is fair to assume that Onias was not the only refugee from the civil war that was being waged in the Land of Israel and from Antiochus Epiphanes' persecution, and that other Jews also were attracted by the welcome that was given them by Ptolemy, just as in the fifteenth century Jews who were persecuted in Spain received a warm welcome from the Ottoman Turks and were given important positions. When the Hasmoneans finally defeated the Syrian Seleucids, the great national enemy of the Ptolemies, the ties, as would be expected, between the Jews of the Land of Israel and the Ptolemies became closer.

It was their meddling in politics, their success in producing ancient versions of cabinet ministers such as the tenth-century Ḥisdai Ibn Shaprut of Cordoba in Spain, the eleventh-century Samuel Ha-Nagid of Granada in Spain, and the twentieth-century Walther Rathenau in Germany and Henry Kissinger in the United States, and their loyalty to the ruler in power during dynastic wars that helped induce charges that the Jews were not truly loyal to the best interests of the state. And yet already an early report by Hecataeus (ca 300 B.C.E.; quoted in Josephus, *Against Apion* 2.43) remarks that, in recognition of the loyalty shown by the Jews, Alexander the Great added to their territory the district of Samaria, free of tribute. Later the Ptolemies in Egypt, as Josephus (*Ant.* 11.318, 12.8) emphasizes, trusted the Jews because of their extraordinary constancy in keeping oaths and pledges. Indeed, Ptolemy VI Philometor (reigned 181–145 B.C.E.) placed his entire army under the command of two Jews, Onias and Dositheos (*Against Apion* 2.49).

But Jewish military influence could be a mixed blessing for the Jews. When, on the death of Ptolemy VI Philometor in 145 B.C.E., his brother, Ptolemy VII Physcon (Euergetes), seized the throne, Onias, true to the legitimate sovereign, Cleopatra II, took up arms against him (*Against Apion* 2.51). Thereupon, at least according to Josephus, Physcon arranged to have the first known organized massacre in Jewish history. He arrested all the Jews of the city—men, women, and children—and exposed them, naked and in chains, to be trampled to death by elephants, whom he is said to have made drunk. The Jews, however, were miraculously saved when the elephants, instead of rushing on them, turned and trampled on some of Physcon's friends. It is this transference of blame from one individual—in this case, the general Onias—to all the Jews, that is a characteristic element in anti-Jewish bigotry.[9] Such an incident of persecution of Jews by a ruler is, however, on the whole exceptional, if it is indeed historical at all;[10] and shortly thereafter, Physcon apparently made his peace with the Jews, because Josephus (*Against Apion* 2.54–55) tells us that Physcon saw a terrible apparition that forbade him to injure the Jews and that his favorite concubine added her entreaty to him not to perpetrate such an enormity. This would seem to be another way of saying that he came to the conclusion that the Jews were too useful to his realm and that it made no sense for him to persecute them. Moreover, we find inscriptions from Lower Egypt containing the regular formula of the dedication of a new synagogue in his honor.[11] Shortly thereafter Cleopatra III, the wife of Ptolemy VII Physcon, entrusted her army to the Jewish generals Helkias and Ananias (Josephus, *Ant.* 13.284–87, 349).

Apparently, the Jews of Egypt retained their religious ties with their brethren in the land of Israel; and this led to the recurring charge, so often found against Jews throughout the ages, that divided loyalties made them less than exemplary citizens of the countries in which they happened to reside. Apion (quoted in Josephus, *Against Apion* 2.65), in accordance with the ancient view that participation in the civic religion was an indication of good citizenship, asked why, if the Jews are citizens, they did not worship the same gods as the Alexandrians did,[12] because in antiquity there was no separation of religion and state; and he proceeded to accuse the Jews of fomenting sedition while plotting together. This charge of double loyalty may well have been fostered by four incidents in connection with the Egyptian Jews.

The first occurred about 102 B.C.E. (Josephus, *Ant.* 13.353–55), when some of the friends of Cleopatra III, disturbed at the expansionism of Alexander Jannaeus, the king of Judaea, advised her, in language clearly anti-Jewish, "not to allow such an abundance of resources to belong to one man, who was a Jew," but to seize Judaea. Her commander-in-chief, Ananias, a Jew, warned her, however, that if she would do such an injustice to Alexander, who was her ally, all the Jews would become her enemies, apparently because the Egyptian Jews felt such a strong bond with their fellow-Jews in the land of Israel, from which many of them or their parents or grandparents had recently emigrated. Inasmuch as there were many Jews serving in the Ptolemaic armies, such a warning could not be dismissed lightly, and indeed Cleopatra listened to Ananias and confirmed her alliance with Alexander. But one may well guess, though Josephus carefully avoids giving us the reaction of Cleopatra's advisers, that they charged the Jews with being more loyal to their fellow religionists in the land of Israel than to their sovereign in Egypt.

A second incident (Josephus, *War* 1.175, *Ant.* 14.99), in which the Egyptian Jews had to choose between loyalty to their sovereign, Archelaus of Pontus, and loyalty to their fellow-Jews in the land of Israel, occurred in 55 B.C.E., when the Roman proconsul of Syria, Gabinius, arrived in Egypt to restore Ptolemy XI Auletes to the throne. The soldiers guarding the Egyptian frontier were Jews, and they were persuaded by Antipater, who was then in control of the Jewish state and who was the ally of the Romans, to allow Gabinius to enter.

A few years later, in 48 B.C.E. (Josephus, *War* 1.190, *Ant.* 14.131–32), when Julius Caesar was in a difficult predicament in Egypt and when a force of allies, including Antipater, came to his aid, the frontier was again being guarded by Jews, and again they were persuaded by Antipater, who this time showed them a letter from the high priest Hyrcanus urging them to receive the Roman army hospitably. Consequently, they allowed the army of Caesar's allies to cross the frontier unmolested. Thus, although our sources provide no specifics for Apion's accusation, the context of his charge is not altogether obscure.[13] But apparently the Jews were so numerous and so influential and the Ptolemies so dependent on them that we do not hear of any persecutions of the Jews as a result of these episodes.

At a somewhat later date the Jews, or at least some Jewish leaders, involved themselves in the complicated politics surrounding the famous Cleopatra VII (reigned 52–31 B.C.E.). It would seem that they originally placed themselves on her side in supporting Julius Caesar; but after the latter's death, when Cleopatra established her liaison with Antony, they apparently sided with his opponent, Octavian, the future emperor Augustus. In any case, we hear (*Against Apion* 2.60) that when a famine afflicted Egypt Cleopatra persecuted the Jews, refusing to give them any rations of grain.

In this case, however, the fact that Cleopatra had oppressed the Jews would almost certainly have aroused sympathy for them, on the part of those loyal to Rome, because of her ruthless acts toward members of her own family but more particularly because of her ability to ensnare Antony and to induce him to fight against his own country and because of her ultimate faithlessness even to him. To a Roman reader, the Jews were thus to be complimented for their ability to see through her cruelty and treachery and thereby avoid any dealings with her. Her refusal to give them food during a famine was, therefore, something of which the Jews had cause to be proud, not ashamed.

Indeed, the disdain that the Romans felt for Cleopatra in the first century B.C.E. is well seen in Virgil's *Aeneid*, where a single word, *nefas* (8.688), "unspeakable abomination," is enough to indicate Virgil's horror at the dishonorable alliance between her and Antony. In Virgil's description of the battle of Actium (*Aeneid* 8.675–713), Cleopatra plays the major, almost the sole, role on the Egyptian side; it is clearly she who is the real enemy, with her timbrel and her dog-headed Egyptian god Anubis, and with her orders to her multitudes. Moreover, Virgil's Dido, in Book 4 of the *Aeneid*, with her wild and passionate nature and her attempts to ensnare Aeneas, would seem to be a poetic version of Cleopatra, though more sympathetically drawn. Similarly, Virgil's friend Horace (*Odes* 1.37) sings a song of fervent rejoicing now that Cleopatra, who together with her contaminated crowd of followers had been preparing mad ruin for Rome, has been defeated, fiercer than ever in her premeditated suicide but still unyielding. Likewise, his contemporary Propertius (3.11.29 ff.) speaks of Cleopatra as a strumpet whose charms brought scandal on Roman arms. To Lucan in the first century C.E., she is the turning point of Roman history: The question was whether the world would be ruled by a woman of alien, that is non-Roman, blood. To Josephus's contemporary Pliny the Younger, moreover, she is the example par excellence of luxury and unbounded ambition.[14] Although Romans would not necessarily have sympathized with Cleopatra's victims when her victims were like Antony, who was ensnared by her charms, they would have more likely sympathized with the Jews inasmuch as Cleopatra was clearly an oppressor.

As for the Seleucids of Syria, because they and their fellow Greeks and Macedonians were a minority in their empire also, they maintained the tradition of the Persians and of Alexander in permitting religious tolerance. After their conquest of the Land of Israel in 198 B.C.E., the Seleucids feared that the Jews of the Land might favor the Ptolemies under whose moderate rule they had lived since Alexander's death; consequently, we find that the Syrian ruler Antiochus III (*Ant.* 12.138–44) gave special privileges to the Jews. He exempted them from all taxation for three years and thereafter reduced their taxes by a third, while exempting the priests, the scribes and temple-singers, and the members of the Jewish governing body, the *gerousia*, from a number of taxes.

The infamous and atypical persecution of the Jews of Judaea by Antiochus IV Epiphanes can hardly be regarded as straightforward Jewhatred, especially when we realize that, so far as we know, Antiochus did not persecute the hundreds of thousands of Jews in other parts of his realm, notably in Syria and in Asia Minor. In fact, he was educated in an atmosphere of religious tolerance and was not a religious fanatic. His actions, particularly his need for money (we may call attention to the statement of Porphyry [quoted in Jerome, *Commentary on Daniel* 11.31 ff.] that Antiochus was impelled by greed), which he found in such abundance in the Temple, may more readily be attributed to his deep involvement in four overwhelming struggles—those against the Parthians, the Ptolemies, and the Romans, as well as dynastic struggles within his own realm. In particular, he was haunted by the defeat his father Antiochus III had encountered at the hands of the Romans and by the humiliation he himself had suffered in 168 B.C.E. at the hands of the Roman general, Popilius Laenas (Polybius 29.27.1–8), who had forced him to withdraw from Egypt. Moreover, we may ask why, if Antiochus were such a fierce persecutor of the Jews, he did not issue his decrees at the beginning of his reign (175 B.C.E.). Indeed, the struggle in Judaea should rather be viewed as a civil war between Jewish factions, each of whom sought to be more Hellenized than the other.[15] In fact, we cannot otherwise explain the apparent speed and thoroughness with which Hellenization spread during this brief period in the Land of Israel. Antiochus, in turn, could not afford to have instability on his southern frontier. We must ask who, if not the extremist Jewish Hellenizers, informed the king about the religious situation in Judaea and advised him that the rebellion of the Jews could not be overcome except by the utterly unique method of religious suppression. In sum, Antiochus has been the victim of a poor "press," particularly from Polybius, who especially despised his egalitarianism.[16] In any case, in the year 162 B.C.E., a mere five years after Antiochus Epiphanes had issued his decrees suppressing the practice of Judaism, his successor, Antiochus V, rescinded them and restored to the Jews the right to live according to their ancestral laws.

We may, however, comment at this point that the right, constantly granted and renewed to the Jews, to live according to their ancestral laws does not imply that the Jews anywhere in the Hellenistic Diaspora had their own independent political units, the *politeumata*, as postulated most notably by Kasher, inasmuch as Zuckerman has pointed out the rather astounding fact that there is no mention of a *politeuma* of this nature in Philo, Josephus, or the *Corpus Papyrorum Judaicarum*, or, for that matter, in any of the statements of the anti-Jewish bigots, who supposedly fought to abolish these Jewish organizations.[17]

3. THE ATTITUDES OF THE ROMAN GOVERNMENT TOWARD THE JEWS

Under the Romans, the Jews maintained and even strengthened their vertical alliance with the ruling power. At the outset it was in the Roman interest to support the Maccabean rebellion (167–141 B.C.E.) against the rule of the Syrian Greeks, Rome's chief rival in the eastern Mediterranean; and, indeed, the Jews were a pawn in the struggle between the two great powers. In fact, Judah Maccabee contracted an alliance with the Romans. Moreover, as Judaism spread through the next two centuries, the realistic Romans no doubt perceived that the Jews were too numerous (perhaps 10 percent of the population of the Roman Empire as a whole during the reign of Augustus[18] and 20 percent of the eastern half of the Empire) to risk antagonizing.

The spread of the idea of spiritual redemption through a Messiah, with the attendant idea of political liberation from the foreign ruling power, during the period from the second century B.C.E. to the first century C.E. must have given a great boost to the spread of Judaism. It is striking that the motive that had led the biblical Pharaoh to enslave the Jews, namely fear of their expansion in numbers, led to the expulsion of Jews from the city of Rome in 139 B.C.E. (as mentioned in the first century C.E. by Valerius Maximus (1.3.3),[19] significantly the first mention of a Jewish community in Rome. The reason given for this action, according to Januarius Nepotianus's epitome of Valerius Maximus (1.3.3), as we have noted, is that the Jews had attempted to transmit their sacred rites to the Romans (*Romanis tradere sacra sua conati sunt*), clearly implying proselytism, or, in the epitome of Julius Paris, that the Jews attempted to infect the Roman customs with the cult of Jupiter Sabazius (*Sabazi* [i.e., *Zevaoth*] *Iovis cultu Romanos inficere mores conati sunt*), implying an attempt at syncretism or, more likely, an endeavor to spread Jewish practices among "sympathizers" without requiring the rite of conversion. The number of Jews in Rome at this time must have been very small;[20] but the precedent was, with this action, established that though the Jews were to be guaranteed the right to practice their religion themselves, the Romans, as they had shown with the suppression of the cult of Bacchus a half century earlier in 186 B.C.E. (Livy 39.8–18), resented the spread of a foreign religion among the Roman natives.

But such an expulsion must have been short-lived. Indeed, it is interesting that the *lex Pappia* of 65 B.C.E., which demanded the general expulsion of all non-citizens from Rome on the grounds that they were too numerous and unworthy to live with the Romans, does not seem to have affected the Jews, because a few years later, in 59 B.C.E., Cicero, in his *Pro Flacco* (28.66), noted how numerous they were, how clannish, and how influential in the assemblies. Cicero was defending a client, and lawyers have been known to exaggerate; but it is self-evident that this courtroom tactic was possible only in a city with a Jewish community of some visibility and at least a modicum of influence.

Shortly after Cicero's remarks, the standing of the Jews in the Roman Republic was enhanced significantly by no less a figure than Julius Caesar himself. Caesar, whose actions served as weighty precedents in the eyes of all his successors, was grateful for Jewish assistance rendered him during his civil war with Pompey, and he consequently granted the Jews numerous privileges.[21] In city after city in Asia Minor, decrees were issued exempting the Jews from military service, permitting them to send money to the Temple in Jerusalem, and allowing them to form corporate groups, a concession granted uniquely to the Jews that must have seemed remarkable and odious to the non-Jewish inhabitants, because such a privilege might well have appeared to be the first step toward challenging Roman authority. Not surprisingly, such preferential treatment did not

leave relations with other groups in the community unscathed. The fact
that no fewer than eight cities in Asia Minor were pressured by the Romans to stop their harassment of the Jews (if we assume, as most scholars
do, that the Roman documents cited by Josephus are authentic)[22] indicates that such privileges were deeply resented. We may likewise infer
that when the Romans gained control of Egypt in 31 B.C.E. the Greeks
resented the fact that from being the ruling class they were now reduced
to a subject status without even their own council, whereas the Jews retained their autonomy, including their *gerousia*, their ethnarch, their
right of assembly in synagogues, and their own judicial system. Indeed,
when the Jews sought to improve their status and to agitate for admission
to the citizenship enjoyed by the Greeks, the latter, seemingly with reason, replied by demanding that the Jews undertake a corresponding increase in their civic responsibilities, such as military service, from which
they had hitherto been exempt. In the end, when the general Marcus
Vipsanius Agrippa in the year 14 B.C.E. was confronted by both sides, he
diplomatically reaffirmed the status quo.

Relations between Jews and the Roman authorities were not, of
course, without grave and ultimately explosive tensions, but before the
great revolt of 66–74 C.E. even the most serious incidents were relatively
short-lived. In 19 C.E., as we have noted, Jews were reportedly expelled
from Rome. Again, the expulsion is apparently connected with Jewish
expansionism, because the reason given, at least in Josephus's account, is
that Jewish embezzlers had defrauded a noble proselyte;[23] and there is
consequently reason to believe, as indeed is explicit in Dio Cassius's version, that Jewish missionary activity played a role in this decision.[24] On
the surface, this expulsion would seem to be an expression of prejudice
against Jews, inasmuch as the punishment meted out to the Jews was far
harsher than that imposed on the adherents of the Isis cult (the two incidents are linked in Tacitus [*Annals* 2.85], Suetonius [*Tiberius* 36.1], and
Josephus [*Ant.* 18.65–84]), who, though they had committed a far more
serious offense, were punished much less severely. But this hardly
marked a reversal of the traditional policy of toleration toward the Jews,
because, in any event, the banishment was brief, though it was apparently
not connected with the evil machinations of Tiberius's minister Sejanus,
who was not the power behind the throne as early as 19.[25] In any case, in
the year 31 Tiberius restored the rights of the Jews (Philo, *Legatio ad
Gaium* 24.160). Moreover, it seems most likely that, as in the expulsion
of 139 B.C.E., only proselytes were expelled, because Tiberius, who was
careful to obey the letter of the law (Velleius Paterculus 2.129.2; Tacitus,
Annals 3.69.6, 4.38.3) and who is praised as an administrator by Josephus
(*Ant.* 18.170–78), would have avoided banishing any citizen without a
trial.[26]

In the same year, 19 c.e., Germanicus, Tiberius's nephew, apparently discriminated against the Jews during his visit to Egypt by not including Jews (Josephus, *Against Apion* 2.63) in his distribution of grain (Tacitus, *Annals* 2.59); but Josephus excuses this slight by saying that it was a barren year and that there was a dearth of grain, though one is surely tempted to ask why, if Germanicus was unable to distribute grain to all the inhabitants of Alexandria, he chose to withhold it from all the Jews. Furthermore, Josephus accounts for this discrimination by noting that it was in accord with the opinion of all the Roman emperors about the Jewish inhabitants of Alexandria, presumably that they were not citizens. We may guess that there is more than a coincidence that this event occurred in the same year that marked the expulsion of Jews from Rome. In any case, the significant point is that Josephus, in an essay in which he goes to great lengths to refute anti-Jewish attitudes, refuses to view Germanicus's action as a case of anti-Jewish prejudice. To support his conclusion, Josephus notes that the administration of the grain supplies was withdrawn not only from the Jews but also from the rest of the Alexandrians, though Tacitus (*Annals* 2.59), in his version of the incident, gives no such indication and says that Germanicus reduced the price of grain by opening the granaries and adopted many practices pleasing to the multitude. Indeed, in defending the Roman emperors against the charge of discrimination, Josephus (*Against Apion* 2.64) stresses that the charge of the Nile and indeed of the entire province, which had been given to the Jews by the Ptolemaic rulers, was continued by the Roman emperors, "who regarded them as not unworthy of such a trust."

Philo (*De Somniis* 2.18.123–32) refers, without mentioning his name, to someone whom he knew of the ruling class who, when he was in charge of Egypt presumably as governor, unsuccessfully attempted, first by force and then by argument, to get Jews to disobey their ancestral customs, and especially the Sabbath, hoping thereby to lead them to irregularity in all other matters pertaining to their Jewish practices. We may remark that the striking thing here is that the governor first tried force and then persuasion, rather than, as one would expect, the reverse order. Apparently, as Philo himself indicates, the reason why the administrator gave up his attempt to compel the Jews was that he aroused general indignation; and the Romans were too pragmatic to disregard such a universal condemnation of their behavior.

Even the concerted attack on the Jews engineered by the Alexandrian mob in 38 c.e., with the connivance of the Roman governor, Flaccus, is blamed by Philo not on Rome's policies, because he fervently believed that it was Rome's mission to establish law and order in the world, but rather on the faithless governor, Flaccus. Indeed, the Emperor Caligula himself may be said to be responsible for the termination of the persecution; and, in fact, the strength of the vertical alliance between the Jews and the emperor was shown by the recall of Flaccus shortly thereafter by Caligula, who, at least in this instance, showed the good sense generally typical of the Roman emperors in their attitude toward the Jews. Flaccus was then put on trial[27] and exiled (Philo, *In Flaccum* 18.146–49).

Not long after this incident, the Alexandrian Jews sent a delegation, headed by Philo, to the Emperor Caligula in Rome to ask him to reassert the traditional Jewish rights granted by the Ptolemies and confirmed by Julius Caesar and Augustus (Josephus, *Ant.* 18.257–60). The opponents of the Jews likewise sent a delegation, headed by the grammarian and intellectual Apion. Here the "Jewish question," for the first time in history, was discussed before a high tribunal.[28] Apion's argument was that the Jews were unpatriotic because they did not pay the honors due to the emperor. Philo, in his treatise *Legatio ad Gaium*, describes the ridicule that the emperor poured on the Jewish delegation; nevertheless, Caligula did not harm the Jewish delegation but merely dismissed them with a joke.[29] Philo clearly presents this as an aberration from traditional Roman policy.

Caligula's attempt to foist his worship as a god on the Jews was regarded by both Philo and Josephus as mad; but even so, we may note that there is no evidence for the assumption that Caligula issued an edict ordering all the inhabitants of the empire, including the Jews, to take part in the worship of the emperor.[30] Moreover, that the Roman governor of Syria, Petronius, in the last analysis was convinced by the Jewish protests to withhold implementation of Caligula's orders shows how the administrative system of the empire could check an occasional unwise emperor. And so great was the influence of the Jewish king, Agrippa I, in the Roman court where he had been raised, that he was able to persuade the mad emperor Caligula himself to abandon his plans (Philo, *Legatio ad Gaium* 42.330–34; Josephus, *Ant.* 18.289–301).[31]

Furthermore, the key role of Agrippa I (Josephus, *Ant.* 19.236–38) in the accession of Claudius as Caligula's successor to the throne in 41 C.E. represents the climax of Jewish influence at court. Claudius himself, to be sure, whom some Alexandrian Jew-baiters declared to have been a cast-off son of the Jewess Salome (*CPJ* 2.156d, lines 11–12), followed an "evenhanded" policy in not enlarging Jewish privileges in Egypt; but, of course, he abolished the restrictions imposed on the Alexandrian Jews during the attack of 38. Indeed, shortly after his accession to the throne, when factional war was renewed in Alexandria between the Jews and their opponents, the new emperor, Claudius, apparently influenced by his friend Agrippa, issued an edict (*Ant.* 19.280–85) reaffirming the equal civic rights of the Jews.

The success of the Alexandrian Jews in winning the favor of the Roman emperor is particularly well illustrated in Claudius's handling of the lawsuit (*CPJ* 2.156) brought by Isidorus, the head of the gymnasium in Alexandria, in 41 c.e. against the Jewish king Agrippa I.[32] In the end the tables were completely turned, and the prosecutor himself and his ally, Lampon, were put to death.

The statement (Suetonius, *Claudius* 25.4, and Acts 18:2)[33] that Claudius expelled from Rome the Jews who persisted in rioting at the instigation of Chrestus (*Iudaeos impulsore Chresto assidue tumultuantis Roma expulit*), as we have suggested, must be understood, in the light of Dio Cassius's remark (60.6.6), to mean that Claudius did not expel the Jews, because, as he says, they had increased so greatly in numbers, but rather that he ordered them, while continuing their traditional mode of life, not to hold meetings. In any case, it was legally impossible to expel those who had any degree of citizenship, as some Jews certainly did.[34] Here again it is the sheer number—and, presumably, influence—of the Jews which served to protect them. In any case, neither Josephus, who is very full at this point, nor Tacitus makes any mention of any expulsion. If, as most scholars believe, the reference to Chrestus is actually to Christus, that is Jesus, perhaps only the Christians were expelled. Or, alternatively, perhaps Claudius did indeed expel all the Jews from Rome and may even have issued an edict to that effect; but under pressure from the Jews, and presumably especially from Agrippa I, he revoked this order and forbade only the right to assemble.[35]

In the land of Israel, the pressures that led to revolution in 66 cannot be perceived in the main as a result of anti-Jewish bigotry, although some of the special characteristics of Judaism certainly contributed both to Jewish resistance and to Roman irritation and repression. In the crucial decades before the revolt, Jews were often successful in pressing appeals to the governor of Syria, under whose jurisdiction the Land of Israel lay, and even to the emperor himself; and there are various indications, as we have indicated, that Jewish and Samaritan influence in the imperial court was not negligible.[36] Thus we may note, for example, the case of the recall of the procurator Pontius Pilate (Josephus, *Ant.* 18.89) because of the Samaritans' complaints that he had used undue force in suppressing them. We may guess that one factor in the rapid turnover of procurators in Judaea was Jewish pressure on the Syrian governor in view of the excesses to which the Jews were subjected, and that the relatively long tenure of Pilate (ten years) was due to the influence of Sejanus, an avowed Jew-baiter,[37] on the Emperor Tiberius during part of this period. That the rabbis could and did send delegations to the emperor would indicate that they must have felt that they would receive a favorable response; and indeed this was usually the case.

The Jews had considerable influence at the imperial court through the friendship between the royal family and Jewish leaders such as Agrippa I and II. Thus, we find that when a dispute between the Jews and the Samaritans was brought before the Emperor Claudius (*War* 2.232–46; *Ant.* 20.118–36), it was the intervention of the young Agrippa II on behalf of the Jews, through his friendship with the emperor's wife Agrippina, that prevailed on Claudius to punish the Samaritans and to dismiss the procurator Cumanus in disgrace for his improper handling of the matter. We may also note that during the first seven years of Nero's reign we know of no fewer than twelve accusations of improper administration made against Roman provincial officials in various parts of the empire, of which six led to condemnations.[38]

Josephus's success in getting Nero to overrule the detention of some priests by the procurator Felix (Josephus, *Life* 13–16) may illustrate the influence that Jews had at the Roman imperial court, because he was able to do so through the intervention of the emperor's wife, Poppaea Sabina, "a worshipper of G-d" ($\theta\varepsilon o\sigma\varepsilon\beta\eta\varsigma$: Josephus, *Ant.* 20.195), perhaps a "sympathizer" with Judaism,[39] to whom Josephus was introduced by Aliturus, an actor of Jewish origin who was a special favorite of Nero (*Life* 16). That Seneca, despite his bitter remarks about the Jews in his writings[40] and despite the fact that he had been a tutor to Nero and was his chief adviser during the first eight years of his reign, was apparently unable to persuade him to impose an anti-Jewish policy, would again illustrate the strength of the Jewish position at court. If Nero finally did annul the equal civic rights of the Jews in Caesarea (*Ant.* 20.183), this is clearly exceptional and is explained by Josephus as due to the large bribe whereby the Greeks prevailed on Beryllus, Nero's tutor and secretary of Greek correspondence, to influence the emperor.

The numerous messianic movements in the Land of Israel, which reached a climax in the first and early second centuries C.E. and which, by definition, sought to establish a Jewish state completely independent of the Romans, must have been a source of great anxiety to the Romans. Josephus (*War* 6.312–13) states that what more than anything else incited the Jews to revolt against the Romans in 66 was an ambiguous oracle, found in their sacred scriptures, to the effect that at that time one from their own country would become ruler of the world. The Jews, says Josephus, understood this to mean someone of their own people, whereas in reality, he insists, it referred to the assumption of imperial authority by Vespasian on Jewish soil. Tacitus (*Histories* 5.13.2) similarly remarks that the ancient priestly writings of the Jews contained the prophecy that the year 66 was the very time when the East should grow strong and that men emanating from Judaea would possess the world. Tacitus, to be sure, interprets this prophecy to refer to the accession to power of Vespasian and Titus, but it is clear that, as he himself says, the masses of the Jews understood it to refer to a Jewish ascendancy of a messianic nature, though he does not use that term itself. Suetonius (*Ves-*

pasian 4.5) uses almost the same language, stating that over all the Orient there had spread an old and established belief that at that time men coming from Judaea were fated to rule the world. He, too, refers the prediction to the emperor of Rome, while noting that the Jews understood it to refer to a Jewish ruler. Suetonius, however, does add one element, namely that this belief had penetrated the entire Orient, in other words, that Jews throughout the East had shared this messianic belief; and hence, we may assume, the Romans must have viewed it with particular apprehension as a revolt that would embrace the entire Jewish community of the eastern Mediterranean, including, presumably, the major Jewish centers of population of Asia Minor, Syria, the Land of Israel, and Egypt.[41]

That the leading rabbi of his day, Johanan ben Zakkai, however, could go over to the Roman general Vespasian and predict that he would gain the throne, and that later his pupil, the great Joshua ben Hananiah, could urge the Jews to accept the Roman suzerainty through his telling the famous Aesopian fable of the lion and the crane (*Genesis Rabbah* 64.10) would indicate that many rabbis were reconciled with Roman rule; and indeed it has been conjectured that some of the differences between Josephus's account in the *Jewish War* and his account in the *Antiquities* may be explained by Josephus's emphasis in the latter that the Romans could rely only on the Pharisees in ruling the Land of Israel.[42]

After the bloody and unsuccessful Jewish revolution of 66–74, one would have thought that the Romans would have reversed their policy of toleration toward the Jews. And yet, though one might well have expected him after the capture of Jerusalem to be vindictive toward the Jews, Titus, when persistently and continuously petitioned by the people of Antioch (Josephus, *War* 7.100–111) to expel the Jews from their city, refused, stating that now that the Jews' country had been destroyed there was no other place to receive them. Thereupon the people of Antioch petitioned Titus to remove the special privileges that the Jews had, but this, too, Titus refused. The non-Jewish inhabitants of Alexandria also, we hear (*Ant.* 12.121–22), asked Vespasian and Titus to deprive the Jews of the rights of citizenship; but these Romans refused this request likewise. Indeed, aside from the admittedly humiliating transformation of the Temple tax into a poll tax called the tax to the *fiscus Iudaicus* for the upkeep of the temple of Jupiter Capitolinus, the privileges of the Jews were not diminished.[43] After the war against the Romans, the Jewish leaders of Alexandria seized six hundred Sicarii who had taken refuge with them and turned over these revolutionaries to the Romans to be put to death (*War* 7.409–19)—a shameful effort to prove loyalty to the Roman rulers and to restore the vertical alliance.

Undoubtedly, there was a great increase in the population of Jews in

Rome after the revolution, because so many captives were taken there and because many of them were apparently freed from slavery by their fellow Jews. That the Jewish king Agrippa II was given the *ornamenta praetoria*, that his sister Berenice became the mistress of the Emperor Titus himself, and that the historian Josephus was given a pension and a residence in the former mansion of the emperor meant that Jewish influence in high places remained.

Under Domitian (81–96) the *fiscus Iudaicus* was collected very strictly (*acerbissime*, "very harshly," "very bitterly") through informers (Suetonius, *Domitian* 12); but this hostile attitude seems to have been prompted again by Jewish (and/or Christian) success in winning converts, especially at the court itself in the persons of the emperor's cousin Flavius Clemens, who was executed, and the latter's wife Flavia Domitilla (Suetonius, *Domitian* 15.1; Dio Cassius 67.14.1–2; Eusebius, *Historia Ecclesiastica* 3.19–20), who was exiled. But, just as before, this hostility was short-lived, and with Nerva (96–98) the persecution for following Jewish ways was ended.

After the death of Domitian, there was again a relaxation of anti-Jewish pressure, perhaps, we may conjecture, because the Romans were so busy waging wars in the East against the Parthians and because they feared that the Jews would form a "fifth column" if they were persecuted. In any case, even the great Diaspora revolt of 115–17 C.E. does not appear to have caused fundamental changes in Roman policy.

One might suppose that Hadrian (who ruled from 117 to 138), as an intellectual, would have been influenced by the anti-Jewish prejudice that was was widely prevalent among Roman writers, but this was not so. Indeed, during his reign, the Jews, at least at first, had high hopes that the traditional formula of the emperors, favorable to the Jews, would be resumed; and indeed this hope seems to have been borne out by his first act, executing the hated governor of Judaea, Lusius Quietus. Whether Hadrian's decree forbidding circumcision was issued before (so *Scriptores Historiae Augustae, Hadrianus* 14.2)[44] and thus contributed to the Bar Kochba rebellion (his edict forbidding circumcision was, in any case, directed not merely against Jews but against all who practiced it) in 132–35 C.E. is uncertain.[45] Most likely, Hadrian's legislation concerning circumcision was a continuation of the legislation concerning castration rather than a specific measure aimed at the Jews.[46] But, in any case, the revolt itself was followed by a series of draconian decrees against many Jewish observances. Yet these, too, were alleviated by his successor Antoninus Pius. That the latter (*Digest* 48.8.11) permitted Jews to circumcise their own children but not converts is another indication that the chief objection was to proselytism. Antoninus Pius's successor, Marcus Aurelius, as he was passing through the Land of Israel on his way to

Egypt, is reported by the fourth-century Ammianus Marcellinus (22.5.5) to have been often disgusted with the "malodorous and rebellious Jews" (*Iudaeorum fetentium et tumultuantium*); nevertheless, it is revealing that this did not lead to persecution of the Jews but rather to a cry of sorrow (*dolenter*): "O Marcomanni, O Quadi, O Sarmatians, at last I have found a people more unruly then you."

Indeed, the official attitude of the Roman government was not merely to tolerate Judaism but positively to protect it, so long as it posed no threat, through attempts at proselytism, to the state cult or to the social and political order.[47] Evidence that the government continued to protect the Jews is to be seen in the sentence to forced labor in the mines of Sardinia imposed (probably during the reign of Commodus [180–92]) by the Roman praetor on a slave named Callistus (or Calixtus), later to become pope, who had broken into a synagogue in Rome and disrupted the Sabbath service.[48]

During the reigns of Septimius Severus (193–211) and Caracalla (211–17), according to Ulpian (*Digest* 50.2.3.3), Jews were permitted to hold governmental, presumably municipal, offices, which apparently had been closed to them previously, perhaps as a result of the Bar Kochba rebellion in 132–35,[49] with the proviso that this right was accompanied by a duty to undertake such responsibilities as did not involve a transgression of their religion.

In the third century the Emperor Elagabalus (218–22), who worshipped the sun-god, was so positively disposed toward the Jews, Samaritans, and Christians that, at least according to the *Historia Augusta* (*Antoninus Heliogabalus* 3.5), he declared that their religion and rites should be transferred to Rome so that all such mysteries could be included in his religion. He is even said (*Antoninus Heliogabalus* 7.2, Dio Cassius 79.1) to have undergone circumcision and to have abstained from pork.

Elagabalus's successor, Alexander Severus (222–35), according to the *Historia Augusta* (*Alexander Severus* 22.4), respected (*reservavit*, "preserved") the privileges of the Jews. So great were his sympathies for the Jews that he was taunted by the people of Antioch, of Egypt, and of Alexandria with the title "Syrian synagogue-chief (ἀρχισυνάγωγος) and high priest (ἀρχιερεύς)."[50] Moreover, so intense was his admiration for Abraham that he is said to have kept a bust of him (*Alexander Severus* 29.2), together with busts of Jesus, Orpheus,[51] and others, in his private sanctuary. Furthermore (*Alexander Severus* 45.6–7), before naming anyone to important administrative or military positions, he would announce his name publicly and invite people to challenge the nomination, declaring that in doing so he was following the example of Jews and Christians, who observed this custom in announcing the names of those who were to be ordained priests. In addition, we are told (*Alexander Sev-*

erus 51.6–8) that he often repeated the statement that he had heard from either a Jew or a Christian, "What you do not wish that a man should do to you, do not do to him"—the Golden Rule ascribed to Hillel (*Shabbath* 31a), to Rabbi Akiva (*Avoth de-Rabbi Nathan* B 26, p. 53 (Schechter), and (and in a positive formulation) to Jesus (Matthew 7:12, Luke 6:31).

Indeed, even after the Roman emperors adopted Christianity as the official state religion, the continuity between the legislation of the pagan emperors and that of the early Christian emperors with regard to the status of the Jews is often as striking as the differences.[52] Furthermore, there is no sudden peripeteia under Constantine, so that even at the end of the fourth century, in the year 393, the Emperor Theodosius I issued a law (*Codex Theodosianus* 16.8.9) that significantly begins, "It is sufficiently established that the sect of the Jews is prohibited by no law," and then proceeds to establish grave concern (*graviter commovemur*) at the interdiction imposed in some places on the assemblies of the Jews.[53] A further law was issued in 412 by the Emperors Honorius and Theodosius II (*Codex Theodosianus* 16.8.20) prohibiting the seizure of synagogues and continuing the exemption of the Jews from appearance in court on Saturdays and Jewish holidays.[54]

4. The Reactions of the Jews to the Roman Government

Now that we have surveyed the attitude of the Roman government toward the Jews, we may examine the reaction of Jews to the Roman administration. The essential toleration, particularly by the Romans, extended to the Jews does not go unappreciated in rabbinic literature.[55] To be sure, it is hardly necessary to point out that various rabbinic comments denounced Rome as a wicked kingdom; but these are balanced in part by a significant number of favorable remarks.[56] Thus, although the rabbis speak of Esau (that is, Rome)[57] as the epitome of wickedness and equate Rome with the hated Amalek,[58] the rabbis (in an anonymous comment) did not forget that Esau was the brother of Jacob (*Genesis Rabbah* 75.4, *Leviticus Rabbah* 15.9) and that the two nations derived from them had complementary missions to perform. Indeed, that Jacob (Israel) and Esau (Rome) are twins is emphasized by the coincidence (*Pesiqta Rabbati* 20.95a–96a) that the Torah was given in the month of Sivan, under the zodiacal sign of Gemini, the twins, to show that it belongs not only to Israel but also to Esau, his twin brother. Presumably this is an allusion to the possibility that any Gentile may become a Jew through conversion, as many Romans actually did.

This parallelism between the two peoples may well have been enhanced by their common view that they had been divinely chosen for a unique destiny, as the Bible, on the one hand, and Livy and Virgil, on the other hand, emphasize. Each was said to have engaged, after great suffering, in a massive national exodus to a promised land, the Israelites from Egypt to Canaan, the Romans from Troy to Rome. Each had a great leader, Moses and Aeneas respectively, who had a very special relationship to the divinity.[59] Moreover, both the Bible and Virgil have an apocalyptic technique that looks forward to a kind of salvation.

There is even sympathy for Esau (Rome), because (*Avoth de-Rabbi Nathan*, Version B, 47.130) we are told that for three tears that Esau shed (Gen 27:38) Israel suffered in three wars (i.e., in 66–74, 115–17, and 132–35). The frequent remark by the rabbis (for example, by the patriarch Rabban Simeon ben Gamaliel in the first half of the second century [*Genesis Rabbah* 65.16]) that Esau was rewarded for his filial piety may be an allusion to the *pietas* for which the ancient Romans were known, particularly as seen in the character of Aeneas in Virgil's *Aeneid*.[60] Indeed, the rabbis (*Genesis Rabbah* 65.16–17) state that the good fortune that the descendants of Esau, that is the Romans, enjoy on earth is due to the great respect that Esau showed toward his father Isaac. In fact, Rabbi Simlai, who lived in the second half of the third century and who spent most of his life in Palestine though he was born in Babylonia, presents a scenario (*Genesis Rabbah* 67.5) in which G-d rebukes Isaac for speaking kind words to Esau after the latter cried when he discovered that Jacob had received Isaac's blessing. Isaac's reply to G-d's charge that Esau is wicked is that Esau acts righteously in honoring his parents. The Midrash (*Genesis Rabbah* 80.14) declares that one of the rewards bestowed on Esau for his filial piety was that princesses sought to marry into his family. There is even a tradition, noted, to be sure, much later (fourteenth century) by Joshua ibn Shu'aib (*Va-yishlaḥ* 16c), that Jacob realized his inferiority to Esau in the honor that Esau showed his father and that he therefore feared that G-d would prefer Esau to himself. The Midrash (*Midrash Psalms* 25.19) is bold enough to state that if Esau hates Jacob for taking away his birthright he is justified. Indeed, the occasional persecution of the Jews by the Romans, the descendants of Esau, is excused by the fact (*Genesis Rabbah* 67.7) that the Romans are merely the agents of G-d.[61]

The very fact, as we have noted, that the Rabbi Levi in the third century[62] synchronizes the founding of Rome with the day when King Solomon married the daughter of the Egyptian Pharaoh Neco and the day when the king of Israel, Jeroboam the son of Nebat, made two golden calves and the day that the prophet Elijah was taken up to heaven, indicates an attempt to link the destinies of the Jews and the Romans. That this chronology pushes back the founding of Rome more than a century and a half before 753 B.C.E., the traditional date of Rome's founding,[63] is a distinct compliment to the Romans, who were very self-conscious about their relatively recent origin.[64] That the founding of Rome is synchronized with a date in the life of King Solomon, the wisest of all men, according to the Bible (1 Kgs 4:31) and the rabbis (*Pesiqta Rabbati* 14.59, *Song of Songs Rabbah* 1.1, no. 9), is likewise a distinct tribute to the Romans. Similarly, the linkage with the prophet Elijah, who is to usher in the Messiah, connects Rome with the messianic aspirations of the Jews; and, indeed, the third-century Babylonian Rav specifically links the coming of the Messiah with the Roman Empire, saying (*Sanhedrin* 98b) that the Messiah will not come until the Roman power has engulfed Israel (that is, the whole world in which Israel is scattered) for nine months (that is, the period of pregnancy), an interpretation of the prophecy in Micah 5:2. There is definite admiration in the statement that the site of Rome was established by none other than the angel Michael (Jerusalem Talmud, '*Avodah Zarah* 1.2.39c; *Song of Songs Rabbah* 1.6),[65] who stuck a stick in the sea, which grew into a large thicket of reeds and became the site of Rome.

Far from casting aspersions on the parentage of Romulus and Remus, the fourth-century Rabbi Yudan (*Midrash Psalms* 10.6, p. 95 Buber; 17.12, p. 134; *Esther Rabbah* 3.5), in the name of Rabbi Judah, refers to them as fatherless children, who, when their mother would not raise them, were nurtured by a she-wolf summoned by G-d to give them suck until they grew up, and who later built two huts on the site of Rome in fulfillment of the passage "Thou hast been the helper of the fatherless" (Ps 10:14). Hence, the founding of Rome is part of a divine plan. We may note that in the alternate version of the passage (*Esther Rabbah* 3.5) Esau, the twin brother of Jacob, is identified as the father of the twins, and consequently there is a further link with the Jews. It should have been tempting, moreover, for the rabbis, in their sermons, to attack the Romans with regard to their origins by comparing Romulus's murder of his brother Remus at the beginning of Roman history with Cain's murder of his brother Abel at the beginning of human history, but there is no such allusion.

In a remarkable passage (*Song of Songs Rabbah* 1.6.4), the third-century Rabbi Levi notes that each time the two huts were built in Rome they collapsed, until an old man named Abba Kolon told the Romans that unless water from the Euphrates were mixed with mortar, the buildings would not stand. He volunteered to get this water and, disguised as a maker of barrels, he journeyed to the Euphrates, where he obtained some water, returned, and mixed it with mortar. The huts now remained standing—hence the proverb "A city without Abba Kolon is unworthy of the name." The city thus built was called Rome-Babylon. A person named Abba Kolon is not otherwise known in the Talmudic corpus; and the best guess seems to be that he is literally "father of a colony."[66]

Indeed, one possible moral of the story is that unless Rome incorporates within itself Jewish wisdom (since Abraham, the ancestor of the Jewish people, came from Ur near the Euphrates in Chaldaea, whence the water was fetched) it cannot stand. The connection of Rome with Babylon is a way of saying that Rome derived its strength from the old civilization of the Orient. One thinks of Juvenal's bitter comment that in his day (in the early second century c.e.) Rome had been so deeply influenced by the Orient, presumably both through immigration of Jews and through conversion of pagans to Judaism, that in effect the Syrian river Orontes had long since been flowing into the Tiber (Juvenal 3.62).

The rabbinic appreciation of Rome is seen in the supreme compliment paid to the Roman genius in law by the third-century rabbi Simeon ben Lakish (Resh Lakish) (*Genesis Rabbah 9.13*). Commenting on the verse "And behold it was very good," he says that this refers to the earthly kingdom, because the Hebrew letters for "very" (*me'od*) and "man" (*adam*) are the same, though in a different order. How then, asks the rabbi, does the earthly kingdom earn such an encomium? He answers that it does so because it exacts justice (the passage uses the Greek word δίκη [or δίκαιον]) for humanity. That the earthly kingdom is Rome is clear from the substitution by the rabbis of Edom (i.e., the Talmudic synonym for Rome) for Adam (which is spelled with the same letters); and this indeed is the reading in the Vilna edition. Of course, Resh Lakish may be using ironic sarcasm, because the phrase "very good" is applied in this Midrash to death (70.1) and to the evil inclination (72.1), but there is no indication of such sarcasm in the passage.

This high regard for the fairness of Roman law was apparently reciprocated, to judge from the anecdote (Jerusalem Talmud, *Baba Qamma 4.4*, *Sifre Deuteronomy* 33.3, and *Baba Qamma* 38a) that the government of Rome sent two commissioners to Rabban Gamaliel II at the end of the first century to investigate the Torah and that these emissaries found it correct in all points except one (that if the ox of an Israelite gores an ox of a Gentile there is no liability, whereas there is liability if the ox of a Gentile gores that of an Israelite). They promised, however, not to report this exception to the government.

That the Romans were truly fair in their administration of justice may be seen from the absence from the Talmudic corpus, even though the rabbis are highly articulate in mentioning their grievances against Roman oppression, of any overt discrimination against Jews in matters pertaining to civil rights.[67] The rabbis, moreover, may well have been acquainted with Roman law, which, in the degree of its development, has often been compared with Talmudic law, because there had apparently been a school of Roman law in Caesarea in the Land of Israel since the third century.[68]

That the rabbis appreciated the *Pax Romana*, though not without ambiguity, is apparent from an otherwise lost Midrashic comment, quoted by medieval authorities, that notes that the numerical value of the name Esau is equal to that of *shalom* ("peace"), that is, 376.[69] The Midrash then adds that but for this name, which appears to be a direct allusion to the *Pax Romana*, no creature would be left in peace by Esau. Of course, we must add that Rabbi Phinehas ben Ḥama and Rabbi Ḥilkiah, dating from the mid-fourth century, in the name of Rabbi Simeon, liken the Roman Empire in its administration to the pig that deceptively stretches out its cloven hoofs as if to say that it is a kosher animal. Similarly, the Roman government robs and extorts and yet maintains the appearance of holding court (*Midrash Leviticus Rabbah* 13.5, *Genesis Rabbah* 65.1).[70] One is reminded of the Briton Calgacus's comment in Tacitus (*Agricola* 30): "Where they make a devastation, they call it peace" (*ubi solitudinem faciunt, pacem appellant*).

None of this should obscure the fact that the Jews, alone among all the subjects of the empire, erupted into revolt three times between the middle of the first and the middle of the second century. This is hardly the symptom of an idyllic relationship. Nevertheless, the revolts were not the norm. They took place against the backdrop of an essentially tolerant policy that was a manifestation, at least in the Diaspora, of a vertical alliance between Jews and the government. Where this alliance did break down, the cause was largely the same kind of fear that led the biblical Pharaoh to his decree, namely that the Jews were becoming so numerous in the Hellenistic period, chiefly through successes in proselytism, and were thus undermining the religion that was directly connected with the state. The reckless confidence that G-d would support their cause in demanding complete independence from Rome seems to have spurred the various revolutionary movements against the Roman Empire. It is especially striking that even in revolt the Jews did not appear to have sought horizontal alliances with other oppressed peoples, though such co-ordination would have made much sense, because so many other nations and tribes fought bitterly against the Romans. Relations between Jews and the Roman government, in particular, were marked by alliance and revolt; but it is the alliance that was dominant, thanks largely, particularly during the imperial period, to the overpowering influence of the rabbis, which increased during the period of Roman rule because of the tremendous prestige of the rabbinic academies. Indeed, we may remark that persecution in general was almost unknown in antiquity. Our survey leads us to conclude that official governmental prejudice against Jews was not a significant phenomenon in the ancient world.

POPULAR PREJUDICE
AGAINST JEWS

1. THE ECONOMIC FACTOR

A major factor in explaining the persistence of the Jews in the Hellenistic and Roman periods, in addition to their inherent strength and their resistance to assimilation to Hellenism, was, paradoxically, the hatred the masses apparently felt toward them. We do not, of course, possess any writings by ordinary people from antiquity except for a few thousand fragments of nonliterary papyri. The literary sources are all the work of the intelligentsia, who generally, if we may take Philo (*Legatio ad Gaium* 18.120) as an example, have the utmost contempt for the mob.

We may wonder that our sources do not indicate the economic causes for the hatred of Jews, especially in view of the prominence of the Jews, at least under the Egyptian Ptolemies, as in the Middle Ages under the Arabs, in the hated position of the tax collector or petty bureaucrat; but we may reply that ancient historians seldom stress or even indicate the economic causes of events: They underline the political and military factors and are strong adherents of the "great man" school of history. Moreover, we have no papyri from Alexandria, the site of the largest and by far the most important and, apparently, the wealthiest Jewish community. To be sure, the Ptolemaic government did not favor private enterprise. Not only did all the land in Egypt belong to the king, but so did all business, inasmuch as those businesses that were not royal monopolies were permitted to exist only through purchase of a license or sharing the product with the king.[1] Moreover, inasmuch as the Ptolemaic banks were a government monopoly, opportunities for moneylending were severely restricted. Fortunately, however, the scanty literary references can now be supplemented by several hundred papyri from the rural regions of Egypt, so that the picture is more nuanced.[2]

Baron cites Josephus's extra-biblical comment (*Ant.* 2.201–2) that the oppression of the ancient Israelites by the Egyptians was due to the Egyptians' envy of the Israelites' abundant wealth and, most appropriately, suggests that this reflects contemporary realties with respect to the masses of the Egyptian peasants.[3] We may further suggest that Josephus, in his version of the Joseph narrative in the *Antiquities*, is replying to the charge of the opponents of the Jews who had apparently claimed that Jews constituted an economic threat to the Egyptians' livelihood. In particular, we may note that in the Bible (Gen 46:33–34) Joseph instructs his brothers that when asked by Pharaoh about their occupation, they should reply not that they are shepherds (as indeed they were)—because shepherds were an abomination to the Egyptians (Gen 46:34)—but rather that they are owners of cattle. Josephus (*Ant.* 2.185–86), on the other hand, has Joseph himself tell Pharaoh directly and apologetically that his brothers are good shepherds and that they follow this calling so that they may not be separated and may look after their father. He then presents the additional and novel economic factor that they follow this calling in order to ingratiate themselves to the Egyptians by not competing with them, because Egyptians were forbidden to occupy themselves with the pasturing of livestock.

Egypt was by far the most important of Rome's provinces, being its granary, the chief source of food for the Roman army and for the masses of the city of Rome; and Alexandria, which within two generations of its founding by Alexander in 332 B.C.E. had displaced Athens as the leading commercial and cultural center of the Mediterranean, was the outlet for the export of this grain. Inasmuch as by far the largest Jewish community in the world of the first century was in Alexandria, with a Jewish population estimated at 180,000,[4] it was, in effect, the New York City of its day, with Jews constituting 30 to 40 percent of the population.

We may gain a picture of the economic activities of the Jews from the Third Book of Maccabees, which (3:4) mentions the alleged persecutions suffered by the Jews under Ptolemy IV (221–203 B.C.E.). In particular, it refers to the favorable attitude toward the Jews, whom some Greeks and other neighbors of the Jews had as their business associates or partners.

Philo (*In Flaccum* 8.57) has given us a valuable picture of the economic life of the Jews in Egypt in his description of the devastation wrought by the attack of 38, noting the losses incurred by tradespeople, farmers, shipowners, shipmen, merchants, and artisans. The tradespeople were actually capitalists who participated in business only by investing their money rather than by buying and selling and were thus distinct from merchants.[5] Josephus (*Ant.* 18.159) refers to such people when he mentions Philo's brother, Alexander, who lent Cypros, the wife of Agrippa I, the huge sum of 200,000 drachmas, partly in cash and partly via a letter of credit to his representative in Italy. In this connection, we may cite a papyrus dated in 41, in which the author, a wholesale dealer in need of money, warns the recipient that if he fails to obtain a loan from the sources the author recommends, "like everyone else, do you, too, beware of the Jews."[6] Inasmuch as the Jews (*Ant.* 19.278) had, shortly before the date of this letter, attacked their enemies on the accession of Claudius, Tcherikover interprets this papyrus as a warning not to enter the Jewish quarter because it was dangerous;[7] but there is no indication in the papyrus of such danger, and the most likely explanation is that it reflects the bitter feeling that the populace generally had against Jews because of their economic dependency on the Jews. The fact that the writer of the papyrus adds the gratuitous phrase "like everyone else" would seem to emphasize that, in his eyes, the warning to beware of *the* Jews is a general one, shared by the Gentile population at large, and seeking loans from Jews was apparently customary.

It is clear from the passage from Philo noted above that Jews were involved in the shipping trade in Alexandria. Indeed, whereas before the last of the Ptolemies, Cleopatra, was defeated in the year 31 B.C.E., the economy was, in effect, a kind of state socialism very closely controlled by the ruler, under the Romans the path was opened for individual initiative; and apparently the Jews took advantage of this opportunity and thereby incurred the envy and wrath of the non-Jews. One might have guessed that there would be a decline in popular anti-Semitism under the Romans, because the Jews no longer held the unpopular position of middlemen economically and could no longer enter careers in the army or in the imperial administration without compromising their Judaism;[8] but there is, if anything, an increase in the ferocity of anti-Jewish feeling, perhaps because of the envy on the part of the non-Jews and their dread of being overwhelmed by the Jews' increasing numbers at a time when the Gentile Roman population was stagnant.

That there was an economic factor, based on Jewish prominence in trade, in popular prejudice against Jews would seem to be indicated by the remark of Claudius Ptolemy, the noted second century C.E. Alexandrian astronomer who is convinced that national characteristics are conditioned by the geographical and astronomical situation. Consequently, his list (*Apotelesmatica* 2.3.65–66.29–31) of those peoples who are more gifted in trade than others starts with Idumaea, Coele-Syria and Judaea; and he remarks that they are more unscrupulous (πανουργότεροι, "more ready to do anything," "more knavish"), despicable cowards, treacherous (ἐπιβουλευτικοί, "scheming"), servile, and in general fickle (ἀλλοπρόσαλλοι, "leaning first to one side and then to the other"), on account of their respective horoscopes. In particular, he singles out the inhabitants of Coele-Syria, Idumaea, and Judaea as more closely familiar to Aries and Ares and concludes that these people are in general bold, godless, and treacherous (ἐπιβουλευτικοί, "scheming" [thus emphasizing this quality by repeating the same word that he had just used above]). Moreover, in referring to the inhabitants of these countries, he really has in mind only the Jews, because all three of these geographical areas are frequently identified with each other.[9]

As to Rome itself, economic factors, we may add, seem to be behind the bitterness evidenced in Cicero's *Pro Flacco* (28.67), because Cicero, speaking in 59 B.C.E., obviously thinks that he can score points with his audience when he asks, "Who is there, gentlemen, who could not honestly praise this action?" referring to Flaccus's act in forbidding the export of gold by the Jews of Asia Minor to Jerusalem after the Roman Senate had on several occasions most urgently forbidden the export of the gold on account of the shortage of gold in Italy. It is significant that even though Cicero's case concerned only the export of gold from the province of Asia he yet saw fit (ibid.) to remind his audience that it was customary to send gold to Jerusalem on the order of *the Jews from Italy and from all our provinces.* This would appear to be an indication that he wanted to broaden the matter to make it a Jewish issue generally and not merely a case involving the Jews of Asia Minor. That the half-shekel tax was levied on all Jews, including proselytes (thus involving the export of a great deal of money from the Roman provinces), may have aroused greater bitterness, inasmuch as there is evidence that at this very time the Jews were extraordinarily successful in winning converts.

We have already noted that the Roman government had to prevent various cities in Asia Minor from interfering with Jewish observance.[10] Thus, for example, Julius Caesar in 46 B.C.E. had to order (Josephus, *Ant.* 14.213) the magistrates, council, and people of Parium in Asia Minor, on appeal from the Jews, to cease preventing the Jews by statute from observing their ancestral customs and sacred rites.[11] Apparently, as is clear from Caesar's decree itself, the people of Parium resented the specially privileged economic position of the Jews, in that the Jews were permitted to assemble and to send money to the Temple in Jerusalem. Again, we hear (*Ant.* 14.242) that the people of Tralles in Asia Minor in 45 B.C.E. objected to the Roman governor's granting to the Jews special privileges to observe the Sabbath and other Jewish rites.[12] Shortly thereafter, a decree of Publius Servilius Galba (*Ant.* 14.244–46) took the magistrates, council, and people of Miletus in Asia Minor to task for behaving contrary to the express wish of the Romans in actually attacking (προσφέρε-σθαι) the Jews and preventing them from observing the Sabbath or performing their ancestral rites.

The several references in Greek and Latin literature to the wealth of the Jews or, at any rate, of Jewish rulers, are a clue that envy of this wealth was a major source of hostility to the Jews throughout the classical period. No fewer than six ancient authors—Theophrastus (*Historia Plantarum* 9.6.1) in the fourth century B.C.E., Diodorus (on two occasions, 2.48.9 and 19.98) in the first century B.C.E., Strabo (16.2.41.763) in the first century B.C.E., Pompeius Trogus (quoted in Justin, *Historiae Philippicae* 36.3.1) in the first century C.E., Dioscorides (*De Materia Medica* 1.19.1) in the first century C.E., and Pliny the Elder (*Natural History* 12.111) in the first century C.E.—mention that balsam is produced nowhere else in the whole world except in Judaea. Theophrastus says that the pure gum sells for twice its weight in silver. Diodorus twice remarks that its use for medicinal purposes was most highly valued by physicians; it is therefore not surprising, as Trogus states, that the income from it because of its scarcity increased the wealth of the nation. Apparently, according to Strabo (17.1.15.800), the value of the balsam was increased through the deliberate limiting of its growth by the Jews to only a few places. So valuable was this balsam, according to Pliny (12.113), that there were pitched battles in defense of it; even its shoots and the bark, he remarks (12.118), fetched huge sums; in no other case, he adds (12.123), is more obvious fraud practiced through adulteration. That, indeed, the balsam was in great demand is manifest from its use in elaborate funeral pyres (so the first-century C.E. Statius, *Silvae* 2.1.159–62 and 5.1.210–14); and it was regarded as one of the representative products of the rich East (3.3.138–41). Its fame was apparently proverbial, as we see in the reference in the second-century C.E. Aelius Aristeides (36 [*Aegyptiacus* 82]) to the famous (ὀνομαστάς) dates and juice [i.e., of balsam] of Palaestina-Syria. The second-century C.E. Galen (*De Antidotis* 1.4) cites it as an example of a medicinal substance of supreme excellence.

The palm groves of Judaea were likewise a source of great wealth, and, we may guess, of envy. Thus, to show how lazy one of two brothers is, Horace (*Epistles* 2.183–84) in the first century B.C.E. says that he prefers idleness to Herod's rich palm groves, thus indicating that the palms of Judaea are a proverbial source of great wealth. Likewise, Lucan (*Pharsalia* 3.216) in the first century C.E. refers to Idume (that is, Judaea), "rich in palm-plantations."

Another source of Jewish wealth was the production of flax, which was considered to be of the finest quality, as we hear from the second-century Pausanias (5.5.2), so that only the flax produced in Elis was comparable to it.[13] In the fourth century we read in the anonymous *Expositio Totius Mundi et Gentium* (31) that among the cities famous for linen clothes the first was Scythopolis in Judaea, which, we are told, exported linen to the whole world and excelled in the richness of all these productions.[14] In the same treatise we also read of several cities in the Land of Israel that exported high-quality purple and were renowned for fertility in wheat, vine, and olive.

That the increasing wealth of the Temple was a major source of the hostility felt by the Romans toward the Jews is clear from (Josephus, *War* 6.335–36) Titus's speech to the leaders of the revolt against the Romans, in which, after enumerating the various privileges granted by the Romans to the Jews, he presents as his climax (τὸ δὲ μέγιστον, "the greatest") the permission given by the Romans to the Jews to collect tribute for the Temple, "without either admonishing or hindering those who brought them—only that you might grow richer at our expense and make preparations with our money to attack us! And then, enjoying such privileges, you turned your superabundance [τὸν κόρον, "satiety," "profusion"] against the donors, and like untamable reptiles spat your venom on those who caressed you." Such a bitter comment, moreover, has particular force when we consider that the masses of the Jews were actually re-garded as poor beggars, at least if we are to judge from the comments of the satirists Martial (12.57.1–14) and Juvenal (3.10–16, 3.296, 6.542–47) at the end of the first and the beginning of the second century c.e. In-deed, when finally the Romans set fire to the Temple, so great was their rancor toward the wealth of the Jews that instead of appropriating it for themselves they chose (Josephus, *War* 6.282) to burn the treasury cham-bers, "in which lay vast (ἄπειρον, "immeasurable," "countless," "infinite") sums of money, vast (ἄπειροι) piles of raiment, and other valuables; for this, in short, was the general repository of Jewish wealth, to which the rich had consigned the contents of their dismantled houses." The repeti-tion of the word *vast* indicates how this wealth of the Temple was viewed.

Baron thinks that Tacitus's passing reference to Jewish wealth (*Histo-ries* 5.5.1) and especially the wealth of the Temple (5.8.1) conveys only the degree to which Jewish cohesiveness had augmented the resources of the Jewish communal organs.[15] But, we may remark, such comments seem to imply envy and animosity, especially when we note that in the first passage Tacitus has chosen to connect the wealth of the Temple with the increase in the number of people sending their annual contribu-tions there due to successful Jewish proselytism. Moreover, in that pas-sage Tacitus speaks not so much of the wealth of the Temple or of Jeru-salem or of Judaea but of the Jews and couples this with his comment, immediately thereafter, that the Jews are extremely loyal to each other but feel only hate and enmity toward every other people. This envy is underlined in the second passage, which speaks of the enormous riches (*immensae opulentiae*) of the Temple.

A further reference to Jewish wealth may be found in the remarks of the Christian interlocutor Antonius Julianus in the first century (quoted in Minucius Felix, *Octavius* 33.3), who comments on the growth of the Jewish people from a small people to a numberless one and from poverty to wealth. A similar comment, implying jealousy of Jewish wealth and power, may be seen in the retort of the second-century Celsus (quoted in Origen, *Against Celsus* 7.18) to the Christians: If the prophets had fore-told that Jesus would be the son of G-d, why did G-d promise the Jews that they would become rich and powerful and fill the earth and massacre their enemies, whereas Jesus condemns the rich and the powerful?

We may also suggest that the several references to the Jews as beggars, most of which occur in the works of satirists of the first and early second centuries, may also reflect economic anti-Jewish bigotry, this time from a sarcastic point of view.[16]

That jealousy of the economic power of the Jews was a factor in preju-dice against Jews would seem to be indicated by the glib comment, noted above and ascribed to the Emperor Hadrian (*Historia Augusta, Quadrigae Tyrannorum* 8.6–7) in the early part of the second century, that the Christians, the Jews, and in fact all nations adore money.

That the economic factor continued to be a source of tension is apparent from a speech of the famous fourth-century orator Libanius (*Oratio de Patrociniis* 13–17), in which he describes a clash with some Jewish tenants, probably near Antioch in Syria,[17] who, after tilling the land for several generations, had refused to continue and either had tried to preserve their former status of freedom or, as Libanius would have it, had tried to impose new conditions on him. Libanius brought the case before a judge who ordered the arrest of the tenants; but to his dismay the tenants bribed the local military commander, who then ruled in their favor. In the speech, which is apparently addressed to the emperor Theodosius I, Libanius aims thus to illustrate the power of the Jewish tactics and its deleterious impact on the economic standing of the Roman Empire, beset, as it was at this time, with such deep financial and military problems. That the case should not be regarded as isolated but rather as an indication of an anti-Jewish outlook would seem to be supported by the phrase "some very typical Jews" (Ἰουδαῖοι τῶν πάνυ) that Libanius uses.[18] What was particularly distressing to Libanius was the success of the Jews in circumventing the Roman system of justice, the greatest pride of the Roman administrative system.

Finally, we may note an encounter in the fifth century of a pagan with a Jew in charge of a fish pond who accused Rutilius Namatianus (*De Reditu Suo* 1.385–86) of damaging his bushes and hitting the seaweed and who bawled about his enormous loss in water that the author and his entourage had sipped. This incident highlights once again the economic charges against the Jews, and particularly their alleged stinginess and sharp and heartless business practices, so that the author concludes that their hearts are chillier than their creed. Of course, such remarks should also be seen from the perspective of the standard Greek and Roman aristocratic disdain for trade and money.

2. The Attack on the Jews in Alexandria in the Year 38

The hatred of the mob came into boldest relief during a series of riots in Alexandria, the most populous of Jewish communities. The first of these, which we have noted briefly above, took place in the year 38 c.e. Philo (*Legatio ad Gaium* 18.120) reports that the hatred of the masses toward the Jews had been smoldering (τυφόμενον) for some time. Thus, when a pretext was offered on the Jews' refusal to obey the decree of Emperor Gaius Caligula that he be worshipped as a god, the promiscuous (μιγάς) mob, carried away with itself (πεφορημένος), let loose. Marcus has already noted that this riot illustrates a typical pattern of ancient massacres of Jews: first, long-standing resentment at the privileged position and influence of the Jews, whether political or economic; second and more immediate, the accusation that the Jews were unpatriotic, inasmuch as they refused to participate in the state cults, which, like a flag, united all the diverse peoples of the empire; third, the rousing of the passions of the mob by professional agitators (though this is perhaps exceptional); and fourth, the intervention of the government to preserve order while blaming the Jews for causing the riot.[19]

In the case of the riot of 38 C.E., there were additional, special circumstances. Even with the mad Caligula as emperor, the attack was hardly inevitable because the Jewish king Agrippa I had so much influence with the emperor, and the Jews might well have persuaded Caligula to permit sacrifices to be sent in his behalf to the Temple in Jerusalem in place of actual worship, as had been the case with his predecessors. Moreover, Caligula himself had attributed Jewish recalcitrance to stupidity rather than to evil intention in not believing that he was a god. What determined the course of events in this instance was the behavior of Flaccus, the Roman governor of Egypt.

In the first five of the six years of his administration, Flaccus (Philo, *In Flaccum* 1.2–3) showed no signs of anti-Jewish animus and indeed was a model administrator—"sagacious and assiduous, quick to think out and execute his plans, very ready at speaking and at understanding what was left unspoken better even than what was said"—who soon mastered the intricate detail involved in governing the large, populous, and complicated province of Egypt. In particular (Philo, *In Flaccum* 1.4), he prevented the promiscuous (μιγάδων) and motley (συγκλύδων) masses from meeting in their political clubs (ἑταιρείας) and associations (συνόδους), in line with the traditional Roman prohibition of meetings of *collegia*. This must have rankled the non-Jews, inasmuch as Flaccus had continued the long-standing policy of permitting the Jews to meet in their associations, known as synagogues, which symbolized the power of the Jews as a "pressure group," precisely the picture drawn by Cicero (*Pro Flacco* 28.66) of the Jews in Rome a century earlier (59 B.C.E.).

Philo (*In Flaccum* 3.9–4.16) conjectures that the change of attitude in Flaccus, and consequently the breakdown of the vertical alliance with the Roman administration, was due to the death of the Emperor Tiberius, who had appointed him and whose close friend he had been, and to the fear that, because Tiberius's successor Caligula had put to death Flaccus's friend Macro, his own position would deteriorate. In desperation, therefore, Flaccus, presumably assuming that the Jews would in their usual fashion remain loyal to the emperor, sought allies among his former enemies.[20] The void was quickly filled by the popularity-hunting (δημοκόποι, *In Flaccum* 4.20) Dionysius and by the intellectuals Isidorus and Lampon, who headed the gymnasium in Alexandria and who, noting that Flaccus had lost standing with the emperor, advised him to win Caligula's favor by surrendering and sacrificing the Jews. Isidorus, in particular, according to Philo (*In Flaccum* 17.135), was a mob courter (ἄνθρωπος ὀχλικός), practiced in producing disturbance and confusion, "an adept at creating factions and tumults where they do not exist and organizing and fostering them when made, ever at pains to keep in contact with him an irregular and unstable horde of promiscuous, ill-assorted people, divided up into sections (μοίρας) or what might be called syndicates (συμμορίας)." As a leader in most of the popular clubs (θίασοι), Isidorus was able, with his gifts of rhetoric, to arouse passions.

The immediate pretext for the riot was the visit of Agrippa I to Alexandria and his ostentatious display of his bodyguard of spearmen decked in armor overlaid with gold and silver. To the Jew-baiters (these were, of course, Greeks rather than native Egyptians, as we can see from the fact that their charismatic leaders were the Greek gymnasiarchs Isidorus and Lampon) this highlighted Jewish wealth and power—another indication of the importance of the economic factor in promoting tension between Jews and non-Jews. Indeed, what must have particularly rankled the opponents of the Jews was that not so very long before this time the same Agrippa had, through his extravagant habits, become penniless and was actually on the verge of suicide (*Ant.* 18.143–67) when he managed successfully to beg Alexander the alabarch (tax administrator) of Alexandria to grant him a loan of 200,000 drachmas and to obtain a further loan of 300,000 drachmas from Antonia, the mother of the future emperor Claudius, as well a loan of a million drachmas from a Samaritan.

The mob responded to Agrippa's majestic appearance by dressing up a lunatic named Carabas in mock-royal apparel with a crown and bodyguards and saluting him as Marin, the Aramaic word for "lord." The implied charge clearly was that the Alexandrian Jews, in giving homage to Agrippa as a king, were guilty of dual loyalty and of constituting themselves, in effect, as a state within a state. The use of the Aramaic word would seem to be intended to emphasize the allegation that the Jews' first loyalty was to the Aramaic-speaking ruler of Palestine. But one guesses that this was intended merely to win the favor of the Romans, whereas the real motive for the riot was economic.

Flaccus's response was not merely to seize the meetinghouse of the Jews but also to emphasize his conviction that the Jews were not loyal to the regime by depriving them of civic rights, denouncing them as foreigners and as aliens, and herding them into a very small part of one of the quarters of the city, the first known ghetto in history. Ancient writers, as we have remarked, rarely stressed or even indicated economic causes of events, and this riot was no exception; nevertheless, the fact that the anti-Jewish bigots then pillaged Jewish homes and shops with abandon may indicate that economic considerations were far from insignificant. Indeed, one immediate result of the riot was the mass unemployment that occurred because Jewish merchants, artisans, and shipmen lost their stocks and were not allowed to practice their usual business. The sheer savagery of the anti-Jewish mob in binding Jews alive, burning them slowly with brushwood, dragging them through the middle of the marketplace, jumping on them, and not sparing even their dead bodies further indicates the release of pent-up fury reminiscent of the massacres of Polish Jews by the followers of Chmielnicki in the seventeenth century and of Russian Jews in the latter part of the nineteenth and early part of the twentieth century.

Flaccus, according to Philo (*Legatio ad Gaium* 20.132), could have halted the riot in an hour if he had desired, but did nothing. Once they knew that the governmental authority would take no action, the mob attacked the synagogues and placed portraits of Caligula in all of them, while Flaccus himself (Philo, *In Flaccum* 10.73–75) made a special point of arresting the members of the *gerousia*, the body of Jews responsible for their self-government, and stripped and scourged them. Both of these acts were intended to underscore Jewish separatism and lack of patriotism; and the charge that the Jews had stored arms (*In Flaccum* 11.88)—an accusation that was disproved when absolutely nothing was found—may be an indication that the Jews were perceived as plotting a revolution, perhaps in conjunction with the revolutionary movement in the Land of Israel, which originated, according to Josephus (*Ant.* 18.1–10), with the census of Quirinius in 6 C.E. To underscore the lack of patriotism of the Jews, the mob desecrated synagogues by introducing into them busts of the emperor. But that the Jew-baiters decried not merely the alleged lack of patriotism but rather simply the fact of Jewishness can be seen in the treatment of the women, whom they seized and forced to eat pork (Philo, *In Flaccum* 11.96) rather than to worship the image of the emperor. In the end, however, what must have seemed to the opponents of the Jews like an instance of "international Jewish power" asserted itself: Flaccus was recalled in disgrace, banished, and eventually executed.[21]

Three years later, on the assassination of Caligula, the Jews, strengthened by the crucial role played by one of them, Agrippa I, in the accession of the Emperor Claudius (Josephus, *Ant.* 19.236–47), armed themselves (*Ant.* 19.278) and attacked the Greeks in Alexandria. At this point the newly crowned emperor intervened (*Ant.* 19.280–85) by reaffirming the rights previously held by the Jews and by demanding that both the Jews and the Greeks avoid disturbances. When the Alexandrian leaders

Isidorus and Lampon made serious charges against King Agrippa, a trial is said to have taken place before the imperial council, the result of which, as we have remarked, was to exonerate Agrippa and to sentence Isidorus and Lampon to death. Once again, it would seem, Jewish power and influence in high places had been reasserted. Shortly thereafter Claudius sent a letter (London Papyrus 1912) in which he adopted an evenhanded stance, warning both the Greeks and the Jews to avoid hostile acts.[22]

That the masses' virulent hatred of the Jews was not confined to Alexandria may be seen in the indecent insults hurled by the non-Jewish inhabitants of Caesarea and Samaria on Agrippa I after his death in the year 44 (*Ant.* 19.356–59), apparently reflecting their resentment of the political power the Jews had gained when he had been named king by the Romans, and this despite the benefactions that Agrippa had bestowed on these non-Jews.

3. Attacks on the Jews in the Year 66

The next major eruption of anti-Jewish violence coincided with the outbreak of the Jewish rebellion against the Romans in 66 c.e. Not unexpectedly, this most violent of all the Jewish outbreaks occurred in Alexandria, with its long history of Greek enmity toward Jews. Our only source, Josephus, was hardly an impartial witness, especially because he had such an antipathy for Jewish revolutionaries.[23] Yet his account should be given serious weight, inasmuch as it is far from a whitewash of the murderous actions of the troops sent by the authorities. In recounting the event, Josephus (*War* 2.487) reminds us that there had always been strife between the native inhabitants and the Jewish settlers ever since the time when Alexander the Great, as a reward for the support that the Jews had given him against the Egyptians, had granted them ἰσομοιρία, that is, rights equal to those of the Greeks. Not only were the Egyptians resentful of these privileges and hateful toward those who aided their conquerors and oppressors, but soon the Greeks themselves developed a strong antagonism toward the Jews. Despite every attempt on the part of the authorities, whether the Ptolemies or their successors, the Romans, to maintain order, there were incessant clashes (*War* 2.489) between the Jews and the Greeks; and the numerous punishments meted out to the rioters of both parties by the governmental authorities merely sharpened the bitterness of the factions. This hostility exploded into serious rioting once word arrived of the Judaean revolt and of the massacres in the cities of Syria and of the Land of Israel. Presumably, the Jew-baiters felt assured that the authorities would favor their cause against people who would now be perceived as unpatriotic rebels. On one occasion (*War* 2.490) when the Alexandrian Greeks met to discuss send-ing a delegation to the emperor, apparently to ask him to curtail Jewish rights, many Jews flocked into the amphitheater where they were meet-ing. The fact that they were greeted with shouts of "enemies" and "spies" should give us a clue that the opponents of the Jews regarded them as unpatriotic rebels.

When a mob seized three Jews with the intention of burning them alive, the whole Jewish community rose to their rescue, and a full-fledged riot ensued. The uprising was put down ruthlessly by the Roman gover-nor, Tiberius Julius Alexander (who was of Jewish origin), whose troops killed fifty thousand Jews, according to Josephus (*War* 2.497).[24] The fact that the Romans were not without casualties (*War* 2.495) would seem to indicate that at least some Jews were armed, perhaps in preparation for assisting their fellow Jews in their revolt against the Romans in the Land of Israel. The fury of the Roman assault, which knew no pity even for infants, would seem to indicate that the Jews fought tenaciously. That the Romans ceased (*War* 2.497), as soon as Alexander gave the signal, illustrates the tremendous discipline of the Roman forces; indeed, Jo-sephus, in citing the incident, drives home the fact that if only the Jews did not antagonize the Roman rulers they could count on their protec-tion. On the other hand, as Josephus (*War* 2.498) remarks, so intense was the hatred of the mob toward the Jews that they were not so easily called off and were only with difficulty torn from the corpses.

Almost simultaneously, a series of riots coincided with the outbreak of the Jewish revolution against the Romans in 66, again indicating that popular resentment against the Jews was deep-seated and long-smolder-ing. Indeed, Josephus (*War* 2.457) makes a point of mentioning that on the very same day and at the very same hour, "as if by divine Providence," when the Roman garrison in Herod's palace in Jerusalem was massacred, the non-Jewish inhabitants of Caesarea slaughtered the Jews resident in that city. The point of this mention is that the break in the tie between the Jews and their rulers meant that the anti-Jewish mobs were, in effect, given carte blanche throughout the empire for their murderous assaults, especially because Caesarea was the Roman provincial capital in the Land of Israel. Indeed, Josephus (*Ant.* 20.184) goes so far as to assign a direct connection between the long-standing quarrel of the Jews and the non-Jews in Caesarea over the civic rights of the Jews and the outbreak of the Jewish revolt against the Romans. Furthermore, Josephus (*Ant.* 20.183–84) makes a point of indicating that the immediate cause of the revolt of 66 was the arrival of a rescript from the Emperor Nero to the disputing parties at Caesarea giving control of the city to the Greeks, thus signaling to the Jews, presumably, the breakdown of the vertical alliance with the authorities in Rome. To be sure, however, Josephus himself tries to deflect the blame from Nero by declaring that it was actually Nero's secretary for Greek correspondence, Beryllus, who had been bribed by the non-Jews of Caesarea and who had managed to persuade the emperor. It was, presumably, the shift of the Romans from their role as "honest brokers" between the two groups to one of favoring the non-Jews that led the Jews to the painful conclusion that they could no longer count on the vertical alliance with their rulers to protect them. The slaughter in Caesarea by the non-Jews of twenty thousand Jews within one hour—a kind of Jewish St. Bartholemew's Day Massacre in more concentrated form—even if the figure is an exaggeration, indicates the premeditated nature of the assault. Indeed, years later, in 74, Eleazar ben Jair at Masada (*War* 7.363) recalled that the non-Jews had always been quarreling with the Jewish inhabitants of Caesarea and that they had seized the opportunity at the outbreak of the war to satisfy their ancient hate.

These attacks on the Jews in 66, in turn, set in motion a series of reprisals by Jews against non-Jews in a number of villages and cities in Syria and in the Land of Israel; and thereafter, in return, the Syrians, in their hatred (*War* 2.461), as Josephus notes, massacred the Jews. Curiously, Josephus gives no specific motive, alleged or actual, on the part of the attackers, as if it were obvious or usual; but significantly Josephus (*War* 2.463) cites the presence of "Judaizers" in each city in Syria who aroused suspicion; and we may guess that one of the causes of the Jew-hatred was precisely the Jewish success not only in winning converts but also in gaining "sympathizers." As to the motives of the Jew-baiters, Josephus lists three (*War* 2.464, 478): hatred ($\mu\tilde{\iota}\sigma o\varsigma$), fear ($\delta\acute{\epsilon}o\varsigma$), and greed ($\pi\lambda\epsilon ov\epsilon\xi\acute{\iota}a$) for plunder—apparently a combination of economic jealousy and fear of Jewish power and expansionism. It is, moreover, revealing to note that in Caesarea, the chief point of conflict, Josephus declares (*War* 2.268, *Ant.* 20.175) that the Jews were superior in wealth—another indication of the importance of the economic factor in explaining the hatred of the Jew-baiters toward the Jews (*War* 2.268 adds that the Jews were superior in physical strength)—while the source of Greek power was the support of the troops who were stationed there and who were mainly from Caesarea and from the nearby city of Sebaste (*Ant.* 20.176). One may infer that the Jewish wealth may well have created jealousy; and indeed we find (*Ant.* 20.177) that when the procurator Felix let loose his soldiers against the Caesarean Jews, he permitted his soldiers to plunder certain houses of the Jewish inhabitants that were laden with very large sums of money. We may furthermore conjecture that the Jews cited their contribution to the city's economic prosperity as an argument that their civic status ought to be improved.[25] Finally, by pointing to the Jews' physical strength, Josephus is doubtless remarking on the sheer number of Jews; and we may surmise that the non-Jews were frightened by the increase in the Jewish population,[26] at least in part due to their success in proselytism.

Even in Scythopolis (Bethshan), where the Jews fought side by side with the non-Jews against outside Jewish invaders, the Jewish inhabitants were lured into a false sense of security and were then massacred to the number of thirteen thousand, with their possessions pillaged (*War* 2.466 and *Life* 26). Likewise, if we may judge from Philo (*Legatio ad Gaium* 30.205), the inhabitants of Ashkelon had "a certain implacable and irreconcilable enmity" to the Jewish inhabitants of the land with whom they shared a frontier. It should not be surprising, therefore, that at the outbreak of the war we hear (*War* 2.477) that the non-Jewish inhabitants of Ashkelon killed twenty-five hundred Jews. In addition, in a number of other cities (ibid.) the Jews were expelled, imprisoned, or slain. The only cities in Syria where there were not massacres were Antioch, Sidon, and Apamea (*War* 2.479), perhaps, as Josephus conjectures, because, with their own vast populations, they did not feel threatened by the Jews.

4. THE AFTERMATH OF THE WAR OF 66–74

Despite this series of disasters, it is striking that the Jews could ultimately count on the support of the rulers against the mob. Antioch, as we have noted, was one of only three Syrian cities that, according to Josephus (*War* 2.479), had not indulged in popular massacres of the Jews on the eve of the war. The Jews of Antioch, like those of Alexandria, had been especially favored by their rulers and had indeed been granted rights on a par with those of the Greeks (*War* 7.44). The number of Jews had increased greatly both through immigration and through conversion of pagans to Judaism. After the outbreak of the fighting, however, the security of the Jews was ended, and a Jew named Antiochus, whom we have cited previously as an apostate, incited a riot when he accused the Jews of planning to burn the city, presumably as an act in concert with their fellow revolutionaries in the Land of Israel. The masses, hearing this, could not control the fury that had apparently, as in Alexandria, been smoldering for a long time and rushed on the Jews in their midst. Now that the revolution had broken out in Judaea, the Roman general no longer protected Jews and instead sent troops to aid Antiochus in forcing the Jews to violate the Sabbath.

After the capture of Jerusalem, when a fire broke out in Antioch, Antiochus accused the Jews of arson (*War* 7.57). The anti-Jewish mob, as if mad, rushed in their insane passion on the accused Jews. This time, however, the results were quite different. Once the revolt of the Jews in Jerusalem was over, the Roman administrator, the deputy governor Gnaeus

Collega, restrained the fury of the mob and, on investigation, learned that the whole affair had been the work of scoundrels who had hoped to get rid of their debts by burning the marketplace and the public records. Here we can plainly see the economic motive of the Jew-baiters, so similar to that of Jew-baiters in more modern times, such as during the French Revolution, when mobs in Alsace burned records of debts that they owed to Jews.

Shortly after the fall of Jerusalem, when the victorious Roman general Titus passed through Antioch, the non-Jewish population greeted him enthusiastically and petitioned him to expel the Jews from the city. Titus, however (*War* 7.104), was unmoved by this request and listened in silence. When the people of the city persisted, Titus declined, stating that because the country of the Jews had been destroyed the latter had nowhere to go. When the people asked that at least the privileges of the Jews be revoked, Titus again refused, leaving the status of the Jews as it formerly was (*War* 7.110–11), thus reaffirming the reliability of the vertical alliance on which the Jews had traditionally depended.

The bitterness of mob hatred and also the ultimate Roman protectiveness were illustrated once again in the great Diaspora revolt of 115 C.E., which was led by the pseudo-Messiah Lukuas-Andreas. Dio Cassius, who elsewhere expresses (49.22.5) respect for the sincere religiosity of the Jews, nevertheless declares (68.32.1–2) that they "would eat the flesh of their victims, make belts for themselves out of their entrails, anoint themselves with their blood and wear their skins as clothing; many they sawed in two, from the head downwards; others they gave to wild beasts, and still others they forced to fight as gladiators." The reports of such atrocities illustrate the extreme bitterness that the Jews' opponents felt toward them; and the charge that, according to Dio, the atrocities were carried out against both Romans and Greeks suggests that the local Greek population bore the brunt of the alleged fury of the Jews. Our sources, both literary and papyrological, all emanate from non-Jewish sources and are one-sided. One papyrus (*CPJ* 2.438) relates how the whole peasantry in an Egyptian district took the field against the Jews. In another papyrus (*CPJ* 2.437), an irascible old lady prays to the invincible Hermes to preserve her son from being roasted, apparently by the Jews (though the Jews are not explicitly mentioned). So bitter were the passions of the non-Jews toward the Jews and so strong was their rancor that even eighty years after the revolt the people of Oxyrhynchos (*CPJ* 2.450) celebrated an annual festival commemorating the victory over the Jews in which they had helped the Roman army.

We do not know the causes, alleged or otherwise, of the hatred felt, in this case, by the non-Jews toward the Jews and, presumably, vice versa; but we may guess that the messianic character of the revolt is a major clue and that the Jews may have sought to establish, under a messianic king, an independent state stretching from Cyrene and Egypt to Cyprus, Judaea, and Mesopotamia, all of which were scenes of revolt. That the revolt lasted for three years (115–17 C.E.) and was so fierce indicates that the fear that the Jews might establish such a state was not without foundation. We may infer from one papyrus (*CPJ* 2.435) that after the Roman victory over the Jews, Greeks in Alexandria, mainly slaves, started an anti-Jewish uprising instigated by people of influence (*CPJ* 2.229). Once again, however, it was the Roman administration that, despite the rebellion of the Jews, took measures against the Greek troublemakers in order to establish law and order. Still, the Jewish community of Egypt had been decimated by these events and was not to be reconstituted in strength until the medieval period.

In Rome itself, despite the insinuations about Jewish clannishness and influence in Cicero's defense of Flaccus (*Pro Flacco* 66), which we have noted, there was apparently no history of virulent hatred of Jews on the part of the mob, noted though it was for its size and unruly nature. We may conjecture that this was fine because the Jews in the city, unlike those in Alexandria or Antioch or Caesarea, did not have or seek special political privileges, so far as we know. Moreover, Rome was the seat of the emperor, who had regarded himself since the days of Julius Caesar as the protector of the Jews; and this factor may have served as a deterrent. Finally, because the emperor constantly had his own bodyguard and a sizable number of troops ready to protect himself from assassination or violent outbreaks, such popular uprisings would have been difficult to carry out. Hence, the Jews, despite the occasional expulsions we have noted, felt reasonably secure in the knowledge that the government would protect them against the passions of the mob.

CHAPTER 5

PREJUDICE AGAINST JEWS AMONG ANCIENT INTELLECTUALS

1. How Much Anti-Jewish Prejudice Was There among Ancient Intellectuals?

If, as we have contended, the vertical alliance of Jews in antiquity with governments was, with relatively few exceptions, successful in protecting the Jews from the often virulent anti-Jewish feelings of the masses of non-Jews, we may well ask what the attitude of non-Jewish intellectuals was toward the Jews and on what grounds those who opposed the Jews based their feelings. To what degree does the bitterness of some of these comments by the intellectuals indicate the success of Jews in maintaining themselves as Jews and even in influencing others to join the Jewish religion? What influence, if any, did these anti-Jewish intellectuals have on the thoughts and actions of rulers, and what impact did they have in fomenting outbreaks of the masses of the people against the Jews?

Though, as we have noted, it is perhaps hard to imagine a time when the world was not preoccupied with the "Jewish question," for many centuries in antiquity, as we have remarked, the Jewish question did not exist. Thus, it is not until Herodotus in the fifth century B.C.E. (though, admittedly, the number of extant Greek writers before him is not great) that any extant Greek writer alludes to the Jews at all; and even he, as we have stated, refers to them only obliquely when he discusses circumcision. A writer such as Cicero, who certainly knew about the Jews, ignores them completely in a work such as *De Natura Deorum*, where he deals at length with various theories concerning theology and where we might well have expected some mention of them, inasmuch as the Jewish view of deity is, from a pagan point of view, so unusual.

Stern's monumental three-volume collection of testimonia[1] seems large, but the truth is that the quotations cover a period of a full thousand years, and many of the quotations pertain only peripherally to the Jews as such. In dealing with this evidence, we should heed several caveats: 1) Most of the passages come from fragments, and thus we are generally not in a position to know the occasion and original context of the remarks. It may be that if we had the full work we should have a different view of the import of the passages; 2) many of the passages occur in

Josephus, particularly in his essay *Against Apion*, or in church fathers, where there is often a question of their authenticity and, in any case, where the polemical nature of the work in which they are embedded is clear. Indeed, if Josephus's reply *Against Apion* had been lost (as it almost was),[2] we would be lacking a large proportion of the most virulent ancient anti-Jewish texts; 3) many passages come from Graeco-Alexandrian writers, all of whom, with the sole exception of Timagenes, are hostile to the Jews; 4) many other passages come from rhetorical historians or satirists, where the references are clearly colored and exaggerated; 5) finally, we may note the patterns of ethnographical treatises which, especially under the influence of the Aristotelian Peripatetic school, had developed an interest in strange, foreign peoples and in their historical origins; hence, the surviving fragments to a great extent reflect this skewed interest.

Scholars who have examined this corpus have emphasized what they consider the almost universal prevalence of virulent anti-Jewish feeling in the remarks of these writers.[3] In the nineteenth and early twentieth centuries in Germany, it became fashionable, as seen in the writings of Felix Stähelin, Ulrich Wilcken, and Hugo Willrich, to cite these passages in promoting the thesis that there was something inherent in the Jews' characteristics that produced hostility toward them wherever they went, especially among those of intellectual attainments. We may, however, remark that, according to my count, 101 (18 percent) of the comments by pagans in Stern's collection are substantially favorable, 339 (59 percent) are more or less neutral, and only 130 (23 percent) are substantially unfavorable,[4] and this despite the fact that the preservation of ancient manuscripts is due, in large part, to the Church, whether in the East or the West. In view of the large number of treatises *Adversus Judaeos*, one might have thought it would seek to preserve passages attacking rather than defending the Jews.[5]

To be sure, Salo Baron, when questioned by Robert Servatius, the chief attorney for the defense at the Eichmann trial, as to the causes of "that negative attitude which had existed for so many hundreds of years and of that war against the Jewish people," replied, "The answer is: dislike of the unlike."[6] But Balsdon has well indicated how the Romans, for example, viewed those who were unlike them.[7] Thus, in India it was said that the people slept in their ears (!); the Brahmans were said to be completely celibate for thirty-seven years, after which they married as many wives as they could; there were medicine men who could determine the sex of unborn children; and there were naked sophists who made prophecies until they had been proved wrong three times, after which time they had to be quiet. This may lead at most to bemused contempt for Indians; it does not lead to hatred, let alone persecution of Indians, though of course there was probably not much of an Indian diaspora. But Sardinians, who were certainly close at hand, were regarded as brigands and congenital liars; and, as the old saying had it, "Sardinians for sale: If one is bad, the others are worse." Yet they were not hated, let alone persecuted; indeed, they were recruited in large numbers for the Roman navy. As for the British, they were said to be hardly civilized and indeed inhospitable, better only than the Irish, who were devoid of any redeeming virtues whatsoever. With regard to the Arabs, there was a story that a cart belonging to the god Hermes, loaded with various kinds of mischief, broke down in their country and was plundered by the natives, whence the result that the Arabs were "liars and impostors, who did not know the meaning of truth." As for the Egyptians, the unknown author of the *Bellum Alexandrinum* writes, "If I were briefed to defend Alexandrians and to establish that they were neither treacherous nor irresponsible, I could make a long speech but it would be a wasted effort." With respect to the Greeks, such writers as Cicero felt that they were irresponsible playboys, sloppy, crooks, sycophants, chatterboxes, full of conceit.[8] Other peoples of antiquity, such as the Syrians, Thracians, Spaniards, Gauls, and Carthaginians, as well as the Romans themselves, were also objects of detestation and derision. Thus, for example, two of the charges made against Jews, that they are lazy and superstitious, are also made by Tacitus against the Germans. But in none of these cases do we have organized hatred or persecution, perhaps, to be sure, because none of these peoples were living among the Romans in such large numbers while also preserving so distinctive a culture as did the Jews and while seeming to have such great loyalty to their own worldwide brotherhood.

Moreover, as we shall note, Jews were admired by some intellectuals, at least, as possessing the four cardinal virtues of wisdom, courage, temperance, and justice.[9] Indeed, the list of their admirers included figures of the stature of Aristotle, his successor Theophrastus, and Varro, who was to be termed by the great literary critic Quintilian (10.1.95) "the most learned of the Romans." Nonetheless, it must be granted that there are a number of serious charges made by the intellectual anti-Jewish bigots, though significantly there are no ethnic connotations, presumably because there were so many converts to Judaism.

2. THE ALLEGED JEWISH MISANTHROPY

The main, most serious, and most recurrent charge by intellectuals against Jews is that they hate Gentiles.[10] The greatest influence on all the philosophies of the Hellenistic and Roman periods was Socrates, who encouraged debate about basic premises. The Jew, on the other hand, at least according to his own theory, could not debate his basic premises, notably the miraculous revelation of the Torah at Sinai. Moreover, the Jew, most intolerantly—at least to the pagan intellectual—asserted that the premises of pagan polytheism were all wrong and indeed insisted that pagans, as children of Noah, were forbidden to worship idols. Jews, ironically, welcomed others into their midst as proselytes—but only on their terms. It is this illiberalism that is constantly attacked by the pagan thinkers. Moreover, intellectuals, almost by definition, seek to persuade others of the validity of their points of view; and, as we shall remark, they must have seen in the Jews dangerous and often successful rivals to their missionary propaganda.

The significance of this issue of illiberalism is underscored by the fact that about the year 300 B.C.E. even Hecataeus (quoted in Diodorus 40.3.4), who was on the whole well disposed toward the Jews, characterized the Jewish mode of life as somewhat unsocial (ἀπάνθρωπον, "inhuman") and hostile to foreigners (μισόξενον). This is the sole remark in his account that may be termed negative, though even it is qualified by the word *somewhat* and justified as a reaction to the Jews' expulsion from Egypt, and though Hecataeus significantly does not himself add any judgment on this Jewish characteristic. Indeed he seems to indicate (quoted in Diodorus 40.3.8) approval of their separation when he remarks, with apparent tribute, that many of their traditional practices were disturbed when they had become subject to foreign rule of the Persians and later of the Macedonians. Nevertheless, the term μισόξενον is clearly hostile, as we see from its occurrence in only one other passage in Greek literature, namely in Josephus (*Ant.* 1.194), where it refers to the hatred of foreigners exhibited by the despised people of Sodom.

Though the Torah (Exod 23:9) commands the Jew to treat the stranger with respect, the dietary laws, Sabbath laws, and rules regarding idolatry were formidable barriers that, to a large extent, prevented the Jews from fraternizing with Gentiles. The prohibition against Gentiles entering the Temple precinct (Josephus, *Ant.* 15.417) and against teaching them the Torah (*Ḥagigah* 13a) may likewise have contributed to rumors and to misunderstanding, including even the blood libel, inasmuch as the Gentile might well ask whether the Jews were trying to hide something embarrassing to themselves in promulgating such rules. This most shocking of all charges of the anti-Jewish bigots is found in the writing of two of the leading intellectuals of the first century B.C.E., Poseidonius[11] and Apollonius Molon (cited in Josephus, *Against Apion* 2.79). They are, it would seem, Apion's sources for the scandalous story that when Antiochus Epiphanes entered the Temple he was hailed with great relief by a Greek who told him how he had been kidnapped and shut up in the Temple, where he was held incommunicado and was fattened up on most lavish feasts. The Greek is said to have soon discovered that this was a practice followed by the Jews each year, and that it would culminate in his being sacrificed in accordance with their customary ritual, after which the Jews would partake of the flesh of the sacrificial victim and swear an oath of hostility to the Greeks. Damocritus (cited in Suda, "Damokritos"), a historian in the first century c.e., like Apion, refers to the sacrifice of a stranger (not specifically a Greek) after he mentions the Jews' worship of an ass's head.[12] Hence we may conclude that these accounts ultimately had a common source, though Damocritus says that the sacrifice occurred every seventh year (presumably an allusion to the Sabbatical year) rather than annually and adds that the Jews used to kill their victim by carding his flesh into small pieces.

The story would appear to be a traditional one of the King of the Saturnalia and of a cannibalistic conspiracy.[13] The fact that human sacrifice was regarded as evidence of barbarian superstition (cf. Cicero, *Pro Fonteio* 14.31), whereas the Roman government abolished it among the nations under its sway, would equate the Jews with other barbarians. Bickermann believes that the story arose in circles close to Antiochus Epiphanes as an effort, that is, noting that the Jews were guilty of an even more heinous sacrilege, to justify the sacrilege he committed in desecrating the Temple.[14] But Tcherikover[15] appears to be on sounder ground when he suggests that the hostility to the Jews was strong enough during the reign of Antiochus Epiphanes that there was hardly any need for his defenders to justify Antiochus's desecration of the Temple.

Furthermore, the Romans, as we can see from their suppression of the Bacchanalia in 186 b.c.e., were very suspicious of secret cults, whose initiates would not reveal the mysteries of their religion to non-initiates. In the case of the Bacchanalia (Livy 39.8–18), we hear that the secrets of this mystery religion were at first revealed to only a few people but soon began to be taught widely to both men and women. When the pleasures of wine and banquets were added to the religious ceremonies in order to attract a larger number of people, the state became suspicious. The analogy with Judaism is rather striking. Thus, Plutarch (*Quaestiones Convivales* 4.6.1.671C), in identifying the Jewish G-d with Dionysus,[16] mentions their secret (ἀπορρήτοις, "unspeakable") rites, corroborating the view found in Philo (*De Somniis* 1.26.164) that Judaism was a mystery cult and Moses was a hierophant or mystagogue.[17] This secrecy may also reflect the well-known exclusion of Gentiles from the Temple area in Jerusalem (Josephus, *Ant.* 15.417) that we have mentioned above. Indeed, Philo (*De Sacrificiis Abelis et Caini* 16.62) had distinguished between the Lesser and the Greater Mysteries and notes that he who has been initiated into the mysteries of Moses is not to divulge them to any of the uninitiated but to conceal them in silence, a reference presumably to the prohibition, noted above, against a Jew teaching the Torah to a non-Jew (*Hagigah* 13a; cf. *Sanhedrin* 59a),[18] just as the initiate into the Bacchanalia is not permitted to divulge the mystery to a noninitiate.

The perception of the Jews as hating other peoples is found in a host of writings of pagan intellectuals. Thus, Manetho in the third century B.C.E. states that by his very first law Osarsiph, whom he identifies with Moses (quoted in Josephus, *Against Apion* 1.250), ordained that the Israelites should have no connection with any except members of their own people. Lysimachus, who lived perhaps in the second or first century B.C.E., reflects the charge of misanthropy when he remarks (quoted in Josephus, *Against Apion* 1.309) that Moses instructed the Israelites to show goodwill to no man, to offer not the best but the worst advice, and to overthrow temples and altars of the gods. Apollonius Molon (cited in Josephus, *Against Apion* 2.258) in the first century B.C.E. condemned the Jews for illiberalism in that they refused admission to persons with other ideas about G-d and would not associate with those who have adopted a different manner of life. His contemporary Diodorus (34 [35].1.1) similarly reports that when King Antiochus Sidetes was laying siege to Jerusalem the majority of his friends advised him to wipe out the Jews, "since they alone of all nations avoided dealings with any other people and looked on all [other] men as their enemies." This hatred of others, they said, went back to the expulsion from Egypt and was demonstrated most clearly by the Jewish refusal to break bread with any other race or to show others any goodwill at all. Pompeius Trogus (quoted in Justin, *Historiae Philippicae* 36, *Epitoma* 2.15), at the beginning of the first century C.E., similarly connects the Jews' alleged misanthropy with their expulsion from Egypt, remarking that they had adopted such an attitude in order to avoid again becoming odious to their neighbors.

Apion (cited in Josephus, *Against Apion* 2.121), at the beginning of the first century C.E., went further in his malice, attributing to the Jews an oath to show no goodwill to any alien, especially to Greeks.[19] The first-century philosopher Euphrates is quoted by Philostratus (*Life of Apollonius of Tyana* 5.33) as noting that the Jews do not mingle with others in common meals, libations, prayers, or sacrifices. Similarly, in his paraphrase of Haman's statement (Esth 3:8) that the Jews' laws are different from those of every other people and that they do not keep the king's laws, Josephus's Haman (*Ant.* 11.212) phrases the charge in terms familiar from the Hellenistic anti-Jewish intellectuals. The Jews, he says, refuse to mingle with others (ἄμικτον, a term used of Centaurs and Cyclopes)[20] and are unsocial (ἀσύμφυλον, "not akin," "incompatible," "unsuitable"). They do not have the same religion, nor do they practice the same laws as other peoples, but both in customs and in practices they are the enemy of the Persians and indeed of all people (ἅπασιν ἀνθρώποις).

Furthermore, Josephus's contemporary Quintilian (3.7.21), at the end of the first century, cites the creator of the Jewish "superstition," that is, Moses, as an example to illustrate his statement that it is notorious for founders of cities to bring together a people bent on the destruction of others. Tacitus (*Histories* 5.5.1), at the beginning of the second century, in a phrase so highly reminiscent of Haman's words as cited by Josephus above, also remarks that the Jews regard the rest of humankind with all the hatred of enemies (*adversus omnes alios hostile odium*); and in immediate juxtaposition he gives the apparent source of this conception, namely that they sit and sleep apart from other peoples and abstain from intercourse with Gentile women.[21] His contemporary Juvenal (*Satire* 14.103–4), in his bitter satirical tone, condemns the Jews for not showing the way or a fountain spring to any but fellow-Jews. It may be that the allusion here is to the prohibition, noted above, against showing the "way" (that is, teaching the Torah) to Gentiles (*Hagigah* 13a).[22]

The stubbornness of the Jews in separating themselves from other peoples was apparently proverbial, as we see in the remark of the second-century C.E. Aelius Aristeides (46 [*De Quattuorviris* 309]) citing the Jews as the stock example of impiety, in that they do not recognize their betters [i.e., they do not believe in the gods] and have in some way ($\tau\rho\acute{o}\pi o\nu$ $\tau\iota\nu\grave{\alpha}$, a phrase reminiscent of Hecataeus's phrase [quoted in Diodorus 40.3.4] "somewhat unsocial and intolerant" [$\grave{\alpha}\pi\acute{\alpha}\nu\theta\rho\omega\pi\acute{o}\nu$ $\tau\iota\nu\alpha$ $\kappa\alpha\grave{\iota}$ $\mu\iota\sigma\acute{o}$-$\xi\varepsilon\nu o\nu$] and hence not vicious in its anti-Jewish innuendo) seceded from the Greeks or rather from all the better people. A similar view of the Jews as a paradigm of a long-standing revolt against all other people is mentioned by Philostratus (*Life of Apollonius of Tyana* 5.33) at the beginning of the third century C.E. He adds that they are "a race that has made its own a life apart and irreconcilable, that cannot share with the rest of humankind in the pleasures of the table nor join in their libations or prayers or sacrifices, and are separated from ourselves by a greater gulf than divides us from Susa or Bactra or the more distant Indies." Indeed, he remarks that the Jews are so far removed from humanity that it would have been better if the Romans had never annexed Judaea. And yet it is clear that such a view was not universally held, inasmuch as these remarks are put into the mouth of the Stoic Euphrates, the opponent of the main subject of the biography, Apollonius. Another person present during this conversation, Dion, disagrees and says that the emphasis should have been placed on deposing Nero rather than on punishing the Jews.

The view that the Jews are somehow divorced from the rest of the human race persists in the early fifth century C.E., as we may see from the letter written by the Neoplatonist Synesius (*Epistulae* 5) describing his sea voyage from Alexandria to Cyrene. The captain of the ship and more than half of the crew were Jews, whom Synesius then proceeds to describe as not a party to the human race (ἔκσπονδον, "not subscribing to a treaty") and as being fully convinced of the piety of sending to their death as many Greeks as possible. This is, indeed, reminiscent of the blood libel that we have already noted, and it may indicate that the bitter antagonism between Greeks and Jews at Cyrene during the revolt of Lukuas-Andreas under Trajan some three centuries earlier had still not subsided.[23]

Furthermore, among the Romans, Cicero was particularly resentful, at least by implication, of the Jewish claim, which appeared to him to be a boast, to enjoy divine protection, presumably as the chosen people of G-d, when he declares sarcastically (*Pro Flacco* 28.67), "The nation [i.e., the Jews]. . . has made it clear how far it enjoys divine protection by the fact that it has been conquered, scattered, enslaved." Similarly, Celsus (quoted in Origen, *Against Celsus* 5.50) in the second century C.E. alluded sarcastically to the "Promised Land" by remarking, "We see what sort of land it was of which they [i.e., the Jews] were thought worthy."[24]

Moreover, that the Jews, comprising in the first century, as we have noted, perhaps a tenth of the total population of the Roman Empire, did not worship the Roman emperor, who was a crucial symbol of unity for a nation comprised of so many different peoples, made them a subject of sharp attack for their lack of patriotism. One can see this, for example, in the bitter comment by the second-century Juvenal (*Satire* 14.100-1) that those who become Jews are wont to flout the Roman laws and instead learn and practice and revere Jewish law. For a nation such as Rome that justly prided itself on the development of an extremely comprehensive and fair system of law, there was almost no charge graver than this.

And yet, as we have remarked, the picture painted by the ancient intellectuals with regard to the Jews is not one-sided. Indeed, even such detractors of the Jews as Tacitus (*Histories* 5.5.1), at the beginning of the second century, grant the legitimacy of certain rites of the Jews, such as the Sabbath, the observance of Passover, and abstention from pork, by virtue of their antiquity. Similarly, the second-century Celsus (quoted in Origen, *Against Celsus* 5.25), though generally critical of the Jews, is ready to grant that their worship may be very peculiar, but at least it is traditional, which is not true of Christianity. Indeed, he notes that in this respect the Jews behave like the rest of humanity, in that each nation follows its traditional customs, whatever kind they may happen to be. He then speculates, in defense of the peculiarities of Jewish practices, that it is probable that from the beginning the various parts of the earth were assigned to different overseers,[25] and that it is consequently impious to abandon the customs that have existed thus in any particular part of the world from the very beginning.[26] In support of his view, he (quoted in

Origen, *Against Celsus* 5.34) cites Herodotus (2.18) and in particular the story (Herodotus 3.38) of the Persian king Darius who asked the Greeks and the Indians how much money they would accept in return for abandoning their traditional practice of disposing of the dead. Similarly, the third-century Porphyry (*Ad Marcellam* 18) insists that the greatest fruit of piety is to honor one's divinity in accordance with one's ancestral traditions. Furthermore, he attacks (cited in Eusebius, *Praeparatio Evangelica* 1.2.3–4) the Christians in particular for deserting the customs of their forefathers and asks, "Must it not be a proof of extreme wickedness and levity to put aside the customs of their own kindred and choose with unreasoning and unquestioning faith the doctrines of the impious enemies of all nations?" A similar attack on the Christians for deserting the time-honored ancestral ways of the Jews is to be found in Julian (*Contra Galilaeos* (238 A–C), who is otherwise generally critical of the Jewish Bible and of Jewish theology.

3. Answers to Charges of Misanthropy in Graeco-Jewish Writers before Josephus

As evidence that the Jews did not hate non-Jews and that, in fact, they had a long history of cordial relations with them, Eupolemus, who lived in the middle of the second century b.c.e., offers a number of statements, which are cited by Alexander Polyhistor (quoted in Clement of Alexandria, *Stromata* 1.21.130.3) but which have no biblical basis, recording letters supposedly sent by King Solomon to Vaphres the pharaoh of Egypt (e.g., cited in Eusebius, *Praeparatio Evangelica* 9.31.1) and to the king of the Tyrians. The cordiality of the reply of the Egyptian king (cited in Eusebius, *Praeparatio Evangelica* 9.32.1) is striking, even to the point that we are told that the entire Egyptian realm observed a day of celebration on Solomon's accession to the throne. This is, therefore, a clear answer to those who charged that the Jews refuse to have friendly dealings with non-Jews. King Solomon, in his letters to the kings of both Egypt and Tyre (cited in Eusebius, *Praeparatio Evangelica* 9.31.1 and 9.33.1) refers to them as friends of his father, that is, as royal advisers.[27] In one of these letters (cited in Eusebius, *Praeparatio Evangelica* 9.34.1), Souron (Hiram), the king of Tyre, shows his great respect for Solomon by addressing him as "the great king" and blessing G-d for choosing for Himself a noble (χρηστόν) man. That Solomon maintained truly cordial relations with his neighbors is seen in the extra-biblical detail (cited in Eusebius, *Praeparatio Evangelica* 9.34.4) that Solomon made a trip to Lebanon, accompanied by Sidonians and Tyrians, in order to formulate the details of the wood to be shipped for the building of the Temple.

Furthermore, the historian Artapanus in the middle of the second century B.C.E., in a statement that seems obviously contrived, clearly answers the charge that the Jews hate non-Jews by stressing (cited in Eusebius, *Praeparatio Evangelica* 9.27.6) that Moses did so much for the Egyptians that he was loved by the Egyptian masses and was deemed worthy of divine honor by the Egyptian priests.

Philo (*De Specialibus Legibus* 2.29.167), at the beginning of the first century C.E., expresses astonishment that some people (τινες) accuse Jews of inhumanity (ἀπανθρωπίαν), whereas the Jews have shown fellowship (κοινωνίας, "communion," "association," "partnership," "joint ownership") and goodwill (εὐνοίας) to all men everywhere through prayers, festivals, and offering of first fruits on behalf of the entire human race. In a show of universalism and tolerance, he says (*De Specialibus Legibus* 1.38.211) that one should give thanks not only for the genus but also for the species and then proceeds to specify that one should give thanks for both men and women, and for both Greeks and barbarians. Indeed, to prove his point, he specifies (*De Specialibus Legibus* 1.17.97) that whereas the priests of other nations offer prayers and sacrifices solely for their countrymen, the high priest of the Jews does so on behalf of the entire human race and, in fact, in a manner reminiscent of a Stoic philosopher, on behalf of all of nature. As an example of this tolerance, he cites (*De Josepho* 40.240) Joseph, who, in a crucial comment, which has no basis in the biblical text, speaks of the natural humanity (φυσικῇ φιλανθρωπίᾳ) that he feels toward all people. Furthermore (*De Virtutibus* 26.140–41), Philo answers the charge of misanthropy by the a fortiori argument that Jews are required by their law to show fair treatment even to irrational animals and all the more so to other human beings. Likewise, Philo (*De Vita Contemplativa* 2.20) is clearly answering the charge of misanthropy when he declares that the ascetic group known as the Therapeutae, who sundered themselves from the community by leading a monastic existence on an island off the coast of Alexandria, did so "not from any acquired habit of savage (ὠμήν, "raw," "fierce," "cruel") misanthropy (μισανθρωπίαν), but because they know how unprofitable and mischievous are associations (ἐπιμιξίας, "mixing with others," "intercourse," "dealings") with persons of dissimilar character." Actually, as he contends elsewhere (*De Abrahamo* 4.22–23), the man of worth who withdraws from the public and loves solitude does so not because he is misanthropic, for he is eminently a lover of mankind (φιλάνθρωπος), but rather because he has rejected vice that is welcomed by the multitude. Indeed, in a counterattack, Philo (*De Vita Mosis* 1.16.95) accuses the Egyptian oppressors of the Israelites of inhumanity (ἀπανθρωπίας) and impiety (ἀσεβείας).[28] Moreover, whereas the Bible (Deut 20:10–14) states that if an enemy refuses the offer of peace, the men are to be slain and the women and children enslaved, Philo (*De Virtutibus* 22.109–10), finding such strong measures antagonistic to his view of Jewish gentleness toward others, stresses that the law commands that pity be shown to such captive women and that their misfortunes should be alleviated by changing their condition for the better in every way.

4. Answers to Charges of Misanthropy in Josephus's *Antiquities*

That Gentiles are Josephus's primary audience for whom he wrote the *Antiquities* is clear from the precedent that he cites (*Ant.* 1.10) for writing his work, namely the translation of the Pentateuch into Greek for King Ptolemy Philadelphus. Indeed, he specifically declares (*Ant.* 1.5) that his work was undertaken in the belief that the whole Greek world would find it worthy of attention. Again, at the end of the work (*Ant.* 20.262), he boasts that no one else would have been equal to the task of issuing so accurate a treatise for the Greeks (εἰς ῞Ελληνας).

In a very real sense, the *Antiquities* is an extended answer to charges that the Jews were guilty of hatred of mankind.[29] Thus, he declares (*Ant.* 1.166) in his narrative of Abraham's visit to Egypt that it is the Egyptians who disparaged each other's practices and who were consequently at enmity with each other, in contrast to Abraham, who, respectful of the opinions of others, patiently conferred with each party and pointed out the flaws in each argument. In addition, Abraham is depicted (*Ant.* 1.181) as graciously reciprocating Melchizedek's lavish hospitality with a more gracious offer of a tithe of all the spoil he had taken in the campaign against the Syrians, whereas in the Hebrew Bible (Gen 14:20) it is not clear whether Abraham gave a tithe or received it. Moreover, it is in answer to such a charge as that repeated by Tacitus, that Jews were devoid of pity for anyone who was not of their religion, that Josephus's Abraham (*Ant.* 1.199) shows pity for his friends, even for the Sodomites.[30] The portrayal, we may add, of the Sodomites in even more derogatory colors in Josephus than in the Bible glorifies still more the figure of Abraham for showing pity toward them nonetheless and for praying on their behalf. Moreover, Josephus (*Ant.* 1.200) remarks that Lot had acquired the lesson of hospitality from Abraham; but the rabbis speak in general terms, whereas Josephus declares that Lot learned to be φιλάνθρωπος, thus answering those critics who claimed that the Jews were misanthropes. Likewise, Abraham (*Ant.* 1.211) shows devotion and kindness to Abimelech in order to demonstrate that he was in no way responsible for the king's illness but, quite the contrary, was eager for his recovery. Furthermore, Josephus (*Ant.* 1.218) completely omits the pathetic scene (Gen 21:16) in which Hagar weeps when cast into the wilderness by Sarah, because this might cast an unfavorable reflection on Abraham as pitiless.

Again, whereas, as we have noted, the Jews had been accused of the blood libel by Apion and by Damocritus, Josephus (*Ant.* 1.233) stresses by implication, as we have noted,[31] the contrast between the sacrifice of Isaac, which was not consummated, and that of Iphigenia, which was actually carried out. In particular, he puts a speech (*Ant.* 1.233–36) into the mouth of G-d, rather than of an angel as in Genesis 22:11, that He does not crave human blood and that He is not capricious in taking away what He has given. This is in direct contrast to Artemis, who (Euripides, *Iphigenia at Aulis* 1524–25) "rejoices in human sacrifices."

Likewise, in answer to the charge that the Jews are illiberal in being unwilling to listen to other points of view, in the episode of Abraham's journey to Egypt Josephus describes his entrance as if it were that of the head of a school of Hellenistic philosophy to dispute with the head of a rival school.[32] In the biblical account (Gen 12:10), the sole reason for Abraham's journey to Egypt is to escape the famine in Canaan; Josephus (*Ant.* 1.161), in characteristic fashion, gives this reason but also adds that he sought to become a student (ἀκροατής, used of becoming a disciple in the philosophic schools) of Egyptian priests in matters of theology.[33] In the spirit of Hellenistic philosophic disputations, Abraham is said to be magnanimously ready to adopt the Egyptian priests' doctrines if he finds them superior to his own (*Ant.* 1.161) or, if he should win the debate, to convert the priests to his beliefs.

Abraham thus emerges as similar to the wise and revered Apollonius of Tyana (cited in Philostratus, *Life of Apollonius* 1.26, 3.16 ff., and 6.10 ff.), Josephus's contemporary, who visited the Magi, the Indians, and the Egyptians both to learn from them and to teach them. Josephus (*Against Apion* 1.176–83) similarly, as we have noted, tells of a learned Jew who came to visit Aristotle in Asia Minor in the fourth century B.C.E. to converse with him and to test his learning, but in the end imparted to Aristotle something of his own. The only comparable passage in the Talmud is the one telling of Joshua ben Ḥananiah's contest with the Athenian sages (*Bekoroth* 8b), in which both parties agreed that the one who was defeated should be left entirely at the mercy of the victor; but there the contest is apparently not for the purpose of conversion but for the sake of physically annihilating the opponent.[34]

The rabbis, like Josephus, speak of Abraham as a missionary, but in the rabbinic writings about him there is no philosophical setting in the Hellenistic style of real debate, including a willingness to be converted if defeated in argument; instead, the picture is of a dogmatic missionary proceeding systematically to win converts.[35] Josephus, sensitive to the charge that the Jews are aggressive missionaries, is careful to modify this picture. Thus, according to Josephus, after Pharaoh discovers the identity of Abraham (*Ant.* 1.165), the latter consorts (or, according to a variant reading, is given permission to consort) with the most learned men of the Egyptians, as a result of which his excellence and reputation, like those of Solon, who similarly is said to have visited Egypt (Plato, *Timaeus* 21E), become more manifest.

Thus, the conclusion of the episode of Abraham and Sarah in Egypt is not, as in the Bible (with its stress on the narrative aspect), their hasty dismissal by Pharaoh or, as in the Genesis Apocryphon (col. 20, a passage reminiscent of the conclusion of the Sarah-Abimelech episode and stressing G-d's role), Abraham's prayer to G-d to remove the plague from Pharaoh. Rather, in the same liberal spirit as that with which Abraham's Egyptian excursion had begun, the narrative ends with the stress on Abraham the scientist and philosopher in converse with the Egyptians. Indeed, at the conclusion of his visit to Egypt, we are shown Abraham, in the fashion of a Hellenistic philosopher reminiscent of Cotta the neo-Academic in Cicero's *De Natura Deorum*, exposing (διαπτύων— "rejecting, dismissing") the arguments the Egyptians present in support of their view and demonstrating that these arguments are without foundation and devoid of truth (*Ant.* 1.166).[36]

Moreover, far from keeping his knowledge to himself, Abraham is presented by Josephus (*Ant.* 1.167) as the one who taught the Egyptians the very sciences for which they later became so famous. He graciously gives (χαρίζεται) them of his knowledge of arithmetic and transmits to them his lore about astronomy, a science of which the Egyptians had previously been ignorant and which was to become the most popular of the four branches of mathematics in Hellenistic times[37]—the one that aroused the most curiosity because of the practical importance of astrology. Hence, it is Abraham's unselfishness in sharing his scientific knowledge with the Egyptians that, according to Josephus, is responsible for Greek competence in these fields, because the Greeks in turn are said to have borrowed from the Egyptians.[38] Artapanus, long before Josephus (cited in Eusebius, *Praeparatio Evangelica* 9.18), had declared that Abraham had taught Pharaoh astrology; but in Josephus it is not Pharaoh but the Egyptian philosophers and scientists whom Abraham instructs; and, far from hoarding his knowledge, indeed with an internationalist scholarly outlook, he shares it cheerfully and freely with his fellow-philosophers and scientists.

Furthermore, Josephus's portrait of Joseph is particularly directed to answer the charge of misanthropy. Thus, in the Bible (Gen 42:2) there is no mention that when Joseph was administering the distribution of grain during the years of famine, the market was open to foreigners, because, presumably, selling grain to outsiders under such circumstances would not have been expected. Josephus (*Ant.* 2.94), however, presents the extra-biblical remark that Joseph opened the market not only to his own nation but also to strangers, because, we are told, Joseph—and, by extension, the Jewish people whom he clearly represents—believed that all people, by virtue of their kinship, should receive aid from those in prosperity. We thus see here the ideal, made so famous by Alexander the Great, that all men are brethren by virtue of having a common father (Plutarch, *Alexander* 27).

Josephus (*Against Apion* 2.146) further stresses that the Mosaic Code was designed to promote humanity toward the world at large, that (*Against Apion* 2.211–13) "our legislator," that is Moses, inculcated into the Jews the duty of sharing with others, and that not only must the Jew furnish food and supplies to those Gentile friends and neighbors who ask for them but that he must show consideration even for declared enemies. He even adds unscriptural provisions, such as that Jews are forbidden to burn up the country of their enemies and to despoil fallen combatants.[39] This gentleness and humanity (φιλανθρωπία) extend even to animals, authorizing their use only in accordance with the Law. It is almost as if Josephus is replying to Juvenal (14.103) when he declares (*Against Apion* 2.211) that the Mosaic law requires the Jew to point out the road to others. Moreover (*Ant.* 4.276), says Josephus, in an addition to the Bible (Lev 19:14), one is not permitted, for the pleasure of laughing oneself, to impede another by misleading him. The Mosaic Law, he says (*Against Apion* 2.291), teaches people not to hate their fellows but rather to share with them. Indeed, Josephus (*Against Apion* 2.237) follows the Septuagint (Exod 22:27) in reading "Thou shalt not revile gods," rather than the rabbinic interpretation (*Sanhedrin* 66a) of the last word as "judges," and deduces therefrom that "our legislator has expressly forbidden us to deride or blaspheme the gods recognized by others, out of respect for the very word " 'G-d.' "[40] In addition, Josephus (*Ant.* 2.304) has discreetly omitted any reference to the passage (Exod 8:21–23) in which Moses seems to show intolerance when he declares that the Israelites sacrifice to G-d what is untouchable to the Egyptians. Likewise, whereas the Bible (Lev 24:15–16) declares that anyone, whether Israelite or Gentile, who curses G-d is subject to the death penalty, Josephus (*Ant.* 4.202), in paraphrasing the passage, omits mention of the applicability of the penalty also to foreigners.

The emphasis placed by Josephus (*Ant.* 4.207) on tolerance is clearly his answer to the charges of narrow-mindedness. Thus, the prohibition (Exod 22:27) against cursing the gods, as cited by Josephus (*Against Apion* 2.237), would seem to be his answer to Manetho's objection (*Against Apion* 1.249, 264, 309) that Moses ordered his people to overthrow temples and altars. Indeed, we may note that Josephus, in his paraphrase in the *Antiquities*, significantly omits the passages (Exod 34:12–13, Deut 12:2–3) in which G-d instructs Moses that when the Israelites enter the land of Canaan they should destroy all the statues, devastate all the high places, and make no covenant with the Canaanites. Balak is concerned with the growing power of the Israelites, but he has not learned, we are told (*Ant.* 4.102), that the Hebrews are not for interfering with other countries and that, in fact, they are forbidden by G-d to do so. Josephus likewise omits any reference to the passage (Num 12:1) that Miriam and Aaron spoke against Moses on account of the Ethiopian woman whom he had married; such murmuring would surely have been regarded by liberal Greek intellectuals as prejudice against the highly respected Ethiopians.[41]

That Moses himself was not prejudiced against Gentiles is clear from the differentiation made by Josephus (*Ant.* 2.315) between Pharaoh and the Egyptians in his comment, in an extra-biblical addition, that when the Israelites departed from Egypt the Egyptians lamented and regretted the harsh way they had treated the Israelites. His lack of prejudice is likewise displayed in the respect shown to Reuel (Jethro), Moses' father-in-law, who is described (*Ant.* 2.258) as a priest held in high veneration by the people of the country. Indeed, whereas the Bible (Exod 2:21) states that Moses was content to dwell with Jethro, Josephus (*Ant.* 2.263) emphasizes that he harbors no prejudice against Gentiles when he says that Reuel actually adopted him as his son. To show the warm feeling that existed between father-in-law and son-in-law, Josephus (*Ant.* 3.63) emphasizes the gladness with which Reuel went to meet Moses after the victory over Amalek and the joy, in turn, that Moses felt at the visit. In the biblical account, Jethro brings back his daughter Zipporah and the children to Moses after a temporary separation. In Josephus, the family had never been parted (cf. Exod 4:20). Furthermore, to show the respect that Jews have for non-Jews, Josephus (*Ant.* 3.64) has an extended description of the banquet given by Moses in honor of his father-in-law, where an ecumenical spirit prevails, with Aaron and his company being joined by Jethro in chanting hymns to G-d as the author and dispenser of their salvation and their liberty. For his part, Jethro is depicted as showing consideration not to embarrass Moses (*Ant.* 3.67) for his inefficient administration of justice; only when all others are gone does he discreetly advise Moses what to do.

The charge of provincialism and intolerance was, we may guess, not confined to the Jew-baiters. As van Unnik[42] has remarked, the words of Zambrias (Zimri) (*Ant.* 4.145–49) would appear to be those of Jewish contemporaries who broke away from the ancestral religion as obscurantist and too confining, indeed as opposing universal opinion.[43] This rebellion objected not merely to Moses's authoritarianism but also to the refusal of Judaism to be open to other religious views. This will explain why Josephus (*Ant.* 4.140) regarded this revolt as far more grave than that of Korah, inasmuch as the latter was directed merely against the leadership of Moses and Aaron, whereas this attacked the very roots of Judaism.

Generosity and magnanimity (μεγαλογνωμοσύνη) were considered to be among the key traits of a great man, as we see in Xenophon's biography of Agesilaus (8.3–4) and in many passages in Aristotle's *Ethics*. Indeed, whereas the Bible (Deut 23:20) simply states the prohibition against charging interest on loans and does not give a reason, Josephus (*Ant.* 4.266) uses the occasion to explain the reason, namely that it is not just or fair to draw a revenue from the misfortune of a fellow-countryman and that, on the contrary, one should welcome the gratitude of such persons and the reward that G-d has in store for such an act of generosity. Although such generosity extends only to Jews, the fruit of the field, according to the Mosaic law as interpreted by Josephus (*Ant.* 4.234), must be made available to all wayfarers, both Jews and non-Jews alike. Indeed, says Josephus in an extra-biblical addition (*Ant.* 4.236–37), one should even invite others, Jews and Gentiles, entreating them to accept as guests the bounty that G-d has given one, "for one must not account as expenditure that which out of liberality (χρηστότητα) one lets men take, because G-d bestows this abundance of good things not for our enjoyment alone, but that we may also share them generously with others; and He is desirous that by these means the special favor that He bears to the people of Israel and the bounty of His gifts may be manifested to others also." In fact, whereas the Bible (Deut 25:3) prescribes whipping the guilty without indicating the offense involved, Josephus (4.238–39) applies this penalty to the case of one who has violated these laws pertaining to generosity, because, as he adds, "through slavery to lucre he has outraged his dignity." After their afflictions in Egypt, he remarks, Jews should take thought of those who are in a similar situation.

Thus, it is significant that in his final eulogy of David's character (*Ant.* 7.391) Josephus stresses that David was just and humane (φιλάνθρωπος), qualities that, he says, are especially applicable to kings. It is in reply to such charges that Josephus's version (*Ant.* 8.117) of King Solomon's prayer at the dedication of the Temple specifically denies that the Jews are "inhuman (ἀπάνθρωποι) by nature or unfriendly to those who are not of our country" and declares that they "wish that all men equally should receive aid from Thee and enjoy Thy blessings." Moreover, Solomon's open-mindedness and magnanimity are shown in the fact, cited by Josephus (*Ant.* 8.147–49, *Against Apion* 1.112–15) from a non-Jewish historian, Dius of Phoenicia, that Solomon sent riddles to King Hiram of

Tyre and asked for others from him on the understanding that the one who failed to solve them should pay a sum of money to the one who succeeded. In this, to be sure, Hiram was bested. But then Josephus (*Ant.* 8.149, *Against Apion* 1.115) demonstrates the honesty and liberalism of Solomon in noting that a certain Abdemon of Tyre propounded riddles Solomon was unable to solve.

Furthermore, in the interests of tolerance, Josephus (*Ant.* 9.138) omits mention of the conversion of a Temple of Baal into an outhouse (2 Kgs 10:27). Again, though Josephus generally follows the Apocryphal Addition C, containing Esther's prayer to G-d, he omits her bitter attack on the idol worship of the non-Jews (Addition C 19–22): "And now they [i.e., the enemies of the Jews] have not been satisfied with the bitterness of our captivity, but they have laid their hands (in the hands of their idols) to remove the ordinance of Thy mouth, and to destroy Thine inheritance, and to stop the mouth of them that praise Thee, and to quench the glory of Thy house and Thy altar, and to open the mouth of the nations to give praise to vain idols, and that a king of flesh should be magnified forever." Furthermore, although additions A and F were available to Josephus[44] he omits them, presumably because in them the struggle between Haman and Mordecai is viewed not as a personal one but as part of the eternal conflict between Jew and non-Jew.

In the Jonah pericope, to be sure, Josephus (*Ant.* 9.206–14) found himself in a dilemma. On the one hand, the biblical account stresses the universalistic attitude of Judaism in that G-d's mercy encompasses not only Israel but also the Gentiles; and this seems to be an effective answer to the charges of misanthropy noted above. Indeed, the fact that G-d shows mercy toward the people of Nineveh, the very Assyrians who had been the bitterest enemies of the Israelites and had been responsible for the destruction of the Kingdom of Israel and the loss of ten of the twelve tribes of Israel, is a dramatic answer to these charges. This is reinforced by the fact that Nineveh is on three occasions in the biblical book of Jonah termed a great city. And yet the scriptural narrative seems to reinforce the charge of misanthropy in that Jonah is angry with G-d for showing mercy toward the people of Nineveh; but, on the other hand, the Jews are cast in a relatively bad light in that the people of Nineveh repent so sincerely. If Josephus were to praise the people of Nineveh, this would show his broad-mindedness; but it might also reflect badly, by comparison, on his fellow-Jews, who had not heeded the admonitions of the prophets.[45] Indeed, such an unfavorable comparison is already to be found in Josephus's older contemporaries, the authors of the Gospels according to Matthew (12:41) and Luke (11:32); and it is just possible that Josephus was aware of this use made by the Christians of the story of Jonah and may have attempted to respond to it by, in effect, not praising the Ninevites.[46] In this respect we may suggest that Josephus is parallel to the Targum of Jonah (3:5), which, in effect, counters the Christian claim, wherein religious conversion and faith are at issue, by stressing that the Ninevites believed in the message brought by Jonah rather than in G-d.[47]

Moreover, the biblical statement (Jonah 4:1) indicating Jonah's extreme anger with G-d because He had forgiven the Ninevites after they had repented might well have been interpreted as chauvinism on the part of Jonah and, through him, on the part of the Jewish people whom he represented. The Septuagint on this verse, we may note, softens Jonah's anger by reading that Jonah was very deeply grieved and confounded rather than that he was displeased and angry. Though Josephus is at this point closely paraphrasing the Book of Jonah, he avoids the problem by omitting the passage completely.

Josephus is particularly sensitive to the charge that Jews are aggressive in converting non-Jews to Judaism. Hence, it is not surprising that he omits (*Ant.* 1.340) the circumcision of the Shechemites by Simeon and Levi. He likwise omits the fact that at Gilgal Joshua performed the rite of circumcision on those Israelites who had been born in the desert (Josh 5:2), even though, according to the Torah (Exod 12:44), the Israelites would not have been able to keep the Passover, as indeed they did (*Ant.* 5.20), if they had not been circumcised.[48] We may guess that the reason for the omission was the implication of the biblical text that all were circumcised regardless of whether they consented or not; and Josephus is eager to tone down the aggressiveness that the Jews apparently displayed during this period in their proselytism.

One of the charges against the Jews, as we see, for example, in Manetho's statement (quoted in *Against Apion* 1.76) about the Hyksos, whom Josephus (*Against Apion* 1.103) identifies with the Israelites, is of exhibiting the utmost cruelty toward the Egyptian natives whom they dominated, "massacring some, and carrying off the wives and children of others into slavery." Lysimachus (quoted in *Against Apion* 1.310) charges that when they came into Canaan they not only maltreated the population but they also committed the gross sacrilege of plundering and setting fire to the temples. Tacitus (*Histories* 5.8.3) remarks that when the Jewish state was re-established in the second century B.C.E. the kings "banished citizens, destroyed towns, killed brothers, wives, and parents, and dared essay every other kind of royal crime without hesitation." Writing in the third century, Dio Cassius (68.32.1–2), who elsewhere expresses respect for the sincere religiosity of the Jews, nevertheless, as in our last chapter, declares that during the uprising led by the pseudo-Messiah Lukuas-Andreas they "would eat the flesh of their victims, make belts for themselves out of their entrails, anoint themselves with their blood and wear their skins for clothing."

It is apparently to counter such charges of cruelty and atrocities that Josephus tones down considerably the Israelite cruelty against the Canaanite kings. Thus, whereas the Bible (Josh 10:28–36) seven times remarks that Joshua smote the various Canaanite towns with the edge of the sword, utterly destroying all the inhabitants, Josephus (*Ant.* 5.61) states very simply that Joshua both captured the kings and punished all the host and made great carnage of the inhabitants and also captured booty. Likewise, whereas the Bible (Josh 11:10–15) describes in vivid terms the apparent ruthlessness with which Joshua captured Hazor and "put to the sword all who were in it, utterly destroying them," so that "there was none left that breathed" (Josh 11:11), Josephus (*Ant.* 5.67) omits this episode completely. Furthermore, whereas in the Bible (Josh 23:1–16) Joshua, in his farewell address, declares that G-d will thrust out all the nations from the land of Canaan, in Josephus (*Ant.* 5.90) Joshua attempts to justify this wholesale slaughter by declaring that he (Joshua) gave such orders because he was convinced that their security and the maintenance of their ancestral institutions demanded such action. In another instance, whereas the Bible (Joshua 8:27) declares that at Ai Joshua did not draw back his hand until he had utterly destroyed all the inhabitants, in Josephus (*Ant.* 5.48) the slaughter apparently is restricted to the men, inasmuch as we are specifically told that a crowd of women, children, and slaves were taken.

One of the charges against the Jews, as we see in such a statement as Tacitus's remark (*Histories* 5.5.2) that Jews abstain from intercourse with foreign women, is their provincialism. In this case, Josephus was confronted with a dilemma, inasmuch as the Bible (Deut 7:3) decisively forbids intermarriage; and yet he was aware that too strenuous an objection to intermarriage would play into the hands of the Jew-baiters who charged the Jews with misanthropy.[49] Josephus, however (*Ant.* 1.241), is proud of the fact that two of Abraham's sons fought alongside Heracles and that the daughter of one of them married Heracles himself. On the other hand, Joshua (23:12–13) in the Hebrew Bible sternly warns the Israelites that if they mix with the Canaanites "they shall be a snare and a trap for you, a scourge on your sides, and thorns in your eyes, till you are driven off this good land which the L-rd your G-d has given you." In Josephus (*Ant.* 5.98) the threat is much reduced in length and in intensity, and Joshua says merely that if the Israelites turn aside to imitate other nations G-d will turn away from them. Likewise, we may note that Josephus (*Ant.* 5.286) tones down considerably the severe objections of Samson's parents to his intermarriage; and in place of "Is there never a woman among the daughters of thy brethren, or among all our people, that thou goest to take a wife of the uncircumcised Philistines?" (Judg 14:3) he has the mere declaration that "they were for refusing because

she was not of their race." It is likewise significant that though he generally follows the Apocryphal Addition C, containing Esther's prayer to
G-d rather closely, Josephus omits the abhorrence of foreigners expressed by Esther (C 26–27): "I detest the bed of the uncircumcised and
of any alien."

We may thus see, from the sheer multitude of instances where Josephus shows sensitivity to pagan charges of intolerance, illiberalism,
and sheer aggressiveness, that the intellectuals with whom he was in constant contact, whether through their writings or presumably in person in
Rome, were pressing these charges. From the vehemence of these contentions, it is clear that the Jews were eminently successful not only in
sundering themselves from the non-Jews but also in converting others to
their way of life and thus undermining what at least some Romans regarded as the basis of the strength that had built the Roman republic and
empire.

5. Answers to Charges of Misanthropy in Josephus's *Against Apion*

Josephus's major and systematic reply to the charges of the anti-Jewish
bigots is to be found in his essay *Against Apion*. He clearly answers the
charge (*Against Apion* 2.259–61) that the Jews are misanthropes when he
says that the Greeks, too, are opposed to foreigners; in particular, he cites
the Spartan practice of expelling foreigners and not allowing citizens to
travel abroad. Indeed, this allegation might well have been viewed more
sympathetically by those who realized that a similar charge was often
brought against the much-admired Spartans.[50] In fact, readers might well
have seen a number of parallels, general and specific, between the Jews
and the Spartans.

In the first place, there is the parallel between their respective lawgivers, Moses and Lycurgus, both of whom (Diodorus 1.94.1–2) claimed a
divine origin for their laws; hence, the implication in Apion's statement
(quoted in Josephus, *Against Apion* 2.25) that Moses ascended Mount
Sinai and remained there in concealment for forty days, after which he
gave the Jews laws, is that those laws were actually Moses' own, but that
he pretended that they were of divine origin. Nevertheless, this charge
might not have been construed by the sophisticated as derogatory, because it couples Moses with such lawgivers as Minos and Lycurgus, who
used such devices to maintain their hold over the masses.[51] We may also
cite Plato's "noble lie" (*Republic* 3.415A–C), which is foisted on the
masses so that they will be content with their lot in life. Moreover, both
Lycurgus and Moses, according to Hecataeus (quoted in Diodorus
40.3.6), instituted a rigorous training program for the youth.

Both the Spartans and Jews likewise had associations with Heracles,

Sparta having been allegedly founded by him (Tyrtaeus 8.1 [Diehl]), and the sons of Abraham by Keturah (Cleodemus-Malchus, cited in Josephus, *Ant.* 1.240–41), the wife who succeeded Sarah, having joined him in his expedition in Africa, during which Heracles married one of their daughters. Likewise, the Jews were said to have formed an alliance with the Spartan king Areus (1 Mac 12:20–23 and Josephus, *Ant.* 12.225–28),[52] who is actually quoted as declaring that the Jews and the Spartans are related, being descended from Abraham. In addressing the Spartans, the Jews were actually seeking respectability in Roman eyes, because Sparta herself had figured prominently in Rome's early history as tied with the Sabines, who had given the Romans wives and even some kings early in their history, notably the revered Numa Pompilius, with whom indeed Plutarch in his *Parallel Lives* compares Lycurgus. Moreover, Sparta's prestige was especially high in first-century Rome, inasmuch as a Spartan squadron had fought for Octavian against Antony at Actium (Plutarch, *Antony* 67), so that Sparta received as a reward the control of several former perioecic cities. The admiration for Sparta may also be seen in the account of the visit of the philosopher Apollonius of Tyana to that city (Philostratus 4.31), during which he was impressed with the institutions of Lycurgus, which were again in full swing.

Both the Spartans and the Jews, moreover, were subjected to distortions arising largely from their reluctance to associate with foreigners (cf. Hecataeus, cited in Diodorus 40.3.4 and Josephus, *Against Apion* 2.257). With regard to the Spartans, Thucydides (5.68) comments on the secret character of their institutions. Plutarch (*Lycurgus* 27.4) notes that alien people introduce alien principles and destroy the internal harmony of the state. Thus, the Jews were accused by Apion (quoted in Josephus, *Against Apion* 2.68) of fomenting sedition. Josephus's reply—oblivious, to be sure, of the difference between concord within a state and concord within a group that has substantial footholds in several host-states—is that if Apion were justified in the accusation how could he at the same time complain about the notorious harmony of the Jews? Indeed, this concord would seem to be a virtue, because, as Josephus (*Ant.* 2.179) declares, the Jews, being thoroughly grounded in the laws, possessing a unity and even an identity of religious belief, and a perfect uniformity in habits and customs, have a beautiful harmony (συμφωνίαν, "symphony") in their character. This concord is admitted by two other ancient writers (Cicero, *Pro Flacco* 28.66 and Tacitus, *Histories* 5.5.1)—both of whom made unfavorable remarks about the Jews—as present among the Jews, the former referring to their harmony (*concordia*) and the latter speaking of their loyal trust in one another.

Manetho (quoted in Josephus, *Against Apion* 1.238) says that Osarsiph-Moses ordained by his first law that his followers should have no connection with any save members of their own confederacy; Lysimachus (quoted in Josephus, *Against Apion* 1.309) declares that Moses exhorted the Jews to show kindness to no Gentile; and Apollonius Molon (cited in Josephus, *Against Apion* 2.258) condemns the Jews for their illiberalism in refusing admission to those who had different views of G-d or who led a different mode of life. Nevertheless, although all these remarks have a negative intent, some of their readers might well have thought of the Spartans, whom Josephus indeed (*Against Apion* 2.259) calls to their attention, because, as we have noted, they made a practice of expelling foreigners and would not allow their own citizens to travel abroad lest they be corrupted by such contacts. Likewise, readers could think of the revered Plato, who also, as Josephus (*Against Apion* 2.257–59) notes, suggested precautions (*Laws*, especially 12.949E ff.) to prevent foreigners from mixing at random with citizens. And, in any case, a reader might well counter with the observation that the Egyptians, of all people, should not frown on those who are contrary to all others, because, as Herodotus (2.91 and 6.35.2 ff.), on the whole a most sympathetic observer of Egyptian life, remarks, everything in Egypt in the way of customs and laws is the reverse of what it is elsewhere. The matter was apparently proverbial, as we see in a speech of Oedipus in Sophocles (*Oedipus at Colonus* 337–41): "They behave as if they were Egyptians, bred the Egyptian way! Down there the men sit indoors all day long weaving, while the women go out and attend to business."

Connected with this charge of exclusiveness is Manetho's charge (quoted in Josephus, *Against Apion* 1.239), perhaps based—if he knew the Bible—on the biblical prohibition against Israelites' walking in "their" (that is, the Egyptians' and Canaanites') statutes (Lev 18:3), that the Jews show intolerance by their deliberate disdain for the gods worshipped by the Egyptians and by their perversity in not abstaining from the flesh of animals held in reverence in Egypt and in their killing and consuming many of them. It is this contrariness, we may comment, that may help to explain the particular repugnance in the Bible for the worship of the golden calf (Exod 32:1–6). Indeed, the Jews are said by Manetho (quoted in *Against Apion* 1.249) to have gone so far in their perversity that they habitually used the very sanctuaries of the Egyptians as kitchens for roasting the venerated sacred animals of the Egyptian religion and forced the Egyptian priests and prophets to slaughter them and then turned these priests and prophets out stark naked.

Yet such a charge, especially from an Egyptian priest, might well have proved ineffective so far as Greek readers were concerned, in view of the similar repugnance to animal worship shown by such philosophers as Sextus Empiricus (*Hypotyposeis* 3.219). Such animal worship appeared to intelligent Greeks and Romans to be at best exotic and at worst repulsive.[53] Thus, Diodorus (1.83.1, 84.1, 86.1, 91.1) is astonished by the Egyptians' worship of living animals and by the Egyptian spinsters' denial to themselves of food for the animals' sake. He notes (1.83) in amazement that a Roman soldier was lynched during the late Republican period because he had accidentally killed a cat. Likewise, Antiphanes (frag. 147; Kock 2.71 = Athenaeus 7.299E) sarcastically remarks that the Egyptians think that eels are gods, indeed the most valuable of gods. Timocles (frag. 1; Kock 2.300 = Athenaeus 7.300A–B) asks of what possible help an ibis-god or a dog-god can be to a human being.[54] The Rhodian poet Anaxadrides (frag. 39; Kock 2.150 = Athenaeus 7.299–300A) bluntly declares that he cannot possibly be an ally of the Egyptians in view of the tremendous gulf between Egyptians and Greeks in beliefs and customs. In particular, he comments that he sacrificed and ate animals that they considered gods. They worship even field mice, he exclaims. Pliny (*Natural History* 30.90), a learned Roman and a contemporary of Josephus, likewise illustrates how a charge by an Egyptian of Jewish perversity in religious belief might have been received by an intellectual, when he attacks the perverse Egyptian worship of beetles—a practice that, he notes, Apion attempts to excuse. Hence, it is not correct to say that Apion's is a literary text that is the product of an elite level of society and has agenda peculiar to discourse at that level, because Pliny was at a similar elite level and with similar agenda and ridicules strange religious practices.

Likewise, Apion's denunciation (quoted in Josephus, *Against Apion* 2.137) of the Jews for their sacrificing of domestic animals would most probably have fallen flat, because, as Josephus remarks (2.138), the Greeks would hardly have been moved to indignation by such a charge, inasmuch as they, like the Jews, sacrificed such animals to the gods and then made a feast of the victims. Indeed, it will be recalled (Hesiod, *Theogony* 535–57) that in classical mythology Prometheus, the god who commanded so much sympathy because he championed the cause of humanity, taught people how to sacrifice animals to the gods. In truth, although association with the Egyptians was an advantage in Josephus's argument for the antiquity of the Jews, he (*Against Apion* 1.252) is careful to distance himself from the theory that the Jews were of Egyptian origin so far as religion is concerned. As to the denunciation of the Jews for not eating pork (*Against Apion* 2.137), such a belief could be matched by the Egyptian abstention from eating lamb (Philo, *Legatio ad Gaium* 45.362); moreover, other peoples—in Asia Minor, Syria, Arabia, and India—likewise abstained from eating pork, and in Egypt it could be eaten only at full moon.

In particular, Apion's charge (quoted in *Against Apion* 2.80), which we have noted, that the Jews kept an ass's head in the Temple and worshipped it, amusing and even shocking as it might have appeared, might have proved unconvincing, first because it appeared inconsistent that the Egyptians, who themselves worshipped animals as gods, should have objected when others did likewise. Second, the mention of the ass might well have produced a positive reaction. Although the ass had negative connotations in the mythological story of Midas, who was given ass's ears as punishment for preferring Pan to Apollo in their musical contest (Ovid, *Metamorphoses* 11.146–93), and although the ass is regarded as a lowly beast in Apuleius's second-century C.E. *Metamorphoses*, still, when the ass is first mentioned in Greek literature (Homer, *Iliad* 11.558), it is in a simile, with distinctly favorable implications, because Ajax's slow retreat is compared to an ass's stubborn resistance in the fields. Moreover, the ass was sacred to Dionysus (Pseudo-Oppianus, *Cynegetica* 4.256; Lactantius, *Institutes* 1.21–27), because both Dionysus and his companion Silenus constantly rode an ass, and to Apollo (Pindar, *Pythian* 10.33, scholia on 10.49).[55] The ass also was sacrificed both at Lampsacus (Ovid, *Fasti* 2.391, 440; 6.345) and at Tarentum[56] and among the Hyperboreans and was associated at Rome with Vesta and crowned at the festival of the Consualia. Furthermore, according to the epic poet Eratosthenes (*Katasterismoi* 11, p. 246, ed. West), the asses on which the satyrs were mounted in the great battle of the gods against the giants were the key to victory, because their braying frightened the enemy. We also hear of a contest between Priapus and a donkey of Dionysus as to which of the two had a more perfect organ of generation. According to Lactantius (*De Falsa Religione* 1.22), Priapus, chagrined at his loss, killed his rival; but according to Hyginus (*Astronomia* 2.3.33) Priapus won but placed the donkey, as compensation, among the constellations of the sky.

Moreover, asses played key roles in military victories. In one case, according to Pausanias (10.18.4), it was their timely braying that led to the routing of the Molossians by the Ambrakiots, who later dedicated a bronze statue of an ass in token of gratitude; and in another instance, according to Herodotus (4.129), it was Darius's contingent of asses that proved most effective in the rout of the Scythian cavalry. Finally, of course, asses were extremely useful in labor and agriculture, as we hear from Josephus (*Against Apion* 2.87). We may add that the fact that, according to Apion (quoted in *Against Apion* 2.80), it was Antiochus Epiphanes who discovered the ass's head in the Temple might well have hurt his cause, inasmuch as Antiochus was regarded as a madman, at least by some. As Polybius (26.1) puts it, "Reasonable folk did not know what to make of him. Some regarded him as a simple and modest man, while others said he was insane." In particular, as we have noted, he was criticized for hobnobbing with the common people and for his arbitrariness in dispensing gifts.[57]

In addition, the very word *concord* (*concordia*, συμφωνία) used by the opponents of Judaism in their charge that the Jews showed concord among themselves would most probably have elicited a positive response from Josephus's Gentile readers, just as its opposite, *dissension*, would have brought forth a negative response. When Josephus (*Against Apion* 2.170) says that Moses made the various virtues—justice, temperance, bravery, and harmony among the members of the community—departments of religion, he substitutes harmony (συμφωνίαν) for wisdom as one of the cardinal virtues; and we are indeed reminded of Plato's question (*Laws* 3.689D), How can there be the least shadow of wisdom when there is no harmony (συμφωνία)? Similarly, Plato (*Republic* 3.401D) speaks of the ideal state as one in which people live in harmony (συμφωνία) and friendship with beauty and reason. Likewise, he contrasts (*Timaeus* 47D) harmony (συμφωνία), which has been given by the Muses to him whose concern with them is guided by intelligence, with inward discord that has come into the soul. Aristotle (*Politics* 7.15.1334B) remarks that when in the training of youth the rational principle and habit are in accord, the result will be the best of harmonies (συμφωνία).

The opposite of harmony is civil strife (στάσις), which is so strongly condemned by Thucydides (3.82–84) in his description of the revolution at Corcyra. We may here note that in his apologetic version of the Bible in the *Antiquities* Josephus (*Antiquities* 1.117) characterizes the punishment inflicted by G-d on the builders of the Tower of Babel as discord (στάσις, a word not found in the Septuagint version of Genesis 11:9) created by causing them to speak various languages. Again, according to Josephus's addition (*Ant.* 1.164), G-d thwarted Pharaoh's passion toward Sarah by bringing about an outbreak of disease and political strife (στάσει τῶν πραγμάτων). Similarly, in his treatment of the rebellion of Korah, Josephus (*Ant.* 4.12) remarks that it was sedition (στάσις), "for which we know of no parallel, whether among Greeks or barbarians," clearly implying that information about seditions was familiar to his readers. Likewise, in discussing the consequences of the seduction of Hebrew youths by Midianite women, Josephus (*Ant.* 4.140) remarks that the whole army was soon permeated by sedition (στάσιν) even worse than that of Korah. Indeed, a good portion of Book 4 (11–66, 141–55) of the *Antiquities* is devoted to accounts that illustrate the degree to which στάσις is the mortal enemy of political states, a subject particularly stressed by Josephus as a comment on the warring factions among the Jewry of his day, especially during the war against the Romans. In particular, unlike the Bible (Deut 19:14), which merely cites the commandment not to remove one's neighbor's landmark, Josephus (*Ant.* 4.225) adds a reason, again in political terms, namely that removal of landmarks leads to wars and seditions (στάσεων). Likewise, in an extra-biblical prayer (*Ant.* 4.294), Moses asks that after they have conquered the Land of Israel the Israelites should not be overcome by civil strife (στάσεως), "whereby ye shall be led to actions contrary to those of your fathers, and ye shall destroy the institutions which they established." Moreover, in an editorial comment, Josephus (*Ant.* 5.231) remarks that Gideon, by his pacifying words to the aggrieved tribe of Ephraim, rescued them from civil strife (στάσεως), thus performing a greater service for them than he did by his military success. Furthermore, whereas the Septuagint (2 Sam 20:1) terms Sheba, who incited the Israelites against David, a transgressor (παράνομος), Josephus chooses political language and calls him one who delighted in dissension (στάσει χαίρων). It is significant, moreover, that in his summary (*Ant.* 7.337) of David's instructions to Solomon concerning the Temple Josephus adds to the biblical account by saying that G-d promised to grant the Hebrews the greatest of all blessings, which are then enumerated as "peace and freedom from war and civil dissension (στάσεων)."

From the alleged Jewish disdain for non-Jews arose the libel (*Against Apion* 2.91–96), which we have noted, that when Antiochus Epiphanes entered the Temple he discovered there a Greek who was being fattened for sacrifice.[58] Bickermann, as we have remarked, believes that this canard arose among Greek literary groups close to Antiochus who sought to defend his apparent sacrilege in desecrating the Temple.[59] But again, in view of the disdain toward Antiochus that prevailed at least in circles of the source or sources of Polybius, Diodorus, and Livy, as we have commented, such a story might well have aroused sympathy for Antiochus's opponents, the Jews. It was Antiochus, we must not forget, who had challenged Roman power in the East by invading Egypt and withdrawing only when the Roman commander Popilius Laenas drew his famous circle around him and told him that he must give an answer to the Senate's decree demanding that he evacuate Egypt before he (Antiochus) stepped out of it (Livy 45.12; Polybius 29.11; Cicero, *Philippics* 8.81; Velleius Paterculus 1.10). In addition, Roman readers were not likely to have forgotten that it was Antiochus's father, Antiochus III, who had given refuge to Hannibal, that most feared and most despised of Roman enemies, when Hannibal fled from Carthage (Livy 33.49). Moreover, readers might well have pointed their fingers at the Egyptians for their hypocrisy in circulating such a tale when they themselves, according to Apollodorus (2.5.11), were said to sacrifice foreigners to their own outlandish gods;[60] but, of course, it is common for a group to deflect a charge against them by accusing another group of the same thing.

Josephus and his critics were skilled rhetoricians; and one of the techniques they learned in the schools was to take the topic of an encomium and transform it into a ψόγος—an invective—and vice versa. In effect, Josephus, in his *Against Apion*, has utilized this technique so that the principal charges of the intellectuals against the Jews might well have proved ineffective.

There is clearly a difference in attitude toward the Jews between Hecataeus in 300 B.C.E. and Apion three centuries later. We may, therefore, suggest that the latter inherited an earlier pro-Jewish tradition, which was widely held and therefore could not be glossed over and which he attempted to interpret in the worst possible way. This will explain why Apion, although undoubtedly unforgiving in his anti-Jewishness, implicitly acknowledges what are certainly some very pro-Jewish beliefs, especially about Moses.

No one will doubt that an Apion was malicious in his intent, but that does not mean that he was necessarily read in that light by others, who may have seen positive elements in his remarks, though admittedly we do not have explicit statements other than those of Josephus. One might argue that no ancient source actually equated, for example, the Jews with the Spartans in their stubborn obedience to the law, internal harmony, and hostility toward outsiders, conservatism, and unyielding courage; with the same technique one could turn the common modern anti-Jewish complaint about the Jews' love of money into a veiled compliment on their deftness in business, which skill is highly valued by our society when not tied to a hated minority. Perhaps we should view these not as veiled compliments but rather as a double standard that is all too familiar to a modern reader. But this is precisely the point: Such remarks might well have turned some—and in view of the known large-scale conversions to Judaism, perhaps many—readers to an admiration, however grudging, of the Jews.

6. Attacks on Jewish Theology

Pagan religion, being polytheistic, tended to be, almost by definition, tolerant, while the Jewish religion, denying as it did the legitimacy of every other religion, was intolerant. And yet, when he speaks of the Jews as philosophers by race, Theophrastus (quoted in Porphyry, *De Abstinentia* 2.26) might speak in laudatory terms about their conversations with each other about the deity while they sacrifice; similarly, Hecataeus (quoted in Diodorus 40.3.4) speaks in laudatory terms of the Jewish avoidance of images of the gods; and likewise Varro (cited in Augustine, *De Civitate Dei* 4.31) could praise the imageless worship of the Jews, noting its parallel with the ancient Roman worship without images[61] and thus making a patriotic point. Moreover, the Jewish attack on the gross anthropomorphism in the way the pagans represented their gods could well find a sympathetic ear among pagan intellectuals, inasmuch as we find a similar attack in the well-known poetry of Xenophanes (fragments 12, 13, and 14) as early as the end of the sixth century B.C.E., who sarcastically asserts that the gods of every people are, in fact, like the people themselves.

As to the censure of images, such writers as Hecataeus and Varro stand in the tradition of the Stoic philosophers starting with Zeno. To Hecataeus (quoted in Diodorus 40.3.4), the Jewish G-d is to be identified with the Heaven, which alone is divine and rules the universe. This error in equating Heaven with G-d and thus making partial pantheists of the Jews is presumably connected with the view of Theophrastus that the Jews contemplated the heavens. So also Strabo (16.2.35.761) speaks of the Jewish G-d as the one force that encompasses everything on land and sea and is the essence of things. Hence, he remarks, no one with sense would be bold enough to fabricate an image of G-d resembling any known creature. Indeed, he says (16.2.36.761) that Moses' views opposing images persuaded not a few thoughtful (εὐγνώμονας, "reasonable," "sensible") men; and Strabo may well be hinting here that in his own day, in the first century B.C.E. and the first century C.E., the high point of Jewish success in winning converts, such views won many adherents to Judaism or at least to "sympathy" with Judaism. Similarly, Juvenal (14.97), to be sure in a derogatory tone, says that the Jews worship nothing but the clouds[62] and the divinity of the heavens. Such a quasi-pantheistic view is clearly reminiscent of the views of the Stoics Zeno, Chrysippus, and Poseidonius (cited in Diogenes Laertius 7.138, 148). Because the ancients had difficulty understanding a conception of G-d which was not to be visually represented at all, they apparently fastened on the Jewish contemplation of the heavens to equate the Jewish perception with the view (e.g., Aristotle, *Metaphysics* 12.8.1074A38 ff.) that the heavenly bodies were gods, that the divine encircled the whole of nature, and that thus the gods do not exist in human form.

That, indeed, the Jews refused to worship idols was known to be a major characteristic of Judaism, as is clear from an anecdote mentioned by Hecataeus (cited in Josephus, *Against Apion* 1.192): When Alexander the Great undertook to restore the ruined temple of Bel in Babylon and ordered all his soldiers to participate, the Jews alone refused, even submitting to chastisement and heavy fines, until finally Alexander pardoned and exempted them. The Persians, too, as we learn from Herodotus (1.131), had rejected images and temples because their deity was not anthropomorphic and because they, in a phrase strongly reminiscent of that of Aristotle, regarded Zeus (or the corresponding Persian god) as the entire circle of heaven.

But though these writers could praise the Jewish view of the non-anthropomorphic nature of the Deity, none of them could approve of the Jews' monotheism, because that would, ipso facto, be unpatriotic, denying the validity of their country's local gods and religion. Even Varro, who is most laudatory, says nothing about Jewish monotheism but seems, by implication, to look on the Jewish religion as a kind of henotheism, that is, a belief in one god as supreme without denying the existence of other gods. The fact that he identifies (cited in Augustine, *De Consensu Evangelistarum* 1.22.30, 1.23.31, 1.27.42) the Jewish G-d with Jupiter, thinking that it made no difference by which name He was called, so long as the same reality is understood, is reminiscent of the passage in the *Letter of Aristeas* (16) in which the Jewish translators equate G-d with Zeus. Similarly, we may remark, Plutarch (*Quaestiones Convivales* 4.6.1–2.671C–D) and Tacitus (*Histories* 5.5.5) indicate that the Jewish G-d had been identified by some with Dionysus. So also, when Valerius Maximus (1.3.3), in the epitome of Julius Paris, declares that the Jews in 139 B.C.E. had been expelled from Rome because they had attempted to infect the Roman customs with the cult of Jupiter Sabazius, he is, in effect, equating the Jewish G-d with Dionysus, who was commonly equated with Sabazius. Hence, these are simply attempts, so common in antiquity, to find an equivalent in the Roman pantheon for a strange god.[63]

It is the Jewish insistence on derogating every other theology that aroused the ire of pagan intellectuals. The anti-Jewish Manetho (quoted in *Against Apion* 1.249) is the first, as we have noted, who explains that the basis of the theology and practices promulgated by Moses is the dictum that the Jews should do everything that is completely opposed to Egyptian custom. Hence, it is not merely that the Jews have their religious beliefs; it is also that the Jews deny and even ridicule the beliefs of others. Indeed, as we have noted, according to Manetho, Moses specifically provided that the Jews should not worship the animal gods of the Egyptians and that they should not refrain from eating any of the animals sacred to the Egyptians.[64] Manetho is apparently aware of the Biblical prohibition not to walk "in their statutes" (Lev 18:3).

Moreover, to such an anti-Jewish bigot as Apion (quoted in Josephus, *Against Apion* 2.65, 73), the failure of the Jews to worship the same gods as those of the Alexandrians was an unpatriotic act, because, in particular, it meant the failure to erect statues of the emperors. In this connection, we may note that the ancient state was based on a community of *sacra*, of cult-observance, especially inasmuch as the alleged kinship of the citizens of the state was clearly a fiction.[65] Whatever tended to discredit or destroy this common bond was therefore subversive of the state. It was not the honor of the gods that was at stake, because the pagans had a maxim, *Deorum iniuriae dis curae*, "Let the injuries of the gods be a concern to the gods." Where we know of indictments of citizens, such as Socrates, Theophrastus, or Phryne, on grounds of impiety, the charge is really that they did not acknowledge the gods that the city-state worshipped and were therefore a threat to the unity of that human community. Hence, there is some justification for Apion's astonishment (cited in Josephus, *Against Apion* 2.38) at the idea of Jews being called Alexandrians[66] (though of course this does not justify the attacks that followed), in anticipation of the principle of *cuius regio eius religio*.

It is this illiberality on the part of the Jews in denying the validity of any other religion and this lack of patriotism in refusing to acknowledge the religion identified with the state that leads to attacks on Jewish theol-

ogy. Thus, the satirist Petronius (fragment 37) says that the Jews worship
a pig-god and that they clamor in the ears of high heaven. The latter part
of this statement reflects the view we have noted in Hecataeus, Strabo,
Tacitus, and Juvenal, identifying the Jewish G-d with heaven itself, and
alludes to the Jewish practice of loud and noisy communal prayer. The
view that the Jews worship a pig would appear to be a satirist's reduction
to absurdity of the Jewish abstention from pork or may reflect the more
serious conjecture, found later in Plutarch (*Quaestiones Convivales* 4.5.1–
2.669F–670A), that the reason why the Jews do not eat pork is that they
worship the pig.

That indeed the pagans largely objected to the Jewish contempt for
other religions is evidenced in Pliny the Elder, who refers relatively
often to the geography and products of Judaea but who has only one
reference to the Jews that may be regarded as anti-Jewish, namely (13.46)
where he describes a variety of dates called *chydaeus* (i.e., "abundant,"
"common") by the Jews and then gratuitously adds "a race remarkable
for their contempt for the divine powers" (*contumelia numinum insignis*).

And yet the pagan intellectuals, in this as in other issues that we have
noted, do not present a monolithic point of view. Thus, we must mention
that in the first or second century the pagan Neo-Pythagorean Pseudo-
Ecphantus seems, like the first-century Pseudo-Longinus (9.9), to have
admired and to have been influenced by the Greek version of the Pentateuch. In particular, Burkert[67] has called attention to two passages that
may have been influenced by Genesis. In the first (quoted in Stobaeus
4.6.22) Pseudo-Ecphantus speaks of "some sort of divine breath which
attached man to the eternal living being, displaying to his better part
the holy aspect of the Creator." This suggests Genesis 2:7, which in the
Septuagint version reads, "And G-d formed man from the earth and
breathed on his face the breath of life, and man became a living soul."
The second passage (quoted in Stobaeus 4.7.64) states that man "was
made by the best craftsman, who wrought him using Himself as a
model." This is reminiscent of Genesis 1:26–27: "And G-d said, Let us
make man according to our image and likeness and let them have dominion. . . . And G-d made man, according to the image of G-d He made
him, male and female he made them."

Furthermore, the Neo-Pythagorean philosopher Numenius (cited in
Lydus, *De Mensibus* 4.53), who lived in the second century, in a clear
encomium of Jewish theology, speaks of the Jewish G-d who is the father
of all the other gods and who consequently deems any other god unworthy of sharing in his cult. He is certainly acquainted with the Bible (Exod
3:14), as we can see from the analogy that he draws between the husbandman and the one who plants, on the one hand, and the First G-d and the
demiurge, on the other hand (cited by Eusebius, *Praeparatio Evangelica*
11.18.14).

In the third century, Porphyry (cited in Lydus, *De Mensibus* 4.53) pays obvious tribute to the Jewish conception of G-d by identifying Him with the Platonic demiurge, that is, the second G-d who is the creator of all things. A similar view is expressed by his pupil Iamblichus (cited in Lydus, *De Mensibus* 4.53), as well as by Syrianus and by Proclus (ibid.) in the fifth century. Apparently the thought was traditional with the Neo-Platonic school.[68]

In the fourth century Julian, though generally critical of Jewish theology—particularly, like Celsus (quoted in Origen, *Against Celsus* 4.71–72), of the anthropopathic nature of G-d (*Contra Galilaeos* 106 E)—speaks (*Contra Galilaeos* 354 A–C) of Abraham, Isaac, and Jacob as Chaldaeans of a sacred race that is skilled in theurgy. He says that he reveres the G-d of these forefathers, "for He is a very great and powerful G-d." In particular, he identifies with the method of sacrifice Abraham employed and notes, with obvious approval, that Abraham used the method of divination from shooting stars and that he augured, as the pagans did, from the flight of birds, an apparent allusion to Genesis 15:9–11. Again, in one of his letters (*Ad Theodorum* 89A, pp. 453 C–454 B), though speaking of the barbarous conceit of the Jews in being unwilling to conciliate the other gods, Julian speaks admiringly of the Jewish G-d as "truly most powerful and most good" and as being worshiped by pagans under other names.[69]

A similar sympathetic view of the Jewish G-d as being identical with the many gods of the pagan world, who are worshipped and called on by different names, as we have noted in the *Letter of Aristeas* (16), is found in the sixth-century Lactantius Placidus in his commentary on Statius's *Thebaid* (4.516), where he ascribes this view to such lofty and obviously admired authorities as the Magi, Orpheus, and Moses, "the priest of the Highest G-d," and Isaiah. The juxtaposition of the much revered Musaeus (either the teacher or student of Orpheus) and Moses, which we have noted in Numenius (quoted in Eusebius, *Praeparatio Evangelica* 9.8.2), is particularly complimentary.

In sum, the ancient intellectuals were far from united in condemning the Jewish views of theology. The attempt to equate these doctrines with those of the Platonists, the Stoics, and the Neo-Pythagoreans clearly won admiration for the Jews, even despite the intolerance of Judaism for other theological ideas.

7. THE ATTACK ON JEWISH CIRCUMCISION

The practices of the Jews that, more than any others, served to differentiate Jews from non-Jews and that indeed successfully served the crucial purpose of keeping them separate were circumcision (though this was admittedly not unique with the Jews), the Sabbath, and diet; and as one would expect, these practices more than any others are attacked by pagan intellectuals. If, in the first relatively long excursus on the Jews in pagan literature, that by Hecataeus of Abdera (quoted in Diodorus 40.3), about the year 300 B.C.E., there is no mention of any of these institutions, the reason would appear to be that he concentrates on the priestly cult centered on the Temple, which was by far the most important institution of Judaism in his day.

It is significant that the very first reference to the Jews that Josephus (*Against Apion* 1.168–71), who clearly, as we have insisted, did a great deal of research, was able to find in pagan literature, was Herodotus's statement (2.104.3) that the Phoenicians and the Syrians of Palestine, whom Josephus identifies with the Jews (though, as we have noted, the reference is disputed), learned the custom of circumcision from the Egyptians.[70] Whether or not Herodotus really had the Jews in mind when he referred to the Syrians of Palestine, the important point is that Josephus in the first century C.E. felt reasonably secure in declaring that he did. Indeed, earlier in the first century Ovid (*Ars Amatoria* 1.416) uses the same phrase "Syrian of Palestine," which is employed by Herodotus, in a clear reference to the Jews, as is manifest from his reference to the "seventh-day feast that the Syrian of Palestine observes."

The association of circumcision with the Jews and the theory that they had derived this practice from the Egyptians is likewise found in the historian Diodorus (1.28.3, 1.55.5) in the first century B.C.E., who draws this conclusion from the fact that the Jews, like the Colchians, had migrated from Egypt. Despite the practice of circumcision, as Herodotus notes, by Ethiopians, Colchians, and Egyptians, it was associated with the Jews above all, as we can see from Diodorus's contemporary, the famous historian and geographer Strabo (16.4.9.771), who, in seeking a parallel to the practice by the tribe of the Creophagi, says that their males have their sexual glands mutilated and that their females have their sexual glands excised "in the Jewish fashion." Again, even though, according to Herodotus, as we have remarked, the Syrians of Palestine acknowledge that they derived the practice from the Egyptians, when Strabo (17.2.5.824) mentions that the Egyptians circumcise their males and excise their females, he adds, "as is also customary among the Jews, who are also Egyptian in origin"—presumably, again, because the practice was most particularly associated with the Jews.

It is significant that Tacitus, despite his marked anti-Jewish prejudice, does not, when he mentions circumcision (*Histories* 5.5.2), indicate that it was borrowed from the Egyptians.[71] Perhaps the reason is that he wishes to indicate that the Jews do everything that is opposed to their Egyptian origin; and to state that they had adopted an Egyptian practice would impute antiquity and legitimacy to this practice. Indeed, Philo (*De Specialibus Legibus* 1.1.2), in answering those who ridicule the practice of circumcision, notes that it is very zealously observed by many other nations, particularly by the Egyptians, "a race regarded as pre-eminent for its populousness, its antiquity, and its attachment to philosophy." The popularity of Egyptian deities and oracles in Rome, as we see from Juvenal (6.528–40), suggests that a kind of "Egyptomania" had swept through some of the most fashionable circles of Roman society in the last half of the first century B.C.E. and throughout the first century C.E.;[72] hence, Philo's retort that circumcision was also practiced by the Egyptians was a most effective reply to those who ridiculed it. The mention of circumcision at the very beginning of the essay *De Specialibus Legibus* may be attributed to Philo's apologetic goal of systematically rationalizing the commandments.[73] The importance of circumcision is said to have been particularly great for Philo because circumcision was being attacked from within by those Jews who were defecting from Judaism;[74] but if so, we may suggest, Philo should have stressed this particularly in his discussion at the beginning of *De Specialibus Legibus*; rather, it would appear, his chief goal is to defend Judaism against the attacks of its critics.

That circumcision was regarded by the anti-Jewish bigots as evidence to support the charge of misanthropy, because it obviously set the Jews apart from other peoples, may be seen in Philo's comment (*Quaestiones in Genesin* 3.62), in answer to the question why Abraham circumcised those who were of foreign birth, that the wise man, in this case Abraham, is actually philanthropic in that he is concerned not only with kinsmen and those of like opinions but also with those of foreign birth, teaching them, as he claims the rite of circumcision does, ascetic continence.

Circumcision was regarded by the Greeks and Romans as a physical deformity, and hence, like others who had various deformities, circumcised men were not permitted to participate in the Olympic Games. Moreover, the practice of circumcision was the butt of many jokes by the pagans. Thus, Philo (*De Specialibus Legibus* 1.1.1–2) begins his description of the special laws of the Jews with the one termed "ridiculous by the great majority, the law concerning circumcision." The very fact that Paul decided not to require circumcision of Christian proselytes and to interpret circumcision allegorically may well have been influenced by the general hostility of the Graeco-Roman world to this practice; and there is reason to believe that circumcision was a major stumbling block that kept "G-d-fearers" from converting completely to Judaism.

That circumcision was indeed the most characteristic sign of the Jews, it has been suggested, may be deduced from the title, *Appella* (or *Apella*), of one of the comedies of the third-century B.C.E. Roman Naevius, because the word *apella* would be the Graeco-Latin equivalent of the Latin *sine pelle*, "without a foreskin."[75] A similar explanation may be the key to understanding the apparently proverbial *credat Iudaeus Apella*, "let the Jew Apella believe it" in Horace (*Satires* 1.5.100).

That circumcision is the most salient external characteristic of the Jew is clear from the Roman satirists, notably Horace (*Satires* 1.9.70) in the first century B.C.E.; Persius (5.184) in the middle of the first century C.E., who use "circumcised" as an apparently stock epithet when mentioning the Jews; and Petronius (68.7–8), Persius's contemporary, who speaks sarcastically of a slave who is perfect except for two faults, that he is circumcised and that he snores. That circumcision is regarded as the most characteristic feature of the Jews is apparent from another passage in Petronius (102.13–14), who has one of his characters remark, "And please circumcise us too, so that we may look like Jews." Indeed, Petronius (fragment 37) knows how important circumcision is, inasmuch as he remarks that unless a Jew is circumcised he is removed (*exemptus*) from his people, emigrates to Greek cities, and does not observe the Sabbath. Stern says that excommunication is probably implied here;[76] but the reference is more likely perhaps to the biblical statement (Gen 17:14) that the uncircumcised male shall be cut off from his people. Thus, Petronius is probably alluding to the assimilation that later takes place on the part of those Jews who are not circumcised or perhaps is referring to the lack of status as a true proselyte of one who does not submit to circumcision, as Tacitus (*Histories* 5.5.2) realized. Indeed, in the debate (*Yevamoth* 46a) between Rabbi Eliezer and Rabbi Joshua ben Ḥananiah as to whether circumcision or immersion in a ritual pool is required for conversion, there can be no question that both are required; and we must conclude, with the Jerusalem Talmud (*Qiddushin* 3.14.64d), that Rabbi Eliezer is merely stressing the fundamental significance of circumcision, whereas Rabbi Joshua is also emphasizing the importance of immersion.[77]

That "circumcised" is a stock epithet of the Jews is seen particularly in Josephus's contemporary Martial (7.30) late in the first century C.E. It is quite clear that a Jew is the subject of Martial's epigram (7.82) about the man who, while exercising himself in public, was unsuccessful in trying to conceal the fact that he was circumcised. In an epigram (11.94) addressed to a circumcised poet, it becomes clear that the reference is to a Jew, because he declares that the poet had been born in the very midst of Solyma, that is, Jerusalem. The Jewish poet swears by the Thunderer's temple, presumably a sarcastic allusion to the Temple in Jerusalem, which was the sanctuary of the Jewish equivalent of Jupiter, the god of thunder. Instead of swearing by the Thunderer, the poet is told by Martial to swear by Anchialus, a name common among slaves and freedmen,[78] though we may here suggest that perhaps the text be emended to read *Antiochum*, so as to make it a sarcastic allusion to Antiochus Epiphanes, who had desecrated the Temple.

The importance of circumcision as the sine qua non for the Jew may be seen in the discussion at the very opening of Philo's treatise *De Specialibus Legibus* (1.1.1–1.2.11), as we have noted, even before he begins his exegesis of the Ten Commandments, though he is able to subsume all the other commandments under the ten. The reason for the unusual position of circumcision in the discussion is that circumcision is properly the "vestibule" or portal through which one must pass in order to understand the true nature of the special laws.[79] Philo then proceeds (*De Specialibus Legibus* 1.1.4–1.2.9) to note its value on grounds of health, purification, hygiene, and fertility (the latter two points being developed at length in *Quaestiones in Genesin* 3.48), as well as on symbolic grounds through the excision of excessive pleasure.[80] He justifies (*Quaestiones in Genesin* 3.47) the restriction of circumcision to males because the male takes more pleasure in the sexual act and hence has to be controlled to a greater degree; moreover, because, according to Philo, the male provides the greater part in the process of procreation, it was necessary for his pride to be checked through circumcision.

From a purely practical point of view, even the family of Herod, who were far removed from Judaism in observance, insisted on circumcision of the non-Jews whom they married. Thus when Syllaeus the Arab wished to marry Salome, the sister of Herod, Herod insisted on Syllaeus's circumcision; but though he was deeply in love with Salome, Syllaeus declined on the grounds that such an operation was so abhorrent to the Arabs of that time that they would stone him to death (*Ant.* 16.225). Similarly, Agrippa II refused to give his sister Drusilla in marriage to Epiphanes, the son of King Antiochus of Commagene, when the latter declined to be circumcised; whereupon he gave her in marriage to Azizus king of Emesa when the latter consented to be circumcised (*Ant.* 20.139). Likewise, Berenice, the sister of Agrippa II, was married to Polemo, the king of Cilicia, only after the latter agreed to be circumcised (*Ant.* 20.145).

The crucial significance of circumcision may similarly be seen in Juvenal's comment (*Satires* 14.96–99) that in the progression from paganism to Judaism, the final step is circumcision. It is also illustrated particularly in the story of the conversion of Izates, the king of Adiabene, to Judaism early in the first century c.e. According to the account of Josephus (*Ant.* 20.38), as corroborated in rabbinic literature (*Genesis Rabbah* 46.11),[81] when Izates decided to convert, he realized that he would not be genuinely a Jew unless he was circumcised, whereupon he decided to act accordingly. Izates' mother, Helena, who had earlier been converted, tried to dissuade him on the ground that such a rite, which was strange and foreign to his subjects, would produce much disaffection toward him. Though temporarily convinced by her and by the Jewish merchant Ananias, who had converted her, he decided to be circumcised when another Jew named Eleazar pointed out to him, while he was reading the Pentateuch, that the law commanded that he be circumcised if he wished to be a Jew.

Furthermore, the crucial importance of circumcision may be seen in the fact that its suppression was either the cause of the Bar Kochba rebellion, as we learn from the *Scriptores Historiae Augustae* (*Life of Hadrian* 14.2), if we may give any credence to this work,[82] or was a means adopted by Hadrian after the revolt in order to exterminate the Jews.[83] And when Hadrian's successor, Antoninus Pius, wished to become reconciled with the Jews, his means (*Digest* 48.8.11.1) were to exempt the Jews from the ban on circumcision.

That circumcision continued to be a most characteristic Jewish practice is clear from the fourth-century philosopher Sallustius (*De Deis et Mundo* 9.5), who, in asking why, if Fate rules all, whole nations—whose members cannot all have the same horoscopes—practice strange customs, cites, as presumably stock examples, the Massagetae eating their fathers, the Jews circumcising themselves, and the Persians practicing incest.

Likewise, Pseudo-Acro (ca 400), in his scholia on Horace's *Satires* (1.9.70), has a snide remark on the origin of circumcision among the Jews, namely that Moses became circumcised through the negligence of a physician and consequently required all other Jewish males to be circumcised so that he might not be inferior. A particularly nasty comment is to be found in Rutilius Namatianus (*De Reditu Suo* 1.387–88) at the beginning of the fifth century c.e. when he speaks of the Jews as a "filthy" (*obscenae*, "repulsive," "abominable," "disgusting") race that infamously (*propudiosa*, "shamefully," "disgracefully") practices circumcision.

In sum, despite the adoption of circumcision by several other peoples besides the Jews, the practice was particularly associated with the Jews in the eyes of pagan intellectuals. It is significant that though, as we have seen, pagan intellectuals are divided in their approach to various other practices of the Jews, none praise circumcision. There can be no doubt that this practice served as a crucial mark of identification separating the Jews from other peoples.

8. THE ATTACK ON THE JEWISH OBSERVANCE OF THE SABBATH

Ahad Ha-Am's comment that more than the Jews have kept the Sabbath, the Sabbath has kept the Jews, illustrates the key importance of this institution in separating the Jews from the non-Jews. Indeed, the frequency with which pagans mention the Sabbath when they refer to the Jews indicates that they were well aware of its centrality in Judaism.[84]

To the earlier pagans the concept of a week of seven days must have appeared strange,[85] because they reckoned only by months and years. The seven-day "Chaldaean" (astrological) week does not appear to have

been introduced until the second century B.C.E., and the Romans themselves do not seem to have adopted the concept of the seven-day week
until the first century C.E. Once the concept of the week was instituted
and the days were named for the various planets, the Sabbath was regarded as the day of Saturn, whose influence was malign. As an evil day,
it was not a good working day and presumably, therefore, according to
this pagan view, had been made into a holiday.[86]

The first pagan to mention the Sabbath is Agatharchides of Cnidus in
Asia Minor, a historian and scholar who lived in the second century B.C.E.
and who apparently derived some knowledge of the Jews from his stay in
Alexandria during the reigns of Ptolemy VI Philometor (180–145 B.C.E.)
and Ptolemy VII Euergetes II (Physcon) (145–117 B.C.E.), under whom
Jews attained a leading military and advisory role in the second century
B.C.E.[87] In a fragment quoted by Josephus (*Against Apion* 1.209–10, also in
an abbreviated form in *Antiquities* 12.5–6), he states that the people
known as Jews, who inhabit the most strongly fortified of cities called
Jerusalem, have a custom of abstaining from work on every seventh day;
and he specifically lists the prohibition as including the bearing of
arms,[88] all agricultural operations, and any other form of public service
(λειτουργίας). During the Sabbath, he says, the Jews pray with out-
stretched arms (as Moses had prayed in Exodus 9:29) in their temple,
apparently an allusion to synagogues, until the evening, presumably an
allusion to the duration of the Sabbath until nightfall on Saturday evening. The failure to specify "most" or "some" Jews would seem to indicate, as we have noted earlier, that the Sabbath was usually, if not universally, observed by the Jews of his era. This would seem to be in line with
the general statement of Hecataeus (quoted in Josephus, *Against Apion*
1.191) that the Jews are so loyal to their laws that they face torture and
even death rather than repudiate their ancestral faith. The identification
of Jews as those who inhabit Jerusalem does not imply that Jews elsewhere do not observe the Sabbath, because Agatharchides does not use
the definite article in his Greek to limit it to the Jerusalem Jews alone.
Presumably, the reason for mentioning Jerusalem is that he seeks, according to Josephus (*Against Apion* 1.205), to deride the folly (εὐηθείας,
"simplicity," "stupidity") of the Jews and hence tells how Ptolemy Soter,
son of Lagus, probably about 302 B.C.E.[89] was able to enter the city with
his army on the Sabbath because the inhabitants refused to fight on
that day.

The context of this passage is apparently Agatharchides' discussion of
dreams, because he tells the story in juxtaposition with his account of the
dream by which Stratonice, the daughter of King Antiochus I of Syria
(reigned 281–261 B.C.E.) and the wife of King Demetrius II of Macedon
(reigned 238–229 B.C.E.), allowed herself to be stopped during her flight

from her husband. Agatharchides concludes that the incident of Ptolemy's entrance into Jerusalem has taught the whole world, except the Jews, the lesson not to resort to dreams and fancies about the law unless its difficulties are such as to baffle human reason, perhaps an allusion to the school of thought among the rabbis (*'Eruvin* 45a) which ultimately prevailed and which permitted defensive fighting on the Sabbath. Thus, concludes Agatharchides (*Against Apion* 1.210), the country was given over to a bitter master, and the defective (φαῦλον, "inefficient," "bad," "inferior") character of their law was exposed. Josephus's emphasis, in one version (*Against Apion* 1.205), that Agatharchides related this story only to ridicule the folly of the Jews, and his claim, in the other version (*Antiquities* 12.5), that Agatharchides reproached the Jews for their superstition (δεισιδαιμονίαν) both indicate how negatively the Sabbath was regarded by non-Jews. Surely, such expressions indicate nascent anti-Jewish prejudice.[90]

Josephus, who quotes Agatharchides' account (*Ant.* 12.6), confirms and supplements it by noting that Ptolemy pretended to enter the city on the Sabbath as if to sacrifice and was able to succeed because the Jews did not fight on the Sabbath. Plutarch (*De Superstitione* 8.169C) likewise apparently (though not indubitably) alludes to this incident and describes how the enemy planted their ladders against the walls, while the Jews, because it was the Sabbath, refused to resist, being "fast bound in the toils of superstition as in one great net." Though he (*De Superstitione* 8.169A–C) is, in general, not unsympathetic to the Jews, he is clearly critical of this Jewish attitude toward the Sabbath, inasmuch as he equates it with what he regards as a similar instance of superstitious folly, namely the Athenian general Nicias's delay in leaving Syracuse with his armada because of an eclipse of the moon, which, he says, cost Athens an army, a navy, and an empire. We may, however, comment that inasmuch as Ptolemy appeared with peaceful intentions to offer sacrifice and inasmuch as the Jews had no organized army, there was no justification, according to Jewish law, for fighting on the Sabbath, because in fact there was actually merely a transfer of control from Macedonian Gentile to Egyptian Gentile rule.

This refusal to fight even in self-defense on the Sabbath led to the slaughter of pious Jews in the time of the persecutions under Antiochus Epiphanes; but Mattathias (1 Mac 2:41; Josephus, *Ant.* 12.276) instructed his army to fight if attacked on the Sabbath. Josephus then adds that "to this day we continue the practice of fighting even on the Sabbath whenever it becomes necessary." And yet, apparently, Mattathias's view was not universally accepted by Jews, inasmuch as we find that more than two centuries later Agrippa II, speaking, at the outset of the war against the Romans in 66, to the Jews generally and not merely to fanatics, declares, according to Josephus (*War* 2.392), "If you observe the Sabbath customs, you will undoubtedly be defeated, as were your forefathers by Pompey."

Another reference to the Jews' refusal to fight on the Sabbath is to be found in Strabo's account (16.2.40.763) of Pompey's capture of Jerusalem in 63 B.C.E. Pompey, he says, seized the city after watching for "the day of fasting [νηστείας], when the Judaeans were abstaining from all work." This day of fasting apparently does not refer to the Day of Atonement, because Josephus (*Ant.* 14.66) says that the city was captured in the third month (of the siege), which started, it seems, in the spring.[91] Dio Cassius (37.16), writing in the early third century and using a source independent of Josephus, confirms that Pompey took advantage of the Sabbath, when Jews, he says, do no work at all, to batter down the walls of Jerusalem. Similarly, Agrippa II, at the beginning of the revolt against the Romans in 66, reminds the revolutionaries (*War* 2.392) that Pompey pressed his siege most vigorously on the days (that is, Sabbaths) when the besieged remained inactive and that they, too, would be similarly hampered in their conduct of the rebellion.[92]

Strabo and several other ancient writers, as we shall see, regarded the Sabbath as a fast day, presumably because they viewed it as a day of abstention from work; and this soon came to be looked on by the pagans as a day of abstention in general, because the verb νηστεύω, corresponding to the noun νηστεία used by Strabo for "fast," came also to mean "to abstain from." As Josephus (*Ant.* 14.63–64) tells it, Pompey actually abstained from attacking the Jews on the Sabbath and merely raised earthworks and brought up his siege engines on that day, because the Jews would have resisted an actual attack on the Sabbath but were not permitted to resist such preparatory activities as those engaged in by Pompey. Inasmuch as one part of the Jews, adherents of Hyrcanus, actually welcomed Pompey and inasmuch as life went on more or less in regular fashion with sacrifices continuing to be brought to the Temple, there was no emergency and hence no reason to violate the Sabbath by taking up arms.

Frontinus (*Strategemata* 2.1.17), in the latter part of the first century C.E., declares that Vespasian (he means Titus) attacked the Jews on the day of Saturn (that is, Saturday), "a day on which it is sinful for them to do any business," and defeated them. Frontinus's statement is, to be sure, not necessarily in contradiction to that of Josephus (*Ant.* 14.63–64), because Frontinus merely identifies the day on which the attack occurred and does not say that Vespasian defeated the Jews because they refused to fight on the Sabbath; but there would hardly be much point in identifying the day of the week on which the attack occurred unless the choice of that particular day had something to do with the victory that followed. Apparently, Frontinus believes that the Jews' attitude toward fighting on the Sabbath had remained the same in the first century c.e. as it had been during the attack by Ptolemy Soter in 320 b.c.e.; or he may have confused the Jews' refusal to fight on the Sabbath during the siege by Pompey with their behavior in 70.

To the pagans the Sabbath was more than a source of ridicule that put the Jews at a military disadvantage; it became a source of derision in general because it placed so many restrictions on the Jew. The pagan ridicule of the Sabbath may be seen, for example, in the comment, at the end of the second century b.c.e., of Meleager of Gadara in Jordan, who lived in Tyre in Phoenicia and who declares in a poem (*Anthologia Graeca* 5.160), "If your lover is some Sabbath-keeper, no great wonder! Love burns hot even on cold Sabbaths." The designation of the Sabbath as cold is presumably derived from the fact that the Jews are forbidden to kindle fires on that day. The word ψυχρός, "cold," is almost a synonym for "dull";[93] and, indeed, we may add, we find that in Aristophanes it often means "flat," "lifeless," or "insipid." A holiday observed by abstention from most ordinary activities and amusements must have seemed to the pagans utterly lifeless. Indeed, we also find the same epithet "cold" as applied to Sabbaths in the fifth-century Latin poet Rutilius Namatianus (*De Reditu Suo* 1.389).

The reference to the Sabbath as a fast day is particularly strange in that the Talmud (*Shabbath* 118b) encourages special feasting on the Sabbath. The rabbis (*Shabbath* 119a) even attribute a special flavor to the food prepared for the Sabbath. Indeed, to fast on the Sabbath requires another fast day to seek forgiveness for this transgression (*Ta'anith* 12b, *Berakoth* 31b).[94]

Strabo's reference to the Sabbath as a day of fasting may also be due in part to the identification of the Sabbath with the day of Saturn, as mentioned by the Roman love poet Tibullus in the second half of the first century b.c.e., who speaks (1.3.18) of the "accursed day of Saturn" (*Saturni sacram . . . diem*). Tacitus (*Histories* 5.4.4), without committing himself, states that some hold that the Sabbath is an observance in honor of Saturn, either because the Jews are said to be derived from the Idaei, the inhabitants of Mount Ida in Crete who are said (*Histories* 5.2.1) to have fled to Africa about the time when Saturn was driven from his throne by Jupiter, or because among the seven planets said to rule the destinies of men Saturn moves in the highest orbit and with the greatest power, or because many of the heavenly bodies complete their revolutions in multiples of seven. The planetary influence of Saturn was said to be gloomy and threatening, as we have noted, and hence it is not surprising that such a day was considered appropriate for fasting. Moreover, inasmuch as the Jews were regarded as deliberately perverse (Tacitus, *Histories* 5.5.2), they made profane whatever others regarded as sacred;

hence their gloomy view of a holiday might well have been regarded as
the very opposite of the pagans' happy view.

Apparently, the view that the Sabbath was a fast day, as well as the
conscientiousness with which it was observed, were proverbial, as we see
from the remark of the Emperor Augustus, in the fragment of a letter
cited by Suetonius (*Augustus* 76.2), that "not even a Jew observes the fast
on Sabbaths as diligently as I did today, for it was not until after the first
hour of the night that I ate two mouthfuls of bread in the bath before I
began to be anointed." This would seem to contradict the assertion that
the pagan view of the Sabbath as a fast day is due to sheer ignorance, inasmuch as here we may see an awareness, at least in Suetonius, that the
fast of the Sabbath extended for an hour into the night following the
Sabbath, approximately the length of time by which the Sabbath is extended into the following night according to the Talmud (*Shabbath*
118b), which encourages the delay of the conclusion of the Sabbath so as
to add from the secular to the holy. Hence, from a pagan point of view,
the "superstition" of the Sabbath was carried by the Jews—who were, in
this sense at least, regarded as fanatics—even beyond the Sabbath day
itself.[95]

Pompeius Trogus (quoted in Justin, *Historiae Philippicae* 36, *Epitoma*
2.14), at the beginning of the first century c.e., explains the origin of the
Sabbath by remarking that Moses, following the Exodus, after suffering
together with his followers from a seven days' fast in the desert of Arabia,
consecrated the seventh day as a fast day because that day had ended both
their hunger and their wanderings.[96] Indeed, Tacitus (*Histories* 5.4.3) also
states that the Jews chose the seventh day for rest because that day
brought an end to their labors, though he does not specifically associate
the Sabbath with fasting. He does, however, say (*Histories* 5.4.3) that the
Jews, by their frequent fasts, still bear witness to the long hunger of former days, presumably during their sojourn in the wilderness; and the fact
that Tacitus almost immediately goes on to explain the origin of the
Sabbath as commemorating the termination of their toils would seem to
confirm a connection between their fasting and the Sabbath. Perhaps, we
may suggest, because it was the custom of the Jews, according to Josephus (*Life* 279), to wait until the sixth hour, that is, approximately
noon, before eating the mid-day meal on the Sabbath, the pagans may
have regarded this as a sign of undue fasting.

The Alexandrian anti-Jewish bigot Lysimachus, without specifically
mentioning the Sabbath, declares (as quoted by Josephus, *Against Apion*
1.308) that the Jews, beset by difficulties after the Exodus, kept a fast and
implored the gods to save them; presumably, the Sabbath is a commemo-
ration of this fast. Apion, his contemporary, likewise speaks (as quoted by
Josephus, *Against Apion* 2.20–21) of a six-day march on the Jews' depar-

ture from Egypt, during which, he says mockingly, the Jews developed tumors in the groin. When they reached Judaea, they rested, he declares, on the seventh day and called it σάββατον, preserving the Egyptian term, because the Egyptian word for a disease of the groin is σαββάτωσις.[97]

Another sneering reference to the Sabbath as a fast day is to be found in the middle of the first century c.e. in Petronius (fragment 37, Ernout), who speaks of the Jews as trembling at the fasts of the Sabbath (*ieiuna Sabbata*) imposed by the law. Again, at the end of the first century, Martial in Epigram 4.4 speaks derisively of the breath of fasting Sabbatarian women.

The contemptuous notion of the Sabbath as a day of affliction is also implied in Juvenal's reference (6.159–60) to the Sabbath day "when kings will go around barefoot," perhaps an allusion to the prohibition of wearing leather shoes on the Day of Atonement or to the fact that the Hasmonean kings also assumed the high priesthood for themselves and hence went barefoot in the Temple, as required for priests.[98]

To be sure, there are several pagan writers who recognize that the Sabbath is not a fast day, but they, too, speak of it in derision. Ovid (*Ars Amatoria* 1.416), at the beginning of the first century, speaks of the seventh-day feasts that the Syrians of Palestine observe. The word he uses for feasts, *festa*, is the normal word for holidays, feasts, or festal banquets and hardly can refer to fast days, though perhaps, like many of the ancients, he regarded the Jews as so perverse that they treated holidays as others would days of mourning.

Again, Persius, in the middle of the first century, speaks (5.176–84) of the floppy tunnies' tails curled around the dishes of red ware on the Sabbath and the white jars swollen out with wine. He then adds that the adherents of Judaism "silently twitch their lips, turning pale at the Sabbath of the circumcised." Indeed, we may remark, the importance of Sabbath meals, and especially of having fish as part of them, is stressed by the Talmud (*Sanhedrin* 65b, 67b). The tunny fish, the largest of the tuna fish family, often exceeds a thousand pounds in weight, and the tail (quite a large portion, even if we allow for the satirist's exaggeration), which was chopped and salted (Mishnah *Nedarim* 6:4) in a form of gefilte fish, was apparently quite a delicacy.[99] On the other hand, Persius may be satirizing the poverty of the Jews in his references to the coarsest part of the fish[100] and to the red earthenware dishes, which were the common dishes of ordinary people. Reinach interprets the phrase "turning pale" as an allusion to the fainting that results from fasting and thus would put the passage in line with the prevalent Gentile classical view that the Sabbath was a day of fasting;[101] but the reference to fish and wine clearly refutes this view. Perhaps the reference is to the fear of a candidate for political office that he will offend the Jews on their Sabbath.[102]

There are a number of other references to the Sabbath in classical literature illustrating the prominence of the day. Horace, in particular, in the first century B.C.E., has an enigmatic reference (*Satires* 1.9.69) to the thirtieth Sabbath (*tricesima Sabbata*) and has one of his characters, Fuscus, ask Horace whether he would risk affronting the circumcised Jews by talking business on this day, an allusion to the prohibition, according to the Talmud (*Shabbath* 150a), of talking about business on the Sabbath.[103]

The degree to which the Sabbath was kept sacred was apparently proverbial, to judge from the comments of Ovid (*Ars Amatoria* 1.75–76), who specifically notes (*Ars Amatoria* 1.413–16) that it was a day unfit for business transactions. Ovid refers also to the restrictions on travel on the Sabbath (*Remedia Amoris* 217–20), perhaps an allusion to the *teḥum Shabbath*, the limits beyond which one may not proceed on the Sabbath, because the context speaks of feet unwilling to run and hence would appear not to allude to the prohibition of traveling in conveyances. Indeed, the Sadducees (Mishnah, *ʿEruvin* 6:1–2), the Essenes (Josephus, *War* 2.147), and early Talmudic law (Mishnah, *Rosh Hashanah* 2:5) prohibited any movement whatsoever on the Sabbath, though the later law (Mishnah, *ʿEruvin* 4:3) reinterpreted Exodus 16:29 to permit walking within the Sabbath limit of two thousand cubits. Ovid's contemporary Tibullus (1.3.13–18) similarly alludes to the prohibition of movement when he declares that his pretext for lingering sick in a foreign land with his loved one was either birds or words of evil omen on the holy day of Saturn, that is, the Sabbath. Such restrictions clearly seemed arbitrary and superstitious, especially to the Romans, with their excellent system of roads.

A striking allusion to the loyalty of the Jews in observing the Sabbath may be seen in Synesius (*Epistulae* 5), who, at the beginning of the fifth century C.E., in describing a harrowing sea voyage, expresses the utmost amazement and indignation at the meticulous observance of the Sabbath by the Jewish captain of the ship, who left his rudder on Friday afternoon and could not be persuaded by any threats—one passenger even drew a sword—to resume it despite the terrible storm; indeed, only when he was convinced that the ship's passengers were clearly in danger of death did he resume the helm.

Another distinctive observance of the Sabbath which provoked ridicule and is alluded to by several of the ancients is the kindling of Sabbath lamps. Persius (*Satires* 5.179–82) mentions the day of Herod, presumably a reference to the Sabbath (which he identifies with Herod because of the fame or notoriety of Herod and of his descendants)[104] on which the lamps wreathed with violets and ranged round the greasy windowsills have spat forth their thick clouds of smoke.[105] That this was a prominent feature of the observance of the Sabbath is clear from the first-century Seneca

(*Epistulae Morales* 95.47), who derides this practice and urges that lamps not be lit on the Sabbath, on the grounds that the gods do not need light nor do they take pleasure in soot. The smoke produced by the lamps in Persius's satire and the soot mentioned by Seneca may allude to the use of cheap oil and may thus be an indirect allusion to the poverty ridiculed by Juvenal and several other ancients as characteristic of the Jews.[106] Lysimachus (quoted in Josephus, *Against Apion* 1.308) apparently seeks to give the origin of this practice when he notes that during the sojourn in the wilderness the Israelites at nightfall lit up a bonfire and torches and mounted guard.

Seneca (cited in Augustine, *De Civitate D-i* 6.11) derides the observance of the Sabbath as inexpedient because the Jews thus lose one-seventh of their lives in idleness and often, indeed, suffer loss through failure to act in times of urgency. The charge that the Jews are lazy (Tacitus, *Histories* 5.4.3; Juvenal 14.105–6) may have originated in this idleness on the seventh day.[107] Tacitus (*Histories* 5.4.3) goes further and ascribes the enactment of the Sabbatical year to the charm of indolence which beguiled the Jews. Indeed Philo (*De Specialibus Legibus* 2.15.60) seems to be answering such a charge when he says, "On this day [the Sabbath] we are commanded to abstain from all work, not because the law inculcates slackness; on the contrary, it always inures men to endure hardship and incites them to labor." Again, in his apologetic work *Hypothetica* (7.14), with which Josephus's essay *Against Apion* corresponds often closely, Philo asks, in obvious response to this charge, "Do you think that this [abstention from work on the Sabbath] marks them [the Jews] as idlers or that any work is equally vital to them?"

Another basic attack on the Sabbath may be seen in the second century C.E. philosopher Celsus (quoted in Origen, *Against Celsus* 6.61), and in the fifth-century Rutilius Namatianus (*De Reditu Suo* 1.392), both of whom asked mockingly why G-d should have had to rest on the seventh day, as if He were exhausted from the first six days of creation.

Finally, the non-Jewish view that the Sabbath is bizarre is illustrated by Pliny the Elder's mention (31.24) of a strange phenomenon, a river in Judaea which dries up every Sabbath. Perhaps this is an allusion to the Sambation River mentioned in the Talmud (*Sanhedrin* 65b), which runs on weekdays but dries up on the Sabbath, or to the river mentioned by Josephus (*War* 7.96–99) as being in Syria (though the river mentioned by Pliny is in Judaea), which is dry for six days and copious only on the seventh. Pliny's account thus may merely be a version of Josephus's description. That the allusion, however, is to the Sabbath and not merely to a cycle of seven days is clear from the use of the word *sabbatis*.

And yet that the Sabbath was not held in universal derision is clear from Plutarch (*Quaestiones Convivales* 4.6.2.671D–672A), who connects the Sabbath with Dionysus, noting that the Bacchants, the devotees of Dionysus, are called Sabi and that they utter that cry when celebrating the god. Another similarity is that the Jews are said to keep the Sabbath by inviting each other to drink and to enjoy wine.

In sum, we may see that the ancient intellectuals almost universally derided the Jewish Sabbath, particularly what they considered the superstitious abstention from work on that day. But that an antiquarian as important as Plutarch could connect the Sabbath with the worship of the ever-popular Dionysus is an indication that this contempt was far from universal; and the allusion to a Sabbatical river that miraculously follows the Sabbath cycle each week is further evidence that the institution of the weekly Sabbath was viewed with considerable awe.

9. The Attack on the Jewish Dietary Laws

Just as the peculiar dietary regulations of the Pythagoreans intrigued the ancients, so did those of the Jews; especially striking was the Jews' abstention from eating pork, a particular delicacy to both the Greeks and the Romans. The Romans, in particular, were fond of pork, as we see from the fact that Latin has more terms to refer to swine than to any other animal. Indeed, the abstinence from their national dish must have struck the Roman nationalists much as a deliberate abstention from roast beef would have affected an English citizen in our day who believes that patriotism and roast beef are somehow connected. We can see such an attitude in the remark ascribed by Plutarch (*Quaestiones Convivales* 4.4.4.669D) to his brother Lamprias, that his grandfather used to say on every occasion, in derision of the Jews, that what they abstained from was precisely the most legitimate meat.

Thus, Diodorus (34 [35].1.4) in the first century B.C.E. tells how Antiochus Epiphanes had sacrificed a great sow in the Temple in Jerusalem and had forced the high priest and the rest of the Jews to partake of the forbidden meat. Again, Apion (quoted in Josephus, *Against Apion* 2.137) denounces the Jews for sacrificing other domestic animals but not eating pork. In his reply, Josephus (*Against Apion* 2.137, 141) reminds Apion that Egyptian priests also abstain from pork (Herodotus 2.47 had already remarked that the Egyptians eat no pork except on special occasions). In the middle of the first century, the Roman satirist Petronius (fragment 37) says that the Jews worship a pig-god (presumably a jeering allusion to the Jews' refusal to partake of pork; Plutarch [*Quaestiones Convivales* 4.5.2.669F] was later to conjecture the reason that the Jews had a special respect for the pig). This abstention is the source of a pun by Cicero (quoted in Plutarch, *Cicero* 7.6.5): When a certain Caecilius, who was suspected of Jewish practices, wanted to thrust aside the Sicilian accusers and denounce Verres, the governor of Sicily, Cicero's response alluded to the fact that *verres* is the Latin word for a male pig: "What has a Jew to do with a Verres?"

This refusal to eat pork is associated with the Jews generally, as we see in the question put by the Emperor Gaius Caligula in the year 40 to the embassy of Alexandrian Jews headed by the philosopher Philo (*Legatio ad Gaium* 45.361): "Why do you refuse to eat pork?" That this abhorrence of pork was a matter of common knowledge is, as we have noted, implied in the remark of Erotianus (*Vocum Hippocraticarum Collectio cum Fragmentis*, F 33), the commentator on Hippocrates in the second half of the first century c.e., that if someone is afflicted with the so-called "Sacred Disease" (epilepsy), the physician should inquire whether the sick person is a Jew, so that he may refrain from giving him pig's flesh, and whether he is an Egyptian, so that the physician may refrain from giving him the flesh of sheep or goats. Similarly, his contemporary Epictetus the Stoic (quoted in Arrian, *Dissertationes* 1.11.12–13) notes that the Jews, Syrians, Egyptians, and Romans differ in their opinions on the subject of food and comments that it cannot be possible that they are all correct, a point of view presumably held by some of his opponents who were more liberal in such matters. Shortly thereafter (1.22.4) he again notes the difference of views among the Jews, Syrians, Egyptians, and Romans in the matter of diet; the point in dispute was not whether holiness should be put before anything else, but whether the particular act of eating swine's flesh is holy or unholy. Indeed, at the end of the second century, the Skeptic philosopher Sextus Empiricus (*Hypotyposeis* 3.24.223), as we have remarked, similarly couples the Jews and the Egyptians in their dietary laws in asserting that any Jew or Egyptian priest would rather die than eat pork. Again, Juvenal (6.159–60) satirically refers to the land where the pigs are free to live to old age and to the tenacity (14.98–99) with which the Jews refrain from eating pork no less than they do from human flesh.[108] Perhaps there is here an echo of Augustus's quip (quoted in Macrobius, *Saturnalia* 2.4.11) that he would rather be Herod's pig than his son (a pun based on the similarity between the Greek word for pig, ὗς, and the Greek word for son, υἱός).[109] Likewise, in the sixth century, we see from the Neo-Platonic philosopher Damascius (*Vita Isidori*, cited in Suda under the entries Δομνῖνος and διαγκωνισάμενος) that abstention from pork was regarded as a sine qua non for a Jew, when he asserts that a Jew would not eat pork even if the pork were prescribed for health reasons.

Abstention from eating pork seemed so strange to the ancients that they speculated as to the reason. Plutarch (*Quaestiones Convivales* 4.5.1–3.669E–671C) is quite respectful toward the Jews in suggesting two possibilities: either they do so out of special respect for hogs, or they do so because they abhor the pig. Plutarch, indeed, seems to justify the Jew's abstention from pork by remarking that the pig is covered on the underside by scaly eruptions and that the very filthiness of the pig's habits produces an inferior quality of meat. With the exception of those animals that have their origin in dirt, no other creature, he admits, is so fond of mud and of dirty, unclean places. Such an explanation and justification of the abstention from pork is not to be found again until Maimonides' *Guide for the Perplexed* (3.48) in the twelfth century.

Another apparent justification for the abstention from pork, as given sympathetically by Plutarch, is that Adonis (whose very name would appear to be Semitic, being derived from '*Adon*, "lord"), who is identified with Dionysus (whom Plutarch cites as the god of the Jews), was slain by a boar, so that consequently the boar is abhorred by the Jews. Perhaps, he says, the Jews have some serious reasons that they do not publish (this may be an allusion to the unwritten Law, that was so important to the Jews and that was the subject of extensive discussions as later codified in the Talmud), implying that perhaps the whole matter is part of a mystery and that they do not impart their Scriptures to Gentiles, as we have noted. One of Plutarch's interlocutors then suggests that the pig is honored because of its benefit to humanity, being the first to cut the soil with its projecting snout and thus teaching man the function of a plowshare.[110]

Tacitus (*Histories* 5.4.2), scoffingly, connects the abstention from pork with the Exodus, remarking that the abstention from swine's flesh commemorates what the Israelites suffered when they were infected by the leprosy conveyed by this animal. Philo (*De Specialibus Legibus* 4.17.101), aware of the apparent inadequacy, especially in the eyes of the non-Jews, of attributing the dietary laws to divine command, remarks that there is no meat as delicious as that of the pig but that the prohibition is due to the need to avoid gluttony. He adds that ten animals are permitted to be eaten because ten is the most perfect number (*De Specialibus Legibus* 4.18.105).

In sum, the dietary laws of the Jews, particularly their refraining from eating pork, aroused considerable curiosity on the part of those who were not prejudiced against them and utter incredulity and contempt on the part of those who despised them. Nevertheless, this contempt was hardly universal among pagan intellectuals, as we may see in particular from Plutarch's complimentary inquiry as to whether this abstention was due to special respect for pigs, abhorrence of pork because of the scaly eruptions on the underside of the pig and the filthiness of the pig's habits, or the association of the pig (boar) with the beloved Adonis.

Moreover, even pagans such as Celsus, who were generally critical of the Jews, pointed out, in all fairness, that the Jews were not unique in having dietary laws. Thus, as Celsus (quoted in Origen, *Against Celsus* 5.41) notes, the Egyptians (that is, the Egyptian priests) abstain from eating pork, as well as goats, sheep, oxen, and fish. In particular, we may remark, he calls the attention of the reader to the abstention of Pythagoras and his disciples from eating beans and all animal food. That Pythagoras had advocated a diet of raw vegetables (cited in Diodorus 10.7), honey, honeycomb or bread, wine only at night, cooked or raw lettuce, rarely seafood (cited in Diogenes Laertius 8.19), would have worked to the advantage of the Jews, inasmuch as the second century, when Celsus lived, was precisely the period when there was a considerable revival of Neo-Pythagoreanism.

10. Contempt for the Jews' Credulity

To those who believed that, in the words of Socrates (Plato, *Apology* 38A), the life uncriticized is not worth living, credulity was hardly admirable, as we see from Herodotus's criticism (1.60) of the ease with which the Athenians allowed themselves to be deceived by Pisistratus's ruse in returning to power. Indeed, the Greeks, says Herodotus, have since olden times been far removed from ridiculous simplicity (εὐηθίης ἠλιθίου) and have been distinguished from non-Greeks by their cleverness.

In view of the nature of the Talmudic discussions (admittedly written down later but reflecting earlier oral discussions and methodology), which put a premium on critical questioning, it seems surprising that the Jews, in the mind of a number of pagans, should have had a reputation for credulity. Hecataeus (quoted in Diodorus 40.3.6), who, as has been noted, was one of the very earliest writers to mention the Jews (ca 300 B.C.E.) and who is hardly anti-Jewish, remarks that the Jews are so docile (εὐπυθεῖς) that they fall to the ground and do reverence to the high priest when he expounds the commandments to them. Perhaps Hecataeus has in mind the readiness of the Israelites to accept the Torah even before they had heard its contents at Sinai (Exod 19:8) or the ease with which Jews believed in the miracles mentioned in the Bible.

The same quality is mentioned in derision by Mnaseas of Patara in Asia Minor (ca. 200 B.C.E.), who, according to Apion (quoted in Josephus, *Against Apion* 2.112–14), told how, during the war between the Jews and the Idumaeans, the Jews believed an Idumaean named Zabidus, who promised to deliver Apollo into their hands if they all departed. Thereupon, in a scene reminiscent of Pisistratus's ruse (Herodotus 1.60) of having a tall woman pose as Athena commanding the Athenians to welcome the tyrant back, Zabidus put on an apparatus of wood with three rows of lamps over his person, presenting the appearance of stars perambulating the earth. The Jews, astounded at this spectacle, kept their distance from him. He was thus able stealthily to enter the Temple and snatch the golden head of a pack ass.

This same credulity is alluded to, as we have noted, in Horace (*Satires* 1.5.97–103) when he says that only the proverbial Jew Apella would believe that frankincense can melt without fire.[111] Significantly, in his comment on Horace's *Satire* 1.5.100, the third-century commentator Porphyrio gives the etymology of Apella as coming from Greek *alpha*-privative ("not") + *pellis* ("skin"), that is, "without a foreskin," a reference to circumcision. Thus, we may see the irony of having Apollo, whose name reminds one so much of the circumcised Jew Apella, rescuing Horace from the circumcised Jews (*Satires* 1.9.69–78). Horace, like the Epicureans, professes that the gods do not intervene in human affairs and thus do not perform such miracles. When, in his version of several miracles, such as that of crossing the Red Sea, Josephus (*Ant.* 2.348) adopts the formula found in Herodotus, Thucydides, and Dionysius of Halicarnassus, "Everyone is welcome to his own opinion," he may well be responding to such a charge.

In the second century c.e., the great Greek physician Galen (*De Pulsuum Differentiis* 2.4, 3.3) is likewise critical of the Jews for accepting everything on faith and compares those who practice medicine without scientific knowledge to Moses, who framed laws for his followers without offering proofs.[112] He is particularly critical (*De Usu Partium* 11.14) of the biblical view that everything in nature is due to G-d's will, in contrast to his scientific view that certain things are actually impossible by nature and that G-d merely chooses the best out of the possibilities of becoming.

Another allusion to the credulousness of the Jews is presented with bitter sarcasm by Rutilius Namatianus (*De Reditu Suo* 1.393–94) when he speaks of the wild ravings of the Jews from the lying lecture platform which not even children can believe, the implication being that Jews appeal to the utterly naive populace to accept their teachings on sheer faith.

And yet even these criticisms of the Jews are for the most part not vicious but more in a spirit of wonder at their naiveté, as we see in the sympathetic remarks of Hecataeus or the bemused disdain we perceive in Horace.

11. Contempt for the Jews as Beggars

Perhaps because of their traditional emphasis on works of charity, the Jews seem to have attracted many proselytes, who presumably realized that by becoming Jews they were assured of food and lodging. Lysimachus, the arch-anti-Jewish bigot (quoted in Josephus, *Against Apion* 1.305) makes retroactive this association of the Jews with beggars when he declares that in the reign of Bocchoris, king of Egypt, the Jews, afflicted with leprosy, made their exodus from Egypt and lived a mendicant existence.

To the epigrammist Martial at the end of the first century (12.57.13), the Jew taught by his mother to beg is a proverbial figure among the many nuisances in the city of Rome. It is the satirist Juvenal who pours the most scorn on the Jews as beggars, noting bitterly (3.10–16) that the grove, once holy to the pious King Numa Pompilius, the successor of Romulus, has now been let out to Jews if they have some straw and a basket, so that the forest is swarming with beggars. Later in this satire (3.296), Juvenal describes a beggar as hanging out in some synagogue with Jews. In still another satire (6.542–47), he speaks of a Jewess who leaves her basket and hay and solicits alms while playing on the credulity of others by telling fortunes and interpreting dreams.[113] That Jewish beggars in the courtyards of synagogues are proverbial is indicated by a chance reference in an astronomical work by Cleomenes (*De Motu Circulari* 2.1.91) in the first or second century. The association of beggars with synagogues may likewise be seen in their juxtaposition in the second-century Artemidorus (*Onirocritica* 3.53); to see beggars in dreams foretells grief, anxiety, and heartache. But such references may be, as we have suggested earlier, a sarcastic way of alluding to the economic power of the Jews, which had aroused so much envy and hatred, or may also allude to the excellent charitable institutions of the Jews, who made sure that beggars in their midst should have decent food and lodging.

12. Alleged Jewish Influence

Cicero (*Pro Flacco* 28.66–67), as we have remarked, describes the Jews, in terms almost reminiscent of modern anti-Jewish bigots, as a passionate "pressure-group," noting how numerous they are, how they stick together, and how influential they are in informal assemblies. Hence, he says sarcastically, he will speak in a low voice so that only the jurors may hear. These remarks are particularly valuable because here we know the *Sitz-in-Leben*, the actual situation in which he made them, namely a trial in which he is defending a client who has been accused of extorting money the Jews had collected in Asia Minor for transmission to the Temple in Jerusalem.

Of course, Cicero was a lawyer accustomed to attacking his opponents in the blackest terms. Similarly, because the evidence against Cicero's client Fonteius had been furnished chiefly by Gauls, Cicero devoted much of his defense to impugning the credibility of their statements on the ground of traditional Gallic inveracity (*Pro Fonteio* 13.30) and concluded that one cannot compare the highest personage in Gaul to even the lowest of Rome's citizens. He thus strengthened his case by appealing to basic piety, of which veracity was a cornerstone, and patriotism. Again (*Pro Archia* 10.25), Cicero classes the Spaniards with the Gauls as being among the wild and barbarous peoples. Similarly (*Pro Scauro* 19.42), he attacks the Phoenicians as a group, regarding them, like their descendants the Carthaginians, as among the most treacherous of nations (note the well-known phrase *fides Punica*, alluding to the faithlessness of the Carthaginians). He considers (*De Provinciis Consularibus* 5.10) the Syrians, like the Jews, as born to slavery. Again, in the *Pro Flacco* (27.65) itself, where it is Cicero's purpose to discredit the Asian accusers of his client, he quotes the proverb "A Phrygian is usually improved by whipping." In addition, alluding to the fact that Carian slaves were considered so worthless that they might be risked in any experiment, he (*Pro Flacco* 27.65) quotes the saying "If it is a risk you wish in any experiment, Caria is the best place for it." As for the other two parts of Asia Minor, Mysia and Lydia, he cites as a byword the remark "He's the lowest of the Mysians" and notes that Lydians are habitually given the leading slave parts in Greek comedies (*Pro Flacco* 27.65). Cicero thus attempts to strengthen his case by ridiculing the Asiatic witnesses as a class. We may thus see, from his quotations of proverbs and bywords, that Cicero is appealing to the widespread prejudices of his listeners.

Furthermore, one is tempted to dismiss such statements on the ground that Cicero is a lawyer who, depending on whom he is defending or attacking, is inconsistent in his presentation of the facts concerning certain personalities and groups.[114] Indeed, in his speech for Cluentius (50.139) Cicero himself points out the differences between his true opinions and those he expressed as a lawyer. Thus, for example, in the *Pro Rabirio* (4.13) Cicero calls Tarquin the proudest and cruelest of kings, but in the *Philippics* (3.4.9–11) he says that Tarquin was neither cruel nor impious, at least compared to Mark Antony. Similarly, Cicero's judgments of the Gracchi varied according to whether he spoke before the people or before the Senate. Thus, in the oration before the people defending the senator Rabirius against the charge of high treason, Cicero (*Pro Rabirio* 5.14–15) speaks of the great courage, sense of duty, and eloquence the Gracchi possessed; but later in the very same year, while addressing the Senate on the Catilinarian conspiracy, he declares (*1 Catiline* 12.29) that the murderers of the Gracchi, like those of Saturninus and of Flaccus, had not been stained but honored by the blood they had shed. Even the infamous Catiline is given a posthumous tribute by Cicero (*Pro Caelio* 5.12).

Indeed, although Jews were among the principal accusers of his client Flaccus, and although he had studied with the arch-anti-Jewish bigot Apollonius Molon at Rhodes, it is significant that Cicero did not resort to such stock anti-Jewish charges as that the Jews hate humankind, that they are the least able among barbarians, and that they have contributed nothing useful to the world.[115] But we may reply that Cicero the lawyer is wise enough to limit himself to the most effective arguments that he can use for his listeners. In this instance he concluded that his case would be most effective if he placed his attack on the plane of patriotism. Hence, he notes (*Pro Flacco* 28.69), for example, that the Jews had recently resisted Roman rule when Pompey intervened in the Land of Israel (63 B.C.E.); that, at a time when the gold resources of the Romans had been low and the Senate had consequently forbidden the export of gold, Flaccus had enforced this edict; and finally, in a most general way, that the sacred rites of the Jews were at variance "with the glory of our empire, the dignity of our name, the customs of our ancestors," that is, the Jewish religion by definition denied legitimacy to every other form of worship, including that of the Romans. Cicero thus strengthened his case by appealing, here as elsewhere, to basic Roman piety and patriotism. Littman argues that the issue is not what the inner feelings of any individual are but rather his public statements, writings, and actions that may influence public opinion and behavior.[116] However, Cicero's statements about the Jews are seldom quoted or alluded to even by church fathers and certainly had no impact in his own day in instigating anti-Jewish attacks.

That Cicero was not alone in citing the power of the Jews may be seen from the comment of the first-century Pompeius Trogus (quoted in Justin, *Historiae Philippicae* 36.2.16), who remarks that "by their justice (*iustitia*), combined (*permixta*) with religion (*religione*), it is incredible (*incredibile*)[117] how powerful (*quantum coaluere*, 'united,' 'consolidated,' 'strong,' 'increased') they became." In this instance, it is significant that the acknowledgment of Jewish strength comes from one who is generally favorably disposed toward the Jews. In any case, there can be no doubt that Jewish influence at the imperial court in Rome was at its height in the first century C.E., particularly during the reigns of Caligula, Claudius, and Nero. Indeed, the fact that a Jew, Agrippa I, was chiefly instrumental in making Claudius emperor surely confirms this power.

Likewise, as Pucci Ben Ze'ev has remarked in discussion of the papyrus (*CPJ* 2.158a), from the so-called *Acts of the Alexandrian Martyrs*, which dates from the year 115 C.E., we see the effectiveness of the Jewish emissaries when they appear before the Roman emperor.[118] On both occasions during the reign of Trajan (before the spring of 113 and before the autumn of 115), the Jewish and Greek communities were involved in armed conflict (*CPJ* 2.158 and 2.435), and in both instances the attitude of the Roman authorities was severe toward the Greeks, thus indicating to the Greeks the great power possessed by the Jews in influencing the imperial policy.

The fact that as late as the third century, when the Jewish community of Egypt had been sharply reduced, the viciously anti-Jewish *Acts of the Alexandrian Martyrs* (so reminiscent of the nineteenth-century *Protocols of the Elders of Zion* in its charge of Jewish domination) was still being copied is an indication of the bitterness at the alleged Jewish influence in high places. It is also evidence of the success of Jews in gaining in numbers and political clout.

In summary, to the intelligentsia it is precisely the unwillingness of Jews to engage in meaningful dialogue with other religious groups on a plane of equality—a sine qua non for the intellectual who welcomes debate—and to be ready to adopt another point of view if it can be shown to be superior to their own attitude that proved that the Jews were illiberal, unscholarly obscurantists. It is precisely to answer such a charge that Josephus (*Ant.* 1.161) puts a liberal attitude into the mouth of Abraham, who descends into Egypt to an international scientific congress, so to speak, with the Egyptians, in which the loser of the debate agrees to adopt the philosophic position of the winner.[119] The intellectuals could not understand the illiberalism of the Jews in failing to accord respect to the religions of others, as Apion (quoted in Josephus, *Against Apion* 2.65), for example, complained; and hence the efforts of the Septuagint, Philo (*De Vita Mosis* 2.38.205 and *De Specialibus Legibus* 1.9.53), and Josephus (*Ant.* 4.207; *Against Apion* 2.237) to show, on the basis of an interpretation of Exodus 22:27, that Jews are actually commanded to accord such respect. But these apologetics were clearly contradicted by the Bible itself and by the oral tradition that the increasingly important Pharisees were expounding during this very period. Furthermore, the fact that it is satirists in particular who single out the distinctive—and, from a pagan point of view, utterly irrational—Jewish observances of circumcision, the dietary laws, and the Sabbath is a clear indication of the degree to which Jews were identified with these practices; and even if a satirist uses a sledgehammer to crack a nut, the force of the satire is lost unless the reader is familiar with the reference and sees at least a kernel of truth in it.

And yet we must make two final remarks. In the first place, not all the intellectuals agreed in viewing the beliefs, practices, and traits of the Jews negatively; indeed, a sizable number among the philosophic schools of the Neo-Pythagoreans and Neo-Platonists admired them. Second, none of the attacks in antiquity of the intelligentsia on the Jews, not even the blood libel, ever led to an organized physical attack on them, so far as we can tell, with the possible exception of the riot of 38 in Alexandria. The influence of the intelligentsia on rulers or assemblies was, to say the least, minimal. Even a Cicero or a Seneca or a Tacitus, who were involved in politics, never, so far as we know, translated his anti-Jewish sentiments into political or other measures against the Jews. In short, the vertical alliance of Jews and rulers was unaffected by the writings or speeches of philosophers or rhetoricians or poets or satirists.

CHAPTER 6

THE ATTRACTIONS OF THE JEWS: THEIR ANTIQUITY

1. The Importance of Antiquity

During the Hellenistic and Roman periods, the general principle seems to have been that the older and more eastern things were, the more divine and the more credible they were, inasmuch as human beings were closest to the gods in the earliest times and in the East.[1]

One recalls the famous conversation of Solon, in the sixth century B.C.E., with an aged Egyptian priest (quoted in Plato, *Timaeus* 22B) who spoke of the Greeks as children because they had no immemorial past: "You ever remain children; in Greece there is no old man." Likewise, Herodotus (2.143) in the fifth century B.C.E. remarks that when his predecessor, the Greek logographer Hecataeus of Miletus, on a visit to Egypt, traced his ancestry back to a god in the sixteenth generation, the Egyptian priests led him, as they later did Herodotus, into the interior of a temple and showed him 345 statues of successive generations of priests without going back to a god. Similarly, in the fourth century B.C.E. Aristotle (*Politics* 7.9.4.1329B25) recognizes that the Egyptian legislator Sesostris lived long before Minos, the first Greek lawgiver.

Such statements, we must remember, in addition to being admitted by the Greeks themselves, were repeated by apologists, who therefore did not dare to say anything false for fear of being found out; consequently, there must have been some basis of truth in what they said. The anonymous author of the pseudo-Platonic *Epinomis* (987E) does attempt to counterattack, so to speak, by asserting that the Greeks actually improved on what they had borrowed;[2] but this was feeble comfort, because most Greeks agreed that those who introduce an idea are the ones who are truly wise.

The Romans also placed a great premium on antiquity. Thus, in the first century B.C.E. Cicero (*De Legibus* 2.10.27) remarks that "the preservation of the rites of the family and of our ancestors means preserving the religous rites which, we can almost say, were handed down to us by the gods themselves, since ancient times were closest to the gods."[3] Elsewhere Cicero (*De Natura Deorum* 3.1.5–4.10) also defends the validity of the Roman religion on the grounds of its antiquity. The importance that the Romans attached to establishing their antiquity may be seen from the determined attempt of his younger contemporary Virgil in his *Aeneid* to trace the ancestry of the Romans back to the famed Trojans and specifically to the Trojan Aeneas, the son of Venus, the daughter of Jupiter.

Indeed, several other peoples claimed remoter antiquity than the Greeks, as seen notably in Berosus's *History of Babylonia* and in Manetho's *Egyptian History*, both written during the third century B.C.E. Moreover, we may note that in the second century C.E. Philo of Byblus in Phoenicia boasts that he had found Phoenician writings dating from even before the Trojan War which claimed that the Phoenician gods and heroes had been the civilizers of humankind.[4]

2. WRITERS MENTIONED BY JOSEPHUS

Thus, in view of the importance both the Greeks and the Romans attached to such antiquity, it is not surprising that in the very first statement in the treatise *Against Apion* Josephus emphasizes that he had, in the *Antiquities*, made clear the extreme antiquity of the Jewish people. The very title of the *Antiquities*, Ἀρχαιολογία, literally "ancient lore," emphasizes this. It is remarkable that during the century before and the century after the beginning of the Common Era, several major works were written with the title *Antiquities*—Varro's *Antiquities of Human and Divine Affairs*, Dionysius of Halicarnassus's *Roman Antiquities*, and Josephus's *Jewish Antiquities*. Furthermore, the title *Against Apion* is not Josephus's own; and one of the titles in the manuscripts, Περὶ Ἀρχαιότητος Ἰουδαίων, *Concerning the Antiquity of the Jews*, again emphasizes this theme. Josephus himself says (*Against Apion* 1.2–3) that his purpose in writing the treatise is to disprove those who discredit the statements in his previous historical work concerning the antiquity (ἀρχαιολογίαν) of the Jews and who claim that the Jews are relatively modern. Indeed, it is noteworthy that in the first four sections of the treatise Josephus uses the word ἀρχαιολογία three times (*Against Apion* 1.1, 2, 4) and the word ἀρχαιότης, likewise meaning "antiquity," once (1.3).

Every nation, says Josephus (*Against Apion* 2.152) in the first century C.E., attempts to trace its origin back to the remotest antiquity in order not to appear merely to imitate other peoples. Although, as Josephus (*Against Apion* 1.7) contends, "in the Greek world everything will be found to be modern and dating, so to speak, from yesterday or the day before," Moses (*Against Apion* 2.154–56) is the most ancient of all legislators in the records of the world. The Greek lawgivers appear to have been born but yesterday or the day before (the same phrase as in *Against Apion* 1.7), whereas an infinity of time (*Against Apion* 2.279) has passed since Moses lived, if one compares his era with that of other lawgivers, including (*Against Apion* 2.154) even the Spartan lawgiver Lycurgus, so much admired and revered by the Greeks.

It is striking that even the opponents of the Jews were ready to concede the antiquity of the Jews. Thus, by declaring, as does the arch-Jew-baiter Apion (cited in *Against Apion* 2.28), that the Jews were Egyptians by race, the opponents of the Jews were actually associating them with what the Greeks regarded as the most ancient of civilizations.[5] As we hear from such writers as Herodotus (2.2) and Diodorus (1.10.1–7), the Egyptians claimed that human beings had been first spontaneously generated in Egypt and that they were the first to look into the sky and to conceive that there were gods.[6] Moreover, the Egyptian priests, by referring to their sacred books, convinced Greek visitors that civilization had arisen in Egypt more than ten thousand years before Alexander the Great (Herodotus 2.142 had said that Egyptian history went back 11,340 years); that their Pharaohs had reigned five thousand years before Cleopatra; that the Egyptian goddess Isis had discovered agriculture; that the Egyptian god Osiris had forced humanity to give up cannibalism; that the Egyptian god Thoth had invented philosophy as well as the alphabet,[7] astronomy, music, and dance 48,863 years before Alexander lived; that it was from Egypt that Erechtheus had brought grain and introduced the Eleusinian mysteries in honor of Demeter; that Heracles—the greatest hero of the Greeks—was born in the Nile valley (Diodorus 1.23.8–25); that (Diodorus 1.29.2, 96.2–98.5) Egyptian priests could prove from written records that they had been visited by such great religious thinkers and philosophers as Orpheus, Musaeus, Daedalus, Melampus, Lycurgus, Pythagoras, and Democritus; and that Athens itself had been founded by Egyptians (Anaximander 72, frag. 20 Jacoby, repeated by Charax 103, frag. 34 Jacoby; Diodorus 1.29.1 ff.). Herodotus (2.4), moreover, credits the Egyptians (rather than the Sumerians, as seems to have been actually the case) with being the first people who reckoned by years and who, indeed, divided the year into twelve months—a great compliment in view of the importance the ancients attached to the reckoning of time.[8]

Likewise, the Greek antiquarian Plutarch (*De Iside et Osiride* 34.364D) notes that Egyptian priests claimed that Homer (*Iliad* 14.201), in declaring that the gods arose out of Ocean, was drawing on Egyptian wisdom; and indeed the Greeks were ready to believe (Plutarch, *De Iside et Osiride* 10.354D–E) that the wisest of the Greeks—Solon, Thales, Plato, Eudoxus, and Pythagoras—were disciples of Egyptian wise men.

The Egyptian priests, moreover, pointed out (cited in Plutarch, *De Iside et Osiride* 34.364D) that Thales, the Greek founder of philosophy, had actually derived from the Egyptians his conception that water was the beginning of all things. Even the great Plato, the most respected of philosophers in the Hellenistic period,[9] refers (*Laws* 2.656E) to ten thousand years of Egyptian history and is said by Egyptian priests (Crantor, cited in Proclus, *In Platonis Timaeum*, p. 73, ed. E. Diehl) to have derived his account of Atlantis from Egyptian texts.

Thus, we can understand how important a role chronology played in the disputes between Jews and their detractors. In fact, as Wacholder[10] has pointed out, a number of pagan historians—Alexander Polyhistor, Varro, Ptolemy of Mendes, and others—were likewise eager to date the main events recorded in the Bible. It is certain, as he notes,[11] that within a century after Eupolemus (ca. 200 B.C.E.) a world chronicle that synchronized Jewish and Greek history had gained international circulation. Indeed, Manetho, although casting aspersions on the Jews as lepers who had been expelled from Egypt, dates this expulsion (cited in Josephus, *Against Apion* 1.231) as having occurred only 125 years after Aegyptus and Danaus, the marriage of whose children produced the ancestors of the Greeks, or even 393 years before then, if we accept Josephus's equation of the Hyksos with the Jews (1.103); thus Manetho actually grants the status of antiquity to the Jews.

Even the arch-enemy of the Jews, Apion (cited in Eusebius, *Praeparatio Evangelica* 10.10.16), admits that the Exodus had occurred in the time of Inachus, the first king of Argos, who was a contemporary of Amosis, the king of Egypt. This would concede tremendous antiquity to the Jews, inasmuch as Inachus[12] was the son of Oceanus and Tethys, both of whom were Titans, and hence he was one of the third generation of the Greek gods. Inachus's daughter Io, who was impregnated by Zeus, became the ancestress of Cadmus and through him of the god Dionysus and perhaps also the hero Oedipus; she was also the ancestress of Europa and through her of the legendary Cretan lawgiver Minos, and finally in the thirteenth generation, through her descendants Aegyptus and Danaus, of the great hero Heracles. Inachus's son Phoroneus was regarded as the first to bring people together to live in communities; that is to say, he introduced civilization into Greece. His descendants founded the famous cities of Argos, Tiryns, and Epidaurus. His grandson Pelasgus was the progenitor of the Pelasgians, whom the Greeks regarded as the original native inhabitants of Greece.[13] It was Pelasgus's son Lycaon whose wicked ways were said to have been one of the causes of the great flood; hence, the date of Inachus would be in the truly remote past.

We may assume, in view of the vast amount of research that Josephus did for his treatise *Against Apion*, as indicated by the great number of authors whom he cites and in view of his apparently thorough knowledge of Apion's works, that Josephus most likely knew that Apion ascribed such great antiquity to the Jews.

Because, as Josephus (*Against Apion* 2.16) says, there were apparently many different dates for Moses, we may ask why he selects, at least when dealing with Apion, not the earlier date Apion cites but rather a date in the eighth century B.C.E., namely (*Against Apion* 2.17) the first year of the seventh Olympiad (754–753 B.C.E.). But Josephus probably preferred this date, late though it was, to an earlier one because it implied that Apion had synchronized the Exodus on the fifteenth of the Jewish month of Nisan with the founding of Rome by Romulus, which, appropriately enough, occurred on the twenty-first of April[14] in the very same year, 754–753 B.C.E., and with the founding of the great city of Carthage, Rome's most potent enemy in her entire history. We may ask whether this synchonization would have been grasped by the casual reader, one who did not have chronological tables handy, and whether in any case the alleged synchronization of the events would have suggested to the reader that the Exodus was as important as the foundation of Carthage and of Rome. In reply, we note that even the rabbis remark on the synchronization of such diverse events as the founding of Rome, the marriage of King Solomon with Pharaoh Neco's daughter, the making of the two golden calves by Jeroboam, and the assumption to heaven of the prophet Elijah.[15]

Similarly, the association of the Jews with the foundation of Carthage seems perfectly natural in view of the geographical proximity of their homelands, Phoenicia and Judaea, and in view of the close relation between their Semitic languages.[16] We may remark that the traditional year for the founding of Carthage was 814 B.C.E., as we may deduce from Dionysius of Halicarnassus (*Roman Antiquities* 1.74.1). Apion (cited in *Against Apion* 2.17) apparently sought to correct Dionysius, whose reputation he envied (cf. the *Suda* under the listing "Apion"), perhaps intending to show Dionysius's anti-Roman bias in dating the founding of Carthage before that of Rome; but ironically, by putting the foundation of both Rome and Carthage in the same year, he unwittingly assigned greater world significance to the event than he had perhaps intended. In any case, to a Roman reader the association of the Jews with the Carthaginians, reluctant though it may be, would improve the Jews' reputation, especially because Carthage's mother-country Phoenicia had been the source of the alphabet (the Cadmean letters), the key to literature for the Greeks, and because the Carthaginians had given the Romans their toughest battle for supremacy over the Mediterranean world.[17] That the antiquity of the Jews was generally granted is clear from the remark of the third-century Origen (*Against Celsus* 1.16) expressing surprise that the second-century Celsus, in enumerating the most ancient and wisest nations of the world, omits the Jews.

3. Other Classical References to the Antiquity of the Jews

One of the greatest tributes to the antiquity and nobility of the Jews is to be found in the first century B.C.E. in Alexander Polyhistor (cited in Stephanus of Byzantium, under the heading Ἰουδαία), who derives the name of Judaea from that of the children of Semiramis, Judas and Idumaea. Presumably this is based on the biblical tradition tracing the origin of the Jews back to Abraham the Chaldaean. To connect the Jews with the legendary Semiramis, the daughter of the goddess Atargatis who conquered so many lands, founded Babylon and Nineveh, and built so many glorious monuments, was a distinct compliment. The connection is repeated later in the century by Pompeius Trogus (quoted in Justin, *Historiae Philippicae* 36.2.1), who traces the origin of the Jews from Damascus, which he calls "the most illustrious city of Syria" and whence, he adds as a revealing afterthought, also the stock of the Assyrian kings through Queen Semiramis had sprung. In the third century Porphyry (cited in Jerome, *Chronica* 7) imputes great antiquity to the Jews by claiming that Semiramis, who reigned one hundred and fifty years before Inachus, lived after Moses and that Moses himself preceded the Trojan War by almost eight hundred fifty years.

In a tremendous tribute, the first-century C.E. encyclopedist Pliny the Elder (5.73), followed by Solinus (*Collectanea Rerum Memorabilium* 35.11) in the third century, speaks of the Jewish sect of the Essenes as having been in existence through thousands of ages—"incredible to relate" (*incredibile dictu*), as he adds.

Likewise in the first century, Claudius Iolaus (cited in Stephanus of Byzantium, under the heading Ἰουδαία) shows even greater admiration for the Jews in tracing their origin back to Udaeus, one of the "Spartoi" ("Sown-men") at Thebes, who was supposedly among the military companions of Dionysus. The Jews are thus connected with Cadmus, the founder of Thebes and the bestower of the alphabet on the Greeks, who was responsible for sowing the serpent's teeth from which sprang armed men. The conjunction with the god Dionysus, which is also found in Plutarch (*Quaestiones Convivales* 4.6.2.671D), is of course another distinct compliment, as we have noted.[18]

In his encyclopedic work, Julius Solinus (*Collectanea Rerum Memorabilium* 34.1) in the third century C.E. speaks of Joppe as the most ancient city of the entire world and claims that it was founded even before the Flood. He and several other writers[19] bring this city into the legendary age by asserting that here Andromeda was rescued by Perseus.

That the antiquity of the Jews was widely acknowledged is implied by Origen (*Against Celsus* 4.21): Celsus, in contending that the biblical account of the Tower of Babel was a corruption of the Greek mythical account of the sons of Aloeus and that the story of destruction of Sodom and Gomorrah was to be compared with the story of Phaethon, had failed to take notice of the evidence of Moses' antiquity.

4. TACITUS'S ACCOUNT OF THE ORIGIN OF THE BRITONS AND THE GERMANS AS COMPARED WITH THE ORIGIN OF THE JEWS

The most complete evidence by a pagan for the antiquity of the Jews is given, significantly and paradoxically, by the writer who is generally re-garded as one of the most vicious Jew-baiters of them all, Tacitus. In order to shed light on his account of the origin of the Jews, we first examine his accounts of the origin of the Britons in his *Agricola* and of the Germans in his *Germania*.

Both the *Agricola* and the *Germania* date from approximately the year 98, a few years before Tacitus composed the *Histories* (which seems to date from between the years 104 and 109),[20] where the excursus about the Jews appears. In all three accounts, Tacitus is concerned with the ques-tion whether the inhabitants are autochthonous or immigrants or a mix-ture of the two.[21]

The ethnographic excursus about the Britons in the *Agricola* (10–12) would seem to supply a good parallel to the passage about the Jews, inas-much as both occur in accounts prior to the suppression of native revolts. However, Tacitus, although spending some time describing the shape of Britain and the nature of the waters that surround it (10), has little about the origin of the inhabitants (11) and indeed disavows information: "Who were the original inhabitants of Britain, whether they were indig-enous or foreign, is, as usual among barbarians, little known." He then proceeds to present three theories as to the origins: The red hair and the large limbs of the inhabitants of Caledonia point to a German origin; the dark complexion and the curly hair of the tribe of the Lures indicate a Spanish origin; the similarity to the Gauls on the part of those living closest to Gaul inclines him to believe in a Gallic origin. What is re-markable is not merely the brevity of the discussion but also the lack of an attempt to connect the Britons with the Greeks generally (as Tacitus seeks to do for the Jews) or with Dionysus or Heracles in particular, as is so often done in speculation about the origin of other barbarians.[22] In any case, none of the three theories imputes antiquity to the Britons, whereas it is only to the Jews that Tacitus imputes great antiquity, so much prized by the ancients, and only the Jews that he tries to connect with other famous peoples, notably the Cretans, the Egyptians, the Ethi-opians, and the Solymi of Homeric fame.

As for the Germans, Tacitus offers few variants of their origin in Gaul.[23] He (*Germania* 2) says very briefly that he regards the Germans as being aboriginal, and offers as presumptive evidence the difficulty in gaining access to Germany by sea; moreover, he adds that it would not make much sense for people living in a favorable climate to move to a country with such unfavorable weather. He then cites, noting only that such freedom of conjecture was permitted by antiquity, the Germans' own account, in their songs, of their founder as being an earth-born god, Tuisco. Such an origin would imply antiquity, whereas for the Jews, despite the obvious richness of their tradition, Tacitus cites none of their own accounts, at least overtly, of their origin; but the key point is that the classical reader of Tacitus's account of the origin of the Germans is given no point of association with the mythology with which he is familiar, whereas, as we shall see, for the origins of the Jews several classical mythological connections are presented.

5. Tacitus's Theories of the Origin of the Jews

The mere fact that Tacitus gives no fewer than six different theories of the origin of the Jews would seem to indicate their importance to him. Apparently, Tacitus did some research into the matter and utilized a number of sources.[24] The only other nation for which we have anything like a large number of accounts of origin in ancient literature is Rome, in which case we have some twenty-five accounts.[25] The Romans, in particular, were sensitive about their lack of antiquity, inasmuch as, after all, the city of Rome was said to have been founded as recently as 753 B.C.E.; hence the attempt on the part of Timaeus, Virgil, and others to add to Rome's antiquity by tracing its history back hundreds of years earlier to the Trojan War and Aeneas.

Emigrants from Crete

In contrast to the accounts of a recent origin of Rome, the first theory of the origins of the Jews presented by Tacitus (*Histories* 5.2.1) is that they were originally exiles from the island of Crete who settled in the furthest parts of Libya at the time when Saturn had been deposed and expelled by Jupiter.[26]

By integrating the origin of the Jews with Greek pre-history, Tacitus would be understood by his readers as not only imputing great antiquity to the Jews[27] but also, in effect, diminishing the gulf between these Jewish barbarians and the Greeks, just as conversely the Table of Nations in the Bible (Gen 10) integrated the Greeks, the descendants of Japheth

(Gen 10:2–4), into the genealogy of humankind. In particular, to be associated with Crete gave enormous prestige to the Jews, inasmuch as the Cretans were acknowledged to have had a great civilization before that of mainland Greece. As Thucydides (1.4) states, Minos, the famous king of Crete, is the earliest of all those known by tradition to have acquired a navy. "He made himself," he adds, "master of a very great part of what is now called the Hellenic Sea, and became lord of the Cyclades islands and first colonizer of most of them, driving out the Carians and establishing his own sons in them as governors." In Homer (*Odyssey* 11.568–71) he is termed "the illustrious son of Zeus" and is described as administering justice in the land of the dead. Moreover, Demeter, the great goddess of the Eleusinian Mysteries, was closely associated with Crete, because we hear that the birth of Plutus, the god of wealth, was the result of the union of Demeter with Iasion "in the rich land of Crete" (Hesiod, *Theogony* 969–71); furthermore, when she wanders everywhere in her search for her daughter Persephone, she asserts (*Homeric Hymn to Demeter*, line 123) that she is from Crete; and indeed, as we hear from Diodorus (5.77), the Eleusinian and other mysteries were sufficiently similar to those of Idaean Zeus that the Cretans claimed that they had been the teachers of the Greeks in all such matters.[28]

That the reputation of the Cretans was very high, at least in certain quarters, is reflected in the writings of both Plato and Aristotle. It is significant that in Plato's dialogue, the *Laws*, his last legacy to the world of philosophy, Socrates no longer appears as a participant, and instead two of the interlocutors are a Cretan and a Spartan, members of nations that Plato admired very much. At the very beginning of that dialogue (*Laws* 1.624–25), Plato compares their systems of laws, noting that both are designed with a view to preparing the population for war, which the respective lawgivers regarded as the natural state of humankind.[29] The Cretan lawgiver, Minos, we hear, went every ninth year to converse with his father Zeus; and Rhadamanthus, his brother, was reputedly the most just of men.[30] In fact, even Zeus, according to legend, was born in Crete (Hesiod, *Theogony* 453 ff.); the mountain where he was hidden in a cave is said to be the Cretan Mount Ida (Hyginus, *Fabellae* 139), which, significantly, Tacitus (*Histories* 5.2.1) here associates with the Idaei, whence, according to him, the Iudaei (Jews). Thus, the connection of the Jews with Mount Ida in Crete would likewise be understood as a distinct compliment. The very reference in Tacitus here (5.2.1) to the mountain as famous (*inclutum*), when there was no particular reason why he had to add this adjective, would lead his readers to ascribe fame to the Jews allegedly associated with this mountain.[31]

Hospers-Jansen contends that the folk etymology of *Iudaei* from *Idaei*, which Tacitus here refers to as a barbarism (*aucto in barbarum cognomen*), is due to an anti-Jewish Latin source; and Herrmann suggests that this author is Antonius Julianus.[32] We may remark that the term *barbarus*, which, to the Greeks, meant "non-Greek-speaking," was used by the Romans in a relatively non-pejorative sense to mean "in a language or manner that is neither Greek nor Latin." Hence, it might have been understood here to mean "in a foreign tongue," where *foreign* could be used in either a neutral or a pejorative sense, just as it is in modern English. Perhaps, then, this is a snide remark on the part of Tacitus, but that does not mean that it was so intended by its originator and that it would be so received by those who heard it.[33] Surely readers of Virgil (*Aeneid* 1.267–68) would have thought of the close and clearly complimentary parallel of the derivation of the name of Iulius (in Julius Caesar) from Iulus (that is, Ascanius, the son of Aeneas), and of the latter from Ilus, the earlier name of Ascanius while Troy (the Ilian realm) was still standing.[34]

The fact that the Jews are here termed refugees (*profugos*) may very well, despite Tacitus's intention, have conjured up sympathetic connotations. The word *profugus* appears often in the epic tradition.[35] One thinks immediately, of course, of its occurrence at the very beginning of Virgil's *Aeneid* (1.2) in sympathetically setting the theme of Aeneas as the refugee from Troy who came to Italy. We may note that Tacitus himself employs the word with a positive connotation with reference to Teucer (*Annals* 3.62.4), the greatest archer among the Greeks attacking Troy, when he fled from the wrath of his father Telamon. Tacitus (*Annals* 16.1.2) also uses the word sympathetically with reference to the Phoenician Dido, when she fled from Tyre and founded Carthage.

The fact that the Jews are said by Tacitus to have settled Africa contemporaneously with the displacement of Saturn by Jupiter is another indication of the great antiquity of the Jews. Saturn was known as a just king of the gods of the early period, under whose rule humanity had its most fortunate times. To be associated, therefore, with Saturn was a high compliment, inasmuch as, according to Rome's national poet, Virgil (*Aeneid* 8.319–27), when Saturn fled from Jupiter, in a scene paralleling, we may suggest, Aeneas's flight from Troy, he came to Latium, the very site of Rome, and gave the unruly race there the highest gift in the eyes of the Romans, namely laws. His rule, we are told, was an age of gold, an era of peace and quiet. Inasmuch as the Saturnian Age, as we may note in Virgil's Fourth Eclogue,[36] is thus synonymous with the golden era of the past, the connection of the Jews with Saturn, despite his connection with the gloomy and saturnine, would be regarded as complimentary by Tacitus's readers.

Moreover, as Tacitus himself (*Histories* 5.4.4) says, of the seven planets that rule the fortunes of humanity, Saturn moves in the highest orbit and has the greatest potency;[37] and the fact that Tacitus here associates Saturn with the Jewish Sabbath may indicate that he or his source connects the Jews' growing power and influence with their association with this powerful planet, though admittedly there is no other place in Tacitus that suggests that he connected human characteristics with individual planets. And yet it is clear that Tacitus knew astrology and that knowledge of astrology was widespread among intellectuals;[38] and it thus seems likely that Tacitus is doing more than merely recording some Hellenistic explanations of the nonexistent link between the Jewish Sabbath and Saturn and of the astronomic number seven. We should recall that already in 139 B.C.E. the expulsion of the Jews from Rome is coupled with the expulsion of the astrologers (Valerius Maximus 1.3.3). Furthermore, Abraham's reputation as an astrologer is already asserted by the Graeco-Jewish historian Artapanus (quoted in Eusebius, *Praeparatio Evangelica* 9.18.1) ca 100 B.C.E., and by his contemporary, Pseudo-Eupolemus (quoted in Eusebius, *Praeparatio Evangelica* 9.17.8). In the second century, not long after the time of Tacitus, Vettius Valens (*Anthologiae* 2.28–29) speaks of the "most wonderful" Abraham, who made clear through astrology the divisions of times of action.[39] Moreover, Tacitus here (5.4.4) presents alternative explanations (*sive . . . sive*) as to the ties between Saturn and the Jews—namely, the connection between Saturn and the Idaean founders of the Jews or the great power of Saturn in the orbits of the planets. Whether Tacitus found both alternatives in the same source or in different sources, it is impossible to say. It is, to be sure, typical of him to offer alternative explanations, possibly as a sign of his learning or his impartiality, without any indication as to which, if any, he regards as the more probable.

Tacitus's statement that the refugees settled in the remotest (*novissima*) part of Libya may well indicate a connection with Ethiopia and hence constitute a link with Tacitus's third version of the origin of the Jews, as Lewy[40] has suggested, because a similar phrase, "the most distant (ἐσχατιαί) parts of the world in Libya," is found in Herodotus (3.115) in reference to Ethiopia. It is their piety, as well as their location at the end of the world, that made the Ethiopians especially suitable as the people to whom Saturn could flee.[41]

A clue that the Jewish association with Libya would be viewed as distinctly complimentary by Tacitus's literate readers may be seen in the passage, which we have noted, in "the prophet" Cleodemus-Malchus of the second century B.C.E. (as cited by Alexander Polyhistor quoted in Josephus, *Antiquities* 1.239–41), in which he states that two of Abraham's sons by Keturah joined with Heracles in fighting against Libya and against the giant Antaeus (the son of Poseidon and Ge) and that Heracles married the daughter of one of these two sons of Abraham. Heracles then proceeded, according to Diodorus Siculus (4.17.4–5) to civilize Libya.[42]

The attempt to link the origins of the Jews with those of the Greeks may have started, or at least found support, among those Jews who were losing their hold on Jewish tradition;[43] but if so, we may ask why we do not find Philo or Josephus or the rabbis, all of whom are so concerned with the survival of the Jewish people, inveighing against such Jews. There is something ironic about the Jews deriving their name from the Idaeans while at the same time being associated with Saturn (Cronus), inasmuch as the Idaeans, who are later identified with the Curetes (Pausanias 5.7.6), attend to the infant Zeus (Jupiter) and protect him against his father Cronus.[44] We may suggest that inasmuch as Saturn stood for a golden age of law, peace, and quiet, perhaps those who originated the association of the Jews with Saturn sought in this way to emphasize that Jews stood for law and order rather than the rule of vengeance.

Superfluous Population of Egypt in the Reign of Isis

A second theory of Tacitus as to the origin of the Jews (*Histories* 5.2.2) is that during the reign of Isis the superfluous population of Egypt, under the leadership of Hierosolymus (i.e., Jerusalem) and Iuda (i.e., Judah), discharged itself on the neighboring lands. One might have thought that Tacitus, with his anti-Jewish prejudice, would have given only one account connecting the Jews with Egypt, namely his sixth hypothesis, asserting that the Jews had been expelled from Egypt during a plague. The fact that the Jews are here spoken of as the superfluous population of Egypt gives them the same motive as many others had for establishing a "colony."[45] Here, we may note, Tacitus (or his source) seems to be reflecting the biblical statement (Exod 1:7) "And the children of Israel were fruitful, and increased abundantly and multiplied and waxed exceedingly mighty, and the land was filled with them." What is significant, however, is that Tacitus does not give the motive for the justification, at least from the Egyptian point of view, of the oppression of the Israelites, namely the Egyptian fear that the Israelites were becoming more numerous and mightier than they themselves. Hence, Tacitus seems, perhaps unwittingly, to be presenting the Israelites in a more favorable light than does the Bible itself.

It is even more significant, however, that Tacitus declares that they left during the reign of the goddess Isis herself, thus imputing great antiquity to the Israelites, whereas, according to Chaeremon's version (cited in *Against Apion* 1.289), the departure of the Israelites occurred much later, during the reign of King Amenophis.

The association of the Jews with the reign of Isis, even if it is merely chronological, would give them prestige, inasmuch as Isis was identified with the revered goddess Demeter (Herodotus 2.59.2) and was regarded

as the greatest deity by the Egyptians. Indeed, Herodotus (2.42.2) remarks that only she and Osiris were worshipped throughout Egypt. She
was said to be (Diodorus 1.27.4) the oldest daughter of Cronus (Saturn);
and this may be a link with Tacitus's first explanation of the origin of the
Jews.[46]

Clearly connected with Tacitus's version is the account of his contemporary Plutarch (*De Iside et Osiride* 31.363D), which has the same
names, Hierosolymus and Iuda (in Plutarch Ἰουδαῖος), of the leaders of
the Jews. There, however, we are told that the evil god Typhon fled from
battle for seven days on the back of an ass, after which he became the
father of Hierosolymus and Judaeus. The role of these two leaders in
Tacitus is at once more important and more honorable. In particular,
in Tacitus the name of Typhon, the demonic god of the Egyptians, the
god of the wilderness, of eclipses, of storms, and of darkness, whose sacred animal was the ass and who himself sometimes took the form of
an ass-headed man, is not mentioned. Likewise, Tacitus has omitted the
ass, which, to the Egyptians, was a symbol of folly, as we see from Plutarch (*De Iside et Osiride* 50.371C). The flight of seven days is likewise
absent. Because seven days is precisely the length of time that it supposedly took the Israelites to reach the Land of Israel after their flight
from Egypt, according to a number of ancient writers including Tacitus,[47] the flight might have provided the occasion for a scurrilous explanation of the Jewish observance of the Sabbath. In sum, Tacitus's account is, in this respect, more positively inclined toward the Jews than
even Plutarch's.

Emigrants from Ethiopia

A third account, reported, significantly, in the name of "very many" (*plerique*), declares that the Jews were of Ethiopian stock, who, in the reign
of Cepheus, were forced by fear and hatred to migrate. Although this
reflects the anti-Jewish attempt, as seen in Manetho and other Graeco-
Egyptian writers, to depict the Jews as having been expelled rather than
as having left voluntarily, and although it also reflects the familiar anti-
Jewish motif that the Jews' refusal to associate with others is due to their
misanthropy, the tradition also has positive elements.[48]

To declare that the Jews go back to the time of King Cepheus of Ethiopia is surely complimentary because it establishes the antiquity of the
Jews and because Cepheus and his famed wife Cassiopeia were placed
among the constellations after their deaths.[49] This antiquity is reinforced
by the mythical tradition that declared that their famed daughter Andromeda had been exposed at Joppa[50] in Judaea, whence she was rescued
by the great hero Perseus, who, according to the Persian version (Herodotus 6.54), was an Assyrian and thus presumably a Semite.[51]

Refugees from Assyria

A fourth theory cited by Tacitus—and significantly without challenge, let alone satirical comment—reports that the Jews were Assyrian refugees, a landless people, who at first invaded Egypt and later established their own cities in the Hebrew territory and the nearer parts of Syria. The Assyrians, as Herodotus (7.63) tells us in his description of Xerxes' army, were called Syrians by the Greeks; and, as Herodotus (1.105 and 2.104) says elsewhere, Palestine was regarded as a part of Syria.

This account in Tacitus is, of course, closest to three major elements of the biblical version,[52] inasmuch as Abraham did originally come from Mesopotamia (Gen 12:4–13:1), the sons of Jacob did descend to Egypt and sojourned there for 430 years (Exod 12:40), and they did eventually enter "Hebrew" territory in the lower part of Syria, namely Judaea. This would seem to be in accord with the view previously expressed in Pompeius Trogus (quoted in Justin, *Historiae Philippicae* 36.2.1) that the Jews came originally from Damascus, the most illustrious city of Syria, from which also the Assyrian kings were said to derive through the legendary Queen Semiramis.[53] It is also in accord with the version found in Nicolaus of Damascus (quoted in Josephus, *Ant.* 1.159), who describes Abram as coming with an army, from the country beyond Babylon called the land of the Chaldees, to Damascus, where he reigned and where his name was still celebrated. The connection with Assyria may be borne out by the statement of the Graeco-Jewish historian Cleodemus-Malchus (cited in Josephus, *Ant.* 1.241) that Abraham had three sons by Keturah, one of whom, Sures, gave his name to Assyria.

Although, to be sure, this Tacitean version depicts the Jews as Hyksos-like invaders, such as those described by Manetho (quoted in Josephus, *Against Apion*, 1.75–91), the fact is that Tacitus reproduces three major elements in the biblical version, as noted above, though this does not, of course, indicate that he viewed them with approval or that he read the Bible firsthand; and his reference to the Jews as Hebrews in connection with their origin from Assyria is perhaps an indication that he knew the significance of the term, namely that the Hebrews are so called because they came from "beyond" (Hebrew *me-'ever*; hence the word *Hebrew*, *'Ivri*) the river Euphrates.[54]

Identification with the Solymi

In presenting his fifth theory of the origin of the Jews, Tacitus, for the first time, explicitly indicates that he is presenting a hypothesis favorable to the Jews (implying that his other accounts, or at least the account immediately preceding, were not favorable to them), inasmuch as he de-

clares that "others say that the Jews are of illustrious origin (*clara* ...
initia), being the Solymi, a people celebrated in Homer's poems, who
founded a city and gave it the name Hierosolyma, formed from their
own."

The word *clarus* that Tacitus uses here to describe the origin of Jews is
a favorite epithet designating the highest praise of the honor-loving Romans.[55] In view of the early attempt, ascribed to Aristotle (quoted by
Clearchus of Soli, cited in Josephus, *Against Apion*, 1.179), to assert that
the Jews are descended from Indian philosophers, it should not be surprising that someone, impressed with their wisdom and antiquity, attempted to associate them with the Solymi, on the basis of the similarity
with the name of the chief city of the Jews, Jerusalem. This theory is,
indeed, complimentary to the Jews, because the Solymi are the people of
Asia Minor against whom the renowned Bellerophon fought. They are
described by the revered Homer (*Iliad* 6.184) as glorious (κυδαλίμοισιν);
and Bellerophon himself in Homer is said to have regarded this as the
hardest battle that he had ever fought. Moreover, putting the Jews in
juxtaposition with the Solymi enhances their claim to antiquity, because,
according to Herodotus (1.173), the Solymi were the ancient inhabitants
of Lycia. These Solymi, moreover, would appear to be the people, mentioned, as we have noted, by the fifth-century B.C.E. epic poet Choerilus
(quoted in Josephus, *Against Apion*, 1.173), who lived in the Solymian
hills near a broad lake and who spoke the Phoenician language.[56] The
identification of the Solymi (referred to as Σολυμῖται, "Solymites") with
the Jews is found even in the anti-Jewish account of Manetho (quoted in
Josephus, *Against Apion*, 1.248). The very fact that apparently in the first
century B.C.E. even the fiercely anti-Jewish Lysimachus (quoted in Josephus, *Against Apion*, 1.311) has an explanation of the name Jerusalem,
as if it were composed of two elements, ἱερός ("sacred," which he interprets as "sacrilegious") and Solyma, would indicate that the identification of Solyma with Jerusalem dated from at least that time.[57]

This theory linking the Jews with the Solymi may be connected with
the view of the Cretan origin of the Jews mentioned earlier by Tacitus,
inasmuch as we are told (Herodotus 1.173) that Sarpedon, the son of the
mythical Phoenician princess Europa, led Cretans to the Milyan territory in Asia Minor, which was occupied by the Solymi.

A connection between the Solymi and the Ethiopians as linked to the
Jews seems possible,[58] because Homer (*Odyssey* 5.282–83) places the two
in juxtaposition, remarking that Poseidon, coming from the Ethiopians,
saw Odysseus from afar from the mountains of the Solymi near the land
of the mythical Phaeacians (perhaps to be identified with the Semitic
Phoenicians). Moreover, Choerilus's description of the Solymi (quoted
in Josephus, *Against Apion* 1.173) accords with the account in the cata-

logue of Xerxes' army (Herodotus 7.70) of the Eastern Ethiopians; both Choerilus's Solymi and Herodotus's Eastern Ethiopians, strikingly, wear on their heads hides of horse heads.

Expulsion from Egypt during a Plague

Tacitus's sixth and final theory of the origin of the Jews (*Histories* 5.3–4) equates the origin of the Jewish nation with the Exodus itself. He declares that most (*plurimi*) authors agree that during a plague in Egypt King Bocchoris, following the advice given to him by the oracle of Ammon, purged his kingdom of the Jews, inasmuch as they were a race (*genus*) hateful (*invisum*) to the gods. One assumes from the amount of space given to this theory by Tacitus that "most" includes Tacitus,[59] especially because he says that it is the view of most authors, because the second and fourth accounts are likewise connected with Egypt,[60] because it is the last of the six explanations, and because he proceeds to explain his notion of the religious usages of the Jews, such as the worship of an ass, the Sabbath, and sacrifices, on the basis of this theory.

According to Tacitus, one of the exiles, Moses by name, warned the Jews not to trust for help from men or gods and taught them to regard as profane all that others held sacred, and vice versa. Under his leadership, they found water during their sojourn and on the seventh day seized a country (presumably Judaea), founded a city (presumably Jerusalem), and dedicated a temple, in which they erected a statue of an ass, because a herd of asses had led them to water during the sojourn.

This account is clearly the least favorable to the Jews; and it seems to be drawn, at least in part, from that arch-Jew-baiter Lysimachus, who also speaks of the expulsion of the Jews during the reign of King Bocchoris, who similarly indicates that Bocchoris consulted the oracle of Ammon and who likewise states that Moses advised the Jews to take their courage into their own hands (quoted in Josephus, *Against Apion*, 1.305–11).[61] He, too, mentions, quite out of accord with the Bible, that Moses led the Jews into Judaea and established the city of Jerusalem. The ascription in this theory of the Exodus to the reign of Bocchoris in the eighth century B.C.E. means that, accordingly, the Jews do not have the claim to remote antiquity associated with the other theories.

That Tacitus does seem to have used Lysimachus for at least some data, found uniquely only in those two writers, would appear to make significant his omissions of a number of details found in Lysimachus's account. In the first place, whereas Lysimachus (quoted in Josephus, *Against Apion* 1.305) says that the Jews were afflicted with disease, Tacitus speaks of a general plague without specifying that it was restricted to the Jews.

Second, whereas Lysimachus specifies that the disease consisted of leprosy, scurvy, and other maladies, Tacitus says vaguely that the plague caused bodily disfigurement (*corpora foedaret*), similar to the Roman view of circumcision.[62]

Third, Tacitus omits Lysimachus's statement that the Jewish lepers begged for food, even though the portrait of Jews as beggars seems to have been an accepted stereotype, as we can see from the satirical comments of Martial (12.57.1–4) and Juvenal (3.10–16, 296; 6.542–47).

Fourth, Lysimachus (quoted in Josephus, *Against Apion*, 1.308–9) indicates that Moses advised the Israelites, after they had implored the gods in vain to save them, to take their courage into their own hands, clearly signifying that they should not look to the gods for help. Tacitus (5.3.1), on the other hand, though remarking that Moses warned the Israelites not to expect help from the gods, adds in apparent contradiction Moses' advice that they should regard "as a guide sent from heaven" (*duce caelesti*), presumably by the gods, "the one whose assistance should first give them escape from their present distress."

Fifth, Tacitus lacks the gruesome detail that the lepers were packed into sheets of lead and sunk in the ocean. The statement in Lysimachus, ascribed to Moses, instructing the Jews to show goodwill to no man is paralleled, to be sure, in Tacitus (5.5.1) in the statement that the Jews feel only hate and enmity toward every other people, but it is not part of Tacitus's account of their origin.

Sixth, Tacitus omits the statement that Moses instructed the Jews to offer not the best but the worst advice.

Seventh, he omits the statement that Moses advised the Jews to overthrow any temples and altars of the pagan gods that they found.

Eighth, whereas Lysimachus says that the Jews maltreated (ὑβρίζοντας, "treated abusively," "insulted", "tortured," "tormented") the inhabitants of the desert through which they passed, and that they plundered and set fire to their temples, Tacitus says nothing at all about what they did to the inhabitants of the desert and says merely that they expelled the former inhabitants of Palestine.

Ninth, Lysimachus sarcastically says that the Jews named the city they founded Hierosolyma (Jerusalem, i.e., [town of] "temple-robbers"), whereas Tacitus says merely that they founded a city, without giving its name.

All of these omissions, however, are subject to the weakness of the *argumentum ex silentio*, especially in view of Tacitus's many indications of bitter prejudice against the Jews as noted above. Or alternatively, we may suggest that Tacitus omits these details in order to give the appearance that he is fair-minded. Indeed, we may note that Tacitus (5.4.3) does explain, disparagingly, as Lysimachus apparently did not, the origin of the Jewish Sabbath from the fact that the seventh day ended their toils, inasmuch as they discovered water in the desert on the seventh day after their exodus; and he adds the snide remark that they were thereafter led by the charms of indolence (*blandiente inertia*) to observe the seventh year as well in inactivity.[63]

There are, however, other elements in the account that might have fostered greater understanding of the Jews. The fact that the Jews were expelled from Egypt might have aroused sympathy among the Romans, inasmuch as the latter-day Egyptians, especially after the Roman encounter with Cleopatra, were regarded by the Romans with hatred and contempt, as we can see from Tacitus's contemporaries Juvenal (Satire 15), Statius (*Silvae* 2.1.74, 5.5.67–68), Pliny the Younger (*Panegyric* 31.2), Florus (4.2.60), and Plutarch (*De Iside et Osiride* 72.380A).[64]

Although there is some reason to think that Tacitus intended his description of the origin of the Jews and of the role of Moses as, in effect, an *Anti-Aeneid*, with the statement (5.3.1) that Moses told the Jews not to trust for help from the gods or men to be contrasted with Aeneas's constant concern with rescuing the household gods,[65] there is reason to think that Tacitus also actually, with a mixture of ambivalence, respected Moses and even to some degree saw a positive parallel with Aeneas.[66] In particular, instead of attacking Moses as a renegade Egyptian priest, as had Manetho (quoted in *Against Apion* 1.235, 250) and several other writers,[67] Tacitus says nothing about Moses' past. Moreover, in view of Philo's statement (*De Vita Mosis* 1.1.2) that the Greeks, in their envy, did not even speak of Moses, we may regard Tacitus's mention of Moses by name as a concession to his importance.

Furthermore, Tacitus (5.5.1) admits that the rites introduced by Moses are defended (*defenduntur*) by their antiquity, which is certainly, as we have seen, a concession to their status.[68] Furthermore, Tacitus notes a close correspondence between these rites (*hi ritus*) and the other institutions (*cetera instituta*). *Antiquitas* is generally a recommendation; and insofar as the origin of the Jews is "ancient," this aspect of the Jews is commendable. By contrast, the way that Jews, and especially proselytes, behaved in Tacitus's own day was generally odious to the Roman ruling class.

Summary

Of Tacitus's six accounts of Jewish origins, four contain distinctly pro-Jewish intimations, all of which impute great antiquity (so much admired by the ancients, especially by the Romans, who lacked it) to the Jews, namely that they came from Crete (note especially the association with Mount Ida, where Zeus was nurtured) at the time of Saturn's expulsion by Jupiter; that their ancestors may be traced back to the reign of Isis in Egypt; that they date from the reign of Ethiopia's King Cepheus, the father of the renowned mythical Andromeda; and that they are identified with the Solymi, who are famous in Homer. Though he does not indicate it in so many words, the fifth account, tracing the Jews back to Assyria, is clearly in consonance with the version of Genesis. And even when he gives, in his last and fullest account, what seems to be an indictment of the Jews, namely that they were expelled from Egypt during a plague, at least nine of the most damaging features in his probable source, Lysimachus, are missing. In truth, the fact that the Jews are termed refugees (*profugos*) may well have aroused sympathetic connotations because this term is applied to Aeneas in Virgil's *Aeneid* (1.2). In particular, the association with Saturn was with the god who was connected with the golden age of humankind and whose return was longed for almost messianically. The ascription to Saturn of the greatest potency among the planets may explain the mixture of respect for and fear of the Jews.

As to the nature of the Exodus, the theory that the Jews were a surplus population would make them parallel with those Lydians who allegedly emigrated to Etruria and with many others who founded colonies. The association with Isis is connected to the golden reign of Saturn and to the rule of justice so much admired by the Romans. The absence in Tacitus, though admittedly this is the *argumentum ex silentio*, of the role of Typhon, the god of evil, the father of Hierosolymus and Iudaius (whom he mentions), again serves to cast the Jews in a more favorable light. The association with the Ethiopians, renowned for their wisdom, piety, and bravery, certainly adds a positive dimension to the Jews.

Finally, we may ask (though it is a misconception of the modus operandi of Greek and Roman historians to envisage them as consulting original authorities as a general rule) why Tacitus—senator, consul, proconsul, close to imperial sources,[69] especially through his famous father-in-law Agricola—did not consult Josephus, who lived in Rome under Imperial auspices during the period when Tacitus began to write. Despite Josephus's prejudices, he was certainly in a position to provide Tacitus with more accurate information than he could obtain from the second- and third-hand accounts that apparently he did use.[70] We can see that in other cases, for example Smyrna, Tacitus (*Ann.* 4.56) does cite what the envoys themselves from the city report (including a claim to divine or heroic ancestry) concerning their origin (though we may note that this comes from a section devoted to senatorial business, and there is at least a strong case for supposing that the material was readily available to Tacitus in the *acta senatus*), whereas he does not present the view of the Jews. Perhaps Tacitus, because of his general prejudice against

Jews, distrusted Josephus because he was a Jew and therefore refused to use him as a source. Or perhaps he regarded as more unbiased the pagan Greek writers he employed, because he found in them, both explicitly and implicitly, comments both positive and negative about the Jews, whereas Josephus was more one-sided.

Granted that the account of Jewish origins that Tacitus prefers is dependent, in part, on Lysimachus, we have asked why Tacitus refrains from reproducing some of the most scurrilous elements in Lysimachus's account. The impression with which we are left is that, hostile as his feelings are toward the Jews, Tacitus does retain enough of his historical conscience to avoid being totally swayed by prejudice or that he seeks to give credibility to his account by pretending to be more evenhanded. It may well be that the statements in Tacitus that are favorable to the Jews should not be interpreted as "pro-Jewish" in view of such a broad horizon of historical, mythological, cultural, and geographical traditions as he presents. There can be no doubt, however, that Tacitus's account does contain a number of positive elements about the Jews; and although these are most likely not Tacitus's own views but those of his sources, the fact is that Tacitus, who is, in general, highly selective in his use of sources, does include them, despite some hostile "packaging." From this and from the widespread success of Jewish proselytism, we can infer that some of Tacitus's sources thought well of the Jews and that their views crept into Tacitus's account.

6. The Importance for Christianity of the Ancient Jewish Connection

The importance of the antiquity that the pagans were ready to grant to the Jews may be seen in the decision of early Christianity to stress its continuity with Judaism. After all, the gulf between Judaism and classical Christianity is really much wider than is generally conceded. Not only does classical Christianity differ in creed, i.e., in believing that Jesus was the Messiah, that he was divine, that he died for man's sins, that salvation can come only through accepting Jesus, and in deed, i.e., in not accepting the Halakhic (legal) basis, whether in the written or in the oral Torah, so central to classical Judaism, but Christianity differs also in its very essence. Jews historically have defined themselves as a people, a nation, a family, whence we can understand the Talmudic formulation (*Qiddushin* 68b) defining the born Jew as one who has a Jewish mother (a biological rather than a credal definition); religion is an accoutrement of the nation. It is not a coincidence that at the very time when Christianity was born Judaism fought no fewer than three wars—in 66–74, 115–17, and 132–

35—to fulfill the crucial national aspect of this definition. Christianity, on the other hand, is the first "pure" *religion* of the ancient world; it would have been inconceivable before 586 B.C.E., the beginning of the Jewish Diaspora, when the destruction of the kingdom of Judah meant that Jews had lost their nationalistic base. True, the Phoenicians had a diaspora before then, as did the Greeks, but their colonies developed their own nation-religions.

The attack on Christianity in pagan literature was on two fronts: First, it was the first religion devoid of a nationalistic connection; and second, it was new and had no real roots in the past. In effect, the Christians had severed many of their links both with their pagan and their Jewish past. The pagans, as we see in the comments of the third-century Porphyry (quoted in Eusebius, *Praeparatio Evangelica* 1.2.2) and the fourth-century Julian (*Contra Galilaeos* 238 A), could understand and appreciate the loyalty of the Jews to an ancient ancestral tradition. But, as Porphyry asked, "How can men fail to be in every way impious and atheistical who have apostasized from those ancestral gods by whom every nation and every state is sustained?" It was only by insisting that Christianity was a continuation, and indeed a logical climax, of Judaism, with its legacy and respectability of antiquity, that Origen was able to meet these charges, just as Eusebius was later to do in his *Praeparatio Evangelica*.

In Josephus's treatise, Manetho and his successors had attempted to deny Judaism's legitimacy by attacking the national origins of the Jews; Celsus, in his treatise *Alethes Logos* ("True Doctrine"), as cited by Origen in his reply, was not much concerned with the fine points of Christian theology; rather, he had attempted to undermine Christianity's legitimacy by arguing that the Christians did not have continuity with Judaism, that their laws had no traditional sanction, and that therefore they lacked national legitimacy.[71] Indeed, if Christianity had gone the way of the Marcionites and had disdained the connection with the Jewish Scriptures, Celsus's charges would have prevailed. The only way that Origen was able to establish Christianity's authenticity was by giving it a historical basis, and the only historical basis was through demonstrating continuity with Judaism and through emphasizing that Christianity marked a religious—Celsus would call it a philosophic—revolt against Judaism, not a break with the Jewish people. Hence Origen had to reply not merely to the external attack of a Celsus but also to the internal attack of a Marcion; and this meant, in effect, that he had to do what Josephus had done in his treatise *Against Apion*, namely to defend the Judaism so crucial to Christianity's credibility. And yet he was confronted with a dilemma, because if he defended Judaism too well the question might well be put to him why Christianity had departed from its Jewish origin.

7. THE IMPORTANCE OF THE ANTIQUITY OF THE
JEWS AS SEEN BY ORIGEN

The third-century church father Origen's defense of Christianity against
the attack of the pagan Celsus is unique among Origen's works in being
directed self-consciously at a pagan audience, though the fact that Origen spends more time attacking paganism than in explaining Christianity
may indicate that part of his audience consisted of Christians who were
on the point of relapse. We may wonder why he seems to go out of his
way to avoid attacking Judaism,[72] though he certainly does attack it in
his other works, notably in his commentary on the Gospel of John. This
reluctance to attack Judaism seems all the more remarkable in view of
his citation of the charge by Celsus's Jew (1.32)[73] that Jesus was born of
an adulterous union.[74] In fact, he even glorifies Judaism, noting how
much Jews and Christians have in common in that they share the belief
in the divine inspiration of the Bible, and this despite the admission that
the Christians do not observe the commandments of the Law and dis-
agree as to the interpretation of the text. Indeed, in answering Celsus's
charges, Origen constantly couples the Christians and the Jews, emphasizing their common theology and morality. One would think that when
Celsus charges that the Jews learned circumcision from the Egyptians
(1.22) Origen would respond by dissociating the Christians from circumcision altogether; but instead he surprisingly defends the originality
of the Jews and then seeks to divert the discussion: "However, it is not my
task here to explain the meaning of circumcision, which began with
Abraham and was stopped by Jesus, as he did not wish his disciples to do
the same. For it is not now the right time to explain his teaching on this
matter, but rather to endeavor to destroy the accusation brought by
Celsus against the doctrine of the Jews."

For Celsus it is axiomatic that nothing can be both new and true (he
apparently does not see the fallacy that everything was once new), and
that consequently Christianity, as a new religion, cannot be true.[75] In the
eyes of Celsus, "ancient" is a synonym for "wise," as we can see from his
statement (1.14) that "there is an ancient doctrine [ἀρχαῖος λόγος, presumably equivalent to the ἀληθὴς λόγος, which is the title of Celsus's
treatise] which has existed from the beginning, which has always been
maintained by the wisest nations and cities and wise men." Indeed,
Celsus himself (4.14) is quoted as saying very proudly that he has "nothing new to say but only ancient doctrine." Consequently, it is not surprising that early Christian apologists tried so hard to establish that
Christians embodied the most ancient and hence authoritative tradition
and that Greek culture depended on it. In fact, even a casual reading of
the Christian apologists of the second and third centuries shows how

preoccupied they were with attempting to prove the antiquity, and hence the superiority, of Christianity, as compared with pagan culture.[76]

It is significant that in the only two instances where Origen (1.16, 4.11) cites Josephus's treatise *On the Antiquity of the Jews* (i.e., *Against Apion*) by name it is to emphasize the antiquity of the Jews. In the first passage (1.16), as we have noted, he expresses surprise that Celsus mentions the Odrysians, Samothracians, Eleusinians, and Hyperboreans (all of whom are remarkable for their obscurity) as among the most ancient and wise nations and yet does not include the Jews. As proof of the antiquity of the Jews, Origen remarks that there are many treatises in circulation among the Egyptians, Phoenicians, and Greeks, but that he regards it as superfluous to quote them. He then refers those interested in examining the evidence to read Josephus's two books *On the Antiquity of the Jews*, which, he correctly declares, contain a considerable collection of writers who testify to the antiquity of the Jews. He likewise directs the reader to the treatise Λόγος πρὸς ῞Ελληνας ("Discourse to the Greeks") by the second-century Christian Tatian, who, he says, quotes with great learning historians who have written about the antiquity of the Jews and of Moses. Origen concludes by remarking that Celsus lists the Galactophagi of Homer, the Druids of Gaul, and the Getae (another group of obscure nations) as very wise and ancient peoples who believe doctrines akin to those of the Jews and yet rejects the claims of the Jews to antiquity and wisdom. Apparently Celsus went to the length (4.33–34) of rejecting the Jewish claim to antiquity that was based on descent from the patriarchs, whom he maligns as sorcerers and deceivers; uneducated and stupid people had accepted such Jewish claims, he asserts.

Celsus's motive in impugning the antiquity of the Jews, says Origen, is his desire to undermine the claim to antiquity of Christianity, "which depended on the Jews." Indeed, Celsus's attack on the origin of the Jews is paralleled by his attack on the origin of Jesus (1.28, 32; as put into the mouth of a Jew), who is presented as the bastard son of a Roman soldier. On the other hand, just as Josephus, not merely in the treatise *Against Apion* but also in his masterwork the *Antiquities*, realizes the importance of establishing the legitimacy of the Jewish people, and consequently of their customs, through proving the antiquity of their history, so also in his *Against Celsus* Origen realized the importance of stressing the Christians' historical, revelatory, and literary continuity with Judaism and consequently their legitimacy.

Because, as we have noted, Celsus equates (1.14) antiquity and wisdom, Origen (4.11) stresses the antiquity of Moses. In particular, he notes that "certain Greek writers" indicate that he lived in the time of Inachus the son [he means the father] of Phoroneus.[77] We may note that among these writers are Ptolemy priest of Mendes (cited by Tatian, *Ora-*

tio ad Graecos 38), Tertullian (*Apology* 19), Clement of Alexandria (*Stromata* 1.101.5), Pseudo-Justin *(Cohortatio ad Graecos* 9), and even, amazingly enough, the arch-enemy of the Jews, Apion (cited by Africanus, in turn cited by Eusebius, *Praeparatio Evangelica* 10.10.16.490B).[78] The last, as we have seen, admits that the Exodus occurred in the time of Inachus. This would concede tremendous antiquity to the Jews, much greater than does the Bible itself, inasmuch as Inachus was said to have been the son of Titans, and hence of the third generation of the Greek gods.

In summary, whereas Celsus had sought to undermine the national legitimacy of the Christians by insisting that Christianity was a new religion that had severed its links with Judaism, Origen might well have gone the way of the Marcionites in severing all ties with Judaism and with the Hebrew Scriptures, but he realized that the result of such an approach would have been to fall prey to the charges of Celsus that Christianity was an upstart religion. Consequently, Origen felt that it was particularly important to establish the antiquity of the Jewish people, with whom the Christians claimed to have a direct link. Christological theology was not of paramount concern to Celsus in his polemic; rather, the attack focused on Jesus the innovator, whose religion lacks respectability because it has no continuity in tradition. By maximizing the common heritage and beliefs of Judaism and Christianity and by minimizing the issues that separated the religions, Origen sought to blunt the attacks of his critics. Hence, we see how important to early Christianity was the concession made by the pagans on the issue of the antiquity of the Jews.

CHAPTER 7

THE ATTRACTIONS OF THE JEWS: THE CARDINAL VIRTUES

1. Early Greek Writers on the Wisdom of the Jews

If the Jews were viewed in antiquity with the disdain and contempt that most scholars claim, we must somehow explain how during the very same period they attracted, as we shall see, so many proselytes and "sympathizers." The attack on the Jews by later pagan intellectuals was, as we have noted, not merely on the ground of their exclusiveness but also their alleged failure to embody the cardinal virtues. And yet the early contacts between Greeks and Jews, prior to Manetho (ca. 270 B.C.E.), led to praise of the Jews for their espousal of the very same four cardinal virtues.[1]

Of the four cardinal virtues—wisdom, courage, temperance, and justice—the wisdom of the Jews was most admired. The semilegendary Pythagoras, who is said to have lived in the sixth century B.C.E., had a reputation so great that Josephus can confidently declare (*Against Apion* 1.162), with no fear of contradiction, that for wisdom and piety he was ranked above all other philosophers, presumably including even Socrates and Plato. Indeed, Plato (*Republic* 10.600A), who was himself probably the most important single intellectual factor in the process of Hellenization in the East during the Hellenistic period,[2] remarks that the followers of Pythagoras have a certain distinction above others. His contemporary Isocrates (*Busiris* 28) remarks that even now (i.e., approximately 390 B.C.E.) persons who profess to be followers of his teaching are more admired even when silent than are those who have the greatest renown for eloquence. Hence, it is particularly impressive that Josephus (*Against Apion* 1.162) can declare with confidence, in an apologetic work where he had to be particularly careful in his claims, that Pythagoras not only knew of the institutions of the Jews but was to a very great degree an admirer (ζηλωτής, "enthusiast," "emulator," "adherent," "imitator") of them.[3] As evidence Josephus (*Against Apion* 1.163–64) cites Hermippus, who lived about 200 B.C.E. and had a reputation as a careful historian and who notes three precepts Pythagoras adopted from "Jews and Thracians," namely not to pass a certain spot on which an ass had collapsed,[4] to abstain from thirst-producing water,[5] and to avoid all calumny (βλασφημίας, "slander," "defamation").[6] Hermippus is then quoted as saying,

"In practicing and repeating these precepts he [i.e., Pythagoras] was imitating and appropriating the doctrines of Jews and Thracians. In fact, it is actually said[7] that that great man introduced many points of Jewish law into his philosophy."[8] Origen (*Against Celsus* 1.15), in the third century, generally a careful scholar, goes even further and, omitting the reference to the Thracians, declares that according to Hermippus Pythagoras brought his own philosophy from the Jews to the Greeks.[9] In any case, Isocrates (*Busiris* 28) brings Pythagoras into juxtaposition with the Near East[10] when he notes that on a visit to Egypt Pythagoras became a student of the Egyptian religion and thereafter brought philosophy to the Greeks.

Pythagoras's indebtedness to the Jews is confirmed by the statement of Antonius Diogenes, who lived at the end of the first century C.E. and who declares (cited in Porphyry, *Vita Pythagorae* 11) that Pythagoras visited the Egyptians, Arabs, Chaldaeans, and Hebrews. From them he is said to have learned the exact knowledge of dreams—a special skill, we may remark, that was particularly associated with the biblical Joseph.[11]

That the Jews in the third century B.C.E. had a reputation as a philosophical people would seem to fit into this picture connecting Pythagoras, with his great reputation in philosophy, and the Jews. Moreover, his introduction of many aspects of Jewish law into his philosophy would seem, from a Greek point of view, to compliment the Jews tremendously for their wisdom and to lead to the conclusion that Jewish law is consonant with the highest ideals of Greek thought. We may also note that Pythagoras's condemnation of the use of images (cited in Diogenes Laertius, *Lives of the Philosophers* 1.6–9) was ascribed to Jewish influence. We may suggest that word had spread of the tremendous impression made on the great Aristotle (whether the meeting was historical or not) by the learned Jew whom, according to Clearchus (quoted in Josephus, *Against Apion* 1.176–83), he had met in Asia Minor and that this wisdom was said to have retroactively influenced Pythagoras also.

As early as the sixth century B.C.E., as we have noted, the Greek poet-philosopher Xenophanes (fragment 10) had criticized Homer, who was, in effect, together with Hesiod, the Bible of the Greeks, for ascribing to the gods "all deeds that are a shame and a disgrace among men—stealing, adultery, and fraud." Mortals," he says, "seem to have begotten gods who have their own dress and voice and form." His henotheistic conclusion was that "there is one god, supreme among gods and men, resembling mortals neither in form nor in mind. He is all eye, all mind, and all ear" (fragments 19–20). This attack on the traditional polytheism and this promulgation of an intellectual monism continue with Xenophanes' pupil Parmenides and with the latter's spiritual heirs, Socrates and Plato. It is not surprising, therefore, that the philosophers, in this attack, should have found allies in the Jews.

Three contemporaries, in the generation after Aristotle's death—the historian Megasthenes and the philosophers Theophrastus[12] and Clearchus of Soli—speak of the Jews, as we have noted, as being philosophers by birth. These writers found in Jewish law a kind of correspondence with the laws of Plato (*Laws*, Book 12), particularly in the concept of the contemplation of the heavens and the rejection of anthropomorphism.[13] Megasthenes (fragment 41, quoted in Clement of Alexandria, *Stromata* 1.15.72.5), who was probably the source of the statement of Clearchus,[14] remarks that the same wisdom found in the old Greek philosophers was also to be seen in the doctrines held by the Hindu Brahmans (whom he had actually visited) and the Jews. Clearchus (cited in Josephus, *Against Apion* 1.179), as we have noted, goes one step further and quotes Aristotle as stating that the Jews are actually descendants of Indian philosophers. The compliment is all the greater in view of Aristotle's statement (*Politics* 1.2.1252B7–8) that it is fitting that Greeks should rule over barbarians (that is, non-Greeks) because barbarians and slaves are by nature one. The compliment likewise takes force from the advice that Aristotle (cited in Plutarch, *De Alexandri Magni Fortuna aut Virtute* 6.329B) is alleged to have given to his pupil Alexander the Great to have the same attitude toward barbarians as toward animals and plants.[15] The implication in all three authors is that all Jews are philosophers or at least are descended from philosophers. Indeed Mélèze-Modrzejewski[16] contends that monotheism itself implied a philosophy. Theophrastus and Clearchus actually supply evidence that Jews are philosophers, namely, in the case of the former, that they converse with each other about the divine during their sacrifices, and, in the case of the latter, that a Jew impressed Aristotle, whom Clearchus quotes, with his learning, endurance, and sobriety.

Theophrastus's phrase (quoted in Porphyry, *De Abstinentia* 2.26) "inasmuch as they [i.e., the Jews] are philosophers by birth"[17] indicates that the pure notions of the Jews with respect to the nature of G-d—which was with the Greeks the chief and highest subject of philosophy—were widely known among intellectuals.[18] That, according to Theophrastus, the Jews converse about the divine (τὸ θεῖον) may well have led him to his conclusion that the Jews are philosophers by birth, inasmuch as in the pre-Socratic systems the term τὸ θεῖον denoted the philosophical concept of the one highest being that governs the world, in contrast to the popular belief in a multitude of mythical deities.[19] That the masses participated in theological discussions—probably, it has been conjectured, in the synagogues, which had come into being several centuries earlier—led Theophrastus to call the Jews philosophers by birth and made them unique in his eyes. That Theophrastus then remarks that the Jews make observations of the stars[20] would be a tremendous tribute to them, ascribing to them knowledge of astronomy, the science that was the most popular of the four branches of mathematics in Hellenistic times[21] and one of the key subjects in the higher education of the philosopher-kings in Plato's ideal state (*Republic* 7.528B–530B). Moreover, in the eyes of the Greek philosophers the orderly motion of the heavenly bodies constituted one of the chief demonstrations of the existence of G-d; and hence a people who systematically observed the heavens were truly philosophers in that they were constantly and scientifically confirming the existence of G-d.[22]

A contemporary of Theophrastus, Clearchus, and Megasthenes, the historian Hecataeus of Abdera presents an idealized portrait of the government of the Jews, remarking (quoted in Diodorus 40.3.5) in obvious admiration that superior wisdom and virtue are the qualities sought in the high priest who rules the Jews. He speaks (quoted in Josephus, *Against Apion* 1.187) in obvious praise of a chief priest named Ezechias, whom he describes as a man "highly esteemed by his countrymen" and an "intellectual" (τὴν ψυχὴν οὐκ ἀνόητος, "not unintelligent in soul").[23] In view of the great premium placed by the ancients on ability in oratory, Hecataeus's description of Ezechias as an able speaker (λέγειν δυνατός) is a great compliment.

2. LATER GREEK AND ROMAN WRITERS ON THE WISDOM OF THE JEWS

Inasmuch as the Bible embodied, more than any other work, the wisdom of the Jews, it is significant that the Pythagorean philosopher Ocellus Lucanus (*De Universi Natura* 45–46), in the second century B.C.E., appears to paraphrase Genesis 1:28, that man should be fruitful and multiply and fill the earth.[24] We have noted the tremendous tribute paid to the Bible by the first-century C.E. pseudo-Longinus (9.9), who paraphrases some of the opening verses of Genesis as an example of the sublime style. There is likewise reason to believe that Pseudo-Ecphantus (cited in Stobaeus 4.6.22), who lived during the first or second century C.E., contains a reminiscence of Genesis 2:7 in referring to the fall of man from his pure nature by his transmigration to the earth; man, he says, would hardly have been released from this condition save that some divine spirit attached him to the Eternal Being. Likewise, in another passage (cited in Stobaeus 4.7.64) he seems to be indebted to Genesis 1:26–27 in referring to the creation of man in the image of G-d.[25]

In antiquity the key to the greatness of a nation, it was thought, was its leadership, as we see notably in the writings of Thucydides. Hence, when the historian Pompeius Trogus (quoted in Justin, *Historiae Philippicae* 36.2.6–10), at the end of the first century B.C.E., pays enormous tribute to Joseph, referring to his extraordinary talent (*excellens ingenium*) and his shrewd (*sollerti*, "skillful," "clever," "ingenious," "inventive") nature (*ingenio*, "talent"), this is a tribute to the Jewish people as a whole and surely an answer to the charge of Apollonius Molon (cited in Josephus, *Against Apion* 2.148) that the Jews are the most untalented of all barbarians. In particular, Trogus states in obvious praise that Joseph made himself master of the arts of magic, whereby within a short time he found great favor with the king. Magic in antiquity, we may remark, served as a bridge between intellectuals and the masses, as we can see from the writings of Apuleius in the second century and from the magical papyri. It served a practical purpose, as we can see from the enormous number of curse tablets that have been found, and a philosophical purpose, in that, according to Apuleius (*Apology* 27, 31), such noted philosophers as Anaxagoras, Leucippus, Democritus, Epicurus, and even the revered Pythagoras had been called magicians because they explored "the origins and elements of material things."

Joseph's wisdom is seen particularly in his interpretation of dreams, a skill the Greeks and Romans especially appreciated. Indeed, dreams and prophecy were regarded as closely related in antiquity; and they, together with omens, signs, and portents, are said to be the means by which the demonic communicated with man.[26] Pompeius Trogus (quoted in Justin, *Historiae Philippicae* 36, *Epitoma* 2.6–10) connects Joseph's extraordinary ability (*excellens ingenium*, his shrewd nature (*sollerti ingenio*), his mastery of the art of magic, and his extreme sagacity (*sagacissimus*, "most shrewd," "keen," "intellectually quick") in interpreting prodigies with his being the first to establish the science (*intellegentiam*) of interpreting dreams, so that nothing of divine or human law—the supreme praise, especially for the law-conscious Romans—seemed to have been unknown to him. In closing his encomium, he states that his admonitions seemed to proceed not from a mortal but from a god.[27]

Because of the great importance attached to dreams in antiquity, as we see, for example, in Homer (*Odyssey* 19.560–66), in Plato (*Phaedo* 60E–61B, *Republic* 9.571–72), and in Virgil (*Aeneid* 6.893–96), and because, according to the standard treatise on dreams, the second-century C.E. Artemidorus's *Oneirocritica*, a morally pure soul can discern the relationship between dreams and the larger order of the universe, Joseph's role in inventing this science was a tremendous tribute. Indeed, a healthy soul has the power of divination, as Cicero declared (*De Divinatione* 1.23.82).

Among the Romans the exclusiveness of the Jews' monotheism, as we have noted, aroused bitter attacks against the Jews on the part of many intellectuals, particularly the Stoics, who felt that they lacked the broad

liberalism toward other religions that was a hallmark of the official
Roman imperial policy. But it was precisely this pure monotheism that is
praised by Varro (who is here clearly echoing Strabo [16.2.35.760–61])[28]
in Augustine's *City of G-d* (4.31.2): "He [Varro] says . . . that the ancient
Romans worshipped the gods without an image for more than 170 years.
'And if the custom,' he says, 'had remained until the present day, the gods
would now be worshipped with greater purity.'" To support this opinion,
he cites as a witness, among others, the Jewish people; nor does he hesitate to conclude this passage by saying of those who first set up images of
the gods for the people that they have both taken away fear from their
fellow-citizens and added error." Because of the high regard throughout
antiquity for his learning and versatility,[29] Varro might quite conceivably
have influenced other intellectuals, whose works are now lost, to look on
the simplicity of Jewish monotheism as reminiscent of their own golden
age, when the Roman religion was imageless. Varro's view would be especially appealing because it so closely parallels Stoic terminology.[30]

That, indeed, Varro's admiration for the pure monotheism of the Jews
was not isolated can be inferred even from Tacitus (*Histories* 5.5.4), who
thus contrasts the Jews with other peoples: "The Egyptians worship very
many animals and images of composite creatures; the Jews conceive of a
single Deity with their minds alone. They regard as impious those who
fashion images of gods in human shape out of perishable materials. Their
G-d is supreme and eternal, neither capable of imitation nor of death."
Tacitus, to be sure, makes these remarks without comment; but the notion of a Supreme Being who is eternal and indestructible is found in many
of the pre-Socratics, Plato, and Aristotle. These, then, were ideas widely
held by the philosophers, several of whom, such as Theophrastus and
Varro, had seen the similarity with the doctrines held by the Jews, whom
they admired for the purity of this conception.

Even those intellectuals who were critical of the Jews made remarks
that might have been construed to concede their virtues. Thus, as we
have noted, the highly influential rhetorician, Apollonius Molon, the
teacher of Cicero, criticized the Jews (cited in *Against Apion* 2.148) as the
most untalented (ἀφυεστάτους, "most lacking in natural talent," "most
witless") of all barbarians and the only people who have contributed no
useful invention to civilization. And yet lack of inventiveness is clearly a
laudatory trait in Herodotus (2.142), where we read that it was the boast
of the Egyptians, whom he so admires, that throughout their history of
11,340 years no change had taken place in their nature, manners, or customs. Similarly, Plato's ideal state, being perfect, admits of no change;
and indeed any change that does occur (*Republic* 8.546A) is degeneration.
Moreover, we may remark, Apollonius's charge might have proved ineffective, because it would couple the Jews with the much admired Spar-

tans (Plato, *Republic* 8.544C),[31] who, as we hear in Thucydides' account of the Lacedaemonian Congress (1.70.2), merely keep what they have and devise nothing new, whereas the Athenians are given to innovation (νεωτεροποιοί). As Plutarch (*Lycurgus* 27.4) notes, "From novelty in principle follows novelty in decisions, something which is bound to give rise to many experiences and policies destructive to the harmony, as it were, of the established government." For a period of five hundred years, he says, Sparta continued to be the leading city of all Greece; and throughout this period, at least in the popular imagination, its people strictly observed Lycurgus's laws and made no alterations at all in them.

Moreover, the Jewish system of education and level of learning won considerable commendation not only from Aristotle and Theophrastus, as noted above, but also from the otherwise anti-Jewish Stoic philosopher Seneca the Younger, who admits (quoted in Augustine, *City of G-d* 6.11) that the Jews "know the reasons for their rites, while most other peoples go through a ritual not knowing why they do so." Seneca here has just expressed surprise that the providence of G-d should have permitted the Jews to conquer the world through conversions to their religion and yet is forced to admit that, in contrast to other peoples, they know why they perform their rites, whereas others do things by rote.[32]

3. ALLEGED GRAECO-JEWISH HISTORIANS BEFORE JOSEPHUS ON THE WISDOM OF THE JEWS

That the historian Eupolemus (quoted in Clement of Alexandria, *Stromata* 1.23.153.4) in the second century B.C.E. can declare that Moses was the first wise man (σοφόν) must have been a source of tremendous pride to the Jews living in the Hellenistic diaspora. Although most scholars[33] assume that Eupolemus was a Jew, Josephus (*Against Apion* 1.218) very definitely regarded him as a pagan (together with Demetrius of Phalerum and Philo the Elder), as we can see from the excuses he offers for errors on the ground of Eupolemus's "inability to follow quite accurately the meaning of our records," though Eupolemus is exceptional in his approximation of the truth.[34] If indeed he was a non-Jew, such praise for the Jews from him would be all the more noteworthy.[35] Furthermore, no greater compliment could be given to a nation, especially by those, such as the Romans, who placed such a premium on their system of laws, than to assert (quoted in Eusebius, *Praeparatio Evangelica* 9.26.1) that it was Moses who first wrote down laws.

Pseudo-Eupolemus, who is generally thought to have lived in the Land of Israel during the middle of the second century B.C.E.,[36] speaks (quoted in Eusebius, *Praeparatio Evangelica* 9.17.3) of Abraham, the progenitor of the Israelites and the Samaritans alike, as excelling all men in nobility of birth and in wisdom. In particular, he ascribes to Abraham the discovery of astrology and Chaldean science (presumably astronomy), which had such importance and prestige in the ancient world. Indeed, Eusebius (*Praeparatio Evangelica* 9.17.4) quotes Pseudo-Eupolemus as saying that even the Phoenicians, who are viewed in antiquity as being so creative, learned from Abraham "the movements of the sun and moon, and everything else as well." Abraham is likewise said (according to Eusebius, *Praeparatio Evangelica* 9.17.8) to have taught many new things to the Egyptian priests, so ancient and so learned, including, in particular, astrology.

As to the historian Artapanus, who lived, it is thought, in the second century B.C.E., even a glance at the fragments that have survived will indicate their syncretistic nature. In particular, it is hard to believe that an observant Jew could have written, with obvious pride, that Joseph established temples (presumably pagan) in Egypt (as cited in Eusebius, *Praeparatio Evangelica* 9.23.4) and that Moses (as cited in Eusebius, *Praeparatio Evangelica* 9.27.4) became the teacher of Orpheus and that he consecrated cats, dogs, ibises, and bulls as gods (as cited in Eusebius, *Praeparatio Evangelica* 9.27.4, 9, 12). Holladay finds, however, that the fragments are so thoroughly committed to the glorification of Jewish heroes and Jewish history that a pagan origin is impossible.[37] But of course this presupposes that non-Jews would not glorify Jewish history and Judaism; and we have cited evidence that there were non-Jews who did praise Jews and glorify Judaism. If, then, Artapanus is indeed a non-Jew, his tribute to the originality and importance of the Jewish contribution to civilization would be all the more effective.

We find in Artapanus (quoted in Eusebius, *Praeparatio Evangelica* 9.18.1) other statements praising the forefathers of the Jews. Thus, in a remark very similar to the one we have noted in Pseudo-Eupolemus, he mentions that Abraham taught astrology to the Egyptian pharaoh. Moreover, inasmuch as one of the charges against the Jews was lack of inventiveness, Artapanus is careful to point out (quoted in Eusebius, *Praeparatio Evangelica* 9.23.3) that Joseph, living in what was undoubtedly the most advanced civilization in his day, discovered methods of measurement and consequently was greatly beloved by the Egyptians.

The historian pseudo-Hecataeus, who most likely dates from the second century B.C.E., praised the Jews' wisdom so highly that Herennius Philo of Byblus (cited in Origen, *Against Celsus* 1.15) expressed doubt that the work was genuine.[38] Moreover, pseudo-Hecataeus illustrates the intelligence of the Jews by relating a story (quoted in Josephus, *Against Apion* 1.201–4) of a Jewish mercenary bowman named Mosollamus, who, noting that the army in which he served was being held up by a seer taking the auspices, proceeded to shoot the bird. To the obvious approval of pseudo-Hecataeus, he then commented that a bird unable to provide for its own safety could hardly provide sound information about the march.

In sum, several historians praise the Jews—and, in particular, their founders, Abraham, Joseph, and Moses—for the quality intelligentsia in antiquity most admired, namely wisdom, and this would surely have garnered admiration for the Jews.

4. PHILO ON THE WISDOM OF THE JEWS

Plato had equated wisdom (σοφία, *Republic* 4.428B) with prudence (φρόνησις, *Laws* 1.631C), whereas Aristotle defines wisdom as dealing with things divine (*Metaphysics* 1.2.983A6–7) and prudence as dealing with things human (*Nicomachean Ethics* 6.5.1140A24–B30).[39] The Stoics (Sextus Empiricus, *Adversus Physicos* 1.13) define wisdom as combining the Aristotelian definitions of wisdom and prudence. Philo, apparently realizing the tremendous prestige of Plato, Aristotle, and the Stoics, combines all three in his definition of wisdom, while claiming at the same time that this wisdom was embodied in the Pentateuch (*Legum Allegoria* 3.15.46).[40] Consequently, the Jews gain through the study of the Pentateuch what the Greeks acquire through the study of philosophy. As Philo (*De Virtutibus* 10.65) puts it, "What the disciples of the most excellent philosophy gain from its teaching, the Jews gain from their customs and laws, that is to know the highest, the most ancient cause of all things, and to reject the delusion of created gods." Philo projects a progression: the culture of the schools (that is, the encyclical studies or the liberal arts) are the bond-servant of philosophy, which, in turn, is the servant of wisdom (*De Congressu Quaerendae Eruditionis Gratia* 14.79). Indeed, the Jews, he says (*Quaestiones in Genesin* 2.58), are a chosen race of men who are desirous of wisdom, which is embodied in the Pentateuch.

Philo apparently felt self-conscious about the implicit charge that the Jews lacked the wisdom of the Greeks. His answer to this is twofold: On the one hand, he asserts (*De Vita Mosis* 1.5.21–24), obviously without biblical basis, that Moses was taught by teachers imported from the neighboring countries, from the provinces of Egypt, and from Greece; but then, realizing that this would lead his readers to conclude that Moses' wisdom was thus indebted to foreigners, he quickly adds, clearly redolent of Plato's theory of ἀνάμνησις, that Moses seemed to be recollecting the wisdom he had known before his birth rather than to be learning from his instructors and that in any case within a short time he advanced beyond their capacities, as shown by his devising and propounding problems they could not easily solve. On the other hand, he asserts (*Quis Rerum Divinarum Heres* 43.214) that the pre-Socratic philosopher Heraclitus, whose greatness, as Philo here remarks, the Greeks celebrated so loudly, claimed as a new discovery his theory of opposites, whereas actually Moses had long before discovered this very concept, namely that opposites are formed from the same whole. Elsewhere (*Quaestiones in Genesin* 3.5), Philo goes even further in asserting that Heraclitus was not merely anticipated by Moses but that he (Heraclitus) actually plagiarized from the Torah "like a thief" (*Quaestiones in Genesin* 4.152).

Likewise, though to be sure he avoids a categorical statement, Philo suggests (*Quod Omnis Probus Liber Sit* 8.57) that the lawbook of the Jews, and in particular the story of Jacob and Esau, was the fountain from which the renowned Zeno, the founder of Stoicism, drew the idea that slavery, which men think is the worst of evils, is actually the best possible boon to the fool, because the loss of independence prevents him from transgressing without fear of punishment. Similarly, without explicitly stating that the Greek philosophers derived from the Pentateuch the idea that virtue is a state of happy feeling, Philo does remark (*De Mutatione Nominum* 31.167–68) that Moses had anticipated this insight. Likewise, Philo claims (*De Specialibus Legibus* 4.10.61) that it was from the tablets of Moses that some Greek legislators had copied the enactment that hearsay evidence should not be accepted. In short, some of the most profound wisdom of the Greeks had been anticipated by the Torah.

5. JOSEPHUS ON THE WISDOM OF THE JEWS

Josephus's *Antiquities*, as we can deduce from his prooemium (*Ant.* 1.10), was directed primarily to non-Jews for apologetic purposes, as we see from the precedent he cites for his work, namely, the translation of the Torah into Greek at the behest of King Ptolemy Philadelphus of Egypt. Apparently he realized that normally it is prohibited to teach the Torah to Gentiles (*Ḥagigah* 13a, *Sanhedrin* 59a). The fact that he asks (*Ant.* 1.9) whether any of the Greeks have been curious to learn "our" history and that he specifically declares (*Ant.* 1.5) that his work was undertaken in the belief that the whole Greek world would find it worthy of attention indicates that he was directing the *Antiquities* to pagans. Again, the boast at the end of the work (*Ant.* 20.262) that no one else would have been equal to the task of issuing so accurate a treatise for the Greeks (εἰς ῞Ελληνας) indicates that he directed the work to the non-Jewish world, because the term *Greeks* for Josephus is used in contrast to *Jews*.

We may note that through a number of extra-biblical additions Josephus stresses the wisdom of the Jews. Thus, he explains (*Ant.* 1.106) the longevity of the early patriarchs by declaring that G-d rewarded them with long life not only for their virtue (ἀρετήν) but also in order to promote the utility of their discoveries in astronomy and geometry.

In particular, we may cite his effective use of the figure of Abraham, who as the first "proselyte" is thus the father of proselytes, the foundation figure as their common father for both Jews and Gentiles, the example par excellence of the man who was able to break away from his previous beliefs and practices and to adopt the way of truth.[41] Thus, Abraham is portrayed as a philosopher whose logic is impeccable (*Ant.* 1.154), who is clever in understanding (*Ant.* 1.154, δεινὸς ὢν συνιέναι, a phrase reminiscent of Oedipus' φρονεῖν . . . δεινόν [Sophocles, *Oedipus Tyrannus*, 316]), and who is able to arrive at an original and unique proof of the existence of G-d (*Ant.* 1.156) from the irregularity of heavenly phenomena, in a form promulgated by the Greek philosophical schools, notably the Stoics.[42] Indeed, his hearers are termed ἀκροωμένοις (*Ant.* 1.154), a word used especially (e.g., Xenophon, *Symposium* 3.6) of those who listen to lectures in the philosophical schools.

In line with the prestige assigned by the Hellenistic Age to science[43]— both Plato and Isocrates, the leaders of the two chief opposing schools of education in the fourth century B.C.E., had emphasized the importance of mathematics not only for its practical value but also as a training for sharpening the mind[44]—Josephus presents Abraham as the one who taught the Egyptians the very sciences for which they later became so famous. Abraham graciously gives (χαρίζεται) them (*Ant.* 1.167) of his knowledge of arithmetic and transmits to them his lore about astronomy, a science of which the Egyptians had previously been ignorant (*Ant.* 1.168) and which was to become, as we have noted, the most popular of the four branches of mathematics in Hellenistic times[45]—the one that aroused the most curiosity because of the practical importance of astrology. Hence, it is Abraham's unselfishness in sharing his scientific knowledge with the Egyptians that, according to Josephus, is responsible for Greek knowledge of these fields, because the Greeks, in turn, borrowed from the Egyptians. Artapanus (quoted in Eusebius, *Praeparatio Evangelica* 9.18.1), as we have seen, had declared long before Josephus that Abraham had taught Pharaoh astrology; but in Josephus it is not Pharaoh but the Egyptian philosophers and scientists whom Abraham instructs, and far from hoarding his knowledge, and with an internationalist scholarly outlook, he shares it cheerfully and freely with his fellow philosophers and scientists. In addition, the true scientist must show his openmindedness by being willing to change his mind if honestly convinced by others. This quality is exhibited, in an extra-biblical addition (*Ant.* 1.161), by Abraham, who visits Egypt not merely, as indicated by the Bible (Gen 12:10), in order to obtain food because of the famine in

Canaan, but also to hear what the famed Egyptian priests said about their gods. His intention, characteristic of all who are truly wise, is either to adopt their views if he finds them more excellent than his own or to convert the Egyptians if his views should prove superior. The picture is reminiscent (although the Jewish visitor is more favorably presented) first of Solon, the wise Athenian (Plato, *Timaeus* 22A), who discovered when he visited Egypt that neither he nor any other Greek had any knowledge of antiquity worth speaking of, and second of the pre-Socratic philosophers, such as Pythagoras, who allegedly visited Egypt to become acquainted with the science and the other esoteric lore of the Egyptians.[46]

Similarly, one of the virtues both of Abraham's sons (*Ant.* 1.238) and of Jacob's children (*Ant.* 2.7) is that they are clever in understanding (δεινοὶ συνιέναι, the same phrase that is used of Abraham, *Ant.* 1.154). Likewise, Isaac is praised (*Ant.* 1.261) for the reasonable calculation (εὐγνώμονι λογισμῷ) he exhibited in settling the dispute over wells with Abimelech's shepherds. Jacob exercises wisdom (σοφία) and intelligence (διάνοια) in understanding the meaning of Joseph's dreams (*Ant.* 2.15).

In turn, Joseph's tremendous understanding (σύνεσιν ἱκανώτατος, *Ant.* 2.80) recommends him to Pharaoh; and in view of his incredible intelligence (πρὸς τὸ παράδοξον τῆς συνέσεως, *Ant.* 2.91), he is given a name by Pharaoh signifying "Discoverer of Secrets." Indeed it is surely significant of Josephus's emphasis on Joseph's wisdom that he uses no fewer than six different synonyms—σοφία, σύνεσις, δεξιότης, φρόνησις, φρόνημα, and λογισμός—in referring to Joseph's wisdom. Because of the quality of wisdom and understanding that Josephus ascribes to Joseph over and over again (*Ant.* 2.9, 46, 87) and his use of φρόνημα (2.40, "reason," "intelligence," "intellect," "thinking") and λογισμός ("skillful calculation," "cool and sensible reflection," "reasonable and deliberate thought"), Greek readers would identify in Joseph the influence of Greek culture and concepts. Indeed, in his brief extra-biblical eulogy of Joseph, the first quality Josephus (*Ant.* 2.198) singles out, after making the general statement that Joseph was a man of admirable virtue, is that he directed all affairs by the dictates of reason (λογισμός).

In view of the importance attached in antiquity to the interpretation of dreams, which we have noted above, it is not surprising that Josephus has notably expanded the accounts of Joseph's dreams.[47] Furthermore it is in interpreting the dreams of the butler, the baker, and Pharaoh that Joseph most clearly shows his sagacity. Thus, we are told (*Ant.* 2.63) in an addition to the biblical narrative, that the butler, as a result of forming a high opinion of the sagacity of his fellow prisoner, Joseph, recounted his dream to him. He then (*Ant.* 2.65) asks Joseph, if he is gifted with any understanding (συνέσεως), to explain the significance of his dream. Hence, we see that the butler assumes that a wise man will ipso facto be adept in interpreting dreams. Likewise, when Pharaoh calls for Joseph to analyze his dreams, it is Joseph's extreme sagacity (σύνεσιν ἱκανώτατος) (*Ant.* 2.80) that had been attested to by the butler and led to the recall of Joseph from prison.

Moses (*Ant.* 4.328), as we shall see at length in our next chapter, is likewise eulogized as having surpassed in understanding (συνέσει) all men who ever lived. Moreover, when introducing Joshua (*Ant.* 3.49) for the first time as Moses' hand-picked adjutant, Josephus, in an extra-biblical addition, singles out among his qualities his great gift of intellect (νοῆσαι, "to perceive," "understand"). Inasmuch as the ability to persuade is intimately connected with intellect, as we see in Thucydides' portrait of Pericles (2.60.5), it is significant that Josephus, in an extra-biblical comment, remarks that Joshua (*Ant.* 5.118) possessed supreme skill in expounding his ideas to the multitude clearly.

Again, when Josephus first makes mention of Saul (*Ant.* 6.45) he describes him as gifted with both mind and understanding (τό τε φρόνημα καὶ τὴν διάνοιαν) surpassing his outward physical advantages. Likewise, David (*Ant.* 7.158) is praised by his relatives and servants for his wisdom and understanding (σοφίαν καὶ τὴν διάνοιαν), the latter being the same word that Josephus had used with respect to Saul; and David is described (*Ant.* 7.391) as being most apt in perceiving and understanding (νοῆσαί τε καὶ συνιδεῖν) the course of future events. David, in turn, prays (*Ant.* 7.381) that his son Solomon may have a sound and just mind (διάνοιαν). Josephus then praises Solomon (*Ant.* 8.34) for his G-dlike understanding (θείαν διάνοιαν) and for mentally grasping with ease the ingenious problems set for him by the Queen of Sheba and solving them more quickly than anyone would have expected (*Ant.* 8.167).[48]

A similar honesty in acknowledging ignorance, such as was characteristic of Socrates, and in eagerness to learn from others, may be seen in the extra-biblical addition (*Ant.* 8.146) that Josephus cites from Menander of Ephesus's Greek translation of Tyrian records, to the effect that Solomon acknowledged that a certain young Tyrian lad named Abdemon, who always successfully solved the problems submitted to him by Solomon, had greater wisdom than he himself possessed. Josephus also (*Ant.* 8.148–49) quotes Dios, the historian of Phoenicia, as referring to an interchange of riddles between King Hiram of Phoenicia and Solomon and mentions that this same Abdemon not only solved Solomon's riddles but also was able to stump Solomon with some riddles that he himself proposed.

Furthermore, in another extra-biblical addition, Josephus (*Ant.* 10.51) praises Josiah for his wisdom (σοφία) and discernment (ἐπινοία). Finally, the disciplined pursuit of purification has brought Daniel in Josephus to the supreme achievement of the Graeco-Roman sage of the type found in Philostratus's *Life of Apollonius of Tyana*—the movement from human to divine wisdom.[49]

6. Second-, Third-, and Fourth-Century Writers on the Wisdom of the Jews

The reputation of the Jews for wisdom may be seen even in the writers who disparage them most. Thus, the satirist Juvenal, who presents some of the nastiest charges against the Jews, states (*Satire* 6.546–47) that a Jew will explain the meaning of dreams for the minutest of coins. And yet, as we have noted above, the ability to interpret dreams was an important ingredient in wisdom and was much prized in antiquity.

To the ancients the ability to express oneself was likewise crucial to wisdom. Hence, the praise accorded to the Bible for its elevated style by the first-century c.e. literary critic Pseudo-Longinus in his *On the Sublime* (9.9) would be regarded as a special compliment.[50]

In view of the tremendous popularity and importance of astrology in antiquity, the comment by the second-century Emperor Hadrian (quoted in *Historia Augusta, Quadrigae Tyrannorum* 8.3) that there is no chief of the Jewish synagogue (*archisynagogus*) who is not an astrologer might very well be regarded as a compliment. Moreover, it would be a tribute to the Jews that the first Jew, Abraham, is referred to by the second-century Vettius Valens in his astrological work (*Anthologiae* 2.28) as "most wonderful" (θαυμασιώτατος), reminding us of the statements of Artapanus (quoted in Eusebius, *Praeparatio Evangelica* 9.18.1) and pseudo-Eupolemus (quoted in Eusebius, *Praeparatio Evangelica* 9.17.8,, 9.18.2) that Abraham had taught the Egyptian pharaoh and the Phoenicians the science of astrology. Vettius speaks of Abraham as the author of books in which he discovered various things and tested them, especially on astrological nativities inclined to traveling (ἀποδηματικῶν μάλιστα γενέσεων). A similar tribute to Abraham as an astrologer is to be found in the fourth-century Firmicus Maternus (*Mathesis* 4, Prooemium 5), who couples Abraham with the much-revered Orpheus as an astrologer, and again (*Mathesis* 4.17.2) calls Abraham "divine." Elsewhere (*Mathesis* 4.18.1), moreover, Abraham is referred to as defining the position of the moon and of the sun.

Inasmuch as the Sibyls were regarded in antiquity as inspired prophetesses, there is clear admiration for the Jews in the reference in the second-century Pausanias (10.12.9) to a Hebrew Sibyl named Sabbe, who is said to have given oracles. That he identifies her as a Hebrew Sibyl while mentioning that some regard her a Babylonian and others call her an Egyptian would add to her praise, because the Babylonians and Egyptians were regarded as among the most ancient of peoples. The Jewish Sibyl is also mentioned by the third-century c.e. Aelian (*Varia Historia* 12.35). According to the *Scholia Platonica* (*In Phaedrum* 244B), this Sibyl, here named Sambethe, is the first of the ten Sibyls. Her antiquity is indicated by the fact that some thought that she was a Chaldaean, as well as by the tradition that she was the wife of one of Noah's sons who prophesied in the Hebrew language about the building of the Tower of Babel. Most complimentary of all is that, even though she lived so long before the time of Alexander the Great, she is said to have foretold the events of his time.

Some of the most remarkable tributes to the Jews come in the second half of the second century c.e. from Numenius of Apamea. We have already noted the impact that Jewish thought is alleged to have had in moulding the ideas of Pythagoras. With the revival of Neo-Pythagoreanism in such a writer as Numenius, we find once again great tribute paid to the Jews. In particular, as we shall note, the oft-repeated statement[51] "What is Plato but Moses speaking in Attic Greek?" coming, as it does, from Numenius, a follower of Plato and the main precursor of Neo-Platonism, is the supreme tribute to Moses and the Bible. Numenius, by mentioning the Jews in immediate juxtaposition with the Brahmans, renews a similar juxtaposition that we have noted in Megasthenes (quoted in Clement of Alexandria, *Stromata* 1.15.72.5). Apparently, to judge from Origen (*Against Celsus* 1.15, 4.51), Numenius even went so far as to quote the sayings of the biblical prophets and to give them an allegorical interpretation.

Moreover, the surprise expressed by the third century c.e. Origen (*Against Celsus* 1.16) that Celsus in the previous century had omitted the Jews from his list of the most ancient and wisest nations is an indication that he expected his audience to grant his point that Celsus was unfair. Indeed, he (*Against Celsus* 4.31) speaks admiringly, in a passage recalling Aristotle's supreme praise of the Jews (quoted in Josephus, *Contra Apionem* 1.179) as a people descended from the Indian philosophers, of the way in which they observed the Sabbath by study: "It was possible to see an entire nation studying philosophy; and in order that they might have leisure to hear the divine laws, the days called Sabbaths and their other feasts were instituted."

In the third century, we likewise find a tremendous compliment given to the Jews by Diogenes Laertius, who, after citing the theory of Clearchus of Soli tracing the descent of the Gymnosophists (a sect of philosophers found in India) from the Magi, adds (1.9) that some unspecified writers trace the Jews back to the same origin. This is a great tribute because the Magi were revered by classical authors as wise men par excellence; and moreover, their reputed power over demons, which gave rise to the word *magic*, added to their standing.

Likewise in the third century C.E., Porphyry (cited in Eusebius, *Praeparatio Evangelica* 9.10.1) is said to have introduced his own god bearing witness to the wisdom of the Hebrew race as well as of other nations renowned for intelligence. The Greeks, he says, had followed the wrong route to the gods, whereas the true road had been ascertained by the Hebrews among others. Furthermore (*De Abstinentia* 4.14), he implies admiration for the wisdom of the biblical laws that do not allow the parent birds to be taken with the nestlings and require work animals to be spared even in enemy country. In promulgating these laws, Porphyry says, the lawgiver was not afraid (as he was wise enough to realize) that the race of animals not liable to sacrifice would multiply and cause people hunger, because he knew that prolific animals have short lives and that other animals would attack those that multiply.

In the fourth century, to be sure, Julian (*Contra Galilaeos* 176A–178C) argues that the Jews have contributed nothing considerable or of great value in the fields of mathematics, science, philosophy, or music, compared with the Egyptians and the Greeks; but as we have seen, some writers such as Pythagoras, Artapanus, Eupolemus, Philo, and Josephus, had contended that the Greeks had borrowed from the Jews.

The epitome of wisdom for the Jews was, of course, King Solomon (1 Kgs 5:9-14, 10:1,3), and indeed the rabbis speak of him as the wisest of all people.[52] And yet Julian (*Contra Galilaeos* 224 C–E) contests this claim, remarking that the exhortations of Isocrates are superior to Solomon's proverbs and that in any case he could not have been very wise if he allowed himself to be deluded by a woman. Moreover, Julian, though he is ready to grant that the Jewish G-d is mighty, yet insists (*Epistulae*, fragment 89b, p. 295 D) that the Jews have neither wise prophets nor interpreters because they are close-minded. We have, however, already seen Josephus's answers to such objections and his aggrandizement (*Ant.* 8.26, 34, 44–45, 143, 165–67, 182) of Solomon's wisdom. We may, moreover, note that Solomon's fame in magic, manifest already in Josephus (*Ant.* 8.47), continues to be evident in the pseudepigraphical second- or third-century *Testament of Solomon*, and in the fourth-century anonymous *Medicina Plinii*, where there is a reference to an amulet against tertian fever on which Solomon's name appears. Similar indication of the high regard for the Jews' knowledge of magic may be seen in the sixth-century pagan Damascius (*Vita Isidori*, quoted in Photius, *Bibliotheca*, cod. 242, p. 339A–B), who tells how an evil spirit was persuaded to leave a woman through an oath when the G-d of the Hebrews was invoked.

It is particularly the early Christian intellectuals who, in their disputations with the Jews, bear witness to the Jewish reputation for learning. Thus, in the second century, Justin Martyr (*Dialogue with Trypho* 115), the greatest of the early Christian disputants, in his controversy with Trypho (whom some have identified with Rabbi Tarphon) remarks that the Jews always manage to hunt up their opponents' weak points like flies that settle on sore places. In particular, in responding to the charge that the Jews are uninventive, he (*Apology* 1.44.59–60) argues that Moses was earlier than any of the Greek philosophers and that the Greeks really depended on the Hebrews for their philosophy.

A number of the Christians, such as Origen, Clement, Eusebius, and Jerome, had Jewish teachers whose learning they recognize and whose interpretations of Scripture they sometimes quote or paraphrase.[53] Indeed, Eusebius (*Praeparatio Evangelica* 12.1), speaking of the δευτερῶται (i.e., the Talmudic rabbis, in all probability), who represent the ἄγραφος παράδοσις (i.e., the unwritten tradition), says that they are people whose faculties have been trained to penetrate to the very heart of Scripture.

Moreover, Origen (*Against Celsus* 1.15), as we have noted, repeats the statement of the third-century B.C.E. Hermippus as quoted by Josephus (*Against Apion* 1.162–65), that the incomparable Pythagoras, who was ranked for wisdom and piety above all other philosophers, had borrowed certain philosophical doctrines from the Jews. Indeed, the criteria for respect for a nation were wisdom and antiquity, as we have noted from Origen's remark (*Against Celsus* 1.16) that Celsus had mentioned the Odrysians, Samothracians, Eleusinians, Hyperboreans, Galactophagi, Druids, and Getae as being "among the most ancient and wise nations." At this point Origen refers the reader to Josephus's treatise *On the Antiquity of the Jews*, that is, the treatise *Against Apion*.

Celsus's charge that the Jews have never done anything important (quoted in Origen, *Against Celsus* 4.31)[54] and that consequently nothing about their history is to be found among the Greeks is taken directly from Josephus's treatise, where he sets forth (*Against Apion* 1.5) as a major part of his agenda his aim to explain why the Jews are mentioned by only a few of the Greek historians. Celsus (*Against Celsus* 4.36), remarking that the Jews were bowed down in obscurity in some corner of Palestine, repeats the charges of Apion (*Against Apion* 2.135) and Apollonius Molon (*Against Apion* 2.148) that the Jews were totally uneducated and were unacquainted with the heroic poetry of Hesiod and others. Indeed, this was a charge to which the Christians were often subjected, because, it was said, they appealed to the uneducated and baser elements of the population—"wool-workers, cobblers, laundry-workers, and the most illiterate and bucolic yokels" (*Against Celsus* 3.55)—and to those who were ready to believe on blind faith.[55]

In reply to the charge that the Jews did nothing to deserve mention by the Greeks, Origen (*Against Celsus* 4.31) notes that if anyone were to study carefully the society of the Jews in their early days when the Law was given, he would find that they came closest to leading a G-dlike life in avoiding the making of images, in living chastely, in showing respect for law and order, in devoting themselves to the study of the Law, and in observing the sacrificial system, with its countless symbolic explanations for those learned enough to understand them.[56] Origen (*Against Celsus* 4.32) also gives another reason, not found in Josephus, why the Jews were of no significance or prominence whatever, namely that they had deliberately withdrawn themselves in order to avoid contact with the multitude, lest their morals be corrupted. In addition, he says (apparently forgetting about the expansion by Kings David and Solomon of their kingdoms), the Jews lacked the ambition, found among so many other nations, to annex other kingdoms, although, on the other hand, they were not so forsaken that they became easy prey for attack by others.

As for Plato, who, as we have noted, ranked so high in influence during the Hellenistic and Roman periods, Josephus (*Against Apion* 2.257) had declared that he followed the example (μεμίμηται, "imitated") of Moses in prescribing as the primary duty of the citizens the study of the laws and in taking precautions to prevent foreigners from mixing with them at random. Origen (*Against Celsus* 4.39) speculates that Plato on his trip to Egypt may have met with those who interpret the Jewish doctrines philosophically and may consequently have been influenced by them in the myth in the *Symposium*; but the fact that he seems dubious about this theory shows his concern not to be ridiculed for exaggerating. He (*Against Celsus* 6.19) has no doubt, however, that Plato in the *Phaedrus* (247C) was influenced by the biblical prophets when he wrote that "no earthly poet either has sung or will sing of the region above the heavens as it deserves" and that "ultimate being, visible only to the mind, lives in this place."[57] Furthermore, he suggests (*Against Celsus* 6.21) that Plato's statement "The way for the souls to and from the earth passes through the planets" (*Phaedrus* 248C–E, *Timaeus* 41D–42E) is derived from Jacob's dream in which he saw a ladder reaching to heaven (Gen 28:12–13). Likewise, he contends (*Against Celsus* 7.30) that Plato (*Phaedo* 110 D–E) borrowed from Isaiah (54:11–12) the idea of the stones that on earth are regarded as precious and that he (Plato) says are an emanation from the stones in the ideal land. Indeed, Origen insists (*Against Celsus* 7.31) that the contrast between the ideal and the sensible world, so central to Plato, is already to be found in Moses and the prophets.

And yet Origen is careful not to go so far as Celsus's contemporary Numenius in asking our previously noted question "What else is Plato than Moses speaking Attic Greek?"[58] Likewise, Origen avoids the hyperbolic claims found in such Hellenistic Jewish writers as Pseudo-Eupolemus (quoted in Eusebius, *Praeparatio Evangelica* 9.17.3), who, as we have noted, states that Abraham excelled all men in wisdom and that he discovered astrology and Chaldean science.

Origen (*Against Celsus* 1.15) follows Josephus (*Against Apion* 1.183–204) in citing Hecataeus of Abdera as an authority for the wisdom of the Jews. Yet he is honest enough to note the doubts of Herennius Philo about the authenticity of the passage, though he declares that if the passage is authentic this is an indication of the powers of persuasion of the Jews. As for the statement that there is nothing novel in the ethical teachings of the Jews, Origen's answer (*Against Celsus* 1.4), far from Josephus's contention that these teachings (*Against Apion* 2.171–75) are truly distinctive, is that inflicting penalties for sins would be groundless unless all men had an a priori conception of moral principles. Indeed, this Stoic idea would undoubtedly make Origen's response all the more appealing. Moreover (*Against Celsus* 7.59), if there are parallels between pagan Greek and biblical passages, this is hardly proof of unoriginality, let alone of invalidity, particularly if the writings of the Jews are proved to be earlier than those of the Greeks; that the literary style of the pagans is more beautiful than the poor and simple language of the Jews is, Origen says, in no way relevant to the question of the superiority of thought.

Even Ambrose, who was so bitterly hostile to the Jews that he exerted the strongest pressure on the Emperor Theodosius in the fourth century not to force the Christians to rebuild a synagogue they had wantonly burned,[59] nevertheless admits (*Commentary on Psalms* 1.41 [*PL* 14.943]) that "some Jews exhibit . . . much diligence and love of study."

Finally, in the fourth century, the learned Jerome, who elsewhere bitterly accuses the Jews of depravity and of persecuting the Christians, pays tribute (*Against Jovinianus* 25) to the Jewish women who undergo great sacrifices to provide religious teachers for their sons. The Jews, he says (*Epistle to Titus* 3:9)—in a tone half of envy and half of reproach—go to great lengths to strengthen their memories: "In childhood they acquire the complete vocabulary of their language and learn to recite all the generations from Adam to Zerubbabel with such accuracy and facility as if they were simply giving their own names." Jerome also alludes to the Jews' love of books: Every synagogue had its library, from which books could be borrowed. The impression gained from reading Jerome is that he regards learning as so universal among Jews that all of them are competent to answer questions on Scripture. Jerome's own Jewish teacher knew Greek and Latin (he quotes Virgil, for example, in Jerome, *Preface to Daniel*), as well as Hebrew and Aramaic.

7. Praise by Pagans of the Courage of the Jews

Courage is always one of the major virtues for the ancients; and the Jews were particularly sensitive to the charge of cowardice made by such a Jew-baiter as Apollonius Molon (cited in *Against Apion* 2.148).

The historian Hecataeus (quoted in Diodorus 40.3.2–3), who about the year 300 B.C.E. presents the first non-Jewish account of the Exodus, makes a point of praising the leader of the Jews, Moses, no less for his courage than for his wisdom in guiding the people to what he asserts was a previously utterly uninhabited land.

Moreover, several of the ancients praise the obstinate courage of the Jews in adhering to their laws. Thus, Hecataeus (quoted in *Against Apion* 1.192–93), according to Josephus, adduces several instances of the Jews' tenaciousness with respect to their laws. In particular, Josephus cites Hecataeus's description of how the Jews submitted to many beatings rather than obeying Alexander the Great's command to have his soldiers, including the Jews, assist in the building of a pagan temple. He quotes Hecataeus as saying that "they deserve admiration on this account."

As for Apollonius's charge, Josephus (*Against Apion* 2.148) notes that Apollonius himself is actually guilty of contradicting himself, for in one place he reproaches the Jews as cowards and in another accuses them of audacity (τόλμαν) and insanity (ἀπόνοια, "loss of all sense"). We may here suggest that to Josephus's audience audacity (τόλμαν, "boldness") may not necessarily have had a pejorative connotation, because Pindar, for example (*Nemean Odes* 7.59), speaks of courage for noble acts, using this same word, τόλμα; and Herodotus (2.121) speaks, again positively, of the amazement and obvious admiration the Egyptian king Rhampsinitus had for the thief's sagacity (πολυφροσύνη) and boldness (τόλμη) in managing to outwit the king and his guards several times.

Moreover, in Josephus himself, the word τόλμα sometimes has a favorable connotation, as, for example, in the statement (*War* 1.333) that Antigonus wished to create an impression of the superiority of his men not only in courage (τόλμη) but also in numbers. Likewise, there is admiration in the attitude of the Romans toward the Sicarii who committed mutual suicide at Masada; and when they listen to the report by a woman survivor as to how the deed was done they are incredulous at such amazing fortitude (τῷ μεγέθει τοῦ τολμήματος, *War* 7.405). That τόλμα might have had a positive connotation in Josephus's day is clear from the positive sense of the corresponding verb τολμάω ("to take courage") in Josephus's contemporary Mark, who in his Gospel (15:43) says that Joseph of Arimathea, "an honorable senator, who himself was expecting the kingdom of G-d, taking courage (τολμήσας), went to Pilate and asked for

the body of Jesus." A similar sense is found in another of Josephus's contemporaries, Plutarch (*Camillus* 22).

Moreover, in the first-century Apion's own words (quoted in *Against
Apion* 2.21), the Israelites, when they made their exodus from Egypt,
reached Judaea in only six days.[60] Yet elsewhere (*Against Apion* 2.23) he
describes them as blind and lame and suffering from all kinds of disease; hence, as Josephus, who is likewise aware of the pro-Jewish intimations in Apion despite the latter's prejudiced intentions, remarks, Apion
is actually complimenting the strength and courage of the Israelites, because they not only traversed a desert but also had to fight against their
enemies.

Even Tacitus (*Histories* 5.13.3), at the beginning of the second century, notes—to be sure, without comment—their contempt for death.
Indeed, speaking of the siege of Jerusalem during the years 66–70, he
says that "all who were able bore arms, and a number, more than propor-
tionate to the population, dared to do so. There was equal stubbornness
on the part of men and women; and if they were to be compelled to leave
their abodes, they were more fearful of life than of death." That Tacitus
must have admired this contempt for death is clear when we recall that
both of the schools of philosophy most popular with Roman intellectuals—Epicureanism and Stoicism—expressed contempt for death; and
Cicero, the greatest of Roman intellectuals, had made contempt for
death the chief theme of his *Tusculan Disputations*.

A century after Tacitus, Dio Cassius (66.5.4) pays an implied tribute to
the bravery of the Jewish defenders of Jerusalem during the war against
the Romans by admitting—what we do not find in the much longer account of Josephus—that some of the Romans came to the conclusion that
the city was impregnable and so defected to the Jewish side. So courageous were the Jews that even after a breach had been made in the wall
the capture of the city did not immediately follow. Indeed, Dio (66.6.2–
3) marvels at the Jewish resistance against Titus before the fall of the
Temple in the year 70: "The Jews resisted [Titus] with more ardor than
ever, as if it were a kind of windfall[61] to fall fighting beside the Temple
and in its defense. . . . Although they were few and fighting against a foe
far outnumbering them, they were not overcome until a part of the Temple had caught fire. Then some impaled themselves voluntarily on the
swords of the Romans, others slew each other, others did away with
themselves or leaped into the flames. They all believed, especially the
last, that it was not a disaster but victory, salvation, and happiness to
perish together with the Temple." Dio (69.12–14) also marvels at the
stubbornness of the Jewish resistance under Bar Kochba.

In the third century Porphyry (*De Abstinentia* 4.13), closely echoing
Josephus (*War* 2.152), expresses admiration for the perseverance of the

Essenes in that, during the war with the Romans, though they were racked and twisted and burned and subjected to every instrument of torture to get them to blaspheme Moses or to eat some forbidden food, they did not cringe before their persecutors or even shed a tear but actually smiled during their agonies.

Moreover, bitter though he is, John Chrysostom (*Homilia de Statuis* 2.3, *PG* 49.37 and *Homilia in Matthaeum* 36.3, *PG* 57.417), in the fourth century, acknowledges the fortitude and perseverance of the Jews in the face of adversity and is forced to admit that many Jews live virtuous lives.

8. JOSEPHUS ON THE COURAGE OF JEWISH HEROES

Josephus was apparently particularly sensitive to the charge of cowardice because he himself (*War* 3.358) had been subjected to such criticism. Thus, it is not surprising that in a number of additions to the biblical narrative he stresses the military prowess and courage of the Jews. In particular, while the rabbis (*Sanhedrin* 96a) stress the miraculous help that Abraham, in attacking the Assyrians, received from an angel named Night, Josephus adds a number of details to enhance Abraham's military excellence, notably that the battle was a stubborn contest (*Ant.* 1.172), that Abraham (*Ant.* 1.177) was determined to help the Sodomites without delay, that he surprised the Assyrians before they had time to arm, and that he slew some in their beds, while others who were drunk took to flight. This military tradition is continued, according to Josephus (*Ant.* 1.240–41), who quotes a certain Cleodemus-Malchus, by two of Abraham's sons by Keturah, who joined Heracles, the most famous of the Greek legendary heroes, in his campaign against Libya and Antaeus, the giant son of Earth. Josephus, who normally inveighs bitterly against intermarriage (e.g., *Ant.* 4.139, 5.306), here seems to record proudly the fact that Heracles married the daughter of one of the sons of Abraham. Moreover, Jacob's sons are described (*Ant.* 2.7) as courageous for their labor and endurance (πρὸς ἔργα χειρῶν καὶ πόνων ὑπομονὴν ἦσαν εὔψυχοι).

The supreme example of military acumen and courage is, as we shall see, Moses, who in a long extra-biblical supplement (*Ant.* 2.238–51) is depicted as the conqueror of Ethiopia, a land that was later to resist successfully invasion by generals of the caliber of Cambyses (Herodotus 3.17–25) and Alexander the Great.

Likewise, it is important to note that Josephus adds to the biblical text on ten occasions by referring to Joshua as a general.[62] His courageous exploits in battle with the Amalekites are attested to by the whole army, and he is consequently praised by Moses himself (*Ant.* 3.59). He shows particular ability in being able to inspire his troops (*Ant.* 5.73). If Joshua fails to complete the conquest, Josephus (*Ant.* 5.90) is careful to ascribe this not to any deficiency on his part but rather to the impediment of advancing age, as well as to the carelessness of those who succeeded him in guarding the commonwealth, a key component, as we see from Thucydides' description (2.60.5–6) of the qualities of a leader. Far different is the picture in rabbinic literature, where Joshua loosens the shoes from off his feet in mourning not for the defeat of Ai but for the neglect of the study of Torah by the people (*Seder Eliyahu Rabbah* [pp. 101–2 Friedmann]), and where an angel reproaches Joshua for having allowed the preparations for war to interfere with the study of Torah ('*Eruvin* 63b).

Moreover, Josephus omits details that would detract from the heroic stature of his biblical personalities. Hence, because the Greeks generally had contempt for menial labor, and the toil of working at the mill was a common and much-dreaded punishment of slaves often referred to in the comic poets, Josephus seems to be careful to omit the fact (Judg 16:21) that Samson "did grind in the prison house." Likewise, in his long appreciation of Saul's character, Josephus (*Ant.* 6.347) declares categorically that the terms "stout-hearted" ($εὔψυχος$), "greatly daring" ($μεγαλό-τολμος$), and "contemptuous of danger" ($τῶν δεινῶν καταφρονητής$) can be justly applied only to such as have emulated Saul, because he, like Hector and Achilles in Homer's *Iliad*, engaged in his exploits knowing beforehand that he was destined to die in the forthcoming battle.[63] Again, when Samuel mistakenly thinks that Jesse's oldest son should be selected as king, G-d tells him (*Ant.* 6.160) that the qualities He seeks in a king are piety, justice, bravery ($ἀνδρεία$) and obedience. Elsewhere the Israelites explain their fear (*Ant.* 7.300) that through his bravery ($ἀνδρείαν$) and zeal ($προθυμίαν$) David may suffer injury and thus deprive them of his protection.[64] Finally, in his eulogy of David (*Ant.* 7.390) Josephus declares that he was brave ($ἀνδρεῖος$) as no one else was.

9. PRAISE BY PAGANS OF THE TEMPERANCE OF THE JEWS

One of the two famous mottoes inscribed at the oracular shrine of Apollo at Delphi was $μηδὲν ἄγαν$, "Nothing in excess." Indeed, one of the divisions of the ethics of the Stoics, the most influential of the philosophical schools in the Hellenistic and Roman periods, was, as noted by Diogenes Laertius (7.84), $περὶ παθῶν$ ("concerning passions").[65] Hellenistic theorists such as Ecphantus insisted that if a ruler was to be truly such he had to begin with self-discipline, because otherwise he would never be able to teach self-control to his subjects.[66]

Temperance among the ancients was shown primarily in one's food and drink habits; and indeed a chief criticism, as we have noted, leveled against the Jews by the pagan writers is that they are guilty of stubborn exclusiveness and separatism largely because of their observance of the dietary laws. And yet this observance of the dietary laws, though mocked at in obvious exaggeration by the Roman satirists such as Juvenal, nevertheless was admired by some of the pagan intellectuals. Confirmation of this is indicated by the statement in the ancient anecdotist and biographer of philosophers, Diogenes Laertius (1.6–9), in the third century C.E., that the food laws of the sixth century B.C.E. philosopher Pythagoras had been borrowed from the Jews.[67] This is corroborated, as we have noted, by Hermippus of Smyrna (cited in Josephus, *Against Apion* 1.164–65) in the third century B.C.E.: "It is correctly stated that that man [Pythagoras] took a great many of the laws of the Jews into his own philosophy." We may note that Celsus, in the second century C.E. (quoted in Origen, *Against Celsus* 5.43), without drawing conclusions as to Jewish influence, cites the similarity between the Jewish dietary laws and the Pythagorean abstention from beans and flesh.

Again in the fourth century B.C.E., Aristotle, according to his disciple Clearchus of Soli (quoted in Josephus, *Against Apion* 1.182), was impressed with the great and wondrous endurance and sobriety (σωφροσύνην) in the manner of life (δίαιτη) of the Jew whom he allegedly met in Asia Minor. The Greek word δίαιτα, which is here employed for "way of life," refers particularly, as does its English derivative, to the diet.

Furthermore, when the first-century Apion (quoted in *Against Apion* 2.137) denounces the Jews for not eating pork, the criticism might well have backfired, because, as Josephus (*Against Apion* 2.137 and 141) indicates in his reply, the Egyptian priests also abstained from pork; in Egypt superstition dictated that pork might be eaten only at the full moon, and there were many other countries where pork was forbidden food.[68]

Moreover, Plutarch (*Quaestiones Convivales* 4.5.2.670 C–D), at the beginning of the second century, we may venture to suggest, represents the Stoic and intellectual norm of tolerance; yet he asks, as we have noted, how one can condemn the Egyptians for irrationality in abstaining from certain animals when the Pythagoreans, who, as we have stressed, were certainly highly respected, especially during the revival of Neo-Pythagoreanism in the first century B.C.E. and in the first century C.E., have regard for a white cock and refrain from eating red mullet and the sea anemone. He likewise calls attention, as we have noted, to the fact that the Magi, the followers of Zoroaster, esteem the hedgehog and abominate water mice. It is interesting indeed that Aelian (*De Natura Animalium* 10.16), at the end of the second century C.E., on the authority of the fourth-century B.C.E. Eudoxus, gives the same explanation for the Egyptian abstention from sacrificing pigs as one of those given by Plutarch (*Quaestiones Convivales* 4.5.2.670A) for the Jewish abstention from eating pork, namely as a tribute to the usefulness of pigs in agriculture.

Moreover, Agathocles (whose date is uncertain) in his *History of Cyzicus* (cf. Athenaeus 9.18.375E–376A), records the service rendered by a pig to Zeus and notes that for this reason the Cretans, in whose island Zeus was said to have been born, abstained from eating pork. Indeed, we may conjecture that this abstention from pork may have been one of the links that led to the theory (Tacitus, *Histories* 5.2.1) that the Jews' origin was in Crete. And to be associated with the Cretans was, as we have noted, hardly a reproach in many circles.

Finally, Pliny the Elder in the first century (5.73) shows extraordinary admiration for the sect of Jews known as the Essenes, who, he says, are remarkable (*mira*, "wonderful," "marvelous," "extraordinary") beyond all other tribes in the whole world, inasmuch as they have no women and have renounced all sexual desire and have no money. The third-century Solinus (*Collectanea Rerum Memorabilium* 35.9–11) closely echoes these sentiments and marvels at the memorable discipline of the Essenes. Likewise, his contemporary Porphyry (*De Abstinentia* 4.13) admires the Essenes for their simplicity and eating habits so scant that on the Sabbath they have no need even of easing themselves.

10. JOSEPHUS ON THE TEMPERANCE OF JEWISH HEROES

Inasmuch as the chief sources of anti-Jewish comments were Greek intellectuals living in Egypt, it is not surprising that in praising Jewish temperance Josephus counterattacks the Egyptians. Thus, he depicts the ancient Egyptians (*Ant.* 2.201), in a considerable addition to the biblical text, as lacking the quality of temperance and, indeed, as being a voluptuous (τρυφεροῖς, "luxurious," "effeminate") people, slaves to pleasure in general and to a love of lucre, slack to labor, and consequently jealous of the prosperity of the Hebrews. In contrast, the biblical text (Exod 1:9–10) says nothing about the excesses of the Egyptians but rather gives as the cause of the Egyptian enslavement of the Israelites the fact that the Israelites were more numerous and mightier than the Egyptians and the fear that they would join an enemy in fighting against the Egyptians. Apparently, Josephus, self-conscious about the vast increase in the number of Jews in his own day largely through proselytism, preferred not to remind his readers of the population explosion of the Jews and the fear of the Romans that their pagan religion would be overwhelmed by Judaism.

Indeed, in his reworking of the Bible, Josephus adds a number of touches to stress the Jews' devotion to temperance and its associated virtue of modesty. Thus, just as the Greeks had to be constantly reminded of this virtue by the motto at Delphi, μηδὲν ἄγαν, so the Israelites had to be exhorted (*Ant.* 4.189) by Moses before his death to practice moderation (σωφρονήσειν); and Josephus notes that Moses himself had refrained from wrath at the moment that he felt most aggrieved by them. Regarding this virtue Moses had an apt pupil in Joshua; and indeed, just as one of the qualities in Pericles so admired by Thucydides (2.65.8) was the ability to restrain the masses and to direct them to a path of moderation, so we find in Joshua a similar ability, as illustrated notably in his success (*Ant.* 5.103), not paralleled in the Bible (Joshua 22:13), in restraining the people's anger at the tribes of Reuben, Gad, and the half tribe of Manasseh, who had erected an altar on the banks of the Jordan.

Modesty is truly a key virtue in Josephus's portrayal of many of his other biblical heroes. Thus, Samson shows the quality of humility in acknowledging (*Ant.* 5.302), after he had been seized by a mighty thirst, that human virtue (ἀρετή) is nothing, because all is attributable to G-d. Likewise, Saul is praised (*Ant.* 6.63) for his restraint (ἐγκράτειαν) and modesty (σωφροσύνην) when he is chosen king.[69] Again, in his eulogy of David, Josephus (*Ant.* 7.391) refers to him as self-controlled (σώφρων) and mild (ἐπιεικής). Finally, Solomon, as we have noted above, exhibits (*Ant.* 8.146–49) his modesty in recognizing that a Tyrian lad, Abdemon, was able to solve riddles that he had prepared, whereas he himself had failed to solve Abdemon's riddles.

11. Praise by Non-Jews of the Justice of the Jews

The queen of the cardinal virtues, as we can see from its being the subject of the most influential of all of Plato's dialogues, the *Republic*, is justice (δικαιοσύνη); and indeed this is the most inclusive term for virtue in general. Aristotle (*Rhetoric* 1.9.1366B) states that people honor most the just and the courageous, and he clearly implies that justice is superior even to courage, because, he remarks, courage is useful to others in war, whereas justice is useful both in war and in peace. Plutarch (*Cato the Younger* 44.8) gives still another reason why justice is superior to courage, namely that some courageous people have a start or advantage supplied by nature, whereas all people start at the same point in their quest for justice. He (*Aristeides* 6.2), moreover, describes the term *just* as the most royal and divine of titles; that it is a term of great praise is clear from its having been applied to the famous Athenian statesman, Aristeides. Plutarch then goes on to remark that people envy the gods because of their incorruptibility; we fear their power, but we love and honor the gods for their justice.

The anti-Jewish Apion (quoted in *Against Apion* 2.125) alleges, without further explanation, that the Jewish laws are unjust. But his older contemporary Pompeius Trogus (quoted in Justin, *Historiae Philippicae* 36.2.16) ascribes justice categorically to the Jews and explains that through this quality, combined with religion, it is incredible[70] how powerful they have become (*coaluere*, "coalesced," "united," "increased," "became strong").

Justice, as we see in Philo,[71] is coupled with the quality of love of humanity (φιλανθρωπία), just as the Latin equivalent of the latter term, *humanitas*, is likewise connected with the virtue of justice.[72] Such Jew-baiters as Apollonius Molon and Lysimachus (cited in *Against Apion* 2.145), as we have seen, had charged the Jews with hatred of humankind. Tacitus (*Histories* 5.5.1) explains this charge by stating that the Jews feel only hatred and enmity toward every other people (*adversus omnes alios hostile odium*). Yet even Tacitus admits (ibid.) that the Jews are inflexibly trustworthy to one another and ever ready to show compassion to their fellow Jews. The word used here by Tacitus for trustworthiness, *fides*, was, to the Romans, as Cicero (*De Officiis* 1.13.39) put it, the foundation of justice. It is the lack of this quality that Livy (21.4.9) attacks more than any other failure in Hannibal, who, he claims, had *perfidia plus quam Punica*—treachery even greater than what one would expect in a Carthaginian.

Perhaps the greatest tribute, however, to the high ethical standards of the Jews is paid by the Emperor Alexander Severus (reigned 222–35 C.E.; possibly, though not probably, to be identified with "Antoninus,"[73] the friend of Rabbi Judah the Prince), who was one of the most cultured of the Roman emperors.[74] In his biography of Alexander Severus, Aelius Lampridius (*Historia Augusta* 51.7–8) remarks that that emperor "used often to exclaim what he had heard and retained from certain Jews or Christians; and when he corrected someone, he would order this to be proclaimed by a public crier: 'What you do not wish done to yourself, do not do to another.' He loved this sentiment so much that he ordered it to be engraved on the palace and on public works." This maxim, of course, is the famous statement in *Shabbath* 31a of Hillel to the proselyte; its negative form makes it likely to be Jewish rather than Christian in origin.[75]

In the fourth century C.E., despite his unpleasant experience with Jewish tenant farmers (*Oratio de Patrociniis* 13–17), Libanius (*Epistulae* 1084.1), in writing to the Jewish Patriarch, compliments the Jews as a people whose habit it is to help everybody, "taking care of all as human beings, but of the best as living a life of virtue."[76]

12. JOSEPHUS ON THE JUSTICE OF JEWISH HEROES

Josephus (*Ant.* 4.217), in expanding on the biblical statement (Deut 16:20) "Justice, only justice shalt thou pursue," gives a theological reason why a judge must show no favoritism, namely that otherwise G-d would appear to be accounted weaker than those to whom, from fear of strength, the judge accords his vote. G-d's strength, he says, is justice, and one who gives this away out of favor to persons of rank makes them appear more powerful than G-d Himself. Justice, he concludes, is the sole attribute of the G-d which is within the power of man to attain. What higher justice is there, exclaims Josephus in his peroration at the end of the essay *Against Apion* (2.293), than obedience to the laws?[77]

In particular, Josephus, in extra-biblical additions, constantly emphasizes the quality of justice in biblical heroes. Thus, in a passage that Josephus quotes from the Babylonian historian Berossus, justice is displayed by Abraham (*Ant.* 1.158), who is termed a just (δίκαιος) man. Again, we read (*Ant.* 3.66) that all the Israelites came to Moses, thinking that only thus would they obtain justice (τοῦ δικαίου), so that (*Ant.* 3.67) even those who lost their cases were convinced that it was justice (δικαιοσύνην) rather than cupidity that determined their fate.

Furthermore, when the people demand that Samuel name a king for them, he (*Ant.* 6.36) is sorely aggrieved because of his innate sense of justice; and in his eulogy of Samuel, Josephus (*Ant.* 6.294) describes him as a just (δίκαιος) and kindly man. Similarly, when Jonathan (*Ant.* 6.212) appeals to Saul, Josephus declares that thus a just cause (δίκαιος λόγος) prevailed over anger and fear. Likewise, one of the qualities G-d declares (*Ant.* 6.160) that Samuel is to look for when he is about to select David as king is justice. Indeed, when David spares Saul's life, Saul compliments him (*Ant.* 6.290) for having shown the righteousness (δικαιοσύνην) of the ancients. Moreover, Josephus editorializes (*Ant.* 7.110) in declaring that David was just (δίκαιος) by nature and that he looked only toward the truth in giving judgment; and in his final eulogy one of his qualities singled out for praise (*Ant.* 7.391) is that he was just. Solomon, Josephus (*Ant.* 8.21) declares, was not hindered by his youth from dispensing justice (δικαιοσύνην); and G-d, in His turn, promised to preserve the kingdom for his descendants if he continued to be just (δίκαιος).

Connected with the virtue of justice is the enormous responsibility to tell the truth. That the Greeks, somewhat ambivalently to be sure, realized its importance is evident in Herodotus's (1.136) obvious admiration for the careful instruction Persian sons are given in speaking the truth and for the Persians' conviction that it is the most disgraceful thing in the world to tell a lie (1.139)—this in contrast to the reputation that the Greeks themselves had, from the figure of Odysseus on down, for cleverness in lying. Indeed, a popular definition of justice, as we see from the aged Cephalus, who represents tradition in Plato's *Republic* (1.331C), is speaking the truth. Hence, Josephus takes pains to explain (*Ant.* 1.162, 1.207) why Abraham has to devise a lying scheme when he comes to Egypt and to Abimelech with his wife Sarah; and he omits (*Ant.* 1.209) the passage (Gen 20:9) in which Abimelech rebukes Abraham for his deceit. Moreover, he describes Moses (*Ant.* 4.303) as one who had in no detail deviated from the truth. We may note that in his apologetic for Samson, Josephus omits Delilah's accusation to Samson that he has told her lies (Judg 16:10, 13), for the Achilles-like hero and the Aristotelian μεγαλόψυχος is truthful. In the case of Joshua,[78] Josephus (*Ant.* 5.57) shows how important it was to Joshua that his oath not be violated, even when given to the deceitful Gibeonites; for we hear (*Ant.* 5.57) that, when he discovered their strategem, Joshua convoked the high priest Eleazar and the council and made them public slaves (Joshua 9:27) so as to avoid violation of his oath to the Gibeonites. Furthermore, we are informed (*Ant.* 5.75) that Joshua tells the Israelites to appoint representatives of approved virtue from each of the tribes to measure out the land faithfully and without fraudulence and to report honestly to the congregation what its dimensions are. Again, Mephibosheth declares his confidence that no calumny enters David's mind, "for it is just and loves the truth" (*Ant.* 7.269).

Inasmuch as justice is closely connected with humanity, as we have noted, Josephus stresses this quality in his biblical heroes. Thus, in particular, Reuben, in his speech to Joseph (*Ant.* 2.101), declares his confidence in his humanity (φιλανθρωπίαν). Moreover, in his final eulogy of David's character, Josephus (*Ant.* 7.391) stresses, among other qualities, that he was just and humane (φιλάνθρωπος), "qualities which are especially applicable to kings." Here again Josephus seems to be answering such anti-Jewish writers as Apollonius Molon and Lysimachus (cited in *Against Apion* 2.145), who had charged the Jews, as we have noted, with hatred of humanity.

Josephus, in his defense of Judaism (*Against Apion* 2.146), notes that humanity is one of the qualities fostered by the law code of the Jews. This virtue is seen particularly in unselfishness and generosity. Thus, Joshua shows the quality of generosity when he distributes all the booty captured at Ai (*Ant.* 5.48) among his soldiers, whereas the biblical text (Josh 8:27) makes no mention of the distribution among the soldiers.

Again, in the case of David, generosity is manifest especially in the famous episode (2 Sam 24:13) where David is given a choice of three punishments: seven years of famine, three months of fleeing before his foes, or three days of pestilence. The Bible (2 Sam 24:14) gives no reason for David's choice; but Josephus (*Ant.* 7.322–23) explains that he chose the last to show that he was not selfish, inasmuch as the pestilence would afflict all alike in his kingdom, whereas the first two would pose no risk to himself.

Josephus devotes attention particularly to refuting Apion's charge (*Against Apion* 2.50) that the Jewish general Onias, to whom the Egyptian king Ptolemy Philometor (reigned 180–145 B.C.E.) had entrusted his

army, had marched against Alexandria, by noting that Onias had demonstrated his justice through remaining true to his oath, in that he turned
against Ptolemy Physcon, who had usurped the throne (2.51–52). The
justice (*iustitiae*) of his action, concludes Josephus (2.53)—although the
authenticity of the event itself may be debated—was attested to by G-d
Himself, inasmuch as when Ptolemy Physcon exposed the Jews to an
elephant stampede so that they might be trampled to death, the beasts
instead turned around and rushed at Physcon's friends. Similarly,
Apion's argument (quoted in *Against Apion* 2.125) that the proof of the
injustice of the Jewish laws is that the Jews have been slaves of one nation
after another, would have been unconvincing, because, as a reader
knowledgeable in Egyptian history would have known, the Egyptians
themselves had for hundreds of years been subject first to the Persians,
then to the Macedonians, and then to the Romans.

13. PRAISE BY PAGANS OF THE PIETY OF THE JEWS

That piety was, in effect, a fifth cardinal virtue we may see from Plato
(*Protagoras* 349B) and from the Stoics (*Stoicorum Veterum Fragmenta*
3.64.40 and Diogenes Laertius 7.119). The former has Socrates ask, "Are
wisdom, self-control, courage, justice, and piety five names which denote
the same thing?"[79] Elsewhere Pseudo-Plato (*Epinomis* 989B) remarks that
"nobody will ever persuade us that there exists for humankind any greater
virtue than piety" (εὐσέβεια). Aristotle (*De Virtutibus et Vitiis* 55.1250
B22–23) defines piety as a part of justice or as an accompaniment to it.
Likewise, Philo (*De Vita Mosis* 2.39.216) clearly regards piety as one
of the five cardinal virtues, inasmuch as he speaks of synagogues as
schools of "prudence and courage and temperance and justice and also
of piety, holiness, and every virtue by which duties to G-d and men
are discerned and rightly performed."[80] Attridge[81] denies that the Hellenistic historians stressed the importance of the specifically religious response (εὐσέβεια) to the acts of providence. Nevertheless, Diodorus
(1.2.2) in his prologue stresses piety and justice as the two virtues historians extol in their heroes. The importance of piety, particularly for the
Romans, may be seen in the fact that the key quality of Aeneas in Virgil's
great national epic is *pietas*, dutiful loyalty, of which piety is an important
element.

Piety is closely related to justice, inasmuch as justice applies to relations among people, while piety pertains to their relationship with G-d.[82]
Thus, Dionysius of Halicarnassus (*Roman Antiquities* 2.62.5) remarks
that the great Roman lawgiver, Numa Pompilius, introduced two virtues
through which the city would be prosperous—justice and piety.[83]

Hecataeus (cited in Josephus, *Against Apion* 1.190–93) specifically declares that the Jews deserve admiration for their regard for their laws and for holding it a major point of honor to endure anything rather than to transgress the laws. That this was a point of high praise is clear from Pericles' Funeral Oration (Thucydides 2.37.3), in which he lauds the Athenians for their reverent fear in restraining themselves from lawlessness and for their obedience to those in authority and to the laws. So also Porphyry (*De Abstinentia* 2.61) says, in obvious admiration, that even when kings strove to force the Jews to eat non-permitted food they preferred to suffer death rather than to transgress the law. The steadfastness of the Jews in rendering obedience to the laws would remind the reader both of the Spartans in general and of the Athenians as idealized in Pericles' Funeral Oration (quoted in Thucydides 2.37.3).

Inasmuch as one of Apion's charges (quoted in *Against Apion* 2.73) against the Jews was that they had shown impiety in not erecting statues to the emperors, Josephus takes great pains to stress that it is an indication of the magnanimity (*magnanimitatem*, "great spiritedness") and moderation of the Romans that they do not require their subjects to violate their own national laws and that they are grateful for such honors as those nations are, according to their own laws, permitted to pay.

Even Julian (*Ad Theodorum* 89A, pp. 453 C–454 B), who is generally not sympathetic to the tenets of Judaism, admires the sincerity of the Jews in their willingness to die for their beliefs and, notably, to endure utter want and starvation rather than to eat pork, in contrast to the apathy of the pagans toward their religious beliefs.

14. JOSEPHUS ON THE PIETY OF JEWISH HEROES

In answering the anti-Jewish attacks of Apollonius Molon, Lysimachus, and the rest, who had charged that the laws of the Jews teach impiety (ἀσέβειαν) (*Against Apion* 2.291), Josephus (*Against Apion* 2.146) emphasizes that the first quality the Mosaic code is designed to promote is piety. He stresses the centrality of piety when he declares (*Against Apion* 2.181) that even Jewish women and children agree that piety must be the motive of all tasks in life. Indeed, Josephus, in his peroration at the end of the essay *Against Apion* (2.293), exclaims, "What greater beauty than inviolable piety?" Thus, Josephus is basically redefining ἀρετή as εὐσέβεια, which was, in fact, an integral part of ἀρετή, according to the Stoics.[84] In truth, it is the related virtues so important in Stoicism (Epictetus, *Dissertationes* 1.6.28–29)—magnanimity (μεγαλοψυχία), courage (ἀνδρεία), patient endurance (καρτερία) and sagacity (σύνεσις)—that bring about the great dividends of freedom from perturbation and freedom from distress.

Through his extra-biblical additions, Josephus has likewise stressed piety. Thus, it is the piety of Abraham and Isaac that Josephus emphasizes in his account of Abraham's readiness to sacrifice his own son (*Ant.* 1.222-36).[85] Again, in his one-sentence eulogy of Jacob (*Ant.* 2.190) the sole virtue he mentions is piety, in which Jacob is said to have been second to none of the forefathers. Josephus's coupling of piety with the other virtues is clear from his statement (*Ant.* 1.6) that under the great Moses the Israelites were trained in piety (εὐσέβειαν) and in the exercise of the other virtues. Furthermore, Josephus indicates the importance of piety when he declares (*Ant.* 1.21) that once Moses won the obedience of the Israelites to the dictates of piety, he had no further difficulty in persuading them to honor all the remaining virtues. Furthermore, when describing (*Ant.* 3.491) the qualities of Joshua, Josephus notes the singular piety he had learned from his mentor Moses.

The importance of piety for Joshua in Josephus[86] is particularly evident in his farewell address to the Israelites. Whereas the biblical Joshua (Josh 24:14) exhorts the people to fear the L-rd and to serve Him in sincerity and faithfulness, Josephus's Joshua (*Ant.* 5.116) not only exhorts the Israelites but specifically explains that only through piety can they retain the friendship of G-d. Moreover, in singling out the qualities Samuel is to look for in a king, G-d first mentions (*Ant.* 6.160) piety (εὐσεβείᾳ) and only then justice, bravery, and obedience, declaring that these are the qualities of which beauty of soul consists. As for Saul's piety, Josephus (*Ant.* 6.124) stresses his respect for an oath, an important matter to the Romans, as we see in Cicero (*De Officiis* 1.13.39); and, indeed, when Jonathan faces death at the hands of his father because of his vow, Jonathan declares that he would be very glad to go to his own death for the sake of his piety (εὐσεβείας, *Ant.* 6.127). Even when the Bible (1 Sam 13:8–14) exhibits Saul's lack of piety in offering a sacrifice before waiting for Samuel, Josephus (*Ant.* 6.103) offers the excuse that he did so out of necessity because of the desertion of his frightened troops. Similar distinctive attributions of piety are to be found in the case of David (*Ant.* 6.160, 7.130, 8.196, 8.315), Solomon (*Ant.* 8.13, 9.22), and the later kings, notably Hezekiah (*Ant.* 9.260, 9.276) and Josiah (*Ant.* 10.50, 10.51, 10.56).

In sum, whether they read testimonies of non-Jewish intellectuals or Josephus, intelligent observers in antiquity would have found much to admire in Judaism, and, in particular, in the great figures of the Bible as paragons of the cardinal virtues so dear to the ancients.

CHAPTER 8

THE ATTRACTIONS OF THE JEWS: THE IDEAL LEADER, MOSES

1. THE PORTRAYAL OF MOSES BY PAGAN WRITERS

In the competition for followers, to a great degree the success of a movement, whether religious or philosophical, depended on the reputation of its founder or lawgiver. We may see this notably in Plutarch's lives of such lawgivers as Lycurgus, Solon, and Numa Pompilius; in the portrayal of Rome's founder, Aeneas, by Virgil; and in the hagiographic-like lives of such notable and seminal philosophers as Socrates, Plato, Zeno, and Diogenes the Cynic by Diogenes Laertius. We may see this also in the figure of Heracles, who was taken as a model by the Cynic-Stoic popular philosophy. Above all, we may perceive this in the crucial importance attached by Plato (*Republic* 5.473) to the philosopher-king if an ideal state is to come into being.

The towering figure of Moses, the one person in Jewish tradition who was well-known to the pagan world, was a tremendous boon to the Jews.[1] His connection with Egypt undoubtedly gave him a certain notoriety, especially during the Hellenistic period, when the Alexandrian scholars dominated the intellectual scene. Philo (*De Vita Mosis* 1.1.1–2), writing within the Alexandrian milieu, asserts that although the fame of his laws had spread throughout the world, not many knew him as he really was, because Greek authors had not wanted to accord him honor, in part out of envy and in part because the ordinances of local lawgivers were often opposed to his. Similarly, Josephus (*Against Apion* 2.145) declares that Apollonius Molon, Lysimachus, and others, due to ignorance and ill will, had cast aspersions on Moses and his code, maligning him as a charlatan (γόητα) and an impostor (ἀπατεῶνα).

Jew-baiters, according to Josephus (*Against Apion* 2.290) had apparently reviled Moses as utterly unimportant (φαυλότατος). Braun[2] has pointed out the significance of the omission of Moses' name from the list of Oriental national heroes cited by Plutarch (*De Iside et Osiride* 24.360B), otherwise a relatively impartial authority. Indeed, in an age and place where grammarians and Homeric scholars were the leaders of the intellectual community, one of the major figures on the intellectual scene in Alexandria in the first half of the first century, Apion, known for his glosses on Homer[3] and Philo's counterpart as a leader of the Alexandrian non-Jewish delegation to the Emperor Gaius Caligula in the year 40 C.E., was a major figure in the revisionist view of Moses.

Let us proceed chronologically through the ancient writers who mention Moses. If we may put any stock in the admittedly questionable reference to Moses in Pseudo-Justin (*Cohortatio ad Gentiles* 9), the historians Hellanicus in the fifth century B.C.E. and Philochorus in the third century B.C.E. had mentioned Moses as a very ancient leader of the Jews.[4]

If, as Philo (*De Vita Mosis* 2.2.8) categorically declares, "He who is to obtain excellence as a legislator should possess all the virtues fully and completely," Moses had to satisfy this model. It is consequently a tremendous compliment that when cited for the first time in the earliest extended mention, that by Hecataeus (ca. 300 B.C.E., quoted in Diodorus 40.3.3), Moses is termed truly outstanding (πολὺ διαφέρων) both for his practical wisdom and his courage (φρονήσει τε καὶ ἀνδρεία). Indeed, this gives him a rank among the greatest lawgivers, because similar phraseology is used by Diodorus (1.94.1–5) to describe three Egyptian lawgivers. Moreover, φρόνησις, that is, sagacity or practical wisdom or prudence, is, as we see in Aristotle (*Politics* 3.4.1277A15–17), the sine qua non for a good ruler. The example par excellence of the person possessing this virtue, cited by Aristotle (*Nicomachean Ethics* 6.5.1140B8–11), is the great statesman Pericles, Thucydides' idol, because, says Aristotle, men like him "can see what is good for themselves and what is good for men in general; we consider that those can do this who are good at managing households or states."

Hecataeus then proceeds to state (quoted in Diodorus 40.3.3–8) that Moses was responsible for all the major institutions of the Jews, including especially those that set them apart from other people. Indeed, Moses was apparently so closely identified with the Jews that he is credited by Hecataeus (quoted in Diodorus 40.3.3), in clear contradiction to the Bible, with founding Jerusalem and with establishing the Temple. Moreover, although the Bible credits G-d with giving the laws to the Israelites at Sinai, Hecataeus (ibid.) says nothing of Divine revelation and instead imputes to Moses the laws, the political institutions, and the religious ritual of the Jews.

It is clear that Hecataeus looked on Moses as a philosopher-king in that he ascribes to him, in a non-biblical remark, the division of the Israelites into twelve tribes, explaining that twelve is regarded as the most perfect number and corresponds to the number of months that make up a year. This is directly in line with Plato's remark (*Laws* 5.745B–D) that the legislator must divide the ideal city, its citizens, and their property into twelve parts.[5]

This emphasis on the number twelve would undoubtedly have impressed a Roman audience as well, inasmuch as they might well have seen a parallel between Moses and Romulus, the founders of their respective nations. Thus, according to Livy (1.8.2) in the first century B.C.E., when Romulus, with his intuitive wisdom, sought to give his people a law code, he realized that it would appear binding only if he would invest his own person with majesty by adopting emblems of authority. The most effective means toward this end, says Livy, was through the assumption of twelve lictors, the number twelve being derived, according to some, from the twelve birds that had given him an augury of kingship or, according to others, from the twelve cities that comprised the Etruscan confederacy (Livy 1.8.3). The importance of the number twelve for the Romans may likewise be seen in the fact that the first action, according to Livy (1.19.6), of the revered Numa Pompilius, upon assuming the kingship, was to divide the year into twelve months.

Moreover, because one major test of a leader is seen in the ability to select outstanding assistants and successors, Hecataeus pays Moses the supreme compliment of saying (quoted in Diodorus 40.3.4) that he chose men of utmost refinement (χαριεστάτους) and of the greatest potential ability (μάλιστα δυνησομένους) to head the entire nation as priests. We may recall that the same word, χαριεστάτους, here used to describe the priests chosen by Moses, is the word used by Aristotle (*Nicomachean Ethics* 1.5.1095B22) to denote the people of superior refinement and of active disposition who identify happiness with honor, which is, adds Aristotle, the end of the political life. Here Hecataeus is, by implication, answering those, such as the biblical Korah,[6] who had attacked Moses for nepotism in selecting his own brother as high priest. In this crucial decision, selecting the proper priests, Moses parallels the founder of Rome, Romulus, as we see in Dionysius of Halicarnassus (*Roman Antiquities* 2.21).[7]

That Hecataeus was impressed with the form of government adopted by Moses is clear from his statement (quoted in Diodorus 40.3.5) that, according to the Mosaic code, the authority over the people is regularly vested in a priest regarded as superior to his colleagues in wisdom and virtue, and that this priest is called the high priest. The compliment is all the greater when we realize that in the time of Hecataeus, to judge from the pages of Josephus, the high priest was far from being necessarily superior to his colleagues in wisdom and virtue. It is also all the greater when we realize that the high priest was, during the period of the Second Temple (538 B.C.E.–70 C.E.), regularly chosen not on the basis of ability, as Hecataeus would have it, but rather in direct succession from father to son.

Moses is praised (by Hecataeus in Diodorus 40.3.7) for assigning greater allotments to the priests than to the rest of the citizens so that they might, by virtue of receiving more ample revenues, be undistracted and apply themselves constantly to the worship of G-d. This is reminiscent of Plato's *Republic* (7.540A–B), where the philosophers, we are told, will, from the age of fifty onward, spend the rest of their lives alternately ruling the ideal state and studying, though spending most of their time in philosophy. In point of fact, what Hecataeus presents is a utopian state similar to that of Panchaia (Diodorus 5.45.5), in which the priests had complete control, as well as to that of Euhemerus (Diodorus 5.45.5), in which the priests received a double share. One would think that, in view of the general contempt that the Greeks had for undue credulity, Hecataeus would make some remark of criticism when he declares (quoted in Diodorus 40.3.6) that the Jews are so docile that they fall to the ground and do reverence to the high priest when he expounds the commandments; but so great is his regard for the high priest as a kind of philosopher-king that he writes no such word of criticism.

Moreover, like Plato's philosopher-king in the *Republic*, Moses is praised (by Hecataeus in Diodorus 40.3.6) for showing foresight (πρό-νοιαν, a key Stoic term) in making provision for warfare and in requiring young men to cultivate "both manliness and steadfastness, and, generally, the endurance of every hardship" (ἀνδρείαν τε καὶ καρτερίαν καὶ τὸ σύνολον ὑπομονὴν πάσης κακοπαθείας; cf. Plato, *Republic* 2.375–3.390). Such a description is highly reminiscent of the Lycurgan constitution of Sparta, which was so much praised in antiquity.[8] Indeed, Moses himself is a role model for his people in that he is said (quoted in Hecataeus's account in Diodorus 40.3.7) to have led out successful military expeditions against the neighboring tribes. In fact, whereas in the Bible it is Joshua who conquered the Land of Israel, in Hecataeus (quoted in Diodorus 40.3.3) Moses is said to have taken possession of the land.

Finally, Hecataeus (quoted in Diodorus 40.3.8) is careful to protect the reputation of Moses by distancing him from the changes in Jewish traditional practices that he, like Strabo (16.2.39.762) at a later point, ascribed to Moses' successors. The fact, we may suggest, that in the earliest mention of Moses, that by Hecataeus, he is given credit for all the major institutions of the Jews, including especially those that set them apart from other people, shows that a tradition had developed, apparently in Alexandria, protecting the reputation of Moses while imputing the extremes of Jewish misanthropy to his successors. We may guess that this attempt to protect the standing of Moses may have been influenced by the potent force that the popular magic of the time attached to the very name of Moses.[9]

The identification by Hecataeus's contemporary, Manetho (quoted in *Against Apion* 1.250), of Osarsiph with Moses, even though the name seems more reminiscent of Joseph, shows how central Moses was to Manetho. The very fact that Manetho[10] (quoted in Josephus, *Against Apion* 1.250) identifies Moses as an Egyptian priest, as do several other writers,[11] and that of this group only Manetho and Chaeremon are anti-Jewish, shows that in itself such a statement does not prove animosity toward Moses. On the contrary, the Egyptian priests were said to possess esoteric knowledge; and Herodotus, for example, as he shows throughout the second book of his *Histories*, was very much impressed with this wisdom. We may conjecture that the basis of this tradition is the upbringing of Moses, according to the Bible, at the court of Pharaoh, who was regarded as a god. Hence, it was readily assumed that Moses must have learned the esoteric lore of the Egyptians. In addition, he had sojourned with Jethro the priest of Midian, whose daughter Zipporah he had married; and, furthermore, he himself was the brother of Aaron, the progenitor of the high priests among the Israelites.

Moses' reputation was further enhanced by Manetho's reference to him (quoted in *Against Apion* 1.235) as one of the learned (λογίων, "erudite") priests, especially because the word λογίων implies not only erudition but also skill and eloquence in words, an attribute much prized among the Greeks. Moreover, Manetho's identification (*Against Apion* 1.238) of Moses as one of the priests of Heliopolis adds considerable status to his person, especially because, as we learn from Strabo (17.1.29.806), both Plato and the famed mathematician and astronomer Eudoxus spent time there with the priests.[12] That the description of Moses as an Egyptian priest is not anti-Jewish is clear from the fact that Strabo, who is not hostile to Jews as such, describes Moses (16.2.35.760) as one of the priests of lower Egypt who left the country because of his disaffection with Egyptian animal worship.

Josephus (*Against Apion* 1.279) comments, though he does not give his source, that the Egyptians wished to regard Moses as remarkable (θαυμαστόν), and even divine (θεῖον), and actually sought to claim him as one of their own, while yet asserting that he was one of the priests expelled from Heliopolis for leprosy. Such a statement could hardly have been made by Josephus in a polemical work unless the Egyptians had indeed made such a remark. Moreover, in Manetho's eyes (*Against Apion* 1.241–42) Moses had standing as a military commander, as seen in his invitation to the Hyksos to join him in an expedition against Egypt and in the ease with which he reduced Egypt to submission.[13]

In general, Alexander Polyhistor, who lived in the first century B.C.E., is well informed about and favorable toward the Jews, but with regard to

Moses he makes the remarkable statement (quoted in Suda, under the entry Ἀλέξανδρος ὁ Μιλήσιος) that the laws of the Hebrews had been composed by a Hebrew woman named Moso. On the surface this would seem to be an attempt to ridicule the lawgiver of the Jews.[14] We may here suggest that perhaps Polyhistor or his source saw a similarity of sound between Moses and Musaeus, the pupil of the revered Orpheus,[15] and Μῶσα (Doric for Μοῦσα, "muse," a feminine noun) and hence drew the conclusion that Moses was feminine. Or alternatively, Polyhistor may have believed that divinely inspired men, like divinities, were bisexual, as we find in the case of such deities as Hermaphroditus and Dionysus.

The historian Diodorus (1.94.1–2) in the first century B.C.E. speaks in praise of Moses as a lawgiver; and although others might have disparaged him for maintaining that Moses had obtained the laws from G-d because they felt that Moses had himself originated them, Diodorus, in citing Moses' assertion, parallels it with the claims of the greatest of all lawgivers in antiquity—Mneves of Egypt, Minos of Crete, Lycurgus of Sparta, Zarathustra of the Persians, and Zalmoxis of the Getans. Diodorus justifies this device as producing much good among those who believed it. "They did it," he says in obvious admiration, "either because they believed that a conception which would help humanity was marvellous and wholly divine, or because they held that the common crowd would be more likely to obey the laws if their gaze was directed towards the majesty and power of those to whom their laws were ascribed."

Strabo, in the first century B.C.E., like Manetho (quoted in Josephus, *Against Apion* 1.250) before him and like Chaeremon (cited in *Against Apion* 1.290) after him, describes Moses as an Egyptian priest. Like Hecataeus (quoted in Diodorus 40.3.2), Strabo (16.2.36.761), in a clearly complimentary remark, ascribes to Moses the establishment of Jerusalem, whither he persuaded not a few thoughtful (εὐγνώμονας) men to settle. He pays Moses the supreme compliment of remaking him in the image of his own Stoic philosophy,[16] ascribing to him a view of G-d as "the one thing alone that encompasses us all and encompasses land and sea—the thing which we call heaven, or universe, or the nature of all that exists." Like Diodorus, Strabo (16.2.38–39.762) bestows on Moses the highest praise of making him parallel to the revered Cretan Minos and the Spartan Lycurgus as a lawgiver who claimed divine sanction for his laws. Moses, he says in obvious admiration, was a prophet (μάντις) like—and the list is an international "Who's Who" of ancient prophets and scientists and philosophers and musicians—Teiresias, Amphiaraus, Trophonius, Orpheus, Musaeus, Zalmoxis, Decaeneus, Achaecarus, the Gymnosophists, the Magi, the Chaldaeans, and the Tyrrhenian nativity-casters. He is thus in the tradition of prophet-kings described by Herodotus (4.94–95),

Plato (*Laws* 1.632D), and Polybius (10.2.1 ff.). Apparently, Moses was part of a canon of ancient and wise men, so that his omission from Celsus's list, as we have remarked, is noted as remarkable by Origen (*Against Celsus* 1.16).

It is significant of the high regard of the ancients for Moses that Strabo (16.2.36–37.761) draws a distinction between, on the one hand, Moses, whom he admires, and the latter's successors, who, he says, at first acted righteously and piously, and, on the other hand, the superstitious men who were later appointed as priests and tyrannical rulers (presumably an allusion to the Hasmonean kings).[17] Elsewhere (16.2.39.762) Strabo repeats this contrast between the prophet-king Moses and his successors, "who, with no bad beginning, turned out for the worse."[18]

Pompeius Trogus (quoted in Justin, *Historiae Philippicae* 36, *Epitoma* 2.11) in the first century c.e. commends Moses not only for the knowledge he had inherited from his father, whom he identifies as Joseph,[19] but also for the beauty of his person, a quality that was so important to the ancients.[20] Most likely, Trogus's remark is a reflection of such a statement as Plato's (*Republic* 7.535A10–12) that, so far as possible, the handsomest persons should be chosen to be philosopher-kings.

Pseudo-Longinus (9.9), in the first century c.e., author of the treatise which, next to Aristotle's *Poetics*, is the most important essay on literary criticism emanating from antiquity, refers to the lawgiver (θεσμοθέτης) of the Jews as no chance person (οὐχ ὁ τυχὼν ἀνήρ), a phrase found also in Strabo (16.2.36.761), "since he understood and gave expression to the power of divinity as it deserved—when he wrote at the beginning of his laws . . . 'G-d said'—what? 'Let there be light.' And there was. 'Let there be earth.' And there was." Apparently Pseudo-Longinus felt that Moses was sufficiently well-known that he did not have to refer to him by name.

Moreover, for Pseudo-Longinus to speak of Moses as a lawgiver was in itself a compliment, putting Moses in a class with Minos and Lycurgus. Pseudo-Longinus, as we have noted, includes this passage, together with four others from Homer and a verbal exchange beween Alexander the Great and Parmenio, to illustrate his point that the basic ingredient of great writing is not literary style but rather a great mind. Because this is the last example cited, it would seem to be the climax, and the compliment is all the greater. It is thus clear from the context that Pseudo-Longinus regarded Moses as at least the equal of Homer in matters concerning the gods.[21]

We may call further attention to the implied compliment in the otherwise anti-Jewish work of the first-century Chaeremon, as cited by Josephus (*Against Apion* 1.290), that the Jewish leaders at the time of the Exodus were two scribes (γραμματέας)—Moses and another sacred scribe (ἱερογραμματέα), Joseph. Indeed, the very mention of Moses is a concession, because, as we have noted from Philo (*De Vita Mosis* 1.1.2), in general the envious Greeks did not even deign to speak of him.

Chaeremon's fellow Jew-baiter, Apion (quoted in *Against Apion* 2.10), the most notorious anti-Jewish writer of the first century, says that he has heard from old people in Egypt that Moses was a native of Heliopolis; he thus follows the tradition, noted above, of Manetho, who had described Moses as a priest of Heliopolis. His assertion that he had heard it from old people aims to emphasize the antiquity of the tradition.[22]

Another compliment paid by Apion (quoted in *Against Apion* 2.11) to Moses, by implication at least, is that he was a scientist,[23] inasmuch as he is said to have set up a model of a boat to serve as a sundial.[24] In view of the Hellenistic emphasis on science,[25] to impute such knowledge to Moses is a distinct compliment.

When Quintilian (3.7.21), at the end of the first century, refers to "the founder of the Jewish superstition," he, like Pseudo-Longinus, does not deem it necessary to name him, because Moses was apparently well-known.[26] The repetition of the same charge of superstition against Moses in Quintilian's younger contemporary Tacitus and in Juvenal is evidence that a new image of Moses, prompted by the conflicts between the Jews and the Roman emperors, starting with Tiberius, had established itself in this period.[27] We must, however, reserve judgment, inasmuch as all three of these critics are rhetoricians or satirists and hence tend to exaggerate.

A curious motif, presumably going back to the Alexandrian anti-Jewish version of the Exodus, that the Jews had been expelled from Egypt because of leprosy (Manetho, quoted in Josephus, *Against Apion* 1.229–33), appears in three extant writers, starting with Nicarchus (cited in Photius, *Lexicon*, under the listing ἄλφα) in his work *On Jews* in the first century and repeated in the early second century by Ptolemy Chennos (cited in Photius, *Lexicon* 190 [p. 151B9, ed. Bekker]) and in the early fourth century by Helladius (cited in Photius, *Lexicon* 279 [p. 529B27, ed. Bekker]). Here we learn that Moses the legislator (νομοθέτης, a term similar to the θεσμοθέτης of Pseudo-Longinus 9.9) was called *alpha* by the Jews because he had much dull-white leprosy (ἀλφούς) on his body. Inasmuch as Moses is nowhere else called *alpha* in extant classical literature, the source may have been the Alexandrian anti-Jewish account of the Exodus.[28] Such a bodily defect was regarded by the ancients as a clear indication of divine disapproval. As we can see from Ptolemy, such puns in connection with letters of the alphabet were common; thus, a certain Satyrus was called *zeta* because of his inquisitiveness (ζητητικόν). From the fact that the Septuagint, Philo, and Josephus (*Ant.* 2.273) on Exodus 4:6 omit the statement that Moses' hand was leprous, and from Photius's reference to Nicarchus's statement as nonsense and to Helladius's as a lie, we may infer that this pun was intended to express hostility toward the Jews.[29] And yet, we may suggest that Moses was, indeed, called *alpha* by the Jews themselves because he was regarded as the greatest prophet, just as in the Book of Revelation (1:8) Jesus, presumably as the new Moses, is spoken of as the Alpha and the Omega.[30]

Even Tacitus, the most bitter of Jew-baiters, early in the second century bestows some respect on Moses. He is the leader (*Histories* 5.3.2) of the exiles in the desert who frees them from their misery by finding water for them. Tacitus (*Histories* 5.4.1) regards his novel legislation as a clever political device to secure his authority over the Jews; and in this respect Moses is presumably like the universally admired Minos. Lest one regard such deceit as a condemnation of Moses, one will recall that in Plato's ideal state (*Republic* 3.414B–415D) the rulers propound a "noble lie" in order to persuade the various classes to accept their status without question.

That Moses had achieved a reputation for wisdom even among those who were critical of him is clear also from the second-century c.e. Celsus (quoted in Origen, *Against Celsus* 1.21), who admits that Moses accepted wise and true doctrines and educated his people with them, and that he, moreover, became famous for his divine power, that is, presumably through magic and sorcery.[31]

Though the eminent second-century physician and philosopher Galen is critical of Moses for framing his laws without offering proofs,[32] there is no venom in this criticism; and it simply confirms the view, which we have noted, of Moses as a divinely inspired lawgiver. That Galen did have regard for Moses as a philosopher is clear from his comment (*De Usu Partium* 11.14) that Moses' way of treating Nature is superior to that of Epicurus, though inferior to that of Plato. In particular, he commends and agrees with Moses' doctrine of the demiurge as the origin of every created thing.

In the second half of the second century c.e., admiration for Moses reached its height in the remark, which we have noted above, of the Neo-Pythagorean Numenius of Apamea, who writes (quoted in Clement of Alexandria, *Stromata* 1.22.150.4), "For what is Plato, but Moses speaking in Attic Greek?" In view of the tremendous reputation enjoyed by Plato and in view of the revival, in modified form, of his teachings in the guise of Neo-Platonism, of which Numenius was the main forerunner, this is a tremendous compliment. We have already noted the traditions connecting Pythagoras himself with Jewish teachings; and apparently this positive attitude toward the Jews continued in his school. The popularity of this dictum may be seen from the fact that it is quoted in no fewer than four other places (Eusebius, *Praeparatio Evangelica* 9.6.9; 11.10.14; The-

odoret, *Graecarum Affectionum Curatio* 2.114; Suda, under the heading
Νουμήνιος) in extant literature.[33]

The fact that Numenius (quoted in Eusebius, *Praeparatio Evangelica*
9.8.2) refers to Moses as Musaeus, the pupil/teacher of Orpheus, recalling Artapanus's statement (quoted in Eusebius, *Praeparatio Evangelica*
9.27.3), is still another indication of his high regard for Moses. His reference there to Moses as "a man who was most powerful in prayer to G-d"
is surely a great tribute. Apparently, to judge from Origen (*Against Celsus*
4.51), Numenius quoted Moses and the prophets in many passages in his
writings and gave them no improbable allegorical interpretations. So
positive is Numenius's view of Moses and of Judaism that it has actually
been suggested that Numenius himself was a Jew.[34] But for someone to
be identified as a Neo-Pythagorean and yet to be also a Jew would be a
remarkable and unparalleled combination.[35]

As late as the sixth century c.e., the scholiast Lactantius Placidus (commentary on Statius, *Thebaid* 4.516), who was apparently one of the last
pagans,[36] in a clear tribute couples Moses with Orpheus—perhaps because of the similarity of the name of Moses to Musaeus, as Numenius
had noted—in their views concerning the knowability of the name of G-d.

2. THE VIRTUES OF MOSES ACCORDING TO
GRAECO-JEWISH HISTORIANS

If, as was especially true in antiquity, the reputation of a people rose or
fell with the reputation of its founder or lawgiver, the fact that the historian Eupolemus (quoted in Clement of Alexandria, *Stromata* 1.23.153.4)
in the second century b.c.e. declared that Moses was the first wise man
(σοφόν) was the supreme compliment.[37] In particular, he notes that
Moses gave the alphabet to the Jews, who in turn taught it to the Phoenicians, who thereafter transmitted it to the Greeks. Only if we compare
the simplicity of this alphabet with the complexity of the syllabic script
of Linear B previously employed by the Greeks can we appreciate the
tremendous importance of this revolutionary innovation.[38] Moreover,
the letters of the alphabet, as instruments of mystery and magic, were
regarded as powerful; and knowledge of the letters was regarded as a
divine gift.[39]

The fact that, according to Artapanus in the second century b.c.e.
(quoted in Eusebius, *Praeparatio Evangelica* 9.27.3–4), Moses was called
Musaeus by the Greeks and was a teacher of Orpheus[40] would elevate
Moses considerably, inasmuch as Orpheus was said to be the founder of
extraordinarily popular mysteries and Musaeus was said to have been his
son or teacher or student, as we have noted. The close association of both
(like that of Moses)[41] with music, which played an enormously important

role among the ancients, as we can see from the education of the guardians in Plato's *Republic*,[42] meant that Moses was raised tremendously in public esteem. One recalls Socrates' remark (Plato, *Apology* 41A6–8), after he has been condemned to death, that if death is a journey to another world he should welcome death, for "What would not a man give if he might converse with Orpheus and Musaeus and Hesiod and Homer?"

In contrast to Apollonius Molon's contention (cited in Josephus, *Against Apion* 2.148) that the Jews had contributed no useful invention to civilization, Artapanus (quoted in Eusebius, *Praeparatio Evangelica* 9.27.4) gives a veritable catalogue of Moses' inventions: ships, machines for lifting stones, Egyptian weapons, devices for drawing water and fighting, and philosophy.[43] So wise was Moses that he was called Hermes because of his ability to interpret the sacred writings. This identification with the god Hermes would, to a pagan, have signified a particular gift in the skill of communication, which was especially the province of Hermes; such an identification is most striking because, as is well known, according to the Bible (Exod 4:10) Moses had a speech impediment. A further compliment may be seen in the sheer popularity of Hermes, who, though a thief and a trickster, is the one god, as we can see from Aristophanes' *Plutus* (admittedly a satirical setting), who was still receiving sacrifices when all the others were being starved out. Moreover, his invention of the lyre made him a general patron of literature, so that in Petronius's *Satyricon*, for example, the wandering scholars are said to be under his special protection.

3. THE VIRTUES OF MOSES ACCORDING TO JOSEPHUS

When we examine the key figures in Josephus's paraphrase of the biblical narrative, we see that, in almost every case, Josephus stresses their external qualities of good birth and handsome stature, and the four cardinal virtues of character—wisdom, courage, temperance, and justice—and the spiritual quality of piety, such as Xenophon described in his biography of Agesilaus (*Agesilaus* 3–6). In general, the hero must be a Platonic-like philosopher-king, a high priest, a prophet, and a veritable Pericles as described by Thucydides.[44] In the case of an outstanding hero such as Moses, his very birth must be attended with extraordinary signs. Moreover, because Josephus is addressing a predominantly non-Jewish audience,[45] his hero must fulfill the qualifications such as Tacitus ascribes to his revered father-in-law Agricola (Tacitus, *Agricola* 44–45): a life ended in its prime but rich in glory, attainment of the true blessings of virtue, honors of political office, wealth sufficient for his desires, death before that of wife and child, integrity of position and reputation, unsevered links of relationship and friendship, and immunity from massacres that followed his death.

Indeed, Josephus's treatment of Moses is an aretalogy—a veritable catalogue of virtues—such as would be appreciated especially by a Roman society that admired the portrait of the ideal Stoic sage. In fact, on no fewer than twenty-one occasions[46] the word ἀρετή is used with reference to Moses. What is particularly effective is that at the very beginning of his long narrative of Moses, one of the Egyptian sacred scribes,[47] a non-Jew who, as Josephus (*Ant.* 2.205) remarks, possessed considerable skill in accurately predicting the future, foretells the birth of a child who will surpass all others in virtue (ἀρετῇ) and win everlasting renown. Indeed, Josephus (*Ant.* 3.187) declares that his subject, the history of the Jewish people, will afford him frequent and ample occasion to discourse on the merits (ἀρετήν) of the lawgiver Moses.

It is particularly effective that when the Israelites arrive at Mount Sinai, Raguel (Jethro), another non-Jew, Moses' father-in-law, praises Moses (*Ant.* 3.65) because he knew that all the salvation of the Israelites had been due to the ἀρετή of Moses. This recognition by non-Jews of the virtues of Moses surely conveyed a clear message to non-Jewish readers of Josephus's works that the constitution Moses promulgated was to be admired and that it would be a distinct honor to join the people whom he led and taught. Indeed, so outstanding was he in his virtue, we are told (*Ant.* 3.96–97), that when Moses did not return from his ascent on Mount Sinai even the sober-minded of the Israelites considered the possibility that he had returned to G-d because of his inherent virtue. It is through the agency of Moses and his merits (ἀρετῆς) that the constitution of the Israelites was established by G-d (*Ant.* 3.322). Finally, we may note that when Josephus (*Ant.* 4.331) describes the impact of Moses' death he presents the extra-biblical comment that his passing was lamented not only by those who had known him directly but also by the very readers of his laws—and these would include non-Jews who read the Septuagint or Josephus's paraphrase—who deduced from these enactments the superlative quality of his virtue (ἀρετή).

Genealogy

The first of the thirty-six stages of praising a person, according to the Greek rhetorician Theon, was to laud his ancestry.[48] Indeed, the *Hippias Maior* (285D), ascribed to Plato, notes, as one of the particular concerns of an "archaeology," the genealogies of heroes and of men. Josephus's Greek readers would have thought of the importance attached to genealogy in Homer, as, for example, in the scene where Glaucus meets Diomedes (*Iliad* 6.123–231) and they exchange genealogies at the point of

engaging in battle.[49] Josephus himself characteristically begins his auto-
biography (*Life* 1–6) with a detailed account of his pedigree, tracing back
both his priestly and his royal ancestry. He likewise stresses (*Against
Apion* 1.31–32) that before marrying a woman a priest must investigate
her pedigree, "obtaining the genealogy from the archives and producing
a number of witnesses." This emphasis on genealogy, he adds, is true not
merely in Judaea but wherever Jews are settled.

When Josephus first introduces us to Moses' father Amram, his initial
remark (*Ant.* 2.210) is that he was a Hebrew "of noble birth" (εὖ γεγονό-
των).[50] Like Demetrius (quoted in Eusebius, *Praeparatio Evangelica*
9.29.2), Philo (*De Vita Mosis* 1.2.7), and the rabbis (*Genesis Rabbah* 19.7,
Song of Songs Rabbah 5.1, *Pesiqta de-Rav Kahana* 2.343–44), Josephus (*Ant.*
2.229) presents the extra-biblical addition that Moses was the seventh
generation after Abraham;[51] and, like the rabbis, he actually mentions
Moses' ancestors by name.

In another addition to the Bible, we are told that the fire at the burning
bush admonished Moses to withdraw from the flame as far as possible
and to be content with what he, as a man of virtue and sprung from
illustrious ancestors, had seen and to pry no further. And when (*Against
Apion* 1.316) Josephus attacks Lysimachus's account of the Exodus, he
makes a point of stressing that Lysimachus should not have been content
with mentioning Moses by name but should have indicated his descent
and his parentage.

The Birth of the Hero

There are many parallels to the predictions and wondrous events attending the birth of both the mythological and the historical hero, including
the motifs of the prediction of his greatness, of his abandonment by his
mother, and his overcoming the ruler of the land.[52] Such motifs were,
undoubtedly, well known to many of Josephus's literate readers. Josephus's additions may best be appreciated when his account is compared
with parallels in classical literature, in the rabbinic Midrashim, and in
Samaritan tradition.[53] Thus, we find (Iamblichus 5.7) a similar annuncia-
tion from the Pythian priestess at Delphi to the father of Pythagoras that
there would be born to him a son of extraordinary beauty and wisdom.
Again, there is a legend in connection with Plato (Diogenes Laertius 3.2)
of the child who will overcome a ruler. Likewise, the apocalyptic technique is seen in Dido's prediction (Virgil, *Aeneid* 4.625) of the birth of
one who would avenge her treatment by Aeneas, namely Hannibal.[54]

From Roman mythology or history the births of Romulus and Remus
may be cited;[55] in their case King Amulius of Alba Longa not only forcibly deprived his older brother Numitor of the throne that was rightfully

his but plotted to prevent Numitor's descendants from seeking revenge by making Numitor's daughter, Rhea Silvia, a vestal virgin, thus preventing her from marrying; but this plot was foiled when she became, by the war god Mars, the mother of twins, who, though thrown into the Tiber River (thus paralleling Pharaoh's orders that male children be drowned), were washed ashore, suckled by a she-wolf, then brought up by the royal herdsman Faustulus, and eventually overthrew Amulius and restored Numitor to the throne.

There are similar historical parallels that were conceivably well known to Josephus and to his readers. Thus, Herodotus (1.107), one of Josephus's favorite authors,[56] tells of the dream of Astyages, the king of the Medes, that his daughter Mandane would have a son who would conquer Asia. When the son, Cyrus, is born, Astyages, like Pharaoh, orders that he be killed; but a herdsman saves him and rears him. The son ultimately becomes king of Persia and defeats Astyages in battle. Moses would thus be equated with Cyrus, the great national hero of the Persians.[57]

In order to heighten expectations for Moses, whereas the Bible (Exod 1:22) merely notes Pharaoh's decree ordering that every newborn Israelite son be cast into the Nile, Josephus (*Ant.* 2.210–16) adds that Moses' father Amram was afraid that the whole race of the Israelites would be extinguished through lack of a succeeding generation and was in grievous perplexity because his wife was pregnant. Josephus then recounts Amram's prayer to G-d beseeching Him to grant deliverance to the Israelites from their tribulations and G-d's response to him in a dream that he should not despair. G-d assures him that just as He had aided his forefathers Abraham and Jacob, so would He enable this child to deliver the Israelites from bondage in Egypt. He predicts (*Ant.* 2.216) that this child will be remembered so long as the universe shall endure (τὰ σύμπαντα τεύξεται);[58] and then in an obvious attempt to impress his non-Jewish audience, Josephus adds the divine prediction that this child will be remembered not only by Hebrews but also by alien nations.

Though Josephus closely parallels the rabbinic tradition with regard to the predictions of Moses' birth, as he does in so many other respects,[59] he does not do so with regard to many other rabbinic expansions on biblical themes, such as the prediction (*Pirqe de-Rabbi Eliezer* 26, *Seder Eliyahu Zuta* 25) from the stars by the notorious King Nimrod that the child Abraham would overthrow the thrones of powerful princes and take possession of their lands. Nor does he parallel the story that Abraham's father Terah hid him until the third or the tenth year of his life when Nimrod sought to kill him. Apparently, Josephus sought to aggrandize the character of Moses to a degree greater than that of Abraham because in the eyes of the Gentiles Moses was most closely identified with the Jewish people. Hence, in Josephus (*Ant.* 2.205) it is an Egyptian sacred scribe who makes the prediction of the future greatness of Moses—surely a more impressive figure to his audience than King Nimrod; and it is to Amram (*Ant.* 2.212–16) in a dream—an element unique in Josephus—that G-d appears with the promise that the child to be born will deliver the Hebrews from bondage; on the other hand, in rabbinic tradition (*Midrash Exodus Rabbah* 1.22; cf. *Megillah* 14a, *Sotah* 12b, *Mekilta Beshalaḥ* 10) it is Moses' sister Miriam who has the dream predicting that Moses will be cast into the waters and that through him the crossing of the Red Sea, as well as other miracles, will be accomplished.[60]

The Upbringing of the Hero

One of the typical motifs, common to the Hellenistic, Roman, Christian, and rabbinic biography of a hero, was his exceptional physical development, beauty, self-control, and precocious intellectual development as a child.[61] Indeed, in the case of a hero such as Romulus, his superiority of stature and strength of body impress his grandfather Numitor when his identity is not yet known (Plutarch, *Romulus* 7.3–4). Again, it is while still a boy that Alexander (Plutarch, *Alexander* 4.8) shows such remarkable self-restraint regarding pleasures of the body and keeps his spirit serious and lofty in advance of his years, despite his tendency to impetuosity and violence in other matters.

As to Moses, according to Josephus (*Ant.* 2.230), already in his third year, presumably after he had completed the standard nursing period of two years (cf. Mishnah, *Nedarim* 2:1 and *Kethuboth* 60a), G-d gave wondrous increase to his stature. Josephus (*Ant.* 2.230) states that his growth in understanding far outran the measure of his years, and his maturity was displayed in his very games; "and his actions then gave promise of the greater deeds to be wrought by him on reaching manhood."[62] We are reminded of Herodotus's description (1.114) of the ten-year-old Cyrus, whose parentage was discovered through an incident that occurred when he was playing with the village boys and ordered one of them to be beaten for disobeying his command.

Josephus (*Ant.* 2.232–36) recounts the tale, which has a clear parallel in the rabbinic tradition, of the infant Moses who is brought to Pharaoh and tramples on Pharaoh's crown.[63] The story has its classical parallel in the anecdote (Herodotus 1.114) noted above, of Cyrus, who already as a child played at being king. But the differences between the Josephan and rabbinic versions are instructive. In the Midrash, it is Moses who takes the crown from Pharaoh's head and places it on his own as a clear prediction that he would some day displace Pharaoh. In Josephus, who was well aware that such an aggressive attitude would not find favor among his readers, it is Pharaoh's daughter who takes the initiative (*Ant.* 2.232) of bringing the infant Moses to him because she is mindful for the succession and because, inasmuch as she has no child of her own, she seeks to adopt Moses as heir apparent. Far from Moses seizing the crown and placing it on his own head, as in the rabbinic tradition, it is Pharaoh who then takes the initiative of placing the crown on Moses' head. Only then do we have the parallel of Moses flinging the crown to the ground and trampling on it. Likewise, Josephus does not include the scene (*Yashar Exodus* 131b–132b) that follows, whereby Moses is then put to the test to see whether he is truly a threat to the throne, namely, of the burning coal and onyx stone placed before him to choose from. Such an incident would have reinforced the view that the Jews are aggressive, because, according to the Midrash, Moses actually stretched forth his little hand toward the onyx stone but was deterred by the angel Gabriel toward the live coal, whereupon he burned his hand, lifted it to his mouth, burned part of his lips and part of his tongue and thus incurred the speech impediment to which the Bible (Exod 4:10) refers.

If Josephus had reproduced the rabbinic tradition of Moses seizing Pharaoh's crown, the parallel (as later described by Nonnus, *Dionysiaca* 6.163–68 and 27.341) with Zagreus, that is Dionysus, who soon after his birth ascended the throne of his father Zeus and mimicked him by brandishing lightning in his little hand, might well have suggested itself to his pagan audience. Josephus, we may guess, was particularly sensitive to this charge of Jewish aggressiveness because the Jews had been at least twice expelled from Rome because of aggressive missionary tactics, first in 139 B.C.E. (Valerius Maximus 1.3.3) and then in 19 C.E. (Dio Cassius 57.18.5a), as we have remarked. Hence, even when Moses removes from his head the crown that Pharaoh had placed on it, Josephus is careful to add that he does so in mere childishness (νηπιότητα). And when the sacred scribe who had foretold that the child's birth would lead to the abasement of the Egyptian empire rushed forward to kill Moses after he had trampled on the crown, the king, we are informed (*Ant.* 2.236), delayed killing him, induced by G-d, whose providence (πρόνοια)—a key Stoic term that would have been appreciated by Josephus's audience— watched over Moses' life.

The Bible (Exodus 2:10) is extraordinarily brief about Moses' education during his youth and states merely that "the child grew up." Philo (*De Vita Mosis* 1.5.21), clearly concerned to portray the legislator of the Jewish people as a kind of philosopher-king in the Platonic tradition, declares that to educate him teachers, some unbidden, arrived from various countries and from the provinces of Egypt, and some, summoned from Greece, arrived under promise of high reward. We are then told that in a short time Moses advanced beyond their capacity to teach him, and that in true Platonic fashion he exemplified the principle of ἀνάμνῆσις, as described in Plato's *Meno*, inasmuch as his seemed a case rather of recollection (ἀνάμνησιν) than of learning; and, indeed, he himself devised and propounded problems his teachers could not easily solve. Philo then (*De Vita Mosis* 1.5.23) proceeds to enumerate the subjects—arithmetic, geometry, and music, as well as hieroglyphics and religion (notably the Egyptian regard for animals, to which they paid divine honors)—that the Egyptian teachers taught him, and informs the reader that the Greeks taught him the rest of the liberal arts, while others taught him Assyrian letters (presumably Aramaic) and the Chaldean science of astronomy.

Though Josephus (*Ant.* 18.259–60) mentions Philo as "no novice in philosophy" and as the head of the Jewish delegation to the Emperor Gaius Caligula, and though there is reason to think that he knew his works,[64] he is content (*Ant.* 2.236) with the briefest of comments about Moses' upbringing (he does not specify education),[65] namely that he was brought up (ἐτρέφετο) with the utmost care (ἐπιμελείας), so that the Hebrews rested their highest hopes on him for their future, while the Egyptians viewed his upbringing with misgiving. One might well assume that Josephus would have recorded with pride the liberal education Moses received; but we may conjecture that he found it embarrassing to state that Moses, who insisted on a monotheism with no representation of the Divine, had been taught hieroglyphics and the details of the Egyptian worship of animals. We may presume that this may have led Josephus to his silence about such Hellenistic Jewish historians as Artapanus (quoted in Eusebius, *Praeparatio Evangelica* 9.27.4), who proudly boasts that Moses invented hieroglyphic writing and taught religion to the Egyptians, assigning divinity to cats, dogs, and ibises.

Handsomeness

The ancients were keenly aware of the importance of physical beauty, as we see notably in Homer, for example, in the scene (*Iliad* 22.370) where the Greeks run to gaze on the stature and admirable form of Hector after he has been slain by Achilles. They would likewise have agreed with Plato's famous comment (*Republic* 7.535A11–12) that in seeking out the guardians of the state "we shall prefer the sturdiest, the bravest, and, so far as possible, the handsomest (εὐειδεστάτους) persons."

In particular, we may note a recurring motif in biographies of famous men—handsomeness from their earliest years. Thus, we are told (Apollonius-Iamblichus 10, p. 11, lines 6–7; cf. Apuleius, *Florida* 15) that the child Pythagoras attracted the attention of everyone because of his beauty. Moreover, in the very earliest of biographies, Isocrates (*Evagoras* 22–23) reports that Evagoras from his youth was endowed with beauty and bodily strength and that these increased as he grew older. Similarly, we hear (Dionysius of Halicarnassus, *Roman Antiquities* 1.79.10) that when the twins Romulus and Remus came to be men, they showed themselves both in dignity of aspect (μορφῆς) and elevation of mind "not like swineherds and neatherds, but such as we might expect those to be who are born of royal race and appear to be the offspring of the gods."

Just as he does in the case of a number of other biblical heroes,[66] so also in the instance of Moses, Josephus emphasizes his beauty. Indeed, almost at the very beginning of his portrait, Moses' beauty plays a key role. Thus, whereas in the Bible (Exod 2:6) Pharaoh's daughter saves the baby in the floating ark because he is crying, in Josephus (*Ant.* 2.224) her motive is that she is enchanted by his size (μεγέθους) and beauty (κάλλους). In fact, when she brings the child Moses to her father (*Ant.* 2.232) with the intention of adopting him and of making him heir to the kingdom, she describes him as being of divine beauty (μορφῇ . . . θεῖον). This is all the more effective, coming, as it does, from a non-Jew, inasmuch as in the Bible (Exod 2:2) it is Moses' mother Jochebed who is said to have seen that her child was goodly (*tov*)—a word the Septuagint renders as ἀστεῖον ("town-bred," "polite," "good," "pretty," "graceful," "charming"). Apparently, this tradition of Moses' beauty had even reached the non-Jewish world, inasmuch we find in Pompeius Trogus (quoted in Justin, *Historiae Philippicae* 36, *Epitome* 2.11), who lived at the end of the first century B.C.E. and at the beginning of the first century C.E., the statement that Moses' "beauty of appearance" (*formae pulchritudo*) recommended him.

Moreover, we are told (*Ant.* 2.231) that none was so indifferent to beauty (κάλλος) as, on seeing him, not to be amazed at his comeliness (εὐμορφίας). Josephus adds that it often happened that persons meeting him as he was borne along the highway neglected their serious affairs to gaze at him; "Indeed, childish charm so perfect and pure as his held the beholders spellbound."[67] We may note that Josephus uses the same nouns (μορφή ["shape," "form," "beauty"] and φρόνημα ["spirit," "intellect," "intelligence"]) in the description by Pharaoh's daughter (*Ant.* 2.232) of the infant Moses that are used by Dionysius (*Roman Antiquities* 1.79.10) in describing Romulus and Remus.

Furthermore, Moses' radiant (γλαῦρος) appearance (*Ant.* 3.83) on descending from Mount Sinai is calculated to appeal to his literate audience. Thus, whereas Exodus 19:25 says merely that Moses went down to the people and spoke to them, Josephus (*Ant.* 3.83) makes a much more dramatic scene, declaring, as he does, that the mere sight of him rid them of their terrors and promised brighter hopes for the future. Even the very air, we are told, became, upon his appearance, serene and purged of its recent disturbances.

Josephus is particularly eager to answer the canard, circulated by Manetho (quoted in *Against Apion* 1.279), among others,[68] that Moses' appearance was marred by leprosy. Josephus, in his elaboration, may have sought to counter Manetho's statement (quoted in *Against Apion* 1.279) that Moses was a leper, as well as the assertion of a Lysimachus (quoted in *Against Apion* 1.305–11) that the ancestors of the Jews were lepers and diseased people who had been banished from Egypt for that reason.[69] That Josephus was sensitive to this charge is clear from his treatment of the passage (Exod 4:6) in which G-d tells Moses, as a sign to help convince the Israelites that He had indeed appeared to him, to put his hand into his bosom. Thereupon his hand was leprous, but when he put it back into his bosom and took it out again it was restored like the rest of his flesh. In Josephus's version (*Ant.* 2.273) there is no mention of leprosy; instead we are told that when Moses drew forth his hand it was "white, of a color resembling chalk."[70] Moreover, Josephus (*Against Apion* 1.279) points out the inherent contradiction on the part of the anti-Jewish Egyptian writers in, on the one hand, claiming Moses as an Egyptian priest and asserting that Moses was remarkable (θαυμαστόν) and even divine (θεῖον), and, on the other hand, charging that he was expelled because of leprosy. Josephus (*Ant.* 3.265), recalling this charge of leprosy, refutes it (3.266–68) by remarking that if this were true Moses would not have issued to his own humiliation statutes banishing lepers, especially because there are nations that honor lepers. In fact, in a significant change, according to Josephus (*Ant.* 3.261, *Against Apion* 1.281), Moses banished lepers not merely from the camp, as the Bible (Lev 13:46, 14:3) would have it, but also from the city, the implication being that there were no lepers in Jerusalem in Josephus's own day.[71]

Moreover, just as Plato had declared that a philosopher-king should, if at all possible, be handsome, so Josephus (*Against Apion* 1.284) remarks that Moses legislated that even the slightest mutilation of the person was reason enough for disqualification for the priesthood and that a priest who during the course of his service met with such an accident was deprived of his position. Josephus then asks (*Against Apion* 1.285) whether it is likely that Moses would have enacted such a stringent law if he himself had been affected by such an an affliction.[72]

The Qualities of Leadership

Josephus is at every point eager to underline Moses' importance as a leader, especially because the race of humanity, according to Josephus (*Ant.* 3.23), is by nature morose (δυσαρέστον, "discontented," "grumbling," "irritable") and censorious (φιλαιτίον, "fond of having reproaches at hand").[73] He stresses the importance of Moses' leadership by noting (*Ant.* 2.204) that the Israelites had endured hardships in Egypt for four hundred years and that the contest was between the Egyptians, striving to kill off the Israelites with drudgery, and the Israelites, ever eager to show themselves superior to their tasks. The details Josephus (*Ant.* 2.203) adds to the biblical account (Exod 1:11) of the hard labor imposed by the Egyptians on the Israelites emphasize the crucial role played by Moses in leading his people out of slavery.

An effective leader must be a great teacher of his people, as we can see from Plato (*Laws* 4.722B). In particular, he must teach his people to obey his laws. In dealing with the rude and uneducated masses, legislators, says Plato, up until his own day, have used only force, whereas persuasion as a means has been totally neglected. Apparently, Josephus is aware of this Platonic view, because he, too, writes (*Against Apion* 2.171) that there are two ways of arriving at any discipline or moral conduct in life, namely by instruction in words and by exercises in practice, and that Moses, as the supreme leader and teacher, succeeded in combining both approaches.[74]

Furthermore, a great leader must be a psychologist; and Moses, in Josephus's portrait, excels in this respect. Thus, whereas the biblical text (Num 21:24) states merely that the Israelites defeated the Amorites, Josephus's Moses (*Ant.* 4.87) finds a good reason, besides the hostile attitude of the Amorites, for getting the Israelites to attack, namely to deliver them from that inactivity (ἀπραξίας) and consequent indigence (ἀπορίας) that had produced their previous mutiny and their present discontent.

Furthermore, an appreciation of Moses' importance to the Israelites as a leader may be seen in Josephus's remark (*Ant.* 3.98), missing from the biblical account (Exod 32:1), that although Moses was absent for forty days on Mount Sinai, the people in their deep distress imagined themselves bereft of a patron (προστάτου, "one who stands out in front as a champion," "leader," "chief," "ruler," "guardian") and protector (κηδεμόνος, "guardian"), the like of which they could never meet again.

Indeed, Josephus (*Ant.* 3.317–18) remarks that admiration for Moses' marvelous power of inspiring faith in all his utterances was not confined to his lifetime but that even in Josephus's own day "there is not a Hebrew who does not, just as if he were still there and ready to punish him for any breach of discipline, obey the laws laid down by Moses, even though in violating them he would escape detection." He notes that only recently when certain non-Jews from Mesopotamia, after a journey of several months, came to venerate the Temple in Jerusalem they could not partake of the sacrifices that they had offered because Moses had forbidden this to those not governed by the laws of the Torah. Again we note here Josephus's introduction of the impression made by Moses' teachings upon non-Jews.

In his encomium of Pericles, Thucydides (2.65.4) points out the truism that the way of the multitude is fickle, as demonstrated by the Athenians, who in their anger at the terrible losses that had befallen them during the great plague, fined their leader Pericles, only to reverse themselves shortly thereafter and to choose him again as general. The ideal government, as Thucydides (2.65.9) stresses, is a government ruled by its foremost citizen rather than a true democracy, which surrenders to the majority whim.

Even more than Pericles, Moses, during the sojourn in the desert, is under constant criticism and the threat of rebellion. Thus, after the spies come back with their pessimistic report about the possibility of conquering Canaan, the people (*Ant.* 3.307) blame Moses and load him and Aaron with abuse, pouring vituperations (βλασφημιῶν) on them with intent to stone them and to return to Egypt. The Bible (Num 14:10), on the other hand, declares merely that all the congregation expressed the desire to stone them. Despite this ugly mood, Moses and Aaron, we are told (*Ant.* 3.310), instead of panicking, show their compassion for the people, their ability to analyze the cause of the people's depression, and their own true leadership by supplicating G-d to rid the people of their ignorance and to calm their spirits; here again the Bible (Num 14:19) simply states that Moses prayed that G-d should pardon them for complaining against Him. Furthermore, when Moses tells them not to fight the Canaanites (*Ant.* 4.1), they proceed to accuse and suspect him of scheming to keep them without resources in order that they may always stand in need of his aid. They refer (*Ant.* 4.3) to Moses as a tyrant (τύραννον) and declare that they are strong enough by themselves to defeat the Canaanites even if Moses should desire to alienate G-d from them. They insist (*Ant.* 4.4) that not only Moses but also all of them are of the stock of Abraham and scorn what they term the arrogance (ἀλαζονείας) of Moses. They assemble (*Ant.* 4.22–23) in disorderly fashion (ἀκόσμως) and with tumult and uproar; and in a great elaboration on the biblical passage (Num 16:3), they shout, "Away with the tyrant, and let the people be rid of their bondage!" The fickle mob, in a scene highly reminiscent of the description in Thucydides (2.65.2–3) of the attitude of the Athenians toward Pericles after the plague, in a tumultuous (θορυβώδη) assembly (Josephus, *Ant.* 4.36), exhibit their "innate delight in decrying those in authority" and, in their shallowness, swayed by what anyone said, are in ferment.

Moses shows his particular skill in his handling of the Israelite masses. Thus, when the people are excited and embittered against him at Elim because of their lack of water (*Ant.* 3.13) and are ready to stone him, Moses fearlessly advances into their midst and by sheer charisma, deriving from his winning presence and his extraordinary influence in addressing a crowd, succeeds, after delivering a long speech, in pacifying their wrath. Again, whereas in the Bible (Exod 16:6) Moses and Aaron merely promise the Israelites food, in Josephus (*Ant.* 3.14–15) Moses alone confronts the unruly mob and exhorts them not to be obsessed by their present discomforts and to have confidence in G-d's solicitude. He thus calms them (*Ant.* 3.22), restraining their impulse to stone him. The scene again is reminiscent of the passage in Virgil (*Aeneid* 1.124–47) in which Neptune calms the seas that have been made turbulent by Aeolus and in which Virgil presents as a simile (*Aeneid* 1.148–56) the effect on a crowd when a great leader assuages their turbulent feelings.

One is reminded of the way in which, according to Thucydides (3.36, 6.19), the Athenian masses were swayed by demagogues such as Cleon and Alcibiades, as well as of the technique by which the gullible captain of the ship, representing the masses, in Plato's parable (*Republic* 6.488A–489A), instead of listening to the true navigator, is won over by the fawning sailors. Indeed, even after Moses is apparently vindicated in his dispute with Korah when the earth swallows up the rebels, the skeptical mob (*Ant.* 4.60–62) conclude that the severity of the punishment inflicted on the rebels is due not so much to their iniquity as to the machinations of Moses. Again, thereafter, Zambrias (Zimri), the Israelite who has relations with a Midianite woman, accuses Moses (*Ant.* 4.149) of tyranny because he attempts to interfere with his free choice. And yet Josephus (*Against Apion* 2.169) is careful to point out that Moses did not, like such Greek philosophers as Pythagoras, Anaxagoras, and Plato, show disdain for the masses but rather addressed his teachings to the many and indeed so firmly implanted his theology in their descendants that it cannot be moved.

Another characteristic of the true leader is his willingness to undergo toil on behalf of his people. This is indeed one of the major characteristics of Plato's philosopher-king, whose first and sole concern must be the well-being of the commonwealth and who must descend into the cave even though life would be much more pleasant in an ivory tower. The picture that we are given is parallel to one of the morals of Plato's Allegory of the Cave (*Republic*, 7.519–20), namely that the philosopher-king, though obviously less than eager to rule, because ruling involves abuse by the citizens, must go down into the cave, inasmuch as the penalty for not governing is to be ruled by those inferior to oneself. Here, too, one is reminded of the glorification of toil in the Cynic-Stoic diatribes and especially in Virgil's *Aeneid* (1.9–10), where, we are told, Aeneas, the founder of Rome, was forced to undergo "so many misfortunes, so many toils."[75] One thinks, furthermore, of the whole array of heroes in early Roman history, such as Lucius Titus Quinctius Cincinnatus (Dionysius of Halicarnassus, *Roman Antiquities* 10.17.1), who left his plough in 458 B.C.E., when called, and worked for the general welfare.

Indeed, in his first editorial comment about Moses, Josephus (*Ant.* 2.229), after describing the rescue of Moses by Pharaoh's daughter, remarks that there is general agreement that Moses excelled all in two respects, namely grandeur of intellect and contempt of toils (πόνων καταφρονήσει). Moreover, when confronting the revolution led by Dathan and Abiram, Moses (*Ant.* 4.42) remarks that, though he could have secured for himself a life of ease, he had chosen to devote himself to sharing the tribulations of his people. "Great," he says, "are the toils (πόνοις) which I have undergone, opposing to every peril all the ardor of my soul." Tacitus (*Histories* 5.4.1) cynically remarks that Moses' purpose in introducing new religious practices, so different from those of other peoples, was to establish his influence over the Israelites for all time. Josephus's Moses is utterly selfless, without ulterior motives. Further (*Against Apion* 2.159), when summarizing the work of Moses as general and as religious educator, Josephus stresses the selflessness of Moses in that he never took advantage of his authority in order to play the despot but sought rather a life of piety, which he believed was the most effective way to provide for the lasting welfare of those who had made him their leader.[76]

And yet, despite this utter altruism, Moses, like Pericles, is unappreciated (*Ant.* 4.42–43) by his people. Whereas they owe their lives to his exertions (καμάτων, "fatigue," "exhaustion," "labor," "effort"), they nevertheless suspect him of knavery. We may add that when Moses selects Joshua as his successor, the qualities in Joshua that he singles out (*Ant.* 3.49) include valor in enduring toils (πόνοις). Indeed, one of the achievements of a great leader is the ability to inculcate into others a readiness to undergo toil, as we see, for example (*Ant.* 3.58), in his success inspiring the Israelites to toil (πονεῖν) after they had defeated Amalek, and to be convinced that by it all things are attainable. Finally, when Moses (*Ant.* 4.178) announces that he must die, he declares that he has deemed it right not to renounce his zeal for the general welfare but to labor to secure for the people the everlasting enjoyment of good things. Whereas in the Bible (Deut 1:11) Moses prays that G-d may multiply the people and bless them, in Josephus (*Ant.* 4.179) Moses is not satisfied to resort to mere prayer but rather takes the initiative to plan ways for the people to attain prosperity. Indeed, in his apologetic treatise *Against Apion* (2.158), Josephus stresses that though Moses succeeded in making the whole people dependent on himself, he did not use his influence for any personal aggrandizement.

The greatest test of leadership comes when sedition arises. It is precisely here (*Ant.* 4.13), when confronted with the great sedition (στασιάζειν) of Korah that Moses shows his true foresight (προενόησε). Indeed, civil strife (στάσις), as Thucydides (3.82–84) stresses, is the great enemy of stability; and Josephus frequently[77] comments on this theme. We may remark that a good portion of Book 4 (11–66, 141–55) of the *Antiquities* is devoted to accounts that illustrate the degree to which στάσις is the mortal enemy of political states;[78] indeed, the two revolts, that of Korah and that of Zambrias, comprise between them more than half of the narrative material in Book 4.[79]

Moses' stature is increased in Josephus because the latter dramatizes, to a much greater degree than does the Bible, the murmuring against Moses. Thus, whereas in the Bible (Num 11:2) the people cry to Moses about their misfortunes in the desert, in Josephus (*Ant.* 3.297) this lament has become a torrent of abuse, whereupon an unnamed individual admonishes them not to be unmindful of what Moses had suffered for the salvation of all. Thereafter, we are told in another unscriptural addition that the multitude is aroused only the more and uproariously and inveighs even more fiercely against Moses.

Again, at Rephidim, when the Israelites find themselves in an absolutely waterless region and vent their wrath on Moses, he, according to the biblical version (Exod 17:4), cries to G-d telling Him that they are on the verge of stoning him; and G-d tells Moses (Exod 17:5) to take with him some of the elders and to pass before the people. Josephus's Moses (*Ant.* 3.34) shuns the onset of the crowd and instead turns to G-d in prayer beseeching that He afford them drink. G-d then promises that He will provide water, and so Moses, fearlessly and alone, without the company of the elders, approaches the people and tells them that G-d will deliver them from their distress. Immediately, in the most dramatic fashion, Moses strikes the rock and water gushes forth.

A great leader must be able to encourage his people. Thus, Moses (*Ant.* 2.327) is described as cheering up (παρορμῶντα, "speeding on," "stimulating," "encouraging") the Israelites and promising them salvation. Likewise, he must be able to console his people. Thus, when the infamous Amalek is approaching to attack them, the biblical narrative declares (Exod 17:9) that it is Joshua whom Moses approaches, bidding him to go out to fight Amalek, whereas in Josephus (*Ant.* 3.47) it is Moses who exhorts the juniors to obey their elders and these latter to hearken to him, their general, whereupon the elders urge Moses to lead them instantly against the enemy. Again, when the Israelites are suffering from thirst during their march through the desert, Moses, the true leader, empathizes to such a degree with his people that he makes the sufferings of all the Israelites his own (*Ant.* 3.5). All look to him as their leader, and it is only to him that they flock in their despondency when they have no water in the desert (*Ant.* 3.6). Finally, in Josephus (*Ant.* 3.44–46) Moses approaches all the people, consoles them, and bids them to take courage and to trust in G-d, remembering the past.

The scene is highly reminiscent of the one in which Aeneas (Virgil, *Aeneid* 1.198–207) consoles his men after they land on the coast of Africa, reminding them that they have endured more grievous obstacles and bidding them to persevere. Similarly, after Moses has told the Israelites that he is to die and they are all in tears, he (*Ant.* 4.195) consoles them and, diverting their minds from his impending death, he exhorts them to put their constitution into practice.

Furthermore, in his treatment of the rebellion of Korah, Josephus (*Ant.* 4.12) remarks that it was a sedition (στάσις) "for which we know of no parallel, whether among Greeks or barbarians," clearly implying that information about seditions was familiar to his readers, as it surely was to readers of Thucydides. The fact (*Ant.* 4.14–15) that Korah was of the same tribe as Moses and indeed was his kinsman, that he was richer than Moses, and that he was very effective in addressing a crowd made him a truly formidable opponent.

Moses shows his mettle by not scorning to take the initiative to go to the rebels Dathan and Abiram. Additionally, in Josephus (*Ant.* 4.32) Moses implores Korah to cease from sedition (στάσεως) and the turbulence (ταραχῆς) arising therefrom. In fact, Moses goes so far in seeking to avoid civil strife that when Korah charges him with nepotism for selecting his brother Aaron to be high priest, Moses states (*Ant.* 4.29) that Aaron is ready to lay down his high priesthood as an open prize to be sued for by any who will. Even after the earthquake has swallowed up Korah and his followers, the sedition does not end. But whereas the Bible (Num 17:6) says merely that the whole Israelite community railed against Moses and Aaron, charging them with having caused the deaths of so many, Josephus (*Ant.* 4.59) exaggerates the seditiousness of the people by stating that the revolt assumed far larger proportions and grew more grievous. "Indeed," he adds, "it found an occasion for proceeding from bad to worse, such that the trouble seemed likely never to cease but to become chronic." By thus exaggerating the seditiousness of the people, Josephus correspondingly increases the stature of Moses in controlling them, just as Thucydides does in the case of Pericles.

Moses' effectiveness as a leader is especially well illustrated in his handling of the unruly mob when the Israelite youths consort with the Midianite women. In the Bible (Num 25:5) Moses sternly instructs the judges of Israel, "Every one of you, slay his men who have yoked themselves to the Ba'al of Pe'or" (the major deity of the Midianites). Josephus' Moses (*Ant.* 4.142), far from commanding that the trespassers be killed, first shows his democratic impulse and his high regard for the people by convening them in assembly.[80] He then very considerately avoids accusing anyone by name, because he does not wish to reduce to desperation any who might be brought back to repentance through gentler means, but seeks rather through mild words to win back the transgressors. His patience in trying to convince them to mend their ways is indicated particularly by Josephus's use of the imperfect tense (*Ant.* 4.144), ἐπειρᾶτο ("he kept on trying").

The dignity of a leader is crucial to his success. Hence, we find that the Septuagint (Exod 4:20) avoids stating that Moses put his wife and his sons on an ass and sent them back to the land of Egypt, and instead, presumably because the ass, at least for the pagans, was usually a lowly animal, declares that Moses mounted them on "beasts," without indicating the identity of the animals.[81] Josephus (*Ant.* 2.277) goes one step further and says that Moses took his wife and sons and hastened away, without mentioning the means. We see a similar avoidance of the association of Moses with asses in Josephus's rendering of the passage (Num 16:15) where Moses protests that he has not taken one ass from the assemblage. Here the Septuagint[82] has Moses say that he has not taken away the desire (ἐπιθύμημα, "object of desire," "dear possession") of any of the Israelites; and likewise Josephus (*Ant.* 4.46) has Moses declare that he has not accepted a present from a single Hebrew to pervert justice. Perhaps a further reason for these changes is that Josephus was sensitive to the charge (*Against Apion* 2.80–88) that the Jews keep an ass's head in the Temple and worship that animal.

Josephus also apparently felt apologetic that Moses was a shepherd, perhaps because shepherds were disqualified as judges or witnesses in the Land of Israel, according to the rabbis (*Sanhedrin* 25b), presumably because they sometimes appropriated the sheep of others. Hence, where the Bible (Exod 3:1) states that Moses kept the flock of Jethro his father-in-law, Josephus (*Ant.* 2.263) adds an explanation, namely that in those days the wealth (κτῆσις) of barbarian races consisted of sheep.

Another of the qualities of the great statesman, as we see in Thucydides' portrait of Pericles (2.60.6), is his refusal to accept bribes. In the Bible (Num 16:15), when confronted with the revolt of Dathan, Abiram, and Korah, Moses bitterly protests to G-d, as we have noted, that he has not taken the ass of any of them and that he has not wronged any of them. In Josephus's elaboration of this (*Ant.* 4.46), Moses indicates that the charge against him is that he has accepted bribes to pervert justice, and he calls G-d Himself to witness that this is not true.

A great leader must be able to choose and train a successor who will carry on his work. In the Bible (Num 27:18) it is G-d who takes the initiative in telling Moses to choose Joshua as his successor. In Josephus (*Ant.* 4.165) we are told that, before choosing Joshua, Moses had already indoctrinated him with a thorough training in the laws and in divine lore.

And yet, great as Moses was as a leader, Josephus takes great pains to make sure that he would not be worshiped as a god. This was particularly necessary in view of the Greeks' frequent apotheosizing of heroes such as Dionysus, Heracles (cf. Diodorus 4.38.3–5, 39.1–2), and Asclepius.[83] Josephus may also be reacting to Sophocles' account of the mysterious disappearance of Oedipus in *Oedipus at Colonus*, which bears a striking resemblance to that of Moses.[84] Even after death the hero was thought to have power to bring good fortune. In particular, founders of cities were objects of religious devotion, as we see in Pausanias (10.4.10).[85]

Josephus, therefore, much as he admired Moses, was careful not to elevate him to divinity.[86] To be sure, in Josephus's account (*Ant.* 3.99) of Moses' ascent on Mount Sinai, he hints that Moses ate heavenly food, inasmuch as, whereas the biblical narrative (Exod 34:28) states that Moses neither ate bread nor drank water during the forty days that he was on the mountain, Josephus (*Ant.* 3.99) says that he tasted no food of the kinds designated for humans. The implication is that Moses partook of heavenly food, that is, drank nectar and ate ambrosia.[87] Moreover, Josephus himself notes (*Ant.* 3.317) that Moses was held in such great admiration for his virtues and his charismatic ability to inspire faith in all his utterances that his words are alive to this day. Indeed, he remarks (*Ant.* 3.320), Moses' legislation, believed to come from G-d, has caused him to be ranked higher than his own human nature. Even a pagan such as Celsus (quoted in Origen, *Against Celsus* 1.21) says that Moses gained a reputation for divine power, presumably through his ability as a magician. But in the very passages (*Ant.* 3.317, 320) where Josephus refers to Moses as so inspiring and as ranking higher than his own nature, he is careful to refer to him as a man (ἀνήρ). Moreover, he is careful to omit G-d's statements that Moses was to be to Aaron as G-d (Exod 4:16) and that G-d was making him as G-d to Pharaoh (Exod 7:1). He is likewise careful to dispel the view held by some (*Ant.* 3.95–96) that Moses tarried on Mount Sinai for forty days because he had been taken back to the divinity. If he refers to Moses (*Ant.* 3.180), as he does, as a "man of G-d" (θεῖον ἄνδρα), it is not to assert Moses' divinity but rather to refute those enemies of the Jews who had charged them (*Ant.* 3.179) with slighting the divinity whom they themselves professed to venerate. Indeed, that Josephus has no intention here of asserting that Moses was actually divine is clear from the proof that Moses was a "man of G-d," namely that the construction of the tabernacle and the appearance of the vestments and vessels of the priests show that Moses was concerned with piety.

Josephus (*Ant.* 4.326) is particularly explicit in stressing that Moses died and in refuting the notion that he was somehow elevated to divine status. Thus, whereas the Bible (Deut 34:5) says simply that Moses died in the land of Moab, Josephus (*Ant.* 4.326) explains why Scripture states this, stressing that Moses "has written of himself in the sacred books that he died, for fear lest they should venture to say that by reason of his surpassing virtue he had gone back to the D-ity."[88] Moreover, very significantly, Josephus does not include the biblical remarks (Deut 34:6) that G-d Himself had buried Moses and that no one knows to this day where he is buried, presumably because he realized that his skeptical readers might have considerable difficulty accepting such statements.[89] He also attempts, more or less scientifically, to give further details of Moses' disappearance, noting that while Moses was bidding farewell to Eleazar the high priest and Joshua his successor, a cloud suddenly descended on him and he disappeared into a ravine. Such an account might well have reminded the reader of the traditional version of the deaths of the two founders of the Romans, Aeneas and Romulus, as described by Dionysius of Halicarnassus, for example.[90] In the case of Aeneas, Dionysius (*Roman Antiquities* 1.64.4) says that his body could nowhere be found, and some conjectured that he had been translated to the gods. As to Romulus, he remarks (2.56.2) that "the more mythical writers[91] say that, as he was holding an assembly in the camp, darkness descended upon him from a clear sky and he disappeared, and they believe that he was caught up by his father Ares." Josephus would thus seem to be equating Moses with these Roman forefathers.

Indeed, the elevation of Moses to divine status seems to be implied in Philo, who remarks (*De Vita Mosis* 1.6.27; cf. 2.51.291) that Moses' associates, struck by his utter asceticism and by the fact that he was so utterly unlike all men, pondered whether he was human or divine or a mixture of both. Josephus, who was excellently educated in the rabbinic tradition (*Life* 8–9), may also be responding to that element in the rabbinic tradition which maintained that Moses did not die but rather continued to administer from above.[92] Quite clearly, Josephus wished to have it both ways: On the one hand, he strongly resisted such contemporary evaluations that deified Moses or Jesus or Aeneas or Romulus; but, on the other hand, the actual scene that he describes—the tears and the weeping, the withdrawal, the cloud descending on Moses and his disappearance, with nothing said of the burial itself—is strikingly reminiscent of the parallels cited above.[93]

Wisdom

As we can see from Plato's *Republic* and *Laws*, whoever is to be the best lawgiver must possess all the virtues in the highest degree.[94] Moreover, the excellence of the laws is measured by wisdom, as we can see in Josephus's editorial remark (*Ant.* 3.223) that the laws of the Torah are excellent beyond the standard of human wisdom.

To the Romans, who placed such a premium on excellence of law and administration, a question like that later posed by Julian (*Contra Gali-*

laeos 221 E) was a serious challenge: "As regards the constitution of the state and the fashion of the law courts, the administration of cities and the excellence of the laws, progress in learning and the cultivation of the liberal arts, were not all these things in a miserable and barbarous state among the Hebrews?" Had the Jews produced musicians, physicians, or philosophers comparable to those produced by the Greeks?

In answer to such challenges, Josephus, as we have noted, consistently stresses the virtue of wisdom in his biblical heroes,[95] especially because the anti-Jewish Apion had charged (*Against Apion* 2.135) that the Jews had not produced any illustrious men, such as men distinguished in wisdom, who were comparable to Socrates, the Stoics Zeno and Cleanthes, or Apion himself.

Josephus (*Ant.* 4.328), in his final encomium of Moses, states that he surpassed in understanding (συνέσει) all men who had ever lived and had put to noblest use the fruit of his reflections (νοηθεῖσιν). Moses exhibited sagacity particularly in his military campaigns, as we can see from the admiration that the Ethiopian princess Tharbis (*Ant.* 2.252) showed at the sagacity (ἐπινοίας, "conception," "thought," "insight," "inventiveness," "craftiness," "artifice") of his maneuvers. Again, when the Israelites complain against Moses because of lack of water and stand ready to stone him, Josephus (*Ant.* 3.12), in an editorial comment, singles out Moses' virtue (ἀρετῆς) and sagacity (συνέσεως) as the two qualities they had completely forgotten.[96]

Inasmuch as Josephus's literate audience was likely to be well versed in philosophy,[97] it should not be surprising that just as Abraham is depicted as a Stoic-like philosopher who proves the existence of G-d (*Ant* 1.156),[98] so Moses (*Ant.* 2.229) is presented as a Stoic sage, remarkable for his contempt for toils (πόνων καταφρονήσει), a typically Stoic phrase. Moreover, a key Stoic term, πρόνοια, plays a crucial role in Josephus's accounts of Abraham[99] and of Moses. We have already noted Amram's confidence in G-d's providence as seen in his decision (*Ant.* 2.219) to place the infant Moses in an ark in the Nile River rather than to continue to rear him in secret. Similarly, Moses, in his speech to the angry Israelites, exhorts them (*Ant.* 3.19) not to despair of G-d's providence (πρόνοιαν). The same juxtaposition of G-d's graciousness (εὐμενῆ) and His providence (προνοίας) which occurs in connection with Abraham is moreover found in Moses' last address to his people, where he renders thanks to G-d for bestowing His concern on him (*Ant.* 4.180, 185). Furthermore, Moses' emphasis on law (νόμος) is in accord with the Stoic view that regarded νόμος as the expression of the cosmos and that viewed man as a κοσμοπολίτης who must arrange his life in accordance with universal law.[100] Hence, by allegorically imputing cosmic significance (*Ant.* 3.181–87) to the tabernacle, the twelve loaves, the candelabrum, the tapestries, and the high priest's garments, Josephus was appealing to the Stoic view that law must have a cosmic dimension.

Even Moses' description of G-d as One, uncreated, immutable to all eternity, and in beauty surpassing mortal thought (*Against Apion* 2.167) is in Greek philosophical dress.[101] Likewise, the simile (*Against Apion* 2.284) of the Law of the Pentateuch finding its way among all humankind as G-d permeates the universe is taken from the Stoics.

The greatest compliment in antiquity, as we have noted, that could be given to a person so far as wisdom is concerned is to call him a philosopher.[102] That Josephus looked on Moses as a thoroughgoing philosopher is to be inferred from the statement (*Ant.* 1.25) that if anyone should desire to consider the reasons for every article in the law transmitted by Moses, he would find the inquiry profound and highly philosophical (φιλόσοφος). Moreover, Josephus clearly implies that Moses is responsible for the profound symbolism attached to the tabernacle and to the vestments of the high priests (*Ant.* 3.179–87). Indeed, according to Josephus (*Against Apion* 2.168), the wisest of the Greeks, including such celebrated philosophers as Pythagoras, Anaxagoras, Plato, and the Stoics, learned their conceptions of G-d from principles Moses supplied to them.[103] Plato, in particular, he notes (*Against Apion* 2.257), imitated Moses in ordaining that citizens should study their laws and that foreigners should be prevented from mixing with citizens.

But the wise leader of his nation must excel not only as a philosopher but also as a lawgiver. The very fact, we may suggest, that Josephus summarizes the Mosaic code at such length in a work that is ostensibly a history shows how important law is for him. Indeed, in large part Josephus's emphasis on Moses as a lawgiver is a reply (*Against Apion* 2.101, 145) to those anti-Jewish bigots, such as Apollonius Molon and Lysimachus, who, whether from ignorance or ill will, had maligned Moses the lawgiver as a charlatan and impostor. Josephus (*Against Apion* 2.147) stresses that Moses exhibits his wisdom particularly as a lawgiver; and the constitution he gave the Israelites is consonant with the reputation he had for virtue (ἀρετή). Indeed, we are told (*Against Apion* 2.159) that Moses provided his people an abundance of good laws in the belief that this was the best means of displaying his own virtue and of ensuring the lasting welfare of those who had made him their leader. We may further remark that the very use of the term *lawgiver* (νομοθέτης) sixteen times in the first four books of the *Antiquities* with regard to Moses, referring to him usually merely as "the lawgiver" without explicitly naming him as Moses,[104] is an indication that to Josephus Moses is *the* wise man *par excellence*, to be bracketed with the revered Spartan Lycurgus, the Athenian Solon, and the Roman Numa Pompilius, though, strictly speaking, G-d alone is the lawgiver.[105] In fact, we may note that on only five occasions do we hear of the laws given by G-d through Moses, whereas on twenty-three occasions we hear of the laws of Moses. But Moses is said (*Ant.* 4.194, 196, 302) to have given the Israelites more than laws: He gave them a πολιτεία, a constitution comparable to that found in the Greek πόλεις. Indeed, the Jewish king, remarks Josephus (*Ant.* 4.224), is required to concede that the laws possess superior wisdom (τοῦ πλείονα τοῦ φρονεῖν).

Furthermore, in a world in which, as we have noted, the antiquity of a nation or a person meant so much,[106] Moses, as Josephus (*Against Apion* 2.154) contends, is the most ancient of all legislators who have ever lived,[107] next to whom such famous lawgivers as Lycurgus of Sparta, Solon of Athens, and Zaleucus of Locris were, so to speak, born yesterday. Indeed, he remarks, the very word *law* (νόμος) is not to be found in Homer. He adds (*Against Apion* 2.279) that an infinity of time has passed since Moses lived, if one compares the age when he lived with those of other legislators. Moreover, the permanence of a code is a measure of its excellence; and by that standard Moses' constitution is the very best, inasmuch as it was promulgated for all time (*Against Apion* 2.156, εἰς ἀεί), a phrase reminiscent of Thucydides' identical phrase (1.22.4) that his history has been composed not as a prize-essay to be enjoyed for the moment but as a possession for all time. Furthermore, as Josephus stresses (*Against Apion* 2.183), the proof of the excellent draftsmanship of these laws is that (like those of Sparta, we may suggest, at least according to tradition) they have not required any amendment.[108] In fact, these laws have excited the emulation of the whole world (*Against Apion* 2.280).[109] Indeed, though the laws in Plato's *Republic* would appear to represent an ideal, they are actually inferior to those of Moses, because they more closely approximate the practice of the masses (*Against Apion* 2.224). Even Lycurgus's laws, so greatly admired, Josephus remarks (*Against Apion* 2.225–26), have hardly endured as long as those promulgated by Moses. Actually, says Josephus (*Against Apion* 2.279), Moses, as compared with other legislators, issued his laws infinitely earlier.

But mere study of the laws is not sufficient; a great statesman, as we see in Plato's *Republic*, must be able to induce his nation to obey these laws. Pericles in his Funeral Oration (Thucydides 2.37.3) praises the Athenians for their obedience to the laws, and Socrates in Plato's *Crito* (50C–51C) refuses to escape from prison because he regards obedience to the laws of the state as being fundamental to its existence. Yet, as Thucydides (2.53.4) notes, during the plague the Athenians were restrained neither by fear of gods nor by the law of men. On the contrary, according to Josephus (*Ant.* 3.223), the Hebrews have transgressed none of Moses' laws in peace, through luxury, or in war, through constraint.

Hence, the great leader must also excel as an educator, as we can see from the tremendous amount of attention given by the philosopher-kings in Plato's *Republic* to the education of the inhabitants of the ideal state. Thus we find, at the very beginning of the *Antiquities* (1.6), the first reference to Moses is as the great lawgiver (νομοθέτη) under whom the Jews were educated (παιδευθέντες) in piety and the exercise of the other virtues. The relationship between legislation and παιδεία is distinctively Greek.[110] What marks the superiority of Moses' laws over other systems of law is that his educational system combined precept and practical training (*Against Apion* 2.171–74). Plato had argued repeatedly in his dialogues that no one errs knowingly and that hence the function of the ruler is to teach the citizens. By this standard, according to Josephus (*Against Apion* 2.175),[111] Moses was supreme, because he left no pretext for ignorance, ordaining uniquely, as he did, the reading of the law every week—a practice other legislators had neglected. Consequently, Josephus is able to boast (*Against Apion* 2.178) that if any Jew is questioned about the laws he knows them more readily than his own name. Indeed, the reason for Moses' success in ordering his own life aright and also legislating for others, according to Josephus in his proem (*Ant.* 1.19), was that he was, in effect, a philosopher who studied the nature of G-d and contemplated His works with the eye of reason (νῷ, "mind"). Time, says Josephus (*Against Apion* 2.279), which is the most truthful judge of worth, has demonstrated the virtue of Moses' philosophy.

Connected with wisdom, as we may see in Thucydides' portrait (2.60) of the ideal statesman, Pericles, is the ability to persuade the masses.[112] In the case of Moses, Josephus was confronted with an obvious problem, inasmuch as the Bible (Exod 4:10 and 6:12), as we have remarked, notes that Moses had a speech impediment. Significantly, Josephus omits both of the biblical references to Moses' speech impairment. Indeed, whereas in the Bible (Exod 5:1) Moses and Aaron go jointly to Pharaoh, with Aaron presumably as the spokesman, to ask him to free the Israelites, in Josephus (*Ant.* 2.281) Moses goes alone, reminds him of the services that he had rendered to the Egyptians in the campaign against Ethiopia, and requests the deliverance of his people. In fact, in his final encomium of Moses, Josephus (*Ant.* 4.328) goes out of his way to declare that Moses found favor in every way in speech (εἰπεῖν) and in addresses (ὁμιλῆσαι) to a crowd.

To the classical Greeks, music was "a second language," of divine origin (Pseudo-Plutarch, *De Musica* 3.1131F–1132A).[113] Indeed, it was a god, Hermes, who was said to have invented the lyre, and a goddess, Athena, who was said to have invented the αὐλός (flute or, rather, oboe). Furthermore, we are told, Heracles, the greatest hero of the Greeks, was instructed by his tutor Chiron in music no less than in the other arts. Music was an integral part of education, as we learn from Plato (*Republic*

3.398C–402D). We are even informed (Cicero, *Tusculan Disputations* 1.2.4) that Themistocles disgraced himself by being unable to play the lyre when his turn came at a banquet. Hence, we should not be surprised that Josephus (*Ant.* 2.346) makes a point of mentioning, in referring to Moses' song (Exod 15:1–21) upon crossing the Red Sea, that Moses himself composed a song to G-d "to enshrine His praise" and the thankfulness of the Israelites for His gracious favor. Josephus, however, realizing the importance attached to poetry, adds to the biblical narrative in order to make more of an impression on his non-Jewish audience. Thus, he asserts (*Ant.* 2.346)—without any biblical basis—that Moses composed his song in hexameter verse, thereby indicating that it was in the same epic meter as the great poems of Homer. Similarly, in referring to Moses' final message to the Israelites, he asserts (*Ant.* 4.303) that Moses recited to them a poem in hexameter verse.[114] But Moses in Josephus (*Ant.* 3.291) is not merely a poet and singer: He is also, on his own initiative, the inventor of a musical instrument, a silver trumpet (βυκάνη), which makes him comparable to Hermes and Athena in this respect. Josephus then proceeds to give an extensive description of the trumpet, noting its length, its mouthpiece, and its extremity. In contrast, we may note, the Bible (Num 10:1–2) declares that it is G-d who bids Moses to make two silver trumpets, and there is no further description of them.

Courage

One of the charges, as we have seen, made against the Jews is that they have not produced any celebrities. In particular, because the ancients attached so much prominence to military leadership, a challenge such as Julian (*Contra Galilaeos* 218 B) was later to pose, namely to point out a single general among the Jews of the caliber of an Alexander or a Caesar, was a source of embarrassment. But Josephus, at least, found an answer, namely the personality of Moses.

The attention of the historian, says Lucian (*Quomodo Historia Conscribenda Sit* 49), should be for the generals first of all. Record should be made of their exhortations, of the dispositions they make, and of the motives and plans that prompted them. Generalship was the key factor in the superiority of the Greeks and Macedonians over the "barbarians";[115] and this superiority began with pre-military training in the gymnasium and progressed through tactics and strategy to the techniques of laying siege. And finally, we may add, his constant reelection to the position of στρατηγός was the means that enabled Pericles, the idol of Josephus's model Thucydides, to dominate Athens for three decades. Lucian, to be sure, warns against focusing attention on generals alone; but he makes an exception in the case of Brasidas and Demosthenes, who were outstandingly inspiring as leaders; and it would therefore seem that Josephus was justified in similarly making an exception of Moses. It is significant that whereas in the Septuagint Moses is never called στρατηγός ("general") or even ἡγεμών ("leader"), in Josephus he is referred to fifteen times in the *Antiquities* (2.241, 268; 3.2, 11, 12, 28, 47, 65, 67, 78, 102, 105; 4.82, 194, 329) and once in the *Against Apion* (2.158) as a στρατηγός; in addition, the verb στρατηγέω, "to be a field-commander," "to lead an army," is used of him once (*Ant.* 2.243); and the noun στρατηγία, "army command," "office of supreme commander," is used with reference to him twice (*Ant.* 2.255, 282). Furthermore, the noun ἡγεμών is used of him six times (*Ant.* 2.268, 4.11; *Against Apion* 1.238, 261; 2.156, 159).[116] Indeed, it is not as teacher or legislator that the voice from the burning bush (*Ant.* 2.268) bids Moses to act but rather as general (στρατηγόν) and leader (ἡγεμόνα).

It is significant that when Josephus (*Ant.* 1.13) enumerates the main topics of the Bible he lists "all sorts of surprising reverses, many fortunes of war, heroic exploits of generals, and political revolutions." One is thus struck by the emphasis on military matters. Indeed, in his final encomium of Moses (*Ant.* 4.329) he remarks that as a general he had few to equal him and that as a prophet he had no rivals. His listing of Moses' achievement as a general before he mentions his role as a prophet would seem to indicate an order of importance; and, in any case, Josephus's attitude is clearly to be contrasted with that of the Bible, which speaks (Deut 34:7–12) only of Moses' supremacy as a prophet. Furthermore, in his apologetic treatise *Against Apion* (2.157–63), in summarizing Moses' achievements, the first point that he makes is that it was Moses who took command of the multitudes who left Egypt and guided them safely through a huge desert and defeated their enemies. Throughout this, says Josephus, he proved the best of generals. Similarly, the offices in which Joshua succeeds Moses (*Ant.* 4.165) are those of prophet and general, whereas, in the corresponding biblical passage (Num 27:18), Joshua is described as a man with spirit, but there is no mention of his military abilities. Finally, after Moses announces to the Israelites that he is to die and proceeds to exhort them to obey the laws he has given them, it is his role as general that they indicate they will miss most (*Ant.* 4.194). At such an emotional point in the history of the nation, Josephus (*Ant.* 4.194–95) tells us that what they remember is his bravery, namely the risks he had run in their behalf and his ardent zeal for their salvation.

Not only are we given in Josephus an extended portrait of Moses as a general, but his people are presented as soldiers. This is especially clear in the exhortation Moses gives to the Israelites before his death (*Ant.* 4.177), where he addresses them as "comrades in arms" (συστρατιῶται) and partners in long tribulation.

Moses' first great exploit as general, according to Josephus, in an extensive extra-biblical addition (*Ant.* 2.238–53), is his campaign on behalf of the Egyptians against the Ethiopians.[117] The biblical basis for this lengthy episode is a single verse in the Bible (Num 12:1): "And Miriam and Aaron spoke against Moses on account of the Ethiopian woman whom he had married; for he had married an Ethiopian woman."[118]

We may suggest that Josephus has resorted to this extraordinary expansion for several reasons. In the first place, Josephus and the Jews generally must have felt considerable embarrassment that, according to the Bible, Moses, the great leader of the Jewish people, was actually a murderer, having taken the law into his own hands in slaying an Egyptian (Exod 2:11–12).[119] Artapanus, in his version (quoted in Eusebius, *Praeparatio Evangelica* 9.27.18), seeks to defend Moses by presenting a scenario in which Moses, in self-defense, slays a certain Chanethothes, who had been designated by the Pharaoh, who was jealous of Moses' fame, to kill him. Josephus, clearly for apologetic reasons, omits both the Bible's and Artapanus's narrative of the slaying by Moses, as well as the slanders brought against Moses by Aaron and Miriam.

In the second place, the episode supplies a case history both in the causes of Jew-hatred and in the benefits that the Jews have given to society. On the one hand, it admirably illustrates Josephus's contention (*Against Apion* 1.224) that the two basic feelings of those prejudiced against Jews are hatred ($\mu\tilde{\iota}\sigma o\varsigma$) and envy ($\varphi\theta\acute{o}\nu o\varsigma$), as indicated when the Egyptians, having appointed Moses as their general in the extremely dangerous campaign against the Ethiopians, hoped, like Proetus with Bellerophon and like David with Uriah, to do away with Moses by guile. On the other hand, the episode shows how much the Egyptians actually owed to the Israelite leader Moses (*Ant.* 2.281–82), inasmuch as, through his successful campaign, he was able to save the Egyptians from the peril of their most dangerous foe. And when the Egyptians were thus saved by Moses, Pharaoh, motivated by envy of Moses' generalship and by fear of seeing himself abased (*Ant.* 2.255), decided to murder Moses. By thus shifting the reason for Pharaoh's wrath from his umbrage at Moses' murder of the Egyptian (which Josephus omits) to envy of his military ability, Josephus here may well be answering such anti-Jewish writers as Manetho by saying that the Egyptians, far from calumniating the Jews, should be grateful to them for the aid they rendered through Moses, and that Jews actually are patriotic, as seen in the instance of Moses, who risked his life to save the Egyptians from the Ethiopian threat.

In the third place, the episode disproves the contention that the Jews are cowards who are militarily inept. On the contrary, Moses turns out to be a brilliant strategist who is fearless in battle against the Ethiopians;

and the Jewish people can thus look back with pride at such a founding father, especially because even so great a military leader as the Persian king Cambyses (Herodotus 3.17–26) had been unsuccessful in his attempt to conquer Ethiopia, had had to make an ignominious retreat to Egypt (Herodotus 3.25), and had succeeded in conquering only the area immediately adjacent to Egypt (Herodotus 3.97). Indeed, the Ethiopians had a reputation for being invincible (Strabo 16.4.4.769), and even Alexander the Great had failed to overcome them.[120]

A major quality of a military leader, as we see, for example, in the portrait of Aeneas in Virgil, is sheer endurance in the face of adversity. Moses exhibits this quality when, for a second time, he must traverse a desert, this time when he is fleeing from Pharaoh, who, in envy, is trying to kill him after the successful campaign against the Ethiopians. Whereas the Bible states simply (Exod 2:15) that Moses fled from Pharaoh and came to the land of Midian, Josephus (*Ant.* 2.256) adds a number of details, namely that he was able to escape despite the fact that the roads were guarded, that he once again adopted the stratagem of going through the desert because he felt that his foes would be less likely to catch him there, that he left without provisions, and that he was, nevertheless, confident (καταφρονῶν, "indifferent," "fearless," "trusting firmly," "having extreme confidence") of his powers of endurance (καρτερία, "perseverance," "steadfastness").

Again, it is his quality of courage (θάρσος, "hardihood") that leads Moses to come near to the burning bush (*Ant.* 2.267), which, according to Josephus's extra-biblical comment, no man, by reason of its divinity, had approached previously. Furthermore, whereas in the Bible (Exod 3:10) the voice tells Moses that he will be sent to Pharaoh to bring forth the Israelites from Egypt, in Josephus (*Ant.* 2.268) the role in which Moses is to be cast is military, because the voice bids him courageously (θαρροῦντα) return to Egypt to act as general and leader (στρατηγὸν καὶ ἡγεμόνα).

Indeed, when Moses appears before the new Pharaoh, he presents himself as a military man. In fact, his first remark (*Ant.* 2.282) to Pharaoh is to remind him of the services that he had rendered to the Egyptians in the campaign against the Ethiopians and of his achievement in commanding and laboring and imperiling himself for his troops—and all this without due reward.

Furthermore, in the Bible (Exod 5:20–23), the Israelites complain to Moses because the Egyptians have now increased their oppression by requiring the Israelites to gather their own straw for the production of bricks; and Moses in turn complains to G-d. Josephus's Moses, however (*Ant.* 2.290), refuses to waver either before the king's threats or before the recriminations of the Israelites and instead steels his soul in his devotion to seeking his people's liberty.

Josephus (*Ant.* 2.310) adds to the portrait of Moses' courage by making more vivid the threat of Pharaoh after the plague of darkness. In the Bible (Exod 10:29), Pharaoh is quoted as saying to Moses merely that he should be gone and that the moment that he looks on his face again Moses will die. Josephus says that Pharaoh was infuriated (ὀργισθείς) by Moses' speech and that he threatened actually to behead him if he should ever come again and pester (ἐνοχλῶν, "annoy," "trouble," "be a nuisance") him on this matter.

Of course, the greatest military achievement of Moses, as Josephus stresses (*Against Apion* 2.157–58), was his leadership of the Israelites during the Exodus. Again, the picture that Josephus paints is that of a general who, like Xenophon in the *Anabasis*, takes command of motley troops—indeed, they are referred to as an army (*Ant.* 3.4)—and brings them safely to their destination through a host of formidable difficulties, overcoming both their lack of water and hostile tribes. It is particularly effective, in answer to the charge of the anti-Jewish bigots that the Jews are cowards, that Moses is admired for his courage (ἀνδραγαθία, "bravery," "manly virtue") by a non-Jew, his father-in-law Raguel (Jethro) (*Ant.* 3.65). "Throughout all this," says Josephus (*Against Apion* 2.158), "he proved the best of generals, the sagest (συνετώτατος, "most intelligent," "sagacious," "wise") of counselors, and the most conscientious of guardians." It is significant that Josephus here stresses that a successful general must be intelligent, even as he later (*Ant.* 4.94) notes, in a comment not found in the Bible (Num 21:25), that the Amorites, in their battle with the Israelites, showed neither skill in counsel (φρονῆσαι δεινούς) nor valor in action.

The high point of Moses' leadership during the Exodus occurs at the Red Sea. Josephus (*Ant.* 2.321) increases the magnitude of Moses' achievement by heightening the drama of the Egyptians' chase of the Israelites and the vigor of their pursuit. In particular, Moses' accomplishment is all the greater, inasmuch as—a remark made twice by Josephus (*Ant.* 2.321, 326)—the Israelites were unarmed, whereas in the Bible, at least according to the Hebrew version (Exod 13:18), they were armed. Moreover, in contrast to the Bible (Exod 14:7), which states that the Egyptians had six hundred chariots but does not indicate the number of horsemen and infantry, Josephus (*Ant.* 2.324) exaggerates the Egyptian threat by giving a round number—50,000—of horsemen and heavy infantry. Furthermore, Josephus (*Ant.* 2.324–25) adds to the danger confronting the Israelites by noting that the Egyptians, by confining them between inaccessible cliffs and the sea, had barred all routes by which they might attempt to escape. Josephus (*Ant.* 2.328) increases the pathos of the situation by remarking on the wailings and lamentations of the women and children "with death before their eyes, hemmed in by mountains, sea, and enemy." At this point, G-d in the Bible (Exod 14:15) berates Moses for crying out to Him instead of telling the people to go forward, and He instructs him to smite the sea. In Josephus (*Ant.* 2.329–33) there is no rebuking of Moses; on the contrary, Moses, we are told (*Ant.* 2.329), firmly trusts in G-d; he takes the initiative, in an extended speech, in exhorting the people; and without any instructions from G-d (*Ant.* 2.338), he smites the sea.

Significantly, Josephus (*Ant.* 2.334) paints the encounter at the Red Sea as a battle. As Josephus puts it, it was only because they were exhausted from the pursuit that the Egyptians deferred the encounter. Again, whereas in the Bible (Exod 14:16) the miracle is at G-d's initiative, in Josephus (*Ant.* 2.337) Moses suggests it to G-d, on the ground that the sea is G-d's and that consequently He can make the deep become dry land.[121] Indeed, it is significant that in seeking a parallel for the supernatural intervention at the Red Sea, Josephus (*Ant.* 2.348) cites the crossing of the Pamphylian Sea, which retired before the army of Alexander the Great. He thus implicitly compares Moses to that greatest of conquerors, while making the miracle itself more credible by indicating that it was not without parallel. But perhaps most important of all, Josephus (*Ant.* 2.339) introduces a totally new element when he states that it was Moses who bravely led the way in entering the sea. With such a leader, we are not surprised to find Josephus's additional remark (*Ant.* 2.340) that the Israelites sped into the sea with zest, assured of G-d's attendant presence, so that the Egyptians, watching this, deemed them mad.

One of the gnawing questions any reader of the biblical narrative of the Exodus will ask is why, if Moses was such a great leader, he chose to lead the Israelites by such a roundabout route to the Promised Land. The Bible's answer (Exod 13:17) is that G-d chose this course lest the people repent when they encounter war from the Philistines and attempt to return to Egypt. Josephus, seeking to heighten the role of Moses, asserts (*Ant.* 2.322) that Moses chose this route. Moreover, Josephus is clearly dissatisfied with the Bible's explanation, presumably because he realized that the alternative, roundabout route likewise presented enormous military obstacles and in addition presented the tremendous problem of thirst in a trackless desert. Hence, a sound leader would surely have chosen the nearer course along the seacoast. Josephus (*Ant.* 2.322–23), keenly aware of this problem, presents, in addition to the biblical answer, two further explanations, namely so that if the Egyptians changed their minds and wished to pursue them they would have to traverse difficult ground and thus should be punished for this malicious breach of their pact, and so that the Israelites might come to Mount Sinai, where G-d had commanded him to do sacrifice.[122]

By amplifying the sufferings of the Israelites in the desert, Josephus (*Ant.* 3.1) increases the stature of their leader Moses. In the first place, it is to his credit (*Ant.* 3.2) that he orders them to take water with them; and when this is exhausted and the water is so bitter that, in an extra-biblical addition (*Ant.* 3.4), not even beasts of burden find it tolerable and the Israelite rabble (ὄχλος) are incapable of meeting the stress of necessity with fortitude (τὸ ἀνδρεῖον), it is to Moses that the multitude turns for salvation. By exaggerating the description of the Israelites' misery because of their lack of water (*Ant.* 3.9–11), in contrast to the brief statement in the Bible, (Exod 15:27) and by likewise expanding on the Israelites' indignation (*Ant.* 3.11–12) at Moses and their readiness to stone him, their general (στρατηγόν), as Josephus significantly terms him, Moses' leadership role is heightened. Indeed, in the face of imminent stoning by the Israelite mob, Moses (*Ant.* 3.21) fearlessly stands up to his critics and tells them that he has no fear for his own safety, inasmuch as, he remarks, it would be no misfortune for him to be unjustly done to death.

In the crucial encounter with Amalek, whereas in the Bible (Exod 17:9) it is, as we have noted, to Joshua that Moses entrusts the leadership in battle, in Josephus (*Ant.* 3.47–48) Moses takes the lead in calling up the heads of the tribes and the other officers and exhorts these subordinates to obey him, their general. Moses then exhibits one of the crucial qualities of a great general, namely the ability to select capable subordinates. In this case, whereas the Bible (Exod 17:9) says simply that Moses told Joshua to select men for the battle, Josephus (*Ant.* 3.49) tells us that Moses selected Joshua and enumerates the qualities that the latter possessed, the first of which was extreme courage and the second of which was valor in endurance of toil. Again, whereas in the Bible (Exod 17:11) all that Moses does in the encounter with Amalek is to hold up his hand, in Josephus (*Ant.* 3.50) Moses plays a much more active role, posting a small force of armed men around the water as a protection for the women and children and for the camp in general. Moses himself stays up all night instructing Joshua how to marshal his forces. Furthermore, at the first streak of dawn he (*Ant.* 3.51), in Aeneas-like fashion, exhorts both Joshua and his men one by one and finally addresses stirring words to the whole army.

Josephus (*Ant.* 3.54) then exaggerates the Hebrew victory over Amalek by remarking that all the Amalekites would have perished had not night intervened to stop the carnage. He adds (*Ant.* 3.55) further details, thus supplementing the praise of Moses as a conquering general: The Israelites, with their most noble (καλλίστην) and most timely (καιρωτάτην) victory, terrified the neighboring nations and in the process acquired vast booty, which Josephus (*Ant.* 3.56–57) describes at length. Moreover, they enslaved not only the persons but also the spirits (φρονήματα) of the Amalekites (*Ant.* 3.56). So inspiring was Moses to his men that after defeating Amalek they began to plume themselves on their valor and to have high aspirations for heroism (*Ant.* 3.58). Furthermore, though the Bible (Exod 17:13) gives no casualty figures, Josephus (*Ant.* 3.59) reports that not a single one of the Israelites was slain, whereas the enemy's dead were past numbering. Finally, presumably because he realized that a good general knows how to cheer up his troops with festivities, Moses (*Ant.* 3.60) after the victory regales his forces with festivity (εὐωχίαις), as he similarly does after the victory over Og (*Ant.* 4.101). And in another supplement to the biblical text (Exod 16:6), Josephus (*Ant.* 3.61–62) states that Moses then rested the Israelites for a few days, presumably so that they might refresh themselves. That the credit for the victory is to be given to Moses is clear from Josephus's comment (*Ant.* 3.65) that after the battle Aaron and Jethro (Raguel) sing the praises of Moses, "to whose merit (ἀρετήν) it was due that all had befallen to their hearts' content."

Even when he looks on Moses as a judge, Josephus (*Ant.* 3.67) refers to him in military language as a general (στραγηγοῦ). Indeed, whereas the Bible (Exod 18:25) delineates Moses' choice of subordinate judges, the advice given to Moses by his father-in-law Raguel (Jethro), according to Josephus (*Ant.* 3.70–71), is to review his *army* diligently and to divide it into groups and to marshal (διακοσμήσουσι, "divide," "muster," a military term) them—not, as in the Bible, in sections of thousands, hundreds, fifties, and tens, but rather in groups of thousands, five hundreds, hundreds, fifties, thirties, twenties, and tens.[123] This organization, says Raguel, again adopting military terminology, will render G-d more propitious to the army (στρατῷ). Indeed, even when Moses ascends Mount Sinai to receive the Law, he is depicted by Josephus (*Ant.* 3.78) as a military leader (στρατηγόν). And when Moses returns with the Law and lists the rewards that the people will receive if they follow the commandments, he urges them to engage in battle (περιμαχητότεροι) for the commandments more jealously than for children and wives, and he points out (*Ant.* 3.88) that they will be redoubtable (φοβεροί) to their foes.

A major quality of a general, as we have already noted, is the ability to inspire his troops. In the Bible (Num 13:17–20), when Moses arrives at the borders of Canaan, he does not speak to the Israelites generally but merely gives direct instructions to the scouts who are to spy out the land. The Josephan Moses (*Ant.* 3.300–301), in an inspiring speech to the entire people, reminds them of the blessing of liberty that G-d has already granted them and of the possession of the Promised Land that is soon to be theirs. He then tells his people to prepare for the task of conquering the land; in an Aeneas-like pose, he reminds them that the task will not be easy. Whereas in the Bible (Num 13:2) it is G-d's idea to send scouts, Josephus (*Ant.* 3.302),[124] ever seeking to build up the stature of Moses as a military planner, attributes the idea to Moses.

Again, Josephus stresses that without Moses' military leadership the Israelites are doomed to defeat. Thus, after the report of the spies, when the Israelites (Num 14:40–45, Deut 1:42) seek to go up to the top of a mountain without Moses' guidance, they suffer a massive defeat, the details of which are expanded considerably by Josephus (*Ant.* 4.7–8), who thereby underlines the indispensability of Moses' generalship. Whereas in the Bible (Num 14:25) at this point, G-d takes the initiative in telling Moses to divert his route into the wilderness, it is Moses, in Josephus' extra-biblical addition (*Ant.* 4.9–10), who takes the initiative in showing the importance of leading a good retreat.

One of the crucial qualities of a general is the ability to inculcate into his troops a lust for battle. This quality is seen in Moses in an extra-biblical detail (Num 21:23–24) in which Josephus states (*Ant* 4.88–89) that before the battle with the Amorites Moses roused the ardor of his soldiers, urging them to gratify their lust for battle. So effective is Moses that immediately thereafter they proceed into action. It is not surprising that, faced with such spirit, the Amorites prove positively fearful. The rout that follows is put very simply in the Bible (Num 21:24): "Israel put them [the Amorites] to the sword." This becomes, in Josephus's version (*Ant.* 4.90–92), an elaborate description of a panic, which draws heavily on Thucydides' account[125] of the Athenian debacle at Syracuse.

Likewise, Josephus (*Ant.* 4.93–94) elaborates on the biblical account (Num 21:24) of the spoil of the Amorites taken by the Hebrews. The victory is all the greater and the credit to be given to Moses the general all the more extraordinary in view of Josephus's comment (*Ant.* 4.96) that by the time Og had come to the aid of his friend Sihon, the latter had already been slain, even though, according to rabbinic tradition (*Song of Songs Rabbah* 4.8 and *Midrash Tannaim* 4), Og was only one day's distance from him.

The battle with Og is a further test of Moses' mettle. That Og was a giant is clear from the Bible (Deut 3:11), which states that his bedstead was nine cubits (13-1/2 feet) in length and four cubits (6 feet) in width. Josephus, realizing that such dimensions would impugn his credibility, omits them, while stressing Og's huge size in more general terms by stating (4.98) that he had a stature and beauty such as few could boast. Moreover, whereas the Bible (Deut 3:4–5) says simply that the Israelites conquered all of Og's cities, which were fortified, Josephus (*Ant.* 4.97) exaggerates the achievement by remarking that the inhabitants of the realm of Og surpassed in riches all the occupants of that area, thanks to the excellence of the soil and an abundance of commodities.

In his last testament to the Israelites, Moses (*Ant.* 4.297), in a passage that has no parallel in the Bible (Deut 20:10–14), gives military advice to the people, namely, that when going to war they should select as their commander and as G-d's lieutenant the one man who is preeminent for valor (ἀρετῇ) and that they should avoid divided control.[126]

Temperance

It is the virtue of temperance that most distinguishes Moses as the Stoic-like sage. In particular, we may call attention to Josephus's final eulogy of Moses, where he is described (*Ant.* 4.328–29) as having found favor with the Israelites in every way, but chiefly through his command of his passions (τῶν παθῶν αὐτοκράτωρ);[127] indeed, the term αὐτοκράτωρ indicates that he was commander-in-chief, so to speak, of his passions.

The opposite of the Stoic sage, in that he does not have command of his passions, is Pharaoh; and this unwillingness to be moderate (σωφρον-εῖν, "to be sound of mind," "to be temperate,"), according to Josephus (*Ant.* 2.296), justifies the infliction of plagues on the Egyptians. This intemperance, coupled with a lack of wisdom (*Ant.* 2.299, 307), impels Pharaoh to prevent the Israelites from departing; and only fear leads this un-Stoic fool, who is oblivious to Divine providence (*Ant.* 2.302), temporarily to submit.[128] Even when, as after the third plague (*Ant.* 2.301–2), Pharaoh is forced (ἠναγκάζετο) to listen to reason (σωφρονεῖν, "to be moderate"), he does so, we are told, only in half measure. Again, in connection with the seventh plague, that of hail, Josephus (*Ant.* 2.305) stresses the contrast between the sobriety of Moses and the lack of this quality (σωφρονιζομένου) on the part of Pharaoh.

Just as the Greeks had to be constantly reminded of the need for moderation, as summarized in the Delphic motto μηδὲν ἄγαν, so Moses, in Josephus's version (*Ant.* 4.189), had to exhort the Jews repeatedly before his death to be moderate (σωφρονήσειν); indeed, he notes that he himself had refrained from wrath at the moment when he felt most irritated by them.

In one episode in the Bible (Exod 32:15–20) that seems to contradict this picture of Moses as self-controlled, Moses, descending from Mount Sinai, sees the people dancing around the golden calf. At this point, Moses's anger (32:19), we are told, burns hot, and in utter exasperation he throws the tablets of the Law to the ground, grinds the calf to a powder, scatters it on water, and forces the Israelites to drink it. Josephus (*Ant.* 3.99) most significantly omits this whole incident, not only, we may suggest, because it reflected badly on the Israelites as a people so fickle that they quickly forgot all the miracles G-d had performed for them, but also because it cast Moses himself in a bad light as a hot-tempered leader.

As to the former reason, Josephus (*Ant.* 3.95–98) tries to explain that the people were seized by great anxiety about Moses because of his delay in returning and by fear lest he had been devoured by a wild beast or had died a natural death. Josephus combines the two ascents of Moses on Mount Sinai; and instead of the scene in which Moses breaks the tablets, we have a description (*Ant.* 3.102) of Moses displaying them to the rejoicing multitude.[129]

Josephus (*Ant.* 4.49), in an editorial comment not found in the Bible (Num 16:30), emphasizes that the chief lesson to be learned from the key challenge to Moses' authority, that of Korah, is the necessity of moderation (σωφροσύνης). Similarly, when the Israelite men consort with the Midianite women, Moses, in a speech not paralleled in the Bible (Num 25:16–18), in effect equates moderation with obedience to authority,[130] stressing (*Ant.* 4.143) that courage (ἀνδρείαν) consists not in violating the laws but in resisting the passions (ἐπιθυμίαις). He then adds (*Ant.* 4.144) that it was not reasonable after the Israelites' sobriety (σωφρονή-σαντας) in the desert to relapse now in their prosperity into drunken riot. Indeed, in his farewell address to the Israelites before his death, Moses (*Ant.* 4.184) indicates that the purpose of the laws he has conveyed to his people is to teach them moderation (σωφροσύνη). Those who know well how to obey, he remarks (*Ant.* 4.186), will also know how to rule. In fact, the lesson Moses hopes (*Ant.* 4.189) the Israelites will learn for the future from their many complaints to and revolts against him is moderation (σωφρονήσειν).

Again, in setting forth the code of laws given at Sinai, Josephus's Moses (*Ant.* 4.244) gives an explanation not found in the biblical (Lev 21:7 and Deut 22:22) prohibition against marrying a female slave, namely that though one may be constrained thereto by love, such passion must be mastered by regard for decorum (τὸ εὐπρεπές).

In particular, Josephus (*Ant.* 6.63) identifies moderation with modesty. In the Bible (Num 12:3), humility is cited as the crowning virtue of Moses: "Now the man Moses was very meek, more than all men that were on the face of the earth." Indeed, the Josephan Moses refers to himself (*Ant.* 4.317) as merely G-d's sub-general (ὑποστρατήγῳ) and underling (ὑπηρέτῃ, "subordinate"). Josephus (*Ant.* 3.74) highlights Moses' modesty in his willingness to take advice from his father-in-law and in his readiness to acknowledge this assistance. Similarly, Moses (*Ant.* 4.157) is said to have modestly recorded the prophecies of Balaam, even though he could just as easily have appropriated them for himself, inasmuch as there were no witnesses to convict him.[131]

Another indication of Moses' humility is the fact (*Ant.* 3.212) that in an era in which clothing was even more important than it is today as a sign of one's standing, Moses dressed like any ordinary person (ἰδιω-

τεύων) and in all else bore himself rather like a simple commoner (δημο-
τικώτερον) who sought in no respect to appear different from the crowd
(τῶν πολλῶν).

And yet Josephus was well aware that the pagans frowned on modesty
and that Aristotle in particular (*Nicomachean Ethics* 4.1125B7–27) is critical of the unduly humble man who, though being worthy of good things,
robs himself of what he deserves. Indeed, Josephus's Moses (*Ant.* 3.188),
in an extra-biblical comment, when he announces the appointment of his
brother Aaron as high priest, very candidly and unashamedly and in a
way that would have appealed to Aristotle (whose ideal was the μεγαλόψυχος, *Nicomachean Ethics* 4.1123A33–1125A35) recounts his own merits
(ἀρετήν), his benevolence (εὔνοιαν), and the perils he had sustained on
the Israelites' behalf. Furthermore, he says (*Ant.* 3.190) that if the choice
had been left to him he would have adjudged himself worthy of the office,
"alike from that self-love that is innate in all, as also because I am conscious of having labored abundantly for your salvation." He reiterates
this point when he is challenged by Korah (*Ant.* 4.27) for his apparent
nepotism. Here he argues that he is a nearer kinsman to himself than is
his brother, and hence would never have passed over himself in bestowing this dignity if kinship were the force guiding him. Finally, he, like
Horace (*Odes* 3.30.1), is not ashamed to say (*Ant.* 4.179) that he has built
through his labors for the public welfare an everlasting memorial.

Justice

Plutarch (*Demetrius* 42.5–9) remarks that justice is the most becoming
function that a king has to carry out. Indeed, says Josephus (*Ant.* 4.223),
a king should have a perpetual care for justice and virtue in every other
form. It is, however, as rare as it is useful (Plutarch, *Titus* 11.4–5). The
reason for its rarity, according to Plutarch (*Cato the Younger* 44.11–14),
is that even though it wins the confidence of the many it provokes the
envy of one's peers, as we also see in the case of Moses, who is envied by
his peer, Korah. But the greatest achievement of the just man, as we
perceive in Plutarch's discussion of Pericles (*Praecepta Gerendae Reipubli-
cae* 10.805C, 13.808C, 14.810D), is that he never uses his position to
destroy his political enemies, as again we deduce in the forbearance with
which Moses deals with his great rivals Dathan, Abiram, and Korah. And
yet, great as justice is, the question arises (Plutarch, *Comparison of Aristeides and Cato* 3–4) whether the just man is useful only to others and not to
himself.

The supreme compliment to Moses' justice is seen in Josephus's addition to Exodus 18:13, when he declares (*Ant.* 3.66–67) that all who came
to Moses did so because they were convinced that they would obtain

justice; and even those who lost their cases before him left satisfied that justice and not greed had determined their fate. Similarly, we may note, Philo (*De Vita Mosis* 1.60.328) remarks that when Moses reproached the tribes of Reuben and Manasseh, they knew that he spoke not out of arrogance but out of solicitude and respect for justice and equality.

Josephus must have been embarrassed by Moses' apparent lack of respect for judicial procedure in his impulsive slaying of the Egyptian overseer (Exod 2:12), but Josephus typically, as we have noted, when confronted with such embarrassing material, omits the incident.[132]

Moses' sense of justice may be seen in his statement to G-d on the occasion of the rebellion of Dathan and Abiram. In the biblical version (Num 16:22), when G-d wishes to annihilate the congregation for associating with them, the people fall on their faces and ask G-d whether if one man sins G-d ought to be angry with the whole congregation. In Josephus (*Ant.* 4.50), Moses takes the lead and, appealing to G-d's sense of justice, asks G-d to exact justice from the sinners but to save the multitude who follow His commandments on the ground that it is not just that all should pay the penalty for the infractions of a few.[133]

Josephus (*Ant.* 4.296) is particularly eager to note that the Mosaic Code requires that every effort be made to avoid war and that, where wars are necessary, they be conducted justly. The biblical passage (Deut 20:10) reads simply, "When you approach a town to attack it, you shall offer it terms of peace." Josephus, in view of his close contacts with the Romans, with their ideals, and with their methods of warfare, was presumably aware of their laws of war, as stated, for example, in Cicero (*De Officiis* 1.11.34–36 and *De Re Publica* 3.23.34–35). As Cicero puts it, the one object in making war is to live in peace unmolested; moreover, he says, international law teaches that a war is just only if it is duly declared after a formal demand for satisfaction has been made. One is reminded also of Virgil's famous statement (*Aeneid* 6.852–53) of the mission of the Romans, *pacisque imponere morem, parcere subjectis et debellare superbos* ("to impose the way of peace, to spare subdued peoples, and to humble haughty ones"). Josephus (*Ant.* 4.296), in his considerable expansion of the biblical passage, is in accord with these ideals and methods. He declares that when the Israelites are on the verge of war they should send an embassy to the enemy to make it clear that, though they have a vast army and armaments, they do not desire to make war and to seize unwanted profit.[134]

Connected with the virtue of justice, as we see here, is the quality of mercy. Indeed, Josephus was confronted with what would seem to be an embarrassing call for no less than genocide, in G-d's statement (Exod 17:14–15) that He will have war with Amalek from generation to generation and that (Deut 25:19) the Israelites are to blot out the remembrance of him. Aware of the embarrassment of such a command, Josephus (*Ant.* 3.39–40) strives mightily to paint the Amalekites in the darkest colors; it is their kings who take the initiative in sending messages to the neighboring peoples to make war on the Israelites and actually to destroy (διαφθείρειν) them. Josephus (*Ant.* 3.43) depicts Moses as expecting no hostility at all, inasmuch as the Israelites had done nothing to provoke it, and Moses is consequently perplexed, especially because his people are destitute of arms and all else. Josephus then adopts (*Ant.* 3.60) the version of Exodus (17:14) that indicates that G-d will utterly blot out the Amalekites, rather than the version of Deuteronomy (25:19) that states that the Israelites are to do so.[135] Thus, according to Josephus's version, Moses predicted (προεφήτευε) that the Amalekites would be utterly exterminated. He does not say by whom or when; indeed, we may comment that this prediction was actually fulfilled, inasmuch as by the time of Josephus they had disappeared.

That Josephus is sensitive to the importance of mercy, however, as a constituent element of justice is clear from his omission (*Ant.* 4.163) of Moses' anger with the commander of his army for sparing the Midianite women who had been guilty of leading the Israelite men astray (Num 31:14–17). There would, however, seem to be a contradiction to this admiration for mercy in the advice, unparalleled in the Bible, given by Moses (*Ant.* 4.191) to the Israelites just before his death that they should leave not one of their enemies alive after defeating them. But here Josephus supplies a justification for this extreme attitude, namely that if the Israelites have but a taste of any of the ways of their enemies they would corrupt the constitution of their ancestors. Any admirer of the Spartan constitution or of Plato's ideal in the *Republic* and of the care they took to preserve the status quo would appreciate such counsel. This will likewise explain Josephus's variation (*Ant.* 4.300) of the biblical injunction (Deut 20:13–14) that in battle the Israelites are to slay the men but to take as booty women, children, and cattle; Josephus enjoins slaying only those who have resisted, reminding one again of Virgil's *Parcere subjectis et debellare superbos* (*Aeneid* 6.853). The Canaanites, however, presumably because of their threat to the very constitution of the Israelites, are to be exterminated wholesale.

If, indeed, G-d is the model of justice, He is also the model of the connected virtue of forgiveness; and we see both of these in Moses. Thus, in exhorting the Israelites just before his death, Moses (*Ant.* 4.188–89), when he reminds them that they have more often imperiled him than has the enemy, adds immediately that he says this with no intent to reproach them, because he is loath to leave them aggrieved by recalling these things to their minds.

Connected also with the virtue of justice is the responsibility to tell the truth.[136] The Greeks were especially sensitive to their reputation as liars, as we can see from Herodotus's remark (1.136), stated in obvious admiration, that the Persians' sons are carefully instructed to speak the truth and that they (1.139) regard it as the most disgraceful thing in the world to tell a lie. Hence, it is not surprising that Josephus takes pains to explain instances of apparent deceit in the Bible.[137] In the case of Moses, Josephus (*Ant.* 4.303), in an editorial comment, remarks that he in no whit strayed from the truth; and indeed, when exhorting the Israelites just before his death, Moses (*Ant.* 4.179) remarks that souls, when on the verge of the end, deliver themselves with perfect integrity, that is, truth. In particular, Josephus commends Moses (*Ant.* 3.73–74) for not claiming as his own the advice given to him by his father-in-law Raguel (Jethro), this in obvious contrast to those Greeks who were guilty of plagiarism.[138]

One of the incidents that would appear to contradict the Israelites' reputation for honesty and presumably Moses' reputation for integrity was Moses' permission to the Israelites to "borrow" jewelry and clothing from the Egyptians. Indeed, a pagan writer, Pompeius Trogus (36.2.12–13), who is generally friendly to the Jews, states that the Jews carried off by stealth the sacred vessels of the Egyptians. Readers usually assume that the Israelites must have practiced deceit in order to obtain these objects, though such theft might perhaps be justified in view of the way in which the Israelites had been treated by the Egyptians for so long.[139] In one of the passages in the Bible (Exod 3:21–22), G-d tells Moses that before departing from Egypt the Israelites were to ask of the Egyptians jewels and clothing, "and ye shall spoil the Egyptians." Indeed, before they actually depart from Egypt, G-d repeats similar instructions to Moses (Exod 11:2–3). Obviously, the Israelites had no intention of returning these "gifts." Josephus resolves the problem by omitting all reference to the first passage; and in his paraphrase of the second passage, he says (*Ant.* 2.314) not that the Israelites approached the Egyptians but rather that the Egyptians took the initiative in honoring the Israelites with gifts, some to speed their departure, others to show their neighborly feelings toward old acquaintances.

Coupled with justice, as we have noted, is the virtue of humanity (φιλανθρωπία, Latin *humanitas*), as we see in Philo and in Macrobius.[140] In his reply to the anti-Jewish critics, Josephus (*Against Apion* 2.146) stresses that the Mosaic Code was designed to promote humanity toward the world at large, that (*Against Apion* 2.211–13) "our legislator," that is, Moses, inculcated into the Jews the duty of sharing with others, and that not only must the Jew furnish food and supplies to those who ask for them but that he must show consideration even for declared enemies. Josephus even adds unscriptural provisions, such as that Jews are forbidden to burn up the country of their enemies and to despoil fallen combatants.[141] This gentleness (ἡμερότητα) and humanity (φιλανθρωπίαν) extend even to animals, authorizing their use only in accordance with the Law.

When he declares (*Against Apion* 2.211) that the Mosaic Law requires the Jew to point out the road to others, it is almost as if he is replying to Juvenal's charge (14.103) that Moses' secret book forbids pointing out the way to any not worshipping the same rites as the Jews do. Moreover, says Josephus (*Ant.* 4.276), in an addition to the Bible (Lev 19:14), one is not permitted, for the pleasure of laughing oneself, to impede another by misleading him. The Mosaic Law, he says (*Against Apion* 2.291), teaches people not to hate their fellows but to share their possessions. Furthermore, in the *Antiquities*, Moses, far from hating humanity, is depicted (*Ant.* 4.11–12) as bearing no malice even toward Korah and his followers, who had rebelled against his authority and were on the verge of stoning him to death.

This emphasis on tolerance is clearly an appeal to his readers for sympathy. Indeed, Josephus (*Against Apion* 2.237) follows the Septuagint (Exod 22:27) in reading, "Thou shalt not revile (κακολογήσεις) gods" and deduces therefrom that "our legislator has expressly forbidden us to deride or blaspheme the gods recognized by others, out of respect for the very word 'G-d.'"[142] His statement (*Ant.* 4.207) that the Law forbids blaspheming the gods other cities revere or robbing foreign temples or taking treasures that have been dedicated in the name of any god would seem to be Josephus's answer (*Ant.* 4.207) to Manetho's objection (*Against Apion* 1.249, 264, 309) that Moses ordered his people to overthrow temples and altars; doing so would seem to be less than tolerant. Indeed, we may note that Josephus, in his paraphrase in the *Antiquities*, significantly omits the passage (Deut 12:2–3) in which G-d instructs Moses that the Israelites, when entering Canaan, should destroy all statues and devastate all high places. In addition, Josephus (*Ant.* 2.304) has discreetly omitted any reference to the passage (Exod 8:21–23) in which Moses seems to show intolerance by declaring that the Israelites sacrifice to G-d what is untouchable to the Egyptians. Furthermore, whereas the Bible (Lev 24:15–16) declares that anyone, whether Israelite or foreigner, who curses G-d is subject to the death penalty, Josephus (*Ant.* 4.202), in paraphrasing the passage, omits mention of the applicability of this penalty also to foreigners.

Likewise, Balak is concerned with the growing power of the Israelites, but he has not learned, we are told (*Ant.* 4.102), that the Hebrews are not for interfering (πολυπραγμονεῖν) with other countries and that, in fact, they are forbidden by G-d to do so. Josephus similarly omits any reference to the passage (Num 12:1) that Miriam and Aaron spoke against

Moses on account of the Ethiopian woman whom he had married; such murmuring would surely have been regarded as prejudice against the highly respected Ethiopians. Moreover, in contrast to such people as the Spartans (*Against Apion* 2.259), who made a practice of expelling foreigners, and even the Athenians (*Against Apion* 2.262–68), who persecuted those who held views at variance with those of the state, Moses (*Against Apion* 2.209–10) most liberally, graciously, and ungrudgingly welcomed into the Jewish fold any who elected to share the ways of the Jews, on the principle that relationships should be based not only on family ties but also on agreement in matters of conduct. Surely such a statement is a gracious and most effective way of indicating to non-Jews that the door is wide open for them to convert to Judaism.

That Moses himself, according to Josephus, was not prejudiced against Gentiles is clear from the fact that he (*Ant.* 2.315) differentiates between Pharaoh and the Egyptians, carefully noting, in an extra-biblical addition, that when the Israelites departed from Egypt the Egyptians lamented and regretted the harsh treatment that they had given to the Israelites. His lack of prejudice is likewise displayed in the respect shown to Raguel (Jethro), his father-in-law, who is described (*Ant.* 2.258) as a priest held in high veneration by the people of his country, Midian. Indeed, whereas the Bible (Exod 2:21) states merely that Moses was content to dwell with Jethro, Josephus (*Ant.* 2.263) emphasizes his lack of bias against non-Jews when he says that Raguel (Jethro) actually adopted him as his son. For his part, Jethro is depicted as showing consideration not to embarrass Moses (*Ant.* 3.67) for his inefficient administration of justice; only when all others are gone does he discreetly advise Moses what to do.

We see an example of Moses' gallantry toward others in his rescue of the daughters of Jethro from ruffians (*Ant.* 2.258–63). Here the Bible (Exod 2:17) says simply that the shepherds came and drove the daughters away, but that Moses helped the latter and watered their flock. Josephus (*Ant.* 2.260–61) vigorously expands on the charity (εὐποιίαν) of this beneficent act (εὐεργετηθεῖσαι) and adds that Moses deemed it monstrous (δεινόν) to overlook the injury to the young women and to allow these men's violence to triumph over their rights (δικαίου), and so he beat off the arrogant intruders.[143]

Akin to the quality of gallantry is that of hospitality, a virtue that was very much prized in the entire ancient world, both in the Near East and in Greece and Rome, as we see, for example, in the episode of Glaucus and Diomedes at the beginning of Book 6 of Homer's *Iliad*. We see this trait in the warm greeting given by Moses (*Ant.* 3.63) to his father-in-law when the latter visits him after the encounter with the Amalekites. The Bible (Exod 18:12) says that Jethro offered sacrifices, and that Aaron and the people joined him in the sacred meal, but nothing is said about a public feast given by Moses. In Josephus, it is Moses who offers the sacrifices and makes a feast for the people.

Connected with the virtue of φιλανθρωπία is the quality of showing gratitude. Thus, Jethro (*Ant.* 2.262), in a considerable amplification of the Bible (Exod 2:20), compliments Moses for his sense of gratitude and for his requiting favors. Furthermore, Moses, in an extra-biblical addition (*Ant.* 3.59), shows how to exhibit gratitude in the way he rewards the valiant soldiers after their victory over Amalek and praises their general Joshua. Finally, in his last speech to the people, Moses (*Ant.* 4.315–16), in a supplement to the Bible (Deut 32), renders personal thanks to G-d for the care He had bestowed on them, for the help He had given him in his struggles, and for the graciousness He had shown toward him.

The literate reader will recall that Plato in his masterwork, the *Republic* (4.443C–445E), defines justice, the very subject of the *Republic*, as a harmony of the virtues of wisdom, courage, and temperance. Likewise, Moses (*Ant.* 4.193), in an extra-biblical addition, exhorts the Israelites before his death to keep the ordered harmony (κόσμον) of the code of laws he has given to the Israelites so that they may be accounted the most fortunate of people. Indeed, as Josephus (*Against Apion* 2.179) declares in the introduction to his summary of the Jewish constitution, the admirable harmony (ὁμόνοιαν) and beautiful concord (συμφωνίαν) that characterize the Jewish people are due to their unity of creed.

Piety

In his very first mention of "the great lawgiver" (*Ant.* 1.6), Josephus states that it was in piety (εὐσέβειαν) and in the exercise of the other virtues (the implication being that, in the scales of value, piety balanced all the other virtues combined) that the Israelites were trained under him. At the very outset of his work (*Ant.* 1.15), he entreats his readers to fix their thoughts on G-d and to test whether Moses was what we might term an orthodox theologian who had a worthy conception of His nature, who had assigned to Him such actions as befitted His power, and who had kept his language free of the unseemly mythology found among other lawgivers, even though in dealing with events of so long ago he would have had ample license to invent fictions. The crucial importance of piety is seen in Josephus's remark (*Ant.* 1.21) that once Moses had won their obedience to the dictates of piety (εὐσέβειαν), he had no further difficulty in persuading the Israelites to strive for the other virtues also.

That Moses was famous for piety may be seen from the statement in the *Life of Claudius* in the *Scriptores Historiae Augustae* (25.2.4–5) that the most learned astrologers had asserted that 120 years was the limit of human life but that Moses alone, "the friend of G-d," had been given 125 years, presumably because of his piety. The introduction of Moses' name without explanation would seem to indicate, as we have noted in our comments on Pseudo-Longinus and Quintilian, that the readers of this work would be expected to know who he was.[144]

The importance of piety in Josephus's account of Moses[145] may be seen in the statement, found even before the narrative of the birth of Moses (*Ant.* 2.212), that G-d makes to Moses' father Amram in a dream, that He had their piety (εὐσέβειαν) in remembrance and consequently would grant them a reward, as He had given their forefathers. The reward, He says, will be the birth of a child who will deliver the Israelites from bondage.

The source of Moses' piety, in the broadest sense, was undoubtedly his upbringing as a priest in the palace of Pharaoh, who was regarded as a god. He thus must have learned the esoteric lore of the Egyptians.[146] Moreover, he had sojourned with Jethro the priest of Midian, whose daughter Zipporah he had married; and he himself was a brother of Aaron, the progenitor of the high priests among the Israelites. Indeed, as we have seen, several writers—Manetho, Pompeius Trogus, Strabo, Chaeremon, and even the supposedly Jewish historian Artapanus—describe him as an Egyptian priest; and the fact that of these writers only Manetho and Chaeremon are anti-Jewish indicates that in itself such a statement does not show animosity toward Moses. On the contrary, the Egyptian priests were said to possess esoteric knowledge; and Herodotus, for example, as he stresses throughout the second book of his *Histories*, was very much impressed with them.

Josephus emphasizes the role of Moses as a prophet, twice identifying him as a prophet when the biblical text does not.[147] Though he realized that to recount all of the plagues would be boring for his readers, he nonetheless does so (*Ant.* 2.293) in order to show that Moses erred in none of his predictions. But his true greatness as a prophet consisted, as Josephus (*Ant.* 4.329) reminds us, in the fact that, whenever he spoke, it seemed that one heard G-d Himself speaking. In his final address to the people, we are told (*Ant.* 4.303, 320), he predicted future events, "in accordance with which all has come and is coming to pass, the seer having in no whit strayed from the truth."[148] Josephus (*Ant.* 4.307) avers that the reason why Moses recorded the blessings and curses of the Torah was that he wished to stress that their lesson should never be abolished by time.

Moreover, Moses' concern to guard against the impious pretensions of false prophets may be seen in Josephus's comment (*Ant.* 3.214) that he, in his piety, left to G-d, through the medium of the oracular stones on the high priest's robes, the "supreme authority whether to attend the sacred rites ... or to absent Himself [from them]."

Moses' piety may be seen in the account of the burning bush (*Ant.* 2.270–71), where he displays unshakable faith in G-d's providence. In an addition to the biblical text (Exod 5 and 7), he shows full confidence in warning Pharaoh that to those who oppose G-d's commands dire calamities arise from all quarters, and no progeny is born to them according to nature's laws. Likewise, before crossing the Red Sea, Moses (*Ant.* 2.330–33), in extra-biblical remarks, exhorts the Israelites, reminding them that G-d has fulfilled far beyond their expectations everything that He has promised and that He lends His aid especially where He sees that people have lost all hope of improving their lot. Furthermore, in a speech that has no parallel in the Bible, Moses reminds the Israelites of G-d's past miracles and lists the rewards that will accrue to them if they follow the commandments.

Again, when Moses appeals (*Ant.* 4.47) to G-d for intervention against the rebellious Korah, he asks Him to prove that all is directed by providence (προνοίᾳ, a key Stoic word), that nothing happens by accident (αὐτομάτως, a key Epicurean word), but that it is G-d's will that overrules and brings everything to its end. Finally, before his death Moses, in a mighty profession of faith, declares (*Ant.* 4.180) that there is for all humanity only one source of felicity, a gracious G-d. Indeed, he looks on himself (*Ant.* 4.317), as we have noted, as merely G-d's subaltern (ὑπο-στρατήγῳ) and subordinate minister (ὑπηρέτη) of the benefactions G-d deigned to confer on the Israelites. We are told (*Against Apion* 2.160) that having first persuaded himself that G-d's will governed all his actions and thoughts, he regarded it as his primary duty to impress that idea on his people. With an attitude such as this, it is not surprising that Moses looked on G-d as his guide and counsellor (ἡγεμόνα καὶ σύμβολον).

That Moses was the most successful legislator in history, more so than Minos or any of the others, is significantly connected by Josephus (*Against Apion* 2.163) with his attainment of the truest conception of G-d. Indeed, the Jewish form of government instituted by Moses is unique in being a *theocracy* (*Against Apion* 2.165), a term apparently invented by Josephus to indicate that Moses placed all sovereignty and authority in the hands of G-d.[149] In particular, Josephus (*Ant.* 4.200) stresses the effectiveness of Moses in underlining the concept of monotheism by noting the consistency of the injunction that the one G-d should have one holy city and one holy temple.[150] Truly, Moses, says Josephus (*Against Apion* 2.170), did not make piety (εὐσέβεια) a part of virtue (ἀρετή) but rather made the various virtues departments of piety, so that piety governs all actions, occupations, and speech of the Jews.

That Jews, moreover, are not guilty of slighting the divinity whom even non-Jews profess to venerate is proved, according to Josephus (*Ant.* 3.179–87), by the symbolism of the tabernacle and its vessels and by the vestments of the priests, every one of which is intended to recall and represent the universe. The fact that, after discussing this symbolism at some length, Josephus (*Ant.* 3.187) says that this will suffice for the moment, because his subject will afford him frequent and ample occasion to discourse on the merits (ἀρετήν) of the lawgiver, implies that the items in the tabernacle and the vestments were Moses' creation and that the symbolism was likewise his.

4. Moses the Magician

The frequency with which Moses' name is connected with magic gave those who used his name considerable power and influence in the ancient world. Thus, Pompeius Trogus (quoted in Justin, *Historiae Philippicae* 36, Epitoma 2.7), at the beginning of the first century C.E., had declared that Joseph had mastered the arts of magic and that Moses, whom he describes as Joseph's son, had inherited his father's knowledge. Pliny (*Natural History* 30.11), in the first century, mentions that one branch of magic is derived from Moses, Jannes, Lotapes, and the Jews.[151] From the fact that a mere seven paragraphs later (30.18) Pliny mentions Apion as the person with whom he has conversed about magic, Gager has plausibly conjectured that Apion was his source for the information about a group of magicians including Moses.[152] If so, it is significant that whereas Apion almost certainly disparaged Moses and the other Jewish magicians, Pliny makes no such negative comment about them.

In the second century C.E., Numenius (quoted in Eusebius, *Praeparatio Evangelica* 9.8.1–2) presents a more accurate version, stating that Jannes and Jambres, Egyptian sacred scribes who are mentioned in the Damascus Document (Zadokite Fragments, lines 17 ff.), in the New Testament (2 Tim 3:8), and in rabbinic literature (Targum Jonathan on Num 22:22; *Yalqut* Exod 168, 176; *Tanḥuma Ki Tissa* 19), and who were judged to be inferior to none in magic, were chosen by the Egyptian people to stand up to Musaeus, the Jewish leader.[153] The references to Moses as "a man most powerful in prayer to G-d" and to Jannes and Jambres as men who were able to avert even the most violent disasters Musaeus attempted to inflict on the Egyptians are likewise a tribute to Moses' power as a magician.

That Moses was indeed famous as a magician is clear from the fact that in the second century, when Apuleius (*Apology* 90) enumerates a number of magicians with whom he is ready to identify himself if proved guilty of having won Pudentilla as his wife through magic, he speaks of "Moses, whom you know." It is possible that Apuleius, who by his own admission (*Apology* 91) took these names from very famous writers (one would guess Pliny, who mentions the names of six of the eight magicians cited by

Apuleius) in public libraries, is simply trying to impress his audience with his erudition; but it is more likely that the phrase "whom you know" is to be taken at face value, because it applies only to Moses.

Likewise in the second century, Celsus (quoted in Origen, *Against Celsus* 1.21) remarks that Moses had acquired fame for "divine power," that is, for his abilities as a magician.[154] Indeed, Moses' fame as a magician is evidently paradigmatic to Celsus (quoted in Origen, *Against Celsus* 1.26), who speaks of the Jews as being addicted to sorcery, "of which Moses was their teacher." The Jews, he says (*Against Celsus* 5.42), have been led on by Moses' sorcery and deceived by him and have learned from him to no good purpose. To be sure, the Egyptians (*Against Celsus* 1.45) maligned him as a sorcerer who appeared to do his miracles by means of trickery, but apparently they were ready to grant that he did perform miracles. The ancient world acknowledged the powers of magic and did not, as Origen (*Against Celsus* 3.5) remarks, entirely deny that wonderful miracles had been performed by Moses; their explanation was, however, that these had been done by sorcery rather than by divine power. On the other hand, a distinction was drawn by Jews and Christians between miracles produced by trickery (as by the Egyptian magicians in Exodus 7:11–12) and those produced with the aid of G-d.[155] Indeed, one of the attractions of Jesus to the multitudes, whether in his own or in later times, was that he was said to have performed feats of magic.[156]

Paradoxically, it was said that Moses derived his ability as a magician from the education that he had received from the Egyptians, who were particularly renowned in this area. This is undoubtedly the significance of Stephen's statement (Acts 7:22) that Moses was instructed in all the wisdom of the Egyptians.

That Moses' renown extended beyond the intelligentia to the masses may be seen in the surviving papyri. In particular, he was said to be the author of several magical books and charms; thus, *Papyri Magicae Graecae* 13, dating from the third or fourth century, bears the title "Holy Book called the Monad or Eighth Book of Moses on the Sacred Name" (lines 343–344 and 1077).[157] Within the text of this book, there are further references to books of Moses, including a *Key of Moses* (which bears a relationship to the *Key of Hermes Trismegistus* in the *Corpus Hermeticum*), an *Archangelical Book of Moses* (which is mentioned in codex 2 of the Nag Hammadi texts), a *Secret Moon Book of Moses*, and a *Diadem of Moses*. These books seem to reflect a rivalry between Moses, who was apparently especially renowned for his knowledge of the divine name, and Hermes, the thief and magician par excellence of the pagans,[158] as masters of magic; and significantly, we shall recall that according to Artapanus (quoted in Eusebius, *Praeparatio Evangelica* 9.27.6), because of his many useful inventions and achievements, Moses was loved by the Egyptian masses and deemed worthy of divine honor (ἰσοθέου, literally, "equal to the gods") by the priests and was called Hermes because of his ability to interpret the sacred writings. Indeed, we are told (*Papyri Magicae Graecae* [ed. Karl L. Preisendanz] 13.14) that Hermes stole from the *Eighth Book of Moses* "when he named the seven sacrificial fumes in his holy book, the *Wing*."

In particular, it is Moses' alleged knowledge of the Divine Name (*Papyri Magicae Graecae* 5.108–18) and of the Divine mysteries which made him so important.[159] Thus, knowledge of the Divine name was thought to make possible the performance of miracles, as we can see, for example, in such a folk treatise as the later *Toledoth Yeshu*. So paradigmatic was G-d's love for Moses that in a third-century Demotic magical papyrus[160] the longing of G-d for Moses is likened to the love that the charm seeks to create between a particular man and a woman. Indeed, the *Diadem of Moses* contained a magical charm that promised success to its user in making him invisible and in securing the love of a woman. To judge from the frequency of such references in the papyri, we may assume that this was one major avenue by which interest in Judaism was aroused. In fact, the name of Moses as a figure of great authority appears so frequently in magical documents and in treatises on alchemy that we are in a quandary as to whether a given document is Jewish or Greek or Egyptian or syncretistic; apparently, the name of Moses had become part of the general vocabulary of writers on magic. So prominent were Jews as practitioners of magic that the number of magical papyri with no Jewish elements at all is exceedingly small.[161] Jews were also said to be masters of alchemy; and here again the name of Moses appears prominently in lists of practitioners.[162] Finally, we must note that almost all of the magical charms containing Jewish elements—even exclusively Jewish elements—have been preserved in collections made by pagans, thus indicating the tremendous influence that Jews exerted in this, to the ancients, all-important area.[163]

CHAPTER 9

THE SUCCESS OF PROSELYTISM BY JEWS IN THE HELLENISTIC AND EARLY ROMAN PERIODS

1. The Idea of Conversion

The only ancient religions with an idea of exclusionary "conversion" were Judaism and Christianity.[1] Polytheism, by definition, tolerates many gods. Moreover, the fact that Judaism is, in the first instance, not so much a religion as a peoplehood or a nation or a family (though, of course, it has all the qualities of a religion as well) meant that conversion to Judaism entailed denying not merely one's ancestral gods but also one's native land and one's parents, brothers, and children.[2] In this respect, as Josephus (*Against Apion* 2.209–10) emphasized, the Jews differed from such ancient peoples as the Athenians and the Spartans, who rarely extended citizenship to non-natives,[3] and shared the attitude of the Romans. In one respect, indeed, entering Judaism was comparable to initiation into the Eleusinian Mysteries, wherein foreigners instantly became members of the Hellenic "nation." To become a Jew would seem to create an immediate conflict in patriotism, inasmuch as public religion in antiquity was always a part of the state; and the Jew ipso facto could not worship the gods of the state. But there was a difference between becoming a Jew and entering the Eleusinian Mysteries or joining Mithraism or the cult of Isis. In those cases one did not necessarily deny the distinctive gods of the Roman Empire; one merely added another god or cult, whereas Judaism alone insisted that the sine qua non for entrance into Judaism was complete disavowal of all other gods. Moreover, Judaism alone insisted that identification with the national aspirations of the Jews was a prerequisite for conversion. Only Rome's special exception of the Jews resolved this conflict, although the question as to whether this exemption extended to proselytes was an issue at various times.

The Pentateuch and the early prophets do not speak of conversion, although the statement (Deut 23:4) prohibiting Ammonites and Moabites from entering "the assembly of the L-rd" seems to imply that other peoples might be permitted to enter the Jewish fold. There is no indication, however, that the Israelites were active missionaries during the biblical period. The Hebrew word *ger*, which later is used of a convert, refers in the Bible to a resident alien, similar to the Greek metic. No biblical text indicates that the mixed multitude of Egyptians who left Egypt with the Israelites converted or that any attempt was made to convert them (Exod 12:38). In the cases where Judah marries a Canaanite, Joseph an Egyptian, Moses a Midianite and an Ethiopian, and David a Philistine, the biblical text nowhere implies the conversion of the non-Israelite spouse.[4]

There is no mention of a formal conversion for Ruth, although the rabbis (*Yevamoth* 47b) understand her statement "Thy people shall be my people" (Ruth 1:16) to indicate that she embraced Judaism. The first instance of actual conversion to Judaism in the Bible is to be found in the Book of Esther (8:17), where we read that in the aftermath of Esther's triumph over Haman many of the peoples of the country became Jews (*mitheyahadim*), "for the fear of the Jews had fallen upon them."[5]

In the latter part of the nineteenth and the early part of the twentieth century, much scholarship, especially in Germany, insisted that Judaism, particularly in the period after Bar Kochba but not restricted to that period, was not interested in gaining converts. In fact, Judaism was said to be hostile to such attempts. Such scholarship was often based on hidden agenda, namely to prove that Christianity, which eagerly sought proselytes, was therefore superior to Judaism. Scholars who responded to this thesis tried either to explain away Judaism's noninvolvement in proselytism or to show that Judaism was actually inherently missionary in nature. Just prior to World War II, the Reform Judaism movement in the United States considered the possibility of seeking out converts; two works of scholarship that appeared at the time concluded that Judaism in the Talmudic period was favorably disposed toward proselytes and indeed sought after them eagerly.[6]

As a matter of fact, a decade earlier the great George Foot Moore, in his classical work, *Judaism*, had stated, "The belief in the future universality of the true religion, the coming of an age when 'the L-rd shall be king over all the earth,' led to efforts to convert the Gentiles to the worship of the one true G-d . . . and made Judaism the first great missionary religion of the Mediterranean world."[7] But Moore was quick to add that the phrase "missionary religion," as applied to Judaism, must be understood with a difference, namely that the Jews did not send out missionaries.

We must therefore address ourselves to two questions: First, Was Judaism in the Hellenistic-Roman period (from Alexander the Great to Bar Kochba [336 B.C.E.–135 C.E.]) a missionary religion? and second, If it was, how can we explain this fact when we neither know the names of any Jewish missionaries (other than a few who preached the Gospel) nor possess, as it seems, a single missionary tract? Indeed, two works, Scot McKnight's *A Light among the Gentiles: Jewish Missionary Activity in the Second Temple Period* and Martin Goodman's forthcoming *Mission and*

Conversion take the position that Judaism was not at all a missionary religion during this period.

2. The Case for Non-Missionary Activity

No one can deny that the Jews, on the whole, had a positive attitude toward, and an acceptance of, proselytes, and no one can disregard the mention in Philo, Josephus, and especially in rabbinic writings of the conversion of a considerable number of individuals to Judaism.[8] Nevertheless, it is striking that there is no mention of proselytes in the 520 papyrus fragments or in the 122 inscriptions from Egypt included in the *Corpus Papyrorum Judaicarum*. Additionally, a number of passages, dating, for the most part, from the second and first centuries B.C.E., speak of conversions as an apocalyptic act on the Last Day, with no traces of missionary activity on the part of Jews of that age.[9] Even when, as in the *Wisdom of Solomon* (18:4), we are told that the light of the Law is to be given to the world, this is seen as indicating a mission to enlighten the world without, however, explaining how to accomplish it.

We may comment, however, that this does not, of course, contradict the notion that there were conversions prior to the last day. Rather, those who had not yet become proselytes would be converted then. Moreover, we would not expect to find records of conversion on papyri because once a Gentile becomes a Jew, Jewish law forbids discrimination against him or her; and in any case there would be no reason for a proselyte to want to advertise, in a document or in an inscription, that he or she was a convert to Judaism.

Martin Goodman, in an as yet unpublished work, *Mission and Conversion*, claims that the notion of a massive surge of proselytism that would account for the population growth of the Jews runs up against a dearth of evidence: No ancient Jewish writer, he says, asserts that such a widespread conversion had taken place, although it would have been an obvious source of pride. In a published article, Goodman remarks on how small a proportion of rabbinic discourse concerns the status of non-Jews.[10] He here asks, moreover, why any Gentile would want to convert to Judaism when, after doing so, he would be obliged to contribute financially to the *fiscus Iudaicus*. Additionally, except for the case of Adiabene (which, being outside the Roman Empire, represented no threat to Rome), Josephus always disapproves of conversion; and large groups of people in antiquity do not convert to Judaism of their own accord.[11] If Philo and Josephus, as we shall see, do speak about the spread of such customs as the Sabbath and dietary laws, this represents, according to Goodman, the spread of Judaizing (that is, observance of certain Jewish practices without actual conversion), not of Judaism.

And yet, despite Goodman's contention, Philo (*De Vita Mosis* 2.5.27) clearly takes pride in the spread of Judaism, because he says that one reason for the translation of the Pentateuch into Greek was that some Jews thought that it was a shame that the Laws should be available to only one half of the human race and denied altogether to the Greeks. Likewise, Josephus (*Against Apion* 2.282) boasts that there is not a single city, Greek or barbarian, nor a single nation to which the practices of Judaism have not spread. The lack of concern among the rabbis about the status of non-Jews is explained by the fact that the Talmud, as a book of *Jewish* law, is primarily concerned with the commandments incumbent on Jews. Moreover, the monetary burden placed on those who became Jews was surely much more than offset by the economic benefit in getting interest-free loans and in being guaranteed care by the community in case of need.

In support of Goodman's thesis, however, we may call attention to a hitherto unnoticed passage in the third-century Porphyry (quoted in Augustine, *Epistulae* 102.8) stating that Judaism originally flourished in a small region of Syria and was gradually extended (*prorepsit*, "crept forth") to the confines of Italy after the time of Julius Caesar, although this comment may refer only to the geographical expansion of Judaism rather than to the increase in the numbers of Jews.

Goodman assumes that the majority of conversions to Judaism in antiquity, as today, took place to facilitate a marriage. He cites the example of Asenath in the Pseudepigraphic *Joseph and Asenath*, dating apparently from the early part of the second century c.e., as the paradigm of the proselyte and notes that the main theme of that narrative is that she cannot marry Joseph so long as she is a heathen, whereas she can and does as soon as she converts to Judaism. However, in their fulminations against proselytism, such writers as Horace, Juvenal, and Tacitus never mention intermarriage as the motivating factor for the conversion. And it is hard to believe that the rabbis would have had so many positive things to say about converts if their motives were usually marriage, especially in view of the rabbinic rule, as cited by Rabbi Nehemiah in the middle of the second century (*Yevamoth* 24b), that one who becomes a proselyte for the sake of marriage is no proper proselyte. Moreover, if we may judge from the case of Antioch (Josephus, *War* 2.559–61), although wives converted to Judaism in large numbers, their husbands remained adherents of pagan worship.

Goodman argues, moreover, that for a missionary philosophy to prevail it is necessary that the unenlightened be viewed as damned,[12] whereas we often find the view that righteous Gentiles are assured their reward in the world to come (Tosefta, *Sanhedrin* 13.2; *Baba Bathra* 10b). Additionally, Gentiles who were in need were to be assisted and discrimination against them forbidden for humane reasons and "for the sake of peace." We may, however, respond that though the attitude toward Gentiles was surely conditioned by the way in which Jews were treated at various times and places, there are numerous places in Talmudic literature where Gentiles as a group are condemned for their cruelty (e.g., *Baba Qamma* 117a, *'Avodah Zarah* 25b), and their morals are considered beneath contempt (cf. *Yevamoth* 98a, *'Avodah Zarah* 22b). Hence, there was ample reason for the Jews to seek to convert them.

Goodman argues that the Septuagint (Exod 22:27), by rendering G-d in the plural in the commandment "Thou shalt not revile G-d," made Judaism tolerant of other religions; and he notes that this rendering is followed by Philo (*De Specialibus Legibus* 1.9.53) and Josephus (*Ant.* 4.207). And yet there are numerous places in the Torah where pagan idols are referred to in the most contemptuous terms (e.g., Deut 29:16, *shikutzehem* ["their abominations"; Septuagint, βδελύγματα, "abominations," "filth," "nastiness," "nausea," "sickness"]). Moreover, the Torah (Deut 7:25) explicitly declares that when the Israelites enter Canaan they are to burn the graven images of the Canaanite gods; it likewise proclaims (Deut 12:2–3) that they are to break down their altars and dash to pieces their pillars. Both of these passages are faithfully rendered in the Septuagint version. Hence, there was ample motivation for the Jews to seek to eradicate the idol worship of the Gentiles and to convert them to Judaism.

Moreover, McKnight, in his recently published work, argues that the absence of firm data regarding initiation rites into Judaism is an argument that Judaism was not a missionary religion, because, if it were, greater attention would have been given to these entrance requirements.[13] But even he admits that this is an *argumentum ex silentio* and hence to be viewed with caution. In any case, we have very little literature prior to the first century, though even McKnight notes that as early as 160 B.C.E. we find reference to someone who is circumcised at the time of his conversion (Judith 14:10).[14] The fierceness of the controversy surrounding Paul's view in the first century that circumcision was not a sine qua non for entrance into Christian Judaism shows that the prevalent view was certainly that it was necessary. As to the relative lack of attention in rabbinic literature to these requirements for conversion, the foundation of this literature, the Mishnah, was not reduced to writing until the beginning of the third century C.E.; but we may note that Hillel and Shammai, who were among the earliest identifiable figures in that tradition, assume that there were such requirements (Mishnah, *'Eduyyoth* 5:2; *Pesaḥim* 8:8).

Finally, although McKnight is ready to admit that the Jews during this period almost universally approved of proselytes and encouraged them to join the Jewish fold, he argues vehemently that this does not constitute evidence that they engaged in missionary activity among Gentiles.[15] However, although there is, in truth, no single item of conclusive evidence, as we shall see, the cumulative evidence—both demographic and literary—for such activity is considerable.

3. THE DEMOGRAPHIC EVIDENCE FOR MISSIONARY ACTIVITY

The Jewish attitude toward proselytism apparently changed from a passive to a more active approach during the Hellenistic period. The chief reason for presuming that there were massive conversions to Judaism during this period is the seemingly dramatic increase in Jewish population at this time. Preexilic Judaea (which contained the major part of the Jewish population at the time of the destruction of the First Temple in 586 B.C.E.), according to Baron's calculations,[16] based on biblical and archaeological data, had no more than 150,000 Jews. By the middle of the first century C.E. he estimates[17] that the total number of Jews in the world had risen to about eight million and that the Jews constituted about one-eighth of the population of the Roman Empire. Even if we accept Harnack's[18] minimum estimate, there were four million Jews in the empire. True, some of this increase can be accounted for by the Jews' superior hygiene (the incidental result of legislation both in the written and in the oral Torah) and their refusal to practice birth control, abortion, or infanticide (see Tacitus, *Histories* 5.5.3). True also, the expansion and intensification of agriculture in Ptolemaic Egypt succeeded in yielding food to a degree unrivaled until a century ago, so that a larger population generally, at any rate in Egypt, could be supported;[19] but the figures demand further explanation. Only proselytism can account for this vast increase, though admittedly aggressive proselytism is only one possible explanation for the numerous conversions.[20]

4. THE LITERARY EVIDENCE FOR MISSIONARY ACTIVITY

The fact that the initial favorable view of Judaism among the fourth century B.C.E. writers Aristotle, Theophrastus, Megasthenes, and Hecataeus eventually gave way to some virulent anti-Judaism would suggest that the Jews aroused resentment in part, as we shall see, because of their success [C4y?] in winning converts.

That Judaism was active in seeking to win proselytes seems evident from the *Letter of Aristeas* (266), dating, it would seem, from the first half of the second century B.C.E. Here King Ptolemy Philadelphus of Egypt, who had, according to that document, commissioned the translation of the Torah into Greek, is represented at a banquet given by the translators as asking, "What is the purpose of speaking?" The answer given is: "To persuade your opponent in debate by pointing out his errors in an orderly list. In this way, you will win over your listener, not being antagonistic but using some commendation to persuade him. And persuasion succeeds through the activity of G-d." The question is a purely secular one, and it is consequently significant that the reply, introducing as it does the role of G-d, has a broader purpose. The opponent here spoken of is clearly a non-Jew; and it would seem, therefore, though admittedly only by implication, that the Jewish interlocutor looks on persuasion—of which conversion is the ultimate form—as a divinely ordained mission. That the Jews take the initiative in evangelizing is clear also from another passage in the *Letter of Aristeas* (227), in which the Jewish interlocutor declares that "we must show liberal charity to our opponents so that in this manner we may lead them to change (μετάγωμεν) to what is proper and fitting to them."[21]

Another passage that seems to refer to proselyting activity is *Sibylline Oracles* 3:5–10, a work that, for the most part, appears to date from the middle of the second century B.C.E.: "Compelled from within to proclaim an oracle to all? But I will utter everything again, as much as G-d bids me say to men. Men, who have the form which G-d molded in his image, why do you wander in vain, and not walk the straight path ever mindful of the immortal creator?" That the author is addressing non-Jews is clear from his proclamation to all men, as is confirmed by his reference to men who have been created in G-d's image—which hardly is confined to Jews alone.

Furthermore, for the author of 2 Maccabees 9:17, dating perhaps as early as the end of the second century B.C.E.,[22] it is a matter of rejoicing that the wicked king Antiochus Epiphanes should have promised on his deathbed to become a Jew. Such a motif makes the story historically dubious and indeed improbable;[23] but the important point is that the author here betrays his positive and even triumphalist attitude toward conversion to Judaism.

An indication that conversion of the Gentiles was regarded as divinely appointed is to found in the Pseudepigraphic *Testament of Levi*[24] (14.4; dating apparently ultimately from the second or first century B.C.E., to judge from its presence in the Dead Sea Scrolls), where we read: "For what will all the nations do if you become darkened with impiety? You will bring down a curse on our nation because you want to destroy the light of the Law which was granted to you for the enlightenment of every man." This concern with the nations, and indeed with universal enlightenment, indicates a burning concern to spread the teachings of the

Torah to all non-Jews. The same such concern is found in the Apocryphal *Wisdom of Solomon* (18.4): "For they [i.e., the Egyptians] had kept in captivity your children, by whom the indestructible light of the Law [i.e., the religion of Israel] was to be given to the world."

Further evidence of proselyting may be found in the Pseudepigraphic *Testament of Joseph*[25] 4:4–5, where Potiphar's wife comes to Joseph with the excuse that she wishes to have instruction in the word of G-d and that she is ready to persuade her husband to forsake paganism and to adopt the Jewish laws. One cannot fail to realize that such a statement is utterly alien to Greek thought but that it is comprehensible against the background of Jewish proselyting activities,[26] though we must note that the initiative comes not from Joseph but from the would-be proselyte herself, Potiphar's wife. The fact, however, that she shows such certainty that she will be able to persuade her husband would seem to indicate the frequency and success of such attempts.

That Philo, in the early part of the first century c.e., was favorably disposed toward conversion of Gentiles to Judaism may be seen in his comment (*De Vita Mosis* 1.27.147) that among those who accompanied the Israelites during the Exodus from Egypt were those who, "reverencing the divine favor shown to the people, had come over to them, and such as were converted (μετεβάλοντο, "underwent a change," "changed courses") and brought to a wiser mind by the magnitude and the number of the successive punishments." Philo is here clearly contrasting these true proselytes with the children resulting from the intermarriages between Hebrew fathers and Egyptian women about which he has spoken in the previous passage; he condemns these offspring as a bastard host who happen to be associated with the true-born Israelites.

He likewise shows his extremely warm disposition toward proselytes when he declares (*De Virtutibus* 20.103–104) that the Pentateuch commands all Jews to love incomers, that is proselytes, as themselves both in body and soul; this passage is especially revealing of Philo's attitude because the biblical text (Lev 19:33–34) on which it is based clearly refers to strangers in the land rather than to proselytes.[27] Likewise, Philo (*De Virtutibus* 33.179) emphasizes that those who turned from polytheism to the creed of one G-d "must be held to be our dearest friends (φιλτάτους) and closest kinsmen (συγγενεστάτους)." We must rejoice with them, he says (in language reminiscent of the passage from ignorance to knowledge in Plato's parable of the Cave in the *Republic* 7.515E–516A), as if they had come from the deepest darkness to behold the most radiant light. Indeed, he (*Legatio ad Gaium* 31.211) significantly ascribes to a non-Jew, Petronius, the Roman governor of Syria, the view that the Jews welcome (ἀποδέχονται, "receive favorably"), on a level with their own citizens, those of other races (ἀλλοφύλους) who pay homage to the Jews (τιμητικῶς ἔχοντας, "doing honor to").”[28] Philo exhibits the same friendly attitude toward proselytes when he declares (*De Specialibus Legibus* 1.9.52) that the Law requires that Jews show special friendship and more than ordinary goodwill toward proselytes; and he adds that there is good reason for this, namely because they have forsaken their country, their kinsfolk, and their friends "for the sake of virtue and holiness."[29]

Elsewhere (*De Praemiis et Poenis* 26.152), Philo wrenches out of context a biblical passage (Deut 28:43) that declares that if the Israelites do not obey the commandments of G-d the stranger (clearly referring to the non-Jew) in their midst will gain ascendancy over them while they will sink lower and lower. He there renders the word *stranger* as proselyte (ἔπηλυς). Philo then paints a picture of the proselyte who is exalted aloft by his happy lot and who rises to a place in heaven that is beyond words, while the born Jew who has proved false to his heritage will be dragged down into the profound darkness of Tartarus. Indeed, when Philo (*De Virtutibus* 35.187) insists that it is not nobility of birth that is the greatest of good gifts but rather the virtue of one's life, he may well be implying that it is not those who are born to Judaism but rather converts who deserve the greatest credit. Likewise, he pays tribute (*De Specialibus Legibus* 4.34.178) to the proselyte because he has turned his kinsfolk, who ordinarily would be his sole confederates, into mortal enemies by leaving the religion of his ancestors for a better home.

Philo (*De Virtutibus* 20.102) also lauds proselytes as those who "have taken a journey to a better home, from idle fables to the clear vision of truth." They should, he says, be accorded every favor and consideration as their due because, as he states in a passage so similar to *De Specialibus Legibus* (1.9.52) cited above, they abandoned their kinsfolk, their country, their customs, and their religion. On the other hand, his condemnation (*De Virtutibus* 41.226), in such strong language, of those who do not convert to Judaism as "enemies of the Jewish nation and of every person in every place" indicates how strongly he believed in the necessity to convert the Gentiles. That Jews must, consequently, take the initiative in seeking converts, even from among those who seem uninterested, is clear from Philo's portrait of Joseph, who (*De Josepho* 16.87) "converted (ἐπέστρεψε, 'turned around,' 'corrected') the favor of even those who seemed to be quite incurable" by setting his virtuous life before his jailers. Finally, when Philo says (*De Vita Mosis* 2.5.27) that Jews comprise half of the human race, even if he is exaggerating, he must be alluding to the extraordinary success that they have experienced in proselytism.

Josephus, at the end of the first century c.e., also remarks on the gracious welcome extended by Jews to all who wish to adopt their laws (*Against Apion* 2.210), though the statement of the Galileans (*Life* 113) that those who wish to live among Jews in the land of Israel must be circumcised may be interpreted to mean that such a requirement was applicable only in the Land of Israel.

Likewise, Josephus (*Against Apion* 2.282) proudly declares that "the masses have long since shown much zeal to adopt our religious observances; and there is not one city, Greek or barbarian, . . . to which our customs have not spread." Josephus's references to the masses (πλήθεσιν) and to their zeal (ζῆλος) indicate that he viewed proselytism as a mass movement. Further evidence of the spread of Judaism throughout the world may be seen in Josephus's analogy (*Against Apion* 2.284) comparing the spread of the Law, that is of Judaism, to the degree to which G-d permeates the universe. Now, because, according to theology, G-d by definition is found literally everywhere in the world, this analogy indicates that Josephus believed that Judaism had similarly spread to the entire race of humankind.

Furthermore, he states (*Against Apion* 2.123) that many (πολλοί) of the Greeks (and he is speaking of the Greeks throughout the Mediterranean world) have agreed to adopt the laws of Judaism, of whom some have remained faithful while others have reverted to their previous ways of life. Commenting (*Against Apion* 2.210) on the gracious welcome extended by Jews to all who wish to adopt their laws, he vehemently refutes (*Against Apion* 2.258) the charge of the renowned rhetorician Apollonius Molon that Jews refuse admission (μὴ παραδεχόμεθα) to persons who retain other preconceived ideas about G-d.[30] Indeed, Josephus goes so far as to recast the Bible in order to emphasize this point. Thus, he (*Ant.* 1.162–68) anachronistically portrays Abraham as a missionary going down to Egypt with the understanding that either he would persuade the Egyptians to adopt his point of view or he would embrace theirs if they were more persuasive.[31]

Another indication of the tremendous growth in numbers of the Jews is to be found in the remarks of the Christian interlocutor of the late second–century Minucius Felix's *Octavius* (33.3). He says that the Jews, so long as they were true to their religion, grew from being few in numbers to become a numberless (*innumeri*) people. We are not told, to be sure, how this vast increase occurred. Nor, for that matter, does the third-century Menander of Laodicea (*Epidictica*)[32] inform us when he says that the greatest multitudes that gather at festivals are to be found among the Hebrews of Palestine, who gather "in very large numbers (πλεῖστοι) from most nations," though the expression is probably an exaggeration in view of the difficult and dangerous conditions of travel.

A number of rabbinical dicta, most of them to be sure from the third and fourth centuries C.E., likewise indicate an eagerness to seek converts. In particular, it has been suggested that the debate (*Yevamoth* 46a) between Rabbi Eliezer and Rabbi Joshua ben Hananiah at the end of the

first century as to whether it is circumcision or immersion in a mikveh
(ritual pool) that is necessary for conversion of males indicates that there
was a view, namely Rabbi Joshua's, that would have increased the number
of converts through eliminating the admittedly difficult operation of
circumcision.[33]

We may also point to the rabbinic portraits of such biblical figures as
Abraham, Isaac, and Joseph as missionaries. Thus, for example, Rabbi
Hoshaya, a third-century rabbi from the Land of Israel (*Genesis Rabbah*
84.4), cites the interpretation of Genesis 37:1 "And Jacob dwelt in the
land of his father's sojournings" by his contemporary Judah bar Simeon.
Instead of *sojournings* (*megurei*) he reads *proselytizings* (*megirei*) and thus
implies that Jacob's father, Isaac, had made proselytes there. Again, Joseph is represented (*Genesis Rabbah* 90.6, 91.5) as refusing to sell grain to
Egyptians who would not be circumcised.

5. EVIDENCE FROM RESENTMENT AGAINST PROSELYTISM

The most striking passage indicating the zeal with which the Jews pursued their missionary activities is to be found in the New Testament
(Matt 23:15), which declares that the Pharisees "compass sea and land to
make one proselyte." The simple meaning is that the Pharisees, who
were most influential in the Jewish religious establishment, would go to
any length to make even a single convert, though admittedly we must
bear in mind Matthew's polemical stance, the cultural context of Matthew's Christian mission, and the hyperbole of this chapter.[34] The bitterness is clear from Matthew's comment that "when he becomes a proselyte you make him twice as much a child (υἱόν) of hell as yourselves," a
passage reminiscent of Juvenal's remark (14.96–99) that whereas the father merely observes certain Jewish practices the child goes further in
even being circumcised. The passage in Matthew may well be tendentious and, because it is not found in the other gospels, may reflect his
special interests. Nevertheless, in order to be credible, polemic, like satire, must be based on reality. Goodman, in his forthcoming *Mission and
Conversion*, argues that the word προσήλυτος here refers not to a proselyte
but to a born Jew, and that Matthew is thus attacking the Pharisees for
their eagerness in trying to persuade other Jews to follow Pharisaic *halakhah*. However, there is no other evidence that Pharisees sought followers for their sect outside the Land of Israel.[35]

Furthermore, in the Septuagint the term προσήλυτος normally refers
to a proselyte, and it surely has this meaning in the three other places
where it appears in the New Testament (Acts 2:10, 6:5, and 13:43).

Moreover, the very fact that Philo (*Quaestiones in Exodum* 2.2) declares that what makes a proselyte is not circumcision indicates that he is differing with the view that the word usually refers to a convert and that circumcision is normally regarded as the sine qua non for the convert.[36] Indeed, it is not surprising that among the audiences of Paul and of other apostles are Jewish proselytes (cf., e.g., Acts 13:43).

A number of Greek and Latin writers allude critically to the eagerness of the Jews to receive proselytes. In the first century B.C.E., Horace (*Satires* 1.4.142–43), with a touch of mild humor rather than with acrimony, refers to the zeal of Jewish missionary activity as if it were proverbial: "We are much more numerous, and like the Jews we shall force you to join our throng," just possibly a satirical allusion to Exodus 23:2: "You shall not follow a multitude to do evil."[37] The recruiting activity is described as a movement, its spread as a sudden attack.[38] The one who is drawn into the clutches of the Jews will be entirely transformed. Nor is there any basis for thinking that the passage in Horace refers to efforts by Jews to influence non-Jews to join them in a political quest, because we know of no such attempts by Jews.[39] Goodman, in his forthcoming *Mission and Conversion*, translates, "We, like the Jews, will compel you to condone it [that is, the writing of satire] with regard to this whole throng of poets." He then argues that this is no evidence for a Jewish mission. But aside from the unusual meaning of *in* in the sense of "with regard to," there would hardly be much point in saying that Jews are compelling others to condone the vice of writing satire, inasmuch as we know of no Jews who wrote satires, whereas we do have references in Tacitus, Juvenal, Dio Cassius, and other Greek and Latin writers to proselytism by Jews, and we do know of forced conversions to Judaism by the Hasmonean kings.

Furthermore, the contrast between the success of Apollo in saving the poet Horace (*Satires* 1.9.78), as against the failure of Fuscus (who, because it is allegedly their "thirtieth Sabbath," is afraid to offend the Jews) to rescue the poet, is all the more significant when we consider that the whole framework of the satire is a battle scene.[40] This martial atmosphere will remind the reader that the Jews were, like the garrulous pest in the satire (who is termed a conqueror [*victore*, line 43]), attempting to conquer the Roman world through proselytism.[41] Horace is, of course, a satirist; but he is relatively gentle, and his satire would fall flat if there were no basis to his obvious exaggeration.

In fact, in bitter allusion to the victorious spread of Judaism throughout the world, the first-century C.E. Seneca the philosopher (quoted in Augustine, *De Civitate D-i* 6.1) declares, "The vanquished have given laws to the victors" (*victi victoribus leges dederunt*). Again, at the beginning of the second century C.E. Tacitus (*Histories* 5.5.1), reflecting the economic factor in contempt for the Jews, remarks with rancor that "the worst ones among other peoples, renouncing their ancestral religions, always kept sending (*congerebant*) tribute and contributing to Jerusalem, thereby increasing the wealth of the Jews." We may note the impact of the imperfect tense of *congerebant*, indicating that the contributions were continuous and repeated. This economic factor in Tacitus's anti-Judaism, to have any meaning, must reflect the half-shekel contributions to the Temple in Jerusalem of a considerable number of converts.

Tacitus (*Histories* 5.5.2) shows similar harshness in remarking that the earliest lesson that proselytes to Judaism receive is "to despise the gods, to disown their country, and to regard their parents, children, and brothers as of little account." This is a clear allusion to the fact that according to Jewish law a proselyte is a like a newborn babe who has no relations in this world (*Yevamoth* 62a). This disdain for country and for family was clearly disruptive to the order of the Roman state and family, which had been the cornerstones of the meteoric rise of Rome. It is significant that Tacitus here, in naming the relations that the proselyte severs, uses the categories similar to those mentioned in the Gospels (Luke 14:26) as required by those who wish to follow Jesus.[42] Indeed, this charge of subversion of state and family was, as we have noted, one that both Philo and Josephus took great pains to refute.

A similar resentfulness is to be seen in Juvenal, Tacitus's contemporary, who, as we have noted, after deriding those who sympathize with Judaism by revering the Sabbath and avoiding pork, denounces their children who worship clouds and a heavenly divinity, who even undergo cicumcision, and who observe all the laws of the Jews. Like Tacitus, he denounces such converts as renegades to the Roman tradition, because they despise Roman statutes while observing the laws Moses handed down in a secret scroll (*Satires* 14.96–106).

6. EXPULSIONS OF JEWS AS EVIDENCE OF MISSIONARY ACTIVITY

That the Jews were aggressive missionaries seems evident from the reports that they were expelled from Rome for such activities on at least two occasions. Jews were regarded as a threat to the political order because they had their own national identification and were therefore a state within a state, and to the social order, because, as both Philo (*De Specialibus Legibus* 1.9.52) and Tacitus (*Histories* 5.5.2) noted, proselytes must cease their association with native land, kinsfolk, and friends. Indeed, the zeal of the Jews in proselyting led, according to Dio Cassius (37.17.1), in a kind of editorial comment, to their frequent repression.[43]

It is surely significant that the very earliest reference to Jews in Rome is in connection with their expulsion in 139 B.C.E. In that year we hear (in the words of the first-century C.E. Valerius Maximus 1.3.3: epitome of Januarius Nepotianus [ca. 500])[44] that the *praetor peregrinus*, the magistrate who decided cases involving foreign residents, banished *(exterminavit)* the Jews[45] from Rome "because they attempted to transmit *(tradere)* their sacred rites to the Romans," although this may mean nothing more than that the Jews had attempted to introduce a new cult without official permission and perhaps had not succeeded. There is no reason to think that this missionary activity was carried on by the delegation of Simon the Hasmonean to Rome (1 Mac 14:24, 15:25 ff.), as Schürer[46] has concluded; and indeed, it is hard to believe that the delegation would have risked their political mission by engaging in religious missionary activity. Here again, although the epitome of the fourth- or fifth-century Januarius Nepotianus asserts that the Jews attempted to *transmit* their sacred rites to the Romans *(qui Romanis tradere sacra sua conati sunt)*, implying proselytism, the epitome of Julius Paris (ca. 400) states that the Jews attempted to *infect* the Roman customs with the cult of Jupiter Sabazius[47] *(qui Sabazi Iovis cultu Romanos inficere mores conati sunt)*, implying an attempt at syncretism or more likely an endeavor to spread Jewish practices among "sympathizers" without requiring the rites of conversion; here, however, there is no indication that they were actually expelled from Rome, because Paris says that the Jews were compelled by the Roman praetor to return to their homes. Although it is not clear whether Jews attempted to convert the Romans to Judaism or whether they sought merely to get the Romans to observe certain Jewish practices, that is, to become "sympathizers," or sought permission to hold their rites in public for their own community, it is evident that the Jews were accused of aggressive tactics. In his forthcoming book, Goodman argues that it is only in Valerius Maximus that we hear of this expulsion; that Valerius lived a century after the event; that we are dependent for his words on two epitomes written several centuries thereafter; that because the two epitomes differ in details, they obviously have not preserved the decree verbatim; and that in any case we have no other evidence that there was a Jewish community in Rome in the second century B.C.E. He also notes that although, according to Nepotianus's summary of Valerius, the private altars of the Jews were removed by the Roman authorities from public places, Jews actually were permitted to erect altars only in the Temple in Jerusalem and that no Jews are recorded as approving of the erection of private altars. We may reply that Valerius is presumably referring to the building of Jewish places of worship, which he would identify as altars.[48] Nor is there evidence contradicting the existence of a Jewish community in Rome in the second century B.C.E. Apparently, however, the expulsion was short-lived, because in 59 B.C.E. Cicero (*Pro Flacco* 28.66), doubtless with the lawyer's characteristic hyperbole, speaks of the "big crowd" (*quanta sit manus*) that the Jews constituted in Rome, "how they stick together" (*quanta concordia*), and how influential they are in informal assemblies (*quantum valeat in contionibus*). Later in the first century B.C.E., Horace (*Satires* 1.4.139–43), as noted above, speaks of the energetic Jewish missionary activities.[49]

The expulsion of the Jews from Rome by the Emperor Tiberius in the year 19 (Josephus, *Ant.* 18.81–84; Tacitus, *Annals* 2.85.4; Suetonius, *Tiberius* 36.1; Dio Cassius 57.18.5a) appears to be connected with their missionary activities, though, to be sure, only Dio explicitly gives this as the reason. Indeed, Dio clearly states that Tiberius banished them because they "were converting (μεθιστάντων, "place in another way," "change," "remove from one place to another") many of the natives to their ways." Suetonius similarly seems to connect the expulsion with religious activity, because he states that those who observed the Egyptian and Jewish cults were forced to burn their religious vestments and other accessories, and he carefully mentions the proselytes as being included in the expulsion. The fact that Tacitus, like Suetonius, couples the expulsion with the proscription of the Egyptian rites[50] would indicate that religion was the factor behind the expulsion, and the fact that he says that the devotees of the Egyptian and Jewish rites were given a deadline by which time they had to renounce their ceremonial would imply that the objection was to converts to these rites, inasmuch as native Jews, at any rate, had been tolerated at Rome for a century and a half prior to this event.

Williams[51] argues that we cannot be sure that the passage in Dio refers to the same event or that it refers to Rome's resident Jewish community, inasmuch as the fragment could fall anywhere between 17 and 20 C.E. and inasmuch as Dio is speaking of the immigration of a group of Jews who were causing trouble through their proselyting activities; but we may reply that it is hard to believe that the same Tiberius, of whom Josephus speaks relatively favorably (e.g., *Ant.* 18.169–79), would have expelled the Jews twice within a few years; and the use of the aorist tense (συν-ελθόντων) by Dio would appear to indicate that the problem was not with those who were flocking to Rome but rather with those who had come to Rome previously and had established the Jewish community there. To conclude, as she does,[52] that the reason for the expulsion was that the Jews were an unruly group who were deemed by Tiberius to pose a threat to law and order is to disregard the fact that in none of the five sources for this event, including the notoriously anti-Jewish Tacitus, is this given as the reason. To put as much stock as she does in Cicero's reference to the turbulence of the Jews at public gatherings (*Pro Flacco* 28.66–67) is to rely on the obvious exaggeration—or rather caricature—of a lawyer defending a client, and over a century and a half earlier at that.[53]

Goodman, to be sure, argues that Josephus does not give missionary activity as the explanation for the expulsion and that, if Jewish missionary activity were well known, Josephus would have been better advised to try to justify such behavior than to hide it; but we may reply that Josephus reports that a certain Fulvia, a woman of high rank who had become a proselyte, was cheated by four Jews who took for themselves the gifts that they had urged her to send to the Temple in Jerusalem. He connects the expulsion with the fact that her husband reported this to Tiberius, who then ordered the whole Jewish community to leave, whereupon the consuls sent four thousand of them to Sardinia for military service. Josephus (*Ant.* 18.81) speaks of the leader of the four as expounding (ἐξηγεῖσθαι) the wisdom of the laws of Moses; and the fact that Fulvia came to them regularly would indicate that they acted as missionaries, perhaps on her initiative, in converting her.[54] Abel concludes that the decree was directed against proselytes alone, because, as we have noted above, Tiberius, a strict adherent of the law, would not have been likely to banish any citizen without a trial, and he insisted merely that Judaism be restricted to those who were Jewish by birth.[55]

A likely allusion to this episode appears in Seneca (*Epistulae Morales* 108.22), who notes, though without mentioning the Jews by name, that in the reign of Tiberius some foreign rites were introduced (*movebantur*, "were set in motion," "were stirred up," "were aroused") and that the proof that a person was an adherent of the new cult was his abstention from eating certain animals, a probable allusion to the Jewish dietary laws. The reference cannot be to the first introduction of Judaism into Rome, inasmuch as we know that Jews had been living in Rome since at least the second century B.C.E., as their expulsion mentioned by Valerius Maximus would indicate. Hence, the passage must allude to conversion of non-Jews to Judaism. Goodman suggests that it is perfectly possible that the incentive to convert came from the proselytes themselves; but we must note that Dio says explicitly that the Jews were "converting" (μεθιστάντων) many (συχνούς) of the natives to their ways. Indeed, the effectiveness of Jewish missionary activities will account, in large part, for ancient pagan anti-Judaism, because pagans resented Judaism's success and feared that it would subvert their old way of life.

As to a third expulsion of the Jews from Rome, during the reign of the Emperor Claudius in the middle of the first century C.E., there is some dispute as to whether this affected only the Christians and whether Claudius's order simply denied the Jews the right of assembly without actually expelling them. According to Suetonius (*Claudius* 25.4), Claudius expelled the Jews, who had been constantly making disturbances (*tumultu-*

antis) at the instigation of Chrestus. Although the absence of a definite article in Latin makes it possible to understand Suetonius's mention of Jews (*Iudaeos*) as referring either to *the* Jews or to Jews (that is, some Jews), the New Testament (Acts 18:2) explicitly states, in support of Suetonius, that Claudius commanded all the Jews to leave Rome. The fifth-century historian Orosius (*Adversus Paganos* 7.6.15) cites Josephus's report that the Jews were expelled by Claudius in the ninth year of his reign (49 C.E.); but there is no such statement in the extant manuscripts of Josephus, and there is reason to believe that this version was created in the mind of Orosius himself.[56] Dio Cassius (60.6.6), immediately after commenting on the vast increase in the number of the Jews, presumably, at least in part, through proselytism, explicitly declares that Claudius did not drive them out—the clear implication being that on other occasions the Jews had been expelled[57]—but rather ordered them not to hold public meetings, while permitting them to continue their traditional mode of life. He, too, speaks of tumult, but says that it would have been hard for Claudius to expel the Jews without raising a tumult. This incident apparently occurred in the year 41, shortly afer Claudius ascended to the throne.[58] Because, according to Josephus (*Ant.* 19.236–44), Claudius owed his throne to the efforts of a Jew, Agrippa I, and because we see that he acceded to the Jewish request (*Ant.* 20.10–14) with regard to the custody of the high priest's vestments and decided the quarrel between the Jews and the Samaritans (Tacitus, *Annals* 12.54) in favor of the Jews, it seems hard to believe that he would have expelled all the Jews because of a single troublemaker.[59] Because most scholars identify Chrestus with Jesus, the most likely explanation is either that the expulsion involved only the Christians or that Claudius at first intended to expel all the Jews but, under pressure from the Jews and perhaps from his friend Agrippa I, reversed the order and restricted it to limiting the right of public assembly by the Jews.[60]

Confronted with the evidence of the expulsion of the Jews from Rome because of proselyting activity, Collins asserts that such active proselyting is not well attested elsewhere.[61] Kraabel dismisses the evidence as unclear.[62] McKnight hazards the suggestion that the evidence from Rome is perhaps only an exceptional and sporadic situation.[63] But, as we have indicated, there is evidence for not merely one but at least two, and perhaps three, expulsions. Our lack of data for other portions of the Roman Empire illustrates the fact that we have very little evidence in general for other areas. Indeed, we may argue that the very fact that the Jews dared to carry on proselyting activity in the capital itself is an indication of their confidence and boldness: In other cities of the empire, it would presumably have been easier to carry on such activity without direct intervention of officials.

7. The Means of Conversion

One of the great puzzles of the proselyting movement is how to explain the existence of a mass movement when we do not know the name of a single Jewish missionary, unless, of course, we except Paul, who is indeed, as Segal has pointed out, a much underutilized source of information for the Judaism of the first century,[64] and the other early Christians who were Jews by birth. Axenfeld has argued that even if the Jews had works of propaganda, they lacked a consciousness of mission and consequently an organization to effect conversions.[65]

The Question of Literacy

Tcherikover, in a seminal article, has questioned the concept of a concerted Jewish literary propaganda in the interests of conversion.[66] He challenges the views that Jewish literary propaganda among the pagans was technically possible and that the distribution of books in the ancient world was similar to that of modern times, that books were produced in large numbers of copies and were sold in thousands of shops and sent to distant countries, and that famous authors had their own "publishers" who profited from these sales. Noting that of literary works found in the papyri in Egypt the vast majority are from the classical period—the most popular writers are Homer, Demosthenes, Euripides, and Hesiod—Tcherikover concludes that the wide reading public in Egypt was interested in famous works of previous generations rather than in "modern" writers, inasmuch as very few works of the Roman period have been found among the many thousands of scraps of papyri that have been discovered thus far. He notes, for example, the absence of scraps of Polybius and (most strikingly because of his broad interests) Plutarch.[67] We may here remark that no fragments of works of the anti-Jewish writings of Manetho, Apion, Chaeremon, or Lysimachus, dating from the Hellenistic-Roman period, have been discovered; nor, for that matter, have any fragments been found of such Graeco-Jewish writers as Demetrius, Eupolemus, Artapanus, Cleodemus-Malchus, Aristeas, Pseudo-Hecataeus, Theophilus, Thallus, Justus of Tiberias, Philo the Elder, Theodotus, Ezekiel the tragedian, or Aristobulus the philosopher. Most important for our purposes, no fragments have thus far been unearthed of Josephus's *Against Apion*.[68]

Further evidence against widespread literary propaganda lies in the rarity in antiquity of "publishers" in the modern sense of the word; thus, for example, Atticus, who is often regarded as Cicero's "publisher," was actually no more than Cicero's close friend who helped him to copy his works. "Publication" consisted of having the author make a few copies for friends; thus Josephus (*Life* 362) presented a copy of his *War* to Agrippa II, as well as to Vespasian and Titus (*Against Apion* 1.51); thereafter copies were made on a larger scale.

In addition, the potential media of propaganda, notably such works as the Septuagint, were in Greek; and there is ample evidence, particularly from inscriptions, that many inhabitants of the Roman Empire knew neither Greek nor Latin; indeed, in a number of provinces knowledge of Greek was confined to a minority of the population.[69]

As Tcherikover correctly notes, the more famous the author and the more respected his social position, the better the prospects for the propagation of his book; a book would be reproduced in a considerable number of copies only when the author had become famous.[70] What militated against "mass production" of copies of Jewish books, according to Tcherikover, was the hostility toward Jews in the Ptolemaic and Roman world.

But Tcherikover can be challenged on almost every basic point. In the first place, literacy was apparently much more widespread than we usually think, certainly by the first century c.e. and definitely in the towns.[71] The fact that book-rolls and writing-tablets appear with much greater frequency in Greek funerary reliefs from the Hellenistic period onward shows that upper-class Greeks attributed much importance to literacy, although literacy may have been higher in a country such as Egypt, where there was a long tradition of bureaucracy and where writing material, namely papyrus, was much more readily available.[72] In the period of the last days of the Roman Republic and during the early empire, it was agreed among the upper classes that a father had an obligation to teach reading and writing to his sons.[73] In the second century, during the reign of Antoninus Pius, the Greek rhetorician Aelius Aristeides (*To Rome* 97) writes, admittedly in exaggeration and presumably of an ideal, that the entire empire is full of schools. A recently discovered inscription from Asia Minor from the same period mentions a generous benefaction by a philanthopist for the education of both boys and girls of his city.[74] Inasmuch as there is good reason to think that there were more women than men converted to Judaism, there is surely significance in the fact that in at least some cities the presence of female pupils is not unusual.[75] In any case, as we can see from Sallust (*Catilina* 25.2) and from Pseudo-Plutarch (*De liberis educandis* 20.14B–C), for example, upper-class women were apparently expected to acquire a good education. If, as we can see (at any rate from later imperial legislation forbidding conversion of slaves to Judaism), many of those who became proselytes were slaves or former slaves, it is relevant to note that many slaves were educated and that many teachers, especially in the higher ranks of the profession, especially in Rome itself, were slaves or freedmen; and, as we see from the case of

Crassus (in Plutarch, *Crassus* 2), to train one's slaves to be readers and clerks certainly enhanced their value.[76]

Even Harris, moreover, who tends to downplay the degree of literacy throughout antiquity, admits that during the Hellenistic Age there was a dramatic increase in the governmental use of writing in the monarchic states, especially in Ptolemaic Egypt, as we can perceive from surviving bureaucratic records.[77] Moreover, as Harris admits, without the wide diffusion of writing, political and administrative control by the Romans of their empire have been much harder, probably impossible, so dependent on writing was the management of the Roman Empire.[78] Surely there is a relationship between the increase in the rate of conversion to Judaism between 250 B.C.E. and the first centuries C.E. and the simultaneous and definite rise in literacy among the inhabitants of the Roman Republic.[79]

Already in the last century of the Roman Republic, writing apparently played a role in political propaganda, as we can see from the inscriptions found at Pompeii. In particular, we may point to Julius Caesar's commentaries on the Gallic and on the Civil wars, the aim of both being clearly to defend Caesar to his contemporaries. Moreover, the large number of electoral endorsements painted on the walls of many houses in Pompeii, although hardly a proof of widespread literacy (especially when we consider the number of spelling mistakes), certainly does indicate that many voters were at least semiliterate.

But the use of writing was not restricted to governmental records and political propaganda. Its use in religious propaganda may be seen in the testimony of cures, presumably to convince doubters, recorded by the priests of the temple of Asclepius at Epidaurus.[80] We know of prayers read from book-rolls and of magical spells in written form. Perhaps one reason for the popularity of the god Hermes (the Roman Mercury) in the ancient world, particularly during the Hellenistic and Roman periods, was that he was the god of communication and indeed was said to have invented letters. The use of writing, as seen in the letters of Paul, to spread doctrines, to answer doubts, and to organize communities is not viewed in the letters themselves as something unique.[81] Such writing could be frequent, as we hear from a soldier (P. Michigan 3.203) who states that he had already written to his mother three times during that month (though, admittedly, there is no evidence that the author himself, rather than a hired scribe, actually wrote the letters).

A striking example of the use of writing in order to spread a philosophical point of view is the sizable Epicurean treatise inscribed by Diogenes of Oenoanda on the wall of his portico in Asia Minor.[82] Surely there was no point for philosophers, who were interested in converting people to their point of view, to write as many tracts as we know they did unless they had some reason to think that those tracts would be read by a reasonable number of people. Nock, in answer to the question why the philosophical schools, which had many of the characteristics of religious groups, held such a dominant place in the spiritual history of the Hellenistic and Roman world, remarks that philosophical literature, especially the works of Plato, exercised no small influence.[83] He notes, in particular, the importance of a large literature of elementary introductions and summaries, such as the Christians were later to use as a vehicle for spreading their teachings. Such introductions and summaries, we may suggest, are also to be found in Josephus, in his summaries of Jewish law in Books 3 and 4 of the *Antiquities* and in the essay *Against Apion* (2.190–219).

Furthermore, we know from Pliny the Younger (*Letters* 4.7.2) of at least one case where a work, the Roman senator Aquilius Regulus's life of his son, was produced in an edition of no fewer than a thousand copies. When Martial (7.88.3–4) at the end of the first century C.E. boasts that every old and young man and every chaste maiden in Vienna reads his epigrams, he is obviously exaggerating, as a satirist would, but the point would be completely lost if there were no basis at all to his claim.

Moreover, it is a mistake to judge the popularity of books on the basis of the literary papyri found in Egypt, a large percentage of which, as it happens, come from a trash heap of the single small town of Oxyrhynchus. There is a very real question whether we would find the same distribution of authors if we were to unearth papyri at Alexandria, for example, let alone in cities in Italy, Greece, Asia Minor, or Syria, where the soil is not conducive to the preservation of papyri. A clue that the Oxyrhynchus papyri may not be typical may be seen in the fact that Epicurus, who is well represented in the charred rolls found at Herculaneum in Italy, remains unattested in Egypt,[84] where the papyri for the most part do not reflect the books found in libraries but rather, in many cases, schoolboy exercises.[85] Hence, in some degree, the frequency with which, for example, fragments of Homer (seven hundred fragments thus far) have been found and published attests to the frequency with which he was commented on by Alexandrian scholars and studied in the schools. Indeed, it cannot be doubted that the schools—where the Septuagint or Jewish missionary tracts would hardly be read—were largely responsible for the preservation of so many literary papyri as we have.[86] The same factors explain the popularity of the authors, all of them classical, who are next most frequent—Demosthenes, Euripides, and Hesiod—each with close to a hundred surviving fragments,[87] and the popularity of handbooks of all sorts, technical and mythological.

Furthermore, the texts of the papyri, for the most part, come from private homes or from the refuse heaps of various provincial towns; they may well represent the books that were discarded rather than the books that were read.[88] "The caution," stresses Kenyon, "must be repeated that our evidence does not give us the whole truth. We have no complete libraries, but only the debris of libraries."[89] Thus, it is probably incorrect to assume that Thucydides, for example, was not read during the Ptolemaic period because he is not represented in the papyri of that period; his frequent appearance subsequently presupposes earlier manuscripts that supplied the exemplars for these later texts. And, lest we think that because of depressed conditions in the empire in the latter part of the second century and during the third century c.e. people could not afford to buy books, the prevalence of papyri dating from precisely these two centuries would seem to indicate that Greek culture flourished at this time.[90]

By the middle of the first century c.e.—the century of Apion and Josephus, we may note—not only public but also private libraries had become numerous.[91] An indication of this may be seen in several satirical remarks, which to be effective must be rooted in reality, made by writers of the period. Thus, Petronius (*Satyricon* 48), in the middle of the first century, has the nouveau riche freedman Trimalchio boast that he has three libraries, one in Greek and two in Latin. His contemporary Seneca (*De Tranquillitate Animi* 9.6–7) speaks of the bibliomania of a man, presumably from the upper classes, who collects the works of obscure writers, sits yawning in the midst of "so many thousands" of books, and gets most of his pleasure from the outside of volumes. A library, he says, is considered as essential an ornament of a house as is a bathroom. The second-century Lucian (*Adversus Indoctum* 4) sarcastically compares the ignorant book collector to a donkey that wags its ears when it hears a lyre being played; his library is nothing but a playground for mice, a home for moths, and a terror for servants. Josephus's contemporary Pliny the Younger (*Letters* 1.8.2) proudly relates that he presented a library to his native city of Como in northern Italy at a cost of a million sesterces and that he bequeathed 400,000 sesterces for its upkeep. The emperors Augustus, Tiberius, Vespasian, and Trajan built libraries in Rome, and we hear that eventually there were no fewer than twenty-six of them in Rome alone.[92] Epaphroditus, to whom Josephus dedicated his treatise *Against Apion*, had, we are informed (the *Suda*, under the listing "Epaphroditus"), a private library of thirty thousand volumes. Much more informative about the distribution of books than the scraps found in the sands of Egypt are the remains of libraries that have been found in Ephesus (in Asia Minor), Timgad (in North Africa), and above all Herculaneum (in Italy). The last, representing a private library that was overwhelmed by the eruption of Mount Vesuvius in the year 79, contained over eighteen hundred rolls and fragments. In view of all this, one has difficulty agreeing with Harris that it is anachronistic to suppose that the sum of all these efforts at libraries had any large-scale effect on the diffusion of the written word.[93]

The vast majority of ancient works, to be sure, have been lost. One thinks, for example, of Didymus, surnamed Chalkenteros ("Bronze Guts") because of his capacity for work, who is said to have written between thirty-five hundred and four thousand books, including commentaries on various poets and prose writers and works on grammar and lexicography, all of which have been lost. Another such prolific writer was the rhetorician Heliodorus, who, according to Horace (*Satires* 1.5.2–3), was the most learned of the Greeks but whose works have utterly perished.

In view of the statements of Seneca, Petronius, and Lucian, we may wonder whether the works of Apion and of Josephus and of Tacitus, even if copied, would have been read or whether they were kept on bookshelves merely for display. As Lewis has remarked, however, "the overriding impression we receive [from the papyri] is that books were sought essentially to be read and reread."[94]

If we are correct in our assumption that readers in antiquity were primarily from the upper classes, we should not be surprised to learn that Judaism, perhaps through the Septuagint and the pro-Jewish intimations in the writings of the ever-popular Apion and Josephus, attracted a number of proselytes and sympathizers from these wealthy groups. We may note, for example, Josephus's account (*Ant.* 18.81–84) of Fulvia, a woman of high rank who became a proselyte to Judaism during the reign of Tiberius. Likewise, during the reign of Tiberius's successor, Gaius Caligula, we hear (Philo, *Legatio ad Gaium* 33.245) that Petronius, the governor of Syria, had shown a considerable interest in Judaism, as indicated by his acquisition of "some rudiments of Jewish philosophy," whether he had developed this interest "through his zeal for culture or after his appointment as governor in the countries where the Jews are very numerous in every city of Asia and Syria, or else because his soul was so disposed." We may likewise conjecture that Pomponia Graecina, the wife of Aulus Plautius, the conqueror of Britain under Claudius, Caligula's successor, became a convert, if the "external superstition" (Tacitus, *Annals* 13.32) to which she became addicted is a reference to Judaism.[95] Moreover, Nero's wife, Poppaea Sabina, is identified by Josephus (*Ant.* 20.195) as a "G-d-fearer" (θεοσεβής), a term usually understood to refer to those Gentiles who adopted certain practices of Judaism without becoming full-fledged Jews. Another aristocratic woman who sympathized with Judaism was Julia Severa (*CII* 2.766), whose husband was Lucius Servenius Capito, a relative of Lucius Servenius Cornutus, who was a senator in the reign of Nero. Furthermore, at the end of the first century we hear (Dio Cassius 67.14.1–3) that the Emperor Domitian put to death his own cousin Flavius Clemens, the consul, and that he banished the latter's wife, Flavia Domitilla, who was likewise related to the emperor, on the ground of "atheism," a charge on which many others who "drifted" (ἐξοκέλλοντες) into Jewish ways had been condemned.

Even if Harris is correct in his conservative estimate that during the late Roman Republic and the High Empire the overall level of literacy was below 15 percent, with male literacy at 20–30 percent and female literacy at 10 percent (and in the provinces well under 5 percent),[96] there were surely many who could read. If we wonder whether literacy extended to women to the point where they were able to read the treatises of Apion and Josephus and Tacitus, the papyri, at least, do indicate that literacy among women was not so unusual and that there were even teachers who were women. Indeed, by the second century B.C.E. in Rome, actual illiteracy is not likely to have been common among female members of the upper orders of society; and an intelligent woman of the upper class was often able to acquire a good conventional education and, in fact, to judge from literary allusions, was expected to do so.[97] The interest in Judaism among the upper classes was not, however, restricted to women. We read in the anti-Jewish *Acta Hermaisci* of the *Acts of the Pagan Martyrs* that the council (or Senate) of Trajan was filled with impious Jews. The report is obviously exaggerated, but such statements, to be effective, as we have repeatedly noted, must be based on some reality.

The Talmudic literature likewise corroborates the picture of upper-class converts. There is even a tradition (*Gittin* 56a) that Nero himself became a convert to Judaism and that Rabbi Meir was a descendant of his. The Midrash (*Deuteronomy Rabbah* 2.24) also relates that a member of the council of the emperor (presumably Domitian) who was a "G-d-fearing man" (and who secretly converted to Judaism) committed suicide in order that the Roman Senate should adjourn for thirty days and thus not carry out its previously ordained decree to kill all the Jews in the empire. Another anecdote (*Tanḥuma* B, *Mishpatim* 3; *Tanḥuma*, *Mishpatim* 5; *Exodus Rabbah* 30.12) tells how Aquila, who is identified as the nephew of the Emperor Hadrian, became a Jew, although he was restrained at first by fear of his uncle.

The Septuagint

If Judaism was so successful in winning converts, where are the missionary tracts? In answer we must first object to the attempt of scholars to distinguish between missionary and apologetic literature.[98]

The most obvious book that could have been used in winning pagans to Judaism was the Septuagint; but Momigliano has remarked that he does not know of any Hellenistic evidence to show that a Gentile became a Jew or a "sympathizer" with Judaism through reading the Bible, and he notes that its bad Greek would have militated against anyone reading it.[99] Nock notes that there is no indication of substantial knowledge of the Septuagint, except as heard by those who frequented synagogues or were concerned to write polemics for or against Christianity, because, as a book, it was bulky, expensive, and inaccessible.[100] Likewise, Tcherikover remarks that the translation of the Torah into Greek made no impression whatsoever in the Greek world, because in the whole of Greek literature there is no indication that the Greeks had read the Bible before the Christian period.[101]

However, the first-century Pseudo-Longinus (*On the Sublime* 9.9), the most celebrated literary critic after Aristotle, not only paraphrases Genesis 1:3 and 1:9–10 but, as we have noted, cites it as an example of the most sublime style. This can hardly be attributed to chance knowledge.[102] In addition, it is unlikely that Pseudo-Longinus would use a quotation utterly unknown to all his readers; and if it were unfamiliar, he should have said more about the work. Finally, from the way that Pseudo-Longinus refers to this passage and to Moses, not bothering to identify him by name, presumably because his readers knew who the "lawgiver of the Jews" was, it seems clear that he was acquainted with much more from the Bible than this passage alone. Of course, this does not mean that Pseudo-Longinus was interested in converting to Judaism; it does, however, indicate that others might have viewed this strong endorsement by a respected literary critic as a good reason to read the Septuagint and perhaps ultimately to adopt the religion advocated there.

Another who seems to have known the Bible was the Pythagorean Ocellus Lucanus, who lived in the second century B.C.E. and who wrote a paraphrase (*De Universi Natura* 46) of the statement (Gen 1:28) "Be fruitful and multiply and fill the earth."[103] Moreover, there are two passages in Pseudo-Ecphantus's treatise *On Kingship* (quoted in Stobaeus, 4.6.22, 4.7.64), dating from the first or second century, which seem to paraphrase Genesis 2:7 ("Then the L-rd G-d formed man of dust from the ground and breathed into his nostrils the breath of life; and man became a living being") and 1:27 ("G-d created man in His own image").[104]

Furthermore, Alexander Polyhistor in the first century B.C.E. wrote a whole treatise *On the Jews*, in which he refers to Abraham, Joseph, Moses, Job, Solomon, and Jeremiah. Others who composed monographs on the Jews (and presumably used the Septuagint) were Apollonius Molon and Teucer of Cyzicus in the first century B.C.E., Apion of Alexandria in the first century C.E., and Herennius Philo of Byblus in the second century C.E. Teucer's work, in particular, seems to have been very extensive, consisting, as it did, of six books. Such works could hardly have been composed without access to the major source of early biblical history, the Bible, presumably in the Greek translation. The Septuagint was also perhaps among the sources of Pompeius Trogus at the end of the first century B.C.E. and Tacitus (*Histories*, Book 5) at the beginning of the second century. In addition, the philosopher Celsus in the second century c.e. was, as we can see from Origen's reply to him, well acquainted with such incidents in the Bible as the stories of the Flood (*Against Celsus* 4.41), the Tower of Babel (4.21), and the interpretation by Joseph of the dreams of the chief butler and baker of Pharaoh (4.47). His contemporary, the Neo-Pythagorean Numenius, is said (cited in Origen, *Against Celsus* 1.15) to have quoted the sayings of the Hebrew prophets.

That the Septuagint was read by Gentiles is implied by Josephus, when he quotes Nicolau of Damascus as stating in his address to the Roman Marcus Agrippa (*Ant.* 16.43) that the Jews do not "make a secret of the precepts that we use as guides in religion and in human relations." It is significant that the remark is put into the mouth of a non-Jew, Nicolaus, in an address to another non-Jew, Agrippa. Josephus's addition (*Ant.* 16.44) that "our customs are excellent in themselves, if one examines them carefully (ἐξετάζει)," is, in effect, an indication that Jews permitted Gentiles to read the Bible.

Indeed, many fragments of the Septuagint have been found on papyri, to be sure dating from various periods.[105] Furthermore, a clue that the Septuagint was used for proselyting purposes and even was successful toward that end, may be seen in Philo's remark (*De Vita Mosis* 2.5.26) that in ancient times the laws (that is, the Pentateuch) were written in the Chaldean tongue (here presumably Hebrew is meant) and remained thus for many years, "so long as they had not yet revealed their beauty to the rest of mankind," the implication being that eventually action was taken in order to reveal the beauty of the Torah to the Gentiles, that is, at least in the ultimate sense, to convert them to Judaism. Before the translation was made, according to Philo (*De Vita Mosis* 2.5.27), people came to be aware of the Torah through observing those who practiced it. But apparently this kind of passive attitude was replaced by a more aggressive attitude, inasmuch as some people (who are unidentified) thought that it was a shame that the laws should be found in only one-half of the human race and denied to the Greeks, whereupon they took steps to have the Pentateuch translated. Additional evidence that the Septuagint was used for proselyting purposes may be seen in Philo's statement (*De Vita Mosis* 2.6.36) that the translation was made so that "the greater part, or even the whole, of the human race might be profited and led to a better life" by the Torah's wise and admirable ordinances.

Furthermore, Philo (*De Vita Mosis* 2.7.41) comments that each year, on the anniversary of the completion of the translation, a festival was held on the island of Pharos, off the coast of Alexandria, where the translation had been made, to which not only Jews but also others "with their whole multitude" (παμπληθεῖς) came. Those who came may well have had their interest aroused in the document that they were celebrating.

That Philo had great hopes that the Septuagint would lead non-Jews to adopt Judaism is clear from his statement of belief (*De Vita Mosis* 2.7.44), put into immediate juxtaposition with his account of the translation of the Septuagint, that "each nation would abandon its peculiar ways and, throwing overboard their ancestral customs, would turn to honoring our laws alone." Indeed, one concrete instance where reading the Bible did affect a candidate for conversion is to be seen in the account of the conversion of Izates, the king of Adiabene, who decided to be circumcised after being told by the Jew Eleazar that he ought to do more than read the Bible (Josephus, *Ant.* 20.44–46). This is corroborated in the *Midrash Genesis Rabbah* (46.10), where we read that the immediate event that led Izates and his brother Monobazus to convert to Judaism was their reading of the verse in Genesis (17:11) "And you shall be circumcised in the flesh of your foreskin."

Apocrypha and Pseudepigrapha

Although one cannot usually determine whether a work was intended for internal apologetic or external missionary propaganda, one may detect missionary motives in certain of the Apocryphal and Pseudepigraphical books, though admittedly they were also needed by Jews to heighten their self-esteem and to define their self-identity.[106] For example, the book of Judith (ca second century B.C.E.) relates (14:5–10) that Achior, an Ammonite[107] and one of Holofernes' generals, became a Jew when he saw the head of Holofernes, thus indicating that Ammonites, who are apparently excluded by the Torah (Deut 23:4–5) from becoming Jews, are acceptable as proselytes. Moreover, the *Sibylline Oracles*, the oldest portion of which dates from the second century B.C.E., speaks (3:195) of Israel's mission "to be the guide of life to all mortals." The strong attack on pagan idolatry and animal worship and the contrast with pure Jewish monotheism fits this stance, which, we may guess, is both apologetic and missionary. Likewise, the exhortation in the *Sibylline Oracles* (3:547–79) to pagans to bring sacrifices to the Temple and to abandon their polytheistic folly (4:162–67), as well as the passage in the apocryphal Wisdom of Solomon (dating from perhaps the first century B.C.E.), attacking idolatry as vain and wicked, would seem to be directed to Gentiles and to serve as propaganda to win proselytes. The fact that the latter book seeks to explain allegorically the biblical miracles, which, if taken literally, might be viewed with incredulity by the Gentiles, may support such a hypothesis.

Moreover, a passage in the Pseudepigraphic 2 Enoch (48:6–9), dating from perhaps the first century B.C.E., declares that one must hand over "the books" not only to one's children but also "among all nations who are discerning, so that they may fear G-d, and so that they may accept them. And they will read them and adhere to them." Although the text is doubtful in places and there is a problem of dating, still this passage suggests that Jews propagandized Gentiles through the use of literature, presumably the Bible.

A number of works, clearly propagandistic in nature, were composed in the second and first centuries B.C.E., probably in Egypt, and ascribed to Gentiles, though their Jewish authorship is generally assumed. Whether or not the *Letter of Aristeas* (probably second century B.C.E.) was written for missionary purposes, certainly its effect is to demonstrate the honor in which the Jewish Scriptures and scholars and their philosophy and ethics were held by King Ptolemy Philadelphus (reigned 283–245 B.C.E.). Indeed, about a third of the *Letter of Aristeas*, as we have noted, deals with a banquet to which the elders are invited by the king, much like the symposia described by Plato, Xenophon, Plutarch, Athenaeus, and Macrobius.

At this symposium the king questions the various elders on a whole series of topics pertaining to politics and ethics, and in every case the king expresses amazement at the great wisdom displayed by the Jews. Yet, as Tcherikover has well remarked, "it is worth noting that the entire wisdom of the Jewish elders as reported by Aristeas is no more than current opinion taken from some compendium of Greek ethics and politics, with the addition of the Jewish belief in one G-d."[108]

The similarity of Judaism and Greek philosophy is stressed in one passage in particular (*Letter of Aristeas* 201) in which the Socratic philosopher Menedemus of Eretria, who is present at the banquet, commends the elders for their belief in divine providence, a belief with which he, like the Stoics and other followers of Socrates, is obviously in agreement. The dietary laws, in a passage anticipating Philo's method,[109] are explained symbolically—a method of explanation for theological problems which, although hardly unique, the Greeks had employed since the days of Heraclitus in the latter part of the sixth century B.C.E. and which was particularly popular with the Stoics;[110] thus, "the 'parting of the hoof' . . . is a symbol to discriminate in each of our actions with a view to what is right" (*Letter of Aristeas* 150). Finally, "Aristeas" (16) goes so far in his apologetics as to identify G-d with Zeus: "G-d . . . is He Whom all men worship (and we, too, Your Majesty, though we address Him differently), as Zeus and Dis." Such remarks were clearly calculated not only to defend Judaism but to make it appealing to non-Jews by showing its consonance, on the one hand, with the highest ideas of philosophy and by demonstrating its uniqueness, on the other hand. The author apparently realized that an obvious question would occur to the reader, namely, why the pagan Greek writers of the classical period make no mention of this great wisdom of the Jewish scriptures. And so, after presenting this question, he states (*Letter of Aristeas* 313) that the historian Theopompus a century earlier had endeavored to refer to the Bible, but that he had been smitten by G-d so as to desist, because the Torah was so holy.

Moreover, Pseudo-Phocylides (ca first century B.C.E.) presents such Pentateuchal laws as dietary regulations (Deut 14:21), apparently in order to show that a pagan poet did not regard such laws as ridiculous.

Finally, in the early part of the second century C.E., the pseudepigraphic work *Joseph and Asenath* glorifies Asenath as the prototype of the proselyte, stresses that she received heavenly recognition of the sincerity of her conversion (15:2–5), and makes a fervent plea for her full acceptance into the Israelite community.[111] This seems like the kind of reassurance proselytes must have welcomed in the light of apparent resistance on the part of some Jews to their complete acceptance on a par with born Jews. Indeed, when Asenath is the intended victim of a murderous conspiracy at the hands of Jews, G-d Himself intervenes to deliver her (16:6, 26:2, 27:11, 28:1, 28:10). Moreover, the description of Asenath as "dead" before her conversion illustrates a major attraction of Judaism, namely its promise of life and, indeed, of immortality.

Graeco-Jewish Writers before Philo

A number of works in Greek, usually said to have been composed by Egyptian Jews, are clearly apologetic and may well have been used in the campaign to overcome Gentile objections to conversion. In particular, the Judaeo-Greek philosophers undoubtedly played an important role in answering the intellectual objections of the Greeks and in winning them to Judaism. Just as the Egyptian priests during the Hellenistic period claimed that Greek philosophy was derived from the Egyptians,[112] so the prevailing approach in Alexandrian Jewish apologetics is to show that the Greek philosophers had borrowed from the Bible.

Thus, in a work now lost except for fragments, attributed to a certain Aristobulus (quoted in Eusebius, *Praeparatio Evangelica* 13.12.1–16), who supposedly wrote it during the reign of Ptolemy VI Philometor (181–145 B.C.E.), the author asserts that the poets Homer and Hesiod and the philosophers Pythagoras, Socrates, and Plato were all acquainted with a translation of the Torah into Greek which had been made before the Persian conquest of Egypt (525 B.C.E.). In making such an assertion, Aristobulus was claiming, in effect, that the Jews had anticipated the Greeks even in their highest achievement, philosophy. This and the fact (2 Mac 1:10) that Aristobulus was a teacher of King Ptolemy would certainly be calculated to enhance the status of Judaism in the eyes of pagan intellectuals. Indeed, the philosopher Aristobulus, in his understanding of

G-d as limited by space or time, in his allegorical explanation of the anthropomorphisms in the Bible, and in his attempted demonstration of a comprehensive ordering of the universe embracing both humanity and nature, was, apparently, consciously trying to adapt the Jewish tradition to a missionary counterattack.[113]

Furthermore, the historian Eupolemus (ca. 150 B.C.E.), presumably in answer to the anti-Jewish charge that the Jews had contributed nothing useful to civilization (cf. Apollonius Molon, cited in Josephus, *Against Apion* 2.148) and indeed had produced no inventors or sages (cf. Apion, quoted in Josephus, *Against Apion* 2.135), states that Moses invented the alphabet, as well as the sciences in general, which he then taught the Phoenicians and Greeks (cited in Clement of Alexandria, *Stromata* 1.23. 153.4). Furthermore, Artapanus (ca. 100 B.C.E.) claims that Abraham taught astrology to the Egyptians, that Joseph improved Egyptian agriculture, and that Moses, whom he identifies with the Greek Musaeus and the Egyptian Hermes-Thoth, originated Egyptian civilization, including navigation, architecture, military strategy, philosophy, religion, and political science (Eusebius, *Praeparatio Evangelica* 9.18.1, 9.23.2, 9.27.3–4). That Eusebius can make such a claim half a millennium after the time of Artapanus is an indication that he, in a polemic work where he had to be careful, believed that it was credible and that others also would find it thus. Likewise, Cleodemus, or Malchus (ca 100 B.C.E.), presumably in answer to the charge that the Jews were cowards, asserts (cited in Josephus, *Ant.* 1.240–41) that Abraham's sons by Keturah joined the legendary Heracles in his campaign against Libya and Antaeus and that Heracles even married the daughter of one of them. Because Heracles was a favorite hero of the Hellenistic Age, particularly to the leading philosophical group, the Stoics, this claim would raise the Jews in the estimation of non-Jews.

Because the ancients were so fond of viewing plays, another vehicle of propaganda may well have been a tragedy such as *The Exodus* (considerable fragments of which have been preserved by Eusebius [*Praeparatio Evangelica* 9.28–29]) by Ezekiel, who apparently lived in the second century B.C.E.[114] Inasmuch as one major attraction to Judaism was the personality of the biblical Moses, as we have suggested, the playwright's glorification of Moses, the central figure of the tragedy, must have been impressive. This appeal must have been all the greater because the author is quite obviously steeped in the giants of Greek literature, most notably Homer, Aeschylus, and Euripides. In particular, we may note the omission or toning down of elements that might presumably prove embarrassing to a pagan audience, as well as the inclusion of non-biblical midrashic-like elements that enhance its attractiveness.[115]

In addition, Jacobson has argued that Ezekiel's drama, *The Exodus*, was composed for non-Jews as well as for Jews and that, in fact, there are indications in the extant fragments of the play that the non-Jews expected to attend the play were Greeks rather than native Egyptians.[116] If, indeed, the play attempts to strengthen the bond of the Jews with the Greeks as against the Egyptians and if, as is the case, there is nothing in the fragments to suggest hostility toward the Greeks or toward paganism in general, this would make for excellent propaganda in seeking converts. Surely the play would impress the audience with the greatness of the heroic leader of the Jewish people, as well as with the nobility of the Jewish people themselves.[117]

Philo

As for the methods of missionaries in spreading the knowledge of the Torah, Philo (*De Specialibus Legibus* 1.59.320) seems to allude to them, for he berates the mystics who restrict their knowledge "to three or four alone" instead of proceeding to the midst of the marketplace so that every man might "share in securing a better and happier life." Philo's statement that these teachings should be extended to every man is a clear indication that they should be given not only to Jews but to non-Jews as well. The analogy he makes with nature (1.59.322–23) is instructive: Just as nature does not conceal any of her glorious works but displays the stars and seas and plants and animals, so one should display all that is profitable—that is, the Torah—for the benefit of all humanity. Indeed, Philo (*De Virtutibus* 39.217) praises the example par excellence of the missionary, Abraham, as one whose voice was invested with persuasiveness and whose hearers were endowed with understanding by the Divine spirit.

Moreover, some of Philo's works are more intelligible when it is recognized that they were directed also or even primarily toward Gentiles,[118] though admittedly it is usually impossible to determine whether Philo is interested in converting Gentiles or in merely explaining the Bible.[119] Such treatises as *De Vita Contemplativa* and *Quod Omnis Probus Liber Sit* are definitely addressed to Gentiles, as Nock admits (the latter being, in substance, a popular Hellenistic diatribe), and as we can see from the approving reference in the latter treatise both to companions of "the Olympian gods" (7.42) and to "the legislator of the Jews" (7.43), phrases one would hardly use in addressing Jews.[120] Moreover, *De Vita Mosis* is an apologetic philosophical and religious biography that paints Moses as a philosopher-king of whom Plato would be proud. Probably intended for a non-Jewish audience are Philo's statements that Moses attained the summit of philosophy (*De Opificio Mundi* 2.8), that the pre-Socratic philosopher Heraclitus stole his theory of opposites from Moses (*Quaestiones in Genesin* 4.152), that Moses excelled the Greek philosophers in assigning the task of giving names not to some of the men of old but to the first man created (*Legum Allegoria* 2.5.15), and that Moses (like Socrates) was opposed to sophistry (*Quod Deterius Potiori Insidiari Soleat* 12.38–39), though admittedly such statements would also have delighted Hellenized Jews. Still, the theory that such treatises and statements were intended primarily for Jews who were on the threshold of apostasy seems less likely in view of the infrequency with which the issue of apostasy is mentioned explicitly by Philo.

An indication that Philo was read by non-Jews may be seen in the third-century romance the *Aethiopica* (9.9) of Heliodorus, who echoes *De Vita Mosis* (2.36.195).[121] Further indications may be found in the fact that papyrus fragments, dating from the third century, have survived of Philo's *Legum Allegoriae*, *Quod Deterius Potiori Insidiari Soleat*, *De Posteritate Caini*, and *De Ebrietate*, as well as of a number of lost treatises, which have been found at Oxyrhynchus.[122]

Josephus

As for Josephus, even Tcherikover, who endeavors to prove that the writings of the Alexandrian Jews were intended for Jews rather than for Gentiles, admits that his conclusions do not apply to him.[123] The very fact, we may note, that Josephus presented a copy of his *War* to the emperor Vespasian, to his son Titus (*Against Apion* 1.51), and to the Jewish king Agrippa II (*Life* 362) shows that he looked for and received support and encouragement in the highest places. Moreover, Josephus explicitly says in these passages that he gave copies of the *War* to *many* of the Romans who had taken part in the campaign, and he adds in the former passage that he sold copies to *many* of his compatriots, "persons well versed in Greek wisdom."

The fact that (*Life* 363) Titus affixed his signature to the work and ordered its publication certainly gave it the authoritative status that guaranteed a wide circulation. Surely Josephus would not have sought help to write the *War* in Greek (*Against Apion* 1.50) if he had not been confident that the resulting work would be widely read.

In the *Antiquities*, which apparently was written shortly before *Against Apion*, Josephus cites (*Ant.* 1.10) as a precedent for his work the translation of the Torah into Greek for King Ptolemy Philadelphus. This is clearly designed as a justification for directing his work to Gentiles with apologetic intent, inasmuch as he apparently realized that teaching the Torah to Gentiles (*Hagigah* 13a, *Sanhedrin* 59a) is normally prohibited, even though he might have justified his enterprise by declaring that he was presenting a history rather than teaching Torah. Indeed, he inquires (*Ant.* 1.9) whether Jews have been willing to communicate such information to Gentiles. His question (*Ant.* 1.9) whether any of the Greeks have been curious to learn "our" history, and his specific declaration (*Ant.* 1.3–4) that his work was undertaken for the public benefit (εἰς κοινὴν ὠφέλειαν) in the belief (*Ant.* 1.5) that the *whole* Greek world would find it worthy of attention indicate that he was directing the *Antiquities* to a wide audience of pagans. Indeed, he expresses his confidence (*Ant.* 1.12) that his work will find many readers among non-Jewish intellectuals when he declares "that there are still today many lovers of learning" like King Ptolemy Philadelphus.[124]

In noting that it has been "our traditional custom to make nothing of what is good into a secret" (*Ant.* 1.11), he perhaps indicates an implicit missionary motive, although he is careful not to stress it lest he anger his Roman patrons. Again, the fact that at the end of the work (*Ant.* 20.262) he boasts that no one else would have been equal to the task of issuing so accurate a treatise for the Greeks indicates that he directed the work to the non-Jewish world, because the term *Greeks* for Josephus is the opposite of *Jews*.

Josephus's contrast of Moses with other legislators (*Ant.* 1.18–26) parallels the portrait in Philo's *De Opificio Mundi* and was clearly intended to impress pagan readers. Moreover, that he intended his work for pagan readers is clear from his omission of several embarrassing episodes, e.g., the cunning of Jacob in connection with Laban's flock (Gen 30:37–38), the Judah–Tamar episode (Gen 38), Moses' slaying of the Egyptian (Exod 2:12), the making of the golden calf (Exod 32), Miriam's leprosy (Num 12), the story of Moses' striking the rock to bring forth water in violation of G-d's command (Num 20:10–12), and the story of the brazen serpent (Num 21:4–9) whereby Moses cured those who had been bitten by the fiery serpents.[125] These passages would certainly have been known to a Jewish audience that had access either to the Hebrew original or to the Greek translation—this despite his statement (*Ant.* 1.17) that he will set forth the precise details of what is written in the Scriptures, neither adding nor omitting anything.

Moreover, as we have noted, Josephus has modified many other biblical passages. In particular, his portrait of Abraham going down to Egypt to engage the Egyptian wise men in conversation (*Ant.* 1.166–68) seems to be a picture of a contemporary Jewish missionary.

Indeed, it seems unlikely that Josephus would have spent close to twenty years writing his *Antiquities* if he did not have good prospects of achieving his goal of attracting a wide readership among pagan intellectuals; and although readership does not necessarily imply conversion, it may well be a first and important step. Inasmuch as his work on the *Jewish War* had the endorsement of none other than the Emperor Titus himself, who gave orders for its publication (*Life* 363), this surely would have given Josephus confidence that both this work and his magnum opus, the *Antiquities*, would be widely read and taken seriously. That his *Antiquities* was, indeed, read by many is clear from Josephus's statement (*Against Apion* 1.2) that a great number of people (συχνούς), "influenced by the malicious calumnies of certain individuals," had sought to discredit statements in his *Antiquities* and that he consequently considered it his duty to devote a treatise to a refutation of them. There would hardly have been much point in doing so if he did not consider it likely that his remarks would be read by his critics and others.

Though the work *Against Apion* was ostensibly merely a defense of Judaism, it seems likely that such a treatise was also employed by missionaries. Thus, by stressing the antiquity of the Jews in contrast to the Greek world, where "everything will be modern and dating, so to speak, from yesterday or the day before" (*Against Apion* 1.7), Josephus gives stature to the Jews so that they do not appear to be mere imitators of other peoples (*Against Apion* 2.152). Apparently, the Jews won this propaganda battle, inasmuch as we find, as we have noted, that even so bitter a Jew-baiter as Tacitus (*Histories* 5.2) mentions complimentary theories of the origin of the Jews, tracing them back to the Golden Age of Saturn or to the reign of the goddess Isis or to King Cepheus of Ethiopia or to the Solymi, renowned in Homer.

Moreover, when Josephus (*Against Apion* 2.168–71) reiterates the theory that had been advanced by Aristobulus and Philo that Pythagoras, Anaxagoras, Plato, and the Stoics had adopted their conceptions of G-d from the principles supplied by Moses, he is indicating to primarily non-Jewish audiences that the supreme fountain of wisdom is to be found in the Jewish Scriptures. Furthermore, Josephus here stresses that the major difference between the Greek philosophers and the Torah is that the former addressed themselves to the esoteric few, whereas the Torah, indeed, addresses the masses by making ethics a department of religion and, unlike the Spartans, Cretans, and Athenians, by combining precept and practice.

Tcherikover argues that polemical works by Jews, at least in the Hellenistic period, were directed to those Jews who had become apostates.[126] But the references in Philo and Josephus that may be interpreted as directed to assimilated or apostate Jews are few. Indeed, the Septuagint, Philo (*De Specialibus Legibus* 1.9.53), and Josephus (*Ant.* 4.207, *Against Apion* 2.237) agree in their interpretation of Exodus 22:27 that the Jew is not permitted to speak in a derogatory fashion about other religions, even those that worship idols. Additionally, the very survival of the writings of Philo and Josephus through a non-Jewish tradition should indicate that they were originally intended for, or in any case reached, the ears of some non-Jews. Finally, if, indeed, the increase in the Jewish population during the Hellenistic-Roman period was far greater than can be accounted for by natural increase, we must conjecture that Jewish literary propaganda had some part in the process.[127]

Conversion through Oral Persuasion

Moreover, all this assumes that people were converted through reading tracts, whereas there is every reason to believe that people were won to various philosophies, particularly Stoicism and Cynicism,[128] as well as to Christianity, for example, for the most part through oral persuasion. Even among the elite, and certainly among the masses, culture had a strong oral component; poets, orators, and lecturers traveled from city to city and regularly gave oral recitations (*recitationes*) of written works (which for many served as a substitute for personal reading) at symposia and at specially arranged sessions at least as early as the time of Asinius Pollio in the first century B.C.E.[129] Again, if we are to judge from Dio Chrysostom (20.10), oral readings of poems and histories took place in such sites as hippodromes. Indeed, the government itself, at any rate in Rome, usually communicated with the masses through town criers (*praecones*).[130]

Generally speaking, the ἀρεταλόγος, the man who described the wonderful deeds and virtues of a god or a hero, did his work orally.[131] In fact, Philo (*De Specialibus Legibus* 1.59.320–23) comes close to suggesting that there were Jewish teachers and preachers who, as it were, like Paul, stood on their soapboxes in the agora. Moreover, Philo (*De Specialibus Legibus* 2.15.62–63) remarks that on each Sabbath day there stand open (ἀναπέπταται, "thrown wide open") in every city thousands of schools, teaching the cardinal virtues with respect to duties to G-d and man. That these Jewish schools (i.e., synagogues) are said to be wide open and that there are said to be thousands of them, would indicate that they attracted large numbers of the general population, and not merely Jews.[132] If the synagogue sermon on the Sabbath, with its exegesis of Scripture, was influenced by the spirit of apologetics, we can understand why the synagogue was thrown open to pagans and why they felt that they were the ones primarily addressed.[133] This will also help to explain why the Sabbath was the chief aspect of Judaism that drew the attention of "sympathizers."

One passage that may well refer to conversion through oral instruction is to be found in the *Testament of Joseph* (4:4) in the Pseudepigrapha, dating in its original form from before the destruction of the Temple in 70 C.E. There Potiphar's wife comes to Joseph seeking to be initiated into the fundamental duties of his religion (ἐπὶ λόγῳ κατηχήσεως), precisely the route followed by a would-be convert beginning a catechism, though, to be sure, here the convert takes the initiative to seek the instruction.

A passage that may well refer to Jewish missionaries is found in Juvenal (6.542–47), who speaks of a Jewess who is a beggar, "an interpreter of the laws of Jerusalem (*interpres legum Solymarum*)" who can explain the significance of dreams. The expression "interpreter of the laws of Jerusalem" is highly reminiscent of the phrase "interpreter of the wisdom of the laws of Moses"[134] (Josephus, *Ant.* 18.81) used by Josephus to describe the Jew who was, apparently, to judge from the parallel passage in Dio Cassius (57.18.5a), a missionary who had defrauded a proselyte named Fulvia in Rome during the reign of Tiberius—an act that resulted in the expulsion of the Jews from the city. This passage in Juvenal would then highlight one of the means by which Jewish missionaries were able to win adherents, namely through interpreting dreams. Georgi adds that the description of the Jewess as a beggar calls attention to a further device by which Jews were able to attract the attention of pagans, namely through offering them alms when they converted to Judaism.[135] Morever, as late as the fifth century c.e. we hear in the poet Rutilius Namatianus (1.393) of the wild ravings (*deliramenta*, "absurdities," "madness") from the lying lecture platforms (*catastae*, "stage," "scaffold," "platform for delivering a lecture") of the Jews.

We may ask why, if missionizing were a normal and widespread function of Judaism, it is not mentioned in the Mishnah, because we would expect a discussion setting forth the *halakhah* of such activity. On the contrary, when the rabbis (*Yevamoth* 47a) do discuss conversion, they describe the procedure to be followed when a Gentile seeks to become a Jew—in other words, when the non-Jew, not the Jewish community, takes the initiative. But in answer we may reply that the Mishnah was not redacted until early in the third century, a considerable amount of time after the height of the proselyting movement. Moreover, in any case, it would seem that missionizing occurred primarily in the Diaspora, whereas the Mishnah reflects conditions in the Land of Israel. Finally, the initiative in seeking converts may have been undertaken principally by people who were not well acquainted with, or who even disagreed with, the rabbis' position.

Why do we hear of no Jewish missions into pagan regions? Why are no missionaries mentioned by name in extant Jewish or pagan literature? The one author whom we would most have expected to name them, Josephus, is not particularly interested in religious history and in any case is careful not to offend his patrons, the Romans, who were very sensitive, as we have seen, about proselytizing. In similar fashion, Philo, as the leader, so to speak, of the Anti-Defamation League of Alexandria, must have been sensitive to the charge of Jewish aggressiveness in proselytizing and consequently avoided alluding to it directly.

As for the rabbis in the Talmudic corpus, most of them were living at a time (after the Bar Kochba rebellion) when proselyting had diminished in volume and had even become dangerous; they, too, in general, were concerned not to antagonize the Romans. The conversations of Rabbi Joshua ben Ḥananiah with the Emperor Hadrian and with the pagan "elders" of Athens (*Ḥullin* 59b–60a, *Bekoroth* 8b) are not for the purpose of converting them and indeed bear the stamp of Greek legend rather than historical fact.[136] Moreover, the case of the royal family of Adiabene (Josephus, *Ant.* 20.49–53) indicates that the conversion was done through contact with itinerant Jewish merchants, that is, amateur missionaries.

The very fact that the New Testament speaks, without further explanation, of Paul (e.g. Acts 9:15, Galatians 2:9), Barnabas (Galatians 2:9), and Peter (Galatians 2:9) as preachers chosen to preach the Gospel before the Gentiles, thus indicating the role of a missionary, would demonstrate that such a function was not considered novel. Indeed, the Book of Acts shows that Gentiles attended synagogue services; and, to judge from the example of Paul, Jewish visitors were apparently invited to address the congregation. When Paul, having been opposed by the Jews, declares (Acts 18:6) that "from now on I will go to the Gentiles," he does not have to explain himself, as if, in his proposed role as missionary, he is doing something unprecedented. The exasperation expressed by Paul in his question (Galatians 5:11) as to why he is being persecuted if he is promoting circumcision (i.e., conversion to Judaism) indicates that he expected his readers and listeners to regard this as nothing unusual.

8. Converts in the Land of Israel and in the Various Lands of the Diaspora

Most other religions of the ancient world, at least before the Hellenistic period, as we have indicated, were not missionary. However, the Jews, Greeks, and Persians, the chief ancient peoples who developed the characteristics of ethnic-cultural nationalism independent of statehood, required religious conversion for membership in the nation.[137] Thus, when foreigners were initiated into the Eleusinian mysteries, they became Greek nationals. Those initiated into Mithraism became Persians. Those who joined the Jewish fold similarly became members of the Jewish nation as well as of the Jewish religion.

Forced Conversions in the Land of Israel

In the Land of Israel we hear of the forced conversions of the Idumaeans and the Ituraeans in the latter part of the second century B.C.E.; and there is reason to think that Josephus's account of their conversion is substantially accurate.[138] Some scholars have gone so far as to theorize that Timagenes' statement implies that the whole of Galilee was forcibly converted; but this view, certainly in its extreme formulation, cannot be accepted, especially because the continuous occupation of parts of Galilee by Jews had never been wholly interrupted.[139]

Most recently, Kasher has argued that the mass conversions of the Idumaeans and of the Ituraeans were voluntary.[140] In the first case, he stresses that Strabo (16.2.34.760) declares that the Idumaeans "joined (προσεχώρησαν, 'went over to') the Judaeans and shared in the same customs with them." This, we may reply, does not imply coersion nor necessarily contradict it. Second, the evidence of Josephus (*Ant.* 13.257–58) is conclusive, that the Jewish king John Hyrcanus permitted the Idumaeans to remain in the land so long as they had themselves circumcised and were willing to observe the laws of the Jews. Similarly convincing is the statement (*Ant.* 15.254) that Hyrcanus transformed (μεταστήσαντος) their way of life to conform with the customs and laws of the Jews. This clearly indicates that the initiative was Hyrcanus's. An apparently independent source, Ptolemy the historian, who perhaps wrote at the end of the first century B.C.E. (cited in Ammonius, *De Adfinium Vocabulorum Differentia* 243), says explicitly that the Idumaeans were forced (ἀναγκασθέντες) to undergo circumcision.

Kasher argues that, in view of Strabo's hostile attitude (16.2.37 and 40.761–62) toward the Hasmoneans as rulers who had destroyed the original Mosaic Judaism and had introduced a regime of tyranny, his silence on the alleged forced conversion is significant, especially because he was not averse to the propagandist anti-Jewish exaggeration (quoted in Josephus, *Ant.* 14.115) that the Jews had made their way into every city. We may respond, however, that in view of Josephus's own strong aversion to forced conversion, as seen in two incidents he reports (*Life* 113 and *War* 2.454), such an action by the Hasmoneans, his direct ancestors (*Life* 2), would have embarrassed him; and yet he does report it not once but twice, as we have seen. Moreover, Strabo's information is clearly flawed, because he makes the mistake (16.2.34.760) of identifying the Idumaeans as Nabataeans. Strabo's statement, quoting the first-century B.C.E. Timagenes (cited in Josephus, *Ant.* 13.319), that Aristobulus I brought over (ᾠκειώσατο, "joined to," "affiliated," "annexed") a portion of the Ituraean nation, whom he joined (συνάψας, "tie," "bind," "attach") by the bond (δεσμῷ, "chain," "shackle") of circumcision, although not specifically saying that Aristobulus applied force, does not contradict Josephus's clear statement (*Ant.* 13.318), which, in language very similar to that which he applies to the Idumaeans, asserts that Aristobulus compelled (ἀναγκάσας) the inhabitants, if they wished to remain in the country, to be circumcised and to live in accordance with the laws of the Jews.

Finally, Kasher argues that forced conversion was in total conflict with Jewish law; but the Talmudic tractate *Gerim* 7, which he cites, dates at the very earliest from the fourth century[141] and probably reflects a much later attitude. In any case, Hyrcanus and Aristobulus were adherents of the Sadducees, and they apparently did not listen to the rabbis any more than did the Zealots, who, according to Josephus (*Life* 113, *War* 2.454), sought forced conversions.

Nor were these isolated instances. Forced conversion was indeed a national policy during the Hasmonean era, a fact evidenced by Alexander Jannaeus (ca. 80 B.C.E.) when he demolished the city of Pella in Moab (Josephus, *Ant.* 13.397) "because the inhabitants would not agree to adopt the national customs of the Jews."

Other Conversions in the Land of Israel

In addition to the mass conversions, we should take note of a few prominent individual proselytes in the latter part of the first and in the early part of the second century C.E., notably Beluria (Beruria, *Rosh Hashanah* 17b), who possessed a considerable number of slaves; Judah the Ammonite (Mishnah, *Yadaim* 4:4, *Berakoth* 28a); and Aquila (*Megillah* 3a, Jerusalem Talmud *Megillah* 1.9.71a).[142]

This period, beginning at least as early as the second century B.C.E., also saw the heightening of Jewish messianic expectations;[143] and a connection between messianic-eschatological hopes and Gentile interest in Judaism developed. To be sure, we have no instance of the word *mashiaḥ* or its equivalents in an eschatological context that can be dated with certainty prior to the first century B.C.E.[144] (although the usage of the term at Qumran may have originated in the second century B.C.E.); yet by the first century B.C.E., both in the Qumran community and in such a work as the *Psalms of Solomon*, we find a strong and developed interest in messianism.

Josephus (*War* 6.312) says that the Jews were incited to revolt against the Romans by an ambiguous oracle, found also in the Bible,[145] that "at that time one from their country would become ruler of the world." That this prophecy of a world-ruler was widespread is manifest from its citation also in Tacitus (*Histories* 5.13.2), who remarks that in the ancient records of the Jewish priests there was a prediction that rulers coming from Judaea were to acquire universal empire, and in Suetonius (*Vespasian* 4.5), who similarly notes an old and established belief (*vetus et constans opinio*) that at that time men coming from Judaea were fated to rule the world. Though Josephus, Tacitus, and Suetonius all refer the prophecy to Vespasian, clearly the revolutionaries thought that it referred to the Jewish Messiah; and the appearance of Menahem, the leader of the Sicarii, one of the groups that led the revolution against Rome in 66 C.E., in royal robes in the Temple (*War* 2.444), indicates the revolt's messianic dimensions, which Josephus otherwise carefully suppressed. It may well be that the spectacle of Gentiles flocking to join the Jewish nation helped to spur such expectations and in turn further aroused missionary activity to bring about the eschatological age in which all people would acknowledge the G-d of Israel.

Conversions in the Diaspora: The Phoenicians

The very dispersion of the Jews, particularly commencing with the invitation to Jews to settle in Alexandria in 332 B.C.E., proved favorable to the extension of Judaism.

The Diaspora provided a more congenial environment for conversion—first of all because there were greater numbers of potential converts living side by side with Jews, engaging in commercial and cultural contact with them and fighting alongside them.[146] Indeed, the Book of Tobit, usually dated in the second century B.C.E., looks forward to the day when "many nations shall come to you [G-d] from afar" (13:13) and when "all the nations in the whole world shall turn and fear G-d" (14:6), that is, will be converted to Judaism.

One theory to explain the widespread success of Jewish proselytism in the Diaspora posits that the Jews had absorbed the far-flung settlements of the Phoenicians, whose language is so similar to Hebrew. Once the mother-cities of Tyre and Sidon and the chief daughter-city, Carthage, had lost their independence, the Phoenician colonies throughout the world were in effect an orphaned Diaspora and may have been attracted to Judaism because of the parallel with the kindred Jewish Diaspora. A number of scholars have been puzzled by the disappearance of the Phoenicians in the first century; and Slouschz has theorized that Phoenician owners of Jewish slaves may have been exposed to Jewish customs and ideas and may easily have passed over into Judaism, because they had practiced circumcision for ages.[147] We may add that Josephus (*Against Apion* 1.166–67) cites, as an illustration of the impact of Jewish customs on various peoples, the prohibition in the laws of the Tyrians (that is, the Phoenicians) of the use of foreign oaths, in enumerating which Theophrastus includes the oath called korban, which, according to Josephus, is found in no other nation except the Jews. We may also cite the statement of Rav in the third century (*Menaḥoth* 110a) that "from Tyre to Carthage they know Israel and their Father in Heaven." In particular, the tremendous growth of the Jewish population of Cyprus, which had a large Phoenician settlement and where the Jews are said to have killed 240,000 persons during the revolt in the time of Trajan (Dio Cassius

68.32), may be due to such conversions. Baron suggests that the success of Jewish missionary activities may help to explain the bitter feelings of Tyre, and to a lesser degree of Sidon, toward the Jews (cf. 1 Mac 5:15; Josephus, *War* 2.478–79; and *Against Apion* 1.70).[148]

Conversions in the Diaspora: Syria

The kindred inhabitants of Syria were similarly attracted to Judaism. On the eve of the great war against the Romans, says Josephus (*War* 2.559–61), the inhabitants of Damascus were fired with a determination to kill the Jews but were afraid of their own wives, "and so their efforts were mainly directed to keeping the secret from them." Eventually they slaughtered the Jews, but they kept their eyes on their wives' reactions. The violence of the Syrians' feelings would appear to indicate the Jews' success as missionaries,[149] inasmuch as Josephus specifically points out, in connection with the onslaught, that the wives had been almost universally converted to Judaism. This fact would be seemingly irrelevant, unless Jewish success in proselytism was indeed a major reason for the attack. That Judaism attracted women in particular may be due largely to the fact that they did not have to undergo excision, a major operation for an adult;[150] but it may also be due to the relatively more elevated and respected position of women in the Jewish community. That Josephus, however, may be thinking primarily of "sympathizers" with Judaism rather than converts may be inferred from the statement (*War* 7.45) that the Jews of Antioch, Syria's chief city, were constantly attracting to their religious ceremonies multitudes of Greeks and that the Antiochean Jews had, *in some measure*, incorporated these Greeks with themselves.

Conversions in the Diaspora: Mesopotamia

The assertions that the Jewish community of Babylonia comprised "countless myriads whose number cannot be ascertained" (Josephus, *Ant.* 11.133) and that in the first century a quasi-independent state was established in a large region near Nehardea under the robber-barons Asinaeus and Anilaeus would indicate that the Jewish population had grown considerably since the days of the Babylonian captivity,[151] whereas the population of the non-Jewish world had apparently not increased during the same period. As late as the third century c.e., we hear (*Qiddushin* 73a) that when Rabbi Zera declared in Mahoza in Babylonia that a proselyte may marry a bastard everyone pelted him with stones, perhaps because Mahoza contained many proselytes, whom such a view offended.

Apparently the most remarkable success of the proselyting movement during this period took place in Adiabene in Mesopotamia in the early part of the first century C.E. The accounts of Josephus (*Ant.* 20.17–96) and of the Talmudic literature are, on the whole, in agreement.[152] According to Josephus's version, Izates, while his father was still king, was brought up in the kingdom of Charax Spasini between the mouths of the Tigris and the Euphrates. There a certain Jewish merchant named Ananias visited the king's wives and taught them to worship G-d after the manner of the Jewish tradition. Again we see that it is women on whom the Jewish emissary had his greatest impact. Through these women Ananias came to the attention of Izates, and through their aid he won him over to Jewish practices, though without circumcision. By chance and without Izates' knowledge, his mother, Queen Helena, had similarly been instructed by another Jew and won over to Judaism. After becoming king, Izates was determined to become a proselyte, but Helena and Ananias tried to stop him on the ground that his subjects would not tolerate the rule of a Jew. Another Jew, however, named Eleazar, later urged him to undergo circumcision, and Izates did so. His older brother, Monobazus, and his kinsmen eventually converted to Judaism. The fears of Ananias were now realized. Indeed, the nobles of Adiabene resented these conversions and invited first the king of Arabia and then the king of Parthia to take over Izates's kingdom. Izates appealed for Divine help and triumphed. When he died, he was succeeded by his brother Monobazus.

The role of the Jewish merchant in the conversion of the wives of the king of Charax Spasini, as well as of Izates himself, suggests that a further motive may have been economic, because conversion to Judaism would give the Adiabenians access to international sources of capital and markets (they would now be able to borrow money without interest [Exod 22:24, Lev 25:35–37, Deut 23:20–21] and would have economic ties with ? Jewish merchants throughout the world).

Josephus says that Izates resolved to convert when Eleazar, finding him reading the law of Moses, remarked that he ought to perform what is there written, namely, to be circumcised. The *Midrash Rabbah* (on Genesis 46:10) similarly reports that Izates (and his brother Monobazus) were reading the book of Genesis and came to the verse (Gen 17:10) commanding circumcision and wept. Thereupon, independently of each other, they secretly decided to undergo circumcision.

Both Josephus and the Talmud stress the piety of the Adiabenian converts. The former (*Ant.* 20.49–53) notes that Helena and Izates (Monobazus in the Talmud, *Baba Bathra* 11a) relieved a great famine in Jerusalem. The latter remarks that Helena lived as a Nazirite, following the biblical prescriptions (Num 6:1–21), for twenty-one years (Mishnah, *Nazir* 3:6), that she had a very tall *sukkah* for the festival of Tabernacles in Lydda which met with the sages' approval (*Sukkah* 2b), that she and Monobazus gave handsome gifts to the Temple (Mishnah, *Yoma* 3:10; Helena alone in Josephus, *Ant.* 20.49), and that the royal family carried a mezuzah with them while traveling, to be affixed to doorposts in accordance with biblical law (Deut 6:9, 11:20). According to Josephus (*War* 2.520), kinsmen of Monobazus, the king of Adiabene, distinguished themselves in the great war against the Romans.[153]

Despite the lack of any indication either in Josephus or in the Talmud that the conversion of the royal house was followed by that of the king's subjects, this has generally been assumed by scholars, though it would seem to have been unusual, especially given Helena's and Ananias's anxieties and the invitation by Izates's opponents to Parthia to overthrow Izates. Inasmuch as Josephus (*War* 1.6) notes that the inhabitants of Adiabene were acquainted, through his original version in Aramaic, with the origin of the great war against the Romans, we may assume that a sizable number of readers, perhaps converts or descendants of converts, were interested in reading his work.

Baron has insightfully theorized that the conversion of the royal family was an act of rich symbolic value, because Adiabene was located in the region of Assyria, and that, in effect, the conversion of the Adiabenians was a poetic revenge for the destruction of the kingdom of Israel by the Assyrians seven and a half centuries earlier. He indicates that the conversion may have encouraged the revolutionaries against Rome in their hope that Rome, too, would, like Assyria, succumb.[154]

Neusner has suggested that, like Constantine three centuries later, Izates had political as well as religious motives in converting.[155] A number of factors may have encouraged the Adiabenian royal dynasty to hope that they might, by conversion to Judaism, assume the hegemony of the Near East through a series of judicious alliances. Shortly before this time, the Jewish robber-barons, Asinaeus and Anilaeus, had established a quasi-independent state of some size and importance in Babylonia. Jewish rulers held power in several nearby lands; one of them, Armenia, was adjacent to Adiabene. Even before the conversion, the Jewish population of Adiabene was probably not inconsiderable, especially because it included the newly acquired Nisibis, with its sizable Jewish population (Josephus, *Ant.* 18.379).

Here, then, in Adiabene we see several characteristics of the proselyting movement: its particular impact on women, the political factor in seeking alliances, the connection with economic goals, the initial stage of winning "sympathizers," and the role of reading the Bible in effecting the final conversion.

Agrippa I's success, a few years after Izates' conversion, in assembling a number of friendly kings at Tiberias (*Ant.* 19.338), which aroused the suspicion of the Roman governor of Syria (*Ant.* 19.340), indicates that an alliance of petty and not such petty states against Rome was not out of the question.[156] Inasmuch as Parthia at this point had been weakened by dynastic violence, Izates may have thought that he could make Adiabene the capstone of such an alliance. Neusner's theory that the Adiabenian royal house hoped to become kings of Judaea is hardly likely, however, because the Torah (Deut 17:15) specifically states that Israelites must choose a born Jew as king. We do not know what eventually became of the proselytes of Adiabene; but, according to the Armenian historian Moses Xorenazi (2.571), a family of Jewish origin descended from a certain Manue (=Monobazus, according to Neusner)[157] came to Armenia during the reign of Trajan; and we may thus conjecture that the Adiabenians fled to Armenia during Trajan's invasion of Adiabene.

Conversions in the Diaspora: Rome

Of the 534 inscriptions of Jews from ancient Rome, seven definitely belong to proselytes. Though such data hardly prove the extent of proselytism (there may have been and most probably were others who did not indicate on their tombstones that they were proselytes), it is admittedly tempting to start with the assumption that proselytism was not as widespread as the Roman satirists would have us believe. Unfortunately, we cannot date these inscriptions precisely, though the catacombs in which they are found were used for interments from the first century B.C.E. to the end of the third century C.E.[158] To the extent that one may cautiously generalize from these seven inscriptions (all of them epitaphs), one may note that five of them belong to females, thus confirming what Josephus (*War* 2.560) says about the particular attraction of the proselyting movement to women elsewhere, namely in Damascus. The fact that five of the seven are in Latin, whereas 76 percent of all Roman Jewish inscriptions are in Greek (with almost all of the others being in Latin), leads Leon to conclude tentatively that proselytes were more frequent in the more Romanized element of the community.[159] Because native Romans were Latin-speaking, we may reasonably assume that the two Greek inscriptions represent people who became proselytes in a Greek-speaking environment or were slaves, whereas the others were converted in Rome. Two of the inscriptions (Leon, nos. 256, 462) were set up by patrons and presumably represent former slaves, the status of much of the Jewish community in Rome. The inscriptions record no details concerning the place and motive of conversion, but the fact that the most famous of the proselytes (Leon, no. 523), Beturia Paulla, became a Jewess at the age of seventy and was honored as the "mother" (hence benefactress) of two synagogues suggests that not all of the proselytes were poor.

One would have thought that the destruction of the Temple by the Romans in 70 c.e. and the attendant and tremendous loss of prestige would have dealt the proselyting movement a blow from which it would not recover, particularly in the capital city of Rome itself. And yet it was after this period that the movement was most successful in official circles in Rome,[160] especially under Domitian, perhaps due in part to the admiration of the heroism the Jews had shown in the great war against the Romans.[161] Indeed, in the reign of Domitian (95 c.e.), we hear (Dio 67.14.1–2)[162] that Flavius Clemens, Domitian's cousin, and his wife, Flavia Domitilla, the emperor's niece, together with many others, were charged with atheism and with having drifted (ἐξοκέλλοντες) into the practices of the Jews (τὰ τῶν Ἰουδαίων ἤθη). In view of Dio's language and especially the word *drifted*, we cannot be sure that they were proselytes; and they may have been "sympathizers" who adopted certain Jewish practices.[163] In any case, as Juvenal (14.96–106) charges in the bitter attack that we have noted, sympathy with certain Jewish practices in one generation sometimes led in the next generation to full conversion to Judaism.

9. Motives of Jews in Seeking Converts

There is, admittedly, no indication in extant literature of organized efforts by the Pharisees to gain converts, but neither is there evidence of organized opposition to such efforts. Inasmuch as the great majority of missionary activity was apparently carried on in the Diaspora, it was individual Jews rather than the Pharisees as a group from the Holy Land who organized the campaigns.

Why were some Jews particularly eager to convert Gentiles? Perhaps, especially after they had achieved an independent state during the Hasmonean period and as their numbers continued to increase dramatically, Jews felt much more secure in admitting outside elements than they had been in the age of Ezra in the fifth century b.c.e., when the community was weak numerically, economically, and spiritually. Moreover, as Goodman has pointed out and as we have noted, the Jews believed—and many thought it would happen very soon—that the Messiah would arrive and bring about the end of the world, at which time the Gentiles would be converted to Judaism (Isa 2:2–4, Mic 4:1–2). And no text indicates that this result would be *preceded* by the conversion of the Gentiles.

In fact, because a sine qua non for this result was the virtuous behavior of the Jews, the prior conversion of Gentiles would, it would seem, delay the Messiah, inasmuch as this would simply produce more Jews, and the presumable possibility of more Jewish sinners. Moreover, the tradition, according to the Talmud (*Yevamoth* 24b), that the Jews will not receive proselytes in the messianic age indicates the rabbinic belief that Gentiles also would be present in the kingdom. Furthermore, the possibility that a Gentile could become a G-d-fearer removed the necessity of his considering conversion to Judaism; indeed, as Goodman has pointed out, unlike the requirement that Christian catechumens be baptized, there is no evidence that pious Gentile G-d-fearers were expected to undergo the rite of initiation, through circumcision, to become fully Jewish. Additionally, texts (e.g., Josephus, *Against Apion* 2.282, Juvenal 14.96–106) that speak of the spread of Jewish customs, such as the Sabbath and dietary laws, are indicative not of conversion but of the alternate path of Judaizing.

Finally, from the liberal attitude toward paganism as seen in the *Letter of Aristeas* (16), which states that pagan worship, in fact, is directed toward the one G-d, we may deduce that there was no incentive to convert the pagans.[164] Moreover, there are indications in Philo (*De Specialibus Legibus* 2.12–13.44–48) and in 2 Baruch (72.4) that righteous Gentiles might be saved; this, too, would, it would seem, remove the incentive to convert them to Judaism.

Yet that the Jews were, nevertheless, motivated to seek to convert the non-Jews is clear, as we have noted, from Philo (*De Virtutibus* 2.26), who indicates that Gentiles who do not convert are the "enemies of the Jews and of every person everywhere—enemies of our nation, because they give their compatriots leave to put their trust in the virtues of their ancestors and despise the thought of living a sound and steadfast life." It is thus clear from Philo's language that the only way for a Gentile to attain a sound life was through conversion to Judaism. Furthermore, there was an incentive for conversion, inasmuch as the Jews viewed the Gentiles as necessarily unclean and consequently excluded from the Temple.[165]

Furthermore, the fact that, after Izates had decided not to undergo circumcision, a Jew named Eleazar from Galilee urged him to do so indicates that there was a view that to become a "G-d-fearer" was not enough. Indeed, we may conjecture that if we had more evidence from the other movements of Judaism of this period and not merely (for the most part) from the Pharisees we might well discover that Eleazar was not alone in taking this more aggressive attitude. A clue to that effect may be seen in the story, recounted by Josephus (*Life* 113), that when two Gentile nobles, subjects of King Agrippa II, came to Josephus while he was general in Galilee, the Jews of the area sought to compel these men to be circumcised as a condition of residence among them.

Moreover, Baron has speculated that economic factors played a major role in many conversions.[166] Jewish merchants such as Ananias, who converted the royal family of Adiabene, might well have found it to their advantage to convert people to gain support for their own commercial ventures, especially if those merchants were engaged in international trade. As Tacitus (*Histories* 5.5.1) notes, wealthy proselytes brought their goods with them to augment those of the born Jews, and presumably those who were less wealthy could and did benefit from this wealth.

10. Reasons for the Success of the Proselyting Movement in the Hellenistic and Early Roman Periods

Bamberger has postulated that the triumph of monotheism in Israel by the close of the biblical period had transformed Judaism into a genuinely universalistic religion in line with the teachings of the prophets, and that such a view won the admiration of some.[167] But the number of converts, certainly in the Greek world, was apparently small, at least in part because the Jews lacked a language in common with that pagan world.

Beginning, however, with the Hellenistic Age ushered in by Alexander the Great, a common international language, the κοινή Greek, which was widely understood throughout the Mediterranean world, was developed. The fact that a considerable number of Jews, especially in the Diaspora, were fluent in it, together with the existence of a translation of the Scriptures into that dialect, surely made proselyting activity easier than it would have been prior to the Hellenistic Age. In an age in which Alexander the Great had proclaimed the brotherhood of all people and the common fatherhood of G-d, the Jews, with their similar Scriptural views, which are stressed alike by Philo, Josephus, and the rabbis,[168] may well have struck a responsive chord.

Moreover, during this period, when Judaism made its greatest inroads, the Oriental religions generally were most successful in gaining adherents, so that, for example, in the year 43 B.C.E. we hear (Dio Cassius 48.15) that the Triumvirate in Rome themselves built temples for public worship of the Egyptian deities Sarapis and Isis. In addition, the rise of Neo-Pythagoreanism shows how impressed the ancients were during this period with a code of behavior, as bizarre as that code might appear.

One basic reason, as we have noted, for the success of proselytism in this period is the spread of the Jewish Diaspora itself. It was now, often for the first time, that Judaism came into direct contact with such missionary philosophies as Epicureanism, Stoicism, and Cynicism; and indeed the philosophical schools resembled religious associations as much as anything else.[169] In fact, philosophers employed the same term, ἐπιστρέφειν or ἐπιστροφή, to describe the conversion process, and this is clearly the source of the Septuagint's usage. This forced the Jews (who could also, as did Josephus when he spoke of the "Fourth Philosophy," for example, look on their religion as a philosophy) to defend themselves. Soon enough the Jews discovered that the best defense is a good offense. They realized that if they wished to avoid rapid assimilation and disappearance they had to clarify and then explain and justify their ideas about religion to the Gentiles. Inasmuch as it was precisely during this period that the Greek Olympian religion was being challenged by philosophers and by mystery cults from both the Orient and Greece, Judaism, if it could present itself as a superior ethical code or as a systematic philosophy predating the Greeks, or as the greatest mystery cult, had an excellent opportunity to win adherents.

Moreover, just as the Athenian victory over Xerxes in the second Persian War led to a surge of great pride among the Athenians and the creation of great works of art and literature, so, we may suggest, the success of the Maccabean revolt led to a rise of Jewish enthusiasm. And yet the victory of the Maccabees did not lead, certainly within its generation or in the generation thereafter, to a surge of artistic creativity; and in any case the creative genius allegedly unleashed by the second Persian War did not include the concept of universalism and proselytism, though in a sense Alexander's victories led to a kind of universalism, namely the spread of Greek culture. Nor, for that matter, did the victory of the Maccabees lead, certainly within its generation or in the generation thereafter, to a surge of creativity comparable to that which followed the extraordinary victory of the Greeks against the Persians.

Finally, paradoxical as it may seem, the apparently catastrophic failure of the attempt to win independence in 70 C.E., by causing a reorientation of Judaism toward a religious rather than a political definition, actually may have aided the proselyting movement in some cases, because this defeat for Jewish nationalism opened the way for conversion even of those who did not seek identification with Israelite nationality.[170] It appears, however, that the great age of proselytizing activities began well before the destruction of the Temple and that Hadrian's decree imposing a death penalty on converts and on those who converted them was undoubtedly a major factor in sharply decreasing the number of proselytes.

11. MOTIVES OF PROSELYTES IN THE HELLENISTIC AND EARLY ROMAN PERIODS

Why would Gentiles convert? As Segal has perceptively remarked, "The phenomenon of Christian conversions, about which we know something because of textual evidence, is better evidence for the conversion of Gentiles to Judaism than is the rabbinic evidence."[171] An analysis of this Christian evidence may thus give us a better clue to the gamut of motives, ranging from contacts with other Jews in international trade to the search for salvation, of converts to Judaism in the first century than does the rabbinic evidence, which dates at the earliest from the beginning of the third century.[172]

Undoubtedly, religious and cultural factors were primary inducements in winning Gentiles to Judaism. We have already commented on the attraction to a strict imageless monotheism, as seen in the highly laudatory remark by the learned and highly respected Varro (cited in Augustine, *De Civitate D-i* 4.31) and the appeal to the Law as a rule by which to live.[173] Still another motive was the search for protection against magic, especially in the light of the continuing demonization of the religious world of the Roman Empire.[174] In particular, one of the appeals of Judaism, as we have remarked, was its antiquity, which even bitter critics of the Jews such as Tacitus (*Histories* 5.2) noted. Another attraction was the Jews' reputation for wisdom, as we see in Aristotle's acknowledgement (quoted in Clearchus of Soli, in turn quoted by Josephus, *Against Apion* 1.176–83).

Economic factors were undoubtedly important in inducing pagans to embrace Judaism. Thus, the devoted labor of Jews in their crafts was widely admired (*Against Apion* 2.283). Moreover, as Strabo (16.2.36.761) points out, Judaism did not put heavy financial burdens (δαπάναις) on its adherents. Poor Gentiles, once converted to Judaism, could benefit from the extraordinarily effective charities of the Jews (cf. Josephus, *Against Apion* 2.283).[175] Those proselytes who were poverty-stricken received the benefit of both municipal and Jewish relief, as well as interest-free loans, because usury is forbidden by the Torah. Indeed, the rabbis (*Sifre Behar* 5.1, *Gerim* 3.4) insisted that if a convert was in financial difficulties it was mandated that other Jews should help him, even to the point of anticipating his duress. Apparently, this reached the point (*Yalqut Shimoni, Emor* 745; *Eleh Devarim Zuta* 1) where some of the sages comment on people who converted simply because they liked to eat or to be supported. Another attraction, as indicated by archaeological evidence, was the accommodation provided by synagogues for travelers.[176] Moreover, inasmuch as Jews were established in important commercial positions in many cities, merchants may have found it profitable to join a group that assured them close economic co-operation throughout the Mediterranean world and beyond. Even an arch-Jew-baiter such as Tacitus (*Histories* 5.5.1) states that though the Jews regard the rest of humanity with all the hatred of enemies they are ever ready to show compassion to one another. Josephus (*Against Apion* 2.283) singles out the unanimity of the Jews (one may express wonder about such a statement in view of the great factionalism during the Great Revolt against the Romans) as a quality that the Gentiles throughout the world sought to imitate.

Many undoubtedly were attracted, in a period of general political, economic, and social instability, to a community that, by closely regulating itself, had found inner security. The very size of the synagogue, such as the one at Sardis, which could have held as many a thousand people, must have given the impression of strength and confidence, as did the fact that some of the Jews in Sardis, at any rate, held positions of considerable influence. The fellowship that came through attending weekly meetings on the Sabbath, reading the same texts, eating together, and avoiding the same foods may have enticed the lonely.

Others may have been attracted to Judaism because they welcomed identification with the national entity or, later, aspirations of the Jews, perhaps because of their disappointment with the Roman or Parthian states. But, on the whole, this factor worked against conversion because the Romans frequently regarded such activities as subversive of the state.

Finally, just as Tertullian (*Apology* 50) was to say, in the traditional rendering, that the blood of the martyrs is the seed of the Church, so the Jews won admiration because of their brave endurance of persecution without flinching,[177] as well as for their cultivation of the cardinal virtues.[178]

Intermarriage, however, was apparently not a major factor, to judge at least from the romance of *Joseph and Asenath*; indeed, we can see from the *Testament of Joseph* (4.4–6) that a proposed conversion based on love is utterly unacceptable to the author. Similarly, both the Jerusalem Talmud (*Qiddushin* 4.1.65b) and the Babylonian Talmud (*Yevamoth* 24b) explicitly exclude those who seek conversion for the sake of marriage or political advancement, or due to fear of the Jews. And yet the Book of Esther (8:17) already notes that after Haman had been discomfited many of the people of the land accepted Judaism (*mitheyahadim*, Septuagint περιετέμνοντο, "were circumcised"), "for fear of the Jews had fallen upon them." Similar motives were clearly responsible for the conversion of the Ammonite Achior in the book of Judith (14.6–10), as noted above. The rabbis, apparently, were realists; and so we hear that Abba Arikha (Rab) declares that if, despite this prohibition, someone has been converted for one of these reasons, that person should be regarded as a proselyte in the full sense of the term.[179]

Moreover, we hear that at the beginning of the Jewish revolt the Roman commander Metilius saved his life by entreating the revolutionaries and specifically by promising to "Judaize" (ἰουδαίσειν), that is, to become a Jew and even to be circumcised (Josephus, *War* 2.454). Finally, slaves were often converted (see, e.g., *Shabbath* 135b, 137b), thus becoming members of the family group. Indeed, the severity of the ruling by the third-century jurist Paul (*Sententiae* 5.22.3–4) subjecting to the death-penalty doctors who circumcised non-Jewish slaves indicates that the practice was apparently widespread.

12. The Status of Proselytes and the
Attitude of Born Jews toward Them in the
Hellenistic and Early Roman Periods

Philo (*De Specialibus Legibus* 1.9.52; cf. *De Virtutibus* 20.102–103) remarks that proselytes are granted all the privileges of native-born Jews.[180]
Though the Torah speaks of *gerim* (Lev 19:33–34, Deut 10:18–19) not in
the sense of proselytes but of strangers, Philo applies these passages to
proselytes, because the Septuagint renders the term *gerim* as προσήλυτοι.
On the basis of the injunction (Lev 19:34) to love such strangers as oneself, Philo, as we have noted, urges born Jews to honor them "not only
with marks of respect but with special friendship and with more than
ordinary goodwill," because "they have left their country, their kinsfolk,
and their friends for the sake of virtue and religion."[181] Moreover, in the
second century, Justin Martyr (*Dialogue with Trypho* 122–23) complains
of the welcome proselytes received from native-born Jews.

Most scholars agree that the Talmudic rabbis were generally favorably
disposed toward proselytism.[182] This positive attitude may be discerned
in the authoritative statement of the patriarch, Rabbi Judah the Prince
(ca 200 C.E.), the redactor of the Mishnah (*Baba Metzia* 4:10), according
to whom it was forbidden to remind a convert's son of his origin or to say
to the convert himself, "Behold who comes to learn Torah! One who has
eaten carcasses and torn thereof" (Tosefta, *Baba Metzia* 3.25). Typical is
the Tannaitic statement (Mekilta, *Nezikin* [*Mishpatim* 18]) "It is said.
'And those that are beloved by Him are compared to the sun when it rises
in all its strength.' Now who is greater—he who loves the king or he
whom the king loves? One must say, he whom the king loves, as the verse
says, 'And He loves the stranger [proselyte].' " Because, as we have seen,
the Septuagint rendered the term *ger* ("stranger") by προσήλυτος,[183] missionaries could underscore the protection and favor the Torah enjoins
toward proselytes. Indeed, the proselytes, such as Onkelos, often were
distinguished for their piety, as we discern in the proverbial statement
(Matt 23:15) "When he [the convert] is made, ye [Pharisees] make him
two-fold more the child of hell than yourselves," which may be interpreted to indicate that the converts of Pharisees were twice as damnable,
that is, twice as careful, in their observance of the commandments as
their teachers.[184] That such great rabbis as Shemaiah, Avtalyon, Akiva,
and Meir in the first two centuries were traced back to proselyte origins
indicates the high regard in which converts were held. Moreover, we
have the statement (*Horayoth* 13a) of the second-century Rabbi Eleazar
ben Zadok that "all rush to marry a proselytess."

Even after proselytism had, it is thought, declined as a movement in the third century, Rabbi Joḥanan and Rabbi Eleazar declared (*Pesaḥim* 87b) that G-d exiled Israel among the nations in order to facilitate proselytism. Again, one may cite the statement (*Tanḥuma Lek Leka* 6) of the third-century Rabbi Simeon ben Lakish that the proselyte is dearer to G-d than the born Jew because the latter would not have accepted the Torah if he had not witnessed the miracles at Sinai (according to tradition, those present at Sinai included all those Jews yet to be born), whereas the proselyte saw none of these things. The rabbinic tradition goes so far as to declare through Amemar (ca 400 c.e.) that, once converted, the proselyte has the status of a newborn babe (*Yevamoth* 22a). Hence, a proselyte might theoretically contract an incestuous marriage, except for the fact that the rabbis were afraid that it might be said that he had exchanged a religion of stricter for one of more easygoing sanctity (ibid.) and hence forbade it. Finally, a late Midrash (*Numbers Rabbah* 8.9) assures the proselyte that he will be blessed in the world to come in accordance with his good deeds and that his descendants who marry priests will serve in the Temple of the future.

It is a mistake, however, to think that the attitude toward proselytes was uniformly favorable.[185] Thus, Rabbi Eliezer at the end of the first century, who, to be sure, was under the ban of excommunication and perhaps may have been influenced by his contacts with the early Christians,[186] comments (*Baba Metzia* 59b) that the reason why the Torah warns against the wronging of proselytes in thirty-six (or, according to others, in forty-six) places is that their original character is bad and they may relapse under evil treatment.[187] Josephus (*Against Apion* 2.123), indeed, admits that although some proselytes have remained faithful, "others, lacking the necessary endurance, have again left the fold." That some proselytes later reneged and even denounced the Jews to the foreign rulers may be the background for the insertion of the benediction for *righteous* proselytes in the Amidah prayer (*Megillah* 17b). During the second century, Rabbi Simeon ben Yoḥai, on beholding a certain Judah ben Gerim (son of proselytes), who had apparently been an informer to the Roman government, is said (*Shabbath* 34a) to have turned him into a heap of bones with his glance. His contemporary Rabbi Jose explained (*Yevamoth* 48b) that the reason why proselytes were oppressed was that they were not so well acquainted with the details of the commandments as were born Jews, while Rabbi Eleazar explained that they convert out of fear rather than out of love; and nameless others declared that proselytes were oppressed because they delayed their conversion to Judaism. At the end of the second century, Rabbi Ḥiyya is quoted as saying (*Midrash Ruth Zuta* on 1.12), "Do not have any faith in a proselyte until twenty-four generations have passed because the inherent evil is still within him."

Furthermore, it is significant that in the hierarchy of status (Mishnah, *Horayoth* 3:8) a bastard takes precedence over a Netin (i.e., a descendant of the Gibeonites who are designated as Temple slaves, according to Joshua 9:27), who, in turn, is superior to a proselyte. Indeed, only an emancipated slave has lower status than a proselyte. In addition, according to the sages (Mishnah, *Yevamoth* 6:5) the category of "whore" applies only to a woman who has been converted to Judaism or to one who has been freed from slavery or to one who has had licentious sexual relations. Likewise, a bastard may not marry a born Israelite but may marry a proselyte (*Yevamoth* 79b, *Qiddushin* 67a). Moreover, a priest is not permitted to marry a proselyte (Mishnah, *Yevamoth* 6:5, *Qiddushin* 4:7, *Bikkurim* 1:5). Furthermore, a proselyte (*Bikkurim* 1:4) is not allowed to call the fathers of Israel his fathers, and he does not have a share in the Land of Israel. Indeed, the Dead Sea Sect (*4Q Florilegium* on 2 Sam 7) forever excludes from the eschatological Temple Ammonites, Moabites (the rabbis made an exception for Ammonite and Moabite women, such as Ruth), bastards, aliens, and proselytes, "for his holy ones are there." The *Fragments of a Zadokite Work* (14.5–6) actually create, for liturgical purposes, a separate group of proselytes, following the priests, Levites, and Israelites. Blidstein argues that this is not merely a sectarian point of view but that it is reflected in the rabbinic statement of the third-century Rabbi Ḥama bar Ḥanina (*Qiddushin* 70b) that "G-d will cause His presence to rest only on genealogically pure families of Israel" and notes that the statement following this speaks of the disability of proselytes. Blidstein also asserts that a substantial body of Jewish exegetical opinion, starting with the Gaon Rabbi Aḥai in the eighth century, understood Rabbi Ḥama's dictum to apply to proselytes.[188] We may also note that a fourfold classification (priests, Levites, Israelites, proselytes), similar to that in the Dead Sea Scrolls, is found in the Tosefta (*Qiddushin* 5.1, p. 293 ed. Lieberman).

The notorious statement of the third-century Rabbi Ḥelbo (*Qiddushin* 70b, *Yevamoth* 47b, *Niddah* 13b) that "proselytes are as injurious to Israel as a scab (*sapaḥat*)" has been interpreted by Braude as a warning against converting Christians;[189] but if so we should have heard much more in the writings of the church fathers about such activities. The statement is, however, best taken as the view of an individual rabbi who aligned himself with the negative opinions noted above. In the same context as Rabbi Ḥelbo's statement (*Niddah* 13b) is one in the name of "our [unspecified] rabbis" that proselytes delay the advent of the Messiah. Apparently, moreover, the rabbis distinguished between conversions in the Land of Israel and those in the Diaspora, inasmuch as the tractate (*Gerim* 4:5) asserts that a proselyte is immediately accepted in the Land of Israel (where, presumably, the courts were more knowledgeable and more careful in matters of particulars), whereas elsewhere he is accepted only if he produces witnesses.

This sharp division of opinion among the rabbis with regard to proselytes reinforces the view that the issue of proselytism was a live one during the Talmudic period even after conversions supposedly ended with the edict of Hadrian. Indeed, as we shall see, Jews continued to make converts in sizable numbers even after the advent of Christianity.

CHAPTER 10

THE SUCCESS OF JEWS IN
WINNING "SYMPATHIZERS"

I. THE PROBLEM

Judaism's success in winning adherents during the Hellenistic and Roman periods is to be measured not merely in terms of the number of converts but also the number of so-called "G-d-fearers" or "sympathizers,"[1] those non-Jews who adopted certain Jewish practices without actually converting to Judaism. Among the many questions about this group is whether they actually existed as an entity.

The discussion about the "sympathizers" usually begins with the eleven passages in Acts (10:2, 22, 35; 13:16, 26, 43, 50; 16:14; 17:4, 17; 18:7) referring to φοβούμενοι τὸν θεόν ("fearers of G-d") and σεβόμενοι τὸν θεόν ("reverencers of G-d"). Lake, Wilcox, and I have contended that these phrases are not necessarily references to "sympathizers" but rather refer to pious people, and our conclusion has been accepted by Robert, among others.[2] In the first century, at least, the term *G-d-fearer*, far from necessarily applying to "sympathizers"—the so-called semi-proselytes—may also refer to Jews by birth or to full converts, as indeed one can see from Acts 13:43, which mentions "G-d-fearing proselytes."[3] Similarly, at the beginning of the second century, the patriarch Jacob's sons—Levi, Benjamin, and Joseph—are termed θεοσεβεῖς, "G-d-worshippers" (another alleged technical term for "G-d-fearers") in the Pseudepigraphic work *Joseph and Asenath*, where it is clear that the reference is not to "sympathizers" but to full-fledged Jews.[4] Even Juvenal, who, as we shall see, does refer to "sympathizers," uses the same verb *metuunt* (14.101), "fear," with clear reference to circumcised full proselytes to Judaism a few lines after he has used it (*metuentes*, 14.96) with reference to "sympathizers." In particular, Wilcox, who has systematically considered each of the references to "G-d-fearers" in the New Testament, appositely asks why, if the terms were technical, Luke changes so abruptly from one term (φοβούμενοι τὸν θεόν) to the other (σεβόμενοι τὸν θεόν). The fact, which he notes, that the apostolic fathers are, on the whole, strangely silent about the identification of the "G-d-fearers" as "sympathizers" is indeed a strong argument in favor of the view that the terms are not technical.[5]

The thesis challenging the existence of "G-d-fearers" as a separate group is not new. As long ago as 1896 Bertholet insisted that the term *G-d-fearer* is merely a synonym for *proselyte*."[6] If, then, the term *G-d-fearer* in Acts does not necessarily imply the existence of such a group, was the class of "sympathizers" therefore small or even nonexistent? MacLennan and Kraabel are surely right when they declare that we must be cautious in utilizing Acts as a historical source, especially when conclusions from Acts are not independently supported by other evidence. They are likewise right in stating that the other evidence has, in the past, almost always been explained with reference to Acts.[7] Hence, we shall here examine the other evidence independently of Acts under five headings: circumstantial evidence; passages in pagan, Jewish, and Christian (other than Acts) writers; and epigraphical-papyrological sources.

2. Circumstantial Evidence

There seems good ground for concluding, as we have attempted to demonstrate, that during the Hellenistic and early Roman periods the Jews were extraordinarily successful in winning converts. A movement of such scope, if we may judge from parallel movements in the growth of Christianity, Mithraism, and Islam, for example, would seem to lead to the existence of intermediate classes of those who went halfway or who tried to effect a syncretism of the old religion and the new one. A precedent for this may be found in the Bible in the case of Naaman (2 Kgs 5:15–18), a Syrian captain, who comes to the realization that there is no G-d but in Israel and who yet continues to bow down in the house of Rimmon, the Syrian storm god, with his master, the King of Syria. Similarly, we hear in the Book of Esther (8:17), as we have noted, that upon the downfall of Haman, the prime minister of the Persian king Ahasuerus, many of the Persians, in their terror of the newly acquired Jewish power, acted as Jews (*mitheyahadim*, "Judaized"), though admittedly the meaning of the term is not clear.[8]

This intermediate state of conversion was somewhat similar to what occurred in Mithraism,[9] where worshippers who were not initiates could attend the cult ceremonies, could pray, and could have a priest offer a sacrifice for them but could not be privy to the actual mysteries themselves. In the case of those who became "sympathizers" with Judaism, we may conjecture that perhaps the later ban on proselytism led people to this halfway station.

If we may point to more modern parallels, even in periods when the Jews were not active missionaries, we hear of the charge of "Judaizers" made against the Albigensians in the twelfth century, against Hussites in

the fifteenth century, and against various Protestant groups in the sixteenth century because they had adopted certain Jewish practices, such as
abstention from certain foods and the observance of the seventh-day
Sabbath.

The history of the Somrei Sabat in Hungary is illuminating: Founded
in the sixteenth century, they passed from denial of the Trinity to observance of the Jewish Sabbath and festivals and abstention from certain
foods to the use of Hebrew in their Christian liturgy to full conversion to
Judaism in many cases. The Molokan, Subbotniki, and Gery sects in
eighteenth- and nineteenth-century Russia likewise illustrate this phenomenon of intermediate stages between Christianity and Judaism. One
may cite also the Indian "Jews" in Mexico, the "Iglesia Israelita" of Chile,
and the Baydaya of Uganda; and it is against such a background that the
"Hebrewisms" of several African tribes may best be understood.[10] Hence,
it would seem reasonable to assume that there was a similar halfway
movement between Judaism and the other religions of its day two thousand years ago.

3. Pagan References

The term *G-d-fearers* or *sympathizers* apparently refers to an "umbrella
group," embracing many different levels of interest in and commitment
to Judaism, ranging from people who supported synagogues financially
(perhaps to get the political support of the Jews) to people who accepted
the Jewish view of G-d in pure or modified form to people who observed
certain distinctively Jewish practices, notably the Sabbath. For some this
was an end in itself; for others it was a step leading ultimately to full
conversion to Judaism.

Pythagoras in the sixth century B.C.E., as we have noted, is said by Hermippus of Smyrna (cited in Origen, *Against Celsus* 1.15) to have brought
his philosophy from the Jews to the Greeks. Specifically, according to
Hermippus (cited in Josephus, *Against Apion* 1.162–65), he imitated
($\mu\iota\mu\text{o}\acute{\upsilon}\mu\varepsilon\nu\text{o}\varsigma$) and appropriated ($\mu\varepsilon\tau\alpha\varphi\acute{\varepsilon}\rho\omega\nu$, "transfer," "translate") the
doctrines of the Jews and the Thracians in his admonition not to pass a
spot where an ass had collapsed, to abstain from thirst-producing water,
and to avoid all calumny.[11] This is not to say that Pythagoras was regarded as a "sympathizer" with Judaism, but the fact that he was so
greatly indebted to Jewish thought might have made the next step, the
actual adoption of Jewish practices, much easier for those who became
his followers.[12]

We have more information about "sympathizers" in Rome than we do
for any other region in the ancient world. Valerius Maximus (in the epitome of Julius Paris, 1.3.3) notes that in 139 B.C.E. Gnaeus Cornelius

Hispalus (actually Gnaeus Cornelius Scipio), as we have remarked, compelled the Jews "who attempted to infect the Roman customs with the cult of Jupiter Sabazius [presumably Zevaoth, 'L-rd of Hosts'] to return to their houses." It is not clear, however, whether Jews attempted to convert the Romans to Judaism or whether they sought merely to get the Romans to observe certain Jewish practices, that is, to become "sympathizers."[13]

In the first century b.c.e., we hear of a freedman, Quintus Caecilius Niger, who had been quaestor under Verres and who sought to win the right to prosecute Verres so as ultimately to let him off the hook. This Caecilius, says Plutarch (*Cicero* 7.6.5), was suspected (ἔνοχος, "liable to," "subject to," "liable to an imputation") of Judaizing ('Ιουδαΐζειν), whence Cicero, who undertook in sincerity to prosecute Verres, is said to have remarked, playing on the word *verres* (a male swine), "What has a Jew to do with a Verres?"[14] The phrase "suspected of Judaizing" implies that Caecilius adhered to some but not all Jewish practices. Inasmuch as this Caecilius had been the quaestor, in effect administrative assistant, of Verres, it seems unlikely, unless the passage in Plutarch is unhistorical, that he was a Jew in the complete sense, because a Jew would have had to compromise his Jewish observance in the service of the Roman state and ipso facto of the state religion.

We hear (Suetonius, *Tiberius* 32.2) of another Sabbath-observer, perhaps a Jew, the grammarian Diogenes, who, in the early part of the first century, used to lecture every Sabbath in Rhodes and who, when the Emperor Tiberius wished to hear him on another day, refused. When this same Diogenes came to Rome to pay his respects to Tiberius, the emperor retorted, "Come back in the seventh year." Such an exchange is meaningful only if we reckon Diogenes as a Jew or as a "sympathizer" who observed the Sabbath. To him the emperor says, in effect, that if the Sabbath means so much to him, let him come back in the Sabbatical year, as described in the Pentateuch.[15]

A probable reference to "sympathizers" that has not hitherto been noticed appears in Suetonius's account (*Tiberius* 36) of the expulsion of the Jews from Rome in the year 19 c.e. There we are told that, in addition to the Jews of military age, whom the Emperor Tiberius assigned to provinces of less healthy climate, he banished others who were of the same race (*gentis*) or who were pursuing (*sectantes*, "following continually," "pursuing eagerly," "chasing") similar beliefs (*similia*, literally "similar things"). The fact that Suetonius distinguishes between those of the Jewish race and those who were pursuing similar beliefs would seem to indicate a difference between Jews, on the one hand, and those who adopted certain Jewish beliefs and practices without becoming full-fledged proselytes, on the other hand.

In the middle of the first century c.e., contemporary with Paul and with the rise of early Christianity, there are several references to "sympathizers." In the reign of Nero, as we have noted, Seneca (quoted in Augustine, *De Civitate D-i* 6.11), after deriding the Jews for their laziness in wasting one seventh of their lives in idleness through the observance of the Sabbath, bitterly notes the spread of Jewish customs that have gained such influence that they are now received throughout the world. "The vanquished have given laws to their victors" (*Victi victoribus leges dederunt*). He then adds that "whereas they [i.e., the Jews] are aware of the origin and meaning of their rites (*sacramentorum*) the greater part of the people go through a ritual not knowing why they do so." Inasmuch as Seneca in this context is deriding the Sabbath, it would seem that he is attacking the spread of the Sabbath, which, as we shall see, is precisely the one aspect of Judaism that seems to have been most attractive to "sympathizers." The contrast, moreover, in the last sentence is between those who are Jews in the full sense and non-Jews who adopt certain Jewish customs without converting completely.[16]

The satirist Petronius (fragment 37, Ernout), in the middle of the first century c.e., distinguishes between, on the one hand, those (presumably "sympathizers") who worship the "pig-god [presumably those who observe the dietary laws] and clamor in the ears of high heaven" and, on the other hand, those who are circumcised and who observe the Sabbath according to the law. Apparently, Petronius here differentiates between those ("sympathizers") who share the Jewish belief in G-d and those (Jews) who observe the Sabbath according to the standard of Halakhah. When Petronius says, as he does here, that the former group "shall go forth from the people," he means that such individuals cannot be accepted as full Jews unless they accept the entire law, including circumcision. Such a passage, we may add, coming from a satirist, has force only if the situation is sufficiently frequent to be recognized by the reader.

Another passage that alludes to sympathizers is found in Epictetus, the Stoic philosopher of the latter part of the first century and the early part of the second century, as quoted by Arrian (*Dissertationes* 2.19–21). "Why," asks the philosopher, "do you act the part (ὑποκρίνῃ, "be an actor," "play a part") of a Jew when you are a Greek?" He then adds, "Whenever we see a man halting between two faiths (ἐπαμφοτερίζοντα, "play a double game," "be ambiguous," "be halfway between," "be of intermediate species") we are in the habit of saying, 'He is not a Jew, he is only acting the part (ὑποκρίνεται).' But when he adopts the attitude of mind of the man who has been baptized and has made his choice, then he both is a Jew in fact and is called one. So we also are counterfeit baptists (παραβαπτισταί), ostensibly (λόγῳ) Jews but in reality (ἔργῳ) something else." Epictetus's use of the word *whenever* (ὅταν) and his citation of this as an example to illustrate a point in a popular exposition of philosophy would seem to indicate that he is describing a frequent occurrence, one that is actually proverbial. He is clearly pointing out a contrast between the part-Jew and the full Jew, as seen by his adoption of the language of the stage (actors) in contrast to reality, and indeed in his adoption of the contrast, so familiar in rhetoric, between appearance (λόγῳ) and reality (ἔργῳ).[17]

A similar distinction is implied in the early part of the second century C.E. in Suetonius's life of Domitian (12.2), who reigned from 81 to 96, that two classes of people were persecuted by Domitian for evasion of the special tax on Jews, namely those who lived as Jews without acknowledging that faith (*vel inprofessi Iudaicam viverunt vitam*) and those who concealed their origin. The first group cannot be Christians, because the Roman government was well aware of the difference between Jews and Christians from the time of Nero.[18] Hence, the first group would seem to refer to the "sympathizers," in contrast to those who acknowledged full adherence to Judaism.

That this reference is indeed to "sympathizers" seems to be corroborated by a passage in the third-century historian Dio Cassius (67.14.2), who notes that during the reign of Domitian, Flavius Clemens, the consul, and his wife, Flavia Domitilla, were accused of atheism, "a charge on which many others who drifted into Jewish ways were condemned." The reference here, too, would seem to be to Judaism rather than to Christianity, because, as we have noted, the distinction between the two was clear in Rome in the days of Nero (and certainly by the time of Dio) and also because no ancient Christian tradition refers to Clemens as a Christian.[19] Moreover, it is hardly likely that a consul would have practiced Judaism fully as a proselyte and have avoided participating in the state religious celebrations that were so integrally a part of the Roman Empire. The key word here, moreover, is *drifted* (ἐξοκέλλοντες), a metaphor that applies to a ship. It can hardly refer to conversion, which is an absolute step; it almost surely refers to step-by-step adoption of one practice of Judaism after another.

The crucial passage differentiating proselytes from "sympathizers" is in the early second-century satirist Juvenal (14.96–99): "Some who have had a father who reveres [*metuentem*] the Sabbath, worship nothing but the clouds and the divinity of the heavens and see no difference between eating swine's flesh, from which their father abstained, and that of man; and in time they take to circumcision." Juvenal is here clearly speaking of a progression of observance: The first generation, that of the "sympathizers," observes the Sabbath and the dietary laws, whereas the second generation accepts the Jewish view of G-d and goes even further in their observance of the dietary laws and eventually adopts Judaism in the fullest sense by undergoing circumcision. Although the term *reveres* (*metu-*

entem) is not necessarily, as Bernays[20] had postulated, a technical term for *sympathizers* equivalent to Acts' φοβούμενοι and σεβόμενοι τὸν θεόν,[21] the passage does differentiate those who observe some practices of Judaism from those who are complete Jews. The "G-d-fearers" must have been numerous if Roman satirists such as Juvenal and popular philosophers such as Epictetus could use them as examples, even if they exaggerate by using sledgehammers to crack a nut. The cutting edge of satire derives from its reflection of reality.[22] Hence, the Sabbath-observing father can hardly be Juvenal's invention and can hardly be an isolated example.

We may here, moreover, call attention to a passage in the fourth-century Julian (*Ad Theodorum* 89A [453C]) which clearly contrasts Jews and "G-d-fearers," where he speaks of those "whose minds were drawn to the doctrines of the Jewish religion." These are, he says, "partly" (ἐν μέρει) "G-d-fearers" (θεοσεβεῖς).

4. JEWISH REFERENCES

There are a number of references to "sympathizers" in Philo, Josephus, Apocrypha and Pseudepigrapha, and the Talmudic writings.

Philo

There are one clear allusion and three somewhat less clear references to "sympathizers" in Philo. In his *Quaestiones in Exodum* 2.2, as we have noted, Philo, commenting on Exodus 22.20 (21) and 23.9, says that the term *proselyte* (Greek προσήλυτος, Hebrew *ger*, "stranger") does not refer to proselytes strictly speaking, inasmuch as the Jews did not practice circumcision in Egypt; and consequently, he concludes, the proselyte who, according to these verses, is not to be wronged must be one who has not undergone circumcision. That such a proselyte is what we would term a "sympathizer" seems indicated from his decision to honor the one G-d; hence, this type of proselyte corresponds to the Rabbis' *ger toshab*, a semi-convert who has embraced monotheism but not other commandments.[23] Perhaps other Alexandrian Jews might have considered such Gentiles to be converts, but Philo insists that they are not.[24]

Philo apparently refers to the "sympathizers" when he remarks (*De Vita Mosis* 2.4.17) that not only Jews but almost every other people "have so far grown in holiness as to value and honor our laws." Whereas other peoples, including the Athenians, Spartans, Egyptians, and Scythians, show disdain for one another's customs, the Jewish institutions "attract (ἐπάγεται, "bring to oneself," "win over") and gain the attention of (συνἐπιστρέφει, "turn at the same time," "help to make attentive") all—of barbarians, of Greeks, of dwellers on the mainland and islands, of nations of the east and the west, of Europe and Asia, of the whole inhabited world (οἰκουμένη) from end to end" (ibid. 2.4.20). In particular, he notes the degree to which the observance of the Sabbath (2.4.21–22), as a day of rest for man, slave, and beast, and of the Day of Atonement (2.4.23–24) has won the awe and reverence of non-Jews, presumably "sympathizers." The fact that Philo singles out the Sabbath and the Day of Atonement, whereas a proselyte is required to observe all the commandments, would seem to indicate that we are dealing with "sympathizers."

Similarly, when Philo (*De Specialibus Legibus* 2.12.42) speaks of the "blameless life of pious men who follow nature and her ordinances" and (*De Specialibus Legibus* 2.12.44) of "all who practice wisdom either in Grecian or barbarian lands and live a blameless and irreproachable life," Wolfson concludes, with some degree of cogency, that the reference is to what he terms "spiritual proselytes," that is, "sympathizers," inasmuch as the ordinances these pious men are said to follow include five laws that are characteristically similar to those described by the rabbis as Noachian, and which are binding on non-Jews.[25]

Finally, there seems some reason to believe, as we have noted, that Petronius, the governor of Syria under Caligula in the middle of the first century C.E. who endeavored to persuade the emperor to rescind his order to place his (the emperor's) statue in the Temple in Jerusalem, may have been a "sympathizer," because Philo (*Legatio ad Gaium* 33.245) states that he had "some rudiments of Jewish philosophy and religion, acquired either in early lessons in the past through his zeal for culture or after his appointment as governor in the countries [Asia and Syria] where the Jews were very numerous in every city, or else because his soul was so disposed (διατεθείς), being drawn to things worthy of serious effort by a nature which listened to no voice or dictation or teaching but its own." The description of Petronius's soul as "disposed" to Jewish religion and the statement that he had been instructed in some of the rudiments (the Greek word indicates *sparks*) of Judaism suggest a picture of a "sympathizer."

Josephus

A number of passages in Josephus allude directly or indirectly to "sympathizers." In his account of the *Jewish War* (2.454), he tells of the massacre of the Roman garrison in Jerusalem, noting that Metilius, the commander, alone saved his life through his promise to turn Jew (ἰουδαΐσειν) and even to be circumcised (μέχρι περιτομῆς, literally "up to [the point of] circumcision"). The fact that Josephus adds "even to be circumcised" indicates that there is probably a distinction between "turning Jew" (i.e., Judaizing) and becoming a full Jew.

Likewise, Josephus (*War* 2.463), in describing the massacres in Syria just prior to the outbreak of the great revolution against the Romans, notes that though all the cities believed that they had rid themselves of their Jews, still they had their Judaizers (᾿Ιουδαΐζοντας), who aroused suspicion; and although they shrank from killing offhand this equivocal (ἀμφίβολον, "doubtful," "ambiguous") element in their midst, they feared this mixed lot (μεμιγμένον)[26] as much as they did pronounced aliens (ἀλλόφυλον), that is, Jews. There is here an evident distinction between Jews and ambiguous Judaizers. The word *mixed* most likely alludes to the fact that these "sympathizers" mixed Jewish customs with those of the pagans.

Elsewhere Josephus (*War* 7.45), as we have stated, notes that the Jews of Antioch had constantly been attracting to their religious ceremonies multitudes of Greeks: His addition that they *in some measure* (τρόπῳ τινὶ) incorporated them with themselves is an indication that these Greeks had become not proselytes but rather "sympathizers," because they had adopted only some Jewish ways.

A key passage is the one (*Ant.* 14.110) in which Josephus describes the great wealth of the Temple in Jerusalem, noting that Jews throughout the inhabited world and those who worshipped G-d (σεβομένων τὸν θεόν), both those from Asia and from Europe, had contributed to it for a very long time. At one time I argued that the reference to those who worshipped G-d is to pious Jews, remarking that if Josephus were referring to "sympathizers" he would have written τῶν σεβομένων, with the definite article, as required by the strict rules of grammar; but I am now convinced by Marcus's argument that the reference is to the "sympathizers," because it is hard to understand why Josephus would refer to Jews throughout the habitable world and then refer to them as coming from Asia and Europe, omitting Africa, where there was such a large Jewish community, particularly in Egypt.[27] It seems more likely that Josephus is distinguishing between the Jews of the habitable world, on the one hand, and the "sympathizers" from Asia and Europe who reverence G-d, on the other hand. Of course, the fact that in this one case the "sympathizers" are referred to as σεβόμενοι τὸν θεόν, the same phrase as that found in Acts, does not definitively prove that this is a technical phrase.

The story of the conversion of Izates (*Ant.* 20.17–96), King of Adiabene in Mesopotamia, to which we have referred previously, likewise illustrates the difference between full converts and "sympathizers." Izates (*Ant.* 20.38) considered that he would not be *genuinely* (βεβαίως, "certainly," "firmly," "surely," "securely") a Jew unless he was circumcised, implying that one might become a Jew in a lesser degree without being circumcised. That this inference is warranted is clear from what follows, because a Jewish merchant named Ananias tried to convince Izates (*Ant.* 20.41), as Paul was later to stress, that he could worship the Divine (τὸ θεῖον σέβειν) even without being circumcised, that is, remain a "sympathizer," "if indeed he had fully decided to be a devoted adherent of Judaism."[28] In this case, however, there was a particular reason for not being circumcised, namely (*Ant.* 20.39) that his subjects, if they discovered that he was circumcised, would not tolerate it. We may conjecture that such an attitude as that of Ananias resulted from the fear of antagonizing the convert's family and relatives or, as in this case, the convert's subjects and led Jews to prefer that non-Jews become merely "sympathizers." It was Ananias's view that "constrained thus by necessity and by fear of his subjects," Izates would be pardoned by G-d Himself. The implication of this view is that normally circumcision was required for full conversion. According to Ananias, in this exceptional case, if Izates had continued to omit the rite of circumcision, he would have been counted not as a "sympathizer" but as a Jew, because he had fully (πάντως, *Ant.* 20.41) decided to be an adherent of Judaism, "for it was this that counted more than circumcision." The fact, however, that another Jew, a certain Eleazar from Galilee (*Ant.* 20.43), disagreed sharply with Ananias and insisted on the necessity of circumcision illustrates that Jews differed among themselves about the desirability of insisting that male proselytes to Judaism fulfill the ritual requirement of circumcision.

Moreover, Nero's wife, Poppaea Sabina, as we have noted above, may well have been a "sympathizer," because Josephus (*Ant.* 20.195) says that when a Jewish embassy asked Nero not to tear down the wall that they had built in the Temple enclosure to block King Agrippa from viewing the sacrifices, Nero consented as a favor to Poppaea, "who was a worshipper of G-d (θεοσεβής)[29] and who pleaded on behalf of the Jews." Smallwood contends that Poppaea could hardly have been attracted to a religion that forbade murder and adultery and asks whether a Roman queen could have repudiated idolatry.[30] But if she became a "sympathizer," she merely selected whatever Jewish practices appealed to her. Josephus's success, on coming to Rome, in obtaining the release of some fellow priests through a Jewish actor at the court named Aliturus, who introduced Josephus to Poppaea (*Life* 16), would seem to reinforce this view that she was a "sympathizer." To be sure, Josephus does not say explicitly that Poppaea was a "sympathizer," but it is hard to understand why she gave him large gifts unless she did, indeed, sympathize with Judaism or unless she sought thereby to defuse the incipient revolution. Moreover, we may wonder why after she had successfully used her influence on behalf of the Jewish embassy she detained two of the members of the embassy as hostages (*Ant.* 20.195). This would seem to contradict her favorable attitude toward them unless we suppose that she detained them not as hostages but as teachers in order to have further instruction about Jewish practices.

Two other references to "sympathizers" may be found in Josephus's apologetic work *Against Apion*. In the first (*Against Apion* 1.166–67) Josephus remarks that many of the Jewish customs have found their way to some cities and here and there have been thought worthy of imitation. He then cites evidence from Theophrastus' *Laws*, which, to be sure, does not speak of individuals who had adopted Jewish practices and indeed, as we have noted, offers as a solitary example the fact that Tyrians prohibit the use of the oath "korban." The statement about *many* customs that had penetrated the world indicates that Josephus is not talking about conversion, because the convert must undertake to obey all the practices of Judaism.

A second passage (*Against Apion* 2.282) triumphantly declares that the masses have been greatly attracted to Jewish observances (εὐσεβείας, "piety," "religious zeal," "reverence") and that there is no city to which the abstention from work on the Jewish Sabbath, the observance of certain fast days, the lighting of lamps, and many of the dietary laws have not spread. Apparently, many Gentiles, however, decided not to become proselytes but instead observed only one or more Jewish practices. The fact that Josephus singles out specific observances as having spread among non-Jews, citing as two of his four examples the laws pertaining to the Sabbath, apparently the most popular Jewish practice among the "sympathizers," and referring to *many* of the dietary laws (rather than *all* of them, the observance of which is required of converts) shows that we are dealing not with full proselytes but with "sympathizers."

There may be another allusion to "sympathizers" in Josephus's statement (*Ant.* 3.318) that "only recently certain persons from beyond the Euphrates, after a journey of four months, undertaken from veneration of our Temple and involving great perils and expense, having offered sacrifices, could not partake of the victims, because Moses had forbidden this to any of those not governed by our laws nor affiliated through the customs of their fathers to ourselves." The passage is apparently referring not to Jews but to non-Jews who wished to worship the Jewish G-d in Jerusalem.

Apocrypha and Pseudepigrapha

The *Testament of Joseph* has a particularly interesting reference to what would appear to be "G-d-fearers." We read there (4:4 ff.), as we have noted previously, that when Potiphar's wife failed to achieve her goal of convincing Joseph to have relations with her, she came to him with the excuse that she wanted instruction in the word of G-d. As an inducement she promised to persuade her husband also to give up his idol worship. Joseph's reply is that G-d did not wish to see those who fear him (τοὺς σεβομένους αὐτόν) live in uncleanness and adultery. The phrase he uses, referring to the σεβόμενοι, is precisely the one found in the Book of Acts and in Josephus with reference to the "G-d-fearers."[31]

Talmudic References

Bertholet, as we have noted, has gone so far as to deny the existence of "G-d-fearers" in the Talmudic period; but this view has been challenged by Lévi, and it may be of value to present the evidence systematically.[32] The rabbinic term for "sympathizers" is not common in the Talmudic literature, perhaps because the "sympathizers" were found not so much in the Land of Israel and in Babylonia, which are the central foci of the rabbis' interest, as in other lands.[33]

Indeed, the rabbis do not use the term *G-d-fearers* as such and instead substitute *Heaven* for *G-d*, as we find also in Daniel 4:23, 1 Maccabees 3:18, and in the Gospels (e.g., Matt 3:2). The term *yirei shamayim* ("Heaven-fearers") itself, which is the rabbinic equivalent for "G-d-fearers," is apparently a coinage of the rabbis, because it is not found in the Bible.[34] This term, however, does not appear in the Mishnah, which dates in all probability from the beginning of the third century. Moreover, although the expression appears seventeen times in the Babylonian Talmud, it nowhere has any meaning other than "pious" or "devout" Jews.[35]

An admittedly problematic passage, however, is to be found in the Babylonian Talmud (*Sanhedrin* 70b), according to which Rabbi Joḥanan said in the name of Rabbi Simeon bar Yoḥai (both of whom lived in the Land of Israel in the middle of the second century) with reference to King Lemuel (Prov 31:1), "All know that your father was a Heaven-fearing man [*yirei shamayim*], and therefore they will say that you inherit [your sinfulness] from your mother." Inasmuch as King Lemuel's father was a non-Jew, the reference here to one who feared Heaven may well be to a "sympathizer." The fact that the text says that "all know" that he was a "sympathizer" would indicate that such "sympathizers" (if Lemuel's father was a "sympathizer") were widely known.

There is a midrashic passage (*Deuteronomy Rabbah* 2.24) that uses the phrase *yirei shamayim* in what appears to be the technical sense of "sympathizers," in connection with a Roman senator, as we have noted above, who committed suicide in order to delay implementation of an imperial decree that within thirty days no Jew should be left in the Roman Empire. The fact that Rabbis Eliezer, Joshua, and Gamaliel were in Rome at that time would enable us to date the incident to approximately 95 C.E. during the reign of Domitian.[36] That the term does not mean merely "pious" but that it probably refers to a person on his way to full conversion would seem to be evidenced by the fact that the rabbis lament that the senator had committed suicide before conversion to Judaism (in their image, "the ship had sailed before paying her dues"); his wife reveals that actually he had taken the step of full conversion, by exhibiting his foreskin.

A clear passage in the *Mekilta de-Rabbi Ishmael* 18 (on Exod 22:20), a Halakhic Midrash that contains traditional material dating from the second century, refers to four categories of true worshippers of G-d—sinless Israelites, righteous (i.e., full) proselytes, repentant sinners, and "Heaven-fearers."[37] The juxtaposition of full proselytes and "Heaven-fearers" indicates that they are related but that they are to be distinguished from each other; and similarly the juxtaposition of sinless Israelites and "Heaven-fearers" indicates that they are to be distinguished from each other.[38]

That the term *yirei shamayim* had become a technical term for "sympathizers" by the third century may be deduced from a passage in the Jerusalem Talmud (*Megillah* 3.2.74a)[39] which quotes Rabbi Eleazar, a third-century rabbi who lived in the Land of Israel, as saying that only the Gentiles who had nothing to do with the Jews during their bitter past will not be permitted to convert to Judaism in the time of the Messiah, but that those "Heaven-fearers" (*yirei shamayim*) who shared the tribulations of Israel would be accepted as full proselytes, with the Emperor Antoninus[40] at their head. The passage clearly indicates that the *yirei shamayim* have been sympathetic to Judaism but have not yet converted, because their conversion is to take place when the Messiah comes. This conclusion is confirmed by the following discussion that raises the question whether Antoninus was a proselyte or not. Those who say that he was point to the fact that he was seen walking on the Day of Atonement with a broken sandal (because it is prohibited to wear normal shoes on that day), whereupon we find the retort, "What can you deduce from that? *Even* fearers of Heaven [*yirei shamayim*] go out wearing such a sandal." The implication is that such "sympathizers" are a degree away from complete conversion. There follows a statement that no one who is uncircumcised may eat of the Paschal Lamb, whereupon, according to one version, Antoninus proceeds to circumcise himself. The inevitable conclusion is that circumcision is what distinguishes the full proselyte from a mere "sympathizer."

Another passage that indicates a clear distinction between proselytes and "sympathizers" is *Genesis Rabbah* 28.5, which quotes the third-century Rabbi Ḥanina as saying: "The cities of the sea are deserving of extermination, and by what merit are they delivered? By the merit of a single convert, or a single fearer of Heaven whom they produce each year." The fact that the fearer of Heaven is paired with the convert and that the context indicates that the merit of either will redeem such cities would seem to support the view that the "Heaven-fearer" is not a pious Jew but a Gentile "sympathizer."

Likewise, the fact that there is a dispute (*Leviticus Rabbah* 3.2; cf. *Midrash Psalms* 22.29 on Psalm 31:8, ed. Buber, p. 191) between the third-century Rabbis Joshua ben Levi and Samuel bar Naḥman as to whether the phrase "Ye that fear the L-rd" refers to "Heaven-fearers" or proselytes would indicate that these two groups are comparable; and the most obvious point of comparison is that proselytes are full converts, whereas "Heaven-fearers" are not. It would also indicate that both disputants recognized that the phrase "Heaven-fearers" is a technical term for a group distinct from proselytes. To be sure, Kuhn and Stegemann cite this passage to support their view that whereas originally the rabbinic term *yirei shamayim* was a technical term for "G-d-fearers," by the third century, when, they claim, there were no longer any "sympathizers," the term was used of proselytes;[41] but there is no indication in *Leviticus Rabbah* that the "sympathizers" had disappeared; the only question was whether the biblical term "Ye that fear G-d" referred to them.

Another passage that clearly differentiates between proselytes and "sympathizers" is *Pesiqta Rabbati* 43, p. 180a (Friedmann), which mentions a dispute as to whether the heathen children suckled by Sarah became full proselytes, as the third-century Rabbi Levi declares, or "Heaven-fearers." Again, the contrast indicates a distinction beween full proselytes and partial proselytes.

The Talmudic category of *ger toshab* (resident alien) would seem to bear a close relationship, moreover, to that of "sympathizer." The second-century Rabbi Meir ('*Avodah Zarah* 64b, Jerusalem Talmud *Yevamoth* 8.1.8d) defines the *ger toshab* as a Gentile who obligates himself not to worship idols, whereas others declare that the *ger toshab* is one who undertakes not merely to abstain from idol-worship but also to observe the other six Noachian commandments; and still others define a *ger toshab* as one who undertakes to observe all the precepts mentioned in the Torah apart from the prohibition of eating the flesh of animals not ritually slaughtered. However, the one common denominator of these definitions is that the *ger toshab* is a non-Jew who observes some of the biblical commandments and has thus completed part of the path to full conversion.

Braude[42] contends that such a discussion has an unmistakable air of unreality; but Lieberman[43] seems to be right in declaring that the clash mirrors the facts of actual life, because apparently there were various gradations of such "sympathizers." The very fact that the third-century Rabbi Johanan (bar Nappaha) ('*Avodah Zarah* 65a; cf. Jerusalem *Yevamoth* 8.1.8d, where the statement is put into the mouth of Rabbi Hanina bar Hama) gives a time limit of twelve months during which the *ger toshab* must make up his mind whether to become a full convert or to be regarded as a Gentile in every respect would seem to indicate that the rabbis, confronted with a widespread phenomenon of "semi-proselytes," had decided to clamp down.[44]

That the question about the permissibility of teaching such "sympathizers" the Torah was a live issue may be inferred from the remark attributed to the third-century Rabbi Johanan (*Sanhedrin* 59a) that a Gentile who engages in the study of Torah is subject to the death penalty. This is in obvious contradiction to the statement (ibid.) by the second-century Rabbi Meir that the pagan who studies the Torah ranks higher than an ignorant high priest, which may be taken as evidence that at least some non-Jews did try to study the Torah.[45]

One of the practices of Judaism most attractive to these sympathizers was the observance of the Sabbath, as we can see from Juvenal (14.96). There is clearly an allusion to this attraction of the Sabbath to non-Jews in the positive statement by the third-century Rabbi Johanan (*Shabbath* 118b) that "he who observes the Sabbath according to its rules, even though he be an idolator like the generation of Enosh, is granted forgiveness of sin." That, however, there were such Gentiles and that their observance of the Sabbath was a debated issue is proved by the vehement statement of the third-century Rabbi Simeon ben Lakish (*Sanhedrin* 58b) that a pagan who rests on the Sabbath deserves death. Indeed, the popularity of the observance of the Jewish Sabbath is further evidenced by the fact that the Church had to fight for the translation of the Jewish Sabbath into the Christian Sunday for almost a millennium.

As to the claim that the term *G-d-fearer* is too elevated to be applied to non-Jews,[46] we may cite as a rabbinic parallel (Tosefta, *Sanhedrin* 13.2) the term *hasidei 'umoth ha-olam* ("the pious ones of the nations of the world"), which has been applied in our own day to righteous Gentiles, especially to those non-Jews who saved Jews from their Nazi persecutors at the risk of their own lives.

5. CHRISTIAN REFERENCES

We may suggest that, by implication, Paul (Galatians 5:3) alludes to the distinction between "sympathizers" and proselytes when he declares that every man who is circumcised (i.e., a proselyte as opposed to a "sympathizer") is obligated to observe the whole law.

The Book of Revelation (3:9) seems to refer to "sympathizers" when it alludes to the presence of "halfway Jews" at Smyrna in Asia Minor at the end of the first century, citing "those of the synagogue of Satan who say that they are Jews and are not."[47]

One passage in the mid-second-century Justin Martyr (*Dialogue with Trypho* 10.2) seems to refer to "sympathizers." There the Jew Trypho charges that Christians do not keep the feasts or Sabbaths nor practice the rite of circumcision, whereas all G-d-fearing persons (φοβούμενοι τὸν θεόν) do so. In this context it makes no sense to look on the "G-d-fearers" as Jews, because the point is that Christians should know better than to disregard the commandments; and the most likely explanation is that because even "G-d-fearers" keep these commandments, certainly Christians, who claim to believe in the Scriptures, should do so.

We may also point to a passage in Tertullian, in his late-second-century work *Ad Nationes* (1.13), in which he attacks pagans who observe Jewish ceremonies, notably the Sabbath and Passover. Moreover, the third-century Christian Latin poet Commodianus, in his *Instructiones* (1.24.11 ff.), likewise alludes to Judaizers who seek to live between both ways"—that is, partaking of both Judaism and Christianity. Commodianus (*Instructiones* 1.37) makes the same point when he exclaims, "What! Are you half a Jew?"

Pines has noted that in at least three Iranian languages—Pahlavi, New Persian, and Sogdian—one of the names for Christians is derived from the Iranian root *tars*, "to fear," and he suggests that when members of the "G-d-fearing" circles showed sympathy for or even adhered to Christianity they continued to be designated as "G-d-fearers." Likewise, in the Mandaean Christian book *Ginza*, one of the designations for Christians is identical in meaning with the Pahlavi term for "fearers." He concludes that the Christians were perhaps so designated because many of them had themselves formerly been or were the sons of "G-d-fearers" or bore a similarity to "G-d-fearers" in their customs.[48] We may recall that whereas the term *G-d-fearers* was originally not a technical term for "sympathizers," by the third century, to judge from Talmudic terms, the phrase had indeed become a technical one for this group.[49]

The fact that the early Christian Church, as we shall see, inveighs so strongly against Judaizers who wear Jewish ritual vestments, follow some of the dietary laws, keep the seventh-day Sabbath, and observe Easter on the Passover or with Jewish rites would indicate the likelihood that these are "sympathizers," though, of course, they may also be Christians who never went through a transitional phase, just as during the Protestant Reformation there were similar Judaizers.

We may here also suggest that the Caelicoli, "Heaven-worshippers," referred to in the Theodosian Code (16.8.19), may be the Latin equivalent of the Talmudic *yirei shamayim* ("Heaven-worshipers"). The members of this mysterious group, who appeared in North Africa toward the end of the fourth century, are unknown outside of the references to them in the laws of Honorius, who was emperor in the West from 395 to 423; but they are clearly Judaizers, because they are reported to be trying "to force certain Christians to adopt the foul and degrading name of Jew."

That there were "G-d-fearers" observing certain Jewish practices without actually converting to Judaism as late as the fifth century may be seen from the observation of Cyril of Alexandria (*PG* 68.281–82), who claims that there were people in Phoenicia and Palestine who called themselves "G-d-fearers" and who worshiped "the Most High G-d" of the Jews, as well as other gods. We may suggest that one reason, in addition to the severe penalties for conversion to Judaism, for the growth of the movement of "G-d-fearers" was that there was apparently no Christian equivalent to a halfway movement, and hence if someone did not wish to go all the way to become a Christian it might have appeared attractive to become a "G-d-fearer" or "sympathizer" with Judaism. It is difficult to believe that these "G-d-fearers" could have collected around synagogues in such numbers, as seems to be the case in the new inscriptions from third-century Aphrodisias, at any rate, without any effort being made by the Jews to attract them.[50]

6. EPIGRAPHICAL AND PAPYROLOGICAL EVIDENCE

MacLennan and Kraabel note that although over a hundred synagogue inscriptions have been uncovered, at most only a single one refers to "sympathizers."[51] In the first place, however, as we shall see, this one inscription almost certainly does refer to "sympathizers," and in the second place the existence of such a class is established by a number of other inscriptions, perhaps totaling as many as fourteen. At least five of these and probably more date from the third century, when the movement seems to have been at its height, to judge from the Aphrodisias inscriptions.[52]

There are few tombstone inscriptions of "sympathizers," perhaps because, as non-Jews, they could hardly be buried in Jewish cemeteries. There are, to be sure, four Roman inscriptions referring to "fearers" (*metuentes*);[53] but these do not come from Jewish catacombs and there is no evidence that they had any relation with Jews.

To be sure, an undated inscription (*CII* 1, no. 228), found in a Jewish setting in Rome, refers to a woman named Eparchia as *theosebes;* another (*CII*, 1, no. 619a),[54] found in Venusia in Apulia, refers to a certain Marcus *theuseves*, likewise in Latin letters. But although these may be the epitaphs of pious Jews, they are more likely those of "sympathizers." The presence of the Greek word *theosebes*, transcribed in Latin letters, in a Latin inscription would seem to indicate that the term is by this time a technical one.

One other reference to a community of "sympathizers" is to be seen in a second-century inscription that appoints the community of Jews *and* the "G-d-fearers" (θεὸν σέβων) as guardians of an enfranchised slave.[55]

One tantalizing undated inscription (*CII* 1, no. 529) found in Rome in the foundations of the Baths of Caracalla, has, at the base of a headless bust, but with *laticlavia*, that is, the toga with the broad stripes of aristocracy, the words "here lies a [G-]d-fearer" [*De]um metuens*). Frey comments that the presence of a bust shows that the person is not a member of the Jewish community; and yet Jewish funerary busts, though rare, do exist.[56] Most likely, however, we may suggest, the inscription is not that of a Jew but of a non-Jewish "sympathizer." Another tombstone inscription of unknown date found in Rhodes speaks of a certain Euphrosyne, "the G-d-fearer" and worthy,[57] though of course this may refer to a pious Jew. One proselyte is referred to as θεοσεβής ("G-d-reverencing"), but the reading is disputed by Leon,[58] and the reference is probably to a pious proselyte rather than to a "G-d-fearer," who would hardly be termed a proselyte.

One of the Sibyls, named Sambethe or Sabbo, was connected with the Jews in particular; indeed, no ancient Oriental goddess was ever associated with her. Consequently, the only reason for pagans worshipping her must be sought in her name, which doubtless reflects the pagan attraction to the Sabbath. Apparently, she was worshipped by a syncretistic association of Sabbath-observers; and hence it is easy to understand why newborn girls were named after the patron goddess.[59] And it is precisely at Karanis in Egypt, where we find ostraka referring to the goddess of the Sabbath, Sambathis, and to the Jewish Sabbatian Sibyl, that we also find a large number of people named Sambation.[60]

The happy fact that the Roman administrators in Egypt recorded the names of not only the inhabitants but also their parents and grandparents enables us to reconstruct the names of whole families. The reference in an inscription at Naukratis in Egypt, for example, to a Sabbatarian (Σαμβαθική) association (σύνοδος) would indicate that the "sympathizers" were not merely individuals but were organized as a group.[61] There can be little doubt that the term denotes those who revere the Sabbath, because σαββατίζειν is the usual word in the Septuagint for "celebrating the Sabbath."[62] They cannot be Jews, because, so far as we know, Jews never refer to their G-d as "the G-d of the Sabbath";[63] and hence they are most likely "sympathizers."

The very name Sambathion (apparently given to male and female children born on the Sabbath) in twenty-nine Egyptian papyri ranging in date from the early first century c.e. to the fifth century[64] apparently refers to adherents of a sect of Sabbath-observers, because their kinsfolk seem to be non-Jews and the papyri were found in villages that are non-Jewish, so far as we know. It is striking that no other Hebrew name was ever borrowed by non-Jews; and the most likely explanation for the choice of the name, consequently, is that the parents were Sabbath-observers. Because the name Sambathion, which occurs so often in these papyri, was given by parents in each instance, we may consider every Sambathion as representing a whole family; and the total number of Sabbath-observers was consequently not inconsiderable, though, of course, we cannot be sure that all members of the families were actually Sabbath-observers.[65]

The name Sambathion occurs frequently in the second century, but as the Jewish community in Egypt declined in numbers the people bearing this name become fewer, so that by the fourth century it disappeared completely. One might object that in the second century, after the Jewish revolts against Trajan and Hadrian had been suppressed, Sabbath observance on the part of a non-Jew must have been fraught with danger, because the Romans had prohibited proselytizing; and this may explain why in that period the name Sambathion was borne only by old people and women.[66]

Tcherikover doubts whether we may call the majority of Sambathions "sympathizers" and prefers to call them "pagan observers of the Sabbath,"[67] but this merely reinforces our flexible picture of the "sympathizers" as people who were attracted to one or another of the practices of Judaism.

There is even evidence (*CPJ* 3.52, note 1) that children who played with dice in the streets of Alexandria knew that the seventh day was the Jewish Sabbath, because we find the word προσάββατον (the day before the Sabbath) in juxtaposition with the number six on such a toy, which was probably (though admittedly not necessarily) not intended for Jewish children, inasmuch as it also contains pagan mythological symbols.[68]

We may also cite an inscription from Cilicia in Asia Minor, apparently dating from the reign of Augustus, which speaks of an "association of the Sambatistae" (ἑταιρέα τῶν Σαμβατιστῶν) worshiping a god called Sabbatistes.[69] They cannot be Jews, because, as we have noted, Jews would never refer to their G-d as "the G-d of the Sabbath," and hence they are most likely "sympathizers."[70] Moreover, an inscription from Lydia in Asia Minor speaks of a woman named Ammias who offers a prayer to Sabathikos, who presumably is the deity of the Sabbath.[71] We have likewise found in Italy inscriptions with the Sabbath-associated names of

Junia Sabatis, Aurelia Sabbatia, and Claudia Sabbathis.[72] The fact that the first appears on a columbarium and hence that the person there interred had been cremated and that the last two inscriptions start with the heathen formula *D.M.*, indicating a dedication to the deified souls of the dead, would show that the inscriptions belong to pagans, most probably Sabbath-observing "sympathizers" or their children.

There are, moreover, a number of other inscriptions and papyri that refer to Sabbath-observers who may well be "sympathizers." The very occurrence of the name Sambation and of reference to brothers who worship the Highest G-d (σεβόμενοι θεὸν ὕψιστον) and to a person with the Hebrew name Azariah in a group of twenty-two inscriptions dating from the first century c.e. found at Tanais on the Sea of Azov in southern Russia seems evidence of Sabbath-observers or their descendants.[73]

A second-century inscription found in the Roman theater in Miletus, in Asia Minor, speaks of the "place of the Jews who are also [called] G-d-fearers (θεοσεβεῖς)." Robert was convinced that the reference was to G-d-fearing, full-fledged Jews, because, he argued, it is a basic contradiction to speak of "sympathizers," that is, non-Jews, who were Jews, and because there would be no point in supposing that Judaizing pagans had their place in the theater with members of the community of which they did not have a part.[74] Likewise, in the case of the third-century inscriptions found at Sardis, referring to two donors named Polyippos and Euligios designated as θεοσεβεῖς, who had fulfilled their pledges, he argues that they were full members of the Jewish community.[75] Furthermore, because an inscription memorializes the gift of a basin to a synagogue in the region of Philadelphia in Asia Minor by a certain Eustathios, who is described as a θεοσεβής, in memory of his brother, even Robert[76] is puzzled by the presence of the definite article before the word θεοσεβής and admits that it may be interpreted in the sense of belonging to a category, though he insists that this is not necessary. Finally, he says, the term θεοσεβής was too honorable, too dignified, and too elevated to be applied to non-Jews. The more likely explanation, however, in view of the clear reference to a class of θεοσεβεῖς at Aphrodisias, is that the reference is to that type of "half-Jew" known as the "G-d-fearer."

We may also note some inscriptions of uncertain date of donors to synagogues in Sardis,[77] Philadelphia,[78] and Tralles[79] in Asia Minor who are described as θεοσεβεῖς ("G-d-fearers") and who are probably "sympathizers."[80]

To be sure, if Lifshitz and Bellen are to be accepted, a manumission inscription from Panticapaeum on the Bosporus dating from the second century suggests a synagogue of Jews and "G-d-fearers,"[81] as does the passage in Acts (17:17), but, we may remark, this does not mean that the "G-d-fearers" were actually members of the synagogues.[82] That the lines

between Jews, Jewish Christians, and "sympathizers" were hazy would
seem to be borne out, for example, by an inscription (*CII* 1.693b, east of
Thessalonica) with a menorah, clearly a Jewish symbol, found in a Christian cemetery, and another (*CII* 1.84*, Italy) containing a menorah and
the Christian Chi-Rho (standing for Christos). Furthermore, several
dedications from Greece have been found containing both crosses and
menorahs, and Christian catacombs have been found with lamps containing menorahs depicted on them. In addition, there are instances of
Christians and Jews buried side by side in Cilicia; and the same curse
formula warning passersby not to molest the dead is used by both Jews
and Christians.[83]

7. Aphrodisias: The Dramatic New Inscriptions and Their Implications

The publication in 1987 of inscriptions from Aphrodisias referring to
θεοσεβεῖς raises the questions 1) whether there was a clearly defined class
of "G-d-fearers" or "sympathizers" who, without embracing Judaism totally, chose to observe Jewish practices; 2) if so, why were these people
turning to Judaism; 3) were there certain areas particularly receptive to
such people; and 4) finally, how were these people related to the emerg-
ing Christianity, particularly in the third and fourth centuries, the presumed date of the Aphrodisias inscriptions.[84]

It is well known that though scholars generally concede a very sizable
Jewish community in Asia Minor in the early centuries of the Common
Era, estimated at more than a million,[85] not only do we lack a Philo for
this important Diaspora community, but we have not a single fragment
of literature written in Asia Minor by Jews of the Hellenistic and Roman
periods, with the exception of portions of the New Testament and the
Sibylline Oracles. Moreover, what little evidence we have about Jews in
Asia Minor often comes from hostile sources, whether pagan or Christian. Modern historians may have been willing to grant the importance
of Judaism in the first Christian century, but all too often they looked on
Judaism as declining to the extent that Christianity rose.[86] As Lane Fox
has remarked, "The more we know from the cities of Greek Asia, the less
it is possible to reduce the Jewish presence to a 'narrow and unsocial'
minority."[87] It would be interesting, he adds, to have a history by a Jewish
Eusebius, describing the Jews' continued prominence and growth in the
Diaspora until 300. Hence, the recent archaeological and epigraphical
discoveries, particularly from Aphrodisias, are especially welcome. We
are now, I believe, in a position to comment, though of course only in a
preliminary way, on the dialogue and debate among pagans, Jews, and
Christians during this period in Asia Minor, an area known for its intense

religious movements, where religious strife had apparently been traditional.[88] Unwarranted would seem to be the excessive caution of Reynolds and Tannenbaum in their statement "As far as the implications of
this Jewish inscription from Aphrodisias for the history of Christianity
itself, *qui tacet, valet.*"[89]

Evidence of the Prosperity of Asia Minor in the Third Century

The third century is often said to be the period of the greatest decline in
the history of the Roman Empire, particularly in view of the barbarian
invasions, natural catastrophes such as plagues and earthquakes, and the
violent history of the imperial throne itself. For Asia Minor, this was the
first time since the Parthian incursion of 40 B.C.E. that the area had been
invaded by an external enemy and the first time since the third century
B.C.E. that it had been penetrated by barbarians from the north. Yet the
greatest damage seems to have been concentrated along the coast, in such
cities as Ephesus and Cyzicus, so that inland cities such as Sardis and
Aphrodisias were spared. Communities such as Sardis[90] seem to have
prospered during this very period. Egypt had its Alexandria, Italy its
Rome, and Greece its Athens, but Asia Minor had numerous cities of size
and stature. Joyce Reynolds has pointed out that the unusually large
number of third-century texts shows how normally the city of Aphrodisias continued to function so far as the Roman government was concerned.[91]

There are other indications of continued prosperity in Asia Minor in
the third century: At Pergamum an agonothete (an officer who presided
over athletic contests) was able to celebrate the festival of Asclepius at his
own expense; at Nicaea the walls damaged by the Gothic invasion were
soon repaired; an imperial mint was established at Cyzicus;[92] at Ephesus
the theater was improved and a porch was built for the goddess Nemesis,
and the square in front of the auditorium and the Library of Celsus was
paved, the harbor was dredged, and a triumphal festival was celebrated;
at Miletus a porch was built for the Temple of Sarapis; in Philadelphia an
awning for a theater was purchased; at Thyateira a triumphal festival was
held; at Panamara and Lagina lavish hospitality was given to worshippers; a large number of contests continued to be held and a gymnasium
was built at Tarnessus.[93]

The very fact that the inhabitants of the inland city of Stratoniceia,
less than half the distance of nearby Aphrodisias from the coast, inquired
of Zeus at Panamara whether the barbarians would attack their city indicates that they expected, or at least had grounds for hoping, on the basis
of previous experience, that the barbarians would restrict their incur-

sions to the area immediately around the coast.[94] And even though this
was a major invasion, the god assured them that their city would not be
destroyed nor they themselves enslaved. It is significant that during the
tumultuous years in the middle of the third century, when the Goths
attacked the coastal cities of Ephesus, Didymna, and Miletus and when
the Persians raided Asia Minor, there is no evidence of devastation in the
community of Sardis; and indeed the Jewish community began its decoration of the synagogue during this period.[95]

Evidence of continuing prosperity at Sardis may be seen in the considerable renovation of the synagogue in the first half of the third century,
with its huge size, magnificence, and many-colored mosaic floor.[96] The
fact that the synagogue building was apparently at first a civic basilica
that was turned over to the Jewish community in the second century is an
indication of the power and influence of the Jews. Indeed, no fewer than
a third of the twenty-seven Jews mentioned in the inscriptions of Sardis
were members of the city council, two were functionaries in the Roman
provincial government, and one was a former Roman procurator.[97] Even
under Christian emperors, the Sardis Jews were permitted to use spoils
from pagan temples in the renovation of their synagogue.[98] In particular,
we may note, Aphrodisias is not far from such major cities—and Jewish
centers—as Laodicea, Hierapolis, Apamea, and Tralles, and not much
further away from such important cities as Sardis, Miletus, Thyateira,
and Ephesus.

In addition to material prosperity, Asia Minor seems to have flourished culturally during the third century, with such figures as Dio Cassius (ca. 155–235) from Nicaea in Bithynia, who wrote a *Roman History* in
eighty books; Diogenes Laertius (flourished 222–35), biographer of the
Greek philosophers, who perhaps came from the town of Laerte in Cilicia; the novelist Xenophon of Ephesus (second or third century); and
Alexander of Aphrodisias (early third century), the most important of the
ancient commentators on Aristotle.

Aphrodisias's Special Relationship with Rome

During the imperial period Aphrodisias itself apparently continued to
enjoy with Rome a special relationship that, like the particular ties with
the Jews, had been established by Julius Caesar and affirmed by Octavian
(Augustus). Perhaps this link was due to its very name, derived, as it was,
from Aphrodite, the Greek equivalent of the Roman Venus, the mother
of Aeneas (who was the founder of Rome and the alleged ancestor of
Julius Caesar through Iulus [Ascanius], the son of Aeneas). Aphrodisias,
as a reward for fighting against Rome's and Caesar's enemies, had been

given ἐλευθερία (freedom) and ἀτέλεια (exemption from taxation).[99] Moreover, the crops of flax, flocks of sheep, and marble quarries in the environs enhanced its prosperity. Such privileges may well have attracted Jewish and other immigrants. Indeed, though smitten by numerous earthquakes, Aphrodisias had such vitality that it seems not only to have recovered but to have replaced the devastated buildings with others of even greater sophistication,[100] and private benefactions continued on a considerable scale. The prosperity of Aphrodisias may be seen in such monuments of architecture as the basilica and the city walls, as well as its glorious sculpture. Its famous school of sculpture, second only to that of Athens for artistic creativity and technical skill, was responsible for inventing important new techniques such as the deep drilling of eyes and hair.[101]

Like several other cities in Caria, Aphrodisias (it is not clear whether it or Antioch was the capital of Caria) was, as we have noted, granted special privileges by the emperors; and the increased importance of the highway along the valley of the Maeander River encouraged both old and new cities.[102] Thus, in one document[103] dating from the third century, we have reference, to be sure with exaggerated rhetoric, to the status of "the most (distinguished) δῆμος, ally of the Romans, of the most glorious city of the Aphrodisians devoted to the emperor, free and autonomous according to the decree of the most holy Senate and the treaty and the divine (imperial) responses." The freedom and special status of Aphrodisias are likewise illustrated in a letter written by the proconsul of Asia under Alexander Severus in the third century to the people of Aphrodisias announcing his intention of visiting the city but only on condition that such a visit was not forbidden by the city's laws, a senatorial decree, or an imperial order.[104] Even when the emperor in 249 ordered that all the inhabitants of the Roman world should offer sacrifice to the deities officially recognized by Rome, a special message[105] to the magistrates, council, and people of Aphrodisias assured them that their freedom and all other rights they had obtained from previous emperors would be maintained.

The Favored Political Position of the Jews

There is a long history of Roman protection of the rights of Jews in Asia Minor, as we have noted. I Maccabees 15:15–23 contains a Roman decree of the second century b.c.e. instructing the rulers of Delos, Caria, Pamphilia, Lycia, Halicarnassus, Myndos, Cnidos, Rhodes, Cos, Phaselis, Side, and Samos, all of them in Asia Minor or on the adjoining islands, not to harm the Jews there. Moreover, Josephus (*Ant.* 14.223–64), who

presumably had access to the emperor's archives, records a number of
Roman decrees issued in the first century B.C.E. to protect the rights of
the Jewish communities of Miletus, Pergamum, Halicarnassus, Tralles,
Laodicea, Sardis, and Ephesus to maintain their religious practices, to
erect synagogues, etc. In his oration *Pro Flacco* (59 B.C.E.) Cicero mentions Jewish communities in Pergamum, Adramyttion, Laodicea, and
Apamea which had the special privilege of being permitted to send to
Jerusalem the half shekels they collected from every Jewish inhabitant. A
hundred years later, obviously encouraged by such conditions, there
were, according to Philo (*Legatio ad Gaium* 36.281–83), Jews living in
great mass throughout Asia Minor. That the Jews of Asia Minor had
made quite an impact is clear from at least three writers from Asia
Minor—Apollonius Molon from Alabanda in Caria, Alexander Polyhistor from Miletus, and Teucer from Cyzicus, all from the first century
B.C.E., who devoted special monographs to the Jews.

In short, Judaism was far from being despised and degraded during
these early centuries.[106] To judge from Sardis, at any rate, at the very
time when the empire was undergoing an economic and political crisis of
the first order, the Jews needed more room. For the Jews, the third century, both in the Land of Israel and in Babylonia, was a period of religious and cultural greatness. Indeed, several of the Roman emperors
showed special regard for the Jews. Thus, the Talmud (*Sanhedrin* 91a–b;
Jerusalem Talmud, *Shevi'ith* 6.1.36d; *Midrash Genesis Rabbah* 20.6 et
alibi) refers to the close friendship of Rabbi Judah the Prince, the Jewish
patriarch of the Land of Israel at the end of the second and at the beginning of the third century, with the Roman Emperor Antoninus, and the
profound reverence the emperor had for Judaism, which was reciprocated in the regard shown by the rabbis for the emperor, who, they said
(Jerusalem Talmud, *Megillah* 3.2.74a), would be the first righteous proselyte to be accepted in the messianic era. Moreover, we have already
noted the favorable attitude of the Emperors Caracalla, Sulpicius Severus, and Alexander Severus toward Jews.

This high regard for the Jews is reflected by a series of coins from
Apamea[107] in Phrygia, dating from the end of the second century, which
bear a representation of Noah's ark, on which sit two figures, with Noah
himself being identified; one bird is perched above and another hovers
over it with a branch. Such coins, in effect like modern commemorative
postage stamps, could not have been issued unless the story of Noah were
well known; the knowledge must have been built up over a period of
many years. Indeed, it is striking that the city of Apamea had a nickname,
ἡ κιβωτός, that is, "box," "chest," or "ark." This nickname may well have
been a Jewish contribution, made possible only because the Jewish community in the city was so large and influential.[108]

Moreover, the fact that Melito, the bishop of Sardis in the latter part of the second century, is so sharp in his attack on the Jews may well be due to resentment against their political and social power, as seen, for example, in their success in getting the city to give them its civic basilica to turn into a magnificent synagogue.

The Inscriptions at Aphrodisias

The chance discovery in 1976 of two inscriptions at Aphrodisias in Asia Minor, dating apparently from the third century,[109] has shed dramatic new light on the "sympathizers." One inscription contains a list of donors with clearly Jewish names, followed by the phrase "and as many as are 'G-d-fearers' " (καὶ ὅσοι θεοσεβεῖς), with clearly Greek or Greco-Roman names. There is important economic information, including the occupations of a number of the donors. It is clear that the "G-d-fearers," with occupations such as mason, marble worker, athlete, portrait painter, fuller, tax collector, and carpenter, are of a higher social group than the Jews, whose occupations are vegetable seller, candymaker, bird seller, and cattle-fodder purveyor. The fact that nine of the "G-d-fearers," are city councillors is evidence that the Jews attracted wealthy people, inasmuch as this office implied heavy financial obligations. A second inscription lists a number of donors who are Jews (as we can see from the names), followed by the names of two proselytes and two "G-d-fearers." Is it possible that these "G-d-fearers" are merely Gentiles who befriended the Jews, and that the nine who are members of the city council did so for merely political reasons? The fact that one of the inscriptions carefully distinguishes proselytes from "G-d-fearers" indicates that these are two separate classes.

As to the attraction that Judaism held for "G-d-fearers" or "sympathizers," the most important conclusion of the Aphrodisias inscriptions is, I believe, that it establishes once and for all that there was a special class, at least at the time of the inscriptions, known as θεοσεβεῖς, because this group is clearly identified as such, in contrast to proselytes and to those presumed to be born Jews.[110] θεοσεβεῖς are now known in several cities in Asia Minor—Aphrodisias (where 54 of the 130 names mentioned are θεοσεβεῖς) and, as we have previously noted, Sardis, Philadelphia (in Lydia), Tralles, and Miletus.[111]

To the Christians, what was particularly irksome, apparently, was that Christians in profusion were adopting Jewish ways, whereas relatively few Jews adopted Christian ways. As John Chrysostom bitterly remarks (*Adversus Judaeos* 1.4.849), "Go into the synagogues, and see if the Jews have changed their days of feasting, if they observe the Paschal Feast at the same time we do."[112] We can now see that the movement of "sympa-

thizers" was indeed widespread, at least in Aphrodisias, where in a single
inscription we find the names of no fewer than fifty-four θεοσεβεῖς, who
are apparently not afraid to be identified as "Jew-lovers."

One interesting question raised by the Aphrodisias inscriptions is
whether the θεοσεβεῖς were organized in an association. We have already
noted an inscription at Naukratis in Egypt, for example, which refers to
a Sabbatarian (Σαμβαθική) association (σύνοδος) and which thus indicates
that the "sympathizers" were not merely individuals but were also organized as a group, as seems to be indicated by the Aphrodisias inscriptions.
There is likewise, as we have noted, an inscription from Cilicia in Asia
Minor mentioning an "association of the Sambatistae" which was worshipping a god called Sabbatistes.[113]

If, in the Aphrodisias inscription, the reading δεκανίας τῶν φιλομαθῶν
(Face a, line 3) is correct, there was a decany, which Reynolds and Tannenbaum identify as a *chevrah*, a benevolent association, which included
sixteen Jews, three proselytes, and two θεοσεβεῖς. Tannenbaum suggests
that the group is a private adult education group, but we may well ask
why so many donors are needed to subsidize a teacher;[114] indeed, other
evidence in the inscription indicates that they subsidized a soup kitchen.

Moreover, if, as Tannenbaum contends, the inscription shows strong
rabbinic influence, we may well ask how such a group would have been
tolerated in the synagogue,[115] where the central feature of the Sabbath
service was the reading of the Torah, when the Talmud, as we have
noted, cites the third-century Rabbi Ammi as prohibiting the teaching of
the Torah to Gentiles (*Ḥagigah* 13a), except presumably to sincere candi-
dates for conversion; and there is no indication that this is the case here
in Aphrodisias. Finally, the reading δεκανίας is very suspect; and indeed
Bowersock read καν(ονίδος), referring to the door frame where the slab
was attached.[116] We may also note the absence of rabbis from the Aphrodisias inscriptions as an indication that the synagogue did not possess
learned leaders or members.

And yet, on the basis of parallels in other cities in Asia Minor, we may
conjecture that Aphrodisias's synagogue(s) had an attraction for Christians, although there can be no doubt that by the third century Christianity was widely disseminated in Asia Minor.[117] Indeed, Judaism, far
from being dead in the third century, that is, superseded by Christianity,
was quite obviously counterattacking, and with considerable success.

We may suggest that the strange charge of atheism, allegedly made by
the Jews of Asia Minor against Christians, which is found in Justin (*Dialogue with Trypho* 17.1) and is repeated by the people of Smyrna against
Polycarp and his community (Eusebius, *Historia Ecclesiastica* 4.15.19),
may be explained if we consider that the opposite of *atheists* is θεοσεβεῖς

("G-d-fearers"). Apparently, even in a much earlier period, Christians (Acts 8:1–2), because they no longer felt safe in Jerusalem, fled to areas where they felt more secure. Frend emphasizes Jewish hostility toward the Church, noting that "synagogues were fountainheads of persecution" (Tertullian, *Scorpiace* 10 and *Ad Nationes* 1.14), as indicated by Justin's reference (*Dialogue with Trypho* 16.4) to Jews cursing the Christians in the synagogue, Eusebius's (*Historia Ecclesiastica* 5.16.12) to Jews beating them in the synagogues, Justin's (*Dialogue with Trypho* 17.1) and Origen's (*Against Celsus* 6.27 and *Commentary on Deuteronomy* 31.21) to the spreading of anti-Christian rumors, and actual assistance by Jews at persecutions and martyrdoms (*Martyrdom of Polycarp* 13 and 17).[118]

On the other hand, one major reason why the Jews so bitterly resented the attraction Paul had exercised on the "sympathizers" was fear that he would draw gifts away from their synagogues;[119] hence Paul's frequent declaration (e.g., Acts 20:33–35) that he had accepted no gifts from his adherents. Indeed, apparently, the "G-d-fearers" made important financial contributions to the synagogues. One such θεοσεβής, a woman named Capitolina from the city of Tralles, not far from Aphrodisias, helped construct a synagogue in her native city (*CIG* 2924).[120]

8. FACTORS THAT ATTRACTED NON-JEWS TO JUDAISM IN THE THIRD CENTURY

In the fourth century John Chrysostom realized the gravity of the challenge that the Judaizers posed to the Church, because, as he says (*Adversus Judaeos* 1.6.852), if the Jewish rites are holy, the way of Christianity must be false. Indeed, even a half century after Constantine had given licit status to Christianity, and with three-quarters of the population of the great city of Antioch professing Christianity, Chrysostom was unable to halt the attraction of Judaism to Christians.

Apparently, so many Christians were attracted to Jewish practices that Chrysostom warns (8.4.933) his listeners not to reveal how many, lest the public reputation of the Church should suffer. Perhaps, we may suggest, Chrysostom's own sermons might have increased Christian interest in the synagogues, especially in view of his stress on ascetic practices that might well have made going to church less "entertaining" than it had been under his predecessors. How much greater, at least ostensibly, the attraction of the synagogues may have been in the previous century, when the Church was being persecuted and when Judaism enjoyed its traditional special privileges! Thus, the *Apostolic Constitutions*, from Syria, remarks on the attraction that the synagogue had for Christians (8.47, 65, and 71). Indeed, we may well ask how, if Christianity had finally, by the second century, come to be distinct from Judaism, there continued to be such steady crossing over into Judaism, at least in certain practices and customs.

What were the factors that led Jewish Christians to continue to practice their formerly Jewish usages and that attracted non-Jews, and perhaps Christians in particular,[121] to the synagogue, whether simply to visit or to become "sympathizers" (θεοσεβεῖς) or even full-fledged proselytes?

In the first place, we may mention the attractions of former centuries, notably the reputation of the Jews for wisdom and the other cardinal virtues, as well as the economic factors that we have already noted. But now there were additional factors, especially applicable at this time.

The third century, in particular, has been termed an "age of anxiety," in which people suffered from a failure of nerve and sought relief through religious experiences.[122] The period saw a quest for identity among both individuals and societies;[123] and this will explain why a relatively large number of intellectuals became believers in various religions during the second and third centuries. Brown describes the new mood of the third century as one that substituted holy people for sacred things and that, consequently, led to an increasing interest on the part of both pagans and Christians in "conversion."[124] Among the special factors that attracted non-Jews to become "sympathizers" with Judaism at this time, we may mention the following:

1) We may suggest, as we have noted above, that even those Jews who stayed in the Church may have influenced Christians toward Jewish ways and were perhaps suspected, as were some of the later Conversos (the so-called Marranos) of fifteenth-century Spain, of pretending conversion in order to subvert Christians.[125] Hence, this seems the most understandable explanation of the reason why conversion to Christianity was made more difficult for Jews than it was for others.[126] In this connection, we may recall Jerome's satirical remark (*Epistulae* 112.13) that if it is permitted for Jewish Christians to continue to observe their Jewish ways "they will not become Christians but they will make us Jews."

2) Another source of attraction to Judaism in Asia Minor was that the Jews were so deeply Hellenized and that they consequently had a common language of discourse with non-Jews. As early as the fourth century B.C.E., we hear of a Jew, as we have noted, who met Aristotle in Asia Minor and who was so deeply Hellenized that Aristotle remarked that he had the soul of a Greek (Clearchus of Soli, quoted in Josephus, *Against Apion* 1.180).[127]

3) The long history of loyalty of the Jews to the state, once the memory of the wars against Rome had faded, may have won them admiration not only from the regime but also from those who saw the empire teetering on the brink of dissolution in the third and following centuries.

Already in the sixth century B.C.E., the Persians had shown their high regard for this loyalty when they entrusted the protection of the highly sensitive border with Ethiopia to a Jewish garrison; and the Ptolemies in Egypt had likewise shown their trust in the Jews by enlisting them in arms and by selecting four of them to be commanders-in-chief.

4) In an era marked by extensive lawlessness and even anarchy, the Jews won respect for their regard for law and order; and even the church father Lactantius (*De Ira* 23.12) in the early fourth century admits that the Jews were praised by the oracle of Apollo for their respect for law. Likewise, Augustine (*De Civitate D-i* 19.23) cites the oracle of Apollo as adducing the Jews to support the view that law is preferable to reason. There are, moreover, a number of passages[128] in the Talmud in which the rabbis praise the Romans as G-d's agents for the administration of law. We may note, in particular, the supreme compliment paid to the Roman genius in law by the third-century Rabbi Resh Lakish (*Genesis Rabbah* 9.13) in his comment on Genesis 1:31: "And behold it was very good." This, he says, refers to the earthly kingdom (Edom, i.e., Rome), because the Hebrew consonants for the words *very* (*me'od*) and *man* (*'adam*) (Edom has the same consonants) are the same, though in a different order. How then, asks the rabbi, does the earthly kingdom merit such a compliment? His answer is that it exacts justice (for which the passage uses the Greek word δίκη [or δίκαιον], transliterated into Hebrew letters).

5) Among the Jews at Sardis, there are no fewer than nine city councillors and three Jews who were members of the Roman imperial administration of the province;[129] and we may conjecture that perhaps one reason why non-Jews adopted the status of θεοσεβεῖς was political, in order to win the support of the apparently populous and influential Jewish community. Apparently, then, the Jews of Asia Minor not only had special privileges but also functioned as full-fledged citizens and agents of government.

6) We may also suggest, as does the author of the *Martyrdom of Pionios* 13.1, a mid-third-century martyr, that prior to the Roman government's granting licit status to Christianity in 313, Christians may have been attracted to the synagogue as a shelter against persecutions, because the Jews continued to maintain their special privileges; hence, at the time of the Aphrodisias inscriptions in the third century, Judaism, being tolerated, was in a much better position than Christianity, which was then a prohibited religion.[130]

7) One of the attractions of Judaism, as we have remarked, was its antiquity, which even bitter opponents such as Tacitus[131] acknowledged. This antiquity was particularly appealing to Christians, inasmuch as critics of Christianity, such as the third-century philosopher Porphyry (in

his book *Philosophy from Oracles*), Celsus (quoted in Origen, *Against Celsus* 5.25), and the fourth-century Julian (*Contra Galilaeos* 43A) had attacked Christianity as an innovation, a latecomer, an upstart, which had chosen to depart from a tradition.

8) Pagans and Christians may also have been attracted to the synagogue because of the reputation of Jews for ethical behavior. Even so bitter an opponent of the Jews as John Chrysostom refers (*Homilia in Matthaeum* 36.3 [*PG* 57.417]) to their fortitude and perseverance in the face of adversity and is forced to admit that many Jews live virtuous lives.

9) In particular, we may note with Origen (*Against Celsus* 4.31) the reputation Jews had for incorruptible judges. Hence, the Christians may well have preferred to go to these courts, particularly in matters concerning business.

10) People may also have been attracted to Judaism out of admiration for the Jews' philanthropy and lack of materialism. Indeed, even Chrysostom (*Homilia in Epistolam ad Philippenses* 9.4 [*PG* 62.251]) laments that many Christians are more materialistically inclined than Jews, pointing out that Jews do not complain about paying high salaries to their religious functionaries, whereas Christians resent having to pay priests.

11) Though there were occasional outbreaks between Jews and Christians, and though Jews and pagans sometimes joined against their common Christian opponents,[132] on the whole the two groups—Jews and Christians—were not hostile to each other. In addition, the social and legal changes of the aging empire must have greatly increased the importance of membership in societies such as Judaism, for mutual protection and self-help.

Moreover, it appears that, at least before 303, during the reign of Diocletian, both the worst anti-Jewish incidents and the most violent persecutions of Christians occurred in cities along the coast of Asia Minor, whereas in inland cities, such as, presumably, Aphrodisias, such incidents are rare. Apparently, bishops and presbyters were even friendly with Jews, so that the *Apostolic Constitutions*, written in Syria in the latter part of the fourth century, sternly declares that if a bishop or another cleric fasts with the Jews or feasts with them or receives gifts, such as unleavened bread for the Passover, from them, the cleric has been defiled and must be purified; if a Christian layman does so, the penalty is no less than excommunication. Indeed, we hear of a fourth-century bishop, Apollinaris of Laodicea, in Syria, whom Basil (*Epistulae* 265.2, 263.4) berates for urging the renewal of the Temple and the observance of worship "according to the Law."

In this connection, we may raise the question whether Christians would have attended services in a synagogue if the liturgy included a prayer cursing them.[133] However, we may note that even if this alleged curse refers to Christians, it is recited only on weekdays and not on Sabbaths and holydays, when apparently, to judge from the references in such church fathers as John Chrysostom, Christians attended the synagogue. Kimelman has argued that among early Christian authors only John (9:22, 12:42, 16:2) mentions exclusion of the Christians from the synagogue.[134] Justin Martyr (*Dialogue with Trypho* 137) states that the Jews scoff at Jesus (he says nothing about Christians) *after* their prayers. Jerome, in a letter to Augustine (112.13), and Epiphanius (*Panarion* 29.9.1) say that the Jews curse not the Christians but a particular group of Jewish Christians known as Nazoraeans.[135] Even if the reference in this benediction is to Christians, we may note that only those writers, namely Justin, Origen, Epiphanius, and Jerome, who had strong connections with Jews in the Land of Israel mention the prayer; Chrysostom, despite his bitter charges against Jews, makes no mention of it.[136]

Apparently, Christians took advantage of the invitation to eat and drink with Jews, as we see from the prohibition set forth in the Council of Elvira, in Spain ca 300, one of the canons (50) of which provides that neither clerics nor laymen should accept Jewish hospitality, on pain of being denied holy communion. Similarly, in the third of the Forged Canons of Nicaea (325), clergy are forbidden to eat with or even converse with Jews, on pain of excommunication. We may also note the strong language against such clergy in pseudo-Ephraem (ca. 410, in Thomas J. Lemy, ed., *Sancti Ephraemi Syri Hymni et Sermones* 2.399 and 411): "He who eats with the magicians shall not eat the body of our Lord, and he who drinks with the Jews shall not inherit life eternal. . . . Everyone who has eaten and drunk and mingled with the Jews enters thereby into the accusation that he has become the comrade of the crucifiers."

One of the inscriptions from Aphrodisias, according to its editors, mentions a πάτελλα, which may refer to a soup kitchen[137] or to some kind of dish for distributing food, to which those on the list of names that follows contributed. This, then, may have been one of the attractions to Judaism, or at any rate to the synagogue, especially on the part of those who were poverty-stricken.[138]

12) We must recognize that Jews were not ghettoized, especially because it appears that they were engaged, at least in the cities for the most part, in business and crafts, in constant contact with non-Jews. In cities where the population was cooped together in close quarters and where the street, as even today in many cases, was the living room, so to speak,[139] Jews and Christians must have had contacts, especially because, as in cities such as Aphrodisias, the Jews were predominantly businessmen and craftsmen. The fact that Hilary of Poitiers is said to have been

so orthodox in his Christianity that he would not eat with a Jew or even answer Jewish salutations in the street[140] is a stark indication that such contacts were usually commonplace.

Apparently, contacts between Christians and Jews were particularly common in communities such as Antioch—and we may guess in the populous cities of Asia Minor—where an orator such as John Chrysostom in the fourth century felt constrained to inveigh against the practice of Judaizing on the part of Christians. Once the same Chrysostom left Antioch for Constantinople, where Jews were apparently much less numerous, his references to Jews become far less frequent. Although at Antioch he tried to persuade the Christians that the number of Judaizers was not so great after all, it seems clear (*Adversus Judaeos* 1.3=PG 48.847) that his repeated attention to this problem indicates that they were indeed numerous, especially because (8.4.930) he warns Christians not to reveal how many the Judaizers were, lest the public reputation of the Church suffer.

13) Another economic reason for the close association of Jews and non-Jews was that Jews were ready and willing to lend money at interest to non-Jews, as we can infer from the prohibition in the third of the forged canons of Nicaea, dating from 325. On the other hand, that some priests lent money at interest to Jews seems indicated by the express prohibition in the forged canons of Nicaea (no. 52); that this was a serious problem is indicated by the punishment of excommunication for those who violated this order.

14) We may also suggest that the synagogues may have been attractive to non-Jewish businessmen for other economic reasons. If indeed it is important, as the inscriptions from Aphrodisias show, to list the occupations of donors, it may be that a particular synagogue attracted those who had certain occupations, just as we hear (*Sukkah* 51b) that in the great synagogue in Alexandria seating was by trade. Hence, people in specific trades may have come to the synagogue to meet those with whom they did business or who were members of the same craft. The omission of certain occupations—such as physicians, rhetoricians, grammarians, teachers, architects, and musicians—may therefore be an indication that this particular synagogue attracted those in certain occupations and not in others.

15) We may conjecture that one factor that may have led non-Jews to identify with Jews was a commercial one, because of the ten Aphrodisian Jews (admittedly a small sample) whose occupations are given, all are engaged in business, six being involved in the production of food (perhaps because of the necessity of adhering to the dietary laws), one being a ragpicker, one a bronze smith, one a goldsmith, and one a dealer in

horse fodder. The Jews' association with food gave them considerable importance, because a major concern of the magistrates of ancient cities was to see to it that bread was sold to the masses at reasonable prices.[141]

16) Religious factors, of course, played a key role in attracting non-Jews to Judaism. The general atmosphere of the third and fourth centuries, and especially in Asia Minor, fostered divergent movements within Christianity, several of which were Judaizing, such as the Hypsistarians of fourth-century Cappadocia, who retained the Sabbath and the dietary laws though they rejected circumcision; the Sabbatists of Cilicia; and the followers of Sambatha at Thyateira.

17) The enthusiasm that must have accompanied Julian's efforts to rebuild the Temple in the fourth century, even though these efforts had been unsuccessful, must have led to a feeling of euphoria. A half century later Jerome (*Commentary on Isaiah* 35:10) bitterly remarks that the Jews and the Judaizers anticipate entering the city of Jerusalem with gladness and renewing the sacrifices. The time is approaching, he adds, when the Jews and the Judaizers expect that all the precepts of the Law will be observed and that Jews will no longer become Christians but that Christians will become Jews. Likewise, in one of his letters (*Epistulae* 112.13), as we have noted, Jerome makes a very similar comment.

18) The Sabbath, as we may perceive from Juvenal (14.96), exercised a particular attraction to those who were "sympathizers" with Judaism. In the second century there were still Christians who observed the Sabbath, as we can surely see from Ignatius of Antioch's *Letter to the Magnesians* (9.1), the allurement being, as he indicates, an opportunity for relaxation of the body, for eating appetizing foods especially prepared for the Sabbath, and for dancing and rejoicing. John Chrysostom (*Adversus Judaeos* 1.5.850, 8.8.940; and *Homiliae* 1.7 [*PG* 61.623]) likewise refers to the many Christians who keep the Sabbath with the Jews. Indeed, Chrysostom (*Homiliae in Romanos* 12.20.3 [*PG* 51.176]) remarks with obvious bitterness that Christians should be ashamed and embarrassed by their religious laxity as compared with the zealousness of the Jews who observe the Sabbath with such devotion and who refrain with such meticulousness from engaging in business as the Sabbath approaches.

We may also suggest that Christians were attracted to attend the synagogue on the Sabbath, where they listened to some of the same passages from the Jewish Scriptures which they heard in Christian churches, but expounded with greater authority because the Jews claimed to have the original text. This was, in any case, part of the "penalty" the Church paid for incorporating the Jewish scriptures as part of their canon, instead of following the lead of the Marcionites in excluding these books. The fact that at the Council of Laodicea in the fourth century it was decreed

(Canon 16) that only the New Testament was to be read on the Sabbath ?
would appear to indicate that many Christians apparently preferred to
hear the Jewish Scriptures read and expounded on that day.

19) Some non-Jews may have discovered the synagogue through acting as "Sabbath *goyim*," that is, performing certain tasks on the Sabbath
and holidays that were prohibited to Jews. This will explain the ruling
(*Apostolic Canons* 62, 65, 70, 71) that forbade Christians to carry oil to a
synagogue or to light lamps on Jewish festivals.

20) In particular, non-Jews were attracted to the celebration of Jewish
festivals, as evidenced notably by the Syrian Church Father Aphrahat,
who in his first homily (ca 345) enjoins his readers to abstain from observing the Sabbaths, new moons, and festivals of the Jews. Likewise,
seven of the eight homilies against Judaizers delivered in such strong
language by Chrysostom preceded the Jewish High Holidays in the autumn, with the remaining one being given immediately before Passover.
The *Apostolic Canons*, similarly dating from the mid-fourth century, warn
(Canon 69) bishops and other clerics not to join the Jews in celebrating
their feasts and fasts. The Council of Laodicea in Asia Minor in 360
(Canon 37) similarly forbids the Christians from accepting gifts from the
feasts of Jews or celebrating feasts with them. Apparently, it was women,
as in the first century, who continued to be especially attracted to Judaism because of the Jewish holidays, so that Chrysostom (*Adversus Judaeos*
2.3.860) charges Christian husbands with the responsibility of keeping
wives from going to the synagogues.

In particular, the Jewish Passover seems to have had an attraction for
Christians, perhaps because it was, according to the Gospels, the occasion for Jesus' Last Supper. So widely prevalent was the joint feasting of
Christians with Jews on the Passover that in 341 the Council of Antioch
(Canon 1) passed legislation prohibiting Christians from dining at Passover with Jews, though perhaps this law is directed merely or mainly at
the Quartodecimans, who celebrated the Christian Passover on the same
date as the Jews did, namely the fourteenth of the Jewish month of Nisan.
Canons 38 and 69 of the Council of Laodicea in Asia Minor in 360 warn
against accepting gifts of unleavened bread from Jews on Passover, which
was apparently a widespread practice, the penalty for clergy being exclusion from the clergy and for laypeople excommunication.

The Quartodecimans were especially strong in Asia Minor,[142] where,
we hear, Polycarp and the bishop Polycrans insisted that this Passover
date, which had been observed of old, should not be discarded, despite all
efforts from the Popes Anicetus and Victor to get him to abandon it. The
fact that Melito, who was a Quartodeciman, attacked the Jews so bitterly
in his *Peri Pascha* may well be an indication that he himself and the Quartodecimans generally were under attack (and perhaps for good reason) as

Judaizers, just as many centuries later the Hussites countered the charge that they were Judaizers by bitterly attacking the Jews.[143] The Church historian Socrates, as late as the fifth century (7.29), notes that the Quartodecimans were centered in the provinces of Asia, Lydia, and Caria (and we should note that Sardis was the capital of Lydia and Aphrodisias of Caria).

Rosh Hashanah, with its prominent blowing of the ram's horn, likewise attracted Christians, as we can see from John Chrysostom (*Adversus Judaeos* 1.5.851). The rabbis, as we have seen, declare that even the *yirei shamayim* join with the Jews in not wearing leather shoes on Yom Kippur; and John Chrysostom (1.2.846) likewise berates those Christians who on that day fast with the Jews and go to the marketplace and watch the Jews "dance with naked feet."[144] The Judaizers likewise, according to Chrysostom, joined the Jews in "pitching their tents," that is, erecting tents for the holiday of Sukkoth (*Adversus Judaeos* 7.1.915).

21) The central feature of the Sabbath service in the synagogue, then as now, was the reading of a portion of the Pentateuch. Apparently, the presence of the scrolls of the Torah and of the prophets must have impressed Christians into believing, as Chrysostom (*Adversus Judaeos* 1.4.848) notes, that the synagogue was a holy place. Books in general aroused awe in antiquity, and Jewish books apparently elicited particular reverence, especially because Christian books were written more and more frequently in the form of a codex similar to a modern book, whereas the Torah of the Jews continued to be written in the form of a parchment scroll. The Jewish scrolls engendered fear and veneration, especially on the part of those Christians, such as Jerome, who realized the implication of the fact that the Septuagint was a mere translation of the Hebrew original, the *Hebraica veritas*.[145] The very fact that the Torah was a secret book (Juvenal, 14.102) that Jews were not permitted, according to the third-century Rabbi Ammi (*Ḥagigah* 13a), as we have noted, to teach to Gentiles, may well have piqued curiosity. Consequently, as John Chrysostom bitterly remarks (*Adversus Judaeos* 1.4.848), "Some think the synagogue is a holy place because the Law and the books of the prophets can be found there." Hence, Chrysostom frequently (1.3.847, 1.5.850, 6.6.913, 6.7.914) found it necessary to combat the belief that these scrolls rendered the synagogue holy. The ark in which the scrolls was kept, he argues (6.7.914), has no tablets of the Law; and the synagogue (which claimed to be the Temple in miniature) possesses no holy of holies, no veil, no high priest, no incense, and no sacrifices. Indeed, during the patristic period, so important were the Jewish scriptures, especially the prophetic books, to the claims of Christianity that at least as many commentaries were written by Christians on the Jewish Scriptures as on the New Testament;[146] and the Psalms became the Christian prayer

book par excellence. The Jews had the ἀρχεῖοι, the ancient archives, as Ignatius (*Letter to the Philadelphians* 8.2) remarks, whereas the Christians apparently felt self-conscious about having firsthand knowledge of only the much more recent κήρυγμα about Jesus.

22) Moreover, non-Jews were apparently impressed by the ancient oaths that were taken before Torah scrolls (*Shevuoth* 38b). Chrysostom (*Adversus Judaeos* 1.3.847) bitterly recalls that he saw a woman who had been forced into a synagogue by a Christian in order to take an oath about some business matters. When asked why he had taken her into a synagogue, the Christian replied that many had told him that the oaths that were taken there were more awesome.

23) In addition to the holy scrolls of the Torah in the synagogue, another attraction was apparently the relics of Jewish martyrs. The Maccabean martyrs, whose tale was prominent in the first two books of the Maccabees, which were part of the Christian canon, had even come to be accepted as saints (indeed, as forerunners of Jesus' martyrdom); they were, after all, Jews who had given their lives for Jewish religious practices, including abstention from pork (Chrysostom, *Homilia de Eleazaro et Septem Pueris* 1.63=PG 525). We hear from John Malalas that there was a synagogue in Antioch built on the supposed remains of the Maccabean martyrs which passed from Jewish to Christian control sometime during the fourth century. For the Christian "the blood of the martyrs is the seed of the Church" (Tertullian, *Apology* 50). Hence, Christians who admired such marytrs and looked for miracles and cures from them, as they did from other saints, might well have sought to emulate them in their observance of the Law. Bickerman finds the enshrining of such relics foreign to Judaism, and attributable to later Christian influence on Antioch's Jews;[147] but this presupposes, perhaps wrongly, that Jews in the Diaspora would not adopt such a practice because it was alien to the Jews of Palestine.

24) Apparently, one of the attractions of the synagogue was what Chrysostom bitterly refers to as its theatricality. He actually accuses the Jews of bringing into the synagogue troupes of actors and dancers (1.2.27.847, 2.3.4.861, 4.7.3.881, 7.1.2.915). He notes the accompaniment of drums, lyres, harps, and other musical instruments at services in the synagogues; we may guess that he is referring to wedding or Purim celebrations. So also Jerome, in his commentary on Ezekiel (34:1), states that Jewish preachers, in a theatrical manner, rouse up applause and shouting.[148]

25) The Mishnah, as exposition of the Bible, also apparently served as a point of attraction, as we may deduce from the exhortation of Christians in the *Didascalia Apostolorum*, dating from somewhere between the middle of the second to the middle of the fourth century, neither to

venerate nor to observe the rites contained in the "Second Legislation" (presumably the Mishnah).[149]

26) The Jewish ritual baths for both women and men, which John Chrysostom (*Catechism* 1.2–3 [*PG* 49.225–26]) admits are more solemn than ordinary baths, also attracted non-Jews, especially in view of the general popularity of baths in the Roman Empire. Theodoret, a fifth-century Christian raised in Antioch in Syria, later bishop in the neighboring city of Cyrrhus, mentions (*In Hebraeos* 6.4 [*PG* 82.717]) Christians who went to ritual baths with the Jews, where they presumably socialized with them; and indeed the *Apostolic Constitutions* (7.44) warns Christians against participation in Jewish baths. The crime of such participation was regarded as particularly heinous because the offending Christians thus sowed disruption in the Church (Chrysostom, *Adversus Judaeos* 3.1.861).

27) Some may have been attracted to Judaism because of their admiration for Jewish astronomers, whose reputation, as the fourth-century Firmicus Maternus (*Mathesis* 4. prooemium 5, 17.2, 17.5, 18.1) attempts to show, went back even to Abraham. Inasmuch as the Jewish calendar was determined by observation of the heavens, they may have felt more confidence in it than in the Christian calendar; and hence, in connection with the date of Easter in particular, as we have seen, they may have been skeptical of the date adopted by the majority of the Church. Thus, Chrysostom bitterly complains (*Adversus Judaeos* 3.3.865) that the Judaizing Christians choose to ignore the date of Easter determined by the Council of Nicaea, thinking "the Jews to be wiser than the fathers of Nicaea." He notes that they justify their stand by arguing that theirs is the older practice of the Church in Antioch. The importance of this issue is apparent from the fact that Chrysostom devoted an entire sermon to it.

28) The Jews' reputed skill in astrology may likewise have proved to be an attraction.[150] Indeed, Hadrian (*Scriptores Historiae Augustae, Quadrigae Tyrannorum* 8.3) in the second century remarks that there is no chief of a synagogue who is not an astrologer (*mathematicus*), soothsayer (*haruspex*), or anointer (*aleptes*). Moreover, in the middle of the second century, Vettius Valens, in his astrological work *Anthologiae* (2.28–29) refers to Abraham as a most wonderful (θαυμασιώτατος) astrological authority. Furthermore, Abraham's skill in astrology is mentioned no fewer than four times in Firmicus Maternus's astrological treatise, the *Mathesis* (4.proemium 5, 17.2, 17.5, and 18.1). Firmicus's contemporary Julian (*Contra Galilaeos* 356C) remarks that Abraham employed the method of divination from shooting stars and from the flight of birds. Because, we may remark, proselytes are regarded as children of Abraham, himself the first proselyte, they would presumably identify with him as an astrologer.

29) Another attraction held out by Jews to non-Jews was the Jewish reputation for magic and the occult.[151] Juvenal (6.544–47), at the begin-

ning of the second century, satirizes Jewish women who sell dream interpretations at bargain prices. Juvenal's younger contemporary Lucian
(*Philopseudeis* 16) tells of a Syrian from Palestine (presumably a Jew) who,
for a large fee, was able to exorcise evil spirits and thus restore people to
sanity.

In catalogues of great magicians, such as those presented by Pliny the
Elder (*Naturalis Historia* 30.11) in the first century and by Apuleius in the
second century (*Apologia* 40), Moses, as we have noted, occupies a prominent place.[152] Likewise, in the second century, Lucian (*Tragodopodagra*
171–73) speaks of Jews who exercise spells. The source of this knowledge
of magic was said (Clearchus of Soli, in his tract *On Education*, cited in
Diogenes Laertius 1.9) to be the Magi.[153] Celsus (quoted in Origen,
Against Celsus 1.26), in the second century, moreover, declares that the
Jews are addicted to sorcery, of which Moses was their teacher. Indeed,
as we have remarked, Moses was reputed to be the author of several magical books and charms. Also, in the magical papyri we find various names
of G-d,[154] as well as appeals to and prayers of Adam, Abraham, Isaac, and
especially Jacob, and a trance of Solomon that is guaranteed to work for
children and adults (*PGM* 4.850–929). Furthermore, Bonner, Goodenough, and Gager[155] have shown that among the tremendous array of
amulets, phylacteries, and recipes on papyri, the number of items with no
Jewish element at all is small. In addition, the Hebrew *Sefer Ha-Razim*[156]
(the *Book of Mysteries*, ed. by Mordecai Margolioth), which dates perhaps
from the third or fourth century, contains the names of countless angels
and other heavenly beings who are likewise mentioned in the magical
papyri. Though written in Hebrew and though showing considerable
acquaintance with rabbinic expression, this work contains many Greek
terms and recipes similar to those we find in Greek and other magical
papyri and in amulets; it even contains directions on how to win at horse
racing and how to find favor with a beautiful woman. Such advice, we
may guess, would seem to be very helpful to Jew and non-Jew alike. Likewise, in the fourth century, Julian (*Contra Galilaeos* 354B) speaks of the
Jews' skill in theurgy, that is, the art of getting a god to do one's bidding
through magic.[157] In the same breath he states that the Jews had learned
the practice of arcane science during their sojourn in Egypt; and one may
guess that he implies that they had also acquired their skill in magic from
the Egyptians, who were renowned for it.[158]

We may guess that a major reason for the eagerness on the part of
Christians to have their fields blessed by Jews, an act expressly prohibited
(Canon 49) by the Council of Elvira in Spain (ca 300) on pain of no less
a penalty than excommunication, was that the recipients believed that
this blessing was more effective than any benediction by a priest. We may
suggest that the prohibition (Canon 36) by the Council of Laodicea in
the fourth century of the making of τὰ λεγόμενα φυλακτήρια ("the objects

called phylacteries" [*tefillin*]) may reflect a view that these phylacteries served as magical amulets. The attraction thus to Judaism because of the Jews' reputation in magic must have been great because magic and alchemy moved up the social ladder in the later empire and in the process became more systematic and less "popular," thus gaining in respectability through the allegedly increased intellectual content.[159]

30) We may note that Jews played a particularly important role in alchemy; and here again the name of Moses appears prominently in lists of practitioners.[160] We hear of a Jewish woman named Maria,[161] who apparently lived at the beginning of the third century and who was well-known among alchemists. Likewise, the name of Solomon is prominent as one who, according to the fifth-century Zosimus, learned his wisdom from the Egyptian king Mambres.[162] The important point is that the contributions of Jewish alchemy were borrowed and preserved by non-Jews in collections designed for general use.

31) Jewish skill in effecting cures[163] may likewise have attracted non-Jews. It is strikingly true that in the relatively long list of occupations of Jews in Aphrodisias, no physician is mentioned;[164] but to judge from John Chrysostom's sharp strictures (*Adversus Judaeos* 8.5.934), Jews were said to possess spells, amulets, and potions that were powerful in curing illnesses. It is better to die than to be healed in this way,[165] he concludes; but apparently there were many who, when actually confronted with the choice, chose to go to these alleged miracle men. It seems, to judge from Chrysostom (8.5.6.935 and 8.8.7–9.940–41), that Christians who sought healing went to the synagogues because they were so sure that the Jews, through their incantations, would cure them; Jesus, he bitterly adds (8.5.936), had no need of charms or incantations or the help of various divine potentates in order to effect his healings. Indeed, we hear (Chrysostom 8.6.936) of Jewish sorcerers coming to the houses of Christians with potions. We are told, moreover, that Christians would sleep over-night in the synagogue of Matrona at Delphne, a suburb of Antioch—a practice clearly reminiscent of what pagans did at the temples of Asclepius. In particular, King Solomon, as we have remarked, was regarded as having magical property to heal, as we see on papyri and amulets and in such a work as the fourth-century *Medicina Plinii*,[166] where his name provides a cure to tertian fever.

As for Aphrodisias itself, there is no certainly pre-Constantine Christian material other than one account of Christian martyrs who are said to have been lynched under the Emperor Decius or Diocletian in the third century.[167] The first bishop from Aphrodisias of whom we hear, Ammonius, appeared at the First Council of Nicaea in 325, but we know nothing further about him. To be sure, Aphrodisias was represented by various bishops at succeeding councils, but we hear nothing specific about the nature of Christianity at Aphrodisias until the fifth century. There is, however, evidence of the existence of what seems to be a fourth-century church south of the theater in Aphrodisias, but no inscriptions have been found in it. We may, nevertheless, comment that if it had not been for the discovery, truly by chance, of the astounding inscriptions described by Reynolds and Tannenbaum, we would have known next to nothing about Aphrodisias's Jews and their supporters. These inscriptions, indeed, highlight the fact that after the Apostolic age Christians may have preached to Jews and converted them but Jews also attracted others, presumably including Christians, as proselytes or, more usually, "sympathizers."

The most likely explanation, however, why in the Aphrodisias inscriptions only three people[168] are designated as proselytes in contrast to fifty-four θεοσεβεῖς is that few attempted or dared to violate the prohibition on proselytism, even if it was hardly enforced. From a letter of Julius Africanus to Aristeides (cited in Eusebius, *Historia Ecclesiastica* 1.7.13), which refers to those called γειώρας (i.e., Hebrew *gerim*, "proselytes") as being of mixed parentage, we may surmise that most proselytes during that period were the result of intermarriage and had one Jewish parent. What is amazing is that despite tremendous losses of perhaps two million lives in the seventy years between the outbreak of the first rebellion against the Romans in 66 c.e. and the end of the Bar Kochba rebellion in 135 c.e.,[169] the Jews were able not only to withstand the challenge of Christianity but also to consolidate their ranks and to produce the great literature of the Talmud and the Midrashim. Finally (perhaps, in part, in response to the challenge of Christianity), even after the empire became Christian and actually legislated against proselytism by Jews, the Jews continued to engage successfully in winning proselytes and especially "sympathizers" to their ranks—a genuine tribute to their inherent vitality.

What kept these "sympathizers" from becoming full proselytes? Baron suggests that one major obstacle was the obligation that good citizens of pagan municipalities were obliged to worship the local deities, whereas Judaism forbade this worship.[170] Apion's accusation (*Against Apion* 2.68) that the Jews fomented sedition may have arisen from the Jews' refusal to show loyalty by worshipping the state's gods. Though born Jews were exempt from this requirement, those converted to Judaism who failed to do so were charged with the crime of "atheism." Nevertheless, the accusation of atheism was made against born Jews as well, as we have noted in the attacks of Apollonius Molon (cited in Josephus, *Against Apion* 2.148). Perhaps these friends of Judaism hesitated to take the final step of associating with the Jewish nation, which might lead to the charge of double loyalties. In any case, the reasons why "sympathizers" did not become full proselytes varied with time and place.[171]

CHAPTER 11

PROSELYTISM BY JEWS IN THE THIRD, FOURTH, AND FIFTH CENTURIES

1. ISSUES

Most scholars hold that for practical purposes, after the massive defeats of the Jews in the uprisings of 66–74, 115–17, and 132–35, proselytism by Jews ceased because of the penalty of death imposed by the Romans for proselytism and because of the Gentiles' tremendous hatred owing to Jewish success in winning converts in the preceding centuries—hatred that drove the Jews into isolation. Moreover, these scholars look on Judaism as "declining" precisely to the extent that Christianity rose. This view has been contested by Simon,[1] but no one has made a systematic study of the evidence to be found in imperial laws, Church councils, the writings of church fathers, the Talmudic corpus, and inscriptions. Over forty years have elapsed since Simon's own study, which must now be corrected and supplemented in view of further evidence, particularly epigraphic. Furthermore, we must distinguish more carefully among the nuances involved in organized, active missionary activities by Jews; readiness by Jews to accept converts but without active measures to do so; grudging acceptance of converts; adoption of certain practices of Judaism without actual conversion; and merely favorable disposition of Gentiles to Jews and Judaism.[2] Indeed, a thorough critical study of Jewish proselytism during this period does not exist.[3]

The third century is one of the great turning points in world history,[4] the period of tremendous decline in the Roman Empire just before the shift from imperial paganism to Christianity. Unfortunately, our chief source for the political events of this period is the *Scriptores Historiae Augustae*, which is, at least in part, a historical romance by a fraudulent author.[5]

We are here concerned with the following issues in particular: 1) To what extent were the Jews active missionaries during the third, fourth, and fifth centuries? 2) To what degree did Jews continue to win proselytes during these centuries without actively seeking them out? 3) To what extent did Judaism withdraw into itself and refuse to confront the Church, restricting itself to a conflict in the realm of theory built around the interpretation of sacred texts?[6] 4) What were the factors that attracted Gentiles to adopt certain Jewish practices or to become full converts? 5) To what degree are the passages in the Talmud that are favorable to proselytism descriptive of the contemporary situation, and to what extent are they applicable to the time of the rabbis who are said to have spoken them? 6) What was the attitude toward proselytism by Jews on the part of the Roman imperial government, the nascent Christian church and its various sects (both leaders and rank and file), and the Jews, particularly the rabbis, themselves? 7) To what degree did these attitudes toward proselytism change with the triumph of Christianity at the beginning of the fourth century? 8) What is the relationship between the tremendous rise of anti-Jewish rhetoric in church fathers in the fourth century and the apparently continued ability of the Jews to win proselytes and "sympathizers" in the very century of Christian triumph?

Our major problem in attempting to answer these questions is the lack of source material. For this period we no longer have a Josephus, nor do we have a Jewish Eusebius to describe the history of the Jews during the centuries when the Church grew; and the rabbis, even in their haggadic discussions, show a singular lack of interest in historical matters, being concerned with exposition of texts and of the laws of Judaism. Pagan writers, to the extent that they do comment on religious currents in their own day, are more concerned with the Christians, presumably because the latter were aggressive missionaries but also because they were until the fourth century completely illegal, whereas the Jews as a corporate body had licit status. If the Jews had any success in winning proselytes or even in attracting Christians to their synagogues without actually converting them, this must have been extremely embarrassing to the Christians; and hence the comment of John Chrysostom (*Adversus Judaeos* 8.4; *PG* 48.933) is significant when he advises Christians to keep silent about the success of the Jews in attracting Christians to their synagogues. As to inscriptions, we would not expect proselytes to advertise the fact that they were converts, especially when such conversions were illegal.

One major question we must attempt to answer is whether the evidence of the laws forbidding conversion to Judaism or the comments of the church fathers attesting to conversion indicate actual pressure or a threat or whether they are merely responding to what they considered theological insults. At this point we must stress the cumulative nature of the evidence. In and of itself each piece of the evidence may perhaps be explained away as a mere response to a theological insult; but when we find law after law and comment after comment by Church canons and fathers and rabbinic authorities, coupled with inscriptions, the likelihood that we are dealing with real threats and not mere theological insults is increased.

2. The Sources: Roman Imperial Legislation

The most important evidence for the continuation of Jewish proselytism (and it is clear that we are here speaking not of active organized missionary activities by Jews but rather of readiness to accept proselytes) during the third, fourth, and fifth centuries is to be found in Roman imperial legislation. The Romans realized that conversion to Judaism meant adherence not merely to a religion but also to a political state; hence, once Judaea was annexed, conversion had dangerous political overtones the Romans could hardly tolerate, especially in view of the three national revolts of the Jews against the Romans in 66–74, 115–17, and 132–35. This sensitivity on the part of the Romans must have been further aggravated by their long frontier and by the constant struggles with the great national enemy, the Parthians, as well as with the barbarians to the north, and no less with the continuing rebellions by native tribes within the empire. The existence of a large Jewish community in the Parthian Empire, one that might have aroused further unrest and even rebellion, must have added to the uneasiness of the Romans.

Indeed, all the fears that the Jews would again rebel came to pass in the year 351, during the reign of the Emperor Constantius, presumably in response to Christian persecution. In that year, under a leader named Patricius,[7] whom, according to Aurelius Victor, the Jews made king, the Jews in the Land of Israel revolted in an uprising of some importance.[8]

According to the *Scriptores Historiae Augustae* (*Vita Hadriani* 14.2), the ban on circumcision had provoked the Jews under Bar Kochba in 132 to revolt against the Romans.[9] But it should be noted that the decree (Modestinus, *Digest* 48.8.11) by Hadrian's successor, Antoninus Pius, permitting circumcision specifically states that Jews are allowed to circumcise their sons; it would appear that the permission did not extend to the circumcision of non-Jewish converts to Judaism.[10] Indeed, in wording his rescript in this fashion, Antoninus Pius was, it would seem, striking a bargain whereby, in return for the right of full practice of their religion, the Jews were to give up proselytism.[11] This conclusion, however, is hard to accept, because if Antoninus really sought to end proselytism by Jews he surely must have realized that prohibiting circumcision, even if enforced, would not stop the Jews from converting women; and all our evidence, such as we have it, indicates that women were converted to Judaism in larger, even much larger, numbers than men—presumably, in part at least, because circumcision was an operation that entailed a considerable amount of pain and a certain amount of danger.[12] Indeed, the fact that Justin Martyr (*Dialogue with Trypho* 8.4, 23.3–5, 123.1), writing during the reign of Antoninus Pius, speaks of circumcision of proselytes as if it were a commonplace occurrence, with no suggestion that it was illegal, indicates either that the law did not prohibit circumcision of proselytes or that the law was not enforced.[13]

The first specific ban on proselytism (both of men and women) was promulgated, apparently in 198/199 during his visit to Judaea, by the Emperor Septimius Severus (*Scriptores Historiae Augustae, Septimius Severus*, 17.1), who, without indicating any reason or motive, forbade people, under heavy penalties (*sub gravi poena*) from becoming Jews (*Iudaeos fieri*). The fact that this law is found in the extremely suspect *Scriptores Historiae Augustae* and does not appear in any of the codifications of law or in any more respectable literary source makes one wonder, to be sure, about its authenticity;[14] but if Stern is correct in accepting its historicity,[15] this is an indication that proselytism had continued. The ban on proselytism issued by Septimius Severus was, however, ineffective. Eusebius (*Historia Ecclesiastica* 6.12.1) cites the example of a certain Domnus, who converted from Christianity to Judaism during the persecution of the Christians in Egypt at the beginning of the third century; quite obviously it was less of a danger at that time to convert to Judaism than to convert to Christianity. The continuation of proselytism is evident also from a passage in Dio Cassius (37.17.1), apparently written in the reign of Caracalla (211–17), which speaks in the present tense of those of "alien race who affect (ζηλοῦσι, "show zeal for") their customs."[16]

That proselytism, in the sense of full conversion, continued until the end of the century is clear from the *Sententiae* (5.22.3–4) of the jurist Paul, who completed his work shortly before the year 300 and who reflects legal conditions just before that time. Constantine granted legal authority to his work, and this status was reaffirmed in the Law of Citations in 426. The law referred to by Paul imposed the punishment of exile and confiscation of property on non-Jews who allowed themselves to be circumcised and condemned to death the ritual circumcisers who performed the operations.

That proselytism, again in the sense of full conversion, continued nevertheless to be practiced by Jews would seem to be evident from the fact that of the 66 laws in the *Codex Theodosianus* (compiled in 438) pertaining to Jews, 14 (21 percent) deal with proselytism of free men and 12 (18 percent) deal with the conversion of slaves. In addition, two (3 percent) pertain to "G-d-fearers." Indeed, we can see that the questions of conversion and of attraction of Gentiles to Judaism were by far the single most important issues pertaining to the Jews on which the emperors legislated and that the issues remained unresolved, at least to the satisfaction of the emperors, for centuries. It was a problem both in the Eastern and in the Western Roman Empire, as we can see from the fact that of those laws issued in the fourth century three are addressed to the *praefectus praetorio* in the East, and three are directed to the *praefectus praetorio* in the West. Of those promulgated in the fifth century, three are directed to the West and four to the East. The sheer vehemence and repetitiousness in the language found in these laws, as against the other laws pertaining to the Jews, is an indication of how much of a threat the emperors and their Church advisers perceived Jewish proselyting to be. Of these twenty-eight laws pertaining to proselytes and "sympathizers," two date from the third century, nine from the fourth century, fourteen from the fifth century, and three from the sixth century. We must bear in mind that we do not have all the legislation of the Roman emperors; thus, for example, the Emperor Julian, in one of his letters (204 [51, Bidez]), states that he has restored the rights taken away from the Jews, but we have no record of this legislation. Of course, one must place this evidence within the framework of what is known from other sources, archaeological and literary;[17] but legislators, whether then or now, in contrast perhaps to individuals, do not generally make a habit of combating abstracts, nor, so far as we know, did Roman emperors legislate merely to combat ideological threats.[18]

On the whole, there was no substantial change in the tradition of toleration of the Jews with the advent of the Christian Empire, inasmuch as the chancellery sought to maintain the appearance of continuity with the legislation of the emperors who had preceded.[19] Moreover, unlike their pagan predecessors, the Christian emperors, who looked on Christianity as the true Judaism, regarded Judaism as a religion rather than as a nationality and were thus eager, it would seem, to continue its toleration. And yet, whereas prior to the Christian triumph in the fourth century the Roman emperors had made only sporadic and ineffective attempts, as we have seen, to restrict proselytism, nevertheless, beginning with Constantine, the legislation, presumably under pressure from the hierarchy of the Church, becomes both more precise and more frequent.

The first in this progression of laws (*CT* 16.8.1) was issued in 329[20] by the Emperor Constantine, seventeen years after his vision of the cross. In it we find the statement that "if one of the people [whether pagans or Christians] shall approach their [i.e., the Jews'] nefarious (*nefariam*) sect and join himself to their conventicles [i.e., synagogues], he shall suffer with them the deserved punishments [presumably the exact punishment was left to the discretion of the judge]." Other than the word *nefariam*, which would seem to reflect the influence of Christian bishops, there appears to be hardly any difference between the tone of this law and that allegedly promulgated by Septimius Severus, which dates from a century before the triumph of Christianity; in fact, the severe punishments indicated in that law are not repeated here, and we are told merely that the punishments are to be those deserved by the violators of the law. It is more inclusive than the edict referred to by the jurist Paul in that it is not restricted to circumcision of men but speaks of conversion generally. This reassertion of the prohibition of proselytism was the first of many such laws issued by Christian emperors that gradually changed the status of the Jews.[21]

That intermarriage of Jewish men with non-Jewish women and the subsequent conversion of the wives to Judaism was a problem and a source of embarrassment to the newly victorious Church may be seen in the legislation (*CT* 16.8.6) decreeing capital punishment for all Jews who married women employed in the imperial weaving factories, "lest they join Christian women to their deeds of disgrace."[22] This law was issued by Constantius II in 339, a mere two years after he became emperor.

The next edict (*CT* 16.8.7) pertaining to proselytism was promulgated by the Emperor Constantius II in 353.[23] It is more explicit than the law issued by Constantine in that it specifies the punishment imposed on the Christian who converts to Judaism, namely confiscation of all his property. This is reminiscent of the law mentioned by the jurist Paul, except that in three respects it is less severe, namely in not prescribing the punishment of exile, in not imposing the death penalty on the physician who performed the circumcision, and in being applicable only to Christians and not to pagans who convert to Judaism; on the other hand, it is more inclusive, in that it applies the penalty of confiscation not only to men who are circumcised but to women as well. Again, the language is more strident, in that the Jews are said to have sacrilegious assemblies. Such modifications in language and especially in the penalties imposed are again clues that we are dealing with a real, not a phantom, threat, far more than with a theological insult.

Thirty years later (383) the Emperor Gratian went further (*CT* 16.7.3) in depriving of the power to bequeath in a will those who convert to Judaism. Unspecified penalties, but harsher ones than usual, were to be imposed on those who convert them.

A law issued in 388 by the Emperors Valentinian II, Theodosius I, and Arcadius (*CT* 3.7.2 and 9.7.5), reminiscent of the canons (16, 78) issued by the Council of Elvira many years earlier in 305 (306), forbade Jews from marrying Christian women and forbade Christians from marrying Jewesses, with the same penalty to be applied as in cases of adultery [i.e., death].[24] One would have thought that, unlike Judaism, which forbade intermarriages in the Torah (Exod 34:16, Deut 7:3), Christianity, in theory at least, should have welcomed intermarriages, which gave the Christians an opportunity to convert their Jewish partners to Christianity; but presumably the reason for such a harsh penalty was that in these cases the non-Jewish partner was not infrequently converted to Judaism.

A strikingly new feature in this law is that the right to accuse was allowed not merely to family members but to the general public, the implication being that such an intermarriage was to be considered a crime against all Christians. Linder conjectures that the assessment of such an act as a crime against the state was due to the influence of Bishop Ambrose, who had launched a vigorous campaign against such intermarriages in 385 (*Epistulae* 19=*PL* 16.982–84).[25]

Apparently, however, the Christian emperors had second thoughts, probably for economic reasons, about the campaign against the Jews. Thus the Emperors Theodosius I, Arcadius, and Honorius in 393 promulgated a law (*CT* 16.8.8) addressed to the master of soldiers in the East which states that the Jewish religion is not prohibited by law and that the emperors are gravely disturbed by the interdiction imposed in some places on assemblies by Jews and directs the Supreme Military Command in the East to protect synagogues from destruction. We may suggest that such a law, worded in such strong language, may well reflect attempts by Christians to attack synagogues. This may, in part, be evidence of a Christian response to the success of the Jews in attracting "sympathizers," because, as we have noted, there is considerable evidence that Christians were attending some synagogues, particularly on Sabbaths and before holidays. It is significant that this law was issued a short time after the Emperor Theodosius in the year 388 was browbeaten by the church father Ambrose to rescind his order to punish those responsible for the pillaging of a synagogue and its transformation into a church. Apparently the attacks continued, inasmuch as we find that in the year 397 the Emperors Arcadius and Honorius issued another law (*CT* 16.8.12) instructing the praetorian prefect of Illyricum to command the governors to assemble in order that they might be told that they must repel the assaults on the Jews and that the Jewish synagogues must remain in their accustomed places.

A law (*Constitutio Sirmondiana* 20.12 =*CT* 16.5.43, 16.10.19) issued in 407 clearly indicates the difficulty of enforcing the laws against heretical groups and the necessity of reissuing them, because it includes the statement that "we consider it necessary to reiterate what we had already ordered." In particular, the emperor singles out the "Heaven-fearers [*Caelicolarum*], who have meetings of a new doctrine unknown to me" (*CT* 16.5.43). These "Heaven-fearers," as we have noted, significantly bear the same name as do the *Yirei Shamayim* referred to by Rabbi Samuel ben Isaac (ca 300 C.E.), who, in raising the question whether or not the royal "Antoninus" was or was not a proselyte, cites the fact that he was seen on the Day of Atonement wearing a cutaway sandal and then adds that from this one cannot draw any definitive conclusion, because even "fearers of Heaven" (*Yirei Shamayim*) go out wearing such a sandal (Jerusalem

Talmud, *Megillah* 3.2.74a). These "Heaven-fearers" are apparently "sympathizers" with Judaism who observe certain Jewish practices without fully converting to Judaism.[26] It would seem that they are Christians, because the emperor warns them (*Codex Justinianus* 1.9.12) that "unless they return to G-d's cult and the Christian veneration, they too shall be attained by those laws with which we ordered that the heretics shall be constrained." We may conjecture that the attitude toward heretics and "G-d-fearers," was a matter of politics, because, in this case at any rate, the general Stilicho, aware of the deterioration of his position in the imperial court, attempted to switch alliances from the senatorial order and the pagan circles to the orthodox Christian circles.[27] The edifices of these "Heaven-fearers," we are informed, are to be turned over to the churches, but the penalty to be inflicted on the worshippers is evidently left to the discretion of the judges because a specific punishment is not indicated.

A year later (408) Stilicho was arrested and executed, but when widespread riots and violent assaults on the Catholic clergy broke out thereafter, a new law (*CT* 16.5.44) was issued accusing the Jews of working with the Donatist heretics in Africa in attacks on the orthodox Church, though again the exact punishment is not indicated. That the problem was not satisfactorily resolved is proved by the issuing, a year later (409), of still another law accusing the Jews of co-operating with heretical Christian groups in persecuting the orthodox Church. It would seem that the previous laws had not been implemented, because we are told that the Jews, the Donatists, and other heretics are not to think that the laws previously issued against them had "cooled down" (*tepuisse*). They are to realize that the judges are to implement the enforcement of all the laws previously passed against them. Again, the phrase "cooled down" in the laws indicates that the threat is real and has not diminished rather than that the issue is a mere theological insult.

That these laws were not enforced is indicated by the issuance in the same year of another law (*CT* 16.8.19) again referring to the "Heaven-fearers" as a "new crime" previously unheard of. It is clear that they are regarded as deviant Christians, because this time they are given a year to return to the orthodox Church. The law recognizes the link between becoming a "G-d-fearer" and taking the next step of becoming a convert to Judaism, because, in immediate juxtaposition to the provision about "G-d-fearers," it specifically refers to those who "force some to cease being Christian and adopt the abominable and vile name of the Jews." The law recognizes that this was a problem of long standing because it declares that those who have committed this crime are to be prosecuted under "the laws of the ancient emperors." Furthermore, the law apologetically states that "it does not bother us to admonish repeatedly" that

Christians shall not be forced to convert to Judaism. Again, such apparently frequent warnings hardly qualify as replies to mere theological insults: They are responding to real threats. That conversions to Judaism were still continuing is manifest from the extremely strong language condemning them, "for it is graver than death and crueler than massacre when someone abjures the Christian faith and becomes polluted with the Jewish incredulity." In apparent exasperation, the law no longer leaves the penalty to the discretion of the court but now goes to the extreme of declaring that such proselytizing is to be regarded as high treason (*maiestatis crimen*).

In a law issued in 415 (*CT* 16.8.22), the Emperors Honorius and Theodosius II accuse the Patriarch Gamaliel VI of fostering conversions to Judaism, because we are told that if he should attempt to defile any Christian or any sectarian with "the Jewish mark of infamy," that is, circumcision, he is to be subjected to the laws' severity—another indication that the law was not being enforced. From the fact that in this rescript the patriarch is deprived of the right to judge Christians, we may conjecture that one of Judaism's attractions for Christians was its court system, which was believed to be fairer than non-Jewish courts. That, indeed, non-Jews during this period did frequent Jewish courts may be seen from the requirement (Jerusalem Talmud, *Mo'ed Qatan* 3.3) that they present an arbitration document in order to be accepted by these courts.

A further indication of nonenforcement of the law and an increase in the severity of the punishment is evident in the issuance of still another law by the Emperors Honorius and Theodosius II in 423 (*CT* 16.8.26) declaring that the penalty to be inflicted on Jews who have circumcised a Christian or who have ordered one to be circumcised is confiscation of property and perpetual exile. The punishment was made even more severe in 438, when the Emperors Theodosius II and Valentinian III (*Novella* 3 = *Breviarium* 3) declared that whoever is guilty of converting a Christian, whether slave or freeborn, is to be subject both to confiscation of property and the death penalty. Such increases in the penalties are strong evidence that the problem is not merely theoretical nor a matter of sheer theological rhetoric. All of these laws, we may add, were incorporated into the Corpus of Justinian, whether in the *Codex* or the *Digest*.

Conversion of Slaves in Roman Imperial Legislation

Though the pagan emperors placed no restrictions on the acquisition of slaves by Jews, the Christian emperors soon attempted to reverse this toleration, though they sought, in general, to maintain continuity with the policies of their pagan predecessors. Indeed, it was on the subject of conversion of slaves to Judaism that the Christian Roman emperors were most insistent and repetitive.

There is ample evidence in rabbinic sources that slavery was practiced by Jews in the Talmudic period (first through fifth centuries).[28] Jewish law required conversion of non-Jewish slaves inasmuch as, among other factors, various tasks in the household, such as cooking and handling of wine, could be performed only by Jews.[29] Indeed, such conversions were considered to be the norm and highly meritorious from biblical times (Genesis 17:12–14, *Shabbath* 135a–b). Hence, laws on this subject represent real situations and can hardly be construed as mere theological insults.

As early as the end of the third century, even before Christianity became the official religion of the empire, we can see that the law (Paul, *Sententiae* 5.22.3–4) prohibited conversion to Judaism. That law also declared that Roman citizens who allowed their slaves to be circumcised in accordance with Jewish custom were to be subjected to exile and confiscation of property, with the death penalty actually being inflicted on the physicians who performed the operation. Moreover, Jews who circumcised the slaves they purchased from another nation were to be punished with banishment or death. That specific penalties are stated and that a choice is indicated also underlines the reality of the situation. The severity of these penalties is evident, in that banishment was harsher than exile—the one who was banished lost both citizenship and property, was usually sent in perpetual banishment to an island, and was liable to suffer capital punishment if he escaped from his place of banishment.[30] Indeed, in Roman penal law it was closest to the death penalty. The slave himself, however, was subject to no penalty, presumably because he was considered not to have free will.

On the matter of slaves, as in almost everything else, there is continuity in the legal tradition between the pagan and the Christian emperors. After Christianity became the official religion of the empire, a series of laws were enacted restricting ownership of non-Jewish slaves by Jews and prohibiting the conversion of slaves. The assumptions behind these enactments were that it was inappropriate for Jews to rule over Christians and that such ownership would normally culminate in conversion of the slaves to Judaism. The idea that it is not proper for Jews to rule over Christians may seem to reflect a theological insult; but the requirement, according to the Torah (Gen 17:27), that heathen slaves be circumcised and the prohibition against selling converted slaves to Gentiles lest they be drawn to apostasy (Mishnah, *Gittin* 4:6) indicate that we are dealing with a real threat. That these imperial laws met with frustration in their enforcement is clear not only from their constant reappearance but also from the fact that the emperors tried various approaches and adopted no clear-cut policy.

That such conversions were a real threat may also be deduced from the enactment of the *Constitutio Sirmondiana* 4 (cf. *CT* 16.9.1) by Constantine in 335, not so very long after his conversion to Christianity, forbidding conversion to Judaism of non-Jewish slaves. It begins by noting that it is a renewal of a repeated law. It declares that if a Jew buys and circumcises a slave, whether Christian or of any other sect, the circumcised slave is to be freed; but it indicates no penalty for the Jew who was guilty of converting the slave, presumably leaving the penalty to the court. Eusebius (*Life of Constantine* 4.27) states that Constantine went further in actually prohibiting the possession of Christian slaves by Jews, but we do not have any law to corroborate this statement.

Four years later, a law was issued by the Emperor Constantine II (*CT* 16.9.2), apparently responding to the failure of the previous law to halt such conversions. The matter had evidently become more serious, because this time the law prescribed the death penalty for the Jew who circumcised a slave whom he had bought.[31] If the failure to state a specific penalty in the previous law might be construed as reflecting a mere theological insult rather than an actual threat, surely the imposition of the death penalty now shows that this was more than a theoretical threat. Moreover, according to this law, for the mere purchase of Christian slaves the Jew was to be deprived of all Christian slaves in his possession.

That Jews continued to purchase Christian slaves and to convert them is clear from the law promulgated by the emperors Gratian, Valentinian II, and Theodosius I in 384 (*CT* 3.1.5) prohibiting both the purchase of Christian slaves by Jews and their conversion to Judaism. Apparently, the harsh law of 335 had been observed in the breach, and so we find here that when the Christian slave has been converted to Judaism, Christians are to redeem him by paying the Jew the price paid for the slave in the first place.

The Emperors Honorius and Theodosius II, in a law (*CT* 16.8.22) issued in Constantinople dated 415, declared, as we have noted, that if the patriarch Gamaliel or any of the Jews should attempt to "defile a Christian or a member of any sect whatsoever, slave and freeman alike, with the Jewish mark of infamy [i.e., circumcision], he shall be subjected to the laws' severity." Moreover, Christian slaves owned by Jews were to be handed over to the Church. That this policy was not working, however, may be seen from the promulgation less than a month later of a new law (*CT* 16.9.3) by the same emperors, this time in the West in Ravenna, permitting the Jews to possess Christian slaves on condition that the slaves be allowed to keep their religion. The law, furthermore, presumably in response to Jewish protests, declared invalid illegal judicial proceedings and confiscations of property of Jews carried out on the pretense that they possessed Christian slaves. Such specific and new details and such changes in the application of the existing laws indicate response to a fluid situation rather than theological insults.

Two years later, however, the Emperors Honorius and Theodosius II reversed themselves in a law (*CT* 16.9.4) that, once again, prohibited the acquisition by Jews, by purchase or gift, of Christian slaves, though it retreated from previous provisions by permitting Jews to inherit Christian slaves and to possess them on condition that they should not convert them to Judaism. Again, the penalty is reiterated for violation of the latter provision, namely death and confiscation of property. But whereas two years earlier the law transferred ownership of Christian slaves from their Jewish owners to the Church, it now stated that the slave would be set free.

The law prohibiting Jews from purchasing Christian slaves is repeated in 423 (*CT* 16.9.5) in even stronger language: "None of the Jews shall *dare* (*audeat*) to buy Christian slaves. For we consider execrable (*nefas*) that the most religious slaves be defiled by the mastery of the most impious (*impiisimorum*) buyers." The law adds that violators are to be punished without any delay—an indication that administrators had been slow in enforcing all the previous laws it was reiterating. And yet it is significant of the Jews' ability to influence the emperors that loopholes were left in the law, which ignored slaves already owned by Jews, as well as those who had been acquired by means other than purchase, such as gift or inheritance or birth.

But these laws were evidently not being enforced, because once again in 438 the emperors Theodosius II and Valentinian III promulgated a law (Theodosius II, *Novella* 3 = *Breviarium* 3) reiterating the death penalty and confiscation of property for converting a Christian slave. Indeed, as late as 527 (*Codex Justinianus* 1.10.2) the law was repeated forbidding a Jew or a Samaritan or anyone who is not a Christian from possessing a Christian slave and providing that the slave thus owned should be freed and that the owner should be fined. A few years later (534) the Emperor Justinian issued another law (*Codex Justinianus* 1.3.54 [56]) forbidding Jews, pagans, and heretics from owning Christian slaves. The law went further, moreover, in declaring that if pagan slaves wished to become Christians they were to be freed without any reimbursement to the owners. One would have thought that such a provision would lead all slaves belonging to Jewish owners to seek their freedom; but apparently many or most preferred to remain slaves under Jewish ownership, presumably because they were treated so well, rather than to become free and to expose themselves to dire economic circumstances. Again, such specific details about reimbursement reveal an actual situation and not mere rhetoric. The following year (535), Justinian (*Novella* 37) repeated the ban on possession and circumcision of Christian slaves.

Nonenforcement of Imperial Laws

The simplest explanation for this constant reiteration of legislation pertaining to conversion by Jews is that the laws were not being obeyed; as MacMullen[32] has so epigrammatically put it, "emperors had to shout to be heard—and were still ignored." Indeed, even when the Roman administrative system was apparently much better organized, a whole province, Egypt, could be dismissed as "ignorant of law, unused to civil rule" (Tacitus, *Histories* 1.11). Especially in the third century, utter chaos was enveloping the Roman Empire at the very time when the challenge of the barbarian invasions was becoming most serious. During the period from 235 to 284, only fifty years, there were twenty-four emperors (only one of whom died a natural death) and eight pretenders. A direct contemporary of these events, the Rabbi Ḥama bar Ḥanina, alluding to the constant wars between Rome and the Germans, states (*Megillah* 6b and *Genesis Rabbah* 75.9) that there were 300 crowned heads in Germany and 365 chieftains in Rome, and that every day they engage in combat and one of them is killed, so that they have the trouble of appointing a new king. These emperors, as the third-century Palestinian Eleazar ben Pedath remarks (Jerusalem Talmud, *Rosh Hashanah* 1.3.57a), regarded themselves as being above the laws. Thus, Ammianus Marcellinus (16.5.12), in the fourth century, has the Emperor Julian declare apologetically that "it is right that an Emperor of most merciful disposition shall rise above the laws." Indeed, these emperors often acted arbitrarily; thus, Rabbi Abbahu, who lived about the year 300 in Caesarea, the seat of Roman administration in Palestine, and who was held in high esteem by the Roman authorities, recounts an incident (*Tanḥuma* B, *Vaethḥanan* 6; *Deuteronomy Rabbah* 9.6) of how a high official found a precious Indian sword and presented it to the emperor, only to have the emperor show his ingratitude and willfulness by decapitating him with it.

No amount of force from above ever succeeded in ironing out all the local differences among the various provinces of the empire,[33] which are reminiscent of the tremendous variations among the provinces of the Ottoman Empire at the beginning of the twentieth century; hence, on many vital questions no decree could ever apply universally. Moreover, there is an obvious lack of clarity in much third- and fourth-century legislation which is due not only to the influence of rhetoricians seeking to outdo themselves and not only to the tradition of tyrannical powers accorded to magistrates but also to a carelessness arising from the necessity for the governors of the various provinces to interpret whatever the legislation said.

Furthermore, delays in the implementation of the law were proverbial; indeed, Constantine in 319 issued four directives seeking to alleviate the problem,[34] two of them concerned with the shortage of lawyers who abandoned cases hopelessly mired in bureaucracy, one concerned with bureaus that neglected to act before the statute of limitations expired, and a fourth dealing with bureau chiefs who spent endless time in deliberate inaction. When one considers how heavy a work load the emperor and his staff had, even a conscientious provincial administrator would have had difficulty getting a response from them in a reasonable period of time. Likewise, from the fact that the Emperor Alexander Severus issued 369 rescripts within a decade, whereas we have only nine for the decade of the 270s, MacMullen justifiably concludes that emperors whose hold on the throne was so insecure and who constantly had to take to the field of battle hardly had time to attend to problems crying out for solution. Moreover, news of the death of an emperor could take up to five months to reach the consciousness of communities far from the capital of a province, thus compounding the chaos.[35]

Furthermore, the venality of the Roman administrative system was notorious. As MacMullen[36] has remarked, "Minor tips and presents had long ruled the contacts of petitioners with those more powerful than themselves in the Roman army camps, in the anterooms of the great, in municipal records offices." Indeed, the Emperor Constantine (*CT* 8.4.6) even set a limit to the "rake-off" that army commanders might demand from civilian officials delivering their supplies. It is in the third century, in particular, that we have a wealth of testimony to venal practices of provincial governors.[37] The third-century Cyprian, bishop of Carthage, writes (*Ad Donatum* 10) sarcastically: "There is nothing to be afraid about the laws. What is for sale is not feared." Similarly, we may read the anonymous comment (*Genesis Rabbah* 67.6) that in the blessing that Isaac gave to his son Esau (Gen 27:39) "Behold thy dwelling shall be from the fatness of the earth," the "fatness of the earth" refers to Italy and to the practice of the Romans of setting up and reducing *duces*. The passage then proceeds to quote the Emperor Antoninus's question to Rabbi Judah the Prince at the end of the second century, "Inasmuch as our *thesaurus* is empty, what shall we do to fill it?" whereupon he began to fill it by promoting and demoting magistrates.

The earlier origins of such practices may be seen from Josephus's praise (*Ant.* 18.170–78) of the Emperor Tiberius in the first century for not replacing governors throughout the empire. In answer to the question why he had not done so, Tiberius narrated a fable about someone who was rebuked by a wounded man from whom he had tried to shoo away bloodsucking flies; similarly, replacing the administrators would simply lead to more exploitation by the new appointees. Likewise, Tacitus (*Histories* 4.14) has Claudius Civilis, a Batavian leader of the German revolt against Rome in 69–70, remark that the constant turnover of provincial administrators results in each administrator being glutted with spoil, only to be replaced by a new governor who obtains the booty for himself.

Moreover, the governors and even lesser officials often arrogated powers to themselves and frequently acted in such an arbitrary manner that the disposition of any request was quite unpredictable, especially in the fourth century. As to provincial magistrates, they often acted on their own, releasing or imprisoning or even executing the accused. Thus, in the first half of the second century, Rabbi Judah ben Bava (*Exodus Rabbah* 15.13) in a parable speaks of a king (who presumably stands, as often in such parables, for a provincial magistrate) who tells his sons (presumably his staff) that he will try capital cases and find everyone guilty, but that on receipt of a gift he will transfer the case to another court. Elsewhere (*Pesaḥim* 118b) we hear, in the name of Rabbi Ishmael, son of Rabbi Jose of the first half of the fourth century, that Rome will offer gifts to the Messiah, hypocritically justifying its claim for recognition on the ground that it is a descendant of Abraham, through his grandson Esau, "the nation that forgives all for the sake of money." Again, the fourth-century Rabbi Phinehas ben Ḥama and Rabbi Ḥilkiah (*Midrash Leviticus Rabbah* 13.5, *Genesis Rabbah* 65.1) accuse the Roman provincial magistrates of hypocrisy and relate an anecdote about a magistrate who was condemning to death thieves and adulterers and magicians while himself admitting to a senator that he had practiced all three crimes in a single night.

3. THE SOURCES: CHURCH CANONS

During the early centuries of the Christian era, and, in particular, during the third and fourth centuries, Judaism, at least in theory, posed a threat from several directions: First of all, it appealed to Christians who, drawing the logical consequences from Christianity's adoption of the Jewish Scriptures, argued that Christianity ought to observe not only the ethical but also the ritual laws stated in those Scriptures; second, some may have been led to adopt Judaism altogether, arguing that the religion that was good enough for Jesus was good enough for them;[38] and third, Jews were accused of associating with some of the numerous Christian heresies, particularly Arianism. It is these threats and charges, whether real or potential, that led to increasing virulence in the statements of church councils and church fathers.

As early as the year 52, we hear (Acts 15) of a synod held in Jerusalem to discuss problems of the nascent Church. How to deal with the Jews and the "Judaizers" is a recurrent question in the canons of such councils. Already in the Synod of Elvira in Spain in 305 (or 306), which was attended by nineteen (or, according to the *Codex Pithoanus* of its acts, forty-three) bishops from various parts of Spain, apparently one of the problems with which the bishops had to contend was the intermarriage of Jewish men with Christian women, presumably because of the consequent conversion of the wives to Judaism. Hence, the Council issued a canon (16) forbidding such marriages and punishing parents of those who violated this canon with interdiction for a period of five years.[39]

That, indeed, there were some, perhaps many, Christian laymen and even clerics who did not share the aversion of their leaders for the Jews and that there were social contacts between the two groups, as we have already noted, may be deduced from another canon of the Council (49), which forbade Christians from allowing their fruits to be blessed by Jews, "lest they make our blessing invalid (*irritam*) and feeble (*infirmam*)." The seriousness with which this was viewed may be perceived from the severity of the penalty for violation, namely, complete exclusion from the Church. Still another canon (50) penalized laymen and clerics who dined together with Jews by forbidding them to take communion. In fact, it was not until the third century that the Church felt confident enough to order its followers to shun Jews;[40] indeed, the *si quis* form used in this canon indicates a legal innovation;[41] but, we may remark, this surely does not indicate that the *problem* was new. Moreover, the use of the term *placuit* in the canon indicates, as always, that the provision was adopted only after some controversy.[42] The promulgations of interdictions against specific practices would seem to indicate that precisely those practices were most common and that the Church feared that socializing by Christians with Jews would lead to heresy or even apostasy.

One of the major problems of the Church throughout this period, as we have remarked above, was that of Christians who were influenced by the Jewish calendar. In particular, we find that many Christians, particularly in Asia Minor (Eusebius, *Historia Ecclesiastica* 5.24), insisted on celebrating Easter at the same time as the Jewish Passover.[43] Thus, we find (Eusebius, *Life of Constantine* 3.18–20) that the Emperor Constantine wrote to all who were absent from the Council of Nicaea (325) that it was unworthy for Christians to follow the calculation of the Jews in determining the date of Easter, "for it is truly shameful for us to hear them boast that without their direction we could not keep this feast."[44] Consequently, the council decided that Easter should never be celebrated at the same time as the festival of Passover.[45] Of course, this does not mean that Christians who observed Easter at the time of Passover were necessarily

"Judaizing." But, by the same token, such agreement in the calendar could serve as a bridge between Christians and Jews. In any case, the very vehemence with which Christians addressed this issue would indicate not merely a theological threat but also fear among the Christian authorities of further emulation of Jewish practices.

Moreover, we find that the Council of Antioch in 341 states, in the strongest terms, that if any layman observes as Easter a day other than the one declared by the Council of Nicaea he is to be excommunicated. And if a cleric "still dares to celebrate Easter *with the Jews* [my italics] and to follow his own perverse will to the ruin of the people and the disturbance of the churches," he is to be separated from the Church. That this was the very first canon adopted by the Council shows how pressing it was; indeed, few things are more important to religious life than the calendar and the calculation of festivals on their proper dates.[46] That the Church, however, was not successful in enforcing this provision seems clear because there were still Quartodecimans, as they were called from the fact that they observed Easter on the fourteenth of the month of Nisan, observing Easter at the same time as the Jewish Passover in the time of Epiphanius (*Panarion* 50), about the year 400, and in the time of Theodoret (*Historia Ecclesiastica* 3.17) a generation later, and because Christian authorities even disagreed among themselves.[47] In fact, in portions of Asia Minor (Socrates, *Historia Ecclesiastica* 4.28, 7.18), where the Quartodecimans were strongest, Christians split with the orthodox Church over this matter. So incendiary was this issue that some Christians even tried to prevent Jews from calculating the date of Passover in order to keep Christians from using this information to set the date of Easter.[48]

This problem of Christians who observed practices similar to those of the Jews was likewise dealt with by the Council of Laodicea in Asia Minor, which was held sometime between 343 and 381. No fewer than four of the sixty canons adopted by the council dealt with this issue. Thus, Canon 16 declares that "on Saturday the Gospels and other portions of the Scripture shall be read aloud." Apparently this provision was meant to counter the practice of some congregations that read portions of the Jewish Scriptures alone on Saturday. Moreover, Canon 36, as we have previously noted, forbade Christians from using τὰ λεγόμενα φυλακτήρια ("the so-called phylacteries" [*tefillin*]),[49] which apparently were viewed by some as magical amulets; the canon couples the use of these amulets with magicians, conjurors, mathematicians, and astrologers and declares that they are chains for the users' own souls. The fact that it specifically forbids their use by higher and lower clergy and declares that those who do use them will be shut out of the Church indicates that phylacteries must have presented a major problem for the Church, inasmuch as even its leaders found them attractive. It would also seem that Christians were particularly drawn to the Jewish festivals; and so we find (Canon 37) the provision forbidding acceptance of festal presents from Jews and the keeping of festivals with them. The Passover, especially, one would surmise, for those Quartodecimans who insisted on observing Easter according to the Jewish calculation of the fourteenth of Nisan, was a source of attraction; and hence, we find a special provision (Canon 38) forbidding anyone to accept unleavened bread from the Jews or to share in the observance of the festival. Such references have clearly passed beyond the stage of merely following the Jewish calendar, because here we have the actual sharing of distinctive Jewish practices. Hefele[50] remarks that about the middle, or at least in the second half, of the fourth century, "Judaizing" no longer flourished; but, as we shall note, there is ample evidence in the writings of the church fathers that "Judaizing" continued to be a major problem for the Church throughout the century.

The Fourth Carthaginian synod, alleged to have taken place in 398, though its canons were apparently not collected until the sixth century,[51] in its pronouncements (Canon 89) shows that "Judaizing" had not ceased, inasmuch as it declares that those who join in "Jewish superstition"—that is, those who observe Jewish practices—are to be excommunicated.

That "Judaizing" was a major problem raised at this council may be seen from the explicit provision (Canon 29) that "Christians shall not Judaize and be idle of Saturday, but shall work on that day," and that instead they should observe Sunday as the Sabbath and, if possible, do no work on that day, with the severe penalty of excommunication being inflicted on those who violated this provision. Two other canons (37, 38) forbade acceptance of festal presents from Jews and the observance of festivals with them or the acceptance of unleavened bread from them, presumably an allusion to the fact that some "Judaizers" chose to observe the practice of the Jewish Passover.

These canons are important because emperors very often incorporated their provisions into Roman law.[52]

4. THE SOURCES: CHURCH FATHERS BEFORE JOHN CHRYSOSTOM

The church fathers, through their vehement attacks on Jewish proselytism, on various sects of Jewish Christians who refused to give up their Jewish practices, and on numerous groups of more orthodox Christians who were attracted to various Jewish practices, give ample evidence of the vitality of Judaism in reaching out to Christians during these centuries. As we shall see as we proceed chronologically through the early church fathers, from Ignatius to John Chrysostom, their polemics against successful Jewish missionary activity had a very real basis, as the new inscriptions from Aphrodisias indicate.[53]

It was almost inevitable that this friction should have occurred because, after all, Christianity had originated with Jews and fought a long and victorious battle against the Marcionites in order to keep the Jewish Scriptures as part of its canon. A church father such as Justin Martyr (*Dialogue with Trypho* 7) had been converted to Christianity by reading the Jewish prophets; and indeed the Jewish Scriptures form approximately three-quarters of the Holy Scriptures of the Christians. During the Patristic period as many (if not more) Christian commentaries were written on the Jewish Scriptures as on the New Testament.[54] The Psalms, which many Christian clergy learned by heart, became the Christian prayer book par excellence. In fact, church father after church father, as we have remarked, kept on insisting that Christianity was the true Judaism in order, among other factors, to obtain for Christianity the benefits of the ancient tradition of Judaism so as to impress the Romans. There can surely be no doubt that Christians felt very sensitive about their rather recent arrival on the scene of history.[55]

The fear of and strong resentment against "Judaizers" may already be seen in the Book of Revelation (3:7–13), dating from the end of the first century, where John addresses the Church of Philadelphia in Asia Minor, "Behold I will make those of the synagogue of Satan who say that they are Jews and are not, but lie—behold I will make them come and bow down before your feet."

Shortly thereafter, Ignatius of Antioch (*Letter to the Philadelphians* 6), who died ca 110 or 117, addressing the same community, declares: "Should anyone expound Judaism, do not listen to him. It is preferable, surely, to listen to a circumcised man preaching Christianity than to an uncircumcised man [presumably a candidate for conversion to Judaism] preaching Judaism." Lest we think that this is mere rhetoric, we may note that Ignatius similarly condemns those Christians who observe Jewish practices when he says (*Letter to the Magnesians* 10) to the people of Magnesia, another city in Asia Minor: "It is absurd to speak of Jesus Christ with the tongue and to cherish in the mind a Judaism which has now come to an end. For where there is Christianity there cannot be Judaism." In particular, Ignatius inveighs against those who maintain the observance of the Jewish Sabbath, which, as we know (cf., e.g., Juvenal 14.96), was so attractive to "sympathizers" with Judaism. Thus, in a remark (*Letter to the Magnesians* 9) reminiscent of the sharp criticism by Seneca the Younger (quoted in Augustine, *De Civitate D-i* 6.11) that those who observe the Sabbath lose a seventh of their life in idleness, Ignatius says, "Let us, therefore, no longer keep the Sabbath after the Jewish manner and rejoice in days of idleness, for 'he that does not work, let him not eat' (2 Thes 3:10)."[56]

The Letter of Barnabas, probably written in the middle of the second century, shortly after the Bar Kochba rebellion, likewise shows bitter concern over those Christians who waver between their Jewish practices—particularly the Sabbath—and the beliefs of Christianity and seeks at all costs to separate Christianity from the synagogue by keeping a different day of the week as the Sabbath.[57]

That outreach by Jews did not cease with the suppression of the Bar Kochba rebellion may be seen from the fact that in the middle of the second century Justin Martyr (*Dialogue with Trypho* 23.3) addresses not only Trypho but also those who wish to become proselytes to Judaism. He likewise (*Dialogue with Trypho* 122–23) complains bitterly about the welcome that proselytes to Judaism receive from native-born Jews. It is these proselytes, he asserts, who, in their desire to become like the Jews in all respects and in contrast with born Jews such as Trypho, attack Christianity violently by blaspheming the name of Christ and by killing and tormenting Christian believers.

As we have already noted, we have a reference to proselytes in a letter, written at the end of the second century or at the beginning of the third century, by Julius Africanus to Aristeides (cited in Eusebius, *Historia Ecclesiastica* 1.7.13), which refers to the so-called γειώρας, that is, proselytes to Judaism, as being of mixed descent (ἐπιμίκτους), the clear implication being that proselytes generally were the results of intermarriage.

At the beginning of the third century, Tertullian (*Adversus Judaeos* 1), who lived in Carthage in northern Africa, describes an all-day dispute between a Christian and a proselyte to Judaism. The very fact that the champion of Judaism is a proselyte may well indicate that proselytism was still going on and was a source of great concern to the Church. Indeed, one is reminded of the statement of Tertullian's contemporary Rav (*Menaḥoth* 110a) that "from Tyre to Carthage they know Israel and their Father in Heaven."[58] Moreover, like his predecessors, Tertullian is upset that some Christians are still observing Jewish practices, such as the Sabbath (*De Jejunio adversus Psychicos* 14.3) and the law (*Apology* 9.13) that forbids meat to be eaten where the blood has not been drawn.[59]

In the middle of the third century, the great church father Origen, who lived in Caesarea in the Land of Israel, commenting on the bitter saying ascribed to Jesus (Matt 23:15) that the Pharisees traverse sea and land to make a single proselyte, indicates (*Commentary on Matthew* 23:15, sermon 16; *PG* 13.1621a; *GCS* 38.29) that proselytism by Jews is still being actively carried on; and he, like Justin Martyr, reports that proselytes to Judaism are often more severe critics of Christianity than born Jews. He insists that the "Judaizing" tendencies within the Christian community are not always spontaneous but that, on the contrary, they are the work of Jewish missionaries. He remarks (*Commentary on Mat-*

thew, sermon 79) that "Judaizers" justify their behavior by noting that Jesus observed Jewish practices and that they, in turn, are merely following in his footsteps. Again, it is the Sabbath and Passover that were of particular attractiveness to Christians; and Origen (*Homily on Jeremiah* 12.13; *PG* 13.395c) attacks those Christians who wash and adorn themselves for the Jewish Sabbath, as well as those who bake unleavened bread for Passover (*Commentary on Matthew*, sermon 79). He is especially critical (*Homily on Genesis* 3.5, *Commentary on Matthew* 11.12, 16.12; *Against Celsus* 2.1, 5.61) of the Ebionite Christians, who continued to observe many Jewish practices, including even circumcision.

Origen (*Against Celsus* 4.31) also alludes to the reputation Jews had for the incorruptibility and "superhuman purity" of their judges,[60] a factor that, as we have conjectured, though admittedly without concrete evidence, may well have attracted Christians not only to Jewish courts but also to Judaism. All of this illustrates the dilemma in which early Christianity found itself: On the one hand, it wished to have the antiquity and the moral reputation of Judaism, and it did so through claiming the Jewish Scriptures for itself; but, on the other hand, it had to proclaim that it was fundamentally different from Judaism and had to attack those in its midst who sought to maintain the Jewish rituals within Christianity.

In the middle of the third century, corresponding closely to the presumed date of the newly discovered inscriptions from Aphrodisias, the Jews of nearby Smyrna are represented, in the account of the martyrdom of Pionius (*Acta Pionii* 13.1, 14.1), as openly teaching Gentiles and as carrying on a proselytizing campaign among Christians as well. The author suggests that Christians have been attracted to the synagogue as a shelter against persecutions, because, until the Christians were granted licit status by the Roman government in 313, the Jews continued to maintain special privileges.

The attraction of the synagogue for Christians may be seen in the *Apostolic Constitutions*, which emanate from the Syrian Church and date from the third or fourth century. Apparently, not merely laymen were attracted to the synagogue and to Jewish practices; and just as we have noted the concern of Church councils to eliminate religious and social contacts between Christians and Jews, so we find in the *Apostolic Constitutions* statements (8.47, 62, 65, 70, 71) that if a cleric should enter a synagogue to pray he is to be deposed, and that if a bishop or another cleric fasts with the Jews or feasts with them or receives gifts, such as unleavened bread, from them on their festivals such a cleric is to be "purified"; and if the offender is a layman, he is to be excommunicated. Such a provision may, of course, be a manifestation merely of *odium theologicum*, but we may surmise that there was reason to fear that the "Shabbos goy," that is, the non-Jew who attends to those needs of the Jew on the Sabbath that

the Jew is forbidden to attend to, might be attracted to the Jewish observances. Thus, we find (*Apostolic Constitutions* 8.71.1) the provision that if
any Christian carries oil into a synagogue or lights lamps on Jewish festivals he is to be suspended. The *Apostolic Constitutions* (7.44) also warn
Christians against participating in Jewish baths,[61] which apparently, as
we have noted, were viewed as having greater solemnity than Christian
baths or which were regarded as a source of danger, inasmuch as there
was presumably some socializing at the baths and hence some opportunity to influence Christians.

In an era of utter lawlessness, as we have seen, Judaism, with its respect
for law and order, attracted many. Indeed, Lactantius (*De Ira* 23.12) in
the early fourth century admits that the Jews were praised by the oracle
of Apollo for their respect for law, as we have noted.

Apparently, as we have remarked, the decision of the Emperor Julian
(361–63), in his revulsion against Christianity, to help the Jews to rebuild
the Temple gave a further impulse to proselytism by Jews. A contemporary of the events, Ephraem Syrus (*Contra Julianum* 1.16, 2.7), says that
the Jews were seized by a frenzied enthusiasm and sounded trumpets
when they learned of Julian's plans to rebuild the Temple in Jerusalem.
Rufinus (*Historia Ecclesiastica* 10.38) reports that some Jews believed that
the era of the prophets had returned and that the rule of the Jews had
been restored. If so, one of the signs of the new era would have been the
flocking of Gentiles to the banner of the Jews. Although there is no evidence of such mass conversion, there is, as we have noted, considerable
evidence of interest in Jewish practices and even, to some degree, in conversion to Judaism.

One of the questions that has always puzzled students of Jewish proselytism is how to explain a movement of such magnitude when, as we have
previously remarked, we do not know of any missionaries as such. We
may, however, note that Ephraem Syrus, in the fourth century (In II Reg.
19.1 [*Opera Syriaca* 1.558]), presumably in exaggeration, bitterly notes
that numerous heathens are deluded by Jewish missionaries.

As late as the latter part of the fourth century, Epiphanius describes a
number of Jewish-Christian sects, such as the Ossaeans (*Panarion* 19.1.5.1),
who observed the Jewish Sabbath, circumcision, and other provisions of
the Law; they even, like the Jews, turned toward Jerusalem when they
prayed. Again, the Jewish Sabbath is of particular attraction, and thus we
find Epiphanius's strong statement (*Panarion* 51.8) condemning a
"philo-Sabbatius, who assails us from among the Jews, a fierce and deceitful serpent." The Cerinthians (*Anacephalaiosis* 2.28–30) are proud of
circumcision; the Nazoraeans, Ebionites, Sampsaeans, and Elkesaites
observe Jewish law generally. Their case is particularly compelling, we
are told, inasmuch as they appeal to the precedent of Jesus himself, who

observed these laws (*Panarion* 28.5.1). Although "Judaizing" tendencies were particularly strong in Judaea, Syria, and Asia Minor, they were found, as we have noted, in all parts of the Roman Empire, including Spain and North Africa. The fathers, in condemning these practices, apparently believed whether rightly or wrongly that it was a small step to pass from such "Judaizing" sects to Judaism itself. Indeed, Jewish practices were said to hold an attraction even for Apollinaris, the bishop of Laodicea in Asia Minor (died 390), whom his contemporary Basil attacks (*Epistulae* 265.2, 263.4) for his positive attitude toward the observance of worship according to the Law. Such an attack may be mere polemic, but it may also reflect still another instance of attraction to Jewish practices.

5. The Sources: John Chrysostom and Subsequent Church Fathers

The prime evidence for the success of the Jews in attracting adherents comes from the bitter diatribes of the most eloquent of the church fathers, John Chrysostom (ca 347–407), bishop of Antioch. It would seem that in 380, when the Emperor Theodosius I established orthodox Christianity as the religion of the empire (*CT* 16.1.2), Christianity's triumph was assured. And yet, in the fall of 386, when he delivered his sermons against the "Judaizers," Chrysostom undoubtedly saw the danger compounded by the growing strength of various Christian heresies, notably that of the Arians; indeed, it was only shortly before this time that the Emperor Valens (364–78), himself an Arian, had persecuted the orthodox Christians with great severity while protecting and honoring the Jews. Apparently, the Jews were attracting so many Christians to their synagogues and to their practices that Chrysostom (*Adversus Judaeos* 8.4.933–34) defensively says that Christians should not spread the information lest it lead to a stampede toward Judaism. In particular, it was women, as we have seen elsewhere, who were drawn to Jewish practices; and so we find that Chrysostom (2.3.860) charges Christian husbands with the responsibility of keeping wives from going to the synagogue. Moreover, though he is probably guilty of rhetorical exaggeration and though he never speaks of the Jews as missionaries as such, he charges (4.1.871) that the Jews actually take the initiative in attracting Christians, calling them "more dangerous than any wolves" and "bent on surrounding my sheep."

The "Judaizers," just as we have previously noted, appealed to the example of Jesus (3.4.866). It is significant that seven of the eight homilies against Judaizers delivered in such strident tones by Chrysostom preceded the Jewish High Holidays (Rosh Hashanah, Day of Atonement, and Sukkoth), with the remaining one being delivered just before Passover. They went to the synagogue on Rosh Hashanah "to watch them blow trumpets" (1.5.851) and, like the Emperor Antoninus who is similarly described in the rabbinic writings, they fasted with the Jews on the Day of Atonement and went to the synagogue to watch the Jews "dance with naked feet" (1.2.846). Furthermore, we are told (7.1.915), they made preparations to join the Jews in "pitching their tents," that is, in setting up their *sukkoth*.

It is, moreover, significant that Chrysostom's sermons against the "Judaizers" come at precisely the time when he is engaged in a bitter controversy with the heretical group known as the Anomoeans, who, he says, agree with the Jews in denying the divinity of Jesus (1.1.845). Indeed, we may surmise that it is precisely because Christianity was so busy fighting such heresies at this time that Judaism felt free to embark again on reaching out.

Apparently, however, far from deterring the Christians from "Judaizing," the sermons seem merely to have made Chrysostom's listeners more curious about Judaism. In the Near East, where people live out of doors almost as much as within their homes,[62] the word about Judaism appears to have spread. Surely, to an onlooker, the fact that Christians were adopting Jewish ways, rather than vice versa, must have seemed remarkable. Even Chrysostom has to admit this (4.3.875–76): "Go into the synagogues," he says, "and see if the Jews have changed their days of fasting, if they observe the Paschal Feast at the same time we do, whether they have ever taken food on that day." Apparently, however, the threat was not so much actual conversion to Judaism, because, as we can see from the Aphrodisias inscriptions, this was relatively uncommon, but rather to the credibility of Christianity.

That actual conversion to Judaism, however, was not indeed the main threat, at least in Italy, where perhaps the imperial authorities were more effective in enforcing their laws, may be seen from a comment of the author known as Ambrosiaster at the end of the fourth century. He remarks (*Quaestiones* 115.14; *PL* 35.2390) that though conversions to Judaism do occur they are nevertheless rare.

The most learned of the Latin fathers, Jerome (c. 347–c. 419), undertook his translation of the Bible because he felt so defensive in colloquies with Jews, inasmuch as Christians had only copies and translations of Jewish books and inasmuch as few of them knew the Hebrew original, the *veritas Hebraica*, to which the Jews always appealed in disputations. Though he encountered much opposition from fellow Christians in the struggle for souls, Jerome concluded that the only way to demolish the arguments of the Jews was to show firsthand knowledge of the Hebrew original. The fact that he had to learn his Hebrew from a Jew and that despite great efforts he never felt completely comfortable in his knowledge of it (at least of the pronunciation)[63] illustrates the handicaps under which Christians labored in their confrontations with Jews.

With, to be sure, obvious rhetorical exaggeration, Jerome, like Chrysostom before him, depicts (*Epistulae* 93; *PL* 22.669) the Jews in their aggressive activities as circling around the Christians seeking to tear them to pieces. He, too (*On Ezekiel* 33.33), is concerned with the multitude of Christians who are attracted to the rites of the synagogue. Like Chrysostom, he notes (*On Matthew* 23.15 [*PL* 26.175]) the presence of "Judaizers" among the women in particular. He also notes with concern (*On Zechariah* 14.10–11), as we have remarked, the belief of the Jews and of the "Judaizers" that the time is coming when all the precepts of the Law will be observed and when Jews will no longer become Christians but rather that Christians will become Jews (*Epistulae* 112.13). Like the other church fathers, he attacks the Jewish Christians, notably the Nazoraeans (*Epistulae* 112.13), declaring that because they want to be both Jews and Christians they are neither Jews nor Christians. The threat of the "Judaizers" and Jewish Christians is seen most graphically in the sarcastic comment by Jerome's contemporary and critic, Rufinus (*Apologia Contra Hieronymum* 1.5, 2.589), that if a few Jews were to institute new rites the Church would have to follow suit and immediately adopt them.

That Jewish Christians continued to be a problem is seen in a passage in Augustine (354–430), who refers (*Epistulae* 196; *PL* 33.894) to a group of Christians in North Africa who call themselves Jews. Though he insists, as do Christians generally, that the Christians are the true Jews, he nevertheless stresses that Christians should not use this name. The sect is given one year to cease to exist. Augustine (*Epistulae* 44) also refers to the presence of "G-d-fearers" in North Africa and refers to the leader of the group as "major," a designation used for the leaders of the Jewish community.[64]

That "Judaizers" did not cease to exist, however, may be seen from the fact that a century later a bishop (*PG* 28.144) apologizes for delivering a homily on the seventh-day Sabbath, lest someone think that he and his congregation were "Judaizing."

Indeed, as late as the middle of the fifth century, Isaac of Antioch (*Homilia de Magis*) bitterly denounces those who, though baptized Christians, go out and receive "the ablutions of demons," that is, of the Jews. Isaac also complains about the attraction of Christians to Jewish magicians and sorcerers, and, in particular, to incantations that use countless names of angels and heavenly beings, as indeed we find in the magical papyri.[65] Isaac here betrays an inferiority complex when he asks, "If we all have one Father, why should anyone feel superior to the nations [i.e., to the non-Jews]?"[66]

6. The Sources: Rabbinic Literature

Most of the rabbinic statements about proselytes date from the period after the Bar Kochba rebellion.[67] Though, to be sure, we do not know the names of any missionaries and though we do not have any missionary tracts as such, we may surmise that the new and very literal translation into Greek in the second century by the famous proselyte Aquila was intended to replace the Septuagint, which had been appropriated by the Church and which now received a negative appraisal from some (unnamed) rabbis (*Soferim* 1.7). Inasmuch as the predominant language of the Roman Empire was Greek and because, presumably, most of those converted were Greek speaking, the movement of outreach to non-Jews must have been aided by the honor in which the Greek language was held by the patriarch Rabbi Judah the Prince at the end of the second century, who declares (*Sotah* 49b), "Why speak Syriac [i.e., Aramaic] in Palestine? Talk either Hebrew or Greek." Indeed, in the middle of the fourth century, Rav Huna (*Genesis Rabbah* 16.4 on Gen 2:14) remarks that the Greeks surpass the Romans in three respects: in law, in books, and in language. The employment of Greek in the synagogues both as a liturgical language and as the language of sermons and even as the language of rabbinic discussions not only in the Diaspora but also in the Land of Israel meant that potential proselytes could be addressed in the language familiar to them.[68]

The fact, moreover, that, in the competition for souls, Christianity almost at the very beginning relaxed the technical requirements for conversion in foregoing circumcision, whereas Judaism did not omit these requirements and still continued to attract converts, must have left the Christians very defensive, as we can see in such works as Justin Martyr's *Dialogue with Trypho*.[69] Indeed, the silence of both pagan and Christian sources, to the extent that they exist, about any reduction by Jews of these requirements would seem to confirm the view that their motivation was not the promotion of proselytism.

That the attitude toward proselytism was a subject of debate in the third century is clear from numerous contemporary statements, both positive and negative. Thus, as we have noted, we have the positive remark of Rabbis Johanan and Eleazar (*Pesaḥim* 87b) that the only reason why G-d dispersed Israel among the nations was so that proselytes might join them. Moreover, Rabbi Johanan (*Nedarim* 32a) declared, in a tremendous tribute to proselytes, that Abraham was punished and his descendants had to undergo tremendous sufferings in Egyptian bondage because "he prevented people from entering under the wings of the Shekhinah [i.e., the Divine Presence]." Rabbi Abbahu (c. 300) likewise interpreted a number of biblical passages in such a way as to encourage proselytizing (*Tanḥuma Genesis Vayetze* 22; *Leviticus Rabbah* 1.2). He even went so far as to state, in the name of Rabbi Johanan, that the daughter of an Ammonite-Israelite marriage was permitted to marry a high priest (Jerusalem *Yevamoth* 8.3.9c), despite the Biblical injunction (Deut 23:4) forbidding an Ammonite to "enter into the congregation of the L-rd forever." He likewise ruled that it was permissible for a proselyte to recite the prayer when bringing first fruits, "which G-d has sworn to our fathers to give to us" (Deut 26:3) (Jerusalem *Bikkurim* 1.4.64a). Another rabbi, Hanina bar Papa, who lived in the Land of Israel at the end of the third and at the beginning of the fourth century, in a compliment to the sincerity of proselytes, predicts (*Pesiqta Rabbati* 35, p. 161a [Friedmann]) that these converts would serve as witnesses against the nations on the Day of Judgment and that their example would justify G-d's punishment of recalcitrant pagans. A further compliment was paid to proselytes by Rabbi Huna at the beginning of the fourth century (*Midrash Genesis Rabbah* 28.5 on Gen 6:7) when he declared that "the evil people are saved by the merits of one proselyte who each year is raised in the midst of them."

The eagerness of the rabbis to win proselytes may be seen particularly in their portrait of Abraham. Thus (*Sifre Deuteronomy* 313 on Deuteronomy 32:10, dating from perhaps the end of the fourth century), Abraham is described as so good a missionary that he succeeds in making G-d known as king of the earth as well as of heaven. In particular, there are a number of references to the success of Abraham and Sarah in Haran, where they "created souls."[70] Even Goodman admits that this function of Abraham as missionary is all the more striking because he lacks this role in the eyes of Philo and Josephus.[71] Similarly, according to the third-century Rabbi Hoshaya, the passage (Gen 37:1) that states that Jacob dwelt in the land of his father's sojournings indicates that Isaac had made proselytes in that area. Jacob (*Midrash Hagadol* 1.397) likewise is depicted as capturing people to turn them toward G-d, in contrast to his brother Esau, who seized people in order to turn them away from G-d. Likewise, the third-century Rabbi Abba bar Kahana (*Genesis Rabbah* 90.6) states that Joseph inspired the Egyptians with a longing to be circumcised so that they might attain to life not only in this world but also in the world to come. Again (*Sifre Numbers* 80, dating likewise from perhaps the end of the fourth century), we read that Jethro won converts by his example.[72] All of this suggests that the rabbis did not look on the conversions as fraught with any great danger; and the warning, dating ca 200 C.E. (Mishnah *Baba Metzia* 4:10, Tosefta *Baba Metzia* 3.25), that it is not permitted to insult a proselyte by reminding him of his pagan past, as well as the very existence of the Talmudic tractate *Gerim* (dating from perhaps the year 400)[73] dealing with the rules governing the reception of converts, are evidence that the matter was of more than mere academic interest.[74] Likewise, the anonymous statement (*Kerithoth* 9a) requiring proselytes to set aside money to be kept for a sacrifice once the Temple is rebuilt indicates that proselytism was still going on during the Amoraic period (200–500).

The fact that Rabbi Joseph ben Ḥiyya of Babylonian Pumbeditha at the beginning of the fourth century explains (*Berakoth* 17b) the verse in Isaiah 46:12, "Hearken to me, you stubborn of heart, you who are far from righteousness," as referring to the Gubaeans, a tribe in the neighborhood of Babylon, on the ground that a proselyte has never yet emerged from them indicates that normally proselytes have emerged from other towns. A similar conclusion may be drawn from the statement of Rabbi Ashi (ibid.), who lived later in the fourth century, who was one of the compilers of the Babylonian Talmud, and who applied the verse of Isaiah to the inhabitants of Mata Meḥasia, a suburb of Sura in Babylonia. The latter, he said, had not yielded a single proselyte even though they saw the glory of the Torah twice a year at the assemblies of scholars.

Simon suggests that it was a concern for successful proselytism that led the sages in these centuries to have a liberal attitude toward pagan culture.[75] Thus, we hear (*Rosh Hashanah* 24b) that the two greatest sages of the third century, Rav and Shmuel, used to pray in a synagogue in Babylonia in which there was a statue of a king and were not afraid of arousing suspicion that they were compromising the biblical prohibition against images. In fact, we are told (*Megillah* 29a) that this synagogue was so sacred that the presence of G-d rested there. Furthermore (Jerusalem *'Avodah Zarah* 3.3), at the time of Rabbi Joḥanan in the third century, Jews began to allow paintings on walls, and the rabbis did not forbid it. An interesting case (ibid.) illustrating the liberalism of the rabbis in this matter may be seen in the question asked by Rabbi Ḥiyya bar Abba, who lived in Babylonia and in the Land of Israel in the third and at the beginning of the fourth centuries, as to whether it was permissible to use a cup on which the Tyche (Fortune) of Rome was painted. The rabbis gave a permissive answer, explaining that because, when the cup is filled with water, the water covers the painting of Tyche, the vessel is considered a common and not a religious object. Indeed, the whole Talmudic tractate of *'Avodah Zarah*, which deals with idol worship, has amazingly little ridicule of idols.[76] This is especially striking when we compare it with the sharp strictures against such worship in the works from the same period by the church fathers Clement of Alexandria (ca 160–215), Athenagoras (latter half of the second century), Theophilus of Antioch (latter half of the second century), Tertullian (flourished 200), Arnobius (died ca 327), and Lactantius (ca 250–ca 325). Even if we say that this attitude reflects their recognition that idolatrous influences did not constitute a real danger to the Jews any longer (*Yoma* 69b, *Sanhedrin* 64a, Judith 8:18),[77] surely the net effect of this liberalism was to make it easier for pagans to make the transition to Judaism.

That proselytism was an issue during the third and fourth centuries is clear from the opposition that it aroused. Thus, we have the remark (*Midrash Ruth Zuta* on 1.12) of Rabbi Ḥiyya the Great at the end of the second century, "Do not have faith in a proselyte until twenty-four generations have passed, because the inherent evil is still within him." We also have the comment (*Qiddushin* 70b), noted above, of the third-century Rabbi Ḥama bar Ḥanina that "G-d will cause his presence to rest only on genealogically pure families of Israel," followed by the statement about the advantage of born Jews over proselytes.

The most negative of statements about proselytism is, as we have remarked, that of Rabbi Ḥelbo, who lived during the latter part of the third and the early part of the fourth century. Repeated no fewer than three times in the Talmud (*Qiddushin* 70b, *Yevamoth* 47b, *Niddah* 13b), his statement is that proselytes are as difficult for Israel as a scab (*sapaḥath*). Moreover, according to Rabbi Ḥelbo, proselytes actually delay the coming of the Messiah (*Niddah* 12b, *Yevamoth* 109b). Of similar import is the statement of Rabbi Isaac bar Joseph, who lived in the first half of the fourth century, that "one evil thing after another befalls those who accept proselytes." But we may comment that the very vehemence and repeated citation of such statements indicates that proselytism was going on and was apparently a subject of sharp debate.

That some rabbis tried to win back to Judaism those Jews who had defected to Christianity is apparent from the remarkably conciliatory saying of the third-century Rabbi Simeon ben Lakish (*Ḥagigah* 27a, *ʿEruvin* 19a) that the fire of Gehenna has no dominion over Jewish apostates, who are as full of good deeds as a pomegranate.[78]

7. The Sources: Inscriptions and Papyri

If, indeed, converts and "sympathizers" continued to be attracted to Judaism in the third and fourth centuries, we would expect some evidence in the inscriptions on tombstones. But of the 731 inscriptions from Italy, most of them from Rome, included by Frey in volume 1 of his Corpus, only eight indicate that these people are proselytes.[79] Moreover, as we have noted, in the 520 papyri included in Tcherikover's corpus (*CPJ*) there is not a single mention of a proselyte or a "G-d-fearer" as such. To say that the *argumentum ex silentio*, when applied to epigraphical data, lacks strength, because everything depends on what happens to have been found and new discoveries may well alter the status of our knowledge,[80] is not a very satisfactory answer, when we consider that we do have several hundred inscriptions and papyri. To be sure, these cover several centuries, and it is very difficult to determine their approximate dates. We may, however, explain this relative lack of mention of proselytes by noting that almost all of the inscriptions in Frey's collection are from the city of Rome, where, it may be, proselytism was relatively curtailed because of the two expulsions of Jews guilty of proselyting activities in 139 B.C.E. (Valerius Maximus 1.3.3) and 19 C.E. (Dio Cassius 57.18.5a)[81] and because, after all, the seat of government was there, where presumably a more careful watch was kept on the activities of the inhabitants. If so, proselytes would hardly have been so imprudent as to reveal that they were converts and thus to bring trouble to their kinfolk and friends. Any attempt, moreover, to identify proselytes by their non-Jewish names would similarly be ineffective, inasmuch as the names of Jews, at least in Rome, which is the source of the majority of our inscriptions, are hardly distinguishable from those of non-Jews.[82]

8. REASONS FOR JEWISH SUCCESS IN WINNING CONVERTS

Though there can be no doubt that Jews were winning converts during this period, the question remains whether they actively sought them out or whether the initiative came from the converts themselves. Though at first glance it would appear that in John Chrysostom's Antioch the Jews were actively seeking Christian converts, in point of fact Chrysostom nowhere unequivocally says that the Jews actually sought them out.[83] Indeed, the whole point of his sermons is that the Christians are taking the initiative. But, in any case, that the Jews were successful in winning either converts or "sympathizers" seems clear from the strident tones of the polemic during this period between Jews and Christians. In this controversy, before the conversion of Constantine, the imperial authorities apparently, at least at times, sided with the Jews, as we can see from the charge (Pseudo-Augustine, *Altercatio Ecclesiae et Synagogae* [*PL* 43.1131]) that the synagogue was being "maintained by the Roman scepter and legions." Judaism and paganism apparently felt much in common as conservative ideologies against the innovative, revolutionary Christianity.[84] There seems little doubt that such an alliance existed under the Emperor Julian (361–63). As the Christians became more and more of a threat, the attention of the imperial authorities was diverted from the Jews, who appeared to be much less of a problem. But even with the triumph of Christianity, the emperors realized the great strength in numbers and in economic power of the Jews and perceived that, beset as they were by internal decay from within and by challenges from barbarians from without, they could not afford to alienate so large and so important an element of their population, which was essentially loyal to them.

It also seems likely that the end of the Jewish state and the destruction of the Temple helped win Jewish adherents in that the political aspect of conversion, namely adherence to the idea of a Jewish state, became secondary, so that the charge of dual loyalty was no longer so prominent. Moreover, in effect, with the end of the sacrificial cult, the Diaspora Jews, proselytes included, became the equals of natives of the Land of Israel.[85] Apparently, we may suggest, to judge from the Tractate *Gerim*, the rabbis in the Land of Israel realized this, inasmuch as they instituted a rule to make conversion more difficult outside the Land than it was within it, namely, as we have noted, through requiring witnesses abroad but being ready to accept proselytes at once without the preliminary hearing of witnesses in the Land of Israel.

9. The Decline of the Outreach Movement and Its Renewal

Simon gives the year 425 as being the end, for practical purposes, of the proselytism and suggests that the chief factor in its demise was the establishment of the Christian state, which was much more concerned than the pagan emperors had been with preventing the expansion of Judaism.[86] But that conversions continued even after this period is clear from the inclusion of numerous provisions, taken over from the Theodosian Code, in the sixth-century Codex of Justinian.

Furthermore, that converts continued to be won (though this may be a new development rather than continuous with the past) may be seen from the conversion to Judaism of the king of the Khazars in southern Russia, together with a sizable number of his subjects, in the eighth century.[87] Moreover, Golb, extrapolating from records in the Geniza in Cairo, where there are names of approximately thirty proselytes, notes that this represents only a small proportion of only one city, Fostat, which had not more than one-fiftieth of the total Jewish population of the medieval Islamic world.[88] He then concludes that there might well have been approximately fifteen thousand proselytes over a span of two centuries, from 1000 to 1200, but hardly less than five thousand during each century. Indeed, that proselytism continued even in the Christian world of the Middle Ages may be seen from the fact that approximately twenty anonymous proselytes are mentioned in the responsa of the German Tosafists during the twelfth and thirteenth centuries, as noted by Wacholder.[89]

10. Summary

That Judaism vigorously continued in the third, fourth, and fifth centuries to attract both converts and "sympathizers" and that it continued to influence "Judaizers" and Jewish Christians is evident from the frequent repetition of imperial laws, canons of the Church councils, comments of church fathers, remarks of rabbis, inscriptions, and papyri, though there is relatively little evidence of active missionaries or of missionary tracts, except for isolated passages in the *Acta Pionii*, Ephraem Syrus, and Jerome, and all of these are perhaps guilty of rhetorical exaggeration. It is clear that far from withdrawing into itself or restricting itself to a conflict built around the interpretation of sacred texts, Judaism boldly confronted the Church. The numerous passages in the Talmud ascribed to rabbis of the third and fourth centuries, indeed, correctly reflect the actual situation in which non-Jews, and especially women, were being attracted to Judaism.

If we examine the imperial laws pertaining to proselytism, we note that on no fewer than five occasions emperors saw the need to repeat a complete ban on proselytism and on two other occasions forbade circumcision in particular. The fact that no fewer than twelve laws repeat the prohibition on conversion of slaves indicates that these provisions were not being enforced.

That proselytism continued is all the more surprising because conversion to Judaism meant not only adherence to a religion but also membership in a nation that, after three desperate attempts in 66–74, 115–17, and 132–35, still looked forward to a messianic redemption. This hope included independence from Rome as a key item in its agenda and hence met firm opposition from the Roman emperors, especially at a time when the empire was fighting for its very life against barbarians to the north and Persians to the east. Undoubtedly the proselyting movement was aided by the fact that, especially during these centuries, laws were often observed in the breach and provincial governors were so frequently corrupt. Indeed, 43 percent of the laws pertaining to the Jews in the Theodosian Code deal with proselytism in one form or another, a clear indication of the continuing presence of the problem even as late as the fifth century.

If, after Christianity had officially become the religion of the empire in 380, a golden-mouthed orator of the capacity of a John Chrysostom was unable to halt the attraction of Judaism to Christians, at least in the year in which in which he delivered the sermons, we can well imagine how much greater their attraction might have been in the previous century, when the Church was being persecuted, when several leading Neo-Platonic and Neo-Pythagorean intellectuals had expressed admiration for Judaism, and when Judaism enjoyed its traditional general privileges. Indeed, there would seem to be a direct correlation between the increased stridency of anti-Jewish remarks by the church fathers of the fourth and fifth centuries and the apparently continued ability of the Jews to win proselytes. This virulence was increased by the alleged cooperation of Jews with pagans and with Christian heretical groups and by the continued presence of "Judaizing" Christians and Jewish Christians.

Even before the official triumph of Christianity, if we may judge particularly from the new inscriptions from Aphrodisias, though the number of proselytes won by Judaism declined, the number of "sympathizers" continued to be large and in fact grew, perhaps because of the increased severity of the punishment for converts. Moreover, the Jews were able to reach non-Jews the more easily because they shared the Greek language, even in the Land of Israel, and, at least in such areas as Asia Minor, were deeply Hellenized. Undoubtedly also, the decision of the Emperor Julian to help the Jews rebuild the Temple gave a further impetus to proselytism. In sum, Judaism in the third, fourth, and fifth centuries not only showed its vigor through the debates constituting its greatest work since the Bible, namely the Talmud, but also met the twin challenges of paganism and Christianity by continuing to win converts and "sympathizers."

CHAPTER 12

CONCLUSION

OUR QUESTION has been how to explain the apparent success of Judaism in the Hellenistic-Roman period in winning so many converts and "sympathizers" at a time when, apparently, Jews were hated by the Gentile masses. Indeed, when Baron[1] counterposes the hatred of Israel and the love of Israel as the two pivots of Jewish history, his thesis, we may say, is particularly applicable to this period. Our answer, basically, is that Judaism was internally strong and was, for this reason, admired by many, even its detractors, especially at a time of general political and economic disarray. Judaism, moreover, took advantage of the fact that ancient religions, being polytheistic, were tolerant of other religious points of view.

The foci of these two great civilizations of antiquity, that of the Greeks in Greece and Asia Minor and that of the Jews in the Land of Israel, are geographically close to each other; and the Bible declares that Shem, the ancestor of the Semites, and Japheth, the ancestor of the Greeks, are brothers. There is, to be sure, a long history of commercial contact between the two peoples, but hardly much more, with the exception of the borrowing of a few words, prior to Alexander the Great in the latter part of the fourth century B.C.E. Indeed, Josephus, who in his apologetic treatise *Against Apion* sought to explain why the Greeks had ignored the Jews for so long and who searched high and low in Greek literature for references to the Jews, was able to find indirect allusions in no authors earlier than Herodotus and Choerilus in the fifth century B.C.E., and it is possible that neither is referring to the Jews.

One explanation for this lack of contact was that the Greeks hardly traveled beyond the coast, whereas the Jews were not living near the Mediterranean and were not a maritime people; but the major reason is that, from the Greek point of view, the Jews were obscurantists who had contributed nothing significant in the realm of the arts and sciences. It is almost as if the Jews, having been inoculated, as it were, by these early minimal contacts, were strengthened for the major confrontations that were yet to come.

The first cultural contact is said to have occurred in the latter part of the fourth century B.C.E., when a learned Jew from the Land of Israel met the great Aristotle in Asia Minor and was complimented for his wisdom, courage, and temperance. There is some question as to whether such a meeting actually took place, and in any case, it represents the contact of a single Jew, rather than of groups of Jews, in Asia Minor, not in the Land of Israel.

To be sure, Aristotle's successor, Theophrastus, seems to refer to the method by which the Syrians, of whom the Jews are said to constitute a part, conduct their sacrifices and speaks of them most laudably as philosophers by race. But inasmuch as he makes one blatant error after another in his description, it seems most likely that either his information came to him secondhand or he is referring not to the Jews but to the Syrians. Likewise, the reference in his contemporary Megasthenes to the Jews as philosophers and the theory connecting them with the Indians are commonplaces and do not indicate direct contact with Jews. As to his contemporary Hecataeus, who likewise speaks about the Jews in generally laudatory terms, doubt about the authenticity of some of these statements had already been expressed in the second century c.e.; and in any case, he could hardly have had firsthand knowledge of the Jews in view of the egregious errors that he makes. Finally, references to the alleged influence of the Jews on the philosopher Pythagoras reflect the romantic tendency during the Hellenistic period of depicting Greek thinkers as coming into contact with Eastern ideas.

It is alleged that Hellenism influenced Jews prior to the Hasmoneans through Jews who served in the armies of Alexander and his successors. And yet, although Jewish apocalypses are couched in military terms, there is no evidence of any influence exercised by Greek armies marching through the Land of Israel. Moreover, though many cities with non-Jewish populations in the Land of Israel had constitutions following Greek models, there is no evidence that Jewish cities had them. In fact, not a single Greek urban community was founded in Judaea. Again, although, to be sure, the Jews had a ruling body known as the *gerousia*, there is no evidence that anything about the *gerousia* other than the name itself was borrowed from the Greeks. Economic ties, as indicated by Greek weights, coins, and trade usage, may have led to social relations in the case of the tax collectors from the Tobiad family, but there is little indication of influence among the masses. There is good reason to believe that Antiochus Epiphanes' attempt in the second century b.c.e. to impose Hellenization on the Jews did not continue a popular process that was in motion effecting a syncretism, and that he consequently encountered substantial resistance. Likewise, his abrupt decision to abandon the attempt forcibly to convert the Jews suggests that his original decree was a whim rather than the climax of a gradual movement.

That the Jews had absorbed the Greek language would seem to be indicated by the presence of Greek inscriptions, but these probably tell us about the use of Greek by Greek-speaking foreigners in Israel rather than about its use by Jews. In any case, the level of Greek here is very elementary. Again, the adoption by Jews of Greek names turns out not to be a very meaningful criterion of their degree of assimilation. Furthermore, there is good reason to believe that the seventy or seventy-two Jews who knew Greek well enough to be able to translate the Pentateuch into Greek in the third century B.C.E. were not from Judaea but from Egypt; and in any case, their Greek is far from the level of a Philo.

As for Greek influence on the biblical books of Ecclesiastes and Daniel and on the Apocryphal book of Ben Sira, prior to the Maccabees, the sources for these alleged Greek ideas may well be found in other books of the Bible or in other Near Eastern sources.

During the Hasmonean and Roman periods, the Jewish masses strongly resisted paganism, as we can see from their passionate opposition to attempts to introduce busts of the emperor into Jerusalem both in the early and in the middle portions of the first century C.E. That the Jews in the Land of Israel frowned on learning the Greek language may be seen from Josephus's remark (*Ant.* 20.264) that the Jews do not favor those people who have learned foreign languages and from the statement that Josephus, though he labored strenuously (*Ant.* 20.263) to master Greek literature, yet had to employ assistants (*Against Apion* 1.50) to help him compose his version in Greek of the *Jewish War*. Indeed, it is quite clear from many sources that the predominant language of the Jews in the Land of Israel throughout the Hellenistic and Roman periods was not Greek but Aramaic. The very fact that the rabbis had the audacity to challenge the patriarch himself for teaching Greek in the first century implies strong discontent.

As for the suggestion that there must have been multitudes of Greek-speaking Jewish pilgrims who came to Jerusalem each year for the pilgrimage festivals and thus must have brought with them their Greek language and ideas, most of the pilgrims came from within the Holy Land. Indeed, we actually know of few pilgrims from abroad, especially in view of the precarious conditions of travel.

In particular, we must draw a distinction in Hellenization between Lower Galilee and Upper Galilee, because the latter, which had a high concentration of Jews, is almost totally devoid of Greek influence.

As for Greek influence on Jewish literature of this period, the Pseudepigraphic 1 Enoch has parallels in Babylonian or Iranian—and thus Gentile but not Greek—sources and is consequently not necessarily derived from Orphic literature. Similarly, such books as Esther, Tobit, Judith, and the *Testament of Joseph* reflect motifs that are found in Egyptian and Iranian—likewise Gentile, though not Greek—sources. Furthermore, it is at least as probable that the Essenes' idea of dualism was derived from Iranian sources as that it came from the Greeks; similarly, the astrological fragments among the Dead Sea Scrolls would seem to show Babylonian rather than Greek influence.

The theory has been presented that Eupolemus, who wrote a history in Greek in the second century B.C.E., was from the Land of Israel. But if he was a Jew, a priest, a historian of the biblical period, a friend of the Hasmoneans, and an inhabitant of the Land of Israel, it is hard to believe that Josephus, who was all of these, should not have used him as a source. In any case, we would have to explain how a Jew from Judaea could have referred to David as the son of Saul. Indeed, there could hardly have been many Jews who wrote in Greek in the Land of Israel, because neither Philo nor Josephus ever refers to any of them.

The fact that Josephus wrote his *Jewish War* originally in Aramaic shows that when he was addressing Jews, as he did in that work, he wrote in the language most familiar to them. It was only when, on the other hand, he sought a non-Jewish audience, as he did with his *Antiquities*, that he wrote in Greek. Moreover, he himself admits that he needed assistants to help him with the Greek of the *Jewish War*.

Furthermore, the most likely vehicle for Greek influence on the educational system in the Land of Israel, the gymnasium, was not established in Jerusalem until 175 B.C.E. The existence of eight sports buildings in the Land of Israel does not prove that Jews frequented them, inasmuch as Josephus states that such buildings as theaters and amphitheaters were alien to Jewish custom. It was, rather, the very large Gentile population of perhaps a million which attended them.

The inclusion of between twenty-five hundred and three thousand words of Greek origin in the Talmudic writings and a number of changes made in the Hebrew language under apparent Greek influence are, to be sure, abundant testimony of Hellenization. And yet these words are almost never from the realm of ideas; and the alleged correspondences with motifs in Stoicism, Epicureanism, and Cynicism are generally commonplaces. Nowhere in the rabbinic corpus do we find the names of Socrates, Plato, or Aristotle; and, in fact, there is not a single Greek philosophical term to be found in this literature. Unlike the Middle Ages, when rabbinic scholars wrote major philosophical works in Arabic, we know of no Talmudic rabbi who distinguished himself in philosophy, let alone wrote a work in Greek. Moreover, though the development of the great system of Roman law is almost exactly contemporaneous with the development of the Talmud, not a single legal term from Latin entered the rabbis' active legal vocabulary. Furthermore, the Greek concept of "oral law" is very different in meaning from that of the Talmud. The one rabbi who was deeply influenced by Hellenism, Elisha ben Avuyah, is roundly condemned. If the study of Greek culture was permitted, it was only under the careful guidance of the patriarch himself.

As for pagan influence on Jewish art in the Land of Israel, the archaeological evidence indicates that prior to the destruction of the Temple the influence of the Pharisees was so strong that the Jews refrained
from any attempts at painting and sculpture. After that time the rabbis'
influence actually increased, but with their heightened confidence that
idolatrous impulses had been eradicated, they became more flexible in
interpreting the laws pertaining to such matters as the occult and art.

In short, Judaism in the Land of Israel proceeded from a position of
strength and confidence. It had encountered Hellenism over a period of
centuries and had successfully resisted the attractions of paganism.
When Hellenism came in earnest with Alexander and his successors, the
power and authority of the rabbis increased as the new challenges were
being met. The development of so many sects of Jews is actually a sign of
the vitality of Judaism.

Judaism in the Diaspora, though it lacked the rabbinic leadership
and the institutions of the Land of Israel, likewise proceeded from a position of strength. The pagans, in their comments on the various details of
Jewish observance, make almost no differentiation among subgroups of
Jews, drawing a distinction only between the laws promulgated by Moses
and those introduced at a later date. The impression they give is that the
Jews, as a people, are universally observant of the most distinctive Jewish
practices, namely circumcision, the Sabbath, and the dietary laws, and
that the Jews are ready to suffer torture and death rather than to repudiate the religion of their forefathers. Again, when we hear of expulsions
from Rome, it is *the* Jews who are banished without distinction, though
the legalistically minded Romans were generally careful not to make facile generalizations.

This unity of the Jews was undoubtedly enhanced by the conscientiousness with which adult males contributed a half shekel each year to
the Temple. A further indication of Jewish Diaspora loyalty to the Jewish
leadership is that on two occasions in the first century B.C.E. Jewish soldiers in the Ptolemaic army, because of the appeal of the head of the
Judaean state or of the high priest, allowed Romans to enter Egypt.

When we ask the same questions about the Jews of the Diaspora that
we have asked about the Jews of the Land of Israel concerning their attitude toward the Greek language and thought, we get very different answers. The 520 papyri, which have supplemented our knowledge of the
Egyptian Jewish community to such a high degree, indicate that within
less than a century of the establishment of the community of Alexandria
in the fourth century B.C.E. the Jews had become Greek-speaking and did
not at all bewail their loss of competence to understand the Hebrew original of the Bible. Of 122 inscriptions of Jews from Egypt, only six are in
Hebrew or Aramaic. Of the 534 inscriptions of Jews from Rome, only

five are in Hebrew or Aramaic. As for Philo, it is hard to believe that if he knew Hebrew he would not have consulted the original text when it differed from the Septuagint translation. Yet the Septuagint, the translation of the Torah into Greek, shows no systematic pattern of Hellenizing and little if any influence of Greek philosophy; on the contrary, in discussions of the Jewish religion, it generally avoids terms used in pagan worship. Moreover, we can gather from Philo's boast that on the Sabbath thousands of schools stand wide open for teaching the cardinal virtues that the Jews as a group (together, it would seem, with potential proselytes) eagerly sought ethical instruction.

To be sure, inasmuch as the Jews were eager to obtain citizenship, which was granted only to those who had received a gymnasium education, the Jews sought admittance to the gymnasium, even though the gymnasiums were dedicated to pagan deities. Furthermore, the athletic games in which students participated were religious festivals. Even Philo, especially in his similes and metaphors, gives ample evidence of firsthand knowledge of sports. If we may judge from the Emperor Claudius's famous letter to the Alexandrians, the Jews of Alexandria as a community sought to participate in the games run by the leaders of the gymnasiums. And yet, if a gymnasium education was acquired at the price of betrayal of Judaism, we would surely have expected Philo to condemn it, whereas he actually praises it. Likewise, if we may judge from Philo, Jews regularly attended the theater, despite its pagan religious associations. We even know of a Jewish tragedian, Ezekiel, who wrote plays in the best style of Euripides, the favorite playwright of the era.

Furthermore, there are syncretistic elements in several apparent Graeco-Jewish writers, such as the statement in the *Letter of Aristeas* (16) that the Jews worship the same god as the Greeks do (Zeus or Dis) under another name. Moreover, Philo speaks of Moses as initiating the Jews into mysteries. Again, several documents in the papyri refer to the Ptolemies as gods. Likewise, inscriptions on tombstones speak in terms of pagan mythology. Furthermore, there are numerous charms and amulets with various names of the biblical G-d side by side with those of pagan deities. And yet there is always a question whether they are of Jewish or pagan origin; and in any case, the possession of amulets apparently did not diminish the loyalty to Judaism of the Jews who possessed them.

In addition, we know from the works of Philo that some Jews were literalists, refusing to resort to allegory and hence encountering severe theological difficulties. Others were extreme allegorists who felt no need to obey the laws in their literal sense. But such interpreters were apparently few and in any case never were organized as a movement.

As for deviations in practice from Jewish law, the papyri present such evidence as loans at interest in direct violation of the Torah, as well as a divorce document that follows non-Jewish formulae and violates the formulae as known to us from the written and the oral Law. Moreover, the community in Egypt had a temple at Leontopolis where sacrifices were brought in violation of the Law of the Torah. But the insignificance of this temple is underscored by Philo's complete silence about it; and there is strong evidence that the Jews of Egypt, as a community, continued to be loyal to the Temple in Jerusalem.

Moreover, Jewish cohesion was promoted by the concentration of Jews in two of the five sections of the city of Alexandria, though they were free to live wherever they wished. The unity of the community during the riots of 38 and 66 is likewise impressive.

In addition, the organization of the Jews in synagogues and in *politeumata* that functioned as Jewish religious, social, cultural, and even political centers, strengthened the community, though we hear of no Torah academies in Egypt, Syria, or Asia Minor, and of only one in Rome. Furthermore, Jews had their own courts. Moreover, Philo states clearly that Jewish children were taught the Laws, written and oral, from their cradles.

The very size of the Jewish communities in Egypt, Syria, and Asia Minor must have militated against assimilation. In Sardis, in particular, we now realize that the Jewish community had far greater wealth, power, and self-confidence, at least in the third century, than we had previously suspected. Indeed, there is reason to think that intermarriage and apostasy were relatively uncommon. We know of only one case of the former from a papyrus and very few cases of the latter from literature or inscriptions. Apparently, the more common method of expressing deviation from the norms of Jewish law was simply nonobservance. Nevertheless, according to Philo, even those who never acted religiously throughout the year observed the fast of the Day of Atonement. In sum, few Jews were lost, while many were gained as proselytes through the ease with which the Jews were able to communicate to non-Jews in the lingua franca of the day, Greek.

How were the Jews able to convert so many to Judaism if, as is commonly thought, they were so universally hated? In the first place, we must distinguish among the attitudes of governments, the masses, and intellectuals. As for the first, Alexander the Great, like the Persians before him, was enough of a realist to understand that he could not rule his vast empire containing relatively few Greeks and Macedonians unless he adopted a tolerant attitude toward the various peoples under his sway. His successors in Egypt, the Ptolemies, who encountered much resentment from the native Egyptians, found the Jews useful as bureaucratic middlemen and as soldiers (in four cases even as commanders-in-chief) and policemen. From the Jewish point of view, this "vertical" alliance with the rulers proved advantageous. If we hear of concerted attacks against Jews, as we do on one occasion, the reason is that a Jewish leader got involved in one of the dynastic wars that characterized so much of Ptolemaic history. But even in this one case, very shortly thereafter the ruler came to his senses, realizing that the Jews were too useful to his realm to be persecuted.

Still, the Jews were always in the anomalous position of claiming, on the one hand, to be loyal to the government, while, on the other hand, being excused from participating in the civic religion, which was never separated from the state, and from serving in the army, at least under the Romans. The charge of double loyalty may well have been fostered by four incidents in which the Jews showed preference for their brethren in the Land of Israel or for the allies of these as against the Egyptian sovereign to whom they claimed loyalty; and yet so numerous and influential were the Jews that they retained their special privileges.

As for the situation of the Jews under the Syrian Seleucids, they were given special privileges by Antiochus III in 198 B.C.E. And even in the instance of the decrees forbidding the practice of Judaism issued by his son, Antiochus Epiphanes, in 167 B.C.E., only if we view the struggle in Judaea as a civil war between Jewish factions can we explain the apparent speed with which Hellenization spread in certain quarters. In any case, a mere five years after Antiochus had issued his decrees, his successor restored their earlier rights to the Jews.

Under the Romans, the Jews maintained and even strengthened their vertical alliance. Cicero, speaking in 59 B.C.E., notes how numerous and how influential in the assemblies the Jews are. We hear of two (or perhaps three) expulsions of the Jews from Rome because of proselytizing, but the expulsions in every case must have been short-lived. The key to the strong position of the Jews was, above all, the gratitude that Julius Caesar, to whom all the emperors looked as their founder, felt to the Jews for their assistance during the civil war with Pompey and the numerous privileges he granted to them. The fact that no fewer than eight cities in Asia Minor were pressured by the Romans to stop their harassment of the Jews indicates both how deeply these privileges were resented locally and how strongly the central Roman government felt about protecting the Jews. The occasional exceptions to this policy are blamed by Philo on a corrupt governor or on an insane emperor. Indeed, the emperor, Caligula, was soon assassinated in 41 C.E.; and his successor, Claudius, in whose accession a Jew, Agrippa I, had played the key role, reaffirmed the civic rights of the Jews.

True, procurators in Judaea, like Roman provincial administrators elsewhere, were frequently corrupt; but Jews were often successful in pressing appeals to the governor of Syria, under whose jurisdiction the procurators functioned; or they could, through their contacts at the imperial court, appeal to the emperor himself. An example of the latter was Josephus's success, through a Jewish actor and through Nero's wife, Poppaea Sabina, in getting the Emperor Nero to overrule the detention of some priests by the procurator Felix.

So strong was the foundation of the policy of toleration toward the Jews that even after the long and bloody revolt of 66–74 the Romans refused to remove the special privileges of the Jews in such important cities as Antioch and Alexandria, despite the insistent request of the non-Jewish population. Again, even after the great Diaspora revolt of 115–17, the Romans did not change the fundamentals of their policy. When, to be sure, after the Bar Kochba rebellion of 132–35 the Emperor Hadrian forbade many Jewish observances, these edicts, too, were soon alleviated by his successor, Antoninus Pius, who came to the throne in 138. In the third century, so great was the admiration for Abraham of the Emperor Alexander Severus, who reigned from 222 to 235, that he kept a bust of the patriarch in his private sanctuary; he was even taunted by the anti-Jewish populace of Alexandria and Antioch with the title "Syrian synagogue-chief." Indeed, the official policy of the Roman government was not merely to tolerate Judaism but positively to protect it, so long as it posed no threat, through attempts at proselytism, to the state cult. Moreover, in the third century Jews were even permitted to hold governmental, presumably municipal, offices. Remarkably, even after the Roman emperors embraced Christianity as the official state religion, there was no sudden change in the official attitude toward the Jews.

Indeed, though the rabbinic leaders denounced Rome as a wicked kingdom, they appreciated for the most part the *pax Romana* and the Romans' devotion to justice and fairness; and in fact we nowhere hear in the Talmudic corpus of any overt discrimination against Jews in matters pertaining to civil rights.

In addition to inherent strength and protection by various governments, a major factor in preserving Jewish existence was the cohesion among the Jews produced by the hatred of the masses toward them. Part of this hatred was due to the importance of the positions occupied by the Jews in the vast bureaucracy, especially in Ptolemaic Egypt, as tax collectors and policemen. Whereas, however, the Ptolemaic economy was a state socialism, under the Romans the path was opened for individual initiative. When the Jews took advantage of this opportunity, they incurred the wrath and envy of the non-Jews. Although the Jews no longer held the hated position of middlemen, there was no decline in popular hatred toward them, apparently because of envy and fear that they would overwhelm the non-Jews in numbers. Moreover, the fact that all adult male Jews everywhere were expected to contribute a half shekel every year to the Temple and that they were overwhelmingly conscientious in doing so resulted in the accumulation of great wealth in the Temple and in resentment among those who were aware of this, especially in view of the shortage of gold in Italy. What added to this envy and created additional bitterness during this period was the rapidly increasing number of contributors due to the success of the Jews in gaining converts.

Moreover, in Egypt the Jews were apparently successfully involved in the lucrative shipping trade. The several references in classical literature to the wealth of the Jews, especially as resulting from the monopoly that they had on the production of balsam in the Land of Israel, are a clue to the envy of this wealth, which was apparently a major source of hostility. In addition, the loyalty of Jews to one another and their isolation from other people due to their restrictive code of law provoked the charge that they hated every other people.

The hatred of the mob reached a climax in a series of riots. The first of these, in 38 c.e. in Alexandria, was occasioned by resentment at the privileged position and influence of the Jews. Normally the government would have prevented the outbreak of the attack, but this time the governor, Flaccus, cooperated with the rioters because he felt that he needed their help to bolster his own deteriorating position. That the economic factor promoted tension is clear—the immediate occasion of the riot was the display of Jewish wealth and power by the visit of Agrippa I to Alexandria. The Jews were accused, moreover, of dual loyalty; but in the end "international Jewish power" asserted itself, and Flaccus was recalled and executed.

The most violent outbreak occurred in Alexandria in 66 c.e., on the eve of the revolt of the Jews against the Romans in Palestine. Apparently, the opponents of the Jews felt assured that the government would favor their cause against a people who were now perceived as unpatriotic rebels. But the Jewish community showed its vaunted unanimity in rescuing three Jews who had been seized by the anti-Jewish mob. The government did not support the Jews because, it would seem, the latter were preparing to assist their fellow Jews in the revolt against the Romans.

That a series of attacks on the Jews broke out, particularly in Caesarea and in Syria, when the revolt began in 66 is an indication of how deepseated was the popular resentment against the Jews. Because the Jews were actually rebelling against the government, the Romans no longer felt a duty to protect them. As for the motives of the opponents of the Jews, Josephus lists three overlapping factors: hatred, fear, and economic greed. The fear was increased by the success of the Jews in winning both proselytes and "sympathizers," the latter being non-Jews who observed some Jewish practices without actually converting to Judaism. And yet once the revolt was over, the Romans restrained the fury of the mob, and

Titus in the year 70 reaffirmed the reliability of the vertical alliance by refusing to alter the privileged status of the Jews of Antioch, despite pressure from non-Jews.

The extreme bitterness felt by the masses toward the Jews may be seen in the reports of vicious atrocities allegedly committed by Jews during the revolt in 115–17 led by the pseudo-Messiah Lukuas-Andreas. The messianic nature of this revolt, like (apparently) that of 66–74 and certainly like that of Bar Kochba (132–35), may well help to explain the fear felt by the non-Jews that the Jews, who were expanding so rapidly in numbers and economic power, would soon dominate the world.

As for the attitude of intellectuals toward the Jews, whereas most scholars have emphasized what they consider the almost universal prevalence of virulent hatred of the Jews among ancient intellectuals, a systematic examination of the comments of non-Jewish writers indicates that the overwhelming majority are either neutral or even favorable. Moreover, many of those who have negative views of the Jews are satirists or rhetorical historians who are clearly exaggerating.

The mere fact that Jews were unlike others in their practices would not have led others to hate them any more than it led to organized hatred or persecution of the people of India or Britain or Arabia, who, from a Greek and Roman point of view, were so idiosyncratic. Nevertheless, the main, most serious, and most recurrent charge against Jews was that they hated humankind, that is, that they were unwilling to grant any legitimacy to any other religious or philosophical point of view. This charge led to a blood libel, that Jews kidnapped Greeks in order to sacrifice them, after which the Jews would partake of the flesh of the sacrificial victim and vow hostility to the Greeks. The report that it was Antiochus Epiphanes who was said to have discovered a Greek in the Temple being fattened for sacrifice would probably have backfired, however, in the eyes of the Romans, inasmuch as it was Antiochus who had challenged Roman power in Egypt and had been forced to withdraw and consequently had been viewed with extreme suspicion by the Romans. Moreover, the Romans were not likely to forget that his father had offered refuge to that most hated of the enemies of the Romans, Hannibal. The prohibition against non-Jews entering the Temple precinct made them particularly suspicious. The pagan intellectuals regarded such illiberalism as especially dangerous, inasmuch as the Jews were regarded as undermining what at least some Roman intellectuals believed was the basis of the religious strength that had built the Roman republic and empire, and inasmuch as the Jews were so often successful rivals to their missionary propaganda.

But Jews were equipped with rebuttals to these charges. Such a Graeco-Jewish writer as the historian Eupolemus calls attention to the friendly dealings of King Solomon with the non-Jewish king of Tyre. The historian Artapanus emphasizes the love the Egyptian masses had for Moses. Philo calls attention to the prayers and sacrifices offered by the high priest not only for his countrymen but also for the entire human race. In particular, Josephus in his *Antiquities* stresses, in his account of the readiness of Abraham to sacrifice his son Isaac, that G-d does not crave human blood. Abraham himself is depicted as debating with Egyptian priests in a manner reminiscent of the spirit of Hellenistic philosophers, magnanimously ready to adopt their doctrines if he finds them superior to his own or, if he should win the debate, to convert the others to his own beliefs. Moreover, Abraham, far from keeping his scientific knowledge to himself, teaches the Egyptians mathematics and astronomy. Again, in his summary of the Mosaic Code in his treatise *Against Apion*, Josephus stresses the duty of Jews to share food and supplies with others. He then counterattacks by noting that it is the Greeks, notably the much-admired Spartans, who expel foreigners, whereas the Jews welcome proselytes. As for narrow-mindedness toward other religions, he adopts the reading of the Septuagint (Exod 22:27) that it is prohibited to curse gods, that is, to speak ill of other religions. Likewise, the harmony Jews were alleged to show among themselves would have been admired by those who deplored the civil strife that was widespread among the Greeks. Furthermore, Josephus is particularly sensitive to the charge that the Jews are aggressive in seeking converts; hence, he omits the circumcision of the Shechemites by Simeon and Levi.

As for the peculiar Jewish view of G-d, the failure of the Jews to worship the gods of the state was, indeed, at least ostensibly, an unpatriotic act, inasmuch as there was, in ancient times, no separation of religion and state. And yet the Jewish attack on pagan anthropomorphism actually found a sympathetic ear among some pagan intellectuals because it had been anticipated by Xenophanes as early as the end of the sixth century B.C.E. Even with regard to the censure of images, the Jews are praised by Hecataeus and Varro and are paired with the Persians, whom Herodotus admired, as well as praised by Stoic philosophers starting with Zeno and by Neo-Pythagoreans, particularly Numenius. Such an intellectual as Strabo is in obvious agreement with the Jewish view of G-d as encompassing everything on land and sea and as being the essence of things.

The practices of the Jews that, more than any others, served to differentiate them from non-Jews and that served so successfully to keep them separate were circumcision, the Sabbath, and the dietary laws. Circumcision was regarded by the pagans as a physical deformity and as such disqualified participation in the Olympic Games. In and of itself, however, it should not have elicited hostility, because it was practiced by several other peoples, including the Egyptian priests, though it was associated particularly with the Jews. If it did produce hostility, the reason was that it was the sine qua non for conversion of males, in contrast to the various other practices adopted by the so-called sympathizers.

Inasmuch as the pagans did not have the concept of a week, they found the idea of the Sabbath, which they realized was so central in Judaism, utterly peculiar and full of folly, especially when it hampered the Jews from fighting on that day. Their derogatory references to the Sabbath as a fast day apparently arose from their view of it as a day of abstention, actually from work rather than from food, as many mistakenly thought. And yet an antiquarian as important as Plutarch could, in clearly laudatory fashion, connect the Sabbath with the worship of the ever-popular Dionysus. Moreover, in answer to the charge that the Sabbath inculcates idleness, Philo replies that the law actually inures men to endure hardship and incites them to labor the other six days.

As for the dietary laws, the Jews' abstention from pork, a particular delicacy to both the Greeks and Romans, seemed strange. But the ancients realized that other peoples, such as the Egyptians, also had peculiar food laws; and the speculations of a Plutarch as to the reasons why the Jews abstain from pork are by no means disrespectful. Moreover, there was a parallel in the even more peculiar diet advocated by the much-admired Pythagoras.

Again, the charge that the Jews kept an ass's head in the Temple and worshipped it might even, to some degree, have produced a positive reaction, inasmuch as the ass was sacred to the gods Dionysus and Apollo and asses had played a key role in several military victories; moreover, asses were extremely useful in labor and agriculture.

To those who believed, in the words of Socrates, that the uncriticized life is not worth living, the credulity of the Jews in accepting the Torah before even being told of its contents and in following the instructions of their priestly leaders was subject to ridicule. And yet even these criticisms of the Jews are, for the most part, more in the nature of wonder at their naïveté, as we can see from the sympathetic remarks of Hecataeus or, at worst, of bemused contempt, as we note in Horace, rather than in the category of vicious attack. Moreover, Josephus, in his paraphrase of the Bible, answers these objections by saying that, as for miracles, everyone is welcome to his or her own opinion.

The Jews are also satirized as beggars, but this may be a sarcastic way of alluding to their economic power or of indicating their attractiveness to those who convert to Judaism because of the well-organized Jewish charities.

Finally, intellectuals such as Cicero, to be sure with rhetorical exaggeration, refer to the power of the Jews as a "pressure group." The influence of the Jews at the imperial court reached its height in the first century during the reigns of the Emperors Caligula, Claudius, and Nero; and the fact that a Jew, Agrippa I, was chiefly responsible for Claudius becoming emperor is sufficient testimony to this power.

We must stress, however, that the intellectuals were far from unanimous in viewing the Jews negatively. In fact, a number of them, particularly among the Neo-Pythagoreans and Neo-Platonists, admired them. Moreover, in any case, anti-Jewish intellectuals as such had relatively little influence in molding either governmental or mass public opinion. Indeed, none of them, with one possible exception, ever took the lead in successfully inciting a physical attack on the Jews.

We must now attempt to explain how the Jews—tolerated, criticized, and hated—managed to attract so many to their religion, whether as proselytes or "sympathizers."

In the first place, inasmuch as antiquity of a nation was so admired in those days, the Jews had a great advantage in that they could claim extreme antiquity, especially as compared with the Greeks and even more with the Romans (who could, at most, trace their history back only to Aeneas and the period of the Trojan War), and could indeed insist that Moses was the most ancient of all legislators in the history of the world. What is particularly important is that even the opponents of the Jews were ready to concede their antiquity. Ironically, by declaring that the Jews were Egyptians by race, the opponents of the Jews were actually associating them with the civilization the Greeks regarded as the most ancient. Even Apion, the arch-enemy of the Jews, admitted that the Exodus had occurred in the time of Inachus, the first king of Argos, who was the son of Titans and hence of the second generation of the Greek gods and the ancestor of the god Dionysus and of the great hero Heracles and the Cretan lawgiver Minos. Elsewhere and in contradiction, Apion synchronized the Exodus with the founding of Rome and of Carthage, a chronology that certainly gave great renown to the Jews.

Other writers greatly honored the Jews by connecting them with the legendary Semiramis, the founder of Babylon and Nineveh, or with Udaeus, one of the Spartoi at Thebes, who was supposedly among the military companions of Dionysus. In particular, the Jewish sect known as the Essenes were said by no less an authority than the first-century Roman encyclopedist Pliny the Elder to have been in existence through multitudes of ages.

Even that arch Jew-baiter, Tacitus, presents no fewer than six accounts of Jewish origins, four of which have distinctly pro-Jewish intimations, and all of which impute great antiquity to the Jews, namely that they came from Crete at the time of Saturn's expulsion by Jupiter, that they go back to the reign of Isis herself in Egypt, that they derive from the reign of King Cepheus of Ethiopia (the father of the renowned mythical Andromeda and associated with the Ethiopians, known for their wisdom, piety, and bravery), and that they are identified with the Solymi (who are famous in Homer as the people against whom the renowned Bellerophon fought). In particular, the association with Saturn was with the god who was connected with the golden age of humankind and whose return was longed for almost messianically. The fact that Saturn was said to have the greatest potency among the planets may explain the mixture of respect for and fear of the Jews, who were at this time winning so many adherents. To be associated with the Cretans gave enormous prestige to the Jews, because the Cretans were acknowledged to have had a great civilization long before the mainland of Greece flourished. Indeed, Tacitus admits that the rites introduced by Moses are defended by their antiquity. Such theories diminished the gulf between the Jewish barbarians and the Greeks. The complimentary nature of Tacitus's remarks about the Jews may be especially appreciated when they are compared with his relative silence about the origins of the Britons and the Germans. Indeed, it is striking that Tacitus, who clearly depends on the anti-Jewish account of Lysimachus, omits some of the most scurrilous elements of that version.

The early Christians realized the value of the antiquity ascribed to the Jews—for as Origen's opponent, the pagan Celsus, put it, nothing can be both new and true—and chose to identify themselves with the Jews. Though this created the problem of how to explain their departure from biblical laws, Christians adopted this path rather than following the lead of the Marcionite Christian heresy and declaring themselves a new religion. This explains why Origen goes out of his way to avoid attacking Judaism in his reply to Celsus.

The Jews were attractive to non-Jews not only because of their antiquity but also because they were conceded by leading intellectuals to possess the cardinal virtues of wisdom, courage, temperance, justice, and piety. In particular, Pythagoras, who for wisdom and piety was ranked above all other philosophers with the possible exception of Socrates, is said to have been indebted to the Jews for some of his doctrines. Furthermore, three contemporaries in the generation after Aristotle's death— the historian Megasthenes and the philosophers Theophrastus and Clearchus—presented the Jews as a people worthy, from a Greek point of view, of the highest of compliments, namely as philosophers by race. Additionally, their contemporary, the historian Hecataeus of Abdera, expressed admiration for the Jews in that superiority in wisdom and virtue were the qualities they sought in their high priests. The Jewish system of education and level of learning likewise won commendation from Aristotle and Theophrastus and even from the otherwise anti-Jewish Stoic philosopher Seneca the Younger.

Inasmuch as the Jews had been accused by Apollonius Molon in the first century B.C.E. of being the most untalented of all barbarians, it is surely significant that at the end of that century the historian Pompeius

Trogus speaks of the biblical Joseph in the most flattering terms as master of magic and as inventor of the science of interpreting dreams, both of which were tremendously admired in antiquity and which, more importantly, served as a bridge between intellectuals and the masses. Moreover, the immensely learned Varro in the first century B.C.E. praises the Jews for their pure monotheism, which he equates with the ancient Roman theology. And even if the Jews were accused of lack of inventiveness, this would simply couple them with the ancient Egyptians and with the much-admired Spartans, as well as with the rulers of Plato's ideal state.

Furthermore, several Graeco-Jewish historians praise the Jews for their wisdom. Thus, Eupolemus declares that Moses was the first wise man. Additionally, the Romans, who placed such a premium on their system of law, must have been impressed by Eupolemus's claim that Moses was the first to reduce laws to writing. Again, Pseudo-Eupolemus speaks of Abraham as excelling all people in wisdom and ascribes to him the discovery of astrology, which had such a high status in the ancient world. Likewise, Artapanus speaks of Joseph as discovering methods of measurement. Moreover, Philo asserts that the famous pre-Socratic philosopher, Heraclitus, was indebted to Moses for his theory of opposites. Finally, in his paraphrase of the Bible, Josephus portrays Abraham as a philosopher whose logic is impeccable and who is able to arrive at an original and unique proof of the existence of G-d. Abraham's unselfishness in sharing his scientific knowledge with the Egyptians is a particular source of praise. Indeed, Josephus stresses the excellence of Jewish leaders in the sciences, particularly mathematics and astronomy. Ancient pagan readers would surely have been impressed by Josephus's extra-biblical remark that the wise King Solomon was so honest intellectually that he admitted that a young Tyrian lad named Abdemon successfully solved all problems that he had put to him and that he was consequently wiser than the king himself.

A number of pagan writers in the second, third, and fourth centuries praise the Jews for their wisdom, particularly in philosophy and astrology. Moreover, inasmuch as Sibyls were regarded by the ancients as inspired prophetesses, acknowledgement by pagan writers that the Jews had Sibyls was surely a compliment. Especially outstanding is the tribute paid to them by the philosopher Numenius of Apamea, who asks, "What is Plato but Moses speaking in Attic?" Likewise, Porphyry introduces his own god as himself bearing witness to the wisdom of the Jews. In particular, the early Christian intellectuals in their disputations bear witness to the Jewish reputation for learning. Indeed, the extremely influential Origen suggests that Plato was indebted to the Jews for his philosophical doctrines. The Jews' lack of prominence, he adds, is due to their having deliberately withdrawn so as to avoid contact with the multitude. Again, Jerome, who is hardly sympathetic to the Jews, pays tribute to Jewish women who undergo great sacrifices in order to provide religious teachers for their sons. He alludes to the Jews' love of books, noting that every synagogue had a library from which books might be borrowed.

Inasmuch as the Jews had been charged with cowardice by Apollonius Molon, several pagan writers as well as the Jews themselves go to great length to provide evidence of their courage. In particular, several of the ancients, notably Hecataeus, praise the obstinate courage of the Jews in adhering to their laws. Their brave defense of Jerusalem in the war against the Romans is cited by Dio Cassius; and even Tacitus notes their contempt for death. Furthermore, in his paraphrase of the Bible, Josephus stresses the military prowess and courage of such heroic figures as Abraham, Moses, Joshua, Saul, and David.

The temperance of the Jews, which is seen particularly in their eating habits, is praised by Aristotle. Again, in having special dietary laws the Jews were no different from such respected peoples as the Egyptians and the Magi. Moreover, Josephus stresses the modesty, humility, and moderation of such Biblical heroes as Moses, Saul, and David.

Philo and Josephus are insistent that justice and love of humanity, with which it is closely joined, are fostered by the law code of the Jews. Again, Josephus embellishes the justice, unselfishness, and generosity of his biblical heroes, notably Abraham, Moses, David, and Solomon. Connected with justice is the responsibility to be truthful; and here Josephus defends Abraham from the charge of lying to the Egyptians and to Abimelech. Even Tacitus admits that the Jews are inflexibly trustworthy to each other. Indeed, the ethical standards of the Jews are praised by such diverse judges as the Emperor Alexander Severus in the third century and the Christian Bishop Ambrose in the fourth century.

Finally, inasmuch as such critics of the Jews as Apollonius Molon and Lysimachus had charged that the laws of the Jews teach impiety, and inasmuch as the Jews' piety—the fifth cardinal virtue according to Plato and the Stoics—was admired by Hecataeus, Porphyry, and Julian, as seen in their regard for the Jewish laws, a point the Romans especially appreciated, Josephus goes to great lengths to emphasize that the first quality the Mosaic code is designed to promote is piety; and he stresses the presence of this quality in Abraham, Jacob, Moses, Joshua, Saul, David, and Solomon.

To a very great degree, the success of a movement in antiquity, whether religious or philosophical, depended on the reputation of its founder or lawgiver. Here Judaism had a great advantage in the personality of Moses, whose connection with Egypt undoubtedly gave him a certain notoriety, inasmuch as Alexandrian scholars dominated the intellectual scene during the Hellenistic Age. Thus, Hecataeus praises him for his practical wisdom and courage and indeed looks on him as a kind of philosopher-king who showed outstanding ability in selecting priestly leaders and in establishing a constitution highly reminiscent of the much-admired Lycurgan constitution of Sparta. Furthermore, he is distanced by Hecataeus, Strabo, and much later by Julian from the changes in Jewish traditional practices that are ascribed to Moses' successors.

The identification of Moses as an Egyptian priest by several writers, including some opponents of the Jews, such as Manetho and Chaeremon, definitely added to his stature, because the Egyptian priests were said to possess esoteric knowledge. As a lawgiver, Moses is paralleled by the historians Diodorus and Strabo in the first century B.C.E. with the greatest of all lawgivers in antiquity, including Minos and Lycurgus. He is likewise compared with the greatest prophets, scientists, philosophers, and musicians. Indeed, Strabo pays Moses the supreme compliment of remaking him in the image of his own Stoic philosophy. Even Tacitus bestows respect on him as the leader who freed his people from their misery by finding water for them.

The greatest tribute to Moses as a lawgiver is found in Pseudo-Longinus's *On the Sublime*, which cites a passage from Genesis to establish the point that the basic ingredient of great writing is not so much literary style as a great mind. Moses was apparently so well known that Pseudo-Longinus and Numenius can refer to him simply as "the lawgiver," and Quintilian can refer to him as "the founder of the Jewish superstition," relying on the reader to supply his name.

Of supreme importance in establishing Moses' reputation are such statements as that Moses invented the alphabet (according to the historian Eupolemus) and that he was called Musaeus, the teacher or student of Orpheus (founder of particularly popular mysteries), and Hermes, the god of communication (according to the historian Artapanus).

The greatest buildup of Moses' virtues is to be found in Josephus, who, in extra-biblical comments, stresses his lofty genealogy, the wondrous events attending his birth, his exceptional physical development and his precocious intellectual development as a child, his handsome stature (he is particularly concerned to answer the charge that Moses had been afflicted with leprosy), and his possession of the four cardinal virtues and of the spiritual quality of piety. Moreover, Josephus portrays him as a Platonic-like philosopher-king, a hero in the mold of an Aeneas and a Romulus, a Stoic-like sage, a high priest, and a prophet. Inasmuch as, according to Josephus, the race of humankind is by nature morose and censorious, the importance of Moses' leadership was all the greater. In his fearless ability to stand up to the fickle multitude and their sedition, he is depicted as a veritable Pericles; and in his willingness to undergo toil on behalf of the people and in his genius in inspiring them, he is reminiscent of Aeneas. It is particularly as an educator, legislator, and poet, and above all as general and prophet that Moses excels. Josephus's modifications of the biblical narrative are occasioned by his apologetic concern to defend the Jews against the charges of their critics, especially cowardice, provincialism, and intolerance, and by his positive desire to portray a personality who would be fully comparable to such great leaders, whether historical or legendary, as Heracles, Lycurgus, Aeneas, and Pericles.

Inasmuch as the Romans placed such emphasis on law, Josephus, though his *Antiquities* is ostensibly a history, summarizes the Mosaic code at great length. Moreover, as compared with other lawgivers, Moses has the advantage of having promulgated his laws far earlier. Moses is also praised for having set up an educational system that combined theoretical precept and practical training. Additionally, Josephus omits the biblical references to Moses' speech impediment and indeed emphasizes his ability, so important as we see in Thucydides' portrait of Pericles, to persuade the masses. Furthermore, inasmuch as music was so important to the ancients, Josephus adds to the biblical portrayal of Moses as poet and singer and actually ascribes to him the invention of a musical instrument. Again, because generalship was the key factor in the superiority of the Greeks and Macedonians over the "barbarians," it should not be surprising that Moses is on fifteen occasions referred to as a general, even though the Septuagint has no such reference. In particular, Josephus has an extensive extra-biblical account of Moses' campaign on behalf of the Egyptians against the famous Ethiopians to emphasize the debt that the Egyptians owed to him for his success against their most powerful enemy. Moses also shows great courage and sagacity in leading the Israelites during the Exodus. Again, in his combination of unrelenting sternness toward a recalcitrant enemy and mercy toward a submissive one, Moses exemplifies Virgil's standard "Parcere subjectis et debellare superbos."

Likewise, Josephus highlights Moses' modesty in his willingness to take advice from his father-in-law and in his readiness to acknowledge this assistance; here he stresses Moses' concern with telling the truth. Josephus is also concerned to make clear that Moses was not prejudiced against Gentiles, as we see in his differentiation between Pharaoh and the Egyptians.

Plato had defined justice as a harmony of the virtues of wisdom, courage, and temperance; similarly, Josephus's Moses exhorts the Israelites to preserve the harmony of the code of laws. Where there is embarrassment, as in the biblical account of the Israelites' "borrowing" of jewelry and clothing from the Egyptians, Josephus either omits the passage or explains that the Egyptians took the initiative in honoring the Israelites with gifts. Moreover, inasmuch as the virtue of humanity was closely related to that of justice, Josephus, in obvious reply to the detractors of the Jews, stresses that Moses inculcated into the Jews the duty of sharing with others and the quality of tolerance for non-Jewish religious beliefs. He also emphasizes Moses' gallantry and hospitality—virtues very much prized in the ancient world.

The crucial importance of piety, actually the fifth of the cardinal virtues, may be seen in Josephus's remark that once Moses had won the obedience of the Israelites to the dictates of piety he had no further difficulties in persuading them to obey all the other commandments. Moreover, it is particularly effective that Moses is praised by a non-Jew, Raguel, his father-in-law, as being responsible for all the salvation of the Israelites.

Finally, the fact that Moses' name is so often connected with magic, which was so popular in the ancient world, gave those who were associated with his name considerable power and influence. His renown as a magician extended beyond his appearance in catalogues listed by intelligentsia to magical books and charms, where he is on a par with Hermes Trismegistos, the magician par excellence in the Greek pantheon. His alleged knowledge of the Divine name and of the Divine mysteries, which allegedly gave him the power to perform such tremendous miracles, attracted Jews and non-Jews alike.

These, then, were some of the strengths of Judaism as it sought to reach out to non-Jews. To be sure, some argue that there was no aggressive missionary activity, that a number of passages speak of conversions only as an apocalyptic act on the Last Day, that no ancient Jewish writer says that such a widespread conversion had taken place (though it would surely have been a source of great pride), that there is no mention of a single proselyte in the 520 papyrus fragments or in the 122 inscriptions from Egypt included in the *Corpus Papyrorum Judaicarum*, that only a small proportion of rabbinic discussion is concerned with the status of non-Jews, that there is an absence in rabbinic literature of firm data regarding initiation rites into Judaism, that we do not know the name of a single missionary (other than a few who preached the Gospel), and that we do not have a single missionary tract. Furthermore, according to this view, for a missionary movement to succeed, it is necessary that the unenlightened be viewed as damned, whereas Judaism assured righteous Gentiles their reward in the world to come and, during this period, adopted a tolerant attitude toward other religions.

And yet there is strong demographic evidence that the number of Jews increased dramatically from 150,000 at the time of the destruction of the First Temple in 586 B.C.E. to eight million at the time of the destruction of the Second Temple in 70 C.E.; and the most likely explanation of this vast increase is the success of proselytism.

There is, moreover, ample literary evidence from the *Letter of Aristeas*, the *Sibylline Oracles*, 2 Maccabees, the New Testament, the *Testament of Levi*, the *Testament of Joseph*, Philo, Josephus, the Christian Minucius Felix, and rabbinic literature that Judaism was active in seeking to win proselytes. Further evidence may be discerned in the resentment that proselytism aroused, as seen notably in Matthew 23:15, Horace's *Satires*, Seneca, Tacitus, and Juvenal. In addition, we have reports that the Jews were expelled from Rome for missionary activities on at least two occasions, in 139 B.C.E. and in 19 C.E., as well as perhaps on a third occasion during the reign of the Emperor Claudius in the middle of the first century.

The question has been raised whether Jewish or anti-Jewish literary propaganda among the pagans was even technically possible. Indeed, among the thousands of scraps of papyri that have been unearthed in Egypt there are no fragments of the anti-Jewish writings of Manetho, Apion, Chaeremon, Lysimachus, or Tacitus; nor have any fragments of any Graeco-Jewish writers been found, with the exception of a few of Philo and one of Josephus. Yet literacy was apparently much more widespread than we usually think, certainly by the first century and definitely in the towns, and most likely in a country such as Egypt, where there was a long tradition of bureaucracy and where writing material, namely papyrus, was readily available. It is precisely when there was a definite rise in literacy that a dramatic increase in the rate of conversion to Judaism occurred. Indeed, one reason for the rise in popularity of Hermes was that he was the Greek god of communication. A major reason why philosophical schools, which had many of the characteristics of religious groups, held such a dominant place in the Hellenistic and Roman world was that they produced tracts to explain their teachings. Moreover, by the middle of the first century libraries, both public and private, had become numerous. In any case, the papyri may not be representative, because they are perhaps the books that were discarded rather than the ones that were read. If readers, including women, came primarily from the upper classes, we should not be surprised to hear, as we do from Philo, Josephus, Tacitus, inscriptions, and rabbinic writings, of a number of proselytes and "sympathizers" from these classes.

The most obvious book that could have been used as a missionary tract was the Septuagint. That it was familiar to readers is clear from the way that Pseudo-Longinus, as we have noted, refers to the "lawgiver of the Jews" without bothering to identify him. Philo clearly implies that the translation was made for proselyting purposes, and he notes that each year, on the anniversary of the translation, a festival was held to which both Jews and whole multitudes of non-Jews came. Josephus also implies that the Septuagint was used by Gentiles.

One may also detect missionary motives in certain Apocryphal and Pseudepigraphical books, notably the book of Judith, the *Sibylline Oracles*, the *Wisdom of Solomon*, 2 Enoch, the *Letter of Aristeas* (especially its attempt to equate the teachings of the Bible with the highest ideas of Greek philosophy), Pseudo-Phocylides, and *Joseph and Asenath* (above all, the glorification of Asenath as the prototype of the righteous proselyte). Likewise, the apologetic works of several Graeco-Jewish writers, notably Aristobulus, Eupolemus, Artapanus, and Cleodemus-Malchus, particularly the claim that the Jews had anticipated the Greeks in making fundamental contributions to civilization, may well have been used in the campaign to overcome Gentile objections to conversion. Similarly, Ezekiel's tragedy, *The Exodus*, with its glorification of Moses, may perhaps have served as a vehicle of propaganda. Several of Philo's works, notably *De Vita Contemplativa*, *Quod Omnis Probus Liber Sit*, and *De Vita Mosis*, especially the view that Greek philosophy was indebted to the Pentateuch, are directed also or even primarily toward Gentiles. Moreover, the fact that Josephus cites as a precedent for his *Antiquities* the translation of the Torah into Greek for King Ptolemy Philadelphus in 270 B.C.E. shows that his work was directed to Gentiles with apologetic intent. This is further indicated by his omission of several embarrassing episodes that would certainly have been known to a Jewish audience acquainted with either the Hebrew original or the Septuagint translation. Indeed, it seems unlikely that Josephus would have spent almost twenty years writing his *Antiquities* in Greek if he did not have hopes of attracting a wide readership among pagan intellectuals. There is also good reason to think that the apologetic essay *Against Apion* might have been employed by missionaries, especially in stressing the antiquity of the Jews and in insisting that the famous Greek philosophers had borrowed their doctrines from the Bible.

People were also converted through oral persuasion. Indeed, Philo's remark that on the Sabbath thousands of schools in every city in Egypt were wide open, teaching the virtues, indicates that they attracted not only Jews but also Gentiles. The Jewess in Juvenal who can explain the significance of dreams may well indicate still another avenue of missionary activity. If we ask why missionizing is not mentioned in the Mishnah, an answer would seem to be that such activities apparently occurred primarily in the Diaspora. If we hear of no Jewish missions into infidel regions, the reason may be that Philo, as the leader of the Jewish community of Alexandria, was sensitive to the charge of Jewish aggressiveness in proselyting and hence declined to publicize them. Likewise, Josephus, the one author who might have been expected to name them, is not particularly interested in religious history and, in any case, is careful not to offend his patrons, the Romans, who were, as we have seen, very sensitive about proselyting. Similarly, the rabbis were concerned not to antagonize the Romans. The fact that the New Testament speaks, without further explanation, of Paul the preacher to the Gentiles, thus indicating his role as a missionary, would indicate that such a function was not considered novel.

Moreover, we hear of two cases of what seem to be forced conversions, for nationalistic reasons, of whole nations, the Idumaeans and the Ituraeans, in the Land of Israel in the latter part of the second century B.C.E. Furthermore, the Jews were, we are told, inclined to revolt in 66 by an ambiguous oracle stating, "At that time one from their country would become ruler of the world." Such messianic speculation may well have spurred conversions, and vice versa.

Undoubtedly, the fact that Jews were now living side by side with Gentiles in large numbers exposed Gentiles to Judaism. Furthermore, Jews were forced to defend themselves because they now came into direct contact with such missionary philosophies as Epicureanism, Stoicism, and Cynicism and with mystery cults from Egypt and the Orient. Moreover, the far-flung Phoenician diaspora, which, by a startling coincidence, disappeared at about this time, may, with its language so similar to Hebrew, have been won over in considerable measure to Judaism. In Syria we hear that large numbers of women were converted to Judaism, perhaps having been attracted by the relatively more elevated position of women in Judaism and by the fact that they did not have to undergo excision.

The most remarkable success of the proselytizing movement took place in Adiabene in Mesopotamia in the early part of the first century, when the royal family was converted. This incident illustrates several characteristics of the movement: its particular impact on women, the political factor in seeking alliances, the connection of conversion with economic goals, the initial winning of "sympathizers," and the role of reading the Bible in effecting the final conversion.

One would have expected that the destruction of the Temple by the Romans in 70 C.E. would have dealt a blow to the prestige of the Jews and to the proselyting movement in particular. And yet the movement reached its greatest success, at least in Roman official circles, under Domitian at the end of the first century.

From the liberal attitude toward pagans in such a work as the *Letter of Aristeas*, one might have deduced that Jews had no incentive to convert the pagans. Nevertheless, that Jews were so motivated seems clear from such a statement as Philo's that Gentiles who do not convert are the enemies of the Jews and of every person everywhere.

The attractions of Judaism in the Hellenistic and early Roman periods, besides its antiquity, its reputation for the cardinal virtues, and its illustrious founder Moses, included economic advantages (especially charitable relief for the poor, accommodations in synagogues that served, in effect, as hostels, interest-free loans, and commercial contacts with Jews in various cities); its reputation for magic, the occult, astrology, the interpretation of dreams; identification with the national aspirations of the Jews; inner security in a close-knit community; and admiration for the Jews' stubbornness in abiding by their tenets. Paradoxically, the loss of the Temple in 70 C.E. may have strengthened the proselyting movement, because it opened the way for conversion even of those who did not seek to identify themselves with a Jewish state. Moreover, at a time when Oriental religions generally were most successful in gaining adherents, Judaism, as an Oriental religion, had a particular appeal. Furthermore, because such missionary philosophies as Epicureanism, Stoicism, and Cynicism were so successful in converting people to their points of view, Judaism discovered that the best defense is a good offense, especially in emphasizing its superior ethical code. In addition, the common international language, the κοινή Greek, made conversion appeals more readily possible.

Once converted, proselytes were granted virtually all the privileges of born Jews. Indeed, the rabbis were generally very favorably disposed toward them. The few negative opinions reflect the failure of some proselytes to carry out their commitment. Such diverse opinions are an indication that the issue of proselytism was a live one during the Talmudic period.

There is good reason for believing that, in addition to winning multitudes of proselytes, the Jews succeeded in gaining many "sympathizers," the so-called "G-d-fearers," who, although observing certain practices of Judaism, notably the Sabbath, did not actually convert. Even if we did not have actual evidence of the existence of such a group, we would postulate it on the basis of parallel movements, which have historically led to the evolution of such intermediate classes.

Furthermore, we have a possible reference to such a group implied in the statement in Valerius Maximus that because the Jews had attempted to "infect" the Roman customs with the cult of Jupiter Sabazius they were expelled from Rome in 139 B.C.E. Other possible references are to be found in such pagan writers as Cicero, Suetonius, Seneca, Petronius, Epictetus, Dio Cassius, and Julian. The key passage, in Juvenal's *Satires*, clearly differentiates "sympathizers," who observe the Sabbath, from proselytes, who submit to circumcision. There are also allusions to "sympathizers" in Philo and especially in Josephus. A key passage in the latter (*Ant.* 14.110) mentions the contributions to the Temple of Jews and of those who worshipped G-d (that is, "sympathizers"). Likewise, the account of the conversion of Izates, King of Adiabene, illustrates the difference between full proselytes and "sympathizers." In addition, a passage in the *Testament of Joseph* seems to refer to "G-d-fearers" who give up their idol worship. There is clear evidence in rabbinic literature for the existence of such a class in the reference (*Mekilta de-Rabbi Ishmael* 18) to four categories of true worshipers of G-d, two of which are proselytes and "Heaven-fearers." Conclusive is the passage (Jerusalem Talmud, *Megillah* 3.2.74a) stating that even "fearers of Heaven" wear broken sandals on the Day of Atonement. Indeed, there is evidence that the question whether it was permissible to teach the Torah to "sympathizers" was a live issue in the third century. Moreover, there seem to be a number of references to "sympathizers" in Christian literature, notably in the Book of Revelation, Justin Martyr's *Dialogue with Trypho*, Tertullian's *Ad Nationes*, Commodianus's *Instructiones*, Cyril of Alexandria, and the Mandaean Christian book *Ginza*, as well as in the Caelicoli in the *Theodosian Code* (16.8.19). Finally, the very name Sambathion in twenty papyri apparently refers to adherents of a sect of Sabbath-observers; and indeed we have an inscription that speaks of a Sabbatarian association.

The discovery in 1976 of two inscriptions from Aphrodisias in Asia Minor referring to θεοσεβεῖς, i.e., those who reverence G-d, would appear to confirm that at least at the time of the presumed date of the inscriptions, the early third century, there was a distinct class of "sympathizers." Despite the general decline in the fortunes of the Roman Empire during this period, apparently there was continued prosperity, both economically and culturally, in inland Asia Minor. Aphrodisias itself continued to enjoy a special relationship with Rome; and the Jews in particular enjoyed considerable political, economic, and social power. Indeed, the sharp attacks on the Jews by Melito, bishop of the neighboring city of Sardis in the latter part of the second century, may well reflect his resentment against their political and social power, as indicated, for example, by their success in getting the city to turn over its civic basilica for conversion into a synagogue.

The inscriptions themselves from Aphrodisias list fifty-four θεοσεβεῖς (we now know, through inscriptions, of θεοσεβεῖς in four other cities as well) and specifically distinguish them from Jews and proselytes. The fact that nine of these "G-d-fearers" are city councillors indicates that the Jews attracted wealthy and influential people. These "G-d-fearers" apparently made important financial contributions to the synagogues, and this may explain one of the causes of mutual bitterness between Jews and Christians.

The factors that attracted non-Jews, including Christians, to Judaism in the third century, whether as proselytes or as "sympathizers" were, in addition to those noted above, the influence toward Jewish ways exercised by Jews who stayed in the Church; the deep Hellenization of Judaism in Asia Minor and hence the existence of a common language of discourse with non-Jews; the admiration won by Jews for their long history of loyalty to the state; the desire of non-Jews to win the political support of the numerous and influential Jewish community; the high regard of the Jews for law and order; the special privileges accorded to them and hence the safety that they afforded against persecution; the reputation of the Jews for ethical behavior; the reputation of the Jews for incorruptibility of their judges; admiration for their philanthropy and their lack of materialism; the generally friendly relationships between Jews and Christians; the fact that Jews were not ghettoized and that there were numerous commercial contacts between Jews and non-Jews; the readiness of Jews to lend money to non-Jews; the usefulness of the synagogue as a meeting place for economic reasons; the importance of Jews in the production and distribution of food; the general atmosphere that fostered divergent movements within Christianity, several of which were "Judaizing"; the short-lived euphoria created by Julian's efforts to rebuild the Temple; the particular attraction of the Sabbath for relaxation; the experience of non-Jews acting as assistants in performing certain tasks on the Sabbath that were prohibited to Jews; the attraction of Jewish festivals, notably Passover; the inspiring presence in synagogues of scrolls of the Torah and of the prophets; the awesomeness created by oaths taken before Torah scrolls; the veneration of relics of Jewish martyrs in at least one synagogue; the theatricality of the synagogue service; the attraction of the Jewish Oral Torah as codified in the Mishnah; the solemnity of Jewish ritual baths; the admiration for Jewish astronomers and astrologers; the reputation of Jews for magic, the occult, and alchemy; and the reputation of Jews as physicians and faith healers. Although we have almost no information as to what led to conversion to Judaism in any particular instance, these factors certainly exposed non-Jews to Judaism in a most positive fashion.

The Jews of Asia Minor were, however, hardly learned and had relatively few contacts with rabbinic Judaism in the Land of Israel or Babylonia; and there is no mention in the rabbinic corpus of a Torah academy in Asia Minor or of a single student from Asia Minor who studied in academies in the Land of Israel or Babylonia. Such Hellenized communities were apparently successful in attracting many "sympathizers" but relatively few proselytes. The fact that only three people in the Aphrodisias inscriptions are designated as proselytes, whereas fifty-four are referred to as "G-d-fearers" is a clue that few in the third century dared to violate the prohibition of proselytism, whereas many were attracted informally to Jewish practices.

The Roman emperors realized that conversion to Judaism meant adherence not merely to a religion but also to a political state; hence conversion had dangerous political overtones. And yet that proselytism continued, in the third, fourth, and fifth centuries, even after the rise and triumph of Christianity, is clear from Roman imperial legislation. The first specific ban on proselytism was promulgated by the Emperor Septimius Severus in 198/199; but there is evidence in both the church father Eusebius and the pagan Dio Cassius that the ban was ineffective. That proselytism continued is evident from the fact that of the sixty-six laws in the *Codex Theodosianus* pertaining to Jews 21 percent deal with proselytism of free men, 18 percent deal with conversion of slaves, and 3 percent pertain to "G-d-fearers." Hence, we may conclude that the question of conversion to Judaism was the single most important issue pertaining to Jews on which the emperors, both in the East and in the West, legislated and that the issue remained unresolved for centuries. Indeed, on no fewer than five occasions emperors saw the need to repeat a complete ban on proselytism and on two other occasions to forbid circumcision in particular. The modifications in language and especially the increased penalties with each new piece of legislation are clues that we are dealing with a real, not a phantom, threat, nor with a mere theological insult. Though the Christian emperors, in general, sought to maintain continuity with the policies of their pagan predecessors, they were most insistent and repetitive on the subject of conversion of slaves to Judaism. The fact that specific penalties are stated, that they are severe, and that a choice is indicated in those penalties is a clue to the reality of the situation. The simplest explanation of this constant reiteration of legislation (no fewer than twelve laws were passed forbidding conversion of slaves) is that the laws were not being obeyed, because the empire was hopelessly mired in bureaucracy; and the venality and the arbitrariness of the system was notorious.

That "Judaizing" and conversions to Judaism were continuing problems for the nascent Church is clear from the frequency with which these issues were raised in Church councils. Thus, the Council of Elvira in Spain in 305 (or 306) prohibited marriages of Jewish men with Christian women, presumably because they led to conversion of the women to Judaism, forbade Christians to allow their fruits to be blessed by Jews, and forbade Christians to dine together with Jews, apparently because such social contacts often led to "Judaizing." The Council of Nicaea in 325 and that of Antioch in 341, in decreeing that Easter should never be celebrated at the same time as the Jewish Passover, realized that the calendar could and sometimes did serve as a bridge between Christians and Jews; the lack of success of these councils in enforcing these rulings is indicated by the fact that as late as the fifth century there were still Quartodecimans observing Easter at the same time as the Jewish Passover. The Council of Laodicea, which was held some time between 343 and 381, in prohibiting the use of phylacteries by Christian laymen and higher and lower clergy, showed that their use, apparently as amulets, even by clergy was a real problem. The Fourth Carthaginian synod in 398, in imposing the severe penalty of excommunication on those Christians who rested on Saturday, demonstrated that the observance of the Jewish Sabbath was still a source of attraction to some Christians.

The vitality of Judaism during the third, fourth, and fifth centuries in reaching out to Christians is manifest from the sharp attacks by church fathers on Jewish proselytism and on "Judaizing." The fact that at the beginning of the third century the champion of Judaism in Tertullian's essay *Adversus Judaeos* is a proselyte may well indicate that proselytism was still continuing and that it was a source of great concern to the fledgling Church. In the middle of the century Origen, in his comment on Jesus' saying (Matthew 23:15) that the Pharisees traverse sea and land to make a single proselyte, remarks that proselytism by Jews is still being actively carried on and adds, though of course we may well be skeptical, that "Judaizing" tendencies within the Christian community were the work of Jewish missionaries. The *Acta Pionii*, dating from the middle of the third century, likewise depicts Jews as openly teaching Gentiles and as carrying on a proselyting campaign among Christians. Ephraem Syrus in the fourth century likewise notes, with bitterness, that numerous heathens are deluded by Jewish missionaries. Jerome also—though, to be sure, he may well be exaggerating—depicts the Jews as active missionaries circling around the Christians and seeking to tear them to pieces.

That Christian clerics were likewise attracted to Jewish practices may be deduced from the *Apostolic Constitutions*, dating from the third or fourth century, which penalizes clerics who enter synagogues to pray or who fast or feast with Jews. It likewise warns Christians against frequenting Jewish baths. In the early fourth century, Lactantius admits that Jews are praised because of their respect for law. Moreover, in the fourth century Epiphanius describes a number of Jewish-Christian sects that appeal to the precedent of Jesus himself in observing such practices as the Jewish Sabbath and circumcision.

The chief evidence for the success of the Jews in attracting adherents is to be found in the diatribes of the eloquent John Chrysostom at the end of the fourth century. Undoubtedly, the danger of the "Judaizers" was compounded by the increasing strength of various Christian heresies, notably those of the Arians and of the Anomaeans, the latter of whom agreed with the Jews in denying the divinity of Jesus. Apparently, women in particular were being drawn to Jewish practices, and so Chrysostom charges Christian husbands to keep their wives from going to the synagogue. He implies that Jews take the initiative in attracting Christians, because he says they are "bent on surrounding my sheep." That his eight discourses were all delivered before Jewish holidays, particularly the High Holidays, indicates the attraction that these holidays held for some Christians. He notes the tremendous impression made on Christians by Jewish scrolls of the Torah and of the prophets, by the solemnity of oaths taken before Torah scrolls, and by the Jews' reputation for powerful amulets and potions. Jews were attracting so many Christians to their synagogues that he advises Christians not to spread this information lest it lead to a veritable stampede to Judaism. We may suggest that his sermons may actually have aroused even greater curiosity among Christians about Judaism.

Jerome, too, depicts the Jews as aggressively circling around Christians, seeking to tear them to pieces, and cites the prominence of "Judaizers" among women in particular. He frantically notes the belief of the Jews and of the "Judaizers" that the time is approaching when the commandments of the Law will be observed and when Jews will no longer become Christians, but rather Christians will become Jews. Augustine refers to a Christian sect who call themselves Jews; and though he insists that the Christians are the true Jews, he gives the sect one year to give up its use of the name. As late as the fifth century, Isaac of Antioch complains about the attraction Jewish magicians have for Christians.

As for the rabbis, the fact that the attitude toward proselytes was debated in the third and fourth centuries indicates that it was a live issue. Significantly, the Talmudic tractate 'Avodah Zarah, which deals with idol worship, has little ridicule of paganism, especially as compared with the attitude toward paganism of the church fathers; this may be due to the concern not to insult pagans and thus to facilitate their transition to Judaism. In particular, the biblical figures of Abraham, Isaac, Jacob, Joseph, and Jethro are cited by third- and fourth-century rabbis in midrashim as examples par excellence of missionaries who succeeded in winning many converts. Moreover, the remarkable statement of the third-century Rabbi Simeon ben Lakish that the fire of Gehenna has no dominion over Jewish apostates may be a deliberate attempt to win them back to Judaism. The very vehemence and the repeated citation of the statement of Rabbi Ḥelbo, who lived in the latter part of the third century and the early part of the fourth century, that proselytes are as difficult for Israel as a scab indicates that proselytism was still going on.

The reason that there is no evidence of converts and "sympathizers" on tombstones may be that most of the extant inscriptions are from the city of Rome, where proselytism was apparently restrained by the two expulsions of Jews that we have mentioned and by the reticence of proselytes to advertise their conversions.

How can we account for the success of the Jews in winning converts? During the period before the triumph of Christianity, Judaism and paganism apparently felt much in common as conservative ideologies combatting the innovative and revolutionary Christianity. With the end of the Jewish state and the destruction of the Temple, the political aspect of conversion became more and more theoretical, and so the charge of dual loyalty became less prominent. Even with the triumph of Christianity, the emperors often realized the great strength in numbers and economic power of the Jews and perceived that, beset as they were with challenges by barbarians from without and by decay from within, they could not afford to alienate so large and important an element of their population, which was basically loyal to them.

In summary, Judaism throughout the Hellenistic and Roman periods and even after the triumph of Christianity showed tremendous vigor not only in strengthening itself internally with the development of that remarkable document, the Talmud, but also in reaching out to pagans and later to Christians and winning large numbers as proselytes and as "sympathizers." The Jews of the Land of Israel were able not only to resist the cultural inroads of Hellenism but even to counterattack. In the Diaspora, to be sure, the Jews were deeply Hellenized but lost relatively few adherents, whether because of their special privileges or because the hatred of the masses for them strengthened their stubbornness. Jews were generally observant of their special laws or, at the very least, were conscious of their identification with the Jewish community.

Governments, on the whole, finding them too numerous, too important economically, and generally loyal, were favorably disposed toward the Jews; and intellectuals, to a much greater degree than hitherto has been acknowledged, admired them, often grudgingly to be sure. Jews such as Philo and Josephus were, moreover, vigorous polemicists against their detractors. The masses, largely for economic reasons, may have resented Jewish privileges and may have envied Jewish wealth and influence, but many of them saw distinct advantages—religious, social, and economic—in adopting Judaism in whole or in part. Even after the three great revolts of 66–74, 115–17, and 132–35, the Jews were hardly powerless[2] and indeed continued to win proselytes and especially "sympathizers." In short, the lachrymose theory of Jewish history, highlighting the weakness and suffering of the Jews, would not, on the whole, seem to apply to the ancient period.

ABBREVIATIONS

AB	*Analecta Bollandia*
Abel	Ernest L. Abel, "Were the Jews Banished from Rome in 19 A.D.?" *REJ* 127 (1968): 383–86
"Abraham"	Louis H. Feldman, "Abraham the Greek Philosopher in Josephus," TAPA 99 (1968): 143–56
AC	*L'Antiquité classique*
AG	*Analecta Gregoriana*
AHDE	*Anuario de historia del derecho español*
AJA	*American Journal of Archaeology*
AJAH	*American Journal of Ancient History*
AJP	*American Journal of Philology*
AJSL	*American Journal of Semitic Languages*
AJS Review	*Association for Jewish Studies Review*
AJT	*American Journal of Theology*
Alberro	Charles A. Alberro, "The Alexandrian Jews during the Ptolemaic Period" (Ph.D. diss., Michigan State University, 1976)
ANRW	*Aufstieg und Niedergang der römischen Welt*
Ant.	Josephus, *Jewish Antiquities*
"Aphrodisias"	Louis H. Feldman, "Proselytes and 'Sympathizers' in the Light of the New Inscriptions from Aphrodisias," *REJ* 148 (1989): 265–305
"'Aqedah"	Louis H. Feldman, "Josephus as a Biblical Interpreter: The 'Aqedah," *JQR* 75 (1984–85): 212–52
AR	*Archiv für Religionswissenschaft*
AS	*Anatolian Studies*
ASTI	*Annual of the Swedish Theological Institute*
Athletics	Harold A. Harris, *Greek Athletics and the Jews* (Cardiff: Univ. of Wales Press, 1976)
Attridge	Harold W. Attridge, *The Interpretation of Biblical History in the Antiquitates Judaicae of Flavius Josephus* (*Harvard Theological*

Review, Harvard Dissertations in Religion 7; Missoula: Scholars Press, 1976)

AUSS *Andrews University Seminary Studies*

Avi-Yonah Michael Avi-Yonah, *Hellenism and the East: Contacts and Inter-relations from Alexander to the Roman Conquest* (Ann Arbor: University Microfilms International, 1978)

Axenfeld Karl Axenfeld, "Die jüdische Propaganda als Vorläuferin und Wegbereiterin der urchristlichen Mission," in Karl Axenfeld et al., eds., *Missionswissenschaftliche Studien: Festschrift zum 70. Geburtstag des Herrn Prof. D. Dr. Gustav Warneck* (Berlin: Warneck, 1904), 1–80

BA *Biblical Archaeologist*

Balsdon John P. V. D. Balsdon, *Romans and Aliens* (London: Duckworth, 1979)

Bamberger Bernard J. Bamberger, *Proselytism in the Talmudic Period* (Cincinnati: Hebrew Union College, 1939)

BAR *Biblical Archaeology Review*

Baron Salo W. Baron, *A Social and Religious History of the Jews*, 2d ed., vols. 1–2 (New York: Columbia Univ. Press and Philadelphia: Jewish Publication Society, 1952)

BASOR *Bulletin of the American Schools of Oriental Research*

BCH *Bulletin de Correspondance hellénique*

Bergmann Judah Bergmann, "Die stoische Philosophie und die jüdische Frömmigkeit," in Ismar Elbogen et al., eds., *Judaica: Festschrift zu Hermann Cohens siebzigstem Geburtstage* (Berlin: Cassirer, 1912), 145–66

Bickerman, *Jews* Elias J. Bickerman, *The Jews in the Greek Age* (Cambridge: Harvard Univ. Press, 1988)

Bickerman, "Origines" Elias J. Bickerman, "Origines Gentium," *CP* 47 (1952): 65–81

BIDR *Bullettino dell'Istituto di diritto romano*

Bilde Per Bilde, "The Roman Emperor Gaius (Caligula)'s Attempt to Erect His Statue in the Temple of Jerusalem," *ST* 32 (1978): 67–93

Braude William G. Braude, *Jewish Proselyting in the First Five Centuries of the Common Era: The Age of the Tannaim and Amoraim* (Providence: Brown Univ. Press, 1940)

Braun   Martin Braun, *History and Romance in Graeco-Oriental Literature* (Oxford: Blackwell, 1938)

Broughton   Thomas Robert S. Broughton, "Roman Asia," in Tenney Frank, ed., *An Economic Survey of Ancient Rome*, vol. 4 (Baltimore: Johns Hopkins Univ. Press, 1938)

BSRLL   *Bulletin de la Société royale des lettres de Lund*

CBQ   *Catholic Biblical Quarterly*

Chadwick   Henry Chadwick, trans. and ed., *Origen: Contra Celsum* (Cambridge: Cambridge Univ. Press, 1965)

CIG   August Boeckh, *Corpus Inscriptionum Graecarum* (Berlin: Reimer, 1828–77)

CII   Jean Baptiste Frey, *Corpus Inscriptionum Iudaicarum*, 2 vols. (Rome: Pontificio istituto di archeologia cristiana, 1936–52)

CIRB   *Corpus Inscriptionum Regni Bosporani*

CJ   *Conservative Judaism*

CO   *Classical Outlook*

Cohen   Shaye J. D. Cohen, "Patriarchs and Scholarchs," PAAJR 48 (1981): 57–85

Collins   John J. Collins, *Between Athens and Jerusalem: Jewish Identity in the Hellenistic Diaspora* (New York: Crossroad, 1983)

CP   *Classical Philology*

CPJ   Victor A. Tcherikover, Alexander Fuks, and Menahem Stern, eds., *Corpus Papyrorum Judaicarum*, 3 vols. (Cambridge: Harvard Univ. Press, 1957–64)

CRINT   Samuel Safrai and Menahem Stern, eds., *The Jewish People in the First Century: Historical Geography, Political History, Social, Cultural and Religious Life and Institutions*, vol. 2 (*Compendia Rerum Iudaicarum ad Novum Testamentum*, Section 1: *The Jewish People in the First Century*; Assen: Van Gorcum, 1976)

CT   *Codex Theodosianus*

"David"   Louis H. Feldman, "Josephus' Portrait of David," HUCA 60 (1989): 129–74

"Dialogue"   John G. Gager, "The Dialogue of Paganism with Judaism: Bar Cochba to Julian," HUCA 44 (1973): 89–118

E-I   *Eretz-Israel*

EJ   *Encyclopaedia Judaica*, 16 vols. (Jerusalem: Macmillan, 1971)

EQ   *Evangelical Quarterly*

"Esther"   Louis H. Feldman, "Hellenizations in Josephus' Version of Esther," TAPA 101 (1970): 143–70

FGH   Felix Jacoby, ed., *Die Fragmente der griechischen Historiker* (Berlin: Weidmann, 1923– and Leiden: Brill, 1954–)

Freyne   Sean Freyne, *Galilee from Alexander the Great to Hadrian: 323 B.C.E. to 135 C.E.: A Study of Second Temple Judaism* (Wilmington: Glazier, 1980)

Gabba   Emilio Gabba, *Greek Knowledge of Jews up to Hecataeus of Abdera* (Berkeley: Center for Hermeneutical Studies, 1981), 1–14

Gager   John G. Gager, *Moses in Greco-Roman Paganism* (Nashville: Abingdon, 1972)

GCS   *Die griechischen christlichen Schriftsteller der ersten drei Jahrhunderte* (Berlin: Akademic Verlag, 1897–)

Georgi   Dieter Georgi, *The Opponents of Paul in Second Corinthians* (Philadelphia: Fortress, 1984; rev. ed. 1986)

Ginzberg   Louis Ginzberg, *The Legends of the Jews*, 7 vols. (Philadelphia: Jewish Publication Society, 1909–38)

Goldstein   Jonathan Goldstein, "Jewish Acceptance and Rejection of Hellenism," in E. P. Sanders et al., eds., *Jewish and Christian Self-Definition*, vol. 2: *Aspects of Judaism in the Greco-Roman Period* (Philadelphia: Fortress, 1981), 64–87, 318–26

Goodenough   Erwin R. Goodenough, *Jewish Symbols in the Greco-Roman Period*, 13 vols. (Princeton: Princeton Univ. Press, 1953–68)

Goodman   Martin Goodman, "Proselytising in Rabbinic Judaism," *JJS* 40 (1989): 175–85

GRBS   *Greek, Roman, and Byzantine Studies*

Green   Peter Green, *Alexander to Actium: The Historical Evolution of the Hellenistic Age* (Berkeley: Univ. of California Press, 1990)

Hadas   Moses Hadas, *Hellenistic Culture: Fusion and Diffusion* (New York: Columbia Univ. Press, 1959)

Harnack   Adolf von Harnack, *The Mission and Expansion of Christianity in the First Three Centuries*. English trans. by James Moffatt, 2d ed., 2 vols. (London: Williams and Norgate, 1908)

Harris   William V. Harris, *Ancient Literacy* (Cambridge, Mass.: Harvard Univ. Press, 1989)

HBD   Paul J. Achtemeier, ed., *Harper's Bible Dictionary* (San Francisco: Harper, 1985)

Hecht   Richard D. Hecht, "The Exegetical Contexts of Philo's Interpretation of Circumcision," in Frederick E. Greenspahn et al., *Nourished with Peace: Studies in Hellenistic Judaism in Memory of Samuel Sandmel* (Chico, California: Scholars Press, 1984), 51–79

Hefele   Charles J. Hefele, *A History of the Christian Councils from the Original Documents.* English trans. by William R. Clark, 2d ed., 5 vols. (Edinburgh: Clark, 1894–96)

"Hellenizations" Louis H. Feldman, "Hellenizations in Josephus' Account of Man's Decline," in Jacob Neusner, ed., *Religions in Antiquity: Essays in Memory of Erwin Ramsdell Goodenough* (*SHR*, 14; Leiden: Brill, 1968), 336–53.

Hengel   Martin Hengel, *Judentum und Hellenismus: Studien zu ihrer Begegnung unter besonderer Berücksichtigung Palästinas bis zur Mitte des 2 Jh. s.v. Chr.* (Tübingen: Mohr, 1969; 2d ed., 1973). English trans. by John Bowden: *Judaism and Hellenism: Studies in Their Encounter in Palestine during the Early Hellenistic Period,* 2 vols. (Philadelphia: Fortress, 1974; references are to the English translation)

Hengel,   Martin Hengel, in collaboration with Christoph Markschies,
Hellenization   *The 'Hellenization' of Judaea in the First Century after Christ* (London: SCM Press, 1989; Philadelphia: Trinity Press International, 1990); translated by John Bowden from the German *Zum Problem der 'Hellenisierung' Judäas im 1. Jahrhundert nach Christus* (1989)

Hengel,   Martin Hengel, "Der Alte und der Neue 'Schürer,'" *JSeS* 35
"Schürer"   (1990): 19–72

HLB   *Harvard Library Bulletin*

Holladay   Carl R. Holladay, *Fragments from Hellenistic Jewish Authors,* vol. 1: *Historians* (Society of Biblical Literature, Texts and Translations, 20; Pseudepigrapha, 10; Chico, California: Scholars Press, 1983)

Holladay, II   Carl R. Holladay, *Fragments from Hellenistic Jewish Authors,* vol. 2: *Poets* (Society of Biblical Literature, Texts and Translations, 30; Pseudepigrapha, 12; Atlanta: Scholars Press, 1989)

van der Horst	Pieter W. van der Horst, "Jews and Christians in Aphrodisias in the Light of Their Relations in Other Cities of Asia Minor," *NTT* 43 (1989): 106–21; reprinted (revised) in his *Essays on the Jewish World of Early Christianity* (Freiburg: Universitätsverlag and Göttingen: Vandenhoeck & Ruprecht, 1990), 166–81
Hospers-Jansen	Anna M. A. Hospers-Jansen, *Tacitus over de Joden, Hist. 5, 2–13* (Groningen: Wolter, 1949)
HSCP	*Harvard Studies in Classical Philology*
HTR	*Harvard Theological Review*
HUCA	*Hebrew Union College Annual*
IOS	*Israel Oriental Studies*
JAC	*Jahrbuch für Antike und Christentum*
"Jacob"	Louis H. Feldman, "Josephus' Portrait of Jacob," *JQR* 79 (1988–89): 101–51
Jacobson	Howard Jacobson, *The Exagoge of Ezekiel* (Cambridge: Cambridge Univ. Press, 1983)
JAOS	*Journal of the American Oriental Society*
JBH	Louis H. Feldman and Gohei Hata, eds., *Josephus, the Bible, and History* (Detroit: Wayne State Univ. Press, 1989)
JBL	*Journal of Biblical Literature*
JCP	*Jahrbücher für classische Philologie*
JEA	*Journal of Egyptian Archaeology*
JEH	*Journal of Ecclesiastical History*
JHI	*Journal of the History of Ideas*
JHS	*Journal of Hellenic Studies*
JJC	Louis H. Feldman and Gohei Hata, eds., *Josephus, Judaism, and Christianity* (Detroit: Wayne State Univ. Press, 1987)
JJML	*Journal of Jewish Music and Liturgy*
JJP	*Journal of Juristic Papyrology*
JJS	*Journal of Jewish Studies*
JMS	Louis H. Feldman, *Josephus and Modern Scholarship (1937–1980)* (Berlin: de Gruyter, 1984)
Jones	Arnold H. M. Jones, *The Cities of the Eastern Roman Provinces* (Oxford: Clarendon, 1937; 2d ed., 1971)

Josephus 9	Louis H. Feldman, ed. and trans., *Josephus*, vol. 9 (*LCL*; London: Heinemann, 1965)
"Joshua"	Louis H. Feldman, "Josephus' Portrait of Joshua," *HTR* 82 (1989): 351–76
JQR	*Jewish Quarterly Review*
JR	*Journal of Religion*
JRS	*Journal of Roman Studies*
JSeS	*Journal of Semitic Studies*
JSJ	*Journal for the Study of Judaism*
JSNT	*Journal for the Study of the New Testament*
JSP	*Journal for the Study of the Pseudepigrapha*
JSS	*Jewish Social Studies*
JTS	*Journal of Theological Studies*
JuR	*Juridical Review*
Juster	Jean Juster, *Les Juifs dans l'empire romain*, 2 vols. (Paris: Geuthner, 1914)
Kasher	Aryeh Kasher, *Jews and Hellenistic Cities in Eretz-Israel: Relations of the Jews in Eretz-Israel with the Hellenistic Cities during the Second Temple Period (332 BCE–70 CE)* (Tübingen: Mohr, 1990)
Kasher, "Gymnasium"	Aryeh Kasher, "The Jewish Attitude to the Alexandrian Gymnasium in the First Century A.D.," AJAH 1 (1976): 148–61
Kraabel	Alf Thomas Kraabel, "Judaism in Asia Minor under the Roman Empire, with a Preliminary Study of the Jewish Community of Sardis, Lydia" (Ph.D. diss., Harvard Univ., 1968)
Kraabel, "Diaspora"	Alf Thomas Kraabel, "The Diaspora Synagogue: Archaeological and Epigraphic Evidence since Sukenik," ANRW 2.19.1 (Berlin: de Gruyter, 1979), 477–510
LCL	Loeb Classical Library
Leon	Harry J. Leon, *The Jews of Ancient Rome* (Philadelphia: Jewish Publication Society, 1960)
Lewis	Naphtali Lewis, *Life in Egypt under Roman Rule* (Oxford: Oxford Univ. Press, 1983)
Lewy	Johanan (Hans) Lewy, *Studies in Jewish Hellenism* [in Hebrew] (Jerusalem: Bialik, 1960)

Lieberman, *Greek*	Saul Lieberman, *Greek in Jewish Palestine* (New York: Jewish Theological Seminary of America, 1942)
Lieberman, *Hellenism*	Saul Lieberman, *Hellenism in Jewish Palestine* (New York: Jewish Theological Seminary of America, 1950)
Lieberman, "How Much Greek"	Saul Lieberman, "How Much Greek in Jewish Palestine?" In Alexander Altmann, ed., *Studies and Texts*, vol. 1: *Biblical and Other Studies* (Cambridge, Mass.: Harvard Univ. Press, 1963), 123–41
Lieberman, "Palestine"	Saul Lieberman, "Palestine in the Third and Fourth Centuries," *JQR* 36 (1945–46): 329–70; 37 (1946–47): 31–54.
Lifshitz	Baruch Lifshitz, *Donateurs et fondateurs dans les synagogues juives: Répertoire des dédicaces grecques relatives à la construction et à la réfection des synagogues* (Paris: Gabalda, 1967)
Linder	Amnon Linder, ed., *The Jews in Roman Imperial Legislation* (Detroit: Wayne State Univ. Press, 1987)
Littman	Robert Littman, "Anti-Semitism in the Greco-Roman Pagan World," in Yehuda Bauer et al., eds., *Remembering for the Future: Working Papers and Addenda*, vol. 1: *Jews and Christians during and after the Holocaust* (Oxford: Pergamon, 1989), 825–35
LQR	*Law Quarterly Review*
LXX	Septuagint
McKnight	Scot McKnight, *A Light among the Gentiles: Jewish Missionary Activity in the Second Temple Period* (Minneapolis: Fortress, 1991)
MacMullen	Ramsay MacMullen, *Roman Government's Response to Crisis A.D. 235–337* (New Haven: Yale Univ. Press, 1976)
MANL	*Memorie dell'Accademia nazionale dei Lincei*
Marcus	Ralph Marcus, "Jewish and Greek Elements in the Septuagint," ed. Alexander Marx et al. *Louis Ginzberg Jubilee Volume* (New York: American Academy for Jewish Research, 1945), 227–45
Marrou	Henri I. Marrou, *Histoire de l'éducation dans l'antiquité* (2d ed., Paris: Editions du Seuil, 1950). English trans. by George Lamb, *A History of Education in Antiquity* (New York: Sheed and Ward, 1956; references are to the English translation)
Matthews	Isaac G. Matthews, "The Jewish Apologetic to the Grecian World in the Apocryphal and Pseudepigraphical Literature" (Ph.D. diss., Univ. of Chicago, 1914)

MB	*Le Musée Belge*
MDAI	*Mitteilungen des deutschen Archäologischen Instituts, Istanbuler Abteilung*
Mendelson	Alan Mendelson, *Philo's Jewish Identity* (Atlanta: Scholars Press, 1988)
MGHAA	*Monumenta Germaniae Historica, Auctores Antiquissimi*
MGWJ	*Monatsschrift für Geschichte und Wissenschaft des Judentums*
"Mikra"	Louis H. Feldman, "Use, Authority, and Exegesis of Mikra in the Writings of Josephus," in Jan Mulder and Harry Sysling, eds., *Mikra, Text, Translation, Reading and Interpretation of the Hebrew Bible in Ancient Judaism and Early Christianity (Compendia Rerum Iudaicarum ad Novum Testamentum*, sect. 2, vol. 1; Assen: Van Gorcum, 1988), 455–518
Momigliano	Arnaldo Momigliano, *Alien Wisdom: The Limits of Hellenization* (Cambridge: Cambridge Univ. Press, 1975)
"Noah"	Louis H. Feldman, "Josephus' Portrait of Noah and Its Parallels in Philo, Pseudo-Philo's *Biblical Antiquities*, and Rabbinic Midrashim," PAAJR 55 (1988): 31–57.
Nock	Arthur D. Nock, *Conversion: The Old and the New in Religion from Alexander the Great to Augustine of Hippo* (Oxford: Oxford Univ. Press, 1933)
Norden	Eduard Norden, "Jahve und Moses in hellenistische Theologie," in *Festgabe von Fachgenossen und Freunden A. von Harnack zum ziebzigsten Geburtstag dargebracht* (Tübingen: Mohr, 1921), 292–301
NT	*Novum Testamentum*
NTS	*New Testament Studies*
NTT	*Nederlands Theologisch Tijdschrift*
OCD	Nicholas G. L. Hammond and Howard H. Scullard, eds., *Oxford Classical Dictionary*, 2d ed. (Oxford: Clarendon, 1970)
OLZ	*Orientalistische Literatur-Zeitung*
"Omnipresence"	Louis H. Feldman, "The Omnipresence of the G-d-Fearers," *BAR* 12.5 (Sept.–Oct. 1986): 58–69
"Orthodoxy"	Louis H. Feldman, "The Orthodoxy of the Jews in Hellenistic Egypt," *JSS* 22 (1960): 212–37
P.	Papyrus (Papyr.)
PAAJR	*Proceedings of the American Academy for Jewish Research*

PEQ *Palestine Exploration Quarterly*

PG Jacques P. Migne, *Patrologiae Cursus Completus Series Graeca.* 161 vols. (Paris: Seu Petit-Montrouge, 1857–66)

"Philo-Semitism" Louis H. Feldman, "Philo-Semitism among Ancient Intellectuals," *Tradition* 1 (1958–59): 27–39

PIASH *Proceedings of the Israel Academy of Sciences and Humanities*

PL Jacques P. Migne, *Patrologiae Cursus Completus Series Latina.* 221 vols. (Paris: Migne, 1841–79)

POxy *Oxyrhynchus Papyri*

"Pro-Jewish" Louis H. Feldman, "Pro-Jewish Intimations in Anti-Jewish Remarks Cited in Josephus' *Against Apion*," *JQR* 78 (1987–88): 187–251

"Prolegomena" Victor A. Tcherikover, "Prolegomena," *CPJ*, vol. 1 (Cambridge, Mass.: Harvard Univ. Press, 1957) 1–111

"Prophets" Louis H. Feldman, "Prophets and Prophecy in Josephus," *JTS* 41 (1990): 386–422

"Proselytism" Louis H. Feldman, "Proselytism and Syncretism" [in Hebrew], in WHJP, 188–207, 340–45, 378–80

RAC Theodor Klauser, ed., *Reallexikon für Antike und Christentum* (Leipzig: Hiersemann, 1941–)

Radin Max Radin, *The Jews among the Greeks and Romans* (Philadelphia: Jewish Publication Society, 1915)

RB *Revue Biblique*

RE August Pauly, Georg Wissowa, Wilhelm Kroll, Karl Mittelhaus, Konrat Ziegler, eds., *Realencyclopädie der klassischen Altertumswissenschaft*, 1st row, 47 vols.; 2d row, 18 vols., 15 suppl. vols. (Stuttgart: Metzler, Druckenmüller, 1893–1978)

Reinach Théodore Reinach, *Textes d'auteurs grecs et romains relatifs au Judaisme* (Paris: Presses universitaires de France, 1895)

REJ *Revue des études juives*

Reynolds Joyce Reynolds and Robert Tannenbaum, *Jews and G-d-Fearers at Aphrodisias: Greek Inscriptions with Commentary* (Cambridge Philological Society, Supplementary Vol. 12; Cambridge: Cambridge University Press, 1987).

RF *Rivista di filologia (Rivista di filologia e di istruzione classica)*

RHR *Revue de l'histoire des religions*

RM	*Rheinisches Museum für Philologie*
Robert	Louis Robert, *Nouvelles Inscriptions de Sardis* (Paris: Librairie d'Amérique et l'Orient, 1964)
RP	*Revue de Philologie*
RQ	*Revue de Qumran*
RS	*Revue sémitique*
RSC	*Rivista di studi classici*
RSR	*Recherches de science religieuse*
Saltman	Ellen S. Saltman, "The Jews of Asia Minor in the Greco-Roman Period: A Religious and Social Study" (M.A. diss., Smith College, 1971)
"Saul"	Louis H. Feldman, "Josephus' Portrait of Saul," HUCA 53 (1982): 45–99
SBB	*Studies in Bibliography and Booklore*
Schürer	Emil Schürer, *The History of the Jewish People in the Age of Jesus Christ (175 B.C.–A.D. 135)*, ed. Geza Vermes and Fergus Millar, 3 vols. (Edinburgh: Clark, 1973–86)
SCI	*Scripta Classica Israelica*
SCO	*Studi classici e orientali*
SEG	*Supplementum Epigraphicum Graecum.* Ed. Pierre Roussel et al. (Leiden: Sijthoff, 1923–)
Segal	Alan F. Segal, *Paul the Convert: The Apostolate and Apostasy of Saul the Pharisee* (New Haven: Yale Univ. Press, 1990)
SH	*Scripta Hierosolymitana*
SHJP	*Studies in the History of the Jewish People and the Land of Israel*
SHR	*Studies in the History of Religions*
Simon	Marcel Simon, *Verus Israel: Etude sur les relations entre chrétiens et juifs dans l'empire romain, 135–425* (Paris: de Boccard, 1948). English trans. by Henry McKeating, *Verus Israel: A Study of the Relations between Christians and Jews in the Roman Empire (135–425)* (Oxford: Oxford Univ. Press, 1986; references are to the English translation)
SJT	*Scottish Journal of Theology*
Smallwood	Edith Mary Smallwood, *The Jews under Roman Rule: From Pompey to Diocletian* (Leiden: Brill, 1976)

Smallwood, Inaugural	Edith Mary Smallwood, *From Pagan Protection to Christian Oppression* (Inaugural Lecture Delivered before the Queen's Univ. of Belfast; Belfast: Mayne, Boyd, 1979)
SMSR	*Studi e materiali di storia delle religioni*
"Solomon"	Louis H. Feldman, "Josephus as an Apologist to the Greco-Roman World: His Portrait of Solomon," in Elisabeth Schüssler Fiorenza, ed., *Aspects of Religious Propaganda in Judaism and Early Christianity* (Notre Dame: Univ. of Notre Dame Press, 1976), 69–98
SP	*Studia Patristica*
SPAW	*Sitzungsberichte der preussischen Akademie der Wissenschaften*
SR	*Studies in Religion/Sciences religieuses*
ST	*Studia Theologica*
Stern	Menahem Stern, ed., *Greek and Latin Authors on Jews and Judaism*, 3 vols. (Jerusalem: Israel Academy of Sciences and Humanities, 1974–84)
SVF	Hans F. A. von Arnim, *Stoicorum Veterum Fragmenta*, 4 vols. (Leipzig: Teubner, 1903–24)
"Sympathizers"	Louis H. Feldman, "Jewish 'Sympathizers' in Classical Literature and Inscriptions," TAPA 81 (1950): 200–208
TAPA	*Transactions of the American Philological Association*
Tcherikover	Victor Tcherikover, *Hellenistic Civilization and the Jews* (Philadelphia: Jewish Publication Society, 1959)
TDNT	Gerhard Kittel and Gerhard Friedrich, eds., *Theologisches Wörterbuch zum Neuen Testament*, 9 vols. (Stuttgart: Kohlhammer, 1933–73); English trans. by Geoffrey W. Bromiley, *Theological Dictionary of the New Testament*, 10 vols. (Grand Rapids: Eerdmans, 1964–76; references are to the English translation).
Thackeray	Henry St. John Thackeray, *Josephus the Man and the Historian* (New York: Jewish Institute of Religion, 1929)
Trebilco	Paul A. Trebilco, *Jewish Communities in Asia Minor* (Cambridge: Cambridge Univ. Press, 1991)
TS	*Theological Studies*
TUGAL	*Texte und Untersuchungen zur Geschichte der altchristlichen Literatur*
VC	*Vigiliae Christianae*
VSW	*Vierteljahrschrift für Sozial- und Wirtschaftsgeschichte*

VT			*Vetus Testamentum*

War			Josephus, *Jewish War*

WHJP			Menahem Stern and Zvi Baras, eds., *World History of the Jewish People*, First Series: *The Diaspora in the Hellenistic-Roman World* [in Hebrew] (Jerusalem: Am Oved, 1984)

Wilken			Robert L. Wilken, *John Chrysostom and the Jews: Rhetoric and Reality in the Late Fourth Century* (Berkeley: Univ. of California Press, 1983)

Williams		Margaret H. Williams, "The Expulsion of the Jews from Rome in A.D. 19," *Latomus* 48 (1989): 765–84

Wolfson			Harry A. Wolfson, *Philo: Foundations of Religious Philosophy in Judaism, Christianity, and Islam*, 2 vols. (Cambridge, Mass.: Harvard Univ. Press, 1947)

YCS			*Yale Classical Studies*

ZAW			*Zeitschrift für die alttestamentliche Wissenschaft*

ZDPV			*Zeitschrift des deutschen Palästina-Vereins*

ZNW			*Zeitschrift für die neutestamentliche Wissenschaft*

NOTES

1. See Stern, 3.1–4. Stern, 3.3, note 10, and Gabba, 13, Supplementary Note A, express doubt that a fragment of a scholion to Alcaeus (*Oxyrhynchus Papyri* 11.1360, fragment 13) contains the name of Jerusalem; but the extant letters, Ἱεροον, point in that direction.

2. For the evidence of Greek pottery in Palestine, see Dominique Auscher, "Les relations entre la Grèce et la Palestine avant la conquête d'Alexandre"; for numismatic evidence of contacts between Greece and Palestine, see pp. 21–27.

3. See Adolf Reifenberg, *Ancient Jewish Coins*, 4th ed., 5–9, nos. 1a–3. To be sure, the coins are all of small denominations and thus intended for local use. Furthermore, the famous Yehud coin depicting a god seated on a winged chariot, which is Greek in artistic style but not an imitation of any one Greek issue nor purely Greek in its iconography, indicates that even in the early part of the fourth century B.C.E. borrowing was going on (though we cannot be sure whether the issuing authority was the Jewish high priest or the local Persian governor), mediated perhaps through the Phoenicians; but this was probably true only in the more assimilated circles of Judaean society. Whether minting of coins by Jews on the Attic standard with the pagan emblem of the owl representing the goddess Athena indicates a more substantial assimilation is questionable. More likely it indicates that the authorities issuing the coins and those to whom they entrusted the production of coins simply followed the pattern of the Athenians—the most important commercial power of the day—and did not regard the depiction of the owl as such as a violation of Jewish law. In any case, we have no evidence, literary or archaeological, that the impact of the Athenians went beyond the matter of coinage.

4. Another such borrowing that has been suggested is *'appiryon* (Cant 3:9) = Greek φορεῖον ("sedan-chair"), but an etymology from the Greek verb φέρω, "to carry," or from Persian seems more likely. For a summary of the evidence of such commercial contacts, see Edwin M. Yamauchi, "Daniel and Contacts between the Aegean and the Near East before Alexander." It has been suggested that linguistic ties between the two peoples go back to an earlier period and that a number of words in the Pentateuch closely parallel Homer or other early Greek writers. Examples that have been cited by such writers as Cyrus H. Gordon, "Homer and Bible: The Origin and Character of East Mediterranean Literature," 60–61, are *'erev* (Gen 1:5), "evening," and Greek ἔρεβος (*Iliad* 16:327), "darkness"; *ketonet* (Gen 37:3), "shirt," and Greek χιτών (*Iliad* 24.580), "man's tunic"; *mekerah* (Gen 49:5), "weapon," "sword," and Greek μάχαιρα (*Iliad* 3.271), "large knife," "dagger"; *mazzah* (Exod 12:39), "unleavened bread," and Greek μᾶζα (Hesiod, *Works and Days* 590), "barley cake"; *'egel* (Lev 9:2), "calf," and Greek ἀγέλη (*Iliad* 19.281), "herd"; *mum* (Lev 23:20), "blemish," and Greek ἀμύμων (*Iliad* 4.194), "blameless." Some of these words, such as ἔρεβος, have Indo-European cognates and hence need not go back to Semitic sources. Words

such as χιτών and ἔρεβος are found in Phoenician and are consequently more easily explained as having been borrowed from the Phoenician language (which is remarkably similar to Hebrew), in view of the fact that Phoenician traders were so active in the Mediterranean area. In other cases, such as the word μάχαιρα, there are various meanings for the word in Hebrew. As for the word ἀγέλη, it appears to be derived from the Greek ἄγω rather than from Hebrew. Likewise, the word ἄκουρος contains the Greek alpha-privative and does not bear a relationship to the biblical word; the phonetic correspondence is coincidental.

5. Cited by Jakob Bernays, *Theophrastos' Schrift über Frömmigkeit: Ein Beitrag zur Religionsgeschichte*, 110, who assumes, though, to be sure, without further proof, that, with the improvement of means of communication, there must have been many Greek travelers in Phoenicia throughout the fourth century B.C.E.

6. See John W. Leopold, response to Gabba, 21.

7. Quoted in Carolus Müller, *Geographi Graeci Minores*, vol. 1, 104, p. 79.

8. Pseudo-Scylax 104; Strabo 1.2.35.42, 16.2.28.758; Conon (quoted in Photius 186, p. 138b); Pomponius Mela (*Chorographia* 1.11.64); Pliny, *Natural History* 5.69, 5.128, 9.11; Pausanias 4.35.9; Josephus, *War* 3.420; Solinus, *Collectanea Rerum Memorabilium* 34.2.

9. Herodotus 2.104.1–3, as cited by Josephus, *Antiquities* 8.262 and *Against Apion* 1.168–71. It is possible that Herodotus is not referring to the Jews at all, inasmuch as he does not mention the Jews by name but rather states that "the Syrians of Palestine" acknowledge that they learned the practice of circumcision from the Egyptians and that other Syrians learned it from the Colchians. Nevertheless, there is a greater likelihood that the reference is to Jews, inasmuch as Diodorus (1.28.1–3), in the first century, when similarly mentioning the Jews and Colchians in juxtaposition as having derived the practice of circumcision from the Egyptians, speaks of the Jewish nation as lying between Arabia and Syria, though, to be sure, he does not use the phrase "Syrians of Palestine."

10. See Stern, 3.38–40.

11. In all fairness, however, we should note that Josephus overlooked the important complimentary, and indisputably authentic, passage in Theophrastus (quoted in Porphyry, *De Abstinentia* 2.26) referring to the Jews as philosophers by race and describing their method of sacrifice. This should perhaps make us realize that Josephus and others may have missed other references, because in antiquity manuscripts were not plentiful and indexes were almost nonexistent.

12. Choerilus's source is apparently Herodotus's description (7.70) of the Ethiopians of Asia, who differed, he says, from the Ethiopians of Africa in speech and hair. The connection of the Solymoi with the Ethiopians may have been occasioned by the juxtaposition, noted by Gabba, 14, Supplementary Note C, of the Solymoi Mountains with the Ethiopians in Homer (*Odyssey* 5.282–83). We may suggest that the connection of the Ethiopians and the Jews may have been based on a tradition that there were black Jews in Ethiopia (the ancestors of the so-called Falashas in Ethiopia in modern times?) whom Herodotus here distinguishes from the (white) Jews from Asia in language and hair. The source of this tradition may be the biblical passage (Num 12:1) that Moses married a Cushite (Ethiopian) woman, which Josephus (*Ant.* 2.238–53), in particular, embellishes considerably.

13. See Hans Lewy, "Aristotle and the Jewish Sage according to Clearchus of Soli." See also Stern, 1.47–52. The likelihood, however, that there was a Jewish community in Asia Minor at this time is increased by the identification of Sepharad, which is mentioned in Obadiah 1.20 as the place to which exiles went from Jerusalem after the fall of the First Temple in 586 B.C.E., with Sardis in Asia Minor, as indicated by two inscriptions found there. See Enno Littmann, *Sardis*, vol. 6, pt. 7, and Anonymous, "Sepharad."

14. See my "Some Observations on the Name of Palestine."

15. Green, xv, 312–25.

16. So Green, 312.

17. So Christian Habicht, "Die herrschende Gesellschaft in den hellenistischen Monarchien."

18. Green, 319–20. Drawing the parallel with the British in India, Green, 322, remarks, "The conquerors' artificial islands of culture were at first no more acceptable than a wrongly matched heart transplant."

19. The word *qorban* in Hebrew means "sacrifice." Because the taking of a vain oath is prohibited in Judaism, if one had transgressed and had sworn an oath he had to bring a *qorban*; and so, by metonymy, *qorban* was apparently used loosely by Theophrastus for "oath." See Solomon Zeitlin, "Korban," 160, who cites the Tosefta, *Nedarim* 1.1, as a source for the connotation of "oath" which the term *qorban* had. Zeitlin, "Korban: A Gift," 133–34, notes that in Mark 7:11, despite the New Testament's explanation of *qorban* as "given to G-d," the meaning in the context is "vow." See also Lieberman, *Greek*, 134–35, who notes that when a person, in ordinary speech, swears by the gold of the Temple or by the gift of the Altar he is regarded as if he had said *keqorban*; and Lieberman cites in support Matthew 23:16. We may also cite in support Josephus, *Antiquities* 4.73, who, in juxtaposition with his discussion of the vows taken by Nazirites, equates *korban* with a gift.

20. Werner Jaeger, *Diokles von Karystos: Die griechische Medizin und die Schule des Aristoteles*, 143, note 1, suggests that the basis of Theophrastus's statement is some vague knowledge of Abraham's attempted sacrifice of his son Isaac; but this seems unlikely because the Torah had not yet in his day been translated into Greek. We may here suggest that the reason Josephus, who sought desperately in his essay *Against Apion* to find references to the Jews in early Greek literature and who cites another passage from Theophrastus (*Against Apion* 1.166–67), does not cite this passage is that he was not convinced that Theophrastus was here talking about Jewish sacrifices.

21. We may here suggest, though with some diffidence, that the connection of the Jews with the Indians may have been fostered by the similarity of the names Ἰνδοί (*Indoi*) and Ἰουδαῖοι (*Ioudaioi*) and by the names Βραχμᾶνες (Brahmans) and Ἄβραμος (Abraham).

22. See the arguments advanced by such scholars as Willrich, Schürer, Jacoby, Stein, Dalbert, Schaller, and Fraser, cited by Stern, 1.23. See now Holladay, 279–90, who concludes that the issue of authenticity of the fragments remains open.

23. Stern, 1.23–24, in answering these doubts, concludes that Josephus had before him a Jewish revision, however slight, of Hecataeus's book.

24. See Stern, 1.44; and Erich S. Gruen's response in Gabba, 16–17. Furthermore, the story of the Jewish soldier Mosollamus (quoted in *Against Apion* 1.201–
4), who killed the bird that was being observed by a seer and then remarked that
if it had been gifted with divination it would not have come to that spot, has a
fully Hellenic flavor, as Gruen (response to Gabba, 18) has remarked, being
highly reminiscent of the attitude toward diviners of Diogenes the Cynic (quoted
in Diogenes Laertius 6.24).

25. Furthermore, Hecataeus's statement (quoted in *Against Apion* 1.188) that
all Jewish priests receive a tithe is inaccurate, for the tithe, at least according to
the Pentateuch (Num 18:21), went to the Levites, who assisted the priests, not to
the priests themselves, though in practice the tithes went to the priests (*Yevamoth*
86b). Moreover, Hecataeus (cited in *Against Apion* 1.194) refers to the Jews as
having been deported to Babylon by the Persians. It is true, as Stern, 1.43 and
2.421, has noted, that we know of a banishment of very many Jews (so Orosius
3.7.6) from the territory of Jericho under Artaxerxes III Ochus in 343 B.C.E.; but
the reference in Hecataeus to many myriads of Jews being exiled would seem to
be describing the great deportation of 586 B.C.E. Doron Mendels, in "Hecataeus
of Abdera and a Jewish 'Patrios Politeia' of the Persian Period (Diodorus Siculus
XL, 3)," argues that Hecataeus reflects a view that emanated from certain priestly
circles of the late Persian era in Judaea at the end of the fourth century B.C.E. and
finds many similarities to the outlook of Exra and Nehemiah. This explains Hecataeus's emphasis on the foundation of Jerusalem and the Temple, as well as the
elevation of Moses and the relative downgrading of the Davidic kingdom and
indeed of monarchy in general. Mendels concludes that Hecataeus's sources, presumably transmitted to him orally, must have been reliable and that he might
have received his information in Egypt.

26. As Goldstein, 73–74, points out, according to Hecataeus (cited in *Against
Apion* 1.193), Jews did not tolerate the existence of pagan altars and shrines in
Judaea, securing the privilege of not having to tolerate pagan worship in their
land in various ways.

27. Stern, 1.93.

28. Josephus is probably thinking of the comment by Aristobulus (quoted in
Eusebius, *Praeparatio Evangelica* 13.12.1–16) in the second century B.C.E., as
noted by Henry St. J. Thackeray, ed. and trans., *Josephus*, vol. 1, on *Against Apion*
1.165.

29. So Gabba, 8.

30. So Hengel, 1.258.

31. Bickerman, *Jews*, 14, suggests that the uniformity of Aramaic as the commercial language of the Persian Empire concealed national distinctions; but if
Herodotus is at all indicative of Greek travelers, such distinctions were made.

32. So Momigliano, 74.

33. So Bickerman, *Jews*, 13.

34. Perhaps, to be sure, the question as to why the Greeks ignored the Jews
has been misconceived. The Greeks before the time of Alexander certainly knew
about Phoenicians and Syrians; but the term *Syrians* may have included what
seemed to them scores of indistinct little tribal and ethnic groups in the area who
had a common language, dressed similarly, and shared many customs. Indeed, it

is not only the Judaeans whom the Greeks ignore, but also the Samaritans, Edomites, Ammonites, Moabites, Galaadites, and Gaulanites. Perhaps they are merely conflated with one another, just as non-Greeks conflated the diverse inhabitants of Greece, Asia Minor, and the Aegean islands into a single group, "Ionians" or "Greeks."

35. See Hengel, 1.88–92.

36. For the evidence see Hengel 1.15–18.

37. See, for example, *'Avodah Zarah* 71a, which states that when a city has been captured by besieging troops, all the wives of priests therein are disqualified to their husbands, the assumption being that they have been violated by the soldiers.

38. See Hengel 1.72. On the ties between Sparta and the Hasmoneans, see Michael S. Ginsburg, "Sparta and Judaea"; S. Schüller, "Some Problems Connected with the Supposed Common Ancestry of Jews and Spartans and Their Relations during the Last Three Centuries B.C."; Menahem Stern, *The Documents on the History of the Hasmonaean Revolt* [in Hebrew] 91–93, 113–16, 126–28; Burkhart Cardauns, "Juden und Spartaner: Zur hellenistisch-jüdischen Literatur" and Ranon Katzoff, "Jonathan and Late Sparta."

39. Hengel 1.23–25.

40. So Kasher, especially 313–15. As Kasher, 1–2, has noted, not only the Jews but also the Hellenistic cities themselves identified the Greek population in the land with the descendants of the ancient Canaanites, as one can see from both literary and numismatic sources. For the evidence see Kasher, 2, note 2a.

41. So Kasher, 315.

42. So Hengel, 1.25–27.

43. See Hugo Mantel, *Studies in the History of the Sanhedrin*.

44. Hengel 1.23–32.

45. Hengel, 1.287. Here Hengel is following Elias Bickerman, *The G-d of the Maccabees: Studies on the Meaning and Origin of the Maccabean Revolt*, especially 76–92.

46. So Fergus Millar, "The Background to the Maccabean Revolution: Reflections on Martin Hengel's 'Judaism and Hellenism,' " 13.

47. Hengel 1.32–57.

48. So noted by Avi-Yonah, 182, and Green, 313.

49. Hengel, *Hellenization*, 7.

50. So Joseph A. Fitzmyer, *A Wandering Aramean*, 33.

51. On the low level of knowledge of Greek among the Palestinian Jews, see Joseph A. Fitzmyer, "The Languages of Palestine in the First Century"; and Jan N. Sevenster, *Do You Know Greek? How Much Greek Could the First Century Jewish Christians Have Known?* 65–71.

52. See Hengel, 1.61–65.

53. So Naomi G. Cohen, "Jewish Names and Their Significance in the Hellenistic and Roman Periods in Asia Minor" [in Hebrew].

54. So Hengel, 1.69–70.

55. The Letter of Aristeas (50) and the Talmud (*Megillah* 9a) give the number of translators as seventy-two. Josephus (*Ant.* 12.57) gives the number as seventy, but in the preceding section (*Ant.* 12.56) he says that there were six from each

tribe, presumably making a total of seventy-two. The readings in the Talmudic tractate *Soferim* (1.9) vary between seventy and seventy-two.

56. Günther Zuntz, "Aristeas Studies II: Aristeas on the Translation of the Torah," 125, commenting on the Letter of Aristeas, says that "any historical reality or any relation to a specific point in the history of the Septuagint is sought in vain."

57. See the discussion by Sidney Jellicoe, *The Septuagint and Modern Study*, 59–63.

58. Goldstein, 73.

59. Hengel, 1.110–15.

60. Hengel, 1.115–30.

61. Hengel, 1.180–210.

62. Hengel, 1.182; Adolf Schlatter, *Geschichte Israels von Alexander dem Grossen bis Hadrian*, 2d ed., 109–10. Another possible parallel is Isaiah 60:17, which mentions gold, silver, bronze, iron, wood, and stones.

63. David Flusser, "The Four Empires in the Fourth Sibyl and in the Book of Daniel," 166–74.

64. See, e.g., Hans-Gustav Güterbock, "The Hittite Version of the Hurrian Kumarbi Myths: Oriental Forerunners of Hesiod." Moreover, Daniel has nothing to parallel the age of heroes.

65. Hengel, 1.131–53. See also his *Hellenization*, 48.

66. The founder of the Stoic school, Zeno, came from Citium in Cyprus, which, according to Diogenes Laertius (7.1), was a Greek city with a Phoenician population; and, indeed, Crates the Cynic addresses him (ibid.) as "my little Phoenician."

67. See Robert A. Stewart Macalister and John Garrow Duncan, *Excavations on the Hill of Ophel, Jerusalem, 1924–1925*, 159ff.

68. So Green, 505.

69. See Hengel, *Hellenization*, 31.

70. See Hengel, *Hellenization*, 8.

71. That this was a mass protest is clear from Josephus's remark (*War* 2.170) that Pilate's action aroused "immense excitement" (μεγίστην ταραχήν) among the Jews, and that the country folk flocked together in crowds (ἄθρους).

72. Note that although the Greek word πρέσβυς initially signifies "elder," in certain periods and places, preference was given to those with connections, regardless of age. Cf. Aristophanes, *Acharnians* 610. We may note that the term *old man* (*zaqen*) is in the Talmud (*Qiddushin* 32b) a synonym for "wise man." This may be the clue to the explanation of the *zaqen* ("old man") acquainted with Greek who, according to the Talmud (*Sotah* 49b, *Baba Qamma* 82b, *Menaḥoth* 64b), told the besiegers of the city of Jerusalem that as long as the besieged continued with their sacrificial service they would not be vanquished. Ernest Wiesenberg, "Related Prohibitions: Swine Breeding and the Study of Greek," 230–31, suggests that the "old man" in this incident may well be Josephus, but he finds a fatal objection to this hypothesis, namely that Josephus was still only in his thirties at the time of Titus's siege of Jerusalem. We may suggest that here, as in *Qiddushin* 32b, the term *zaqen* means "wise man" (although, in this passage, it obviously does not carry a compliment) rather than "old man."

73. To be sure, Josephus may here be trying to forestall (justified) criticism of his inferior Greek by appealing to class snobbery.

74. Jan N. Sevenster, *Do You Know Greek? How Much Greek Could the First Jewish Christians Have Known?* 70.

75. Hengel, *Hellenization*, 17. However, though the Gospels are written in Greek, there is no indication in any of them that Jesus knew Greek; on the contrary, he seems to have had a contempt for pagans, as we see in the incident with the Phoenician woman (Mark 7:25–30).

76. Cited by Gerard Mussies, "Greek in Palestine and the Diaspora," 1055.

77. Hannah M. Cotton and Joseph Geiger, eds., *Masada II: The Latin and Greek Documents*, note that the widespread use of Greek (and with no evident barbarisms) on papyri, ostraca, inscriptions on jars, and the like at Masada, dating for the most part, so far as we can tell, from the Herodian period, would seem to indicate that this is extensive evidence for the use of Greek during this period. But the evidence at Masada that Italian wine was imported would confirm that Masada is not typical of Palestine during this period. Rather, as the editors remark (page 8), "Repeated shipments of luxury items to such a remote location would not have been made unless the king and his court stayed there occasionally." Similarly, we may suggest, the use of Greek reflects the fact that Masada during much of this period was occupied by Herod and his family and, presumably after his son Archelaus was deposed in 6 C.E., by a Roman garrison, which was probably stationed there until the fortress was seized by Jewish revolutionaries in 66 C.E.

78. For the letter see Baruch Lifshitz, "Papyrus Grecs du désert de Juda."

79. Baron, 2.387, note 25.

80. From the insistence in the *Letter of Aristeas* (121) that the pious translators were well versed in Greek literature and from the great pains taken by the author (180–294) to display the translators as participating with Greeks in seven days of Greek-style banqueting, Jonathan A. Goldstein ("The Message of *Aristeas to Philokrates*: In the Second Century B.C.E., Obey the Torah, Venerate the Temple in Jerusalem, but Speak Greek, and Put Your Hopes in the Ptolemaic Dynasty"), 14, suggests that we may infer that there was a large group, particularly in Judaea, although the evidence of their existence is the polemic against them here, that held the opposite point of view—namely, that Jews must not live in the Diaspora (and certainly not in Egypt), that they must not use Greek, that they must certainly not read Greek literature, that they must not associate with Greeks, and that they must not follow Greek ways. Of course, as Goldstein there notes, the author of the *Letter of Aristeas* was not an extreme Hellenizer, because he is convinced that knowledge of the Greek language and literature is not incompatible with the observance of the laws of the Torah.

81. Except perhaps Cleopatra; see Plutarch, *Antony* 27.4.

82. Jonathan A. Goldstein, in an unpublished article, suggests that the phrase here used, *hokmath yevanith*, should not be taken as a synonym for *hokmah yevanith*; according to him it means not "Greek wisdom" but "the artfulness of Greek," that is, Greek rhetoric.

83. See Hengel, *Hellenization*, 8.

84. Hengel, 1.59.

85. See Benjamin Isaac, "A Donation for Herod's Temple in Jerusalem."

86. Hengel, *Hellenization*, 9.

87. It has been argued that if, indeed, there are few Greek inscriptions from this period, there are also few Hebrew and Aramaic ones, and that surely one should not conclude from this that the knowledge of Hebrew and Aramaic was not strong in Palestine. But Joseph Naveh and Jonas C. Greenfield ("Hebrew and Aramaic in the Persian Period," 128), have remarked: "The epigraphic finds have made clear the dominant role of Aramaic in the commercial, legal and administrative spheres. The official name *Yehud* for Judea, rather than the traditional *Yehuda*, known from earlier and later periods, is the best example of the pervasiveness of the impact of Aramaic on the Jews." Moreover, the *Targum to Job* from Qumran has been dated on linguistic grounds in the second century B.C.E. by Michael Sokoloff, *The Targum to Job from Qumran Cave XI*, 25.

88. Hengel, *Hellenization*, 66–67. Hengel, 9–11, cites data from a catalogue of Jewish ossuaries from Jerusalem soon to be published by L. Y. Rahmani, namely that 138 are in Jewish (Hebrew or Aramaic) script, 71 in Greek, 15 (or 16) in both, 2 in Latin, and 1 in Palmyrene. But we are not given the dates of these ossuaries, nor are we informed how many of them are of Jews from outside the Land of Israel (though we are told that several are from such places as Alexandria, Cyrene, and Capua in Italy) who chose to be buried there. Moreover, as Rahmani notes, several of the inscriptions contain warnings to passers-by not to molest the deceased; such warnings would naturally be couched in the language, namely Greek, of those who were suspected of seeking to rob the graves. But even if we neglect all of these factors, we must note that almost twice as many of the inscriptions are in Hebrew or Aramaic as in Greek. Moreover, Rahmani remarks that the inscriptions reveal little systematic knowledge of Greek language, grammar, or literature, but rather a knowledge of everyday speech.

89. So Bezalel Bar-Kochva, *Judas Maccabaeus: The Jewish Struggle against the Seleucids*, 119, note 12.

90. Moreover, just as in our own day, many Jews from abroad sought to be buried in the Holy Land; hence some (admittedly not the majority) of those interred there are from the Diaspora, where Greek was, indeed, firmly entrenched as the language of the Jews.

91. Goldstein, 72.

92. Megasthenes, quoted in Clement of Alexandria, *Stromata* 1.15. 72.5; Theophrastus, quoted in Porphyry, *De Abstinentia* 2.26; Clearchus of Soli, quoted in Josephus, *Against Apion* 1.179.

93. Actually, 2,556,000, according to Josephus's own arithmetic, plus menstruating women and those otherwise defiled.

94. 25,000: Joachim Jeremias, "Die Einwohnerzahl Jerusalems zur Zeit Jesu"; 82,500: Magen Broshi, "La population de l'ancienne Jérusalem"; 220,000: Anthony Byatt, "Josephus and Population Numbers in First Century Palestine."

95. For a detailed discussion of the evidence and of the relevant modern scholarship, cf. Baron, 1.370–72, note 7.

96. Hengel, *Hellenization*, 11–12.

97. So Martin Hengel, "Schürer," 42.

98. So also ibid., 42. Hengel, however, is incorrect in saying that the duty to

make the pilgrimage to Jerusalem was incumbent on the Jews of Palestine alone. The Mishnah, *Ḥagigah* 1:1, and the Gemara that follows (2a–7b) make no such distinction.

99. 700,000: Harnack, 1.8; 5,000,000: Juster, 1.210, note 2; 2,000,000: Baron, 1.370–72, note 7.

100. Mussies, "Greek in Palestine and the Diaspora," 1059, has correctly noted that from as late as the third and fourth centuries C.E. we have some information, precisely about such Hellenistic towns as Scythopolis, Jerusalem, and Gaza, which indicates that Aramaic was still the prevalent language there even among Christians.

101. See Tcherikover, 90–116.

102. Tcherikover, 114.

103. Given crop yields, there is surely a degree of exaggeration in Josephus's statistics here.

104. So Freyne, 152.

105. To be sure, some Jews chopped down the golden eagle that Herod had placed in the Temple (Josephus, *War* 1.648–55); but Josephus clarifies that only in the Temple was it unlawful, according to Jewish law, to place such images (1.650).

106. James F. Strange, quoted in Eric M. Meyers, "Galilean Regionalism as a Factor in Historical Reconstruction," 97; Strange, "Archaeology and the Religion of Judaism in Palestine," 661; Eric M. Meyers and James F. Strange, *Archaeology, the Rabbis, and Early Christianity*; Eric M. Meyers, "Galilean Regionalism: A Reappraisal," 125–28. Whereas in Lower Galilee 40 percent of the inscriptions are in Greek, only a few Greek inscriptions of Jewish origin have been found in Upper Galilee, most notably from Qatsyon (and it is not clear whether this is a Jewish site). On the other hand, Aramaic is attested in nearly two-thirds of the inscriptions. Freyne, 141, is not convinced of the validity of this thesis and notes that the conclusions of Meyers and Strange, *Archaeology, the Rabbis, and Early Christianity*, are based on epigraphic material from only seventeen sites, all of them from the western shore of the Sea of Galilee and the southern half of Lower Galilee.

107. Meyers, "Galilean Regionalism as a Factor in Historical Reconstruction," 99.

108. Meyers, "Galilean Regionalism"; idem, "The Cultural Setting of Galilee: The Case of Regionalism and Early Judaism," 697–98; idem, "Ancient Synagogues in Galilee: Their Religious and Cultural Setting." In one of his most recent publications, "Galilean Regionalism: A Reappraisal," 115–31, Meyers effectively refutes the thesis of Freyne, especially 141, that all Galilee was Hellenized, and insists that one must differentiate Upper from Lower Galilee.

109. Meyers, "Galilean Regionalism," 97.

110. Meyers, "Ancient Synagogues in Galilee": 97–108; idem., "Galilean Regionalism as a Factor in Historical Reconstruction": 97. See also Meyers and Strange, *Archaeology, the Rabbis, and Early Christianity*, 38–40; and Carol L. Meyers and Eric M. Meyers, "The Ark in Art: A Ceramic Rendering of the Torah Shrine from Nabratein," 185*, note 27.

111. Michael Avi-Yonah, *The Holy Land from the Persian to the Arab Conquests (536 B.C. to A.D. 640): A Historical Geography*, 191.

112. So Meyers, "The Cultural Setting of Galilee," 697; and "Ancient Synagogues in Galilee, 106.

113. Stephanus of Byzantium, *Ethnica*, ed. August Meineke (Berlin: Reimer, 1849), 132. Cited by Hengel, *Hellenization*, 20.

114. Hengel, 1.68; Shimon Applebaum, review [in Hebrew] of *CPJ*, vol. 1, 423–24. See "Orthodoxy," 223–26.

115. *Athletics*, 44.

116. Freyne, 142, argues that the presence of a stadium in Tiberias suggests that the Greek passion for sports was shared by the Jews there; but surely the stadium may have been built for and patronized by non-Jews. Furthermore, according to 2 Maccabees 4:7–14, prior to the Hellenizers in the reign of Antiochus Epiphanes there had been no gymnasiums in Jerusalem, and even the wearing of the Greek sunhat (πέτασος) was regarded as an outrageous novelty; hence the stadium represented a break with the past rather than the culmination of it, as Hengel would have us believe. Indeed, as we have noted, archaeologists have thus far found not a single trace of gymnasiums or stadia or theaters in Judaea for the period prior to Antiochus.

117. Morton Smith, *Palestinian Parties and Politics That Shaped the Old Testament*, 75–76.

118. Cf. John R. Hinnells, "The Zoroastrian Doctrine of Salvation in the Roman World: A Study of the Oracle of Hystaspes," who concludes (p. 146) that the oracle of Hystaspes, where this motif occurs, is a genuine Iranian—specifically Zoroastrian—work, dating from the first century B.C.E., if not earlier.

119. See Martin Braun, *History and Romance in Graeco-Oriental Literature*, 44–104.

120. See George W. E. Nickelsburg, "Apocalyptic and Myth in I Enoch 6–11," especially 395–97 and 399–404.

121. So Paul D. Hanson, "Rebellion in Heaven, Azazel, and Euhemeristic Heroes in 1 Enoch 6–11."

122. Matthews, 7.

123. Hengel, 1.218–47.

124. See Martin Hengel, "Qumran und der Hellenismus."

125. Isidore Lévy, *La légende de Pythagore de Grèce en Palestine*, suggests that the Essenes were directly influenced by the Pythagoreans; but this seems most unlikely, in view of the zeal of the Essenes in other respects in defending their Jewish heritage against all alien influences.

126. See Hengel, 1.230.

127. Hengel, 1.234–39.

128. Moshe Weinfeld, *The Organizational Pattern and the Penal Code of the Qumran Sect: A Comparison with Guilds and Religious Associations of the Hellenistic-Roman Period*, has presented a point-by-point examination of the organization of the Qumran community and has noted congruences with the rules of seventeen religious associations (θίασοι) and guilds of the Hellenistic-Roman world, notably those of Ptolemaic Egypt, ranging from the third century B.C.E. to the second century C.E. However, though he finds a certain amount of similarity between the two, especially in disciplinary matters, he stresses that the Qumran sect differs from the pagan associations in its distinctly Jewish character. He cautiously and

convincingly concludes that no direct influence of one on the other can be proved. Moreover, we know of no adequate Jewish or Israelite precedent for the laws of organization of the Qumran community because we have no Jewish or Israelite writings of this genre that might be expected to deal with such subjects. We may guess that if we knew more about the Rechabites, the monastic-like group mentioned by the prophet Jeremiah (chapter 35), we might well find that the Qumran sect had modeled itself on them.

129. Philo, *Quod Omnis Probus Liber Sit* 12.75; Josephus, *Ant.* 18.20.

130. Hengel, 1.92–95.

131. Holladay, 99, note 3. See my review in *CO* 62 (1985): 101–2.

132. So Francis T. Fallon, "Eupolemus," 862–63.

133. See David Rokeah, "A New Onomasticon Fragment from Oxyrhynchus and Philo's Etymologies."

134. Among those who identify this Eupolemus with the ambassador of the Maccabees are Jacob Freudenthal, *Hellenistische Studien: Alexander Polyhistor und die von ihm erhaltenen Reste jüdischer und samaritanischer Geschichtswerke*, 127; Emil Schürer, *Geschichte des jüdischen Volkes im Zeitalter Jesu Christi*, 4th ed., vol. 3, Part 4, 475–76; Felix Jacoby, "Eupolemos (11)"; Hengel, 2.63, note 269; Ben Zion Wacholder, *Eupolemus: A Study of Judaeo-Greek Literature*, 1–7; Holladay, 93; and Francis T. Fallon, "Eupolemus," 863. The alternate reading, γαμβρός, in Manuscript B, which properly identifies David as the son-in-law of Saul, is clearly a correction made by a scribe who realized the factual error of the original, as Wacholder, in *Eupolemus* . . . , 130, realizes.

135. Hengel, 1.96.

136. See, for example, Hengel, 1.95.

137. See, most recently, Robert Doran, *Temple Propaganda: The Purpose and Character of 2 Maccabees*, 112–13.

138. Doran, *Temple Propaganda*, 113. Furthermore, Solomon Zeitlin (ed., *The Second Book of Maccabees*, 19) notes that one of the letters with which the book opens (1:10) gives as its date 188 of the Seleucid Era (i.e., 125–124 B.C.E.). Inasmuch as Judaea was then an independent state, it seems hardly likely that someone in Judaea would have dated a document according to the Seleucid Era; a provenance from Antioch in Syria would seem more likely.

139. Eusebius, *Praeparatio Evangelica* 9.24.1, cites a fragment on Joseph from the fourteenth book; but Jacob Freudenthal, *Alexander Polyhistor*, 100, finds it incredible that Philo could have composed fourteen books of epic verse celebrating Jerusalem, inasmuch as brevity was the norm for epic poetry in the Hellenistic period, and consequently emends ιδ' to δ'. Holladay (II, 207 and 266–67, note 36), however, notes that recent scholarship has reopened the question as to whether Callimachus's preference for brevity should be regarded as the norm during this period.

As for the suggestion that Theodotus, the author of a poem *On Shechem*, is both from the Land of Israel and Jewish, we may remark that the fact that he calls Shechem a holy city would indicate that he was a Samaritan. Inasmuch as there was a Samaritan colony in Egypt, most scholars have classified him as an Alexandrian. In any case, we are not sure of his date; and the guess of most scholars is that he flourished about 100 B.C.E., well after the Maccabean revolt.

140. Hengel, *Hellenization*, 25.

141. Ben Zion Wacholder, in "Greek Authors in Herod's Library," lists forty-four works, nineteen of them "well-attested" and fourteen based on fragments of Alexander Polyhistor; but, aside from the fact that neither Josephus nor his presumed major source and Herod's adviser, Nicolaus of Damascus, asserts that Herod had such a library, the "well-attested" books are merely works cited by Nicolaus, there being no indication that Nicolaus, let alone Herod, had read them firsthand. Furthermore, there is no indication that Nicolaus consulted Alexander Polyhistor's sources firsthand. One thinks of the long list of authorities cited by Josephus's contemporary Pliny the Elder in the first book of his *Naturalis Historia*, representing the bibliography that he ought to have consulted. In antiquity, in many cases, one author simply copied a list of citations from another.

142. See my *JMS*, 121–91, 907–12; "Flavius Josephus Revisited: The Man, His Writings, and His Significance," 788–804; "Mikra," 455–518; "A Selective Critical Bibliography of Josephus," 355–66; "Josephus' *Jewish Antiquities* and Pseudo-Philo's *Biblical Antiquities*"; "Josephus' Commentary on Genesis"; "Hellenizations"; "Josephus' Portrait of Noah and Its Parallels in Philo, Pseudo-Philo's *Biblical Antiquities*, and Rabbinic Midrashim"; "Hellenizations in Josephus' *Jewish Antiquities*: The Portrait of Abraham"; "Abraham"; "Abraham the General in Josephus"; "'*Aqedah*"; "Jacob"; "Joshua"; "Josephus' Portrait of Deborah"; "Josephus' Version of Samson"; "Saul"; "David"; "Solomon"; "Esther"; and "Prophets."

143. So Henry A. Fischel, "Story and History: Observations on Greco-Roman Rhetoric and Pharisaism."

144. *Bekoroth* 8b, *Niddah* 69b, *Sanhedrin* 90b.

145. Gadara, we may note, was very close to the area where the rabbis lived, being a city a little to the east of the Jordan River. It produced three other famous ancient Greek writers—Menippus the satirist (third century B.C.E.), Meleager the poet (first century B.C.E.), and Philodemus the Epicurean philosopher (first century B.C.E.).

146. Lieberman, *Greek*; idem, *Hellenism*; idem, "How Much Greek"; David Daube, "Alexandrian Methods of Interpretation and the Rabbis"; Yitzhak Baer, *Israel among the Nations*; Elimelekh Epstein Halevi, *The Aggadah in the Light of Greek Sources*; Henry A Fischel, *Rabbinic Literature and Greco-Roman Philosophy*; and idem, ed., *Essays in Greco-Roman and Related Talmudic Literature*.

147. See Henry A. Fischel, "Greek and Latin Languages, Rabbinical Knowledge of," 885–86.

148. Goldstein, 70–71.

149. Bergmann; Wilhelm Bacher, *Die Agada der Tannaiten*, vol. 1; Armand Kaminka, "Les rapports entre le rabbinisme et la philosophie stoicienne"; Yitzhak Baer, *Israel among the Nations*. Cf. most recently Hengel, "Schürer," 58–59, who remarks that Josephus is not wholly wrong in comparing the Pharisees to the Stoics and that the Stoic views of the creation of the world and of the fate of the soul after death must have been of interest to cultured Jews.

150. See Henry A. Fischel, "Stoicism"; and Bergmann.

151. Lieberman, "How Much Greek."

152. Bergmann, 145–66.

153. See Henry A. Fischel, "Epicureanism." Fischel also suggests that the "Pardes" (*Hagigah* 14b) that four great rabbis—Ben Azzai, Elisha ben Avuyah, Ben Zoma, and Akiva—are alleged to have entered may have reference to the school of Epicurus; but the mystic doctrines that are there associated with "Pardes" would seem to fit better the school of Gnosticism than that of Epicureanism.

154. Henry A. Fischel, "Cynics and Cynicism."

155. Yitzhak Baer, *Israel among the Nations*.

156. Wolfson, 1.92; Lieberman, "How Much Greek," 130.

157. See Daniel Sperber, *A Dictionary of Greek and Latin Legal Terms in Rabbinic Literature*; and Ranon Katzoff, "Sperber's Dictionary of Greek and Latin Legal Terms in Rabbinic Literature—A Review Essay," 202.

158. Samuel Krauss estimated the ratio of entries of Greek to Latin loanwords in rabbinic Hebrew at a hundred to one, although in the Greek and Latin index in his *Griechische und lateinische Lehnwörter im Talmud, Midrasch und Targum*, vol. 2, 655–84, the ratio is approximately ten to one. In Sperber's volume the ratio is about three to one. See Katzoff, 204.

159. Katzoff, "Sperber's Dictionary," 204–5.

160. Matthews, 11.

161. See Lieberman, *Hellenism*, 58–62.

162. *Progymnasmata* 8 (ed. Hugo Rabe; Leipzig: Teubner, 1913), 19. Cited by Lieberman, *Hellenism*, 59, note 96.

163. Diogenes Laertius 3.41–43, 5.11–16, 5.51–57, 5.61–64, 5.69–74, 10.16–21; Cohen, 57–85.

164. Cohen, 76–79. We may suggest that a closer parallel to the entrance requirement to Rabban Gamaliel's study hall is the prayer of Socrates to Pan with which Plato closes the *Phaedrus* (279B): "May my outer qualities be consonant with my inner qualities." But this is a prayer rather than an entrance requirement, and even this would not seem to be sufficiently distinctive.

165. Hengel, 1.81.

166. Arnaldo Momigliano, review of Martin Hengel, *Judentum und Hellenismus*, 152.

167. Hengel, 1.76. Henry A. Fischel, in "Greek and Latin Languages, Rabbinical Knowledge of," 885, states that this ruling is probably legendary; but Ernest Wiesenberg, "Related Prohibitions: Swine Breeding and the Study of Greek," argues that the decree is probably historical and identifies Josephus as the old man (*Baba Qamma* 82b, *Sotah* 49b, *Menahoth* 64b) who was learned in Greek wisdom and who gave the advice to send up a pig instead of cattle for the sacrifice in the Temple.

168. Hengel, 1.75–76.

169. See Lieberman, *Hellenism*, 108.

170. See Lieberman, *Hellenism*, 113.

171. For the alternate readings, see Lieberman, *Hellenism*, 106, note 39. The matter is thoroughly discussed by Lieberman, in *Hellenism*, 108–113, who, after noting serious objections to the identification with Homer, concludes that the reference is, indeed, to Homer, but that the books of Homer were probably not included in the category of "Greek wisdom," and that they were employed in exercises for those children who did not in any case study Torah.

172. Lieberman, *Hellenism*, 113–14.

173. To be sure, David Goodblatt, in "The Talmudic Sources on the Origins of Organized Jewish Education" [in Hebrew], casts doubt on the reliability of the Talmudic source concerning both Simeon ben Shetah and Joshua ben Gamla, primarily on the ground that Josephus says nothing about these traditions. But we may note that Josephus is a historian who concentrates on political and military events and has extraordinarily little to say about education and culture.

174. So Green, 325.

175. So ibid., 315.

176. Goodenough, *Jewish Symbols in the Greco-Roman Period*; George F. Moore, *Judaism in the First Centuries of the Christian Era: The Age of the Tannaim*.

177. Shaye J. D. Cohen, "Epigraphical Rabbis."

178. Stern, 1.21–24, questions the authenticity of this passage, inasmuch as Hecataeus, a pagan, expresses admiration for the Jews' destruction of pagan shrines; but Hecataeus appears to have shared Plato's admiration for peoples who adhered tenaciously to their own laws, however un-Greek. Moreover, the very fact that Josephus can attribute such words to Hecataeus would indicate that this was regarded as the attitude of the Jews of Palestine toward pagan shrines.

179. So Goldstein, 74.

180. Morton Smith, "Palestinian Judaism in the First Century," 74–78; and Jacob Neusner, "Josephus' Pharisees." For a challenge to these views, see Francis X. Malinowski, "Galilean Judaism in the Writings of Flavius Josephus," 172–73; and Daniel R. Schwartz, "Josephus and Nicolaus on the Pharisees." David Goodblatt, in "The Place of the Pharisees in First Century Judaism: The State of the Debate," has upheld the position of Smith and Neusner; but most recently Steve Mason, in *Flavius Josephus on the Pharisees*, has convincingly shown that Josephus is consistent in his presentation of the Pharisees, that Josephus's assumption of Pharisaic predominance appears even in his incidental references to the Pharisees in the *War* and the *Life*, that such stories about the Pharisees must have had a traditional non-Josephan origin, that Josephus was directly acquainted only with the pre-70 state of affairs in Palestine, and that Josephus's tendency throughout his works is to lament the popularity and influence of the Pharisees.

181. See David W. Suter, "Judith."

182. Lieberman, *Hellenism*, 116. Luitpold Wallach, "A Palestinian Polemic against Idolatry: A Study in Rabbinic Literary Forms," argues that *Mekilta Bahodesh* 6 (ed. Lauterbach, 2.244–46) shows that the rabbis vigorously polemicized against polytheism and idolatry; but the passage is exceptional and, even by Wallach's own argument, is more a defense of the fate of Judaism in the face of pagan triumph than it is an attack on idolatry. In any case, the polemic is notably mild.

183. Morton Smith, "Goodenough's *Jewish Symbols* in Retrospect," 60.

184. Ibid., 60, where Smith notes that the sequence of painting styles in Pompeii, as well as the growth of florid architectural decoration, confirms the military details found in liberal sources.

185. Shaye J. D. Cohen, "Epigraphical Rabbis."

186. Moses Aberbach, in *The Roman-Jewish War (66–70 A.D.): Its Origin and Consequences*, 42, presents the interesting hypothesis that the Roman attitude toward the Jews changed under Augustus because Herod had failed to Hellenize

the Jews and, ironically, from the Roman point of view, had enhanced Judaism through rebuilding the Temple. But there is no definite evidence to support this theory.

187. So Freyne, 143–44.

188. Glen W. Bowersock, *Hellenism in Late Antiquity*, 6–7.

189. Cf., e.g., Hecataeus, quoted in Diodorus 40.3.4, and Tacitus, *Histories* 5.5.1.

190. Uriel Rappaport, "The Relations between Jews and Non-Jews and the Great War against Rome" [in Hebrew]; and idem, "Notes on the Causes of the Great Revolt against Rome" [in Hebrew]. Both of these articles have been reprinted in Aryeh Kasher, *The Great Jewish Revolt: Factors and Circumstances Leading to Its Outbreak* [in Hebrew], 159–72, 417–21.

191. The text reads, "Rabbi Joḥanan [third century c.e.] said, 'Israel was not exiled until twenty-four sects [*kithoth*, "parties, classes"] of heretics [*minim*, "sectarians"] came into being.'" That this reflects the pluralism in Jewish beliefs and practices in the first century is indicated by Louis Ginzberg, *An Unknown Jewish Sect*, 1; Saul Lieberman, *Texts and Studies*, 199; and Ephraim E. Urbach, "Class-Status and Leadership in the World of the Palestinian Sages," 39. Ronald Reuven Kimelman, in "Rabbi Yohanan of Tiberias: Aspects of the Social and Religious History of Third Century Palestine," 178–79, disagrees, noting that it was a popular rabbinic preoccupation, especially in the third century and thereafter, to speculate on the causes of the destruction of Jerusalem, and that a third-century source discovered in Egypt in 1945 mentions a plethora of heresies that had spread among the Jews "to this very day." He consequently concludes that Rabbi Joḥanan is reflecting a third-century setting. We may, however, suggest that he may both be reflecting a first-century tradition and be citing it because it is so relevant to his own day.

192. Samuel Sandmel, "Hellenism and Judaism," 32. Some may regard the description of the *shtetl*, as depicted by Mark Zborowski and Elizabeth Herzog in their book *Life Is With People: The Jewish Little-town of Eastern Europe* as an exaggerated and romanticized myth. Even Ruth Gay, however, in her article "Inventing the Shtetl," *American Scholar* 53 (1984): 329–49, who criticizes this idealized picture because it neglects the poverty and fear in which Jews lived, does not imply that the authors are wrong in indicating that there was relatively little assimilation. One should not confuse assimilation, which increased rapidly in the twentieth century in the cities, with the relative remoteness from "enlightened" ideas that was characteristic of the Jews of the small towns of Eastern Europe even in the twentieth century.

CHAPTER 2

1. Note that this is the word used by Aristotle (quoted in Clearchus of Soli, quoted in Josephus, *Against Apion* 1.182) when he praises the endurance and sobriety in the manner of life (δίαιτῃ) displayed by the Jew whom he met.

2. So in the epitome of Januarius Nepotianus. According to the epitome of Julius Paris, the praetor compelled the Jews, who had attempted to infect the Roman customs with the cult of Jupiter Sabazius, to return to their homes.

3. Or "Jews," because Latin has no definite article and hence does not distinguish between "Jews" and "the Jews."

4. Josephus dates the story toward the end of the procuratorship of Pontius Pilate (26–36 C.E.); but, as Stern, 2.70, correctly notes, the date of 19 C.E., as given by Tacitus, is supported by Dio Cassius.

5. See Stern, 2.116–17.

6. Eight hundred talents would be equal to 4,800,000 drachmas or denarii and hence contributions from 2,400,000 adult male Jews. Josephus (*Ant.* 14.113) insists that this money was transferred to Cos by the Jews of Asia Minor generally. Smallwood, 125, suggests that eight hundred may be an error for eighty or that large voluntary gifts may have been included. Jacob Liver, in "The Half-Shekel Offering in Biblical and Post-Biblical Literature," argues that the half-shekel tax was not fixed as an obligation on every Jew until the end of the Hasmonean period or somewhat later and insists that the half-shekel tax mentioned in the Pentateuch (Exod 30:11–16) had a different character and purpose. But inasmuch as we have no significant historian extant before Josephus and inasmuch as he says nothing about the origin of the tax, we may assume that it had been in force ever since Sinai. See Smallwood, 125, note 18.

7. One may ask whether perhaps there is circular reasoning here, in that if a Jew did join in pagan worship he would no longer be considered a Jew. But if the point of view codified in the Talmud (*Qiddushin* 68b), namely that one born of a Jewish mother is a Jew regardless of his or her beliefs or actions, was applicable at this time, the answer would be that he was a Jew, according to Jewish law. Moreover, although non-Jews would probably have considered such a renegade to be a non-Jew, he would, in this context, in all probability, have been referred to as a former Jew.

8. Apparently Tacitus is unaware that the Sabbatical year is observed only in the Land of Israel.

9. Goodenough, 12.15. Alberro, 211, is persuaded that Philo is speaking for the majority of the Jews of Alexandria on the grounds that Alexandria was a cosmopolitan city where Greek culture was at its height, and that the degree of Hellenization there was much greater than in the rural districts of Egypt. But inasmuch as we have no papyri from Alexandria, such a comparison seems premature.

10. Tcherikover, 355–56.

11. Solomon Zeitlin, editor of *The Second Book of Maccabees*, argues on pages 31–40 against the authenticity of the letters as they stand; but the important point is that the author of the book was confident that readers would regard as credible the sending of such letters by the Jews of Judaea to those of Egypt.

12. See especially Green, 318–19.

13. Avi-Yonah, 136–66, especially 163.

14. See Arthur E. Cowley, ed., *Aramaic Papyri of the Fifth Century B.C.*, nos. 81–82.

15. Gustav A. Deissmann, *Bibelstudien: Beiträge, zumeist aus den Papyri und Inscriften, zur Geschichte der Sprache, des Schrifttums und der Religion des hellenistischen Judentums und des Urchristentums*, 72. So also August Bludau, *Juden und Judenverfolgungen in alten Alexandria*, 35–43. Albert Harkavy, "Contribution à la littér-

ature gnomique," and Solomon Schechter, "Genizah Fragments 1: Gnomic," have published a collection of anonymous wisdom sentences having clear affinities with Ecclesiastes, written in Hebrew and found in the Genizah in Cairo. Klaus Berger, in *Die Weisheitsschrift aus der Kairoer Geniza: Erstedition, Kommentar und Übersetzung*, noting parallels with Philo and with other Hellenistic Jewish writers, ascribes the document to the Egyptian Diaspora and assigns it a date of 100 C.E. If so, this would be a notable exception to our view that knowledge of Hebrew, for practical purposes, disappears among the Egyptian Jews after 300 B.C.E. But the parallels are hardly striking; there are parallels at least as striking to be found in Qumran and in other sources in the Land of Israel.

16. See Henry B. Swete, *Introduction to the Old Testament in Greek*, 19–20; Henry St. John Thackeray, *The Septuagint and Jewish Worship*, 41, 47–48; and Marcus, 233. Elias J. Bickerman, "The Septuagint as a Translation," 9–11, however, accepts the statement of Aristeas that the translation was made by order of the Ptolemaic government. We may suggest that Ptolemy wanted to show favor to the Jews, inasmuch as he needed their help as bureaucrats in order to control the native Egyptian masses, who quite obviously resented the rule of an interloper.

17. Though some of the later rabbis were favorable to the translation (cf. *Megillah* 9b, which applies to the Septuagint the passage "The beauty of Japheth shall dwell in the tents of Shem" [Gen 9:27]), others (see *Soferim* 1.7) drew a parallel with the incident of the golden calf, asserting that the translation had been completed on the anniversary of the day when the golden calf had been built.

18. See the *Letter of Aristeas* generally, especially 30.

19. See, for example, Henry A. Redpath, "Mythological Terms in the LXX"; and Marcus, 227–45.

20. Henry St. John Thackeray, "The Poetry of the Greek Book of Proverbs," 65, points out that all the features of the collection of Zenobius, a Sophist of the time of Hadrian who published an anthology of Greek proverbs, also appear in the Greek translation of Proverbs. In particular, the translation employs the two metres, iambic and hexameter, that had long been considered appropriate for such maxims. The translator shows the same partiality as do his pagan predecessors for half-lines ending with the caesura and the same disregard for distinctions between long and short vowels. There is, moreover, a close correspondence in the actual wording between the Greek translation of Proverbs and some famous pagan proverbial phrases—e.g., 7:22 (κύων ἐπὶ δεσμούς) and 23:31 (γυμνότερος ὑπέρου).

21. So Marcus, 236. When, however, Marcus expresses the opinion that "there are relatively as many allusions to Greek gods, festivals, myths, oaths, etc., in early rabbinic literature as in the Septuagint," he fails to realize, as an examination of Samuel Krauss, *Griechische und lateinische Lehnwörter im Talmud, Midrasch und Targum*, vol. 2, would show, that the Talmudic literature uses these terms in denunciation of pagan idolatry and not in translation of traditional Jewish concepts.

22. See Charles H. Dodd, *The Bible and the Greeks*, 33–34, followed, for example, by Samuel Sandmel, *The Genius of Paul*, 46–47.

23. So Alan F. Segal, "Torah and Nomos in Recent Scholarly Discussion."

24. So Bickerman, *Jews*, 114–15.

25. See Bickerman, *Jews*, 113–14.

26. See Bickerman, *Jews*, 114.

27. To the 116 inscriptions from Egypt in *CII*, 2 (1952), numbers 1424–1539, David M. Lewis, in "The Jewish Inscriptions of Egypt," has added six more.

28. So Leon, 76. It is very difficult to date these inscriptions with any degree of precision; but it would appear that there are no significant changes in language or other respects throughout the ancient period. Smallwood, 133, suggests that the preponderance of Greek in epitaphs does not necessarily indicate that the Jewish community remained Greek-speaking, inasmuch as Jews may have retained Greek for epitaphs as the language of their former home and of their ancestors. We may remark, however, that if the Jews had so much regard for their ancestors they should have used Aramaic in their epitaphs, as indeed they did not. Hence, the Greek used in epitaphs probably represents the language in actual use.

29. For the text, translation, and discussion of the fragments see Holladay, 51–91.

30. See Holladay, 189–90 and 194–95, notes 6–9.

31. See the discussion by Shaye J. D. Cohen, "Sosates the Jewish Homer."

32. Holladay, 2, 209–10.

33. This is the view of Jacobson, 13–17, though Holladay, 2, 312–13, is non-committal.

34. So Jacobson, 8–13.

35. Wolfson, 1.90.

36. So Samuel Sandmel, *Philo's Place in Judaism: A Study of Conceptions of Abraham in Jewish Literature*, 13. On the basis of a study of Philo's treatment of the story of Abraham, Sandmel concludes that Philo's knowledge of Hebrew was at best useless and at worst nonexistent.

37. See David Rokeah, "A New Onomasticon Fragment from Oxyrhynchus and Philo's Etymologies."

38. To be sure, the author of the *Letter of Aristeas* never explicitly says that he is a pagan, but Josephus (*Ant.* 12.23), in his close paraphrase of the *Letter*, does say so clearly.

39. Moses Hadas (ed. and trans., *Aristeas to Philocrates [Letter of Aristeas]*) 3–54, after a thorough analysis, assigns a date shortly after 132 B.C.E. for its composition. Sidney Jellicoe, in *The Septuagint and Modern Study*, 47–50 favors a *terminus ante quem* of about 170 B.C.E. Hugo Willrich, in *Urkundenfälschung in der hellenistisch-jüdischen Literatur* 86–91, however, contends that the *Letter of Aristeas*, especially section 28, shows that it was written after the fall of the Ptolemies (31 B.C.E.), and that the data about the Land of Israel indicate that it was written in the time of Augustus before the struggle under Caligula.

40. The work could, of course, still be aimed at a Jewish audience, because Jews would be more confident of the validity of their religious beliefs and practices if they were confirmed by a pagan.

41. So Joseph Reider, ed., *The Book of Wisdom*, 29–38.

42. So Reider, 12.

43. So Green, 317.

44. The scholars of the Museum were particularly concerned with the higher

and lower criticism of Homer; but throughout antiquity such criticism was not of concern to Jews. Green, 815, note 31, cites one passage in Callimachus (*Palatine Anthology* 6.148) that may depend on Isaiah 14:12; but the passage is too short and the language not sufficiently distinctive to be conclusive.

45. See *CPJ* 1. 38. Wolfson, 1. 79, follows Harold Idris Bell (*Jews and Christians in Egypt: The Jewish Troubles in Alexandria and the Athanasian Controversy*), 25, lines 92–93, and p. 29, in stating that because Egyptians were excluded, so undoubtedly were the Jews. There is much to commend the view of Kasher, "Gymnasium," 151–56, that Claudius's warning does not refer to Jewish infiltration into the list of ephebes but was actually meant to deter Jews not from "entering" (ἐπισπαίειν, an emendation made by Schwartz) but from "harassing" (ἐπισπαίρειν, the original reading) the public games organized by the gymnasiarchs.

46. This is disputed by Aryeh Kasher, "Gymnasium," 148–51, and *The Jews in Hellenistic and Roman Egypt: The Struggle for Equal Rights*, 204–5; he notes that the assumption that the Jew had received a gymnasium education depended on a doubtful reconstruction of lines 13–14. In particular, he notes ("Gymnasium," 158, note 24) that the word γυμνάσιον, reconstructed by Schubart in his original edition of this papyrus, is a neuter noun, whereas the definite article used here is τόν, which is masculine; but, we may remark, the reading of every letter in the word γυμνάσιον is doubtful. Moreover, in the papyrus the appellant, Helenos, complains that he runs the risk of being deprived of his native country (πατρίδος); this would appear to indicate that he was threatened with losing something dependent on the appropriate education he claims to have received. That the scribe has crossed out the word Ἀλεξανδρέως ("Alexandrian") and substituted Ἰουδαίου τῶν ἀπὸ Ἀλεξανδρε(ίας) would seem to indicate a challenge to the status of the applicant; and the most likely point at issue would seem to be his citizenship. That several other words in the document have been crossed out by the scribe would seem to confirm this. The connection between the contested status of the applicant and his "appropriate education" appears to indicate that such an education, which would be most likely in the gymnasium, would automatically acquire the status that the appellant claims. Kasher suggests that Helenos might have been educated in a Jewish gymnasium, but we know of no such institution in Egypt.

47. So "Prolegomena," 39, note 99.

48. See "Prolegomena," 11–15.

49. This is the conclusion of Thomas A. Brady, "The Gymnasium in Ptolemaic Egypt," 16–17. Jones, 311, mentions two gymnasiarchs who were not Greek, one a Thracian and the other a Persian; but this does not, of course, necessarily mean that Jews could hold such an office.

50. See Louis Robert, "Un Corpus des Inscriptions Juives," 85–86, and *Hellenica* 3, 100, cited by Tcherikover, 526, note 33.

51. Cited by Tcherikover, 350. There may be a reference to Jewish senior ephebes in an inscription found at Aphrodisias and published by Reynolds, 132.

52. Marrou, 109.

53. Cf. Michael Rostovtzeff, *The Social and Economic History of the Hellenistic World*, 2.1059, who notes the existence, within these alumni associations, of sub-associations of alumni of particular years.

54. Marrou, 104. This seems to have been true until the time of the Roman

Empire, when the gymnasiums in Egypt, like most of those outside Egypt, came under public control.

55. Jones, 310.

56. See Francis H. Colson and George H. Whitaker, eds., *Philo*, vol. 4, 198–99, note b. Marrou, 158, remarks that this committee of "controllers of wisdom," the σωφρονισταί, disappeared at some unknown date in the Hellenistic period but that it began to function again under the Roman Empire. Alan Mendelson, in *Secular Education in Philo of Alexandria*, 31, conjectures consequently that Philo may be alluding to the σωφρονιστής as a contemporaneous official of the local gymnasium.

57. Ralph Marcus, "An Outline of Philo's System of Education" [in Hebrew], 231. Marcus thinks that this praise may be due to the circumstance that Philo is here addressing a Greek audience; but even he admits that it is very possible that Jews visited the pagan Greek gymnasium from time to time.

58. See *Athletics*, 134–35.

59. Wolfson, 1.79.

60. Noted by Thomas A. Brady, "The Gymnasium in Ptolemaic Egypt," 18. Marrou, 392–93, mentions one gymnasium that had no fewer than forty-one marble statues of Hermes.

61. Marrou, 109.

62. So Shimon Applebaum, pp. 424–25 of rev. of *CPJ*, vol. 1 [in Hebrew].

63. Marrou, 130–31.

64. Marrou, 116.

65. Wolfson, 1.80.

66. See Arnold H. M. Jones, *The Greek City from Alexander to Justinian*, 230; and Edward Norman Gardiner, *Athletics of the Ancient World*, 45.

67. Gardiner, *Athletics*, 22.

68. Cf. *'Avodah Zarah* 18b, which inveighs against those who visit stadia, where such contests were held.

69. So Harold A. Harris, in *Greek Athletics and the Jews*, 51–95.

70. So Harris, *Greek Athletics*, 73, who, to be sure, cites the parallel from Plato (*Phaedrus* 239C).

71. So Harris, *Greek Athletics*, 77.

72. So Alan Mendelson, *Secular Education*, 31–32.

73. This is the interpretation of *CPJ* 2, no. 153, p. 53, and of Harris, *Greek Athletics*, 92. The latter suggests that for some time the rule demanding that competitors be Greek had come to be disregarded and that Jews had been entering, but that when the riot of 38 occurred the Alexandrian Greeks used the occasion as an excuse to demand that Jews be excluded. Aryeh Kasher, in *The Jews in Hellenistic and Roman Egypt: The Struggle for Equal Rights*, 314–21, however, insists that Claudius's letter does not deal with any surreptitious infiltration by Jews into the Alexandrian gymnasium but rather simply warns the Jews not to harass (reading μηδὲ ἐπισπαίρειν) the games arranged by the gymasiarchs and cosmetae (see note 45 above).

74. This is the most likely explanation of Claudius's order (*CPJ*, 2.153, lines 88–92) to the Jews not to send separate embassies "as if they lived in a separate city, a course of action never before adopted."

75. Cf. the enumeration of the types of clowns, mimics, and buffoons in *'Avodah Zarah* 18b.

76. Roy C. Flickinger, *The Greek Theater and Its Drama*, 120.

77. Arthur E. Haigh and Arthur W. Pickard-Cambridge, *The Attic Theatre: A Description of the Stage and Theatre of the Athenians and of the Dramatic Performances at Athens*, 3d ed. 2. Suicides were permissible on stage, because this taboo did not protect the actor against himself.

78. Reynolds, 54, notes that the inscription itself speaks of the "place of Jews who are also G-d-fearers," and she notes three possible interpretations: keeping the text as it stands and referring to G-d-fearing Jews; declaring that the reference is to "G-d-fearers" who, because of their close association with Jews, are referred to as such; or emending the text to indicate "Jews and G-d-fearers." In any case, the reference is to a special place in the theater for a Jewish group of one sort or another.

79. Quoted in Eusebius, *Praeparatio Evangelica* 9.29.7 ff. Jacobson, 20, notes, however, that Ezekiel, for theologico-religious reasons, deliberately avoids bringing G-d on stage and that all one hears is a voice. He admits that this in itself may be sacrilegious but argues (pp. 19–20) that we lack evidence for this period and for the Alexandrian Jewish milieu in particular as to standards of orthodoxy. Surely, however, the intimate association of both tragedies and comedies with the god Dionysus would ipso facto have made attendance at the theater objectionable. Moreover, although he admits that it is not quite exact, Jacobson draws an analogy between the voice of G-d speaking in the play and the phenomenon of speaking the words of G-d in the first person in Jewish liturgy and in public Bible-reading; but there is a major difference, namely that in the latter it is clear that the reader is not impersonating G-d, whereas in the play the audience is asked to make the willing suspension of disbelief and to imagine that G-d Himself is speaking. And yet Jacobson himself (20–21) argues for the antiquity and continuity of Aggadah as seen in the Septuagint and in Ezekiel's play itself. If so, what would have been offensive to the rabbis would most likely have been offensive to Ezekiel and to his circle. In this connection, it is surely significant that we know of no plays that were composed in the Land of Israel; and, for that matter, we know of no successor to Ezekiel in Alexandria. Hadas, 100, asserting that unity of scene seems not to have been preserved, suggests that the play was not intended for performance. He notes that the practice of writing closet dramas, plays to be read as pamphlets rather than to be acted, goes back to at least the fourth century B.C.E., and that Alexandria itself had a number of tragedians whose works were apparently never performed. On the other hand, Carl R. Holladay, in *Fragments from Hellenistic Jewish Authors*, vol. 2: *Poets*, 315, suggests that Ezekiel has recast the biblical material with a view to the technical demands of production and performance.

80. Wolfson, 1.81.

81. So Tcherikover, "Prolegomena," 7–8, and literature cited in notes 21 and 22 there; and Aryeh Kasher, *The Jews in Hellenistic and Roman Egypt: The Struggle for Equal Rights*, 106–7. See also Salo W. Baron, *The Jewish Community, Its History and Structure to the American Revolution*, vol. 1, 87–93.

82. See Salo W. Baron, *The Jewish Community: Its History and Structure to the*

American Revolution, vol. 1, 92; vol. 3, note 19; and Samuel Klein, "Das Fremdenhaus der Synagoge."

83. So Kasher, 106.

84. See Tcherikover, 303, and citations; 508, note 28.

85. See the list in "Prolegomena," 8.

86. So Edith Mary Smallwood, ed., *Philonis Alexandrini Legatio ad Gaium*,
208–9.

87. So Kasher, passim.

88. Constantine Zuckerman, "Hellenistic *politeumata* and the Jews: A Reconsideration," especially 172–73. Kasher, in a letter to the present author, notes
that Strabo (quoted in Josephus, *Ant.* 14.115–17) remarks that the Jews of Alexandria had an ethnarch of their own who governed the Jewish people just as if he
were the head of a sovereign state (πολιτείας ἄρχων αὐτοτελοῦς). See Dorothy J.
Thompson Crawford, "The Idumaeans of Memphis and the Ptolemaic Politeumata."

89. Philo, *In Flaccum* 10.74, refers to him as a genarch.

90. See Tcherikover, 302; *Josephus* 9, on 19.283; and Stern, 1.280–81.

91. This is also implied by Strabo's comment (quoted in Josephus, *Ant.* 14.117)
that the Jews in Alexandria were ruled by an ethnarch, "who governs the people
and adjudicates suits and supervises contracts and ordinances, just as if he were
the head of a sovereign state."

92. Henry A. Green, *The Economic and Social Origins of Gnosticism*, 89–90. See
also his "Interpersonal Relations, Ethnic Structure and Economy—A Sociological Reading of Jewish Identification in Roman Egypt."

93. Jacob Liver, "The Half-Shekel Offering in Biblical and Post-Biblical Literature," argues (pp. 190–98) that the annual offering did not become an established institution and was not fixed as an obligation on every Jew until the end of
the Hasmonean period or even somewhat later. He cites as evidence a fragment
from the Dead Sea Scrolls which interprets the regulation, as stated in the Pentateuch, as a ransom offering made only once in a lifetime; but in response we may
note that if the Dead Sea Sect consisted of Essenes they were excluded from the
Temple (Josephus, *Ant.* 18.19) and hence presumably did not contribute to it.

94. So Kraabel, "Diaspora."

95. Alf Thomas Kraabel, "Social Systems of Six Diaspora Synagogues," 88.

96. See Kraabel, "Diaspora," 486.

97. So Mendelson, 23.

98. Ibid., 23–24.

99. Leo Fuchs, *Die Juden Aegyptens in ptolemäischer und römischer Zeit*, 127.

100. Erwin R. Goodenough, *By Light, Light*, 4–5, believes that Philo interprets Judaism as a mystery; but Wolfson, 1.45–46, believes that Philo borrows
merely the terminology of the mysteries, just as he borrows that of popular religion and mythology. But although, undoubtedly, Goodenough goes too far,
Wolfson does not sufficiently estimate the importance of language, particularly
in antiquity, as an integral part of a system of thought.

101. We may here mention the intriguing document, which contains a version
of Psalm 20:2–6 from the Aramaic text in demotic script, dating, apparently, from
the end of the second century B.C.E. and calling on the Egyptian god Horus, side

by side with the Hebrew G-d, for help "in our troubles." Charles F. Nims and Richard C. Steiner, in "A Paganized Version of Psalm 20:2–6 from the Aramaic Text in Demotic Script," conclude that this is a pagan adaptation of a prayer based on Psalm 20 rather than a Jewish adaptation of a pagan prayer; but they themselves admit that the spelling of the divine names, as well as other features of the language of the document, contains a distinct Hebrew component and hence points to a Jewish origin. That the document is in Aramaic at a time when Aramaic had practically ceased to be spoken in Egypt and that the people were so devoted to Horus, the arch-rival of Seth, both indicate that Edfu, a leading center of Horus worship and the site of an important Jewish community, was the place of origin. If, then, the document is of Jewish origin, it would be evidence both of the survival of Aramaic in Ptolemaic Egypt and of considerable syncretism.

102. *CPJ* 1.23, 24, etc.

103. *CII* 2.1537 and 1538 (= David M. Lewis, "The Jewish Inscriptions of Egypt," 165–66).

104. *CII* 2.1508, 1511, 1530 (= David M. Lewis, "The Jewish Inscriptions," 156, 157, 161–162). The location of the inscriptions in the necropolis of Leontopolis (Tel el-Yehoudieh), as well as the names of the deceased, argue for a Jewish origin.

105. Arnaldo Momigliano, "Un documento della spiritualità dei Giudei Leontopolitani," concludes that the terminology and thoughts in this inscription are altogether pagan, but he supplies no reasons for his views.

106. *CPJ* 3.475. Tcherikover says that this Jacob is "obviously a Jew, in spite of the fact that he performs his duty as a guard in the temple of Sarapis." But there is no evidence other than his name. Another possibility is that he is a Christian.

107. Goodenough, 2.153–295.

108. Goodenough, 2.154.

109. Goodenough, 2.191.

110. Campbell Bonner, *Studies in Magical Amulets Chiefly Graeco-Egyptian*, 30–31, who is generally much more reluctant than is Goodenough to identify a charm as Jewish, admits that such a charm is more likely to be Jewish than Gentile or Gnostic.

111. Goodenough, 2.191, 194–95.

112. Goodenough, 2.194. Helios, we may note, was particularly popular in Jewish prayers and is actually depicted on five synagogue floors found in the Land of Israel, as well as on Jewish sarcophagi dating from the second to the fourth centuries. This may be connected with the revival of the worship of Helios in the third century. We may also call attention to Mordecai Margalioth, ed., *Sefer Ha-Razim* [in Hebrew]. This work, the dating of which is disputed (though he tentatively dates it in the third century), shows profound knowledge of Greek magic, even including technical terms. It contains Greek etymologies for some of its seven hundred angels and has prayers to pagan deities, including Helios, who are conceived of as deities subordinate to the Jewish G-d. One is reminded of the Emperor Constantine, who, at the time of his conversion, ordered prayers to Sol Invictus as a generic enough name for the Divine so as to satisfy pagans, Jews, and Christians.

113. Goodenough, 2.229.

114. Goodenough, 2.291–94.

115. Goodenough, 2.199; 8.5, etc.

116. Goodenough, 8.20.

117. Goodenough, 2.237.

118. Karl L. Preisendanz, *Papyri Graecae Magicae*, 2, lines 115–28. On the magical papyri containing the name of Moses, see Gager, 140–52.

119. Cf. Goodenough, 2.194.

120. Goodenough, 2.153–55. Undoubtedly, as Goodenough's many critics have noted, he went too far in accepting papyri as Jewish merely because they included Jewish names, whereas such names may merely reflect the phenomenon, frequently found today, of the adoption, whether knowingly or unknowingly, of Jewish names by non-Jews.

121. So Gager, 136.

122. Goodenough, 2. 261–69.

123. On the authenticity of this letter, see the convincing discussion by Ralph Marcus, ed. and trans., *Josephus*, vol. 7, 764–66.

124. This privilege should be especially appreciated in the light of Julius Caesar's decree prohibiting most collegia to meet in Rome.

125. On the authenticity of these decrees, see Tessa Rajak, "Was there a Roman Charter for the Jews?" 109; *contra* but unconvincing, Horst R. Moehring, "The *Acta Pro Judaeis* in the *Antiquities* of Flavius Josephus: A Study in Hellenistic and Modern Apologetic Historiography."

126. See the discussion by Trebilco, 14–15.

127. See Trebilco, 20–27.

128. See Reynolds and "Aphrodisias."

129. Reynolds, 78–84.

130. Ibid., 79. Of the 125 names of born Jews in the Aphrodisias inscriptions eleven are of biblical origin, whereas the names of all three proselytes are biblical. On the other hand, of the 54 names of θεοσεβεῖς, only one and possibly a second are biblical. One should not, however, draw too much significance from this, because, as Naomi G. Cohen, in "Jewish Names and Their Significance in the Hellenistic-Roman Period in Asia Minor," has shown, names, at least in Asia Minor, are not an indication of religious intensity, and the biblical names found in the inscriptions often actually reflect Christian influence. In particular, the names of two of the proselytes, Joseph and Samuel, found in the Aphrodisias inscriptions, are inexplicably common in both the *Corpus Papyrorum Judaicarum* and in the Talmud, but they are also common in the Christian tradition; hence, there is a possibility but hardly a proof that these proselytes started out as Christians and then converted to Judaism.

131. Naomi G. Cohen, "Rabbi Meir, a Descendant of Anatolian Proselytes: New Light on His Name and the Historic Kernel of the Nero Legend in Gittin 56a."

132. See Lifshitz, no. 10. We may assume, with good reason, that the patriarch is the patriarch of the Land of Israel and not some local official and note that the penalty is extremely high even for the inflation of the third century. See Martin Hengel, "Die Synagogeninschrift von Stobi," 158–59.

133. Julian, *Ad Communitatem Iudaeorum*, no. 204, pp. 396D–398 (in Stern, 2, no. 486a, pp. 559–68).

134. Libanius, *Epistulae* 1251.1–2 (in Stern, 2, no. 504, pp. 598–99).

135. See Lee I. Levine, "The Jewish Patriarch (Nasi) in Third Century Palestine"; and Reuven Kimelman, "The Conflict between R. Yohanan and Resh Laqish on the Supremacy of the Patriarchate."

136. Trebilco, 3, while noting the advantages of archaeological evidence, namely its directness, immediacy, and independence, also calls attention to the problems of interpretation, particularly the problem of dating and of coordinating archaeological finds with literary and historical evidence. Trebilco, 2–3, has given us a useful caveat on the use of epigraphical sources, namely that the evidence is at best only partial, because we have only those inscriptions that happen to have survived (and often in fragmentary form), and that inscriptions tend to be formal public documents that are not indicative of the range of human activity in everyday life. Moreover, there is often a serious problem of dating the inscriptions. Additionally, as he notes, the collection of inscriptions by Frey, *CII*, is both inaccurate and incomplete. See further the bibliography cited by Trebilco, 191, note 8.

137. So Saltman, 42. Saltman's explanation that the differences in attitude and observance between the Jews of the coast and those of inland Asia Minor are due to the survival in the interior of religious and social traditions of pre-exilic and exilic settlements, in contrast to the newer traditions brought to the coast by normative Jews of the Second Temple Period, has little evidence to support it. The more likely explanation is that travel inland was difficult and that consequently rabbinic visitors to the area restricted their stays to coastal cities.

138. So Saltman, 8–9.

139. So Robert L. Wilken, "Melito, the Jewish Community at Sardis, and the Sacrifice of Isaac," 55–56.

140. One of the inscriptions from Sardis mentions a σοφοδιδάσκαλος, and this has been taken to refer to a rabbi and to confirm the presence of Pharisaic influence; but aside from the fact that only one such inscription has been found, the word that we should expect for the Greek equivalent of the rabbinic *talmid hakham* should have the meaning "wise student" rather than "wise teacher."

141. See Alf Thomas Kraabel, "The Synagogue and the Jewish Community," 178; and, most recently, Trebilco, 38–54.

142. So Van der Horst, 175.

143. See, for example, Alf Thomas Kraabel, "Social Systems of Six Diaspora Synagogues," 87.

144. So Harnack, 2.182–229, and especially 327–28.

145. See Harnack, 2.225.

146. Notably Franz Cumont, *Les Religions orientales dans le paganisme romain*, 3d ed., 99; and Martin P. Nilsson, *Geschichte der griechischen Religion*, vol. 2, 636–40.

147. On the identity of these officials as Jews, see Kraabel, 74, n. 2. Moreover, the Talmud (*Shabbath* 147Â) may perhaps be alluding to the sundering of the communities in Asia Minor from the Jews in the Land of Israel when it declares that "the wines and baths of Phrygia have separated the ten tribes from Israel";

but the allusion here most likely is to a place in northern Israel famous for its wine.

148. So Trebilco, 143.

149. So Trebilco, 129–30, 144.

150. Alf Thomas Kraabel, "Paganism and Judaism: The Sardis Evidence," 29–33.

151. These literalists were probably not Gentiles, for we have no evidence that Gentiles used this line of attack during Philo's time.

152. Montgomery J. Shroyer, "Alexandrian Jewish Literalists," 278. Several of these difficulties are similar to those listed by such a Jewish heretic as Ḥiwi al-Balkhi in the ninth century. See Judah Rosenthal, *Ḥiwi al-Balkhi: A Comparative Study*.

153. See Joseph Klausner, *From Jesus to Paul*, 28–92.

154. See Wolfson, 1.69 and "Prolegomena," 77, note 61.

155. So Collins, 13.

156. So Erwin R. Goodenough, *The Jurisprudence of the Jewish Courts in Egypt*, 13–14. Note especially his replies to the contentions of Juster, Bréhier, and Heinemann that there is no practical value in Philo's remarks on law. In his view that Philo based his law on the decisions of local Jewish courts in Egypt, Goodenough is supported by Samuel Belkin, *Philo and the Oral Law*, 5–8.

157. See "Prolegomena," 32, note 34, where a number of reasons for not accepting Philo as such a source are offered.

158. For the six papyri, see Arthur E. Cowley, *Aramaic Papyri of the Fifth Century B.C.*, no. 81; *CPJ* 1.20, 1.23, 1.24, 2.148, 2.149; for the loan at an unknown rate of interest, see Cowley, no. 81, line 47; for the loan without interest, see *CPJ* 1.23. Cf. Rafal Taubenschlag, *The Law of Greco-Roman Egypt in the Light of the Papyri, 332 B.C.–640 A.D.*, vol. 1, 260, who remarks that both the Egyptian and the Greek law permitted loans with or without stipulation of interest. The permissible maximum on money loans was 2 percent a month throughout the Ptolemaic period.

159. There is here, in the use of the term *partnership* (κοινωνία) perhaps a hint of the Talmudic device of the *hetter iska*, a legal contrivance that created a formal partnership between creditor and debtor, in which half of the furnished capital constituted a loan to the "businessman," or active partner, while the other half was held by him in the form of a deposit, and which provided that the active partner enjoyed some greater benefit than the silent partner did (Mishnah Baba Mezia 5:4 and Gemara 104b).

160. For the Jewish divorce document, see *CPJ* 2.10–12 (no. 144). For non-Jewish divorce documents, see Orsolina Montevecchi, "Ricerche di sociologia nei documenti dell' Egitto greco-romano." For the comparison of Jewish and non-Jewish divorce documents, see Jean Lesquier, "Les Actes de divorce gréco-égyptiens: Etude de formulaire"; and Rafal Taubenschlag, *The Law of Greco-Roman Egypt in the Light of the Papyri, 332 B.C.–640 A.D.*, vol. 1, 91.

161. *CPJ* 1.34. Cf. Taubenschlag, *The Law*, p. 36: "It is a matter of fact that these [the papyri], apart from the mention of a Jewish notary's office in no. 143 and the possible hint of some 'political law' of Jews in no. 128, never refer to Jewish law."

162. In Responsa of R. Meir b. Baruch of Rothenburg (ed. Cremona, 1557), no. 78.

163. The matter is, however, debated in the Talmudic passages just cited.

164. Scholars have debated whether the Jews of Egypt at the same time looked on the Temple of Onias as their particular religious center. Heinrich H. Graetz, *Geschichte der Juden von den ältesten Zeiten bis auf die Gegenwart*, vol. 3.1, 5th ed., 32–33, argues that Judaea did not lay an interdict on the Temple of Onias because this temple had taken such firm root in Egypt that the rabbis decided to be more lenient toward it, as we see from their ruling that sacrifices in the Temple of Onias are not to be regarded as idolatry. But Samuel A. Hirsch, "The Temple of Onias," 56–57, argues that the Temple of Onias was utterly insignificant even for the Egyptian Jews, because it is not mentioned by any of the Hellenistic writers except Josephus. However, inasmuch as the Talmud sees fit to mention it in several places and to issue special rules pertaining to the priests who served in it and the animals vowed to be brought there, we may conclude that it was not utterly insignificant. Moreover, when Hirsch argues from the complete silence about it observed by all Hellenistic writers except Josephus—who, we must note, thought it worthy of frequent mention—we must remember that almost all Hellenistic Jewish literature has perished except for Philo, Josephus, several books of the Apocrypha and Pseudepigrapha, and scanty fragments of Graeco-Jewish writings.

165. So Alan Mendelson, *Philo's Jewish Identity*, 73.

166. So Mendelson, 74. This is also the view of Alberro, 210.

167. Tcherikover, 353.

168. Cf. the remark of Theodor Mommsen, *The Provinces of the Roman Empire from Caesar to Diocletian*, vol. 2, 177, who describes the city of Alexandria as almost as much a city of the Jews as of the Greeks.

169. Gerhard Kittel, in "Das Konnubium mit der Nicht-Juden im antiken Judentum," *Forschungen zur Judenfrage* 2 (1937): 30–62, argues that intermarriage of Jews with non-Jews was frequent in the first century: but his whole research is suspect because of its blatant attempt to seek the endorsement of Hitler. As to the remark of McKnight, 17, seeking to find significance in Josephus's failure (*Ant.* 2.91–92) to condemn Joseph's marriage with a non-Jew, in this Josephus is merely following the Bible. Similarly, we may add, Josephus (*Ant.* 2.263) does not condemn Moses' marriage with a non-Jew, inasmuch as the Bible itself refrains from any criticism at this point. Likewise, Josephus (*Ant.* 11.199–203) does not condemn Esther's marriage with the non-Jewish king Ahasuerus, inasmuch as the Bible does not.

170. Baron, 2.233.

171. Tcherikover, 353.

172. Tcherikover, 20–21.

173. Tcherikover, 528, note 52.

174. Berlin Papyrus no. 11641 (unpublished), cited by Wilhelm Schubart, *Einführung in die Papyruskunde*, 330. Even this is only probably a case of intermarriage.

175. Wolfson, 1.73–78.

176. Ibid., 1.74.

177. Ibid., 1.75.

178. For citations see ibid., 1.75, note 76.

179. Ibid., 1.78. In this group, presumably, should be included those who gave up their Judaism to become citizens of Alexandria, inasmuch as full citizenship involved worship of the city gods, as William W. Tarn and Guy T. Griffith, in *Hellenistic Civilisation*, 3d ed., 221, have pointed out. It is against this group that the author of 3 Maccabees inveighs as traitors.

180. Wolfson, 1.78.

181. Goodenough, 1.35, note 7.

182. Inasmuch as Philo refers to him merely as Alexander, there is some doubt as to whether this is Philo's nephew, Tiberius Julius Alexander, but the consensus among scholars favors this identification. So, for example, Francis H. Colson, ed., *Philo*, vol. 9, 447.

183. However, neither Tacitus (*Histories* 1.11.1, 2.74.1; 2.79; *Annals* 15.28.3) nor Suetonius (*Vespasian* 6.3), who mention Tiberius Alexander, refer to his Jewish birth. This would appear to reflect the pagan point of view that the failure to abide by Jewish laws and customs did indicate that a person had ceased to be a Jew.

184. So *CPJ* 1.127, p. 231. *CPJ* 1.127, p. 230, notes that Hugo Willrich (*Juden und Griechen vor der Makkabäischen Erhebung*, 131–32; *Judaica: Forschungen zur hellenistisch-jüdischen Geschichte und Litteratur*, 19–28; "Der historische Kern des III Makkabäerbuches," 257; and "Dositheos (4)") had argued that the whole story of the saving of Ptolemy's life by Dositheos had been fabricated and was based on the narrative of the saving of the life of King Ahasuerus by Mordecai in the Book of Esther. But, as Tcherikover points out, the discovery of five papyri and a demotic ostrakon show that at this very time there was a Dositheos son of Drimylos at the court of Ptolemy. Because the name Drimylos is very rare, it seems very likely that this is the man referred to in 3 Maccabees.

185. Dositheos is also mentioned as a priest in a Demotic ostrakon; see *CPJ* 1.127d, p. 236.

186. McKnight, 19, cites as an apostate the Jew whom Aristotle is said to have met in Asia Minor and who "not only spoke Greek but had the soul of a Greek" (quoted in Josephus, *Against Apion* 1.180). But it is clear that this is simply Aristotle's compliment that this Jew had a philosophical temperament. Aristotle also declares (*Against Apion* 1.179) that the Jews as a group were descended from the Indian philosophers, but surely this does not mean that Aristotle regarded all Jews as apostates.

187. Cited by Smallwood, 234, note 59, and 507. The precise date is uncertain, but Smallwood suggests 123.

188. So Smallwood, 507.

189. So Joseph Reider, ed., *The Book of Wisdom*, 12–14.

Chapter 3

1. See especially Joseph Mélèze-Modrzejewski, who in "Sur l'antisémitisme païen," challenges the concept that anti-Judaism is eternal.

2. In the Bible, Hebrew is referred to as *Sefath Kenaan*, that is, the language of

Canaan; and yet the Bible (Gen 10:6) designates Canaan as the son not of Shem but of Ham, another of Noah's sons.

3. Josephus (*Against Apion* 1.90) quotes Manetho, the Egyptian historian, as stating that the Hyksos, after being expelled from Egypt, founded the city of Jerusalem. He then quotes Manetho (*Against Apion* 1.241) as saying that the Israelites sent an embassy to the Hyksos inviting them to join in an expedition against Egypt.

4. See, e.g., W. Lee Humphreys, "Ahasuerus."

5. Diana Delia, "The Population of Roman Alexandria," 286–87, calls attention to the figure of 180,000 Jews in Alexandria and its immediate environs, according to her reading of the *Acta Alexandrinorum* (*P. Giessen Univ.* 5.46), though the text at this point is badly damaged. Inasmuch as Diodorus (17.52.6) states that in his own day, approximately 60 B.C.E., more than three hundred thousand people resided in Alexandria, and inasmuch as, according to Philo (*In Flaccum* 8.55), two of the five quarters of the city were called Jewish because most of the Jews inhabited them, though, he adds, there were not a few Jews in the other sections of the city, we can postulate a Jewish population of at least 120,000. Delia then estimates that the total population of Alexandria ranged between 500,000 and 600,000 persons during the Roman principate. This would appear to be not inconsistent with the figure of 50,000 Jews who were supposedly massacred by the troops of the Roman governor of Egypt, Tiberius Julius Alexander, in the year 66 (Josephus, *War* 2.497). Moreover, a generation earlier, Philo (*In Flaccum* 6.43) had declared that a million Jews were living in Egypt.

6. See "Prolegomena," 11–15, 17–19.

7. "Prolegomena," 11–12.

8. At the end of the *Letter of Aristeas* (308–11), we see that the Jewish community of Alexandria not only authorized but also accepted the translation.

9. If indeed we find that in 217 B.C.E. Ptolemy IV Philopator (3 Mac 5–6) ordered the Jews to be massacred in Alexandria by a horde of elephants, the story is too similar to the tale told by Josephus (*Against Apion* 2.53–54) about Ptolemy Physcon (145 B.C.E.); and the account of Josephus seems to be less improbable, as Henry St. John Thackeray, trans. and ed., *Josephus*, vol. 1, 314, note a, has remarked.

10. Cf. Smallwood, 224, note 18: "The tale in any case has a legendary ring." Harold Idris Bell, "Anti-Semitism in Alexandria," 3, concludes that such an incident reflects the motives of a propagandist writing at a later time, when relations between the Jews and Greeks were becoming embittered by religious, as well as political, factors.

11. *CII* 2.1441–42, 1449.

12. An excellent question from an Alexandrian point of view, as Shaye J. D. Cohen, in "'Anti-Semitism' in Antiquity: The Problem of Definition," 46, remarks.

13. Aryeh Kasher, in *The Jews in Hellenistic and Roman Egypt: The Struggle for Equal Rights*, 14–17, noting Hirtius's statement (*Bellum Alexandrinum* 7.3) that in part of the city the residents proved openly loyal to Caesar, suggests that these residents should be identified with the members of the Jewish community and points to the privileges granted by him to the Jews after his victory. But the

silence of the *Bellum Alexandrinum* and especially of Josephus, for whom it is crucial to establish Caesar's indebtedness to the Jews, argue against this hypothesis.

14. See Ilse Becher, *Das Bild der Kleopatra in der griechischen und lateinischen Literatur*; and my "Pro-Jewish," 229–30.

15. See Tcherikover, 175–203.

16. Note, for example, Polybius's statement (26.7) that all respectable men were entirely puzzled about Antiochus, some looking on him as a plain and simple man, while others viewed him as a madman (ἐπιμανής, a pun on his surname ἐπιφανής, "illustrious"). In particular, Polybius, with his aristocratic sympathies, is critical of him for his egalitarianism in bathing in the public baths when they were full of common people and in conversing not only with common people but even with the meanest of foreigners.

17. Aryeh Kasher, *The Jews in Hellenistic and Roman Egypt*; Constantine Zuckerman, "Hellenistic *Politeumata* and the Jews: A Reconsideration." When *politeumata* are mentioned in papyri, they are in the nature of Landsmannschaften; what unites them is their common origin and hence their common worship. The one Jewish *politeuma* of which we have information, that of Berenice in Cyrenaica, as Zuckerman, "*Politeumata*," 179, has noted, is not the political organization of the entire Jewish community but rather the social organization of a group within the community. Likewise, the mention in the *Letter of Aristeas* (310) of the *politeuma* of Alexandria which prohibited the alteration of the text of the Septuagint is, as Zuckerman, "*Politeumata*," 181–84, remarks, a reference not to the political organization of the Jews of Alexandria but rather to a private group. Moreover, as Diana Delia, in "Roman Alexandria: Studies in Its Social History," 33–40, has indicated, the assertion of Philo (*Legatio ad Gaium* 29.194) and of Josephus (*Against Apion* 2.39) that the Alexandrian Jews were Alexandrians refers not to their being citizens but rather to their origin or place of residence.

18. See Baron, 1.370–72.

19. There is no persuasive reason to think that this missionary activity was carried on by the delegation of Simon the Hasmonean to Rome (1 Mac 14.24, 15.25 ff.), as Emil Schürer, in *Geschichte des jüdischen Volkes im Zeitalter Jesu Christi*, 4th ed., vol. 3, part 4, 59, and Leon, 2–4, have concluded. Indeed, it is hard to believe that the delegation would have risked jeopardizing their political mission by engaging in religious missionary activity, especially because such activity would, ipso facto, have involved denying the Roman gods, who were regarded as an integral part of the state.

20. So Smallwood, 130.

21. See Josephus, *Ant.* 14.185–267.

22. See the comments on the literature concerning this topic in my *JMS* 273–76, 922.

23. Josephus, *Ant.* 18.81–84; cf. Suetonius, *Tiberius* 36; Dio Cassius 57.18.5a; Tacitus, *Annals* 2.85.

24. See Leon, 17–19; *Josephus* 9.60–61.

25. So Smallwood, 208–9.

26. See Abel, 383–86.

27. To be sure, Isidore and Lampon, who had previously urged Flaccus to secure his position by persecuting the Jews, now joined his accusers.

28. So "Prolegomena," 67.

29. So Bilde, 72. There is surely no viciousness in Caligula's remark (Philo, *Legatio ad Gaium* 45.367), "They seem to me to be people unfortunate rather than wicked and to be foolish in refusing to believe that I have got the nature of a god."

30. So Bilde, 72. In arguing that Caligula did not depart from the traditional Roman policy of tolerance toward the Jews, Bilde disagrees with the great majority of scholars, notably Juster, 1.351–52; Leo Fuchs, *Die Juden Aegyptens in ptolemäischer und römischer Zeit*, 19; Vincent M. Scramuzza, "The Policy of the Early Roman Emperors towards Judaism," vol. 5, 284; and Lucien Cerfaux et al., *Le culte des souverains dans la civilisation gréco-romaine*, 343–46.

31. Anthony A. Barrett, *Caligula: The Corruption of Power*, 191, argues that Caligula's reign marked a turning point in the relations of the Romans with the Jews, that events during his reign showed how difficult the position of the Jews had become and how they could find themselves at the mercy of what they considered an arbitrary tyrant, and that all this strengthened the hands of the Jewish nationalists. A more plausible conclusion is that the reign of Caligula marks a very temporary aberration, and that the rise of the Jewish nationalists had effect only in the Land of Israel itself, and then primarily during the rule of the procurators that followed.

32. This is the interpretation of Tcherikover, *CPJ* 2.156, pp. 68–69.

33. Suetonius's statement may mean only that Jews who had rioted were expelled, and hence there would be no necessary contradiction between it and Dio; but Acts declares that all the Jews were expelled. Another question is whether the passages in Suetonius and in Acts refer to the same incident or to two separate expulsions. See Smallwood, 211, note 29. She concludes (210–16) that there were two separate episodes.

34. So Smallwood, 216.

35. So Stern, 2.116.

36. Josephus, *War* 2.232–46; *Ant.* 20.118–36; *Life* 13–16; *Ant.* 20.195. See also Lee I. Levine, "The Jewish-Greek Conflict in First-Century Caesarea," 383, note 15.

37. See Philo, *Legatio ad Gaium* 24.159–61; Edith Mary Smallwood, ed., *Philonis Alexandrini Legatio ad Gaium*, 243–45; Smallwood, "Some Notes on the Jews under Tiberius,"; Stern, 2.70–71.

38. So Lee I. Levine, "The Jewish-Greek Conflict," 383, note 15.

39. But cf. my comment, *Josephus* 9, on *Ant.* 20.195. We may remark that it would seem strange that after pleading successfully on behalf of the Jews Poppaea Sabina then proceeded to bid ten of the Jewish ambassadors from Judaea to depart, while detaining Ishmael the high priest and Helcias the keeper of the treasury. One possible explanation for this action may be that she, a "sympathizer," wanted them to instruct her further in the beliefs and practices of Judaism.

40. Note, for example, Seneca's bitter comment (quoted in Augustine, *De Civitate Dei* 6.11): "The customs of this most accursed [*sceleratissimae*] race have gained such influence that they are now received throughout the world. The vanquished have given laws to their victors."

41. Connected with these prophecies, as Stern, 2.118, suggests, is the promise made by some astrologers to Nero (Suetonius, *Nero* 40.2) that when he was cast

off he would have the rule of the East, with a few expressly naming the sovereignty of Jerusalem.

42. So Morton Smith, "Palestinian Judaism in the First Century."

43. Suetonius, *Domitian* 12. Even this tax, which would appear to be humiliating, was not imposed uniquely on the Jews, because, as Michael Rostowzew (Rostovtzeff), in "Fiscus," 2403–2404, has pointed out, a *fiscus Alexandrinus* and a *fiscus Asiaticus* were similarly levied on the Alexandrians and Asiatics respectively.

44. Ronald Syme, in *Ammianus and the Historia Augusta*, 219, argues at length that the *Historia Augusta* is a historical romance by a fraudulent author; but he admits (p. 177) that a wealth of valuable details can be disengaged from it. The author, he remarks (p. 204), "comports himself as the new Suetonius, and he enters into competition with the historians, modestly adding novel and precise detail, the product of scholarly research."

45. See my discussion in "Some Observations on the Name of Palestine," 14–23.

46. So Stern, 2.621.

47. So Smallwood, Inaugural, 6. Bilde, 74, argues that the demolition of the imperial altar at Jamnia by the Jews was a political act that, from the Roman point of view, expressed political disloyalty. In this respect it was similar to the interruption of the sacrifice for the emperor in the Temple in the year 66, which, indeed, is interpreted by Josephus (*War* 2.409–10 and 417) as a sign of revolt. Maurilio Adriani, in "Note sull' antisemitismo antico," argues that Roman prejudice against Jews was based on two accusations, impiety and political disloyalty (through failure to participate in the state religion); but, as we have indicated, the Roman government, beginning with Julius Caesar, had a long tradition of tolerance on both these counts.

48. See Hermann Vogelstein and Paul Rieger, *Geschichte der Juden in Rom*, vol. 1, 32. Leon, 43, comments, however, that this tale, which is related by an opponent of the papacy, probably Hippolytus, may be apocryphal.

49. So Linder, 103–4. As Linder notes, this opening of municipal offices to Jews is confirmed in Jewish sources.

50. Stern, 2.630, calls attention to a Jewish dedication to Alexander Severus in an inscription from Intercisa (*CII* 1.677), as well as to a synagogue of Severus cited in a medieval commentary on the Bible by David Qimhi and in *Midrash Bereshith Rabbati* (ed. Albeck, p. 209). Arnaldo Momigliano, in "Severo Alexandro Archisynagogus," 151–53, suggests that Alexander Severus took upon himself the role of protector of synagogues and was designated honorary *archisynagogus* of one of them.

51. Stern, 2.631, says that it is suspicious that the names of Abraham and Orpheus are coupled in the same way as in Firmicus Maternus (*Mathesis* 4, Prooemium 5).

52. So Smallwood, Inaugural, 4.

53. So Smallwood, 7.

54. The protection of synagogues is reaffirmed in 420 and 423 by the Emperors Honorius and Theodosius II (*Codex Theodosianus* 16.8.21, 16.8.25).

55. We may here comment on the crucial methodological question as to whether we may speak collectively of the rabbis or whether we should examine

the rabbinic treatises document by document, differentiating among them on the basis of the date of the document, or whether we may take at face value comments of rabbis that are quoted in works edited at a much later date. Those who are skeptical of the ascription of comments assume that a given work, once edited, has an organic unity that requires remolding of these opinions. Jacob Neusner, in a challenging series of works, has contended that we must proceed document by document and notes (see, for example, his *From Enemy to Sibling: Rome and Israel in the First Century of Western Civilization: An Experiment in Method*) that whereas in the Mishnah, redacted ca 200 C.E., there are no references to Rome or to its alternative Talmudic names of Edom, Esau, or Ishmael, and only a trivial comment in the Tosefta, redacted at about the same time, yet when we come to the midrashim *Genesis Rabbah* and *Leviticus Rabbah*, redacted in about 400 C.E., approximately a century after Christianity's triumph, we find recurrent references to the struggle between Rome and Israel. We may, however, reply that the difference is to be explained by the legalistic nature of the Mishnah and the Tosefta, which have little historical or aggadic content, whereas the midrashim deal primarily with non-Halakhic material, often alluding to contemporary historical situations, as do so often modern sermons today that deal with biblical texts.

The present author starts with the assumption—always subject to challenge— that when a statement is quoted in the Talmud or in a Midrash in the name of a particular rabbi we must take this ascription seriously. That the same or a similar comment is so often found in midrashim that were redacted centuries apart would seem to indicate that the key point is not when the work was redacted but rather which rabbi said it and when. Here, it would seem, one should be guided by the statement (*Megillah* 15a), based on the verse (Esther 2:22) "And Esther told the king in the name of Mordecai," of Rabbi Eleazar ben Pedah, the third-century scholar who lived in both the Land of Israel and Babylonia, in the name of Rabbi Ḥanina bar Ḥama, who lived earlier in the same century in both lands, that whoever reports a saying in the name of its originator brings deliverance to the world. The importance of this statement, we may note, is indicated by its occurrence in the Baraitha (*Avoth* 6.6) and by its repetition in another place in the Talmud (*Ḥullin* 104b). Most recently Richard Kalmin, in "Rabbinic Attitudes toward Rabbis as a Key to the Dating of Talmudic Sources," has concluded, in opposition to the view frequently expressed by Jacob Neusner (e.g., *Making the Classics in Judaism: The Three Stages of Literary Formation*, 19–44), that aspects of Amoraic attitudes, at least so far as expressions of praise and special respect, most likely originate close to the time of the rabbis involved and are not later editorial fabrications.

56. So also Mireille Hadas-Lebel, *L'Image de Rome dans la littérature juive d'époque hellénistique et romaine jusqu'au début du IVe siècle*, especially 172–271.

57. That the Romans were thought of as descendants of Esau is possibly to be seen in 4 Ezra (6:8–9), dating, according to most scholars, from about 100 C.E., which speaks of Esau as "the end of this age" and Jacob as "the beginning of the age that follows." The first rabbi who is cited as clearly identifying Rome with Esau and Edom is Rabbi Akiva (ca. 50–135 C.E.), who explains (Jerusalem Talmud, *Ta'anith* 4.8.68d, *Genesis Rabbah* 65.21) the verse (Gen 27:22) "The voice is the voice of Jacob, but the hands are the hands of Esau" as illustrating the an-

guished cry of Jacob, that is, of the Jewish people, caused by what the hands of Esau, that is presumably the Romans, had done to them. In my "Jacob," 130–33, I have suggested that the equation is to be found in Josephus at the end of the first century and have called attention to his extra-biblical comment (*Ant.* 1.275) in which Isaac predicts that Esau's descendants, through strength of body in arms and through labors of all kinds, will reap an agelong (δι᾽ αἰῶνος) reputation. It would seem likely that Josephus here has Rome, Virgil's *urbs aeterna*, in mind. As to the equation of Esau = Rome, see Mireille Hadas-Lebel, "Jacob et Esau ou Israel et Rome dans le Talmud et le Midrash," who, however, emphasizes the enmity between Israel and Rome as portrayed in the references to Jacob and Esau. It is only, nevertheless, in the third century that the rabbis saw fit to stress the ambiguity of this relationship. Thus, it is significant that not until the middle of the third century c.e. did Rabbi Ḥama bar Ḥanina (*Exodus Rabbah* 21.7) name Samael, who is usually identified with Satan, the greatest of all the angels, as Esau's guardian angel; and Samael is indeed later specifically identified as the angel of Mars, the red planet (presumably because of the connection of Edom = red = Esau; see Abraham Epstein, "The Beasts of the Four Kingdoms" [in Hebrew]), and consequently as the guardian angel of Rome, Mars's alleged descendants. Elsewhere (*Song of Songs Rabbah* 3.6) it is the same Ḥama bar Ḥanina who declares that Jacob says to Esau, "Your countenance resembles that of your guardian angel."

58. *Midrash Tannaim* 72 and *Mekilta Amalek* 2.56a, cited by Ginzberg, 5.272, note 19.

59. On this parallelism see Hadas, 249–63. We may here note that the book of Josippon (1.2), written in 953 and dependent apparently on good sources of information, some of which are no longer extant, has a story about Esau's grandson, Zepho, who accompanies Aeneas on his expeditions in Italy, becomes king of the Kittim, has a grandson named Latinus (Aeneas's father-in-law in Virgil's *Aeneid*), is killed by Turnus (Aeneas's greatest opponent in the *Aeneid*), and eventually has a descendant Romulus, who founds the city of Rome, so that Romulus is, indeed, in the direct line from Esau. We may remark that the identification of Kittim with the Romans is found at least as early as the second century (Targum Onkelos on Numbers 24:24). Moreover, a strong case for such an identification can be made in a number of Qumran texts, where the Kittim appear as the last Gentile world power to oppress the people of G-d. See Frederick F. Bruce, "Kittim."

60. Cf., e.g., at the very beginning of the *Aeneid* (1.10): "insignem pietate virum."

61. It is not always clear whether Esau refers to the Romans or to the Christians. Thus, as Ginzberg, 6.68, note 350, remarks, when the rabbis (Jerusalem Talmud, *Nedarim* 3.38a) note Esau's pride in his descent from Abraham and in his relationship with Jacob-Israel, the reference may well be to the Christians.

62. Jerusalem Talmud, '*Avodah Zarah* 1.2.39c, *Song of Songs Rabbah* 1.6, *Shabbath* 56b, *Sanhedrin* 21b, *Sifre Deuteronomy* 52, p. 86a. In *Shabbath* 56b this passage is given in the name of Rabbi Judah in the name of Samuel and is cited in the form of a rabbinic Baraitha and hence dates probably from the first two centuries.

63. Neco was actually king of Egypt from ca 609 to 593 b.c.e., approximately three and a half centuries after Solomon.

64. Note, for example, Livy's highly self–conscious comment (Book 1, Preface 7) that if any people deserve to consecrate their origins and refer them to a divine source—the implication being that the Romans actually have utterly ignominious beginnings from the bastard Romulus—the Roman people, by virtue of their military glory, merit this.

65. The name of the angel is Gabriel in the passage as cited in *Shabbath* 56b, *Sanhedrin* 21b, and *Sifre Deuteronomy* 52, p. 86a.

66. In my article "Abba Kolon and the Founding of Rome," I note and comment on sixteen theories that have been presented in the attempt to identify Abba Kolon. My own conclusion is that the constant collapse of the huts reflects the chaos in the Roman Empire in the middle of the third century, with no fewer than twenty-four emperors (including colleagues in imperial power) being recognized in Rome within a span of fifty years (235–284), only one of whom died a natural death. The trip to the Euphrates to get water so as to enable the huts of Rome to remain standing may reflect the achievement of the Palmyrene nobleman Odaenathus, who, after the Romans had suffered an ignominious defeat at the hands of the Persians, managed to defeat the Persians. The equation of Rome and Babylon may reflect the fact that the two temples had been destroyed respectively by the Babylonians and the Romans, as well as the fact that now an ally in the East, Palmyra, had saved the West.

67. So Baron, 2.109.

68. Cf. Ludwig Mitteis, *Reichsrecht und Volksrecht in den östlichen Provinzen des Römischen Kaiserreichs*, 194; Paul Krüger, *Geschichte der Quellen und Litteratur des römischen Rechts*, 2d ed., 153 and 393, note 7; Bernhard G. A. Kübler, "Rechtsschulen," 388, and *Geschichte des römischen Rechts*, 426, note 12.

69. See Menahem Kasher, *Torah Shelemah*, vol. 4 , 1022, note 143, cited by Saul Lieberman, "Palestine," 354, note 185.

70. Cf. *Midrash Psalms* 80.6: "Wicked Esau displays himself so openly on the seats of the justice that the legal tricks whereby he robs, steals, and plunders appear to be just proceedings." Similarly, *Sekhel Tov, Toledoth* 6.33: "So does the wicked state rob and oppress and pretend to dispense loving-kindness." On the identification of Rome with the pig or wild boar, see Jerome on Daniel 7:7 and *Avoth de-Rabbi Nathan* A 34 and other rabbinic passages cited by Jay Braverman, in *Jerome's Commentary on Daniel: A Study of Comparative Jewish and Christian Interpretations of the Hebrew Bible*, 90–93. That the wild boar was a favorite food of the Romans and that in Rome several distinguished families had the name Aper ("wild boar") made the analogy all the more telling. One may also recall the Talmudic passage (*Baba Qamma* 82b and *Menahoth* 64b) about the old man, learned in Greek wisdom, on whose advice the Romans sent a pig instead of a kosher animal to the Jews for the Temple sacrifice when the latter were being besieged.

CHAPTER 4

1. So William W. Tarn and Guy T. Griffith, *Hellenistic Civilisation*, 3d ed., 193.

2. The papyri have been collected, translated, and commented on, with a long and valuable prolegomenon by Victor A. Tcherikover, in *CPJ*.

3. Baron, 1.383, note 35.

4. See Diana Delia, "The Population of Roman Alexandria," 287–88, who bases this estimate on a passage in the *Acta Alexandrinorum*, as we have noted.

5. So "Prolegomena," 48. On wealthy Jewish businessmen in Alexandria, see Alexander Fuks, "Notes on the Archive of Nicanor."

6. *CPJ* 2.33 (no. 152).

7. Tcherikover, 339–40. Ulrich Wilcken, *Grundzüge und Chrestomatie der Papyruskunde*, 1.2.60, on the other hand, regards this as the most ancient evidence of commercial anti-Judaism.

8. So Adrian N. Sherwin-White, *Racial Prejudice in Imperial Rome*, 99.

9. So Stern, 2.163.

10. On the authenticity of these decrees, see my *JMS* 273–76, 922. Horst R. Moehring, in "The *Acta Pro Judaeis* in the *Antiquities* of Flavius Josephus: A Study in Hellenistic and Modern Apologetic Historiography," argues that the acceptance or nonacceptance of the authenticity of the documents cited by Josephus in *Antiquities*, Books 14 and 16, has depended not so much on intrinsic factors as on the apologetic concerns of modern historians themselves. He imputes significance, however, to Josephus's silence about the fire of 69 that destroyed about three thousand documents in the Roman archives, some of which must have pertained to Jewish rights. He cites instances where decrees of the Senate were forged, asserts that in antiquity historians probably did not bother to check the original texts of decrees and were content with secondhand opinions about them, and notes a number of instances where the texts of documents are unusually corrupt and where Josephus's versions of decrees do not correspond to the standard known to us from epigraphical evidence. He very cynically contends that if Josephus did include forged documents he would illustrate thereby how well he had learned the methods of historians. He notes how much information was necessary in order to find a given decree in the archives; and this, we may assume, must have deterred not only Josephus and his assistants but also anyone else who sought to check up on them. He concludes that Josephus's invitation to the reader to check his accuracy is a matter of literary courtesy. We may add that even if someone were to take all the trouble to check up on Josephus and were to discover a discrepancy, Josephus could always have claimed that the original document, which was destroyed in the fire of 69 and a copy of which he had seen in the archives of the city the decree pertained to, was worded in accordance with the quotation in his work rather than the language of Vespasian's copy. Tessa Rajak, in "Jewish Rights in the Greek Cities under Roman Rule," rejects Moehring's view that the documents quoted by Josephus are apologetic Jewish forgeries. Josephus, she says, deployed the documents as part of his literary design and for apologetic purposes to contribute to mutual understanding between Jews and Greeks. In the case of Josephus, we may remark, because lively contacts existed among Jewish communities, he would have had no difficulty obtaining official documents from their archives; or alternatively, the documents may have been assembled in Josephus's major source, Nicolaus of Damascus, or by Josephus's close friend, Agrippa II, the son of Agrippa I, who may have had access to them because of his close association with the Emperors Caligula and Claudius. Moreover, according to Josephus's own words, twice repeated (*Ant.* 14.188, 266), these decrees were still to be found engraved on bronze tablets in the Capitol in Rome;

surely he had too much to lose being caught red-handed with a forgery or even being accused of such, in an apologetic treatise.

11. So Friedrich Ritschl, Ludwig Mendelssohn, and Paul Viereck, as cited by Ralph Marcus, ed. and trans., *Josephus*, vol. 7, 561, note c.

12. So Juster, 1.146, note 7, as cited by Marcus, 7.577, note d.

13. Stern, 2.194, calls attention to the skill of the Jews in the production of flax, which was considered suitable for the rich, as we find in the Talmud (*Baba Metzia* 29b).

14. Similarly, in the Jerusalem Talmud (*Kethuboth* 7.31c and *Qiddushin* 2.62c) and in the Midrash (*Bereshith Rabbah* 19), as noted by Stern, 2.498, we hear of the fame of the linen industry of Scythopolis.

15. Baron, 1.383, note 35.

16. Lysimachus, quoted in Josephus, *Against Apion* 1.305; Martial, 12.57.1–4; Juvenal, 3.10–16, 3.296, 6.542–47.

17. So Stern, 2.587, though others have suggested the Land of Israel.

18. There is some dispute as to the exact meaning of the phrase, but this seems to be the most likely explanation. See Stern, 2.587.

19. Ralph Marcus, "Antisemitism in the Hellenistic-Roman World," 72.

20. Adrian N. Sherwin-White, "Philo and Avilius Flaccus: A Conundrum," suggests that Flaccus allied himself with the opponents of the Jews in order to conciliate the most dangerous of his local enemies so as to forestall prosecution for extortion.

21. On this riot and its aftermath, see Philo, *In Flaccum*, passim, and cf. *Legatio ad Gaium* 18.122, 19.131–20.132. A report by the sixth-century chronicler John Malalas (244.15 ff.) that a similar riot took place in Antioch two years later may also indicate how widespread and deep anti-Jewish feelings were.

22. For a detailed discussion of Claudius's two edicts and his letter on the Jewish question, see "Prolegomena," 1.69–74; Aryeh Kasher, *The Jews in Hellenistic and Roman Egypt: The Struggle for Equal Rights*, 310–26; and the bibliography and my remarks in *JMS*, 331–38, 928.

23. So noted by "Prolegomena," 1.78.

24. In the *War* (7.369) Josephus gives the number slain as more than sixty thousand. But this refers to the victims in all of Egypt, whereas the figure of fifty thousand (*War* 2.497) is for Alexandria alone.

25. So Smallwood, 286.

26. Lee I. Levine, "The Jewish-Greek Conflict in First Century Caesarea."

CHAPTER 5

1. See Stern.

2. See my "Pro-Jewish," 192–93.

3. Cf., e.g., Baron, 1.194: "Almost every note in the cacophony of medieval and modern anti-Semitism was sounded by the chorus of ancient writers." Likewise, Jerry L. Daniel, "Anti-Semitism in the Hellenistic-Roman Period," 45: "A survey of the comments about Jews in the Hellenistic-Roman literature shows that they were almost universally disliked, or at least viewed with an amused contempt." Most recently Kasher, 2, remarks that the literary evidence included in Stern's

collection comprises, for the most part, a "cacophonous choir" of libels against the Jews, with only a very few words of praise for Israel and its historical tradition.

4. The percentages in the first two volumes of Stern's collection (the third contains merely a few addenda plus an index) are substantially the same. In volume 1, from Herodotus in the fifth century B.C.E. through Plutarch in the first century C.E., 47 notices are favorable (16 percent), 69 are unfavorable (24 percent), and 165 are neutral (60 percent). In volume 2, covering the period from the second through the sixth century, 54 are favorable (20 percent), 61 are unfavorable (21 percent), and 174 are neutral (59 percent).

5. For a conjecture as to why the Church permitted all the anti-Jewish writings of Manetho, Chaeremon, Lysimachus, Apion, Apollonius Molon, and Posidonius to be lost, see my "Pro-Jewish," 193–94. Littman, 834, disputes the value of my statistics on the grounds that the survival of material from antiquity is uneven and that, in any case, when the major writers of Rome, who were the ones read by medieval Europe, mention Jews, they do so unfavorably. We may reply that the number of authors included in Stern's collection is 178, which is hardly inconsiderable; and what is even more remarkable is that the Church, hardly the most hospitable medium for preserving comments about the Jews, is responsible, as we have noted, for most of what we have. As to the fact that it is the major writers, such as Cicero, who were read and had the greatest influence, and that they are anti-Jewish, we may reply that medieval Jew-baiters seldom quote or cite ancient classical authors to support their anti-Jewish views, which are almost always based on selected passages from the New Testament.

6. Salo W. Baron, "Changing Patterns of Antisemitism: A Survey," 5.

7. Balsdon, 60–61, and sources cited on page 269, note 12.

8. See Balsdon: Sardinians, 64; British, 66; Arabs, 67–68; Egyptians, *Bellum Alexandrinum* 7.2, cited by Balsdon, 69; Greeks, 31–33.

9. See my "Philo-Semitism."

10. Jan N. Sevenster, *The Roots of Pagan Anti-Semitism in the Ancient World*, 89, argues that the self-isolation of the Jews, which was perceived as hatred of the rest of humanity, more than any other single factor was at the heart of the pagan intellectual attacks upon the Jews. Hans Conzelmann, *Heiden-Juden-Christen: Auseinandersetzungen in der Literatur der hellenistisch-römischen Zeit*, 43–120, disagrees with Sevenster and argues that hatred of Jews is local, not universal.

11. In a forthcoming work, Bezalel Bar-Kochva, *Poseidonius of Apamea and Ancient Anti-Semitism*, traces Posidonius's original version to Diodorus (34 [35].2.34 ff.) and argues that Apion has falsely named Posidonius as his reference and that Josephus did not consult Posidonius's version directly. He contends, finding further evidence that Strabo's source was Posidonius, that on the contrary Posidonius's version was actually very favorable to Judaism; that it shows respect for the Jewish faith; that it deplores the harsh treatment of the Temple by Antiochus Epiphanes; that it praises Antiochus VII Sidetes, who sent a magnificent sacrifice to the Temple, as "great-souled" and pious (Josephus, *Ant.* 13.243); that it shows understanding by ascribing Jewish separateness from other nations to the Jews' piety; and that it depicts Moses and his followers as philosopher-theologians. In addition, Bar-Kochva shows how Posidonius, as paraphrased in Strabo, consistently altered Hecataeus's version of Judaism in order to accord

with Stoic conceptions and ideals, some of them—notably the building of temples, divination in the "holy of holies," the requirement that a temple be built so that people who have a tendency for auspicious dreams may sleep in its "holy of holies" and experience divination, the distinction between the two major periods in the history of civilization, and a society without laws—being characteristic of Poseidonius exclusively. Finally, Posidonius chose Mosaic Judaism to illustrate his Stoic ideas because the ground had been laid for him by such predecessors as Clearchus, Theophrastus, and Megasthenes, who had described the Jews as a nation of philosophers. As to the hostility toward Judaism that existed in his own day, Poseidonius (cited in Strabo 16.2.39.762) overcame this by drawing a clear distinction between Mosaic Judaism and that of its successors, the Hasmoneans.

12. The remarkable canard that the Jews worshiped an ass in the Temple is found for the first time in the rhetorical historian Mnaseas of Patara in Lycia in 200 B.C.E., to be sure at third hand, inasmuch as he is cited by Apion, who is cited by Josephus (*Against Apion* 2.114).

Poseidonius (cited in Josephus, *Against Apion* 2.79) is said to have asserted that the Jews worshiped the ass, deeming it worthy of the deepest reverence. According to Diodorus (34 [35].1.3) and Apion (quoted in Josephus, *Against Apion* 2.80), Antiochus Epiphanes found an image in the Temple, but Diodorus adds that it was a marble statue of a heavily bearded man seated on an ass with a book in his hands, which suggested to Antiochus that it was an image of Moses. Perhaps this reflects merely the Greek view that the founder of a nation deserved special honors and even apotheosis. Possibly, too, there is here an allusion to and ridiculing of the Jewish expectation that the Messiah would come riding on an ass. Finally, there may be here a hint of the story of Balaam and his ass or of the story, noted by Tacitus (*Histories* 5.3.2), that a herd of wild asses had led Moses to an abundant spring of water. It seems strange that the ancients, some of whom, at any rate, were aware of the fact that the Jews forbade images, should have originated such a canard. Indeed, the same Tacitus, who admits (*Histories* 5.9.1) that when Pompey entered the Temple he found it devoid of all images, repeats, in almost immediate juxtaposition (*Histories* 5.4.2), the story that the Jews had consecrated in the Temple the image of an ass, by whose guidance they had found deliverance from their long and thirsty wanderings in the wilderness. Perhaps the explanation is simply that there was speculation among the Gentiles as to the reason why they were prohibited from entering the precincts of the Temple (Josephus, *Ant.* 15.417) and why even the high priest could enter the Holy of Holies only on the Day of Atonement. Inasmuch as the whole matter of what was in the Holy of Holies was shrouded in mystery, such a canard could be disseminated without much fear of contradiction, and the admiration (see Varro, cited in Augustine, *City of G-d* 4.31) for the allegedly imageless cult of the Jews could be counteracted.

A number of theories have been presented to explain the source of the charge of ass-worship. One is that the ass was to the Egyptians the symbol of folly, as we see in Plutarch (*De Iside et Osiride* 50.371C). More negatively, it was the cruel and vindictive enemy of the Egyptians, the Persian king Artaxerxes III Ochus, who deified the ass (cf. Aelian, *De Natura Animalium* 10.28). Perhaps, as Tcherikover, 365, has suggested, the origin of the canard is to be found in the tale related by

Plutarch (*De Iside et Osiride* 31.363C–D), that Typhon or Set, the Egyptian god of the wilderness, of eclipses, storms, darkness, and evil, who was the opponent of Osiris, the god of good, after a battle fled on the back of an ass, his sacred animal (he was himself sometimes depicted as ass-headed), for seven days and thereafter became the father of two sons, Hierosolymus and Judaeus. Typhon was the symbol of superstitious fear and hatred (Pseudo-Plutarch, *Septem Sapientium Convivium* 5.150F; Apuleius, *Metamorphoses* 11.6; Aelian, *De Natura Animalium* 10.28). He is thus regarded as the ancestor of the Jews, especially because the flight took seven days, precisely the length of time, according to a number of ancient writers (Apion, quoted in Josephus, *Against Apion* 2.20–21; Pompeius Trogus, quoted in Justin, *Historiae Philippicae* 36, *Epitoma* 2.14; Tacitus, *Historiae* 5.4.3), that it supposedly took the Israelites to reach the Land of Israel after their flight from Egypt.

The fact that Manetho (quoted in Josephus, *Against Apion* 1.78) associates the Jews with the city of Auaris, which was consecrated to Typhon, further develops this connection. This story would apparently make Typhon the ancestor of the Jews and would equate Typhon with Moses, who, according to the version in Diodorus, was depicted as riding on an ass. The Jews would thus stand accused of, in effect, devil worship. Adolf Jacoby, "Der angebliche Eselkult der Juden und Christen"; Ralph Marcus, "Antisemitism in the Hellenistic-Roman World," 74, note 6; and Lukas Vischer, "Le prétendu culte de l'âne dans l'Église primitive," have presented the appealing suggestion that the canard may have been reinforced by the similarity between the Egyptian word for ass, *yao*, and the Hebrew Tetragrammaton, which, according to Diodorus (1.94.2) and Varro (cited in Lydus, *De Mensibus* 4.53, pp. 110–11), was pronounced *Iao*. Erik Goldschmidt, "Die Israel-Quellen bei Tacitus," 175–78, has offered the ingenious, if unconvincing, suggestion that by changing the vowel points under the Hebrew word for city (*'ir*) in reference to Jerusalem (*'ir ha-qodesh*, "the holy city"), an anti-Jewish writer who knew Hebrew, or more likely was an apostate, spoke of *'ayir ha-qodesh*, "the sacred wild ass." In like manner, the charge that the Jews hated humankind may have arisen from changing the vowel points under *sin'ah be-'Edom* ("hatred for Edom," i.e., Rome) to *sin'ah be'adam* ("hatred of humanity," *odium generis humani* [Tacitus, *Annals* 15.44.4]).

We may also suggest a possible sarcastic connection between the Greek word for ass, ὄνος, and the Jewish high priest Onias, who took refuge in Egypt, built a temple at Leontopolis, and was named commander-in-chief of the Ptolemaic army. Still another theory, advanced by Norman Bentwich (*Josephus*, 228) notes that the Hebrew word for "ass" also signifies an upper millstone (presumably because it performed a service similar to that of the ass as a beast of burden); the mystery surrounding the *'even shetiyah*—the stone on which the world was said to have been created and on which the Holy Ark in the Temple was placed, and where the blood of the burnt offering was sprinkled by the high priest on the Day of Atonement—would be the source of this double entendre. Finally, Elias Bickermann, "Ritualmord und Eselkult. Ein Beitrag zur Geschichte antiker Publizistik," 255–64, has suggested that it is unnecesary to look for reasons why the story arose, inasmuch as the opponents of the Jews merely took the details of the Idumaean tale, utterly unconnected with the Jews, about the theft of a golden ass's head from an enemy shrine. A parallel, we may suggest, would be the origin of the *Protocols of the Elders of Zion*, which was adapted from a pamphlet by Maurice Joly written in 1864 ascribing ambitions of world domination to Napoleon III and having nothing to do with the Jews.

Joseph Halévy, "Le Culte d'une tête d'âne," has suggested that the origin lies in the fact that the Hebrew word for ass, *ḥamor*, is identified with the Samaritans through the Biblical Hamor (Gen 34:2), whose son Shechem bears the same name as the sacred city of the Samaritans. A simple explanation would be that just as, according to Plutarch (*Quaestiones convivales* 4.5.2.670A), one reason why the Jews refrain from eating pork is that they honor the pig for being the first to cut the soil with its protruding snout, so the ass was said to have been revered because during the Israelites' sojourn in the wilderness after the exodus from Egypt a herd of wild asses (Tacitus, *Histories* 5.3.2) are said to have led Moses to abundant streams of water when the Israelites were parched with thirst. On the whole, the theory connecting the canard with Typhon seems most persuasive: It has been adopted by, among others, Eduard Meyer, *Ursprung und Anfänge des Christentums*, 5th ed., vol. 2, 35; Louis Finkelstein, "Pre-Maccabean Documents in the Passover Haggadah," 300–1; and Tcherikover, 365–66.

13. Cf. Plutarch, *Publicola* 4; Diodorus 22.5; and Sallust, *Conspiracy of Catiline* 22.

14. Bickermann, "Ritualmord und Eselkult," 171–87 and 255–64. Cf. also David Flusser, "The Ritual Murder Slander against the Jews in the Light of Outlooks in the Hellenistic Period" [in Hebrew], who notes the similarity with the description of human sacrifice in the Dionysiac cult as described by Porphyry (*De Abstinentia* 2.55).

15. Tcherikover, 367, notes that Polybius, who is highly critical of Antiochus, declares (31.11) that Antiochus met his death deservedly in punishment for profaning the temple of Artemis-Nanaiah in Elam, while he (Polybius) mentions nothing of his desecration of the Temple in Jerusalem, which was so celebrated that Polybius (quoted in Josephus, *Antiquities* 12.136) says that he will treat it separately. It was convenient to associate the name of Antiochus with the story of the fattened Greek only because he had once entered the Temple. To the Alexandrians he was a hero who was the prototype of the champion of the Jew-baiters.

16. Another clue, noted here by Plutarch, to the reason for the identification with the wine-god may be that the Festival of Tabernacles is celebrated at the height of the vintage and that the Jews observe the Sabbath by drinking wine. Furthermore, the most conclusive evidence for the identification of the Jewish G-d with Dionysus includes the facts that the high priest is dressed in a miter, fawnskin, and buskins resembling those of Dionysus's devotees, that noise is an integral part of their noctural festivals, and that there is a carved thyrsus on the pediment of the Temple. Moreover, as noted by Plutarch (*Quaestiones Convivales* 4.5.3.671B) just before this passage, some people regarded Adonis as identical with Dionysus; and this, too, may likewise account for the identification, because the name Adonis is so similar to the Hebrew word for L-rd, *'Adon*. That Plutarch is not alone in making this association of Adonis with the Jews may be seen from Ovid's juxtaposition of Adonis and the Jewish Sabbath (*Ars Amatoria* 1.75–76) a century before Plutarch: "Nor let Adonis, bewailed of Venus, escape you, nor the

seventh day that the Syrian Jew holds sacred." Tacitus (*Histories* 5.5.5), to be sure, noting that some have identified the Jewish G-d with Dionysus, discounts the evidence they cite, namely that their priests chant to the music of flutes and cymbals and wear garlands of ivy and that a golden vine was found in the Temple (cf. Josephus, *Ant.* 15.395; *War* 5.210; Mishnah *Middoth* 3:8).

17. The unspeakable aspect of Judaism may be a reference to the prohibition against pronouncing the name of G-d (cf. Dio Cassius 37.17.2) except on the Day of Atonement, when the High Priest himself did so.

18. There may here also be an allusion to the esoteric philosophy about which the rabbis (*Ḥagigah* 14b) were so wary, as seen in the incident about the four scholars in the early second century who entered the "garden" (*pardes*), that is, engaged in esoteric speculation, from which only one of them, Rabbi Akiva, emerged intact.

19. To be sure, his contemporary Philo (*In Flaccum* 5.29, 11.96) attacks the Egyptians as jealous and oppressive, as well as hypocritical and addicted to sensuality. See citations in McKnight, 22. We may reply, however, that Philo is even more critical of the Jews themselves on these same grounds.

20. Sophocles, *Trachiniae* 1095; Euripides, *Cyclops* 429. See "Esther," 163.

21. McKnight, 27, says that Jews criticized Gentiles for basically one reason, namely that pagan religion led to unacceptable ethical practices. This, he says, gives the statement of Tacitus (*Histories* 5.5.2) the "ring of truth": Jews, according to this passage, "despise gods, deplore their fatherland, and regard parents, children and kin as nothing." But Tacitus is here referring not to Jews as a whole but to proselytes, who, according to Jewish law, have no relatives among their previous kin.

22. The allusion in the phrase that the Jews will lead only the circumcised to the fountain may be to the dispute beween Rabbi Eliezer and Rabbi Joshua ben Hananiah (*Yevamoth* 46a–b) as to whether circumcision or baptism is required for conversion to Judaism. The fountain here may be the *miqvah*, and Juvenal may be alluding to the final conclusion that both are necessary. Or alternatively, the fountain may be another allusion to the Torah, which is frequently compared to water and termed a fountain.

23. So Stern, 3.50.

24. Likewise, Julian (*Contra Galilaeos* 209 D–218 A), in the fourth century C.E., ridicules the low political status of the Jews as slaves and subjects, throughout most of their history, in contrast to the sovereign power of Rome.

25. Cf. Chadwick, xx, note 1, and the literature there cited with regard to the idea that each nation is under a special angel.

26. Stern, 2.303, cites, as further parallels to this view, Porphyry, *Ad Marcellam* 18, and Minucius Felix, *Octavius* 6.1.

27. See Holladay, 145, note 49.

28. See the discussion of Philo's answer to the charge of misanthropy in Alan Mendelson, *Philo's Jewish Identity*, 103–13.

29. Lucio Troiani, in "I lettori delle Antichità giudaiche di Giuseppe. Prospettive e probleme," argues that Josephus's readers are not primarily Gentiles but rather the innumerable Hellenized Jews who were exercising important religious functions throughout the empire. However, as we have noted, it is clear from the proem of the *Antiquities* (1.10) that his primary audience consisted of Gentiles.

30. We may remark that it is only in the Zohar (1:112b), which was codified in the thirteenth century, that we hear of Abraham's friendship with the Sodomites.

31. See my "*'Aqedah*," 245–46.

32. So Abraham Schalit, trans. and ed., Josephus, *Antiquitates Judaicae*, vol. 1 [in Hebrew], introduction, lxx.

33. In this, Josephus makes Abraham parallel to Pythagoras, who, according to Aristoxenus (frag. 13 Wehrli), traveled to Egypt and, according to Isocrates (*Busiris* 28), became a disciple of the priests there, studying their sacrifices and cult practices and later introducing their philosophy to the Greeks. To be sure, Isocrates later (33), in effect, admits that this tale was invented; but that it was accepted as true is indicated by a certain Antiphon (cited in Diogenes Laertius 8.3), who tells how Pythagoras learned the secrets, especially the mathematical secrets, of the Egyptian priests. See Kurt von Fritz, "Pythagoras," 180–86; and James A. Philip, *Pythagoras and Early Pythagoreanism*, 189–91.

34. A similar parallel in Greek mythology (Ovid, *Metamorphoses* 6.382–400) is the contest between Apollo and Marsyas the satyr, in which the condition imposed by Apollo is that the victor should be able to do what he liked with the vanquished. Apollo wins and decides to flay Marsyas alive.

35. See citations in Ginzberg, 5.220, note 61.

36. It is true that the rabbinic midrashim also know of disputations carried on by Abraham, but these are, characteristically, not with other philosophers but with his father Terah and with Nimrod (*Genesis Rabbah* 38.13). Again, Abraham's powers of persuasion are likewise celebrated by the rabbis, though not in disputations with other philosophers but with visitors to his tent whom Abraham seeks to convert to monotheism (*Genesis Rabbah* 39.14).

37. Marrou, 182.

38. See, for example, the bitter attack by Pseudo-Plutarch, in his *De Herodoti Malignitate* 13–14.857B–F, on Herodotus for attempting to assert that the Greeks had learned from the Egyptians about processions and national festivals and to make of Heracles either an Egyptian or a Phoenician.

39. The latter remark would appear to be contradicted by the fact that the Israelites, before leaving Egypt, despoiled the Egyptians (Exod 12:36) and by the further fact (Josephus, *Ant.* 3.59) that, after the victory over the Amalekites, Moses ordered the corpses of the enemies to be stripped. So also *Antiquities* 4.93, after the victory over the Amorites, and 4.162, after the defeat of the Midianites. Philo, *De Vita Mosis* 1.44.249, emphasizes the humanity (φιλανθρωπία) shown by Moses in not even having the will to take revenge against the Canaanites, because they were his kin. Inasmuch as Moses is depicted as the greatest of legislators, Philo's discussion (*De Vita Mosis* 2.2.8–11) of the virtues of the legislator is particularly relevant. There he enumerates four: love of humanity, of justice, and of goodness, and hatred of evil.

40. So also Philo, *De Vita Mosis* 2.38.205, *De Specialibus Legibus* 1.9.53, and *Quaestiones in Exodum* 2.5. Philo, *De Vita Mosis* 1.27.149, says that the Jews are a nation destined to be consecrated above all others to offer prayers forever on behalf of the human race that it may be delivered from evil and may participate in what is good. We may note that Strabo (16.2.36–37.761), attempting to defend Moses against the charge of misanthropy, says that Moses and his immediate successors acted righteously and piously toward G-d, but that at a later time

superstitious people introduced various laws and customs that separated the Jews from other peoples. Similarly, as late as the fourth century C.E. the Emperor Julian (*Contra Galilaeos* 238C) asserts that though Moses taught the Israelites to worship only one god he was tolerant toward other religions, but that later generations had the shamelessness and audacity to insult other religions.

41. See Diodorus 3.2; Pomponius Mela 3.85; Seneca, *Hercules Furens* 38–41; Lactantius Placidus on Statius, *Thebaid* 5.427. Cf. Frank M. Snowden, *Blacks in Antiquity: Ethiopians in the Greco-Roman Experience*, 144–47; and his *Before Color Prejudice: The Ancient View of Blacks*, 46 and passim.

42. Willem C. van Unnik, "Josephus' Account of the Story of Israel's Sin with Alien Women in the Country of Midian (Num. 25.1 ff.)," 259.

43. Cf. Ruth Schian, *Untersuchungen über das argumentum e consensu omnium.* To form an exception is, ipso facto, to be completely wrong.

44. See my "Esther," 164.

45. This is actually the view expressed in the *Midrash Lamentations Rabbah*, introduction, no. 31: "I sent one prophet to Nineveh, and he brought it to penitence and conversion. And these Israelites in Jerusalem—how many prophets have I sent to them!" See my "Josephus' Interpretation of Jonah."

46. Etan Levine, in *The Aramaic Version of Jonah*, 14, remarks that several early church fathers (e.g., Justin Martyr, *Dialogue with Trypho* 107; Jerome, *Commentary on Jonah* 1:3 and 4:1), in their anti-Jewish polemics, used the motif of the Ninevites' sincere repentance to contrast the Ninevites' piety with the stubbornness of the Jews. We may also suggest that Josephus's omission of Jonah's statement (Jonah 4:8) "It is better for me to die than to live" may be a response to Christian exegesis, which cited this verse with reference to the Christian view that death was better for Jesus than life, because while alive he could save only one nation but with his death he saved the whole world. See Robert H. Bowers, *The Legend of Jonah*, 58–59, and Levine, *Aramaic Version*, 14, who notes that the Targum has, by subtle paraphrase, altered the "proof-text" in Jonah through rendering it "It is better that I die than that I live." Cf. also André Paul, "Flavius Josephus' 'Antiquities of the Jews': An Anti-Christian Manifesto," 473–80, who suggests that Josephus substitutes (*Ant.* 1.103) the word παῦλαν ("truce") for the word *berith* (Gen 9:9, Septuagint διαθήκην) due to his desire to dissociate himself from the New Testament's emphasis on the doctrine of the "new covenant." But, as I have noted ("Noah," 56, note 30), if indeed Josephus is writing an anti-Christian manifesto, we would have expected him to be more open about it, because he had nothing to fear from the Christians at the time that he wrote the *Antiquities*, inasmuch as they were few in number and were hardly held in favor by the Emperor Domitian, during whose reign Josephus issued his work. Moreover, the fact that Josephus (*Ant.* 20.198–200) is so highly laudatory of James, the brother of Jesus (a passage whose authenticity has seldom been questioned), is not consistent with the view that he was carrying on a polemic against Christianity.

47. We may also note that the rabbis, clearly seeking to protect the reputation of the Jews, have a tradition (*Pirqe de-Rabbi Eliezer* 10, *Tanḥuma Vayikra* 8, *Midrash Jonah* 96) that the reason why Jonah boarded the ship was that he hoped that he would lose his life on the voyage and thus be spared the pain of seeing the heathens repent while the Jews failed to do so.

48. The rabbinic *Midrash Aggadath Bereshith* 17:8 notes that the Israelites would never have been able to enter the Holy Land if Joshua had not circumcised them, inasmuch as the Land had been promised to the patriarchs on condition that their descendants would observe the rite of circumcision.

49. We may here note, of course, that "marrying out" was frowned on by many ancient nations. In particular, the Greeks even disapproved of marrying citizens of other Greek cities.

50. Cf., e.g., the speech by the Corinthians (Thucydides 1.70.4) at the Lacedaemonian Congress before the outbreak of the Peloponnesian War.

51. So Strabo 16.2.38–39.762. Similarly, Tacitus (*Histories* 5.4.1) remarks that it was in order to establish his influence over the people for all time that Moses introduced new religious practices quite opposed to those of all other religions.

52. On the common ancestry of the Spartans and the Jews which the letter of Areus alleges, see S. Schüller, "Some Problems Connected with the Supposed Common Ancestry of Jews and Spartans and Their Relations during the Last Three Centuries B.C."; and Ranon Katzoff, "Jonathan and Late Sparta." Whether the correspondence between the Jewish king Jonathan and the Spartan king Areus is authentic (Schüller thinks it is; Katzoff is noncommittal) or not, the important point is that Josephus thought that such an alliance would seem credible to his readers.

53. So Arthur S. Pease, *Cicero, De Natura Deorum*, vol. 1, 289–91, on *De Natura Deorum* 1.43, who lists twenty-nine references in classical literature to the attack against the worship of animals.

54. Cf. Philo, *De Decalogo* 16.76–80, who, apparently basing himself on the theory that the best defense is a good offense, charges the Egyptians with worshipping oxen, rams, goats, lions, crocodiles, asps, dogs, cats, wolves, ibises, hawks, fishes, and even parts of fishes.

55. Cf. Alexander H. Krappe, "Ἀπόλλων Ὄνος [Apollo the Ass]," 223–34, who concludes that the famous story of the donkey ears of Midas reveals the true nature of the mythical king as an ass-headed divinity. Commenting on Lycophron's *Cassandra* (1397–1408), he notes that when Midas, on his expedition against Thrace, put on donkey's ears, he assimilated himself to the ass-shaped god of his people.

56. Cf. Aelian, *Varia Historia* 12.34; Callimachus, frags. 187 and 188; Simmias of Rhodes, cited in Antoninus Liberalis, *Metamorphoses* 20 [ed. Martini].

57. Cf. also Polybius 28.22, 29.24, 30.25.1–26.9; Diodorus 29.32, 31.16; Livy 41.20. Heinrich Graetz, "Ursprung der zwei Verleumdungen gegen das Judenthum vom Eselkultus und von der Lieblosigkeit gegen Andersgläubige," suggests that it was Antiochus's friends who, in order to justify the persecution of the Jews, originated the story of his discovery of the ass's head and of the fattened Greek to be sacrificed.

58. Apion (quoted by Josephus, *Against Apion* 2.95), as we have noted, says that the sacrifice was performed annually. Damocritus (cited in Suda, under the entry "Damokritos") says that this was done every seventh year and does not mention Antiochus.

59. Elias J. Bickermann, "Ritualmord und Eselkult," 255–64.

60. David Flusser, "The Ritual Murder Slander against the Jews" [in Hebrew], 104–24, notes the similarity to the description of human sacrifice in the Di-

onysiac cult as described by Porphyry (*De Abstinentia* 2.55). We may note here that Josephus (*Ant.* 1.233), by implication, stresses the contrast between the sacrifice of Isaac, which was not consummated, and that of Iphigenia, which, according to Euripides' *Iphigenia at Aulis*, was actually carried out. In particular, he puts a speech (*Ant.* 1.233–36) into the mouth of G-d, rather than of an angel, as in Genesis 22:11, to the effect that He does not crave human blood and is not capricious in taking away what he has given. This is, as we have noticed ("*'Aqedah*, 245–46), in direct contrast to Artemis, who (Euripides, *Iphigenia at Aulis*, 1524–25) "rejoices in human sacrifices."

61. In this connection we may suggest that the mysterious god (Livy 5.50) who in 390 B.C.E. warned the Romans of the disaster that awaited them from the Gauls is a god wihout name and hence is given the name Aius Locutius ("Speaking Speaker"). Livy (quoted in *Scholia in Lucanum* 2.593), like Varro, notes that the Jews believe that G-d is not to be represented by any figure, and that therefore there is no image to be found in the Temple in Jerusalem. Hence, the Scholiast states that Judaea is given over to the worship of an unknown G-d and that the Jews do not give the name of the deity to whom the Temple is dedicated. The phrase "unknown G-d" (cf. Paul's reference in Acts 17:23 to the unknown G-d whom the Athenians ignorantly worship) was adopted from Neo-Platonism (see Proclus, *The Elements of Theology*, 2d ed., 310–13) and appears again as *incertus deus* in Lucan (2.592–93), as ἄδηλος θεός in Lydus (*De Mensibus* 4.53) quoting Lucan, and as *incertum numen* in the *Historia Augusta* (*Vita Claudii* 2.2). It presumably reflects the fact that in the Bible there is no specific name given to G-d and that when Moses (Exod 3:13–14) attempts to learn His name G-d describes His essence rather than names Himself.

62. There may actually be an implied compliment here, whether Juvenal realized it or not, inasmuch as Socrates in Aristophanes' *Clouds* is depicted as worshipping the clouds; and hence some readers might well have equated the Jews, in this respect, with the much revered Socrates. This would reinforce the picture that we have noted in Aristotle and in Theophrastus of the Jews as a nation of philosophers.

63. This identification of Sabazius with the Jewish G-d may have been aided by the similarity between Sabazius and the Hebrew epithet *Ẕeva'oth*, "L-rd of Hosts," applied to G-d.

64. Despite Manetho, however, we may note that in the attack on the Egyptian animal worship the Jews were in agreement with the philosophical Greeks, as we see in Sextus Empiricus (*Hypotyposeis* 3.219).

65. So Radin, 163.

66. So Shaye J. D. Cohen, "'Anti-Semitism' in Antiquity: The Problem of Definition," 46.

67. Walter Burkert, in *Pseudepigrapha*, vol. 1, 49–51.

68. So Stern, 2.667.

69. Already in the second century B.C.E., according to the *Letter of Aristeas* (16), the chief of the translators of the Torah into Greek, at the symposium sponsored by King Ptolemy Philadelphus in their honor, similarly explains to the king that the Jewish G-d is simply another version of Zeus.

70. The Phoenicians were not circumcised, to judge from Ezekiel 32:30, who specifically speaks of the Sidonians as uncircumcised; but compare the evidence of Philo as cited by Eusebius, *Praeparatio Evangelica* 1.10. If, indeed, as Henry St. John Thackeray, ed., *Josephus*, vol. 1, 231, note c, on *Against Apion* 1.169, surmises, the reference to the Phoenicians is actually to the Philistines (because their coastal territory is the only part of Palestine that Herodotus [2.106] apparently visited), Herodotus seems to be mistaken, inasmuch as they were uncircumcised, at least in the biblical era (Judg 14:3, 1 Sam 17:26). Reinach, 2, note 1, who declares that the passage refers solely to the Philistines and not to the Jews at all, says that Aristophanes, who speaks (*Birds* 507) of the Phoenicians as circumcised, confirms Herodotus's statement and concludes that by the time of Herodotus the Philistines also had begun to practice circumcision (see Philo of Byblos, cited in Eusebius, *Praeparatio Evangelica* 1.10). It seems unlikely, however, that they would change their ancestral custom and thus conform to that of their long-time enemy, the Jews. A more likely explanation is that Aristophanes is referring to the Jews but has not differentiated them from their geographical neighbors, the Phoenicians. Herodotus apparently refers vaguely to the people from this geographical area as Palestinian Syrians, perhaps because of the early association of the Jews with the Syrians, as we see in Deuteronomy 26:5 ("a wandering Aramaean was my father"), as well as in Nicolaus of Damascus (quoted in Josephus, *Ant.* 1.159–60), Pompeius Trogus (36.1–3), and Ovid (*Ars Amatoria* 1.415). As for the alleged borrowing of the rite from the Egyptians, Herodotus could hardly have had a Jewish source for such a view; but inasmuch as he spent a great deal of time in Egypt, he might have heard from one of the priests, with whom he was in close contact and who did practice circumcision, that Moses, who had given the Jews their laws, including circumcision, had been born in Egypt and had derived his ideas from Egyptian priests.

71. So Reinach, 307, note 2.

72. So Hecht, 77–78.

73. So Hecht, 79.

74. So Alan Mendelson, *Philo's Jewish Identity*, 58.

75. Stern, 3.13, remains skeptical that Naevius's play is about a Jew, because we have no reference to Jews in Rome before 139 B.C.E. and because he doubts that in the third century B.C.E., even if *Apella* means "circumcised," the Jew should be considered the circumcised par excellence. He prefers to take Apella as the Greek name Apelles; but Joseph Geiger, "The Earliest Reference to Jews in Latin Literature," persuasively argues that inasmuch as Horace (*Satires* 1.5.100) refers to the proverbial Jew as Apella and inasmuch as he mentions the *curtis Iudaeis* (*Satires* 1.9.70), the reference to Apella by Naevius is to a Jew, especially when we consider that ridicule of the Jewish practice of circumcision was a favorite motif among the Roman satirists.

76. Stern, 1.444.

77. See the discussion by Bamberger, 45–52.

78. For various theories to explain the name Anchialus, see the literature cited by Stern, 1.528.

79. So Hecht, 75.

80. See the discussion by Hecht, 51–79, especially 62–79, who notes (p. 63) that Philo's treatment is remarkable not so much for what he says about circumcision as for his omission of the covenant, which, after all, is central in the biblical statement.

81. For a review of the literature on this incident, see my *JMS*, 730–32. See now Lawrence H. Schiffman, "The Conversion of the Royal House of Adiabene in Josephus and Rabbinic Sources."

82. Ronald Syme, in *Ammianus and the Historia Augusta*, argues that the *Historia Augusta* is a historical romance by a fraudulent author, though he admits (p. 177) that many reliable details can be disengaged from it, as we have noted.

83. See Max Wilcox (reviser), "From the Destruction of Jerusalem to the Downfall of Bar Kokhba," in Schürer, 1.537; and my "Some Observations on the Name of Palestine," 19–20.

84. Robert Goldenberg, "The Jewish Sabbath in the Roman World up to the Time of Constantine the Great," 429, correctly remarks that the Sabbath was the most conspicuous Jewish observance in the ancient world.

85. See Francis H. Colson, *The Week: An Essay on the Origin and Development of the Seven-Day Cycle*; John P. V. D. Balsdon, *Life and Leisure in Ancient Rome*, 61–65; Balsdon, 232–34.

86. See Balsdon, 232–33.

87. Agatharchides was better informed than several other pagan writers about the Sabbath in that, as Stern, 1.105 points out, he does not make the mistake of which they are so frequently guilty, namely, viewing it as a fast day.

88. Radin, 179–81, contends that there were never any restrictions on fighting on the Sabbath. "It is not easy," he says, "to imagine one of the grim swordsmen of David or Joab allowing his throat to be cut by an enemy because he was attacked on the Sabbath." He thinks that the references to the capture of Jerusalem on the Sabbath by various rulers are based on the stories of martyrdom related in the books of the Maccabees. He also finds it hard to believe that the Ptolemies would have employed as many Jews as they did as mercenaries if they would not fight on the Sabbath. Yet the several pagan references to the refusal of the Jews to fight on the Sabbath seem decisive. As to the religious observance of the biblical period, the Jews may well have deviated from the practice that prevailed in the postexilic period. Finally, the Jewish mercenaries in the army of the Ptolemies may have been unobservant, as many Egyptian Jews were in other respects. See my "Orthodoxy" and now also Bezalel Bar-Kochva, *Judas Maccabaeus: The Jewish Struggle against the Seleucids*, 474–93, who argues that the problem of self-defense on the Sabbath must have arisen before religious persecutions occurred and must have led to practical regulations permitting Jews to defend themselves.

89. On the date see Tcherikover, 57–58, and Stern, 1.108.

90. *Pace* Stern, 1.105.

91. Cf. Ralph Marcus, ed. and trans., *Josephus*, vol. 7, 475, note d, on *Antiquities* 14.53.

92. Some have interpreted this as a reference to the Day of Atonement, which is called the Sabbath of Sabbaths (Lev 16:31, 23:32); but there would be no point in Pompey's waiting for the Day of Atonement, because the same laws regarding abstention from work apply to the Sabbath as to the Day of Atonement.

93. So Radin, 177.

94. In attempting to explain the serious error that the Jews fast on the Sabbath, Radin, 399–400, suggests that the pagans may have confused the Sabbath with the Day of Atonement. Yet the pagan references to the Sabbath as commemorating the Exodus hardly fit such a theory, because there is no overt indication in the Bible that the Day of Atonement is connected with a historical event; but they do fit the biblical statement connecting the Sabbath and the Exodus.

95. We may here suggest that another reference to the Sabbath as a fast day is to be found in the statement in Fronto (*Epistulae ad M. Caesarem et Invicem* 2.9) that the author looks forward to the first of September as the superstitious to the star at the sight of which they break their fast. The allusion would then be to the sighting of three stars to indicate the end of the Sabbath (*Shabbath* 35b).

96. The source of this connection of the Sabbath with the Exodus may well be the statement in Scripture (Deut 5:15) declaring that the Sabbath is to commemorate the Exodus.

97. Meinrad Scheller, "σαββώ und σαββάτωσις," expresses the view that *sabbatosis* is an Alexandrian slang term referring to an illness that requires abstention from sexual relations.

98. Juvenal, however, refers here to festal sabbaths, perhaps an allusion to the fact that Yom Kippur is a festive day.

99. The prominence of fish is attested by tiles from the ceiling of the Dura Europos synagogue which show pictures of fish as part of the Sabbath meal.

100. The tunny was a common fish eaten by the proletariat.

101. Reinach, 265, note 3.

102. So Hugh J. Michael, "The Jewish Sabbath in the Latin Classical Writers," 120. Plutarch (*Quaestiones Convivales* 4.6.2.671E), in the early second century, likewise realized that Jews do not fast on their Sabbath; he has one of his interlocutors remark that "the feast of the Sabbath is not completely unrelated to Dionysus." He notes that the Jews themselves testify to this connection, because they celebrate the Sabbath by inviting each other to drink and to enjoy wine and that unless something more serious interferes with this custom (perhaps a reference to the fact that Yom Kippur transcends the Sabbath) they themselves regularly take at least a sip of neat wine. This is apparently a reference to the practice of ushering in the Sabbath with the benediction over wine, as prescribed by the Men of the Great Assembly (*Berakoth* 33a). The statement that the Jews carry out their Sabbath activities unless something more serious interferes may indicate merely that Jews invite guests whenever possible, or it may have reference to the entire passage, implying that Jews observe the Sabbath except when prevented by life-threatening emergencies (Mishnah, *Shabbath* 18:3 etc.).

103. No fewer than seven major solutions have been proposed to solve the riddle of Horace's thirtieth Sabbath. See my "The Enigma of Horace's Thirtieth Sabbath," in which I conclude that Horace's allusion is more effective if it refers not to some meaningless nonsense but rather to the thirtieth day of the month, a Sabbath, that is the New Moon, so prominently celebrated in Horace's time. Hence, the rescue of Horace by Augustus's favorite, Apollo, the sun-god and hence the moon's enemy, is particularly fitting. It is appropriate that Apollo, rather than Mercury—otherwise the poet's protector—should rescue Horace

here, because Apollo's great antagonist, Dionysus, was associated with the Jews, at least in the mind of an intellectual such as Plutarch (*Quaestiones Convivales* 4.5.3.671B and 4.6.1.671C). The statement in the satire (1.9.74) that Horace has been left under the knife (*cultro*, so similar in sound to the word *curtis*, line 70, "circumcised," perhaps alludes to the use of a knife in circumcision) may refer to circumcision, the distinctive mark of the Jews, and would likewise refer to the zeal, noted elsewhere by Horace (*Satires* 1.4.142–43), of the Jews in seeking to convert others to their religion. Finally, we may note that the New Moon holiday, like all Sabbaths and holidays, ends with the setting of the sun, as presided over by Apollo, the deus ex machina who signals the end of this Sabbath and thus rescues Horace from the superstitious and moon-struck Jews and their supporters (Horace, *Satires* 1.9.78).

104. It seems unlikely that the reference is to Herod's birthday or to the celebration of a special day by the Herodians mentioned in the New Testament (Mark 3:6, 12:13; Matt 22:16), in view of the generic reference in line 184 to the Sabbath of the circumcised, which must be an allusion to the Jewish Sabbath generally.

105. The mention of violets is apparently an allusion to the custom of having flowers in the home to give a festive air to the Sabbath. The Talmud (*Shabbath* 33b and 119a) mentions the use of myrtle on the Sabbath table and tells the story of Rabbi Simeon bar Yoḥai meeting with a man carrying two bunches of myrtle for the Sabbath. The Midrash (*Leviticus Rabbah* 23.6) mentions roses for Sabbaths and holidays. As for the Sabbath lamps, presumably, as with Hanukkah lamps, they were placed on windowsills so that the public might more readily see them, though there is no such law with respect to Sabbath lamps.

106. The rabbis, as we see from the Mishnah (*Shabbath* 2:2), were concerned that the oil of the Sabbath lamps should produce a good flame (as well as not cause a bad odor) so as to avoid the danger of fire and the need to tamper with the lamp. Similarly, Josephus (*Against Apion* 2.282), in singling out Jewish practices that have spread among the Gentiles, makes specific reference to the lighting of lamps.

107. The charge is repeated as late as the beginning of the fifth century by Rutilius Namatianus (*De Reditu Suo* 1.391), who remarks that each seventh day is condemned to ignoble sloth.

108. Such a remark, especially coming from an anti-Jewish bigot, would seem to refute the blood libel that had been foisted on the Jews by Damocritus and Apion.

109. Although such apparent extremism generally engendered ridicule, some intellectuals were more tolerant. Thus, Plutarch (*Quaestiones Convivales* 4.5.2.670C–D) asks how one can blame the Egyptians for irrationality in abstaining from eating certain animals, when the Pythagoreans respect even a white cock and abstain from eating the red mullet and the sea anemone among marine animals, and when the Magi, the followers of Zoroaster, esteem the hedgehog and abominate water mice. Plutarch then speculates as to why the Jews avoid eating pigs. If they hated them, he says, the Jews would kill them just as the Magi kill water mice; but in fact, he correctly comments, it is just as unlawful for Jews to

destroy pigs (presumably an allusion to the prohibition of causing anguish to living creatures [*Shabbath* 128b]) as to eat them.

110. This would be consistent with the view that the Jews honor the ass because it first led them to water during their sojourn in the wilderness (cf. Tacitus, *Histories* 5.3.2). This reason for abstention from eating these animals thus accords with the view of the Egyptian priests in Diodorus (1.87), that the Egyptians worship animals, though he does not specify the pig, that had benefited them. Aelian (*De Natura Animalium* 10.16), in the third century c.e., on the authority of Eudoxus, does specify that the Egyptians abstain from sacrificing pigs because they are useful to agriculture, inasmuch as they press seeds into the moist soil, thus preventing consumption of the seeds by birds. Agathocles (of uncertain date), in his *History of Cyzicus*, similarly records the service rendered by the pig to Zeus and notes that for this reason the Cretans, on whose island Zeus was said to have been born, abstained from eating pork.

111. We may suggest that Apollo, who rescues Horace from the bore in *Satires* 1.9, might well—and ironically—remind the reader of the very similarly named Apella in the apparently proverbial phrase *credat Iudaeus Apella* (*Satires* 1.5.100), alluding to the Jews' credulity. We know of no Jew named Apella in Rome, despite the fact that we have over five hundred tombstone inscriptions containing a host of names. To be sure, there is a Christian named Apelles mentioned in Paul's Epistle to the Romans (16:10), as well as a Jew named Apella in a first-century ostracon from Egypt (in *CPJ* 2. 126, no. 188) and another named Apella in an inscription from Phrygia (in *CII* 2, no. 761). Now, the similarity of the names Apella and Apollo, unnoticed by previous commentators, is striking, especially when we consider that the name Apollo is said by Plutarch (*Lycurgus* 6), himself a priest of Apollo at the end of the first century, to be derived from *apella*, the very name of the proverbial Jew in the Fifth Satire.

112. There are two passages on this theme in fragments from a lost work on Hippocrates' *Anatomy* extant only in Arabic translation. These are quoted in Richard R. Walzer, *Galen on Jews and Christians*, 11 and 15. The example Galen gives is, interestingly enough, the same as that given by Pseudo-Longinus, 9.9, namely, "G-d said" (Gen. 1:3, 9, 10). But Pseudo-Longinus and Galen draw opposite conclusions—the former, from the point of view of style, praising the Bible, and the latter, from the point of view of content, criticizing the Bible for unscientific method.

113. Begging as a Jewish characteristic may also be seen in the scholia on Juvenal 4.117 (Wessner, p. 64) referring to those who go begging at the Arician gate (on the Appian Way) or at the hill among the Jews.

114. See my "Cicero's Conception of Historiography," 133–34.

115. So Stern, 1.194.

116. Littman, 831.

117. Stern, 1.338, translates "almost incredible," but the word *almost* has been introduced without any basis into the Latin.

118. Maria Pucci Ben Ze'ev, "Greek Attacks against Alexandrian Jews during Emperor Trajan's Reign."

119. See my "Abraham."

CHAPTER 6

1. See Georgi, 160, and the literature cited on page 223, notes 492–94.

2. So Elias J. Bickerman, "The Jewish Historian Demetrios," 74.

3. Cf. a similar sentiment in Plato, *Philebus* 16C, "The ancients are better than we, for they dwelt nearer to the gods." On the appeal to antiquity to prove the truth of tradition, see Robert L. Wilken, *The Christians as the Romans Saw Them*, 122–23.

4. Cf. Arnaldo Momigliano, "The Origins of Universal History." Cf. Arthur Hilary Armstrong, "Pagan and Christian Traditionalism in the First Three Centuries," who correctly notes that reverence for antiquity was a conviction shared by pagans and Christians.

5. Cf. Philo, *De Specialibus Legibus* 1.1.2, where, despite his contempt elsewhere for the Egyptians because of their anti-Judaism, he refers to them as "a race most populous, most ancient (ἀρχαιότατον) and most deeply attached to philosophy."

6. See Herodotus 2.4, Diodorus 1.11.5–6.

7. Cf. Pliny, *Natural History* 7.193, who notes the claim of some Egyptians that their king Menes had invented the alphabet fifteen thousand years before Phoroneus, the son of Inachus (the founder of Argos), did.

8. See Herbert J. Rose, "Time-Reckoning."

9. Cf. Moses Hadas, "Plato in Hellenistic Fusion"; idem, *Hellenistic Culture*, 72–82.

10. Ben Zion Wacholder, "Biblical Chronology in the Hellenistic World Chronicles," especially pp. 477–81 on anti-Jewish biblical chronology.

11. Idem, 463.

12. See Philip Mayerson, *Classical Mythology in Literature, Art, and Music*, 286. We may assume that Josephus knew the passage in Ptolemy of Mendes, who is cited by Apion (who is referred to by Tatian, *Oratio ad Graecos* 38) in synchronizing the Exodus with Amosis, who lived in the time of Inachus.

13. See Herbert J. Rose, "Pelasgus."

14. See Ovid, *Fasti* 4.731–805, concerning the festival called Parilia, which came to be regarded as the birthday celebration of Rome. A similar linkage is found in the tradition (Jerusalem *Taʿanith* 4.8.68d, *Genesis Rabbah* 65.21) that the Romans were descended from Esau, the elder twin brother of Jacob. Indeed, from the coincidence that the Torah was given in the month of Sivan, under the zodiacal sign of Gemini (the Twins), the rabbis (*Pesiqta Rabbati* 20.95–96) concluded that it belongs not only to Israel but also to Esau, presumably alluding to the fact that any Gentile may become a Jew through conversion. Moreover, the close association of the Romans with the Jews is stressed in the Talmud (*ʿAvodah Zarah* 8b) in the statement of Rabbi Dimi, who traveled in the first half of the fourth century C.E. from the Land of Israel to Babylonia and back, that the Romans fought thirty-two inconclusive battles against the Greeks, but only after they had made an alliance with the Jews (presumably a reference to the Hasmoneans) were the Romans able to prevail over the Greeks (that is, apparently, over the Syrian Seleucids).

15. Jerusalem, *'Avodah Zarah* 1.2.39c, *Song of Songs Rabbah* 1.6, *Shabbath* 56b, *Sanhedrin* 21b, *Sifre Deuteronomy* 52, p. 119 (variant reading in Finkelstein's edition), *Pesiqta Rabbati* 14.59. The statement is ascribed to the Rabbi Levi, who lived in the third century C.E., but it is clearly of more ancient origin. The rabbis thus push back the founding of Rome to at least a century and a half before 753 B.C.E.

16. It is surprising that Apion does not use the occasion to press the charge that the Jews had displaced the Phoenicians and the Canaanites, who had emigrated to Egypt and eventually to the vicinity of Carthage. Indeed, the tradition lasted well into Byzantine times, as we can see from the statement of the sixth-century Procopius (*History of the Wars* 4.10.22) that there was an inscription in Carthage declaring that Joshua was a thief. See Johanan Lewy, *Studies in Jewish Hellenism* [in Hebrew], 60–78, who traces this tradition back to Hasmonean times and suggests that it may have arisen when the Hasmonean state expanded to include the coastal plains.

17. Another possible association of the Jews with the Carthaginians may have come about because, as has been conjectured, many Phoenicians had converted to Judaism. See Baron, 1.374, and the literature cited there.

18. The connection with the Spartoi, as we have noted, may explain the tradition of a relationship between the Jews and Sparta (1 Mac 12:20–23; 2 Mac 5:9; and Josephus, *Ant.* 12.226–27).

19. Pseudo-Scylax (quoted in Carolus Müller, *Geographi Graeci Minores*, vol. 2), 104, p. 79; Strabo 1.2.35.42, 16.2.28.758; Pomponius Mela 1.11.64; Pliny, *Natural History* 5.69, 9.11; Josephus, *War* 3.420; Conon, *Narrationes* (quoted in Photius 186, p. 138b); Pausanias 4.35.9.

20. Lewy, 128, note 69, asserts that Tacitus composed the chapters on the Jews about the year 100.

21. So Eduard Norden, *Die Germanische Urgeschichte in Tacitus Germania*, 47. He and Wilhelm Kroll, in *Studien zum Verständnis der römischen Literatur*, 160, insist that the ethnographic excursus on the Jews in the *Histories* is no different from the excursuses on the Britons in the *Agricola* and on the Germans in the *Germania*; but they are alluding to outward form only.

22. See Bickerman, "Origines," 75.

23. *Pace* Karl Trüdinger, *Studien zur Geschichte der griechisch-römischen Ethnographie*, 152.

24. A number of scholars have argued, from the verbal similarities and from the order of topics, that the excursus on the Jews has been taken from Pliny the Elder's *Natural History*: Heinrich Nissen, "Die Historien des Plinius," 541; Edmund Groag, "Zur Kritik von Tacitus' Quellen in den Historien," 783–84; Philippe Fabia, *Les sources de Tacite dans les Histoires et les Annales*, 247–59; and Gavin P. Townend, "Claudius and the Digressions in Tacitus," 363. They contend that Tacitus would naturally have sought out the account of Pliny, who was a contemporary of the events, a friend of the emperor, and an officer, and who had written a continuation, now lost, of the history of Aufidius Bassus. In any case, as Townend remarks, it would be less to the credit of "the skeptical historian" to have produced this farrago from his own research than to have borrowed

it from the polymath Pliny. A number of scholars have, however, argued against Tacitus's dependence on Pliny: Declef Detlefsen, "Über des älteren Plinius Geschichte seiner Zeit und ihr Verhältniss zum Tacitus"; Camille Thiaucourt, "Ce que Tacite dit des Juifs," 58; and Ettore Paratore, *Tacito*, 2d ed. In particular, Detlefsen notes that Pliny (5.70 ff.) omits discussion of the source of the Jews, although elsewhere he dwells on the question of the origin of peoples, and that Pliny and Tacitus differ in their mention of Cepheus, the king of Ethiopia. Menahem Stern, "The Jews in Greek and Latin Literature," 1156, concludes that there is no reason to assume that all of Tacitus's versions of the origin of the Jews had already been collected in a single source and that it seems more probable that he used more than one source. As Bernhard Blumenkranz, in "Tacite: Antisémite ou xénophobe? (A propos de deux livres récents)," 188, remarks, Tacitus's vague expressions in introducing each of his versions—*memorant, quidam, plerique, sunt qui, alii,* and *plurimi auctores*—lead one to suppose that Tacitus is repeating ideas that are very common.

25. So Bickerman, "Origines," 65. These accounts have been diligently collected by Dionysius of Halicarnassus (*Roman Antiquities* 1.72–73), Plutarch (*Romulus* 2), and various Latin authors (Festus, under the entry "Roma"; Servius, on *Aeneid* 1.273). Most of these versions attempt to account for the name of the founder or the name of the city of Rome. Few are concerned with the origin of the Roman people; and only those who present Remus as the son of Zeus (see the fragments of Antigonus, in Carolus Müller, ed., *Fragmenta Historicorum Graecorum,* 4.305 [Festus]) or who indicate that Rome was a Pelasgian foundation (Plutarch, *Romulus* 1) impute great antiquity to the city. Most prevalent are the views (Plutarch, *Romulus* 2) relating Rome to Heracles, Aeneas, and Odysseus and consequently attributing a more recent date to the founding of the city.

The only other case where we find a considerable number of accounts of the origin of a people is in Ammianus Marcellinus (15.9.1), in his six accounts of the origin of the Gauls. There, too, associations are mentioned with famous heroes, such as Heracles, or famous events, such as the Trojan War. What is striking about these accounts is that none is negative and that two of them are said to derive from the inhabitants themselves.

26. The connection of the Jews with Crete may very well reflect the historical fact, as noted by Herodotus (7.171), that originally all Crete was inhabited by non-Greeks and only later, after Minos's expedition to Sicily, was peopled by Greeks. Inasmuch as the Phoenician language is so similar to Hebrew, Tacitus's theory may reflect a source who knew of the Phoenician contact with Crete, as Franz X. Leonhard, *Über den Bericht des Tacitus über die Juden, Hist.* 5, 2–6, 12–13, suggested long ago. Readers might also recall the statement of Herodotus (1.2) that some Greeks, whose name the Persian historians had failed to record but who, according to Herodotus, were probably Cretans, carried off Europa, the daughter of the king of Tyre in Phoenicia, in vengeance for the abduction of Io from the Greek city of Argos. They might also recall the famous mythological account (Ovid, *Metamorphoses* 2.836–75) telling how Zeus, disguised as a bull, carried off Europa to Crete, where she bore him three famous sons—Minos, later king of Crete; Rhadamanthus, who appears with Minos in the exalted position as one of the judges of the dead in the Lower World (Homer, *Odyssey* 4.564 and

Diodorus Siculus 5.79); and Sarpedon, who plays such a prominent role on the Trojan side of the Trojan War in Homer's *Iliad*, especially in Book 16. Another connection is in the fact that Europa's brother is the Phoenician Cadmus, the founder of Thebes responsible for giving the alphabet to the Greeks.

27. Josephus himself says (*Against Apion* 1.2–3) that his purpose in writing the treatise against Apion is to disprove those who discredit the statements in his previous historical work concerning the antiquity (ἀρχαιολογίαν) of the Jews and who claim that the Jews are relatively modern (νεώτερον). See further my "Pro-Jewish."

28. In fact, so prestigious were the Cretans that whereas normally a tribe preferred to be known as autochthonous, the Caunians (Herodotus 1.172) actually preferred to be known as originally from Crete rather than of native stock, as Herodotus believed them to be. Moreover, inasmuch as they wanted to impress Euhemerus, the priests in Panchaia, the imaginary island in the Indian Ocean that is presented as a kind of utopia, informed Euhemerus (*Euhemerus* 63, frag. 1, *FGH*, part 1) of their Cretan origin.

The famous statement of the Cretan religious teacher and miracle worker Epimenides (fragment 1, quoted by Callimachus's *Hymn to Zeus* 8 and the New Testament's *Epistle to Titus* 1:12) of the sixth century B.C.E., that the Cretans are always liars would seem to indicate that the Cretan reputation was not unmixed. But aside from the logical puzzle this remark raises, because the author himself is a Cretan, we may note that at least among the Greeks lying was hardly a negative attribute but rather an indication of cleverness; we find it ascribed, for example, to the great hero Odysseus (though admittedly Odysseus's later reputation, as seen in such plays as Sophocles' *Philoctetes* and Euripides' *Hecuba*, was mixed) and even to Athena and other deities. Moreover, the source of this remark is the reference, as indicated by the epigram of the first-century Gaetulicus (quoted in the *Palatine Anthology* 7.275), by the Cretans to the tomb of Zeus, which would seem to be a falsehood because Zeus was regarded as one of the immortals. Furthermore, inasmuch as the quotation goes on to describe the Cretans as "evil beasts and lazy bellies," we may surmise that the author is simply a bitter and disgruntled Cretan; he does not tell us what non-Cretans thought of the Cretans.

29. One can hardly think of a greater compliment in antiquity than to be associated with the Spartans (though admittedly there is a bias toward them in much of our surviving literature because most of our authors reflect an aristocratic predisposition in general), but it turns out that even they are indebted to the Cretans. Aristotle, who, we know, made an exhaustive study of the constitutions of the various states of the Greek world and beyond, states (*Politics* 2.10.1271B20–24) that the Spartan constitution "is said to be, and probably is, in a very great measure, a copy of the Cretan." Indeed, he remarks (*Politics* 2.10.1272A13–27) that there can be no doubt that the common meals, surely one of the most distinctive features of the Spartan constitution, are less well managed in Sparta than in Crete. Furthermore, he notes the tradition that the Spartan lawgiver Lycurgus, when he went abroad, spent most of his time in Crete. The historian Ephorus (cited in Strabo 10.4.17–18.481–82) in the fourth century B.C.E. notes the view expressed by various writers that most Cretan institutions are Spartan in origin; but Ephorus himself disagrees and insists that they were

actually invented by the Cretans and only perfected by the Spartans. Apparently, this parallelism of Cretan and Spartan institutions was well known, inasmuch as Polybius (6.45.1–47) indicates that such learned and generally reliable writers as Plato, Xenophon, Aristotle, Ephorus, and Callisthenes agree in praising Crete for its constitution that was so similar to that of Sparta. See further R. F. Willetts, *Ancient Crete: A Social History from Early Times until the Roman Occupation*, 59–65.

30. See Willetts, *Ancient Crete*, 150–51.

31. The word, apparently a poetical term, is found in writers such as Sallust who are influenced by poetical vocabulary. See Otto Prinz, "Inclutus."

32. Hospers-Jansen, 112 and 191; Léon Herrmann, rev. of Hospers-Jansen, *Tacitus over de Joden*. Hospers-Jansen's contention is that this cannot have been an old and well-known etymology, because, if it were, Josephus would certainly have cited it and refuted it in his essay *Against Apion*. We may, however, reply that Josephus may not have cited it because his essay is concerned with answering canards and there is nothing vicious about such an etymology: on the contrary, even if false, it is quite complimentary.

33. On the meaning of *barbarus* in Tacitus, see Gerold Walser, *Rom, das Reich, und die fremden Völker in der Geschichtsschreibung der frühen Kaiserzeit*, 71.

34. Another parallel that might have suggested itself is found in the first-century author Claudius Iolaus (cited in Stephanus of Byzantium, under the entry Ἰουδαία [Meineke F 124 R = *FGH* 3 C 788 F 4]), who derived the name Judaea from Udaeus, one of the Spartoi ("Sown-men") at Thebes, who was a military companion of Dionysus. This connection may have come about through Cadmus, the Phoenician who founded Thebes, whose daughter was Semele, the mother of Dionysus. The association with the Spartoi may have originated from the tradition of friendship between the Jews and Sparta (1 Mac 12:20–23; Josephus, *Ant.* 12.225–28; 2 Mac 5:9). See the literature cited by Stern, 1.535, to which add Ranon Katzoff, "Jonathan and Late Sparta." Apparently, as Hans Lewy, "Aethiopier und Juden in der antiken Literatur," 66, note 2, remarks, there was nothing unusual about explaining the name of a people in recounting the legend of their founding; and indeed Hellanicus (*FGH* 4 F 66–70) and the Sophist Hippias of Elis (*FGH* 6 F 1) composed works with the title Ἐθνῶν ὀνομασίαι ("Names of Nations"). Examples are not far to find, as numerous as they are fantastic: Mauri (Moors) from Medii (Medes) (Sallust, *Jugurtha* 18.10); Cimbri from Cimmerii (Poseidonius cited in Diodorus 5.32.4, Strabo 7.2.293, Plutarch *Marius* 11.7); Numidae (Numidians) from Nomades (Nomads, "wanderers") (Sallust, *Jugurtha* 18.7–8). This may be the explanation of the strange statement ascribed to Aristotle (quoted in Clearchus of Soli, *On Sleep*, in turn quoted in Josephus, *Against Apion* 1.179) that the Jews are descended from the Indian philosophers. We may guess, though admittedly with diffidence, that such a view was derived from a fancied etymology of Ἰουδαῖοι from Ἰνδοί, or perhaps of Abram from Brahman, as we have noted.

35. So Frederick Kuntz, "Die Sprache des Tacitus und die Tradition der lateinischen Historikersprache."

36. According to Ovid (*Metamorphoses* 1.89–90), the Golden Age of Saturn needed no laws or punishments, inasmuch as all people inherently acted justly. We may here suggest that the reference in Virgil's Fourth Eclogue (line 6), the so-called "Messianic Eclogue," to the return of the Saturnian realms may rein-

force, because of the connection between Saturn and the Jews, the possible connection with the Messianic prophecy of Isaiah which this poem resembles.

37. On Saturn as the most powerful planet, see Diodorus 2.30.3; Chrysippus (*SVF* 2. F 527, p. 169; Epigenes, cited in Seneca, *Naturales Quaestiones* 7.4; Diodorus of Tarsus, cited in Photius [ed. Bekker, cod. 223, p. 211b, 1.29]), cited by Stern, 2.38.

38. Cf. Frederick H. Cramer, *Astrology in Roman Law and Politics*, 154, who remarks that a searching interest in astrology was characteristic of the higher socio-economic strata in Rome at the turn of the first century c.e. "For Rome's intellectuals," he says, "a minimum knowledge of the various cosmological theories, including, of course, astronomical hypotheses and established facts, had long become a standard part of the higher educational curriculum." Moreover, in the circles of the emperors from Augustus to Nerva a fierce faith in astrology prevailed. Tacitus himself (*Annals* 6.22) closely allied himself with the great majority of men (*plurimis mortalium*) in believing that astrology was nothing less than a science, "clear testimonies to which have been given both by past ages and by our own" that each person's future is fixed from the day of his very birth, and that the failure of any predictions to come true was due solely to the inaccuracies of astrologers. Indeed, Tacitus (*Annals* 6.22; cf. Cramer, p. 162) notes as an example of a correct astrological prophecy that of one of the sons of Thrasyllus (i.e., Balbillus) concerning the succession of Nero to the throne. That Tacitus was aware of the claims of astrology seems likely, because astrology, as Benjamin Farrington, in "Astrology," 134, remarks, commanded the ardent allegiance of the best minds of the ancient world and was particularly favored by the Stoic philosophers, with whose views Tacitus had much in common. Cf. Marrou, 182, who remarks that of the four branches of mathematics, astronomy, which, of course, included astrology, was the most popular in the Hellenistic Age.

39. On the reputation of Jews as astrologers, see Hengel, 2.62, note 264; and Holladay, 180–81, note 12, and 184, note 27.

40. Hans Lewy, "Aethiopier und Juden in der antiken Literatur," 67.

41. We may also note that in Ezekiel the Tragedian (ca 100 b.c.e.; quoted in Eusebius, *Praeparatio Evangelica* 9.28.4b), Moses' wife Zipporah declares that Libya is inhabited by Ethiopians.

42. Perhaps, we may suggest, the Jewish association with Africa was furthered by the fact that the most famous and most powerful city of northern Africa was Carthage, which had been founded by the Phoenicians, whose language is so similar to Hebrew.

43. So George LaPiana, "Foreign Groups in Rome during the First Centuries of the Empire," 382.

44. See Hans Lewy, "Aethiopier und Juden," 69.

45. Stern, 2.33–34, cites as parallels Livy 10.6.2 and Seneca, *Consolatio ad Helviam* 7.4. Stern, 2.33, notes that the motif of the overpopulation of Egypt and its establishment of colonies in many parts of the world is found in Diodorus 1.29.5 (presumably from Hecataeus) and 1.31.6, as well as in Aristotle, *De Animalium Generatione* 770A34 f., Strabo 15.1.22.695, and Pliny, *Natural History* 7.33. Philo, *De Specialibus Legibus* 1.1.2, also remarks that the Egyptians are a race preeminent in populousness.

46. On the enormous antiquity of Isis, see Rolf E. Witt, *Isis in the Graeco-Roman World*, 21. To be sure, Tacitus himself may have shared the negative opinion of Juvenal (6.526–28) toward Isis, but she is viewed favorably, as noted here, in much of the literature available to his readers. Isis was also said to be the inventor of writing, both hieroglyphic and demotic. See the inscription in *BCH* 51 (1927): 379–80 (cited in Frederick C. Grant, ed., *Hellenistic Religions: The Age of Syncretism*, 131–33). Like her father, she stands for justice. Her popularity was very great: In Apuleius's *Metamorphoses* she appears to the hero and tells him that she is called, among other names, the mother of the gods in Phrygia, Athena in Athens, Aphrodite in Cyprus, Dictynna in Crete, Persephone in Sicily, and Demeter in Eleusis, while only the Ethiopians and the Egyptians worship her by her true name, Isis. A papyrus (Oxyrhynchus 11.1380) similarly alludes to her omnipresence and versatility by remarking that she is called Themis in Chalcedon, Selene in Thessaly, Helen in Bithynia, and Hecate in Caria. Moreover, she was worshiped as Tyche Agathe ("Good Luck"), as the Holy, as the Truth, as Justice, as the Savior of Man, as Phronesis ("Wisdom"), as Providence, as Mistress of the Sea, and even as Leader of the Muses. For a discussion of this papyrus, see Friedrich Solmsen, *Isis among the Greeks and Romans*, 54–56. Her names (and consequently her powers) were said to be infinite and her wisdom immeasurable. Adding to her popularity was her reputation as a great sorceress, said to possess great magical power and viewed as the mistress of the art of medicine. Her popularity was particularly great because, as Apuleius (*Metamorphoses* 11.25.1) puts it, "To the troubles of people in misfortune, you bring the sweet love of a mother." Thus, she was, in effect, a forerunner of the later cult of the Virgin Mary. Her worship was hardly confined to foreigners and the poorer classes, as we can see from the story of the extraordinary devotion to her of the noble lady Paulina in Josephus (*Ant.* 18.65–80). Despite intermittent governmental opposition to her in Rome and despite the general unpopularity of all things Egyptian after the defeat of Antony and Cleopatra at Actium in 31 B.C.E., her worship remained popular, offering, as Herbert J. Rose, *Religion in Greece and Rome*, 284, remarks, "the prestige of an immemorial antiquity," so that eventually the Emperor Caligula even erected a temple to her in the Campus Martius about the year 38. Indeed, as Solmsen, vii, remarks, of all the Oriental deities whose power expands in late antiquity, she established by far the closest contacts with the traditions of classical civilization.

47. Apion, quoted in *Against Apion* 2.20–21; Pompeius Trogus, quoted in Justin, *Historiae Philippicae* 36, *Epitoma* 2.14; Tacitus, *Histories* 5.4.3.

48. Thus, to say that the Jews are descended from the Ethiopians, who were renowned for their wisdom, piety, and bravery and who are termed blameless by Homer (*Iliad* 1.423), is clearly to praise them. This connection with Ethiopia may reflect Moses' military campaign against Ethiopia, his marriage to the Ethiopian princess, and his alleged sojourn in Ethiopia, as found in the Graeco-Jewish historian Artapanus (quoted in Eusebius, *Praeparatio Evangelica* 9.27.7–10.432D–433A), in Josephus (*Ant.* 2.238–53), and in Jewish midrashic literature of the late Middle Ages. It presents a simple explanation of how the Jews managed to come to Egypt; and, inasmuch as there were almost certainly Jews (the so-called Falashas) in Ethiopia before Hellenistic times, it may explain the

connection between the two groups of Jews. On the Ethiopians see Diodorus 3.2; Pomponius Mela 3.85; Seneca, *Hercules Furens* 38–41; Lactantius Placidus on Statius, *Thebaid* 5.427. Cf. Frank M. Snowden, *Blacks in Antiquity: Ethiopians in the Greco-Roman Experience*, 144–47; and his *Before Color Prejudice: The Ancient View of Blacks*, 46 and passim. But although mythology idealizes the Ethiopians, we must, on the other hand, in all fairness, note that the Greeks and Romans did not always admire blackness, as we can see in Philodemus's use of Andromeda (in *Palatine Anthology* 5.121) as an example of a woman loved despite her race.

49. On Cepheus see Stern, 2.34, who cites the following on the connection between Cepheus and Ethiopia: Euripides, *Andromeda* (in August Nauck, *Tragicorum Graecorum Fragmenta*, no. 113); Agatharchides, *De Mari Erythraeo* 1.4 (Carolus Müller, *Geographi Graeci Minores*, vol. 1, 1.112); Ovid, *Metamorphoses* 4.669; and Lucian, *Dialogi Marini* 14. Cassiopeia, according to Hesiod, was the daughter of Arabus, the ancestor of the Arabs, and the wife of Phoenix, the ancestor of the Phoenicians—in both cases, therefore, related to Semites.

50. Philo of Byblus, quoted by Stephanus of Byzantium, under the entry Ἰόπη, in a folk etymology, derives the name of Joppa from the name Αἰθιόπη and hence finds another link between the Jews and the Ethiopians.

51. Hospers-Jansen, 193, argues that the connection of Joppa and the Ethiopians with the Jews can date only from the Jewish expansion in the time of the Hasmoneans, when Joppa became a Jewish possession (cf. Pliny the Elder, *Natural History* 9.15), which it remained, with a few interruptions, until it was conquered by Vespasian. Hence, she declares, this *origo* arose after the time of the Maccabees. We may counter, however, that the passages, dating from the fifth century B.C.E., in Herodotus (2.104.3), who notes that both the Ethiopians and the Syrians of Palestine practiced circumcision, and in Choerilus (quoted in *Against Apion* 1.172–74), who seems to allude to Ethiopians speaking a Semitic tongue, argue for an earlier connection between Jews and Ethiopians. Furthermore, as Israel Lévi, "Tacite et l'origine du peuple juif," 332, indicates, already at the beginning of the second half of the fourth century B.C.E. Pseudo-Scylax (quoted in Carolus Müller, *Geographi Graeci Minores*, vol. 1, 104, p. 79 = Stern, 3.10) does indicate that Joppa is the site where Andromeda was exposed to the monster.

This confusion of the Jews and the Ethiopians may perhaps also be seen in the passage from Choerilus about the Phoenician-speaking people from the Solymian hills. Presumably these are the Solymi, who constitute Tacitus's fifth theory as to the origin of the Jews and who are mentioned by Choerilus. Josephus (*Against Apion*, 1.172–74), in quoting this passage, as we have noted, claims that Choerilus is referring to the Jews. This connection may have been fostered by the fact that the East Ethiopians spoke Phoenician, according to Herodotus (7.89); in any case, Ethiopic is certainly a Semitic language. The connection with Ethiopia may also have been enhanced by the tradition (Varro, *Antiquities* 18.3) that Isis had traveled as queen from Ethiopia to Egypt. See Frank M. Snowden, "Ethiopians and the Isiac Worship." An alternative explanation is that the name Ethiopia is also found in Samothrace and Lesbos. Indeed, according to Homer (*Odyssey* 1.23), part of the Ethiopians live toward the setting, while part live toward the rising of the sun. In fact, we hear (*Odyssey* 4.83–84) that Menelaus wandered over Cyprus, Phoenicia, and Egypt and came to the Ethiopians, Sidonians, and Erembi; the juxtaposition of Ethiopians and Sidonians (Phoenicians) would again seem to indicate a connection between these two Semitic peoples.

We may also comment that the fact that the Jews were forced by fear and hatred to leave Ethiopia, though apparently a nasty allusion, may well have recalled, to the literate reader, the very same words, *metus* and *odium*, in Virgil's *Aeneid* (1.361; cited by Lewy, 143, note 121), where we read that fierce hatred of another Semitic ruler, the Phoenician tyrant Pygmalion, and keen fear led those who had been oppressed by him to flee to Carthage under the leadership of Dido.

52. Cf. Lewy, 119, note 9, who remarks that there is no doubt that Tacitus, the author of this account, drew it from the Bible.

53. This association of the Jews with Queen Semiramis would be a distinct compliment, inasmuch as Semiramis, the alleged daughter of the goddess Atargatis, had a tremendous reputation as a conqueror and as a builder of great cities, especially Babylon.

54. Stern, 2.34 notes that the term *Hebrews* is also attested by Statius and Antonius Diogenes at the end of the first century and by three writers of the second century—Appian, Pausanias, and Charax of Pergamum. But we must note that it is only Tacitus who uses the term in connection with the origin of the Hebrews from Assyria, which is precisely whence they derived their name.

55. It seems extremely unlikely that this theory has a Jewish origin, inasmuch as a Jew would hardly contradict the biblical account deriving the Jews from the Chaldaean Abraham, and inasmuch as a Jew, unless he happened to be highly assimilated, would hardly seek to associate the origin of his people with a nation celebrated in a pagan epic. Bickerman, "Origines," 79, note 32, expresses doubt that the identification of the Jews with the Solymi derives from a Jewish source, but he gives no reason for his doubt. Stern, 3.6, on the contrary, says that only a Jew could have been inspired by the Homeric passages about the Solymi to interpret them as referring to the Jews. It is true that there were, in the second century B.C.E., Graeco-Jewish writers such as Artapanus (quoted in Eusebius, *Praeparatio Evangelica* 9.27.3–4), who identified Moses with the Greek mythical Musaeus and who claimed that he was the teacher of the mythical Orpheus, as well as Cleodemus-Malchus (cited in Josephus, *Ant.* 1.241), who apparently is proud of the claim that Heracles married the granddaughter of Abraham; but there is a very real question as to whether these writers were Jewish in the first place. There are other attempts to connect the name of a people with a mythical people: We may cite Diodorus (5.24.1–3), who derives the name of the Galatae (Gauls) from Heracles' son Galates by a Celtic princess.

56. George Huxley, "Choirilos of Samos," 18–19, argues that the contingent speaking a Phoenician tongue, said to come from the Solymian hills and described by Choerilus as marching in Xerxes' army, are not Jews, despite Josephus's conclusion (1.174), because the round tonsure ascribed to the Solymi was against Jewish practice (Lev 19:27). Moreover, if they were Jews, they should have been marching with the contingent of Syrians from Palestine (Herodotus 7.89), who would have included Canaanites and Philistines. He notes that the

Milyans, who were once called Solymi (Herodotus 1.173), are said by Herodotus (7.77) to have helmets made of hide, precisely the headgear ascribed to the Solymians by Choerilus (quoted in *Against Apion* 1.173). They, like Choerilus's Solymians, who are said to have lived near a broad lake, apparently dwelt in the lakeland on the borders of the Pisidian territory in southwestern Asia Minor. The name Solymi is likewise applied to the Kabaleis of southwestern Asia Minor, and Strabo (13.4.16.630) places a Mount Solymos near Termissos in Pisidia; moreover, Pliny the Elder (*Natural History* 5.94) and Stephanus of Byzantium (under the entry Πεισιδία) state that the Pisidians were formerly called Solymi. The fact that, according to Choerilus, the Solymi spoke a Phoenician language, may be explained by the story, mentioned by Herodotus (1.173), that Sarpedon, the son of the Phoenician Europa, led a group of Cretans to the territory of the Milyans. Alternatively, as Stern, 3.6, suggests, the statement in Choerilus that the Solymi spoke a Phoenician language may be explained by the view that the Phoenicians, according to Herodotus (1.1), dwelt on the shores of the Erythrean Sea (i.e., the Indian Ocean and the Persian Gulf) before they migrated to the Mediterranean, "freighting their vessels with the wares of Egypt and Assyria." Herodotus (7.89) repeats this statement, noting that the Phoenicians themselves declare that they at one time dwelt by the Erythrean Sea.

57. Josephus, too, influenced, it would seem, by the similarity of sound between the words *Jerusalem* and *Solyma*, appears to have adopted this etymology of Jerusalem from Solyma (*Ant.* 1.171–80; 7.67; *War* 6.438). He bases himself on the biblical tradition (Ps 76:3) that Salem, the district where Melchizedek was king (Gen 14:18), is the later Jerusalem. The text in *Ant.* 7.67 reads, "David . . . named the city after himself [i.e., "the city of David," as in 1 Kings 3:1]; for in the time of our forefather Abraham it was called Solyma; but afterwards they named it Hierosolyma, calling the temple Solyma, which, in the Hebrew tongue, means 'security.'" The manuscripts then add, "But some say that afterwards Homer called it Hierosolyma." Vincenzo Ussani, "Questioni Flaviane," and Henry St. John Thackeray and Ralph Marcus, trans. and ed., *Josephus*, vol. 5, ad loc., following Benedict Niese, regard these words as a gloss, although they do accord with Josephus's interpretation (*Against Apion* 1.174) of Choerilus identifying the Solymian hills with the Land of Israel. Moreover, we should note that these words do appear in the Latin translation dating from the sixth century ascribed to Cassiodorus.

We find a similar identification of Solyma with Jerusalem in Josephus's contemporaries Valerius Flaccus (*Argonautica* 1.13), Statius (*Silvae* 5.2.138), Martial (7.55 and 11.94), and Juvenal (6.544), and his immediate second-century successors Pausanias (8.16.5) and Philostratus (*Life of Apollonius of Tyana* 6.29). The similarity in sound between Jerusalem and Solyma has been noted by Theobald Labhardt, *Quae de Iudaeorum Origine Iudicaverint Veteres*, 33.

Israel Lévi, "Tacite et l'origine du peuple juif," 339, concludes that the name Solyma for Jerusalem was invented by the historians of the Jewish War against the Romans, because it is chiefly used in connection with the fall of the city in the year 70, and that it was they who spread this theory of the origin of the Jews. Hospers-Jansen, 195, attempts to refute this theory by noting that Tacitus does not use the name Solyma in describing the conquest of Jerusalem. We may add that the reference to the Jews as Solymites in Manetho (quoted in *Against Apion* 1.248) in the third century B.C.E. would indicate that the usage antedated the war against the Romans.

58. So Henry St. John Thackeray, trans. and ed., *Josephus*, vol. 1, 232–33, on *Against Apion* 1.174.

59. So also Lewy, 144, who notes, as a parallel, Dionysius of Halicarnassus (*Roman Antiquities* 1.10–11), who likewise, in citing several origins, gives three briefly and then the fourth at length. Menahem Stern, "The Jews in Greek and Latin Literature," 1155, notes that Tacitus formally refrains from stating his preference among the six versions of the origin of the Jews, in keeping with the ethnographic tradition of ancient times. Nonetheless, as he comments, only this version includes aetiological explanations of existing phenomena in the Jewish religion; hence, this last version has added weight.

60. See Franz X. Leonhard, *Über den Bericht des Tacitus über die Juden, Hist. 5*, 2–6, 23.

61. Reinach, 304, note 1, remarks that in this entire paragraph Tacitus has merely abridged the account of Lysimachus, which he probably read in Apion or in Antonius Julianus. Likewise, Hospers-Jansen, 195, states that the composition of Tacitus's narrative shows a remarkable resemblance to that of Lysimachus. Stern, 2.35 correctly remarks that the writings of Lysimachus are known to us only through Josephus, and hence his exact (and, we may add, full) language cannot be known; but Josephus is definitely quoting at this point, and because he is engaged in a polemic it would seem that he would have had to be extremely careful not to quote inaccurately or incompletely or out of context.

62. Stern, 2.35 says that Tacitus's failure to specify leprosy is in line with his well-known avoidance of vulgar and common words; this attitude is thus in contrast to that of Pompeius Trogus (quoted in Justin 36.2.12), who defines the disease as *scabies* and *vitiligo*, though to be sure Tacitus does later refer to the *scabies* from which the Jews suffered.

63. Lewy, 120, n. 13, argues that because Tacitus agrees with Lysimachus in most but in not in all respects, the version had been transmitted to him orally. But, as we have noted, the differences are considerable and apparently deliberate.

64. See further Balsdon, 68–69.

65. So Lewy, 149, note 148.

66. Cf. Lewy, 145, note 132, who notes parallels between 5.3.1—"Adsensere atque omnium ignari fortuitum iter incipiunt"—and *Aeneid* 2.130— "Adsensere omnes"—and 3.7—"incerti quo Fata ferant."

67. Pompeius Trogus (quoted in Justin, *Historiae Philippicae* 36, *Epitoma* 2.16), Strabo (16.2.35.760), Chaeremon (quoted in Josephus, *Against Apion* 1.290), and even the allegedly Graeco-Jewish historian Artapanus (quoted in Eusebius, *Praeparatio Evangelica* 9.27.4,6).

68. Apparently, like Strabo (16.2.35.761–37.762), Tacitus draws a distinction between, on the one hand, Moses, whom he, to be sure grudgingly, respects, and the latter's successors, who, according to Strabo, at first acted righteously and piously but later acted superstitiously and tyrannically.

69. See Ronald Syme, "Tacitus: Some Sources of His Information."

70. So Frederick F. Bruce, "Tacitus on Jewish History," 35.

71. This theme is emphasized by Albert Wifstrand, "Die wahre Lehre des Kelsos."

72. Of course, it is biblical Judaism that Origen is discussing: he does, however, refer to the sins of the postbiblical Jews.

73. Unless otherwise noted, all references in Origen in this chapter are to his *Contra Celsum*.

74. The fact that Origen does not dwell at any length on the bastard origin of Jesus that is alleged by Celsus would seem to indicate that his audience included Christians.

75. See Henry Chadwick, *Early Christian Thought and the Classical Tradition: Studies in Justin, Clement, and Origen*, 23.

76. So Arthur J. Droge, *Homer or Moses? Early Christian Interpretations of the History of Culture*, especially 9.

77. Origen's erroneous statement that Phoroneus was the father, rather than the son, of Inachus would seem to indicate that he does not have a text before him but rather is relying on memory or that he made a slip of the pen.

78. Eusebius (*Chronica*, p. 7 [ed. Helm]) is also aware of this tradition, but he apparently did not accept it. For some reason, he chose to date Inachus earlier than Moses; in his *Chronicle* he makes Cecrops Moses' contemporary and Inachus a contemporary of Isaac and Jacob (*Chronica*, pp. 10, 27B, 41A–B [Helm]). Indeed, Syncellus (70–71, ed. Mosshammer) later criticizes him sharply for departing from the earlier tradition. It is curious that the pagan Porphyry gives Moses an antiquity even greater than that of Inachus, declaring that Moses was a contemporary of Ninus and Semiramis. This would give Moses a tremendous antiquity, because Greek chronicles, following Castor of Rhodes, considered Ninus the first datable king in Asia. In Eusebius's *Chronicle*, Ninus is said to be contemporary with Abraham, from whose birth Eusebius dates all subsequent events.

CHAPTER 7

1. See my "Philo-Semitism."

2. So Moses Hadas, "Plato in Hellenistic Fusion"; idem, *Hellenistic Culture*, 72–82.

3. It is indeed ironic, as Günther Zuntz ("Aristeas Studies II: Aristeas on the Translation of the Torah," 125) has remarked, that we have two utterly contradictory views with regard to the indebtedness of the Greeks to the Jews. On the one hand, we are told (*Letter of Aristeas* 313–16) that when Theopompus and Theodectes in the fourth century B.C.E. attempted to introduce material from the Torah into their works they were smitten with illness. On the other hand, we find statements, such as this one concerning Pythagoras, that the greatest Greek thinkers were profoundly indebted to the Torah. Cf. the Jewish philosopher, Aristobulus, who (quoted in Eusebius, *Praeparatio Evangelica* 13.12) in the second century B.C.E. declared that the most famous of the Greeks, from Homer and Orpheus to Pythagoras and Plato, had derived their ideas from the Torah.

4. Howard Jacobson, in "Hermippus, Pythagoras and the Jews," 146, suggests that the reference is to Exodus 23:5: "If you see the ass of one who hates you lying

under its burden, you shall refrain from leaving him with it; you shall help him to lift it up." He notes that Iamblichus (*De Vita Pythagorica* 18.84), Porphyry (*Vita Pythagorae* 42), and Diogenes Laertius (8.17) indicate that the dictum applies to helping a man carry a burden.

5. Stern, 1.96, understands this to refer to salty water; in that case, we may suggest, the reference might be to the brackish water that the Israelites encountered during their sojourn in the Sinai desert after leaving Egypt. Saul Lieberman, in *Ha-Yerushalmi Kiphshuto*, vol. 1.1, 49, thinks that the reference is to the prohibition (Mishnah, *Terumoth* 8:4) against drinking certain liquids that have been left uncovered because they may have been poisoned by a snake. Howard Jacobson, in "Hermippus, Pythagoras and the Jews," 148–49, suggests that water is here a metaphor and that the reference is to falsehood (Exod 23:7), which, like bad water, at first appears attractive but in the end leaves a person in worse condition. However, we know of no such metaphor current in the period of Pythagoras.

6. Presumably the reference here is Exodus 22:27: "The judges thou shalt not revile; and a ruler among thy people thou shalt not curse." Indeed, Jacobson, in "Hermippus," 146, notes that Philo (*Quaestiones in Exodum* 2.6) in his explication of this verse designates the forbidden behavior as βλασφημία. Perhaps the reference is to Leviticus 19:16: "Thou shalt not go up and down as a talebearer among thy people."

7. Josephus does not tell us who actually said this, but we do have such a statement by the Alexandrian Jewish philosopher Aristobulus, who lived in the second century B.C.E., as quoted by Eusebius (*Praeparatio Evangelica* 13.12.664A).

8. The word μετενεγκεῖν, which is translated "introduced" by Thackeray in the Loeb Library edition of Josephus's writings, often has the meaning "translate," as in Josephus's *Antiquities* 1.7 and 11.29. Stern (1.93) presents the view that there is nothing specifically Jewish in the passage cited by Josephus and hence that there is no reason to suppose that a Jewish writer invented it. He remarks that it hardly enhances the glory of the Jewish people, inasmuch as the Jews are put on the same level as the Thracians. Nevertheless, Josephus's addition, after the statement about the Jews and Thracians, and while still quoting from Hermippus, that Pythagoras introduced many points of Jewish law into his philosophy is a clear indication that Pythagoras drew on Judaism in particular and not merely on the Jewish and Thracian teachings. We may discern what a great compliment it was to assert that Pythagoras was indebted to the Jews when we hear that there was a tradition (cited in Cicero, *De Re Publica* 2.15; Livy 1.18.2), obviously anachronistic, that the greatly revered Roman King Numa Pompilius, who supposedly lived in the late eighth and early seventh centuries B.C.E., was a pupil of Pythagoras. That Cicero and Livy here go to the trouble of denying this report is due to their desire, as they both put it, to prove that Roman civilization was not brought from overseas but grew from its own native excellence.

9. That Josephus's readers might have been ready to accept such a tradition is possible in view of the statement of the third-century B.C.E. historian Neanthes (quoted in Carolus Müller, *Fragmenta Historicorum Graecorum*, vol. 3, 2) that Pythagoras himself was a Syrian or Tyrian by birth.

10. Other passages indicating Pythagoras's indebtedness to the East are Porphyry, *Vita Pythagorae* 6; Iamblichus, *De Vita Pythagorica*; Clement of Alexandria, *Stromata* 1.15.66.2; 6.2.27.2; and Suda, under the word δογματίζει. See Theodor Hopfner, *Orient und griechische Philosophie*, 3–6; and Isidore Lévy, *La légende de Pythagore de Grèce en Palestine*.

11. According to Pompeius Trogus (quoted in Justin, *Historiae Philippicae* 36, *Epitoma* 2.8), who lived at the end of the first century B.C.E. and at the beginning of the first century C.E., Joseph was the first to establish the science of interpreting dreams.

12. To be sure, as we have noted, Theophrastus (quoted in Porphyry, *De Abstinentia* 2.26) does not explicitly state that the Jews are philosophers by race. He is speaking here of "the Syrians, of whom the Jews constitute a part." But the very fact that he sees fit to bring in the Jews at all, inasmuch as he could have spoken simply about the Syrians, is perhaps an indication that he regarded the Jews as a type of philosophical caste within the Syrians, as Jakob Bernays, in *Theophrastus' Schrift über Frömmigkeit: Ein Beitrag zur Religionsgeschichte*, 111, postulated. Werner Jaeger, in *Diokles von Karystos: Die griechische Medizin und die Schule des Aristoteles*, 139, and "Greeks and Jews," 132, note 14, however, objects.

13. So Pierre M. Schuhl, "Sur un fragment de Cléarque: Les premiers rapports entre savants grecs et juifs."

14. So Werner Jaeger, *Diokles von Karystos*, 140–42; and "Greeks and Jews," 132, note 14. Stern, 1.45, however, is skeptical about the theory of Clearchus's dependence on Megasthenes, inasmuch as Clearchus (quoted in *Against Apion* 1.179) mentions the Indian tribe as the Calani, whereas Megasthenes refers to the Brahmans. Moreover, as Louis Robert, *Comptes rendus de l'Académie des Inscriptions et Belles Lettres*, 451 ff., has shown, we have epigraphical evidence that Clearchus had spent time in Bactria (modern Afghanistan); hence we may suppose that he had the opportunity of directly observing the religions of India. In reply to Stern, nevertheless, we may remark that the Brahmans represent a priestly group, whereas the Calani represent a philosophical group, and that consequently one might belong to both at the same time.

15. Another exception to Aristotle's negative attitude toward barbarians may be seen in his admiration for the constitution of Carthage (*Politics* 2.11.1272B24–1273B26).

16. Joseph Mélèze-Modrzejewski, "L'Image du juif dans la pensée grecque vers 300 avant nôtre ère," 107, and works cited in his note 12.

17. Idem, 107, rightly objects to the usual translation, "philosophers by race."

18. So Radin, 86.

19. So Werner Jaeger, "Greeks and Jews," 133.

20. The equation of Jews with philosophers may have been aided by the fact that Xenophanes, who, according to Aristotle (*Metaphysics* 1.5.986B21–24), was the first Greek who spoke of the unity of the divinity, came to his view through looking at the sky. We may note that Pseudo-Eupolemus (quoted in Eusebius, *Praeparatio Evangelica* 9.17.3) ascribes to Abraham the invention of astrology, and that Josephus (*Ant.* 1.167) declares that Abraham taught astronomy to the Egyptians.

21. Marrou, 182.

22. See Stern, 1.11, who notes that a similar tribute is paid by Caesar (*Bellum Gallicum* 6.14.6) to the Druids, who spend much time in the discussion of the stars and their motion.

23. Berndt Schaller, "Hekataios von Abdera über die Juden. Zur Frage der Echtheit und der Datierung," concludes that the fragments of Hecataeus in Josephus are not authentic; the work was written not by a known Greek historian-philosopher but by one close to the missionary author of the *Letter of Aristeas* some time between 165 and 100 B.C.E.

24. This is the conclusion of Richard Harder, *Ocellus Lucanus—Text und Kommentar*, 128–132, and is regarded as probable by Stern, 1.131.

25. So Walter Burkert, "Zur Geistesgeschichtlichen Einordung einiger Pseudopythagorica," 53 ff. Philo also (*Quod Omnis Probus Liber Sit* 1.2) stresses the affinity of Judaism and Pythagoreanism when he refers to the society of Pythagorean philosophers as "most sacred."

26. Thus, we find that in Homer (*Iliad* 1.63) none other than Zeus himself is the sender of dreams. Likewise, in Hesiod's *Theogony* (211–13), dreams have a divine origin: we see that at the very beginning of things Night, the child of primordial Chaos, gives birth to the family of dreams. As for the Romans, as Shaye J. D. Cohen, in *Josephus in Galilee and Rome: His Vita and Development as a Historian*, 109, has remarked, their autobiographies (note, for example, those of Sulla and Augustus) are always filled with dreams as indications of divine concern for the subject. That the ability to interpret dreams was much prized is clear, furthermore, from Aeschylus's inclusion (*Prometheus Bound* 485) of the discovery of the rules of oneiromancy as one of the chief inventions for which we are indebted to Prometheus. Pagan prophets (μάντεις) and "Chaldaeans" were supposed to be expert in interpreting dreams. Indeed, according to the much revered Diotima in Plato (*Symposium* 203A), a person who knows how to judge dreams is a "spiritual man" (δαιμόνιος ἀνήρ), in contrast to one who is versed in anything else, whether a science or a trade, and therefore a mere technician. That there were professional dream-interpreters is clear from Theophrastus's statement (*Characters* 16.11) that it is characteristic of a superstitious person to go to a dream-interpreter when he has a dream. Indeed, there were handbooks of dream interpretation, one of which, that of the second-century Artemidorus, has come down to us. In the third century in Ptolemaic Egypt, the interpretation of dreams had developed into an almost stereotyped technique in direct succession to ancient Egyptian tradition. Thus, we hear that the cult of the Egyptian god Sarapis at Athens included an ὀνειροκριτής, who interpreted dreams. See Nock, 54; Hengel, 2.162, note 846; and Morton Smith, "The Occult in Josephus," 246.

27. Joseph's fame for the interpretation of dreams may also be seen in the statement of Philo the Epic Poet (ca 100 B.C.E.; quoted in Alexander Polyhistor, in turn cited by Eusebius, *Praeparatio Evangelica* 9.24.1), who refers to Joseph as an interpreter (θεσπιστής, "prophet") of dreams. This skill in dream interpretation explains the identification of Joseph with the Hellenistic Egyptian god Sarapis, who was so prominent during this period and in whose cult the interpretation of dreams was developed into a fixed technique. Cf. the anonymous

comment in *'Avodah Zarah* 43a, which punningly states that Sarapis alludes to Joseph, who became a prince (*sar*) and appeased (*hefis*) the whole world.

28. So Norden, 298.

29. Cicero (*Ad Atticum* 13.17.2), referring to his enormous productivity as a writer, calls Varro πολυγραφώτατος. Quintilian (10.1.95) praises him as the most erudite of the Romans. Augustine (*De Civitate Dei* 6.2) says of him that he "read so much that we wonder when he had time to write, wrote so much that we can scarcely believe anyone could have read it all."

30. Norden, 298–99, has convincingly shown this by merely translating Varro's words into Greek.

31. Cf. Karl R. Popper, *The Open Society and Its Enemies*, vol. 1, 41: "Through his doctrine of the similarity between Sparta and the perfect state, Plato became one of the most successful propagandists of what I should like to call 'the Great Myth of Sparta'—the perennial and influential myth of the supremacy of the Spartan constitution and way of life."

32. Robert Turcan, *Sénèque et les religions orientales*, 23, says that the contrast is between the Jewish priests and the rest of the Jewish people; and Stern, 1.432, says that the contrast is between the Jews and the non-Jews ("G-d-fearers") who adopt Jewish customs. But there is no mention of Jewish priests at all; and it is clear that Seneca is at this point begrudgingly complimenting the Jews, because Augustine, who is quoting him, says before this comment that Seneca adds a statement regarding his opinion of their system of sacred institutions generally. Hence, the contrast is between Jews and non-Jews generally rather than between Jews and proselytes. Stern says that Reinach, 263, note 2, interprets the passage as contrasting Jews and non-Jews who adopt Jewish customs; but Reinach contrasts Jews and non-Jews generally, his statement being "Seneca opposes the Jews as a group, who know why they practice certain rites, to the mass of the superstitious ignorant people who are content to follow a routine."

33. E.g., Holladay, 93 and 98–99, note 2. Eupolemus is referred to as a Jew by Eusebius (*Historia Ecclesiastica* 6.13.7) and by Jerome (*De Viris Illustribus* 38). For a detailed discussion of the debate as to whether or not Eupolemus was a Jew, see Ben Zion Wacholder, *Eupolemus: A Study of Judaeo-Greek Literature*, 1–5. For a careful edition of the text, translation, and commentary on the fragments of Eupolemus, see Holladay, 93–156.

34. Undoubtedly what Josephus has in mind are such errors on the part of Eupolemus as the statements that David was the son of Saul (quoted in Eusebius, *Praeparatio Evangelica* 9.30.3) and that Eli was high priest at the time of King Solomon's accession (quoted in Eusebius, *Praeparatio Evangelica* 9.30.8). Further reasons for questioning his Jewishness are that he alters the measurements of the Temple (in *Praeparatio Evangelica* 9.34.4) and that he introduces such syncretistic tendencies as Solomon's gift of a golden pillar to Hiram to be displayed in Tyre in the temple of Zeus (in *Praeparatio Evangelica* 9.34.18). Holladay, 139, note 19, explains such errors by postulating that they are due to Alexander Polyhistor, who is quoting Eupolemus; but these seem to be errors that would characterize non-Jews who have a certain amount of familiarity with the Bible but are not thoroughly versed in it.

35. This encomium of the Jews would be especially effective because the Greeks placed such emphasis on the originators of the arts and sciences. The effectiveness would be particularly great because Apollonius Molon (cited in *Against Apion* 2.148) had castigated the Jews as the only people who had made no useful contribution to civilization; and Apion (quoted in *Against Apion* 2.135), as we have noted, had disparaged the Jews for producing neither inventors in the arts and crafts nor eminent sages.

36. See Holladay, 157–59. His identity is shrouded in mystery, but he is generally thought to have been a Samaritan. The allegedly blatant syncretism (see Holladay, 99, note 2) identifying Enoch with Atlas (quoted in Eusebius, *Praeparatio Evangelica* 9.17.9) is not necessarily syncretistic at all. The text may be translated either: "The Greeks say that 'Atlas discovered astrology,' and Atlas and Enoch are the same" or "The Greeks say that 'Atlas discovered astrology and that Atlas and Enoch are the same.'" In the latter case, it is the Greek view, not pseudo-Eupolemus's view, that is cited.

37. Holladay, 189.

38. Pseudo-Hecataeus's date and identity are still very much disputed. See the summary of various positions by Holladay, 277–90.

39. So noted by Wolfson, 2.211.

40. So ibid., 2.212.

41. Note the similar importance of Abraham for Paul in seeking proselytes, particularly in his epistle to the Romans, especially chapter 4.

42. See my "Abraham," 145–50.

43. Cf. Marrou, 176–85.

44. Ibid., 73, 83.

45. Ibid., 182.

46. See my "Abraham," 151–52.

47. In the Hebrew (Gen 37:1–35: I use a standard edition with the commentary of Meir Loeb Malbim [New York: Friedman, s.a.]) the narrative dealing with Joseph's dreams and subsequent enslavement has 57 lines, whereas Josephus (*Ant.* 2.9–38: I use the Loeb Classical Library edition by Henry St. John Thackeray, *Josephus*, vol. 4) has 186. This gives a ratio of Josephus to the Hebrew of 3:26. As points of comparison, we may note that the ratio of Josephus's version to the Hebrew for the pericope of Nehemiah is .24, for Hezekiah .97, for Ezra 1.20, for Daniel 1.32, for Samson 1.54, for David 1.95, and for Saul 2.70.

48. On Solomon's wisdom, see my "Solomon."

49. So David Satran, "Daniel: Seer, Philosopher, Holy Man."

50. This would seem to be contradicted by a writer on astronomy named Cleomedes (*De Motu Circulari* 2.1.91), who lived somewhere in the Mediterranean world during the first or second century, when he speaks of the vulgar Greek spoken from the midst of the synagogue and by the beggars in its courtyards. But, as Lieberman (*Greek*, 29–30) points out, the passage does not indicate that the Jews in the Diaspora spoke bad Greek like foreigners but rather that they used vulgar but good Greek, similar to that spoken by the lowest classes of society or by women celebrating the Thesmophoria at the festivals of Demeter. It does not, as Stern (2.158) notes, indicate that the Jews spoke some special Graeco-Jewish language similar to the later development of Yiddish and Ladino.

51. Quoted in Clement of Alexandria, *Stromata* 1.22.150.4; Eusebius, *Preparatio Evangelica* 9.6.9, 11.10.14; Theodoret, *Graecarum Affectionum Curatio* 2.114; Suda, under the entry Νουμήνιος.

52. *Pesiqta Rabbati* 14.59; *Song of Songs Rabbah* 1.1., no. 9.

53. See Samuel Krauss, "The Jews in the Works of the Church Fathers."

54. Chadwick, 207 (ad loc.), comments that the phrase used here by Celsus, οὔτ᾽ ἐν λόγῳ οὔτ᾽ ἐν ἀριθμῷ, refers to the anecdote that the Megarians asked the oracle who were the most important people in Greece and were told that they were not even in the reckoning at all.

55. On the social world of early Christianity see, most recently, Robin Lane Fox, in *Pagans and Christians*, who notes that the hard core of the membership of the early Church "lay in the humbler free classes, people who were far removed from higher education and at most controlled a very modest property of their own. It is against this silent majority that the exceptions should be seen, although the exceptions generally wrote the surviving texts and addressed exceptional Christians."

56. The Jews' emphasis on study is Origen's answer to Celsus's charge (*Against Celsus* 4.35) that Judaism appeals to uneducated and stupid people. It is significant that Origen does not counterattack, as does Josephus (*Against Apion* 1.12), who belittles the greatness of Homer by remarking that his date is clearly later than the Trojan War and that he did not leave his poems in writing, presumably because he was illiterate. (This statement by Josephus, we may remark, became the basis of the theory of Friedrich August Wolf in his *Prolegomena* to Homer [1795], as later elaborated by Milman Parry in the twentieth century, of Homer as an oral poet.) The Jews, says Origen (*Against Celsus* 2.34), though they are zealous students of their own Scriptures, are not very well [or at all] versed in Greek literature; hence, this would seem to give credence to the charge that the Jews are, indeed, obscurantist.

57. Eric R. Dodds, in *Pagan and Christian in an Age of Anxiety: Some Aspects of Religious Experience from Marcus Aurelius to Constantine*, 118, cites the statement of Augustine, *De Vera Religione* 23, that most of the Platonists of his day have been converted to Christianity with the change of only a few words and sentiments. Chadwick, xx, remarks that even the title itself of Celsus's work, *The True Doctrine*, has a strong Platonic ring.

58. Quoted in Clement of Alexandria, *Stromata* 1.22.150.4; Eusebius, *Praeparatio Evangelica* 9.6.9 and 11.10.14; Theodoret, *Graecarum Affectionum Curatio* 2.114; and the *Suda*, under the listing Νουμήνιος.

59. Ambrose, *Epistulae* 40 and 41, in Migne's *PL* 16.1148–71. Cf. the discussion by James E. Seaver, *Persecution of the Jews in the Roman Empire (300–438)*, 41–44.

60. Apion is here indirectly confirming one of the purposes of the Sabbath, as stated in Deuteronomy 5:15, to commemorate the Exodus.

61. The Greek word here is ἕρμαιον—"a gift of Hermes," i.e., an unexpected piece of luck.

62. *War* 4.459; *Ant.* 3.59, 4.165, 4.324, 6.84, 7.68, 7.294, 9.207, 9.280, 11.112. See my "Joshua," 358–61.

63. See my "Saul."

64. Similarly, we may suggest, Hector's wife Andromache (Homer, *Iliad* 6.407–10) declares that his prowess will bring about his death and will widow his wife and orphan his son. This is repeated like a leitmotif throughout the *Iliad*.

65. See Attridge, 165–66.

66. So Erwin R. Goodenough, "The Political Philosophy of Hellenistic Kingship," 95.

67. The Pythagoreans abstained from flesh, eggs, and beans and subsisted on vegetables, cheese, and coarse bread.

68. Cf. Balsdon, 223–24.

69. See my "Saul," 79–82.

70. Stern, 1.338, translates "almost incredible," but there is no word *almost* in the Latin original, as we have noted.

71. Philo, *De Mutatione Nominum* 40.225; *De Vita Mosis* 2.2.9; *De Decalogo* 30.164. See the discussion by Wolfson, 2.218–20.

72. Cf. Macrobius on Cicero's *Somnium Scipionis* 1.8 in the latter's *De Re Publica*, Book 6, cited by Wolfson, 2.220, note 146.

73. See Joshua Gutmann, "Antoninus Pius: In Talmud and Aggadah."

74. Severus (*Historia Augusta, Alexander Severus*, 30.2) was so deeply interested in ethical philosophy that he devoted part of every day to a study of Plato's *Republic* and Cicero's *On Moral Duties* and *Republic*.

75. See Albrecht Dihle, *Die goldene Regel: Eine Einführung in die Geschichte der antiken und frühchristlichen Vulgärethik*.

76. Admittedly, this may be sheer flattery for the sake of gaining a favor for a friend. However, even Bishop Ambrose (*Commentary on Psalms* 1.41 [*PL* 14.943]), whose anti-Judaism was notorious in the fourth century, admitted that the ethical standards of some Jews was high.

77. Christoph Schäublin, in "Josephus und die Griechen," stresses the influence of Plato's *Laws* on Josephus.

78. See my "Joshua," 362–64.

79. Cf. Aristotle, *De Virtutibus et Vitiis* 55.1250B22–23, who defines piety as either a part of justice or an accompaniment to it.

80. Cf. also Philo, *De Specialibus Legibus* 4.25.135 and 4.27.147, who speaks of piety as the queen of the virtues.

81. Attridge, 183.

82. See Attridge, 115.

83. So also the terms are used together by Xenophon, *Memorabilia* 4–8, 11; Dionysius 1.5.2, 1.53, 2.18, 4.92, 6.62, 13.5.3; Diodorus 1.2.2, cited by Attridge, 115; and Diodorus 12.20.1–3.

84. Holladay, 98.

85. See my "'*Aqedah*.'"

86. See my "Joshua," 364–66.

CHAPTER 8

1. See Gager. Abraham, to be sure, is mentioned by Apollonius Molon (cited in Eusebius, *Praeparatio Evangelica* 9.19.2–3), Alexander Polyhistor (quoted in Josephus, *Ant.* 1.240; Eusebius, *Praeparatio Evangelica* 9.19.17–23), Nicolaus of

Damascus (quoted in Josephus, *Ant.* 1.159–60), Pompeius Trogus (quoted in Justin, *Historiae Philippicae* 36.2.3), Claudius Charax of Pergamum (cited in Stephanus of Byzantium, under the heading ʾΕβραῖοι), Celsus (quoted in Origen, *Against Celsus* 4.43), Alexander of Lycopolis (*Contra Manichaei Opiniones Disputatio* 24), Julian (*Contra Galilaeos* 209D, 343D, 354A–C, 356C–357A, 358D–E), *Scriptores Historiae Augustae* (*Alexander Severus* 29.2), and Damascius (in Photius 242, p. 345B). It is surprising that Jacob (Israel), who plays such a prominent role in the Bible, is mentioned only by Pompeius Trogus (quoted in Justin, *Historiae Philippicae* 36.2.3–5), Celsus (quoted by Origen, *Against Celsus* 4.43–46, 5.60), and Julian (*Contra Galilaeos* 209D–E, 354A). Joseph is mentioned by Apollonius Molon (cited in Eusebius, *Praeparatio Evangelica* 9.19.3), Pompeius Trogus (quoted in Justin, *Historiae Philippicae* 36.2.6–10), and Chaeremon (cited in Josephus, *Against Apion* 1. 290). Despite his importance in Jewish history, David is mentioned only by Alexander Polyhistor (cited in Clement of Alexandria, *Stromata* 1.21.130.3), Nicolaus of Damascus (cited in Josephus, *Ant.* 7.101, 16.181–83), Julian (*Contra Galilaeos* 253D), and Simplicius (*Commentaria in Aristotelis de Caelo* [in Heiberg, *Commentaria in Aristotelem Graeca*, 7 (Berlin, 1894), p. 90]). Solomon is mentioned by Menander of Ephesus (quoted in Josephus, *Against Apion* 1.120), Dius (quoted in Josephus, *Against Apion* 1.114–15), Theophilus (cited in Eusebius, *Praeparatio Evangelica* 9.34.19), Laetus (cited in Tatian, *Oratio ad Graecos* 37), Alexander Polyhistor (cited in Clement of Alexandria, *Stromata* 1.21.130.3), Nicolaus of Damascus (cited in Josephus, *Ant.* 16.181–83), Dio Cassius (69.14.2), Julian (*Contra Galilaeos* 224C–D), Pelagonius (*Ars Veterinaria* 451), and *Medicina Plinii* (3.15.7).

2. Martin Braun, *History and Romance in Graeco-Oriental Literature*, 68.

3. Some of Apion's glosses on Homer have been found in a papyrus fragment (P. Rylands 1.26) dating from the first century. A few first-century scholia on Homer's *Odyssey* (Literary Papyri, London 30; British Museum inv. 271) mention his name among other commentators. See my "Pro-Jewish," 238–39.

4. A major reason for doubting that Hellanicus and Philochorus referred to Moses is that Josephus, who looked everywhere for references in early Greek literature to the Jews in order to prove the antiquity of the Jews and who is familiar with Hellanicus (*Against Apion* 1.16), does not have this reference; similarly, Clement of Alexandria (*Stromata* 1.15.72.2) in the early third century knows of Hellanicus but not of this passage. See Gager, 26, note 3; and Stern, 3.38–41.

5. So Gager, 32–33. Likewise, Herodotus (1.145, 148) comments on the recurrence of the number twelve in noting the number of settlements established by the Ionians in Asia. Similarly, Aristotle (fragment 385 [Rose]) speaks of a division into twelve parts corresponding to the twelve months of the year. Philo (*De Fuga et Inventione* 33.184) is also aware of the connection of the number twelve with astronomy, which was, as we have noted, regarded as the queen of the sciences in Hellenistic times, and remarks that twelve is a perfect number, as attested by the number of constellations in the zodiac, the number of months, and the number of hours in the day. Specifically, like Hecataeus, he connects Moses (*De Fuga et Inventione* 33.185) with the number twelve, noting that Moses celebrates this number in several places; telling us, as had Hecataeus, of twelve

tribes; and adding that Moses directed that twelve loaves be set forth on the table in the Tabernacle and bade the Israelites weave twelve stones on the "oracle" of the high priest's garment.

6. Cf. Josephus, *Ant.* 4.26–28.

7. The importance of the appointment of priests may likewise be seen in the fact that, according to Livy (1.20.1), the first act of Numa Pompilius, after establishing the calendar, was his appointment of priests.

8. Cf. Polybius 6.48.3–4, cited by Stern, 1.32.

9. See Gager, 134–61.

10. There is a very real question as to Manetho's authorship of some of the statements quoted by Josephus. Indeed, Isaak Heinemann, "Antisemitismus," 27, insists that modern Josephan scholarship has refuted the thesis that Manetho was an anti-Jewish writer, because, he says, in truth he never even spoke of the Jews as such. See my discussion in "Pro-Jewish," 194–96. I conclude that Josephus is more credible precisely because he cites Manetho in a polemical work, where he had to be especially careful not to misrepresent his opponents lest he be laughed out of court.

11. Pompeius Trogus (quoted in Justin, *Historiae Philippicae* 36, *Epitoma* 2.16), Strabo (16.2.35.760), Chaeremon (cited in Josephus, *Against Apion* 1.290); cf. even the allegedly Graeco-Jewish historian Artapanus (quoted in Eusebius, *Praeparatio Evangelica* 9.27.4–6).

12. Because Heliopolis was the city of the sun-god, whence the name, perhaps such a tradition is an oblique reference to the connection of Moses with Aton, the sun-god of the hated religious rebel Akhenaton, whose henotheism Moses may have been thought to have borrowed, as Freud in his *Moses and Monotheism* was later to suggest. Moreover, inasmuch as a Jewish temple had been established at Leontopolis in the district of Heliopolis in the second century B.C.E., this connection may have seemed more credible.

13. So also Abraham was remolded to accentuate his ability as a general. See my "Abraham the General in Josephus."

14. Some scholars, for example, Jacob Freudenthal, *Hellenistische Studien: Alexander Polyhistor und die von ihm erhaltenen Reste jüdischer und samaritanischer Geschichtswerke*, vol. 1, 29, and Reinach, 65, note 2, have suggested that the notion of a female lawgiver had originated in the history of the Sibyls; but the Sibyls, we may note, were not lawgivers but prophetesses. We may here suggest, as a parallel, the passage in Juvenal (6.544–45) that speaks of the interpreter of the laws of Jerusalem, the great priestess of the tree (perhaps an allusion to the grove of Numa Pompilius, where he had been instructed by the nymph Egeria, and which had now become a gathering-place for begging Jewesses), "the faithful messenger of the decrees of the sky" (an allusion to the fact that the Jews worshiped only the divinity of the sky [*caeli numen*], as Juvenal put it elsewhere [14.97]). Isaak Heinemann, "Moses," 360, has described the tradition as malevolent and cites as parallels the transformation of the name Cleomenes to Cleomene in Aristophanes' *Clouds* (680) and Chrysippus to Chrysippa in Cicero's *De Natura Deorum* (1.34.93).

15. Moses is thus identified by Artapanus, quoted in Eusebius, *Praeparatio Evangelica* 9.27.3, and his name is spelled thus in Numenius, quoted in Eusebius, *Praeparatio Evangelica* 9.8.2.

16. See Gager, 41–43.

17. Tacitus (*Histories* 5.5.1) similarly, we may note, though generally very critical of the Jews, distinguishes between the Jewish observance of the Sabbath, which, he says, is upheld by its antiquity, and all other customs, which were introduced at a later period. Among these other customs, Tacitus notes particularly the practice whereby proselytes contribute two drachmas annually (a reflection, presumably, of Tacitus's bitterness at the success of the Jews in winning proselytes), the xenophobic separation of the Jews, and their refusal to set up statues of the emperor.

This tradition of a distinction between Moses' legislation and that of a later era, we may remark, was still alive as late as the fourth century, for we read in Julian (*Contra Galilaeos* 238C) that though Moses taught the Israelites to worship only one G-d, he added, "Thou shalt not revile gods" (so in the Septuagint version of Exodus 22:27, in Philo's *Quaestiones in Exodum* 2.5 and *De Specialibus Legibus* 1.9.53, and in Josephus's *Against Apion* 2.237); later generations had the shamelessness and audacity to insult other religions.

18. These superstitious men, says Strabo, originated the Jewish abstention from certain types of flesh, as well as the practice of circumcision and excision (that is, of females), as well as other observances of this kind. This may perhaps reflect the view that the Torah as we have it did not originate in its entirety with Moses (cf. *Baba Bathra* 15a) and perhaps the sentiment of those excessive allegorists mentioned by Philo (*De Migratione Abrahami* 16.89) that the Torah is essentially an ethical document and that ritual provisions are not to be taken literally. The statement that circumcision was introduced after the time of Moses may reflect Moses' own negligence in not circumcising his sons (Exod 4:24–26).

19. This is perhaps an allusion to Moses' great concern (Exod 13:19) to carry out Joseph's wish to be buried in the land of Israel.

20. Gager, 50, cites this as evidence that Pompeius or his source was familiar with Jewish sources, noting that the Bible (Exod 2:2) describes the newly born Moses as beautiful. But in view of Pompeius's egregious errors in making Moses the son of Joseph and in making Arruas (presumably Aaron) the son rather than the brother of Moses (presumably he had heard that Aaron was subordinate to Moses), it seems more likely that he had no direct knowledge of the Septuagint.

21. So Gager, 57. Some scholars, such as Konrat Ziegler, "Das Genesiscitat in der Schrift *Peri Hupsous*," have argued that the citation from Genesis breaks the train of Pseudo-Longinus's thought and that the parallels with Jewish thought and vocabulary could not possibly stem from him. But Hermann Mutschmann, "Das Genesiscitat in der Schrift *Peri Hupsous*," has correctly noted that the passage in question is very much in place and is, indeed, the climax of Pseudo-Longinus's argument. Eduard Norden, "Das Genesiscitat in der Schrift vom Erhabenen," has suggested that Pseudo-Longinus was a pagan Greek author who knew and used Jewish writings, especially those of Philo. Theodor Mommsen, *Römische Geschichte*, vol. 5, 494; Wilhelm von Christ, *Geschichte der griechischen Literatur bis auf die Zeit Justinians*, 788; and Walter B. Sedgwick, "Sappho in 'Longinus' (X, 2, Line 13)," have called him a hellenized Jew. George P. Goold, "A Greek Professorial Circle at Rome," 177, says that he belonged to the same environment that produced Philo and that he is in some sense a Jew. Gager, 63, plausibly states that because the line of demarcation between Greeks with Jewish

sympathies and hellenized Jews was extremely vague in cultural, philosophical, and religious matters, we cannot draw any convincing conclusion in the matter.

22. Apion records that Moses ascended a mountain called Sinai, remained there in concealment for forty days, and then descended and gave the Jews their laws. Gager, 124, concludes that Apion, as an official of the Museum, may have been familiar with the Septuagint, but this remains nothing more than a possibility, because the motif of Moses' stay on the mountain is frequent in the magical papyri; or alternatively, Apion and other non-Jewish Alexandrian writers may have been familiar with such Graeco-Jewish historians as Artapanus and Eupolemus, or with the tragedy by Ezekiel on the exodus from Egypt. We may respond, however, that Apion knows that Moses was on Mount Sinai for forty days, precisely the length of time that he was there according to the Pentateuch (Exod 24:18); and this would seem to indicate that he knew the Septuagint or that, at any rate, he had oral contact with a Jew. Stern, 1.397 suggests that Apion's attempt to show that Moses' sojourn on Sinai was part of his plan to deceive the Israelites into thinking that the laws were of divine origin is in line with the rationalistic criticism of other revelations, such as those of Minos and Lycurgus, as indicated in Strabo (16.2.38–39.762). Unlike the other Alexandrian versions of Moses, which stress his opposition to the Egyptian religion, Apion asserts that it was the basis of his new religious outlook in Jerusalem, and that Moses was, in effect, a plagiarist who had appropriated the doctrines of Egyptian predecessors—perhaps another allusion to Akhenaton, who was so despised that he had become a non-person and whose very name was anathema to the Egyptians.

23. Josephus has similarly enhanced his portrait of Abraham by presenting him (*Ant.* 1.167) in an extra-biblical detail as a mathematician and astronomer who taught these sciences to the famed Egyptians, who in turn taught them to the Greeks. The early Greek philosophers, notably Thales, are depicted as well versed in science, especially astronomy (one of the subjects of higher education in Plato's ideal state [*Republic* 7.528B–530B])—a field of which the Egyptians had supposedly been ignorant prior to Abraham and which was to become the most popular of the four branches of mathematics in Hellenistic times. See Marrou, 182. Pseudo-Eupolemus (quoted in Eusebius, *Praeparatio Evangelica* 9.17.8) and Artapanus (quoted in Eusebius, *Praeparatio Evangelica* 9.18.1), like Josephus, declare that Abraham taught astronomy and astrology to the Egyptians. This may reflect the oral tradition found in the *Midrash ha-Gadol* (ed. Schechter, 1.189–90) that Abraham came to his belief in one G-d through reasoning that because the sun and moon alternately disappear, they must both have a single Master, G-d.

24. Although the columns of the Temple (apparently the structure to which Apion is referring) were celebrated, we know of no sundial other than that of the steps of King Ahab (2 Kgs 20:8–11, Isa 38:7–8), which the Targum, Symmachus, and the Vulgate understood to be an actual sundial. The source of the statement that Moses devised a sundial may be the tradition, based on statements such as are found in Artapanus (quoted in Eusebius, *Praeparatio Evangelica* 9.27.4), that Moses bestowed on humanity many useful contributions through his invention of such devices as ships, machines for lifting stones, weapons, and devices for drawing water. A clue that the sun-clock, the sundial, and the twelve divisions of the day did not come from Egypt but from Babylonia (or Chaldaea—Abraham,

too, we should note, came from Chaldaea) may be found in Herodotus's statement (2.109) to this effect. We may also note the importance attached to time-
reckoning by the pre-Socratics, because we are told (Pliny, *Natural History* 2.187)
that Anaximenes first exhibited a *horologium*, what the Spartans call a σκιοθήρικον
(sundial). Cf. Strabo 2.5.24.126; Cleomenes 1.8; Plutarch, *Marcellus* 19; Diogenes Laertius 2.1; Ptolemy, *Geography* 1.2.2; Vitruvius 1.6.6. See Wilhelm A.
Becker, *Gallus; or Roman Scenes of the Time of Augustus*, 4th ed., 317–21. That such
an invention would have been especially appreciated by the Romans is apparent
from the fact that, according to Pliny (*Natural History* 7.60), there was no sundial
in Rome until eleven years before the war with Pyrrhus (ca 293 B.C.E.). The water
glass (*clepsydra, solarium,* or *gnomon*) was, according to Athenaeus (4.174), invented by Ctesibos about the year 145 B.C.E. during the reign of Ptolemy Euergetes II, although Pliny (7.69) declares that the first water glass was set up by
Scipio Nasica in Rome in 158 B.C.E. Its importance to the Romans is indicated by
Pliny's remark (36.73) that a magnificent *horologium*, a *gnomon* in the shape of an
obelisk, was erected by Augustus in the Campus Martius, but Pliny complains
that eventually it became incorrect in its keeping of time. Elsewhere, we may
remark, the eighth-century Byzantine Christian Georgius Syncellus (*Ecloge Chro-
nographia,* ed. Alden A. Mosshammer [Leipzig, 1984], 377) asserts that Abraham instructed the Egyptians in calendar reckoning and that the Greeks derived
this art from them. Here the anti-Jewish Apion ascribes to Moses inventiveness
in astronomy and chronography, which the Egyptians admired so much, and thus
implicitly admits the baselessness of his own charge (*Against Apion* 2.135) that the
Jews have not produced any geniuses, inventors in arts and crafts, or eminent
sages.

25. See Marrou, 176–85; and my "Abraham," 154–56.

26. Likewise in the second half of the second century, Numenius sees no need
to inform the reader that it is Moses of whom he is speaking when he refers to the
Lawgiver (νομοθέτης) as one who plants and distributes and transplants for people
the germs that have been previously deposited from a higher source. Similarly,
the *Scriptores Historiae Augustae* (*Divus Claudius* 2.4), dating perhaps from the
fourth century, mentions Moses by name as living 125 years, without bothering
to introduce him further to the reader, as if he were well-known.

Quintilian's use of the word *superstition* would indicate that he apparently felt
that Judaism had gone beyond the usual bounds of religion. Of course, Quintilian
was a rhetorician, and such vituperation need not be taken at face value, as is
perhaps also true of the anti-Jewish remarks in Cicero's *Pro Flacco,* as we have
suggested, or in the works of the Roman satirists. Indeed, the fact that Quintilian
(4.1.19) acted as attorney for the Jewish Queen Berenice would indicate that he
was probably not innately anti-Jewish, for Berenice, who had intervened on behalf of the Jews (Josephus, *War* 2.310–14), would hardly have chosen an anti-
Jewish bigot to represent her.

27. So Gager, 81.

28. So Isaak Heinemann, "Moses," 361.

29. Gager, 132, disagrees and concludes that it is nothing more than a rhetorical exercise, a clever witticism.

30. The special virtue of the *aleph* is recognized in the debate (2 *Alphabet of*

Rabbi Akiva 50–55) as to which letter G-d should choose in beginning the Torah. Although a *beth* is finally chosen, the claim of the letter *aleph* is also acted on favorably, and it is placed at the beginning of the Ten Commandments. In this debate, it may be noted, the *aleph* is the only letter that is modest enough to refrain from pressing its claim; and it is this virtue of modesty that Moses similarly (Num 12:3) is declared to possess, because he is the most modest of all men on the face of the earth. It is possible, we may suggest, that there is a double entendre in calling Moses *alpha*, which is so similar to the Hebrew word *aluph*, "ruler," "general," alluding to these functions that Moses filled. There may also be an answer here to a possible Christian claim that Jesus, as the Alpha and Omega, was the revived Moses (in Mark 6:14–15 and Luke 9:7–8 it is conjectured and then denied that Jesus may be one of the old prophets).

31. See also Celsus, quoted in Origen, *Against Celsus* 5. 41–42.

32. The passage, preserved only in Arabic, is from Galen's *On Hippocrates' Anatomy*; see Richard R. Walzer, *Galen on Jews and Christians*, 10–11, 18–23.

33. The *Suda* actually accuses Plato of plagiarizing from the works of Moses his views of G-d and creation; but the statement, as simply construed, seems to indicate merely that their teachings are similar. In point of fact, Philo had stressed the affinity of Judaism with Platonism when he termed Plato "most sacred" and "most clear-toned" (*Quod Omnis Probus Liber Sit* 2.13).

34. So Charles Bigg, *The Christian Platonists of Alexandria*, 300, note 1.

35. Gager, 68–69, has correctly pointed out that a Jew could hardly have written (frag. 34) that the Jewish G-d was the father of all the gods, that (frag. 9a) the Egyptians were equal to the Jews in knowledge of the gods, and that (frag. 18) Jannes and Jambres matched Moses in a contest of magic. True, Numenius might have been an unorthodox Jew; but in view of the sympathetic view of Judaism held by another emergent Neo-Platonist, Porphyry, in the following century, it seems more likely that he was a non-Jew who admired Judaism.

36. See Stern, 2.682, note 1.

37. For a careful edition of the text, translation, and commentary on the fragments, see Holladay, 93–156.

38. On the degree to which the introduction of the alphabet into Greece was indeed revolutionary, see Harris, 45–47, 331.

39. See Franz Dornseiff, *Das Alphabet in Mystik und Magic*; and Georgi, 161.

40. Usually Musaeus is mentioned as Orpheus's son (e.g., Diodorus 4.25.1) or disciple (e.g., Tatian, *Oratio ad Graecos* 41). The fact that Moses, identified with Musaeus, is here termed by Artapanus the teacher of Orpheus would add still more to his stature.

41. According to Josephus (*Ant.* 2.346) it was in hexameter verse that Moses composed his song on the occasion of the miraculous crossing of the Red Sea, as well as his final song (*Ant.* 4.303) before his death.

42. One is also reminded of Socrates' dream (Plato, *Phaedo* 60E6–7), just before his death, telling him to cultivate and make music, whereupon, even though he was convinced that philosophy, which he had pursued throughout his life, was the noblest and best music, he composed a hymn in honor of Apollo and versified some fables of Aesop.

43. This catalogue is paralleled by similar claims for numerous pagan heroes. See Holladay, 232–33, note 46.

44. See my "Mikra," 485–94.

45. See my "Mikra," 470–71.

46. *Ant.* 2.205, 238, 243, 257, 262; 3.12, 65, 67, 69, 74, 97, 187, 188, 192, 317, 322; 4.196, 320, 321, 326, 331.

47. It is significant that Josephus here (*Ant.* 2.205) refers to the Egyptian prophet as a "sacred scribe" (ἱερογραμματεύς) rather than a soothsayer (μάντις). Josephus, as I have noted elsewhere ("Prophets," 416–17), like the Septuagint, uses the word μάντις and its cognates when referring to heathen soothsayers. The μάντις, as Herbert J. Rose, "Divination (Greek)," 796, remarks, is not an inspired prophet but a craftsman (δημιουργός), coupled with physicians and carpenters in Homer (*Odyssey* 17.384). Thus, Josephus uses the term μάντις with reference to Balaam (*Ant.* 4.104 [*bis*], 112, 157) or to Egyptian seers in general (*Ant.* 2.241; *Against Apion* 1.236, 256, 257, 258 [*bis*], 267, 306).

48. Quoted in Leonardus Spengel, ed., *Rhetores Graeci*, vol. 2 (Leipzig: Teubner, 1854), 60–130.

49. Likewise, readers might have thought of the importance attached to genealogies in Herodotus (7.204), who makes a special point of tracing the family tree of King Leonidas of Sparta twenty generations back to Heracles. The Egyptians, if we may judge from Plato (*Timaeus* 22B), had sneered at the genealogies of the Greeks as being little better than nursery tales. We may also note that when Cornelius Nepos (*Epaminondas* 1) begins his life of Epaminondas, he speaks of his family and then goes on to discuss his education and qualities of character. Similarly, note the genealogies of famous heroes in the following: Plutarch, *Theseus* 3; *Fabius Maximus* 1; *Brutus* 1–2; *Pyrrhus* 1; *Lycurgus* 1; Philostratus, *Life of Apollonius* 1.4; *Scriptores Historiae Augustae, Hadrianus* 1.1–2; *Antoninus Pius* 1.1–7, cited by Charles H. Talbert, "Prophecies of Future Greatness: The Contribution of Greco-Roman Biographies to an Understanding of Luke 1:5–4:15," 135.

50. So also in rabbinic tradition (*Sifre Numbers* 67, *Exodus Rabbah* 1.8).

51. Henry St. John Thackeray, in his note on this passage (*Josephus*, vol. 4, 264, note a), remarks that the sentence stating that Moses was the seventh generation after Abraham and enumerating these seven generations has been condemned by some editors as an interruption of the narrative and that it may be a postscript of the author; but in view of Josephus's emphasis elsewhere on genealogy, as we have noted, the greater likelihood is that it is authentic. Moses Gaster, in *The Asatir: The Samaritan Book of the "Secrets of Moses" Together with the Pitron or Samaritan Commentary and the Samaritan Story of the Death of Moses*, 74, notes that the fact that Moses is the seventh generation from Abraham is a distinct feature of Samaritan chronology.

52. See Otto Rank, *Der Mythus von der Geburt des Helden: Versuch einer psychologischen Mythendeutung*; Eduard Norden, *Die Geburt des Kindes: Geschichte einer religiösen Idee* (Leipzig: Teubner, 1924); and Stith Thompson, *Motif-Index of Folk-Literature*, 5.50, M 311, under the heading "Prophecy, future greatness of unborn child," for numerous references in various mythologies.

53. On Josephus's knowledge of Greek literature, see the literature cited in my *JMS*, 392–419, 819–22, and 935–37. On his knowledge of Latin literature, see Thackeray, 119–20; Beniamin Nadel, "Josephus Flavius and the Terminology of Roman Political Invective" [in Polish]; and David Daube, "Three Legal Notes on Josephus after His Surrender." As to whether ancient readers would have appreciated the parallels to classical literature in Josephus's additions to the biblical text, see my discussion in "Pro-Jewish," 230–43.

As to whether Josephus might have been acquainted with traditions found in later rabbinic tradition, we may note that Josephus himself (*Life* 8–9) remarks on his excellent education, presumably in the legal and aggadic traditions of Judaism, which he received in his native city of Jerusalem, which was then the center of Jewish learning; on the reputation he achieved for his excellent memory and understanding (μνήμη τε καὶ σύνεσις); and on the fact that when he was only fourteen years of age he had already won universal applause for his love of learning (φιλογράμματον). To be sure, Josephus may well be guilty of boasting; but in view of the numerous and bitter enemies that he had, it is unlikely that he would have attempted to make such statements unless there was a considerable foundation to them. Moreover, see Bernard J. Bamberger, "The Dating of Aggadic Materials," who has argued convincingly that the Talmud and Midrashim are compilations of traditional material that had existed orally for a considerable time before they were written down. He notes that extra-rabbinic sources, notably the Septuagint, the Apocrypha, the Pseudepigrapha, Hellenistic Jewish writings, and the New Testament—all apparently older than rabbinic writings in their present form—contain innumerable parallels to the rabbinic aggadah. For example, inasmuch as the second-century Rabbi Meir (*Megillah* 13a) states, as does the Septuagint (Esther 2:7), that Mordecai had married Esther, it is more likely that the translators of the Septuagint were acquainted with this ancient tradition than that Rabbi Meir consulted the Septuagint. Similarly, the plague of '*arob* is understood by the second-century Rabbi Nehemiah to consist of stinging insects (*Exodus Rabbah* 11.3), whereas the Hebrew is generally understood to refer to varied wild beasts; again, this is the explanation of the Septuagint (Exod 8:17). Furthermore, one of the paintings of the third-century C.E. Dura Europos synagogue depicts Hiel (1 Kgs 16:34), a confederate of the priests of Baal, crouching beneath the altar while a snake approaches to bite him; but such a story is not mentioned in a Hebrew source until much later Midrashim (*Exodus Rabbah* 15.15, *Pesiqta Rabbati* 4.13a). Hence, that tradition must have been more ancient. See further Salomo Rappaport, *Agada und Exegese bei Flavius Josephus*.

54. So Moses Hadas, "Aeneas and the Tradition of the National Hero," 413.

55. See Dionysius of Halicarnassus, *Roman Antiquities* 1.76.1. On Josephus's knowledge of Dionysius, see my *JMS*, 407–8, 935–36.

56. See my "'*Aqedah*," 224, note 38.

57. Similarly, prior to the birth of Alexander the Great, his father Philip (Plutarch, *Alexander* 2.5) dreamed that he was putting a seal in the figure of a lion into his wife's womb; and the seer Aristander of Telmessus interpreted this to mean that Philip's wife Olympias was pregnant with a son who would someday prove as stout and courageous as a lion. Cf. Quintus Curtius, *History of*

Alexander 1, who notes a portent plus an interpretive prophecy. Vernon K. Robbins, "Laudation Stories in the Gospel of Luke and Plutarch's *Alexander*," 295–96, compares this passage to Luke 1:31–33, where the angel Gabriel predicts to Mary the forthcoming birth of a child who will reign over the house of Jacob forever.

Konradin Ferrari d'Occhieppo, *Der Stern der Weisen: Geschichte oder Legende?* 2d ed., 13, comments on the affinity between Josephus's version of the birth of Moses (2.205–9) after an Egyptian sacred scribe has predicted the birth of an Israelite child who will abase Egyptian sovereignty and the Egyptian Pharaoh orders the destruction of all male children born to the Israelites, on the one hand, and the story of the birth of Jesus and the slaughter of the innocents, on the other hand.

Likewise, in his *Life of Augustus* (94), Suetonius gives an account of the omens that occurred before Augustus was born, as well as those that appeared on the very day of his birth and afterward, from which, he concludes, it was possible to anticipate his future greatness and uninterrupted good fortune. In particular, he relates (94.4) that Augustus's mother fell asleep in the Temple of Apollo and that the birth of Augustus nine months later suggested a divine paternity. Similarly, Dio Cassius (45.1) reports the belief that Apollo engendered Augustus. He includes three dreams among fourteen such items; for example, a man dreamed of the savior of the Roman people and then on meeting Augustus for the first time declared that he was the boy about whom he had dreamed. Philostratus (*Life of Apollonius of Tyana* 1.5) also tells of a portent at the birth of the philosopher Apollonius: "No doubt," he remarks, "the gods were giving a revelation—an omen of his brilliance, his exaltation above earthly things, his closeness to heaven." See Charles H. Talbert's, "Prophecies of Future Greatness: The Contribution of Greco-Roman Biographies to the Understanding of Luke 1:5–4:15," where the author cites similar examples from Suetonius's lives of the emperors Tiberius, Claudius, Nero, Vespasian, and Titus, as well as from Plutarch's lives of Pericles (6.2–3), Marius (3.3–4.1), and Lycurgus (5), and from the lives of the Emperors Hadrian (2.4, 8, 9), and Antoninus Pius (3.1–5) in the *Scriptores Historiae Augustae*. This well-known convention, as Talbert remarks, being subject to perversion, could be ridiculed in satire, as in Lucian's *Alexander*. Such analogies might support the arguments of Hugo Gressmann (*Mose und seine Zeit: Ein Kommentar zu den Mose-sagen*) and of Sigmund Freud (*Moses and Monotheism*) that Moses was the son of Pharaoh's daughter and that the real intention of Pharaoh's command was not to drown the Hebrew children but rather to secure the death of his daughter's child. But neither Josephus nor any of the Jew-baiters whom he cites in the essay *Against Apion* makes such a statement, and it is hazardous to conjecture. Another analogy would be with Oedipus.

58. Cf. Virgil, *Aeneid* 1.607–9, where Aeneas expresses his gratitude to Queen Dido of Carthage for her hospitality: "So long as rivers will run into seas, so long as shadows will traverse the slopes on mountains, so long as the sky will feed the stars, always will your honor and name and praises remain."

59. With regard to Moses' birth, see Hendrik W. Obbink, "On the Legends of Moses in the Haggadah," 252–53; Charles Perrot, "Les recits d'enfance dans

la Haggada antérieure au IIe siècle de nôtre ère," 497–504. For rabbinic parallels to Josephus's overall account of Moses, see Salomo Rappaport, *Agada und Exegese bei Flavius Josephus*, 24–39.

60. Similarly, in Pseudo-Philo's *Biblical Antiquities* (9.10), which so often parallels Josephus, the birth of Moses is predicted in Miriam's dream. See my "Prolegomenon," in reprint of Montague R. James, *The Biblical Antiquities of Philo*, lviii–lxvi.

61. One may note the examples of Plutarch's *Theseus* (6.4), *Solon* (2), *Themistocles* (2.1), *Dion* (4.2), *Alexander* (5.1), *Romulus* (8), and *Cicero* (2.2); Quintus Curtius's *History of Alexander* (1); Philostratus's *Life of Apollonius of Tyana* (1.7.11); Pseudo-Callisthenes' *Alexander Romance*; 1 Enoch 106.11 (where Noah blesses G-d while still in the hands of a midwife); Philo's *De Vita Mosis* (1.5.20–24, 1.6.25–29); and Jubilees 11–12 (Abraham as a child prodigy). Cited by Charles H. Talbert, "Prophecies of Future Greatness," 135. See Ludwig Bieler, θεῖος ἀνήρ, *das Bild des "göttlichen Menschen" in Spätantike und Frühchristentum*, vol. 1, 34–38; Hermann K. Usener, *Kleine Schriften*, vol. 4, 127–28. The latter cites the examples of Evangelos of Miletus (Conon, *Narrationes* 44), Amphoteos, and Akarnan the son of Callirhoe (Apollodorus, *Bibliotheca* 1.7.4). See Hans Scherb, *Das Motif vom starken Knaben in der Märchen der Weltliteratur: Eine religionsgeschichtliche Bedeutung und Entwicklung*, cited by Isidore Lévy, *La légende de Pythagore de Grèce en Palestine*, 141, note 4. For parallels in rabbinic literature, see Charles Perrot, "Les recits d'enfance dans la Haggada antérieure au IIe siècle de nôtre ère," who has collected the haggadic materials relating to the childhood of Noah, Abraham, Isaac, Moses, Samson, Samuel, and Elijah. Thus, we hear, for example, that Abraham in his third year (*Midrash Genesis Rabbah* 38, Pseudo-Jonathan on Genesis 11:28) recognized that all the idols of his father were naught and destroyed them. Cf. Luke 2.40, 52, where we are told that the child Jesus "grew and became strong, filled with wisdom, and the favor of G-d was upon him. . . . And Jesus increased in wisdom and in stature and in favor with G-d and man."

62. Philo (*De Vita Mosis* 1.5.18–24) discourses at even greater length than does Josephus on the physical and mental precociousness of the child Moses. Philo is more eager to present Moses as the prototype of the philosopher-king and hence stresses that even as an infant he did not engage in fun, frolic, and sport but rather applied himself to learning and discovering what was sure to profit the soul.

63. *Tanḥuma Exodus* 8, *Midrash Exodus Rabbah* 1.26, *Midrash Deuteronomy Rabbah* 11.10, *Yashar Exodus* 131b–132b. David Flusser, "*Palaea Historica*: An Unknown Source of Biblical Legends," notes a similar narrative in a Byzantine work dating from not before the ninth century (in Afanasii Vassiliev, *Anecdota Graeco-Byzantina*). There Moses takes Pharaoh's crown (as in the rabbinic tradition) and tramples on it. Then one of the noblemen who advise Pharaoh suggests that gold and a burning torch (rather than an onyx stone and a burning coal, as in the rabbinic tradition) be placed before Moses, whereupon Moses chooses the torch and puts it into his mouth (and there is no mention of the role of the angel Gabriel in saving Moses, as in the rabbinic tradition).

64. See my "Mikra," 474–75.

65. To be sure, Étienne Nodet, ed., *Flavius Josèphe: Les Antiquités Juives*, vol. 1, 91, on *Antiquities* 2.230, reads παιδείαις with some of the manuscripts in place

of παιδιαῖς, the reading of one manuscript which has been adopted by all other editors, including Niese, Naber, and Thackeray. If Nodet is correct, the meaning would be that Moses showed his maturer excellence in his educational activities rather than in his childish games. But the sixth-century Latin version ascribed to Cassiodorus, reading *infantia*, clearly favors the other editors, as does the context, which speaks of Moses' extraordinary precociousness in his early years.

66. See my "Mikra," 486–88.

67. Similarly, the Midrash (*Exodus Rabbah* 1.26 on 2:10, *Tanḥuma Exodus* 8.9; cf. Sir 44:22–45:1) states that because Moses was so beautiful everyone wished to look at him, and whoever saw him could not turn away from him. Philo (*De Vita Mosis* 1.2.9, 1.4.15, 1.4.18) stresses his beauty in a number of places. Rabbinic tradition (*Pirqe de-Rabbi Eliezer* 38) has a similar remark in connection with Joseph, to the effect that when Joseph traveled through Egypt as viceroy, maidens threw gifts at him to make him turn his eyes in their direction so as to give them an opportunity to gaze at his beauty. Josephus, however, in his appeal to his rationalistic readers, avoids the exaggeration of the rabbis (*Pirqe de-Rabbi Eliezer* 48.21), who compare his beauty to that of an angel.

68. See above, note 28.

69. So Gohei Hata, "The Story of Moses Interpreted within the Context of Anti-Semitism," 183.

70. Similarly, the Septuagint avoids the mention of leprosy and declares that his hand became as snow. Philo (*De Vita Mosis* 1.14.79) avoids mentioning that Moses' hand became leprous and instead asserts that the hand appeared whiter than snow.

71. Noted by Gohei Hata, "The Story of Moses," 190.

72. Similarly, we may note, in canon law "Nemo admirandus ordinandus est." A person with a disfigurement that would be gaped at by the congregation is not to be ordained a Catholic priest.

73. We may note that even Tacitus (*Histories* 5.3.1), despite his bitter attack on the Jews, stresses more than do any of his predecessors the role of Moses in inspiring the Israelites in the desert. He adds that Moses urged them to rely on themselves rather than on men and gods, perhaps an allusion to the biblical statement (Exod 14:15) of G-d to Moses when the Israelites complained while being pursued by the Egyptian troops: "Why do you cry to me? Tell the people of Israel to go forward." Again, in Tacitus (*Histories* 5.3.2) Moses is the leader who enables the Israelites to be free of their misery by finding water for them. Lord Fitz R.R.S. Raglan, "The Hero of Tradition," in listing twenty-two characteristic features of the hero in folklore, notes that the Moses of the Bible has more of them (twenty-one) than does any other hero. We may note that in Josephus these twenty-one points are emphasized even further.

74. Noted by Yehoshua Amir, in "Θεοκρατία as a Concept of Political Philosophy: Josephus' Presentation of Moses' *Politeia*," 102–3.

75. On the comparison of Aeneas and Moses as leaders of their peoples, see Moses Hadas, "Aeneas and the Tradition of the National Hero."

76. So also Philo (*De Vita Mosis* 1.27.151) stresses that Moses' constant aim was to benefit his subjects, "and, in all that he said or did, to further their interests and neglect no opportunity which would forward the common well-being."

77. See my "Mikra," 496–97.

78. We may also note that when discussing the biblical prohibition (Deut 19:14 and 27:17) of removing one's neighbor's landmark, Josephus (*Ant.* 4.225) adds that the reason for this prohibition is to avoid wars and seditions (στάσεων).

79. Noted by Attridge, 128.

80. Willem C. van Unnik, "Josephus' Account of the Story of Israel's Sin with Alien Women in the Country of Midian (Num. 25. 1 ff.)," 252–53, indicates that such a tactic is often found in the works of Greek historians, notably Dionysius of Halicarnassus in his *Roman Antiquities*, who notes that when there is civil strife among the Romans they are called into assembly, where the matter is discussed.

81. This is one of the changes noted by the Talmud (*Megillah* 9a) as instituted by the translators under divine inspiration. On the ass as a lowly animal note, e.g., the disdain implicit when the mythical Midas is punished for challenging the verdict of Tmolus that Apollo is superior to Pan as a musician, and Midas's ears are lengthened into the form of those of an ass (Ovid, *Metamorphoses* 11.172–93).

82. The rabbinic version (*Megillah* 9a) of the change indicates that the translators read *ḥemed* ("valuable") for *ḥamor* ("ass").

83. See Lucian, *Cynicus* 13, where Heracles is called a divine man (θεῖον ἄνδρα). Cf. Friedrich Pfister, *Der Reliquienkult im Altertum*, and Lewis R. Farnell, *Greek Hero Cults and Ideas of Immortality*. Moreover, stories were told of Alexander the Great's attempt to throw himself into the Euphrates River so that he might be thought to have passed directly to the gods. Likewise, it was told of the philosopher Empedocles (Heracleides of Pontus, quoted in Diogenes Laertius [8.68]) that after an evening party he disappeared and was nowhere to be found, and that one of those present at the party claimed to have heard a voice from heaven declaring that he was now a god. Apollonius of Tyana (quoted in Philostratus, *Life of Apollonius of Tyana* 1.2, 2.17, 2.40, 5.24, 7.21, 7.38, 8.5, 8.7) is depicted as a godlike man (θεῖος ἀνήρ), whose divinity is manifest in his wisdom and virtue. Again, when speaking of the death of Apollonius, Philostratus adds (8.29), "if he did actually die," and then declares that no one ventured to dispute that he was immortal. Furthermore, a certain nameless ex-praetor (quoted in Suetonius, *Augustus* 100.4) swore that he had seen Augustus's spirit after his death ascend to heaven as his body was burned on the funeral pyre. Indeed, the motif of the apotheosis of rulers and philosophers became so widespread that it was made the subject of satire in Seneca's *Apocolocyntosis* (describing the "pumpkinification" of the Emperor Claudius) and in Lucian's *Deorum Concilium* and *De Morte Peregrini*.

84. This is particularly significant, inasmuch as Josephus is definitely indebted to Sophocles elsewhere. See Thackeray, 116–17; and my "Solomon," 83–89. It is also just possible that Josephus is reacting against the Christian tradition of the apotheosis of Jesus (Luke 24; Acts 1). See Pierpaolo Fornaro, "Il cristianesimo oggetto di polemica indiretta in Flavio Giuseppe (Ant. Jud. IV 326);" and André Paul, "Flavius Josephus' 'Antiquities of the Jews': An Anti-Christian Manifesto."

85. See Charles Bradford Welles, "The Hellenistic Orient," in Robert C. Dentan, ed., *The Idea of History in the Ancient Near East*, 157; and Charles H. Talbert, "Prophecies of Future Greatness: The Contribution of Greco-Roman Biographies to an Understanding of Luke 1:5–4:15."

86. Josephus's care to avoid deifying Moses may have been a deliberate reaction against the Samaritans, who looked on Moses as the most perfect of men, without any blemish at all, whether physical or moral, a priest among angels, one for whose sake the very world had been created, as Moses Gaster, has remarked in *The Asatir: The Samaritan Book of the "Secrets of Moses" Together with the Pitron or Samaritan Commentary and the Samaritan Story of the Death of Moses*, 75. Far from being the amanuensis that he seems to be in the rabbinic tradition, he is termed by the Samaritans the light of knowledge and understanding, as John MacDonald, in *The Theology of the Samaritans*, 153–54, has remarked. Indeed, when he ascended Mount Sinai he is said to have gone to the very heart of heaven. In addition to the laws intended for ordinary humans, he received esoteric knowledge to be restricted in its transmission solely to those of deep spiritual insight. It is he who, on G-d's behalf or acting as spokesman for G-d, said the creative words "Let there be light." He, unlike all other creatures, is said to have been in existence prior to the initial creation process; and indeed, like the Jesus of the Fourth Gospel, he was begotten in order to bring creation to pass. He is the great intercessor, and only through him can prayer be accepted. Indeed, this exaltation of Moses, as MacDonald, in "The Samaritan Doctrine of Moses," has remarked, is a unique Samaritan doctrine, unmatched in Jewish, Christian, or Moslem belief.

Moreover, Moses is for the Samaritans the Taheb ("Restorer"), the expected Messiah-like eschatological figure who will bring about a golden age and who will pray for the guilty and save them. It is among the Samaritans alone that the title "man of G-d" receives prominence as applied to Moses. See Carl R. Holladay, *Theios Aner in Hellenistic Judaism: A Critique of the Use of This Category in New Testament Christology*, 101, note 344, who cites the Samaritan *Memar Marqah* 6.6. Indeed, the Samaritan depiction of Moses is highly reminiscent of the New Testament's description of Jesus as the first begotten being, materialized from his pre-existent bodiless state. Moses is a second G-d, G-d's vice-regent on earth (*Memar Marqah* 1.2), whose very name includes the title "Elokim" (G-d)(*Memar Marqah* 5.4) and of whom it is said that he who believes in him believes in his L-rd (*Memar Marqah* 4.7).

So prominent is Moses for the Samaritans that we hear (Josephus, *Ant.* 18.85) that an unnamed man was able to gather a large following by promising that he would show them the sacred implements buried on Mount Gerizim by Moses. What is particularly striking is that Moses could not possibly have buried them there, inasmuch as he never entered the Land of Israel, as Wayne A. Meeks has remarked in *The Prophet-King: Moses Traditions and the Johannine Christology*, 248.

87. So Wayne A. Meeks, *The Prophet-King*, 141.

88. Similarly, Pseudo-Philo, *Biblical Antiquities* (19.16) and *Assumption of Moses* (1.15) express the view that Moses' death took place in public and that G-d buried him.

89. See James D. Tabor, "'Returning to the Divinity': Josephus's Portrayal of the Disappearances of Enoch, Elijah, and Moses," 237. Christopher Begg, in "Josephus's Portrayal of the Disappearances of Enoch, Elijah, and Moses: Some Observations," 692, comments on Josephus's statement (*Ant.* 4.326) that Moses

wrote of himself that he died for fear that any might say that "by reason of his surpassing virtue he had gone back to the divinity." He explains Moses' fear as arising from his extraordinary modesty, as seen in Josephus's extra-biblical statement (*Ant.* 3.212) that Moses "bore himself as a simple commoner, who desired in nothing to appear different from the crowd." We may suggest that Josephus is here drawing a deliberate contrast between Moses and the philosophers Empedocles and Heraclitus of Pontus, as well as such kings as Alexander and Augustus. See Arthur S. Pease, "Some Aspects of Invisibility," HSCP 53 (1942): 17–21. Perhaps Josephus is also, by implication, contrasting Moses' death with the alleged apotheosis of Jesus, as claimed in the Gospels.

90. See Henry St. John Thackeray, *Josephus the Man and the Historian*, 57.

91. One of these is Ovid, in *Metamorphoses* 14.805–85, where Jupiter fulfills the promise that he had made to lift Romulus up to heaven. Cf. Ovid, *Fasti* 2.481–509 and Livy 1.16.

92. See *Sotah* 13b, *Sifre Deuteronomy* 357, *Midrash Tannaim* 224. See Ginzberg, 6.163–64, note 452. The *Palaea Historia* (Afanasii Vassiliev, *Anecdota Graeco-Byzantina* 257–58; see David Flusser, "*Palaea Historica*: An Unknown Source of Biblical Legends," 72) recounts a tradition that when Moses died alone on the mountain Samael the devil tried to bring the body of Moses down to the people so that they might worship him as a god. G-d then commanded the archangel Michael to take Moses' body away. Samael objected and they quarreled, whereupon Michael was vexed and rebuked the devil.

93. See James D. Tabor, "'Returning to the Divinity': Josephus's Portrayal of the Disappearances of Enoch, Elijah, and Moses," 237–38.

94. So also Philo, *De Vita Mosis* 2.1.3.

95. See my "Mikra," 488–90.

96. Likewise, Moses' hand-picked successor, Joshua, is described (*Ant.* 3.49) as highly gifted in intellect (νοῆσαι); and again, in his final appraisal of Joshua, Josephus (*Ant.* 5.118) remarks that he was not wanting in intelligence (συνέσεως).

97. For Josephus's use of Hellenizations to appeal to the philosophic interest of his audience, see my "Mikra," 498–500.

98. See my "Abraham," 145–50.

99. See my "'Aqedah," 229–30.

100. Carl R. Holladay, *Theios Aner in Hellenistic Judaism*, 102.

101. David L. Tiede, *The Charismatic Figure as Miracle Worker*, 210, compares Cleanthes' "Hymn to Zeus" (Stobaeus, *Eclogues* 1.112).

102. See, for example, Aristotle's account, noted above, of the Jew whom he met in Asia Minor and who led him to generalize (*Against Apion* 1.179) that the Jews are descended from Indian philosophers.

103. Philo, *De Specialibus Legibus* 4.10.61, also asserts that Greek legislators copied from the laws of Moses.

104. In addition, Moses is the subject of the verb νομοθετέω three times (*Ant.* 3.266, 268, 317); and the noun νομοθεσία is applied to him twice (*Ant.* 3.287, 320). So also in Philo the most common title for Moses is "the lawgiver." See Francis H. Colson, trans. and ed., *Philo*, vol. 10, 386. On the usage of this term in pagan and Hellenistic Jewish literature, see Walter Gutbrod, "νομοθέτης." Philo (*De Vita Mosis* 1.28.162) speaks of Moses as the "reasonable and living

impersonation of law," but Josephus avoids such a representation. Moreover, Pseudo-Longinus, *On the Sublime* 9.9, refers to Moses as θεσμοθέτης, "lawgiver." Pseudo-Longinus, as Gager, 59, has remarked, is the first author, whether pagan, Jewish, or Christian, to use the archaic term θεσμοθέτης of Moses. We may suggest that Josephus does not use the term θεσμοθέτης because it represents a deliberate attempt to underline Moses' theological excellence, which Josephus does not wish to emphasize. Cf. Philo, *De Vita Mosis* 1.1.1, who declares that he proposes to write the life of Moses, "whom some describe as the legislator (νομοθέτης) of the Jews, others as interpreter of the holy laws."

105. The rabbis, as Heinrich Bloch (*Die Quellen des Flavius Josephus in seiner Archäologie*, 139–40, correctly points out, do not refer to Moses as "lawgiver" but rather as "our teacher." Josephus himself (*Ant.* 3.322) is careful ultimately to state that the constitution of the Jews was established by G-d Himself, through the agency of Moses.

106. The importance that the Romans attached to establishing their antiquity may be seen from the determined attempt of Virgil in his *Aeneid* to trace the ancestry of the Romans back to the famed Trojans and specifically to Aeneas, the son of Venus, the daughter of Jupiter. Likewise, we may recall Livy's famous comment in his preface (7) that if any nation deserves the privilege of claiming a divine ancestry, that nation is Rome. On the other hand, in the Greek world, says Josephus (*Against Apion* 1.7), "everything will be found to be modern and dating, so to speak, from yesterday or the day before." See my "Pro-Jewish," 199–206.

107. So also Eupolemus, quoted in Eusebius, *Praeparatio Evangelica* 9.26.1.

108. Cf. Philo, *De Vita Mosis* 2.3.12–14, who contrasts the permanence of Moses' laws with the laws of other nations, unsettled by countless causes—such as wars, tyrannies, and luxury—that fortune has lavished on them.

109. Philo, *De Vita Mosis* 2.4.17–18, had used very similar language in stating that almost every other people, particularly those who take more account of virtue, had valued and honored the laws of the Jews.

110. So Wayne A. Meeks, *The Prophet-King: Moses Traditions and the Johannine Christology*, 133.

111. So also Philo, *Hypothetica* (quoted in Eusebius, *Praeparatio Evangelica* 8.7.12): "He [Moses] required them [the Israelites] to assemble in the same place on these seventh days and sitting together in a respectful and orderly manner hear the laws read so that none should be ignorant of them."

112. See my "Mikra," 490. We may note that Korah (*Ant.* 4.14) is also singled out as a capable speaker (ἱκανὸς . . . εἰπεῖν) and very effective in addressing a crowd (δήμοις ὁμιλεῖν πιθανώτατος).

113. See Isobel Henderson, "Ancient Greek Music," 385.

114. Cf. Josephus's addition (*Ant.* 7.305) to the Bible (2 Sam 22:1 and 1 Chr 16:7), that David composed songs and hymns to G-d in various meters, some in trimeters and others in pentameters.

115. So Hengel, 1.13.

116. We should also note, as Wayne A. Meeks, *The Prophet-King*, 134, remarks, that in the Hellenistic and Roman world ἡγεμών also connoted a provincial governor.

117. In the *Palaea Historica*, as David Flusser, in *"Palaea Historica*: An Unknown Source of Biblical Legends," 67–68, points out, Moses leads an expedition against the people of India and carries three thousand storks to overcome the immense number of serpents that are to be found along the way. This is clearly a variant of the version in Josephus. India is substituted for Ethiopia, we may suggest, because India, at the time of the composition of the *Palaea Historica*, was relatively more exotic than Ethiopia. One view, found in *Yelammedenu* in *Yalqut* 1.738, *Exodus Rabbah* 1.27, and *Avoth de-Rabbi Nathan* 39, is that the Cushite woman is Zipporah the Midianite, Moses' first wife; this would be supported by Demetrius (quoted in Eusebius, *Praeparatio Evangelica* 9.29.3) and Ezekiel the Tragedian (quoted in Eusebius, *Praeparatio Evangelica* 9.28.4b), who identify Midian and Ethiopia. That a single word (*Kushith*, "Ethiopian") could have given rise to so far-reaching a legend is the assumption of Abraham Geiger, *Urschrift und Übersetzungen der Bibel in ihrer Abhängigkeit von der inneren Entwicklung des Judenthums*, 199; and Meyer A. Halévy, *Moise dans l'histoire et dans la légende*, 114. Salomo Rappaport, *Agada und Exegese bei Flavius Josephus*, 117, note 141, disputes this and contends, rather, that the legend merely leaned on this word. But midrashic exegesis is full of such lengthy explanations.

This is hardly the place to enter into the discussion of Josephus's source for this episode, on which the literature is considerable: See, in particular, the following: Isidore Lévy, "Moise en Ethiopie"; idem, *Moise dans l'histoire*; Rappaport, *Agada und Exegese*; Martin Braun, *History and Romance in Graeco-Oriental Literature*; David Flusser, *"Palaea Historica*: An Unknown Source of Biblical Legends"; Daniel J. Silver, "Moses and the Hungry Birds"; Tessa Rajak, "Moses in Ethiopia: Legend and Literature"; Avigdor Shinan, "Moses and the Ethiopian Woman: Sources of a Story in *The Chronicles of Moses*"; and Donna Runnalls, "Moses' Ethiopian Campaign." Alfred Wiedemann, in "Zu den Felsgraffiti in der Gegend des ersten Katarakts," mentions a graffito in which we learn that under the Nineteenth Dynasty, in the time of Rameses II, Ethiopia, then an Egyptian province, had an Egyptian governor named Mesui, whose identification with Moses has been proposed; Wiedemann thinks that the two were interchanged in an Egyptian half-historical tale. This may be the historical basis of Josephus's tale, though Lévy, in "Moise en Ethiopie," 205, objects on chronological and other grounds to the identification of Mesui and Moses. Nevertheless, he postulates (p. 206) that Artapanus's account reflects a historic conquest of the Upper Nile.

118. As to Josephus's source, there are four major theories:

(1) Josephus derived it from a now-lost midrashic source. This is the view of Leopold von Ranke, *Weltgeschichte*, vol. 3.2, 18; Bernhard Heller, rev. of Meyer A. Halévy, *Moise dans l'histoire et dans la légende*, 631; Salomo Rappaport, *Agada und Exegese bei Flavius Josephus*, 28–29 and 117, note 143; Abraham Schalit, trans. and ed., *Josephus, Antiquitates Judaicae* [in Hebrew], vol. 1, lxxi. The fact that a parallel for the marriage with the Ethiopian princess is not found in Artapanus but is found only in Midrashim would argue for this explanation. As to why it is not found in the older Midrashim and indeed does not appear in rabbinic literature (*Targum Yerushalmi* on Numbers 12:1, *Sefer Hayashar*, *Shalsheleth Haqqabala*, *Divre Hayamim shel Moshe*, *Chronicles of Jerahmeel* 45–56)

until the eleventh century, Rappaport, *Agada und Exegese*, 117, note 143, suggests that perhaps Moses, the Levite, the war hero, was expunged by the opponents of the war-leading Levite Hasmoneans; but we may reply that the Hasmoneans looked on themselves not as Levites but as Kohanim (priests), though, to be sure, they sprang from the tribe of Levi, and in any case Moses was such a national hero that such censorship seems unlikely. Another possible view is that the legend was expunged at a time when there was opposition to a Jew leading a war in foreign service, but we know of no such opposition. Another problem with this theory is that these rabbinic sources depict Moses as fighting on the side of the Ethiopians, whereas Josephus presents him as attacking them; still other problems are that in these sources Moses marries the widow of the Ethiopian king, that he refrains from having relations with her, and that he reigns as king of Ethiopia for forty years and then separates from her, whereas in Josephus he marries the daughter of the king and there is no mention of the other details. On the other hand, Zacharias Frankel, *Über den Einfluss der palästinischen Exegese auf die alexandrinische Hermeneutik*, 119, note k, far from suggesting that Josephus borrowed the legend from Midrashim, conjectures that the Ethiopian episode in the late Midrashim was borrowed from Josephus through Josippon; but Josippon, as we have it, does not have any such episode. The assignment of a seemingly impossible task to the hero, in the hope that he will meet his death along the way, is paralleled in the stories of Heracles, Bellerophon, Jason, and Psyche.

(2) Josephus had an Alexandrian Jewish source, which was, as Martin Braun, in *History and Romance in Graeco-Oriental Literature*, 26–27, postulates, a pro-Jewish reply to an anti-Jewish Egyptian account such as is found in (pseudo-) Manetho. The replier is usually said to be Artapanus (quoted in Eusebius, *Praeparatio Evangelica* 9.27. 7–10); so Heinrich Bloch, *Die Quellen des Flavius Josephus in seiner Archäologie*, 60–62; Jacob Freudenthal, *Hellenistische Studien: Alexander Polyhistor und die von ihm erhaltenen Reste jüdischer und samaritanischer Geschichtswerke*, 1.169–70; Ginzberg 5.409–10, note 80; and Isaak Heinemann, "Moses," 372. We may note, incidentally, that both Artapanus and Josephus are silent about Moses' slaying of the Egyptian overseer. But Artapanus omits the crucial story of Moses' marriage with the Ethiopian princess. Meyer A. Halévy, in *Moïse dans l'histoire et dans la légende*, 115, endeavors to attribute this omission to apologetic reasons, inasmuch as Artarpanus did not want to ascribe a love story to Moses; but, in that he attributes to Moses such un-Jewish conceptions as the introduction of the worship of cats, dogs, and ibises (quoted in Eusebius, *Praeparatio Evangelica* 9.27.4), we may assume that Artapanus was seeking to impress his pagan audience; and such a love story as that of Moses with Tharbis would certainly impress them. Moreover, he attributes to Moses the foundation of Meroe, so named from Merris, his adoptive mother, whereas Josephus (*Ant.* 2.249) says that Meroe drew its name from the sister of Cambyses. Josephus never mentions Artapanus, though he surely had ample opportunity to do so, particularly in his apologetic treatise *Against Apion*. Isidore Lévy, in "Moïse en Ethiopie," 201, postulates that both Artapanus and Josephus borrowed from Pseudo-Hecataeus, who tells (quoted in Diodorus 1.54) of the campaign of Sesostris against the Ethiopians. Braun, in *History and*

Romance, 99–100, agrees that Josephus's story of Tharbis originates from a pre-Artapanean version and that the omissions in Artapanus can be explained by noting that it was Artapanus's habit to be selective in abbreviating his sources by citing only religious and cultural data rather than warlike and erotic events. Hugo Willrich, *Juden und Griechen vor der makkabäischen Erhebung*, 168–69, adopted this view but retracted it in his *Judaica: Forschungen zur hellen-istich-jüdischen Geschichte und Litteratur*, 111–14. Gustav Hölscher, "Josephus," 1959, postulates a lost Alexandrian Midrash as Josephus's source both for this addition and for many other changes in his paraphrase of the Bible. Abraham Schalit, in *Josephus, Antiquitates Judaicae*, vol. 1, xlviii–xlix, concludes that both Artapanus and Josephus derive from a common source (he suggests Alexander Polyhistor), but that Josephus shows a later stage of development. Ben Zion Wacholder, in *Nicolaus of Damascus*, 58, suggests that the source was Nicolaus of Damascus, because the interweaving of romance and warfare and an anti-Egyptian bias are salient characteristics of Nicolaus's style. The view that Josephus had an Alexandrian Jewish source has plausibility, inasmuch as a story about a war between Egypt and Ethiopia would be of particular relevance to the Egyptians, to whom the Ethiopians were a perpetual foe, never con-quered. Still, we may wonder, though admittedly the *argumentum ex silentio* is hardly conclusive, why Philo, who writes at such length apologetically about Moses in his *De Vita Mosis* and is particularly concerned to answer the charges of Jew-baiters, does not repeat this story, which would have answered so many of their contentions. The romantic motif may have come from the Ninus Ro-mance, which, according to Robert M. Rattenbury, "Romance: Traces of Lost Greek Novels," and Braun, *History and Romance*, 9, dates from the first century B.C.E.

(3) Josephus modeled the legend, or at least the Tharbis episode, on one or more popular stories drawn from mythology or legend: Salia, the Etruscan princess who was abducted by Cathetus, who was madly in love with her (Alex-ander Polyhistor, quoted in Plutarch, *Parallela Graeca et Romana* 40.315E-F); the Amazon Antiope, who fell in love with Theseus and surrendered the city to him (Pausanias 1.2.1); the Roman Tarpeia, who opened the gate of the Roman fortress to the Sabine Titus Tatius, whom she loved (Livy 1.11; Ovid, *Fasti* 1.259–76; Dionysius of Halicarnassus, *Roman Antiquities* 2.38; Propertius 4.4); Scylla, who pulled out the purple hair which grew on her father's head and on which his life depended, so that Minos, whom she loved, might capture her city of Megara (Apollodorus 3.15.8); Polycrita, who, in direct reversal of the story of Moses and Tharbis, saved her country by taking advantage of the love for her of the general who was besieging her city (Parthenius 9; Plutarch, *Mulierum Virtutes* 17.254B-F; Aulus Gellius, *Noctes Atticae* 3.15; Polyaenus 8.36); Peisidice, who betrayed her city because of her love for Achilles, who was besieging it (Parthenius 21); Leucophrye, who betrayed her father to her lover (Parthenius 5); Nanis, the daughter of Croesus, who betrayed her father to her lover Cyrus, king of the Persians (Parthenius 22); Demonice, who be-trayed her city because of her love for Brennus, king of the Galatians, who was besieging it (Plutarch, *Parallela Graeca et Romana* 15.309 B-C); Comaitho

(Apollodorus 2.4.7); Pieria (Polyaenus 8.35; Plutarch, *Mulierum Virtutes* 16.253; cf. Erwin Rohde, *Kleine Schriften*, vol. 2 [Tübingen: Mohr, 1901], 43, note 1), who followed Phrygius, the leader whom she loved, on condition that he make peace.

(4) Josephus invented it himself. This is the view of Isaak Heinemann, "Moses," 374. He notes from the way that Josephus has embellished the story of Joseph and Potiphar's wife how much such a romance would correspond to Josephus's taste; but as Martin Braun, in *Griechischer Roman und hellenistische Geschichtsschreibung*, and Hans Sprödowsky, "Die Hellenisierung der Geschichte von Joseph in Ägypten bei Flavius Josephus," have shown, Josephus's portrait of Joseph depends largely on older legendary products.

119. Philo (*De Vita Mosis* 1.8.43–44), clearly aware of the problem, adds that the Egyptian overseers were exceedingly harsh and ferocious, comparable in their savagery to venomous animals, and that the Egyptian whom Moses slew was the cruelest of all. Moses killed him, says Philo (1.8.44) "because he not only made no concession but was rendered harsher than ever by his exhortations, beating with breathless promptness those who did not execute his orders, persecuting them to the point of death and subjecting them to every outrage." Philo is conscious of the controversy that surrounded Moses' unilateral action and therefore adds: "Moses considered that his action in killing him was a righteous action. And righteous it was that one who only lived to destroy men should himself be destroyed."

120. Consequently, as Holladay, 235, note 56, points out, victories over the Ethiopians became a frequent motif in enhancing the standing of heroes and heroines, e.g., Osiris (Diodorus 1.17.1, 18.3–4), Sesostris (Diodorus 1.55.1, 1.94.4; Herodotus 2.110; Strabo 16.4.4.769), and Semiramis (Diodorus 2.14.4). Another reason for the insertion of this episode is that, including, as it does, the love affair of Moses and the Ethiopian princess, which is not present in Artapanus, it provides romantic interest for Josephus's readers. Indeed, Ethiopia always had a romantic interest for the Greeks and Romans, inaccessible as it was and hence, as seen, for example in the later novel by Heliodorus, associated with all sorts of marvels in the Greek and Roman mind. See Frank M. Snowden, *Blacks in Antiquity: Ethiopians in the Greco-Roman Experience*. We may add that here, too, there is an apologetic strain, in that Moses abides by his agreement and marries the Ethiopian princess, whereas in the parallel stories in the Graeco-Roman legendary and historical traditions, the hero systematically betrays the traitoress.

121. Even though generally Josephus downgrades or rationalizes miracles, here, whereas the Bible (Exod 14:21) declares that it took all that night for G-d to drive back the sea, in Josephus (*Ant.* 2.338) we are told that the miracle was instantaneous and that the sea recoiled at Moses' very stroke. Moreover, very uncharacteristically, Josephus (*Ant.* 2.343) adds to the miracle by remarking that rain fell in torrents from heaven and that crashing thunder accompanied the flash of lightning. Furthermore, he heightens the miracle by stating (*Ant.* 2.346) that the Egyptians were punished in such wise as within men's memory no others had ever been before. See Horst R. Moehring, "Rationalization of Miracles in the Writings of Flavius Josephus."

122. Philo, *De Vita Mosis* 1.29.164, gives, in addition to the biblical reason, a factor unmentioned by Josephus, namely that Moses sought, by leading the Israelites through a long stretch of desert, to test the extent of their loyalty when supplies were not abundant.

123. See Judith R. Baskin, *Pharaoh's Counsellors: Job, Jethro, and Balaam in Rabbinic and Patristic Tradition*, 66, who remarks that the reorganization of Moses' forces is strikingly close to the formation of Roman troops, where each officer took his title from the number of men whom he commanded. Similarly, we may add, when Josephus (*Ant.* 3.289) describes the Israelite camp, he follows the pattern of the Roman camp, with the tabernacle (as Henry St. John Thackeray, trans. and ed., *Josephus*, vol. 4, 459, note a, remarks) replacing the *praetorium*.

124. So also Philo, *De Vita Mosis* 1.40.221. On this point Pseudo-Philo, *Biblical Antiquities* 15.1, agrees with the biblical text.

125. See the comments of Henry St. John Thackeray, trans. and ed., *Josephus*, vol. 4, 521, notes b and c, who cites in particular the parallel with Thucydides' account (7.83–84) of the retreat of the Athenians from Syracuse.

126. Here, too, as in Thackeray, 4. 619, notes a and b, Josephus is indebted for his language to Thucydides (6.72).

127. Similarly, Philo (*De Vita Mosis* 1.6.25) praises Moses for his temperance, noting that though, having been brought up in the palace of Pharaoh, he had abundant opportunities to submit to the temptations of lust, "he kept a tight hold on them [the lusts of adolescence] with the reins, as it were, of temperance (σωφροσύνῃ) and self-control (καρτερίᾳ)." He adds (1.6.29) that Moses made a special practice of frugal contentment and had an unparalleled scorn for a life of luxury. His enumeration of the virtues to which Moses devoted particular attention (1.27.154) starts with exhibitions of self-restraint (ἐγκράτειαι), continence (καρτερίαι), and temperance (σωφροσύναι). Moses' moderation reaches the point of asceticism, as we can see from Philo's comment (2.14.68) that he abstained from food and drink and sexual relations in order to hold himself ready at all times to receive oracular messages. So also Philo (*Legum Allegoria* 3.44.129, 46.134) declares that Moses cut off all passions everywhere, in contrast to Aaron (3.44.128), who attempted rather to control them. Philo (3.45.131) considers that only such a man as Moses was able, through a special grace of G-d, to suppress his emotions completely.

128. See Carl R. Holladay, *Theios Aner in Hellenistic Judaism: A Critique of the Use of This Category in New Testament Christology*, 96.

129. See the discussion by Levy Smolar and Moshe Aberbach, "The Golden Calf Episode in Postbiblical Literature."

130. We may note that when Josephus enumerates his canon of the cardinal virtues (*Ant.* 6.160) he lists obedience (πειθοῖ) as one of them. A similar equation of sobriety (σωφρονεῖν) with obedience may be seen in Josephus's editorial comment (*Ant.* 4.264) about the rebellious son. The same point is made in Josephus's discussion (*Ant.* 4.289) of individual responsibility, namely, that one should not impute to the fathers the sins of the sons, inasmuch as the young, in their disdain for discipline, permit themselves much that is contrary to the instruction of the laws.

131. Thus, Moses avoids the charge of plagiarism so frequently practiced in antiquity. For examples, see Aristophanes' accusation of Eupolis (*Clouds* 553–54) and Eupolis's accusation of Aristophanes (fragment 78 Kock). Plato, we may note, was accused of deriving the ideas of the *Republic* from the Sophist Protagoras; and in Hellenistic Alexandria investigations of plagiarism were apparently frequent. See my "Mikra," 492, note 140. Josephus's statement about Balaam is to be compared with that of the Baraitha quoted in the Talmud (*Baba Bathra* 14b), that Moses wrote his own book (that is, the Torah) and the section of Balaam.

132. Philo, *Legum Allegoria* 3.12.37, does not suppress the passage but interprets it allegorically.

133. So also Philo (*De Vita Mosis* 1.60.328) remarks that when Moses reproached the tribes of Reuben and Manasseh, they knew that he spoke not out of arrogance but out of solicitude for them all and out of respect for justice and equality, and that his detestation of evil was never meant to cast reproach but always to bring those capable of improvement to a better mind.

134. Cf. Philo, *De Vita Mosis* 1.43.243, who similarly notes, in an expansion of the biblical passage (Num 20:14–21), Moses' efforts to persuade the king of the Edomites to allow the Israelites to pass through their land peacefully.

135. Similarly, Josephus (*Ant.* 6.136) defends what most humane readers would have found well nigh incomprehensible, namely the slaughter by Saul of the Amalekite women and infants, noting two reasons why Saul did not deem this savage or too cruel for human nature: first that they were enemies, and, second, that it was, as in the case of Moses' battle with the Amalekites, G-d who bade him to destroy them. See my "Saul," 86–87.

136. We see this connection when Josephus (*Ant.* 7.110) editorializes about David; there he stresses that David was just (δίκαιος) by nature and that he looked only toward truth in giving judgment.

137. See my "Mikra," 493.

138. See my "Mikra," 492, note 140. We may remark that Philo, apparently feeling that inclusion of Jethro's visit to Moses and of Moses' acceptance of his advice would detract from the authoritativeness of Moses, omits this incident.

139. So Philo, *De Vita Mosis* 1.25.141, and Jubilees 48:18. In *Berakoth* 9b the rabbis emphasize that the Israelites did not want to "borrow" from the Egyptians and were satisfied merely with regaining their freedom; but G-d insisted that they do so in order to fulfill the promise that He had made to Abraham (Gen 15:13–14) that they would leave Egypt with great substance.

140. Philo, *De Mutatione Nominum* 40.225, *De Vita Mosis* 2.2.9, *De Decalogo* 30.164; Macrobius on Cicero's *Somnium Scipionis* (*De Re Publica*, Book 6), cited by Wolfson, 2.220, note 146.

141. The latter remark would appear to be contradicted by the fact that the Israelites, before leaving Egypt, despoiled the Egyptians (Exod 12:36) and by the further fact (*Ant.* 3.59) that, after the victory over the Amalekites, Moses ordered the corpses of the enemies to be stripped. So also *Antiquities* 4.93, after the victory of the Amorites, and *Antiquities* 4.162, after the defeat of the Midianites. Likewise, Philo, *De Vita Mosis* 1.44.249, emphasizes the humanity (φιλανθρωπίας) shown by Moses in not even having the will to take revenge against the

Canaanites, because they were his kin. Inasmuch as Moses is depicted as the greatest of legislators, Philo's discussion (*De Vita Mosis* 2.2.8–11) of the virtues of the legislator is particularly relevant. There he enumerates four: love of humanity (φιλάνθρωπον), of justice, and of goodness, and hatred of evil.

142. So also Philo, *De Vita Mosis* 2.38.205, *De Specialibus Legibus* 1.9.53, and *Quaestiones in Exodum* 2.5. Philo, *De Vita Mosis* 1.27.149, says that the Jews are a nation destined to be consecrated above all others to offer prayers forever on behalf of the human race that it may be delivered from evil and may participate in what is good. Josephus (*Ant.* 8.117) not only repeats Solomon's prayer to G-d at the dedication of the Temple that He listen to non-Jews when they come to pray in His temple, but he adds his hope that G-d will do so in order to prove that Jews are "not inhumane by nature nor unfriendly to those who are not of our country but wish that all men equally should receive aid from Thee and enjoy Thy blessings." Strabo, 16.2.36–37.761, says that Moses and his immediate successors acted righteously and piously toward G-d, but that later superstitious people introduced various laws and customs that served to separate the Jews from other peoples.

143. Philo, *De Mutatione Nominum* 22.128–29, also takes the opportunity to remark that Moses earned his title "G-d's man" through his beneficence (εὐεργετεῖν), which is a peculiarly divine prerogative.

144. So also Gager, 23.

145. On the importance of piety for the various key figures in Josephus's paraphrase of the Bible, see my "Pro-Jewish," 228, note 71. Attridge, 116, note 2, cites twelve major biblical characters who are said to possess this virtue but does not list Moses. Similarly, for Philo (*De Praemiis et Poenis* 9.53 and *De Vita Mosis* 2.13.66) piety is the key virtue of Moses.

146. Philo (*De Specialibus Legibus* 1.8.41, 2.32.201, 4.34.176; *De Virtutibus* 11.75, 32.174) refers to Moses as a hierophant (ἱεροφάντης), the technical term that designates the highest officer of the heathen mysteries and the demonstrator of its sacred knowledge. Philo (*De Sacrificiis Abelis et Caini* 38.130) also refers to him as high priest. The most essential quality required of a priest, as Philo (*De Vita Mosis* 2.13.66) notes, is piety; and this, he says, Moses possessed to a very high degree.

147. *Ant.* 2.327 vs. Exod 14:13; *Ant.* 4.320 vs. Deut 33:1. See my "Prophets." So also Philo, *Legum Allegoria* 2.1.1, and Wolfson, 2.16–20.

148. This statement, that Moses' final song contains a prediction of events to come, agrees with rabbinic tradition; see *Sifre Deuteronomy* 307–33, *Midrash Tannaim* 192–204, and Yerushalmi Targumim ad loc., cited by Ginzberg, 6.155, note 920.

149. In arriving at this term, Josephus, as Yehoshua Amir, "Θεοκρατία as a Concept of Political Philosophy," 93–105, has noted, was undoubtedly influenced by Plato (*Laws* 4.712B), who remarks that the ideal state should bear the name of G-d, who is the true ruler of rational man.

150. So also Philo, *De Specialibus Legibus* 1.12.67: "He [Moses] provided that there should not be temples built either in many places or many in the same place, for he judged that since G-d is one, there should be also only one temple."

151. From this context it would appear that Jannes and Lotapes were Jews,

though other sources refer to Jannes as an Egyptian magician and as an opponent of Moses. The name Lotapes is an enigma, because the Egyptian magician with whom Jannes is usually coupled is Jambres. Reinach, 282, note 1, says that the name Lotapes should be understood to refer to Iambres or Mambres or perhaps Artapanus, who would be the inventor of the story of Jannes. In a postscript Reinach, 363, mentions an ingenious, if unconvincing, explanation by Joseph Derenbourg, that Lotapes is due to *Lat-ob* from the phrase *ba'alat 'ob* ("medium," 1 Sam 28:7). Charles C. Torrey, "The Magic of 'Lotapes,'" tries to show that it is a corrupt form of the Tetragrammaton. On Moses' reputation as a magician, see Gager, 134–61.

152. Gager, 138.

153. The fact that Moses is referred to as Musaeus is a clear compliment, as we have previously noted, in view of Musaeus's standing as a supreme poet and musician, the son or teacher or pupil of the renowned Orpheus himself, many of whose characteristics he assumed.

154. So Chadwick, 21, note 2.

155. So Origen, *Against Celsus* 2.50.

156. This is acknowledged by those who were opposed to him, as we see in rabbinic references (e.g., *Sanhedrin* 107b) and in the medieval *Toledoth Yeshu* admitting his ability as a magician. On Jesus as a magician, see Morton Smith, *Jesus the Magician*.

157. See "Dialogue," 111.

158. See Norman O. Brown, *Hermes The Thief: The Evolution of a Myth*.

159. See Gager, 142–43. Cf. Philo's statement (*De Cherubim* 14.49)—one of the very few that are autobiographical in his works—that he himself had been initiated "under Moses the G-d-beloved into his greater mysteries."

160. Francis L. Griffith and Herbert Thompson, eds., *The Demotic Magical Papyrus of London and Leiden*, 3 vols., cited by Gager, 144–46.

161. So Gager, 135.

162. See Gager, 152–53, and "Dialogue," 111, which cites Marcellin P. E. Berthelot and Charles-Emile Ruelle, *Collection des anciens alchimistes grecs*, vol. 1, 2–3.

163. So Gager, 136.

CHAPTER 9

1. The literature on proselytism is enormous. The most important works are Heinrich H. Graetz, *Die jüdischen Proselyten im Römerreiche unter den Kaisern Domitian, Nerva, Trajan und Hadrian*; Alfred Bertholet, *Die Stellung der Israeliten und der Juden zu den Fremden*; Harnack, 1–8; Joachim Jeremias, *Jerusalem zur Zeit Jesu. Kulturgeschichtliche Untersuchung zur neutestamentlichen Zeitgeschichte*, 3d ed., 246–67 (English trans. by F. H. and C. H. Cave, *Jerusalem in the Time of Jesus: An Investigation into Economic and Social Conditions during the New Testament Period*, 320–34); George F. Moore, *Judaism in the First Centuries of the Christian Era: The Age of the Tannaim*, vol. 1, 323–53; Samuel Bialoblocki, *Die Beziehungen des Judentums zu Proselyten und Proselytentum*; Frederick M. Derwachter, *Preparing the Way for Paul: The Proselyte Movement in Later Judaism*; Bamberger; Braude;

Wolfson, 2.352–74; Peter Dalbert, *Die Theologie der hellenistisch-jüdischen Missionsliteratur unter Ausschluss von Philo und Josephus*; David Bosch, *Die Heidenmission in der Zukunftsschau Jesu: Eine Untersuchung zur Eschatologie der synoptischen Evangelien*; Ernst Lerle, *Proselytenwerburg und Urchristentum*; Karl G. Kuhn and Hartmut Stegemann, "Proselyten"; Ferdinand Hahn, *Das Verständnis der Mission im Neuen Testament*; Uriel Rappaport, "Jewish Religious Propaganda and Proselytism in the Period of the Second Commonwealth" [in Hebrew]; Karl G. Kuhn, "Προσήλυτος"; R. De Ridder, *The Dispersion of the People of G-d* (1971; reprinted in 1975 as *Discipling the Nations*); Edward P. Sanders, "The Covenant as a Soteriological Category and the Nature of Salvation in Palestinian and Hellenistic Judaism," 25–38; Joseph R. Rosenbloom, *Conversion to Judaism: From the Biblical Period to the Present*, 40–60; Shaye J. D. Cohen, "Conversion to Judaism in Historical Perspective: From Biblical Israel to Postbiblical Judaism"; Louis H. Feldman, "Proselytism and Syncretism" [in Hebrew], 188–207, 340–45, 378–80; Georgi; Fergus Millar, "Gentiles and Judaism: 'G-d-Fearers' and Proselytes"; Simon, 271–305; Shaye J. D. Cohen, "Crossing the Boundary and Becoming a Jew"; and Scot McKnight, *A Light among the Gentiles: Jewish Missionary Activity in the Second Temple Period*.

2. Both the rabbis (*Yevamoth* 22a) and their opponents, such as Tacitus (*Histories* 5.5.2), realized this.

3. The citizenship law of 451–450 B.C.E., attributed to Pericles (Aristotle, *Athenian Constitution* 26.4; Plutarch, *Pericles* 37.3; Aelian, *Varia Historia* 6.10), actually tightened up on the extension of citizenship by bestowing it only on those who could prove that both their parents were citizens of Athens.

4. See Shaye J. D. Cohen, "Conversion to Judaism in Historical Perspective," 31–34.

5. Solomon Zeitlin, "Proselytes and Proselytism during the Second Commonwealth and the Early Tannaitic Period," 873, contends that the word *mitheyaḥadim* does not mean "became Jews" but rather "pretended to be Judaeans." His evidence is that at the time of the composition of the Book of Esther there could not have been conversions to Judaism. But this is begging the question, inasmuch as we have no evidence one way or the other, aside from this statement, as to whether conversion was possible at that time.

6. The chief work that attempted to establish this thesis was Bamberger's. Almost simultaneously, with the same conclusion, the work by another Reform rabbi, Braude, appeared.

7. George F. Moore, *Judaism in the First Centuries of the Christian Era: The Age of the Tannaim*, vol. 1, 323–24.

8. For a list and discussion, see Bamberger, 174–226.

9. 1 Enoch 48:4, 90:30–33; Tobit 13:11; Ben Sira 66:11–17; *Testament of Simeon* 7:2; *Testament of Levi* 18:2–9; *Testament of Judah* 24:6, 25:5; *Testament of Zebulon* 9:8; *Testament of Benjamin* 9:2, 10:5–10; *Sibylline Oracles* 5:493–500; 4 Ezra 6:26; 2 Baruch 68:5. See McKnight, 35–38.

10. Goodman, 184.

11. So Shaye J. D. Cohen, "Respect for Judaism by Gentiles according to Josephus."

12. Such a conclusion does not necessarily follow, if we may look at the stand taken by the Roman Catholic Church, especially since Vatican II, in its interpretation of *extra ecclesiam nulla salus*.

13. McKnight, 88.

14. Ibid., 79.

15. Ibid., 43.

16. Salo W. Baron, "Population," 869.

17. Baron, 1.170, and especially 370–72, note 7.

18. Harnack, 1–8.

19. See Karl W. Butzer, *Early Hydraulic Civilization in Egypt: A Study in Cultural Ecology*, 91–92.

20. Among those who have accepted the view that Judaism was an active and successful missionary religion during this period are Karl G. Kuhn, "Προσήλυτος"; and Georgi, 83–84 and notes 1–15. In a most recent study, Scot McKnight, "Jewish Missionary Activity: The Evidence of Demographics and Synagogues," 10, cites the words of Salo W. Baron, in "Population," 866: "In the eyes of demographers bent on scientific precision and certainty all demographic research undertaken for any period before the eighteenth century runs the risk of appearing as a mere fantasy. . . . Ancient and medieval censuses, even when recorded, were taken too far apart, and used unknown or, at least, variable statistical methods. Hence they furnish almost no guidance for the prevailing trends." McKnight, 29, note 40, cannot believe that 1,650,000 Jews were wiped out, as Baron postulates, between 1000 and 586 B.C.E.; but he has apparently forgotten that for practical purposes ten of the twelve tribes of Israel were eliminated in 722–721 B.C.E. But even McKnight, 11, is ready to concede a figure of six million Jews in the first century C.E. He says that until we can discern other important contributing factors—among which he suggests importation and survival rate—we lack the evidence needed to permit inferences about trends. As to importation, this would involve merely shifts of Jews from one area to another; and although we have no specific data on changes in life expectancy from one period to another, even a casual examination of the many thousands of tombstone inscription that have come down to us and very frequently do give the age at death confirms the conclusion that there were no major changes during the period of antiquity. McKnight, 12, stresses that at no point does Baron suggest that demographic changes from the period 586 B.C. to 70 C.E. can be explained only on the basis of proselytism; but if not proselytism, what other factor can account for such an astounding increase? Moreover, although Baron, 1.370, note 7, is careful to stress that his population estimates are based on scattered documentary evidence, often very dubious in itself, a series of hypotheses, supplementing this evidence, support one another in their convergence. In particular, we may cite the statement of Bar-Hebraeus, a thirteenth-century Christian writer, who reports that there were 6,944,000 Jews, according to the census taken by the Emperor Claudius in the middle of the first century, to which Baron, 1.170, despite Bar-Hebraeus's late date, gives credence. Such a figure is supported by statements of Josephus, who, as general in Galilee, must have had an awareness of the population of the area where he was commander. His figures, which cannot be total figments

of imagination, indicate that there were 204 villages in Galilee (*Life* 235), of which the smallest had 15,000 inhabitants (*War* 3.587–88), making a total of 3,060,000. Furthermore, on the basis of the number of lambs consumed at Passover in the year 66, he states that there were 2,700,000 (actually 2,556,000) Jews in Jerusalem (*War* 6.425; this in addition to those who were ritually defiled and who could not therefore partake of the lambs) and that 1,100,000 Jews perished during the siege of Jerusalem (*War* 6.420).

We must add Josephus's claim (*Ant.* 11.133) that in Mesopotamia there were countless myriads of Jews, "whose number cannot be ascertained." Furthermore, Philo, who as the head of the Alexandrian Jewish community must have had considerable knowledge as to the number of Jews in Egypt, explicitly states (*In Flaccum* 6.43) that the governor of Egypt knew that in Egypt there were no fewer than a million Jews. See my discussion, *JMS*, 366–69. Thomas H. Hollingsworth, in *Historical Demography*, 295–319, whom McKnight, 26, note 25, cites to support his skepticism with regard to population estimates, does indeed caution the student to be aware of the limits of demographic research for historical analysis. To be sure, Hollingsworth, 252, notes that copying errors in figures cited in records are by no means uncommon. On 307–8 he cites, with some degree of confidence, figures that indicate tremendous fluctuations in the population of ancient Egypt, from between twenty and twenty-five million in 525 B.C.E. to between twelve and thirteen million in 50 B.C.E. to seven and a half million in 75 C.E. to thirty million in 541 C.E. But even these figures do not come close to the changes in Jewish population charted by Baron; and in any case the key factor is how to account for the tremendous increase in population within a comparatively short period of time.

21. Cf. a similar view in the Pseudepigraphic *Testament of Benjamin* 5.1–5, dating from the second or first century B.C.E.

22. See Robert Doran, *Temple Propaganda: The Purpose and Character of 2 Maccabees*, 111–13.

23. So Solomon Zeitlin, ed., *The Second Book of Maccabees*, 184.

24. Though some passages in the *Testament of Levi* are clearly Christian additions, the *Testament* as a whole, including this passage, is pre-Christian. See James H. Charlesworth, *The Pseudepigrapha and Modern Research with a Supplement*, 212.

25. Like the *Testament of Levi*, the *Testament of Joseph*, in its present form, is a Christian work dating from the second half of the second century C.E. Nevertheless, the discovery of portions of the *Testaments of the Twelve Patriarchs*, to which these belong, among the Dead Sea Qumran scrolls is an indication that the original version is a Jewish work that dates from before the destruction of the Qumran community in 70 C.E. and may be as early as the second century B.C.E. Braun, 54, note 3, concedes that the passage in the *Testament of Joseph* in which Potiphar's wife offers to convert and to get her husband to convert to Judaism may be a later interpolation; but he sees no compelling reason for accepting this hypothesis. We may add that there is every reason to believe that the height of the proselyting movement was reached before the destruction of the Temple in 70 and that the movement, although certainly continuing thereafter, had started to decline in numbers.

26. See Braun, 52.

27. That the reference in Philo is to proselytes is clear from his statement (*De Virtutibus* 20.102) that the incomers have abandoned "their kinsfolk by blood, their country, their customs and the temples and images of their gods" and "have taken the journey to a better home, from idle fables to the clear vision of truth and the worship of the one and truly existing G-d."

28. The reference here may be not only to proselytes but also to "sympathizers," as Edith Mary Smallwood, ed., *Philonis Alexandrini Legatio ad Gaium*, 269–70, indicates.

29. Philo gives a similar reason in *De Specialibus Legibus* 1.57.309, where he has an attack on pagan "customs packed with false inventions and vanity." Such an outburst is most uncharacteristic of Philo in view of his sensitivity to the charge of Jewish aggressiveness in proselytizing.

30. Josephus apparently felt that he had to be extremely careful not to offend his Roman hosts by referring to the inroads the Jews had made through proselytism into the Roman populace. It is surely significant that in the *Antiquities*, aside from the passage (*Ant.* 20.17–96) about the conversion of the royal family of Adiabene (which was, after all, under Parthian domination, and hence of no immediate concern to the Romans), Josephus nowhere propagandizes openly for proselytism. An interesting case in point may be seen in Josephus's treatment of the Book of Jonah. The picture of the non-Jewish sailors in the biblical book is of pious men who shift from the worship of their own pagan gods (Jonah 1:5) to the worship of the Hebrew G-d. In fact, we are told (Jonah 1:16) that they feared the L-rd exceedingly and that they offered a sacrifice to the L-rd and made vows. The picture in Josephus is very different. There is no indication in Josephus that the sailors were or were not Jews or that they prayed to their own individual gods; instead (*Ant.* 9.209), we are told very simply that the sailors began to pray, without being told to whom they were praying. The rabbinic tradition (*Pirqe de-Rabbi Eliezer* 10, *Tanḥuma Vayikra* 8, *Midrash Jonah* 97), on the other hand, stresses the non-Jewish origin of the sailors by noting that on the vessel were representatives of the seventy nations of the world. See now my "Josephus's Interpretation of Jonah."

31. See my "Abraham," 143–56.

32. In Leonhard Spengel, *Rhetores Graeci*, 3.366.

33. Of the 534 inscriptions from the Jewish congregations of ancient Rome, as noted by Leon, 253–54, only seven indubitable proselytes are to be counted. But this relative paucity of evidence from inscriptions about proselytes may well be explained by the reluctance of proselytes to advertise on tombstones their religious status.

34. Among others who have affirmed at length that this statement in Matthew reflects reality, we may cite Axenfeld, 36–46.

35. McKnight, 106–7, interprets Matthew 23:15 to refer to the attempt of the Pharisees to impose their understanding of the Law on Gentile "G-d-fearers." But there is no indication in the word *proselyte* that is here used that the reference is to such a group.

36. For other possible interpretations and a convincing refutation thereof, see Bamberger, 267–71.

37. We may have another allusion to proselytes in Horace's description (*Satires* 1.4.10) of a poet scribbling bad verses while "standing on one foot," which was the phrase used by the proselyte who approached Rabbi Hillel, Horace's contemporary (*Shabbath* 31a), and asked to be taught the entire Torah while standing on one foot.

38. So Georgi, 97.

39. John Nolland, "Proselytism or Politics in Horace, *Satires* I, 4, 138–143?" is followed by McKnight, 64, in arguing that Horace is here referring not to proselyting activities but to political influence, such as Cicero imputes to the Jews (*Pro Flacco* 28.66); but their skepticism is based on their unwillingness to believe that Horace has in mind the kind of forced acceptance of Judaism that was imposed on the Idumaeans in the Maccabean period. If, however, the Jews were as eager and as successful in proselytism as we have indicated, such a reservation seems unjustified. In any case, the passage in Horace speaks clearly of forcing others, that is, non-Jews, to join the Jews in their activities. There is nothing in the passage in Cicero that speaks of Jews seeking to get non-Jews to join them as a pressure group.

40. So William S. Anderson, "Horace, the Unwilling Warrior, *Satire* I, 9." Indeed, throughout the satire, Horace employs a large number of epic and martial expressions, reminding the reader of the Homeric scene (*Iliad* 20.443) where Hector is saved from Achilles by the intervention of Apollo.

41. Apollo might well—and ironically—remind the reader of the very similarly named Apella in the apparently proverbial phrase *credat Iudaeus Apella* (*Satires* 1.5.100), which we have noted above, alluding to the Jews' credulity. This connection takes on additional significance when we consider that in his remarks on this passage, the commentator Porphyrio gives the etymology of Apella as coming from alpha privative + *pellis*, that is, without a foreskin, hence a reference to circumcision, the most prominent identifying symbol of the Jew, as we find in numerous snide remarks by ancient writers. Consequently, we can appreciate the irony of having Apollo, whose name reminds one so much of the circumcised Jew Apella, rescuing Horace from *curtis Iudaeis* ("the circumcised Jews") mentioned in the line (*Satires* 1.9.70) after the *tricesima Sabbata*. We may also suggest that there is a deliberate pun in Horace's remark that, in deferring to the religious sensibilities of the Jews, his friend has left him under the knife (*cultro*, line 74, so similar in sound to the word "circumcised," *curtis*, line 70, and perhaps alluding to the use of a knife in circumcision). Moreover, in the statement that Apollo has "saved" (*servavit*) the poet, Horace is alluding to his being saved by medical skill, a meaning (*Oxford Latin Dictionary*, under the listing *servo* 9) that *servo* does have; and hence it is Apollo the god of medicine who is here referred to. This significance may be further enhanced by the allusion to the surgical knife, *cultro* (line 74), under which the poet finds himself, another mock reference perhaps to circumcision, as we have noted.

42. So Abraham J. Malherbe, *Social Aspects of Early Christianity*, 51–52.

43. Dio's words are: "I do not know how this title [i.e., "Jews"] came to be given them, but it applies also to all the rest of mankind, although of alien race, who affect their customs. This class exists even among the Romans, and though often repressed (κολουσθέν, "put down," "cut short," "abased") has increased to a very great extent and has won its way to the right of freedom in its observances."

The fact that Dio, in the same breath, so to speak, mentions the spread of Judaism to non-Jews and their frequent suppression would seem to indicate a cause-and-effect relationship.

44. We should note that the two epitomists of Valerius Maximus are both very late, approximately half a millennium after the time of Valerius Maximus.

45. Perhaps, as we have noted, simply "Jews," inasmuch as Latin does not have an article.

46. Emil Schürer, *Geschichte des jüdischen Volkes im Zeitalter Jesu Christi*, 4th ed., vol. 3, part 4, 59; Leon, 2–4. Because of the stark contrast between the favorable answer given to the envoys of the Maccabees and the expulsion of the Jewish community from Rome, Salvatore Alessandri, in "La presunta cacciata dei Giudei da Roma nel 139 a. Cr.," concludes that the expulsion never took place, especially in view of the excellent relations then existing between Rome and Judaea. But Stern, 1.359–60, convincingly points out, on the basis of the fragments of the epitome of Livy found at Oxyrhynchus (*POxy* no. 668, 1.191), that the praenomen Lucius in Julius Paris's epitome of Valerius Maximus is mistaken, that the Hasmonean embassy should be dated to 142 B.C.E., and that there was no connection between the embassy and the expulsion of the Jews in 139 B.C.E. Smallwood, 130, takes an intermediate position in suggesting not that the envoys engaged in proselyting activities but rather that the Jewish community of Rome, seeing the favorable reception that the envoys received, concluded that the Romans approved of their religion as well as of their nation and thus felt inspired to engage in missionary activity. But it is hard to believe that a new and small community would have been so ignorant of the Roman attachment to their cult and so self-confident as to undertake such proselyting, especially in view of the vigorous Roman reaction to the Bacchanalian rites a half century before. Surely they must have realized that the only reason why the Romans had formed an alliance with the tiny nation of Judaea was that they had a common enemy, the Syrian Seleucids.

47. Eugene N. Lane, "Sabazius and the Jews in Valerius Maximus: A Reexamination," argues against the thesis that the Jews were accused of attempting to spread Jewish practices or to promote a syncretism, noting that such a view depends on a tenth-century manuscript of a late-antique epitomist of Valerius Maximus and is contradicted by our other manuscripts. The fact, however, that we have two separate epitomes, neither of them dependent on the other, that declare that the Jews had attempted (*conati erant*) to foist their religion on the Romans would seem to argue against Lane. As for the date of the manuscript of the epitomist, as late as the tenth century, many, if not most, of our classical texts depend on manuscripts that are no older.

48. Or alternatively, we may call attention to the statement (*Berakoth* 19a and *Pesaḥim* 53a) of the third-century Rabbi Joseph that a certain Roman Jew named Thaddeus accustomed the Roman Jews to eat kids roasted whole on the eve of Passover, even though, as Simeon ben Shetaḥ in the first century B.C.E. reminded him, it was prohibited to do so outside the Temple of Jerusalem.

49. Franz Dornseiff, "Verschmähtes zu Vergil, Horaz, und Properz," 65, has even suggested, on the basis of innuendo, though without any proof, that Horace's father was a proselyte.

50. Josephus also, significantly it would seem, places this expulsion in immedi-

ate juxtaposition with a scandal at the temple of Isis in Rome (*Ant.* 18.65–80). This scandal, he says (*Ant.* 18.65), occurred simultaneously with the incident that led to the expulsion of the Jews.

51. Williams, 767–68.

52. Williams, 779–84.

53. See A. J. Marshall, "Flaccus and the Jews of Asia—Cicero Pro Flacco 28.67–69."

54. Josephus sought to win the favor of the emperor himself, as well as of the intellectuals, who, as we know, decried conversionary activity. Therefore, as Georgi, 95, remarks, he suppressed as far as possible the fact that the expulsion was due to Jewish missionary activity. For the same reason he omits the assertion, found in Suetonius (*Tiberius* 36), that not only Judaism but also the Egyptian and other foreign cults were abolished, inasmuch as this might have led the reader to conclude that the Jews, being thus grouped with other missionary cults, were similarly guilty of aggressive proselytism.

55. Abel, 383–86. Cf. Horst R. Moehring, "The Persecution of the Jews and the Adherents of the Isis Cult at Rome A.D. 19."

56. After quoting Suetonius's statement that Claudius expelled the Jews who were constantly making disturbances at the instigation of Chrestus (he reads Christus rather than Chrestus), Orosius shows his tendentious nature when he proceeds to add, "As to whether he had commanded that the Jews rioting against Christ to be restrained and checked or also had wanted the Christians as persons of a cognate religion to be expelled, it is not at all to be discerned." Suetonius, it will be recalled, speaks of the Jews as rioting not *against* Christ but rather at the *instigation* of Chrestus. As to ascription to Josephus by Christians of statements that he did not write, one is reminded of Origen's remark (*Commentary on Matthew* 10:17, *Against Celsus* 1.47 and 2.13) that Josephus placed the blame for the destruction of the Temple in Jerusalem on the execution of James by the Jews. This statement is not to be found in our manuscripts of Josephus, although he does recount the death of James (*Ant.* 20.200–203).

57. Of course, it is distinctly possible that Suetonius and Dio Cassius are speaking of two different events, inasmuch as Suetonius speaks of an expulsion and Dio specifically denies this; but it may well be that Dio is here contesting the view that an expulsion had occurred in that year. In any case, the important point for our purposes is the reason for Claudius's action, whether or not he expelled the Jews, and that is the tumult that they had aroused, presumably through their proselyting activities.

58. See Dixon Slingerland, "Suetonius *Claudius* 25.4 and the Account in Dio Cassius," 307–16. Another possible reference to this expulsion of the Jews may be found in an enigmatic passage in Philo (*Legatio ad Gaium* 23.157), in which he praises the Emperor Augustus for not expelling the Jews from Rome or depriving them of their Roman citizenship. Because it is most likely, despite Slingerland, 315–16, that the *Legatio ad Gaium* was written in or soon after the year 41, as E. Mary Smallwood, ed., *Philonis Alexandrini Legatio ad Gaium* 151 and 238, indicates, the digression about Augustus would seem to have been brought in to compare unfavorably Claudius, who had just become emperor, with the great Augustus, who should have been his model. The scholiast (ca. 400) on Juvenal, as

Stern, 2.655, remarks, speaks of an expulsion of Jews from Rome, but there is some dispute as to whether it is the expulsion under Tiberius or that under Claudius, or whether it may not even refer to still another expulsion.

59. Tcherikover, however ("Prolegomena," 73–74), successfully contests the view that Claudius was pro-Jewish and points out that his edict (*Ant.* 19.280–85) with respect to the Jews and especially his famous letter (*CPJ* 2, no. 153) show that he was actually evenhanded and that he vigorously opposed any attempt by the Jews to upset the status quo with regard to their rights and privileges.

60. See the discussion by Stern, 2.113–17.

61. John J. Collins, "A Symbol of Otherness: Circumcision and Salvation in the First Century," 170.

62. Alf Thomas Kraabel, "The Roman Diaspora: Six Questionable Assumptions," 451–52.

63. McKnight, 74.

64. As Segal, xiv, correctly remarks, there is little evidence in Paul's letters that he thought of himself as leaving Judaism. Paul, dating from the middle of the first century, would seem to be more nearly contemporary evidence for first-century Judaism than the Mishnah, which dates from about 220 C.E. The Galilean Jew Eleazar (Josephus, *Ant.* 20.43–45), who was responsible for arousing in Izates, the king of Adiabene, the need for circumcision, is sometimes regarded as a missionary; but there is no indication of this in Josephus, who declares (*Ant.* 20.44) that he came to Izates to pay him his respects.

65. Axenfeld, 46, 53–54.

66. Victor Tcherikover, "Jewish Apologetic Literature Reconsidered." Tcherikover's view is endorsed by Nikolaus Walter, "*Pseudepigraphische jüdisch-hellenistische Dichtung: Pseudo-Phokylides, Pseudo-Orpheus, Gefälschte Verse auf Namen griechischen Dichter,*" 178.

67. As to Tcherikover's amazement that no fragments of Plutarch have thus far been discovered, see Eric G. Turner, *Greek Papyri: An Introduction,* 97, who notes that in the last few years, for the first time, pieces of both Plutarch and Libanius have been recognized and published.

68. Only one fragment of any of the works of Josephus (*War* 2.576–79, 582–84) has been found so far. It has been published by Hans Oellacher, *Griechische literarische Papyri,* 61–63. As to the Graeco-Jewish and anti-Jewish writers, we may note that prose fragments are notoriously difficult to identify.

69. So Harris, 175–90.

70. So Victor Tcherikover, "Jewish Apologetic Literature Reconsidered," 173.

71. Lewis, 61–63.

72. See Harris, 145.

73. See, for example, Nepos, *Atticus* 1; Cicero, *Ad Atticum* 8.4.1; Valerius Maximus 2.7.6; Plutarch, *Cato the Elder* 20; and Suetonius, *Augustus* 48, 64. So also Plautus (*Mostellaria* 126), in enumerating what parents do in raising their children, says that they teach them letters (*litteras,* "literature"), though there is some question whether this reflects the time and place of the Greek comedy (Athens in the fourth century B.C.E.), from which the plot of his play was taken, or Rome at the time of Plautus at the end of the third century B.C.E.

74. André Balland, *Fouilles de Xanthos*, 7, no. 67 (= *Supplementum Epigraphicum Graecum* 30 [1980]: no. 1535).

75. See Martial 8.3.15–16 and 9.68.1–2; and Valerius Maximus 6.1.3. Harris, 239, admits that this is probably enough evidence for the city of Rome in Martial's own time, though he refuses to agree with Marrou that as many girls attended school as did boys.

76. For the evidence, see Harris, 255–59.

77. Harris, 121.

78. Harris, 206.

79. Even Harris, 282, is ready to admit the latter fact.

80. Emma J. Edelstein and Ludwig Edelstein, *Asclepius: A Collection and Interpretation of the Testimonies*, 1, no. 423, cited by Harris, 124.

81. See Wayne A. Meeks, *The First Urban Christians: The Social World of the Apostle Paul*, 143, 146.

82. See Martin F. Smith, "Fifty-five New Fragments of Diogenes of Oenoanda," 44.

83. Nock, 179.

84. John G. Winter, *Life and Letters in the Papyri*, 266. As to the unrepresentative nature of the papyri, because we have them from only villages and towns of Middle and Upper Egypt, see William H. Willis, "Greek Literary Papyri from Egypt and the Classical Canon," 24. Willis, "A Census of the Literary Papyri from Egypt," 205–6, correctly stresses that Egypt was in many ways, notably in geography, tradition, and political isolation, a province atypical of the rest. The unrepresentative nature of the fragments is also stressed by Eric G. Turner, "Roman Oxyrhynchus," 90–91, who notes that thus far no papyri have been found of such important writers as Lucian, Dio Cassius, Appian, Athenaeus, and Diogenes Laertius.

85. Winter, *Life and Letters*, 194–95.

86. So Charles H. Oldfather, *The Greek Literary Texts from Greco-Roman Egypt: A Study in the History of Civilization*, 67.

87. Lewis, 59.

88. So Winter, *Life and Letters*, 274.

89. Frederic G. Kenyon, "The Library of a Greek at Oxyrhynchus," 131.

90. So Kenyon, 130.

91. So Frederic G. Kenyon, *Books and Readers in Ancient Greece*, 2d ed., 80–81. For a complete listing of the literary fragments, see Roger A. Pack, *The Greek and Latin Literary Texts from Greco-Roman Egypt*, 2d ed., who enumerates 2,771 literary papyri that had been discovered by 1964. Eric G. Turner, *Greek Papyri: An Introduction*, 45, remarks that at least as many texts still await an editor as have been published and that (p. 128) papyri are still being discovered in Egypt faster than scholars can transcribe and edit them.

92. See Frederic G. Kenyon and Colin H. Roberts, "Libraries."

93. Harris, 228–29.

94. Lewis, 61.

95. So Stern, 2.383.

96. Harris, 266–67.

97. So Harris, 173, 252. See Lewis, 62–63. Harris, 140, points out that Herodas's small audience of educated urban Greeks apparently found nothing startling in the fact that in his third mime, "The Schoolmaster," dating from the third century B.C.E., the mother of the schoolboy is literate.

98. See Segal, 85, who suggests the possibility that apologetic works were used for missionary purposes as well as for their more obvious use in Gentile education. He there argues that apologetics were the primary motivation of Jews living under Hellenized influence, whereas missionary literature was characteristic of less acculturated Jews. But the greatest success of proselytism would seem to have been in the Diaspora, where the more acculturated Jews lived, who presumably were capable of communicating more readily with the pagans.

99. Momigliano, 91.

100. Nock, 79.

101. Victor Tcherikover, "Jewish Apologetic Literature Reconsidered," 177.

102. *Pace* Nock, 79.

103. Cf. Stern, 1.133.

104. See Walter Burkert, "Zur Geistesgeschichtlichen Einordnung einiger Pseudopythagorica," 49–51. Burkert also maintains that the Neo-Pythagorean philosopher Onatas was aware of the challenge of Jewish monotheism.

105. For a listing and extended discussion of the more important of these papyri, see Sidney Jellicoe, *The Septuagint and Modern Study*, 224–42. As of 1949, Colin H. Roberts, in "The Christian Book and the Greek Papyri," 155, note 2, had counted 116 papyrus fragments of the Septuagint dating from the second through the fourth century.

106. For a survey of apologetic literature from a Jewish point of view, see Moritz Friedländer, *Geschichte der jüdischen Apologetik als Vorgeschichte des Christentums*; and Judah Bergmann, *Jüdische Apologetik im neutestamentlichen Zeitalter*.

107. Despite the apparently explicit injunction (Deut 23:4) that Ammonites and Moabites are not permitted to "enter into the congregation of the L-rd forever," that is, to be converted to Judaism, the rabbis (Mishnah, *Yevamoth* 8:3) ruled that this prohibition was restricted to males and even (*Berakoth* 28a) went so far as to declare that the inhabitants of these countries in later times were not descended from the original Ammonites and Moabites, inasmuch as the Assyrian king Sennacherib had long ago "mixed up all nations."

108. "Prolegomena," 42.

109. Cf. Philo, *De Specialibus Legibus* 4.18.105–19.109.

110. Cf. Wolfson, 1.132–33.

111. On *Joseph and Asenath* as missionary propaganda, see Victor Aptowitzer, "Asenath, the Wife of Joseph: A Haggadic Literary-Historical Study," 305–6; Marc Philonenko, *Joseph et Aséneth*, 106–7; and George W. E. Nickelsburg, *Jewish Literature between the Bible and the Mishnah: A Historical and Literary Introduction*, 262. *Contra* McKnight, 60–62, who stresses that it is Asenath who takes the initiative in seeking conversion to Judaism and that it is not Joseph who seeks her out. But precisely such a theme would have proved most effective in the hands of a missionary, because it would show that a wise Gentile would eagerly take the initiative in seeking conversion to Judaism. In "The Social Setting and Purpose

of Joseph and Asenath," Randall D. Chesnutt argues against the thesis that *Joseph and Asenath* was a missionary tract, stressing that the author presupposes too much in assuming that his readers are familiar with the biblical story of Joseph as well as with other patriarchal narratives; but, as Nickelsburg remarks, the fact that the story is told from the point of view of the proselyte Asenath indicates that it is written for a Gentile audience. Even Chesnutt agrees, moreover, that the central purpose of the treatise is to enhance the status of Gentile converts in the Jewish community.

112. So Diodorus 1.96–98; Plutarch, *De Iside et Osiride* 10.354 D-E.

113. Hengel, 1.167–69.

114. So Howard Jacobson, *The Exagoge of Ezekiel*, 8–13.

115. Ibid., 20–23.

116. Ibid., 8.

117. Ibid., 17. Victor Tcherikover, "Jewish Apologetic Literature Reconsidered," 179, says that the play has nothing in common with apologetics; but, as Jacobson, 181, note 4, correctly remarks, he is demonstrably wrong, because the modifications in the biblical narrative are clearly apologetic and in particular are intended to counteract the anti-Jewish Exodus-traditions of Manetho and others that were current in Alexandria at the time the play was composed, which Jacobson (pp. 5–13) assigns to the second century B.C.E.

118. So Erwin R. Goodenough, "Philo's Exposition of the Law and His *De Vita Mosis*."

119. Georgi, 182, concludes that both Jews and Gentiles are being addressed throughout Philo's works.

120. Nock, 79.

121. Ibid., 286.

122. The remark of Georgi, 65, that the method of proselyting was through inviting pagans into synagogues to hear displays of preaching rests on his quotation of Philo (*De Specialibus Legibus* 2.15.62) that synagogues "stand wide open to outsiders."

123. Victor Tcherikover, "Jewish Apologetic Literature Reconsidered," 183.

124. Lucio Troiani, "I lettori delle Antichità giudaiche di Giuseppe. Prospettive e problemi," argues that the readers for whom the *Antiquities* is intended are, for the most part, not Gentiles but the numerous Hellenized Jews, who exercised important religious functions throughout the empire. We may, however, reply that we do not have a single fragment of any Hellenized Jewish author quoting from or otherwise indicating indebtedness to Josephus's work or even mentioning him by name.

125. See my "Hellenizations," 337–38.

126. Victor Tcherikover, "Jewish Apologetic Literature," 181.

127. So Robert McL. Wilson, "Jewish Literary Propaganda," 71.

128. See Nock, *Conversion*, 164–86; and Georgi, 99–100 and 187–88, notes 111 and 112.

129. So Seneca the Elder, *Controversiae* 4, praef. 2. See Margherita Guarducci, "Poeti vaganti e conferenzieri dell' età ellenistica," cited by Harris, 125.

130. So Harris, 208.

131. So Martin P. Nilsson, *Geschichte der griechischen Religion*, vol. 2, 3d ed., 228–29.

132. McKnight, 63, argues that there is nothing in the context to argue for Gentile attendance in these synagogues. But Philo's emphasis that there are *thousands* of schools in every city and that they stand wide open would surely imply this. It is hard to believe that there would be need of thousands of schools (an obvious exaggeration, to be sure) in every city for Jews alone.

133. So Georgi, 89.

134. Georgi, 96, calls attention to the similarity of phraseology.

135. Georgi, 99. Similarly, as Georgi, 99–100, points out, the Cynic-Stoic wandering preachers were regarded as beggars by their pagan Roman critics. Begging, says Georgi, 152, was a generally recognized religious phenomenon found among other religions and cults. The pleading for support by itinerant pneumatics who recruited for their deity or for their philosophical beliefs must have been part of that.

136. So Judah Bergmann, *Jüdische Apologetik im neutestamentlichen Zeitalter*.

137. See Baron 1.181.

138. Victor Aptowitzer, *Parteipolitik der Hasmonäerzeit im rabbinischen und pseudoepigraphischen Schrifttum* 47, theorizes that the thirteenth benediction of the Amidah, which refers to righteous proselytes, was intended as an indirect protest against the forcible conversion of the Idumaeans; but inasmuch as the benediction was included long after this event, it more probably seeks to exclude the general group of those insincere in their conversion.

139. See Stern, 1.225.

140. Aryeh Kasher, *Jews, Idumaeans, and Ancient Arabs: Relations of the Jews in Eretz-Israel with the Nations of the Frontier and the Desert during the Hellenistic and Roman Era (332 B.C.E.–70 C.E.*, 46–77, 79–85.

141. So Aaron Rothkoff, "Minor Tractates."

142. Aquila (whether he is to be identified with Onkelos, the author of the Aramaic paraphrase of the Torah who was the disciple of Rabban Gamaliel or, more probably, is a different person) translated the Bible literally into Greek under the supervision of Rabbi Eliezer and Rabbi Joshua. Alec E. Silverstone, in *Aquila and Onkelos*, regards the two as identical; but see Louis I. Rabinowitz, "Onkelos and Aquila."

143. See James H. Charlesworth, "The Concept of the Messiah in the Pseudepigrapha," who cites (p. 190) references to an eschatological Messiah in the Dead Sea Scrolls and in the Targumim. He notes (p. 217) the presence of references to the Messiah in eleven of the fifty-one books of the Pseudepigrapha, notably, among Jewish writings, in Psalms of Solomon, 2 Baruch, 4 Ezra, 1 Enoch, and 3 Enoch, dating from the second century B.C.E. to the first century C.E., for the most part.

144. So John J. Collins, "Messianism in the Maccabean Period," 98.

145. This was apparently the interpretation given to Daniel 7:13–14, 9:11–12, or 24–27; or to Micah 5:2 or perhaps to Genesis 49:10.

146. For the evidence and an evaluation thereof, see "Prolegomena," especially 11–15, 25–39.

147. Nahum Slouschz, *Hébraeo-Phéniciens et Judéo-Berbères: Introduction à l'histoire des juifs et du judaisme en Afrique* and his *Travels in North Africa*. Baron, 1.374, however, cautions that careful investigation into the ever-increasing epigraphical and archaeological materials is needed before a definitive solution can be found.

148. Baron, 1.374–75. We may add that if the relative density of inscriptions is any guide to the degree of literacy, the province with the highest density of inscriptions in Latin, at any rate, is Africa, including the area of Carthage, which was founded as a Phoenician colony. See the table in Harris, 268.

149. So Baron, 1.176–77.

150. This view is expressed by Philo (*Quaestiones in Genesin* 3.48), who contrasts the Jewish practice of circumcision on the eighth day with that of the Egyptians in the fourteenth year. He says that it is very much better and more far-sighted to perform the circumcision on infants, "for perhaps one who is full-grown would hesitate through fear to carry out this ordinance of his own free will."

151. In the first century, we may note, there was a Jewish dynasty ruling in Armenia descended from Herod. In addition, there were Jewish rulers in Chalcis, Cappadocia, Ituraea, and Abilene.

152. Josephus's lengthy account is in an easy-flowing style very different from Books 17–19 of the *Antiquities*, and we are thus tempted to suggest that Josephus had a special source for it. See Daniel R. Schwartz, "*KATA TOYTON TON KAIPON*: Josephus' Source on Agrippa II"; and Lawrence H. Schiffman, "The Conversion of the Royal House of Adiabene in Josephus and Rabbinic Sources." The latter suggests that Josephus presents the account at such length as part of his polemic against Hellenistic anti-Judaism and in particular against the charge that Jews hated all others. Another reason, we may add, is to emphasize, as Josephus had done in the *War*, the stupidity of going to war against the Romans, because Izates (*Ant.* 20.69–70), when the Parthians try to convince him to join in war against the Romans, argues that so great is the might and good fortune of the Romans that to hope to defeat them was to expect the impossible. Abraham Schalit, "Evidence of an Aramaic Source in Josephus' 'Antiquities of the Jews,' " has cited some indications to support his theory that the account is based on a source in Aramaic, but his evidence is hardly conclusive. On the embellishments in Josephus's account, see my "Introduction," *JJC*, 51. Whereas elsewhere in the *Antiquities* Josephus frowns on conversion, presumably because he did not wish to offend his Roman patrons, he glamorizes it here, apparently because the conversion occurred outside the Roman Empire and because Adiabene opposed the Parthians, the great national enemy of the Romans. Indeed, the Adiabenians' abandonment of the Parthian gods could well be understood and applauded by the Romans, because a nation was generally identified with its gods. We may also suggest that the fear expressed by Izates' mother, Helena (*Ant.* 20.39), that the Adiabenians would not tolerate the rule of a Jew over themselves may reflect the view that Parthian subjects would look askance at a Jew because the Jewish people were subjects of the Romans and, so far as Josephus was concerned, with the exception of some diehards, were loyal subjects.

153. The many troops from co-religionists in lands across the Euphrates who, according to the third-century Dio Cassius (66.4), assisted the Jewish revolutionaries, undoubtedly included numerous Adiabenians.

154. Baron, 1.210.

155. Jacob Neusner, "The Conversion of Adiabene to Judaism."

156. Cf. Daniel R. Schwartz, *Agrippa I: The Last King of Judaea*, who notes that the six kings at the conference included two pairs of brothers and that there is a good deal of evidence for Agrippa's ties with all but one of these kings.

157. Cited by Jacob Neusner, "The Jews in Pagan Armenia."

158. Leon, 66.

159. Leon, 256.

160. See Heinrich H. Graetz, *Die jüdischen Proselyten im Römerreiche unter den Kaisern Domitian, Nerva, Trajan und Hadrian.*

161. Even Tacitus, though showing contempt for the Jews, grudgingly admits (*Histories* 5.13.3) that during the siege "both men and women showed the same determination, and if they were to be forced to change their home, they feared life more than death." Dio Cassius (66.5), in a detail intentionally omitted, one would guess, by the pro-Roman Josephus, notes that a number of Roman soldiers defected to the Jews during the course of the siege, persuaded that the city was actually impregnable. We may further suggest that Josephus's extensive account (*War* 7.252–406) of the defenders of Masada, which was relatively unimportant from a military point of view, and of their grisly act of committing mutual suicide rather than submitting to the Romans might have aroused the admiration of the Romans, as indeed it did of the Roman soldiers who entered Masada and were "incredulous of such amazing fortitude" (*War* 7.405).

162. Cf. Suetonius, *Domitian* 15.1.

163. Christian tradition makes of Clemens and Domitilla martyrs during Domitian's persecution of the Christians; but by the time of Dio (150–235) the distinction between Jews and Christians was probably clear to the Roman world, as Leon, 252, remarks, though Dio himself never mentions the Christians by name.

164. The same liberal attitude toward paganism may be seen in the pressure applied by Josephus (*Life* 113) to his subordinates in Galilee not to circumcise two of Agrippa II's courtiers, on the ground that everyone should be allowed to worship G-d as one pleases.

165. See citations in McKnight, 23 and 130, note 67.

166. Baron, 1.175.

167. Bamberger, 17.

168. For the passages see McKnight, 13–14.

169. So Segal, 84.

170. Bamberger, 17.

171. Segal, 106.

172. Most recently, McKnight, 93–95, has commented on the statement of Philo (*De Vita Mosis* 1.27.147) referring to the mixed multitude who accompanied the Israelites in the Exodus from Egypt as a promiscuous, nondescript, and menial crowd who had been "converted (μετεβάλοντο) and brought over to a wiser

mind by the magnitude and the number of the successive punishments." We see here that Philo, already at the beginning of the first century, had taken a negative stand toward those who converted for dishonorable reasons. Indeed, from the vehemence of this passage one can infer that the attitude toward such converts was a live issue.

173. See John G. Gager, *The Origins of Anti-Semitism: Attitudes toward Judaism in Pagan and Christian Antiquity*; and Schürer, 3.1.150–76.

174. See Segal, 109.

175. Indeed, at a later period in the fourth century, the Emperor Julian (*Ad Arsacium Archiereum Galatiae* 84a, p. 430 D) remarks that it is disgraceful that, when no Jew ever has to beg, all men see that pagans lack aid from their fellows.

176. See Georgi, 188–89, note 117.

177. Cf. Solomon Zeitlin, "Anti-Semitism," 134, who appositely remarks that the Jews of the Diaspora who shed their blood upholding the idea of a universal G-d were in great measure responsible, at least indirectly, because of the example they set, for the later spread of Christianity through the pagan world. Hence, as he concludes, we may truly say that the blood of the Jews of the Diaspora was the seed of the Church.

178. See my "Philo-Semitism."

179. Cf. the anecdote found in *Menaḥoth* 44a of a man whose scrupulousness about *ẓiẓith* saved him from having relations with a prostitute, who, in turn, was so impressed with him that she decided to become a proselyte. When she did so, Rabbi Ḥiyya asked whether she had laid eyes on one of his disciples. When she admitted that she had indeed done so, he, most exceptionally, sanctioned the conversion and her marriage to his disciple.

180. However, as we have noted, they were prohibited by the Torah (Deut 17:15) from becoming kings of Judaea.

181. Tacitus (*Histories* 5.5.2) similarly—and bitterly—remarks that proselytes are taught as their first lesson to despise the gods, to disown their country, and to disregard their parents, children, and brothers. Cf. the remark attributed to Jesus (Luke 14:26): "If anyone comes to me and does not hate his own father and mother and wife and children and brothers and sisters, yes, and even his own life, he cannot be my disciple."

182. Most notably Bamberger and Braude. The notion that the Jews were not active missionaries during this period is found in Joseph Derenbourg, *Essai sur l'Histoire et la Géographie de la Palestine*, vol. 1; Adolf Jellinek, "Eine alte Schutzrede für die Proselyten"; Isaac Weil, *Le Prosélytisme chez les Juifs selon la Bible et le Talmud*; and Heinrich H. Graetz, *Die jüdischen Proselyten im Römerreiche unter den Kaisern Domitian, Nerva, Trajan und Hadrian*. As Bamberger, 299, note 3, however, has remarked, this assumption was undoubtedly influenced by the view of Moses Mendelssohn, who in his letter in 1770 to the Christian Lavater (who had challenged him to embrace Christianity) and in his *Jerusalem* (1783) had denied that Judaism was a missionary religion. Moreover, as Bamberger remarks, such a view was further influenced by nineteenth-century conditions in Western Europe, when the idea of proselytism was disgusting to loyal Jews at a time when apostasy among Jews in Western Europe was so widespread.

183. Moïse Ohana, "Prosélytisme et targum palestinien: Données nouvelles pour la datation de Néofiti 1," notes that Targum Neofiti 1 preserves the meaning "foreigner" for *ger* and hence must be pre-Mishnaic, because the Mishnah already uses *ger* in the sense of "proselyte." Inasmuch as the Septuagint probably reflects the Palestinian tradition of the third century B.C.E., the Neofiti tradition either predates this or, more likely, represents a parallel and independent tradition that survived until a later date. Cf. Theophile J. Meek, "The Translation of *Ger* in the Hexateuch and Its Bearing on the Documentary Hypothesis," 180.

184. The fact that the reference is to conversion indicates that the subject is conversion to Judaism, because the word *convert* is never used of mere adoption of the Pharisaic point of view.

185. See Ephraim Urbach, "*Ger*" [in Hebrew].

186. Cf. *'Avodah Zarah* 16b–17a, which notes that Rabbi Eliezer was arrested because of *minuth* ("heresy," with special reference to Christianity).

187. Yet even Rabbi Eliezer (Mekilta, *Amalek* 3) is quoted as saying that one should not reject a sincere proselyte but rather should encourage him.

188. Gerald Blidstein, "4Q Florilegium and Rabbinic Sources on Bastard and Proselyte." Joseph M. Baumgarten, in "Exclusions from the Temple: Proselytes and Agrippa I," argues that there is no conclusive evidence that proselytes were actually excluded from the Temple and that, on the contrary, rabbinic texts presuppose that proselytes may enter the Temple area.

189. Braude, 42–44.

CHAPTER 10

1. The literature on "G-d-fearers" is enormous. The following, in particular, may be cited: Hermann L. Strack and Paul Billerbeck, *Kommentar zum neuen Testament aus Talmud und Midrasch*, vol. 2, 715–23; Kirsopp Lake, "Proselytes and G-d-fearers"; "Sympathizers"; Louis Robert, *Nouvelles Inscriptions de Sardis*, 39–45; Kazimierz Romaniuk, "Die G-ttesfürchtigen im Neuen Testament"; Heinz Bellen, "Συναγωγὴ τῶν Ἰουδαίων καὶ θεοσεβῶν. Die Aussage einer bosporanischen Freilassungeinschrift (CIRB 71) zum Problem der 'G-ttesfürchtigen' "; Georg Bertram, "θεοσεβής"; Baruch Lifshitz, "De nouveau sur les 'sympathisants' "; Folker Siegert, "G-ttesfürchtige und Sympathisanten"; Hildebrecht Hommel, "Juden und Christen im kaiserzeitlichen Milet. Überlegungen zur Theaterinschrift"; Alf Thomas Kraabel, "The Disappearance of the 'G-d-Fearers' "; Max Wilcox, "The 'G-d-fearers' in Acts—A Reconsideration"; Marcel Simon, "G-ttesfürchtiger"; *JMS*, 732–34; John J. Collins, "A Symbol of Otherness: Circumcision and Salvation in the First Century," 179–85; Thomas M. Finn, "The G-d-fearers Reconsidered"; John G. Gager, "Jews, Gentiles, and Synagogues in the Book of Acts"; Fergus Millar, "Gentiles and Judaism: 'G-d-Fearers' and Proselytes," 164–72; Robert S. MacLennan and Alf Thomas Kraabel, "The G-d-Fearers—A Literary and Theological Invention"; Robert E. Tannenbaum, "Jews and G-d-Fearers in the Holy City of Aphrodite"; "Omnipresence"; Shaye J. D. Cohen, "Respect for Judaism by Gentiles according to Josephus"; M. R. Diffenderfer, "Conditions of Membership in the People of

G-d: A Study Based on Acts 15 and Other Relevant Passages in Acts," 291–308; Laurence H. Kant, "Jewish Inscriptions in Greek and Latin," 687–90; Joyce M. Reynolds and Robert Tannenbaum, *Jews and G-d-Fearers at Aphrodisias: Greek Inscriptions with Commentary*; J. Andrew Overman, "The G-d-Fearers: Some Neglected Features"; Shaye J. D. Cohen, "Crossing the Boundary and Becoming a Jew," 31–33; "Aphrodisias"; van der Horst; Trebilco, 145–66.

2. Lake, "Proselytes and G-d-Fearers," 85–88; Wilcox, "The 'G-d-Fearers' in Acts"; "Sympathizers"; Louis Robert, *Nouvelles inscriptions de Sardis*, 41–45.

3. So Neil J. McEleney, "Conversion, Circumcision and the Law," 326.

4. So Marc Philonenko, *Joseph et Aséneth*, 142.

5. Max Wilcox, "The 'G-d-Fearers' in Acts.

6. Alfred Bertholet, *Die Stellung der Israeliten und der Juden zu den Fremden*, 331–34.

7. Robert S. MacLennan and Alf Thomas Kraabel, "The G-d-Fearers."

8. The Septuagint reads περιετέμνοντο, "were circumcised."

9. See Nock, 117.

10. On these various groups, see Cecil Roth and Yehuda Slutsky, "Judaizers," *EJ* 10 (1971): 397–402, especially 398 and 401.

11. It is not possible, as Stern, 1.96, remarks, to determine whether Hermippus intended to connect all three of these prohibitions with both the Jews and the Thracians.

12. Stern, 1.93, confirms the authenticity of the passage in Josephus on the ground that it hardly enhances the glory of the Jews to be compared with the Thracians.

13. The suggestion of Franz Cumont, in "A Propos de Sabazius et du Judaisme," that those who tried to spread the worship of Jupiter Sabazius were devotees of a superstitious Jewish-pagan cult is contradicted, as Stern, 1.359, has remarked, by the explicit statement that they were Jews; but the reason may be that our pagan source did not draw fine distinctions.

14. Stern, 1.566, says that the pun may be apocryphal, because Cicero, whose anti-Judaism should have led him to mention Caecilius's Jewishness, has no reference to it, and that it derives from the fact that Caecilius's namesake, a Greek writer in the Augustan Age, was a Jew.

15. Francis H. Colson, *The Week: An Essay on the Origin and Development of the Seven-Day Cycle*, 86, explains that there were so many people at leisure on the Sabbath that Diogenes found it a suitable day to collect an audience.

16. So Stern, 1.432.

17. That Epictetus is referring to Jews rather than to Christians seems clear from the fact that his discourses are dated to about 108 c.e., by which time he should have known the difference between Jews and Christians, especially because he himself refers to Christians as Galileans. See Stern, 1.543–44.

18. So Stern, 2.130.

19. So Stern, 2.380–81.

20. Jakob Bernays, "Die G-ttesfürchtigen bei Juvenal."

21. See my "Sympathizers."

22. So Thomas M. Finn, "The G-d-fearers Reconsidered," 81.

23. So Samuel Belkin, *Philo and the Oral Law*, 47.

24. Finn, "The G-d-fearers Reconsidered," 82–83.

25. Wolfson, 2.373–74.

26. Henry St. John Thackeray, trans. and ed., *Josephus*, vol. 2, on *War* 2.463, renders this word incorrectly as "neutrals."

27. See my "Sympathizers" and Ralph Marcus, "The *Sebomenoi* in Josephus."

28. The fact that the phrase for "worshipping G-d" is similar to Acts' σεβόμενοι τὸν θεόν is hardly conclusive evidence that this is a technical term, especially inasmuch as here the active, rather than the middle, voice of the verb is used and inasmuch as the word for G-d is not the same but rather "the Divine."

29. The term θεοσεβής is at this time hardly a technical term, because it sometimes is used of pious people generally, whether Jews or non-Jews. Max Wilcox, "The 'G-d-Fearers' in Acts—A Reconsideration," 121, remarks that it is strange that Josephus nowhere else uses the term θεοσεβής in reference to "sympathizers," and suggests that he would have done so if the term had existed and had been widely understood. The reason, we may reply, why Josephus does not use it elsewhere is that there was not yet in his time a single technical term for the "sympathizers."

30. Edith Mary Smallwood, "The Alleged Jewish Tendencies of Poppaea Sabina."

31. As Braun, 53, remarks, this refusal, in a relatively early document (dating from before the year 70 C.E.), on the part of Joseph to accept the conversion of Potiphar and his wife presages a tendency that was to be characteristic of rabbinic Judaism as seen in the Talmud.

32. Alfred Bertholet, *Die Stellung der Israeliten und der Juden zu den Fremden*, 331–34; Israel Lévi, "Le prosélytisme juif."

33. So Hermann L. Strack and Paul Billerbeck, *Kommentar zum neuen Testament aus Talmud und Midrasch*, vol. 2, 716–21.

34. So Folker Siegert, "G-ttesfürchtige und Sympathisanten," 112.

35. So Max Wilcox, "The 'G-d-Fearers' in Acts," 122, note 55.

36. So Folker Siegert, "G-ttesfürchtige und Sympathisanten," 110ff.

37. A similar passage is also found in *Numbers Rabbah* 8.2; *Avoth de-Rabbi Nathan* A 36 (ed. Schechter, 54a); *Avoth de-Rabbi Nathan* B 18, p. 40; and *Seder Eliyahu Rabbah* 18 (p. 105 Friedmann). *Mishnath Rabbi Eliezer*, p. 303, has patriarchs, converts, penitents, and fearers of Heaven. In some versions of the *Midrash on Psalms* 118.11, a statement is added that the "Heaven-fearers" are the proselytes, but Buber, in his edition, refuses to accept this reading.

38. Wolfson, 2.373, suggests that these "Heaven-fearers" are probably to be identified with "resident aliens" (*gerei toshab*) who observe the Noachian laws or with "sympathizers." He notes that Maimonides (*Mishneh Torah, Issure Biah* 14.7, *Melakim* 8.10–11) identifies the "pious of the nations" with "resident aliens." Max Wilcox, "The G-d-Fearers in Acts," 116–17, argues that the *yirei shamayim* in this passage are not "sympathizers" and that the passage is rather referring to two kinds of Jews, proselytes and Jews by birth; but if so, we may respond that the fact that two types of proselytes are mentioned indicates that the members of one type were not full proselytes.

39. See the discussion of this passage by Lieberman, *Greek*, 78–80.

40. Attempts to identify "Antoninus" with any of the Antonine or Severan emperors at the end of the second and at the beginning of the third century have proved unsuccessful. See Joshua Gutmann, "Antoninus Pius."

41. Karl G. Kuhn and Hartmut Stegemann, "Proselyten," 1279.

42. Braude, 136.

43. Lieberman, *Greek*, 81.

44. The close connection between the *ger toshab* and the "sympathizer" may be deduced from the fact that there is a *baraitha* (*Gittin* 57b, *Sanhedrin* 98b) that describes Naaman as a *ger toshab*, whereas Naaman was not a resident alien but one who accepted Jewish monotheism "in fear of heaven." See Bamberger, 137.

45. So Arthur Marmorstein, "Judaism and Christianity in the Middle of the Third Century," 222.

46. So Louis Robert, *Nouvelles inscriptions de Sardis*, 41–45.

47. Cf. the apparently proverbial saying, closely contemporary with the Book of Revelation (ca 100), in Epictetus (quoted in Arrian, *Dissertationes* 2.9.20), "He is not a Jew, he is only acting the part."

48. Shlomo Pines, "The Iranian Name for Christians and the 'G-d-fearers,' " 150–51. In this connection we may note in Justin Martyr (*Dialogue with Trypho* 10.2) that the Jew Trypho declares that the Christians do not observe the precepts that were kept by the "G-d-fearers" (φοβούμενοι).

49. Cf. Lieberman, *Greek*, 81–82.

50. See Simon, 393.

51. Robert S. MacLennan and Alf Thomas Kraabel, "The G-d-Fearers—A Literary and Theological Invention," 49.

52. Laurence H. Kant, "Jewish Inscriptions in Greek and Latin," 689, note 109, lists the following: *CII* 1.642 (Pola, Istria, Italy, third century), *CII* 1.5 (*metuens*, Rome, Roman period); *CII* 1.285 (*metuens*, Rome); *CII* 1.500 (θεοσεβής, Rome, Roman period), *CII* 1.524 (*metuens*, Rome, Roman period), *CII* 1.529 (*metuens*, Rome, Roman period); *CII* 1.731 (θεοσεβής, Rhodes, Greece), *CII* 2.754 (θεοσεβής, Philadelphia, Lydia, third or fourth century); Baruch Lifshitz, *Donateurs et Fondateurs dans les Synagogues Juives*, no. 17 (θεοσεβής, Sardis, third century); Lifshitz, no. 18 (θεοσεβής, Sardis, third century); *CIG* 14.9852 (=*IG* 14.2259 =*CIL* 11.3758, θεοσεβής); and Paton and Hicks, *Inscriptions of Cos*, no. 278 (θεοσεβής). To these we may add *CIG* 2924 (=Lifshitz, 30, θεοσεβεστάτη, Tralles, third century) and *CII* 2.748 (θεοσεβεῖς, Miletus, second century). Simon refers to four inscriptions of *metuentes* ("G-d-fearers"), but Leon, 253, notes that none of these is known to have come from a Jewish catacomb. We may, however, remark that we would not expect "G-d-fearers" to be buried in Jewish cemeteries inasmuch as they are not Jews, though at least one inscription (*CII* 1.619a) from Venusia in Apulia, dating from the fourth or fifth century, shows that "G-d-fearers" could be buried with "normal" Jews, as Kant, "Jewish Inscriptions," 688, note 104, indicates.

53. Leon, 253–54.

54. See Baruch Lifshitz, "Les Juifs à Venosa," 368; and Laurence H. Kant, "Jewish Inscriptions in Greek and Latin," 688.

55. Baruch Lifshitz, Prolegomenon to *CII* (reprint), vol. 1, 65–66, no. 683a.

56. So Goodenough, 2.44–45.

57. Baruch Lifshitz, Prolegomenon to *CII* (reprint), vol. 1, 89, no. 731a.

58. Leon, 292, no. 202.

59. See Victor Tcherikover, "The Sambathions," 94.

60. See Leiv Amundsen, *Greek Ostraca in the University of Michigan Collection*, Part 1, Texts, 657.

61. Friedrich Preisigke, *Sammelbuch griechischer Urkunden aus Ägypten*, vol. 1, 12.

62. See Fergus Millar, "Gentiles and Judaism: 'G-d-Fearers' and Proselytes," 161.

63. Victor Tcherikover, "The Sambathions," 84.

64. See Tcherikover, *CPJ* 3.43–87.

65. See *CPJ* 3.54–55. Victor Tcherikover, "The Sambathions," 88–89, doubts whether we may call the majority of Sambathions "sympathizers" and prefers to call them "pagan observers of the Sabbath"; but this merely reinforces the picture of the "sympathizers" as people who were attracted to one or another of the practices of Judaism.

66. Cf. *CPJ* 3.54: "If the Russian Subbotniki [non-Jews who observed the Sabbath according to the Bible but not according to the Talmud] could profess Judaism in nineteenth-century Russia, when severe punishments were permanently threatening them, why not in Egypt, in a world not yet accustomed to religious persecution?"

67. Victor Tcherikover, "The Sambathions," 88–89.

68. An intriguing papyrus that may have been written by sympathizers (or by syncretizing Jews) has been published by Charles F. Nims and Richard C. Steiner, "A Paganized Version of Psalm 20:2–6 from the Aramaic Text in Demotic Script," as we have noted. It contains a prayer in Aramaic but written in Egyptian demotic script addressed jointly to Horus and to the Jewish G-d and closely paralleling Psalm 20. The editors conclude that it is a pagan adaptation of a prayer based on Psalm 20, though they admit that it may be a Jewish syncretistic prayer. If it is the former, we would have here a possible instance of a "sympathizer" who still retains his allegiance to Horus while also calling on the Jewish G-d for help in his straitened circumstances.

69. Wilhelm Dittenberger, *Orientis Graeci Inscriptiones Selectae*, 573.

70. Tcherikover, "The Sambathions," 84.

71. Ibid., 85.

72. *CII* 1, Appendix, nos. 63, 68, 71.

73. See Emil Schürer, "Die Juden im bosporanischen Reiche und die Genossenschaften der σεβόμενοι θεὸν ὕψιστον ebendaselbt." Cf. Erwin R. Goodenough, "The Bosporus Inscriptions to the Most High G-d."

74. Louis Robert, *Nouvelles inscriptions de Sardis*, 41.

75. Ibid., 39.

76. Ibid., 43.

77. Lifshitz, 24, nos. 17 and 18. Lifshitz, 25, follows Louis Robert, "Sur un Dicton relatif à Phasélis. La vente du Droit de Cité," 39, in insisting that the term is not technical but merely indicates that the person is "pious," and cites "Sympa-

thizers" to support this view. But the latter article attempts to show that the references in Acts to σεβόμενοι τὸν θεόν and φοβούμενοι τὸν θεόν are not necessarily to "sympathizers," whereas the inscriptions from Sardis date from the third century, when, as we can see from the rabbinic references cited above, the term *yirei shamayim* (*Heaven-fearers*) had become a technical term referring to "sympathizers."

78. *CII* 2.754 (= Lifshitz, no. 28).

79. Lifshitz, no. 30.

80. Lifshitz, 24–26, 31, 32.

81. Baruch Lifshitz, "Prolegomenon," in reissue of *CII*, vol. 1, 65–66; Heinz Bellen, "Συναγωγὴ τῶν Ἰουδαίων καὶ Θεοσεβῶν. Die Aussage einer bosporanischen Freilassungeinschrift (cirb 71) zum Problem der 'G-ttesfürchtigen.'" Cited by Laurence H. Kant, "Jewish Inscriptions in Greek and Latin," 688.

82. *Contra* Kant, "Jewish Inscriptions," 689–90 and note 110.

83. See Kant, ibid., 685–86.

84. See Reynolds.

85. So Salo W. Baron, "Population," 871.

86. See the confession by Robert L. Wilken, *Judaism and the Early Christian Mind: A Study of Cyril of Alexandria's Exegesis and Theology*, ix.

87. Robin Lane Fox, *Pagans and Christians*, 318.

88. See William H. C. Frend, *Martyrdom and Persecution in the Early Church: A Study of a Conflict from the Maccabees to Donatus*.

89. Reynolds, 89.

90. So Adolf Neubauer, *La Géographie du Talmud: Mémoire couronné par l'Académie des Inscriptions et Belles-lettres*, 310. To be sure, the passage speaks of "Asia," but Neubauer concludes that the reference is to Sardis, which was probably the most important city in Asia Minor.

91. Reynolds, 108.

92. David Magie, *Roman Rule in Asia Minor to the End of the Third Century after Christ*, vol. 1, 712.

93. Ibid., 1.692–93.

94. See ibid., 1.706.

95. See George M. A. Hanfmann, *Sardis from Prehistoric to Roman Times: Results of the Archaeological Exploration of Sardis 1958–1975*, 146.

96. See Andrew R. Seeger, "The Building History of the Sardis Synagogue."

97. Alf Thomas Kraabel, "*Hypsistos* and the Synagogue at Sardis," 87.

98. George M. A. Hanfmann, *From Croesus to Constantine: The Cities of Western Asia Minor and Their Arts in Greek and Roman Times*, 89–90.

99. Reynolds, 1.

100. See ibid., 109.

101. See Maria Floriani Squarciapino, *La Scuola di Afrodisia*.

102. Broughton, 713.

103. Reynolds, 168 (no. 43).

104. See David Magie, *Roman Rule in Asia Minor*, vol. 1, 691.

105. Idem, 1.703–4.

106. Moshe D. Herr, "The Historical Significance of the Dialogue between Jewish Sages and Roman Dignitaries," takes a contrary point of view.

107. William M. Ramsay, *The Cities and Bishoprics of Phrygia; being an essay of the local history of Phrygia from the earliest times to the Turkish Conquest*, vol. 2, 673–74; Jones, 70.

108. So Trebilco, 92–93.

109. Published and commented on by Reynolds.

110. See my "Omnipresence," 58–69, for the evidence in pagan and Christian writers, in Philo and Josephus, in the Talmudic corpus, and in inscriptions. Alf Thomas Kraabel, in "Synagoga Caeca: Systematic Distortion in Gentile Interpretations of Evidence for Judaism in the Early Christian Period," 231–32, argues that the θεοσεβεῖς are non-Jews who are well-disposed toward the Jews. But as Trebilco, 250–51, retorts, it is hard to understand why such people would be called "pious" rather than simply "good neighbors."

111. Sardis: Lifshitz, nos. 17 and 18; Philadelphia: Lifshitz, no. 28; Tralles: Lifshitz, no. 32; Miletus: *CII* 2.748.

112. Chrysostom (*Homiliae in Romanos* 12.20.3; *PG* 51.176) likewise remarks on the loyalty of Jewish businessmen in the observance of the Sabbath, even to the point of refusing the offer of a haggling customer when the Sabbath approaches. Similarly, Epiphanius (*Panarion* 30.11) remarks on the loyalty of Jews to Jerusalem.

113. Wilhelm Dittenberger, ed., *Orientis Graeci Inscriptiones Selectae*, 573.

114. Quoted in Reynolds, 34. If the reading is correct, we may suggest that the δεκανία was like a guild. We may note that some large guilds were divided into *centuriae*, or more commonly *decuriae* (having thus the same root as the word δεκανία); and in a few a committee of *decuriones* appears to have been the effective governing body. Many guilds possessed a hall (*schola*) or chapel (*templum*) in which they held their business meetings, conducted religious exercises, and met for social occasions. See Jean Pierre Waltzing, *Etude historique sur les corporations professionelles chez les Romains depuis les origines jusqu'à la chute de l'Empire d'Occident*, 357–62, 379–83.

115. To be sure, a synagogue has not yet been found in the excavations at Aphrodisias; but inasmuch as approximately 80 percent of the city has not yet been unearthed, we may expect one or more to be found. See the comment by Pieter van der Horst, "Jews and Christians in Aphrodisias in the Light of Their Relations in Other Cities of Asia Minor," 172.

116. In an unpublished paper Bowersock comments as follows: "Καν may perhaps be considered as an abbreviation for κανονίδος, τῆσδε κανονίδος, i.e., a door frame. In short, the line near the beginning would indicate the use to which the large stone was put, as the door frame of the synagogue. And if one examines the side text closely, it will be apparent that the writing is organized together near the top so that it stops exactly at a point where presumably a wooden door would be affixed. And indeed, there are two holes in the side of the stone which seem to have been made for that purpose. The shape of the door, the squeezing of the text at the top, and the two holes tend to persuade me that this must be a door frame even if the word containing *kan* would be better resolved in some other way."

117. Harnack, 2.222–26.

118. William H. C. Frend, "The Persecutions: Some Links between Judaism and the Early Church."

119. William M. Ramsay, *Pauline and Other Studies in Early Christian History*, 58.

120. Cf. Louis Robert, *Etudes anatoliennes; recherches sur les inscriptions grecques de l'Asie Mineure*, 409–12; and Lifshitz, 32, no. 30. Though she is not specifically referred to as a "G-d-fearer," Julia Severa (*CII* 2.766; Lifshitz, 34–36, no. 33), a wealthy woman who erected a synagogue in Akmonia in Phrygia in Asia Minor in the first century, was most probably a "G-d-fearer," inasmuch as another inscription (William M. Ramsay, *The Cities and Bishoprics of Phrygia*, vol. 1.2, 647, no. 550) speaks of her as a chief priestess, presumably of a pagan cult. We may conclude that she later converted to Judaism and then built the synagogue or that she became a "sympathizer." Alf Thomas Kraabel, "Greeks, Jews, and Lutherans in the Middle Half of Acts," 153–54, asserts that such a mixture of pagan and Jewish is inappropriate among Jews associated with synagogues, and he prefers to look on Julia Severa as a pagan benefactor of the synagogue; but the inscriptions from Aphrodisias show precisely such a combination among people in Asia Minor who are specifically referred to as "G-d-fearers."

121. Robert L. Wilken, *John Chrysostom and the Jews: Rhetoric and Reality in the Late Fourth Century*, 69–70, notes that there is a distinction between Jewish Christians, who are Jews who believe in Jesus yet observe certain parts of Jewish law, and Judaizing Christians, who are Christians, usually Gentiles, who while practicing Christianity adopt certain aspects of Jewish law, even though they had not observed them before becoming Christians. Yet, as Wilken correctly points out, these groups share one important aspect, namely their attitude toward the observance of Jewish laws.

122. Eric R. Dodds, *Pagan and Christian in an Age of Anxiety: Some Aspects of Religious Experience from Marcus Aurelius to Constantine*.

123. So John G. Gager, *Kingdom and Community*.

124. Peter Brown, *The Making of Late Antiquity*.

125. So R. E. Taylor, "Attitudes of the Fathers toward Practices of Jewish Christians," especially 508–9.

126. So Juster, 1.109–10.

127. Naomi G. Cohen, in "Jewish Names and Their Significance in the Hellenistic-Roman Period in Asia Minor," concludes that most of the Jews in Asia Minor belonged to the Hellenistic stratum of society, rather than to the autochthonous Phrygian or foreign immigrant status, and that this may well have been a contributing sociological factor in positively disposing interested pagans toward Judaism.

128. See *Genesis Rabbah* 9.13, 49.9; *Leviticus Rabbah* 13.5; *Midrash Psalms* 80.6.

129. See George M. A. Hanfmann, "The Ninth Campaign at Sardis," 32.

130. So James Parkes, *The Conflict of the Church and Synagogue: A Study in the Origins of Antisemitism*, 139; and Simon, 153–54. Disputed by Kraabel, 34, n. 1.

131. Cf. Tacitus, *Histories* 5.2.1, and my discussion above.

132. Fergus Millar, in his review of William H. C. Frend, *Martyrdom and Persecution in the Early Church*, rightly objects, however, that there is no evidence other than general statements in Christian sources about the hostility of the Jews.

133. See Morris Goldstein, *Jesus in the Jewish Tradition*, 45 and the literature there cited.

134. Reuven Kimelman, "*Birkat Ha-Minim* and the Lack of Evidence for an Anti-Christian Prayer in Late Antiquity."

135. Lawrence H. Schiffman, in *Who Was a Jew? Rabbinic and Halakhic Perspectives on the Jewish-Christian Schism,* 53–61, argues that Jerome distinguished betwen Nazarenes (or Christians) and Nazoreans, and that Epiphanius mistook the Hebrew *noserim* as a reference to the Nazorean sect of his day. We may remark that it seems unlikely that the rabbis would have referred to the Nazoreans, a sect so insignificant that they are, as Schiffman, p. 60, notes, a curiosity even to the church fathers.

136. Indeed, as the sixth-century Venantius Fortunatus (*Vita Sancti Hilarii* 3; MGHAA 4.2, p. 2) remarks, "Abstention from Jewish hospitality is something which has hitherto seemed difficult among mortal men."

137. So Reynolds, 27.

138. The photographs of this inscription included by Reynolds and Tannenbaum in their monograph are notoriously obscure, but Bowersock, who had better photographs, remarks in a private communication that he has grave doubts about this reading. Moreover, this particular inscription, according to Bowersock, seems to come from a much later hand, rather crudely aligned and with somewhat erratic spelling, as is often the case with later Byzantine texts, and hence may not be much earlier than the fifth century c.e. Tannenbaum (in his chapter in Reynolds, 27) equates this πάτελλα with the Talmudic institution of *tamḥui,* literally "dish," which is used in the Mishnah (e.g., *Peah* 8:7) and Tosefta and both Talmudim (e.g., *Baba Bathra* 8b) in reference to a daily collection (in a dish) and distribution of cooked food to the poor. But if the reading πάτελλα is correct, this would seem to have its parallel in the Talmudic *petaleya'* (*petaleyah, petileyah*), which is a wicker basket, especially a sort of bale for packing dates or figs, as we can see from the passage in Tosefta, *Shabbath* 12 (13): 15, which declares it permissible to cut open a *patella* of figs on the Sabbath (cf. Jerusalem *Shabbath* 15.1.15a, *Kilayim* 16.5, *Ma'aser Sheni* 1.2.52d; Tosefta *Ma'aser Sheni* 1:10).

To be sure, the word πάτελλα is used in Greek by the second-century grammarian Pollux (6.85) with reference to a dish; and similarly, in Latin a *patella* is a small pan or dish or plate, or a vessel used in cooking, and also one in which food was served (Varro, *Grammar* 85); but if indeed this is the meaning here, it would seem significant that the Jews of Aphrodisias are using the term in a sense different from that of their Talmudic brethren, and hence that Tannenbaum's claims of Talmudic influence are not well founded. But in either case, the reference, which would seem to be to food that is given to the poor, would emphasize another attraction offered by Jews to non-Jews. This would be particularly significant, inasmuch as, with the exception of Rhodes and perhaps of Samos, Greek cities had no permanent arrangements for feeding the poor; at best, in other cities, such distributions occurred at festivals or on special occasions. The Emperor Julian (*Ad Arsacium Archiereum Galatiae* 84a.430B–D) likewise stresses that no Jew ever has to beg (though admittedly the rest of the passage imputes an even broader philanthropy to the Church), in contrast to the picture drawn by the satirists Martial (12.57.1–14) at the end of the first century and Juvenal (3.10–16, 296, and 6.542–47) at the beginning of the second century, and in contrast to the lack of support shown by pagans to one another. Once again we see here the importance of the economic factor, this time in winning people to Judaism.

139. Ramsay MacMullen, *Roman Social Relations, 50 B.C. to A.D. 284*, 62–65.

140. Venantius Fortunatus, *Vita Sancti Hilarii* 3; MGHAA 4.2, p. 2; cf. Amolo, *Liber contra Judaeos* 3; *PL* 116.180 ff.

141. See Arnold H. M. Jones, *The Greek City from Alexander to Justinian*, 215–19.

142. See Eusebius, *Historia Ecclesiastica* 5.23–24.

143. Alf Thomas Kraabel, in "Melito the Bishop and the Synagogue at Sardis: Text and Context," insists that one of Melito's main reasons for attacking the Jews was to ward off the charge that Quartodecimans were by definition sympathetic to Judaism. But the very fact that Melito is constrained to defend himself so vehemently against such a charge would seem to indicate that there was some substance to it. An additional reason for Melito's vehemence, as Kraabel points out, was undoubtedly the size and status of the Jewish community of Sardis, which now has been so strikingly confirmed by the excavations of Hanfmann and his team.

144. According to the Mishnah (*Ta'anith* 4:8) none of the Jews' festive days compared in joy with the Fifteenth of Av and the Day of Atonement, on which days the daughters of Jerusalem would go forth, dressed in white, and dance in the vineyards.

145. See Goodenough, 4.111–36.

146. So Robert L. Wilken, *John Chrysostom and the Jews*, 68.

147. See Elias Bickerman, "Les Maccabées de Malalas."

148. Georgi, 114, cites, as a contradiction to this, Philo's statement (*De Vita Mosis* 2.39.211) denying that any theatrical performance was given in Jewish worship; but a closer examination of the passage in Philo indicates that Jewish worship merely avoided the *extremes* of bursts of laughter, sports, mimes, and dances rather than conviviality and dancing as such.

149. The Mishnah is referred to as the δευτέρωσις, literally the "second" law in Justinian, Novella 146, a term apparently derived from the literal meaning of the word *mishnah*, that is, "repetition."

150. The Graeco-Jewish historian Artapanus (ca 100 B.C.E.; quoted in Eusebius, *Praeparatio Evangelica* 9.18.1), as we have noted, states that Abraham taught the Egyptian pharaoh the science of astrology. Similar statements are found in pseudo-Eupolemus (quoted in Eusebius, *Praeparatio Evangelica* 9.17.8) and Josephus (*Ant.* 1.167).

151. Already in the first century B.C.E., as we have remarked, Pompeius Trogus (36.2.8) describes the Jews as highly skilled in the art of interpreting dreams. On the relationship between Judaism and paganism in magic, see in particular Goodenough, 2.153–295.

152. For the important role played by the Jewish names of G-d and angels, see Goodenough, 2.153–295 and Simon, 339–68.

153. Celsus, quoted in Origen, *Against Celsus* 6.80, likewise states that the Magi are the source of magic for various nations, though he does not mention the Jews specifically.

154. See "Dialogue," 110.

155. Campbell Bonner, *Studies in Magical Amulets, Chiefly Graeco-Egyptian*, 28; Goodenough, 2.206; Gager, 134–61.

156. Mordecai Margalioth, ed., *Sepher Ha-Razim* [in Hebrew]. See the discussion of this work by Judah Goldin, "The Magic of Magic and Superstition," 132–38.

157. Wilken, 85, notes that in the index to the *Papyri Magicae Graecae* there are more references to the Jewish G-d than to any other divine name.

158. Likewise, in the first half of the sixth century, the pagan Neo-Platonic philosopher Damascius (*Vita Isidori*, quoted in Photius, *Bibliotheca*, cod. 242, p. 339A–B [Zintzen 55–56]) relates that a certain Theosebius was able to expel an evil spirit from the wife of the fifth-century Neo-Platonist philosopher Hierocles through invoking the rays of the sun and the G-d of the Hebrews. We have already noted the positive attitude toward Judaism of such Neo-Platonist philosophers as Numenius and Julian.

159. So Alfons A. Barb, "The Survival of Magic Arts."

160. "Dialogue," 111, citing Marcellin P. E. Berthelot and Charles-Emile Ruelle, *Collection des anciens alchimistes Grecs*, 3 vols.

161. Berthelot and Ruelle, *Collection des anciens alchimistes grecs*, 2, 240; and Raphael Patai, "Maria the Jewess—Founding Mother of Alchemy."

162. Cited in "Dialogue," 111.

163. See "Aphrodisias," 297.

164. We may, however, note that the physician Galen, in the second century, apparently relied on either the compendium of the wealthy Jew Rufus of Samaria, who came to Rome in his time, or on earlier commentaries on Hippocrates. See Franz Pfaff, "Rufus aus Samaria, Hippokrates kommentator und Quelle Galens."

165. This must have been particularly irksome in view of the fact that much of Christianity's initial appeal, to judge from the miraculous cures ascribed to Jesus in the Gospels, was to Christian claims of cures in the name of Jesus. Jews were apparently aware of such claims and were even ready to give them credence. One is reminded ironically of the remark of Rabbi Ishmael (Tosefta *Ḥullin* 2.23, cf. *'Avodah Zarah* 27b), who did not allow his nephew Rabbi Eleazar ben Damah to be healed in the name of Yeshu ben Pandera (presumably Jesus, as we can see from Celsus, quoted in Origen, *Against Celsus* 1.32) after a serpent had bitten him, even though Ben Damah was ready to bring proof that he was actually able to heal him. When Ben Damah died before the cure could be applied, Rabbi Ishmael remarked, "Happy are you, Ben Damah, not to have broken down the fence of the Sages."

166. See Nock, 117.

167. See Paul Peeters, in *AB* 23 (1904): 255–57.

168. Kraabel, 149–54, notes the prominence of women in the Jewish communities of Asia Minor, which fits in with Anatolian culture, where women played such an important part in pagan religious cults and in civic life; and in view of the predominance of women among proselytes, at least in an earlier era, as noted by Josephus (*War* 2.560), we should expect an indication of the prominence of women among those converted or attracted to Judaism at Aphrodisias. But inasmuch as the inscription, in its long lists, mentions only men (with the possible

exception of a Jew named Iael [see Reynolds, 101]), it is possible that it names only donors, rather than adherents, of the respective groups of Jews, proselytes, and "sympathizers."

169. Even if the figures are exaggerated, the losses certainly were high. According to Josephus (*War* 2.497), in 66 C.E. fifty-thousand Jews in Alexandria were slaughtered by the Roman troops on orders of the Roman governor, the renegade Jew Tiberius Julius Alexander, during a riot. In the great Jewish war against the Romans in the Land of Israel, Josephus (*War* 6.420–21) says that the number of those who perished during the siege of Jerusalem alone was 1,100,000. Again, during the revolt led by the pseudo-Messiah Lukuas-Andreas during the reign of Trajan (115–17), many tens of thousands of Jews were killed in Egypt, according to Eusebius (*Historia Ecclesiastica* 4.2); the fact that the Jews are said to have originally killed 220,000 persons in Cyrene and 240,000 in Cyprus (Dio Cassius 68.32) would indicate tremendous losses ultimately for the Jews, inasmuch as the revolt was finally suppressed in bitter fighting. Georgius Syncellus (347–48) in the eighth century states categorically that the Jews who fought against the Greeks in Libya, Cyprus, and Egypt were exterminated. So great was the destruction of Egyptian Jewry that for several decades after 117 Jewish names disappear from the extant lists of taxpayers; and even in Alexandria, where some Jews survived, the Jewish court was suspended (Tosefta, *Kethuboth* 3:1; Tosefta, *Peah* 4:6), and the community far from succeeded in recovering its former strength. Finally, in the Land of Israel the Jews suffered terrible losses in the revolt of the pseudo-Messiah Bar Kochba (132–35 C.E.); according to Dio Cassius (69.14), "580,000 men were slain in the various raids and battles, and the number of those that perished by famine, disease, and fire was past finding out."

170. Baron, 1.179.

171. Hengel, 313, states that the existence of "G-d-fearers" or "sympathizers" illustrates "the insoluble dilemma of the Jewish religion in ancient times" in that, because "it could not break free from its nationalist roots among the people, it had to stoop to constant and ultimately untenable compromises." He then adds that this is where the primitive Church set in. We may, however, remark that there is quite a difference between the attitude of Judaism toward its "sympathizers" and that of Christianity toward its "sympathizers," in that Judaism steadfastly refused to grant to these "sympathizers" the status of "Jews," whereas Christianity, early in its career, did make compromises with its converts, notably on the question of circumcision, granting them full status as Christians.

CHAPTER 11

1. Simon, 272.

2. For a somewhat different formulation, see Shaye J. D. Cohen, "Respect for Judaism by Gentiles according to Josephus," especially 410.

3. So Wilken, 91, note 9. As Wilken notes, Bamberger and Braude deal extensively with the attitude toward proselytism during this period, but their conclusions are drawn almost exclusively from the statements of the rabbis and disregard almost completely the other sources listed in this chapter. Cf. the critique of Braude's book on these grounds by Gedaliahu Alon, *Studies in Jewish History in the Times of the Second Temple, the Mishna and the Talmud*. To Alon's criticism we

may add that Bamberger and Braude make almost no attempt to differentiate between the attitudes of the rabbis in the various centuries of the Talmudic period, let alone to consider the impact of both the changes in the Roman Empire and the rise and triumph of Christianity on the proselytizing movement.

4. See Albert T. Olmstead, "The Mid-Third Century of the Christian Era."

5. So Ronald Syme, *Ammianus and the Historia Augusta*, 219.

6. Cf., e.g., Alfredo Mordechai Rabello, "The Legal Condition of the Jews in the Roman Empire," 745: "Under the Christian Emperors, Judaism, unable to acquire converts, was compelled to withdraw into itself." So also Louis M. O. Duchesne, *Histoire ancienne de l'Eglise*, vol. 1, 6th ed., 568, English trans. by Claude Jenkins, *Early History of the Christian Church, from Its Foundations to the End of the Fifth Century*, 412: "The religious life now became very narrow. The day of liberal Jews, who coquetted with hellenism and with the government, was past and gone for good. There is no longer any desire to stand well with other nations, nor to make proselytes. That field is left to the Nazarenes. The Jews retired within themselves, absorbed in the contemplation of the law."

7. The revolt is mentioned by a number of Christian writers: Jerome, *Chronica*. (ed. Helm, 2d ed.) 238; Socrates, *Historia Ecclesiastica*. 2.33; Sozomenus, *Historia Ecclesiastica*. 4.7.5; Theophanes (ed. Carl de Boor; Leipzig: Teubner, 1883) 1.40; Cedrenus (ed. Bekker) 1.524; Nicephorus Callistus 9.32 (*PG* 146.353); Michael the Syrian, *Chronica*. (ed. Jean B. Chabot; Paris: Leroux, 1899) 1.268; Agapius [in *Patrologia Orientalis*] 7.571–72). The revolt is cited by only one pagan writer, the fourth-century Aurelius Victor (*Liber de Caesaribus*. 42.11), who has merely one sentence, "And meanwhile the revolt of the Jews, who impiously raised Patricius to royalty, was crushed." The revolt has echoes in the Midrash, as noted by Stern, 2.501.

8. This is disputed by Lieberman, "Palestine," 340–41; but see Stern, 2.501.

9. See Edith Mary Smallwood, "The Legislation of Hadrian and Antoninus Pius against Circumcision." Max Wilcox, in his revision of Schürer, 1.537, accepts this version of the cause of the Bar Kochba rebellion as found in the *Scriptores Historiae Augustae*, despite his general skepticism as to the reliability of that work, and declines to accept the attempt by Hugo Mantel, in "The Causes of the Bar Kochba Revolt," to refute this thesis. Of course, it may well be, as Alfredo Mordechai Rabello, in "The Legal Condition of the Jews in the Roman Empire," 698, suggests, that the ban extended only to male Gentiles who underwent circumcision, whereas female converts escaped any penalty.

10. Inasmuch as the entire passage in Modestinus (*Rules*, Book 6) deals with slaves, Siro Solazzi, "Fra norme romane antisemite," 396–97, suggests a textual emendation that would restrict the application of this passage to circumcision of slaves alone. Joseph Geiger, "The Ban on Circumcision and the Bar-Kokhba Revolt" [in Hebrew], looks on the rescript not as granting freedom to circumcise where it was previously forbidden but rather as restricting the right to circumcise where it had been previously unlimited. Linder, 99, however, concludes that Antoninus Pius's rescript represents a repeal, in regard to the Jews, of Hadrian's general interdiction of circumcision.

11. So Smallwood, 472, who suggests that the law became a dead letter because of ambiguities in its administration, such as in resolving the questions whether circumcision was permitted to Jewish apostate or Christian families,

whether it was permitted to proselyte families of long standing, and whether it was permitted for sons of a mixed Jewish-Gentile marriage. If credence is given to the *Scriptores Historiae Augustae* (*Antoninus Pius* 5.4), the decree of Antoninus Pius failed to satisfy at least some of the Jews, inasmuch as we find that they revolted against him.

12. Cf., e.g., Josephus's remark (*War* 2.559–61), noted above, that on the eve of the great war against the Romans in 66, the inhabitants of Damascus were fired with a determination to kill the Jews but were afraid of their own wives, "who, with few exceptions, had all become converts to the Jewish religion."

13. Smallwood, 471.

14. Anthony R. Birley, *Septimius Severus: The African Emperor*, rev. ed., 135 and 250, note 12, regards this statement as implausible and almost certainly spurious, in view of the claim in the *Scriptores Historiae Augustae* (*Septimius Severus* 17.1) that Septimius granted "very many privileges to the Palestinians on his journey." We may, however, remark that Septimius, stickler for law and realist as he was, may well have been favorably disposed toward the Jews while at the same time insisting that they should not attempt, through proselytism, to destroy the paganism that he felt had built and maintained the Roman Empire.

15. Stern, 2.625.

16. It is clear that Dio Cassius is here speaking of full converts to Judaism, inasmuch as he has just referred to the people called Jews and then applies this name to aliens who adopt their ways: "I do not know how this title [Jews] came to be given them, but it applies also to the rest of mankind, although of alien race, who affect their customs."

17. So Wilken, 51–52.

18. So Simon, 250.

19. So Linder, 68.

20. Linder, 124–25, convincingly shows that the date 315, given by the editors of the *Codex Theodosianus*, is impossible.

21. Simon, 290–91, states that of the privileges guaranteed by the emperors to the Jews only one was explicitly and immediately withdrawn from them, namely the right to propagate their faith. But we have noted that such restrictions were placed on the Jews by Septimius Severus at the end of the second century and reaffirmed in Paul's *Sententiae* at the end of the third century.

22. Walter Pakter, in "Canonical Jewry-Law in the Age of Eusebius" (forthcoming), remarks that in the Eastern Empire, purple cloth, linen, and silk manufactured in the imperial factories were not mere economic commodities but were also symbols of prestige whose manufacture and sale were rigidly controlled. Inasmuch as there were secrets involved in their manufacture, the ban on intermarriage to Jewish men was thus meant to keep these secrets out of the hands of the Jews, especially those in the Land of Israel, which was well known for its textile industry then as in later times.

23. Wilken, 52, comments on the absence of legislation during the years from 340 to 380 and concludes that Constantine's impact on the status of the Jews was less profound than is usually supposed; but, as we have noted, there was legislation in 353 which went beyond that of Constantine.

24. See *CT* 9.40.1 and Linder, 181.

25. Linder, 178.

26. See "Omnipresence," 58–69. Although Reynolds, 20, prefers a date in the early third century for the new inscriptions from Aphrodisias listing fifty-four "G-d-fearers," she admits that a date in the late fourth or fifth century is possible. This later date would accord with the statement in *Codex Theodosianus* 16.5.43, issued in 407, that the "Heaven-fearers" (*Caelicolarum*) represent a new doctrine, as corroborated by the statement in *Codex Theodosianus* 16.8.19 that the "Heaven-fearers" represent a "new crime." If we then ask how such a date will fit in with the fact that the rabbinic citations refer to rabbis in the third century, we may then suggest, to be sure with diffidence, that the ascriptions may be anachronistic and that the references are actually to the scene current in the fifth century, when the rabbinic works were codified.

27. So Linder, 228.

28. See, e.g., Mishnah *Berakoth* 2:7; *Pesaḥim* 7:2; *Sukkah* 2:1; *Rosh Hashanah* 1:7; and Babylonian Talmud, *Gittin* 46b–47a.

29. See Linder, 82; and Bernhard Blumenkranz, *Juifs et Chrétiens dans le Monde Occidental, 430–1096*, 184.

30. Noted by Linder, 119.

31. Linder, 149–50, commenting on the provision of the law that women, formerly occupied in the state weaving establishments "whom the Jews led to their fellowship in turpitude," are to be restored to the weaving establishment, states that the law deals with proselyting of women slaves, in analogy with the preceding paragraph; but the imposition of capital punishment indicates that the law is not referring to bondwomen, inasmuch as slaves who converted to Judaism were not penalized, on the ground that they had no will of their own. Rather, the passage would seem to refer to intermarriage between Jewish men and non-Jewish women, as Peter Browe, in "Die Judengesetzgebung Justinians," has shown.

32. MacMullen, 92.

33. So ibid., 203.

34. Ibid., 182.

35. Ibid., 93–94.

36. Ibid., 91–92.

37. See ibid., 252–53, note 67, who cites *Codex Justinianus* 7.64.7 (285); Firmicus Maternus, *Mathesis* 3.7.26 (early fourth century); and Louis Robert, "Epigrammes relatives à des Gouverneurs," 108.

38. Cf. the argument of Celsus, quoted in Origen, *Against Celsus* 2.6.

39. Cf. the similar edict issued in 388 by the Emperors Valentinian II, Theodosius, and Arcadius (*CT* 3.7.2 and 9.7.5), which we have noted above, forbidding intermarriage between Jews and Christians. Cf. Pedro Lombardia, "Los Matrimonios mixtos en el Concilio de Elvira." Marriages to Jewish women were apparently not a problem; and ancient statutes, as David Daube, in "The Self-Understood in Legal History," 127, has remarked, do not attempt to cover every eventuality.

40. Walter Pakter, "Canonical Jewry-Law in the Age of Eusebius."

41. So David Daube, *Forms of Roman Legislation*, 6.

42. So Pakter, "Canonical Jewry-Law."

43. It is precisely in Asia Minor, as we have noted above, where inscriptions, notably at Aphrodisias, have been discovered referring to the largest number of "G-d-fearers."

44. As if to clinch his point, Constantine remarks that Christians cannot rely on Jewish calculations to determine the date of Easter, inasmuch as the Jews frequently celebrate two Passovers in the same year. But what has misled Constantine, we may suggest, is either the fact that in the Diaspora an extra day of the holiday is celebrated, or that there is, in the Jewish calendar, a *Pesah sheni*, "a second Passover," for the benefit of those who are unable to observe Passover on the original date of the fourteenth of Nisan because of ritual defilement or because of unavoidable absence from Jerusalem.

45. See Hefele, 1.325.

46. So Wilken, 77, 92–93. Cf. Louis Ginzberg, *An Unknown Jewish Sect*, 105, who cites a similar remark by Jacob ben Ephraim, a disciple of Saadia Gaon, who, as late as the tenth century, when asked about a Christian sect that followed Jesus yet kept the Jewish calendar, replied that Jews do not repel people who ascribe prophetic power to those who are not prophets—including Jesus, Mohammed, and the pseudo-Messiah Abu Isa—"because they agree with us about the festival calendar."

47. Epiphanius (*Panarion* 70) makes note of the Audians (Odians), a monastic group founded about the time of the Council of Nicaea (325), who insisted that Easter must be celebrated at the same time as the Jewish Passover, even if the Passover came before the time of the equinox.

48. So Saul Lieberman, *Texts and Studies*, 116.

49. Although the term φυλακτήριον may refer to any kind of amulet, the reference to τὰ λεγόμενα φυλακτήρια ("the so-called phylacteries") indicates a special kind of amulet. To a Christian this would surely be the phylacteries worn by Jews, especially in view of the usage in Matthew 23:5, where the reference is clearly to such phylacteries.

50. Hefele, 2.311.

51. See Hefele, 2.410.

52. Alfredo Mordechai Rabello, "The Legal Condition of the Jews in the Roman Empire," 676.

53. See Hengel, "Schürer," 36.

54. Wilken, 68.

55. See my "Origen's *Contra Celsum* and Josephus' *Contra Apionem*: The Issue of Jewish Origins," and the discussion above in Chapter 6.

56. Ignatius here shows awareness of and mentions several specific practices of the Sabbath that were observed by Jewish Christians, namely, eating things that had been prepared on the previous day, drinking lukewarm drinks, walking only within a prescribed distance from their dwelling place, and dancing. We may be tempted to remark that Christians, no less than Jews, lose a seventh of their lives in idleness, but it is clear from his remarks that at least in Ignatius's time the Christian Sunday was not observed as a day of rest.

57. See J. Alvarez, "Apostolic Writings and the Roots of Anti-Semitism."

58. See Nahum Slouschz, *Hébraeo-Phéniciens et Judéo-Berbères: Introduction à l'histoire des juifs et du judaisme en Afrique*, and his *Travels in North Africa*.

59. See William H. C. Frend, "A Note on Tertullian and the Jews," 292–93.

60. When he declares that judges were said to be gods, "in conformity with an ancient Jewish usage of speech," Origen (*Against Celsus* 4.31) here shows his awareness of the rabbinic exegesis (*Sanhedrin* 66a) of Exodus 22:27 (28), "You shall not revile *Elokim*, which the Septuagint on this passage, Philo (*De Vita Mosis* 2.38.205, *De Specialibus Legibus* 1.9.53), and Josephus (*Ant.* 4.207, *Against Apion* 2.237) all interpreted to mean that one is not permitted to insult other people's gods but which the rabbis understood to mean that one may not curse judges.

61. So also in John Chrysostom (*Catechism* 1.2–3; *PG* 49.225–26) and Theodoret of Antioch (*In Hebraeos* 6.4; *PG* 82.717).

62. See Ramsay MacMullen, *Roman Social Relations, 50 B.C. to A.D. 284*, 62–65, cited by Wilken, 78.

63. See Jay Braverman, *Jerome's Commentary on Daniel: A Study of Comparative Jewish and Christian Interpretations of the Hebrew Bible*, 4–5.

64. Linder, 257, refutes the theory, based on this passage in Augustine, that the "G-d-fearers" were restricted to North Africa, noting that the law of 407 was directed at Italy and Spain, as well as at Africa.

65. Isaac of Antioch, *Opera Omnia*, ed. Gustav Bickell (Giessen: Ricker, 1873–77). Cf., in particular, *Papyri Magicae Graecae*, 13, and "Aphrodisias," 294–96.

66. So Wilken, 90.

67. That ascription of statements to rabbis is to be taken at face value rather than to be regarded as views originating from the much later redactors of the rabbinic works would seem to be indicated by such a remark (commenting on the verse [Esther 2:22] "And Esther told the king in the name of Mordecai") as that of the third-century Rabbi Eleazar in the name of Rabbi Ḥanina that "whoever reports a saying in the name of its originator brings deliverance to the world" (*Megillah* 15a). The rabbis had too much respect for the chain of tradition, which was so crucial an article of faith in their belief in the Oral Law, to have misrepresented statements by their predecessors in the process of recalling them.

68. See Jerome, *Epistles* 121, *ad Algasiam* 10. See Lieberman, *Greek*, 29–67.

69. Simon, 277–78, cites the passage (*Yevamoth* 46a) in which Rabbi Joshua ben Ḥananiah, who flourished in the early second century, declares that a proselyte who has performed the prescribed ablution but has not been circumcised is a proper proselyte, as well as the passage (*Yevamoth.* 46b) in which the second-century Rabbi Judah bar Ilai declares that either circumcision or ablution suffices as the initiation rite for proselytes. He concludes that such leniency must have removed one of the most powerful obstacles to the spread of Judaism. But see Gedaliahu Alon, rev. of Braude [in Hebrew], 282–83, who concludes that the correct version of the controversy between Rabbi Eliezer and Rabbi Joshua ben Ḥananiah as to whether circumcision or immersion in a ritual pool is required of a convert is not to be found in the Babylonian Talmud but rather the Jerusalem Talmud (*Qiddushin* 3.14.64d) and the tractate *Gerim*, according to which both circumcision and ablution are required.

70. *Avoth de-Rabbi Nathan* B 26; *Numbers Rabbah* 14.11; *Pesiqta Rabbati* 43, p. 181a. According to *Sifre Deuteronomy* 32, Abraham and Sarah brought men and women under the wings of the Divine Presence by converting them.

71. Goodman, 179. In the case of Josephus (*Ant.* 1.161, 166–67), we find that Abraham, when he went down to Egypt, taught not Judaism but arithmetic and astronomy. We find a similar picture in Artapanus (quoted by Eusebius, *Praeparatio Evangelica* 9.18) who depicts Abraham as teaching astrology to the Egyptians.

72. See Judith R. Baskin, *Pharaoh's Counsellors: Job, Jethro, and Balaam in Rabbinic and Patristic Tradition*, 59.

73. See Aaron Rothkoff, "Minor Tractates."

74. See Smallwood, 502.

75. Simon, 347–48.

76. So Lieberman, *Hellenism*, 116.

77. So David Rokeah, *Jews, Pagans and Christians in Conflict*, 44.

78. See Arthur Marmorstein, "Judaism and Christianity in the Middle of the Third Century," 220, who argues that the apostates are Jews who have been converted to Christianity. He suggests that the harangues of luminaries of the Church, such as John Chrysostom, to Christians to avoid visiting Jewish places of worship are motivated by exasperation with Jewish Christians who had survived even after the official triumph of Christianity.

79. Simon, 284, says that there are nine inscriptions mentioning proselytes, but the independent reading of inscription number 72 by Leon, 273–74, shows no reference to a proselyte.

80. So Simon, 284.

81. As we have noted, there may have been a third expulsion in the middle of the first century (Suetonius, *Claudius* 25.4; Acts 18:2).

82. So Leon, 93–121.

83. So Wilken, 91.

84. Cf. Lieberman, *Greek*, 85.

85. So Simon, 273.

86. Simon, 395.

87. See Omeljan Pritsak and Norman Golb, *Documents of the History of the Khazars*; D. M. Dunlop, *The History of the Jewish Khazars*; and Peter B. Golden, *Khazar Studies: An Historio-Philological Inquiry into the Origins of the Khazars*.

88. Norman Golb, *Jewish Proselytism—A Phenomenon in the Religious History of Early Medieval Europe*, 32–37.

89. Ben Zion Wacholder, "Cases of Proselytizing in the Tosafist Responsa."

CHAPTER 12

1. Salo W. Baron, "World Dimensions of Jewish History," in Aaron Steinberg, ed., *Simon Dubnow: The Man and His Work* (Paris: French Section of the World Jewish Congress, 1963) 36.

2. See David Biale, *Power and Powerlessness in Jewish History*, 11.

BIBLIOGRAPHY

[Anonymous], "Sepharad." *EJ* 14 (1971): 1164.

Abel, Ernest L. "Were the Jews Banished from Rome in 19 A.D.?" *REJ* 127 (1968): 383–86.

Aberbach, Moses. *The Roman-Jewish War (66–70 A.D.): Its Origin and Consequences*. London: The Jewish Quarterly, 1966.

Abrahams, Israel. *Studies in Pharisaism and the Gospels*. Vol. 1. Cambridge: Cambridge University Press, 1917.

Adriani, Maurilio. "Note sull' antisemitismo antico." SMSR 36 (1965): 63–98.

Alberro, Charles A. "The Alexandrian Jews during the Ptolemaic Period." Ph.D. diss., Michigan State University, 1976.

Alessandri, Salvatore. "La presunta cacciata dei Giudei da Roma nel 139 a. Cr." *SCO* 17 (1968): 187–98.

Alon, Gedaliahu. Review [in Hebrew] of William G. Braude, *Jewish Proselyting in the First Five Centuries of the Common Era*. In *Studies in Jewish History in the Times of the Second Temple, the Mishna and the Talmud*, vol. 2. [in Hebrew] Tel-Aviv: Hakibutz Hameuḥad, 1958. 278–84.

Alvarez, J. "Apostolic Writings and the Roots of Anti-Semitism." *SP* 13 (1975): 69–76.

Amir, Yehoshua. "Θεοκρατία as a Concept of Political Philosophy: Josephus' Presentation of Moses' *Politeia*." SCI 8–9 (1985–88): 83–105.

Amundsen, Leiv. *Greek Ostraca in the University of Michigan Collection*, Part 1, Texts. Univ. of Michigan Studies, Humanistic Series, vol. 34. Ann Arbor: University of Michigan, 1935.

Anderson, William S. "Horace, the Unwilling Warrior, *Satire* I, 9." *AJP* 77 (1956): 148–66.

Applebaum, Shimon. Review [in Hebrew] of *CPJ*, vol. 1, by Victor A. Tcheriko-ver and Alexander Fuks. *Tarbiz* 28 (1958–59): 418–27.

Aptowitzer, Victor. "Asenath, the Wife of Joseph: A Haggadic Literary-Historical Study." HUCA 1 (1924): 239–306.

———. *Parteipolitik der Hasmonäerzeit im rabbinischen und pseudepigraphischen Schrifttum*. Wien: Kohut-Foundation, 1927.

Armstrong, Arthur Hilary. "Pagan and Christian Traditionalism in the First Three Centuries." *SP* 15 (1984): 414–31.

Attridge, Harold W. *The Interpretation of Biblical History in the Antiquitates Judaicae of Flavius Josephus*. HTR, Harvard Dissertations in Religion, vol. 7. Missoula: Scholars Press, 1976.

Auscher, Dominique. "Les relations entre la Grèce et la Palestine avant la conquête d'Alexandre." *VT* 17 (1967): 8–21.

Avi-Yonah, Michael. *The Holy Land from the Persian to the Arab Conquests (536 B.C. to A.D. 640): A Historical Geography*. Grand Rapids, Michigan: Baker, 1966.

Avi-Yonah, Michael. *Hellenism and the East: Contacts and Interrelations from Alexander to the Roman Conquest.* Ann Arbor: University Microfilms International, 1978.

Axenfeld, Karl. "Die jüdische Propaganda als Vorläuferin und Wegbereiterin der urchristlichen Mission." In *Missionswissenschaftliche Studien. Festschrift zum 70. Geburtstag des Herrn Prof. D. Dr. Gustav Warneck*, ed. Karl Axenfeld et al. Berlin: Warneck, 1904. 1–80.

Bacher, Wilhelm. *Die Agada der Tannaiten*, vol. 1. Strassburg: Trübner, 1903.

Baer, Yitzhak. *Israel among the Nations* [in Hebrew]. Jerusalem: Bialik, 1955.

Balland, André. *Fouilles de Xanthos*, vol. 7. Paris: Klincksieck, 1981.

Balsdon, John P. V. D. *Life and Leisure in Ancient Rome.* London: Bodley Head, 1969.

———. *Romans and Aliens.* London: Duckworth, 1979.

Bamberger, Bernard J. *Proselytism in the Talmudic Period.* Cincinnati: Hebrew Union College, 1939.

———. "The Dating of Aggadic Materials." *JBL* 68 (1949): 115–23.

Barag, Dan, and David Flusser. "The Ossuary of Yehohanah Granddaughter of the High Priest Theophilus." *IEJ* 36 (1986): 39–44.

Barb, Alfons A. "The Survival of Magic Arts." In *The Conflict between Paganism and Christianity in the Fourth Century: Essays*, ed. Arnaldo Momigliano. Oxford: Clarendon, 1963. 100–25.

Bar-Kochva, Bezalel. *Judas Maccabaeus: The Jewish Struggle against the Seleucids.* Cambridge: Cambridge University Press, 1989.

———. *Poseidonius of Apamea and Ancient Anti-Semitism* (forthcoming).

Baron, Salo W. *The Jewish Community, Its History and Structure to the American Revolution.* 3 vols. Philadelphia: Jewish Publication Society, 1942.

———. *A Social and Religious History of the Jews*, 2d ed., vols. 1–2. New York: Columbia Univ. Press and Philadelphia: Jewish Publication Society, 1952.

———. "World Dimensions of Jewish History." In *Simon Dubnow: The Man and His Work*, ed. Aaron Steinberg. Paris: French Section of the World Jewish Congress, 1963. 26–40.

———. "Population." *EJ* 13 (1971): 866–903.

———. "Changing Patterns of Antisemitism: A Survey." *JSS* 38 (1976): 5–38.

Barrett, Anthony A. *Caligula: The Corruption of Power.* New Haven: Yale University Press, 1989.

Baskin, Judith R. *Pharaoh's Counsellors: Job, Jethro, and Balaam in Rabbinic and Patristic Tradition.* Chico, California: Scholars Press, 1983.

Baumgarten, Joseph M. "Exclusions from the Temple: Proselytes and Agrippa I." *JJS* 33 (1982): 215–25.

Becher, Ilse. *Das Bild der Kleopatra in der griechischen und lateinischen Literatur.* Deutsche Akademie der Wissenschaften zu Berlin: Schriften der Sektion für Altertumswissenschaft; Berlin: Akademie-Verlag, 1966.

Becker, Wilhelm A. *Gallus; or Roman Scenes of the Time of Augustus*, 4th ed. Trans. Frederick Metcalfe. London: Longmans, 1873.

Begg, Christopher. " 'Josephus's Portrayal of the Disappearances of Enoch, Elijah, and Moses': Some Observations." *JBL* 109 (1990): 691–93.

Belkin, Samuel. *Philo and the Oral Law.* Cambridge: Harvard Univ. Press, 1940.

Bell, Harold Idris. *Jews and Christians in Egypt: The Jewish Troubles in Alexandria and the Athanasian Controversy.* London: British Museum, 1924.

———. "Anti-Semitism in Alexandria." *JRS* 31 (1941): 1–18.

Bellen, Heinz. "Συναγωγὴ τῶν Ἰουδαίων καὶ θεοσεβῶν. Die Aussage einer bosporanischen Freilassungeinschrift (CIRB 71) zum Problem der 'G-ttesfürchtigen.'" *JAC* 8–9 (1965–66): 171–76.

Bentwich, Norman. *Josephus.* Philadelphia: Jewish Publication Society, 1914.

Berger, Klaus. *Die Weisheitsschrift aus der Kairoer Geniza: Erstedition, Kommentar und Übersetzung (Texte und Arbeiten zum Neutestamentlichen Zeitalter.* Tübingen: Francke, 1989.

Bergmann, Judah. *Jüdische Apologetik im neutestamentlichen Zeitalter.* Berlin: Reimer, 1908.

———. "Die stoische Philosophie und die jüdische Frömmigkeit." In *Judaica (Festschrift Hermann Cohen),* ed. Ismar Elbogen et al. Berlin: Cassirer, 1912. 145–66.

Bernays, Jakob. *Theophrastus' Schrift über Frömmigkeit: Ein Beitrag zur Religionsgeschichte.* Berlin: Hertz, 1866.

———. "Die G-ttesfürchtigen bei Juvenal." In *Commentationes philologae in honorem Theodori Mommseni.* Berlin: Weidmann, 1877. 563–69. Reprinted in *Gesammelte Abhandlungen von Jacob Bernays,* vol. 2, ed. Hermann K. Usener. Berlin: Hertz, 1885. 71–80.

Berthelot, Marcellin P. E., and Ruelle, Charles-Emile. *Collection des anciens alchimistes grecs.* 3 vols. Paris: Steinheil, 1887–88.

Bertholet, Alfred. *Die Stellung der Israeliten und der Juden zu den Fremden.* Freiburg and Leipzig: Mohr, 1896.

Bertram, Georg. "Θεοσεβής." *Theologisches Wörterbuch zum Neuen Testament,* vol. 3, ed. Gerhard Kittel. Stuttgart: Kohlhammer, 1938. 124–28. Trans. Geoffrey W. Bromiley. TDNT, vol. 3. Grand Rapids: Eerdmans, 1966. 123–28.

Biale, David. *Power and Powerlessness in Jewish History.* New York: Schocken, 1986.

Bialoblocki, Samuel. *Die Beziehungen des Judentums zu Proselyten und Proselytentum.* Berlin: Brecker, 1930.

Bickermann (Bickerman), Elias. "Ritualmord und Eselkult. Ein Beitrag zur Geschichte antiker Publizistik." MGWJ 71 (1927): 171–87, 255–64. Reprinted in his *Studies in Jewish and Christian History,* vol. 2. Leiden: Brill, 1980. 225–55.

———. "Les Maccabées de Malalas." *Byzantion* 21 (1951): 63–83. Reprinted in his *Studies in Jewish and Christian History,* vol. 2. Leiden: Brill, 1980. 192–209.

———. "Origines Gentium." *CP* 47 (1952): 65–81.

———. "The Septuagint as a Translation." PAAJR 28 (1959): 1–39. Reprinted in his *Studies in Jewish and Christian History,* vol. 1. Leiden: Brill, 1976. 167–200.

———. "The Jewish Historian Demetrios." In *Christianity, Judaism, and Other Greco-Roman Cults: Studies for Morton Smith at Sixty,* Part 3: *Judaism before 70,* ed. Jacob Neusner. Leiden: Brill, 1975. 72–84. Reprinted in his *Studies in Jewish and Christian History,* vol. 2. Leiden: Brill, 1980, 347–58.

———. *The G-d of the Maccabees: Studies on the Meaning and Origin of the Maccabean Revolt.* Leiden: Brill, 1979. Esp. 76–92.

Bickermann, Elias. *The Jews in the Greek Age*. Cambridge, Mass.: Harvard Univ. Press, 1988.

Bieler, Ludwig. Θεῖος ἀνήρ, *das Bild des "göttlichen Menschen" in Spätantike und Frühchristentum*, vol. 1. Wien: Höfels, 1935.

Bigg, Charles. *The Christian Platonists of Alexandria*. Oxford: Clarendon, 1913.

Bilde, Per. "The Roman Emperor Gaius (Caligula)'s Attempt to Erect His Statue in the Temple of Jerusalem." *ST* 32 (1978): 67–93.

Birley, Anthony R. *Septimius Severus: The African Emperor*, rev. ed. New Haven: Yale Univ. Press, 1989.

Blidstein, Gerald. "4Q Florilegium and Rabbinic Sources on Bastard and Proselyte." *RQ* 8 (1972–74): 431–35.

Bloch, Heinrich. *Die Quellen des Flavius Josephus in seiner Archäologie*. Leipzig: Teubner, 1879.

Bludau, August. *Juden und Judenverfolgungen im alten Alexandria*. Münster: Aschendorff, 1906.

Blumenkranz, Bernhard. "Tacite: Antisémite ou xénophobe?" *REJ* 11 (111) (1951–52): 187–91.

———. *Juifs et Chrétiens dans le Monde Occidental, 430–1096*. Paris: Mouton, 1960.

Bonner, Campbell. *Studies in Magical Amulets, Chiefly Graeco-Egyptian*. Ann Arbor: Univ. of Michigan Press, 1950.

Bosch, David. *Die Heidenmission in der Zukunftsschau Jesu: Eine Untersuchung zur Eschatologie der synoptischen Evangelien*. Zürich: Zwingli, 1959.

Bowers, Robert H. *The Legend of Jonah*. The Hague: Nijhoff, 1971.

Bowersock, Glen W. *Hellenism in Late Antiquity*. Ann Arbor: Univ. of Michigan Press, 1990.

Brady, Thomas A. "The Gymnasium in Ptolemaic Egypt." *Univ. of Missouri Studies* 11.3 (1936): 9–20.

Braude, William G. *Jewish Proselyting in the First Five Centuries of the Common Era: The Age of the Tannaim and Amoraim*. Providence: Brown Univ. Press, 1940.

Braun, Martin. *Griechischer roman und hellenistische Geschichtsschreibung*. Frankfurt: Klostermann, 1934.

———. *History and Romance in Graeco-Oriental Literature*. Oxford: Blackwell, 1938.

Braverman, Jay. *Jerome's Commentary on Daniel: A Study of Comparative Jewish and Christian Interpretations of the Hebrew Bible*. CBQ Monograph Series, 7. Washington: Catholic Biblical Association of America, 1978.

Broshi, Magen. "La population de l'ancienne Jérusalem." *RB* 82 (1975): 5–14.

Broughton, Thomas Robert S. "Roman Asia." In *An Economic Survey of Ancient Rome*, vol. 4, ed. Tenney Frank. Baltimore: Johns Hopkins Univ. Press, 1938. 499–950.

Browe, Peter. "Die Judengesetzgebung Justinians." *AG* 8 (1935): 118–23.

Brown, Norman O. *Hermes the Thief: The Evolution of a Myth*. Madison: Univ. of Wisconsin Press, 1947.

Brown, Peter. *The Making of Late Antiquity*. Cambridge: Harvard Univ. Press, 1978.

Bruce, Frederick F. "Kittim." *EJ* 10 (1971): 1080–82.

———. "Tacitus on Jewish History." *JSeS* 29 (1984): 33–44.

Burkert, Walter. "Zur Geistesgeschichtlichen Einordnung einiger Pseudopythagorica." In *Pseudepigrapha*, vol. 1, ed. Kurt von Fritz. *Fondation Hardt pour l'étude de l'antiquité classique, Entretiens* 18 (1971). Geneva: Vandoeuvres-Geneva, 1972. 23–55.

Butzer, Karl W. *Early Hydraulic Civilization in Egypt: A Study in Cultural Ecology.* Chicago: Univ. of Chicago Press, 1976.

Byatt, Anthony. "Josephus and Population Numbers in First Century Palestine." *PEQ* 105 (1973): 51–60.

Cardauns, Burkart. "Juden und Spartaner: Zur hellenistisch-jüdischen Literatur." *Hermes* 95 (1967): 317–24.

Cerfaux, Lucien, J. Cerfaux, and Julien Tondriau. *Le culte des souverains dans la civilisation gréco-romaine.* Tournai: Desclée, 1957.

Chadwick, Henry, trans. and ed. *Origen: Contra Celsum.* Cambridge: Cambridge Univ. Press, 1965.

———. *Early Christian Thought and the Classical Tradition: Studies in Justin, Clement, and Origen.* New York: Oxford Univ. Press, 1966.

Charlesworth, James H. "The Concept of the Messiah in the Pseudepigrapha." ANRW 2.19.1. Berlin: de Gruyter, 1979. 188–218.

———. *The Pseudepigrapha and Modern Research with a Supplement.* Chico, California: Scholars Press, 1981.

Chesnutt, Randall D. "The Social Setting and Purpose of Joseph and Aseneth." *JSP* 2 (1988): 21–48.

von Christ, Wilhelm. *Geschichte der griechischen Literatur bis auf die Zeit Justinians*, 4th ed. München: Beck, 1905.

Cohen, Naomi G. "Jewish Names and Their Significance in the Hellenistic and Roman Periods in Asia Minor." Ph.D. diss. [in Hebrew], Jerusalem: Hebrew University, 1969.

———. "Rabbi Meir, a Descendant of Anatolian Proselytes: New Light on His Name and the Historic Kernel of the Nero Legend in Gittin 56a." *JJS* 23 (1972): 51–59.

Cohen, Shaye J. D. *Josephus in Galilee and Rome: His Vita and Development as a Historian.* Leiden: Brill, 1979.

———. "Patriarchs and Scholarchs." PAAJR 48 (1981): 57–85.

———. "Sosates the Jewish Homer." *HTR* 74 (1981): 391–96.

———. "Epigraphical Rabbis." *JQR* 72 (1981–82): 1–17.

———. "Conversion to Judaism in Historical Perspective: From Biblical Israel to Postbiblical Judaism." *CJ* 36.4 (Summer 1983): 31–45.

———. " 'Anti-Semitism' in Antiquity: The Problem of Definition." In *History and Hate: The Dimensions of Anti-Semitism*, ed. David Berger. Philadelphia: Jewish Publication Society, 1986. 43–47.

———. "Respect for Judaism by Gentiles according to Josephus." *HTR* 80 (1987): 409–30.

———. "Crossing the Boundary and Becoming a Jew." *HTR* 82 (1989): 14–33.

Collins, John J. *Between Athens and Jerusalem: Jewish Identity in the Hellenistic Diaspora.* New York: Crossroad, 1983.

Collins, John J. "A Symbol of Otherness: Circumcision and Salvation in the First Century." In *"To See Ourselves as Others See Us": Christians, Jews, "Others" in Late Antiquity*, ed. Jacob Neusner and Ernest S. Frerichs. Chico, California: Scholars Press, 1985. 163–86.

———. "Messianism in the Maccabean Period." In *Judaisms and Their Messiahs at the Turn of the Christian Era*, ed. Jacob Neusner et al. Cambridge: Cambridge Univ. Press, 1987.

Colson, Francis H. *The Week: An Essay on the Origin and Development of the Seven-Day Cycle*. Cambridge: Cambridge Univ. Press, 1926.

———, and George H. Whitaker, eds. *Philo*, 10 vols. LCL; London: Heinemann, 1929–62.

Conzelmann, Hans. *Heiden-Juden-Christen: Auseinandersetzungen in der Literatur der hellenistisch-römischen Zeit*. Tübingen: Mohr, 1981.

Cotton, Hannah M., and Joseph Geiger, eds. *Masada II: The Latin and Greek Documents*. Jerusalem: Israel Exploration Society, The Hebrew University of Jerusalem, 1989.

Cowley, Arthur E., ed. *Aramaic Papyri of the Fifth Century* B.C. Oxford: Clarendon, 1923.

Cramer, Frederick H. *Astrology in Roman Law and Politics*. Philadelphia: American Philosophical Society, 1954.

Crawford, Dorothy J. Thompson. "The Idumaeans of Memphis and the Ptolemaic Politeumata." *Atti del XVII Congresso Internazionale di Papirologia* (Napoli, 1984): 1069–75.

Cumont, Franz. "A Propos de Sabazius et du Judaisme." *MB* 14 (1910): 55–60.

———. *Les Religions orientales dans le paganisme romain*, 3d ed. Paris: Librairie Leroux, 1929.

Dalbert, Peter. *Die Theologie der hellenistisch-jüdischen Missionsliteratur unter Ausschluss von Philo und Josephus*. Hamburg: Reich, 1954.

Daniel, Jerry L. "Anti-Semitism in the Hellenistic-Roman Period." *JBL* 98 (1979): 45–65.

Daube, David. "Alexandrian Methods of Interpretation and the Rabbis." *Festschrift Hans Lewald*. Basel: Helbing and Lichtenhahn, 1953. 27–44.

———. *Forms of Roman Legislation*. Oxford: Oxford Univ. Press, 1956.

———. "The Self-Understood in Legal History." *JuR* 18 (1973): 126–34.

———. "Three Legal Notes on Josephus after His Surrender." *LQR* 93 (1977): 191–94.

Deissmann, Gustav Adolf. *Bibelstudien: Beiträge, zumeist aus den Papyri und Inscriften, zur Geschichte der Sprache, des Schrifttums und der Religion des hellenistischen Judentums und des Urchristentums*. Marburg: Elwert, 1895.

———. *Licht vom Osten. Das Neue Testament und die neuentdeckten Texte der hellenistischen-römischen Welt*, 4th ed. Tübingen: Mohr, 1923. Trans. Lionel R. M. Strachan. *Light from the Ancient East: The New Testament Illustrated by Recently Discovered Texts of the Graeco-Roman World*, 4th ed. London: Hodder and Stoughton, 1927.

Delia, Diana. "Roman Alexandria. Studies in Its Social History." Ph.D. diss., Columbia University, 1983; published as *Alexandrian Citizenship during the Roman Principate*. Atlanta: Scholars Press, 1991.

Delia, Diana. "The Population of Roman Alexandria." TAPA 118 (1988): 275–92.

Derenbourg, Joseph. *Essai sur l'Histoire et la Géographie de la Palestine*, vol. 1. Paris: Imprimerie Impériale, 1867.

De Ridder, R. *The Dispersion of the People of G-d*. 1971. Reprinted as *Disciplining the Nations*. Grand Rapids: Baker, 1975.

Derwachter, Frederick M. *Preparing the Way for Paul: The Proselyte Movement in Later Judaism*. New York: Macmillan, 1930.

Detlefsen, Declef. "Über des älteren Plinius Geschichte seiner Zeit und ihr Verhältniss zum Tacitus." *Philologus* 34 (1876): 40–49.

Diffenderfer, M. R. "Conditions of Membership in the People of G-d: A Study Based on Acts 15 and Other Relevant Passages in Acts." Ph.D. diss., University of Durham, 1987.

Dihle, Albrecht. *Die goldene Regel: Eine Einführung in die Geschichte der antiken und frühchristlichen Vulgärethik*. Göttingen: Vandenhoeck and Ruprecht, 1962.

Dittenberger, Wilhelm. *Orientis Graeci Inscriptiones Selectae*. 2 vols. Leipzig: Hirzel, 1903–5.

Dodd, Charles H. *The Bible and the Greeks*. London: Hodder and Stoughton, 1935.

Dodds, Eric R., ed. *Proclus, The Elements of Theology*, 2d ed. Oxford: Clarendon, 1963.

——— . *Pagan and Christian in an Age of Anxiety: Some Aspects of Religious Experience from Marcus Aurelius to Constantine*. Cambridge: Cambridge Univ. Press, 1965.

Doran, Robert. *Temple Propaganda: The Purpose and Character of 2 Maccabees*. CBQ Monograph Series, 12. Washington: The Catholic Biblical Association of America, 1981.

Dornseiff, Franz. *Das Alphabet in Mystik und Magic*. Leipzig: Teubner, 1922.

——— . "Verschmähtes zu Vergil, Horaz, und Properz" (*Berichte über die Verhandlungen der Sächsischen Akademie der Wissenschaften zu Leipzig, Philologisch-historische Klasse* 97.6. Berlin: Akademie-Verlag, 1951.

Droge, Arthur J. *Homer or Moses? Early Christian Interpretations of the History of Culture*. Tübingen: Mohr, 1989.

Duchesne, Louis M. O. *Histoire ancienne de l'Eglise*, vol. 1, 4th ed. Paris: Fontemoing, 1908. Trans. Claude Jenkins. *Early History of the Christian Church from Its Foundations to the End of the Fifth Century*. London: Murray, 1909.

Dunlop, D. M. *The History of the Jewish Khazars*. Princeton: Princeton Univ. Press, 1954.

Eddy, Samuel K. *The King Is Dead: Studies in the Near Eastern Resistance to Hellenism 334–31 B.C.* Lincoln: Univ. of Nebraska Press, 1961.

Edelstein, Emma J., and Ludwig Edelstein. *Asclepius: A Collection and Interpretation of the Testimonies*. Baltimore: Johns Hopkins Univ. Press, 1945.

Epstein, Abraham. "The Beasts of the Four Kingdoms" [in Hebrew]. *Beth Talmud* 4 (1885): 173–77.

Fabia, Philippe. *Les sources de Tacite dans les Histoires et les Annales*. Paris: Imprimerie nationale, 1893. 247–59.

Fallon, Francis T. "Eupolemus." In *The Old Testament Pseudepigrapha*, vol. 2, ed. James H. Charlesworth. Garden City: Doubleday, 1985. 861–72.

Farnell, Lewis R. *Greek Hero Cults and Ideas of Immortality*. Oxford: Clarendon, 1921.

Farrington, Benjamin. "Astrology." *OCD* (1970). 133–34.

Feldman, Louis H. "Jewish 'Sympathizers' in Classical Literature and Inscriptions." TAPA 81 (1950): 200–208.

———. "Cicero's Conception of Historiography." Ph.D. diss., Harvard University, 1951.

———. "Philo-Semitism among Ancient Intellectuals." *Tradition* 1 (1958–59): 27–39.

———. "The Orthodoxy of the Jews in Hellenistic Egypt." *JSS* 22 (1960): 212–37.

———, ed. and trans. *Josephus*, vol. 9. *LCL*; London: Heinemann, 1965.

———. "Abraham the Greek Philosopher in Josephus." TAPA 99 (1968): 143–56.

———. "Hellenizations in Josephus' Account of Man's Decline." In *Religions in Antiquity: Essays in Memory of Erwin Ramsdell Goodenough*, ed. Jacob Neusner. Leiden: Brill, 1968. 336–53.

———. "Hellenizations in Josephus' Version of Esther." TAPA 101 (1970): 143–70.

———. "Prolegomenon." In reprint of Montague R. James, *The Biblical Antiquities of Philo* (London: S.P.C.K., 1917). New York: Ktav, 1971. vii–clxix.

———. "Josephus as an Apologist to the Greco-Roman World: His Portrait of Solomon." In *Aspects of Religious Propaganda in Judaism and Early Christianity*, ed. Elisabeth Schüssler Fiorenza. Notre Dame: Univ. of Notre Dame Press, 1976. 69–98.

———. "Hengel's *Judaism and Hellenism* in Retrospect." *JBL* 96 (1977): 371–82.

———. "Josephus' Commentary on Genesis." *JQR* 72 (1981–82): 121–31.

———. "Josephus' Portrait of Saul." HUCA 53 (1982): 45–99.

———. "Abraham the General in Josephus." In *Nourished with Peace: Studies in Hellenistic Judaism in Memory of Samuel Sandmel*, ed. Frederick E. Greenspahn et al. Chico, California: Scholars Press, 1984. 43–49.

———. "Flavius Josephus Revisited: The Man, His Writings, and His Significance." ANRW 2.21.2. Berlin: de Gruyter, 1984. 763–862.

———. "The Jews in Greek and Roman Literature" [in Hebrew]. In *World History of the Jewish People*, First Series: *The Diaspora in the Hellenistic-Roman World*, ed. Menahem Stern and Zvi Baras. Jerusalem: Am Oved, 1984. 265–85, 361–65, 383–84.

———. "Proselytism and Syncretism" [in Hebrew]. *World History of the Jewish People*, First Series: *The Diaspora in the Hellenistic-Roman World*, ed. Menahem Stern and Zvi Baras. Jerusalem: Am Oved, 1984. 188–207, 340–45, 378–80.

———. *Josephus and Modern Scholarship (1937–1980)*. Berlin: de Gruyter, 1984.

———. "Josephus as a Biblical Interpreter: The 'Aqedah." *JQR* 75 (1984–85): 212–52.

———. Review of Carl R. Holladay, *Fragments from Hellenistic Jewish Authors*. *CO* 62 (1985): 101–2.

———. "How Much Hellenism in Jewish Palestine?" HUCA 57 (1986): 83–111.

———. "Josephus' Portrait of Deborah." In *Hellenica et Judaica: Hommage à Valentin Nikiprowetzky*, ed. André Caquot et al. Leuven-Paris: Editions Peeters, 1986. 115–28.

Feldman, Louis H. 'Anti-Semitism in the Ancient World," in David Berger, ed., *History and Hate: The Dimensions of Anti-Semitism*. Philadelphia: Jewish Publication Society, 1986. 15–42.

―――. "The Omnipresence of the G-d-Fearers." *BAR* 12.5 (Sept.-Oct. 1986): 58–69.

―――. "Philo's Views on Music." JJML 9 (1986–87): 36–54.

―――. "Hellenizations in Josephus' *Jewish Antiquities*: The Portrait of Abraham." In *JJC*, 133–53.

―――. Introduction to *JJC*, 23–67.

―――. "Torah and Secular Culture: Challenge and Response in the Hellenistic Period." *Tradition* 23.2 (Summer 1987): 1–15.

―――. "Pro-Jewish Intimations in Anti-Jewish Remarks Cited in Josephus' *Against Apion*." *JQR* 78 (1987–88): 187–251.

―――. "Josephus' Portrait of Noah and Its Parallels in Philo, Pseudo-Philo's *Biblical Antiquities*, and Rabbinic Midrashim." PAAJR 55 (1988): 31–57.

―――. "Josephus' Version of Samson." *JSJ* 19 (1988): 171–214.

―――. "Use, Authority, and Exegesis of Mikra in the Writings of Josephus." In *Mikra, Text, Translation, Reading and Interpretation of the Hebrew Bible in Ancient Judaism and Early Christianity (Compendia Rerum Iudaicarum ad Novum Testamentum*, sect. 2, vol. 1), ed. Jan Mulder and Harry Sysling. Assen: Van Gorcum, 1988. 455–518.

―――. "Josephus' Portrait of Jacob." *JQR* 79 (1988–89): 101–51.

―――. Introduction to *JBH*, ed. Louis H. Feldman and Gohei Hata. 17–49.

―――. "Josephus' *Jewish Antiquities* and Pseudo-Philo's *Biblical Antiquities*." In *JBH*, 59–80.

―――. "Josephus' Portrait of David." HUCA 60 (1989): 129–74.

―――. "Proselytes and 'Sympathizers' in the Light of the New Inscriptions from Aphrodisias." *REJ* 148 (1989): 265–305.

―――. "A Selective Critical Bibliography of Josephus." In *JBH*, 330–448.

―――. "Josephus' Portrait of Joshua." *HTR* 82 (1989): 351–76.

―――. "The Enigma of Horace's Thirtieth Sabbath." *SCI* 10 (1989–90): 87–112.

―――. "Origen's *Contra Celsum* and Josephus' *Contra Apionem*: The Issue of Jewish Origins." *VC* 44 (1990): 105–35.

―――. "Prophets and Prophecy in Josephus." *JTS* 41 (1990): 386–422.

―――. "Some Observations on the Name of Palestine." HUCA 61 (1990): 1–23.

―――. "Abba Kolon and the Founding of Rome." *JQR* 81 (1990–91): 448–82.

―――. "Josephus' Portrait of Moses." *JQR* 82 (1991–92).

―――. "Josephus' Portrait of Samuel." *Abr-Nahrain* 30 (1992): 1–29.

―――. "Proselytism by Jews in the Third, Fourth, and Fifth Centuries." *JSJ* 23 (1992).

―――. "Was Judaism a Missionary Religion in Ancient Times?" In *Jewish Assimilation, Acculturation, and Accommodation: Past Traditions, Current Issues, and Future Prospects*, ed. Menahem Mor. Lanham, New York: University Press of America, 1992. 24–37.

―――. "The Palestinian and Diaspora World: Judaism in the First Century." In *Christianity and Rabbinic Judaism: A Parallel History of Their Origin and Early Development*, ed. Hershel Shanks (forthcoming).

Feldman, Louis H. "Jewish Proselytism." In *Eusebius, Judaism, and Christianity*, ed. Harold W. Attridge and Gohei Hata (forthcoming).

————. "Josephus' Portrait of Joseph." *RB* (forthcoming).

————. "The Contribution of Salo W. Baron to the Study of Ancient Jewish History: His Appraisal of Anti-Semitism and Proselytism." AJSR (forthcoming).

————. "Josephus' Portrait of Hezekiah." *JBL* (forthcoming).

————. "Josephus' Portrait of Daniel." *Henoch* (forthcoming).

————. "Josephus' Portrait of Nehemiah." *JJS* (forthcoming).

————. "Josephus' Portrait of Ahab." *Ephemerides Theologicae Lovanienses*.

————. "Josephus' Portrait of Jeroboam." AUSS (forthcoming).

————. "Josephus' Portrait of Ezra." *VT* (forthcoming).

————, and Gohei Hata, eds. *Josephus, Judaism, and Christianity*. Detroit: Wayne State Univ. Press, 1987 (abbreviated in this volume as *JJC*).

————, and Gohei Hata, eds. *Josephus, the Bible, and History*. Detroit: Wayne State Univ. Press, 1989 (abbreviated in this volume as *JBH*).

Ferrari d'Occhieppo, Konradin. *Der Stern der Weisen: Geschichte oder Legende?* 2d ed. Wien: Herold, 1977.

Finkelstein, Louis. "Pre-Maccabean Documents in the Passover Haggadah." *HTR* 35 (1942): 291–332; 36 (1943): 1–38.

Finn, Thomas M. "The G-d-fearers Reconsidered." *CBQ* 47 (1985): 75–84.

Fischel, Henry A. "Story and History: Observations on Greco-Roman Rhetoric and Pharisaism." In Denis Sinor, ed., *American Oriental Society, Middle West Branch, Semi-Centennial Volume, Asian Studies Research Institute, Oriental Series* 3 (1969): 59–88.

————. "Cynics and Cynicism." *EJ* 5 (1971): 1177–78.

————. "Epicureanism." *EJ* 6 (1971): 817.

————. "Greek and Latin Languages, Rabbinical Knowledge of." *EJ* 7 (1971): 884–87.

————. "Stoicism." *EJ* 15 (1971): 409–10.

————. *Rabbinic Literature and Greco-Roman Philosophy*. Leiden: Brill, 1973.

————, ed. *Essays in Greco-Roman and Related Talmudic Literature*. New York: Ktav, 1977.

Fitzmyer, Joseph A. "The Languages of Palestine in the First Century." *CBQ* 30 (1972): 501–31.

————. *A Wandering Aramean*. Missoula, Montana: Scholars Press, 1979.

Flickinger, Roy C. *The Greek Theater and Its Drama*, 4th ed. Chicago: University of Chicago Press, 1938.

Flusser, David. "The Ritual Murder Slander against the Jews in the Light of Outlooks in the Hellenistic Period" [in Hebrew]. In *Lewy Memorial Volume*, ed. Moshe Schwabe and Joshua Gutman. Jerusalem: Magnes, 1949. 104–24.

————. "*Palaea Historica*: An Unknown Source of Biblical Legends." *SH* 22 (1971): 48–79.

————. "The Four Empires in the Fourth Sibyl and in the Book of Daniel." *IOS* 2 (1972): 148–75.

Fornaro, Pierpaolo. "Il cristianesimo oggetto di polemica indiretta in Flavio Giuseppe (Ant. Jud. IV 326)." *RSC* 27 (1979): 431–60.

Fox, Robin Lane. *Pagans and Christians*. New York: Knopf, 1987.

Frankel, Zacharias. *Über den Einfluss der palästinischen Exegese auf die alexandrinische Hermeneutik*. Leipzig: Barth, 1851.

Frend, William H. C. "The Persecutions: Some Links between Judaism and the Early Church." *JEH* 9 (1958): 141–58.

―――. *Martyrdom and Persecution in the Early Church: A Study of a Conflict from the Maccabees to Donatus*. Oxford: Oxford Univ. Press, 1965.

―――. "A Note on Tertullian and the Jews." *SP* 10 (1970): 291–96.

Freud, Sigmund. *Moses and Monotheism*. London: Hogarth, 1939.

Freudenthal, Jacob. *Hellenistische Studien: Alexander Polyhistor und die von ihm erhaltenen Reste jüdischer und samaritanischer Geschichtswerke*, vols. 1–2. Breslau: Grass, Barth, 1874–75.

Frey, Jean Baptiste. *Corpus Inscriptionum Iudaicarum*, 2 vols. Rome: Pontificio Istituto di Archeologia cristiana, 1936–52.

Freyne, Sean. *Galilee from Alexander the Great to Hadrian: 323 B.C.E. to 135 C.E.: A Study of Second Temple Judaism*. Wilmington: Glazier, 1980.

Friedländer, Moritz. *Geschichte der jüdischen Apologetik als Vorgeschichte des Christentums*. Zürich: Schmidt, 1903.

von Fritz, Kurt. "Pythagoras." *RE* 47 (1963): 171–209.

Fuchs, Leo. *Die Juden Aegyptens in ptolemäischer und römischer Zeit*. Wien: Rath, 1924.

Fuks, Alexander. "Notes on the Archive of Nicanor." *JJP* 5 (1951): 207–16. Reprinted in his *Social Conflicts in Ancient Greece*. Jerusalem: Magnes, 1984. 312–21.

Gabba, Emilio. *Greek Knowledge of Jews up to Hecataeus of Abdera*. Berkeley: Center for Hermeneutical Studies, 1981. 1–14.

Gager, John G. *Moses in Greco-Roman Paganism*. Nashville: Abingdon, 1972.

―――. "The Dialogue of Paganism with Judaism: Bar Cochba to Julian." HUCA 44 (1973): 89–118.

―――. *Kingdom and Community*. New York: Prentice-Hall, 1975.

―――. *The Origins of Anti-Semitism: Attitudes toward Judaism in Pagan and Christian Antiquity*. New York: Oxford Univ. Press, 1983.

―――. "Jews, Gentiles, and Synagogues in the Book of Acts." In *Christians among Jews and Gentiles: Essays in Honor of Krister Stendahl on His Sixty-fifth Birthday*, ed. George W. Nickelsburg and George W. MacRae. Philadelphia: Fortress, 1986. 91–99.

Gardiner, Edward Norman. *Athletics of the Ancient World*. Oxford: Clarendon, 1930.

Gaster, Moses. *The Asatir: The Samaritan Book of the "Secrets of Moses" Together with the Pitron or Samaritan Commentary and the Samaritan Story of the Death of Moses*. London: Royal Asiatic Society, 1927.

Gay, Ruth. "Inventing the Shtetl." *American Scholar* 53 (1984): 329–49.

Geiger, Abraham. *Urschrift und Übersetzungen der Bibel in ihrer Abhängigkeit von der inneren Entwicklung des Judenthums*. Breslau: Hainauer, 1857.

Geiger, Joseph. "The Ban on Circumcision and the Bar-Kokhba Revolt" [in Hebrew]. *Zion* 41 (1976): 139–47.

―――. "The Earliest Reference to Jews in Latin Literature." *JSJ* 15 (1984): 145–47.

Georgi, Dieter. *The Opponents of Paul in Second Corinthians*. Philadelphia: Fortress, 1984, rev. ed. 1986.

Ginsberg, S. "Sparta and Judea." *CP* 29 (1934): 117–22.

Ginzberg, Louis. *The Legends of the Jews*. 7 vols. Philadelphia: Jewish Publication Society, 1909–38.

———. *An Unknown Jewish Sect*. New York: Jewish Theological Seminary of America, 1976.

Golb, Norman. *Jewish Proselytism—A Phenomenon in the Religious History of Early Medieval Europe*. Cincinnati: Univ. of Cincinnati Judaic Studies Program, 1987.

Golden, Peter B. *Khazar Studies: An Historico-Philological Inquiry into the Origins of the Khazars*. 2 vols. Budapest: Akademiai Kiado, 1980.

Goldenberg, Robert. "The Jewish Sabbath in the Roman World up to the Time of Constantine the Great." ANRW 19.1. Berlin: de Gruyter, 1979. 414–47.

Goldin, Judah. "The Magic of Magic and Superstition." In *Aspects of Religious Propaganda in Judaism and Early Christianity*, ed. Elisabeth Schüssler Fiorenza. Notre Dame: Univ. of Notre Dame Press, 1976. 115–47.

Goldschmidt, Erik. "Die Israel-Quellen bei Tacitus." *Der Morgen* 11 (1935–36): 175–78.

Goldstein, Jonathan A. "Jewish Acceptance and Rejection of Hellenism." In *Jewish and Christian Self-Definition*, vol. 2: *Aspects of Judaism in the Greco-Roman Period*, ed. E. P. Sanders et al. Philadelphia: Fortress, 1981. 64–87, 318–26.

———. "The Message of *Aristeas to Philokrates*: In the Second Century B.C.E., Obey the Torah, Venerate the Temple of Jerusalem, But Speak Greek, and Put Your Hopes in the Ptolemaic Dynasty." In *Eretz Israel, Israel and the Jewish Diaspora: Mutual Relations*, ed. Menachem Mor (*Studies in Jewish Civilization*, 1). Lanham, New York: University Press of America, 1991. 1–23.

Goldstein, Morris. *Jesus in the Jewish Tradition*. New York: Macmillan, 1950.

Goodblatt, David. "The Talmudic Sources on the Origins of Organized Jewish Education" [in Hebrew]. SHJP 5 (1980): 83–103.

———. "The Place of the Pharisees in First Century Judaism: The State of the Debate." *JSJ* 20 (1989): 12–30.

Goodenough, Erwin R. "The Political Philosophy of Hellenistic Kingship." *YCS* 1 (1928): 55–104.

———. *The Jurisprudence of the Jewish Courts in Egypt*. New Haven: Yale Univ. Press, 1929.

———. "Philo's Exposition of the Law and His De Vita Mosis." *HTR* 27 (1933): 109–25.

———. *By Light, Light*. New Haven: Yale Univ. Press, 1935.

———. *Jewish Symbols in the Greco-Roman Period*. 13 vols. Princeton: Princeton Univ. Press, 1953–68.

———. "The Bosporus Inscriptions to the Most High G-d." *JQR* 47 (1956–57): 221–44.

Goodman, Martin. "Proselytising in Rabbinic Judaism." *JJS* 40 (1989): 175–85.

———. *Mission and Conversion* (forthcoming).

Goold, George P. "A Greek Professorial Circle at Rome." TAPA 92 (1961): 168–92.

Gordon, Cyrus H. "Homer and Bible: The Origin and Character of East Mediterranean Literature," HUCA 26 (1955): 43–108.

Graetz, Heinrich H. "Ursprung der zwei Verleumdungen gegen das Judenthum vom Eselkultus und von der Lieblosigkeit gegen Andersgläubige." MGWJ 21 (1872): 193–206.

———. *Die jüdischen Proselyten im Römerreiche unter den Kaisern Domitian, Nerva, Trajan und Hadrian.* Breslau: Schottlaender, 1884.

———. *Geschichte der Juden von den ältesten Zeiten bis auf die Gegenwart,* ed. Marcus Brann. Vol. 3.1, 5th ed. Leipzig: Leiner, 1905.

Grant, Frederick C., ed. *Hellenistic Religions: The Age of Syncretism.* New York: Liberal Arts, 1953.

Green, Henry A. *The Economic and Social Origins of Gnosticism.* Atlanta: Scholars Press, 1985.

———. "Interpersonal Relations, Ethnic Structure and Economy—A Sociological Reading of Jewish Identification in Roman Egypt." *Ninth World Congress of Jewish Studies, Jerusalem, August 4–12, 1985, Division B.* Jerusalem: World Union of Jewish Studies, 1986. 15–22.

Green, Peter. *Alexander to Actium: The Historical Evolution of the Hellenistic Age.* Berkeley: Univ. of California Press, 1990.

Gressman, Hugo. *Mose und seine Zeit: Ein Kommentar zu den Mose-sagen.* Göttingen: Vandenhoeck and Ruprecht, 1913.

Griffith, Francis L., and Herbert Thompson, ed., *The Demotic Magical Papyrus of London and Leiden.* 3 vols. London: Grevel, 1904–9.

Groag, Edmund. "Zur Kritik von Tacitus' Quellen in den Historien," JCP 23 (1897): 709–99.

Gruen, Erich S. Response to Emilio Gabba, *Greek Knowledge of Jews up to Hecataeus of Abdera.* Berkeley: Center for Hermeneutical Studies, 1981. 15–18.

Guarducci, Margherita. "Poeti vaganti e conferenzieri dell' età ellenistica." MANL, ser. 6.2 (1929): 629–65.

Gutbrod, Walter. "νομοθέτης." TDNT 4 (1967): 1089.

Güterbock, Hans-Gustav. "The Hittite Version of the Hurrian Kumarbi Myths: Oriental Forerunners of Hesiod." *AJA* 52 (1948): 123–34.

Gutmann, Joshua. "Antoninus Pius: In Talmud and Aggadah." *EJ* 3 (1971): 165–66.

Habicht, Christian. "Die herrschende Gesellschaft in den hellenistischen Monarchien." *VSW* 45 (1958): 1–15.

Hadas, Moses. "Aeneas and the Tradition of the National Hero." *AJP* 69 (1948): 408–14.

———, ed. and trans. *Aristeas to Philocrates [Letter of Aristeas].* New York: Harper, 1951.

———. "Plato in Hellenistic Fusion." *JHI* 19 (1958): 3–13.

———. *Hellenistic Culture: Fusion and Diffusion.* New York: Columbia Univ. Press, 1959.

Hadas-Lebel, Mireille. "Jacob et Esau ou Israel et Rome dans le talmud et le midrash." *RHR* 201 (1984): 369–92.

———. "L'Image de Rome dans la littérature juive d'époque hellénistique et romaine jusqu'au début du IVe siècle." Ph.D. diss., Univ. of Paris: Sorbonne, 1987.

Hahn, Ferdinand. *Das Verständnis der Mission im Neuen Testament.* Neukirchen-Vluyn: Neukirchener Verlag des Erziehungsvereins, 1963.

Haigh, Arthur E., and Arthur W. Pickard-Cambridge. *The Attic Theatre: A Description of the Stage and Theatre of the Athenians and of the Dramatic Performances at Athens,* 3d ed. Oxford: Clarendon, 1927.

Halevi, Elimelekh Epstein. *The Aggadah in the Light of Greek Sources* [in Hebrew]. Tel-Aviv: Dvir, 1972.

Halévy, Joseph. "Le Culte d'une tête d'âne." *RS* 11 (1903) 154–64.

Halévy, Meyer A. *Moise dans l'histoire et dans la légende.* Paris: Rieder, 1927.

Hanfmann, George M. A. "The Ninth Campaign at Sardis." BASOR 187 (Oct. 1967): 9–62.

———. *From Croesus to Constantine: The Cities of Western Asia Minor and Their Arts in Greek and Roman Times.* Ann Arbor: Univ. of Michigan Press, 1975.

———. *Sardis from Prehistoric to Roman Times: Results of the Archaeological Exploration of Sardis 1958–1975.* Cambridge: Harvard Univ. Press, 1983.

Hanson, Paul D. "Rebellion in Heaven, Azazel, and Euhemeristic Heroes in I Enoch 6–11." *JBL* 96 (1977): 195–233.

Harder, Richard. *Ocellus Lucanus—Text und Kommentar.* Berlin: Weidmann, 1926.

Harkavy, Albert. "Contribution à la littérature gnomique." *REJ* 24 (1903): 298–305.

von Harnack, Adolf. *The Mission and Expansion of Christianity in the First Three Centuries,* 2d ed., 2 vols. Trans. James Moffatt. London: Williams and Norgate, 1904–5.

Harris, Harold A. *Greek Athletics and the Jews.* Cardiff: Univ. of Wales Press, 1976.

Harris, William V. *Ancient Literacy.* Cambridge, Mass.: Harvard Univ. Press, 1989.

Hata, Gohei. "The Story of Moses Interpreted within the Context of Anti-Semitism." In *JJC,* 180–97.

Hecht, Richard D. "The Exegetical Contexts of Philo's Interpretation of Circumcision." In *Nourished with Peace: Studies in Hellenistic Judaism in Memory of Samuel Sandmel,* ed. Frederick E. Greenspahn et al. Chico, California: Scholars Press, 1984. 51–79.

Hefele, Charles J. *A History of the Christian Councils from the Original Documents,* 2d ed., 5 vols. Trans. William R. Clark. Edinburgh: Clark, 1894–96.

Heinemann, Isaak. "Antisemitismus." *RE,* Supplement 5 (1931): 3–43.

———. "Moses." *RE* 31 (1935): 359–75.

Heller, Bernhard. Rev. of Meyer A. Halévy, *Moise dans l'histoire et dans la légende.* MGWJ 72 (1928): 631–33.

Henderson, Isobel. "Ancient Greek Music." In *New Oxford History of Music,* vol. 1, ed. Jack A. Westrup et al. London: Oxford Univ. Press, 1957. 336–403.

Hengel, Martin. "Die Synagogeninschrift von Stobi." *ZNW* 57 (1966): 145–83.

———. *Judentum und Hellenismus: Studien zu ihrer Begegnung unter besonderer Berücksichtigung Palästinas bis zur Mitte des 2 Jh.s. v Chr.* Tübingen: Mohr, 1969; 2d ed., 1973. Trans. John Bowden. *Judaism and Hellenism: Studies in Their Encounter in Palestine during the Early Hellenistic Period.* 2 vols. Philadelphia: Fortress, 1974 (references are to the English translation).

————. "Qumran und der Hellenismus." In *Qumran. Sa piété, sa théologie, et son milieu*, ed. Matthias Delcor. Paris: Duculot, 1978. 333–72.

————, in collaboration with Christoph Markschies. *Zum Problem der 'Hellenisierung' Judäas im 1. Jahrhundert nach Christus.* 1989. Trans. John Bowden. *The 'Hellenization' of Judaea in the First Century after Christ.* London: SCM Press; Philadelphia: Trinity Press International, 1989.

————. "Der Alte und der Neue 'Schürer.'" *JSeS* 35 (1990): 19–72.

Herr, Moshe D. "The Historical Significance of the Dialogue between Jewish Sages and Roman Dignitaries." *SH* 22 (1971): 121–50.

Herrmann, Léon. Review of *Tacitus over de Joden*, by Anna M. A. Hospers-Jansen. *Latomus* 9 (1950): 472–73.

Hinnells, John R. "The Zoroastrian Doctrine of Salvation in the Roman World: A Study of the Oracle of Hystaspes." In *Man and His Salvation: Studies in Memory of S.G.F. Brandon*, ed. Eric J. Sharpe and John R. Hinnells. Manchester: Manchester Univ., 1973. 125–48.

Hirsch, Samuel A. "The Temple of Onias." In *Jews' College Jubilee Volume*, ed. Isidore Harris. London: Luzac, 1906. 39–80.

Holladay, Carl R. *Theios Aner in Hellenistic Judaism: A Critique of the Use of This Category in New Testament Christology.* Missoula, Montana: Scholars Press, 1977.

————. *Fragments from Hellenistic Jewish Authors*, vol. 1: *Historians.* Society of Biblical Literature, Texts and Translations, 20; Pseudepigrapha, 10. Chico, California: Scholars Press, 1983.

————. *Fragments from Hellenistic Jewish Authors*, vol. 2: *Poets.* Society of Biblical Literature, Texts and Translations, 30; Pseudepigrapha, 12. Atlanta: Scholars Press, 1989.

Hollingsworth, Thomas H. *Historical Demography.* Ithaca: Cornell Univ. Press, 1969.

Hölscher, Gustav. "Josephus." *RE* 18 (1916): 1934–2000.

Hommel, Hildebrecht. "Juden und Christen im kaiserzeitlichen Milet. Überlegungen zur Theaterinschrift." *MDAI* 25 (1975): 167–95.

Hopfner, Theodor. *Orient und griechische Philosophie.* Leipzig: Hinrichs, 1925.

van der Horst, Pieter W. "Jews and Christians in Aphrodisias in the Light of Their Relations in Other Cities of Asia Minor." *NTT* 43 (1989): 106–21. Reprinted (revised) in his *Essays on the Jewish World of Early Christianity.* Freiburg: Universitätsverlag and Göttingen: Vandenhoeck and Ruprecht, 1990. 166–81.

Hospers-Jansen, Anna M. A. *Tacitus over de Joden, Hist. 5, 2–13.* Groningen: Wolter, 1949.

Humphreys, W. Lee. "Ahasuerus." *HBD* (1985): 16.

Huxley, George. "Choirilos of Samos." *GRBS* 10 (1969): 12–29.

Isaac, Benjamin. "A Donation for Herod's Temple in Jerusalem." *IEJ* 33 (1983): 86–92.

Jacobson, Howard. "Hermippus, Pythagoras and the Jews." *REJ* 135 (1976): 145–49.

————. *The Exagoge of Ezekiel.* Cambridge: Cambridge Univ. Press, 1983.

Jacoby, Adolf. "Der angebliche Eselkult der Juden und Christen." *AR* 25 (1927): 265–82.

Jacoby, Felix. "Eupolemos (11)." *RE* 11 (1907): 1227–29.
Jaeger, Werner. *Diokles von Karystos: Die griechische Medizin und die Schule des Aristoteles.* Berlin: de Gruyter, 1938.
———. "Greeks and Jews." *JR* 18 (1938): 127–43.
Jellicoe, Sidney. *The Septuagint and Modern Study.* Oxford: Clarendon, 1968.
Jellinek, Adolf. "Eine alte Schutzrede für die Proselyten." In his *Zeitstimmen*, vol. 2. Wien: Herzfeld and Bauer, 1871. 17–28.
Jeremias, Joachim. *Jerusalem zur Zeit Jesu. Kulturgeschichtliche Untersuchung zur neutestamentlichen Zeitgeschichte.* Leipzig: Pfeiffer, 1923; 3d ed., Göttingen: Vandenhoeck and Ruprecht, 1962. Trans. F. H. and C. H. Cave. *Jerusalem in the Time of Jesus: An Investigation into Economic and Social Conditions during the New Testament Period.* Philadelphia: Fortress, 1969.
———. "Die Einwohnerzahl Jerusalems zur Zeit Jesu." ZDPV 66 (1943): 24–31.
Jones, Arnold H. M. *The Greek City from Alexander to Justinian.* Oxford: Clarendon, 1940.
———. *The Cities of the Eastern Roman Provinces*, 2d ed. Oxford: Clarendon, 1971.
Juster, Jean. *Les Juifs dans l'empire romain.* 2 vols. Paris: Geuthner, 1914.
Kalmin, Richard. "Rabbinic Attitudes toward Rabbis as a Key to the Dating of Talmudic Sources," paper delivered to the Society of Biblical Literature, Kansas City, 26 November 1991.
Kaminka, Armand. "Les rapports entre le rabbinisme et la philosophie stoicienne." *REJ* 82 (1926): 233–52.
Kant, Laurence H. "Jewish Inscriptions in Greek and Latin." ANRW 2.20.2. Berlin: de Gruyter, 1987. 671–713.
Kasher, Aryeh. "The Jewish Attitude to the Alexandrian Gymnasium in the First Century A.D." AJAH 1 (1976): 148–61.
———, ed. *The Great Jewish Revolt: Factors and Circumstances Leading to Its Outbreak* [in Hebrew]. Jerusalem: Merkaz Zalman Shazar, 1983.
———. *The Jews in Hellenistic and Roman Egypt: The Struggle for Equal Rights.* Tübingen: Mohr, 1985.
———. *Jews, Idumaeans, and Ancient Arabs: Relations of the Jews in Eretz-Israel with the Nations of the Frontier and the Desert during the Hellenistic and Roman Era (332 B.C.E.–70 C.E.).* Tübingen: Mohr, 1988.
———. *Jews and Hellenistic Cities in Eretz-Israel: Relations of the Jews in Eretz-Israel with the Hellenistic Cities during the Second Temple Period (332 BCE–70 CE).* Tübingen: Mohr, 1990.
Kasher, Menahem. *Torah Shelemah*, vol. 4. Jerusalem: Azriel, 1934.
Katzoff, Ranon. "Jonathan and Late Sparta." *AJP* 106 (1985): 485–89.
———. "Sperber's Dictionary of Greek and Latin Legal Terms in Rabbinic Literature—A Review Essay." *JJS* 20 (1989): 195–206.
Kenyon, Frederic G. "The Library of a Greek at Oxyrhynchus." *JHS* 8 (1922): 131.
———. *Books and Readers in Ancient Greece*, 2d ed. Oxford: Clarendon, 1951.
———, and Colin H. Roberts. "Libraries." *OCD*, 607–8.
Kimelman, Ronald Reuven. "Rabbi Yohanan of Tiberias: Aspects of the Social and Religious History of Third Century Palestine." Ph.D. diss., Yale Univ., 1977.

Kimelman, Ronald Reuven. "The Conflict between R. Yohanan and Resh Laqish on the Supremacy of the Patriarchate." In *Seventh World Congress of Jewish Studies*. Jerusalem: The World Union of Jewish Studies, 1981. 1–20.

———. "*Birkat Ha-Minim* and the Lack of Evidence for an Anti-Christian Prayer in Late Antiquity." In *Jewish and Christian Self-Definition*, vol. 2: *Aspects of Judaism in the Graeco-Roman Period*, ed. E. P. Sanders et al. Philadelphia: Fortress, 1981. 226–44, 391–403.

Kittel, Gerhard. "Das Konnubium mit der Nicht-Juden im antiken Judentum." *Forschungen zur Judenfrage* 2 (1937): 30–62.

———, and Gerhard Friedrich, eds. *Theologisches Wörterbuch zum Neuen Testament*. 9 vols. Stuttgart: Kohlhammer, 1933–73. Trans. Geoffrey W. Bromiley. *Theological Dictionary of the New Testament*. 10 vols. Grand Rapids: Eerdmans, 1964–76.

Klausner, Joseph. *From Jesus to Paul*. Trans. William F. Stinespring. New York: Macmillan, 1943.

Klein, Samuel. "Das Fremdenhaus der Synagoge." MGWJ 76 (1932): 545–57, 603–4; 77 (1933): 81–84.

Kraabel, Alf Thomas. "Judaism in Asia Minor under the Roman Empire, with a Preliminary Study of the Jewish Community of Sardis, Lydia." Ph.D. diss., Harvard University, 1968.

———. "*Hypsistos* and the Synagogue at Sardis." GRBS 10 (1969): 81–93.

———. "Melito the Bishop and the Synagogue at Sardis: Text and Context." In *Studies Presented to George M. A. Hanfmann*, ed. David G. Mitten et al. Mainz: Philipp von Zabern, 1971. 77–85.

———. "Paganism and Judaism: The Sardis Evidence." In *Paganisme, judaisme, christianisme: Influences et affrontements dans le monde antique: Mélanges offerts à Marcel Simon*, ed. André Benoit et al. Paris: de Boccard, 1978. 13–33.

———. "The Diaspora Synagogue: Archaeological and Epigraphic Evidence since Sukenik." ANRW 2.19.1. Berlin: de Gruyter, 1979. 477–510.

———. "The Disappearance of the 'G-d-Fearers.'" *Numen* 28 (1981): 113–26.

———. "Social Systems of Six Diaspora Synagogues." In *Ancient Synagogues: The State of Research*, ed. Joseph Gutmann. Chico, California: Scholars Press, 1981. 79–91.

———. "The Roman Diaspora: Six Questionable Assumptions." *JJS* 33 (1982): 445–64.

———. "The Synagogue and the Jewish Community." In *Sardis from Prehistoric to Roman Times*, ed. George M. A. Hanfmann. Cambridge, Mass.: Harvard Univ. Press, 1983. 168–90.

———. "Synagoga Caeca: Systematic Distortion in Gentile Interpretations of Evidence for Judaism in the Early Christian Period." In *'To See Ourselves as Others See Us.' Christians, Jews, 'Others' in Late Antiquity*, ed. Jacob Neusner and Ernest S. Frerichs. Chico, California: Scholars Press, 1985. 219–46.

———. "Greeks, Jews, and Lutherans in the Middle Half of Acts." HTR 79 (1986): 147–57.

Krappe, Alexander H. "Ἀπόλλων Ὄνος." CP 42 (1947): 223–34.

Krauss, Samuel. "The Jews in the Works of the Church Fathers." JQR 5 (1892–93): 122–57; 6 (1893–94): 82–99, 225–61.

Krauss, Samuel. *Griechische und lateinische Lehnwörter im Talmud, Midrasch und Targum*, vols. 1–2. Berlin: Calvary, 1899.

Kroll, Wilhelm. *Studien zum Verständnis der römischen Literatur*. Stuttgart: Metzler, 1924.

Krüger, Paul. *Geschichte der Quellen und Litteratur des römischen Rechts*, 2d ed. München: Duncker and Humblot, 1912.

Kübler, Bernhard G. A. "Rechtsschulen." *RE*, 2nd Reihe (1920): 380–94.

———. *Geschichte des römischen Rechts*. Leipzig: Deichert, 1925.

Kuhn, Karl G. "Προσήλυτος." TDNT 6 (1968): 727–44.

———, and Hartmut Stegemann. "Proselyten." *RE*, Supplement 9 (1962): 1248–83.

Kuntz, Frederick. "Die Sprache des Tacitus und die Tradition der lateinischen Historikersprache." Ph.D. diss., Heidelberg, 1962.

Labhardt, Theobald. *Quae de Iudaeorum Origine Iudicaverint Veteres*. Augsburg: Pfeiffer, 1881.

Lake, Kirsopp. "Proselytes and G-d-fearers." In Frederick Foakes-Jackson and Kirsopp Lake, *The Beginnings of Christianity*, I: *The Acts of the Apostles*. London: Macmillan, 1933. 74–96.

Lane, Eugene N. "Sabazius and the Jews in Valerius Maximus: A Reexamination." *JRS* 69 (1979): 35–38.

LaPiana, George. "Foreign Groups in Rome during the First Centuries of the Empire." *HTR* 20 (1927): 183–403.

Lemy, Thomas J., ed. *Sancti Ephraemi Syri Hymni et Sermones*. 4 vols. Mechlinia: Dessain, 1882–1902.

Leon, Harry J. *The Jews of Ancient Rome*. Philadelphia: Jewish Publication Society, 1960.

Leonhard, Franz X. *Über den Bericht des Tacitus über die Juden, Hist. 5, 2–6*. Ellwangen: Kaupert, 1852.

Leopold, John W. Response to Emilio Gabba, *Greek Knowledge of Jews up to Hecataeus of Abdera*. Berkeley: Center for Hermeneutical Studies, 1981. 19–25.

Lerle, Ernst. *Proselytenwerbung und Urchristentum*. Berlin: Evangelische Verlagsanstadt, 1960.

Lesquier, Jean. "Les Actes de divorce gréco-égyptiens: Etude de formulaire." *RP* 30 (1906): 5–30.

Lévi, Israel. "Le prosélytisme juif." *REJ* 50 (1905): 1–9; 51 (1906): 1–31; 53 (1907): 56–61.

Levine, Etan. *The Aramaic Version of Jonah*. Jerusalem: Jerusalem Academic Press, 1975.

Levine, Lee I. "The Jewish-Greek Conflict in First-Century Caesarea." *JJS* 25 (1974): 381–97.

———. "The Jewish Patriarch (Nasi) in Third Century Palestine." ANRW 2.19.2. Berlin: de Gruyter, 1979. 649–88.

Lévy, Isidore. "Moïse en Ethiopie." *REJ* 53 (1907): 201–11.

———. *La légende de Pythagore de Grèce en Palestine*. Bibliothèque de l'Ecole des hautes Etudes. Sciences historiques et philologiques, 250. Paris: Champion, 1927.

Lévy, Israel. "Tacite et l'origine du peuple juif." *Latomus* 5 (1946): 331–40.

Lewis, David M. "The Jewish Inscriptions of Egypt." *CPJ*, vol. 3. Cambridge, Mass.: Harvard Univ. Press, 1964), 138–66.

Lewis, Naphtali. *Life in Egypt under Roman Rule*. Oxford: Oxford Univ. Press, 1983.

Lewy, Hans (Johanan). "Aethiopier und Juden in der antiken Literatur." MGWJ 81 (1937): 65–71.

———. "Aristotle and the Jewish Sage according to Clearchus of Soli." *HTR* 31 (1938): 205–35.

———. *Studies in Jewish Hellenism* [in Hebrew]. Jerusalem: Bialik, 1960.

Lieberman, Saul. *Ha-Yerushalmi Kiphshuto*, vol. 1.1. Jerusalem: Darom, 1934.

———. *Greek in Jewish Palestine*. New York: Jewish Theological Seminary of America, 1942. Esp. "Gentiles and Semi-Proselytes," 68–90.

———. "Palestine in the Third and Fourth Centuries." *JQR* 36 (1945–46): 329–70; 37 (1946–47): 31–54.

———. *Hellenism in Jewish Palestine*. New York: Jewish Theological Seminary of America, 1950.

———. "How Much Greek in Jewish Palestine?" In *Studies and Texts*, vol. 1: *Biblical and Other Studies*, ed. Alexander Altmann. Cambridge, Mass.: Harvard Univ. Press, 1963. 123–41.

———. *Texts and Studies*. New York: Ktav, 1974.

Lifshitz, Baruch. "Les Juifs à Venosa." *RF* 40 (1962): 367–71.

———. "Papyrus Grecs du désert de Juda." *Aegyptus* 42 (1962): 240–56.

———. *Donateurs et fondateurs dans les synagogues juives: Répertoire des dédicaces grecques relatives à la construction et à la réfection des synagogues*. Paris: Gabalda, 1967.

———. "De nouveau sur les 'sympathisants.' " *JSJ* 1 (1970): 77–84.

———. Prolegomenon to *CII* (reprint), vol. 1. New York: Ktav, 1975. 21–107.

Linder, Amnon, ed. *The Jews in Roman Imperial Legislation*. Detroit: Wayne State Univ. Press, 1987.

Littman, Robert. "Anti-Semitism in the Greco-Roman Pagan World." In *Remembering for the Future: Working Papers and Addenda*, vol. 1: *Jews and Christians during and after the Holocaust*, ed. Yehuda Bauer et al. Oxford: Pergamon, 1989. 825–35.

Littmann, Enno. *Sardis*, vol. 6, pt. 7. Leiden: Brill, 1916. 23–28.

Liver, Jacob. "The Half-Shekel Offering in Biblical and Post-Biblical Literature." *HTR* 56 (1963): 173–98.

Lombardia, Pedro. "Los Matrimonios mixtos en el Concilio de Elvira." AHDE 24. 543–58.

Macalister, Robert A. Stewart, and John Garrow Duncan. *Excavations on the Hill of Ophel, Jerusalem, 1924–1925*. London: Palestine Exploration Fund, 1926.

MacDonald, John. "The Samaritan Doctrine of Moses." *SJT* 3 (1960): 149–62.

———. *The Theology of the Samaritans*. London, SCM Press, 1964.

McEleney, Neil J. "Conversion, Circumcision and the Law." *NTS* 20 (1973–74): 319–41.

McKnight, Scot. *A Light among the Gentiles: Jewish Missionary Activity in the Second Temple Period*. Minneapolis: Fortress, 1991.

———. "Jewish Missionary Activity: The Evidence of Demographics and Synagogues." In *Jewish Proselytism*, ed. Amy-Jill Levine and Richard I. Pervo. Lanham, Maryland: Univ. Press of America, forthcoming. 1–33.

MacLennan, Robert S., and Alf Thomas Kraabel. "The G-d-Fearers—A Literary and Theological Invention." *BAR* 12.5 (Sept.–Oct. 1986): 46–53.

MacMullen, Ramsay. *Roman Social Relations, 50 B.C. to A.D. 284*. New Haven: Yale Univ. Press, 1974.

———. *Roman Government's Response to Crisis, A.D. 235–337*. New Haven: Yale Univ. Press, 1976.

Magie, David. *Roman Rule in Asia Minor to the End of the Third Century after Christ*. 2 vols. Princeton: Princeton Univ. Press, 1950.

Malherbe, Abraham J. *Social Aspects of Early Christianity*, 2d ed. Philadelphia: Fortress, 1983.

Malinowski, Francis X. "Galilean Judaism in the Writings of Flavius Josephus." Ph.D. diss., Duke University, 1973.

Mantel, Hugo. *Studies in the History of the Sanhedrin*. Cambridge, Mass.: Harvard Univ. Press, 1961.

———. "The Causes of the Bar Kochba Revolt." *JQR* 58 (1967–68): 224–42, 274–96.

Marcus, Ralph. "An Outline of Philo's System of Education" [in Hebrew]. In *Sefer Touroff (Turov)*, ed. Eisig Silberschlag. Boston: Hebrew Teachers College, 1938. 223–31.

———, ed. and trans. *Josephus*, vol. 7. *LCL*; London: Heinemann, 1943.

———. "Jewish and Greek Elements in the Septuagint." In *Louis Ginzberg Jubilee Volume*, ed. Alexander Marx et al. New York: American Academy for Jewish Research, 1945. 227–45.

———. "Antisemitism in the Hellenistic-Roman World." In *Essays on Antisemitism*, 2d ed., ed. Koppel S. Pinson. New York: Conference on Jewish Relations, 1946. 61–78.

———. "The *Sebomenoi* in Josephus." *JSS* 14 (1952): 247–50.

Margalioth, Mordecai, ed. *Sefer Ha-Razim* [in Hebrew]. Jerusalem: American Academy for Jewish Research, 1966.

Marmorstein, Arthur. "Judaism and Christianity in the Middle of the Third Century." In his *Studies in Jewish Theology*. London: Oxford Univ. Press, 1950. 179–224.

Marrou, Henri I. *Histoire de l'éducation dans l'antiquité*, 6th ed. Paris: Editions du Seuil, 1965. Trans. George Lamb. *A History of Education in Antiquity*. New York: Sheed and Ward, 1956 (references are to the English translation).

Marshall, Anthony J. "Flaccus and the Jews of Asia—Cicero Pro Flacco 28.67–69." *Phoenix* 29 (1975): 139–54.

Mason, Steve. *Flavius Josephus on the Pharisees*. Leiden: Brill, 1991.

Matthews, Isaac G. "The Jewish Apologetic to the Grecian World in the Apocryphal and Pseudepigraphical Literature." Ph.D. diss., University of Chicago, 1914.

Mayerson, Philip. *Classical Mythology in Literature, Art, and Music*. Waltham, Mass.: Xerox, 1971.

Meek, Theophile J. "The Translation of *Ger* in the Hexateuch and Its Bearing on the Documentary Hypothesis." *JBL* 49 (1930): 172–80.

Meeks, Wayne A. *The Prophet-King: Moses Traditions and the Johannine Christology. Supplements to NT*, 14. Leiden: Brill, 1967.

———. *The First Urban Christians: The Social World of the Apostle Paul*. New Haven: Yale University Press, 1983.

Mélèze-Modrzejewski, Joseph. "Sur l'antisémitisme païen." In *Le Racisme, mythes et sciences, pour Léon Poliakov*, ed. Maurice Olender. Bruxelles: Editions Complexe, 1981. 411–39.

———. "L'Image du juif dans la pensée grecque vers 300 avant notre ère." In *Greece and Rome in Eretz Israel: Collected Essays*, ed. Aryeh Kasher et al. Jerusalem: Yad Izhak Ben-Zvi: the Israel Exploration Society, 1990. 105–18.

Mendels, Doron. "Hecataeus of Abdera and a Jewish 'Patrios Politeia' of the Persian Period (Diodorus Siculus XL, 3)." *ZAW* 95 (1983): 96–110.

Mendelson, Alan. *Secular Education in Philo of Alexandria*. Cincinnati: Hebrew Union College, 1982.

———. *Philo's Jewish Identity*. Atlanta: Scholars Press, 1988.

Meyer, Eduard. *Ursprung und Anfänge des Christentums*, 5th ed., vol. 2. Stuttgart: Cotta, 1925.

Meyers, Carol L., and Eric M. Meyers. "The Ark in Art: A Ceramic Rendering of the Torah Shrine from Nabratein." *E-I* 16 (1982): 176*–185*.

Meyers, Eric M. "Galilean Regionalism as a Factor in Historical Reconstruction." BASOR 220–21 (1976): 93–101.

———. "The Cultural Setting of Galilee: The Case of Regionalism and Early Judaism." ANRW 2.19.1. Berlin: de Gruyter, 1979. 686–702.

———. "Ancient Synagogues in Galilee: Their Religious and Cultural Setting." *BA* 43 (Spring 1980): 97–108.

———. "Galilean Regionalism: A Reappraisal." In *Approaches to Ancient Judaism*, vol. 5, ed. William S. Green. Chico, California: Scholars Press, 1985. 125–31.

———, and James F. Strange. *Archaeology, the Rabbis, and Early Christianity*. Nashville: Abingdon, 1981. 42–47.

Michael, Hugh J. "The Jewish Sabbath in the Latin Classical Writers." AJSL 40 (1923–24): 117–24.

Millar, Fergus. Review of William H. C. Frend, *Martyrdom and Persecution in the Early Church*. *JRS* 56 (1966): 232–36.

———. "The Background to the Maccabean Revolution: Reflections on Martin Hengel's 'Judaism and Hellenism.' " *JJS* 22 (1978): 1–21.

———. "Gentiles and Judaism: 'G-d-Fearers' and Proselytes." In Emil Schürer, *The History of the Jewish People in the Age of Jesus Christ (175 B.C.–A.D. 135)*, vol. 3.1, ed. Geza Vermes and Fergus Millar. Edinburgh: Clark, 1986. 150–76.

Mitteis, Ludwig. *Reichsrecht und volksrecht in den östlichen provinzen des Römischen kaiserreichs*. Leipzig: Teubner, 1891.

Moehring, Horst. "The Persecution of the Jews and the Adherents of the Isis Cult at Rome A.D. 19." *NT* 3 (1954): 293–304.

———. "Rationalization of Miracles in the Writings of Flavius Josephus." TUGAL 112 (1973): 376–83.

———. "The *Acta Pro Judaeis* in the *Antiquities* of Flavius Josephus: A Study in Hellenistic and Modern Apologetic Historiography." In *Christianity, Judaism and Other Greco-Roman Cults: Studies for Morton Smith at Sixty: Judaism before 70*, ed. Jacob Neusner. *Studies in Judaism in Late Antiquity*, vol. 12, part 3. Leiden: Brill, 1975. 124–58.

Momigliano, Arnaldo. "Un documento della spiritualità dei Giudei Leontopolitani." *Aegyptus* 12 (1932): 171–72.

———. "Severo Alexandro Archisynagogus." *Athenaeum* 12 (1934): 151–53.

———. Review of *Judentum und Hellenismus*, by Martin Hengel. *JTS* 21 (1970): 149–53.

———. *Alien Wisdom: The Limits of Hellenization*. Cambridge: Cambridge Univ. Press, 1975.

———. "The Origins of Universal History." In *The Poet and the Historian: Essays in Literary and Historical Biblical Criticism*, ed. Richard E. Friedman. Chico, California: Scholars Press, 1983. 133–54.

Mommsen, Theodor. *Römische Geschichte*, vol. 5. Berlin: Weidmann, 1885.

———. *The Provinces of the Roman Empire from Caesar to Diocletian*, vol. 2. Trans. William P. Dickson. London: Bentley, 1886.

Montevecchi, Orsolina. "Ricerche di sociologia nei documenti dell' Egitto greco-romano." *Aegyptus* 16 (1936): 20.

Moore, George F. *Judaism in the First Centuries of the Christian Era: The Age of the Tannaim*. 3 vols. Cambridge, Mass.: Harvard Univ. Press, 1927–30.

Müller, Carolus. *Geographi Graeci Minores*, vols. 1–2. Paris: Firmin Didot, 1855.

———. *Fragmenta Historicorum Graecorum*, vols. 3–4. Paris: Firmin Didot, 1874.

Mussies, Gerard. "Greek in Palestine and the Diaspora." CRINT, 1040–64.

Mutschmann, Hermann. "Das Genesiscitat in der Schrift Περὶ Ὕψους." *Hermes* 52 (1917): 161–200.

Nadel, Beniamin. "Josephus Flavius and the Terminology of Roman Political Invective" [in Polish]. *Eos* 56 (1966): 256–72.

Nauck, August. *Tragicorum Graecorum Fragmenta*. Leipzig: Teubner, 1889.

Naveh, Joseph, and Jonas C. Greenfield. "Hebrew and Aramaic in the Persian Period." In *The Cambridge History of Judaism*, vol. 1: *Introduction: The Persian Period*, ed. William D. Davies and Louis Finkelstein. Cambridge: Cambridge Univ. Press, 1984. 115–29.

Neubauer, Adolf. *La Géographie du talmud: Mémoire couronné par l'Académie des inscriptions et belles-lettres*. Paris: Michel Lévy, 1868.

Neusner, Jacob. "The Conversion of Adiabene to Judaism." *JBL* 83 (1964): 60–66.

———. "The Jews in Pagan Armenia." *JAOS* 84 (1964): 230–40.

———. "Josephus' Pharisees." In *Ex Orbe Religionum: Studia Geo Widengren Oblata*, vol. 1, ed. J. Bergman et al. Leiden: Brill, 1972. 224–44.

———. *From Enemy to Sibling: Rome and Israel in the First Century of Western Civilization: An Experiment in Method*. Flushing, N.Y.: Queens College, 1986.

———. *Making the Classics in Judaism: The Three Stages of Literary Formation*. Atlanta: Scholars Press, 1989.

Nickelsburg, George W. E. "Apocalyptic and Myth in I Enoch 6–11." *JBL* 96 (1977): 383–405.

———. *Jewish Literature between the Bible and the Mishnah: A Historical and Literary Introduction*. Philadelphia: Fortress, 1981.

Nilsson, Martin P. *Geschichte der griechischen Religion*, vol. 2: *Die hellenistische und römische Zeit (Handbuch der Altertumswissenschaft*, 5.2), 3d ed. München: Beck, 1974.

Nims, Charles F., and Richard C. Steiner. "A Paganized Version of Psalm 20: 2–6 from the Aramaic Text in Demotic Script." JAOS 103 (1983): 261–74.

Nissen, Heinrich. "Die Historien des Plinius." *RM* 26 (1871): 497–548.

Nock, Arthur D. *Conversion: The Old and the New in Religion from Alexander the Great to Augustine of Hippo*. Oxford: Oxford Univ. Press, 1933.

Nodet, Etienne, ed. *Flavius Josèphe: Les Antiquités Juives*, vols. 1–2: Livres I à III. Paris: Les Editions du Cerf, 1990.

Nolland, John. "Proselytism or Politics in Horace, *Satires* I, 4, 138–143?" *VC* 33 (1979): 347–55.

Norden, Eduard. *Die Germanische Urgeschichte in Tacitus Germania*. Leipzig: Teubner, 1920.

———. "Jahve und Moses in hellenistische Theologie." In *Festgabe von Fachgenossen und Freunden A. von Harnack zum siebzigsten Geburtstag dargebracht.* Tübingen: Mohr, 1921. 292–301.

———. "Das Genesiscitat in der Schrift vom Erhabenen." *Abhandlungen der deutschen Akademie der Wissenschaften zu Berlin, Klasse für Sprache, Literatur und Kunst*, 1954, no. 1. Berlin: Akademie Verlag, 1955.

Obbink, Hendrik W. "On the Legends of Moses in the Haggadah." In *Studia Biblica et Semitica Theodoro Christiano Vreizen . . . dedicata*, ed. Willem C. van Unnik and Adam S. van der Woude. Wageningen: Veenman and Zonen, 1966. 252–64.

Oellacher, Hans. *Griechische literarische Papyri*. Baden bei Wien: Rohrer, 1939.

Ohana, Moïse. "Prosélytisme et targum palestinien: Données nouvelles pour la datation de Néofiti 1." *Biblica* 55 (1974): 317–32.

Oldfather, Charles H. *The Greek Literary Texts from Greco-Roman Egypt: A Study in the History of Civilization. University of Wisconsin Studies in the Social Studies and History*, no. 9. Madison: University of Wisconsin, 1923.

Olmstead, Albert T. "The Mid-Third Century of the Christian Era." *CP* 37 (1942): 241–62, 398–420.

Overman, J. Andrew. "The G-d-Fearers: Some Neglected Features." *JSNT* 32 (1988): 17–26.

Pack, Roger A. *The Greek and Latin Literary Texts from Greco-Roman Egypt*, 2d ed. Ann Arbor: Univ. of Michigan Press, 1965.

Pakter, Walter. "Canonical Jewry-Law in the Age of Eusebius." In *Eusebius, Judaism, and Christianity* (forthcoming), ed. Harold W. Attridge and Gohei Hata.

Paratore, Ettore. *Tacito*, 2d ed. Roma: Edizioni dell' Ateneo, 1962. 596–612.

Parkes, James. *The Conflict of the Church and Synagogue: A Study in the Origins of Antisemitism*. London: Soncino, 1934.

Patai, Raphael. "Maria the Jewess—Founding Mother of Alchemy." *Ambix* 29 (1982): 177–97.

Paul, André. "Flavius Josephus' 'Antiquities of the Jews': An Anti-Christian Manifesto." *NTS* 31 (1985): 473–80.

Pease, Arthur S. "Some Aspects of Invisibility." *HSEP* 53 (1942): 17–21.

———, ed. *Cicero, De Natura Deorum*. 2 vols. Cambridge, Mass.: Harvard Univ. Press, 1955.

Peeters, Paul. *Analecta Bollandiana* 23 (1904): 255-57.

Perrot, Charles. "Les recits d'enfance dans la Haggada antérieure au IIe siècle de nôtre ère." *RSR* 55 (1967): 481–518.

Pfaff, Franz. "Rufus aus Samaria, Hippokrates kommentator und Quelle Galens." *Hermes* 67 (1932): 356–59.

Pfister, Friedrich. *Der Reliquienkult im Altertum*. Giessen: Töpelmann, 1909–12.

Philip, James A. *Pythagoras and Early Pythagoreanism*. Toronto: University of Toronto Press, 1966.

Philonenko, Marc. *Joseph et Aséneth*. Leiden: Brill, 1968.

Pines, Shlomo. "The Iranian Name for Christians and the 'G-d-fearers.' " PIASH 2.7 (1968): 143–52.

Popper, Karl R. *The Open Society and Its Enemies*, vol. 1. London: Routledge, 1945.

Preisendanz, Karl L. *Papyri Graecae Magicae*. Leipzig: Teubner, 1928.

Preisigke, Friedrich. *Sammelbuch griechischer Urkunden aus Ägypten*. Strassburg: Trübner, 1913.

Prinz, Otto. "Inclutus." *Glotta* 29 (1942): 138–47.

Pritsak, Omeljan, and Norman Golb. *Documents of the History of the Khazars*. Berkeley: Univ. of California Press, 1977.

Pucci Ben Ze'ev, Maria. "Greek Attacks against Alexandrian Jews during Emperor Trajan's Reign." *JSJ* 20 (1989): 31–48.

Rabello, Alfredo Mordechai. "The Legal Condition of the Jews in the Roman Empire." ANRW 2.13. Berlin: de Gruyter, 1980. 662–762.

Rabinowitz, Louis I. "Onkelos and Aquila." *EJ* 12 (1971): 1405–6.

Radin, Max. *The Jews among the Greeks and Romans*. Philadelphia: Jewish Publication Society, 1915.

Raglan, Lord Fitz R. R. S. "The Hero of Tradition." *Folklore* 45 (1934): 212–31.

Rajak, Tessa. "Moses in Ethiopia: Legend and Literature." *JJS* 29 (1978): 111–22.

———. "Was There a Roman Charter for the Jews?" *JRS* 74 (1984): 107–23.

———. "Jewish Rights in the Greek Cities under Roman Rule." In *Approaches to Ancient Judaism*, vol. 5: *Studies in Judaism and Its Greco-Roman Context*, ed. William S. Green. *Brown Judaic Studies*, 32. Atlanta: Scholars Press, 1985. 19–35.

Ramsay, William M. *The Cities and Bishoprics of Phrygia; being an essay of the local history of Phrygia from the earliest times to the Turkish Conquest*. 2 vols. Oxford: Clarendon, 1895–97.

———. *Pauline and Other Studies in Early Christian History*. London: Hodder and Stoughton, 1906.

Rank, Otto. *Der Mythus von der Geburt des Helden: Versuch einer psychologischen Mythendeutung*. Wien: Deuticke, 1909. Trans. F. Robbins and Smith E. Jelliffe. *The Myth of the Birth of the Hero: A Psychological Interpretation of Mythology*. New York: Journal of Nervous and Mental Disease Publishing Co., 1914.

von Ranke, Leopold. *Weltgeschichte*, vol. 3.2. Leipzig: Duncker and Humblot, 1883. 12–33.

Rappaport, Salomo. *Agada und Exegese bei Flavius Josephus*. Wien: Alexander Kohut Memorial Foundation, 1930.

Rappaport, Uriel. "Jewish Religious Propaganda and Proselytism in the Period of the Second Commonwealth" [in Hebrew]. Ph.D. diss., Jerusalem: Hebrew University, 1965.

———. "The Relations between Jews and Non-Jews and the Great War against Rome" [in Hebrew]. *Tarbiz* 47 (1977–78): 1–14. Reprinted in Aryeh Kasher, *The Great Jewish Revolt* [in Hebrew], 159–72.

———. "Notes on the Causes of the Great Revolt against Rome" [in Hebrew]. *Cathedra* 8 (1978): 42–46. Reprinted in Aryeh Kasher, *The Great Jewish Revolt* [in Hebrew], 417–21.

Rattenbury, Robert M. "Romance: Traces of Lost Greek Novels." In *New Chapters in the History of Greek Literature*, 3d series, ed. John U. Powell. Oxford: Clarendon, 1933. 211–57.

Redpath, Henry A. "Mythological Terms in the LXX." *AJT* 9 (1905): 34–45.

Reider, Joseph, ed. *The Book of Wisdom*. New York: Harper, 1957.

Reifenberg, Adolf. *Ancient Jewish Coins*, 4th ed. Jerusalem: Mass, 1965.

Reinach, Théodore. *Textes d'auteurs grecs et romains relatifs au Judaisme*. Paris: Presses Universitaires de France, 1895.

Reynolds, Joyce M. *Aphrodisias and Rome: Documents from the Excavation of the Theatre at Aphrodisias Conducted by Professor Kenan T. Erim, Together with Some Related Texts*. London: Society for the Promotion of Roman Studies, 1982.

———, and Robert Tannenbaum. *Jews and G-d-Fearers at Aphrodisias: Greek Inscriptions with Commentary*. Cambridge Philological Society, Supplementary Vol. 12. Cambridge: Cambridge Univ. Press, 1987.

Robbins, Vernon K. "Laudation Stories in the Gospel of Luke and Plutarch's *Alexander*." In *Society of Biblical Literature 1981 Seminar Papers*, ed. Kent H. Richards. Chico, California: Scholars Press, 1981. 293–308.

Robert, Louis. *Études anatoliennes; recherches sur les inscriptions grecques de l'Asie Mineure*. Paris: de Boccard, 1937.

———. "Un Corpus des Inscriptions Juives." *REJ* 101 (1937): 73–86.

———. "Sur un Dicton relatif à Phasélis. La vente du Droit de Cité." *Hellenica* 1. Limoges: Bontemps, 1940: 37–42.

———. "Épigrammes relatives à des Gouverneurs." *Hellenica* 4. Paris: Librairie d'Amérique et d'Orient Adrien-Maisonneuve, 1948: 35–114.

———. *Nouvelles Inscriptions de Sardes*. Paris: Librairie d'Amérique et l'Orient, 1964.

———. *Comptes rendus de l'Académie des Inscriptions et Belles Lettres*, 1968. 451 ff.

Roberts, Colin H. "The Christian Book and the Greek Papyri." *JTS* 50 (1949): 155–68.

Rohde, Erwin. *Kleine Schriften*. vol. 2. Tübingen: Mohr, 1901.

Rokeah, David. "A New Onomasticon Fragment from Oxyrhynchus and Philo's Etymologies." *JTS* 19 (1968): 70–82.

———. *Jews, Pagans and Christians in Conflict*. Jerusalem/Leiden: Magnes/Brill, 1982.

Romaniuk, Kazimierz. "Die Gottesfürchtigen im Neuen Testament." *Aegyptus* 44 (1964): 66–91.

Rose, Herbert J. "Divination (Greek)." In *Encyclopaedia of Religion and Ethics*, vol. 4, ed. James Hastings. New York: Scribner's, 1914. 796–99.

Rose, Herbert J. *Religion in Greece and Rome.* New York: Harper, 1959.

———. "Pelasgus." *OCD* (1970): 794.

———. "Time-Reckoning." *OCD* (1970): 1075–76.

Rosenbloom, Joseph R. *Conversion to Judaism: From the Biblical Period to the Present.* Cincinnati: Hebrew Union College Press, 1978.

Rosenthal, Judah. *Ḥiwi al-Balkhi: A Comparative Study.* Philadelphia: Dropsie College, 1949.

Rostowzew (Rostovtzeff), Michael. "Fiscus." *RE* 12 (1909): 2385–2405.

———. *The Social and Economic History of the Hellenistic World.* 3 vols. Oxford: Clarendon, 1941.

Roth, Cecil, and Yehuda Slutsky. "Judaizers." *EJ* 10 (1971): 397–402.

Rothkoff, Aaron. "Minor Tractates." *EJ* 12 (1971): 49–50.

Runnalls, Donna. "Moses' Ethiopian Campaign." *JSJ* 14 (1983): 135–56.

Safrai, Samuel, and Menachem Stern, eds. *The Jewish People in the First Century: Historical Geography, Political History, Social, Cultural and Religious Life and Institutions,* vol. 2 (*Compendia Rerum Iudaicarum ad Novum Testamentum,* Section 1: *The Jewish People in the First Century.* Assen: Van Gorcum, 1976 (abbreviated as CRINT in this volume).

Saltman, Ellen S. "The Jews of Asia Minor in the Greco-Roman Period: A Religious and Social Study." M.A. diss., Smith College, 1971.

Sanders, E. P. "The Covenant as a Soteriological Category and the Nature of Salvation in Palestinian and Hellenistic Judaism." In *Jews, Greeks, and Christians: Studies in Honor of W. D. Davies,* ed. Robert Hamerton-Kelly and Robin Scroggs. Leiden: Brill, 1976. 11–44.

Sandmel, Samuel. *Philo's Place in Judaism: A Study of Conceptions of Abraham in Jewish Literature.* Cincinnati: Hebrew Union College, 1956.

———. *The Genius of Paul.* New York: Farrar, Straus, and Cudahy, 1958.

———. "Hellenism and Judaism." In *Great Confrontations in Jewish History,* ed. Stanley M. Wagner and Allen D. Breck. The J. M. Goodstein Lectures on Judaica, 1975; Denver: Univ. of Denver, 1977. 21–38.

Satran, David. "Daniel: Seer, Philosopher, Holy Man." In *Ideal Figures in Ancient Judaism: Profiles and Paradigms,* ed. John J. Collins and George W. E. Nickelsburg. Society of Biblical Literature, Septuagint and Cognate Studies, 12. Chico, California: Scholars Press, 1980. 33–48.

Schalit, Abraham, trans. and ed., *Josephus, Antiquitates Judaicae.* 3 vols. [in Hebrew]. Jerusalem: Bialik, 1944–63.

———. "Evidence of an Aramaic Source in Josephus' 'Antiquities of the Jews.'" ASTI4 (1965): 163–88.

Schaller, Berndt. "Hekataios von Abdera über die Juden. Zur Frage der Echtheit und der Datierung." *ZNW* 54 (1963): 15–31.

Schäublin, Christoph. "Josephus und die Griechen." *Hermes* 110 (1982): 316–41.

Schechter, Solomon. "Genizah Fragments 1: Gnomic." *JQR* 16 (1904): 425–42.

Scheller, Meinrad. "σαββώ und σαββάτωσις." *Glotta* 34 (1955): 298–300.

Scherb, Hans. *Das Motif vom starken Knaben in der Märchen der Weltliteratur: Eine religionsgeschichtliche Bedeutung und Entwicklung.* Stuttgart: Kohlhammer, 1930.

Schian, Ruth. *Untersuchungen über das argumentum e consensu omnium.* Hildesheim: Olms, 1973.

Schiffman, Lawrence H. *Who Was a Jew? Rabbinic and Halakhic Perspectives on the Jewish-Christian Schism.* Hoboken: Ktav, 1985.

———. "The Conversion of the Royal House of Adiabene in Josephus and Rabbinic Sources." In *Josephus, Judaism, and Christianity,* ed. Louis H. Feldman and Gohei Hata. Detroit: Wayne State Univ. Press, 1987. 293–312.

Schlatter, Adolf. *Geschichte Israels von Alexander dem Grossen bis Hadrian.* 2d ed. Stuttgart: Calwer, 1906.

Schubart, Wilhelm. *Einführung in die Papyruskunde.* Berlin: Weidmann, 1918.

Schuhl, Pierre M. "Sur un fragment de Cléarque: Les premiers rapports entre savants grecs et juifs." *RHR* 147 (1955): 124–26.

Schüller, S. "Some Problems Connected with the Supposed Common Ancestry of Jews and Spartans and Their Relations during the Last Three Centuries B.C." *JSeS* 1 (1956): 257–68.

Schürer, Emil. "Die Juden im bosporanischen Reiche und die Genossenschaften der σεβόμενοι θεὸν ὕψιστον ebendaselbt." SPAW (Berlin, 1897): 200–25.

———. *Geschichte des jüdischen Volkes im Zeitalter Jesu Christi,* 4th ed., vol. 3, part 4. Leipzig: Hinrichs, 1909.

———. *The History of the Jewish People in the Age of Jesus Christ (175 B.C.–A.D. 135),* ed. Geza Vermes and Fergus Millar. 3 vols. Edinburgh: Clark, 1973–86.

Schwartz, Daniel R. "*KATA TOYTON TON KAIPON*: Josephus' Source on Agrippa II." *JQR* 72 (1981–82): 241–68.

———. "Josephus and Nicolaus on the Pharisees." *JSJ* 14 (1983): 164–71.

———. *Agrippa I: The Last King of Judaea.* Tübingen: Mohr, 1990.

Scramuzza, Vincent M. "The Policy of the Early Roman Emperors towards Judaism." In *The Beginnings of Christianity,* vol. 5, ed. Frederick J. Foakes-Jackson and Kirsopp Lake. London: Macmillan, 1933. 284.

Seaver, James E. *Persecution of the Jews in the Roman Empire (300–438).* Lawrence, Kansas: Univ. of Kansas Press, 1952.

Sedgwick, Walter B. "Sappho in 'Longinus' (X, 2, Line 13)." *AJP* 69 (1948): 198–99.

Seeger, Andrew R. "The Building History of the Sardis Synagogue." *AJA* 76 (1972): 425–35.

Segal, Alan F. "Torah and Nomos in Recent Scholarly Discussion." *SR* 13 (1984): 19–28. Reprinted in his *The Other Judaisms of Late Antiquity.* Atlanta: Scholars Press, 1987. 131–45.

———. *Paul the Convert: The Apostolate and Apostasy of Saul the Pharisee.* New Haven: Yale Univ. Press, 1990.

Sevenster, Jan N. *Do You Know Greek? How Much Greek Could the First Jewish Christians Have Known?* Leiden: Brill, 1968.

———. *The Roots of Pagan Anti-Semitism in the Ancient World.* Supplements to *NT,* 41. Leiden: Brill, 1975.

Sherwin-White, Adrian N. *Racial Prejudice in Imperial Rome.* Cambridge: Cambridge Univ. Press, 1967.

———. "Philo and Avilius Flaccus: A Conundrum." *Latomus* 31 (1972): 820–28.

Shinan, Avigdor. "Moses and the Ethiopian Woman: Sources of a Story in *The Chronicles of Moses*." *SH* 27 (1978): 66–78.

Shroyer, Montgomery J. "Alexandrian Jewish Literalists." *JBL* 55 (1936): 261–84.

Siegert, Folker. "G-ttesfürchtige und Sympathisanten." *JSJ* 4 (1973): 109–64.

Silver, Daniel J. "Moses and the Hungry Birds." *JQR* 64 (1973–74): 123–53.

Silverstone, Alec E. *Aquila and Onkelos*. Manchester: Manchester Univ. Press, 1931.

Simon, Marcel. "G-ttesfürchtiger." *RAC* 11 (1981): 1060–70.

——— . *Verus Israel: Etude sur les relations entre chrétiens et juifs dans l'empire romain, 135–425*. Paris: de Boccard, 1948. Trans. Henry McKeating. *Verus Israel: A Study of the Relations between Christians and Jews in the Roman Empire (135–425)*. Oxford: Oxford Univ. Press, 1986.

Slingerland, Dixon. "Suetonius *Claudius* 25.4 and the Account in Dio Cassius." *JQR* 79 (1988–89): 305–22.

Slouschz, Nahum. *Hébraeo-Phéniciens et Judéo-Berbères: Introduction à l'histoire des juifs et du judaisme en Afrique*. Paris: Leroux, 1908.

——— . *Travels in North Africa*. Philadelphia: Jewish Publication Society, 1927.

Smallwood, Edith Mary. "The Alleged Jewish Tendencies of Poppaea Sabina." *JTS* 10 (1959): 329–35.

——— . "Some Notes on the Jews under Tiberius." *Latomus* 15 (1956): 314–29.

——— . "The Legislation of Hadrian and Antoninus Pius against Circumcision." *Latomus* 18 (1959): 334–47; 20 (1961): 93–96.

——— , ed. *Philonis Alexandrini Legatio ad Gaium*. Leiden: Brill, 1961.

——— . *The Jews under Roman Rule: From Pompey to Diocletian*. Leiden: Brill, 1976.

——— . *From Pagan Protection to Christian Oppression*. Inaugural Lecture delivered before the Queen's University of Belfast. Belfast: Mayne, Boyd, 1979.

Smith, Martin F. "Fifty-five New Fragments of Diogenes of Oenoanda." *AS* 28 (1978): 39–92.

Smith, Morton. "Palestinian Judaism in the First Century." In *Israel: Its Role in Civilization*, ed. Moshe Davis. New York: Harper, 1956. 67–81. Reprinted in Henry A. Fischel, ed. *Essays in Greco-Roman and Related Talmudic Literature*. New York: Ktav, 1977. 183–97.

——— . "Goodenough's *Jewish Symbols* in Retrospect." *JBL* 86 (1967): 53–68.

——— . *Palestinian Parties and Politics That Shaped the Old Testament*. New York: Columbia Univ. Press, 1971.

——— . *Jesus the Magician*. New York: Harper, 1978.

——— . "The Occult in Josephus." In *JJC*, 236–56.

Smolar, Levy, and Moshe Aberbach. "The Golden Calf Episode in Postbiblical Literature." HUCA 39 (1968): 91–116.

Snowden, Frank M. "Ethiopians and the Isiac Worship." *AC* 25 (1956): 112–16.

——— . *Blacks in Antiquity: Ethiopians in the Greco-Roman Experience*. Cambridge: Belknap, 1970.

——— . *Before Color Prejudice: The Ancient View of Blacks*. Cambridge, Mass.: Harvard Univ. Press, 1983.

Sokoloff, Michael. *The Targum to Job from Qumran Cave XI*. Ramat-Gan: Bar-Ilan Univ. Press, 1974.

Solazzi, Siro. "Fra norme romane antisemite." BIDR 3 (1936–37): 396–406.

Solmsen, Friedrich. *Isis among the Greeks and Romans*. Cambridge, Mass.: Harvard Univ. Press, 1979.

Spengel, Leonardus, ed. *Rhetores Gracci*. vols. 2–3. Leipzig: Teubner, 1854–85.

Sperber, Daniel. *A Dictionary of Greek and Latin Legal Terms in Rabbinic Literature*. Ramat-Gan: Bar-Ilan Univ. Press, 1984.

Sprödowsky, Hans. "Die Hellenisierung der Geschichte von Joseph in Ägypten bei Flavius Josephus." Ph.D. diss., Greifswald, 1937.

Squarciapino, Maria Floriani. *La Scuola di Afrodisia*. Roma: Governatorato di Roma, 1945.

Stern, Menahem. *The Documents on the History of the Hasmonaean Revolt* [in Hebrew]. Tel Aviv: Hakibbutz Hameuḥad, 1965.

———, ed. *Greek and Latin Authors on Jews and Judaism*. 3 vols. Jerusalem: Israel Academy of Sciences and Humanities, 1974–84.

———. "The Jews in Greek and Latin Literature." CRINT (1976): 1101–59.

———, and Zvi Baras, eds. *World History of the Jewish People*, First Series: *The Diaspora in the Hellenistic-Roman World* [in Hebrew]. Jerusalem: Am Oved, 1984 (abbreviated in this volume as WHJP).

Strack, Hermann L., and Paul Billerbeck. *Kommentar zum neuen Testament aus Talmud und Midrasch*. 4 vols. München: Beck, 1924.

Strange, James F. "Archaeology and the Religion of Judaism in Palestine." ANRW 2.19.1. Berlin: de Gruyter, 1979. 646–85.

Suter, David W. "Judith." *HBD* (1985): 518.

Swete, Henry B. *Introduction to the Old Testament in Greek*. Cambridge: Cambridge Univ. Press, 1902.

Syme, Ronald. *Ammianus and the Historia Augusta*. Oxford: Clarendon, 1968.

———. "Tacitus: Some Sources of His Information." *JRS* 72 (1982): 68–82.

Tabor, James D. " 'Returning to the Divinity': Josephus's Portrayal of the Disappearances of Enoch, Elijah, and Moses." *JBL* 108 (1989): 225–38.

Talbert, Charles H. "Prophecies of Future Greatness: The Contribution of Greco-Roman Biographies to an Understanding of Luke 1:5–4:15." In *The Divine Helmsman: Studies on G-d's Control of Human Events, Presented to Lou H. Silberman*, ed. James L. Crenshaw and Samuel Sandmel. New York: Ktav, 1980. 129–41.

Tannenbaum, Robert E. "Jews and G-d-Fearers in the Holy City of Aphrodite." *BAR* 12.5 (Sept.–Oct. 1986): 54–57.

Tarn, William W., and Guy T. Griffith. *Hellenistic Civilisation*, 3d ed. London: Arnold, 1952.

Taubenschlag, Rafal. *The Law of Greco-Roman Egypt in the Light of the Papyri, 332 B.C.–640 A.D.* 2 vols. New York: Herald Square, 1944–48.

Taylor, R. E. "Attitudes of the Fathers toward Practices of Jewish Christians." *SP* 4 (1961): 504–11.

Tcherikover, Victor. "The Sambathions." *SH* 1 (1954): 78–98

———. "Jewish Apologetic Literature Reconsidered." *Eos* 48 (1956): 169–93.

Tcherikover, Victor. "Prolegomena." In his *CPJ*, vol. 1. Cambridge, Mass.: Harvard Univ. Press, 1957. 1–111.

————. *Hellenistic Civilization and the Jews*. Philadelphia: Jewish Publication Society, 1959.

————, Alexander Fuks, and Menahem Stern, eds. *CPJ*. 3 vols. Cambridge, Mass.: Harvard Univ. Press, 1957–64.

Thackeray, Henry St. John. "The Poetry of the Greek Book of Proverbs." *JTS* 13 (1912): 46–66.

————. *The Septuagint and Jewish Worship*. London: Milford, 1921.

————, ed. and trans. *Josephus*, vols. 1, 2, 4. *LCL*; London: Heinemann, 1926, 1927, 1930.

————. *Josephus the Man and Historian*. New York: Jewish Institute of Religion, 1929.

————, and Ralph Marcus, trans. and ed. *Josephus*, vol. 5. *LCL*; London: Heinemann, 1934.

Thiaucourt, Camille. "Ce que Tacite dit des Juifs au commencement du livre des *Histoires*." *REJ* 19 (1889): 57–74 and 20 (1890): 312–14.

Thompson, Stith. *Motif-Index of Folk-Literature*. 6 vols. Bloomington: Indiana Univ. Press, 1957.

Tiede, David L. *The Charismatic Figure as Miracle Worker*. Missoula, Montana: Scholars Press, 1972.

Torrey, Charles C. "The Magic of 'Lotapes.' " *JBL* 68 (1949): 325–27.

Townend, Gavin P. "Claudius and the Digressions in Tacitus." *RM* 105 (1962): 358–68.

Trebilco, Paul R. "Studies on Jewish Communities in Asia Minor." Ph.D. diss., Univ. of Durham, 1987. Revised and abbreviated as *Jewish Communities in Asia Minor*. Cambridge: Cambridge Univ. Press, 1991.

Troiani, Lucio. "I lettori delle Antichità giudaiche di Giuseppe. Prospettive e problemi." *Athenaeum* 64 (1986): 343–53.

Trüdinger, Karl. *Studien zur Geschichte der griechisch-römischen Ethnographie*. Basel: Birkhäuser, 1918.

Turcan, Robert. *Sénèque et les religions orientales*. Bruxelles: Latomus, 1967.

Turner, Eric G. "Roman Oxyrhynchus." *JEA* 39 (1952): 78–93.

————. *Greek Papyri: An Introduction*. Oxford: Clarendon, 1980.

van Unnik, Willem C. "Josephus' Account of the Story of Israel's Sin with Alien Women in the Country of Midian (Num. 25. 1 ff.)." In *Travels in the World of the Old Testament: Studies Presented to Professor M. A. Beek*, ed. Matthieu S. H. G. Heerma von Voss. *Studia Semitica Nerlandica*, 16. Assen: Van Gorcum, 1974. 241–61.

Urbach, Ephraim E. "Ger" [in Hebrew]. *Encyclopedia Ivrit* 11 (Jerusalem: Encyclopedia Publishing Co., 1957): 172–84.

————. "Class-Status and Leadership in the World of the Palestinian Sages." PIASH 2.4 (1968): 38–74.

Usener, Hermann K. "Italische Mythen." *RM* 30 (1875): 182–229. Reprinted in his *Kleine Schriften*, vol. 4. Leipzig: Teubner, 1913. 93–143.

Ussani, Vincenzo. "Quaestioni Flaviane." *RF* 39 (1911): 397–99

Vassiliev, Afanasii. *Anecdota Graeco-Byzantina*. Moscow: Universitas Caesarea, 1893.

Vischer, Lukas. "Le prétendu culte de l'âne dans l'Eglise primitive." *RHR* 139 (1951): 14–35.

Vogelstein, Hermann, and Paul Rieger. *Geschichte der Juden in Rom*, vol. 1. Berlin: Mayer and Müller, 1896.

Wacholder, Ben Zion. "Cases of Proselytizing in the Tosafist Responsa." *JQR* 51 (1960–61): 288–315.

———. "Greek Authors in Herod's Library." *SBB* 5 (1961): 102–9. Reprinted in his *Nicolaus of Damascus*. Berkeley: Univ. of California Press, 1962. 81–86.

———. *Nicolaus of Damascus*. Berkeley: Univ. of California Press, 1962.

———. "Biblical Chronology in the Hellenistic World Chronicles." *HTR* 61 (1968): 451–81. Reprinted in his *Essays on Jewish Chronology and Chronography*. New York: Ktav, 1976. 106–36.

———. *Eupolemus: A Study of Judaeo-Greek Literature*. Cincinnati: Hebrew Union College, 1974.

Wallach, Luitpold. "A Palestinian Polemic against Idolatry: A Study in Rabbinic Literary Forms." HUCA 19 (1946): 389–404.

Walser, Gerold. *Rom, das Reich, und die fremden Völker in der Geschichtsschreibung der frühen Kaiserzeit*. Baden-Baden: Verlag für Kunst und Wissenschaft, 1951.

Walter, Nikolaus. "Pseudepigraphische jüdisch-hellenistische Dichtung: Pseudo-Phokylides, Pseudo-Orpheus, Gefälschte Verse auf Namen griechischer Dichter." In *Jüdische Schriften aus hellenistisch-römische Zeit* 4.3, ed. Werner G. Kümmel. Gütersloh: Mohn, 1983. 175–278.

Waltzing, Jean Pierre. *Etude historique sur les corporations professionelles chez les romains depuis les origines jusqu'à la chute de l'empire d'Occident*. Louvain: Peeters, 1895–1900.

Walzer, Richard R. *Galen on Jews and Christians*. London: Oxford Univ. Press, 1949.

Weil, Isaac. *Le Prosélytisme chez les Juifs selon la Bible et le Talmud*. Strasbourg: Derivaux, 1880.

Weinfeld, Moshe. *The Organizational Pattern and the Penal Code of the Qumran Sect: A Comparison with Guilds and Religious Associations of the Hellenistic-Roman Period*. Fribourg: Editions Universitaires and Göttingen: Vandenhoeck and Ruprecht, 1986.

Welles, Charles Bradford. "The Hellenistic Orient." In *The Idea of History in the Ancient Near East*, ed. Robert C. Dentan. New Haven: Yale Univ. Press, 1955. 133–67.

Wiedemann, Alfred. "Zu den Felsgraffiti in der Gegend des ersten Katarakts." *OLZ* 3 (1900): 171–75.

Wiesenberg, Ernest. "Related Prohibitions: Swine Breeding and the Study of Greek." HUCA 27 (1956): 213–33.

Wifstrand, Albert. "Die wahre Lehre des Kelsos." BSRLL (1941–42): 391–431.

Wilcken, Ulrich. *Grundzüge und Chrestomathie der Papyruskunde*, 1.1–2. Leipzig: Teubner, 1912.

Wilcox, Max, reviser. "From the Destruction of Jerusalem to the Downfall of Bar Kokhba." In Emil Schürer, *The History of the Jewish People in the Age of Jesus*

Christ (175 B.C.–A.D. 135), ed. Geza Vermes and Fergus Millar, vol. 1. Edinburgh: Clark, 1973. 514–57.

Wilcox, Max. "The 'G-d-fearers' in Acts—A Reconsideration." JSNT 13 (1981): 102–22.

Wilken, Robert L. *Judaism and the Early Christian Mind: A Study of Cyril of Alexandria's Exegesis and Theology*. New Haven: Yale Univ. Press, 1971.

———. "Melito, the Jewish Community at Sardis, and the Sacrifice of Isaac." *TS* 37 (1976): 53–69.

———. *John Chrysostom and the Jews: Rhetoric and Reality in the Late Fourth Century*. Berkeley: Univ. of California Press, 1983.

———. *The Christians as the Romans Saw Them*. New Haven: Yale Univ. Press, 1984.

Willetts, R. F. *Ancient Crete: A Social History from Early Times until the Roman Occupation*. London: Routledge and Kegan Paul, 1965.

Williams, Margaret H. "The Expulsion of the Jews from Rome in A.D. 19." *Latomus* 48 (1989): 765–84.

Willis, William H. "Greek Literary Papyri from Egypt and the Classical Canon." *HLB* 12 (1958): 5–34.

———. "A Census of the Literary Papyri from Egypt." GRBS 9 (1968): 205–41.

Willrich, Hugo. *Juden und Griechen vor der Makkabäischen Erhebung*. Göttingen: Vandenhoeck and Ruprecht, 1895.

———. *Judaica: Forschungen zur hellenistisch-jüdischen Geschichte und Litteratur*. Göttingen: Vandenhoeck and Ruprecht, 1900.

———. "Der historische Kern des III. Makkabäerbuches." *Hermes* 39 (1904): 244–58.

———. "Dositheos (4)." *RE* 10 (1905): 1605.

———. *Urkundenfälschung in der hellenistisch-jüdischen Literatur*. Göttingen: Vandenhoeck and Ruprecht, 1924.

Wilson, Robert McL. "Jewish Literary Propaganda." In *Paganisme, Judaisme, Christianisme: Influences et effrontements dans le monde antique: Mélanges offerts à Marcel Simon*, ed. André Benoit et al. Paris: de Boccard, 1978. 61–71.

Winter, John G. *Life and Letters in the Papyri*. Ann Arbor: Univ. of Michigan Press, 1933.

Witt, Rolf E. *Isis in the Graeco-Roman World*. Ithaca: Cornell Univ. Press, 1971.

Wolfson, Harry A. *Philo: Foundations of Religious Philosophy in Judaism, Christianity, and Islam*, vols. 1–2. Cambridge, Mass.: Harvard Univ. Press, 1947.

Yamauchi, Edwin. "Daniel and Contacts between the Aegean and the Near East before Alexander." *EQ* 53 (1981): 37–47.

Zborowski, Mark, and Elizabeth Herzog. *Life Is With People: The Jewish Littletown of Eastern Europe*. New York: International Universities, 1952.

Zeitlin, Solomon. "Anti-Semitism." *Crozer Quarterly* 22 (1945): 134–49.

———, ed. *The Second Book of Maccabees*. New York: Harper, 1954.

———. "Korban." *JQR* 53 (1962–63): 160–63.

———. "Proselytes and Proselytism during the Second Commonwealth and the Early Tannaitic Period." *Harry Austryn Wolfson Jubilee Volume on the Occasion of His Seventy-fifth Birthday*, English Section, vol. 2. Jerusalem: American Academy for Jewish Research, 1965. 871–81.

Zeitlin, Solomon. "Korban: A Gift." *JQR* 59 (1968–69): 133–35.

Ziegler, Konrat. "Das Genesiscitat in der Schrift Περὶ "Υψους." *Hermes* 50 (1915): 572–603.

Zuckerman, Constantine. "Hellenistic *Politeumata* and the Jews: A Reconsideration." *SCI* 8–9 (1985–88): 171–85.

Zuntz, Günther. "Aristeas Studies II: Aristeas on the Translation of the Torah." *JSeS* 4 (1959): 109–26.

INDEXES

2. Apocrypha, Pseudepigrapha, and Dead Sea Scrolls

APOCRYPHA

PSEUDEPIGRAPHA

OTHER (ALLEGED) GRAECO-JEWISH WRITERS

Ezekiel the Tragedian
ap. Clement of Alexandria, *Stromata*
1.23.155.1, p. 62; *ap.* Eusebius, *Praeparatio Evangelica* 9.28.4b, pp. 517n.41,
546n.117; *ap.* Eusebius, *Praeparatio
Evangelica* 9.28–29, p. 317; 9.28.1, p. 62;
9.29.7 ff., p. 481n.79

Hecataeus (Pseudo-)
ap. Diodorus 1.54, p. 547n.118; *ap.* Josephus, *Against Apion* 1.201–4, pp. 208–9

Philo the Epic Poet
ap. Eusebius, *Praeparatio Evangelica*
9.24.1, p. 526n.27

5. *Rabbinic and Allied Literature (Tannaitic,
Amoraic, later Jewish, and Samaritan)*

TANNAITIC LITERATURE
(MISHNAH, BARAITHA, TOSEFTA,
MEKILTA, TARGUMIM)

MISHNAH
'*Avodah Zarah* 3:4, p. 42
Avoth 1:1 ff., p. 36; 1:3, p. 15; 1:6, p. 34;
    1:10, p. 13; 1:10–11, p. 34; 1:16, p. 34;
    2:3, p. 34; 2:15, p. 34; 3:2, p. 13; 4:1, p. 34
Baba Metzia 4:10, pp. 338, 409; 5:1 ff., p. 76;
    5:4, p. 486n.159
Berakoth 2:7, p. 583n.28
Bikkurim 1:4, p. 340; 1:5, p. 340
'*Eduyyoth* 5:2, p. 292
'*Eruvin* 4:3, p. 165; 6:1–2, p. 165
Gittin 4:6, p. 392
Hagigah 1:1, p. 469n.98
Horayoth 3:8, p. 340
Menahoth 13:10, p. 77
Middoth 3.8, p. 502n.16
Nazir 3:6, p. 329
Nedarim 2:1, p. 247; 6:4, p. 164
Peah 8:7, p. 577n.138
Pesahim 7:2, p. 583n.28; 8:8, p. 292
Qiddushin 4:7, p. 340
Rosh Hashanah 1:7, p. 583n.28; 2:5, p. 165
Shabbath 2:2, p. 510n.106; 4:2, p. 42; 18:3,
    p. 509n.102
Shevi'ith 8:5, p. 42
Sotah 9:14, p. 20 (*bis*)
Sukkah 2:1, p. 583n.28
Ta'anith 4:8, p. 578n.144
Terumoth 8:4, p. 524n.5

Yadaim 4:4, p. 326; 4:6, p. 37
Yevamoth 6:5, p. 340 (*bis*); 8:3, p. 563n.107
Yoma 3:10, p. 330

BARAITHA
Avoth 6:1, p. 34; 6:6, p. 493n.55

TOSEFTA
Baba Metzia 3.25, pp. 338, 409
Hullin 2.23, p. 579n.165
Kethuboth 3.1, pp. 64, 580n.169
Ma'aser Sheni 1.10, p. 577n.138
Peah 4.6, pp. 64, 580n.169
Qiddushin 5.1, p. 340
Sanhedrin 7, end, p. 35; 13.2, pp. 291, 356
Shabbath 12 (13).15, p. 577n.138
Sukkah 4.6, p. 63

MEKILTA
Mekilta Amalek 2.56a, p. 494n.58; 3, p.
    569n.187
Mekilta Bahodesh 6, p. 474n.182
Mekilta Beshalah 10, p. 247
Mekilta de-Rabbi Ishmael 18, pp. 354, 440
Mekilta Nezikin [Mishpatim] 18, p. 338

TARGUMIM
Jonah 3:5, p. 140
Jonathan on Numbers 22:22, p. 285
Pseudo-Jonathan on Genesis 11:28, p.
    540n.61
Onkelos on Numbers 24:24, p. 494n.59
Yerushalmi on Numbers 12:1, p. 546n.118

AMORAIC LITERATURE
(JERUSALEM TALMUD, BABYLONIAN
TALMUD, MINOR TRACTATES,
MIDRASHIM)

JERUSALEM TALMUD
'*Avodah Zarah* 1.2.39c, pp. 104, 494n.62,
    513n.15; 3.3, p. 410 (*bis*)
Baba Qamma 4.4, p. 105
Bikkurim 1.4.64a, p. 409
Gittin 7.1.48c, p. 34
Kethuboth 7.31c, p. 497n.14; 8.11.32c, p. 38;
    13.35c, p. 38
Kilayim 16.5, p. 577n.138
Ma'aser Sheni 1.2.52d, p. 577n.138
Megillah 1.9.71a, p. 326; 3.73d, p. 38;
    3.2.74a, pp. 354, 366, 389–90, 440
Mo'ed Qatan 3.3, p. 391

Alexander of Lycopolis, *Contra Manichaei Opiniones Disputatio* 24, p. 531n.1
Alexander Polyhistor, *ap.* Clement of Alexandria, *Stromata* 1.21.130.3, p. 531n.1; *ap.* Eusebius, *Praeparatio Evangelica* 9.19.17–23, p. 530n.1; *ap.* Josephus, *Ant.* 1.240, p. 530n.1; *ap.* Plutarch, *Parallela Graeca et Romana* 40.315E–F, p. 514n.118; *ap.* Stephanus of Byzantium, s.v. Ἰουδαία, p. 182; *ap.* Suda, s.v. Ἀλέξανδρος ὁ Μιλήσιος, pp. 237–38
Anaxadrides, frag. 39 (Kock 2.150 [= Athenaeus 7.299–300A]), p. 145
Anaximander 72 (frag. 20 Jacoby), p. 179
Antigonus, *ap.* Carolus Müller, ed., *Fragmenta Historicorum Graecorum* 4.305, p. 514n.25
Antiphanes, frag. 147 (Kock 2.71 [= Athenaeus 7.299E]), p. 145
Antonius Diogenes, *ap.* Porphyry, *Life of Pythagoras* 11, pp. 9, 202
Apion, *ap.* Eusebius, *Praeparatio Evangelica* 10.10.16, pp. 180, 200; *ap.* Josephus, *Against Apion* 2.10, p. 240; 2.11, p. 240; 2.17, p. 181; 2.20–21, pp. 163, 500n.12, 518n.47; 2.21, p. 221; 2.23, p. 221; 2.25, p. 142; 2.28, p. 179; 2.38, p. 151; 2.65, pp. 89, 151, 175; 2.68, pp. 143, 382; 2.73, pp. 151, 231; 2.80, p. 145, 146, 499n.12; 2.95, p. 505n.58; 2.114, p. 499n.12; 2.121, p. 128; 2.125, pp. 226, 230; 2.135, pp. 217, 317, 528n.35, 535n.24; 2.137, pp. 145, 167, 224; *ap.* Literary Papyri, London 30; British Museum inv. 271, p. 531n.3; *ap. Rylands Papyri* 1.26, p. 531n.3; *ap.* Tatian, *Oratio ad Graecos* 38, p. 512n.12
Apollodorus, *Bibliotheca* 1.7.4, p. 540n.61; 2.4.7, p. 549n.118; 2.5.11, p. 148; 3.15.8, p. 548n.118
Apollonius-Iamblichus 10 (p. 11, lines 6–7), p. 249
Apollonius Molon, *ap.* Eusebius, *Praeparatio Evangelica* 9.19.2–3, p. 530n.1; 9.19.3, p. 530n.1; *ap.* Josephus, *Against Apion* 2.79, p. 126; 2.145, pp. 227, 229; 2.148, pp. 205, 206, 217, 220 (*bis*), 243, 317, 382, 528n.35; 2.258, pp. 46, 128, 144
Aristophanes, *Acharnians* 610, p. 466n.72; *Birds* 507, p. 507n.70; *Clouds* 553–54, p. 551n.131; 680, p. 532n.14
Aristotle, *De Animalium Generatione* 770A34 f., p. 517n.45; *Athenian Constitution* 26.4,

p. 554n.3; *Metaphysics* 1.2.983A6–7, p. 209; 1.5.986B21–24, p. 525n.20; 12.8.1074A38 ff., p. 150; *Meteorologica* 2.359A, p. 6; *Nicomachean Ethics* 1.5.1095B22, p. 235; 4.1123A33–1125A35, p. 276; 4.1125B7–27, p. 276; 6.5.1140A24–B30, p. 209; 6.5.1140B8–11, p. 234; *Politics* 1.2.1252B7–8, p. 203; 2.10.1271B20–24, p. 515n.29; 2.10.1272A13–27, p. 515n.29; 2.11.1272B24–1273B26, p. 525n.15; 3.4.1277A15–17, p. 234; 7.9.4.1329B25, p. 177; 7.15.1334B, p. 147; *Rhetoric* 1.9.1366B, p. 226; *De Virtutibus et Vitiis* 55.1250B22–23, pp. 230, 530n.79; *ap.* Josephus, *Against Apion* 1.176–83, pp. 5, 202, 336; 1.179, pp. 5, 8, 46, 191, 203, 215, 488n.186, 516n.34, 544n.102; 1.180, pp. 370, 488n.186; 1.182, pp. 224, 475n.1; frag. 385 (Rose), p. 531n.5
Aristoxenus, frag. 13 (Wehrli), p. 503n.33
Artemidorus, *Onirocritica* 3.53, p. 172
Athenaeus 4.174, 535n.24

Callimachus, frag. 187, p. 505n.56; frag. 188, p. 505n.56; *ap. Palatine Anthology* 6.148, p. 479n.44
Celsus, *ap.* Origen, *Against Celsus* 1.14, pp. 198, 199; 1.21, pp. 241, 259, 286; 1.22, p. 198; 1.26, pp. 286, 380; 1.28, p. 199; 1.32, pp. 198, 199, 579n.165; 1.45, p. 286; 2.6, p. 583n.38; 3.55, p. 217; 4.14, p. 198; 4.21, p. 313; 4.31, p. 217; 4.33–34, p. 199; 4.36, p. 217; 4.41, p. 313; 4.43–46, p. 531n.1; 4.47, p. 313; 4.71–72, p. 153; 5.25, pp. 130, 372; 5.34, p. 131; 5.41, p. 170; 5.41–42, p. 536n.31; 5.42, p. 286; 5.43, p. 224; 5.50, p. 130; 5.60, p. 531n.1; 6.61, p. 166; 6.80, p. 578n.153; 7.18, p. 112
Chaeremon, *ap.* Josephus, *Against Apion* 1.289, p. 188; 1.290, pp. 238, 239, 522n.67, 531n.1, 532n.11
Charax, Claudius of Pergamum 103 (frag. 34 Jacoby), p. 179; *ap.* Stephanus of Byzantium, s.v. Ἑβραῖοι, p. 531n.1
Choerilus, *ap.* Josephus, *Against Apion* 1.172–73, p. 5; 1.172–74, p. 519n.51 (*bis*); 1.173, pp. 191 (*bis*), 521n.56; 1.174, p. 520n.56
Chrysippus, *SVF* 2. F 527 (p. 169), p. 517n.37

(Bailey), p. 34; Vatican frag. 10, p. 34; Vatican frag. 45, p. 34

Epigenes, *ap.* Seneca, *Natural Quaestiones* 7.4, p. 517n.37

Epimenides, frag. 1, *ap.* Callimachus, *Hymn to Zeus* 8, p. 515n.28; *ap.* New Testament, *Epistle to Titus* 1:12, p. 515n.28

Eratosthenes, *Katasterismoi* 11 (p. 246, ed. West), p. 146

Erotianus, *Vocum Hippocraticarum Collectio cum Fragmentis* F 33, pp. 49, 168

Euhemerus 63, frag. 1, *FGH*, part 1, p. 515n.28

Eupolis, frag. 78 Kock, p. 551n.131

Euripides, *Andromeda, ap.* August Nauck, *Tragicorum Graecorum Fragmenta*, no. 113, p. 519n.49; *Cyclops* 429, p. 502n.20; *Iphigenia at Aulis* 1524–25, pp. 134, 506n.60

Gaetulicus, *ap.* Palatine Anthology 7.275, p. 515n.28

Galen, *De Antidotis* 1.4, p. 111; *De Pulsuum Differentiis* 2.4, p. 171; 3.3, p. 171; *De Usu Partium* 11.14, pp. 171, 241

Hecataeus of Abdera, *ap.* Diodorus Siculus 1.46.8, p. 9; 40.3, pp. 8 (*bis*), 154; 40.3.2, p. 238; 40.3.2–3, p. 220; 40.3.3, pp. 234 (*ter*), 236; 40.3.3–8, p. 234; 40.3.4, pp. 46, 126, 129, 143, 149 (*bis*), 235, 475n.189; 40.3.5, pp. 8, 204, 235; 40.3.6, pp. 142, 170, 236 (*bis*); 40.3.7, p. 236 (*bis*); 40.3.8, pp. 46, 126, 236; ap. Josephus, *Against Apion* 1.183, p. 8; 1.187, p. 204; 1.188, p. 464n.25; 1.190–93, p. 231; 1.191, pp. 48, 159; 1.192, pp. 48, 150; 1.192–93, p. 220; 1.193, pp. 39, 464n.26; 1.194, p. 464n.25; 1.198, p. 8; 1.201–4, p. 464n.24; 2.43, pp. 8, 88

Heliodorus, *Aethiopica* 9.9, p. 319

Helladius, *ap.* Photius, *Lexicon* 279 (p. 529B27, ed. Bekker), p. 240

Hellanicus, *ap.* Josephus, *Against Apion* 1.16, p. 4; *ap.* Ps.-Justin, *Cohortatio ad Gentiles* 9, p. 4; *ap. FGH* 4 F 66–70, p. 516n.34

Heracleides of Pontus, *ap.* Diogenes Laertius 8.68, p. 542n.83

Hermippus of Smyrna, *ap.* Josephus, *Against Apion* 1.162–65, pp. 217, 344; 1.164–65, pp. 9, 224; 1.165, p. 201–2; *ap.*

Origen, *Against Celsus* 1.15, pp. 9, 202, 344

Hermogenes, *Progymnasmata* (ed. Hugo Rabe) 8, p. 473n.162

Herodotus 1.1, p. 521n.56; 1.60, p. 170 (*bis*); 1.105, p. 190; 1.105.2–4, p. 3; 1.107, p. 246; 1.114, p. 247 (*bis*); 1.131, p. 150; 1.136, pp. 228, 279; 1.139, pp. 228, 279; 1.145, p. 531n.1; 1.148, p. 531n.1; 1.171, p. 514n.26; 1.172, p. 515n.28; 1.173, pp. 191 (*bis*), 521n.56; 2.1, p. 514n.26; 2.2, p. 179; 2.4, pp. 179, 512n.6; 2.18, p. 131; 2.42.2, p. 189; 2.47, p. 167; 2.59.2, p. 188; 2.91, p. 144; 2.104, p. 190; 2.104.1–3, p. 462n.9; 2.104.3, pp. 154, 519n.51; 2.106, p. 507n.70; 2.110, p. 549n.120; 2.121, p. 220; 2.142, pp. 179, 206; 2.143, p. 177; 3.5.1–2, p. 3; 3.17–25, p. 222; 3.17–26, p. 268; 3.25, p. 268; 3.38, pp. 52, 131; 3.95, p. 86; 3.97, p. 268; 3.115, p. 187; 4.94–95, p. 238; 4.129, p. 146; 6.35.2 ff., p. 144; 6.54, p. 189; 7.63, p. 190; 7.70, pp. 192, 462n.12; 7.77, p. 521n.56; 7.89, pp. 519 n.51, 520n.56, 521n.56; 7.204, p. 537n.49

Hesiod, *Theogony* 211–13, p. 526n.26; 453 ff., p. 185; 535–57, p. 145; 969–71, p. 185; *Works and Days* 109–201, p. 16; 252–53, p. 16; 590, p. 461n.4

Hippias of Elis, *FGH* 6 F 1, p. 516n.34

Homer, *Iliad* 1.63, p. 526n.26; 1.423, p. 518n.48; 3.271, p. 461n.4; 4.194, p. 462n.4; 6.123–231, p. 244; 6.184, pp. 5, 191; 6.407–10, p. 530n.64; 11.558, p. 146; 14.201, p. 179; 16.327, p. 461n.4; 19.281, p. 461n.4; 20.443, p. 558n.40; 22.370, p. 249; 24.580, p. 461n.4; *Odyssey* 1.23, p. 519n.51; 4.83–84, p. 520n.51; 4.564, p. 514n.26; 5.282–83, pp. 191, 462n.12; 11.568–71, p. 185; 17.384, p. 537n.47; 19.560–66, p. 205; *Homeric Hymns, Hymn to Demeter* 123, p. 185

Iamblichus, *De Vita Pythagorica* 5.7, p. 245; 18.84, p. 524n.4; *ap.* Lydus, *De Mensibus* 4.53, p. 153

Isaeus 4.7, p. 4

Isocrates, *Busiris* 28, pp. 201, 202, 503n.33; 33, p. 503n.33; *Evagoras* 22–23, p. 249

Julian, *Ad Arsacium Archiereum Galatiae* 84a (p. 430B–D), p. 577n.138; 84a (p. 430D), p. 568n.175; *Ad Communitatem Iudae-*

CORPORA OF ROMAN LAW

NAMES AND SUBJECTS

Geographical Place-Names

Greek Words

Latin Words

Hebrew and Aramaic Words

MODERN SCHOLARS